A Dictionary of
Psychology

Andrew M. Colman is Professor of Psychology at the University of Leicester and is a Fellow of the British Psychological Society. He graduated from the University of Cape Town, where he was appointed to his first lecturing position, and he then lectured at Rhodes University before moving to Leicester. His previous publications include more than 150 journal articles and several books, among which are *Facts, Fallacies and Frauds in Psychology* (1987), *Game Theory and its Applications in the Social and Biological Sciences* (2nd edn, 1995), and *What is Psychology* (3rd edn, 1994). He edited the 12-volume *Longman Essential Psychology* series (1995) and is the founder and former editor of the journal *Current Psychology* (1981–).

Oxford Paperback Reference

The most authoritative and up-to-date reference books for both students and the general reader.

*forthcoming

A Dictionary of
Psychology

ANDREW M. COLMAN

OXFORD
UNIVERSITY PRESS

OXFORD

UNIVERSITY PRESS

Great Clarendon Street, Oxford OX2 6DP

Oxford University Press is a department of the University of Oxford.
It furthers the University's objective of excellence in research, scholarship,
and education by publishing worldwide in

Oxford New York

Auckland Bangkok Buenos Aires Cape Town Chennai
Dar es Salaam Delhi Hong Kong Istanbul Karachi Kolkata
Kuala Lumpur Madrid Melbourne Mexico City Mumbai
Nairobi São Paulo Shanghai Taipei Tokyo Toronto

Oxford is a registered trade mark of Oxford University Press
in the UK and in certain other countries

Published in the United States
by Oxford University Press Inc., New York

First published 2001
First published as an Oxford University Press paperback 2002
Reissued with corrections and new cover 2003

British Library Cataloguing in Publication Data
Data available

Library of Congress Cataloging in Publication Data
Data available

ISBN 0-19-860761-X

1 3 5 7 9 10 8 6 4 2

Typeset in 8.75 on 10.25pt Swift by SNP Best-set Typesetter Ltd., Hong Kong
Printed in Great Britain by Clays Ltd, St Ives plc

Contents

Preface

The Red Queen shook her head. 'You may call it "nonsense" if you like,' she said, 'but *I've* heard nonsense, compared with which that would be as sensible as a dictionary!'

Lewis Carroll: *Through the Looking-Glass*

The aim of this dictionary is to provide sensible and informative definitions of the most important and difficult words that a reader is likely to encounter in books and articles on psychology. Other dictionaries of psychology are available, but in general they provide only superficial coverage of the more technical terminology of neuroanatomy, neurophysiology, psychopharmacology, and statistics, and most of them make no systematic attempt to cover the specialized vocabulary of psychoanalysis. This dictionary provides systematic coverage of these areas, in addition to the basic terminology of psychology and psychiatry, and the definitions contain more explicit factual information and explanation than is available in other dictionaries.

The definitions are as simple as possible, but no simpler than that. Many of the concepts of psychology are inherently difficult and, if they are to be treated seriously, they ought not to be oversimplified or trivialized. In recognition of this, the definitions attempt to provide enough information to enable the serious reader to grasp the fundamental meaning and significance of even the more difficult concepts. Thus, for example, the entry under the headword **blood–brain barrier** avoids defining it in the usual, but misleading, way as a membrane and instead provides a detailed description of this remarkable but complex mechanism. In the same vein, the **peg-word mnemonic** is explained in enough detail to enable the reader to use it in practice; the **lateral geniculate nucleus** is not dismissed in a single sentence as a type of nerve cell, as in other dictionaries, but is described more accurately in terms of its structure and functions; and the **visual cortex** is not merely identified with vision and located at the back of the head but is given a full and detailed description. The entries under **information theory**, **prospect theory**, and **signal detection theory** provide enough information for the reader to grasp the fundamental ideas behind the theories and to understand how they actually work, and the same approach is adopted with other difficult terms. The aim is always to respect genuine difficulties and complexities but to provide the clearest possible definitions using the simplest possible language relative to the ideas being discussed.

Two unusual features of this dictionary deserve mention here. First, in many cases important terms and concepts are attributed to their originators or discoverers and, at the request of the publisher, when individuals are mentioned by name, their birth and death dates are usually supplied, although some dates, especially death dates, have been impossible to discover—people sometimes make significant contributions and then fade away into obscurity. Second, the entries are far more extensively cross-referenced than has been customary in earlier dictionaries. For example, the entry under **visual illusion** includes cross-references to every particular visual illusion described (and often illustrated) elsewhere in the dictionary, and the entry under **cranial nerve** is cross-referenced to all twelve of the human cranial nerves, each of which has its own separate entry. The purpose of the cross-references is to enable a reader who has looked up a word to obtain additional information that is either directly or indirectly relevant to it, and in general to encourage the use of the dictionary as an aid to serious scholarship.

The selection of headwords for this dictionary was not an easy task. I had to discard many words that could have gone in, and hard choices had to be made. Dilemmas were resolved by asking the following two questions: Is the word used in psychological books and articles? Are readers likely to want to look it up? Speaking on BBC radio in September 1999, the England football coach, Kevin Keegan, commented memorably: 'Picking the team isn't difficult; what's difficult is deciding which players to leave out.' I faced the same problem picking headwords for this dictionary; the difficult part was deciding which words to leave out.

The headwords that were finally selected include the core terminology of psychology, together with technical words that originate from other disciplines but are often used by psychologists. Psychology is a uniquely diverse discipline, ranging from biological aspects of behaviour to social psychology, and from basic research to various applied professional fields, such as clinical and counselling psychology, educational and school psychology, industrial/organizational and occupational psychology, and forensic and criminological psychology. Many of the technical terms of psychiatry, psychoanalysis, neuroanatomy, neurophysiology, pharmacology, computing, optometry, ethology, genetics, statistics, philosophy, linguistics, sociology, and anthropology have migrated into psychology and become partly naturalized there, and the most important ones are included in this dictionary.

Mental disorders are covered systematically and comprehensively, and definitions in this area are based on the widely accepted criteria of the American Psychiatric Association's *Diagnostic and Statistical Manual of Mental Disorders* (DSM-IV) and the World Health Organization's *Diagnostic Criteria for Research* (ICD-10).

The basic vocabulary of psychoanalysis is included in this dictionary, although—in fact, partly because—other dictionaries of psychology omit most psychoanalytic terms and concepts altogether and treat the ones that are included only superficially. In this dictionary, terms introduced by Sigmund Freud are defined in sufficient detail to convey their meanings without trivialization, and key terms coined by subsequent psychoanalysts, including Jung, Adler, Erikson, Klein, Fairbairn, Winnicott, Kohut, Lacan, and Reich, are also included. Citations of Freud's writings are given by reference to *The Standard Edition of the Complete Psychological Works of Sigmund Freud*, translated and edited by James Strachey, using the usual convention in Freud scholarship of roman numerals for volume numbers and arabic numerals for page numbers, and citations of Jung's writings are referenced to *The Collected Works of C. G. Jung*, edited by Read, Fordham, and Adler, using arabic volume and paragraph numbers, as is conventional in Jungian literature.

Appendix I, at the back of the dictionary, contains a list of phobias and phobic stimuli that is, as far as I am aware, the most comprehensive yet compiled and one of the few to include etymologies. Appendix II contains an extensive list of over 700 abbreviations and symbols commonly used in psychology, cross-referenced to corresponding entries in the main body of the dictionary.

The definitions in the main body of the dictionary include occasional comments about careful usage: see, for example, **adrenalin rush** (based on a misconception), **anorexia** (not the same as **anorexia nervosa**), **basal ganglia** (best reserved for ganglia involved in voluntary movement), **innate** (not the same as **hereditary**), **monosynaptic reflex** (a physical impossibility), **narcotic** (not just an addictive drug), **paradox** (more than something merely surprising), **phi phenomenon** (not just any form of apparent movement), and so on. Occasional suggestions are made for renaming concepts that seem to be misnamed. For example, this dictionary suggests the term **Dircks's ghost** instead of the misnomer **Pepper's ghost**, **Luckiesh illusion** instead of **Sander parallelogram**, and **Merkel's law** instead of **Hick's law**, for reasons that are explained in the relevant entries, though it seems too late to change **TAT** back to its original name.

Scattered throughout the dictionary are suggestions for practical demonstrations of dramatic or interesting psychological phenomena that can be observed under home conditions. The following entries, among others, include easy demonstrations, some trivial and others illustrating profound ideas: **afterimage**, **Aristotle's illusion**, **Aubert effect**, **Bidwell's ghost**, **blind spot**, **Cheshire Cat effect**, **conservation**, **Craik–O'Brien effect**, **Dollar Auction game**, **Emmert's law**, **filling-in illusion**, **flight of colours**, **floating-finger illusion**, **Gelb effect**, **hole-in-the-hand illusion**, **Kohnstamm effect**, **lightness**, **phi movement**, **Pulfrich effect**, **Purkinje figure**, **Purkinje shift**, **randomization**, **size–weight illusion**, **Stroop effect**, **successive contrast**, **teacup illusion**, **tilt aftereffect**, **winner's curse**.

Friends, relatives, and colleagues have asked me where I found the headwords and the information used to define them. The answer is—everywhere. In some cases I managed to access the required information close to home in my own long-term memory store; more often, I looked in journal articles, textbooks, and reference works; in many cases I asked leading authorities in the relevant research areas for help; and occasionally I was driven to trawl the Internet. I wrote this dictionary in circumstances that were difficult for me at work, and I am lucky to have had a lot of support and advice. Acknowledgements to people who helped me are provided elsewhere in these preliminary pages, though I take responsibility for errors that have no doubt remained. A list of the textbooks and reference works that I found most useful is provided at the back of the dictionary.

Andrew M. Colman

Advisory Editors

Biological aspects of psychology: Daniel P. Kimble, University of Oregon

Cognitive psychology: Robert J. Sternberg, Yale University

Mental disorders: Robert L. Spitzer, New York State Psychiatric Institute

Neurology and cognitive neuropsychology: Andrew Mayes, Royal Hallamshire Hospital

Psychoanalysis: Richard Stevens, The Open University

Psychopharmacology: Leonard W. Hamilton, Rutgers University

Sensation and perception: Harvey R. Schiffman, Rutgers University

Acknowledgements

Thanks are due to Rob Hemmings, Kathy Smith, and Philip W. Lee, for help with the preparation of the figures, most of which were created from scratch, and to Janice Smith for further technical assistance. Kathy Smith and Caroline Salinger also provided other forms of help and support for which I am especially grateful.

In addition to the Advisory Editors, who corrected errors, pointed out gaps or omissions, and made numerous other useful suggestions for improvement, and the copy-editor Linda Antoniw, who was also responsible for many substantive improvements, the following deserve thanks for helping with specific definitions or obscure factual information: Lyn Abramson (University of Wisconsin), Sally Blount (University of Chicago), Tamsin Carlisle (Dow Jones Canada/The Wall Street Journal), Rachel Charnock (University of Aberdeen), Edward Crossman (University of California, Berkeley), David Crystal (University of Wales, Bangor), Roy Davies (University of Leicester), Joanne Dunham (University of Leicester Medical Sciences Library), Susan Dye (Sun Bank), Walter Ehrenstein (Institut für Arbeitsphysiologie, Dortmund), Elaine Engst (Cornell University), Nigel Foreman (University of Middlesex), Pumla Gobodo-Madikizela (University of the Transkei), Gabriele Griffin (Kingston University), Horst Gundlach (Institut für Geschichte der Psychologie, Universität Passau), Michel Jouvet (Université Claude Bernard), Bob Lockhart (University of Toronto), George Loewenstein (Carnegie-Mellon University), Geoff Lowe (University of Hull), Helmut Lück (FernUniversität Hagen), Howard Margolis (University of Chicago), Jack Mayer (University of New Hampshire), Michael Molnar (Freud Museum), Serge Moscovici (University of Paris), Kazuo Ohya (Nagoya University), John Palmer (University of Washington), Stephen Palmer (University of California, Berkeley), Angus Phillips (Oxford University Press), Ian Pountney (Oracle Corporation UK Ltd), Briony Pulford (University of Wolverhampton), Richard Rawles (University College London), Roddy Roediger (Washington University), Lee Ross (Stanford University), Karl Rumelhart (Stanford University), Sverker Runeson (University of Uppsala), Peter Salovey (Yale University), Dan Schacter (Harvard University), Francine Shapiro (EMDR Institute, Pacific Grove, California), Ann Silver (University of Cambridge), John Simpson (Oxford University Press), Peter Smith (Stanford University), Gerhard Stemberger (Österreichische Arbeitsgemeinschaft für Gestalttheoretische Psychotherapie, Vienna), David Stretch (University of Leicester), Susan Sutcliffe (Greenhill College), Stephen Taylor (Vision Consultants), Peter Thompson (York University), Anne Treisman (Princeton University), John Vandenbergh (North Carolina State University), Neil Weinstein (Rutgers University), Gary Wells (Iowa State University), Wes Whitten (Australian National University), Margaret Woodhouse (University of Wales, Cardiff), and Marisa Zavalloni (Université de Montréal).

Illustration Acknowledgements

The author and publisher wish to thank Market House Books Ltd. for the use of the following illustrations from *A Dictionary of Biology*, 4th ed., and *A Dictionary of Science*, 4th ed. (both Oxford University Press).

A Dictionary of Biology
- Autonomic nervous system: The parasympathetic and sympathetic systems
- Ear: Main structures of the mammalian ear
- Genetic code
- Lipid bilayer
- Meiosis: Stages in a cell containing two pairs of homologous chromosomes
- Mitosis: The stages of mitosis in a cell containing two pairs of homologous chromosomes
- Pyramid of numbers: A woodland food chain
- Retina: Basic structure (light enters from the bottom of the diagram)
- Skin: Structure of mammalian skin
- Synapse: Basic structure

A Dictionary of Science
- DNA: Molecular structure
- Eye: Main structures of the vertebrate eye
- Harmonic: Fundamental and two overtones
- Motor neuron
- RNA: Molecular structure
- Sensory neuron

Layout of Entries

1. Every headword is printed in boldface type. Alphabetization is strictly letter by letter, ignoring spaces between words and punctuation marks. Numbers are listed as if they were spelt out in words: for example, **16PF** is positioned as if it were written 'sixteen PF', between **situationist critique** and **size constancy**.

2. The headword is followed by an abbreviation in italic type indicating the part of speech and occasionally (when there is likely to be confusion) whether it is singular or plural. The abbreviations are *abbrev.* (abbreviation), *adj.* (adjective), *adv.* (adverb), *conj.* (conjunction), *n.* (noun), *pl.* (plural), and *sing.* (singular).

3. If the headword has two or more sharply distinctive senses, then they are separated and labelled with boldface numerals (**1**, **2**, and so on), but closely related meanings are defined together without numbering. When two or more senses are defined, the one that is most common in the literature of psychology is generally defined first.

4. Within a definition, an asterisk attached to a word or phrase indicates a cross-reference, directing readers to a separate entry that will help them to understand the definition or provide more information about the term or concept. Only cross-references that are thought to be especially helpful are asterisked, and terms are often used in the definitions without asterisks although they are included as headwords elsewhere in the dictionary. A degree of cross-referential integrity has been maintained: obscure or technical words that are used in the definitions are usually asterisked and included elsewhere as headwords with their own definitions, to ensure that the dictionary is reasonably self-contained.

5. In some cases, synonyms or alternative names for the concept and alternative or variant spellings are given after the definition, in italic type.

6. After the definition and its synonyms and alternative spellings, additional entries that should be consulted for further information are introduced with one of the following directions in italic type: *See*, *See under*, *See also*, or *Compare*.

7. Next, derivative or subsidiary forms are occasionally listed in boldface type, usually in alphabetical order. For example, under the headword **mesomorph** are listed the derivative forms **mesomorphic** and **mesomorphy**, and under **meme** are listed **memeplex**, **meme pool**, **memetic**, **memetic engineering**, and **memetics**. As a general rule, the most common form of the word appears as the headword and the less common forms as derivatives or subsidiaries: thus, **diploid** appears as a headword although it is an adjective, and the noun **diploidy** is listed under it as a subsidiary form, because the adjectival form is far more common in

psychological usage. If the term has a common abbreviation, it is shown in bold-face type and marked *abbrev.*

8. A partial or full etymology is provided at the end of an entry, in square brackets, if it illuminates or clarifies the headword. The study of etymologies is often helpful, fixing the meaning of a word such as **migraine** and helping with spelling by, for example, insulating against the surprisingly common misspelling of a word such as **autotopagnosia**. Etymologies are omitted where the word is familiar or its derivation is obvious or implicit in the definition, or has not been determined with confidence.

Greek Alphabet

Letter name	Greek letter	English equivalent
alpha	A α	A a
beta	B β	B b
gamma	Γ γ	G g
delta	Δ δ	D d
epsilon	E ε	E e
zeta	Z ζ	Z z
eta	H η	E e
theta	Θ θ	TH th
iota	I ι	I i
kappa	K κ	K k
lambda	Λ λ	L l
mu	M μ	M m
nu	N ν	N n
xi	Ξ ξ	X x
omicron	O o	O o
pi	Π π	P p
rho	P ρ	R r
sigma	Σ σ	S s
tau	T τ	T t
upsilon	Y υ	U u
phi	Φ φ	PH ph
chi	X χ	CH ch
psi	Ψ ψ	PS ps
omega	Ω ω	O o

abaissement du niveau mental *n*. In *analytical psychology, a reduced state of concentration and attention, accompanied by a loosening of inhibitions and relaxation of restraints, in which unexpected contents may emerge from the *unconscious (2). It usually occurs spontaneously but can be deliberately encouraged in preparation for *active imagination. Carl Gustav Jung (1875–1961) borrowed the term from his teacher, the French psychologist and neurologist Pierre Janet (1859–1947).
[French: literally reduction of mental level]

abasia *n*. Inability to walk. *Compare* dysbasia.
[From Greek *a*- without + *basis* a step, from *bainein* to step or go + *-ia* indicating a condition or quality]

abbreviated reaction time *n*. Another name for *central reaction time.

ABC *abbrev*. **1.** A model used in *rational emotive behaviour therapy (REBT) for analysing a client's problems systematically into: *A*, the *activating event; *B*, the mediating evaluative *beliefs; and *C*, behavioural and emotional consequences. It is sometimes extended to *ABCDE*, with the addition of: *D*, disputing; and *E*, effect of practising rational thinking. **2.** Shorthand for the sequence of effects in *behaviour therapy: antecedent, behaviour, consequence.

abderite *n*. A simpleton.
[Named after Abdera, a town in the ancient country of Thrace whose inhabitants were reputed to be stupid]

abducens nerve *n*. Either of the sixth pair of *cranial nerves controlling the lateral *rectus muscles of the eyes, turning the eye outwards for a sidelong direction of gaze. Paralysis of this nerve causes convergent squint of the affected eye. Also called the *pathetic nerve*.
[From Latin *abducere* to lead away, from *ab*-away + *ducere* to lead or carry]

aberration *n*. **1.** A deviation from what is normal, usual, or right. *See also* chromosomal aberration. **2.** A temporary lapse of behaviour or mental function. **3.** A defect of the *crystalline lens of the eye, or of any other lens or mirror, also called *astigmatism* or *dioptric aberration*, in which rays of light do not all converge on to a single focal point. In *chromatic aberration*, different wavelengths of light are refracted through different angles and focused at different distances, leading to blurred images with coloured fringes—*see also* achromatic (2), refraction. In *spherical aberration* light passing through the lens near its edge is focused at a different point from light passing near the lens's centre, resulting in a distorted visual image, the defect arising from the surface of the lens being spherical.
[From Latin *aberrare* to wander away, from *ab* away + *errare* to wander + *-ation* indicating a process or condition]

ability *n*. Developed skill, competence, or power to do something, especially (in psychology) existing capacity to perform some function, whether physical, mental, or a combination of the two, without further education or training, contrasted with *capacity, which is latent ability. *See also* cognitive ability. *Compare* aptitude.
[From Latin *habilitas* ability, from *habilis* able, from *habere* to have or to hold]

ability test *n*. A test that measures a person's current level of performance or that estimates future performance. The term sometimes denotes an *achievement test, sometimes an *aptitude test, and sometimes an *intelligence test.

abiogenesis n. The generation of living from non-living matter. *Compare* biogenesis.
[Coined in 1870 by the English biologist Thomas Henry Huxley (1825–95), from Greek *a-* without + English *biogenesis*]

abiosis n. Absence of life. **abiotic** adj. Lifeless or inanimate.
[From Greek *a-* without + *bios* life + *-osis* indicating a process or state]

ablation n. Surgical removal of a structure or part of the brain or other organ of the body. **ablate** vb.
[From Latin *ab-* from + *latum* taken + *-ion* indicating an action, process, or state]

ablation experiment n. A basic research method of physiological psychology based on *ablation, especially during the first three-quarters of the 20th century, in which an attempt is made to determine the functions of a specific region of the nervous system by examining the behavioural effects of its surgical removal. It was pioneered in 1824 by the French physiologist Marie Jean Pierre Flourens (1794–1867) and is also called a *lesion experiment*.

ablaut n. A change in the quality of a *vowel serving to indicate a grammatical distinction, as in the forms *sing/sang/sung/song* or *foot/feet*. *Compare* umlaut (2).
[Coined by the German philologist Jakob Ludwig Karl Grimm (1785–1863) from German *ab* off + *Laut* a sound]

ableism n. Discrimination against people who are not able-bodied, or an assumption that it is necessary to cater only for able-bodied people. The term was coined by US feminists in the 1980s and was later used by the Council of the London Borough of Haringey in a press release in 1986. Also spelt *ablism*. *Compare* ageism, ethnocentrism, fattism, heterosexism, racism, sexism, speciesism. **ableist** or **ablist** n. 1. One who practises or advocates *ableism. adj. 2. Of or relating to *ableism.
[From *able* + Greek *-ismos* indicating a state or condition, on the model of words such as *ageism*]

Abney effect n. 1. The slight change in the *hue of *monochromatic light when its *lightness changes as a result of white light being added to it. 2. A perceptual phenomenon whereby a large surface that is suddenly illuminated appears to brighten first near its centre and then near its edges, and if the illumination is suddenly extinguished it appears to darken first near its edges and then near its centre.
[Named after the English chemist and physicist Sir William de Wiveleslie Abney (1843–1920)]

Abney's law n. The principle according to which the total luminance of light composed of several wavelengths is equal to the sum of the luminances of its *monochromatic components.
[Named after the English chemist and physicist Sir William de Wiveleslie Abney (1843–1920)]

abnormal adj. Departing from what is usual or what is the rule or *norm (1, 2).
[From Latin *ab* from + *norma* a rule + *-alis* of or relating to]

abnormality n. Anything that is *abnormal. A psychological abnormality is a manifestation of *cognition, *emotion, or *behaviour that deviates from an accepted norm or is a *sign (1) or *symptom of a *mental disorder. *See also* abnormal psychology.

abnormal psychology n. A branch of psychology devoted to the study of the classification, aetiology, diagnosis, treatment, and prevention of *mental disorders and disabilities. Also called *psychopathology*. *Compare* clinical psychology.

abortion n. An operation to terminate a pregnancy prematurely (also called an *induced abortion*), or a premature expulsion of an embryo or foetus occurring naturally (also called a *spontaneous abortion*). **abort** vb.
[From Latin *ab-* badly or wrongly + *oriri* to appear or arise + *-ion* indicating an action, process, or state]

ABO system *See under* blood group.

aboulia n. A variant spelling of *abulia.

Abraham Lincoln effect n. The tendency for a *block portrait to be difficult to recognize as a meaningful image when viewed close up but to become more recognizable when viewed

from a distance or when blurred by half closing the eyes, for example, loss of information paradoxically increasing the recognizability of the image. *See* block portrait (and accompanying illustration).
[Named by the US biomedical engineer Leon D(avid) Harmon (born 1922) after Abraham Lincoln (1809–65), the 16th US president, whose image he used to construct the first block portrait published in a technical report in 1971 and in an article in *Scientific American* magazine in 1973]

abreaction *n*. In *psychoanalysis, a release or discharge of emotional energy following the recollection of a painful memory that has been repressed. It can occur spontaneously or during psychotherapy, especially under *hypnosis, and may lead to *catharsis. As a therapeutic procedure, it was discovered in 1880–82 by the Austrian physician Josef Breuer (1842–1925), and during the infancy of psychoanalysis it was believed to be therapeutic in itself. *See also* principle of constancy.
[From German *abreagieren* to abreact or (metaphorically) let off steam, from Latin *ab* from + German *reagieren* to respond, coined in 1893 by Breuer and Sigmund Freud (1856–1939) in an article 'On the Psychical Mechanism of Hysterical Phenomena: Preliminary Communication' (*Standard Edition*, II, pp. 3–17]

absence *n*. The state or condition of being away from a place. In abnormal psychology and neurology, a brief period of loss of attention or consciousness, often followed by *amnesia for the period of absence, characteristic of minor (formerly called *petit mal*) *epilepsy. *Compare* tonic–clonic.

absent-mindedness *n*. Preoccupation to the point of being inattentive to one's own behaviour and surroundings, often characterized by *action slips arising from *open-loop control of actions that demand *closed-loop control for accurate implementation. *See also* Cognitive Failures Questionnaire.

absolute acuity *n*. The maximum keenness or sharpness of a sense organ to detect weak stimuli, usually expressed in terms of the *absolute threshold. *See also* acuity. *Compare* differential acuity.

absolute error *n*. In *psychophysics, the difference between the judged value of a stimulus and its true value, ignoring the direction of the difference. *Compare* relative error.
[Alluding to the mathematical sense of *absolute*, referring to a magnitude disregarding its positive or negative sign]

absolute judgement method *See* method of absolute judgement.

absolute limen *n*. Another name for the *absolute threshold.
[From Latin *limen* a threshold]

absolute pitch *n*. The ability to identify the *pitch of a musical tone, or to produce a specified tone at its correct pitch, without reference to another tone. *See also* perfect pitch. *Compare* relative pitch.

absolute reflex *n*. The name given on occasions by the Russian physiologist Ivan Petrovich Pavlov (1849–1936) to what is usually called the *unconditioned response.

absolute refractory period *n*. A *refractory period (2), lasting up to 2 milliseconds after the onset of an *action potential, during which no *stimulus (5) can initiate another nerve impulse in the neuron. *Compare* relative refractory period.

absolute scale *n*. In statistics and measurement theory, a *ratio scale in which the unit of measurement is fixed. In practice, values on an absolute scale are usually if not always obtained by counting. *See also* measurement level, scale (1). *Compare* interval scale, log-interval scale, nominal scale, ordinal scale, ratio scale.

absolute thinking *n*. Interpreting personal fears and desires in absolutes (for example, describing oneself as being absolutely devastated by a setback); regarded in some branches of *counselling as a cognitive error that limits *insight (3).

absolute threshold *n*. In *psychophysics, the smallest intensity of a sensory stimulus that can be detected or can reliably evoke a sensation, a typical example being the average human absolute threshold for sound intensity at 1,000 hertz (about two octaves above Middle C), which is an intensity of about 6.5 dB SPL (*see under* decibel). The original concept of a sharply defined limit below which nothing can be perceived was discredited and largely abandoned after the development of *signal detection theory, the absolute threshold being redefined as the magnitude that can be detected on a specified proportion of presentations (often 50 or 75 per cent, though other percentages are sometimes used). Also called the *absolute limen* or *Reiz limen (RL)*. *See also* acuity, audibility function, audiogram, bone conduction threshold, contrast sensitivity function, contrast threshold, dark adaptation, decibel, Heimdallr sensitivity, light adaptation, Piper's law, psychophysics, Ricco's law, subliminal. *Compare* difference threshold.

absorbance *See under* reflectance.

abstinence *n.* **1.** Avoidance of alcohol or some other drug of dependence, or more generally self-restraint from some indulgence. *See also* abstinence syndrome, withdrawal. **2.** In psychodynamic counselling and therapy, the practice of the counsellor or therapist of holding back from uninhibited interaction and conversation with the client or patient.
[From Latin *abstinere* to abstain]

abstinence rule *n.* In *psychoanalysis, the organization of treatment to minimize the substitutive satisfaction of needs related to symptoms that the patient finds outside the analytic situation, in spite of the frustration and suffering that can result. Sigmund Freud (1856–1939) introduced the rule in an article on 'Observations on Transference-Love' (1915): 'I shall state it as a fundamental principle that the patient's need and longing should be allowed to persist in her, in order that they may serve as forces impelling her to do work and to make changes, and that we must beware of appeasing these forces by means of surrogates' (*Standard Edition*, XII, pp. 159–71, at p. 165).

abstinence syndrome *n.* A pattern of signs and symptoms associated with *withdrawal in a drug-dependent person who is suddenly deprived of a regular supply of the drug and is forced to practise *abstinence (1).

abstract attitude *n.* A term introduced by the German psychiatrist Kurt Goldstein (1878–1965) to denote the ability to use conceptual categories in order to classify things according to their attributes and to think symbolically rather than concretely. This ability is impaired in many forms of brain damage and mental disorder. Also called *categorical attitude*.

abstraction *n.* **1.** The act or process of formulating a general concept by identifying common *features (1) from specific instances or examples, or a concept formed in this way. **2.** A state of *absent-mindedness or preoccupation. **3.** In general, the act of withdrawing or removing something.
[From Latin *abstractus* drawn off, from *ab* away from + *trahere, tractum* to draw + *-ion* indicating an action, process, or state]

abstract measurement theory *n.* Another name for *axiomatic measurement theory.

absurdity test *n.* Any psychological test in which the respondent attempts to identify what is wrong or illogical about a verbal or a pictorial stimulus, such as a missing leg in a drawing of a spider or a missing numeral in a drawing of a clock face. It is often included as an item or subtest of an *IQ test.

abulia *n.* A deficit of will or motivation, often leading to an inability to make decisions or plans.
[From Greek *a-* without + *boule* will + *-ia* indicating a condition or quality]

abuse (alcohol, child, elder, spouse, substance) *See under* alcohol abuse, child abuse, elder abuse, spouse abuse, substance abuse.

ABX paradigm *n.* In *psychophysics, a method of determining a *difference threshold by presenting two stimuli (A and B) and a third (X) that is the same as one of the others, the observer's task being to decide whether it matches A or B.

academic problem *n.* A *learning difficulty, usually in a schoolchild, that does not amount to a *learning disability.

academic skills disorders *n.* An alternative name for *learning disabilities.

acalculia *n.* Impairment of ability to do arithmetic. *See also* agraphia, alexia, specific disorder of arithmetic skills. *Compare* dyscalculia.
[From Greek *a-* without + Latin *calculare* to count, from *calculus* diminutive of *calx* a stone + *-ia* indicating a condition or quality]

acatamathesia n. An obscure synonym for *agnosia; an inability to comprehend sensory information. Also spelt *akatamathesia*. *Compare* agnosia.
[From Greek *a-* without + *katamathanein* to observe or understand, from *kata* thoroughly + *mathanein* to learn + *-ia* indicating a condition or quality]

accent n. **1.** A characteristic pronunciation of a language, especially one associated with a geographical region or social group, to be distinguished from a *dialect. **2.** The *stress (2) or prominence given to a spoken syllable, usually through a rise in pitch, loudness, or sound quality, or a written mark to indicate this.
[From Latin *ad* to + *cantus* a song]

acceptor n. A chemical substance that receives and combines with another substance, as in an oxidation–reduction reaction where the oxygen is the acceptor of the substance that is oxidized and hydrogen is the acceptor of the substance that is reduced.

accessibility n. **1.** In cognitive psychology, the ease with which information in long-term memory can be retrieved. An *accessible memory* is one that can be retrieved without *cues (3) or *prompts. *Compare* availability. **2.** In *modal logic, the property of a *possible world of being open to scrutiny from some other world in such a way that the truth value of *propositions (1) about it can be known. **3.** In general, the ease with which something can be approached, reached, or obtained. **accessible** adj.
[From Latin *accessus* an approach + *-ibilitas* capacity, from *habilis* able]

accessory cell n. Any of a number of cells in the nervous system that contribute to the support, maintenance, and repair of *neurons. *See* astrocyte, ependymal cell, microglia, oligodendrocyte, Schwann cell.

accessory nerve n. Either of two pairs of eleventh *cranial nerves, the motor nerves arising partly from the lateral walls of the medulla oblongata and partly from the cervical (neck) region of the spinal cord, divided into the cranial accessory nerves, distributed by the *vagus nerve to the muscles of the larynx and pharynx, and the spinal accessory nerves, supplying muscles in the neck, shoulder, and upper back.

accidence n. Inflections of words or changes in the forms of words to indicate different grammatical functions, as in *write*, *wrote*, *writing*.
[From Latin *accidentia* accidental matters]

accidental sample n. A *non-probability sample drawn haphazardly from a population by a procedure such as stopping the first hundred passers-by on a particular street corner. *See also* convenience sample, opportunity sample, quota sample, self-selected sample, snowball sample. *Compare* cluster sample, probability sample, random digit dialling, simple random sample, stratified random sample.

accommodation n. **1.** The voluntary or involuntary adjustment of the curvature of the *crystalline lens of the eye to keep an image focused on the fovea with changes in the distance of the object being viewed; more specifically, one of the monocular cues of visual *depth perception, the degree of curvature of the lenses providing information about the distances of objects focused on the retinas. Also called *visual accommodation*. *See also* accommodation reflex, dark focus, far point, near point, Purkinje–Sanson image, range of accommodation. **2.** In the writings of the Swiss psychologist Jean Piaget (1896–1980) and his followers, a form of *adaptation (3) in which psychological structures or processes are modified to fit the changing demands of the environment, as when an infant adapts its perceptual processes and behavioural repertoire to a new toy that is introduced into its milieu. *See also* equilibration. *Compare* assimilation (2). **3.** A decrease in a neuron's propensity to produce an action potential, the reduced responsiveness being caused by repeated stimulation. **accommodate** vb. **accommodative** adj. *Compare* assimilation (2).
[From Latin *accommodare* to accommodate, from *ad* to + *commodus* fitting + *-ation* indicating a process or condition]

accommodation reflex n. A reflex adjustment of the eyes for *near vision that occurs in response to an object appearing suddenly in front of the face and that consists of pupillary constriction, ocular convergence, and increased convexity of the lenses. *See also* accommodation (1), ciliary reflex.

acculturation *n*. The process of assimilating the ideas, beliefs, customs, values, and knowledge of another culture through direct contact with it, usually after migration from one place to another.

acculturation difficulty *n*. Any problem of *acculturation that falls short of being an *adjustment disorder.

accumbens nucleus *n*. Another name for the *nucleus accumbens.

accuracy test *n*. Any test in which the correctness of responses, rather than the speed of performance, is measured. *Compare* power test.

acephalous *adj*. Headless, or having only an indistinct or degenerate head, like certain insect larvae. Figuratively, without a ruler or leader.
[From Greek *a-* without + *kephale* a head + *-ous* having or characterized by]

acetaldehyde *n*. A colourless volatile noxious liquid that accumulates in the body of a person who drinks alcohol while taking the drug *Antabuse, resulting in nausea, vomiting, pounding of the heart, shortness of breath, and other unpleasant symptoms. Formula CH_3CHO. *See also* paraldehyde.
[From Latin *acet(um)* vinegar + *al(cohol) dehyd(rog)e(natum)* dehydrogenated alcohol]

acetic acid *n*. A colourless pungent-tasting liquid that occurs in the fermentation of alcohol, and as a *metabolite of *acetylcholine and *serotonin. It can be diluted with water to form vinegar and is widely used in the manufacture of vinyl acetates, plastics, and pharmaceuticals. *See also* acetyl.
[From Latin *acetum* vinegar]

acetyl *n*. The *radical (2) group —$COCH_3$ formed by removing —OH from *acetic acid.
[From *acet(ic) acid* + *-yl* indicating a chemical group or radical, from Greek *hyle* wood]

acetylcholine *n*. A *neurotransmitter substance secreted from the ends of many neurons and functioning as the main chemical messenger for *motor neurons in the *peripheral nervous system, including the *autonomic nervous system, and as a significant neurotransmitter in the *central nervous system, functioning to excite *skeletal muscles and to inhibit *cardiac muscle, remaining in existence only long enough for the impulse to cross from one cell to another before being broken down by *acetylcholinesterase into acetic acid and choline. *See also* Alzheimer's disease, carbachol, cholinergic, cholinomimetic, muscarine, muscarinic receptor, nicotinic receptor, *Vagusstoff*. **ACh** *abbrev*.
[From Latin *acetum* vinegar + Greek *hyle* wood or material + *chole* bile + *-ine* indicating an organic compound]

acetylcholinesterase *n*. An enzyme that hydrolyses *acetylcholine to acetic acid and choline. By destroying acetylcholine after its release from the terminal *boutons of *presynaptic neurons and from *postsynaptic receptors after a nerve impulse has been triggered, it stops further postsynaptic nerve impulses. Also called *cholinesterase*. *See also* nerve gas, physostigmine. **AChE** *abbrev*.
[From *acetylcholine* + *ester* + *-ase* denoting an enzyme, from Greek *diastasis* separation]

acetylsalicylic acid *n*. The chemical name for *aspirin.

achievement motivation *n*. Another name for *need for achievement.

achievement test *n*. Any test of acquired ability or skill, a typical example being a test of scholastic attainment. *See also* competency test. *Compare* ability test, aptitude test.

Achilles tendon reflex *n*. A *deep tendon reflex occurring in response to a tap on the Achilles tendon at the back of the ankle. It is often absent in people with diabetes, diseases of the peripheral nervous system, pyramidal tract disease, or hyperthyroidism. Also called the *ankle reflex*.

achromatic *adj*. **1.** Without *hue, or represented in black, white, and grey. An *achromatic colour*, also called a *neutral grey* or *neutral colour*, is a mixture of black and white without any *chroma and is the *lightness component of any colour. *See also* Hering grey, saturation (1). **2.** Capable of refracting or reflecting light without chromatic *aberration (3).
[From Greek *a-* without + *chroma* colour]

achromatic interval n. For light of a particular *hue, the range of light intensities from its *absolute threshold to the lowest intensity at which its hue can be detected; analogously, for a *pure tone of a particular frequency, the range of *amplitudes from its absolute threshold to the lowest intensity at which its pitch can be detected.

achromatic system n. In the *opponent-process theory of colour vision, the pathway that carries information about an object's lightness. Compare chromatic system.

achromatopsia n. Total *colour-blindness resulting from lesions, usually in areas V2 and V4 of the *visual cortex, resulting in an inability to see colours, with an intact ability to see shapes and movement. People who acquire this condition usually lose the ability even to imagine colours. See also colour agnosia (under agnosia), dyschromatopsia, monochromatism, parachromatopsia. Compare chromatopsia. **achromatopsic** adj. [From Greek a- without + chroma colour + ops an eye + -ia indicating a condition or quality]

acid n. **1.** Any substance that when dissolved in water releases positively charged hydrogen *ions and produces a corrosive solution having a *pH of less than 7. Compare alkali. **2.** A common street name for *LSD. **acidic** adj. Of, relating to, or consisting of an acid (1). **acidity** n. The degree to which a solution is *acidic. [From Latin acidus sharp or sour]

acid odour n. One of the primary odours in the *Crocker–Henderson system. US acid odor.

acoustic adj. Of or relating to sound. Also called acoustical. **acoustics** n. The study of sound. [From Greek akoustikos of or relating to sound, from akouein to hear + -ikos of, relating to, or resembling]

acoustic coding n. Remembering something by storing the sound of its verbal expression rather than its meaning or the physical movements required to articulate it. Compare articulatory coding, semantic coding.

acoustic confusion n. Erroneous perception or memory resulting from the substitution of an incorrect but similar-sounding word, as when someone mishears or misremembers it's my turn to cook when in fact it is that person's turn to book theatre tickets. Compare semantic confusion.

acoustic cue n. **1.** An acoustic property of a speech sound, such as a *formant, used to identify the sound and to distinguish it from other speech sounds. See also distinctive feature, minimal pair, neutralization. **2.** A *cue (3) that prompts recall of a remembered word by evoking its sound.

acoustic feature n. Any physical property or *feature (1) of a sound, such as its *fundamental frequency or its *amplitude. Compare acoustic cue (1), distinctive feature.

acoustic generalization n. *Stimulus generalization of auditory stimuli, as when a response to a sound (such as a word or a tune) that has been learned, is evoked by a similar sound.

acoustic–mnestic aphasia See under aphasia.

acoustic nerve n. Another name for the *vestibulocochlear nerve.

acoustic reflex n. An involuntary contraction of the *tensor tympani and *stapedius muscles within the middle ears, occurring simultaneously in both ears in response to intense noise presented to either ear, stiffening the eardrum and restricting movements of the *ossicles, causing a *temporary threshold shift and protecting against damage to the organs of hearing. It is similar to the pupillary light reflex in response to bright light. Also called the tympanic reflex.

acoustic similarity effect n. The tendency for lists of similar-sounding words to be more difficult to remember than lists of dissimilar-sounding words.

acoustic store n. A general term for the *postcategorical acoustic store and the *precategorical acoustic store, though there is some doubt about their existence. More generally, a hypothetical repository of memories produced by *acoustic coding. Compare subvocal rehearsal loop.

acquaintanceship knowledge n. A category of *knowledge that is distinct from both *declarative knowledge (knowing that) and *procedural knowledge (knowing how). It consists of knowledge of people, places, and things, and although it may include declarative knowledge it need not necessarily do so, as when one knows a colour, or a smell, or a face, but cannot state any facts about it. This class of knowledge was discussed by the Welsh philosopher Bertrand (Arthur William) Russell (1872–1970) in *The Problems of Philosophy* (1912) and is poorly understood in psychology.

acquiescence response set *n*. In psychometrics, a consistent tendency to respond to yes/no questionnaire items by answering *Yes*, irrespective of the content of the questions. Properly constructed questionnaires generally control for this response set by *counterbalancing (2). Also called *acquiescence response style*. *See also* balanced scale, counterbalancing (2), response set (2).

acquired distinctiveness *n*. A learnt differentiation or discrimination between items that were previously indistinguishable, as when a person attends a wine-tasting course and acquires the ability to discriminate wines that previously tasted the same. *Compare* acquired similarity.

acquired dyslexia *n*. One of the two major categories of *dyslexia, this form of the disorder resulting directly from brain damage, usually to the left cerebral hemisphere. *See also* cognitive neuropsychology, deep dyslexia, surface dyslexia. *Compare* developmental dyslexia.
[From Greek *dys-* bad or abnormal + *lexis* a word + *-ia* indicating a condition or quality]

acquired similarity *n*. A tendency for items that were previously perceived as dissimilar to be perceived as the same as a result of learning to use them for the same purpose or to classify them in the same category or with the same label. For example, in Japanese, /r/ and /l/ are *allophones that do not give distinct meanings to different words, and as a result Japanese speakers often lack the ability to distinguish between them, but this causes problems for native Japanese speakers of English, because in English /r/ and /l/ distinguish *minimal pairs such as *right* and *light* and are therefore different *phonemes. *Compare* acquired distinctiveness.

acrasia *See* akrasia.

acrolect *n*. The most prestigious variety of a language within a speech community, such as *Received Pronunciation in Britain. *See also* dialect, idiolect, lect. *Compare* basilect, mesolect.
[From Greek *akros* highest + *legein* to speak]

acromegaly *n*. Enlargement of the bones in the head, hands, and feet, caused by an excessive secretion of growth hormone by the pituitary gland, sometimes associated with *cerebral gigantism. **acromegalic** *adj*.
[From Greek *akros* highest + *megas* big]

acronym method *n*. A memory aid based on acronyms. *See under* mnemonic.
[From Greek *akros* topmost + *onoma* a name]

acroparaesthesia *n*. A persistent sensation of numbness, tingling, or pins and needles in the extremities (hands or feet), sometimes caused by compression or inflammation of nerves in the affected area. US *acroparesthesia*. *See also* paraesthesia.
[From Greek *akron* extreme, alluding to the hands and feet (extremities) + *para* beside or beyond + *aisthesis* sensation + *-ia* indicating a condition or quality]

acrotomorphilia *n*. A *paraphilia characterized by recurrent sexually arousing fantasies, sexual urges, or behaviour associated with having a partner with an amputated leg. It is found among both heterosexual and homosexual men and women and should be carefully distinguished from *apotemnophilia. People with acrotomorphilia often refer to themselves as *devotees*. Also called *monopede mania, monopedophila,* or *unipedophilia,* but the latter two forms are liable to cause confusion with *paedophilia*.
[From Greek *akron* a tip + *tome* a cut + *morphe* a form or shape + *philos* loving, from *phileein* to love + *-ia* indicating a condition or quality]

ACT* *abbrev*. (pronounced *act-star*). Adaptive Control of Thought, an advanced version of a *network model of *information processing first put forward in 1976 by the Canadian-born US psychologist John R(obert) Anderson (born 1947). It includes two distinct *long-term memory stores: (a) a *declarative memory, modelled by a semantic network of interconnected *concepts represented by *nodes (2), containing *declarative knowledge, the active part of the declarative memory system constituting *working memory;

and (b) a *procedural memory, modelled by a *production system, containing the system's procedural knowledge. *See also* fan effect.

actin *n*. A protein that interacts with *myosin to form the contractile protein *actomyosin in muscles and is also involved in other physiological processes.
[From *act* + Latin *-in(a)* indicating an organic compound]

acting in *n*. A term sometimes used in *psychoanalysis to denote *acting out (1, 2) when it occurs within an analytic session rather than in ordinary life.

acting out *n*. **1.** In *psychoanalysis, the enactment rather than recollection of past events, especially enactments relating to the *transference during therapy. It is often impulsive and aggressive, and it is usually uncharacteristic of the patient's normal behaviour. The concept was introduced by Sigmund Freud (1856–1939) in *An Outline of Psycho-Analysis* (1938/40): the patient 'acts it [the past event] before us, as it were, rather than reporting it to us' (*Standard Edition*, XXIII, pp. 144–207, at p. 176). *See also* acting in. **2.** A *defence mechanism in which unconscious emotional conflicts or impulses are dealt with by actions, including *parapraxes, rather than thought or contemplation. **act out** *vb*.

action (drug) *See* drug action.

action potential *n*. The momentary change in the voltage difference across the membrane of a *neuron, usually triggered by nerve impulses from several other neurons at *synapses (1), characterized by an influx of positively charged sodium ions through the cell membrane, resulting in an impulse being propagated along the neuron's *axon, reversing its *resting potential of approximately –70 millivolts (mV), the inner surface being negative relative to the outer surface and the membrane more permeable to potassium ions than to sodium ions, and changing it to approximately +40 mV, increasing the permeability of the membrane to sodium ions and resulting in the influx of positively charged ions, thereby propagating the potential from the *axon hillock down the axon at a speed ranging from about 0.1 to 10 metres per second. Also called a *nerve impulse*. *See also* all-or-none law, depolarization, excitatory post-

synaptic potential, inhibitory postsynaptic potential, refractory period (2), saltation (1), sodium pump. *Compare* graded potential.

action research *n*. A term coined in the 1940s by the Polish/German-born US psychologist Kurt Lewin (1890–1947) for a form of *applied research in which experimental techniques are combined with programmes of social action to bring about desired social changes. *See also* participatory action research. *Compare* basic research, descriptive research, evaluation research, exploratory research.

action slip *n*. An unintended action or behavioural sequence, often resulting from failure of attention in *absent-mindedness, and generally involving *open-loop control of an action that requires *closed-loop control for its correct implementation. *See also* parapraxis.

activated gene *n*. A gene whose expression has been enhanced by a *gene activator.

activating event *n*. In *rational emotive behaviour therapy (REBT), something that is believed to happen, to have happened, or to be about to happen, and that triggers irrational beliefs leading to emotional problems. *See also* ABC (1).

activator gene *n*. A *regulator gene that synthesizes a *gene activator capable of binding to a *gene operator and enhancing the expression of a *structural gene by increasing the synthesis of its protein product. *Compare* repressor gene.

active analysis *n*. A style of *psychoanalysis in which the analyst offers frequent *interpretations (2). *Compare* passive analysis.

active avoidance conditioning *n*. Learning to respond in a way that results in the avoidance of a punishing or aversive stimulus, as when a rat is trained to jump over a barrier whenever a light comes on in order to avoid electric shock that follows shortly after. Also called *active avoidance learning*. *Compare* escape conditioning, passive avoidance conditioning. *See also* avoidance conditioning.

active imagination *n*. In *analytical psychology, a term introduced by Carl Gustav Jung (1875–1961) in the Tavistock lectures, delivered in London in 1935, to denote a process of allowing *fantasies (2) to run free, as if dreaming with open eyes. He had expounded the concept (though not the terminology) earlier (*Collected Works*, 6, paragraphs 712–14, 723n). *See also* abaissement de niveau mental.

active sleep *n.* Another name for *REM sleep.

active technique *n.* In *psychoanalysis, a set of technical procedures presented by the Hungarian psychoanalyst Sandor Ferenczi (1873–1933) to the 1920 Psychoanalytic Congress in The Hague, with the approval of Sigmund Freud (1856–1939), in which the analyst is encouraged to go beyond *interpretation (2) and on occasions to issue instructions and prohibitions to patients.

active transport *n.* The movement of particles up an electrochemical potential gradient, such as the movement of sodium ions across a *cell membrane from a region where they are in a low concentration to a region of high concentration. This process requires metabolic energy and is assisted by *enzymes, often called pumps when they serve this function. *See* carrier protein, ionophore, sodium pump.

active vocabulary *n.* The set of words that a person uses in speech and writing. *Compare* passive vocabulary.

activity wheel *n.* A drum, suspended horizontally and free to rotate, into which an animal may be placed to measure arousal or activity.

actomyosin *n.* A protein synthesized from *actin and *myosin in skeletal muscles that, when stimulated, shrinks and causes muscle contraction, the energy being supplied by *ATP.

actor–observer difference *n.* An *attributional bias tending to cause people to attribute their own actions to situational factors and observers to attribute those same actions to internal personality dispositions. It is explained partly by the greater amount of information available to actors than observers, partly by differences between actors and observers in perceptual focus, and partly by motivational factors that might induce actors to emphasize external causes and observers internal causes. The phenomenon was first reported in 1972 by the US psychologists

Edward Ellsworth Jones (1926–93) and Richard E. Nisbett (born 1941). *See also* attribution, attribution theory.

act psychology *n.* A doctrine, first propounded by the German psychologist and philosopher Franz Brentano (1838–1917), according to which psychology should study not merely the elements of consciousness as in *structuralism (2) but also mental acts and the way they are directed towards entities other than themselves. Brentano published his ideas in 1874 in his book *Psychologie vom empirischen Standpunkt* (Psychology from an Empirical Standpoint), and was an important forerunner of *phenomenology. *See also* intentionality (1). *Compare* content psychology.

actualization *n.* The realization of latent potential. *Compare* self-actualization. **actualize** *vb.*
[From Latin *actualis* of or relating to acts, from *actus* an act + Greek *-izein* cause to become or to resemble]

actual neurosis *n.* In *psychoanalysis, a form of *neurosis that does not have its origin in infantile conflicts but in the present, the *symptoms resulting directly from the absence or inadequacy of sexual satisfaction and not appearing as symbolic forms of expression. Sigmund Freud (1856–1939), who introduced the concept in 1898 in an article on 'Sexuality in the Aetiology of the Neuroses' (*Standard Edition*, III, pp. 263–85, at p. 279), originally identified anxiety neurosis (*generalized anxiety disorder) and *neurasthenia as the actual neuroses, and he later added *hypochondria. *Compare* psychoneurosis.
[From German *aktual* present-day]

actuarial prediction *n.* Any prediction of behaviour based on purely statistical information and not subjective judgement. It is characterized by mechanical processing of information, leading to probabilities representing empirically determined relative frequencies, as when psychometric test scores are compared with tables of *normative (2) data to make a prediction that the probability is p that an individual will succeed on a training programme, reoffend when released from prison, develop a certain mental disorder, or commit suicide, the prediction being based on the relative frequencies of such outcomes among people with similar test scores. It was

first systematically analysed and compared with *clinical prediction by the US psychologist Paul Everett Meehl (born 1920) in his book *Clinical Versus Statistical Prediction: A Theoretical Analysis and a Review of the Evidence* (1954). Meehl was the first to point out that it is almost always more accurate than clinical prediction. Also called *statistical prediction*. *See also* bootstrapping.
[From Latin *actuarius* a keeper of records, from *acta* chronicles or records]

actus reus *n.* A legal term denoting a criminal act in contradistinction to a criminal intent and knowledge of the wrongness of the criminal act, which in turn is called *mens rea. For a defendant to be convicted of a crime, both an actus reus and a mens rea must normally be proved.
[From Latin *actus* act + *reus* guilty]

acuity *n.* Keenness or sharpness, especially of sensation. *See also* absolute acuity, absolute threshold, acuity grating, audiogram, difference threshold, differential acuity, dynamic visual acuity, König bars, Landolt circle, minimum audible angle, minimum audible field, minimum separable, minimum visible, receiver operating characteristic, signal detection theory, Snellen fraction, stereoscopic acuity, two-point threshold, vernier acuity, visual acuity.
[From Latin *acutus* sharp, from *acus* a needle]

acuity grating *n.* A device for measuring *visual acuity by displaying a light background with a set of evenly spaced dark bars whose width and distance apart can be reduced simultaneously until the *minimum separable is reached. *See also* grating, König bars, vernier acuity.

acupuncture *n.* A technique of Chinese origin for inducing anaesthesia or treating various disorders by inserting needles into the skin at carefully specified points to stimulate nerve impulses. Also called *stylostixis*. *See also* gate-control theory.
[From Latin *acus* a needle + English *puncture*]

acute *adj.* Sharp or pointed; penetrating or piercing; important or critical; of or relating to sensation or perception that is finely discriminating; of or relating to a disorder or symptom that begins abruptly and subsides quickly. *Compare* chronic.

[From Latin *acutus* sharpened, from *acuere* to sharpen]

acute confusional state *n.* **1.** A form of *delirium characterized by *amnesia, *clouding of consciousness, and problems of orientation. **2.** An *acute stress disorder, especially during adolescence, resulting from a sudden change in circumstances or the environment.

acute pain *n.* Severe short-term *pain often following injury, surgery, dental problems, or heart attack (myocardial infarction). *Compare* chronic pain.

acute stress disorder *n.* A transient *anxiety disorder following exposure to a traumatic event, with a similar pattern of symptoms to *post-traumatic stress disorder plus symptoms of *dissociation (such as *dissociative amnesia, *depersonalization, *derealization) but occurring within four weeks of the traumatic event. If the symptoms persist beyond four weeks, then a diagnosis of post-traumatic stress disorder may be considered.
[From Latin *acutus* sharpened, from *acuere* to sharpen, from *acus* a needle]

acute stress reaction *n.* A form of *acute stress disorder in which exposure to the *psychosocial stressor is followed immediately (within one hour) by the onset of the symptoms, which begin to subside after no more than eight hours.

Adam *n.* A common street name of *ecstasy (2).
[A near-anagram of *MDMA]

adaptation *n.* **1.** In the theory of *evolution, a feature of an organism's structure, physiology, or behaviour that solves a problem in its life or helps it to pass its genes on to the next generation. **2.** In physiology and sensation, a temporary reduction in the responsiveness of a *sensory receptor other than a *pain receptor as a result of repeated or continuous stimulation. Also called *sensory adaptation*. *See also* auditory adaptation, chromatic adaptation, cross-adaptation, dark adaptation, light adaptation, odour adaptation, prism adaptation, thermal adaptation, transient tritanopia, visual adaptation. **3.** In the writings of the Swiss psychologist Jean Piaget (1896–1980), the modification of an organism's psychological structures or processes in

response to environmental demands, comprising *accommodation (2) and *assimilation (2). *See also* equilibration. **4.** A general term for any process whereby behaviour or subjective experience alters to fit in with a changed environment or circumstances or in response to social pressure. Often mistakenly written or pronounced as *adaption*. *See also* alloplastic, autoplastic. **adaptive** *adj*.
[From Latin *adaptare* to adjust or to fit, from *ad* to + *aptus* fitting + *-ion* indicating an action, process, or state]

adaptation level *n*. A hypothesized neutral position or region in a bipolar stimulus dimension, functioning as a reference point for subjective judgements, stimuli above the adaptation level being judged to have a particular *attribute (such as large, heavy, or loud), stimuli below it being judged to have the opposite or complementary attribute (small, light, or soft), and stimuli in its vicinity being judged to be neutral with respect to the attribute. *See also* adaptation-level theory. **AL** *abbrev*.

adaptation-level theory *n*. A theory proposed by the US psychologist Harry Helson (1898–1977) in an article in the *American Journal of Psychology* in 1947, according to which the *adaptation level is determined for a class of stimuli by members of the class already sampled or attended to, by stimuli having a background or contextual influence, and by recollections of past judgements of similar stimuli, the adaptation level being the logarithm of the mean of the relevant stimuli, weighted according to their effectiveness in terms of nearness, recency, salience, and so on. According to the theory, subjective judgements are necessarily relative to the prevailing norm or adaptation level, so that a 4 ounce (113 gram) pen is heavy, but a baseball bat must weigh over 40 ounces (1.13 kilograms) to be judged heavy. The phenomenon is a type of *context effect. Also called *AL theory*. *Compare* assimilation-contrast theory.

adaptation syndrome *See* general adaptation syndrome.

adaptive control of thought *See* ACT*.

adaptive radiation *n*. The evolutionary process whereby species that are descended from a common ancestor diverge to exploit different *ecological niches.

adaptive testing *n*. A sequential testing procedure in which successive test items are selected for administration to a respondent on the basis of that person's responses to earlier items.

adaptor *n*. Something or someone that adapts or adjusts to a changed situation or helps a person or other organism to adjust, especially (in social psychology) a *gesture (1), usually involving self-touching, that helps one to cope with an emotional reaction, typical examples being self-grooming behaviour, covering the eyes for fear, or putting a hand over the mouth for surprise. *See also* displacement activity, kinesics.

addiction *n*. A state of dependency on a chemical substance, especially on a drug such as *alcohol, *nicotine, or *caffeine, or a narcotic such as *morphine or *heroin, characterized by a strong physiological and/or psychological need and a compulsive inability to resist taking the drug despite anticipation of probable adverse consequences, *withdrawal if there is an abrupt deprivation of the substance, and in some cases drug *tolerance (3). *See also* dependence (2), nucleus accumbens, substance dependence. **addictive** *adj*.
[From Latin *addictus* given over, from *addicere* to assent to, from *ad* to + *dicere* to declare + *-ion* indicating an action, process, or state]

additive alleles *n*. A pair of *alleles combining to produce a *heterozygote that is phenotypically the average of the two corresponding *homozygotes.

additive colour mixture *n*. A colour formed by the combination of *additive primaries, or the process of forming such a colour. US *additive color mixture*. *See also* colour mixing. *Compare* subtractive colour mixture.

additive model *n*. Any statistical or mathematical model in which an effect can be expressed as a weighted sum of *independent variables, so that the portion of the effect contributed by one independent variable does not depend on the value of any other independent variable. A classic example of a linear additive model is *multiple regression. *See also* additivity. *Compare* multiplicative model.

additive primary *n*. Any of the shades of red, green, or blue that can be mixed to form white and to match all other *spectral colours and also certain *non-spectral colours such as purple. Primary red, green, and blue are often defined as light with wavelengths of 670, 535, and 470 nanometres respectively, but any three shades may be used, provided that none is equivalent to a combination of the other two. Also called a *primary colour*, though that term is ambiguous. *See also* CIE colour system, chromaticity, colour equation, Grassmann's laws (perception), primary colour (1), Rayleigh equation, tristimulus values. *Compare* psychological primary, secondary colour, subtractive primary.

additivity *n.* In *analysis of variance (ANOVA), the property of having only *main effects and no *interaction effects and thus being represented by an *additive model without multiplicative terms. In *axiomatic measurement theory, a property of a quantitative *attribute such that for any two levels of the attribute, a third always exists such that the greatest of the three levels is the sum of the other two. The absence of this property is called *non-additivity*. **additive** *adj.*

addressed phonology *n.* The sound of a word or verbal expression as it is stored in memory. *Compare* assembled phonology.

adelphogamy *n.* **1.** A form of *polyandry in which two or more brothers share the same wife or wives. **2.** Marriage between brothers and sisters, as occurred in royal families in ancient Egypt, or mating between brothers and sisters, as occurs in some ants.
[From Greek *adelphos* a brother + *gamos* marriage]

adenine *n.* One of the constituent *bases (1) of ATP and the nucleic acids, having an affinity for thymine in DNA and uracil in RNA. **A** *abbrev.*
[From Greek *aden* a gland + *-ine* indicating an organic compound]

adenohypophysis *n.* The anterior lobe of the hypophysis (pituitary gland), usually called the *anterior pituitary. *Compare* neurohypophysis.
[From Greek *aden* a gland + *hypophysis* an attachment underneath, from *hypo* under + *phyein* to grow]

adenosine *n.* A compound of *adenine and *ribose, present in all cells in a combining form and functioning in the nervous system as a *neurotransmitter. *See also* ADP, AMP, ATP.
[A blend of *adenine* and *ribose* + Greek *-ine* indicating an organic compound]

adenosine diphosphate *See* ADP.

adenosine monophosphate *See* AMP.

adenosine triphosphate *See* ATP.

adenylate cyclase *n.* An enzyme in a cell membrane that responds to a hormone by initiating the conversion of *ATP to *cyclic AMP as a *second messenger.
[From *adenyl(ic acid)* + *-ate* indicating a salt or ester of an acid + *cycl(ic AMP)* + Greek *-ase* denoting an enzyme, from *diastasis* separation]

adenylic acid *n.* Another name for *AMP.

adequate stimulus *n.* The type of *stimulus (1) to which a specified sensory receptor is adapted to respond, such as visible light for the photoreceptors or audible sound for the auditory receptors in the organ of Corti. *Compare* inadequate stimulus.

adiadochokinesia *n.* An inability, sometimes classified as a form of *apraxia, to perform rapid rhythmic movements such as finger tapping, often indicative of damage to the *cerebellum. *Compare* dysdiadochokinesia.
[From Greek *a-* without + *diadochos* a successor + *kinesis* movement + *-ia* indicating a condition or quality]

adipose *adj.* Of, relating to, or consisting of fat.
[From Latin *adiposus* fatty, from *adeps* fat]

adipose tissue *n.* Structures in a human or animal body composed of fat cells.

adipsia *n.* Absence of thirst or abstention from drinking. *Compare* polydipsia.
[From Greek *a-* without + *dipsa* thirst + *-ia* indicating a condition or quality]

adjacency pair *n.* Any sequence of a single stimulus utterance followed by a single response utterance, as in a question and answer.

Adjective Check List *n.* In psychometrics, any list of adjectives that can be marked as applicable or not applicable to oneself, to one's ideal self, to another person, or to some other entity or concept. When written with initial uppercase letters, the term denotes more specifically a measure consisting of a list of 300 adjectives, from *absent-minded* to *zany*, selected by the US psychologist Harrison G. Gough (born 1921) and introduced as a commercial test in 1952. The test yields 24 scores, including measures of personal adjustment, self-confidence, self-control, lability, counselling readiness, some *response styles, and 15 personality needs, such as achievement, dominance, and endurance. Gough discussed its psychometric properties in an article in the journal *Psychological Reports* in 1960. Also called the *Gough Adjective Check List*. **ACL** *abbrev.*

adjustment *n.* Adaptation, (in psychology) especially behavioural adaptation to a particular environment or set of circumstances.

adjustment disorder *n.* A mental disorder, the essential feature of which is the development of clinically significant emotional or behavioural symptoms as a reaction to an identifiable *psychosocial stressor (such as termination of a romantic relationship, marked business problems, marital difficulties, a natural disaster, failing to attain an important goal, or becoming unemployed), involving greater distress than would normally be expected from the stressor and significant impairment in social, occupational, or academic functioning. *See also* culture shock, grief reaction.

adjustment method *n.* Another name for the *method of average error.

Adlerian *adj.* Of or relating to the school of *psychoanalysis, called *individual psychology, founded in 1911 by the Austrian psychiatrist Alfred Adler (1870–1937). *See* compensation, Diana complex, fictional finalism, guiding fiction, inferiority complex, life lie, masculine protest, neurotic character, will to power.

admissible alternative/strategy *n.* In decision theory and game theory, an alternative or *strategy (2) that is not dominated by a *dominant alternative/strategy.

adolescence *n.* The period of development from the onset of *puberty to the attainment of adulthood, beginning with the appearance of *secondary sexual characteristics, usually between 11 and 13 years of age, continuing through the teenage years, and terminating legally at the age of majority, usually 18 years of age.
[From Latin *adolescentia* adolescence, from *adolescere* to grow up, from *ad* to + *alescere* to grow, from *alere* to feed or nourish]

adolescent *n.* **1.** A person in a period of *adolescence. *adj.* **2.** Of, relating to, or peculiar to *adolescence, or in a state or period of adolescence.

adoption study *n.* In behaviour genetics, an investigation of the correlations between adopted children and either their natural parents or their adoptive parents (or both) on a measurable *trait in order to estimate the *heritability of that trait, the assumption being that the higher the heritability of the trait, the greater will be the correlation with natural parents, and the lower the heritability the greater will be the correlation with adoptive parents. Since the late 1970s some adoption studies have examined correlations between natural and adoptive siblings within the same households, the assumption being that if the heritability of the trait is high, then the natural children's scores will correlate more highly with those of other natural children, who share half their genes, than with the scores of the adoptive children to whom they are not genetically related, whereas if heritability is low, the reverse should hold. *Compare* kinship study, twin study.

ADP *abbrev.* Adenosine diphosphate, a (nucleotide) compound formed when stored energy is released from *ATP by *ATPase in the performance of muscular contractions or the transmission of nerve impulses.

adrenal cortex *n.* The outermost layer of the *adrenal gland, which releases *corticosteroid hormones such as *cortisol (hydrocortisone) into the bloodstream in response to *stress (1). *See also* adrenocorticotrophic hormone (ACTH), DHEA, zona fasciculata, zona glomerulosa, zona reticularis.
[From the Latin *ad* at + *renes* kidneys + *cortex* bark or outer layer]

adrenal gland *n.* An *endocrine gland situated just above each kidney, secreting *adrenalin (epinephrine), *noradrenalin (norepinephrine), and other *hormones into the bloodstream. *See also* adrenal cortex, adrenal medulla.

adrenalin *n*. A *biogenic amine and *hormone belonging to the group of *catecholamines, also functioning as a *neurotransmitter, synthesized from tyrosine in the presence of the cofactor vitamin C and secreted by the *chromaffin cells of the *adrenal medulla and by nerve fibres in the *sympathetic nervous system, causing an increase in blood pressure, accelerated heart rate, deepened respiration, sweating, dilation of the pupils, release of sugar from stores in the liver, diversion of blood from the intestines to the skeletal muscles, closure of the sphincter of the bladder leading to retention of urine, and other physiological reactions typical of *fear, *anxiety, or *stress (1). Formula: $(HO)_2C_6H_3CH(OH)CH_2NHCH_3$. Also spelt *adrenaline*. Also called *epinephrine*, especially in the US. *See also* adrenergic, fight-or-flight response. *Compare* noradrenalin.
[From the Latin *ad* at + *renes* kidneys + *-in(a)* indicating an organic or chemical substance]

adrenalin rush *n*. A sudden increase in competitive drive displayed by an athlete or sports competitor, supposedly associated with the release of *adrenalin into the bloodstream. This expression is based on a misunderstanding of the effects of adrenalin and is avoided in careful usage: *noradrenalin rush* or even *serotonin rush* would be marginally more apt.

adrenal medulla *n*. The inner part of the *adrenal gland, containing *chromaffin cells that release *adrenalin (epinephrine) and *noradrenalin (norepinephrine) into the bloodstream in response to fear or stress.

adrenergic *adj*. Releasing *adrenalin (epinephrine) or a similar substance; also activated by or responding to adrenalin or a similar substance, this extended usage being widespread but consistently rejected by the English physiologist Sir Henry Hallet Dale (1875–1968), who coined the suffix *-ergic*, and by many other authorities. *Compare* cholinergic, dopaminergic, GABAergic, noradrenergic, serotonergic.
[From *adrenalin* + Greek *ergon* work + *-ikos* of, relating to, or resembling]

adrenergic receptor *n*. Either of two types of *neuroreceptor for *adrenalin (epinephrine)

and *noradrenalin (norepinephrine) situated on a neuron, muscle, or gland. Alpha-adrenergic (or *α*-adrenergic) receptors, which are found in smooth muscles that line blood vessels, can raise blood pressure by constricting them, and beta-adrenergic (or *β*-adrenergic) receptors, which are found in membranes surrounding the heart muscle and the smooth muscles of the lungs and intestines, function by activating slightly different *second messenger pathways. In most cases, alpha receptors are associated with excitation of the smooth muscles, and beta receptors with inhibition, but the muscles of the heart have beta receptors that are excitatory and some of the alpha receptors in the intestines are inhibitory.

adrenocorticotrophic hormone *n*. A *hormone secreted by the *anterior pituitary that stimulates the *adrenal cortex to secrete *steroid hormones such as *cortisol (hydrocortisone) into the bloodstream, especially in response to *stress (1) or injury. Also spelt *adrenocorticotropic hormone*. Also called *adrenocorticotrop(h)in* or *corticotrop(h)in*. *See also* dexamethasone, POMC. **ACTH** *abbrev*.

adultomorphic fallacy *n*. The error of attributing to infants and children the thoughts and feelings of adults.
[From *adult* + Greek *morphe* a form or shape + *-ikos* of, relating to, or resembling]

advantage by illness *n*. Another name for *secondary gain.

adverse (drug) reaction *n*. Another name for a *side-effect.

adynamia *n*. Flaccid paralysis resulting from muscular weakness. **adynamic** *adj*.
[From Greek *a-* without + *dynamis* strength + *-ia* indicating a condition or quality]

aerial perspective *n*. One of the monocular cues of visual *depth perception, a form of *perspective closely related to *linear perspective and *texture gradient, great distances being suggested by a haziness of outline and surface detail coupled with diminution of colour intensity or a bluish haze, effects that are caused by the scattering of light by dust and vapour particles in the atmosphere. Also called *atmosphere perspective*. *See also* Aubert–Förster phenomenon.

[From Greek *aerios* of or relating to air, from *aer* air]

aerobic *adj.* Of or relating to the generation of energy by a form of metabolism requiring oxygen or air. *See also* glycolysis, Krebs cycle. *Compare* anaerobic.
[From Greek *aer* air + *bios* life + *-ikos* of, relating to, or resembling]

aerophagia *n.* Spasmodic swallowing of air, a nervous habit resulting in stomach pains and belching.
[From Greek *aer* air + *phagein* to consume + *-ia* indicating a condition or quality]

aesthesiometer *n.* A device for measuring sensory discrimination, especially a device for determining the *two-point threshold. US *esthesiometer*.
[From Greek *aisthesis* sensation, from *aisthanesthai* to feel + *metron* a measure]

aetiology *n.* The cause of a particular disorder, or the study of the causes of disorders in general. US *etiology*. **aetiological** *adj.* US *etiological*.
[From Greek *aitia* cause + *logos* word, discourse, or reason]

affect *n.* Emotion or subjectively experienced feeling, such as happiness, sadness, fear, or anger. *Blunted affect* is emotional expression that is significantly reduced in intensity; *flat affect* is absence or near absence of emotional expression and is also called *flattening of affect* or *affective flattening*; *inappropriate affect* or *incongruity of affect* is a mismatch between emotional expression and what one is speaking or thinking about; *labile affect* is instability or fluctuation of emotions; and *restricted affect* or *constricted affect* is diminution in the range of emotional expression. *See also* emotion, primary emotions. *Compare* mood.
[From Latin *affectus* past participle of *afficere* to influence, from *ad* to + *facere* to do]

affect display *n.* A form of *non-verbal communication in which an *emotion or *affect is communicated, chiefly in humans by a *facial expression. *See also* display rule, expressive behaviour, kinesics, primary emotions. **affective** *adj.*

affectional bond *n.* The emotional tie between an infant and its mother or caretaker,

forming the basis of the relationship with which *attachment theory is concerned.

affective disorder *n.* Another name for a *mood disorder.

affective flattening *n.* Reduced or absent expression of *affect, associated with certain mental disorders, notably some forms of *schizophrenia, indicated by unchanging and unresponsive facial expression, *aprosodia, avoidance of eye contact, and diminished body language.

afferent *adj.* Towards the centre; of or relating to a nerve impulse from a *sense organ to the *central nervous system, or to a neuron or nerve that transmits such impulses. *See also* sensory nerve. *Compare* efferent.
[From Latin *aferre* to carry to, from *ad* to + *ferre* to carry]

affiliation need *n.* Another name for *need for affiliation.

affirming the antecedent *n.* In *conditional reasoning, arguing validly from a hypothetical proposition of the form *If p then q* that, because *p* therefore *q*. For example, given the proposition *If the burglars entered by the front door, then they forced the lock*, it is valid to deduce from the fact that the burglars entered by the front door that they must have forced the lock. Also called *modus ponens. Compare* affirming the consequent, denying the antecedent, denying the consequent.

affirming the consequent *n.* In *conditional reasoning, arguing invalidly from a hypothetical proposition of the form *If p then q* that, because *q* therefore *p*. For example, given the proposition *If the burglars entered by the front door, then they forced the lock*, it is invalid to conclude from the fact that the burglars forced the lock that they must have entered by the front door. *Compare* affirming the antecedent, denying the antecedent, denying the consequent.

affordance *n.* A term coined in 1977 by the US psychologist James Jerome Gibson (1904–79), to refer to a resource or support provided by the environment to an organism, furnishing or affording the organism with an opportunity to act in a particular way. Examples of affordances include a surface that affords physical support, an edible substance that affords an opportunity to eat, and the positioning of an outstretched hand that affords the prospect of shaking hands. *See also* direct perception.

affricate *n.* A complex *consonant speech sound the *articulation of which involves a *plosive followed immediately by a *fricative at the same place of articulation. English has two affricate *phonemes, the first and last sounds in *church*, which is the unvoiced affricate, and the first and last phonemes in *judge*, which is the voiced affricate. *See also* manner of articulation.
[From Latin *affricare* to rub against, from *fricare* to rub]

aftereffect *n.* Any phenomenon occurring some time after its cause, especially (in psychology) a delayed sensory or perceptual experience. *See also* afterimage, Aubert effect, contingent aftereffect, figural aftereffect, McCollough effect, motion aftereffect, postural aftereffect, spiral aftereffect, successive contrast, tilt aftereffect, visual aftereffect, waterfall illusion.

afterimage *n.* A sensory experience, especially a visual image, that persists after the stimulus has ceased, also called a *primary afterimage*, or one that appears after a primary afterimage. The first in the sequence of visual afterimages following brief exposure to a bright stimulus is called a *Hering image and is normally a *positive afterimage, dark areas of the original image appearing dark, and light areas appearing light, usually appearing in the same colours as the original stimulus but sometimes colourless, and persisting for only a fraction of a second. The subsequent *Purkinje image is a *complementary afterimage, colours of the original stimulus appearing in approximate complementary colours in the image, and it is more persistent than the Hering image but also tends to disappear if the gaze is shifted, though it can often be briefly restored by blinking. The third afterimage is positive and is called a *Hess image. These effects can be demonstrated by adapting one's eyes to darkness for at least 15 minutes and then setting off a camera's electronic flash, which for safety reasons should not be looked at directly with dark-adapted eyes, or by briefly switching on a bright light. *See also* aftersensation, Aubert effect, Bidwell's

ghost, Emmert's law, flight of colours, iconic store, McCollough effect, visual illusion. *Compare* eidetic image.

aftersensation *n.* Any *sensation persisting after the cessation of the *stimulus (1, 3), especially an *afterimage or an *aftertaste.

aftertaste *n.* A sensation of *taste or *flavour that lingers after a sapid (tastable) food or drink has been in the mouth. The term is also used metaphorically for any lingering impression, especially a nasty one.

agape *n.* Brotherly or Christian *love.
[From Greek *agape* brotherly love]

agapic love *n.* A secondary type of brotherly love that is altruistic and selfless and is a combination of *erotic love and *storgic love. *Compare* ludic love, manic love, pragmatic love.

age-equivalent score *n.* A measure of a person's ability, skill, or knowledge, expressed in terms of the age at which the average person attains that level of performance. Also called an *age score*. *Compare* grade-equivalent score.

ageism *n.* The belief in the intrinsic superiority of people within a certain age range, often accompanied by *prejudice, *stereotyping, and discrimination on the basis of age, usually against old people. Also spelt *agism*, especially in the US. *Compare* ableism, ethnocentrism, fattism, heterosexism, racism, sexism, speciesism. **ageist** or **agist** *n.* **1.** One who practises or advocates *ageism. *adj.* **2.** Of or relating to *ageism.
[Coined in 1969 by the US gerontologist Robert N. Butler (born 1927) from *age* on the model of *racism*]

age regression *n.* The adoption of a pattern of behaviour characteristic of an earlier stage of development, observed occasionally in certain forms of mental disorder. In *hypnotic age regression* this occurs as a direct response to suggestions from the hypnotist.
[From *age* + Latin *regressus* a retreat, from *regradi* to go back, from *re-* again + *gradi* to go + *-ion* indicating an action, process, or state]

age-related cognitive decline *n.* Diminution in cognitive functions occurring naturally as part of the ageing process. *See also* age-related memory impairment.

age-related memory impairment *n*. A form of age-related cognitive decline, the predominant symptom of which is a decline in memory occurring naturally as part of the ageing process.

age scale *n*. In psychometrics, any measuring scale that yields *age-equivalent scores.

age score *n*. In psychometrics, another name for an *age-equivalent score.

ageusia *n*. Absence of the sense of taste. *Compare* cacogeusia, dysgeusia, hypergeusia, hypogeusia, parageusia, taste blindness. **ageusic** *adj*.
[From Greek *a-* without + *geusis* taste + *-ia* indicating a condition or quality]

agglomerative hierarchical clustering *n*. In statistics, any technique of *cluster analysis in which each individual or case starts out as a cluster, and at each step of the analysis clusters are combined until all cases belong to a single cluster. Once formed, a cluster cannot be split but can be combined with other clusters.

agglutinative language *n*. A language such as Finnish, Japanese, Turkish, or Swahili in which grammatical relationships are indicated by building up words out of long sequences of units, each of which indicates a particular grammatical meaning. Also called an *agglutinating language. Compare* inflecting language, isolating language.
[From Latin *agglutinare* to glue together, from *ad* to + *gluten* glue]

aggression *n*. Behaviour whose primary or sole purpose or function is to injure another person or organism, whether physically or psychologically. *See also* frustration–aggression hypothesis.
[From Latin *aggredi, aggressus* to attack, from *ad* to + *gradi* to step + *-ion* indicating an action, process, or state]

aggression, displaced *See* displaced aggression.

aggression, instinctual *See under* Thanatos.

agitated depression *n*. A form of *depression accompanied by *psychomotor agitation.

agitation *See* psychomotor agitation.

agnosia *n*. A term introduced in 1891 by the Austrian neurologist and founder of psychoanalysis Sigmund Freud (1856–1939), nowadays denoting an *impairment of ability to recognize or identify familiar objects, entities, or people, usually as a result of a *neurological deficit or disorder. The major forms are: *ahylognosia* (impaired ability to discriminate by touch such physical properties of objects as their weight, density, or texture; *compare* amorphognosia, tactile agnosia); *amorphognosia* (impaired ability to recognize by touch the size and shape of objects; *compare* ahylognosia, tactile agnosia); *anosognosia* (impaired ability or refusal to recognize that one has a sensory or motor impairment or, in some cases following a massive *stroke and *hemiplegia, even to recognize part of one's body as one's own); *apperceptive agnosia* (impaired ability to identify and discriminate between objects, usually associated with right hemisphere brain damage, also called *visual shape agnosia*, in contrast to associative agnosia); *asomatagnosia* (impaired ability to recognize one's own body or part of it; *compare* anosognosia, autotopagnosia); *associative agnosia* (impaired ability to interpret or give meaning to objects, as in failing to understand that a 4-inch-long hollow cylinder, closed at one end, with a loop attached to the outside, is a mug, in contrast to apperceptive agnosia); *auditory agnosia* (impaired ability to recognize or identify familiar sounds or spoken words); *autotopagnosia* (see also separate entry, impaired ability to identify parts of one's own body, often indicative of lesions in the pathway between the thalamus and the parietal lobes; *compare* asomatagnosia, finger agnosia, topagnosia); *colour agnosia* (impaired ability to recognize or identify colours in spite of intact colour discrimination and adequate language skills; *compare* achromatopsia); *finger agnosia* (see also separate entry; impaired ability to recognize, identify, differentiate, name, select, or indicate individual fingers of either hand, hence a form of autotopagnosia); *gustatory agnosia* (impaired ability to recognize or identify tastes); *haptic agnosia* (another name for *tactile agnosia); *horologagnosia* (impaired ability to tell the time); *integrative agnosia* (intact ability to recognize elements of perceptual forms with impaired ability to integrate the elements into perceptual wholes); *logagnosia* (another name for Wernicke's aphasia, *see under* aphasia); *object blindness* (impaired ability to identify objects that are clearly perceived); *olfactory agnosia* (impaired ability to recognize or identify smells); *optic agnosia* (impaired ability to identify objects by sight, with intact ability to identify them by touch); *phonagnosia* (see also separate entry; impaired ability to identify people by their voices); *prosopagnosia* (see also separate entry; impaired ability to recognize or identify previously familiar faces, sometimes even those of close relatives, such faces being identified as faces but not as belonging to particular known people, this form of agnosia usually being associated with damage to the posterior right hemisphere); *simultanagnosia* (see also separate entry; impaired ability to perceive more than one object at the same time, often occurring as a symptom of *Bálint's syndrome); *tactile agnosia* (see also separate entry; impaired ability to recognize or identify objects by touch alone, also called *haptic agnosia, tactoagnosia, compare* ahylognosia, amorphognosia); *topagnosia* (impaired ability to identify which part of one's body has been touched, *compare* autotopagnosia); *topographagnosia* (see also separate entry; impaired ability to find one's way around, read maps, draw plans, and perform similar tasks, often associated with damage to the right hemisphere parietal lobe, comparable to *visuospatial agnosia); *transformational agnosia* (impaired ability to recognize objects viewed from unusual angles, such as a tennis racket seen from its side, based on the assumption that the impairment derives from a deficit in the ability to transform the major or minor axis—length or width—when it appears foreshortened, often associated with damage to the right parietal lobe, also called *apperceptive agnosia); *visual agnosia* (impaired ability to recognize or identify visual images or stimuli); *visual shape agnosia* (impaired ability to identify and discriminate between objects, usually associated with right hemisphere brain damage, also called *visual apperceptive agnosia*, in contrast to *associative agnosia; *visuospatial agnosia* (impaired ability to count a small number of scattered objects, coupled with peculiar alignment of handwriting, such as confining the words to only one half of a page, impairment in reading ability, impaired ability to copy simple drawings, often

associated with damage to the right hemisphere at the junction of the occipital and parietal lobes, *compare* topographagnosia). Also called *acatamathesia*.
[From Greek *a-* without + *gnosis* knowledge + *-ia* indicating a condition or quality]

agonist *n.* **1.** A person or animal engaged in a struggle. *Compare* antagonist (1). **2.** A muscle that contracts in the same direction as another. *Compare* antagonist (2). **3.** A substance that binds to *neuroreceptors and has the same effects in exciting or inhibiting the *postsynaptic cells as the *neurotransmitter that would otherwise bind to those sites. *See also* synergist. *Compare* antagonist (3).
[From Greek *agon* a festival of competitions, from *agein* to lead]

agoraphobia *n.* A *phobia or cluster of phobias associated with *anxiety or fear of leaving home, being in a crowd, visiting public places such as shopping areas, travelling alone in buses, trains, or aircraft, or being in other situations from which escape might be awkward or where a *panic attack would be difficult to handle. It is usually regarded as a *specific phobia, but some classifications (such as *ICD-10) assign it to a subcategory on its own.
[From Greek *agora* a market-place + *phobos* fear + *-ia* indicating a condition or quality]

agrammatism *n.* A form of *aphasia in which there is an impairment in ability to arrange words in their correct order, to use *function words properly, and/or to use *accidence appropriately in an *inflecting language. There is evidence to suggest that these deficits can occur separately.

agraphia *n.* An impairment in the ability to write, resulting from neurological damage to the language centres in the brain. The major forms are: *apraxic agraphia* (impaired ability to write in spite of an ability to spell words orally); *agraphia for numbers* (impaired ability to write numbers, also called *agraphic acalculia*); *ideational agraphia* (impaired ability to select appropriate letter forms in spite of an ability to copy written text); *orthographical agraphia* (impaired ability to translate spoken sounds into appropriate written forms, also called *lexical agraphia*); *phonological agraphia* (impaired ability to spell by sound, coupled with over-reliance on established spelling vocabulary); *spatial agraphia* (impaired ability to

arrange and orient writing appropriately on a page); *surface agraphia* (spelling by sound coupled with an impaired ability to spell irregular words). *See also* dysgraphia.
[From Greek *a-* without + *graphein* to write + *-ia* indicating a condition or quality]

agraphic acalculia *See under* agraphia.

agreeableness *n*. The quality of being pleasant. Also, one of the *Big Five personality factors, characterized by *traits such as kindness, generosity, warmth, unselfishness, and trust. Also called *pleasantness*. **agreeable** *adj*.

agrypnia *n*. An unusual name for *insomnia.
[From Greek *agrypnos* wakeful, from *agrein* to pursue + *hypnos* sleep + *-ia* indicating a condition or quality]

aha experience *n*. The feeling that accompanies sudden *insight (2). Also called an *aha reaction*.

ahedonia *n*. A variant form of *anhedonia.

ahylognosia *n*. Impaired ability to discriminate by touch such physical properties as weight, density, or texture, with intact ability to recognize size and shape. Also spelt *ahylagnosia*. *See also* agnosia. *Compare* amorphognosia, tactile agnosia.
[From Greek *a-* without + *hyle* matter + *gnosis* knowledge + *-ia* indicating a condition or quality]

AIDS *abbrev*. Acquired immune (or immuno-) deficiency syndrome, a disorder believed to be caused by the *HIV retrovirus and transmitted by infected blood entering the body, especially through transfusion or the sharing of needles by injecting drug users, by sexual intercourse, or from a mother to her unborn child via the placenta. It is characterized by destruction of *T lymphocytes and consequent loss of immunity to opportunistic infections. Almost half of all AIDS patients develop *HIV dementia. Also written as *Aids*.

AIDS dementia complex *n*. Another name for *HIV dementia. **ADC** *abbrev*.

AIDS-related complex *n*. A cluster of flu-like symptoms that are often premonitory of full-blown *AIDS: inflammation of lymph nodes, night sweats, persistent fevers, coughs, throat infection, and prolonged diarrhoea. **ARC** *abbrev*.

aim-inhibition *n*. In *psychoanalysis, the quality of an *instinct (3) that fails to achieve its direct mode of satisfaction or *instinctual aim but that obtains partial satisfaction from remote approximations of the behaviour or activity that would satisfy it. Sigmund Freud (1856–1939) introduced the concept in 1921 in his book *Group Psychology and the Analysis of the Ego* (Standard Edition, XVIII, pp. 69–143, at pp. 138–9) to explain the origin of sociable feelings of affection, the assumption being that if friendships and affection between relatives were not subject to aim-inhibition, then they would be overtly sexual. **aim-inhibited** *adj*.

aim of instinct *See* instinctual aim.

air crib *n*. A closed, electrically heated, sound-insulated compartment, about the size of an ordinary crib, in which a baby can be kept without clothing or blankets, one wall containing a panel of safety glass that can be opened like a window and across which a curtain can be drawn to darken the compartment, the floor consisting of tightly stretched moveable canvas operated like a roller towel, stored on a spool outside the compartment on one side and passing into a wire hamper on the other. Toys, including musical boxes, can be placed in the compartment, within which the baby is protected from airborne infections, dust, and allergens, and an advantage claimed for the air crib is that, because the baby's crying is almost inaudible from the outside and there are no hazards within it, *reinforcement (1) of crying is unlikely to occur. The device was invented by the US psychologist B(urrhus) F(rederic) Skinner (1904–90), who raised his second daughter Deborah in it and described the results in an article in the *Ladies Home Journal* in October 1945. The device attracted a great deal of controversy, but a study of 50 former air-crib babies and their parents, published in 1995, reported wholly positive results. Also called a *Skinner crib*.

air encephalogram *n*. Another name for a *pneumoencephalogram.

air theory *n*. A term used by the US psychologist James Jerome Gibson (1904–79) to refer to any theory of perception that explains perceptual phenomena such as object and space perception without reference to the surrounding context in which perceptions are embedded. *See also* direct perception.

[Alluding to something suspended in mid air without support]

akatamathesia *See* acatamathesia.

akathisia *n.* Restless *psychomotor agitation, indicated by fidgeting, inability to sit or stand still, pacing up and down, or rocking from foot to foot when standing, usually as a side-effect of *neuroleptic (1) medication.

[From Greek *a-* not + *kathizein* to sit still + *-ia* indicating a condition or quality]

akinaesthesia *n.* Absence of *kinaesthesis or muscle sense, usually resulting from damage to the central nervous system. Also called *akinaesthesis*. US *akinesthesia, akinesthesis*.

[From Greek *a-* without + *kineein* to move + *aisthesis* sensation, from *aisthanesthai* to feel + *-ia* indicating a condition or quality]

akinesia *n.* A decrease in spontaneous motor activity and a reduction in normal gestures, sometimes caused by a lesion in the supplementary motor area (*see under* motor cortex). *See also* neuroleptic-induced, parkinsonism. *Compare* bradykinesia.

[From Greek *a-* not + *kinesis* movement + *-ia* indicating a condition or quality]

akinetic apraxia *See under* apraxia.

akinetopsia *n.* A perceptual defect characterized by an inability to perceive motion, objects being visible while at rest but movement causing them to disappear, invariably associated with a lesion in Area V5 (also called MT) of the *visual cortex, towards the back of the *middle temporal gyrus. **akinetopsic** *adj.*

[From Greek *a-* without + *kinetikos* of or relating to motion, from *kineein* to move + *opsis* sight, from *ops* an eye + *-ia* indicating a condition or quality]

akrasia *n.* Weakness of will, or acting against one's principles. Also spelt *acrasia*.

[From Greek *a-* without + *kratos* power + *-ia* indicating a condition or quality]

alarm call *n.* A vocal *alarm signal.

alarm pheromone *n.* A *pheromone that is released by an animal as an *alarm signal and

that induces a fear or fright response in members of the same species.

alarm reaction *n.* The first stage of the *general adaptation syndrome to *stress (1), characterized by an initial fall in body temperature and blood pressure, followed by a countershock phase during which hormones such as *cortisol (hydrocortisone), *adrenalin (epinephrine), and *noradrenalin (norepinephrine) are secreted into the bloodstream and a biological defensive reaction begins. *See also* exhaustion stage, resistance stage.

alarm signal *n.* A sound or other communication that is emitted by a bird or an animal in response to a danger or threat and that is recognized by other members of the same species as a signal to take evasive action. It is sometimes classified as a type of *altruism, because it draws attention to the individual giving the alarm signal and sometimes exposes it to added danger. *See also* alarm call, alarm pheromone.

albedo *n.* Reflectivity, indexed by the proportion of incident light that an object reflects.

[From Latin *albedo* whiteness, from *albus* white]

alcohol *n.* Ethyl alcohol, a colourless volatile liquid and central nervous system *depressant drug that is produced by fermentation of sugar and is the psychoactive constituent of intoxicating beverages. Its pharmacological action, though not fully understood, is in part at least through the facilitation of the inhibitory neurotransmitter *GABA, probably through stimulation of the GABA receptor complex. Although the absorption and *bioavailability of alcohol depends on body weight, sex, how recently one has eaten, plus several other factors, roughly one unit of alcohol (one half pint of beer, one glass of wine, or one measure of spirits) taken by an average 150 lb (68 kg) person generally leads to a *blood alcohol concentration (BAC) of about 20 mg/dl and produces measurable deterioration in performance on complex hand–eye coordination tasks; two units taken in quick succession (alcohol normally being metabolized at about one unit per hour) leads to a BAC of 40 mg/dl and produces in addition a deterioration in visual acuity; three units leads to BAC 60 mg/dl and a loss of coordination;

seven units leads to 140 mg/dl and confusion, slurred speech, and *ataxia; 12 units leads to BAC 240 mg/dl and coma; and 14 units leads to 280 mg/dl and death. When a person drinks alcohol, inhibitory processes decline first, resulting in an exaggeration of spinal reflexes and the appearance of forms of behaviour (talkative, boisterous, aggressive) that are normally under the influence of social inhibition—this accounts for the mistaken notion that it is a central nervous system stimulant. Also called *ethanol*. Formula C_2H_5OH. **alcoholic** *adj.* **1.** Of or relating to *alcohol. *n.* **2.** A person addicted to *alcohol. **alcoholism** *n.* Addiction to *alcohol. *See also* alcohol-related disorders, drink-driving.
[From Arabic *al-koh'l*, antimony sulphide, a powder used in the Middle East as a cosmetic to darken the eyelids, from *al* the + *koh'l* finely divided, alluding to the fine vapour given off by liquids containing alcohol]

alcohol abuse *n.* A form of *substance abuse associated specifically with drinking alcohol, leading to serious problems of functioning at home, school, or work. When there is evidence of *tolerance (3), *withdrawal, or compulsive drinking, *alcohol dependence rather than alcohol abuse may be diagnosed. Preferred usage *alcohol misuse*.

alcohol amnestic disorder *n.* Another name for *Korsakoff's psychosis. Also called *alcohol amnesic syndrome*.

alcohol dependence *n.* A form of *substance dependence in which physiological *dependence (2) on alcohol is manifested by *tolerance (3) and *withdrawal symptoms. Also called *alcoholism*. *Compare* dipsomania.

alcohol hallucinosis *n.* An organic disorder characterized by auditory *hallucinations without *clouding of consciousness, usually during the first few days of *withdrawal from alcohol following prolonged alcohol misuse. *Compare* delirium tremens, hallucinosis, organic hallucinosis.

alcohol-related disorders *n.* *Substance-related disorders associated specifically with drinking alcohol, including *alcohol abuse, *alcohol dependence, *Korsakoff's psychosis, and a range of alcohol-induced disorders. *See* substance-induced disorders.

aldehyde dehydrogenase *n.* An enzyme that is involved in the metabolism of *alcohol and is blocked by the drug *Antabuse (disulfiram), leading to the accumulation of *acetaldehyde in the body.

aldosterone *n.* A *corticosteroid hormone belonging to the *mineralocorticoid group, secreted by the adrenal cortex in response to the kidney hormone *angiotensin II, involved in the regulation of mineral and water balance by its reciprocal action in causing the kidneys to retain sodium and excrete potassium while forming urine from venous blood.
[From *ald(ehyde)* + *ster(ol)* + *(ket)one*]

alethia *n.* Inability to forget.
[From Greek *a-* without + *lethe* forgetfulness + *-ia* indicating a condition or quality]

Alexander technique *n.* A technique for improving posture, bodily movements, and breathing, thereby reducing stress and increasing confidence, popular especially with actors, musicians, and other performing artists. *See also* body therapies.
[Named after the Australian actor and physiotherapist Frederick Mathias Alexander (1869–1955) who developed and promoted it in the 1930s]

alexia *n.* An inability to read written or printed words, usually called *dyslexia, also called *visual aphasia* or (non-technically) *word blindness*. *See also* dyslexia.
[From Greek *a-* without + *lexis* a word + *-ia* indicating a condition or quality]

alexic acalculia *n.* Selective impairment in ability to read numbers, also called *alexia for numbers*.

alexithymia *n.* A disturbance of affect and cognition indicated by difficulty in describing or recognizing one's own emotions, and a reduced affective and fantasy life.
[From Greek *alexein* to avert + *thymos* spirit + *-ia* indicating a condition or quality]

algaesthesia *n.* Sensitivity to pain. Also written *algaesthesis*. US *algesthesia*, *algesthesis*.
[From Greek *algesis* the sense of pain, from *algos* pain + *aisthesis* feeling + *-ia* indicating a condition or quality]

algesia *n.* The pain sense.

[From Greek *algesis* the sense of pain, from *algos* pain + *-ia* indicating a condition or quality]

algesimeter *n.* An instrument for measuring the acuteness of *pain sensations, usually by means of a needle that can be inserted into the skin to varying measured depths until a specified pain response is evoked. *See also* cold pressor pain, dolorimeter, ischaemic pain.
[From Greek *algesis* the sense of pain, from *algos* pain + *metron* a measure]

algolagnia *n.* Another name for *sadomasochism. Also called *algophilia*.
[From Greek *algos* pain + *lagneia* lust + *-ia* indicating a condition or quality]

algorithm *n.* Any well-defined computational procedure that takes a value or set of values as input and, after a finite sequence of computational steps, produces a value or set of values as output. Computer programs are the most familiar examples of algorithms, and another useful definition of an algorithm is any operation that can be carried out by a *Turing machine. Also more generally and informally, any step-by-step procedure for finding the unique solution to a problem. *Compare* heuristic.
[From Arabic *al-Khwārazmi* a native of Khwārazm (Khiva), the name by which the ninth-century Arab mathematician Abu Ja'far Mohommed ben Musa came to be known]

algorithmic *adj.* Of or relating to an *algorithm, or more generally having a definite path to a solution.

aliasing *n.* In a visual or auditory signal or any periodic or oscillating variable or time series, a distortion resulting from insufficiently high resolution when the variable is sampled at a frequency that is too low in relation to the signal's frequency, a familiar cinematographic example being the *wagon wheel illusion in which the wheels of a stagecoach appear to turn slowly one way, then slowly the other way as it gathers speed. A sine wave of 1,000 hertz would appear stationary if it were sampled exactly once per millisecond (thousandth of a second) or once every two milliseconds, and so on, and it would appear to be cycling very slowly if sampled at a frequency very close to once per millisecond. *See also* stroboscope.

[Coined by the US statistician John Wilder Tukey (1915–2000) from Latin *alias* at another time, from *alius* other]

alienation *n.* **1.** Turning away; inducing someone to become indifferent or hostile or causing their affections to be diverted. **2.** The state of being an outsider or feeling detached from society. **3.** A state in which one's emotions are experienced as foreign so that the self and the outside world appear unreal. *See also* depersonalization, derealization.
[From Latin *alienus* foreign, from *alius* other + *-ation* indicating a process or condition]

alien hand sign *n.* A form of *apraxia, usually resulting from a lesion in the *corpus callosum, in which a hand (usually the left) performs actions independent of its owner's will.

alienist *n.* An old-fashioned word for a *psychiatrist.

alimentary *adj.* Pertaining to nutrition or providing nourishment.
[From Latin *alimentum* food or nourishment, from *alere* to nourish]

alimentary canal *n.* The tubular passage from the mouth to the anus through which food passes and within which digestion takes place, comprising the *pharynx, *oesophagus, *stomach, *small intestine, and *large intestine. Also called the *digestive tract* or *gastrointestinal tract*.

alimentation *n.* Nourishment, sustenance, or support.

aliphatic *adj.* Fatty, belonging to the class of non-aromatic methane derivatives or open-chain organic compounds. Aliphatic and *aromatic hydrocarbons in petrol or gasoline, glue, paint thinners, and some aerosol propellants are *psychotropic when inhaled. *See also* inhalant, inhalant-related disorders, solvent abuse.
[From Greek *aleiphar, aleiphatos* oil + *-ikos* of, relating to, or resembling]

alkali *n.* Any substance that when dissolved in water accepts positively charged hydrogen *ions and produces a corrosive solution having a *pH value more than 7. *See also* base (1). *Compare* acid. **alkaline** *adj.* **alkalinity** *n.* The degree to which a solution is *alkaline.
[From Arabic *al-qili* the ashes]

alkaloid n. Any of a group of physiologically active and often *psychotropic nitrogenous *bases (1) occurring naturally in plants, being usually colourless, crystalline in structure, and bitter-tasting, including *apomorphine, *atropine, *belladonna, *bromocriptine, *capsaicin, *cocaine, *codeine, *crack, *ergot, *hyoscyamine, the *indole alkaloids (psilocybin and DMT), *mescaline, *morphine, *muscarine, *nicotine, *physostigmine, *quinine, *reserpine, *scopolamine, *strychnine, and the *xanthine derivatives (caffeine, theobromine, and theophylline). [From alkali + -oid indicating likeness or resemblance, from Greek eidos shape or form]

allaesthesia n. A disturbance of body *schema in which tactile stimulation on one side of the body is perceived on the other, usually as a result of a lesion in the cerebral cortex, brainstem, or spinal cord. Also spelt allesthesia. Also called allochiria. [From Greek allos other + aisthesis sensation, from aisthanesthai to feel + -ia indicating a condition or quality]

Allais paradox n. A *paradox of decision making that usually elicits responses inconsistent with *expected utility theory. First, a choice is made between

- A $500,000 with probability 1 (certainty)
- B $2,500,000, $500,000, or $0 with probabilities 10 per cent, 89 per cent, and 1 per cent respectively

Second, a choice is made between

- C $500,000 or $0 with probabilities 11 per cent and 89 per cent
- D $2,500,000 or $0 with probabilities 10 per cent and 90 per cent respectively.

Most people prefer A to B, because they prefer the certainty of winning a large amount to the small probability of winning an even larger amount coupled with a risk of winning nothing at all. But most of the same people prefer D to C, because the chances of winning are nearly the same in both cases but the prize is much larger in D than in C. Writing $u(2,500,000)$, $u(500,000)$, and $u(0)$ for the utilities that a person attaches to the corresponding amounts of money, the first preference implies that

$$0.11u(500,000) > 0.10u(2,500,000) + 0.01u(0),$$

and the second implies that

$$0.11u(500,000) < 0.10u(2,500,000) + 0.01u(0),$$

a contradiction, showing that expected utility theory does not accurately describe human choice behaviour. See also revealed preference, risk aversion. Compare common ratio effect, Ellsberg paradox, modified Ellsberg paradox, St Petersburg paradox. [Named after the French economist Maurice (Félix Charles) Allais (born 1911) who formulated it in 1953]

allegro speech n. Rapid speaking exhibiting features typical of fluent, casual, connected speech, such as strue for it's true. See also elision, haplology, intrusion. Compare lento speech. [From Italian allegro rapid, from Latin alacer brisk]

allele n. Short for allelomorph, one of two or more alternative versions of a *gene that can occupy a particular locus on a chromosome, each responsible for a different characteristic or *phenotype, such as a different eye colour. A pair of alleles are often represented by upper-case and lower-case forms of the same roman letter, such as A and a. See also additive alleles, antimorph, balanced polymorphism, complementation, dominant gene, epistasis, genetic polymorphism, Hardy–Weinberg law, heterozygous, homozygous, recessive gene, segregation of alleles. [From Greek allel one another]

allergen n. Any substance, usually a foreign protein, that functions as an *antigen and causes an allergic reaction. See allergy. [From Greek allos other + ergon activity or work]

allergy n. An acquired hypersensitivity of the body to certain *antigens or *allergens. A typical example is hay fever, which is an allergy to certain types of pollen. Also, colloquially, any aversion or dislike. **allergic** adj. [From Greek allos other + ergon activity or work]

allesthesia See allaesthesia.

alliaceous adj. Of or relating to the taste or smell of garlic or onion. [From Latin allium garlic + -aceus of a certain kind, related to, or resembling]

allochiria n. Another name for *allaesthesia. [From Greek allos other + cheir a hand + -ia indicating a condition or quality]

allocortex *n.* All parts of the *cerebral cortex that do not belong to the six-layered *neocortex. *See* archaecortex, mesocortex, palaeocortex.
[From Greek *allos* other + Latin *cortex* bark or outer layer]

allo-erotism *n.* In *psychoanalysis, sexual satisfaction through an external *instinctual object, in contrast to *auto-erotism. Also called *allo-eroticism*.
[From Greek *allos* other + *eros* love or sexual desire + *-ismos* indicating a state or condition]

allomone *n.* Any of a number of chemical substances with communicative functions, secreted externally by an organism and affecting the behaviour or physiology of members of one or more other species. *See also* kairomone. *Compare* pheromone.
[From Greek *allos* other + *horman* to stimulate]

allomorph *n.* One of the variant forms assumed by a single *morpheme in different circumstances, such as each of the forms of the negating prefix *in-* in the words *indirect*, *irreducible*, *improbable*, and *ignoble*. **allomorphic** *adj.*
[From Greek *allos* other + *morphe* form]

allopathy *n.* Orthodox pharmacological therapy for physical and mental disorders, using drugs having effects that are opposite to those of the disorder, in contradistinction to *homeopathy.
[From Greek *allos* other + *pathos* suffering]

allophone *n.* One of the variant forms of a single *phoneme, such as the voiced non-fricative form of the phoneme /r/ in the word *row* or the voiceless fricative form of the same phoneme in the word *tree*. Further examples are the allophones of the phoneme /t/ in *tip* (aspirated), *stay* (unaspirated), *button* (nasalized), and *bottle* (laterally articulated). *See also* phone. **allophonic** *adj.*
[From Greek *allos* other + *phone* a sound]

alloplastic *adj.* Of or relating to *adaptation (1) through alteration of the external environment. *Compare* autoplastic.
[From Greek *allos* other + *plastikos* mouldable, from *plassein* to form + *-ikos* of, relating to, or resembling]

all-or-none law *n.* A fundamental proposition about nerve impulses according to which the strength or intensity of a *stimulus (1) does not affect the properties of an *action potential that it initiates, although it may affect the frequency with which action potentials occur. Also called the *all-or-none principle* or the *all-or-nothing law* or *principle*. *See also* relative refractory period.

Allport–Vernon–Lindzey Study of Values *n.* A test designed to measure the relative strengths of the six basic values identified by the German psychologist and educator Eduard Spranger (1882–1963) in his book *Lebensformen* (1914, English translation *Types of Men*, 1928), namely theoretical, economic, aesthetic, social, political, and religious. It consists of a series of multiple-choice questions referring to alternative activities or occupations from which the respondent chooses the ones that are most appealing. It is often interpreted as essentially an *interest inventory. Also called the *Study of Values*.
[Named after the US psychologist Gordon W(illard) Allport (1897–1967), the English psychologist Philip E(wart) Vernon (1905–87), and the US psychologist Gardner Lindzey (born 1920) who published it jointly in its revised version in 1951, a preliminary version having been published by Allport and Vernon in 1931]

alogia *n.* Literally wordless, but usually (in relation to one of the *negative symptoms of schizophrenia, for example) taken to mean impoverishment of thought inferred from *poverty of speech or *poverty of content.
[From Greek *a-* without + *logia* words, from *logos* word + *-ia* indicating a condition or quality]

alpha-adrenergic receptor *See under* adrenergic receptor.

alpha blocking *n.* Suppression of the *alpha wave in an *EEG trace of a person who pays *attention to or concentrates on something.

alpha element *n.* In *psychoanalysis, a term introduced by the Indian-born British psychoanalyst Wilfred R(uprecht) Bion (1897–1979) to denote any mental element that is available for transformation by the *alpha function into a *beta element.

alpha fibre *n.* A large-diameter, thickly myelinated type of *efferent somatic nerve fibre,

such as the fibre supplying a *skeletal muscle, composed of alpha motor neurons and having high conduction velocity. US *alpha fiber*. Also written α *fibre*. *Compare* C fibre, gamma fibre, Ia fibre, Ib fibre, II fibre.
[From *alpha* (α) the first letter of the Greek alphabet]

alpha-foetoprotein *n*. A protein produced in the liver of a human foetus. Unusually low levels in the amniotic fluid or blood of an expectant mother may indicate *Down's syndrome in the foetus, and unusually high levels spina bifida. *See also* amniocentesis. Also spelt *alphafetoprotein*. **afp** *abbrev*.

alpha function *n*. In *psychoanalysis, a term introduced by the Indian-born British psychoanalyst Wilfred R(uprecht) Bion (1897–1979) to denote the process whereby the raw material of sensory experience, namely *beta elements, are transformed into elements suitable for mental 'digestion' in the form of *alpha elements.

alpha male *n*. The highest-ranked male member of a *dominance hierarchy, *hook order, or *pecking order. Also written α *male*.

alpha-methylparatyrosine *n*. A chemical closely related to *tyrosine that attaches to the enzyme *tyrosine hydroxylase, preventing the enzyme from metabolizing tyrosine into *dopa, causing a decrease in the synthesis of dopa, and therefore also of the *catecholamines dopamine, adrenalin (epinephrine), and noradrenalin (norepinephrine). **AMPT** *abbrev*.

alpha motor neuron *n*. The largest type of spinal *motor neuron, supplying *skeletal muscles and forming *alpha fibres. Also called an *alpha motoneuron*. *Compare* gamma motor neuron, Renshaw cell.

alpha movement *n*. A form of *apparent movement that is produced when stimuli of different sizes, such as bars of different lengths, are presented in an alternating pattern with an interstimulus interval of about 60 milliseconds, the visual illusion being created of a single object increasing and decreasing in size. Also called *alpha motion*. *See also* Korte's laws. *Compare* beta movement, delta movement, gamma movement.

alphanumeric *adj*. Of or relating to a character set, data set, or variable, consisting of letters of the alphabet, numerals, and usually a few other symbols such as punctuation marks and basic mathematical symbols. *See also* byte. [From *alphabet* + *numeric*]

alpha receptor *n*. Another name for an alpha *adrenergic receptor.

alpha reliability coefficient *n*. Another name for *Cronbach's alpha.

alpha wave *n*. A high-amplitude *EEG wave with a frequency of 8–12 hertz, characteristic of relaxed wakefulness, usually in a person whose eyes are closed. Also called an *alpha rhythm*. *See also* alpha blocking.

alprazolam *n*. A member of the *benzodiazepine group of drugs, used as a sedative and anxiolytic. Also called *Xanax* (trademark). *See also* sedative-, hypnotic-, or anxiolytic-related disorders.

altered state of consciousness *n*. Any abnormal form of *consciousness, including *derealization, *depersonalization, *hypnosis, *oceanic feeling, *peak experience, or intoxication with a *hallucinogen or *euphoriant drug. **ASC** *abbrev*.

alternating personality *n*. Another name for *multiple personality disorder. *See* dissociative identity disorder.

alternating perspective *n*. A *perspective reversal, or change in the apparent angle from which something is being viewed, that occurs while viewing certain *ambiguous figures such as the *Necker cube, *Schröder staircase, or *Scripture's blocks.

alternative forms *n*. In psychometrics, two or more similar versions of a psychometric test. If they are similar in content but have not been shown to have similar psychometric properties, then they are also called *comparable forms*; if they have similar *means, *standard deviations, and *correlations with other tests, then they are also called *parallel forms*; and if they are similar in all important psychometric properties, then they are also called *equivalent forms*. Also, especially in the US, called *alternate forms*.

alternative hypothesis n. In statistics, a hypothesis that functions as an alternative to the *null hypothesis and typically asserts that the *independent variable has an effect on the *dependent variable that cannot be explained by chance alone. Also called an *experimental hypothesis*.

altricial adj. Of or relating to species of birds whose young are hatched naked, blind, and dependent on their parents for feeding in the nest. Compare precocial. **altrices** n. *Altricial birds.
[From Latin altrices nurses, from altrix a nurse, from alere to nourish]

altruism n. In social psychology and sociobiology, behaviour that benefits another individual or other individuals in terms of direct advantages or chances of survival and reproduction at some cost to the benefactor. See also alarm signal, prosocial behaviour, reciprocal altruism. **altruist** n. One who acts with *altruism. **altruistic** adj. Compare selfish.
[French altruisme, from Italian altrui others, from Latin alteri huic to this other]

altruistic suicide See under suicide.

alveolar adj. Pertaining to the alveolar ridge, the hard, bony part of the palate immediately behind the upper front teeth, and descriptive of speech sounds articulated with the tongue tip against the alveolar ridge, such as the initial sounds in the words date, late, name, say, tea, and zoo. See also place of articulation. **alveolus** n.
[From Latin alveolus a small depression, referring to the tooth sockets]

alveolar hypoventilation syndrome See central alveolar hypoventilation syndrome.

Alzheimer's disease n. A degenerative brain disease with insidious onset beginning before 65 years of age, followed by slow development over several years, characterized by *dementia called dementia of the Alzheimer type (DAT), loss of memory, and emotional instability, accompanied by postmortem evidence of *amyloid plaques, *neurofibrillary tangles, and other brain pathology, usually leading to death between four and twelve years after the onset of the disease. Some authorities believe that the amyloid plaques are responsible for the symptoms and that the neurofibrillary tangles are secondary; others believe that the neurofibrillary tangles are primary and the amyloid plaques are secondary. The disorder is associated with a deficit of the neurotransmitter *acetylcholine and may be caused by *mutations in *mitochondrial DNA, by defects in *chromosome 21, or by a *prion. See also Down's syndrome, nucleus basalis of Meynert. Compare Pick's disease, SDAT. **AD** abbrev.
[Named after the German neurologist Alois Alzheimer (1864–1915) who first described the brain lesions associated with it in 1907]

amacrine adj. Lacking a conspicuous *axon, referring especially to neurons in the middle layer of the *retina that link *bipolar cells and retinal *ganglion cells and that make only lateral connections, their cell bodies lying in the *inner nuclear layer and connecting with other cells in the *inner plexiform layer. There are many different kinds, the functions of which are not well understood. Compare horizontal cell.
[From Greek ama as soon as + krinein to separate]

amafufunyane n. The plural form of the word *ufufunyane in Nguni languages; a *culture-bound syndrome found mainly among young women in Xhosa-speaking communities of southern Africa, exhibiting the same signs and symptoms as ufufunyane, and distinguished locally from thwasa (see spell).
[From Xhosa amafufunyane characters or voices that have entered and taken control of a person, from ukufuya to possess (such things as herds of cattle) or to treat a person as a possession]

Amanita muscaria n. The *fly agaric mushroom, sometimes eaten for its *psychedelic effects. See also hallucinogen, magic mushroom, teonanactyl. Compare cohoba.
[Latin]

amantadine n. Amantadine hydrochloride, an antiviral drug that blocks the uptake of *dopamine in the brain, increasing the amount that remains available, and is used in the treatment of *Parkinson's disease and *neuroleptic-induced conditions. Also called Symmetrel (trademark). See also antiparkinsonian.
[An anagram of adamantine impregnable, impenetrable, or unbreakable]

amaurosis *n.* *Blindness without damage to the eyes, usually associated with lesions in the optic nerves. *Compare* amblyopia, anopia. **amaurotic** *adj.*
[From Greek *amauros* dark]

amaurotic familial idiocy *n.* Another name for *Tay–Sachs disease.

ambient system *n.* The aspect of vision that governs spatial orientation, using information from both *central vision and *peripheral vision. *Compare* focal system.
[From Latin *ambiens* going around, from *ambi-* round or about + *ire* to go]

ambiguity tolerance *See under* intolerance of ambiguity.

ambiguous figure *n.* An image such as the *Mach illusion, *Necker cube, *reversible goblet, *Schröder staircase, *Scripture's blocks, or *young girl/old woman figure, the perception of which appears to oscillate or flip involuntarily between (usually) two alternatives, one perception or interpretation completely excluding the other while it persists. Although such figures are not strictly illusory, they are almost invariably included in discussions of visual illusions. Also called an *oscillating figure* or a *reversible figure*. *See also* figure–ground reversal, perspective reversal, top-down processing, visual illusion. *Compare* impossible figure.

ambilingual *adj.* **1.** Able to speak two languages equally fluently. *n.* **2.** A person who can speak two languages with equal facility. Also called a *balanced bilingual*. *Compare* unbalanced bilingual.
[From Latin *ambi-* both + *lingua* tongue + *-alis* of or relating to]

ambivalence *n.* The coexistence in one person of two opposing emotions, desires, beliefs, or behavioural tendencies directed towards the same *instinctual object, especially love and hate. The term was coined in 1910 by the Swiss psychiatrist Eugen Bleuler (1857–1939), who considered ambivalence to be a major sign of *schizophrenia, and Sigmund Freud (1856–1939) introduced it into *psychoanalysis in an article in 1912 on 'The Dynamics of Transference' (*Standard Edition*, XII, pp. 98–108). *See also* defusion of instincts, depressive position, paranoid-schizoid position. **ambivalent** *adj.*

[From Latin *ambi-* both + *valens* being strong, from *valere* to be strong]

amblyacusia *n.* Any impairment of the sense of hearing. Also spelt *amblyacousia*. Also called *amblyacusis* or *amblyacousis*. **amblyacusic** *adj.*
[From Greek *amblys* dull + *akousis* hearing, from *akouein* to hear + *-ia* indicating a condition or quality]

amblyaphia *n.* Any impairment of the sense of touch.
[From Greek *amblys* dull + *haphe* touch + *-ia* indicating a condition or quality]

amblygeustia *n.* Any impairment of the sense of taste.
[From Greek *amblys* dull + *geusis* taste + *-ia* indicating a condition or quality]

amblyopia *n.* Impaired vision without any apparent damage to the eye or the optic nerve. *Compare* amaurosis, anopia.
[From Greek *amblys* dull + *ops* an eye + *-ia* indicating a condition or quality]

amblyopia ex anopsia *n.* *Amblyopia caused by disuse of an eye, especially monocular blindness associated with *strabismus and consequent suppression of the image from one eye through *binocular rivalry, the most common cause of amblyopia and of *blindness in general. Also spelt *amblyopia ex anoopsia*. Also called *suppression amblyopia*.
[From Greek, literally dull vision from sightlessness]

amenorrhoea *n.* Pathological absence of menstruation. US *amenorrhea*.
[From Greek *a-* without + *men* month + *rhoia* a flow, from *rhein* to flow]

amentia *n.* Severe *mental retardation. *Compare* dementia.
[From Latin *a-* without + *mens, mentis* a mind + *-ia* indicating a condition or quality]

American College Testing Program *n.* An *achievement test, designed to measure academic ability, used to select candidates for admission to some colleges and universities in the US. It comprises four subtests in English, mathematics, natural sciences, and social sciences. *Compare* Scholastic Aptitude Test. **ACTP** *abbrev.*

American Sign Language *n.* A communication system for deaf people in the US in which meaning is conveyed by hand signals and the positions of the hands relative to the upper part of the body. *See also* sign language. *Compare* British Sign Language. Also called *Ameslan*. **ASL** *abbrev.*

Ameslan *n.* Another name for *American Sign Language.

Ames room *n.* A distorted room that appears almost normal when viewed with one eye through a peephole in one of its walls, but the floor, ceiling, and side walls of which are actually trapezium-shaped (US *trapezoidal*) rather than rectangular, resulting in visual illusions relating to the sizes of objects or people within the room. Some viewers experience an ineffable strangeness that is believed to result from trying to accommodate the focal length of the eye to the far corners of the room that appear to be the same distance from the peephole but are not. Also called the *Ames illusion* or the *distorted-room illusion. See also* Honi phenomenon, transactionalism. *Compare* trapezoidal window.
[Named after the US painter and psychologist Adelbert Ames, Jr (1880–1955) who constructed the first such room in 1946, although the idea had been conceived in the late 19th century by the German physiologist, physicist, and mathematician Hermann Ludwig Ferdinand von Helmholtz (1821–94)]

Ames window *n.* Another name for the *trapezoidal window.

ametropia *n.* An imperfection in the refractive properties of the *crystalline lens of the eye, resulting in an inability to focus images on the retina and causing partial blindness.
[From Greek *ametros* unmeasured, from *a-* without + *metron* a measure + *ops* an eye + *-ia* indicating a condition or quality]

amfetamine *See* amphetamine.

amimia *n.* Inability to make meaningful *gestures (1) or to understand the gestures of others. *See also* kinesics.
[From Greek *a-* without + *mimos* mime + *-ia* indicating a condition or quality]

amine *n.* An organic compound formed from ammonia by replacing one or more of the hydrogen atoms with one or more hydrocarbon *radicals (2). Amines such as *adrenalin (epinephrine), *noradrenalin (norepinephrine), *dopamine, *histamine, *serotonin, and *tryptamine are of special importance in neurobiology because of their function as *neurotransmitters. *See also* biogenic amine, catecholamine, imidazoleamine, indoleamine, monoamine.

amino acid *n.* Any of a group of organic compounds containing at least one amino group (NH_2) and one carboxyl group (COOH), just 20 of which from among more than 100 that occur in nature forming the component molecules of all *peptides, *polypeptides, and *proteins of which living cells are composed. They include non-essential amino acids, which can be synthesized in the body, and essential amino acids, which cannot be synthesized in the body and must therefore be supplied in the diet. *See* aspartic acid, creatine, dopa, glutamic acid, glycine, phenylalanine, tryptophan, tyrosine. *See also* codon, genetic code.

Amitril *n.* A proprietary name for the tricyclic antidepressant drug *amitriptyline.
[Trademark]

amitriptyline *n.* Amitriptyline hydrochloride, one of the most commonly prescribed of the *tricyclic antidepressant drugs, used in the treatment of depression, and of anorexia nervosa and bulimia nervosa when accompanied by depression, and as an adjunctive treatment of neurogenic pain. It acts by blocking the reuptake mechanism of amine *neurotransmitters, allowing them to accumulate at *synapses (1) in the central nervous system. Also called *Amitril, Elavil, Endep, Laroxyl, Saroten,* and *Triptafen* (trademarks). Formula: $C_{20}H_{23}N$.

Ammon's horn *n.* Another name for the main part of the *hippocampus. The entire hippocampal formation includes not only Ammon's horn but also the subiculum and the dentate gyrus. Also called *cornu ammonis.*
[Named after the Egyptian deity Ammon, often depicted with a ram's head, somewhat resembling the shape of the hippocampus]

amnesia *n.* Loss of memory, the most common forms generally affecting *declarative memory rather than *procedural memory.

See also anterograde amnesia, confabulation, global amnesia, infantile amnesia, mnemonic, retrograde amnesia, source amnesia, transient global amnesia. *Compare* hypermnesia.

[From Greek *amnesia* oblivion, from *a-* without + *mnasthai* to remember + *-ia* indicating a condition or quality]

amnesic syndrome *See* amnestic disorder.

amnestic disorder *n.* A *mental disorder characterized by a significant decline in the capacity to learn and recall new information, and often also a decline in the recall of previously learnt information or experiences, leading to impairment in social or occupational functioning, the symptoms not occurring exclusively during delirium or dementia. The disorder may result from a *general medical condition, including head injury, medication, or exposure to a toxin, and there is a variant form of substance-induced persisting amnestic disorder often caused by a deficiency of vitamins (especially thiamine) following prolonged alcohol misuse. Also called *amnesic syndrome. See also* cognitive disorders.

[From Greek *amnestos* forgetting, from *a-* not + *mnasthai* to remember]

amniocentesis *n.* Extraction of a small amount of amniotic fluid through a hollow needle from the uterus of a pregnant woman to detect foetal abnormalities such as *Down's syndrome. See also* alpha-foetoprotein.

[From Greek *amnion* the innermost membrane enveloping an embryo + *kentesis* a puncture, from *kentein* to prick]

amobarbital *n.* Amylobarbital sodium, a short-acting *barbiturate drug and central nervous system *depressant, used as a sedative and hypnotic drug, and sometimes taken as a street drug. Also called *amylobarbitone, Amytal* (trademark). Formula $C_{11}H_{18}N_2O_3Na$.

[From *amyl*, from Greek *amylon* starch + *hyle* matter, amyl having been originally synthesized from starch + *barbit(uric) (acid)* + *-al* indicating a pharmaceutical product]

amodal completion *n.* Perceptual *filling-in of an occluded region of an object or image. *Compare* phonemic restoration.

[From Latin *a* from or away from + *modus* a measure or manner + *-alis* of or relating to]

amok *n.* A *culture-bound syndrome originally reported in Malaysia but later also in Indonesia, Laos, the Philippines, Papua New Guinea, Polynesia, Puerto Rico, and among the Navajo in North America, characterized by a period of hostile brooding, often precipitated by a perceived insult or affront, followed by an outburst of uncontrolled aggression directed at people and objects in the vicinity (*running amok*) with *paranoid ideation and *automatism, followed by exhaustion and *amnesia for the violent behaviour. It is often interpreted in Western cultures as a *dissociative disorder. Also called *amuck. See also* cafard, iich'aa, mal de pelea.

[From Malay *amoq* a furious assault]

amorphognosia *n.* Impaired ability to recognize by touch the size and shape of objects. Also called *amorphognosis. See also* agnosia. *Compare* ahylognosia, tactile agnosia.

[From Greek *a-* without + *morphe* form + *gnosis* knowledge + *-ia* indicating a condition or quality]

AMP *abbrev.* Adenosine monophosphate, a constituent *nucleotide of *DNA and *RNA consisting of *adenine, *deoxyribose, and a *phosphate group. Also called *adenylic acid. See also* cyclic AMP.

amphetamine *n.* A synthetic *sympathomimetic drug that is often used as a street drug and as a medication to control the symptoms of narcolepsy in adults and attention-deficit/hyperactivity disorder and hyperkinetic disorders in children, and that acts as a central nervous system *stimulant, causing the release of *noradrenalin (norepinephrine) and *dopamine from noradrenergic and dopaminergic neurons and blocking the reuptake of dopamine, leading to feelings of euphoria that can last for several hours, with occasional unpleasant side-effects such as panic, anxiety, paranoia, and insomnia. Also called *Benzedrine* (trademark) or *speed* (street name). Formula $C_9H_{13}N$. *See also* amphetamine-related disorders, dextroamphetamine, methamphetamine, methylphenidate. *Compare* cocaine, ecstasy (2).

[From its chemical composition *a(lpha)* + *m(ethyl)* + *ph(enyl)* + *et(hyl)* + *amine*]

amphetamine psychosis *n.* A condition resembling *schizophrenia caused by an overdose of *amphetamine.

amphetamine-related disorders *n.*
*Substance-related disorders associated
specifically with *amphetamine and amphet-
amine-like substances such as *dextroamphetamine and *methamphetamine (speed).
Included among these disorders are amphetamine misuse, amphetamine dependence, and
a range of amphetamine-induced disorders.
See substance-induced disorders.

amphipathic *adj.* Pertaining to a molecule
that has one hydrophilic end (attracted to
water) and one hydrophobic end (repulsed by
water), such as are found in the *lipid components of *cell membranes and in detergents.
See also lipid bilayer.
[From Greek *amphi* both + *pathos* feeling + *-ikos*
of, relating to, or resembling]

amplification *n.* Enlargement: expressing an
idea more expansively, or increasing the *amplitude of a sound. In *analytical psychology,
*interpretation (2) of a dream-image through
*directed association and exploration of
mythology, mysticism, folklore, and cultural
symbols.
[From Latin *amplificare* to make more copious]

amplitude *n.* Size, extent, or magnitude, especially of a vibratory movement or the displacement of a periodic oscillation or wave,
its *instantaneous amplitude* being its displacement at a specific moment from the zero or
mean position and its *peak amplitude* being the
maximum displacement that it attains, peak
amplitude usually being implied when the
term is unqualified. It is the physical counterpart of the psychological sensations of loudness in a sound wave and of lightness or
brightness in a light wave. *See also* decibel.
[From Latin *amplitudo* breadth, from *amplus*
spacious]

ampulla *n.* A small vessel such as a miniature
two-handled ancient Roman flask; also any
membranous *vesicle, especially the bulge in
each *semicircular canal with its crest-shaped
inner surface or crista containing *hair cells.
It is part of the *vestibular system and plays a
part in sensations of body orientation.
[From Latin *ampulla* a small flagon, irregular
diminutive of *amphora* a flagon]

amputee *See under* acrotomorphilia,
apotemnophilia.

amuck *See* amok.

amurakh *See* latah.

amusia *n.* Inability to recognize or reproduce
tunes.

amygdala *n.* An almond-shaped brain structure in the *limbic system at the base of the
inside of each *temporal lobe, contiguous
with the olfactory cortex, controlling the experience and expression of emotion and involved in motivation, aggression, feeding,
and (through its links with the hippocampus)
long-term memory. Electrical stimulation of
this area usually produces an intense emotion
of fear. Ablation of the amygdala has been
used to treat *intermittent explosive disorder
or other forms of *impulse-control disorder.
Also called the *amygdaloid body* or *amygdaloid
complex. See also* kindling. **amygdalae** *pl.*
[From Latin *amygdala* an almond, from Greek
amygdale an almond]

amygdalohippocampectomy *n.* A neurosur-
gical procedure that is used for the treatment
of certain forms of *temporal lobe epilepsy
and that involves the removal of most of the
*amygdala and the *anterior part of the *hip-
pocampus, the brain structures where the
focus of the epilepsy is located.

amyl nitrite *n.* The best known of the *nitrite
inhalants, an amber-coloured, fruity-smelling
liquid that acts as a peripheral *vasodilator,
functioning for some users as an *aphrodisiac, and that also causes a decrease in oxygen in the brain. A common street name for
amyl nitrite capsules is *poppers*.
[From Greek *amylon* starch + *hyle* matter, amyl
having been originally synthesized from
starch + *nitrite* a salt or ester of nitrous acid]

amylobarbitone *n. See* amobarbital.

amyloid plaque *n.* A deposit of insoluble beta-
amyloid protein (BAP) occurring in the brains
of most people over 70 years old, causing degeneration of neurons, and found abundantly
in people with *Alzheimer's disease, especially in the cerebral cortex, hippocampus,
amygdala, and entorhinal cortex. The protein
is made up of approximately 40 amino acids
and is an abnormal breakdown product of a
larger precursor protein that is encoded by
a gene on *chromosome 21 and is present in

healthy brains, though with an unknown function. Also called a *senile plaque*. *See also* neurofibrillary tangle, progressive supranuclear palsy.

[Named in 1853 by the German pathologist Rudolf Ludwig Karl Virchow (1821–1902) from Greek *amylon* starch + *-oeides* denoting resemblance of form, from *eidos* shape or form, based on the false assumption that it consists of a starchy substance]

amyotrophic lateral sclerosis *n*. A type of *motor neuron disease beginning in middle age and progressing rapidly, causing death within five years, characterized by weakness and *atrophy of the muscles initially of the hands, forearms, and legs, but spreading to most of the body and face, with *dysarthria and *dysphagia. Also called *Lou Gehrig's disease*. **ALS** *abbrev*.

[From Greek *a-* without + *mys* muscle + *trophe* nourishment]

Amytal *n*. A proprietary name for the short-acting barbiturate drug *amobarbital (amylobarbitone).
[Trademark]

anabolic steroid *n*. Any of several synthetic *steroid hormones, specifically *androgens, used in the treatment of injuries and (illegally) by some athletes for body building. They sometimes induce a sense of euphoria and exaggerated self-importance, but after repeated use this may give way to listlessness, irritability, and general dysphoria. *See also* performance enhancer, substance abuse, substance-related disorders. *Compare* steroid.
[From Greek *anabole* a heaping up, from *ana* up + *bole* a throw]

anabolism *n*. A constructive form of *metabolism involving the synthesis of proteins and storage of energy. *Compare* catabolism. **anabolic** *adj*.
[From Greek *anabole* a heaping up, from *ana* up + *bole* a throw + *-ismos* indicating a state or condition]

anaclitic *adj*. In *psychoanalysis, of, relating to, or characterized by strong emotional dependence on another person, exemplified by the behaviour of an infant at the mother's breast. Sigmund Freud (1856–1939) introduced the concept in 1905 in his book *Three Essays on the Theory of Sexuality* (*Standard Edition*,

VII, pp. 130–243, at pp. 181–5). *See also* anaclitic depression, anaclitic object-choice.
anaclisis *n*. The state or condition of being *anaclitic.
[From Greek *anaklitos* leaning up against, from *ana* up + *klinein* to lean + *-ikos* of or relating to]

anaclitic depression *n*. A form of *depression manifested by infants, usually triggered by sudden separation from a parent after having had a normal relationship for at least six months, characterized by crying, apprehension, withdrawal, *anorexia, and *dyssomnias. The disorder was introduced and named in 1946 by the Austrian psychoanalyst René A. Spitz (1887–1974). *See also* anaclitic, attachment theory, hospitalism, maternal deprivation, separation anxiety, separation anxiety disorder.

anaclitic object-choice *n*. In *psychoanalysis, a form of *object-choice in which one chooses a love-object to resemble a parental figure, being attracted to people who have the ability to feed, care, and protect one. It is usually explained by the fact that the sexual instinct initially develops *anaclitically on the instinct of self-preservation. The concept was introduced in 1914 by Sigmund Freud (1856–1939) in an article 'On Narcissism: An Introduction' (*Standard Edition*, XIV, pp. 73–102, at pp. 87–90). *See also* anaclitic. *Compare* narcissistic object-choice.

anacoluthon *n*. A sentence showing a lack of grammatical sequence, or a grammatical construction in which one part of a sentence does not fit grammatically with another, such as the following utterance: *The main reason for my feeling of guilt—and I'm not the sort of person given to wallowing in guilt, although I have had periods in my life when I felt depressed, probably because both my parents tended to be depressives.* **anacolutha** *pl*. **anacoluthic** *adj*.
[From Greek *an-* not + *akolouthos* following]

anacusia *n*. Total *deafness. Also spelt *anacousia*. Also called *anacusis* or *anacousis*. **anacusic** *adj*.
[From Greek *an-* without + *akousis* hearing, from *akouein* to hear + *-ia* indicating a condition or quality]

anaerobic *adj*. Of or relating to the generation of energy by a form of *metabolism not requiring oxygen or air. *See also* fast glycolytic fibre, glycolysis. *Compare* aerobic.

[From Greek *an-* without + *aer* air + *bios* life + *-ikos* of, relating to, or resembling]

anaesthesia *n*. Absence of sensation or feeling, often resulting from a disorder or induced by *anaesthetic (1) drugs or *hypnosis, called *general anaesthesia* when it involves loss of consciousness and *local anaesthesia* when it affects only a restricted area of the body. US *anesthesia*. *See also* acupuncture, bathyanaesthesia, conversion symptom, epidural anaesthetic, gate-control theory, glove anaesthesia, narcotic, pallanaesthesia, rausch, shoe anaesthesia, stocking anaesthesia. *Compare* analgesia.
[Coined in 1846 by the US anatomist and writer Oliver Wendell Holmes (1809–94) from Greek *anaisthesia* absence of sensation, from *an-* without + *aisthesis* feeling + *-ia* indicating a condition or quality]

anaesthetic *n*. **1.** Any drug or substance that induces *anaesthesia. *adj*. **2.** Inducing or characterized by *anaesthesia. US *anesthetic*.

Anafranil *n*. A proprietary name for the drug *clomipramine.
[Trademark]

anaglyph *n*. A stereoscopic image composed of two separate images of the same object or scene, taken from slightly different positions, represented in two different colours, usually red and green or cyan (blue–green) that, when viewed through spectacles having one lens of each colour, merge to produce a three-dimensional effect. The term is also applied to any artwork such as a cameo that is designed to stand out in low relief. *See also* Cyclopean perception, random-dot stereogram, stereopsis, visual illusion. **anaglyphic**, **anaglyphical**, **anaglyptic**, or **anaglyptical** *adj*.
[From Greek *anaglyphe* carved in low relief, from *ana-* backwards or up + *glyphe* an engraving or carving, from *glyphein* to engrave or carve]

anaglyptoscope *n*. An instrument that alters the angle of incident light on a three-dimensional object, reversing the areas of light and shadow, used in research into *chiaroscuro.
[From *anaglyph* + Greek *skopeein* to view]

anagogic interpretation *n*. In *psychoanalysis, a mode of *interpretation of dreams, myths, and other symbolic representations in order to reveal their higher allegorical or spiritual meaning. It is considered to be the opposite of ordinary analytic interpretation, which on the contrary reduces such material to its basic and often sexual content. Carl Gustav Jung (1875–1961) incorporated anagogic interpretation into his *analytical psychology, but Sigmund Freud (1856–1939) rejected it as merely a reversion to pre-analytic notions ('Dreams and Telepathy', 1922, *Standard Edition*, XVIII, pp. 197–220, at p. 216).
[From Greek *anagoge* a lifting up, from *ana* up + *agein* to lead]

anal character *n*. In *psychoanalysis, a personality pattern determined by *fixation (2) at the *anal stage and characterized by the adult personality traits of orderliness, frugality, and obstinacy, sometimes called the three Ps: pedantry, parsimony, and petulance. Also called the *anal personality*. *See* anal triad. *See also* obsessive–compulsive personality disorder.

analeptic *adj*. **1.** Restorative or invigorating. *n*. **2.** A restorative or invigorating drug, especially one that helps to restore consciousness after a general anaesthetic. *See also* psychoanaleptic.
[From Greek *analeptikos* restorative, from *analambanein* to take up, from *ana* up + *lambanein* to take + *-itikos* resembling or marked by]

anal erotism *n*. In *psychoanalysis, sensuous pleasure derived from stimulation of the anus, and focusing of *libido on the anus during the *anal stage. Also called *anal eroticism*. **anal-erotic** *adj*.

anal-expulsive phase *n*. A subdivision of the *anal stage suggested in 1924 by the German psychoanalyst Karl Abraham (1877–1925) in his book *Versuch einer Entwicklungsgeschichte der Libido* (A Study of the Developmental History of the Libido). In this first phase, *anal erotism is linked to evacuation of the bowels, and the sadistic instinct is satisfied through destruction of faeces; whereas in the second *anal-retentive phase, anal erotism is associated with retention of faeces, and the sadistic instinct is linked to possessive control. Abraham believed that the progression from the first to the second of these two phases is crucial for the later development of the ability to form loving relationships. Also called the *anal-expulsive stage*.

analgesia

analgesia *n.* Absence or diminution of *pain sensation, often induced by *analgesic drugs or *hypnosis. *See also* audioanalgesia, hidden observer, neodissociation theory, thermoanalgesia. *Compare* anaesthesia.
[From Greek *an-* without + *algesis* sense of pain, from *algos* pain + *-ia* indicating a condition or quality]

analgesic *n.* **1.** Any drug or substance that induces *analgesia. *See* aspirin, beta-endorphin, carbamazepine, codeine, narcotic analgesic, quinine. *See also* phenylquinine writhing test. *adj.* **2.** Inducing or characterized by *analgesia.

analogies test *n.* A type of *intelligence test item requiring logical thinking, usually presented in the form *A is to B as C is to . . .* , sometimes followed by a number of alternatives from which a selection must be made, the right answer in this example being *D.* Another easy example is *Bird is to air as fish is to . . .* , the right answer being *water.* A typical hard example with response alternatives is: *C is to X as F is to . . . (M, U, L, V, or H).* Although arguments could be developed to justify various answers, the 'right' answer to this item is *U,* because *C* and *X* are three letters from either end of the alphabet, and *F* and *U* are six letters from either end.

analogue *n.* **1.** Something that is seen as comparable to another; specifically, a physical representation, such as a pointer on a dial, of a quantity being measured; an organ or body part resembling another; an organic compound related to another by the replacement of hydrogen atoms by alkyl groups. *adj. n.* **2.** (Of or pertaining to) a form of *knowledge representation in which continuously varying dimensions or relations between elements of the thing being represented correspond to continuously varying dimensions or relations between parts of the representation, so that the representations resemble the things that they represent. Also spelt *analog,* especially in the US, where it is a variant form, and in computing terminology. *Compare* digital, symbolic representation. **analogical** or **analogic** *adj.*
[From Greek *analogos* proportionate, from *ana* up + *logos* word, discourse, or reason]

anal-retentive phase *n.* The second phase of the *anal stage according to a suggestion made in 1924 by the German psychoanalyst

Karl Abraham (1877–1925) in his book *Versuch einer Entwicklungsgeschichte der Libido* (A Study of the Developmental History of the Libido). In the first *anal-expulsive phase, *anal erotism is linked to evacuation of the bowels and the sadistic instinct is satisfied by destruction of faeces, whereas in this second anal-retentive phase, anal erotism is associated with retention of faeces, and the sadistic instinct is satisfied by possessive control. Also called the *anal-retentive stage.*

anal sadistic stage *n.* Another name for the *anal stage.

anal stage *n.* According to the *psychoanalytic theory of Sigmund Freud (1856–1939), the second *libidinal stage of *psychosexual development, from about 2 to 3 years of age, characterized by a focusing of *libido on the anal *erotogenic zone, an investment of *object-relationships with meanings associated with faeces and defecation, and a strengthening of *sadomasochistic tendencies. In an article entitled 'The Disposition to Obsessional Neurosis' (1913), Freud mentioned it for the first time: 'And now we see the need for yet another stage to be inserted before the final shape is reached—a stage in which the component instincts have already come together for the choice of an object and that object is already something extraneous in contrast to the subject's own self, but in which the primacy of the genital zones has not yet been established' (*Standard Edition,* XII, pp. 317–26, at p. 321). When in 1915 Freud revised his book *Three Essays on the Theory of Sexuality* (1905, *Standard Edition,* VII, pp. 130–243), he placed the anal stage between the *oral stage and the *phallic stage. In his 1917 article 'On Transformations of Instinct as Exemplified in Anal Erotism' (*Standard Edition,* XVII, pp. 127–33), he famously interpreted the symbolic meaning of giving and withholding: faeces = gifts (to parents or caretakers), and gifts = money, hence such phrases as *filthy lucre.* Also called the *anal-sadistic stage* or *phase. See* anal-expulsive phase, anal-retentive phase. *See also* anal character, genital stage, latency period.

anal triad *n.* In *psychoanalysis, the three personality *traits of orderliness, parsimony (or meanness), and obstinacy, first identified by Sigmund Freud (1856–1939) as the distinctive adult traits associated with imperfect negotiation of the *anal stage of development ('Character and Anal Erotism', 1908, *Standard Edition*, IX, pp. 169–75). The traits are sometimes called the three Ps: pedantry, parsimony, and petulance. *See also* anal character, fixation (2), obsessive–compulsive personality disorder.

analysand *n.* A person undergoing *psychoanalysis.
[From *analysis* + *-and*, following the model of *multiplicand*, a number that is to be multiplied]

analysis *n.* The action or process of analysing; also, an abbreviated name for *psychoanalysis.

analysis by synthesis *n.* A recognition process in which hypotheses are formulated and compared with input data until one of the hypotheses produces a match. This is how experienced crossword-puzzle solvers often identify words with missing letters, for example, if the clue is *Via the middle route in South America*, a solver who knows that the answer is a four-letter word with the form —E—U may be unable to work out the logic of the clue but may guess that the answer is the name of a South American city or country and may test various hypotheses until finding one that fits, namely *PERU*. It involves both *bottom-up processing and *top-down processing.

analysis of covariance *n.* In statistics, a technique of data analysis based on *analysis of variance (ANOVA) that uses statistical control to remove the effect of an *extraneous variable, known or assumed to be correlated with the *dependent variable, and analyses the portion of the variance in the dependent variable explained by one or more *independent variables excluding the extraneous variable. In psychology, it is often used to suppress extraneous subject variables such as intelligence or age that cannot be controlled by *randomization. *See also* analysis of covariance structures, covariate. **ANCOVA** *abbrev.*

analysis of covariance structures *n.* A statistical method, combining techniques of *factor analysis and *multiple regression, for analysing *causal models derived from *correlational studies. It generally involves *structural equation modelling and sometimes *path diagrams. *See also* analysis of covariance (ANCOVA).

analysis of variance *n.* A statistical procedure for testing the significance of differences among several group means by partitioning the total variance in the *dependent variable into effects due to the *independent variable (in *one-way ANOVA*) or each of the two or more independent variables (in *multifactorial ANOVA*) plus error variance. In multifactorial designs the proportion of the total variance due to *interaction effects involving two or more independent variables is also estimated. *See also* a posteriori test, multiple comparisons, planned comparison, repeated-measures analysis of variance. *Compare* analysis of covariance (ANCOVA), multivariate analysis of variance (MANOVA). **ANOVA** *abbrev.*

analyst *n.* One who analyses. In *psychoanalysis, another name for a *psychoanalyst.

analytical psychology *n.* A term introduced by Carl Gustav Jung (1875–1961) in 1913, the year he left the *psychoanalytic movement, to denote the new approach that he saw as having evolved out of psychoanalysis under his leadership. Also called *Jungian analysis*. *See abaissement du niveau mental*, active imagination, amplification, anagogic interpretation, anima, animus (3), archetypal form, archetype (2), collective unconscious, complex indicator, directed association, directed thinking, Electra complex, enantiodromia, extraversion, fantasy thinking, function type, God-image, horme, imago (1), individuation, inflation of consciousness, introversion, mana, mandala, *numinosum*, objective psyche, *participation mystique*, persona (1), personal unconscious, primordial image, psychoid, psychopomp, *puer aeternus*, reductive interpretation, shadow (2), synchronicity, syzygy, uroboros, word-association test.

analytic language *n.* Another name for an *isolating language.

analytic statement *n.* In *logic, a declarative statement in which the predicate is contained in the subject. Such a statement cannot be confirmed or refuted by observation or experience, and its negation is either directly or implicitly self-contradictory. One example is the statement *All bachelors are unmarried*; another is *God is omnipotent*, provided that omnipotence is part of the definition of God. The truth or falsity of an analytic statement or

proposition is *a priori. Also called an *analytic proposition*. *Compare* synthetic statement.
[From Greek *analytikos*, analytic, from *analyein* to break down or dissolve, from *ana-* down + *lyein* to loosen]

anamnesis n. **1.** *Reminiscence, or the ability to recall past experiences. **2.** The account of a patient or client of the antecedents and course of a disorder. *Compare* catamnesis. **anamneses** pl. **anamnestic** adj. Easily recalled.
[From Greek *anamimneskein* to recall, from *ana* up + *mimneskein* to remind]

anamorphic adj. Of, relating to, or consisting of a distorted image that regains its correct proportions when viewed from a particular angle or in a curved mirror. An anamorphic picture or image is usually so distorted that it is difficult or impossible to interpret with normal viewing, but when examined with an *anamorphoscope* (usually a polished cylinder or cone), or when viewed at a steep slant, the distortion is corrected and the normal proportions of the image are restored, the most famous example in fine art being *The Ambassadors* painted in 1533 by the German artist Hans Holbein the Younger (1497–1543), which contains an elongated human skull that becomes recognizable only when the painting is viewed from its edge at a downward angle of 27 degrees.
[From Greek *ana* back or again + *morphe* a shape or form + *-ikos* of, relating to, or resembling]

anandamide n. A naturally occurring substance in the brain that stimulates the same receptors as the psychotropic substances in *cannabis.
[From Sanskrit *ananda* perfect bliss, from *a-* intensive prefix + *nandi* joy + *amide* an organic compound containing the group —$CONH_2$, from *am(monia)* + *-ide* indicating membership of a particular group of chemical compounds]

anankastic neurosis *See* obsessive–compulsive disorder.
[From Greek *ananke* necessity]

anankastic personality disorder n. Another name for *obsessive–compulsive personality disorder.

anaphase n. The third phase of cell division by *mitosis, when the paired chromosomes move apart to the poles of the spindle, or either of the two phases when this occurs during *meiosis (1).
[From Greek *ana* up + *phasis* an aspect, from *phainein* to show]

anaphia n. Absence of the sense of touch.
[From Greek *a-* without + *haphe* touch + *-ia* indicating a condition or quality]

anaphora n. In speaking or writing, the use of a pronoun or other word to refer back to something already mentioned in the sentence. In the sentence *When Wundt founded the world's first psychological laboratory in 1879, he did it in Leipzig*, the words *he*, *did*, and *it* all exemplify anaphora, because they refer back to *Wundt*, *founded*, and *founded the world's first psychological laboratory*, respectively. *See also* deixis. *Compare* cataphora. **anaphoric** adj.
[From Greek *ana-* backwards + *pherein* to carry]

anaphrodisiac adj. n. (Of or relating to) any substance that diminishes sexual desire. Many therapeutic drugs, including the selective serotonin reuptake inhibitors such as Prozac, have anaphrodisiac side-effects. *Compare* aphrodisiac.
[From Greek *an-* without + *aphrodisiakos* aphrodisiac, from *Aphrodite* the Greek goddess of love]

anaphylaxis n. Heightened sensitivity to a foreign substance, such as penicillin or bee sting, often but not necessarily a *protein, resulting from earlier exposure to it.
[From Greek *ana* back + *phylaxis* protection]

anaphylactic shock n. A form of *traumatic shock caused by *anaphylaxis.

anarthria n. Inability to speak coherently.
[From Greek *an-* without + *arthron* articulation + *-ia* indicating a condition or quality]

anchoring and adjustment n. A judgemental *heuristic through which a person makes an estimate by starting from an initial value and then adjusting it to yield a final estimate, the adjustment typically being insufficient and the estimate therefore biased towards the initial value. The initial value may be suggested by the formulation of the problem, as in a classic experiment in which people were asked to estimate the number of African countries in the United Nations by first indicating whether a number suggested by the experimenter was too high or too low and then estimating the actual number; those who began from a suggested number of 10 gave a median estimate of 25 (too low), and those who began from 65 gave a median estimate of 45 (too high). Alternatively, the initial value may result from partial computation, as in another classic experiment in which high school students who were given five seconds to estimate the value of the product $1 \times 2 \times 3 \times 4 \times 5 \times 6 \times 7 \times 8$ produced a median estimate of 512 (too low), whereas those asked to estimate the product $8 \times 7 \times 6 \times 5 \times 4 \times 3 \times 2 \times 1$ produced a median estimate of 2,250 (too high), apparently because members of both groups calculated the first few steps and then extrapolated without sufficient adjustment. When *revealed preferences are determined empirically, the technique of asking decision makers whether they prefer various gambles to a fixed alternative tends to lead to anchoring and adjustment on the probability scale, whereas asking them how much they would be willing to stake on the gamble tends to lead to anchoring and adjustment on the money scale. The heuristic was first introduced in 1971 by the US psychologists Paul Slovic (born 1938) and Sarah C. Lichtenstein (born 1933). *See also* overconfidence effect, preference reversal (1).

anchor test *n.* In psychometrics, a common set of test items administered in combination with two or more *alternative forms of the test with the aim of establishing the equivalence of the scores on the alternative forms.

ancient mariner effect *n.* A tendency for people to be more willing to disclose intimate details of their lives to strangers than to acquaintances. Also called the *passing stranger effect*.
[Named after Samuel Taylor Coleridge's poem *The Rime of the Ancient Mariner* (1798), in which the aged sailor tells his horrific story over and over again to strangers]

androgen *n.* A male sex hormone such as *testosterone or *androsterone that is produced by the testes and that promotes the development of male sexual organs and masculine *secondary sexual characteristics, or a synthetic substance with a similar pharmacological action. **androgenic** *adj.* Of or relating to *androgens.

[From Greek *andros* a man + *genes* born or produced]

androgenization *n.* The process whereby exposure to *androgens causes male sex organs to develop in an embryo.

androgenous *adj.* Producing only male offspring. Often confused with *androgynous, which has a different meaning and a different etymology.
[From Greek *andros* a man + *genes* born or produced + *-ous* having or characterized by]

androgynous *adj.* Having both male and female characteristics. Often confused with *androgenous. *See also* Bem Sex Role Inventory, epicene (1). **androgyny** *n.* The condition or state of being *androgynous.
[From Greek *andros* a man + *gyne* a woman + *-ous* having or characterized by]

andromania *n.* Another name for *nymphomania.
[From Greek *andros* a man + *mania* madness + *-ia* indicating a condition or quality]

androsterone *n.* An *androgen steroid hormone, less active than *testosterone, produced in the testes and detectable in men's urine and synthesized artificially from cholesterol.
[From *andro(gen)* + *ster(ol)* + *(horm)one*]

anecdotal evidence *n.* Evidence obtained informally from isolated observations rather than from systematic investigation, seldom collected with sufficient care or reported in sufficient detail to be trusted as a basis for generalization, but often a source of hypotheses for further investigation.

anechoic room *n.* A room specially designed to minimize the penetration of sounds from outside and reflections of sounds from surfaces on the inside.

anergasia *n.* Loss of function, especially in relation to *organic disorders.
[From Greek *an-* without + *ergasia* work or business]

anergia *n.* Listlessness or lack of activity. **anergic** *adj.*
[From Greek *an-* without + *ergon* work + *-ia* indicating a condition or quality]

anesthesia See anaesthesia.

aneurysm n. An abnormal dilation of a blood vessel at a point where its wall is weakened, either in the brain (where it can lead to a *stroke) or elsewhere in the body. Also spelt aneurism.
[From Greek aneurysma an aneurysm, from ana up + eurys wide]

angel dust n. A common street name for the depressant drug *phencyclidine.

angina n. Short for angina pectoris, a sudden and intense chest pain, generally following physical exertion, often radiating towards the left shoulder and arm and accompanied by feelings of suffocation, caused by an inadequate blood supply to the heart muscle. See also referred pain.
[From Latin angina quinsy, from Greek anchone a strangling]

angiogram n. An X-ray image of the blood vessels of the brain or other organ made after injecting a contrast medium, usually containing iodine, that is opaque to X-rays. See also brain imaging. **angiography** n. The process of producing *angiograms.
[From Greek angeion a (blood) vessel + gramme a line]

angiotensin II n. A polypeptide hormone that causes constriction of the blood vessels, raising blood pressure, precipitates *adrenalin release and blocks its reuptake, and stimulates the release of *aldosterone, thereby promoting sodium retention. The hormone *renin, which is secreted by the kidneys in response to a decline in blood pressure, converts a plasma protein to angiotensin I, and this in turn is converted to angiotensin II by angiotensin converting enzyme.
[From Greek angeion a (blood) vessel + Latin tensus tight, from tendere to stretch + -in(a) indicating an organic compound]

angst n. **1.** An unfocused feeling of anxiety. **2.** In *existentialism in general and *existential therapy in particular, the dread arising from the realization that one's existence leads to an undetermined future, the emptiness of which must be filled by freely chosen actions. **3.** In *psychoanalysis, anxiety, which is distinguished from fright (Schreck), and fear (Furcht) according to Sigmund Freud (1856–1939) in

his book Beyond the Pleasure Principle (1920). Anxiety 'describes a particular state of expecting the danger or preparing for it, even though it may be an unknown one'; fright 'is the name we give to the state a person gets into when he has run into danger without being prepared for it'; and fear 'requires a definite object of which to be afraid' (Standard Edition, XVIII, pp. 7–64, at pp. 12–13). **angsty** adj.
[From German Angst fear]

angstrom n. One ten billionth of a metre (10^{-10} metre) or one ten millionth of a millimetre, used mainly for expressing wavelengths of light and other electromagnetic radiation. The *visible spectrum extends from approximately 3,900 angstroms at the violet end of the spectrum to 7,400 angstroms at the red end. Also called an angstrom unit, but that usage is obsolescent. Also written Ångström, Ångström unit. Compare nanometre.
[Named after the Swedish physicist Anders Jonas Ångström (1814–74) who introduced it]

angular gyrus n. The *gyrus immediately behind *Wernicke's area that curves round the back of the *lateral sulcus of each cerebral hemisphere, on the border of the parietal and temporal lobes. It is implicated in the control of visual gaze, and in the left hemisphere it has a specialized language function, lesions in this area being associated with nominal aphasia (see under aphasia).

angular size n. The magnitude of an object or image expressed in terms of the *visual angle that it subtends at the eye. See also size constancy.

anhedonia n. Inability to experience pleasure or interest in formerly pleasurable activities. Compare hypohedonia. **anhedonic** adj.
[From Greek an- without + hedone pleasure + -ia indicating a condition or quality]

aniconia n. Absence of mental imagery.
[From Greek an- without + eikon an image + -ia indicating a condition or quality]

anima n. In *analytical psychology, the feminine principle as represented in the male unconscious, an *archetype (2) forming part of the *collective unconscious, representing the feminine aspect of human nature, characterized by imagination, fantasy, and play, manifesting itself in personified form in dreams and fantasies, and acting as a *psychopomp connecting the *ego and the unconscious. As Carl Gustav Jung (1875–1961) described it: 'Every man carries with him the eternal image of woman, not the image of this or that particular woman, but a definitive feminine image. This image is fundamentally unconscious, an hereditary factor of primordial origin engraved in the living organic system of the man, an imprint or "archetype" of all the ancestral experiences of the female, a deposit, as it were, of all the impressions ever made by woman' (*Collected Works*, 17, paragraph 338). *See also* imago (1), syzygy. *Compare* animus (3). [From Latin *anima* air, breath, or spirit]

animal magnetism n. A term introduced in 1779 by the Viennese physician Franz Anton Mesmer (1734–1815) for a substance resembling ordinary magnetism (believed also to be a substance) that he claimed to have discovered in human bodies and that could be channelled, stored, and transmitted between people. Two Royal Commissions in France, where Mesmer was then practising, investigated this claim in 1784 and declared that the effects that Mesmer had reported were in fact due to touch, imagination, and imitation. Mesmer's work is often cited as the basis for later research into *hypnosis, but animal magnetism was not hypnosis, and there is no evidence that Mesmer ever hypnotized anyone. Also called *mesmerism*.

animal psychology n. The study of animal behaviour through laboratory experimentation. *See also* comparative psychology. *Compare* ethology.

animism n. **1.** The ascription of psychological *attributes such as desires and intentions to plants, inanimate objects, or natural phenomena. The term was first used in this sense by the British social anthropologist Sir Edward Burnett Tylor (1832–1917) in his book *Primitive Culture* (1871) to describe the beliefs of the 'ruder tribes' of India, who believed, for example, that the sun shines in order to provide warmth. Although the French anthropologist Lucien Lévy-Bruhl (1857–1939) criticized such usage in 1910 in his book *Les Fonctions Mentales dans les Sociétés Inférieures* (translated into English under the less provocative title *How Natives Think*), the Swiss psychologist Jean Piaget (1896–1980) adopted the term to describe the thinking of children who have not yet learned to distinguish animate from inanimate objects and popularized this usage in his book *La Représentation du Monde chez l'Enfant* (The Child's Conception of the World), first published in 1926. According to Piaget, animistic thinking undergoes four stages of development: first, between 4 and 6 years of age, children believe that everything is alive; second, between 6 and 7 years, they believe that everything that moves is alive; third, between 8 and 10 years, they believe that everything that moves by itself is alive; and fourth, from about 11 years, they distinguish correctly between animate and inanimate objects. The ascription of specifically human attributes to non-human animals and objects is a form of animism called *anthropomorphism. **2.** The doctrine that the soul is the vital principle (*anima mundi*) on which all organic development depends, propounded most influentially by the German physician Georg Ernst Stahl (1660–1734) in his book *Theoria Medica Vera* in 1707. **3.** A doctrine promoted by the Greek philosophers Pythagoras (?580–?500 BC) and Plato (?427–?347 BC) according to which an immaterial force organizes and animates the material world. **animist** n. One whose thinking is characterized by *animism. **animistic** adj.
[From Latin *anima* air, breath, or soul + -*ismus* indicating a state or condition]

animus n. **1.** Antipathy or animosity. **2.** Intention, purpose, or motivation. **3.** In *analytical psychology, the masculine principle present as an *archetype (2) in the female *collective unconscious, characterized by focused consciousness, authority, and respect. It is the counterpart of the *anima in the male unconscious, and it functions as a *psychopomp connecting the *ego and the unconscious. According to Carl Gustav Jung (1875–1961), 'In its primary *unconscious* form the animus is a compound of spontaneous, unpremeditated opinions which exercise a powerful influence on the woman's emotional life' (*Collected Works*, 16, p. 521). *See also* imago (1), syzygy.
[From Latin *animus* mind or spirit]

anion n. A negatively charged *ion such as *chloride. *Compare* cation.
[From Greek *ana* up + *ion* going, from *ienai* to go]

anion channel *n*. An *ion channel across a cell membrane permitting the transport of *anions across it.

anisotropic *adj*. Having different physical properties in different directions or with respect to different axes. *Compare* isotropic. **anisotropy** or **anisotrophy** *n*.
[From Greek *anisos* unequal, from *an-* without + *isos* equal or the same + *tropos* a turn, from *trapein* to turn]

ankle reflex *n*. Another name for the *Achilles tendon reflex.

Anna O *n*. The name used by the Austrian physician Josef Breuer (1842–1925) to refer to his patient Bertha Pappenheim (1860–1936), the first person ever to undergo *psychoanalysis. She suffered from various symptoms of *hysteria, which were made to disappear by enabling her under *hypnosis to recall the traumatic events that precipitated them, her recollections of these events being accompanied by violent outbursts of emotion that Breuer labelled *catharsis. Breuer described the case in 1895 in *Studies on Hysteria*, co-authored with Sigmund Freud (1856–1939) (*Standard Edition*, II, at pp. 21–47), but the veracity of the account, and in particular the claim that Anna O was cured, have been questioned by later researchers.

annealing *n*. **1.** In *connectionism (1) and *parallel distributed processing, the use of random shocks to alter the states of units in a network of connected units until they are all responding as consistently as possible to signals received from one another and no further adjustments in connections and firing rates can lead to further improvements. The random shocks are designed to overcome the problem of entrapment in local minima after *gradient descent or in local maxima after *hill climbing procedures. The technique is analogous to tapping or shaking a toaster to get the crumbs to fall to the bottom. *Compare* relaxation technique. **2.** In *genetic engineering, heating double-stranded *DNA so that the strands separate and then allowing them to cool in the presence of single strands from another organism to form *heteroduplex DNA. *See also* DNA hybridization, hybridization, recombinant DNA. **anneal** *vb*.
[Alluding to *annealing*, making metal easier to work by heating it and allowing it to cool slowly, thereby removing internal stresses and realigning the molecules or crystals within the microstructure of the material, from Old English *onaelan* to set on fire, from *on* on + *aelan* to burn, from *al* fire]

anniversary reaction *n*. An emotional reaction on the anniversary of a traumatic event or experience such as a *bereavement.

anoesia *n*. An obsolescent term for *mental retardation. US *anesia*. Also called *anoia*.
[From Greek *a-* without + *nous* intellect or sense + *-ia* indicating a condition or quality]

anomaloscope *n*. A device for mixing light from the red and green parts of the *visible spectrum and comparing the result with a standard yellow to measure defects in colour vision according to the *Rayleigh equation.
[So called because it is used to detect *colour anomalies]

anomalous dichromacy *n*. A form of *colour-blindness caused by a defect in the functioning of one of the three *visual pigments in the cones of the retina, leading to a form of colour vision in which only two of the three *primary colours (1) can be perceived and therefore any spectral hue can be matched by only two primary colours, the most common form being *deuteranopia. Also called *anomalous dichromasy, anomalous dichromatism, anomalous dichromatopsia, anomalous dichromopsia. See also* protanopia, tritanopia. *Compare* anomalous trichromacy. **anomalous dichromat** *n*. A person with *anomalous dichromacy.

anomalous myopia *n*. A transient form of *myopia caused by the temporary absence of adequate stimuli for *accommodation (1). *See also* dark focus.

anomalous sentence *n*. A sentence that is syntactically well formed but semantically meaningless. The best-known example, suggested by the US linguist and philosopher (Avram) Noam Chomsky (born 1928), is *Colourless green ideas sleep furiously*.

anomalous trichromacy *n*. A form of *colour-blindness in which the proportions of three *primary colours (1) that are mixed to match a comparison colour deviate from the normal. Also called *anomalous trichromasy, anomalous trichromatism, anomalous trichromatopsia, anom-*

alous trichromopsia. See also Rayleigh equation. *Compare* anomalous dichromacy. **anomalous trichromat** *n.* A person with *anomalous trichromacy.

anomia *n.* Inability to name common objects or pictures of common objects; another name for anomic *aphasia.
[From Greek *a-* without + *onomia* a name + *-ia* indicating a condition or quality]

anomic aphasia *See under* aphasia.

anomic suicide *See under* suicide.

anomie *n.* A state of society in which rules and standards of belief and conduct have weakened or broken down, or an analogous condition in an individual, characterized by hopelessness, disorientation, loss of belief and sense of purpose, and social isolation. The concept was introduced by the French sociologist Émile Durkheim (1858–1917), who provided evidence in his book *Suicide* (1897) of correlations between suicide rates and indicators of anomie such as divorce rates. Also spelt *anomy.* **anomic** *adj.*
[From French *anomie*, from Greek *anomia* lawlessness or normlessness, from *a-* without + *nomos* a law + *-ia* indicating a condition or quality]

anoopsia *n.* *Strabismus, especially the common form in which one or both eyes are deviated upwards. Also spelt *anopsia.* Also called *hypertropia. See also* amblyopia ex anopsia.
[From Greek *ano* upwards, from *ana* up + *ops* an eye + *-ia* indicating a condition or quality]

anopia *n.* *Blindness, especially when caused by a defect in one or both eyes. Also called *anopsia. See also* amblyopia, hemianopia, homonymous hemianopia, nyctalopia, object blindness. *Compare* amaurosis, amblyopia.
[From Greek *an-* without + *ops* an eye + *-ia* indicating a condition or quality]

anopsia *n.* **1.** A variant spelling of *anoopsia. **2.** A variant form of *anopia.
[From Greek *ano* upwards or *an-* without + *ops* an eye + *-ia* indicating a condition or quality]

anorexia *n.* Absence of appetite, distinguished in careful usage from the disorder *anorexia nervosa, which should not be short-ened to *anorexia. See also* aphagia, dysphagia. *Compare* pseudoanorexia. **anorectic** *adj.*
[From Greek *an-* not or without + *orexis* appetite + *-ia* indicating a condition or quality]

anorexia nervosa *n.* An *eating disorder usually (but not exclusively) occurring in adolescent girls and young women, characterized by intense fear of becoming fat even though underweight, a refusal to maintain body weight at a normal level (at least 85 per cent of expected weight for sex, age, and height), disturbances in body image, and amenorrhoea. People with the disorder avoid eating even though hungry, and it is distinguished in careful usage from *anorexia. It is popularly (and misleadingly) known as the *slimmers' disease. See also* lanugo. *Compare* bulimia nervosa.
[From Greek *an-* not or without + *orexis* appetite + Latin *nervus* a nerve]

anorgasmia *n.* Failure of orgasmic response during sexual activity. Also called *anorgasmy. See* female orgasmic disorder, male orgasmic disorder.

anorthopia *n.* Abnormal or defective vision.
[From Greek *an-* without + *orthos* right + *ops* an eye + *-ia* indicating a condition or quality]

anorthoscope *n.* A 19th-century device for studying *anorthoscopic perception, consisting of a pair of circular discs mounted one behind the other, capable of rotating at different speeds and in opposite directions, enabling images attached to the rear disc to be viewed through a slit in the front disc.

anorthoscopic *adj.* Abnormally viewed, of or relating to perception of a figure that is revealed one section at a time through a narrow slit behind which the figure moves. If images such as simple geometric shapes or letters of the alphabet are presented anorthoscopically, form perception occurs and the shapes of the images are clearly perceived in spite of the absence of any retinal image of the corresponding shapes. The other major example of form perception without a corresponding retinal image is a *Kanizsa triangle. See also* anorthoscope, illusory contour, retinal painting. *Compare* void mode.
[From Greek *an-* without + *orthos* right + *skopeein* to view + *-ikos* of, relating to, or resembling]

anosmia *n.* Absence of the sense of smell. *See also* specific anosmia. *Compare* cacosmia, dysosmia, hyperosmia, hyposmia, parosmia. [From Greek *an-* without + *osme* a smell + *-ia* indicating a condition or quality]

anosognosia *n.* Impaired ability or refusal to recognize that one has a sensory or motor impairment or, in some cases following a massive *stroke and *hemiplegia, even to recognize part of one's body as one's own. Also spelt *anosagnosia*. *See also* Anton's syndrome, agnosia. [From French *anosognosi*, named in 1914 by the French neurologist Josef F(rançois) F(élix) Babinski (1857–1932), from Greek *an-* without + *nosos* a disorder + *gnosis* knowledge + *-ia* indicating a condition or quality]

Antabuse *n.* A proprietary name for the drug disulfiram that is used in the treatment of *alcohol dependence. It interferes with the normal metabolism of ethyl alcohol by blocking the action of the enzyme *aldehyde dehydrogenase that normally converts it into acetic acid, allowing the noxious metabolite *acetaldehyde to accumulate, resulting in nausea, vomiting, pounding of the heart, shortness of breath, and other unpleasant symptoms. [Trademark]

antagonist *n.* **1.** An opponent or adversary in a struggle. *Compare* agonist (1). **2.** A muscle that opposes the action of another. *Compare* agonist (2). **3.** A substance that depresses the effect of an *agonist (3) either by acting at different *neuroreceptor sites from those of the agonist (a *non-competitive antagonist) or by binding to the same neuroreceptors as the agonist without exciting or inhibiting the *postsynaptic neurons (a competitive antagonist, also called a *receptor blocker*), a typical example being the narcotic antagonist *naloxone, which binds to neuroreceptors in the brain that would otherwise be occupied by morphine, and thereby prevents morphine from exerting its usual effects. *See also* dopamine antagonist. *Compare* agonist (3). [From Greek *anti* against + *agon* a festival of competitions, from *agein* to lead]

antecedent *See under* conditional reasoning.

anterior *adj.* In front or before. *Compare* posterior. [From Latin *anterior* in front, from *ante* before]

anterior commissure *n.* A round bundle of nerve fibres connecting the anterior or front parts of the left and right *temporal lobes and *olfactory bulbs. *See also* commissure. [From Latin *commissura* a joining together, from *com-* together + *mittere* to send]

anterior funiculus *See under* funiculus.

anterior horn *n.* Either of the two *ventral ends of the H-shaped column of grey matter that runs throughout the length of the spinal cord and to which most of the motor neurons are attached. *Compare* posterior horn.

anterior pituitary *n.* The front part or lobe of the *pituitary gland that, in response to hormones from the *hypothalamus, secretes *trophic hormones controlling most of the other *endocrine glands in the body, and that also acts directly on *somatic cells by secreting *growth hormone, affecting bodily growth and *metabolism, and *melanocyte-stimulating hormone, affecting skin and other pigmentation. Also called the *adenohypophysis*. *See* adrenocorticotrophic hormone (ACTH), beta-endorphin, beta-lipotropin, follicle-stimulating hormone, luteinizing hormone, prolactin, thyroid-stimulating hormone. *Compare* posterior pituitary.

anterograde amnesia *n.* Loss of memory for events or experiences after the traumatic event or incident that caused the amnesia. It generally affects *declarative memory but not *procedural memory. *See also* global amnesia, transient global amnesia. *Compare* retrograde amnesia. [From Latin *anterior* previous + *gradus* a step]

anterograde degeneration *n.* Another name for *Wallerian degeneration. [From Latin *anterior* in front or forward + *gradi* to go]

anterograde transport *n.* The movement of freshly synthesized components of neurons along *microtubules into *axons and *dendrites. *Compare* retrograde transport.

anthrax *n.* A highly infectious disease of warm-blooded animals, especially cattle and sheep, caused by the bacterium *Bacillus anthracis*, transmissible to humans and formerly called *woolsorter's disease*, occasionally stockpiled as a potential biological weapon.

[From Greek *anthrax* coal, charcoal, or a carbuncle, alluding to the dark scabs that form on the skin of an infected person]

anthropobiology *n.* The biology of human beings.
[From Greek *anthropos* man or the human species + English *biology*]

anthropocentrism *n.* Viewing or considering an issue from a narrowly human perspective, especially when disregarding or disdaining other animals, or an exaggerated conception of the significance of the human species in the universe. *Compare* anthropomorphism. **anthropocentric** *adj.*
[From Greek *anthropos* man or the human species + *kentron* the centre]

anthropogenic *adj.* Of or relating to the origins of the human species. **anthropogenesis** or **anthropogeny** *n.* The study of the origins of the human species.
[From Greek *anthropos* man or the human species + *genesis* birth or origin + *-ikos* of, relating to, or resembling]

anthropography *n.* The study of the geographical distribution of humans.
[A blend of Greek *anthropo(s)* man or the human species and English *(geo)graphy*]

anthropoid *adj.* **1.** Resembling the human species in form, applied especially to the *Anthropoidea or higher primates (humans, apes, and monkeys) or more narrowly to the highest apes (gorillas, chimpanzees, orangutans, and gibbons). *n.* **2.** An *anthropoid (1) primate or ape. *Compare* prosimian.
[From Greek *anthropos* man or the human species + *-oeides* denoting resemblance of form, from *eidos* shape]

Anthropoidea *n.* A suborder of higher primates, including humans, apes, and monkeys, within the order of Primates. *See also* anthropoid (1, 2). *Compare* prosimian.

anthropology *n.* The study of humans, including their origins, physical attributes, and cultures. *See also* cultural anthropology, ethnography (1, 2), ethnology, physical anthropology, social anthropology. **anthropological** *adj.* **anthropologist** *n.* One who practises *anthropology.

[From Greek *anthropos* man or the human species + *logos* word, discourse, or reason]

anthropomorphism *n.* The attribution of human characteristics to non-human entities, especially animals. *See also* animism (1). *Compare* anthropocentrism. **anthropomorphic** *adj.* Of, relating to, or characterized by *anthropomorphism. **anthropomorphize** *vb.* To attribute human characteristics to non-human entities, especially animals.
[From Greek *anthropos* man or the human species + *morphe* a form or shape + *-ismos* indicating a state or condition]

anthroponomastics *n.* The study of personal names. The study of names in general is called *onomastics*, and it is usually divided into *anthroponomastics* and *toponomastics* or *toponymy*, the study of place names.
[From Greek *anthropos* man or human + *onoma* name]

anthropophagus *n.* A cannibal. **anthropophagi** *pl.* **anthropophagous** *adj.* Cannibalistic. **anthropophagy** *n.* Cannibalism.
[From Greek *anthropos* man or the human species + *phagein* to eat]

anthropophonics *n.* The study of the full range of speech sounds of which the human vocal apparatus is capable, irrespective of the sounds actually used in *natural languages.
[From Greek *anthropos* man or human + *phone* sound]

anthroposophy *n.* The spiritualistic and mystical doctrine of the Austrian philosopher Rudolf Steiner (1861–1925), emphasizing the educational and psychological value of creative activities, such as the types of myth-making that played a larger part in life in earlier times.
[From Greek *anthropos* man or the human species + *sophia* wisdom]

anti-anxiety drug *n.* Another name for an *anxiolytic drug.

antibody *n.* A protein of the *immunoglobulin class, produced in the blood of an organism in response to the presence of an *antigen. By attaching itself to an antigen, it may render the antigen innocuous or cause it to be destroyed by other cells of the immune system. *See also* B lymphocyte, immune response, T lymphocyte.

anticathexis *n.* Another name for *counter-cathexis.

anticholinergic *adj.* Of or relating to any drug such as *atropine or *scopolamine that blocks nerve impulses in the *parasympathetic nervous system or counteracts the effects of *acetylcholine, such blocking also resulting from the action of certain *antiparkinsonian drugs, *neuroleptics (1), and *tricyclic antidepressants. Effects include dilation of the pupils of the eyes and preparation for far vision, dry mouth, quickening of the heart, reduction of gastric juice secretion, and retention of urine. *See also* benztropine, biperiden, cycloplegia, procyclidine, trihexyphenidyl. *Compare* cholinergic.
[From *anti* + *(acetyl)cholin(e)* + Greek *erg(on)* work + *-ik(os)* of, relating to, or resembling]

anticholinesterase *n.* A drug such as *physostigmine or *sarin that blocks the action of *acetylcholinesterase in mopping up *acetylcholine in the *peripheral nervous system. *Nerve gases are based on such agents.
[From *anti* + *(acetyl)cholin(e)* + *ester* + Greek *-ase* denoting an enzyme, from *diastasis* separation]

anticipation method *n.* Another name for the *serial anticipation method.

anticipatory socialization *n.* Adoption of attitudes and values of a group to which one does not belong, serving the twin functions of facilitating a move into that group and easing the process of adjustment after becoming a member of it. The concept was popularized by the US sociologist Samuel Stouffer (1900–60) and several co-authors of the monumental study of the US Army entitled *The American Soldier* (1949), in which it was reported that privates in the army who accepted the attitudes and values of the officer ranks were more likely than others to be promoted, and it was subsequently analysed in detail, in relation to *reference groups, by the US sociologist Robert K(ing) Merton (born 1910) in his book *Social Theory and Social Structure* (1957). Subsequent researchers found evidence that the working-class parents of children who are destined to be upwardly mobile within the class structure tend to hold, and to pass on to

their children, the attitudes and values of the class into which the child is destined to move. *See also* socialization (1).

anticonformity *n.* Behaviour that deliberately goes against the *norms (1) or social pressure of a group. It differs from independence inasmuch as the person responds to the group pressure rather than remaining unaffected by it. *Compare* conformity.

anticonvulsant *adj. n.* (Of or relating to) a drug such as *phenytoin, *carbamazepine, or any of the *benzodiazepines that prevents or reduces the severity of epileptic or other *convulsions or *seizures. *See also* hemeralopia. *Compare* convulsant.

antidepressant *adj. n.* (Of or relating to) any drug that tends to alleviate *depression and that is used in the treatment of *mood disorders, including the *monoamine oxidase inhibitors (MAOIs), the *tricyclic antidepressants and *tetracyclic antidepressants, the *selective serotonin reuptake inhibitors (SSRIs), and *St John's wort. Also called a *thymoleptic. See also* GHB, inositol, stimulant drug.

antidiuretic hormone *n.* Another name for *vasopressin. **ADH** *abbrev.*

antidromic *adj.* Of or relating to a nerve impulse conducted in the opposite direction to normal, towards the cell body rather than away from it, as when the axon of a sensory neuron responds to injury of the skin by sending impulses backwards to branching points, triggering the release of *substance P. *See* axon reflex. *Compare* orthodromic.
[From Greek *anti* against + *dromos* a course or run + *-ikos* of, relating to, or resembling]

antigen *n.* Any entity or substance, including a *bacterium, *virus, or *toxin, that mobilizes an *antibody when it enters or invades an organism, or a protein on the surface of an invading entity that has such an effect.
[From *anti(body)* + Greek *gen(es)* born or produced]

antigen–antibody response *n.* Another name for an *immune response.

antihistamine *n.* Any substance that counteracts the physiological and pharmacological effects of *histamine, including non-prescription drugs that block histamine receptors without stopping the release of histamine and that are used for the treatment of allergies (including hay fever) and the prevention of *motion sickness. **antihistaminic** *adj.*

anti-intraception *n.* A dislike of subjectivity and imagination. *See* F scale.
[From Greek *anti* against + Latin *intra* within + *capere, ceptum* to take + *-ion* indicating an action, process, or state]

antimanic *adj. n.* (Of or relating to) a drug such as *lithium carbonate or *carbamazepine that is used in the treatment of acute *manic episodes and *bipolar disorders. *Compare* mood stabilizer.

antimorph *n.* A *mutant (2) gene that has the opposite effect to its normal *allele and competes with it in a *heterozygous organism.
[From *anti* + Greek *morphe* a form or shape]

anti-Müllerian hormone *n.* Another name for *Müllerian inhibiting substance. **AMH** *abbrev.*

antinomy *n.* A type of *paradox consisting of a contradiction between two apparently unassailable propositions. **antinomic** *adj.*
[From Greek *anti* against + *nomos* a law]

antiparkinsonian *adj. n.* (Of or relating to) any drug that alleviates *parkinsonism or the pseudo-parkinsonian side-effects of neuroleptic drugs such as the *phenothiazines. In particular, *L-dopa or *bromocriptine compensates for the shortfall of dopamine in the substantia nigra and striatum of the brains of people with *Parkinson's disease; *deprenyl inhibits the action of a monoamine oxidase enzyme that destroys cells in the substantia nigra in people with Parkinson's disease; the antiviral drug *amantadine is believed to increase *dopamine release; and *anticholinergic drugs such as *benztropine, *biperiden, *procyclidine, and *trihexyphenidyl counteract the relative overabundance of *acetylcholine in the striatum.

antipsychiatry *n.* A radical critique of traditional (especially medical) approaches to mental disorders, influenced by *existentialism and *sociology, popularized by the Scottish psychiatrist Ronald D(avid) Laing

(1927–89) and others during the 1960s and 1970s.

antipsychotic *n.* Another name for a *neuroleptic (1).

anti-Semitism scale *n.* Any scale designed to measure prejudice against Jews, especially the *A-S scale.

antisocial personality disorder *n.* A *personality disorder characterized by a pervasive pattern of disregard for and violation of the rights of others, beginning in childhood or early adolescence and continuing into adulthood, with such signs and symptoms as failure to conform to social norms, manifested by repeated unlawful behaviour; deceitfulness, as indicated by repeated lying or swindling for pleasure or personal gain; impulsivity or failure to plan ahead; irritability and aggressiveness involving frequent assaults or fights; reckless disregard for the safety of self or others; consistent irresponsibility involving failure to hold down jobs or to honour financial obligations; and lack of remorse for the mistreatment of others, as indicated by indifference and rationalization. Also called *sociopathy* or (in *ICD-10 and elsewhere) *dissocial personality disorder*. *Compare* conduct disorder, psychopathy, XYY syndrome. **APD** *abbrev.*

Anton's syndrome *n.* A rare form of *anosognosia in which a person who is totally blind, usually as a result of extensive damage to the visual cortex or the optic nerves, is unaware of the blindness, typically either guessing at the appearance of objects from non-visual cues while believing that they are being perceived visually, or believing that for some reason the surroundings are plunged in darkness. Also called *blindness denial*. *Compare* blindsight (which may be interpreted as the inverse of Anton's syndrome).
[Named after the Czech neurologist and psychiatrist Gabriel Anton (1858–1933) who first described it in a case study published in 1899 in the journal *Wiener klinische Wochenschrift*, translated into English in the journal *Cognitive Neuropsychology* in 1993]

antonym *n.* A word that has the opposite meaning to another word, such as *high*, which is an antonym of *low*. Some authorities, notably the British linguist John Lyons (born 1932), reserve the term for *graded antonyms*,

such as the example just given, in which degrees of difference exist, and refer to *ungraded antonyms*—words that are either/or opposites, such as *male* and *female*, or *single* and *married* —as *complementaries*. *See also* antonym test. *Compare* synonym. **antonymous** *adj.* **antonymy** *n.* The relationship between words that are *antonyms.
[From Greek *anti* against + *onoma* a name]

antonym test *n.* A type of *intelligence test item in which the respondent is presented with a word and is asked to supply a word with the opposite meaning to it, often by choosing from a set of response alternatives. Also called an *opposites test*. *See also* antonym. *Compare* synonym test.

anvil *n.* A non-technical name for the *incus of the middle ear. *See also* hammer.
[So called because of its resemblance to a blacksmith's anvil]

anxiety *n.* A state of uneasiness, accompanied by dysphoria and somatic signs and symptoms of tension, focused on apprehension of possible failure, misfortune, or danger. *See also* anxiety disorders, anxiolytic, automatic anxiety, neurotic anxiety, performance anxiety, primal anxiety, primary anxiety, realistic anxiety, separation anxiety, signal anxiety, state anxiety, stranger anxiety, trait anxiety.
[From Latin *anxietas* anxiety, from *angere* to press tightly]

anxiety disorders *n.* A class of *mental disorders in which *anxiety features prominently. *See* acute stress disorder, agoraphobia, generalized anxiety disorder, obsessive–compulsive disorder, overanxious disorder, panic disorder, post-traumatic stress disorder, separation anxiety disorder, social phobia, specific phobia. *See also* anxiolytic.

anxiety hysteria *n.* In *psychoanalysis, a *neurosis with a *phobia as its central symptom. The term was introduced in 1908 by the Austrian psychiatrist Wilhelm Stekel (1868–1940) in his book *Nervöse Angstzustände und ihre Behandlung* (Neurotic Anxiety States and their Treatment) specifically to emphasize its structural resemblance to conversion hysteria (now called *dissociative disorder). *See also* transference neurosis (1).

anxiety neurosis *n.* Another name for *generalized anxiety disorder. The term was intro-

duced by Sigmund Freud (1856–1939) in the title of an article in 1894 'On the Grounds for Detaching a Particular Syndrome from Neurasthenia Under the Description "Anxiety Neurosis"' (*Standard Edition*, I, pp. 315–44), in which he distinguished it from *neurasthenia, because of the predominance of anxiety, and from *hysteria, because unlike hysteria, he interpreted it as an *actual neurosis.

anxiolytic *adj. n.* (Of or relating to) any of the drugs that reduce *anxiety or tension, especially the *benzodiazepines and *buspirone. Also called an *anti-anxiety* drug, and formerly called a *minor tranquillizer*. *See also* sedative-, hypnotic-, or anxiolytic-related disorders.
[From *anxiety* + Greek *lysis* dissolution, from *lyein* to loose + *-itikos* resembling or marked by]

anxious personality disorder *n.* Another name for *avoidant personality disorder.

apathy *n.* Absence of emotion, interest, or enthusiasm.
[From Greek *apatheia* indifference, from *a-* without + *pathos* feeling]

Apgar score *n.* An index of the physical and psychological condition of a newborn infant obtained by adding points (0, 1, or 2) for heart rate, respiratory effort, muscle tone, response to stimulation, and skin coloration, a score of 10 representing perfect condition on the test.
[Named after the US anaesthesiologist Virginia Apgar (1909–74) who introduced it in 1953]

aphagia *n.* Inability or lack of desire to eat, sometimes caused by damage to the *glossopharyngeal nerve or *hypoglossal nerve, making swallowing difficult or impossible, or a lesion in the *lateral hypothalamic feeding centre, and sometimes due to *psychogenic causes. *See also* lateral hypothalamic syndrome. *Compare* anorexia, dysphagia.
[From Greek *a-* without + *phagein* to consume + *-ia* indicating a condition or quality]

aphakia *n.* Absence of the *crystalline lens of an eye resulting in severe *hyperopia, whether congenital or due to some other cause, such as surgical removal of the lens to treat a *cataract.
[From Greek *a-* without + *phakos* a lentil + *-ia* indicating a condition or quality]

aphanisis *n.* A term used in *psychoanalysis to denote the disappearance of sexual desire. It was coined in 1927 by the Welsh psychoanalyst Ernest Jones (1879–1958) in his *Papers on Psycho-Analysis* (5th ed., pp. 438–50).
[From Greek *aphanes* invisible]

aphasia *n.* An *impairment of expression or comprehension of language caused by injury or disease in the language centres of the brain. The major forms related specifically to speech (*see also* agraphia, dyslexia) are: *acoustic–mnestic aphasia* (impaired ability to recall lists of words or to repeat long sentences, caused by a lesion in the left *temporal lobe of the brain); *agrammatism* (impairment in ability to arrange words in their correct order, to use *function words properly, and/or to use *accidence appropriately in an *inflecting language; *amnesic aphasia* (impaired ability to retrieve words that are required for fluent speech, also written *amnestic aphasia*); *anomic aphasia* (impaired ability to name objects or representations of objects, also called *anomia*; *compare* amnesic aphasia); *aphemia* (another name for Broca's aphasia); *ataxic aphasia* (another name for Broca's aphasia); *auditory aphasia* (another name for Wernicke's aphasia); *Broca's aphasia* (impaired ability to speak, with intact ability to comprehend speech, associated with damage to *Broca's area of the brain); *conduction aphasia* (impaired ability to repeat spoken words, together with errors in word selection in spontaneous speech, resulting from damage to the links between auditory and motor areas of the brain; *compare* mixed transcortical aphasia, transcortical motor aphasia, transcortical sensory aphasia, *see also* arcuate fasciculus); *dynamic aphasia* (a variant of non-fluent aphasia characterized by almost total failure to initiate speech but an intact ability to name objects, to read, and to repeat sentences); *dysprosody* (impaired ability to produce the appropriate *prosody required in speech); *expressive aphasia* (another name for Broca's aphasia); *fluent aphasia* (any form of aphasia, such as Wernicke's aphasia or conduction aphasia, in which language flows without difficulty, but either language comprehension is impaired or the speech is unintelligible); *ideomotor aphasia* (a generic term for transcortical motor aphasia, transcortical sensory aphasia, and mixed transcortical aphasia); *jargon aphasia* (copious unintelligible speech); *laloplegia* (a form of aphasia resulting from paralysis of the muscles of the *vocal tract and not those of the tongue); *mixed transcortical aphasia* (a blend of transcortical motor aphasia and transcortical sensory aphasia, with impaired spontaneous speech but intact ability to repeat spoken language; *compare* conduction aphasia); *motor aphasia* (another name for Broca's aphasia); *nominal aphasia* (a form of amnesic aphasia in which there is an impaired ability to retrieve the names of people or things); *non-fluent aphasia* (any form of aphasia, such as Broca's aphasia, in which speech is impaired); *optic aphasia* (selective impairment in ability to name objects presented visually, with intact ability to name them after touching them); *paraphasia* (habitual substitution of one word for another); *receptive aphasia* (another name for Wernicke's aphasia); *sensory aphasia* (another name for Wernicke's aphasia); *spasmophemia* (speech that is impaired by *spasms of the muscles in the vocal tract); *standard aphasia* (sparse speech with *content words but few *function words); *syntactic aphasia* (impaired ability to arrange words in grammatical sequence); *tactile aphasia* (selective impairment in ability to name objects by touch alone, with intact ability to name them after seeing them); *transcortical motor aphasia* (any form of aphasia resulting from disconnection of fibre tracts across the cortex to motor areas, resulting in impaired spontaneous speech but intact ability to repeat spoken language; *compare* conduction aphasia); *transcortical sensory aphasia* (any form of aphasia resulting from disconnection of fibre tracts across the cortex to sensory areas, resulting in impaired spontaneous speech but intact ability to repeat spoken language; *compare* conduction aphasia); *visual aphasia* (another name for *alexia); *Wernicke's aphasia* (impaired ability to understand speech, with intact ability to speak fluently, though not always intelligibly, associated with damage to *Wernicke's area in the brain). *Compare* dysphonia, mutism, selective mutism.
[From Greek *a-* without + *phasis* speech, from *phanai* to speak + *-ia* indicating a condition or quality]

aphemia *n.* Loss of ability to speak; Broca's aphasia (*see under* aphasia).
[From Greek *a-* without + *phanai* to speak + *-ia* indicating a condition or quality]

aphonia *n.* Loss of the voice resulting from damage to the vocal tract. If the inability to

speak is of psychological origin or caused by a lesion in the central nervous system, then the condition is not properly called *aphonia*.
[From Greek *a-* without + *phone* voice + *-ia* indicating a condition or quality]

aphorism *n.* A succinct, pithy adage or maxim expressing a universal truth, such as *Procrastination is the thief of time* or, more pointedly, *Punctuality is the thief of time*.
[From Greek *aphorizein* to define, from *apo* from + *horos* a limit]

aphrasia *n.* Another name for *mutism.
[From Greek *a-* without + *phrazein* to express + *-ia* indicating a condition or quality]

aphrodisiac *adj. n.* (Of or relating to) any substance such as *amyl nitrite, *bufotenin, *cantharides, *ginkgo, *ginseng, *L-dopa, or *yohimbine that stimulates or excites sexual desire. A central nervous system *depressant drug such as alcohol tends to lower sexual inhibitions, *cannabis generally increases the intensity of sensations, including sexual sensations, and *empathogens such as *ecstasy (2) or *GHB cause people to feel intensely benevolent to one another, but such substances are not true aphrodisiacs, because they do not directly affect sexual desire. *Compare* anaphrodisiac.
[From Greek *aphrodisiakos* aphrodisiac, from *Aphrodite* the Greek goddess of love]

Aplysia *n.* The sea hare, a marine snail approximately 25 centimetres long with only a vestigial shell, widely studied in neuroscience because of its large *neurons and comparatively simple neural circuits.
[From Greek *aplytos* unwashed, from *a-* without + *plynein* to wash + *-ia* indicating a condition or quality]

apnoea *n.* Cessation of breathing. US *apnea*. *See also* sleep apnoea.
[From Greek *apnoia* cessation of breathing, from *a-* without + *pnein* to breathe]

apocrine *adj.* Of or relating to a gland such as the mammary, the secretion of which contains part of the secreting cell. *Compare* holocrine, merocrine.
[From Greek *apo* off + *krinein* to separate]

Apollonian *adj.* Rational and controlled; in the philosophy of the German philosopher

Friedrich Wilhelm Nietzsche (1844–1900), of or relating to static qualities of form, reason, harmony, and sobriety. *Compare* Dionysian.
[Named after Apollo, the Greek god of light, poetry, music, healing, and prophecy]

apomorphine *n.* An *alkaloid that is prepared by dehydrating *morphine and that acts as a *dopaminomimetic drug, used as a powerful emetic, expectorant, and hypnotic.
[From Greek *apo* from + English *morphine*]

apoplexy *n.* Abrupt loss of consciousness, often followed by paralysis, usually caused by a rupture or thrombosis of a blood vessel in the brain. **apoplectic** *adj.* Of, relating to, or resembling *apoplexy; colloquially (arising from a misapprehension of the nature of the disorder), enraged or infuriated.
[From Greek *apoplexia* paralysis from a stroke, from *apo* away + *plessein* to strike]

apoptosis *n.* Programmed cell death, an active process requiring RNA and protein synthesis, that in the nervous system sometimes results from cytotoxic substances or a decrease in nerve growth factor, but that also occurs naturally as part of neuronal *pruning during development and growth. *See also* neural Darwinism.
[From Greek *apo* off + *ptosis* a falling, from *piptein* to fall + *-osis* indicating a process or state]

apostatic selection *n.* A *frequency-dependent form of *natural selection in which a *predator selects the most common type in a population of *prey. *See also* disruptive selection. *Compare* stabilizing selection.
[From Greek *apo* off + *stasis* a standing]

a posteriori *adj. adv.* Of, relating to, or denoting *propositions (1), arguments, or *concepts that proceed from observation or experience rather than from theoretical deduction; proceeding from observation rather than inference. *See* a priori. *See also* synthetic statement.
[Latin: from what comes after]

a posteriori test *n.* A statistical test that was not planned before the data were collected, especially a *multiple comparison corrected for the bias that can arise when tests are made of differences that emerge from inspecting data. Also called a *post hoc test*. *See* Bonferroni correction, Duncan's multiple range test, least-

significant difference test, Newman–Keuls test, Scheffé test, Tukey-HSD test. *Compare* planned comparison.
[From Latin *a* from + *posteriori* the latter]

apostrophe *n.* **1.** A *figure of speech involving a sudden deviation from the ordinary course of speech to address an object, a place, or a person present or absent, dead or alive, as in *Milton! Thou shouldst be living at this hour* (William Wordsworth, *Written in London, Sept. 1802*, I.13). **2.** A typographical mark usually indicating the omission of letters in the contraction of a word, as in the formation of genitive or possessive case (*John's*, a contraction of *John his*).
[From Greek *apo* from + *strophe* a turn]

apotemnophilia *n.* A *paraphilia characterized by recurrent sexually arousing fantasies, sexual urges, or behaviour associated with having one of one's own limbs (usually a leg) amputated. It should be carefully distinguished from *acrotomorphilia.
[From Greek *apo* away + *temnein* to cut + *philos* loving, from *philein* to love + *-ia* indicating a condition or quality]

apparent movement *n.* A sensation of movement in the absence of actual movement, especially a class of visual illusions that arise when two visual stimuli a few centimetres apart are exposed or displayed in an alternating pattern, first studied systematically in 1912 by the German Gestalt psychologist Max Wertheimer (1880–1943), who distinguished the following stages (*Stadien*). If each stimulus is exposed for about 50 milliseconds, then with an interstimulus interval below about 25 milliseconds the stimuli, though possibly flickering, appear to be simultaneous (this is called the *Simultanstadium*); with an interstimulus interval over about 400 milliseconds there is no illusion and the stimuli are seen to alternate (the *Sukzessivstadium*); but between approximately 25 and 400 milliseconds, under certain conditions defined by *Korte's laws, powerful illusions of movement are created: first *partial movement when the interstimulus interval is relatively short, then *optimal movement when the interval is increased, and finally *phi movement when the interval is increased further. These phenomena underlie the effects created by illuminated signboards with arrows or other elements that appear to move, and they also explain the motion pictures of cinema and television. The concepts of *alpha movement, *beta movement, *gamma movement, and *delta movement, denoting different forms of apparent movement, were introduced by other German Gestalt psychologists between 1913 and 1915. Apparent movement is also called *apparent motion*, *phenomenal motion*, or the *phi phenomenon*, but in careful usage this latter term is reserved for the phenomenon of phi movement in particular. *See also* autokinetic effect, iconic store, motion capture, phantom grating, random-dot kinematogram, Ternus phenomenon, vection, waterfall illusion.

appeasement behaviour *n.* Submissive behaviour of an animal, discouraging an attack by a hostile aggressor. US *appeasement behavior*.
[From Old French *apeser* to bring peace, from Latin *ad* to + *pax* peace]

apperception *n.* The process of comprehending a *perception by integrating it with similar or related perceptions or previously acquired knowledge; also, the awareness of the act or experience of perceiving, or self-consciousness in contrast to perception—first used in this sense by the German philosopher and mathematician Gottfried Wilhelm von Leibniz (1646–1716). *See also* apperceptive mass, TAT. **apperceive** *vb.* **apperceptive** *adj.*
[From Latin *ad* to + *percipere, perceptum* to perceive, from *per* through or thoroughly + *capere, ceptum* to take + *-ion* indicating an action, process, or state]

apperceptive agnosia *See under* agnosia.

apperceptive mass *n.* The previously acquired perceptions and knowledge with which a new perception is integrated in the process of *apperception.

appestat *n.* A mechanism in the *hypothalamus that is sensitive to *glucose levels in the blood and that regulates eating. It is located in the *lateral hypothalamic feeding centre, where stimulation of it increases eating and destruction inhibits eating, and in the *ventromedial hypothalamus, where stimulation inhibits eating and destruction increases eating.
[From *appetite* + Greek *statikos* causing to stand, from *histanai* to stand + *-ikos* of, relating to, or resembling]

appetite n. Desire for food; more generally, desire to satisfy any physical craving; more generally still, any enthusiasm or inclination, such as an appetite for war.
[From Latin *appetitus* a craving, from *appetere* to desire ardently]

appetitive behaviour n. Behaviour motivated by desire for food or drink. US *appetitive behavior*.

appetitive phase n. The first phase of the *sexual response cycle.

apples n. An edible fruit; also, a branded version of the stimulant designer drug *ecstasy (2).
[Identified by a symbol of an apple]

applied psychology n. An umbrella term covering various branches of psychology in which research findings are applied to practical problems. In *clinical psychology and *counselling psychology, research into mental disorders is applied with the ultimate aim of helping people with those disorders. In *educational psychology and *school psychology, research into problems of learning, adjustment, and behaviour among schoolchildren is applied in an effort to provide practical help to children, their parents, and their teachers. In *occupational psychology and *industrial/organizational psychology, the results of research into the well-being and efficiency of people in work is used to tackle problems arising in the workplace and in organizations generally. In *forensic psychology and *criminological psychology, problems associated with criminal behaviour, criminal investigation, and legal processes in court are addressed. In *health psychology, research findings are applied to psychological aspects of health promotion and the prevention and treatment of illness.

applied research n. Research undertaken with the primary goal of solving practical problems, often contrasted with *basic research. *See* action research, evaluation research. *See also* descriptive research, exploratory research.

apprehension span *See* span of apprehension.

approach–approach conflict n. A choice between two or more equally attractive goals,

one of the three main types of conflict identified in 1931 by the Polish/German-born US psychologist Kurt Lewin (1890–1947), though he did not name any of the types. He published his classification in a monograph that was translated into English and issued in 1935 under the title *A Dynamic Theory of Personality*. Lewin mentioned *Buridan's ass as a typical example of this type of conflict. *See also* approach–avoidance conflict, avoidance–avoidance conflict.

approach–avoidance conflict n. Ambivalence towards a goal that embodies both positive and negative characteristics, one of the three main types of conflict identified in 1931 by the Polish/German-born US psychologist Kurt Lewin (1890–1947), though he did not name any of the types. When a goal is simultaneously satisfying and threatening, pleasant and unpleasant, attractive and anxiety-arousing, people's behaviour tends to vacillate at a point near but not too near the goal. Further from the goal the tendency to approach predominates, nearer the goal the tendency to avoid predominates, and equilibrium occurs where the approach and avoidance functions cross. *See also* approach–approach conflict, avoidance–avoidance conflict, Rosencrantz and Guildenstern effect.

approximant n. A *consonant speech sound in which the organs of articulation approach each other, but not so closely as to cause audible friction. There are two major classes of approximants: *semivowels such as the initial *phonemes in the English words *win* and *yes*, and *liquids such as the initial phonemes in the English words *love* and *road*.
[From Latin *proximare* to draw near or approach]

approximate answers *See* Ganser syndrome.

approximation to language n. A random string of words in which the relative frequencies of words or word sequences correspond to their relative frequencies in the language. A *zero-order approximation* is a random string of words that takes no account of relative frequencies; in a *first-order approximation*, the relative frequencies of words correspond to their relative frequencies in the language, so that the most common words, such as *the* and *is* in English, occur relatively frequently; in a *sec-*

ond-order approximation, the relative frequencies of word pairs correspond to their relative frequencies in the language, and so on. The US psychologist George A(rmitage) Miller (born 1920) and J. A. Selfridge introduced a psychological technique, published in the *American Journal of Psychology* in 1950, for constructing a slightly different type of approximation: for a zero-order approximation, words are selected at random from a dictionary (*Combat callous irritability migrates depraved temporal prolix . . .*); for a first-order approximation, words are selected from published word counts in proportion to their frequencies (*Day to is for they have proposed I the it materials of are . . .*); for a second-order approximation, a word is chosen at random and is shown to a person, who is asked to suggest the most likely word to follow it, then this second word alone is shown to another person, who suggests the most likely word to follow it, and so on (*Gone down here is not large feet are the happy days and so what is dead weight that many were constructed . . .*); for a third-order approximation, each person sees the two preceding words (*Happened to see Europe again is that trip to the end is . . .*); and for a fourth-order approximation, each person sees the three preceding words (*We are going to see him is not correct to chuckle loudly and depart for home . . .*). Each successive order of approximation is more meaningful and is easier to learn, to recall after learning, and to hear when spoken softly or with background noise. *See also* stylostatistics.

appurtenance *n.* In *Gestalt psychology, the mutual influence of parts of the *visual field, a typical example being the influence of two adjacent patches of colour on each other in simultaneous *colour contrast, other areas of the visual field not affecting the phenomenon.
[From Old French *apertenir* to appertain, from Latin *appertinere* to appertain, from *ad* to + *pertinere* to belong]

apraxia *n.* A loss or diminution in ability, caused by neurological impairment usually in the left hemisphere of the brain, to perform purposeful bodily movements or *gestures (1) on request, though often with apparently unimpaired ability to perform them when they arise in natural contexts (such as when circumstances call for waving goodbye to someone), the impairment not being due to paralysis or poor comprehen-

sion. The major forms are: *akinetic apraxia* (impaired ability to perform a spontaneous gesture); *amnesic apraxia* (impaired ability to perform purposeful bodily movements or gestures on request because of amnesia for the request, also written *amnestic apraxia*); *constructional apraxia* (impaired ability to copy simple drawings or patterns); *dressing apraxia* (impaired ability to dress); *gait apraxia* (impaired ability to walk); *ideational apraxia* (impaired ability to repeat previously well-established actions); *ideomotor apraxia* (impaired ability to imitate unfamiliar actions, also called *motor apraxia* or *ideokinetic apraxia*); *left-sided apraxia* (impaired ability to carry out verbal requests with the left side of the body, resulting from damage to the *corpus callosum preventing impulses from the left hemisphere reaching the right motor cortex, also called *callosal apraxia, sympathetic apraxia, unilateral limb apraxia*); *oculomotor apraxia* (impaired ability to make eye movements, also called *ocular apraxia* or *optic apraxia*); *oral apraxia* (impaired ability to perform actions of the mouth and tongue, such as opening the mouth or protruding the tongue); *paramimia* (impaired ability to gesture); *sensory apraxia* (another name for ideational apraxia); *speech apraxia* (impaired ability to speak, without other language impairments). *See also* adiadochokinesia, alien hand sign, kinesics.
[From Greek *apraxia* inaction, from *a-* without + *praxis* a deed or action + *-ia* indicating a condition or quality]

a priori *adj. adv.* Of, relating to, or denoting *propositions (1), arguments, or *concepts that proceed from theoretical deduction rather than from observation or experience, hence being based on inference rather than observation. An a priori proposition can be known to be true or false without reference to observation or experience, whereas the truth or falsity of an *a posteriori proposition is contingent and can be established only by *empirical test. An a priori argument seeks to deduce conclusions from a priori premises, whereas an a posteriori argument proceeds from a posteriori premises. An a priori concept is one that is not derived from experience: the *empiricist philosophers claimed that all concepts are empirical and a posteriori, but the Greek philosopher Plato (?427–?347 BC) and *rationalists such as the German philosopher and mathematician Gottfried Wilhelm von Leibniz (1646–1716)

claimed that some concepts, such as those of substance, cause, equality, likeness, and difference, are a priori, and the German idealist philosopher Immanuel Kant (1724–1804) argued that observation and experience themselves presuppose a priori knowledge. The terms *a priori* and *a posteriori* were introduced by scholastic philosophers of the late medieval period and were popularized in the 17th century by Leibniz and the French philosopher René Descartes (1596–1650). *See also* analytic statement. *Compare* a posteriori.
[Latin: from what comes before]

a priori probability *n*. Another name for a *prior probability (2).

a priori test *n*. Another name for a *planned comparison.

a priori validity *n*. Another name for *face validity.

aprosexia *n*. Inability to concentrate. *Compare* hyperprosexia, hypoprosexia.
[From Greek *a-* without + *prosexis* heedfulness, from *prosechein* to heed + *-ia* indicating a condition or quality]

aprosodia *n*. A flat, unmodulated speaking voice, lacking the normal range of *prosody, often indicative of *affective flattening or a lesion in the *frontal lobe of the right *cerebral hemisphere. *Compare* dysprosody.
[From Greek *a-* without + *prosoidia* a song set to music, from *pros* towards + *oide* a song + *-ia* indicating a condition or quality]

aptitude *n*. Suitability, natural ability, or capacity to learn; especially (in psychology) potential rather than existing capacity to perform some function, whether physical, mental, or a combination of the two, given the necessary education or training. *See also* aptitude test. *Compare* ability.
[From Latin *aptus* suitable or adapted, from *apere* to fasten + *-tudo* indicating a state or condition]

aptitude test *n*. A test designed to measure an *aptitude. *See also* vocational aptitude test. *Compare* ability test, achievement test.

aptronym *n*. A name that befits a person's nature, occupation, or activities. Examples relevant to psychology include the Austrian neurologist Sigmund Freud (1856–1939), who based his theory of psychoanalysis on the *pleasure principle (pleasure is *Freude* in German), his rival the Swiss psychologist Carl Gustav Jung (1875–1961), who was almost 30 years younger than Freud (young is *jung* in German), and his feminist disciple, the German-born US psychoanalyst Karen Horney (1885–1952), who rejected his theory of *penis envy. Other aptronyms include Sir Henry Head, the English neurologist; Iris C. Love, the US archaeologist who excavated the temple of Aphrodite (the Greek goddess of love) at Cnidus in Turkey in 1969; Gay Search, author of *The Last Taboo: Sexual Abuse of Children* (1988); and J. J. C. Smart, the clever Australian philosopher. *See also* folk etymology (2) for the aptronym *Crapper*.
[Irregular formation from Latin *aptus* fitting + *nomen* a name]

aqueduct of Sylvius *n*. Another name for the *cerebral aqueduct.
[From Latin *aqua* water + *ducere*, *ductum* to lead, named after the French anatomist Sylvius (1478–1555), also called Jacques Dubois, who discovered it]

aqueous humour *n*. The watery fluid in the space between the cornea and crystalline lens of the eye. US *aqueous humor*. *See also* glaucoma. *Compare* vitreous humour.
[From Latin *aqua* water + *-osus* having or characterized by + *umor* bodily fluid, from *umere* to be moist]

arachnoid membrane *n*. The middle of the three *meninges, being a thin, transparent, non-vascular membrane covering the brain and spinal cord, attached tightly to the dura mater. Sometimes called the *arachnoid layer* or the *arachnoid mater*. *Compare* dura mater, pia mater.
[From the Greek *arachne* a spider, alluding to its delicate weblike structure]

arachnoid space *n*. The space, filled with *cerebrospinal fluid, between the *arachnoid membrane and the inner *pia mater.

Arago phenomenon *n*. The relatively greater sensitivity of *peripheral vision as compared to *central vision in dim light, owing to the physiological characteristics of *scotopic vision, in particular the distribution of *rods on the retina. Ancient astronomers were the first to notice that when observing the night sky, stars can be seen in peripheral vision that disappear when fixated directly. *See* fovea.

[Named after the French astronomer and physicist (Dominique) François (Jean) Arago (1786–1853) who first examined it in detail]

arboreal *adj.* **1.** Tree-like in form or appearance. **2.** Tree-dwelling.
[From Latin *arbor* a tree]

arborization *n.* Any branching tree-like formation or structure.
[From Latin *arbor* a tree + *-izare* from Greek *-izein* to cause to become + *-ation* indicating a process or condition]

archaecortex *n.* The type of cortex that is found mainly in the *hippocampus and that evolved in humans earlier than any other part of the human *cerebral cortex. Also spelt *archicortex* or *archecortex*. Also called the *archaepallium* or *archipallium*. *See also* neocortex. *Compare* mesocortex, palaeocortex.
[From Greek *archaios* ancient, from *arche* beginning + Latin *cortex* bark or outer layer]

archetypal form *n.* In *analytical psychology, an image, motif, pattern, or theme associated with an *archetype (2), the archetype itself not being susceptible to direct representation. *See* God-image, mandala, primordial image. *See also* collective unconscious.

archetype *n.* **1.** A perfect or typical example of its class, or another name for a *prototype (2). **2.** In *analytical psychology, an inherited mental structure or pattern, forming part of the *collective unconscious, observable only through its manifestations in behaviour, especially that associated with ancient and universal experiences such as birth, marriage, motherhood, and death. Carl Gustav Jung (1875–1961) introduced the term into his technical vocabulary in 1919 and later defined it as 'an irrepresentable, unconscious, pre-existent form that seems to be part of the inherited structure of the psyche and can therefore manifest itself spontaneously anywhere, at any time' (*Collected Works*, 10, paragraph 847). Also (originally) called a *primordial image*. *See also* anima, animus (3), archetypal form, collective unconscious, imago (1), primordial image, *puer aeternus*, shadow (2). **archetypal** *adj.*

[From Greek *archetypon* an original, from *arche* the beginning + *typos* a model]

Archimedes spiral *n.* A plane curve whose equation is $r = a\theta$ in polar coordinates, meaning that the length of the curve's radius r from its centre is always a constant ratio of the angle that the radius forms with a fixed axis, and as a consequence the coils of the spiral are a constant distance apart like the grooves of old-fashioned vinyl phonograph records, which are in fact Archimedes spirals. The term is sometimes used as a synonym for a *Plateau spiral, but this is avoided in careful usage because a Plateau spiral is merely a device based on it and often on some other spiral. Also called an *Archimedean spiral*.
[Named after the ancient Greek mathematician and physicist Archimedes of Syracuse (?287–212 BC) who was the first to study it and whose treatise *On Spirals* is devoted mainly to it]

arctic hysteria *See* pibloktoq.

arcuate fasciculus *n.* A small bundle of nerve fibres in each cerebral hemisphere that curves round the back of the lateral sulcus and that in the (usually) left hemisphere connects *Broca's area with *Wernicke's area. Lesions to it often result in conduction aphasia (*see under* aphasia). *See also* disconnection syndrome.
[From Latin *arcuatus* bent like a bow, from *arcuare* to bend like a bow, from *arcus* a bow + *fasciculus* a little bundle, diminutive of *fasculus* a bundle]

arcuate nucleus *n.* A small nucleus near the base of the *hypothalamus containing the cell bodies that produce hypothalamic *hormones.

area postrema *n.* An area of the brain in the roof of the fourth *ventricle at its posterior tip, outside the *blood–brain barrier, functioning as a chemoreceptor trigger area and controlling the vomiting reflex, also containing *serotonergic nerve fibres.
[From Latin *postremus* hindmost]

Areas V1, V2, V3, V4, V5 *See under* visual cortex. *Compare* Brodmann area.

argot *n.* A secretive form of *jargon (1) or *slang peculiar to a specific group, originally

a band of thieves. *See also* back slang, cant (2), register (2), rhyming slang.
[French, origin unknown]

Argyll Robertson pupil *n.* A *pupil of the eye that constricts in response to *accommodation (1) but not in response to light, a neurological sign of damage to the midbrain relays of the *oculomotor nerve. **ARP** *abbrev.*
[Named after the Scottish physician Douglas M. C. L. Argyll Robertson (1837–1909) who drew attention to it]

ARIMA *abbrev.* Autoregressive integrated moving average, a widely used class of models developed in 1970 by the English statisticians George Edward Pelham Box (born 1919) and Gwilym Meiron Jenkins (1933–82) for *time-series analysis, also called *Box–Jenkins models.* *See also* Type III error.
[Named after the three components of the model, namely the *a*utoregression, *i*ntegration (differencing), and *m*oving *a*verage coefficients]

Aristotle's illusion *n.* A tactile illusion that is created when the eyes are closed, two fingers of one hand are crossed, and a small object such as an acorn is pressed (especially by another person) into the cleft between the tips of the crossed fingers. The sensation is that of touching two objects rather than one. The first written account of it was given by the Greek philosopher Aristotle (384–322 BC) in the essay *On Dreams* in the *Parva Naturalia*: 'When the fingers are crossed, one object seems to be two; but yet we deny that it is two; for sight is more authoritative than touch. Yet, if touch stood alone, we should actually have pronounced the one object to be two' (Chapter 2). Aristotle mentioned it also in *Metaphysics*: 'Touch says there are two objects when we cross our fingers, while sight says there is one' (Book 4, Chapter 6). The explanation for the illusion, apparently overlooked by Aristotle, is that when the fingers are crossed the outsides of two fingers are touched simultaneously, and in ordinary circumstances and past experience that requires stimulation by two separate objects. This explanation was first advanced in *Problems*, a spurious work often attributed to Aristotle, probably written by one of his followers: 'When we hold the hand in its natural position, we cannot touch an object with the outer sides of two fingers' (Book 35, Chapter 10). Further references to the illusion are to be found in Book 31, Chapters 11 and 17 of *Problems*. Also called *Aristotle's experiment. See also* diplaesthesia.

arithmetic mean *n.* In descriptive statistics, the average value, calculated (for a finite set of scores) by adding the scores together and then dividing the total by the number of scores. Often referred to simply as the *mean*, this is the most commonly used measure of *central tendency. *See also* median, mode, trimmed mean. *Compare* geometric mean, harmonic mean. **M** *abbrev.*
[From Old French *moien*, from Latin *medianus* median]

armchair experiment *n.* Another name for a *Gedankenexperiment*.

arms race *n.* A competition between military powers building up armaments; hence figuratively in evolutionary theory, a sequence of evolutionary changes in two (or more) species competing for survival and reproduction, often a *predator and its *prey, in which each advantageous *adaptation (1) in one is countered by a corresponding adaptation in the other.

Army Alpha and Beta tests *n.* The first *group tests of intelligence, providing the prototypes of many that were to follow, intended to improve selection, placement, and training for specific occupations within the US army during the First World War, constructed by a group of US psychologists under the leadership of Robert Mearns Yerkes (1876–1956), including Lewis Madison Terman (1877–1956), and applied to approximately 1,750,000 recruits in just over one year. The test and the results that it generated were kept secret until the war ended, eventually being published by the National Academy of Sciences in 1921 in a book edited by Yerkes entitled *Psychology Examining in the United States Army*, and in 1919 Yerkes published a version of the tests called the *National Intelligence Test*, which was widely used by schools, universities, and commercial companies. The Army Alpha test included the earliest examples of *analogies tests, *number-completion tests, *synonym tests, and *antonym tests, and the Army Beta test, designed specifically for people who were illiterate, introduced the first *incomplete-pictures test and *coding test, all the subtests being strictly timed.

Army General Classification Test n. An *intelligence test used during the Second World War and after, suitable for literate adults. **AGCT** abbrev.

aromatic adj. Spicy or fragrant, belonging to the class of benzene derivatives or closed-chain organic compounds. *Aliphatic and aromatic hydrocarbons in petrol or gasoline, glue, paint thinners, and some aerosol propellants are *psychotropic when inhaled. See also inhalant-related disorders, solvent abuse. [Greek aroma, aromatos spice + -ikos of, relating to, or resembling]

arousal n. Short for physiological arousal: excitation of the *ascending reticular activating system, leading to a condition of alertness and readiness to respond, as evidenced by such physiological signs as increased heart rate and blood pressure, *galvanic skin response (GSR), and *desynchronized EEG activity. See also arousal phase, cognitive–appraisal theory, Yerkes–Dodson law.

arousal phase n. The second phase of the *sexual response cycle, when sexual excitement develops.

arrangement problem n. A measure of problem-solving ability in which the respondent tries to arrange a number of elements in the correct sequence, the most common version being a *picture-arrangement test.

Arrow's impossibility theorem n. A theorem introduced in 1951 by the US economist Kenneth J(oseph) Arrow (born 1921) and modified in 1963 to correct an error that had been found in it, showing that no voting system or any other social choice function could ever guarantee to aggregate the individual preferences of a group into a collective preference ranking so as to satisfy the following four seemingly necessary but mild conditions of fairness. (U) Unrestricted domain: the social choice function must generate a collective preference order from any logically possible set of individual preference orders; (P) Pareto condition: whenever all individuals prefer an alternative x to another y, x must be preferred to y in the collective preference order; (I) Independence of irrelevant alternatives: the collective preference order of any pair of alternatives x and y must depend solely on the individuals' preferences between these alter-

natives and not on their preferences for other (irrelevant) alternatives; (D) Non-dictatorship: the collective preference order must not invariably correspond to the preferences of any single individual, regardless of the preferences of the others. The proof of the theorem relies on the profile of individual preferences that gives rise to *Condorcet's paradox of *intransitive preferences and shows that any social choice function that satisfies U, P, and I necessarily violates D and is therefore dictatorial. Also called Arrow's paradox.

artefact n. **1.** An article, such as a tool or a work of art, made by a person or people. **2.** Something that is observed in an empirical investigation and is not a natural occurrence but a by-product of the investigation itself. Also (especially in US) spelt artifact. **artefactual** or **artifactual** adj. [From Latin arte by art, from ars skill or art + factum made, from facere to make]

arteriogram n. Another name for an *angiogram. **arteriography** n. Another name for *angiography. [From Greek arteria an artery + gramme a line]

arteriosclerosis n. Hardening or *sclerosis of the arteries. See also atherosclerosis, cerebral arteriosclerosis. **arteriosclerotic** adj. **arteriosclerotic dementia** n. Another name for *vascular dementia or *multi-infarct dementia. [From Greek arteria an artery + sklerosis a hardening, from skleros hard + -osis indicating a process or state]

articulation n. The production of speech sounds by using the speech organs to modify the airstream, usually from the lungs. *Consonants are classified chiefly by *place of articulation and *manner of articulation. [From Latin articulus a little joint, hence articulare to provide with joints + -ation indicating a process or condition]

articulation disorder n. Another name for *phonological disorder.

articulatory coding n. Remembering something by storing the physical movements required to produce its verbal expression, rather than by storing its sound or its meaning. Compare acoustic coding, semantic coding.

articulatory loop n. Another name for a *subvocal rehearsal loop. Also called an *articulatory rehearsal loop*.

articulatory store n. Another name for a *subvocal rehearsal loop.

artifact See artefact.

artificial insemination n. Introduction of sperm into the *vagina or uterus by any method other than coitus.

artificial intelligence n. The design of hypothetical or actual computer programs or machines to do things normally done by minds, such as playing chess, thinking logically, writing poetry, composing music, or analysing chemical substances. The most challenging problems arise in attempting to simulate functions of intelligence that are largely unconscious, such as those involved in vision and language. The term was introduced in 1956 by the US computer engineer John McCarthy (born 1927). See strong AI, weak AI. See also case grammar, Chinese room, computer vision, default reasoning, expert system, frame (2), frame problem, fuzzy logic, General Problem Solver, Gödel's theorem, knowledge representation, neural network, non-monotonic reasoning, optical character recognition, Pandemonium, SHRDLU, Turing machine, Turing test. Also called *machine intelligence*. **AI** abbrev.

artificial language n. A language deliberately invented or constructed, especially as a means of communication in computing or information technology. See also language (1). Compare natural language.

artificial neural network n. Another name for a *neural network. Also called an *artificial neural net*. **ANN** abbrev.

artificial pupil n. Another name for a *reduction screen.

art therapy n. A form of *psychotherapy in which clients or patients are encouraged to express their feelings and inner conflicts through art.

ascending reticular activating system n. The ascending fibres of the *reticular formation in the brainstem, defined functionally rather than anatomically according to their control of the level of physiological *arousal or activation of the cerebral cortex, essential for wakefulness, attention, and concentration. Also called the *reticular activating system* (RAS). See also cerveau isolé. Compare descending reticular formation. **ARAS** abbrev.

Asch experiment n. A classic experiment on *conformity introduced in 1951 by the Polishborn US psychologist Solomon E(lliott) Asch (1907–96) and subsequently used by numerous researchers. A group of people (usually seven to nine in Asch's original series) were seated around a table and told that they were to take part in an experiment on visual discrimination. They were shown 18 pairs of cards, and in each case were asked to say out loud, one at a time, which of the three lines on one card was the same length as the comparison line on the other. The task was deliberately made sufficiently easy to ensure that errors were virtually zero when people were tested alone, without any conformity pressure, but in the experiment there was only one real subject or participant in the group, usually sitting at the end of the row and therefore having to formulate judgements after hearing those of the other group members, and the rest of the group were accomplices of the experimenter, trained to give unanimous wrong answers on 12 critical trials out of the 18. About 37 per cent of judgements on critical trials were conforming responses—the real subject going along with the incorrect unanimous majority. The experience was rather stressful for those who remained independent, and conformity was found to increase with the size of the unanimous majority ranged against the real subject, but only up to a majority of three against one, after which further increases produced no significant increases in conformity.

ascorbic acid See vitamin C.

asemia n. Impaired ability to encode or comprehend signs such as *gestures (1) or the spoken and written signs and symbols of human languages. Also called *asemasia* or *asymbolia*. [From Greek a- without + semeion a sign + -ia indicating a condition or quality]

asexual reproduction n. Procreation as it occurs in some species without formation of male or female *gametes, usually by *fission

(2). In careful usage it is distinguished from *parthenogenesis.

asonia n. Impaired ability to discriminate between tones of different pitches. Also (nontechnically) called *tone deafness*.
[From Latin *a-* away or away from + *sonus* a sound]

aspartame n. The intensely sweet non-carbohydrate crystalline compound $C_{14}H_{18}N_2O_5$ formed from the amino acids *phenylalanine and *aspartic acid, used as an artificial sweetener that is 200 times sweeter than sucrose (table sugar).
[From *aspart(ic) (acid)* + *(phenyl)a(lanine)* + *me(thyl) (ester)*]

aspartate n. Another name for *aspartic acid.

aspartic acid n. A non-essential *amino acid that is a component molecule of proteins and that functions as a *neurotransmitter. Also called *aspartate. See also* aspartame. **Asp** *abbrev*.
[From *aspar(agus)*, in which it is found, + Greek *-ikos* of, relating to, or resembling]

Asperger's disorder n. A *pervasive developmental disorder characterized by severe and sustained impairment in social interaction together with restricted, repetitive, or stereotyped patterns of behaviour, interests, or activities, causing clinically significant impairment in everyday living, without the language and cognitive deficits characteristic of *autistic disorder but in other ways similar to it, usually found in males. *Compare* schizoid personality disorder.
[Named after the Austrian psychiatrist Hans Asperger (1906–80) who first described it in 1944]

aspiration n. Audible breath that may accompany the articulation of a speech sound. For example, in most *accents (1) of English, the initial *consonants in the words *pen, ten,* and *ken* are followed by a brief sound like /h/ before the voicing of the vowel begins, but when /p/, /t/, or /k/ is preceded by /s/, as in *spy, sty,* and *sky,* it is not aspirated. *See also* Grassmann's law (linguistics). **aspirate** *vb.* **1.** To pronounce a speech sound with *aspiration. *n.* **2.** A speech sound pronounced with *aspiration.

aspirin n. Acetylsalicylic acid, a white, crystalline compound originally derived from the bark of the willow tree *Salix alba,* identified and first synthesized by the German chemist Felix Hoffmann (1868–1946) at the Bayer division of the German chemical company I. G. Farben in 1898, widely used as an *analgesic (1). It consists of an acetyl group linked to a salicylic acid group, and its powerful anti-inflammatory and antipyretic (fever-reducing) effects result from its inhibition of *prostaglandin synthesis. When it enters the molecule prostaglandin H_2 synthase or PGHS, the enzyme that produces prostaglandins, its acetyl group binds to a site within the enzyme and blocks the channel through which arachidonic acid from the *endoplasmic reticulum is converted to prostaglandins. It also shuts down forms of the PGHS enzyme that protect the lining of the stomach. Signs and symptoms of aspirin overdose include gastrointestinal bleeding, dizziness, sweating, thirst, tinnitus, visual disturbances, confusion, drowsiness, breathlessness, nausea, vomiting, coma, and death. Formula: $CH_3COOC_6H_4COOH$. *See also* ototoxic.
[The original proprietary name given to it by Bayer, from *a(cetyl)* + German *Spir(säure)* spiraeic (now salicylic) acid + *-in(e)* indicating an organic compound]

A/S ratio *abbrev*. Association/sensation ratio, an index of the comparative *intelligence of mammalian species formulated by the Canadian psychologist Donald O(lding) Hebb (1904–85), defined as brain volume devoted to *association areas divided by brain volume devoted to sensory and motor areas. *Compare* encephalization quotient, progression index.

A–S Reaction Study n. An early personality inventory designed to measure ascendance versus submissiveness in everyday social relationships, constructed by the US psychologists Gordon W(illard) Allport (1897–1967) and Floyd H(enry) Allport (1890–1978) and published in their book *The A–S Reaction Study* (1928). Not to be confused with the *A-S scale.

A–S scale *abbrev*. A scale to measure anti-Semitism (prejudice against or hostility to Jews), especially the scale first published by the German philosopher, sociologist, and psychologist Theodor W(iesengrund) Adorno (1903–69) and several colleagues in the book *The Authoritarian Personality* (1950). Not to be confused with the *A–S Reaction Study. *See also* authoritarianism.

assembled phonology *n.* The sound of a word or verbal expression as it is built up from knowledge of the usual sounds of letters and sequences of letters. This method fails with irregular words such as *yacht* in English, but in regular languages such as German or Spanish the correct pronunciation can always be worked out in this way. *Compare* addressed phonology.

assertiveness training *n.* A form of *counselling or *psychotherapy developed in 1949 by the US psychologist Andrew Salter (born 1914) in which people learn to express their needs, wishes, and feelings frankly, honestly, and directly, in a way that causes others to take them into account. Also called *assertion training*. *See also* modelling, social skills training.

assimilation *n.* **1.** Absorption or incorporation of information or of a substance, or more generally the act or process of making things similar or alike. **2.** In the writings of the Swiss psychologist Jean Piaget (1896–1980) and his followers, a form of *adaptation (3) in which novel experiences are incorporated into existing psychological structures or processes, as when an infant responds to a new toy that is introduced into its environment by treating it like an already familiar object, interpreting it on the basis of past experience as something to be grasped, shaken, put in the mouth, and so on. *See also* equilibration. *Compare* accommodation (2). **3.** The influence on a speech sound by one of its neighbours, making the two sounds more alike than they would otherwise be. For example, the plural-forming /s/ is pronounced with a voiced [z] *allophone when it follows a voiced *consonant, as in the English word *dogs*, but with a voiceless [s] allophone when it follows a voiceless consonant as in *cats*. **4.** Decreasing the discrepancy between one's own attitude and that of a persuasive source or message. *See also* assimilation-contrast theory, false-consensus effect. *Compare* contrast (4). **5.** The distortion of a memory through making it similar to already existing memories, a phenomenon that also occurs in *serial reproduction and *rumour transmission. *Compare* levelling (1), sharpening. **6.** A tendency for the perception of objects or images to take on perceptual characteristics of adjacent objects or images. *See* colour assimilation. **assimilate** *vb.* **assimilative** *adj.*

[From Latin *assimilare* to make similar or alike, from *ad* to + *similis* like + *-ation* indicating a process or condition]

assimilation–contrast theory *n.* A theory of judgement and *attitude change according to which a judge's initial judgement or attitude acts as an anchor, so that items of information or persuasive communications that are not very discrepant from the anchor and that therefore fall within the person's *latitude of acceptance* are assimilated, the person's judgement or attitude changing in the direction of the communication, whereas items of information or persuasive communications that are highly discrepant produce either minimal change if they fall within the person's *latitude of neutrality* or produce contrast effects if they fall within the *latitude of rejection*, the person's judgement or attitude changing in the opposite direction. Attitudes associated with high *ego involvement tend to have narrow latitudes of acceptance and wide latitudes of rejection, and the reverse applies to attitudes of low ego involvement. A consequence of this theory is that an extreme and ego-involving judgement or attitude tends to be polarized (to become even more extreme) in response to most types of information or persuasive communications. The theory was formulated in 1961 by the US-based Turkish psychologist Muzafer Sherif (1906–88) and the US psychologist Carl I(vor) Hovland (1912–61). *See also* boomerang effect, contrast (5), discrepancy effects, false-consensus effect. *Compare* adaptation-level theory.

association area *n.* Another name for a *tertiary projection area, or more loosely any area of the cerebral cortex not devoted to primary sensory or motor functions, or to primary and secondary sensory or motor functions (usage is not consistent). Also called an *association centre* or an area of the *association cortex*.

association fibre *n.* Any of the nerve fibres that pass from one *gyrus to another within or between lobes of the same cerebral hemisphere. US *association fiber*.

association, free *See* free association.

associationism *n.* A psychological doctrine concerning the attraction between mental elements or ideas, first suggested in a chapter entitled 'Of the Association of Ideas' that the

English empiricist philosopher John Locke (1632–1704) added in 1700 to a new edition of his *Essay Concerning Human Understanding*, originally published in 1690, the doctrine later being elaborated by the Scottish philosopher James Mill (1773–1836) and his English son John Stuart Mill (1806–73). According to the Mills, mental experiences consist of elementary *sensations* when sense organs are stimulated, and *ideas* are thoughts and memories experienced in the absence of sensory stimulation. Ideas have a tendency to become associated with one another: complex ideas arise from the association of simple ideas, and once two ideas have become associated, it is then difficult to experience one without the other, as when the idea of redness, associated in most people's minds with warmth, tends to come to mind whenever we think of warmth. James Mill believed that the single *contiguity law (elements become associated when they are close to one another in time or space) explained all mental associations and complex ideas. John Stuart Mill added the *similarity law (similar ideas tend to become associated), and the *frequency law (the more frequently ideas occur together, the more strongly they become associated), and also introduced what he called *mental chemistry, according to which simple ideas combine to form complex ideas that are qualitatively different from their constituent elements. The Scottish mental philosopher Alexander Bain (1818–1903) was the first to suggest that behavioural actions can also form associations with ideas. *See also* grouping law. *Compare* connectionism (2).

association/sensation ratio *See* A/S ratio.

association test *n.* Another name for the *word-association test. Also called the *association method*.

association value *n.* A property of *nonsense syllables and other materials that are themselves meaningless of being, to varying degrees, suggestive of meaningful words or ideas. For example, according to empirical studies, the nonsense syllables *BAL*, *FUT*, and *MOD* have very high association value, whereas *CIJ*, *VAF*, and *XEJ* have very low association value.

associative illusion *n.* Any *visual illusion in which one part of an image or object is mis-perceived because of the effect of another. Also called a *geometric illusion*. *See* Baldwin illusion, Craik–O'Brien effect, curvature illusion, Delboeuf illusion, Ebbinghaus illusion, Ehrenstein's brightness illusion, Ehrenstein's square illusion, filled-space illusion, filling-in illusion, Fraser spiral, Helmholtz illusion, Hering illusion, Hermann grid, hollow squares illusion, horizontal-vertical illusion, irradiation illusion, Jastrow illusion, Land effect, Margaret Thatcher illusion, Morinaga misalignment illusion, Müller-Lyer illusion, Münsterberg illusion, Orbison illusion, Ouchi illusion, pattern-induced flicker colour, Poggendorff illusion, Ponzo illusion, Sander parallelogram, star illusion, teacup illusion, top hat illusion, twisted-cord illusion, Wundt illusion, Zanforlin illusion, Zöllner illusion. *See also* context effect, field effect, visual induction.

associative interference *n.* An umbrella term for *proactive interference and *retroactive interference. Also called *associative inhibition*.

associative laws *n.* The principles governing *associative learning. *See also* associationism.

associative learning *n.* The learning of contingencies between events such as occurs in *conditioning (1). In *classical conditioning, associations between *conditioned stimuli and *unconditioned stimuli are learned; in *operant conditioning, associations between *responses and *reinforcers are learned. *See also* autoshaping, shaping (1).

associative memory *n.* Memory for links or connections between items, often studied through *paired-associate learning.

associative priming *See* under priming (1).

assortative mating *n.* Preference for sexual partners with similar *phenotypes, as when humans select mates who tend to resemble themselves in wealth, social class, intelligence, or attractiveness, or when other organisms choose mates that resemble themselves on specific criteria. *See also* heritability, population genetics. *Compare* disassortative mating.
[From French *assortir* to classify, from Latin *ad* to + *sors, sortis* a lot]

astereognosis *n.* Inability to identify or recognize objects by touch, often resulting from a lesion in the somatosensory association area (*see* somatosensory cortex). The unimpaired ability is called *stereognosis*.
[From Greek *a-* without + *stereos* solid + *gnosis* knowledge]

asthenia *n.* Listlessness, debility, or tendency to fatigue. *See also* neurasthenia. **asthenic** *adj.*
[From Greek *astheneia* weakness, from *a-* without + *sthenos* strength + *-ia* indicating a condition or quality]

asthenic body type *n.* A slender, long-limbed *somatotype believed by the German psychiatrist Ernst Kretschmer (1888–1964) and his followers to be prone to *schizophrenia. *See also* Kretschmer constitutional type. *Compare* athletic body type, dysplastic body type, pyknic body type.
[From Greek *a-* without + *sthenos* strength]

astigmatism *n.* A defect in a lens or mirror in which rays of light from a single point do not all focus at the same point but are drawn into a line; hence a visual defect resulting from astigmatism of the *crystalline lens of the eye, characterized by lines oriented in a certain direction being perceived more distinctly than lines in the transverse direction. *See also* aberration (3).
[From Greek *a-* without + *stigma*, *stigmatos* a point or focus]

astonishing hypothesis *n.* The name given in 1994 by the Nobel prizewinning English molecular biologist Francis H(arry) C(ompton) Crick (born 1916) to the proposition that a person's mental experiences are entirely explained by the behaviour of neurons, glial cells, and the atoms, ions, and molecules that constitute and influence them.

astrocyte *n.* Any of the large *neuroglial cells shaped like many-pointed stars that support the rigid structure of the brain, mop up *potassium ions during periods of intense neuronal activity, recycle glutamate and GABA after release, function as phagocytes by engulfing debris from decaying cells, and possibly play a role in the *blood–brain barrier by surrounding capillaries in the brain with the terminal boutons of their dendrites. Also called *astroglia*.

[From Greek *astron* a star + *kytos* a vessel or hollow]

astrocytoma *n.* A tumour in the central nervous system composed of proliferating *astrocytes, the main type of brain tumour in humans.
[From Greek *astron* a star + *kytos* a vessel or hollow + *-oma* indicating an abnormality]

asymbolia *n.* Another name for *asemia.
[From Greek *a-* without + *symbolon* a token, from *syn* together + *ballein* to throw]

asyndeton *n.* A form of sentence construction in which a conjunction is omitted for economy of expression or rhetorical effect. A double asyndeton occurs in the usual English translation of Julius Caesar's sentence: *I came, I saw, I conquered*.
[From Greek *a-* not or without + *syndetos* bound together, from *syn* together + *detos* bound or tied]

ataque de nervios *n.* A *culture-bound syndrome found mainly among Latino communities in the Caribbean, but also in many Latin American and Mediterranean cultures, characterized by outbursts of uncontrollable shouting, crying, trembling, a sensation of heat in the chest rising to the head, and aggression, both verbal and physical, accompanied by a sense of loss of control, generally precipitated by a *psychosocial stressor such as bereavement, divorce, or a family conflict. It is sometimes interpreted as a form of *panic attack. **ataques de nervios** *pl.*
[From Spanish *ataque* attack + *de* of + *nervios* nerves, hence literally an attack of nerves]

ataraxia *n.* Tranquillity or freedom from anxiety. **ataractic** *adj.* Capable of calming or tranquillizing. An ataractic drug is a *tranquillizer.
[From Greek *ataraktos* undisturbed, from *a-* without + *tarassein* to trouble + *-ia* indicating a condition or quality]

ataxia *n.* Diminution or loss of the ability to coordinate voluntary movements, caused by a lesion in the *cerebellum or another area of the *central nervous system. *See* gait ataxia, locomotor ataxia, optic ataxia, sensory ataxia. *See also* posturography, Romberg's sign. *Compare* dystaxia, pseudoataxia.

[From Greek *a*- without + *taxis* order + -*ia* indicating a condition or quality]

ateleiosis *n*. Dwarfism without loss of proportion between body parts.
[From Greek *a*- without + *telos* an end + -*osis* indicating a process or state]

atherosclerosis *n*. The major form of *arteriosclerosis, involving *sclerosis and thickening of the inner walls of the arteries through the deposit of *cholesterol and other fatty substances. In the coronary arteries, this may lead to coronary heart disease; in the brain, to *neurological impairments such as *vascular dementia or multi-infarct dementia.
[From Greek *athera* porridge or gruel + *sklerosis* a hardening, from *skleros* hard + -*osis* indicating a process or state]

athetosis *n*. A neuromuscular condition characterized by involuntary, slow, writhing movements, especially of the fingers, hands, head, and tongue, associated with some forms of *cerebral arteriosclerosis, *cerebral palsy, lesions in the *basal ganglia, or *tardive dyskinesia. **athetoid** *adj*.
[From Greek *athetos* not in place, from *a*- not + *tithenai* to place + -*osis* indicating a process or state]

athletic body type *n*. A muscular, well-built *somatotype believed by the German psychiatrist Ernst Kretschmer (1888–1964) and his followers to be prone to *schizophrenia. *See also* Kretschmer constitutional type. *Compare* asthenic body type, dysplastic body type, pyknic body type.
[From Greek *athletes* an athlete, from *athlos* a contest]

Ativan *n*. A proprietary name for the benzodiazepine drug *lorazepam.
[Trademark]

atmosphere effect *n*. In *person perception, the tendency for one characteristic of a person to influence the way the person's other characteristics are perceived by others. *See* halo effect, trait centrality.

atmosphere hypothesis *n*. The conjecture that errors in judging the validity of *syllogisms sometimes arise from a bias in favour of judging a conclusion as valid if it contains the same *quantifiers (1, 2) or other logical terms

as the premises. For example, the following syllogism is often wrongly judged to be valid: *Some professors are logicians; Some logicians are absent-minded; Therefore, some professors are absent-minded*. The reasons for the plausibility of this invalid syllogism are the repetition of the form *Some P are Q* and the fact that the conclusion seems plausible. *Compare* conversion hypothesis.

atmosphere perspective *n*. Another name for *aerial perspective.

atonia *n*. Absence of normal muscle *tonus. Also called *atony*. *See also* cataplexy (1, 2), dystonia, REM atonia, sleep paralysis.
[From Greek *a*- without + *tonos* tension or tone + -*ia* indicating a condition or quality]

ATP *abbrev*. Adenosine triphosphate, a nucleotide synthesized in the mitochondria of all animal and plant cells during the *Krebs cycle. Its main function is to store energy, which it liberates when it is converted by *ATPase to *ADP during nerve impulses or muscular contractions. It is also converted by *adenylate cyclase into *cyclic AMP, which functions as a *second messenger.

ATPase *abbrev*. Adenosine triphosphatase, an *enzyme that converts *ATP to *ADP when energy is consumed in a nerve impulse or muscular contraction.
[From *ATP* + Greek -*ase* denoting an enzyme, from *diastasis* separation]

atrophy *n*. Degeneration or wasting away of an organ, structure, or body part through disease, inadequate nutrition, or disuse. *Compare* hypertrophy.
[From Greek *a*- without + *trophe* nourishment]

atropine *n*. A poisonous *alkaloid obtained from the deadly nightshade plant *Atropa belladonna*, being a *muscarine *antagonist (3) that blocks the action of *acetylcholine in the parasympathetic nervous system, paralysing smooth muscles, and is used as a pre-anaesthetic medication and an antidote to chemical nerve agents. It was popular with medieval poisoners, and because a few drops of it in the eyes cause the pupils to dilate, it has been used throughout history by women as a cosmetic and is still used medicinally for eye examinations. *See also* belladonna, BZ gas, hyoscyamine, Lomotil, methyl atropine, muscarinic receptor. *Compare* curare, scopolamine, strychnine.

[From Greek *Atropos* the eldest of the three Fates and the one who cuts the thread of life, from *atropos* that may not be turned away from, from *a-* without + *tropos* a turn, from *trapein* to turn]

attachment disorder *See* reactive attachment disorder.

attachment theory *n*. A theory advanced in 1951 by the English psychiatrist (Edward) John (Mostyn) Bowlby (1907–90) according to which an infant has an inborn biological need for close contact with its mother (or other main caretaker), a normal bond developing within the first 6 months of life through the mother's responsiveness to these needs, and *maternal deprivation during this critical period having adverse effects on psychological development. *See also* anaclitic depression, hospitalism, love, separation anxiety, separation anxiety disorder. *Compare* imprinting.

attensity *n*. A term introduced by the English psychologist Edward Bradford Titchener (1867–1927) for the type of sensory clarity distinguishing a sensation that is the focus of attention from one that is not.

[From *at(tributive)* + *tensity* stretching, from Latin *tendere*, *tensus* to stretch]

attention *n*. Sustained concentration on a specific stimulus, sensation, idea, thought, or activity, enabling one to use information-processing systems with limited capacity to handle vast amounts of information available from the sense organs and memory stores. *See also* alpha blocking, attention operating characteristic, attention span (1, 2), attenuation theory, automatic processing, bottleneck theory, cocktail party phenomenon, controlled processing, dual-task performance, filter theory, hypercathexis, late selection, marginal consciousness. *Compare* attensity, consciousness.

[From Latin *attentio* attention, from *attendere* to apply the mind to something, from Latin *tendere*, *tensus* to stretch]

attentional dyslexia *n*. A rare form of *dyslexia characterized by normal reading of individual words and naming of individual letters presented in isolation but an impaired ability to read more than one word or to name more than one letter when two or more are presented simultaneously on the page. *See also* hyperlexia.

attention-deficit/hyperactivity disorder *n*. A *mental disorder of childhood affecting between two and ten per cent of school-age children worldwide, at least three times as common in boys as in girls, characterized by persistent inattention, hyperactivity, or impulsivity, with some of these signs and symptoms appearing before age 7, causing problems at school or work and in the home, and interfering significantly with social, academic, or occupational functioning. The disorder may be manifested as a predominantly inattentive subtype, a predominantly hyperactive–impulsive subtype, or a combined subtype. It is not a disorder of attention per se, as formerly believed, but a developmental failure in areas of the brain responsible for inhibition and self-control, especially the *caudate nucleus, the *globus pallidus, the *prefrontal cortex, and the *vermis of the cerebellum, areas that use *dopamine to communicate with one another and that tend to be shrunken in people with the disorder. Also called *attention-deficit disorder* (*ADD*), *minimal brain dysfunction* (*MBD*). *Compare* hyperkinesis, hyperkinetic disorders. **ADHD** *abbrev*.

attention operating characteristic *n*. A type of *performance operating characteristic used in the study of *attention, consisting of a graph in which the level of performance of one task is plotted against the level of performance of the other, the tasks being performed simultaneously and attention shifted periodically from one task to the other. **AOC** *abbrev*.

attention span *n*. **1.** The length of time for which a person can attend to something. **2.** Another name for the *span of apprehension. *See also* chunking, magical number seven.

attenuation *n*. Reducing the force, effect, or value of something. In statistics, a reduction in the magnitude of a *correlation below its theoretical true value as a result of measurement error in one or both of the sets of scores entering into the relationship. A widely used *correction for attenuation*, which assumes that the errors are uncorrelated with the true scores and with each other, states that the true correlation is equal to the correlation be-

tween the observed scores divided by the *geometric mean of their *reliabilities.
[From Latin *attenuare* to make thin, from *ad* to + *tenuis* thin + *-ation* indicating a process or condition]

attenuation theory *n*. Any theory of *attention according to which information that is not attended to is processed, though at a shallower *level of processing than the information receiving attention. The mechanism that implements this process is called an *attenuating filter*. The theory was formulated in 1960 by the US-based English psychologist Anne (Marie) Treisman (born 1935). *See also* cocktail party phenomenon, filter theory, selective attention. *Compare* bottleneck theory.
[From Latin *attenuare* to make thin or to weaken, from *tenuis* thin]

attitude *n*. **1**. An enduring pattern of evaluative responses towards a person, object, or issue. According to a frequently quoted classical definition, it is a more or less consistent pattern of affective, cognitive, and *conative or behavioural responses (or of feeling, thinking, and behaving) towards a psychological object, but the consistency implied by this definition is a supposition that is frequently unmatched by reality, and it is possible to have an attitude towards something without having ever having the opportunity to express it in behaviour. *See also* attitude change, attitude scale, dual-process model, elaboration likelihood model, expectancy-value theory, self-perception theory, theory of planned behaviour, theory of reasoned action. **2**. A bodily posture, especially one indicative of a mental state (*She assumed an attitude of dejection, holding her head in her hands*). **3**. Informally, truculent or cheeky demeanour or behaviour (*My teenage son was sulking and gave me nothing but attitude*). **attitudinal** *adj*. Of or relating to an *attitude (1, 2) or to attitudes.
[From Italian *attitudine* disposition, from Latin *aptitudo* fitness, from *aptus* fit or apt]

attitude change *n*. The process whereby an *attitude (1) towards a person, object, or issue becomes more or less favourable, usually as a consequence of *persuasion. *See also* assimilation-contrast theory, balance theory, cognitive consistency theory, congruity theory, elaboration likelihood model, forced compliance, group polarization, ingratiation, inocu-

lation theory, law of social impact, rhetoric (1), sleeper effect.

attitude scale *n*. An instrument for measuring *attitudes (1), often but not necessarily consisting of some form of *questionnaire. *See* Guttman scale, Likert scale, semantic differential, Thurstone scale, unfolding technique, unobtrusive measure.

attitude similarity hypothesis *n*. The proposition that people tend to be attracted to others who share their attitudes and values in important areas. This hypothesis has received strong and consistent support from empirical investigations. Also called the *similarity-attraction hypothesis*. *Compare* need complementarity hypothesis.

attribute *n*. A quality, property, aspect, or *feature (1) of any *phenomenon, whether an object, event, *concept, *schema, or person. *See* integral attribute, separable attribute.
[From Latin *attribuere* to associate with, from *ad* to + *tribuere* to give]

attribution *n*. The assignment of causes to behaviour, or the perception or inference of the causes of behaviour, such causes including personal dispositional factors and external situational factors. The term was introduced in this sense in 1958 by the Austrian-born US psychologist Fritz Heider (1896–1988). *See also* actor–observer difference, áttributional bias, attribution theory, covariation principle, false-consensus effect, fundamental attribution error, Kelley's cube, person perception, positivity bias (1), self-serving bias. **attributional** *adj*.

attributional bias *n*. Any systematic distortion in the assignment of causes to behaviour or in inferring the causes of behaviour. The most important ones so far discovered are the *actor–observer difference, *base-rate fallacy, *fundamental attribution error, *positivity bias (1), and *self-serving bias. *See also* attribution, attribution theory.

attribution error *See* fundamental attribution error.

attribution theory *n*. A theory designed to explain how people perceive, infer, or ascribe causes to their own and other people's behaviour. Basic research in this area has established that we tend to attribute another person's behaviour to internal, dispositional causes rather than external, situational causes if the behaviour seems different from how other people would behave in the same situation but characteristic of that person's behaviour in similar and dissimilar situations in the past; but if the behaviour seems similar to that of others in the same situation but uncharacteristic of that person's past behaviour in similar and different situations, then we are likely to attribute it to external causes. The theory was first formulated by the Austrian-born US psychologist Fritz Heider (1896–1988) in articles published in 1944 and 1946 and in his book *The Psychology of Interpersonal Relations* in 1958, and it was developed from the 1960s onwards especially by the US psychologists Edward Ellsworth Jones (1926–93) and Harold H. Kelley (born 1921), the most influential theory being *Kelley's cube. See also actor–observer difference, attributional bias, causal schema, cognitive-appraisal theory, covariation principle, false-consensus effect, fundamental attribution error, impression formation, person perception, positivity bias (1), self-perception theory, self-serving bias. **AT** abbrev.

attributive *adj.* Of or relating to an adjective or adjectival phrase occurring within the same noun phrase as the noun that it modifies. For example, the adjective *good* is attributive in the phrase *the good terrorist*, but it is *predicative in *the terrorist is good*.
[From Latin *attribuere* to associate with + *-ivus* indicating a tendency, inclination, or quality]

attuition *n.* A hypothetical form of apprehension lower than human *perception but higher than simple *sensation. *Compare* intuition.
[From Latin *ad* towards + *intuitio* a contemplation, from *intueri* to gaze at, from *tueri* to look or gaze at]

atypical antipsychotic *n.* Any of a class of drugs that are used in the treatment of *schizophrenia and other psychotic disorders and that have fewer *neuroleptic-induced side-effects than conventional *neuroleptic (1) drugs. *See* clozapine, olanzapine, risperidone, sertindole.

Aubert effect *n.* The phenomenon that occurs after fixating one's gaze on an illumi-

nated vertical bar in a dark room for a minute or two and then tilting one's head to one side through an angle of 30 degrees or more. This creates the illusion that the bar is tilted in the opposite direction and shows that the *semicircular canals of the vestibular system provide insufficient information for full orientation in the vertical dimension. A stimulus for demonstrating this effect is most easily constructed by placing a battery torch or flashlight in a cardboard box with a vertical slit cut into one of its sides and covered with tissue paper to diffuse the light.
[Named after the German physiologist and psychologist Hermann Ludimar (Rudolf) Aubert (1826–92) who first drew attention to it]

Aubert–Fleischl paradox *n.* The tendency for a moving stimulus to appear to move more slowly when the eyes track it with *smooth eye movements than when the gaze is fixated on the static background. It is a slightly surprising phenomenon rather than a true *paradox.
[Named after the German physiologist and psychologist Hermann Ludimar (Rudolf) Aubert (1826–92) and the Austrian physiologist Marxow Ernst Fleischl (1846–91) who discovered it]

Aubert–Förster law *n.* The proposition that the minimum size at which a stimulus such as a printed letter of the alphabet is just recognizable is directly proportional to its *angular distance from the *fixation (1) point or, equivalently, to the distance from the *fovea of its projection on the *retina. The law holds from 2 to 40 angular degrees. *Compare* Aubert–Förster phenomenon.
[Named after the German physiologist and psychologist Hermann Ludimar (Rudolf) Aubert (1826–92) and the Polish-born German ophthalmologist Carl Friedrich Richard Förster (1825–1902) who formulated it and published it briefly in 1856 and fully in 1857]

Aubert–Förster phenomenon *n.* The proposition that near objects are perceived with greater acuity than objects further away, even if they subtend the same *visual angle. Also called the *Förster phenomenon. See also* aerial perspective. *Compare* Aubert–Förster law.

auction game *See* Dollar Auction game.

audibility function *n.* A graph depicting a listener's *absolute threshold for sound inten-

sity across the range of audible frequencies.
AF abbrev.

audibility range n. The frequencies of sound waves that a listener can hear as *tones (1), between the audibility limits of the lowest to the highest frequencies that can be perceived. For a person with normal hearing, the range is more than 10 *octaves, from 16 hertz to about 20,000 hertz, but for most people the upper audibility limit decreases sharply throughout adulthood. Also called the auditory spectrum. See also frequency theory, Galton whistle, infrasound, ultrasound.

audible thought n. A *hallucination in which one hears one's own thoughts being spoken.

audience effect n. The effect of passive onlookers or spectators on an individual's task performance. Depending on the nature of the task, the effect on performance may be positive or negative. See also drive theory of social facilitation, next-in-line effect, overlearning, response competition, social facilitation. Compare coaction effect.

audile adj. **1.** Another word for *auditory. n. **2.** A person whose characteristic style of mental imagery is auditory rather than visual, tactile, or motor. Compare motile (2), tactile (2), visualizer.

audioanalgesia n. Diminished sensation of *pain during exposure to loud sounds; also, the use of music to distract a person's attention from pain, as during dentistry. See also analgesia.
[From Latin audio I hear, from audire to hear + Greek an- without + algos pain + -ia indicating a condition or quality]

audiogenic seizure n. A *convulsion brought about by prolonged exposure to high-frequency sounds, especially in rats, mice, hamsters, and rabbits. See also infrasound, ultrasound.
[From Latin audio I hear, from audire to hear + generare to produce]

audiogram n. A graphic record of a listener's *absolute threshold for *pure tones as a function of the frequency of the tones, a full description of auditory acuity as measured by an *audiometer. It is often plotted in terms of hearing loss (deviations from average thresholds) in decibels as a function of frequency.
[From Latin audio I hear, from audire to hear + Greek gramme a line]

audiogravic illusion n. An error in *sound localization arising from the body being tilted out of the upright position in the absence of visual cues, resulting in the sound source being perceived where it would be in relation to the body if the body were upright. Compare audiogyral illusion.
[From Latin audio I hear, from audire to hear + gravis heavy + -icus of, relating to, or resembling]

audiogyral illusion n. An error in *sound localization that occurs when a sound source on the end of a boom attached rigidly to a listener's head is thus kept at a fixed point relative to the head, usually a few feet in front of the nose, even when the head is turned from side to side, the invariable consequence being that the sound is heard as coming from a point directly overhead. A second version of the same illusion occurs when a person is seated on a slowly rotating platform and a sound source some distance in front rotates with the person's body, again creating the illusion that the sound source is directly overhead. A closely related version occurs when a person sits motionless inside a slowly rotating striped drum that induces *vection, a sensation that the body is rotating in the opposite direction, and a sound source is located at a fixed point outside the drum, creating the illusion once again that the sound source is directly overhead. The illusion in its various forms was discovered by the German-born US psychologist Hans Wallach (1904–98) and published in the Journal of Experimental Psychology in 1940. It is explained by the fact that in ordinary circumstances rotation of the body or head produces changes in *transient disparities, *phase delays, and *sonic shadows, except when the sound originates from directly above or below, and experience teaches us that in such circumstances, because we are terrestrial creatures, it almost invariably originates from above. See also sound localization. Compare audiogravic illusion.
[From Latin audio I hear, from audire to hear + gyrus a circle + -alis of or relating to]

audiokinetic response n. An automatic movement of the eyes in response to a change in the position of the body relative to a

continuous sound source, its effect being to maintain fixation of gaze on an object of potential interest.
[From Latin *audio* I hear, from *audire* to hear + *kinetikos* of or relating to motion, from *kineein* to move + *-ikos* of, relating to, or resembling]

audiometer *n.* A device for measuring a person's auditory acuity across a range of sound intensities and frequencies. *See also* audiogram. **audiometric** *adj.*
[From Latin *audio* I hear, from *audire* to hear + Greek *metron* a measure]

audiometric zero *n.* The normal or average intensity threshold for sound of a specified frequency.

audiometry *n.* The measurement of auditory acuity with an *audiometer.

audio-oculogyric reflex *n.* A *reflex turning of the head and eyes towards a sudden or unexpected sound.
[From Latin *audio* I hear, from *audire* to hear + *oculus* the eye + *gyrus* a circle or turning + *-icus* of, relating to, or resembling]

audition *n.* **1.** The act or experience of *hearing. **2.** A trial performance by a musician or other performing artist applying to join a group, gain a place on a course, or take part in a performance.
[From Latin *auditio, -onis* a hearing, from *audire* to hear + *-ion* indicating an action, process, or state]

auditory *adj.* Of or relating to the sense of hearing or *audition (1). Also called *audile*.
[From Latin *auditorius* relating to hearing, from *audire* to hear]

auditory acuity *n.* Keenness or sharpness of hearing. *See also* acuity, audiogram, audiometer.

auditory adaptation *n.* Transient loss of hearing sensitivity to tones of certain frequencies following prolonged exposure to an unchanging sound wave. When the sound that causes the effect is loud and the hearing loss is more than transient it is usually called *auditory fatigue. See also* adaptation (2).

auditory agnosia *See under* agnosia.

auditory aphasia *See under* aphasia.

auditory association cortex *See under* auditory cortex.

auditory beat *n.* The periodic waxing and waning of sound, produced when two tones with slightly different *frequencies (1) are sounded simultaneously, caused by wave interference as the two tones alternately reinforce and cancel each other's amplitude, as when a tone of 256 hertz (Middle C) is sounded simultaneously with a tone of 260 hertz, generating a beat frequency of 4 hertz (cycles per second). Piano tuners work by counting beats. Beats occur even if the tones are presented separately to the two ears via headphones (*see* binaural beat).

auditory canal *n.* Either of two passages in each ear, the *external auditory canal* (also called the *external meatus*) leading from the *outer ear to the *tympanic membrane, and the *internal auditory canal* (also called the *internal meatus*) located in the *temporal bone and containing the *vestibulocochlear nerve that transmits impulses from the *inner ear to the brain. When unspecified, the external canal is usually meant, but such ambiguity is avoided in careful usage. *Compare* Eustachian tube.

auditory cortex *n.* Areas of the *cerebral cortex, namely the primary auditory cortex and the auditory association cortex, devoted to processing information from the organs of hearing. In each cerebral hemisphere, the primary auditory cortex occupies *Heschl's gyrus, a small gyrus running transversely across the superior temporal gyrus, the upper gyrus of the temporal lobe (temporal operculum). It is divided into separate bands responding to particular tonal frequencies, and projections from the *basilar membranes of both ears are represented in a *tonotopic map in each hemisphere. In the (usually) left hemisphere it includes *Wernicke's area, and the auditory association cortex is adjacent to it in the superior temporal gyrus. *See also* inferior colliculus, medial geniculate nucleus.

auditory egocentre *n.* The point in the centre of the skull where auditory sensations are perceived or felt to converge. US *auditory egocenter*. *See also* egocentre.

auditory fatigue *n.* Temporary loss of hearing sensitivity resulting from exposure to a loud tone, the loss usually extending from the frequency of the fatiguing tone to about one *octave above it. *Compare* auditory adaptation.

auditory flutter *n*. The sensation produced by sound that is periodically interrupted at a rate below the frequency of *auditory flutter fusion and that can therefore be heard as intermittent by the listener. Also called *auditory flicker*. *Compare* flicker.

auditory flutter fusion *n*. The lowest interruption frequency at which a listener ceases to hear *auditory flutter and begins to hear a continuous sound. Also called *auditory flicker fusion*. *Compare* critical flicker frequency. **AFF** *abbrev*.

auditory fusion *n*. Hearing two or more sounds as one. When the sounds are presented to different ears it is also called *binaural fusion*. *Compare* precedence effect.

auditory hallucination *n*. A *hallucination of a sound, usually of voices speaking. The definition sometimes (but not in *DSM-IV or *ICD-10) excludes sounds perceived as emanating from inside the head.

auditory illusion *n*. Any *illusion of *hearing. *See* audiogravic illusion, audiogyral illusion, auditory staircase illusion, binaural shift, melodic paradox, missing fundamental illusion, phonemic restoration, semitone paradox, tritone paradox, ventriloquism effect, verbal transformation effect. *See also* Doppler effect (which is not strictly illusory). *Compare* postural aftereffect, tactile illusion, visual illusion.

auditory localization *See* sound localization.

auditory masking *n*. The obscuring of one sound, sometimes called a *test stimulus*, by another, called a *masking stimulus*, causing the *absolute threshold of the test stimulus to increase or its perceived *loudness to decrease. The masking stimulus is presented either before the test stimulus (*forward masking), at the same time as the test stimulus (*simultaneous masking), or after the test stimulus (*backward masking), and backward or forward masking has been found to occur when the masking stimulus is presented within 100 milliseconds of the test stimulus. *See also* central masking, critical band, masking.

auditory meatus *n*. Another name for the external or internal *auditory canal.
[From Latin *meatus* a course]

auditory nerve *n*. Another name for the *vestibulocochlear nerve.

auditory receptive field *n*. An area of space around the head from which auditory stimuli elicit responses from a specified auditory neuron, the spatial area being the auditory neuron's receptive field. The auditory cortex and midbrain of the barn owl, which is capable of more accurate *sound localization than any other species that has been tested, have been found to contain neurons that respond only to sounds in very specific spatial areas. *See also* receptive field.

auditory receptor *n*. A *sensory receptor consisting of *hair cells in the *basilar membrane of the *organ of Corti that translate sound waves—pressure waves with frequencies between 16 hertz and 20,000 hertz—into nerve impulses. Also called a *phonoreceptor*.

auditory space perception *n*. Another name for *sound localization.

auditory spectrum *n*. Another name for the *audibility range.
[So called by analogy with the spectrum of visible light]

auditory staircase illusion *n*. A sound equivalent of the *staircase illusion, discovered in 1964 by the US psychologist Roger N. Shepard (born 1929) in the perception of musical tones that are clearly defined in terms of pitch class (the twelve tones of the octave that are usually labelled C, C#, D, . . . , B) but are ambiguous as regards the octaves to which they belong, each tone being composed of equal-intensity *sinusoidal waves from several octaves. If a sequence of such tones moving up or down through the twelve tones of the octave is played repeatedly, then instead of hearing a sequence of twelve tones being repeated, listeners hear a single sequence apparently rising or descending endlessly. Also called the *illusion of circular pitch*. *See also* melodic paradox, semitone paradox, tritone paradox.

auditory suffix effect *n*. The impairment of memory for a list of words caused by the presentation at the end of the list, during the learning process, of further words or speech sounds that need not be committed to memory. Non-speech sounds do not normally produce such an effect. *See also* precategorical acoustic store.

auditory system *n.* A generic name for the totality of structures in the nervous system that are involved in hearing.

auditory tube *n.* Another (informal) name for the Eustachian tube.

Aufgabe *n.* A task or assignment, whether self-imposed or resulting from external instructions or an experimental manipulation, that creates a particular mental set or behavioural predisposition. *See also Einstellung*, set (2), water-jar problem.
[From German *Aufgabe* task, job, or assignment, from *auf* on + *Gabe* something given, from *geben* to give]

aura *n.* **1.** A distinctive ambience or quality generated by a person or thing. **2.** A brief sensation, such as a flash of light (*phosphene), a blind spot (*scotoma), or a sound, experienced as a *prodromal warning of an attack of (especially) *epilepsy or *migraine. **3.** In occultism and *parapsychology, an emanation supposedly surrounding a person or other living thing and said to be visible only to a person with a special psychic ability or gift.
[From Latin *aura* a breeze]

aural *adj.* Of, relating to, or perceived through the ear.
[From Latin *auris* an ear]

aural harmonic *n.* A *harmonic generated by the auditory system.

auricle *n.* **1.** Another name for the *pinna or external part of the ear. **2.** The atrium or upper chamber of the heart, or a small sac in the atrium of the heart. **3.** Any ear-shaped biological structure. **auricular** *adj.*
[From Latin *auricula* the external ear, from *auris* an ear]

australopithecine *adj. n.* (Of or relating to) any member of the extinct genus of human-like *hominids *Australopithecus*, believed to have lived between 4 million and 1 million years ago in southern and eastern Africa, including *Australopithecus africanus*, *A. robustus*, and *A. afarensis*.

[From Latin *australis* southern + Greek *pithekos* ape]

authoritarianism *n.* A personality characteristic associated with a potentiality for fascism first identified in 1950 by the German philosopher, sociologist, and psychologist Theodor W(iesengrund) Adorno (1903–69) and several colleagues in a monumental study entitled *The Authoritarian Personality*, usually measured with the *F scale or a modification of it. It correlates positively with anti-Semitism, *ethnocentrism, political and economic conservatism, and *intolerance of ambiguity. *See also* A-S scale, E scale, PEC scale. **authoritarian** *adj.*

autism *n.* **1.** A pathological self-absorption and preoccupation with the self to the exclusion of the outside world, characteristic of some forms of *autistic disorder and *schizophrenia. **2.** An alternative name for *autistic disorder. *See also* autistic disorder. **autistic** *adj.*
[From Greek *autos* self + *-ismos* indicating a state or condition]

autistic disorder *n.* A *pervasive developmental disorder characterized by gross and sustained impairment of social interaction and communication; restricted and stereotyped patterns of behaviour, interests, and activities; and abnormalities manifested before age 3 in social development, language acquisition, or play. Symptoms may include emotional non-responsiveness, lack of reciprocity in social interaction, failure to develop peer relations, delay or failure of speech development, stereotyped and idiosyncratic language usage or non-verbal behaviour (including *gaze aversion), insistence on sameness, and ritualized mannerisms. The disorder was first described in 1943 by the Austrian-born US child psychiatrist Leo Kanner (1894–1981). Also called *autism, childhood autism, infantile autism, Kanner's syndrome*. *See also* idiot savant, theory of mind. *Compare* Asperger's disorder.

autobiographical memory *n.* Another name for *episodic memory.

autochthonous *adj.* Indigenous; originating from within a person or an organ rather than from external stimulation. It is applied to functions such as heartbeat that originate within the organ and also to psychological phenomena such as an *autochthonous Gestalt* that is generated by the perceiver rather than being inherent in the stimulus.

[From Greek *autochthon* from the Earth, from *autos* self + *chthon* the Earth + *-ous* having or characterized by]

autocorrelation *n*. A *correlation between values of a *time series and values of the same time series shifted backwards or forwards by a fixed amount, called a *lag*. A typical example would be a correlation between a migraine patient's daily ratings of headache severity with the ratings one day earlier, each rating being paired with the one given on the previous day. In this case, the rating on the first day is paired with the rating on the second day, the rating on the second day with the rating on the third day, and so on. This is called the *first-order autocorrelation*, and it tends to be positive if score *t* tends to be predictive of score *t* + 1. The autocorrelation of scores *t* with scores *t* + 2 is the *second-order autocorrelation*, and so on. *See also* autoregression, correlogram.

[From Greek *autos* self + English *correlation*]

auto-erotic *adj*. Of or relating to sexual stimulation of one's own body or *masturbation. In *psychoanalysis, of or relating to *auto-erotism.

auto-erotism *n*. In *psychoanalysis, a form of behaviour characteristic of early infancy in which an *instinct (3) is satisfied without recourse to an external *instinctual object. The word was first used in 1898 by the English sexologist Havelock Ellis (1859–1939) in his book *Studies in the Psychology of Sex* (vol. 1), where he defined it as 'spontaneous sexual emotion generated in the absence of an external stimulus proceeding, directly or indirectly, from another person' (p. 110). Also called *auto-eroticism*. *See also* allo-erotism, narcissism.

[From Greek *autos* self + *eros* love or sexual desire + *-ismos* indicating a state or condition]

autogenic training *n*. A form of *psychotherapy in which the client is taught self-hypnosis and *biofeedback as techniques of managing stress. It involves a sequence of graded mental exercises (concentrating in turn on feelings of heaviness in the limbs, a sense of warmth in the limbs, heart rate, breathing, warmth of the upper abdomen, and coolness of the forehead) designed to promote physical relaxation. It was developed in Germany from the 1930s to the 1950s and popularized by the German psychiatrist and neurologist Johann Heinrich Schultz (1884–1970). Also called *autogenics*.

[From German *das autogene Training*, from Greek *autogenes* self-generated, from *autos* self + *genein* to produce]

autohypnosis *n*. Self-induced *hypnosis. Also called *self-hypnosis*.

[From Greek *autos* self + *hypnos* sleep + *-osis* indicating a process or state]

autointoxication *n*. Self-poisoning by a substance produced within the body.

[From Greek *autos* self + Latin *intoxicare* to poison, from *toxicum* a poison + *-ation* indicating a process or condition]

autokinetic effect *n*. The *apparent movement of a stationary point of light when viewed in a totally dark environment, resulting from *physiological nystagmus that the visual system cannot compensate for in the absence of any visible frame of reference. Also called the *autokinetic phenomenon* or the *autokinetic illusion (AKI)*.

[Coined in 1887 by the German physiologist and psychologist Hermann Aubert (1826–92) from Greek *autos* self + *kinetikos* of or relating to motion, from *kineein* to move or *kinesis* movement + *-ikos* of, relating to, or resembling]

autological *adj*. Of or relating to an adjective that is self-descriptive, such as the adjective *short* (which is short), *English* (which is English), and *polysyllabic* (which is polysyllabic). *See also* Grelling's paradox. *Compare* heterological.

[From Greek *autos* self + *logos* a word + Latin *-icalis* of, relating to, or resembling]

automatic anxiety *n*. In *psychoanalysis, an infant's psychological feeling of helplessness, arising from biological helplessness, experienced as a form of *anxiety, or a reproduction of such anxiety in an older child or an adult when confronted with a situation with which it is difficult to cope. The concept was introduced by Sigmund Freud (1856–1939) in his book *Inhibitions, Symptoms and Anxiety* (1926, *Standard Edition*, XX, pp. 77–175, at p. 138). *See also* anxiety.

automaticity *See* automatic processing.

automatic priming See under priming (1).

automatic processing n. Any *information processing that occurs involuntarily and without conscious intention or control, as in the performance of well-practised activities such as seeing, reading, riding a bicycle, playing a game, or driving a car. Compared to *controlled processing, automatic processing is generally much faster, can be carried out with less effort, is less easily impaired by fatigue or alcohol, and can involve parallel processing of information from more than one sensory channel, but its development is slower and involves much more practice than controlled processing, and once established it is less controllable. The *Stroop effect provides a dramatic illustration of automatic processing. Also called *automaticity*, *preconscious processing*, or *pre-attentive processing*. See also absent-mindedness, attention, centipede effect, dual-process model, Humphrey's law, hyper-reflection, open-loop control, principle of least effort.

automatism n. Behaviour executed without conscious awareness or control, as for example in *sleepwalking, *hypnosis, *fugue states, and certain forms of *epilepsy. Also called *automaticity*. See also dissociation theory.

automaton n. A machine or mechanical device that can perform tasks intelligently; a person who behaves mechanically, without emotion, like a robot. See also zombie (1). **automata** pl.
[From Greek *automatos* self-moving, from *autos* self]

automnesia n. Spontaneous revival of memories from an earlier phase of life.
[From Greek *autos* self + *mneme* memory + -*ia* indicating a condition or quality]

automorphic perception n. A tendency to perceive others as physically more similar to oneself than they actually are. An example from fine art is the work of the Italian painter and sculptor Amedeo Modigliani (1884–1920) who depicted, and therefore presumably perceived, most of his subjects with elongated features resembling his own. See also egocentrism, false-consensus effect.
[From Greek *autos* self + *morphe* a form or shape]

autonomic adj. **1.** Self-governing or self-regulating. **2.** Of or relating to the *autonomic nervous system.
[From Greek *autonomos* living under one's own laws, from *autos* self + *nomos* a law + -*ikos* of, relating to, or resembling]

autonomic arousal disorder n. A disorder characterized by persistent or recurrent signs and symptoms mediated by the *autonomic nervous system, excluding pain but including palpitation, hyperventilation, or nausea. It is not diagnosed if it is caused by a *general medical condition.

autonomic nervous system n. The largely self-regulating division of the *nervous system of vertebrates, controlling the involuntary and vegetative *cardiovascular, digestive, reproductive, and respiratory functions of the body, itself subdivided into the *sympathetic nervous system and the *parasympathetic nervous system (see illustration). Compare somatic nervous system. **ANS** abbrev.

autonomous speech n. An invented language understood only by its inventor(s), such as the secret languages sometimes used by twins, especially in their second year of life. Also called *idioglossia* or *cryptophasia*.

autonomy, functional See functional autonomy.

autonomy versus shame and doubt n. One of the crises in the developmental theory of the German-born *ego psychologist Erik H. Erikson (1902–94). See developmental crises.

autopagnosia n. A common misspelling of *autotopagnosia.

autoplastic adj. Of or relating to *adaptation (1) through alteration of the self. Compare alloplastic.
[From Greek *autos* self + *plastikos* mouldable, from *plassein* to form + -*itikos* resembling or marked by]

autopsy, psychological See psychological autopsy.

autoradiography n. A technique for showing the distribution of radioactively labelled molecules in a tissue specimen by exposing a pho-

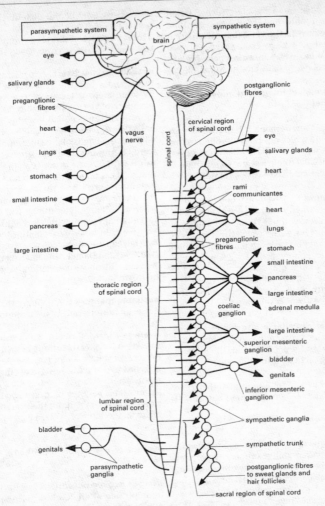

Autonomic nervous system. The parasympathetic and sympathetic systems.

tographic plate to radiation from the specimen.
[From Greek *autos* self + English *radiography*]

autoradiograph *n.* A photograph produced by *autoradiography.

autoreceptor *n.* A *neuroreceptor for a *neurotransmitter located on the neuron that se-

cretes it, such as one of the receptors that are located in the membranes of *presynaptic cells and that monitor the amount of neurotransmitter synthesized and secreted.

autoregression *n.* A property of a *time series in which each score is a linear function of the preceding score (first-order autoregression) or of more than one of the preceding scores

(higher-order autoregression). Such a series, even with only first-order autoregression, has a memory in the sense that each score is correlated with all preceding scores. *See also* ARIMA, autocorrelation. **autoregressive** *adj*.
[From Greek *autos* self + English *regression*]

autoregressive integrated moving average model *See* ARIMA.

autoscopic phenomena *n*. Hallucinatory experiences in which one perceives one's face or body in front of one like a mirror reflection, though usually colourless and transparent.
[From Greek *autos* self + *skopeein* to watch]

autoshaping *n*. A type of *conditioning (1) that occurs when an animal learns to respond to a *stimulus without *reinforcement (1) of the response but with *associative learning of a contingency between a *conditioned stimulus and the reinforcement. For example, in pigeons, brief illumination of a plastic key before the delivery of food results in the pigeon learning to peck the key whenever it is illuminated. *Compare* shaping (1).

autosomal disorder *n*. A disorder such as Huntington's disease or phenylketonuria that is *genetic but not *sex-linked, the relevant gene being carried on an *autosome.

autosome *n*. Any *chromosome other than the X and Y *sex chromosomes. **autosomal** *adj*.
[From Greek *autos* self + *soma* a body]

autotopagnosia *n*. A form of agnosia involving an impaired ability to identify parts of one's own body, often indicative of a lesion in the pathway between the *thalamus and the *parietal lobe. Often misspelt *autopagnosia*. *See also* agnosia, finger agnosia. *Compare* asomatagnosia (*see under* agnosia), topagnosia.
[From Greek *autos* self + *topos* place + *a-* without + *gnosis* knowing + -*ia* indicating a condition or quality]

availability *n*. The property of being accessible or obtainable, especially (in cognitive psychology) the property of information in long-term memory of being retrievable provided that *cues (3), *prompts, or appropriate retrieval strategies can be implemented. An *available memory* is one that can potentially

be retrieved. *See also* availability heuristic. *Compare* accessibility (1).
[From Latin *ad* to + *valere* to be strong or to prevail + -*abilitas* capacity, from *habilis* able]

availability heuristic *n*. A cognitive *heuristic through which the frequency or probability of an event is judged by the number of instances of it that can readily be brought to mind. It can generate biased or incorrect judgements, as when people are asked whether the English language contains more words beginning with the letter *k* or more words with *k* as the third letter, most people finding it easier to think of instances of words beginning with *k* and therefore concluding that there are more words beginning with *k*, whereas in fact a typical long text contains twice as many words with *k* as the third letter. The heuristic was first identified in 1973 by the Israeli psychologists Amos Tversky (1937–96) and Daniel Kahneman (born 1934). *See also* illusory correlation, simulation heuristic.

available memory *n*. A memory that potentially can be retrieved. *See* availability.

average *n*. An informal term for a score or value that is typical of a group or distribution of scores or values. When a precise meaning is attached to this term, it is usually the *arithmetic mean.
[From Arabic *awariyah* damaged goods, referring to damage to ships or their cargoes leading to losses that were shared equally among traders]

average error method *See* method of average error.

average evoked potential *n*. The fluctuation in amplitude of an *evoked potential, averaged over a large number of separate readings to eliminate random *noise (2). Also called an *average evoked response (AER)*. *See also* N140, P200, P300, string length. **AEP** *abbrev*.

average heterozygosity *n*. A measure of the genetic variability within a population, being the average proportion of organisms that are *heterozygous for a specified set of *gene loci. Low genetic variability, such as is found for example among cheetahs in Africa, can result from an *evolutionary bottleneck and can make the species vulnerable to extinction.

average linkage between groups method
n. In statistics, a popular technique of *cluster analysis in which the distance between two clusters is defined as the average of the distances between all pairs of individuals or cases formed by taking one from each cluster. In contrast to single and complete linkage methods, it uses information about all pairs of distances, not just the nearest or the furthest. Also called the *unweighted pair-group method using arithmetic averages (UPGMA)*.

average linkage within groups method *n*. In statistics, a technique of *cluster analysis in which clusters are combined in such a way that the average distance between all individuals or cases in the resulting cluster is minimized. Also, the distance between two clusters is defined as the average distance between all possible pairs of individuals in the cluster that would result if they were combined.

aversion therapy *n*. A technique of *behaviour therapy used to eliminate undesirable habits, like cigarette smoking, by repeatedly pairing unpleasant or painful stimuli such as electric shock, or responses such as nausea (induced by a drug such as *Antabuse), with the unwanted behaviour or associated stimuli. [From Latin *aversus* turned away, from *avertere* to turn away, from *vertere* to turn]

aversive *n*. Tending to repel or deter; unpleasant.
[From Latin *aversus* opposed, from *avertere* to turn from, from *ab* from + *vertere* to turn + *-ivus* indicating a tendency, inclination, or quality]

avoidance–avoidance conflict *n*. Conflict arising from the simultaneous presence of two or more approximately equal threats, one of the three main types of conflict identified in 1931 by the Polish/German-born US psychologist Kurt Lewin (1890–1947), though he did not name any of the types. Such conflicts tend to be stable and to remain unresolved, because approach towards one of the horns of the dilemma increases the tendency to retreat towards the other, and fear or anxiety is therefore minimized at a point where distances from both are greatest. *See also* approach–approach conflict, approach–avoidance conflict, double bind.

avoidance conditioning *n*. In *operant conditioning, a form of *negative reinforcement in which an organism avoids an aversive stimulus by making a particular response. Typically, a rat is placed in a long, narrow alleyway with a grid floor that becomes electrified and delivers a shock a few seconds after the presentation of a *conditioned stimulus such as a light, and the rat can avoid the painful stimulation by running to the end of the alley and stepping into a non-electrified goal box in the time interval between the signal and the shock. In *active avoidance conditioning* the organism has to make a positive response in order to avoid the aversive stimulus, whereas in *passive avoidance conditioning* it has to abstain from making the response in order to avoid the aversive stimulus. Also called *avoidance learning. See also* Kamin effect, Sidman avoidance conditioning, two-way avoidance conditioning. *Compare* escape conditioning.

avoidant personality disorder *n*. A *personality disorder characterized by a pervasive pattern of social inhibition, feelings of inadequacy, and hypersensitivity to criticism, disapproval, or rejection, beginning by early adulthood and indicated by such signs and symptoms as avoidance of work involving significant interpersonal contact; unwillingness to associate with people unless certain of being liked; restraint in intimate relationships for fear of being shamed or ridiculed; preoccupation with criticism or rejection; inhibition in new social situations arising from feelings of inadequacy; self-image as inept, unappealing, and inferior to others; and reluctance to engage in activities carrying the risk of embarrassment. Also called *anxious personality disorder. Compare* schizoid personality disorder.

avolition *n*. Inability to initiate or sustain purposeful activities; one of the *negative symptoms of *schizophrenia.
[From Greek *a-* without + English *volition* the exercise of will, from Latin *volo* I will]

axiom *n*. A statement or proposition that can be accepted without proof or evidence and that may therefore occur as a premise but not the conclusion of an argument. In formal proofs in logic and mathematics, axioms are stipulated as true for the purposes of the

chain of argument that follows. Also called a *postulate*. **axiomatic** *adj*.
[From Greek *axioma* a self-evident truth, from *axioein* to consider worthy, from *axios* worthy]

axiomatic measurement theory *n*. A branch of mathematics and mathematical psychology concerned with the correspondence between measurements of psychological or other *attributes and the attributes themselves. Also called *abstract measurement theory*. *See also* additivity, measurement, measurement level, measurement model, multiplicative model, scale (1). *Compare* conjoint measurement theory.

axoaxonic *adj*. Of or relating to a comparatively rare type of *synapse (1) between the *axon of an *inhibitory neuron and the axon of a neuron that it inhibits. *Compare* axodendritic, axosomatic, dendrodendritic. **A-A** *abbrev*.

axodendritic *adj*. Of or relating to a *synapse (1) between the *axon of one *neuron and the *dendrite of another, usually excitatory in its effect on the target neuron. *Compare* axoaxonic, axosomatic, dendrodendritic. **A-D** *abbrev*.

axolemma *n*. Another name for a *neurolemma.

axon *n*. A long, threadlike *process (2) or extending fibre of a *neuron, capable of conducting a nerve impulse away from the cell body towards the neuron's terminal *bouton, from where it is transmitted via a *synapse (1) to another neuron, a muscle, or a gland. Also called a *nerve fibre*. *See also* microtubule. *Compare* dendrite. **axonal** *adj*.
[From Greek *axon* an axis]

axonal transport *n*. The movement of chemical substances such as *neurotransmitters and sometimes small objects such as *organelles along the *axon of a neuron, either away from the cell body (anterograde axonal transport) or towards it (retrograde axonal transport). *See also* microtubule.

axon hillock *n*. The small protuberance on the cell body of a neuron where the *axon arises and where a nerve impulse is normally (except in certain large neurons) initiated.

axon reflex *n*. A *reflex response to scratching of the skin with a sharp object: a red line appears within seconds, followed by a red flare in the surrounding skin, and finally a white weal, these phenomena constituting the *triple response*. The weal and flare result from the activity of *pain receptors that transmit impulses along their *axons not only in the normal *orthodromic direction towards the central nervous system but also in the *antidromic direction from axon forking nodes into the neighbouring skin, where the free nerve endings respond by releasing *substance P, which binds to artery walls causing them to dilate and to produce the flare response, and which binds to *mast cells and stimulates them to release *histamine, resulting in the accumulation of fluid that constitutes the weal response.

axosomatic *adj*. Of or relating to a *synapse (1) between an *axon and a *soma (1) or cell body, usually inhibitory in its effect on the target neuron. *Compare* axoaxonic, axodendritic, dendrodendritic. **A-S** *abbrev*.

azimuth *n*. The direction of an object or image in the horizontal plane, relative to a fixed point such as an object immediately in front or to the north pole. *Compare* zenith distance.
[From Arabic *as-sumūt* azimuth, from *al* the + *sumūt* directions, from *samt* direction]

babbling *n*. The speech sounds, generally characterized by repeated syllables such as *bababa* and *dada*, produced by infants immediately before the onset of recognizable speech, restricted largely to *phonemes of the language being acquired. *Compare* cooing.

Babinski reflex *n*. The involuntary fanning of the toes when the sole of the foot is stroked with a hard object such as a metal key, observed in normal infants below 2 years of age but considered an abnormal neurological sign in older children and adults, suggestive of a lesion in the *corticospinal tract. It is normally replaced around 2 years of age by the *plantar response, which is a curling inwards of the toes. The *Babinski sign* is the presence of the Babinski reflex in a person over 2 years of age, an indication of neurological damage.
[Named after the French neurologist Josef F(rançois) F(élix) Babinski (1857–1932) who is credited with having discovered it]

baby talk *n*. An ambiguous term referring both to the style of speech used by young children and that of older people when speaking to them. *See also* caretaker speech, motherese.

back cross *n*. In genetics, a cross between a *hybrid (1) of the first generation and one of its parents, or the offspring resulting from such a mating.

back formation *n*. The creation of a new word on the basis of a familiar word that is mistakenly assumed to be derived from it. For example, the verb *to edit* is a back formation from the noun *editor*, which is not derived from the verb but is a Latin word meaning producer, derived from the prefix *e-* out and the word *datum*, meaning given, from the verb *dare* to give; similarly *to burgle* is a back formation from *burglar*, *to peddle* from *pedlar* or *peddler*,

and *to sculpt* from *sculptor*. *Compare* folk etymology (2), metanalysis.

back mutation *n*. The restoration of a *mutant (2) phenotype to the normal form by a further mutation of the same gene. Also called a *reversion*.

backprop *n*. A colloquial name for the *back-propagation algorithm.

back-propagation algorithm *n*. In *parallel distributed processing, a method of adjusting the output of a multi-layered *neural network to produce a desired state for a given input, by first checking the input and computing the required output for that input, then comparing the current output to the required output and adjusting the connection weights to reduce the discrepancy between the required output and the current output, and then repeating this process of adjustment for the next level down in the system and for each lower level of the system in turn down to the lowest level, thus causing the system to learn to produce the required output. It implements a method of learning by *gradient descent. It was discovered simultaneously and independently by several researchers in 1982 and became well known after an influential publication by the US psychologist David E(verett) Rumelhart (born 1942) and his colleagues in 1986, the term itself having been introduced in 1962 by the US psychologist Frank Rosenblatt (1928–71) in connection with his work on the *perceptron. Also called *backward propagation* or *backprop*. *See* delta rule. *See also* algorithm, connectionism.

back slang *n*. A secret language in which words are spelt and spoken backwards or approximately backwards. A familiar British example is *yob* instead of *boy*, and less well-known examples include *tekram* instead of *market* and *tenip* instead of *pint*. Back slang has been reported in the UK among soldiers, labourers, shopkeepers, thieves, and public school pupils, and it has also been found in several other parts of the world, including France, Java, and Thailand. *See also* slang.

back vowel *n.* A *vowel (see the diagram accompanying that entry) articulated towards the back of the mouth with the back of the tongue raised, such as the vowels in *goose, lot, thaw*, and *heart*. *Compare* central vowel, front vowel.

backward association *n.* A learned association between a *stimulus (1) and either another stimulus or a *response occurring before it in time. Also called a *retroactive association*. *Compare* forward association.

backward conditioning *n.* A modified form of *classical conditioning in which the *conditioned stimulus does not precede the *unconditioned stimulus but follows it. *Compare* forward conditioning.

backward masking *n.* A form of *masking that occurs when perception of a stimulus called the *test stimulus* is reduced or eliminated by the presentation of a second stimulus called the *masking stimulus* which, in the case of *visual masking, follows the test stimulus up to 500 milliseconds later—as when a row of printed letters is exposed for 50 milliseconds, long enough to make them easily legible in normal circumstances, and this is followed after 150 milliseconds by a dark ring surrounding the position of one of the letters, completely masking the letter and causing it to vanish from the array. When the test stimulus and masking stimulus do not overlap spatially, the phenomenon is called *metacontrast. *See also* auditory masking. *Compare* forward masking, simultaneous masking.

backward propagation *See* back-propagation algorithm.

backward span *n.* A test of *short-term memory in which the respondent is presented with a sequence of items, usually numbers, and then tries to repeat them back in reverse order. The *Wechsler scales include both backward span and *ordered recall subtests.

bacteria *n. pl.* Unicellular or threadlike microorganisms that reproduce by *fission (2) and are often parasitic and liable to cause diseases. **bacterial** *adj.* **bacterium** *sing.*
[From Greek *bakterion* a little rod, diminutive of *baktron* a rod]

bad breast *See under* good breast.

bad faith *n.* In the *existentialism of the French philosopher Jean-Paul Sartre (1905–80), a form of self-deception and deception of others in which people refuse to acknowledge responsibility for their own freely chosen actions and perceive or depict themselves as the passive victims of circumstance. *See also* existential therapy.

bad object *See under* good object.

bah tschi *See* latah.

balanced bilingual *n.* Another name for an *ambilingual (2). *Compare* unbalanced bilingual.
[From *balanced* + Latin *bis* two + *lingua* a tongue + *-alis* of or relating to]

balanced polymorphism *n.* A type of *genetic polymorphism characterized by a relatively permanent equilibrium with different *alleles of a gene present at fixed relative frequencies in the population. Also called a *Hardy–Weinberg equilibrium*. *See also* Hardy–Weinberg law, heterosis. *Compare* transient polymorphism.

balanced scale *n.* In psychometrics, any scale designed to control for potential sources of bias by *counterbalancing (2); especially a questionnaire that controls for *acquiescence response set by ensuring that half the items are keyed positively, affirmative answers increasing a respondent's score on the attribute being measured, and half the items are scored negatively, negative answers increasing the score—the net effect being that scores on the test are not biased systematically in either direction by acquiescence.

balance theory *n.* A *cognitive consistency theory of *person perception and *attitude change in which the elements, often depicted as vertices of a triangle, are a person (*p*), another person (*o*), and an attitude object (*x*), the relations between the three elements, represented by the sides of the triangle, being either positive or negative according to *p*'s attitudes and beliefs. The model represents *p*'s cognitions, and it can exist in a state of either *balance*, if none of the relations is negative or if two are negative, or *imbalance*, if just one of the relations is negative. In some later versions of the theory, the state of the model with three negative relations is considered ambiguous or *non-balanced*. According to the theory, an imbalanced state of the model, with just one negative relation, is dynamically unstable and has a tendency to become balanced, which means that one or more of the relations tends to change. For example, if Peter (*p*) hates classical music (*x*) but falls in love with Olivia (*o*), who tells him that she loves classical music, then there is one negative and two positive relations, and Peter's attitude towards either classical music or Olivia is likely to change, unless he can change her attitude towards classical music or his belief about her attitude. The theory was developed by the Austrian-born US psychologist Fritz Heider (1896–1988), first published in an article in 1946, and later presented in his book *The Psychology of Interpersonal Relations* in 1958, and the US psychologist Theodore M(ead) Newcomb (1903–84) contributed to its development in 1953. *See also* positivity bias (2).

Baldwin illusion *n*. A visual illusion in which a line spanning the distance between two large squares appears shorter than a line of the same length spanning the distance between two smaller squares (see illustration). It is a close relative of the Zanforlin illusion.
[Named after the US psychologist James Mark Baldwin (1861–1934) who first drew attention to it]

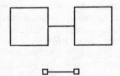

Baldwin illusion. The horizontal lines between the squares are equal in length.

Bálint's syndrome *n*. A syndrome caused by bilateral brain damage in the area where the *parietal and *occipital lobes meet, characterized by *optic ataxia, ocular *apraxia (in-

ability to shift gaze on command), and *simultanagnosia.
[Named after the Hungarian physician Rezsoe Bálint (1874–1929) who first described it in 1907]

ballism *n*. A condition usually resulting from damage to the *subthalamic nucleus characterized by involuntary violent flailing of the limbs, resembling throwing movements, which are exhausting and incapacitating. *Compare* hemiballism.
[From Greek *ballein* to throw]

ballistic movement *n*. A movement such as a *saccade that cannot be controlled once it has been initiated and that is thought to be programmed by the *cerebellum. *See also* open-loop control. *Compare* ramp movement.
[From Latin *ballista* a Roman military weapon for projecting heavy objects, from Greek *ballein* to throw]

band-pass filter *n*. A type of *filter (2) for screening light, sound, alternating current, or other oscillating signals and transmitting frequencies only or mainly within a specified range. A *high-pass filter* transmits frequencies above a specified threshold, and a *low-pass filter* those below a specified threshold.

bandwagon effect *n*. An accelerating diffusion through a group or population of a pattern of behaviour, the probability of any individual adopting it increasing with the proportion who have already done so. It occurs in situations in which people believe that their interests are served by joining a fashionable movement, as when soldiers decide during a revolution or civil war to defect to the rebel faction because many others have already defected.
[So called because a bandwagon is a vehicle that carries the band in a circus procession and drums up popular support]

bandwidth *n*. The range of frequencies over which a sense organ or any other communication channel functions or responds. Thus the human auditory system responds within a bandwidth corresponding to the *audibility range from about 16 hertz to 20,000 hertz (cycles per second). *See also* spectrum.

baraesthesia *n*. The sensation of pressure. US *baresthesia*.

[From Greek *baros* weight + *aisthesis* sensation, from *aisthanesthai* to feel + *-ia* indicating a condition or quality]

baragnosis *n.* An impaired ability to judge weight with the cutaneous and muscle senses. Often confused with *baragnosis.

[From Greek *baros* weight + *a-* without + *gnosis* knowledge]

Bárány nystagmus *n.* Another name for *caloric nystagmus. *See* Bárány test.

Bárány test *n.* A method for detecting diseases of the *semicircular canals by irrigating the ears alternately with warm water or air and cold water or air, the stimulus eliciting *caloric nystagmus towards the stimulated side if the stimulus is warm and away from the stimulated side if it is cold. Also called the *caloric test*.

[Named after the Nobel prizewinning Austrian physician Robert Bárány (1876–1936) who devised it]

barber's paradox *n.* A close relative of *Russell's paradox, expressed in terms of a village in which there is a barber who shaves all and only those men who do not shave themselves. From this it follows that if this barber shaves himself, then he does not, and if he does not, then he does. It was first published in 1918 by the Welsh philosopher Bertrand (Arthur William) Russell (1872–1970), who attributed it to an unnamed source.

barber's pole effect *n.* The phenomenon whereby a rotating pole painted with spiral stripes of alternating colours, if viewed through a horizontal slit, is seen as marks moving horizontally, and if viewed through a vertical slit as marks moving vertically, although the movement of the stripes themselves is the same in both cases.

barbiturate *n.* Any of a number of drugs derived from barbituric acid, including the long-acting *phenobarbital and the short-acting *amobarbital, *pentobarbital, *secobarbital, and *thiopental, that generally act as central nervous system *depressants (although stimulant barbiturates have also been synthesized) by stimulating the *GABA receptor complex and are used as *sedative–hypnotic drugs or *anaesthetics (1) and are frequently taken as street drugs.

Street names for barbiturates in general include *barbs*, *candy*, *dolls*, *goofers*. *See also* sedative-, hypnotic-, or anxiolytic-related disorders; truth drug.

[From German *Barbitursäure*, from the name *Barbara* + *uric* + *Säure* acid, coined by the German chemist Adolf von Bayer (1835–1917) who discovered the drug on Saint Barbara's Day, 4 December 1864]

barbiturism *n.* Acute or chronic poisoning by a *barbiturate, leading to depressed respiration, disorientation, bluish discoloration of the skin and mucous membranes caused by a deficiency of haemoglobin in the blood, and possibly coma and death.

barbs *n.* A street name for *barbiturate drugs in general.

bar chart *n.* In descriptive statistics, a graph resembling a *histogram but having a base (usually horizontal) axis representing values of a qualitative variable such as gender or religion rather than a quantitative variable such as age. Also called a *block diagram*.

Bard–Cannon theory *n.* Another name for the *Cannon–Bard theory.

bar detector *n.* A type of cell in the *primary visual cortex (Area V1) that responds maximally to a bar (lighter than the surround for some cells, darker than the surround for others) oriented at a particular angle on the retina, the response being strongest for a moving bar-shaped stimulus. *See also* complex cell, end-stopped receptive field, feature detector, hypercomplex cell, simple cell. *Compare* edge detector.

Barnum effect *n.* A tendency for people to accept vague, ambiguous, and generalized statements as being accurate descriptions of their own personalities. The effect was first demonstrated empirically in 1949 by the US psychologist Bertram R(obin) Forer (1914–2000), who constructed a personality profile consisting of the following 13 statements, drawn largely from an astrology book: 'You have a great need for other people to like and admire you. You have a tendency to be critical of yourself. You have a great deal of unused capacity which you have not turned to your advantage. While you have some personality weaknesses, you are generally able to compensate for them. Your sexual adjust-ment has presented problems for you. Disciplined and self-controlled outside, you tend to be worrisome and insecure inside. At times you have serious doubts as to whether you have made the right decision or done the right thing. You prefer a certain amount of change and variety and become dissatisfied when hemmed in by restrictions and limitations. You pride yourself as an independent thinker and do not accept others' statements without satisfactory proof. You have found it unwise to be too frank in revealing yourself to others. At times you are extraverted, affable and sociable, while at other times you are introverted, wary and reserved. Some of your aspirations tend to be pretty unrealistic. Security is one of your major goals in life.' People who are presented with this profile and are told that it is based on a personality test, hand-writing analysis, or some other plausible data typically rate it quite highly as being applica-ble to them personally. In Forer's original ex-periment, the profile was supposedly based on a personality questionnaire that a group of 39 students had filled in a week earlier. The students were asked to 'rate on a scale of zero to five the degree to which the personality de-scription reveals the basic characteristics of your personality', and most of them chose 4 or 5, with a mean of 4.26. They were also asked to 'check each statement as true or false about yourself'; the average number of statements accepted as true was 10.23 out of 13. *See also* illusory correlation.

[The term *Barnum effect* was introduced in 1956 in an article in the journal *American Psychologist* by the US psychologist Paul Everett Meehl (born 1920), quoting an unpublished comment by the US psychologist Donald G(ildersleeve) Paterson (1892–1962) about 'personality description after the manner of P. T. Barnum', alluding to the US showman P(hineas) T(aylor) Barnum (1810–91), co-founder of the Barnum and Bailey circus, and by implication to one or both of the following quotations attributed to him: 'My secret of success is always to have a little something for everyone' and 'There's a sucker born every minute']

barognosis *n*. The sense of weight or the abil-ity to judge lifted weights. Often confused with *baragnosis.

[From Greek *baros* weight + *gnosis* knowledge]

baroreceptor *n*. Any of the pressure-sensitive receptors in the right atrium of the heart and in certain large blood vessels that respond to decreases in blood volume or pressure, result-ing from loss of extracellular fluid, by sending impulses to the *hypothalamus, leading to the release of *angiotensin II and a sensation of *thirst. Also called a *baroceptor. See also* hy-povolaemic thirst, subfornical organ. *Compare* blood-flow receptor.

[From Greek *baros* weight + English *receptor*]

Bartholin's gland *n*. Either of a pair of *ex-ocrine glands in a woman's vagina that se-crete a lubricating mucus when she is sexually aroused.

[Named by its discoverer, the Danish anatomist Caspar Bartholin (1655–1738), in honour of his father, Thomas]

Bartlett–Box *F* test *n*. In statistics, a test that several groups come from populations with the same *variance. For sufficiently large sam-ple sizes, a non-significant probability allows a researcher to reject the hypothesis that the variances differ. The test assumes that the ob-servations come from *normal distributions.

[Named after the English statisticians Maurice Stevenson Bartlett (1910–2002) and George Edward Pelham Box (born 1919) and the *F statistic that it uses]

basal forebrain *n*. An ill-defined region at the bottom of the forebrain, dorsal to the hypo-thalamus, including the *preoptic nucleus, *septum pellucidum, and the *nucleus basalis of Meynert.

basal ganglia *n. pl.* Structures containing clusters of neuron cell bodies in and around the thalamus near the base of the brain, some-times taken to include the amygdala and claustrum, but in careful usage restricted to structures involved in the control of volun-tary movement, namely the *caudate nu-cleus, *lenticular nucleus (including the *putamen and *globus pallidus), *subthal-amic nucleus, and *substantia nigra. The caudate nucleus and putamen together constitute the *striatum. Lesions in these areas can lead to movement disorders such as *athetosis, *ballism, *chorea, *dystonia, *hemiballism, *Huntington's disease, *Parkinson's disease, *tardive dyskinesia, and *tremor. **basal ganglion** *sing*.

[From Greek *ganglion* a cystic tumour]

basal metabolic rate *n*. The rate at which *metabolism occurs in the body at rest, 12 to 14 hours after eating, usually measured in kilocalories of heat generated per square metre of body surface area per hour. *See also* Calorie. **BMR** *abbrev*.

base *n*. **1.** An *alkaline chemical compound that reacts with an acid to form a salt and water; in biochemistry often denoting the constituent nitrogenous bases of DNA and RNA, namely *adenine, *cytosine, *guanine, and either *thymine (in DNA) or *uracil (in RNA). *See also* purine, pyrimidine. **2.** In biology, the part of an organ closest to its point of attachment. **3.** The bottom, root, or supporting foundation of anything. **basal** or **basilar** *adj*. Pertaining to the bottom or root. **basic** *adj*. Of, relating to, or consisting of a chemical base, or pertaining to the bottom, root, or supporting foundation of anything.
[From Latin *basis* a pedestal]

basement effect *n*. Another name for the *floor effect.

base pairing *n*. Another name for *complementary base pairing.

base rate *n*. The natural value or level of a *variable when it is unaffected by any special or unusual influences, especially the *prior probability (1) of an event, or the average number of times an event occurs in a given time period divided by the maximum number of times it could occur. *See also* base-rate fallacy.

base-rate fallacy *n*. A failure to take account of the *base rate or *prior probability (1) of an event when subjectively judging its *conditional probability. A classic experiment in 1973 by the Israeli psychologists Daniel Kahneman (born 1934) and Amos Tversky (1937–96) showed that people's judgements as to whether a student who was described in a personality sketch was more likely to be a student of engineering or of law tended to ignore the additional information that the student was drawn randomly from a group of 70 engineering students and 30 law students or from a group of 30 engineering students and 70 law students, although that information was highly relevant to the question in hand. The fallacy is usually explained by the use in problems of this kind of the *representativeness heuristic, which is insensitive to prior probabilities. *See also* attributional bias, Bayesian inference, taxicab problem, Wells effect. *Compare* conjunction fallacy, sample size fallacy.

base sequence *n*. Another name for a *DNA sequence.
[So called because it is made up of bases]

BASIC-ID *abbrev*. Behaviours, affective processes, sensations, images, cognitions, and interpersonal relationships springing from drugs or biological factors. This acronym summarizes the core elements of human life and basic modalities of response to situations in *multimodal therapy, according to which an intervention is most likely to be effective if it follows the order of the response pattern of the patient or client. Thus, if the first-order anxiety response is in the sensory modality (for example, churning of the stomach), then sensory techniques such as relaxation or biofeedback are used as initial treatments.

basic-level category *n*. The level of specificity/generality of a *concept within a conceptual hierarchy at which most people tend naturally to categorize it, usually neither the most specific nor the most general available category but the one with the most *attributes distinctive of the concept in question. Thus, in most ordinary circumstances a cat is conceptualized and referred to as a *cat* rather than a *quadruped* (which would include dogs and other four-legged animals) or a *tabby cat* (which would exclude ginger toms and other cats). Also called a *basic-level concept*, a *natural-level category* or *concept*, or a *natural category*, but this latter term is avoided in careful usage. *See also* prototype theory.

basic mistrust *n*. In *psychoanalysis, an initial relationship lacking trust, developed by an infant with its mother or caretaker as a result of bad mothering when basic trust does not develop. Also called *basic distrust*. *See* basic trust versus basic mistrust.

Basic Orthographic Syllabic Structure *See* BOSS.

basic research *n*. Research undertaken with the primary goal of contributing to knowledge or understanding of some phenomenon or phenomena by testing explicit *hypotheses, generally contrasted with *applied research. Also called *theoretical research. Compare* action research, descriptive research, evaluation research, exploratory research.

basic rest–activity cycle n. A *biological rhythm of waxing and waning alertness with a period of approximately 90 minutes in humans. During sleep it controls the cycles of *REM and *slow-wave sleep. Also called the *rest–activity cycle.* **BRAC** *abbrev.*

basic rule of psychoanalysis n. Another name for the *fundamental rule of psychoanalysis.

basic trust versus basic mistrust n. One of the crises in the developmental theory of the German-born *ego psychologist Erik H. Erikson (1902–94). The English psychoanalyst Donald Woods Winnicott (1896–1971), and the British-based Hungarian psychiatrist Michael Balint (1896–1970), among others, also use the term *basic trust* to denote the initial trusting relationship normally developed by an infant with its mother or caretaker. *See* developmental crises. *Compare* basic mistrust.

basilar *adj.* Situated at the base.

basilar artery n. An unpaired artery at the base of the brain, supplying the pons, cerebellum, posterior part of the cerebrum, and inner ears.

basilar membrane n. The membrane of the *organ of Corti in the inner ear, containing *hair cells that convert sound waves into nerve impulses. *See also* place theory, travelling wave.

basilect n. The least prestigious variety of a language within a speech community, or the variety furthest away from the *acrolect. *See also* dialect, idiolect, lect. *Compare* acrolect, mesolect.
[From Greek *basis* bottom + *legein* to speak]

basket cell n. Any of a class of inhibitory *interneurons found in the *cerebral cortex and the *cerebellum, having a short axon that divides into a large number of processes and forms basket-like networks round the cell bodies of numerous *Purkinje cells, whose action it inhibits. *Compare* Golgi cell, stellate cell.

basulca n. Coca paste, a crude extract of the coca plant, consumed as a drug in cocaine-producing countries in South America. *See* cocaine.
[Spanish]

Batesian mimicry n. A form of *mimicry in which a species that is harmless or palatable to a *predator is protected from predation by its resemblance in shape or coloration to a harmful or unpalatable species. *Compare* Müllerian mimicry.
[Named after the English naturalist and explorer Henry Walter Bates (1825–92) who first described it in 1861]

bathyaesthesia n. Sensation from receptors inside the body. US *bathyesthesia.* Also called *bathaesthesia* or *bathesthesia. Compare* bathyanaesthesia.
[From Greek *bathys* deep + *aisthesis* sensation, from *aisthanesthai* to feel + -*ia* indicating a condition or quality]

bathyanaesthesia n. Impairment or loss of sensation from receptors within the body. US *bathyanesthesia.* Also called *bathanaesthesia* or *bathanesthesia. See also* anaesthesia. *Compare* bathyaesthesia.
[From Greek *bathys* deep + *anaisthesia* absence of sensation, from *an-* without + *aisthesis* feeling + -*ia* indicating a condition or quality]

battered baby syndrome n. A term coined by the German-born US paediatrician Charles Henry Kempe (born 1922) in an article in the *Journal of the American Medical Association* in 1962 to denote the pattern of physical and psychological injuries inflicted on a baby by intentional neglect or repeated excessive beating by a parent or caretaker. *See also* battered child syndrome, child abuse. *Compare* battered wife syndrome.

battered child syndrome n. An extension of the term *battered baby syndrome, used when the victim is an older child. **BCS** *abbrev.*

battered wife syndrome n. A non-technical term used loosely to denote the physical and psychological consequences of physical abuse, usually of a woman by her husband or partner, sometimes involving *post-traumatic stress disorder. *See also* spouse abuse. *Compare* battered baby syndrome. **BWS** *abbrev.*

battery *See* test battery.

baud *n.* A unit of information transmission speed corresponding to one unit or *bit per second. *See also* bit, information (2). **Kbaud** or **kilobaud** *n.* Thousands of bits or units per second.
[Named after the French engineer and inventor of the first successful teleprinter, Jean M. E. Baudot (1845–1903)]

Bayesian inference *n.* A form of statistical reasoning in which *prior probabilities (2) are modified in the light of data or empirical evidence in accordance with *Bayes' theorem to yield *posterior probabilities, which may then be used as prior probabilities for further updating in the light of subsequent data. Bayesian inference is often based on *subjective probabilities, and the following example shows how Bayesian updating is done. Suppose a physician begins with a prior probability $P(H)$ that a certain patient has HIV infection. This prior probability may be the base rate of HIV infection in the community or may be a subjective estimate derived from anywhere; let us assume that it is 0.001. The physician then observes a relevant symptom, dementia, and needs to determine the posterior probability $P(H|D)$ that the patient has HIV infection, given this new datum. Using Bayes' theorem, the physician multiplies the prior probability $P(H)$ by $P(D|H)/P(D)$, which is the *likelihood ratio (1) of the subjective probability of the symptom occurring if the patient has the disorder (let us say 0.50) divided by the subjective probability of the symptom irrespective of the disorder—let us say 0.002. Thus the posterior probability $P(H|D) = (0.001)(0.50/0.002) = 0.25$, and the physician's subjective probability that the patient has HIV infection has risen from 0.001 to 0.25. This posterior probability can then be used as a prior probability for updating in the light of further evidence, and so on. Also called *Bayesian statistics* or *conditioning*. *See also* insufficient reason.

Bayes' rule *n.* The proposition that the *conditional probability of an event H, given another event D, is equal to the joint probability of both events divided by the probability of the conditioning event: $P(H|D) = P(H$ and $D)/P(D)$. It follows immediately from the fourth of *Kolmogorov's axioms of probability, and in spite of its apparent triviality it is impor-

tant because *Bayes' theorem is easily derived from it, eliminating the necessity to memorize Bayes' theorem.
[Named after the English mathematician and Presbyterian clergyman Thomas Bayes (1702–61) who introduced it]

Bayes' theorem *n.* In statistics, a theorem, easily proved from *Bayes' rule, expressing the *conditional probability of an event H given an event D, written $P(H|D)$, in terms of the conditional probability of D given H, written $P(D|H)$, the probability of D, and the probability of H. In its simplest form, $P(H|D) = P(D|H)P(H)/P(D)$. The theorem enables the *prior probability (2) of a hypothesis (H) to be updated repeatedly to produce *posterior probabilities in the light of data (D) derived from observation or experience, and it underpins the whole edifice of *Bayesian inference. In its most general form, the theorem states that if H_n is one of a set H_i of mutually exclusive and exhaustive events, then $P(H_n|D) = P(D|H_n)P(H_n)/\Sigma_i[P(D|H_i)P(H_i)]$.
[Named after the English mathematician and Presbyterian clergyman Thomas Bayes (1702–61) and published posthumously in 1763]

Bayley Scales of Infant Development *n.* A popular instrument for measuring infant development, comprising three subscales: a mental scale, measuring memory, perception, and other cognitive functions; a motor scale, measuring the quality of motor performance; and an infant behaviour scale, measuring social behaviour, persistence, and other general factors.
[Named after the US psychologist Nancy Bayley (1899–1995) who introduced an early version of the scales in 1924 and a revised version in 1965]

B cell *n.* Another name for a *B lymphocyte.

beat (auditory) *See* auditory beat.

Beck Depression Inventory *n.* A widely used questionnaire, originally designed to be administered by a trained test administrator but widely used as a self-report scale, comprising 21 items, each describing a behavioural manifestation of *depression together with between four and six self-evaluative statements from which the respondent is asked to choose the one that is most applicable. The question-

naire provides a total score between 0 and 60 indicating the depth of the respondent's depression. A revised version called the Beck Depression Inventory-II was published in 1993. Other Beck inventories designed to measure suicide ideation, hopelessness, and anxiety have also been constructed. **BDI** or **BDI-II** *abbrev*.
[Named after the US psychiatrist Aaron (Temkin) Beck (born 1921) who, together with four colleagues, first discussed it in an article in the *Archives of General Psychiatry* in 1961]

bee dance *See* round dance, waggle dance.

behaviour *n*. The physical activity of an *organism, including overt bodily movements and internal glandular and other physiological processes, constituting the sum total of the organism's physical *responses to its environment. The term also denotes the specific physical responses of an organism to particular *stimuli or classes of stimuli. US *behavior*.

behavioural contagion *n*. Another name for *social contagion, especially when applied to overt behaviour such as yawning. US *behavioral contagion*.

behavioural decision theory *n*. An approach to judgement and decision making focusing on *subjective expected utility and on departures from *normative (1) theories such as *Bayes' theorem and *utility theory. It was first put forward by the US psychologist Ward (Dennis) Edwards (born 1927) in an influential article in 1954, and many authorities interpret it to include *psychological decision theory. US *behavioral decision theory*. *Compare* decision theory. **BDT** *abbrev*.

behavioural ecology *n*. A branch of study devoted to understanding behaviour in terms of *natural selection and *adaptation (1). US *behavioral ecology*. *See also* ecology (1).

behavioural oscillation *n*. In *Hullian learning theory, momentary fluctuations in an organism's propensity to respond to a *stimulus (1). US *behavioral oscillation*. $_sO_R$ *abbrev*.

behavioural pharmacology *n*. The branch of *pharmacology concerned with the study of the effects of drugs on behaviour, with particular emphasis on the development and classification of drugs. US *behavioral pharmacology*.

behavioural science *n*. The application of scientific principles to the study of the behaviour of organisms. The term is applied to disciplines such as psychology, anthropology, sociology, behavioural zoology, and any other discipline devoted to studying behaviour scientifically. US *behavioral science*.

behaviour contrast *n*. The phenomenon whereby if an organism is given a small reward for a particular response, and then the reward is increased, the organism's rate of responding tends to increase to a level higher than it would have been if the larger reward had been given from the start. Also, if a large reward is replaced by a smaller one, the rate of responding tends to fall below the level that would have occurred if the smaller reward had been given from the outset, but this version of the phenomenon is less robust. In its positive form it is also called the *elation effect* or the *Crespi effect*. US *behavior contrast*.

behaviour genetics *n*. An interdisciplinary field of study concerned with the *genetic or hereditary bases of animal and human behaviour. US *behavior genetics*. Also called *behavioural genetics* or *behavioral genetics*. *See* adoption study, DF extremes analysis, kinship study, twin study.

behaviourism *n*. A school of psychology launched in 1913 by the US psychologist John B(roadus) Watson (1878–1958) with the theoretical goal of the 'prediction and control of behavior', representing a radical break with the classical experimental psychology of *structuralism (2), which emphasized neither prediction nor control nor behaviour. Watson considered the introspective methods of structuralism to be unscientific, he excluded everything except behaviour from psychology, and he borrowed the doctrine of *operationalism from *logical positivism, defining the meaning of psychological concepts as literally the operations through which they are measured. According to behaviourism, virtually all behaviour can be explained as the product of *learning (1), and all learning consists of *conditioning (1). The contemporary work on *classical conditioning of the Russian physiologist Ivan Petrovich Pavlov (1849–1936), of which Watson was apparently unaware, added further impetus to the behaviourist movement when it became known in the US. The most influential proponent of neobehaviourism since the 1940s was the US psychologist B(urrhus) F(rederic) Skinner (1904–90), who initiated the study of *operant conditioning. As a complete explanation of all forms of behaviour, the doctrines of classical and operant conditioning have lost much of their force in the face of mounting attacks from various sources and the decline of positivist dogmas, but neobehaviourism is still influential in the English-speaking world. US *behaviorism*. *See also* associationism, connectionism (2). **behaviourist** or **behaviorist** *adj. n.* (Of or relating to) a member or follower of the school of behaviourism or one who advocates or practises behaviourism.

behaviour modification *n.* Another name for *behaviour therapy. US *behavior modification*.

behaviour therapy *n.* A collection of *psychotherapeutic techniques aimed at altering maladaptive or unwanted behaviour patterns, especially through the application of principles of *conditioning (1) and *learning (1), the basic assumptions being that most forms of mental disorder can be interpreted as maladaptive patterns of behaviour, that these patterns result from learning processes, and that the appropriate treatment involves the unlearning of these behaviour patterns and the learning of new ones. US *behavior therapy*. Also called *behaviour modification*. *See* ABC (2), aversion therapy, contingency management, flooding, modelling, paradoxical intention, reciprocal inhibition, shaping (1), systematic desensitization, token economy. *Compare* cognitive behaviour modification, multimodal therapy.

bel *n.* A unit for comparing the intensity of any two power levels, given by the logarithm to the base 10 of the ratio of the two levels. Hence a ratio of 10 : 1 corresponds to 1 bel and a ratio of 100 : 1 to 2 bels. For sound measurements, the more common unit is the *decibel, which is equal to one-tenth of a bel.
[Named after the Scottish-born US scientist Alexander Graham Bell (1847–1922), inventor of the telephone]

belief *n.* Any *proposition (1) that is accepted as true on the basis of inconclusive evidence.

A belief is stronger than a baseless *opinion but not as strong as an item of *knowledge. More generally, belief is conviction, faith, or confidence in something or someone. **believe** *vb.*

belladonna *n.* Either of two *alkaloid drugs, *atropine or *hyoscyamine, extracted from the leaves and roots of the deadly nightshade plant *Atropa belladonna*.
[From Italian *bella donna* fair lady, because one of its pharmacological effects is to enlarge the pupils of the eyes, thereby enhancing a woman's sexual attractiveness]

bell curve *n.* A colloquial name for the *normal distribution, so called because of its appearance, though many other probability distributions are also approximately bell-shaped.

belle indifférence, la *See* la belle indifférence.

Bellevue–Wechsler scales *n.* Another name for the *Wechsler–Bellevue scales. *See under* Wechsler scales.

Bell–Magendie law *n.* The principle that *afferent neurons enter the spinal cord dorsally (from the back), whereas *efferent neurons issue from the spinal cord ventrally (from the front). *See also* dorsal root, ventral root.
[Named after the Scottish anatomist Sir Charles Bell (1774–1842) who discovered it in 1811 and the French physiologist François Magendie (1783–1855) who rediscovered it independently in 1822]

Bell's palsy *n.* Paralysis of one side of the face caused by inflammation of the *facial nerve, often accompanied by *hyperacusis on the affected side owing to loss of the nerve's dampening effect on the *stapedius muscle. It is temporary in 80 per cent of cases. *Compare* Möbius syndrome.
[Named after the Scottish anatomist Sir Charles Bell (1774–1842), who first described it]

Bem Sex Role Inventory *n.* A questionnaire designed to measure psychological *androgyny, developed by the US psychologist Sandra (Lipsitz) Bem (born 1944) and published in articles in the *Journal of Consulting and Clinical Psychology* in 1974 and the *Journal of Personality and Social Psychology* in 1975. It is based on the finding that masculinity–femininity is not a single bipolar dimension but is better conceptualized as two unipolar dimensions: people with high scores on the measure of masculinity and low scores on the measure of femininity are labelled *masculine*, and those with high scores on the measure of femininity and low scores on the measure of masculinity are labelled *feminine*; but some people obtain high scores on both measures and are labelled *androgynous*, and some score low on both measures and are labelled *undifferentiated*. Bem reported evidence that androgynous people are able to act in a masculine fashion when circumstances demand, such as maintaining independence when subjected to pressures to conform, and in a feminine fashion in situations requiring femininity, such as playing with a kitten.

Bender Gestalt Test *n*. A neurological test, designed to help in the diagnosis of loss of function and organic brain damage in children and adults, consisting of nine geometrical figures that are copied by the respondent, the drawings being evaluated according to the overall quality of the reproductions, their organization in relation to Gestalt *grouping laws, and the errors made. It was constructed by the US neurologist Lauretta Bender (1897–1987) and first described by her in an article in the *American Orthopsychiatric Association Research Monographs* in 1938. It is sometimes used as a *projective test. Also called the *Bender Visual-Motor Gestalt Test* or the *Visual-Motor Gestalt Test*. **BGT** *abbrev*.

benefit–cost analysis *n*. Another name for *cost–benefit analysis.

benefit–cost ratio *n*. The ratio of total present benefits (*B*) to total present costs (*C*), sometimes used in *cost–benefit analysis with the assumption that a project is worthwhile if and only if *B/C* is greater than 1, but this ratio leads to ambiguities. Consider a proposed wind farm that is judged to produce benefits worth 5m (in any currency), to result in environmental damage worth 2m, and to cost 1m to build. If the environmental damage is classified as a negative benefit, then $B = 5\,m - 2\,m = 3\,m$, $C = 1\,m$, and the benefit–cost ratio $B/C = 3/1 = 3$, suggesting that the project is very worthwhile. But if the environmental damage is classified as a positive cost, then $B = 5\,m$, $C = 2\,m + 1\,m = 3\,m$,

and the benefit–cost ratio $B/C = 5/3 = 1.67$, and the project is much less worthwhile. The *net benefit index* $B - C = 5\,m - 3\,m = 2\,m$ without any ambiguity. Also written *benefit/cost ratio* or *benefit : cost ratio*.

Benham's top *n*. A black-and-white patterned disc that induces perceptions of colours, called *pattern-induced flicker colours (PIFCs), when rotated in white or monochromatic light. The basic design (on which there are many variations) consists of a disc divided into black and white halves, with a triplet of concentric black arcs in each of four equal sectors of the white half, the arcs in the first sector being close to the circumference, and the arcs in each of the succeeding sectors being closer to the centre than the arcs in the previous sector (see illustration). The top produces visual illusions of bright colours, especially when rotated at 5–10 hertz (cycles per second), the colours of the arcs from the circumference to the centre being either red, green, blue, and violet; or violet, blue, green, and red, depending on the direction of rotation. The top stimulates adjacent areas of the retina at the same frequency but with slight phase differences, black following white at different points in each revolution of the top, and the perception of colours is believed to originate from retinal neurons that form lateral connections between such areas and are phase-sensitive, although research using *dichoptic stimuli has shown that brain processes may also play a part. The top was marketed as a toy in Victorian England. Also called *Benham's wheel*. *See also* colour induction, Fechner–Benham colours.

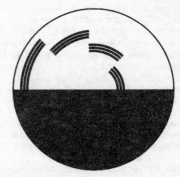

Benham's top

[Named after the English amateur scientist and polymath Charles Edwin Benham (1860–1929), whose 'artificial spectrum top' was discussed in the journal *Nature* in 1894, although unknown to Benham it had already been discovered by the German philosopher, physician, psychologist, and mystic Gustav Theodor Fechner (1801–87), who published his findings in 1838]

bennies *n*. A street name for *benzodiazepine drugs.

Benzedrine *n*. A proprietary name for *amphetamine.
[Trademark]

benzilic acid *See* BZ gas.

benzodiazepine *n*. Any member of a class of drugs with chemical structures based on 1,4-benzodiazepine or 1,2-imidazo-benzodiazepine that all have *anxiolytic, *hypnotic (1), *anticonvulsant, *muscle relaxant, and *anaesthetic (2) effects and are sometimes taken as street drugs. They have a strong affinity for *neuroreceptors belonging to the *GABA receptor complex, and they lower arousal by virtue of their interaction with neurons that release GABA, thereby acting as central nervous system *depressants. Common street names for benzodiazepines include *bennies* and *benzos*. *See* alprazolam (Xanax), chlordiazepoxide (Librium), diazepam (Valium), flunitrazepam (Rohypnol), lorazepam (Ativan), temazepam (Restoril), triazolam (Halcion). *See also* sedative-, hypnotic-, or anxiolytic-related disorders. *Compare* buspirone, picrotoxin.
[From *benzo-* of or relating to benzene + *di-* two, from Greek *dis* twice + *az-* denoting nitrogen, from Greek *a-* not + *zaein* to live + *ep(oxide)* a compound containing oxygen joined to other atoms, from Greek *epi* on or above + *oxide* a compound of oxygen and another element]

benzos *n*. A street name for *benzodiazepine drugs.

benztropine *n*. Benztropine mesylate, an *anticholinergic and *antihistaminic drug that is used in the treatment of *parkinsonism. *See also* antiparkinsonian.
[From *benz(o)-* of or relating to benzene + *(a)tropine*]

bereavement *n*. Loss of a relative or friend through death; the *grief reaction that often follows such a loss.
[From Old English *bereafian* to plunder]

Bernoulli trial *n*. In the theory of probability, any of a sequence of independent random experiments each of which has two possible outcomes, often labelled success (*S*) or failure (*F*), with unchanging probabilities, a standard example being a sequence of coin tosses. *See also* binomial test.
[Named after the Swiss mathematician Jacob (or Jacques or James) Bernoulli (1654–1705) who developed it in his book *Ars Conjectandi* (1713)]

Bernreuter Personality Inventory *n*. The first multi-score personality questionnaire, published by the US psychologist Robert Gibbon Bernreuter (1901–95) in his book *The Personality Inventory* (1931). It comprises 125 items to be answered *Yes*, *No*, or *?* and yields scores on six variables: Neurotic Tendency, Self-Sufficiency, Introversion–Extraversion, Dominance–Submission, Sociability, and Confidence. *Compare* Personal Data Sheet.

Bertrand's box paradox *See under* Monty Hall problem.

bestiality *n*. **1**. A *paraphilia characterized by sexual intercourse between a person and an animal. Also called *zoophilia* or *zooerasty*. **2**. Brutal or savage behaviour or character. **bestial** *adj*.
[From Latin *bestia* a beast]

beta-adrenergic receptor *See under* adrenergic receptor.

beta-blocker *n*. A drug such as *propranolol that inhibits the action of neurons that respond to *adrenalin (epinephrine) by blocking their (beta-) *adrenergic receptors, and thus subdues the activity of the heart; used as a medication in the treatment of cardiac arrhythmias, hypertension, migraine, tremor caused by anxiety, *akathisia caused by neuroleptic medication, *social phobia, *panic disorder, and *withdrawal from alcohol and other substances; also used by musicians and actors to suppress the effects of *performance anxiety and by athletes as a *performance enhancer to moderate excessive arousal.

beta-carotene *See under* carotene.

beta coefficient *n*. In *multiple regression, a name for a standardized regression coefficient, calculated after first transforming the independent variable into *standard scores or *z scores. This makes the regression coefficients more comparable by removing differences due to differing units of measurement of the independent variables. When the independent variables are uncorrelated with one another, beta coefficients are equal to the simple correlations with the *dependent variable. Beta coefficients are sometimes called *beta weights* or *standardized regression coefficients*. Symbol: β.

beta element *n*. In *psychoanalysis, a term introduced by the Indian-born British psychoanalyst Wilfred R(uprecht) Bion (1897–1979) to denote any of the raw elements of *emotion that are transformed by the *alpha function into *alpha elements suitable for mental 'digestion'.

beta-endorphin *n*. An *endogenous opioid, secreted by the *anterior pituitary, that is more powerfully *analgesic (2) than morphine, also causing rigidity and alterations of mood and behaviour. It occurs both in free form and as a terminal polypeptide chain of 31 amino acids in a *beta-lipotropin molecule. Also written β-endorphin. *See also* endorphin, POMC.

beta-lipotropin *n*. A lipotropin (a fat-mobilizing protein hormone) that is released by the anterior pituitary and that contains *beta-endorphin as the final sequence of 31 amino acids of its polypeptide chain. Also written *beta-lipotrophin*, β-*lipotropin*, or β-*lipotrophin*.

beta movement *n*. A form of *apparent movement that is produced when identical stimuli are presented in an alternating pattern with an interstimulus interval of about 60 milliseconds, the visual illusion being created of a single object moving back and forth. Also called *beta motion, optimal movement*, or *stroboscopic movement*. *See also* Korte's laws. *Compare* alpha movement, gamma movement, delta movement.

beta receptor *n*. Another name for a beta *adrenergic receptor.

[From *beta* (β) the second letter of the Greek alphabet]

beta wave *n*. A low-voltage *EEG wave with a frequency of 13–30 hertz, usually occurring in a state of arousal. Also called a *beta rhythm*.

betel *n*. The leaf of the betel pepper *Piper betle* or the nut of the betel palm *Areca catechu*, sometimes chewed, especially by people of the Indian subcontinent and South-East Asia, as a digestive and for its *psychotropic effects of mild euphoria. *See also* euphoriant.
[Portuguese, from Malayalam *vettila*]

between-groups variance *n*. In *analysis of variance (ANOVA), the part of the total *variance in the *dependent variable that can be explained by differences between group means.

between-subjects design *n*. Any research design in which different groups of research participants or subjects are tested under different *treatment conditions. *Compare* within-subjects design.

Betz cell *n*. Any of the giant *pyramidal cells in the primary *motor cortex, the axons of which form the major part of the *corticospinal tract involved in voluntary movements.
[Named after the Russian anatomist Vladimir Aleksandrovich Betz (1834–94) who discovered it]

Bezold–Brücke phenomenon *n*. The shift in hue with a change in the physical intensity of illumination, objects and images appearing relatively red or green in dim light and relatively blue or yellow in bright light, the *psychological primary colours themselves being largely unaffected. *See also* Purkinje shift.
[Named after the German meteorologist Wilhelm von Bezold (1837–1907), who described it briefly in 1873, and the German physiologist Ernst Wilhelm von Brücke (1819–92) who studied it thoroughly in 1878]

bhang *n*. The dried leaves, flowering tops, and young stems of the female *cannabis plant, used as a psychotropic drug, usually prepared as an infusion and taken as a drink. Also spelt *bang*.
[From Hindi *bhang*, from Sanskrit *bhanga*]

bibliotherapy *n*. Any form of *psychotherapy in which the reading of prescribed texts forms an important part of the therapeutic process. [From Greek *biblion* a book]

biceps reflex *n*. A *deep tendon reflex occurring in response to a tap on the tendon of the biceps muscle near the elbow.
[Named after the biceps brachii muscle, from Latin *bis* twice + *caput* a head, alluding to the fact that it has two heads at its origin]

biconditional *n*. In logic and mathematics, a statement of the form *p if and only if q*. This means that *q* is a necessary and sufficient condition of *p*, and it is sometimes written *p iff q*. An example is: *A number is prime iff it can be evenly divided only by itself and 1*. It is called a biconditional because it is equivalent to the double (bi-) statement *If p then q and if q then p*. A biconditional is true if both of its component statements are true or if both are false, and otherwise it is false.

bidialectal *adj*. Proficient in the use of two *dialects.

Bidwell's ghost *n*. An afterimage trailing behind a moving spot of light that is observed with dark-adapted eyes and fixated gaze in a dimly lit room. Behind the moving spot, with a delay of about 0.2 second, there appears to follow a ghost light leaving a trail that glows for several seconds. If the original stimulus is white, blue, or green, then the ghost is violet; if the original stimulus is orange or yellow, then the ghost is blue or blue-green; and if the original stimulus is red, then no clear ghost appears. The effect can be demonstrated by adapting one's eyes in darkness for 15 minutes and then moving a spot of light from a small torch or flashlight rapidly over a light-coloured surface while keeping the gaze fixated rather than tracking the movement of the spot; if the spot is moved through a tortuous path, the ghost will follow the same tortuous path one-fifth of a second later. The term is also used loosely as a synonym for a static *afterimage or a *Purkinje image, but in careful usage it is reserved for the moving afterimage described by Bidwell.
[Named after the English physicist and barrister Shelford Bidwell (1849–1909) who described it in his book *Curiosities of Light and Vision* (1899)]

Big Five *n*. The following factors, derived from *factor analysis and widely accepted since the 1980s as the fundamental dimensions of human personality: *extraversion, *agreeableness, *conscientiousness, *neuroticism, and *openness to experience or intellect. The evidence for the Big Five was reviewed by the US psychologist Lewis Robert Goldberg (born 1932) in an influential article in the journal *American Psychologist* in 1993. *See also* little thirty, NEO.

bilabial *adj*. Of, relating to, or denoting a speech sound articulated with the lower lip touching the upper lip, as in the initial *phonemes in *may*, *pay*, and *bay*. *See also* place of articulation.
[From Latin *bis* twice + *labium* a lip + *-alis* of or relating to]

bilateral transfer *n*. *Transfer of training from one side of the body to the other, as when practising a skill with one hand improves its performance with the other.

bile *n*. A viscous bitter greenish or golden brown alkaline fluid secreted by the liver, stored in the gall bladder, and discharged into the duodenum during digestion for the emulsification and absorption of fats. *See also* humour (3).
[From Latin *bilis* bile]

bilingual *adj*. **1.** Able to speak two languages. *Compare* ambilingual (1). *n*. **2.** A bilingual person. **bilingualism** *n*.
[From Latin *bis* twice + *lingua* a tongue + *-alis* of or relating to]

bilis *n*. A *culture-bound syndrome found in many Latin American communities, characterized by intense anger or rage, accompanied by acute nervous tension, headache, trembling, screaming, stomach upset, and even loss of consciousness, often followed by chronic fatigue or asthenia, interpreted locally as a result of a disturbance in the balance of *humours (3) in the body. Also called *colera* or *muina*.
[Spanish *bilis* bile, from Latin *bilis* bile]

bimodal distribution *n*. Any *probability distribution or *frequency distribution with two *modes, therefore appearing visually with two peaks, indicating a clustering of scores around two different values.

binary code n. A system of representing information by using the digits 0 and 1, so that each number, letter, or other item of information is represented by a unique sequence of *bits.

binary colour n. Another name for a *secondary colour. US binary color.

binaural adj. Of, relating to, or involving the simultaneous use of two ears or the presentation of the same audible stimulus to both ears. Often confused with *dichotic. Compare monaural.
[From Latin bis twice, bini two by two + auris an ear + -alis of or relating to]

binaural beat n. An *auditory beat that is heard when two tones with slightly different *frequencies (1) are presented separately to the two ears via headphones, proving that the waves can reinforce and cancel each other in the auditory cortex rather than in the ear. Compare central masking.

binaural cue n. In *sound localization, a *cue (2) that helps to determine the location of a sound source and that depends on *binaural information. See interaural intensity difference, interaural time difference, phase delay, sonic shadow, transient disparity.

binaural disparity n. Any difference in the sound reaching the two ears from a single source, providing a *binaural cue for *sound localization.

binaural fusion n. Hearing sounds presented to different ears as a single sound. See also auditory fusion.

binaural intensity difference n. Another name for a *sonic shadow. Also called an interaural intensity difference.

binaural ratio n. The relative sound intensities reaching the two ears from a single source affected by a *sonic shadow cast by the listener's head.

binaural shift n. An *auditory illusion that arises when two low-pitched tones with frequencies close to each other are presented separately to the two ears, resulting in the impression of a single sound source whose location seems to swing periodically from one side to the other as the *phase delay and *transient disparity changes continuously.

binaural sound localization See sound localization.

binaural summation n. The relatively greater perceived loudness of a sound that is heard binaurally rather than monaurally, the *absolute threshold for loudness being 3 dB lower when it is heard binaurally.

binaural time difference n. A generic name for *phase delay and/or *transient disparity. Also called an interaural time difference.

binaural unmasking n. A phenomenon in which a *monaural sound that masks another monaural sound loses its masking property when it is heard *binaurally. See also auditory masking, masking.

binding n. Tying, securing, or constraining. In *psychoanalysis, an operation tending to restrict the flow of *libidinal energy, usually by the *ego exerting a restraining influence on the *primary process. For example, in an article on 'Project for a Scientific Psychology', published in 1895, Sigmund Freud (1856–1939) cited the example of a painful memory that needs to be tamed: 'particularly large and repeated binding from the ego is required before this facilitation to unpleasure can be counterbalanced' (Standard Edition, I, pp. 177–397, at pp. 380–1). Freud developed the idea further in his book Beyond the Pleasure Principle (1920, Standard Edition, XVIII, pp. 7–64), and in An Outline of Psycho-Analysis (1938/40, Standard Edition, XXIII, pp. 144–207, at p. 148) he described binding as a preservative operation that is a primary aim of *Eros, in contrast to *Thanatos, whose primary aim is to destroy things. See also bound energy.

binding problem n. Within the field of *knowledge representation, the problem of how to represent conjunctions. In visual perception, in order to pick out a blue square from a display including a collection of red squares and blue triangles, it is not enough to isolate its non-unique shape or its non-unique colour; it is necessary to bind each shape to its colour and then to isolate the unique conjunction (blue + square). In language comprehension, in order to understand a sentence such as *The cause of Mary's hatred of John, in Peter's opinion, was John's betrayal of her trust*, it is necessary to bind the noun phrase *John's betrayal of her trust* to *The cause of Mary's hatred of John*. The problem of binding underlies symbolic representation in general. *See also* feature integration theory, government and binding.

Binet–Simon scale *n.* The first *standardized (2) *intelligence test, constructed in 1905 by the French psychologists Alfred Binet (1857–1911) and Théodore Simon (1873–1961). It included items designed to measure ability to follow instructions, to exercise judgement, and to solve a wide variety of problems. The final version contained 54 items arranged in order of difficulty, from following the movement of a lighted match with the eyes, through pointing to named parts of the body and counting backwards from 20, to working out what time a clock face would show if the hour and minute hands swapped places. Also called the *Binet scale*, though this is unfair to Simon, who played a major part in its development. *See also* mental age, Stanford–Binet intelligence scale.

binge-eating disorder *n.* A condition (included in the *DSM-IV appendix of conditions meriting further study, but not in the *ICD-10 classification) characterized by recurrent episodes of binge eating, with similar signs and symptoms to *bulimia nervosa but without the compensatory behaviour intended to prevent weight gain, such as self-induced vomiting, misuse of laxatives or diuretics, enemas, fasting, or excessive exercise.

binocular *adj.* Of, relating to, or involving the simultaneous use of both eyes. *Compare* dichoptic, monocular.
[From Latin *bis* twice, *bini* two by two + *oculus* an eye]

binocular cell *n.* A neuron in the *visual cortex that receives inputs from both eyes. Approximately half the neurons in the *primary visual cortex are binocular. *See also* disparity-selective cell, ocular dominance.

binocular cue *n.* Either of the *cues (2) of distance, known as *ocular convergence and *stereopsis, that contribute towards visual *depth perception and that depend on integration of information from both eyes. *Compare* monocular cue.

binocular disparity *n.* The slight discrepancy between the two retinal images of a three-dimensional object or scene, caused by *binocular parallax and providing the basis for *stereopsis, certain *disparity-selective cells in Areas V1, V2, and V5 (MT) of the *visual cortex responding selectively to particular disparities and thus being selectively tuned to stimuli at specific distances. If the disparity lies within *Panum's fusion area, then *binocular fusion occurs and stereopsis results, whereas if the disparity is greater, then *diplopia occurs. Binocular disparity is usually expressed in terms of the difference between the *visual angles subtended by points on the object or surface being viewed, the visual system being capable of responding with sensations of three-dimensional depth to retinal disparities as small as 2 seconds of arc, corresponding to 1/1,800 of a degree, and near the fovea the maximum binocular disparity resulting in fusion corresponds to a visual angle of about 10 minutes of arc or 1/6 of one degree. Also called *retinal disparity* or *visual disparity*. *See also* anaglyph, correspondence problem, corresponding retinal points, horopter, Panum's limiting case, random-dot stereogram, stereoblindness, stereoscopic acuity.

binocular fusion *n.* Merging of slightly different images from the two eyes, arising from *binocular disparity, into a single stereoscopic perception. Also called simply *fusion* or *binocular interaction*. *See also* corresponding retinal points, horopter, Panum's fusion area, Panum's limiting case. *Compare* binocular rivalry.

binocular interaction *n.* Another name for *binocular fusion.

binocular parallax *n.* The disparity between the two retinal images of a three-dimensional object or scene arising from the slightly different vantage points of the two eyes, such *binocular disparity functioning as one of the binocular cues of visual *depth perception and providing the basis for *stereopsis. *See also* corresponding retinal points, disparity-selective cell, parallax. *Compare* monocular parallax.

binocular rivalry *n.* Inability to perceive two markedly different images presented to the left and right eyes simultaneously, one invariably dominating over the other for the whole or part of the percept at any particular time. Also called *binocular suppression* or *retinal rivalry. See also* amblyopia ex anopsia, Cheshire Cat effect, hole-in-the-hand illusion. *Compare* binocular fusion.

binocular summation *n.* Stimulation of corresponding areas of the two retinas with light, the perceived *lightness being approximately the average lightness of the two stimuli perceived monocularly. *See also* Fechner's paradox.

binocular suppression *n.* Another name for *binocular rivalry.

binomial test *n.* In inferential statistics, a simple test of whether a sample of dichotomous scores, labelled success/failure (or male/female, remember/don't remember, and so on) comes from a binomial probability distribution. The binomial distribution represents the probability, given a sequence of *Bernoulli trials with a fixed probability of success on each trial, of achieving a number of successes as extreme as the number observed in a specified number of trials. For example, a string of guesses (hits/misses) with a pack of 25 ESP or Zener cards, which contains five cards with each of five different symbols, entails a 1/5 probability of a hit on each trial. Application of the binomial test shows that, for a statistically significant result (conventionally, a probability of less than $p < 0.05$), leading to a rejection of the null hypothesis that the scores come from a binomial distribution, more than eight (or fewer than two) hits in 25 guesses would be required.
[From Latin *bis* twice, *bini* two by two + *nomen* a name]

bioacoustics *n.* The study of the relation between organisms and sound.
[From Greek *bios* life + *akoustikos* of or relating to sound, from *akouein* to hear + *-ikos* of, relating to, or resembling]

bioavailability *n.* The proportion of a drug or of its active ingredient that is absorbed and that therefore becomes available at its target *neuroreceptor sites after ingestion or administration. It is usually estimated by comparing the concentration of the drug in the blood after intravenous injection (full bioavailability) with its concentration after administra-

tion by the usual route, such as eating or swallowing, drinking in an infusion, snorting, or smoking. **bioavailable** *adj.*

biodemography *n.* The science dealing with the interface between *ecology (1) and *population genetics.
[From *bio(logy)* + *demography*]

bioenergetics *n.* **1.** The study of energy relationships in living organisms. **2.** A technique of *psychotherapy developed by the US psychiatrist Alexander Lowen (born 1910), influenced by *psychoanalysis and Reichian *orgone therapy. *See also* body therapies.
[From Greek *bios* life + *energeia* activity, from *ergon* work + *-itikos* resembling or marked by]

bioengineering *n.* The design and provision of devices such as artificial limbs, hearing aids, and spectacles to replace lost bodily functions or to rectify or supplement defective functioning of body parts or organs. Also called *biological engineering.*

biofeedback *n.* A technique whereby a person learns to control a normally involuntary *autonomic response (such as blood pressure, heart rate, or alpha wave EEG activity) by attending to the output of a device that monitors the response continuously (such as a blood pressure monitor, an electrocardiograph, or an electroencephalograph, respectively). It is sometimes used to treat stress disorders such as *migraine headaches and *hypertension.
[From Greek *bios* life + English *feedback*]

bioflavinoids *See* vitamin P.

biogenesis *n.* The biological principle according to which living organisms originate from parent organisms similar to themselves, in contrast to the 19th century doctrines of spontaneous generation and *abiogenesis.
[From Greek *bios* life + *genesis* birth]

biogenic amine *n.* Any member of a group of *amines that are produced in the body and that play important roles in nervous system functioning, including catecholamines such as *dopamine, *adrenalin (epinephrine), and *noradrenalin (norepinephrine); indoleamines such as *serotonin; and imidazoleamines such as *histamine. *See also* neurotransmitter.

[From Greek *bios* life + *genein* to produce, referring to the fact that they are produced naturally in the body, unlike amines such as amphetamine]

biological clock *n*. Any mechanism or process responsible for a *biological rhythm. *See also* pacemaker neuron, suprachiasmatic nucleus, telomere, *Zeitgeber*.

biological engineering *n*. Another name for *bioengineering.

biological motion *n*. Another name for the perception created by a *point-light display. Also called *biological movement* or *biomechanical motion*.

biological rhythm *n*. Any periodic, more-or-less regular fluctuation or cycle in a biological system or process that is not wholly under the control of environmental cues but is controlled centrally by a *biological clock. It may be an *ultradian rhythm such as a *circannual rhythm or a *menstrual cycle; a *circadian rhythm such as the *sleep–wake cycle; or an *infradian rhythm such as an *alpha wave, *basic rest–activity cycle, *beta wave, *delta wave, *gamma wave, *sensorimotor rhythm, or *theta wave. *See also* chronobiology, pacemaker neuron, suprachiasmatic nucleus, *Zeitgeber. Compare* biorhythm.

biology *n*. The study of living *organisms; or a generic term for the life sciences, including botany, zoology, anatomy, physiology, biochemistry, and related disciplines.
[From Greek *bios* life + *logos* word, discourse, or reason]

bioluminescence *n*. The emission of light by certain living organisms, including insects such as fireflies, certain bacteria and fungi, and especially deep-sea marine organisms. It is achieved by the oxidation of the light-producing compound *luciferin by the enzyme *luciferase. **bioluminescent** *adj*.
[From Greek *bios* life + Latin *lumen* light]

biomechanical motion *n*. Another name for the perception created by a *point-light display. Also called *biomechanical movement* or *biological motion*.

Bio-Medical Data Package *See* BMDP.

biometry *n*. The statistical analysis of biological data. Also called *biometrics*. **biometric** *adj*.
[From Greek *bios* life + *metron* a measure]

bionics *n*. The study of brain functions and other biological processes applied to the design of electronic devices such as computers that can perform similar operations; or the process of replacing or augmenting the function of body parts with artificial (especially electronic) devices. **bionic** *adj*. Of, relating to, or resembling *bionics.
[From *bio(logical) (electro)nics*]

biophysics *n*. The physics of biological processes, and the application of the techniques and concepts of physics to biology.

biopsychology *n*. A branch of biology or psychology that deals with the interaction of mind and body and the effects of this interaction.

biorhythm *n*. According to a discredited doctrine developed by the German ear, nose, and throat specialist Wilhelm Fliess (1848–1928), any of three precisely periodic rhythms of 23 days (physical cycle), 28 days (emotional cycle), and 33 days (intellectual cycle), supposedly fixed at the time of birth for a person's entire life, the interaction between the three cycles determining critical days on which problems are likely to occur throughout life. *Compare* biological rhythm.

biosonar *n*. A system of object detection, location, identification, and ranging by means of *echolocation, the emission of sound or *ultrasound and the analysis of returning echoes. It has evolved independently in two groups of bats and also in dolphins, whales, oilbirds (*Steatornis caripensis*) of South America and Trinidad, and cave swiftlets of the Asian genus *Collacalia*, and is also used in a primitive form and to a small extent by shrews, rats, seals, and blind human beings (*see* facial vision). In its most sophisticated form as used by dolphins, whales, and some bats, the time delay of an echo provides information about the distance of the target object; *transient disparities, *phase delays, and *sonic shadows enable the target's direction to be pinpointed, the amplitude of an echo indicates the target's overall size; the amplitudes of the echo's component frequencies provide clues as to the sizes of the target's features; and the

*Doppler effect indicates whether the target is coming closer or moving away. The bottlenose dolphin (*Tursiops truncatus*) can detect a steel ball the size of a walnut under water at a range of 64 metres (210 feet).

[From Greek *bios* life + English *sonar* an acronym for *so(und) na(vigation and) r(anging)*]

biostatics *n*. The branch of biology devoted to studying the structure of organisms in relation to their function. **biostatic** *adj*.

[From Greek *bios* life + *stasis* a standing + *-itikos* resembling or marked by]

biotechnology *n*. **1.** The industrial use of living organisms, especially bacteria, to manufacture substances such as beer, wine, cheese, antibiotics, hormones, or vaccines, to recycle waste, or to create energy. *See also* monoclonal antibody. **2.** In the US, another name for *ergonomics.

biotin *See* vitamin H.

biotope *n*. A small ecological environment or microhabitat, such as the bark of a tree, that supports a distinct biological community.

[From Greek *bios* life + *topos* place]

biperiden *n*. A synthetic *anticholinergic drug that is used in the treatment of *Parkinson's disease, biperiden hydrochloride being administered orally and biperiden lactate by intramuscular or intravenous injection. *See also* antiparkinsonian.

bipolar *adj*. Having two poles, as in a *bipolar cell or bipolar neuron; or more generally having two extremes or extremities, as in a bipolar adjective pair such as *good–bad*, frequently used in rating scales.

bipolar affective disorder *See* bipolar disorders.

bipolar cell *n*. A *neuron, usually a sensory nerve cell, with two *processes (2), an *axon and a *dendrite, extending in opposite directions from its cell body or soma. It is found abundantly in the middle layer of the *retina, where retinal bipolar cells with *centre-surround receptive fields—the centre being supplied by direct inputs from *photoreceptors and the surround by *horizontal cells, or vice versa—relay information to retinal *ganglion cells, but in general it is the least common

type of neuron in the nervous system, although it is the one usually depicted in the standard textbook diagram of a supposedly typical neuron. Also called a *bipolar neuron*. *See also* off-centre cell, on-centre cell.

bipolar disorders *n*. A class of *mood disorders characterized by *manic episodes or *mixed episodes and usually, but not necessarily, also *major depressive episodes. Some classifications, including *DSM-IV, also distinguish bipolar II disorders, characterized by major depressive episodes together with *hypomanic episodes, rather than manic episodes as in bipolar I disorders. The third major form of bipolar disorder is *cyclothymic disorder. Also called *manic–depressive psychosis*. *See also* antimanic, mood stabilizer. *Compare* cyclothymia.

[From Latin *bis* twice + *polaris* of or relating to a pole, from *polus* a pole]

bipolar rating scale *n*. Any *rating scale in which the response alternatives provided for each item are anchored by pairs of opposites or *antonyms, often adjective pairs such as *good ------- bad*, or *useful ------- useless*. *See also* semantic differential.

birth trauma *n*. The supposedly distressing aspect of the process of being born, according to the Austrian psychoanalyst Otto Rank (1884–1939) and later therapists, including the US psychoanalyst Phyllis Greenacre (1894–1989) and the US psychologist Arthur Janov. Rank argued in his book *The Trauma of Birth* (1929) that the shock of birth creates a reservoir of anxiety and that all neuroses stem from birth anxiety. *See also* primal anxiety.

bisection method *See* method of bisection.

bisexual *n*. **1.** A person who is sexually attracted to both men and women. *Compare* heterosexual (1), homosexual (1). *adj*. **2.** Being sexually attracted to both men and women. *Compare* heterosexual (2), homosexual (2). **3.** Of, relating to, or showing characteristics of both sexes, *androgynous, or having both male and female reproductive organs. *See* hermaphrodite (2). **bisexuality** or, especially in the US, **bisexualism** *n*. Attraction to or sexual activity with members of both sexes.

[From Latin *bis* twice + *sexus* sex + *-alis* of or relating to]

bit *n.* In computer technology, a single digit in binary notation symbolized by either 0 or 1, represented by a switch that is either off or on, a location on a disk or a tape that is either not magnetized or magnetized, or the absence or presence of an electrical or electronic pulse. In *information theory, it is the standard unit of *information (2), representing the information required to specify one of two alternatives, the number of bits in a given signal being defined by the minimum number of binary digits required to encode it. The binary equivalents of the decimal digits 0, 1, 2, 3, 4, 5, 6, 7, 8, and 9 are 0, 1, 10, 11, 100, 101, 110, 111, 1000, and 1001, respectively; therefore, if the information specifies a choice of one out of just two alternatives, then one bit of information is sufficient to encode the information, three or four alternatives require two bits, five to eight alternatives require three bits, nine or ten alternatives require four bits, and so on. *See also* baud, binary code, Boolean, byte, nybble.
[A blend of *b(inary)* and *(dig)it*]

bite bar *n.* A device containing a hollow mould of a person's teeth that can be bitten on to in order to keep the head completely still during an experiment.

bitter *n.* One of the primary tastes in *Henning's tetrahedron, the characteristic taste of *quinine or orange peel.

bivariate statistics *n.* The branch of statistics devoted to analysing the relationship between pairs of variables when neither is an *independent variable in an experiment. The prototypical example of bivariate statistics is the *product-moment correlation coefficient. *Compare* multivariate statistics, univariate statistics.
[From Latin *bis* twice + English *variate*]

black bile *See under* humour (3).

blackboard memory *n.* Another name for a *buffer store.

Black English Vernacular *n.* A speech style, nowadays thought to be *creole in origin, characteristic of inner-city African-American communities in the United States, recognizable through such expressions as: *It's just the same old same old* (It's just the same old thing); *I be done fed the baby soon*; *I been know your address*, *mister*; *They real fine*; *Don't nobody understand me?* Also called *Ebonics* or (colloquially) *soul talk*. *See also* vernacular. **BEV** *abbrev.*
[From Latin *vernaculus* belonging to a household slave, from *verna* a household slave]

blacking out *n.* Another name for *falling out.

Blacky pictures *n.* A *projective test resembling the *TAT but designed for children, comprising a series of twelve cartoon drawings in which a dog called Blacky, designated as male or female to match the sex of the respondent, is depicted playing human roles with other dogs called Mama and Papa and a sibling of indeterminate age and sex called Tippy. The respondent is asked to make up a vivid, imaginative story about each picture and then to respond to a series of multiple-choice and short-answer questions about the picture. The test was constructed by the US psychologist Gerald S. Blum (born 1922) in the course of postgraduate research and first published by him in the journal *Genetic Psychology Monographs* in 1949. Also called the *Blacky Test*. *Compare* Children's Apperception Test.

blaming the victim *n.* A pervasive tendency to assume that a person who has suffered a misfortune must have done something wrong to deserve it. It is explained by the *just world hypothesis.

blastocyst *n.* An early form of an embryo, consisting of a hollow ball of cells one cell thick, that develops from a *morula. *See also* embryo, foetus, zygote.
[From Greek *blastos* a bud + *kystis* a bladder]

blend *n.* A word formed by joining the end of one word on to the beginning of another, or more generally part of one word on to part of another, typical examples being *brunch*, which is formed from the beginning of *breakfast* and the end of *lunch*, *moped* from *motor* and *pedal*, *motel* from *motorcar* and *hotel*, *napalm* from *naphthene* and *palmitate*, *prissy* from *prim* and *sissy*, and *smog* from *smoke* and *fog*. Also called a *portmanteau word*.

blending inheritance *n.* A once-popular doctrine, subsequently discredited following the general acceptance of *Mendelian genetics, that the intermediate characteristics of *hybrids (1) result from a physical merging or mixing of the substances carrying the parental characteristics rather than from the recombination of unchanged particulate hereditary factors (genes). *Compare* particulate inheritance.

blindness *n*. Inability to see. Total blindness, which is a comparatively rare condition, is unambiguously defined as an inability to perceive light in either eye; partial blindness in which there is some residual vision is comparatively common, affecting approximately 90 per cent of registered blind people in the US and the UK, and is variously defined. The American Foundation for the Blind proposed a twofold criterion: either a *Snellen fraction of 20/200 or less in the better eye with maximum correction (spectacles), or *tunnel vision limiting the visual field to a *visual angle of no more than 20 degrees. Blindness is usually an acquired condition, congenital causes accounting for only about one per cent of registered blind people, the major cause among registered blind people in the US and the UK being *diabetes, although blindness in one eye, among people not usually registered blind, is most often caused by *amblyopia ex anopsia. Also called *visual impairment*, especially when there is some residual vision. *See also* amaurosis, ametropia, anopia, Anton's syndrome, blindsight, Braille, cataract, chromatopsia, colour-blindness, conversion symptom, cortical blindness, facial vision, glaucoma, hemeralopia, hemianopia, homonymous hemianopia, nyctalopia, object blindness, optacon, optohapt, retinitis pigmentosa, scotoma, spatial neglect, stereoblindness, strabismus, Tadoma method, Tay–Sachs disease, thermoform. **blind** *adj*. [From Old English *blind* and Old Norse *blindr* sightless, cognate with Old Norse *blunda* to close one's eyes]

blindness denial *n*. Another name for *Anton's syndrome.

blindsight *n*. Residual vision in the absence of a functioning *primary visual cortex in primates and possibly other animals. More specifically, a capacity possessed by some people who appear to be totally blind, owing to lesions in the primary visual cortex, to respond to visual stimuli. Such people have no conscious experience of vision, but if forced to guess they can correctly direct their eyes towards light sources, identify objects moving in particular directions, or even discriminate between simple visual shapes, and they are often surprised that their guesses are correct. This phenomenon is explained by small but direct connections, bypassing the primary visual cortex, between the *lateral geniculate nuclei and areas of the prestriate *visual cortex that are specialized for colour, movement, and form perception. The term was introduced in 1974 by the British neuropsychologist Lawrence Weiskrantz (born 1926) and several colleagues in a case report of a patient with the condition, and became widely known after the publication of Weiskrantz's book *Blindsight: A Case Study and Implications* (1986). Also written *blind sight*. *Compare* Anton's syndrome (which may be interpreted as the inverse of blindsight).

blind spot *n*. **1**. A small oval area on the *retina of each eye, approximately 2 millimetres in diameter, where the ganglion cells in the inner retinal layer, nearest the front of the eye, feed backwards through the retina into the optic nerve, and where there are therefore no photoreceptors and vision is absent. Squids and octopuses do not have blind spots, because their eyes have evolved with the retinal layers arranged the other way round, with the ganglion cells in the outer retinal layer at the back of the eye. A person is not ordinarily aware of a blind spot because the gap is covered by vision from the other eye, and if one eye is closed it is not noticed because of the *filling-in phenomenon, but its location can be mapped as follows. Gaze fixedly at a distant object with one eye, keeping the other eye closed, and hold a small distinctive stimulus such as a cotton bud or Q-tip at arm's length directly in front of the object, then slowly move the stimulus horizontally outwards from the direction of gaze until it vanishes approximately 18 degrees out—about the width of one's hand at arm's length. Also called an *optic disc*. **2**. Any part of the visual field in which vision is absent. Also called a *scotoma*. **3**. Any place where vision, hearing, or reception of broadcast signals is difficult or impossible. **4**. A topic on which a person is notably ignorant or lacking in insight or ability.

blind study *n*. A research design planned so that, in order to control for the influence of *demand characteristics, the research participants or subjects do not know the details of the investigation or the *experimental hypothesis being tested, at least until after the data have been collected. *See* double-blind study, randomized double-blind experiment, single-blind study.

blind watchmaker *n*. A term coined in 1986 by the British ethologist Richard Dawkins (born 1941) to denote *natural selection, alluding to the Argument from Design, an argument for the existence of God put forward in 1802 by the theologian William Paley (1743–1805). Paley argued that if he found a watch while crossing a heath he would conclude that it must have had a maker, because it is too intricate and precise to have arisen by accident, and that for the same reason the intricacy and precision of the works of nature forced him to conclude that they too must have had a maker, namely God; but Dawkins argued that natural selection operates like a blind watchmaker in fashioning the complicated structures of nature.

blink reflex *n*. An involuntary reflex blinking of both eyes when an object or puff of air touches the cornea of one eye. The *afferent pathway is the *trigeminal nerve and the *efferent pathway is the *facial nerve.

blivet *See* impossible trident.

blob *n*. Any of the ovoid (egg-shaped) areas in the *primary visual cortex (Area V1), about a quarter of a millimetre in diameter and separated by half-millimetre interblobs, containing neurons with *double-opponent receptive fields sensitive to light of a specific wavelength (red–green and blue–yellow), and others with ordinary *centre-surround receptive fields (white–black), not at all sensitive to shape or movement, responsible for perception of colours including *achromatic shades of black, white, and grey. Blobs are found in layers 2 and 3 of the primary visual cortex, receiving projections from sublayers $4C\alpha$ and $4C\beta$ and projecting to Area V2 of the *visual cortex, which in turn projects to Area V4 in the *fusiform gyrus, an area specialized for colour vision. *See also* W cell.
[So called because it shows up as a blob when the cerebral cortex is stained for the enzyme cytochrome oxidase]

Bloch's law *n*. Another name for the *Bunsen–Roscoe law.

block design test *n*. A type of *intelligence test item or subtest in which the respondent tries to arrange a number of painted wooden blocks to copy a design formed by the examiner or shown on a diagram.

block diagram *n*. Another name for a *bar chart, a *histogram, or a *flow chart.

blocking memory *n*. A memory that intrudes into consciousness and impedes or obstructs retrieval of a different though related memory. *See* ugly sister effect. *Compare* screen memory.

block portrait *n*. A degraded image, usually of a face, divided into large rectangles or blocks, the lightness of each block being set to the average of the image in that region, so that a block overlaying an area of dark hair becomes uniformly black, a block overlaying an area of light skin becomes uniformly light, and a block straddling light skin and a dark eyebrow becomes uniformly grey (see illustration). Coarse block portraits, made up of approximately 16 × 16 rectangles using eight or sixteen lightness values or shades of grey, have information of high *spatial frequency filtered out and are impossible to recognize when viewed close up in clear detail, but they are easy to recognize when viewed from a distance or blurred by half-closing the eyes or overlaying the portrait with tissue paper or frosted glass, the result-

Block portrait

ing loss of information paradoxically increasing the recognizability of the image. The first block portrait was constructed by the US biomedical engineer Leon D(avid) Harmon (born 1922) and published in a technical report in 1971, followed by an article in *Scientific American* magazine in 1973. *See also* Abraham Lincoln effect.

blood *n.* The fluid that is pumped through the arteries and veins by the heart to supply the tissues of the body with nutrients and oxygen, to remove waste products, and to transport *hormones and other substances. In vertebrates it is red and is composed of a pale yellow fluid called *plasma (1) in which are suspended *erythrocytes, *leucocytes, and *platelets. *See also* blood–brain barrier, blood group, erythropoietin, humour (3).

blood alcohol concentration *n.* The amount of alcohol in a given volume of blood, usually expressed in units of mass per units of volume, as milligrams or grams of alcohol per decilitre (100 millilitres) of blood. *See also* alcohol, drink-driving. Also called *blood alcohol level (BAL)*. **BAC** *abbrev.*

blood alcohol level *See* blood alcohol concentration.

blood–brain barrier *n.* A protective mechanism that allows blood to flow freely to the brain but prevents most substances in the bloodstream from reaching the brain tissue. It is effected through the unique structure of the capillaries that supply blood to the brain, such capillaries being composed of *endothelial cells sealed together in continuous tight junctions to form solid walls not found anywhere else in the body. These capillaries are also almost completely encircled by *astrocytes, forming a jigsaw pattern on their outer walls and providing *glial sheaths around them. *Lipid-soluble substances such as *alcohol, *nicotine, *caffeine, and *heroin easily cross the barrier and enter the brain, because the *cell membranes and glial sheaths are composed of lipid molecules, whereas water-soluble substances are generally kept out, but certain water-soluble substances such as *glucose (in its dextral form only), *phenylalanine, and *L-opa are carried across the barrier by specialized *active transport processes. *See also* circumventricular organ. **BBB** *abbrev.*

blood-flow receptor *n.* Any of a number of sensory receptors in the kidneys that respond to a decrease in blood flow by releasing *renin, which acts as an *enzyme for the synthesis of *angiotensin II.

blood group *n.* Any of the blood types identified by the many classification systems, especially one of the four types of the ABO system based on the presence or absence of two genetically determined *antigens, A and B, on the surface of red blood cells. Type A shows the A antigen and an *antibody to the B antigen called anti-B agglutinin, Type B shows the B antigen and anti-A agglutinin, Type AB shows both antigens and neither agglutinin, and Type O shows neither antigen and both agglutinins. Also called *blood type*. *See also* race (2).

blue–yellow cell *n.* A neuron that is located in the visual system and is excited by blue light and inhibited by yellow light or vice versa. Such *opponent-process cells are not found in the retina, where the *trichromatic theory applies, but at higher levels in the visual system. *See also* red–green cell. *Compare* cone.

blunted affect *See under* affect.

B lymphocyte *n.* A type of *lymphocyte that is synthesized in bone marrow and secreted from the spleen and that mobilizes *antibodies of *immunoglobulin and plays an important part in the *immune system. Also called a *B cell*. *See also* monoclonal antibody, stem cell. *Compare* T lymphocyte.
[From *b(one marrow) lymphocyte*]

BMDP *abbrev.* Bio-Medical Data Package, a suite of statistical computer programs often used by psychologists, distributed by the University of California Press, USA. *Compare* SAS, SPSS, SYSTAT.

body adjustment test *n.* Another name for the *tilting-room test. **BAT** *abbrev.*

body cell *n.* A somatic cell as opposed to a *germ cell.

body dysmorphic disorder *n.* A *somatoform disorder characterized by a pathological preoccupation with an imagined or exaggerated defect in physical appearance. Also called *dysmorphophobia*. **BDD** *abbrev.*

[From Greek *dys-* bad or abnormal + *morphe* form]

body image *n.* A mental representation of one's own physical appearance, based partly on self-observation and partly on the reactions of others. *See also* image (3), schema.

body language *n.* Another name for *kinesics or, loosely speaking, of *non-verbal communication in general.

body therapies *n.* Techniques of *psychotherapy that emphasize physical approaches to psychological problems, especially *Alexander technique, *bioenergetics, *orgone therapy, *primal therapy, and *rolfing.

Bogardus social distance scale *n.* Another name for a *social distance scale.

bogus pipeline *n.* A technique designed to reduce *response bias in self-report measures of attitudes or emotions by convincing the respondent that the researcher has a reliable and valid means, usually in the form of a sham *lie detector attached to the respondent's body, of checking the truthfulness of the verbal responses. The technique was introduced by the US psychologists Edward Ellsworth Jones (1926–93) and Harold Sigall (born 1943) in an article in the journal *Psychological Bulletin* in 1971. *See also* nonreactive measure.

bonding *n.* The formation of close personal attachment, especially by an infant or child with its mother. *See* attachment theory.

bone conduction *n.* The transmission of sound waves to the auditory receptors in the inner ear through the bones of the skull rather than through the air in the outer ear, eardrum, and middle ear. **bone-conducted** *adj.*

bone conduction threshold *n.* The *absolute threshold of *bone-conducted sound, bypassing the outer ear and middle ear and therefore used to determine whether hearing loss is caused by damage to the inner ear.

Bonferroni correction *n.* In statistics, a procedure whereby the significance level of a statistical test is adjusted in order to protect against

*Type I errors when *multiple comparisons are being made. Thus if 10 *t tests need to be performed on a set of scores, a researcher may use a Bonferroni-corrected significance level of $0.05/10 = 0.005$ instead of the conventional 0.05. This procedure is extremely conservative inasmuch as it may lead to *Type II errors, but it is safe, easy to understand, and can be used with a wide variety of tests. A Bonferroni-corrected t test is sometimes called simply a *Bonferroni t test* or a *modified LSD test*. A Bonferroni-corrected *Mann–Whitney U test is sometimes called a *Bonferroni Mann–Whitney U test*, and so on. *Compare* Duncan's multiple range test, least-significant difference test, Newman–Keuls test, Scheffé test, Tukey-HSD test.
[Named after the Italian mathematician Carlo Emilio Bonferroni (1892–1960) who, in 1935 and 1936, published inequalities on which the procedure is based]

bong *n.* A water pipe used for smoking *cannabis and other drugs.
[From Thai *baung* a wooden cylinder]

bony labyrinth *n.* The cavity in the temporal bone that contains the *membranous labyrinth of the inner ear, with the *vestibular system and the *semicircular canals, and the *cochlea with the *organ of Corti. Also called the *osseous labyrinth*.

Boolean *adj.* Of, relating to, or comprising a system of algebra or symbolic logic in which *propositions (1) are represented by the binary digits 0 (false) and 1 (true), used especially in computing and electronics. A *Boolean algebra* comprises a set of elements together with two binary operations (the *Boolean sum* denoted by the symbol + and the *Boolean product* denoted by .) obeying certain axioms. In *Boolean set theory* the Boolean sum is interpreted as set union, the Boolean product as set intersection, 0 as the null set, and 1 as the universal set; in *Boolean logic* the Boolean sum is interpreted as *or*, the Boolean product as *and*, 0 as *false*, and 1 as *true*, so that $0 + 0 = 0$, $0 + 1 = 1$, $1 + 1 = 1$, $0 . 0 = 0$, $0 . 1 = 0$, and $1 . 1 = 1$. Boolean set theory and Boolean logic are *isomorphic. *See also* bit, fuzzy logic, set theory.
[Named after the English mathematician George Boole (1815–64) who formulated the ideas in his books *Mathematical Analysis of Logic* (1847) and *An Investigation of the Laws of Thought* (1854)]

boomerang effect *n*. An attitude change in a direction opposite to that of a persuasive message, supposedly resulting from the persuasive message being too discrepant from the target person's original attitude. It is often feared by persuasive communicators but seldom if ever occurs in practice. *See also* assimilation-contrast theory, discrepancy effects.

bootstrapping *n*. Constructing a *linear model of a judge's predictions of a criterion variable and then using the linear model instead of the judge to make further judgements or predictions. Such linear models consistently outperform the judges from whose judgements they are derived, because the coefficient weights are distillations of the judges' underlying principles, free of the extraneous variables that inevitably influence each of their specific judgements. This technique became widely known in the early 1970s under the leadership of the US psychologists Lewis Robert Goldberg (born 1932) and Robyn Mason Dawes (born 1936). In one typical study, a group of judges studied ten background, aptitude, and personality measures taken from graduate students and predicted the students' grade point averages in the first year of graduate study. Linear models of every one of the judges performed better than the judges themselves in predicting the students' grade point averages. *See also* actuarial prediction. **bootstrap** *adj. vb*.
[So called because it is reminiscent of lifting oneself up by one's own bootstraps]

borderline intelligence *n*. An *IQ in the range from 71 to 84.
[So called because it is just above the margin of *mental retardation]

borderline personality disorder *n*. A *personality disorder characterized by a pervasive pattern of impulsivity and unstable personal relationships, self-image, and affect, beginning in early childhood, and indicated by such signs and symptoms as frantic attempts to avoid real or imagined abandonment; intense and unstable personal relationships; continuously fluctuating self-image; impulsivity (in spending, unsafe sex, substance abuse, reckless driving, binge eating, and the like); recurrent suicidal or self-mutilating gestures or behaviour; emotional instability; chronic feelings of emptiness; intense and inappropriate anger (such as frequent outbursts of temper); and transient, stress-related *paranoid ideation or *dissociation. **BPD** *abbrev*.
[So called because it cannot easily be assigned to any of the other personality disorders]

Boring figure *n*. Another name for the most familiar version of the *young girl/old woman figure.
[Named after the US psychologist Edwin Garrigues Boring (1886–1968) who published it in 1930, although he did not create it]

BOSS *abbrev*. The initial syllable of a word as it is pronounced, such as the syllable *ne-* in the word *nevertheless*.
[From *B(asic) O(rthographic) S(yllabic) S(tructure)*, a model of syllabic recognition]

bottleneck (evolutionary) *See* evolutionary bottleneck.

bottleneck theory *n*. Any theory of *attention according to which all incoming information is subjected to some *level of processing before a portion of it is selected for attention. *See also* cocktail party phenomenon, filter theory, selective attention.
[So called because the quantity of incoming information is narrowed like the neck of a bottle]

bottom-up processing *n*. Any form of *information processing that is initiated, guided, and determined by input and that proceeds in sequential stages, with each stage coming closer to a final interpretation than the last, as in *computational theories of vision that proceed from raw sensory data to more abstract cognitive operations. A clear example of bottom-up processing is provided by *feature detection theory. This form of processing allows the possibility of learning from experience during the processing procedure. *Bottom-up theories* of perception are theories according to which low-level sensory *features (1) of a stimulus are first recognized and then built up, with the help of memory and existing *schemata, into higher-order perceptions. The term was introduced in 1975 by the US psychologists Donald A. Norman (born 1935) and David E(verett) Rumelhart (born 1942). Also called *data-driven processing*. *See also* analysis by synthesis. *Compare* top-down processing.

bouffée délirante *n*. A *culture-bound syndrome of Francophone West Africa and Haiti, characterized by sudden outbursts of violent behaviour, accompanied by confusion, *psychomotor agitation, and sometimes also *paranoid ideation and *hallucinations. It is sometimes interpreted as a *brief psychotic disorder.
[From French *bouffée* explosion + *délirante* raving]

boulimia *n*. A variant spelling of *bulimia.

bounded rationality *n*. A concept introduced in influential articles in 1955 and 1956 by the US economist and decision theorist Herbert A(lexander) Simon (1916–2001) to refer to human cognitive capacities and decision processes that are not strictly *rational and are therefore not guaranteed to produce optimal results. The bounds on human rationality arise from limitations of our information-processing abilities and the costs involved in exhaustive comparison of all available options; furthermore, perfectly rational choice is often impossible to achieve in practice, as (for example) in the *travelling salesman problem. Cognitive *heuristics, including Simon's own *satisficing, and *elimination by aspects are among the most thoroughly investigated bounded-rationality choice procedures. *See also* psychological decision theory.

bound energy *n*. In *psychoanalysis, psychic energy in the *secondary process, contained and accumulating within particular groups of neurons, its flow being subject to checks and controls through *binding. Sigmund Freud (1856–1939) attributed the concept to the Austrian physician Josef Breuer (1842–1925), but Breuer, although he discussed a related concept, never used the term, and the version of the concept that Freud published in 1895 in his 'Project for a Scientific Psychology' (*Standard Edition*, I, pp. 177–397) is quite different from Breuer's, although both based their notions on the *principle of constancy. *See also* nirvana principle, reality principle. *Compare* free energy.

bound form *n*. A *morpheme that cannot occur on its own as a word, such as the prefix *un-* or the suffix *-tion* in English. Also called a *bound morpheme*. *Compare* free morpheme.

bouton *n*. The swollen tip of an *axon that forms a *synapse (1) with part of another nerve fibre, muscle, or gland. Also called a *synaptic terminal*, *terminal bouton*, *end foot*, or *end bulb*.
[From French *bouton* a button, alluding to its appearance]

bovine spongiform encephalopathy *n*. The full name of the disease *BSE.
[From Latin *bos*, *bovis* an ox or cow + *spongia* a sponge + *forma* form + Greek *enkephalos* brain, from *en* in + *kephale* head + *pathos* suffering]

bow-wow theory *n*. A dismissive name for the *onomatopoeic theory of the origin of language. Also called the *ding-dong theory*.
[From the sound of a dog barking]

box-and-whisker plot *n*. In statistics, a graph representing the distribution of a variable, showing a box to represent the *interquartile range, with a mark inside it representing the *median, and from each end of the box a line (whisker) extending as far as the smallest and largest scores (see illustration). Also called a *box plot*.

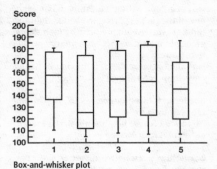

Box-and-whisker plot

Box–Jenkins model *n*. Another name for an *ARIMA model.
[Named after the English statisticians George Edward Pelham Box (born 1919) and Gwilym Meiron Jenkins (1933–82), who co-authored a book describing the model, entitled *Time-Series Analysis: Forecasting and Control* (1970)]

box plot *n*. Another name for a *box-and-whisker plot.

brachygraphy *n.* An obsolescent form of shorthand writing. *Compare* stenography, tachygraphy.
[From Greek *brachys* short + *graphein* to write]

brachymetropia *n.* Another name for *myopia.
[From Greek *brachys* short + *metron* a measure + *ops* an eye + *-ia* indicating a condition or quality]

bracketing *n.* Another name for *epoche.

bradycardia *n.* Abnormally slow pulse, often defined as less than 60 beats per minute. *Compare* tachycardia.
[From Greek *bradys* slow + *kardia* the heart]

bradykinesia *n.* Abnormal slowing of bodily movements, notably as a feature of *Parkinson's disease and of *parkinsonism. *See also* neuroleptic-induced. *Compare* akinesia.
[From Greek *bradys* slow + *kinesis* movement + *-ia* indicating a condition or quality]

bradykinin *n.* A *kinin that is formed in injured tissue in human and animal bodies, causing contraction of most smooth muscles but dilation of blood vessels.
[From Greek *bradys* slow + *kineein* to move, so called because it causes slow muscle contractions]

Braille *n.* A writing system designed for blind people in which text is encoded in raised dots that can be read by touch, each dot or group of dots standing for a letter, numeral, or punctuation mark. *Compare* optacon, optohapt.
[Named after Louis Braille (1809–52), French musician and teacher, blind from an early age, who invented the system in 1829]

brain *n.* The part of the *central nervous system that is enclosed within the skull, comprising, from the top down, the *cerebrum, *midbrain, *cerebellum, *pons, and *medulla oblongata. The remainder of the central nervous system is the *spinal cord. The adult human brain weighs 1300–1400 grams (about 3 pounds), contains about 80 billion neurons (50 billion of them in the *cerebral cortex), each typically forming *synapses (1) with hundreds or thousands of other neurons, and consumes about 20 per cent of the body's total oxygen intake. *See also* cerebral cortex.

[From Old English *brægen* a brain, cognate with Greek *bregma* the front part of the head]

brain fag *n.* A *culture-bound syndrome originally reported among English-speaking school and university students in West Africa, who attributed it to overwork, characterized by loss of ability to concentrate, learn, remember, or think, usually accompanied by sensations of pain, pressure, or tightness around the head or neck and blurred vision.
[From *fag* in the sense of being fagged out or exhausted, perhaps from *flag* to droop]

brain imaging *n.* Any of several techniques for imaging or visualizing the structure or function of the brain, including electroencephalography or *EEG, computed tomography or *CT scans, magnetic resonance imaging or *MRI, *magnetoencephalography, positron emission tomography or *PET scans, and single photon emission computed tomography or *SPECT scans. *See also* angiogram, nuclear magnetic resonance, radioisotope scan, regional cerebral blood flow, ultrasound.

brainstem *n.* The stalklike structure at the bottom of the brain between the cerebral hemispheres and the spinal cord, consisting of the *midbrain, the *pons, and the *medulla oblongata, containing the nuclei of most of the cranial nerves and controlling consciousness and certain vegetative functions such as breathing and the operation of the heart and lungs. Also written *brain stem*.

brainstem reticular formation *n.* Another name for the *reticular formation. **BSRF** *abbrev.*

brainstorming *n.* A method of generating ideas and solving problems through the encouragement of intensive spontaneous group discussion.

brain tissue transplantation *See* foetal brain transplantation.

brainwashing *n.* The process of attempting to produce radical changes in a person's attitudes or beliefs through the application of techniques such as *sensory deprivation, induced hunger, pain, extreme physical discomfort, and the alternation of interrogations by kind and cruel inquisitors.

Brazelton assessment *n.* Another name for the *Neonatal Behavioral Assessment Scale. Also called the *Brazelton scale*.
[Named after the US paediatrician T(homas) Berry Brazelton (born 1918)]

breakage and reunion *n.* In genetics, another name for *crossing over.

breathing-related sleep disorder *n.* One of the *dyssomnias, characterized by sleep disruption leading to *hypersomnia or *insomnia judged to be a result of a sleep-related breathing condition, most commonly *sleep apnoea or *central alveolar hypoventilation syndrome.

breeding size *n.* The number of animals in a population actively involved in breeding.

bregma *n.* The point at the top of the skull where the *coronal sutures meet the *sagittal suture, or where the frontal bone joins the two *parietal bones; in infants it corresponds to the anterior *fontanelle. **bregmata** *pl.*
[From Greek *bregma* the front of the head]

bricolage *n.* A term used especially in writings on *qualitative research to characterize the use of multiple diverse research methods, such as observation, interviewing, interpretation of textual material, and introspection, together with multiple theoretical approaches. **bricoleur** *n.* One who practises *bricolage.
[From French *bricolage* DIY (do-it-yourself) or the hobby of constructing and repairing household objects and systems, first applied to research by the French social anthropologist Claude Lévi-Strauss (born 1908) in a publication in 1966]

bridge of Varolius *n.* An obsolescent name for the *pons.
[Named after the Italian anatomist Costanzo Varolius (?1543–75) who first identified it]

brief psychotherapy *n.* Any form of *psychotherapy limited to a small number of sessions (often 15), usually aimed at dealing with a circumscribed symptom or achieving a narrow and specific objective. *See also* cognitive–analytic therapy, crisis intervention, focal therapy.

brief psychotic disorder *n.* A *mental disorder characterized by the sudden appearance of *delusions, *hallucinations, *disorganized speech, or grossly disorganized behaviour such as *catatonia, the episode lasting at least one day but less than four weeks. *Compare* schizophrenia.

bright light therapy *See* phototherapy.

brightness *n.* The experienced or subjective intensity of light; also another name for *lightness, but some authorities believe that this second sense confuses two distinct though closely related phenomena. *See also* luminance.

brightness constancy *n.* Another name (avoided in careful usage) for *lightness constancy.

brightness contrast *n.* Another name (avoided in careful usage) for *lightness contrast.

brightness enhancement *n.* The greater brightness of a light flickering at about 10 hertz than the same light presented with steady luminance, the phenomenon being explained by the fact that there is more activity in retinal *ganglion cells stimulated by light flickering below the *critical flicker frequency than by light flickering above this frequency or by continuous light.

brightness masking *n.* *Visual masking with a flash of bright light.

bril *n.* A unit of *brightness in which light of 1 millilambert (*see* lambert) is arbitrarily assigned a value of 100 bril.

Briquet's syndrome *n.* Another name for *somatization disorder.
[Named after the French psychiatrist Paul Briquet (1796–1881), who described it in 1859]

British Ability Scales *n.* An *intelligence test, first published in 1979, designed for use with children and adolescents up to 17 or 18 years of age, comprising a set of 23 subtests designed to measure a wide diversity of mental abilities and yielding three scores: visual IQ, verbal IQ, and general IQ. Its subtests are designed to measure the following six mental processes: speed of information-processing, reasoning, spatial imagery, perceptual matching, short-term memory, and retrieval and application of knowledge. The correlations between the subtests are all moderate or high, and general IQ scores derived from the test correlate well with independent measures of scholastic and academic attainment. *See also* Rasch scale. **BAS** *abbrev.*

British Sign Language *n.* A communication system for deaf people in the UK in which meaning is conveyed by hand signals and the positions of the hands relative to the upper part of the body. *See also* sign language. *Compare* American Sign Language. **BSL** *abbrev.*

broad heritability *See under* heritability.

Broca's aphasia *See under* aphasia.

Broca's area *n.* A region of the *cerebral cortex towards the back of the inferior (lowest) gyrus of the frontal lobe, immediately anterior to the tip of the temporal lobe, usually in the left cerebral hemisphere in both left-handed and right-handed people, involved in the production of spoken and written language. Lesions in this area are associated with Broca's aphasia, also called *expressive aphasia* or *motor aphasia* (*see under* aphasia). Also called *Broca's centre* or *Broca's speech centre*. *Compare* Wernicke's area.
[Named after the French surgeon and anthropologist Paul Broca (1824–80), who discovered its function in 1861]

Brodmann area *n.* Any of the 47 numbered areas of the *cerebral cortex, such as Area 17, the primary visual cortex, in the most widely used reference map of the brain (see illustra-

tion). It was constructed as a *cytoarchitectonic map based on differences in cell layers and structures, but the areas turned out in general to correspond to different psychological functions.
[Named after the German neurologist Korbinian Brodmann (1868–1918), who developed an early version of it in 1903 and published it in an influential book in 1909]

bromocriptine *n.* Bromocriptine mesylate, an *alkaloid drug derived from *ergot that mimics the activity of *dopamine and is used in the treatment of *Parkinson's disease and is also used to treat certain forms of amenorrhoea and female infertility, because it selectively inhibits the secretion of *prolactin by the anterior pituitary. Also called *Parlodel* (trademark). *See also* antiparkinsonian, dopaminomimetic.
[From Greek *bromos* a bad smell + English *ergocryptine* a type of ergot, from *ergot* + Greek *kryptos* hidden + *-ine* indicating an organic compound]

Bruce effect *n.* The failure of a recently mated female mouse to produce offspring if housed near a strange male, although the presence of her own stud male or a strange castrated male does not have this effect. The destruction of the female's olfactory bulbs eleminates the effect, because it is caused by the presence in the strange male's urine of a *pheromone that inhibits the female's secretion of prolactin and implantation of the fertilized ovum. Also called *pregnancy blockage*.
[Named after the British reproductive biologist Hilda M(argaret) Bruce (1903–74), who first reported it in 1959]

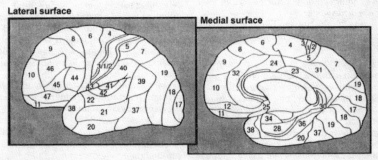

Lateral surface

Medial surface

Brodmann areas

brujeria *n.* A name for *rootwork in Spanish-speaking communities of the Caribbean and the southern United States, where it is also called *mal puesto*.
[Spanish *brujeria* witchcraft, from *bruja* a witch]

Brunswik faces *n.* Schematic drawings of faces, with simplified representations of eyes, nose, and mouth that can be varied from one face to another, used for research into perceptual discrimination and cognitive categorization.
[Named after the Hungarian-born US psychologist Egon Brunswik (1903–55), who introduced them]

Brunswikian *adj.* Of, relating to, or resembling the theory of perception introduced by the Hungarian-born US psychologist Egon Brunswik (1903–55). *See also* Brunswik faces, Brunswik ratio, ecological criterion, ecological fallacy, ecological validity (2), ecology (2), lens model, probabilistic functionalism, ratiomorphic.

Brunswik ratio *n.* An index of *perceptual constancy given by $(R-S)/(A-S)$, where R is the physical magnitude or intensity of the stimulus chosen as a match, S is the physical magnitude or intensity for a stimulus match with zero constancy, and A is the physical magnitude or intensity that would be chosen under 100 per cent constancy. The ratio is equal to zero when there is no perceptual constancy and 1 when there is perfect constancy. Because sensation increases as the logarithm of physical magnitude or intensity, according to *Fechner's law, a modified version called the *Thouless ratio was introduced in 1931. *See also* Brunswikian.
[Named after the Hungarian-born US psychologist Egon Brunswik (1903–55), who introduced it in 1929]

brute force algorithm *n.* A method of *problem solving in which every possibility is examined and the best one (or a best one) is chosen. It is often implemented by computers, but it cannot be used to solve complex problems such as the *travelling salesman problem or the game of chess, because the number of alternatives is too large for any computer to handle.

bruxism *n.* The habit of grinding the teeth, either unconsciously while awake or in Stage II *NREM sleep.
[From Greek *brychein* to gnash]

BSE *abbrev.* Bovine spongiform encephalopathy, a progressive and ultimately fatal disease that attacks the nervous system of cattle and may infect human beings, causing new-variant *Creutzfeldt–Jakob disease. It is believed by most authorities to be a *prion disease, but according to an alternative theory it is an autoimmune disease, similar to *multiple sclerosis, caused by the immune system's reaction to the bacterium *Acinetobacter*, a common microbe found in water, soil, sewage, and in the skin of cattle and human beings, where it infects open wounds and cuts and mimics the molecular structure of a brain tissue protein, causing the immune system to attack both the bacteria and normal brain tissue. Its non-technical name is *mad cow disease*.

buccal *adj.* Of or relating to the cheek or mouth.
[From Latin *bucca* a cheek]

buffer store *n.* A temporary memory store that holds information for short periods, for example the *phonological loop or the *visuo-spatial sketchpad of *working memory. Also called *blackboard memory*.

bufotenin *n.* A psychoactive drug found in *cohoba snuff, in the mushroom *Amanita muscaria*, and in the poisonous secretions from the skin glands of toads. It is an *indole alkaloid and an analogue of *serotonin, but unlike true serotonin it has *psychedelic or *hallucinogenic effects and also functions as an *aphrodisiac. The metabolism of serotonin into bufotenin instead of 5-hydroxyindoleacetic acid is believed to be of significance in the aetiology of schizophrenia. Also spelt *bufotenine*. *See also* phantasticant.
[From Latin *bufo* a toad + *-ten* origin unknown, perhaps from Latin *tenus* a snare + *-ine* indicating an organic compound]

bulbar *adj.* Of, relating to, or attached to the *medulla oblongata or the medulla oblongata and the *pons.
[From Greek *bolbos* an onion or garlic bulb, so

called because of the bulbous appearance of these structures]

bulimia *n*. **1.** Pathologically voracious appetite, including cases caused by a brain lesion. Also called *hyperorexia*, *hyperphagia*, or loosely speaking *polyphagia*. **2.** A shortened name for *bulimia nervosa.
[From Greek *boulimia* bulimia, from *bous* ox + *limos* hunger + -*ia* indicating a condition or quality, indicating the condition of someone who is hungry enough to eat an ox, not (as often stated) one who is as hungry as an ox, the ox being a creature not known for its voracity]

bulimia nervosa *n*. An *eating disorder characterized by recurrent episodes of binge eating, often carried out in secret, accompanied by a sense of loss of control, followed by feelings of shame and compensatory behaviour intended to prevent weight gain, such as self-induced vomiting, misuse of laxatives or diuretics, enemas, fasting, or excessive exercise, together with undue emphasis attached to body shape and weight in self-evaluation. *Compare* anorexia nervosa, binge-eating disorder. *See also* bulimia (1, 2).
[From *bulimia* + Latin *nervus* a nerve]

bundle hypothesis *n*. The notion, attacked in *Gestalt psychology, that a complex perception is nothing more than the sum of its component elements.

Bunsen–Roscoe law *n*. A basic principle of photochemistry according to which the reaction of any light-sensitive pigment, including a *visual pigment in the retina of the eye, is a multiplicative function of the intensity of the light exposure and its duration, the photochemical effect on pigment molecules depending simply on the total number of incident light quanta. It is usually expressed as $I \times t = k$, where I is the physical intensity of the flash, t is its duration, and k is a constant. It is valid up to about 100 milliseconds for *absolute thresholds and *difference thresholds or just noticeable differences in visual sensations, and is valid over a far wider range of durations for photographic emulsions. Also called *Bloch's law*.
[Named after the German chemist Robert Wilhelm Eberhard Bunsen (1811–99) and the English chemist Henry Enfield Roscoe (1833–1915) who formulated it]

Buridan's ass *n*. A problem of decision making typified by a hungry ass standing between two equidistant and equally attractive bales of hay who starves to death because *reason provides no grounds for choosing one rather than the other. *See also* approach–approach conflict.
[Named after the French scholastic philosopher Jean Buridan (?1295–1356) to whom the example is attributed]

burnout *n*. An *acute stress disorder or reaction characterized by exhaustion resulting from overwork, with anxiety, fatigue, insomnia, depression, and impairment in work performance.

burnt odour *n*. One of the six primary odours in *Henning's prism, and one of the four in the *Crocker–Henderson system, resembling the odour of tar oil. US *burned odor*.

buspirone *n*. Buspirone hydrochloride, an *anxiolytic drug that is chemically unrelated to most other anxiolytic drugs in common use (the benzodiazepines) and does not manifest *cross-tolerance with them. Its pharmacological action is poorly understood but is known to involve *serotonin receptors. Also called *Buspar* (trademark).

butyrophenone *n*. Any of a small number of *neuroleptic (1) drugs with *dopamine antagonist action, especially *haloperidol, *droperidol, and *spiroperidol, used in the treatment of *schizophrenia, *Huntington's disease, and *Tourette's disorder.
[From Greek *boutyron* fat, from *bous* ox + *tyros* cheese + English *phene* an old name for benzene, from Greek *phainein* to show, alluding to its use in manufacturing illuminating gas + -*one* indicating a ketone, from Greek -*one* a feminine name suffix]

bystander effect *n*. The reluctance of bystanders to intervene in an emergency, especially when a person appears to be in distress or when a crime is being committed. Scores of experiments have shown that people are much less likely to intervene in an emergency, and are generally slower to respond, when other people are present than when they are alone, and this phenomenon is sometimes called *group inhibition of helping*. It was discovered by the US psychologists Bibb Latané (born 1937) and John M(cConnon) Darley (born 1938), who reported an experiment in the *Journal of Personality and Social Psychology* in 1968 in which people found themselves either alone or in a group in a waiting-room when smoke started billowing through a vent in the wall, quickly filling the room and making breathing difficult. Of the people who were alone when the smoke appeared, 55 per cent reported the fire within 2 minutes of first noticing it, and 75 per cent reported it within 6 minutes; but when groups of three were tested together, in only 12 per cent of cases did any of the three report the fire within 2 minutes, and in only 38 per cent of cases within 6 minutes. Also called the *bystander apathy* effect. *See also* diffusion of responsibility.

byte *n.* A measure of *information (2) equivalent to (usually) eight *bits, sufficient to encode a character from a basic set of letters, numbers, and other symbols. *Compare* nybble.
[An arbitrary formation, based on *bit* and *bite*, possibly influenced by *b(inar)y (digi)t e(ight)*]

BZ gas *abbrev.* Benzilic acid gas, an *atropine-like substance that when inhaled produces incapacitating physical and psychological effects. *See also* incapacitant. *Compare* CN gas, CS gas, Mace, pepper spray, tear gas.

cachexia *n.* General debilitation resulting from any chronic disorder.
[From Greek *kakos* bad + *hexis* condition + *-ia* indicating a condition or quality]

cachinnation *n.* Loud, raucous laughter, without appropriate cause, most often found in *hebephrenic schizophrenia. **cachinnate** *vb.*
[From Latin *cachinnare* to laugh loudly + *-ation* indicating a process or condition]

cacogeusia *n.* The *hallucination or *illusion of an unpleasant taste in the mouth, often found in people with idiopathic *epilepsy, people receiving *tranquillizer therapy, and some people with *delusional disorders. *Compare* ageusia, dysgeusia, hypergeusia, hypogeusia, parageusia, taste blindness.
[From Greek *kakos* bad + *geusis* taste + *-ia* indicating a condition or quality]

cacography *n.* Bad handwriting or incorrect spelling. *Compare* orthography (1).
[From Greek *kakos* bad + *graphein* to write]

cacology *n.* Bad or faulty speech or choice of words.
[From Greek *kakos* bad + *logos* a word or discourse]

cacophony *n.* Unpleasant, harsh, or discordant sounds, especially disagreeable speech sounds.
[From Greek *kakos* bad + *phone* sound]

cacosmia *n.* The *hallucination or *illusion of an unpleasant smell in the nostrils. Also spelt *kakosmia*. *See also* anosmia, dysosmia, hyperosmia, hyposmia, parosmia, specific anosmia.
[From Greek *kakos* bad + *osme* a smell + *-ia* indicating a condition or quality]

cafard *n.* A variant name for *amok in Polynesia. Also called *cathard*.
[From French *cafard* a cockroach or hypocrite]

cafeteria feeding *n.* A procedure in which organisms are permitted to choose from a range of different foods. It is used to study their ability to select a balanced diet or to correct for dietary deficiencies.

cafe wall illusion *n.* Another name for the *Münsterberg illusion, so called because a cafe in Bristol city, England, is tiled on the outside with the pattern that creates a vivid example of the illusion. *See also* lavatory wall illusion.
[Named by the English psychologist Richard L(angton) Gregory (born 1923) in an editorial in the journal *Perception* in 1972]

caffeine *n.* The white crystalline *alkaloid central nervous system *stimulant that is present in coffee, tea, cocoa, cola, chocolate, and many analgesic and tonic medicines and that dilates blood vessels and prevents adenosine from inhibiting glutamate release. It is the most common and the most potent of the three pharmacologically active *xanthine derivatives, the others being *theobromine and *theophylline. Its major psychological effects when taken in moderate dosages include a decrease in fatigue and drowsiness, an increase in speed and efficiency, and a reduction in the number of errors (especially in an overlearned task such as typing); large dosages cause insomnia, tachycardia, diuresis, tremor, and possibly cardiovascular and respiratory failure, and there is evidence of caffeine *dependence (2), abrupt discontinuation after repeated and regular moderate or high dosages tending to lead to headaches, drowsiness, depression, and sometimes nausea and vomiting. Formula $C_8H_{10}N_4O_2$. **caffeinated** *adj.* Containing *caffeine. **caffeinism** or **caffeism** *n.* Addiction to *caffeine, or habitual excessive caffeine ingestion. **decaffeinated** *adj*. With all or most of the *caffeine removed. Also spelt *caffein*. *See also* caffeine-related disorders.

[From German *Kaffee* coffee + *-ine* indicating an organic compound]

caffeine-related disorders *n*. *Substance-related disorders associated specifically with the consumption of *caffeine, including caffeine *intoxication, caffeine-induced *anxiety disorder, and caffeine-induced *sleep disorder. *See also* substance-induced disorders.

CAGE *abbrev*. A four-item questionnaire constructed in 1970 by John A. Ewing and Beatrice A. Rouse as a quick screening device for *alcohol dependence: (1) Have you ever felt you should *Cut* down on your drinking? (2) Have people *Annoyed* you by criticizing your drinking? (3) Have you ever felt *Guilty* about your drinking? (4) Have you ever used a drink as an *Eye-opener* first thing in the morning?

Calabar bean *n*. The dark brown poisonous seed of the tropical African plant *Physostigma venenosum* from which the drug *physostigmine is extracted.

[Named after Calabar, the Nigerian port that is the capital of the Cross River state where it grows abundantly]

calcarine sulcus *n*. A deep horizontal groove that bisects the inner or *medial surface of the *occipital lobe of each *cerebral hemisphere, running from the *parieto-occipital sulcus to the back of the lobe. The *gyri on both sides of this sulcus are occupied by the *primary visual cortex (Area V1). Also called the *calcarine fissure*.

[From Latin *calcar, calcaris* a spur, alluding to the wishbone or spur shape formed by both calcarine sulci taken together]

calcitonin *n*. A hormone that is secreted by the *thyroid gland and that regulates the level of calcium in the blood and restricts the loss of calcium from the bones of the skeleton resulting from the effects of *parathyroid hormone.

calcium *n*. A white–grey metallic element found in sea water, limestone, chalk, marble, and gypsum; an essential constituent of teeth and bones, occurring most often in the form of calcium carbonate, required as an *electrolyte for human physiology. *See also* calci-

tonin, calcium antagonist, calcium channel, calpain, parathyroid hormone. **Ca** *abbrev*.

[From Latin *calx, calcis* lime or limestone]

calcium antagonist *n*. Any of a number of drugs that prevent the transport of calcium ions across calcium channels into the heart and smooth muscles, thereby causing the muscles to relax, and that are used in the treatment of hypertension and angina. Also called a *calcium blocker* or a *calcium channel blocker*. *See also* antagonist (3).

calcium channel *n*. An *ion channel across a cell membrane allowing the passage of calcium ions and believed to be implicated in the *long-term potentiation of memory traces.

calcium (channel) blocker *n*. Another name for a *calcium antagonist.

California F scale *n*. Another name for the *F scale. **California A-S scale** *See* A-S scale. **California E scale** *See* E scale. **California PEC scale** *See* PEC scale.

California Psychological Inventory *n*. A widely used *personality test in the form of a *self-report questionnaire containing 434 (originally 480, then 462) yes/no questions (including 12 duplicates), such as 'I enjoy social gatherings just to be with people', constructed by the US psychologist Harrison G. Gough (born 1921) and first published in 1956/57. It is designed to measure the lay concepts that are used in personality description in everyday life, and originally yielded 18 scores: Dominance (Do), Capacity for status (Cs), Sociability (Sy), Social presence (Sp), Self-acceptance (Sa), Sense of well-being (Wb), Responsibility (Re), Socialization (So), Self-control (Sc), Tolerance (To), Good impression (Gi), Community (Cm), Achievement via conformance (Ac), Achievement via independence (Ai), Intellectual efficiency (Ie), Psychological-mindedness (Py), Flexibility (Fx), and Femininity (Fe). In 1987 Independence (In) and Empathy (Em) were added to the scale. **CPI** *abbrev*.

callosal apraxia *n*. Another name for *left-sided apraxia. *See also* apraxia.

caloric nystagmus *n*. A form of *nystagmus resulting from the introduction of warm or cold fluid into the ear, stimulating the *dynamic labyrinth and eliciting a rotation of the eyeballs towards the stimulated side if the stimulating fluid is warm, and away from the stimulated side if it is cold. Also called *Bárány nystagmus*. *See also* Bárány test, vestibulo-ocular reflex.

[From Latin *calor* heat + Greek *nystagmos* nystagmus, from *nystazein* to nap]

caloric test *n*. Another name for the *Bárány test.

Calorie *n*. A unit of heat, energy, or food value, equal to 1,000 calories (with lower-case initial *c*, see below). Also (preferably) called a *kilocalorie*, a *large calorie*, or a *kilogram calorie*. **Cal.** or **kcal** *abbrev*. **calorie** *n*. Formerly defined as the heat required to raise the temperature of one gram of water by one degree centigrade, now defined in standard SI units as 4.1868 joules. Also called a *small calorie* or *gram calorie*. **cal.** *abbrev*. There is much confusion, *calorie* often being written when *Calorie* is meant. In psychology, and in writing about food and nutrition, *calorie* usually denotes *kilocalorie*. **caloric** or **calorific** *adj*.

[From Latin *calor* heat]

calpain *n*. A protein that is activated by *calcium ions found in some synapses and that has been hypothesized to erode the membranes of *postsynaptic neurons, allowing pre-existing *dendritic spines to emerge, or bringing hidden receptors to the surface of dendritic spines, thus strengthening certain synaptic connections and providing a physical substrate for *long-term potentiation and memory *consolidation without requiring any new neural growth, which does not normally occur in the central nervous system. It is synthesized from papain, a proteolytic enzyme present in papaya latex, and is used as a protein digestant and meat tenderizer.

[From *cal(cium)* + *(pa)pain*]

calque *n*. A word or phrase borrowed from another language by translating its component parts separately and literally, such as the English word *superman* taken from the German word *Übermensch*, or the English phrase *power politics* taken from the German word *Machtpolitik*. Also called a *loan translation*.

[From French *calque* a tracing, from Latin *calcare* to tread, from *calx* a heel]

canalizing selection *n*. A form of *natural selection that is relatively insensitive to fluctuations in the environment.

cancellation heuristic *n*. A judgemental and decision-making *heuristic that involves discarding the components that are shared by the available alternatives. The Israeli psychologists Daniel Kahneman (born 1934) and Amos Tversky (1937–96), who introduced the heuristic in 1979, illustrated it with the following two-stage game. In the first stage, there was a 0.75 probability of the game terminating without any prize and a 0.25 probability of moving on to the second stage. Participants who reached the second stage had a choice between (a) 3,000 Israeli pounds with certainty, and (b) a 0.80 probability of winning 4,000 Israeli pounds, but they had to make their decisions for the second stage before the result of the first stage was known. Most ignored the first stage, which is common to both alternatives, and 80 per cent preferred (a), which they considered a certainty in spite of the chance element in the first stage. But in (a) there is a $0.25 \times 1.00 = 0.25$ probability of winning 3,000 Israeli pounds, and in (b) there is a $0.25 \times 0.80 = 0.20$ probability of winning 4,000 Israeli pounds, and when the choice was framed in this way, 65 per cent of the research participants chose (b). In fact, the *expected utility is higher in (b). *See also* framing effect.

cancellation method *n*. A technique for measuring the subjective loudness of a *combination tone by delivering a real tone, of the same frequency as the combination tone but with exactly opposite phase, called a *cancellation tone*, and increasing its intensity until the combination tone is no longer heard.

candela *n*. A basic unit of *luminous intensity, equal to that of a source emitting monochromatic light of frequency 540×10^{12} hertz in a given direction with a radiant intensity in that direction of 1/683 watts per steradian—a stereo radian or solid angle with its vertex at the centre of a sphere cutting off an area of the sphere's surface equal to the square of its radius. *See also* bril, lumen, luminance, luminous flux. **cd** *abbrev*.

[From Latin *candela* a candle]

candlepower *n*. A unit of luminous intensity, now replaced by the *candela.

candy *n.* **1.** Confectionary in general. **2.** A street name for *barbiturate drugs.
[From Old French *sucre candi* candied sugar, from Arabic *qandi* candied, from *qand* cane sugar, from Dravidian]

cannabis *n.* The *psychotropic drug *delta-9-tetrahydrocannabinol (THC) and related substances called *cannabinoids* that are found in the leaves, flowering tops, and young stems of the female common hemp plant *Cannabis sativa*, and whose biochemical action remains largely unknown. The earliest record of its use as a drug is found in a compendium of medicines of the Chinese Emperor Shen Nung dated 2737 BC, and it is now a popular street drug, inducing euphoria, relaxation of inhibitions, and intensification of perceptions, with potential medicinal benefits, alleviating painful muscular spasms in people with multiple sclerosis, reducing the nausea and vomiting accompanying chemotherapy for cancer, and reducing intra-ocular pressure in people with glaucoma. The cut and dried leaves, tops, and stems of the plant, rolled into cigarettes and smoked, are generally called *marijuana*; the dried resinous exudate of the flowering tops of the female hemp plant and the undersides of its leaves, when smoked with tobacco or added to foods and eaten, is called *hashish*; and the drink made from an infusion of cannabis is called *bhang*. The common street names of cannabis include *dope*, *ganja*, *grass*, *joint*, *pot*, *reefer*, *spliff*, and *weed* (see separate entries for specific meanings). *See also* anandamide, cannabis-related disorders, endocannabinoid, substance abuse, substance-related disorders.
[From Latin *Cannabis* the biological name of the common hemp genus, perhaps from an expression used in ancient Mesopotamia *kah nah bah* cane with two, denoting a cane-like plant with male and female forms]

cannabis-related disorders *n.* *Substance-related disorders associated specifically with the use of *cannabis. *See* substance abuse, substance-induced disorders, substance use disorders.

cannibal *n.* A human being who eats the flesh of other human beings, or an animal that eats the flesh of others of its own species (conspecifics). **cannibalism** *n.* The act or practice of eating flesh of one's own species. **cannibalistic** *adj.*

[From Spanish *Canibales*, the word used by the Italian-born navigator Christopher Columbus (1451–1506) for the Carib people of Cuba and Haiti]

cannibalistic stage *n.* Another name for the *oral sadistic phase.

Cannon–Bard theory *n.* The proposition that the quality of an emotion is determined by the pattern of stimulation sent from the *thalamus to the *cerebral cortex, and that the bodily expression of emotion is governed by signals from the thalamus to muscles and glands. Also called *Cannon's theory* or the *Bard–Cannon theory*. *Compare* James–Lange theory.
[Named after the US physiologist Walter Bradford Cannon (1871–1945) and the US psychologist Philip Bard (1898–1977) who were the first to suggest it in the 1930s]

canonical correlation *n.* A statistical procedure that seeks to discover and describe the relationship between a set of *predictor variables and a set of *dependent variables. Pairs of linear combinations of the two sets of variables are found that are maximally correlated, and the proportion of the total *variance in the criterion set that is explained by the predictor set is extracted. *Compare* discriminant function analysis, in which there is usually only one dependent variable.
[From Greek *kanon* rule, measuring rod, standard, related to *kanna* a reed + *correlation*]

canonical sequence *n.* In genetics, another name for a *consensus sequence.
[From Latin *canonicus* living under a rule, from *canon* a rule, from Greek *kanon* a rule or measuring rod]

cant *n.* **1.** Insincere or hypocritical speech or the repetition of trite phrases that have lost their original meanings. **2.** The *argot of a particular social group, such as thieves, journalists, lawyers, or gypsies. **3.** A rare word for the sing-song, mewling style of speech occasionally used by people pleading for something.
[From Latin *cantare* to sing]

cantharides *n.* A poisonous urogenital irritant and diuretic made from the dried bodies of the blister-beetle *Lytta vesicatoris* belonging to the family Meloidae, and not Cantharidae

as often stated, used mainly as a blistering agent or *aphrodisiac. Also called *Spanish fly*. **cantharis** *sing.*
[From Greek *kantharis* Spanish fly]

capacity *n.* The ability to contain or the amount that can be contained or absorbed. In psychology, it usually refers to latent *ability or the capability to learn.
[From Latin *capacitas* capacity, from *capax* spacious, from *capere* to take]

Capgras syndrome *n.* A *delusional misidentification of familiar people, usually relatives or friends, who are believed to have been replaced by exact doubles or impostors; thus a delusion of underidentification, in contrast to *Frégoli syndrome, which involves overidentification. The poet John Cowper was afflicted with Capgras syndrome, believing as he did that his friend, the Reverend John Newton, had been supplanted by an impersonator. Also called *l'illusion de sosies* or the *illusion of doubles*. Compare Doppelgänger, intermetamorphosis, reduplicative paramnesia.
[Named after the French psychiatrist Jean Marie Joseph Capgras (1873–1950) who, together with the French psychiatrist Jean Marie Joseph Reboul-Lachaux (1873–1950), first described it in 1923]

caprylic odour *n.* One of the primary odours in the *Crocker–Henderson system, goat-like or putrid. US **caprylic odor**.
[From Latin *caper* a goat, cognate with *Capricorn* the Goat, the tenth sign of the zodiac]

capsaicin *n.* A bitter *alkaloid present in capsicums, hot peppers, and chillis that excites peripheral nerve endings of the *trigeminal nerve and causes certain neurons to release *substance P. *See also* common chemical sense.
[From Latin *capsa* a box or case + *-in(a)* indicating an organic compound]

carbachol *n.* A synthetic drug that acts as a *parasympathomimetic and *cholinergic agent but is immune to the inactivating effects of *acetylcholinesterase. It is used in the treatment of urinary retention, abdominal distention, and glaucoma. *See also* cholinomimetic.
[From its chemical name *carba(moyl)-chol(ine) (chloride)*]

carbamate *n.* A salt or ester of carbamic acid, used in certain *psychotropic medications, including *glutethimide (Doriden) and *meprobamate (Miltown).
[From *carbamic* + *-ate* indicating chemical compound]

carbamazepine *n.* An *antimanic, *anticonvulsant, and *analgesic (2) drug that is often used instead of or in addition to *lithium carbonate in the treatment of acute manic episodes, bipolar disorders, neuralgia affecting the trigeminal nerve, and epilepsy. Also called *Tegretol* (trademark).
[From its chemical name *carbam(oyl)* + *-azepine* as in *benzodiazepine*]

carcinogen *n.* Any substance or agent that causes cancer. **carcinogenic** *adj.*
[From Greek *karkinoma* a cancer, from *karkinos* a crab + *genein* to produce]

carcinoma *n.* A type of malignant tumour originating in epithelial tissue; more loosely, any cancer, but this meaning is avoided in careful usage.
[From Greek *karkinoma* a cancer, from *karkinos* a crab + *-oma* indicating an abnormality]

cardiac muscle *n.* A specialized type of involuntary striated muscle that is found only in the heart and that is exceptional inasmuch as involuntary muscles are generally smooth. It consists of contractile fibres that resemble those of *skeletal muscles but are much smaller in diameter. Compare smooth muscle, striped muscle.
[From Greek *kardia* the heart]

cardinal humour *See under* humour (3).

cardinal vowels *n.* A set of idealized speech sounds devised by the British phonetician Daniel Jones (1881–1967), usually represented by their location in a *vowel quadrilateral* representing the mouth (see vowel), used as reference points to classify the vowel sounds of any language. *See also* back vowel, central vowel, close vowel, front vowel, mid vowel, open vowel.

cardiovascular *adj.* Of, relating to, or involving the heart and blood vessels.
[From Greek *kardia* the heart + Latin *vasculum* a little vessel, diminutive of *vas* a vessel]

caretaker speech *n.* A speech style often used by adults and older children when talking to infants or young children, characterized by shortened sentences, simplified grammar, restricted vocabulary, slow speech with many repetitions, diminutive and reduplicative words, such as *doggy* and *choo-choo*, raised pitch and exaggerated pitch variation, and many utterances ending in questions with a rising tone (*some more?*, *go walkies?*). Also called *child-directed speech*, *motherese* (misleadingly, because it is not restricted to mothers) and *baby talk* (ambiguously, because it is used by adults).

caricature advantage *n.* The enhanced recognizability of caricatured images of familiar faces relative to undistorted or veridical images of the same faces, the distorted images being paradoxically easier to recognize. Like the *differential inversion effect, it is not confined exclusively to faces but is found also with other classes of stimuli that differ only in configuration provided that the viewers have expert knowledge of the stimuli, as when bird-watchers view images of songbirds.

carnivore *n.* Any animal of the order Carnivora of flesh-eating mammals, including dogs, cats, bears, raccoons, hyenas, civets, and weasels. *Homo sapiens* is not a carnivore but an omnivore. *See also* predator. *Compare* herbivore, omnivore. **carnivorous** *adj.* Flesh-eating.
[From Latin *caro, carnis* flesh + *vorare* to devour]

carotene *n.* Any of four different reddish-orange pigments that are found in many plants and are converted to *vitamin A in the liver. The most important is beta-carotene or *β*-carotene, the yellow-orange pigment of carrots that is also found in other vegetables and in milk.
[From Latin *carota* a carrot + *-ene* indicating an unsaturated compound with double bonds, from Greek *-ene* a feminine name suffix]

carpentered world *n.* The built environment of industrial societies, containing numerous *artefacts (1) constructed from straight lines and right angles. The absence of such objects in tribal cultures of sub-Saharan Africa was put forward in 1967 by the South African psychologist William Hudson (born 1914) as an explanation for the apparent inability of tribal Africans to interpret *linear perspective in *pictorial depth perception and their relative lack of susceptibility to the *Müller-Lyer illusion and related visual illusions, this notion being called the *carpentered-world hypothesis*.

carrier (genetic) *n.* In genetics and pathology, an organism that does not itself manifest a particular trait or disease but is capable of passing it on to others.

carrier protein *n.* Any *protein in a cell membrane that binds to molecules and transports them across the membrane. *See also* active transport, ionophore.

carrying capacity *n.* In *ecology (1) and the theory of *evolution, the maximum number of individuals that a habitat or area can support indefinitely, the limit usually being determined by the available food supply.

Cartesian *adj.* Of or relating to the writings or doctrines of the French philosopher René Descartes (1596–1650). *See* a priori, Cartesian dualism, mind–body problem, rationalism (1).

Cartesian dualism *n.* An approach to the *mind–body problem introduced by the French philosopher René Descartes (1596–1650), who believed that mental experiences are functions of the soul and, because the soul is immaterial, that they cannot be located in any particular organ of the body, but that the soul and the body influence each other, and that the seat of soul–body interaction is the *pineal gland. Descartes' reasons for choosing the pineal gland were that it is close to the centre of the head, that it was believed at the time to be found only in human beings—and that human beings are the only creatures with rational souls—and that the pineal gland is the only part of the main structure of the brain that is not divided into two halves and that therefore seemed to Descartes to be the only organ capable of integrating the images from the two eyes into a single percept. He believed that the pineal gland operates like a valve, controlling the flow of 'vital spirits' through the body, enabling the soul and body to influence each other. Descartes appears to have been oblivious to the philosophical problem underlying this conception until it was pointed out to him in 1643 by Princess Elizabeth of Bohemia

(1596–1662), the daughter of King James I of England and VI of Scotland, in a letter that has survived.

cascade processing n. The implementation of later stages of *information processing before the completion of earlier stages. For example, in retrieving the meaning of a printed word, a person may have to identify all the letters and match the word against an internal *lexicon (2) in order to extract its meaning. According to *discrete processing models, information is not passed on to the next stage until processing at the current stage is complete, but in a cascade processing model a word may, for example, be matched against items in the lexicon, by way of hypotheses or guesses, before all the letters have been identified, and conjectures about meaning may be made before a complete lexical match has been established. The concept was introduced in 1979 by the US cognitive scientist James L(loyd) McClelland (born 1948) and has been influential in *connectionist models of information processing. *See also* parallel processing, serial processing.

case grammar n. A form of *generative grammar introduced in the late 1960s by the US linguist Charles Fillmore (born 1929) in which linguistic elements are categorized according to their *semantic roles. In the theory, the *deep-structure cases of noun phrases do not correspond to the *surface structure or the *syntax. The cases originally suggested were *agentive* (a person or entity causing a verb's action to be performed), *instrumental* (an inanimate entity causally involved in a verb's action), *dative* (a person or animal affected indirectly by a verb's action), *factitive* (an entity resulting from a verb's action), *locative* (the location of a verb's action), and *objective* (an entity affected directly by a transitive verb's action). Later, further cases were suggested: *source* (the place from which something moves), *goal* (the place to which something moves), *counter-agent* (the force of resistance against which a verb's action is performed), *experiencer* (a person or thing affected by a verb's action, replacing dative), and *result* (an entity or state resulting from a verb's action, replacing factitive). For example, in the sentence *The child opened the door with a key*, the noun phrase *the child* is agentive, *the door* is objective, and *a key* is instrumental. Case grammar has been

incorporated in some *artificial intelligence programs designed to accept *natural language input.

case study n. A research method involving a detailed investigation of a single individual or a single organized group, used extensively in clinical psychology and also, though less often, in other branches of the discipline. In case studies of organized groups, *participant observation is often used. Also called a *single-case design*.

castrate vb. To emasculate or remove the testicles from; or, figuratively, to deprive of power. **castration** n. The act or process of *castrating. **castrato** n. A male singer *castrated before puberty to preserve his unbroken soprano or alto voice, especially in the 17th and 18th centuries (**castrati** pl.).
[From Latin *castrare* to emasculate or geld]

castration complex n. In *psychoanalysis, a *complex (2), closely linked with the *Oedipus complex, focusing on fantasies of one's penis being cut off, evoked in a child by the discovery of the anatomical difference between the sexes. In a boy, it induces anxiety about being castrated and initiates the *latency period; in a girl, it is experienced as a loss that she has suffered and initiates a desire for the paternal penis and attempts to deny or compensate for the loss. Sigmund Freud (1856–1939) introduced the concept in 1908 in an article 'On the Sexual Theories of Children' (*Standard Edition*, IX, pp. 209–26, at pp. 215–17) and developed it further in his famous case of *Little Hans, 'Analysis of a Phobia in a Five-Year-Old Boy', first published in 1909 (*Standard Edition*, X, pp. 5–149). *See also* phallic stage.

catabolism n. A destructive form of *metabolism in which complex molecules are broken down into simpler ones with the release of energy. *Compare* anabolism. **catabolic** adj. **catabolite** n. Any substance produced by *catabolism.
[From Greek *kataballein* to throw down, from *kata* down + *ballein* to throw]

catachresis n. Any misuse or wrong application of a word, often by assuming its meaning to be that of a word with a similar sound, as in the utterance *I suffer from prostrate trouble*, seeming to imply that I can't get up from a lying position, when *prostate* is meant. *Compare* malapropism.

[From Greek *katachresis* a misuse, from *kata* down + *chresthai* to use]

catalepsy *n*. A state of myotonia in which a person's muscles are partly rigid, sometimes manifested in *hypnosis, in people with *catatonia, and in people with certain forms of brain damage, notably *cerebellar lesions. People in such a state tend to leave their arms, legs, or bodies in whatever positions they are placed by another person. Sometimes confused with *cataplexy (1). Also called *cerea flexibilitas*. *See also* myotonia, tonus. *Compare* clasp-knife rigidity, cogwheel rigidity. **cataleptic** *adj*.

[From Greek *kata* down + *lepsis* a seizure, from *lambanein* to seize]

catalexia *n*. A form of *dyslexia in which the same word or phrase is read repeatedly.

[From Greek *kata* down + *lexis* a word + *-ia* indicating a condition or quality]

catamnesis *n*. The follow-up medical history of a patient or client after recovery from a disorder. *Compare* anamnesis (2). **catamneses** *pl*. **catamnestic** *adj*.

[From Greek *kata* back + *mnesis* memory]

cataphora *n*. In speaking or writing, the use of a pronoun or other word to refer forward to something mentioned later in a sentence or linguistic expression. In the sentence *When I was questioned, this is what I told the police: I heard a loud argument at about midnight*, the word *this* exemplifies cataphora, because it refers forward to *I heard a loud argument at about midnight*. *See also* deixis. *Compare* anaphora. **cataphoric** *adj*.

[From Greek *kata* down + *pherein* to carry]

cataplexy *n*. **1.** A sudden loss of muscle *tonus, without loss of *consciousness, leading to collapse, immobility, and a state closely resembling *REM sleep without loss of consciousness, induced by laughter or strong emotions such as fear, anger, or surprise, sometimes confused with *cataplexy. A propensity for cataplexy is genetic in origin, and strains of cataplexic dogs have been bred. *Compare* narcolepsy. **2.** A death-like state of immobility adopted by some animals to deter predators. **cataplectic** or **cataplexic** *adj*.

[From Greek *kata* down + *plessein* to strike]

cataract *n*. A waterfall or downpour, hence figuratively a partial or total opacity of the *crystalline lens of the eye leading to *blindness, characterized by a greyish white appearance of the lens visible through the pupil, usually caused by degenerative changes after 45 years of age, treated by excision of the lens and the prescription of spectacles or contact lenses. *See also* aphakia, cornea.

[From Latin *cataracta* a waterfall, from Greek *katarrhaktes* a waterfall]

catastrophe theory *n*. A mathematical theory, developed by the French mathematician René Frédéric Thom (1923–2002) and first published in 1972, devoted to the classification of surfaces according to their shape. Aspects of the theory that describe abrupt changes occurring when gradually changing variables reach critical points, as when the locus of a point moving along the topmost fold of a smoothly folded surface suddenly drops to the surface below, have been used to model psychological phenomena such as gradually increasing anger abruptly erupting into a temper tantrum.

catastrophism *n*. **1.** A theory that gradual processes of *evolution have been modified by the effects of great natural cataclysms. Also (preferably) called *neocatastrophism* to distinguish it from sense 2. **2.** An obsolete theory of biological and geological development, widely accepted in the 18th and 19th centuries, according to which the fossil record represents a series of sudden abrupt changes brought about by divine creations and extinctions rather than gradual evolutionary processes.

[From Greek *katastrephein* to overturn, from *kata* down + *strephein* to turn + *-ismos* indicating a state or condition]

catathymia *n*. A state in which mental processes are under the control of the emotions. **catathymic** *adj*.

[From Greek *kata* according to + *thymos* spirit or temper + *-ia* indicating a condition or quality]

catathymic amnesia *n*. Another name for *episodic amnesia.

catatonia *n*. Marked abnormality of muscle *tonus or behaviour including motor immobility, excessive and apparently purposeless motor activity, *catalepsy or cerea flexibilitas, extreme *negativism (1) or *mutism, posturing or stereotyped movements, *echolalia, or *echopraxia. *See* catatonic disorder due to general medical condition, schizophrenia. **catatonic** *adj.*

[From Greek *kata* down + *tonos* tension, from *teinein* to stretch + *-ia* indicating a condition or quality]

catatonic disorder due to general medical condition *n.* A form of *catatonia arising as a secondary or symptomatic effect of a *general medical condition, characterized by catatonic signs such as motor immobility, excessive and purposeless motor activity, *catalepsy or cerea flexibilitas, extreme *negativism (1) or *mutism, peculiarities of voluntary movement, *echolalia, or *echopraxia.

catatonic schizophrenia *n.* One of the major types of *schizophrenia, the essential feature of which is pronounced *psychomotor disturbance, manifested as physical immobility evidenced by *catalepsy or cerea flexibilitas, *stupor, excessive (apparently purposeless) motor activity or peculiarities of voluntary movement, *negativism (1), *mutism, and *echolalia, or *echopraxia.

catch trial *n.* In a series of trials used to determine an *absolute threshold in *psychophysics, a trial in which no stimulus is presented, usually included a number of times to estimate the individual's baseline tendency to give positive responses. *See also* signal detection theory.

catecholamine *n.* A group of *biogenic amines that are derivatives of catechol (2-hydroxyphenol) and that also contain an *amine group, including the *neurotransmitters *adrenalin (epinephrine), *noradrenalin (norepinephrine), and *dopamine. **CA** *abbrev.*
[From *catechol* a substance found in resins and lignins, named after the *Acacia catechu* tree + English *amine*]

catechol-o-methyl-transferase *n.* An *enzyme that metabolizes free *catecholamines in the space between and around synapses. *Compare* monoamine oxidase (MOA). **COMT** *abbrev.*

Catego *n.* Computer software for processing *SCAN data according to categories of *signs (1) and *symptoms, introduced by the English psychiatrist John Kenneth Wing (born 1923) and several co-authors in their book *The Description and Classification of Psychiatric Symptoms* (1974).
[From *catego(ries)*]

categorical attitude *n.* Another name for *abstract attitude.

categorical imperative *n.* A principle of morality first formulated in 1785 by the German idealist philosopher Immanuel Kant (1724–1804) in *Grundlegung zur Metaphysik der Sitten* (Foundations of the Metaphysics of Morals). His first formulation, most often quoted is: 'Act only on such a maxim that you can at the same time will to become a universal law' (*Immanuel Kants Werke*, Volume IV, p. 52). According to Kant, a *maxim* is a personal rule of conduct, and it is a hypothetical imperative if it takes the form 'If you want X, then do Y', assuming that Y is the only or the best means of obtaining X and the reason for doing Y is actually contingent on your desire for X. A maxim is a categorical imperative if it takes the form 'Always do Y', where the reason for doing Y is not contingent on any desire in the sense of being your means of obtaining some end that you desire. A categorical imperative is intended not only to be rational, but also to serve as a fundamental principle of morality. Only certain maxims can be categorical imperatives. Kant's clearest example of one that cannot is: 'Always borrow money when in need and promise to pay it back without any intention of keeping the promise' (p. 54). One cannot rationally will this maxim to be a universal law, because it cannot be universalized without generating a contradiction. If everybody habitually broke promises, then there could be no promises; nobody would believe them, because a promise needs a promisee as well as a promiser, and there would be no promisees.

categorical perception *n.* Perception of stimuli as belonging to two or more distinct classes when in physical terms they vary along a *continuum, as when light varying in wavelength within the *visible spectrum is perceived as four (or sometimes five, six, or seven) qualitatively different colours, in contrast to musical tones varying in wavelength within the *audibility range, which are heard by most listeners as points on a continuum.

The perception of *phonemes tends to be categorical, so that if voicing is gradually added to the unvoiced initial consonant in the word *tie*, the listener hears no significant change until a critical point at which the word abruptly changes to *die*. *See also* metathetic stimulus dimension, type fallacy.

categorical syllogism *n*. A conventional *syllogism of the type introduced by the Greek philosopher Aristotle (384–322 BC), and used by almost all his successors, in which the *propositions (1) are expressed in terms of category membership, using the four standard categorical proposition forms *All S are P, No S are P, Some S are P*, and *Some S are not P*. Examples of propositions that might be used in a categorical syllogism are *All men are mortal, No wombats play tennis, Some thunderstorms are thrilling*, and *Some swans are not white*. A categorical syllogism cannot express a logical argument containing non-categorical propositions such as *Elizabeth is the mother of Charles*. *See also* modal logic.

categorical variable *n*. In statistics, any *discrete variable that has a limited number of distinct values, such as gender—which has two values, namely male and female. *Compare* continuous variable.

category mistake *n*. A statement about something that belongs to one category but is intelligible only of something belonging to another category, as when the mind is referred to as if it were a physical entity. The concept was introduced by the English philosopher Gilbert Ryle (1900–76) on page 17 of his book *The Concept of Mind* (1949), where he used the example of someone who can see a university library, lecture halls, and other university buildings but wonders where the university is. Ryle described *Cartesian dualism as the dogma of 'the ghost in the machine'.

catharsis *n*. A word used by the Greek philosopher Aristotle (384–322 BC) to denote the purging of emotions that results from watching a staged performance of a tragedy. The key passage is as follows: 'A tragedy, then, is the imitation of an action that is serious and also, as having magnitude, complete in itself; in language with pleasurable accessories, each kind brought in separately in the parts of the work; in a dramatic, not in a narrative form;

with incidents arousing pity and fear, wherewith to accomplish its catharsis of such emotions' (*Poetics*, Chapter 6, Bekker edition, p. 1449b). Aristotle may well have returned to this topic in the lost Book 2 of this work. In *psychoanalysis, catharsis is the bringing to consciousness of repressed ideas, accompanied by the expression of emotions, thereby relieving tension. The Austrian physician Josef Breuer (1842–1925) first investigated it in the context of therapy in his case of *Anna O, after which he and Sigmund Freud (1856–1939) imported the concept into psychoanalysis in 1895 in *Studies on Hysteria* (*Standard Edition*, II, pp. 21–47), and it became a therapeutic technique designed to produce *abreaction. It was at first closely associated with *hypnosis, but Freud soon began to use *free association as a basic therapeutic procedure instead of hypnosis, and as a consequence catharsis receded into the background. The term has been used loosely in psychology to denote the supposed reduction of aggressive urges resulting from exposure to violence enacted in television programmes, films, or computer games. **cathartic** *adj*.
[From Greek *katharsis* purgation, from *kathairein* to purge or purify]

cathexis *n*. In *psychoanalysis, the emotional charge associated with an *instinct (3), or the process of investing psychic energy in a part of the body or an *instinctual object. The Austrian physician Josef Breuer (1842–1925) and Sigmund Freud (1856–1939) introduced the concept in 1895 in their book *Studies on Hysteria* (*Standard Edition*, II). The original German word used by Breuer and Freud was *Besetzung*, an everyday word meaning occupation; the word *cathexis* was coined in 1922 by Freud's translator James Strachey (1887–1967), who revealed that Freud considered it too technical (*Standard Edition* III, p. 63, note 2). A word more in harmony with the German is *investment*. *See also* economic, hypercathexis. *Compare* countercathexis, decathexis. **cathect** *vb*. To load with psychic energy through *cathexis.
[From Greek *kathexis* occupation, from *kathechein* to hold fast]

cation *n*. A positively charged *ion such as an ion of sodium, potassium, or calcium. *Compare* anion.
[From Greek *kata* down + *ion* going, from *ienai* to go]

cation channel n. An *ion channel across a cell membrane permitting the transport of *cations across it. See also sodium channel. Compare anion channel.

catnip n. A herb resembling mint, the smell of which has the effect on cats of a euphoriant and intoxicant. When consumed by humans, it can produce effects that are similar to those of *cannabis or even *LSD. Also called catmint or catnep.
[From its biological name, Latin Nepeta cataria]

Cattell Culture-Fair Test n. An *intelligence test designed specifically to avoid the *test bias assumed to affect scores on more conventional tests, such as the *Wechsler scales and the *Stanford–Binet test, by excluding items requiring linguistic skills and general knowledge. See also culture-fair. Compare Raven's Progressive Matrices. **CCFT** abbrev.
[Named after the English-born US psychologist Raymond B(ernard) Cattell (1905–98) who first published it in the Journal of Educational Psychology in 1940, describing it as 'culture-free']

Cattell 16-PF See 16PF.

caudal adj. Towards the tail or the *posterior part of the body, organ, or part or, in the human brain, towards the brainstem. Compare rostral.
[From Latin cauda a tail]

caudate adj. Having a tail or a tail-like appendage.
[From Latin cauda a tail]

caudate nucleus n. One of the *basal ganglia in the *corpus striatum: a crescent-shaped mass of grey matter in each cerebral hemisphere, near the thalamus, concerned with inhibitory control of movement. See also attention-deficit/hyperactivity disorder.
[From Latin cauda a tail, alluding to its shape]

caudatolenticular adj. Of or belonging to the *caudate nucleus and *lenticular nucleus of the basal ganglia in the brain.

causal adj. Of, relating to, or acting as something that brings about a particular result.
[From Latin causalis causal, from causa a cause]

causal effect n. A change in a *dependent variable brought about directly by an *independent variable.

causalgia n. A condition in which burning pain is experienced along the course of a peripheral nerve without the application of heat. Also called thermalgia.
[From Greek kausos fever + algos pain + -ia indicating a condition or quality]

causal inference n. A conclusion based on evidence and reasoning that an event or process brought about a certain consequence.

causal schema n. A concept introduced in 1958 by the Austrian-born US psychologist Fritz Heider (1896–1988) to denote a conceptual organization of a sequence of events in which some are identified as causes and others as effects. The concept was elaborated in 1977 by the Israeli psychologists Amos Tversky (1937–96) and Daniel Kahneman (born 1934), whose conceptual schemas include causal data (perceived as causes of the events of interest), diagnostic data (perceived as consequences of the events of interest), and also incidental data (perceived as neither causes nor consequences of the events of interest). See also attribution theory, covariation principle, Kelley's cube, schema.

causal texture n. A term introduced in 1935 by the US psychologist Edward C(hace) Tolman (1886–1959) and the Hungarian-born US psychologist Egon Brunswik (1903–55) to denote the regular pattern of dependency of events in the environment on one another.

causal variable n. An *independent variable that produces a *causal effect.

cautious shift See under risky shift.

CCC trigram abbrev. Another name for a *consonant trigram.
[An acronym of c(onsonant) c(onsonant) c(onsonant)]

ceiling effect n. In statistics and measurement theory, an artificial upper limit on the value that a *variable can attain, causing the distribution of scores to be skewed. For example, the distribution of scores on an ability test will be skewed by a ceiling effect if the test is much too easy for many of the respondents and many of them obtain perfect scores. *Compare* floor effect.

celestial illusion *n.* Another name for the *moon illusion, especially when referring to other heavenly bodies apart from the moon.
[From Medieval Latin *celestialis*, of or relating to the heavens, from *caelum* heaven]

cell *n.* The smallest independently functioning unit of an *organism, consisting of a *nucleus (1) containing genetic information, surrounded by a *cytoplasm containing various organelles including *mitochondria, *ribosomes, and *lysosomes, bounded by a *cell membrane. *See also* eukaryote, prokaryote. **cellular** *adj.*
[From Latin *cella* a room, from *celare* to hide]

cell assembly *n.* A collection of neurons that have become functionally interrelated, through repeated excitation, into a circuit capable of responding as a unit, providing a neural basis for perception, learning, and other mental activities, according to a hypothesis of the Canadian psychologist Donald O(lding) Hebb (1904–85). *See also* Hebb synapse, phase sequence, reverberating circuit.

cell body *n.* The central part of a neuron or other cell containing the *nucleus (1) and other structures that keep the cell alive, as distinct from a cell *process (2). Also called a *soma (1).

cell division *n.* The process whereby a cell splits into two new cells by *fission (2) in bacteria and other prokaryotes and by *mitosis or *meiosis (1) during growth or reproduction, respectively, in other organisms.

cell membrane *n.* A double layer of *amphipathic *lipid molecules (a lipid bilayer), plus various protein molecules, punctured by tiny pores approximately 60 nanometres (billionths of a metre) in diameter, forming a *semipermeable membrane that segregates the fluid inside a cell from the fluid outside it and maintains the structural integrity of the cell. Molecules smaller than the pores can cross the membrane by passive diffusion; larger molecules that are lipid soluble can dissolve in the membrane and cross it by diffusion; and larger molecules that are not lipid soluble can cross the membrane only by *active transport. Also called a *plasma membrane*. *See also* osmosis, sodium pump.
[From Latin *membrana* a thin skin]

cellular automaton *n.* A mathematical *model of self-replication and destruction, usually represented by a checkerboard of either fixed or infinite dimensions, each cell of which has a finite number of states, usually including a quiescent or empty state, and a finite set of neighbouring cells that can influence its state, the pattern of changes being determined by transition rules that apply simultaneously to all cells in each discrete time unit. The concept was introduced in the early 1950s by the Hungarian-born US mathematician John von Neumann (1903–57), whose cellular automata incorporated universal *Turing machines and whose articles on the subject were published posthumously under the title *Theory of Self-Replicating Automata* (1966). *See also* microtubule. **cellular automata** *pl.*
[From Greek *automatos* spontaneous or self-moving, from *autos* self]

censored variable *n.* In statistics, any *variable showing a *floor effect or a *ceiling effect owing to the fact that observations could not be made beyond the most extreme value.

censorship *n.* The policy or practice of examining publications, television programmes, or other forms of communication with a view to suppressing or altering those that are considered unacceptable or offensive. In *psychoanalysis, the suppression of unconscious wishes and their modification before entering consciousness. Sigmund Freud (1856–1939) first used the term in its psychoanalytic sense in a letter to Fliess in 1897 (*Standard Edition*, I, p. 273), and he developed the concept further in his book *Interpretation of Dreams* (1900, *Standard Edition*, IV–V), where he used it to explain the distortion of meaning in dreams. According to Freud, the *first censorship* operates between the *unconscious (2) and the *preconscious, and the *second censorship* between the preconscious and *consciousness: 'To every transition from one system to that immediately above it (that is, every advance to a higher stage of psychical organization) there corresponds a new censorship' (p. 192). *See also* free association.

centile *n.* Another name for a *percentile.

centipede effect *n.* A term occasionally used to denote *hyper-reflection. It alludes to the following poem, usually attributed to Anonymous but in fact published in 1871 by the US poet Mrs Edmund Craster (died 1874): 'The Centipede was happy quite, / Until a Toad in fun / Said, 'Pray, which leg goes after which?' / And worked her mind to such a pitch, / She lay distracted in a ditch / Considering how to run.' *See also* Humphrey's law.

central alveolar hypoventilation syndrome *n.* A *breathing-related sleep disorder, occurring usually in overweight people, characterized by loss of breathing control and insufficient oxygen intake, resulting in abnormally low blood oxygen level, especially during sleep, and often leading to *hypersomnia or *insomnia. *Compare* sleep apnoea.
[From Latin *alveolus* a small depression, referring to the terminal air cavities in the lungs + Greek *hypo* under + Latin *ventilare* to ventilate, from *ventus* a wind]

central auditory processing disorder *n.* An impairment in the interpretation of sound stimuli in the absence of any peripheral hearing loss, usually caused by a lesion in the *brainstem or *auditory cortex, usually resulting in reading or learning difficulties in children with this disorder. Also called *central deafness* or *cortical deafness*. **CAPD** *abbrev.*

central canal *n.* A narrow duct filled with *cerebrospinal fluid running through the length of the *spinal cord. *See also* lumen (2).

central deafness *n.* Another name for *central auditory processing disorder.

central dogma *n.* In genetics, the principle according to which genetic information is transferred from DNA to the proteins that it encodes, and not from protein to DNA, therefore implying that although genes can influence the form of an organism's body or its behaviour, the form of the organism's body or its behaviour cannot influence its genes. In a stronger formulation of the dogma, information supposedly flows unidirectionally from DNA to RNA and from RNA to proteins, but that version had to be abandoned with the discovery of *retroviruses. *See also* Weismannism.

central dyslexias *n.* A general term for forms of *dyslexia that are thought to depend on cognitive processing operations occurring in the central nervous system after the words have been visually analysed. One major subtype of central dyslexias is *surface dyslexia; another is *deep dyslexia.

central executive *n.* A part of *working memory containing both a short-term memory store and an executive processor that operates on and briefly stores information and plays an important part in language comprehension. It is aided by two *buffer stores, a *phonological loop and a *visuospatial sketchpad.

central fissure *n.* Another name for the *central sulcus.
[From Latin *fissus* split, from *findere* to split]

central grey matter *n.* Another name for the *periaqueductal grey matter. US *central gray matter*.

central limit theorem *n.* In statistics, a theorem showing (roughly) that the sum of any sufficiently large number of unrelated variables tends to be distributed according to the *normal distribution, irrespective of how the individual variables are distributed, except in certain special cases. It explains why psychological and biological variables that are due to the additive effects of numerous independently acting causes are often distributed approximately normally. The earliest version of it was proved in 1818 by the French mathematician Pierre Simon Marquis de Laplace (1749–1827).

central masking *n.* A form of *auditory masking in which the test stimulus is presented to one ear and the masking stimulus to the other, the masking being interpreted as central because it cannot be ascribed to any peripheral process occurring in the ear but must arise centrally at or beyond the point where information from the two ears is combined. Also, an analogous form of *visual masking usually called *dichoptic masking that leads to similar conclusions. *Compare* binaural beat.

central nervous system *n.* The part of the *nervous system that in humans and other vertebrates comprises the *brain and *spinal cord. *Compare* peripheral nervous system. **CNS** *abbrev.*

central nystagmus n. A form of *nystagmus resulting from damage to a *vestibular nerve or one of its nuclei.

central processing unit n. The part of a computer that executes programs. Also called a *central processor*. **CPU** *abbrev.*

central processor n. **1.** Another name for a *central processing unit. **2.** In *cognition, a *hypothetical construct analogous to the *central processing unit of a computer that receives information, allocates resources to subsystems, takes decisions, and controls voluntary behaviour. *See also* filter theory.

central reaction time n. According to an analysis introduced in 1868 by the Dutch ophthalmologist Franciscus Cornelius Donders (1818–89), the fraction of *reaction time that remains after subtracting the time taken up by the passage of a nerve impulse from the *sensory receptor to the brain and for another nerve impulse from the brain to the muscle. *Compare* physiological time. Also called *abbreviated reaction time* or *reduced reaction time*.

central sleep apnoea n. A form of *sleep apnoea, occurring usually in elderly people, in which the episodes of breathing cessation during sleep are not associated with any obstruction to the upper airway or loud snoring but arise from cardiac or neurological disorders. US *central sleep apnea*. *Compare* obstructive sleep apnoea.

central sulcus n. The deep vertical cleft in each of the two cerebral hemispheres separating the *frontal lobe from the *parietal lobe. Also called the *central fissure*, the *fissure of Rolando*, or the *Rolandic fissure*.
[From Latin *sulcus* a furrow]

central tendency n. In descriptive statistics, the middle or typical value of any *probability distribution or set of scores, usually measured by the *arithmetic mean, *median, or *mode.

central trait *See under* trait centrality.

central vision n. Vision that results from stimuli in the centre of the field of vision, the images of which fall on the *macula lutea of the retina. *See also* ambient system, Arago phenomenon. *Compare* peripheral vision.

central vowel n. A *vowel (see the diagram accompanying that entry) produced in the middle of the mouth with the central part of the tongue raised, such as the vowel in *girl* or the initial vowel in *alone*, which is phonetically the same as the vowel in *the* and is called a schwa. *Compare* back vowel, front vowel.

centration n. A term introduced by the Swiss psychologist Jean Piaget (1896–1980) to refer to the tendency of young children to focus attention on only one salient aspect of an object, situation, or problem at a time, to the exclusion of other potentially relevant aspects. A classic example is provided by an experiment first described by Piaget in 1941 in *The Child's Conception of Number* in which a child watches while a number of objects are set out in a row and then moved closer together, and the child is asked whether there are now more objects, fewer objects, or the same number of objects. Most children in the *pre-operational stage of development focus on the relative lengths of the rows without taking into account their relative densities or the fact that nothing has been added or taken away, and conclude that there are fewer objects than before. The process of cognitive development by which a child develops from centration to a more objective way of perceiving the world is called *decentration* or *decentering*. *See also* conservation.

centre-surround receptive field n. A type of *receptive field characteristic of retinal *ganglion cells and *bipolar cells with a central ON area in which stimulation tends to excite neural responses and a surrounding OFF area in which stimulation tends to suppress neural responses by *lateral inhibition, so that the strongest response occurs when only the central region is stimulated; the term also applies to a receptive field with a central OFF area and a surrounding ON area. US *center-surround receptive field*. *See also* blob, double-opponent receptive field, Hermann grid, off-centre cell, on-centre cell, Ouchi illusion.

centring n. Another name for *centration.

centroid method n. In statistics, a technique of *cluster analysis in which the distance between two clusters is defined as the distance between their means.

centromere n. The part of a *chromosome that attaches to a *nuclear spindle during

*mitosis. Like a *telomere, it consists of hundreds of stuttering units of *repetitive DNA.
[From German *Zentromer* a centromere, from Latin *centrum* the middle, from Greek *kentron* a sharp point + *meros* a portion]

cephalic *adj.* Of, relating to, or situated in or near the head.
[From Greek *kephale* a head + -*ikos* of, relating to, or resembling]

cephalic index *n.* A numerical indication of the broadness of a head, obtained by dividing its maximum breadth by its maximum length and then multiplying by 100. The cephalic index of long (*dolichocephalous*) heads is below 76, of medium (*mesocephalous*) heads is between 76 and 80, and of broad (*brachycephalous*) heads is above 80. *Compare* cranial index (which is a measure of narrowness).

cephalocaudal *adj.* From the head to the tail, referring to the development of an embryo, and also later stages of development, in which growth is fastest at the head and progressively slower in parts of the body distant from the head. *Compare* proximodistal.
[From Greek *kephale* a head + *cauda* a tail]

cerea flexibilitas *n.* A wax-like malleability of the body, sometimes manifested in *hypnosis and in people with *catatonia and certain forms of brain damage, notably *cerebellar lesions. People in such a state tend to leave their arms, legs, or bodies in whatever positions they are placed by another person. Also called *catalepsy, flexibilitas cerea. Compare* cogwheel rigidity, clasp-knife rigidity.
[From Latin *cera* wax + *flexus* bent, from *flectere* to bend]

cerebellar peduncle *n.* Any of three paired bundles of nerve fibres connecting the *cerebellum to the midbrain and the medulla oblongata. The superior, middle, and inferior cerebellar peduncles receive afferent inputs from most of the external sense organs (touch, vision, and hearing) and the vestibular system and send efferent outputs to the thalamus and various nuclei in the midbrain and brainstem. *Compare* cerebral peduncle.
[From Latin *pedunculus*, a corruption of *pediculus* a little foot, from *pes, pedis* a foot]

cerebellar syndrome *n.* A pattern of signs and symptoms associated with damage to the *cerebellum, including unsteady body movements, a characteristic cerebellar gait with feet wide apart and difficulty turning, *ataxia, *adiadochokinesia, *dysmetria, *intention tremor, *postural tremor, and mispronunciation of words. Also called *Nonne's syndrome. See also* Gerstmann–Sträussler–Scheinker syndrome, vestibulocerebellum.

cerebellospinal tract *n.* A bundle of motor nerve fibres running from the cerebellum to the spinal cord, concerned with the regulation of muscle tonus and posture. *Compare* spinocerebellar tract.

cerebellum *n.* One of the main structures in the brain, situated at the back of the skull, behind the brainstem and beneath the back of the cerebrum, consisting of two deeply fissured lateral hemispheres separated by a narrow central girdle, the *vermis, connected to the brainstem by three pairs of *cerebellar peduncles. The vermis on the upper surface, containing an inverted *topographic map of the body, is involved in trunk and eye movements; the intermediate zones and hemispheres on either side of the vermis, containing separate topographic maps (not inverted) of each side of the body, regulate limb movements by the same side; and the deep *flocculonodular lobe, separated by a deep fissure from the base of the cerebellum, is concerned chiefly with posture, balance, and *ballistic movements. Unlike the cerebral hemispheres, each hemisphere of the cerebellum is associated with the same side of the body. Lesions in the cerebellum produce deficits of movement and balance but do not affect sensory functions. *See* neocerebellum, spinocerebellum, vestibulocerebellum. *See also* adiadochokinesia, basket cell, catalepsy, cerea flexibilitas, cerebellar syndrome, cerebellospinal tract, climbing fibre, dentate nucleus, dysmetria, folium, gait ataxia, Gerstmann–Sträussler–Scheinker syndrome, glomerulus, Golgi cell, granule cell, medulloblastoma, metencephalon, mossy fibre, parallel fibre, Purkinje cell, spinocerebellar tract, stellate cell. **cerebellar** *adj.*
[From Latin *cerebellum* a little brain, diminutive of *cerebrum* a brain]

cerebral *adj.* Of or relating to the *cerebrum, or more loosely to the brain as a whole.
[From Latin *cerebrum* the brain + -*al*, from -*alis* of or relating to]

cerebral angiogram

cerebral angiogram *n.* An *angiogram of the brain. Also called a *cerebral arteriogram*.
[From Greek *angeion* a (blood) vessel + *gramme* a line]

cerebral angiography *n.* The process of producing *angiograms of brains. Also called *cerebral arteriography*.

cerebral aqueduct *n.* A canal filled with cerebrospinal fluid connecting the third and fourth ventricles of the brain. Also called the *aqueduct of Sylvius* or *Sylvian aqueduct*.
[From Latin *aqua* water + *ducere, ductum* to lead]

cerebral arteriogram *n.* Another name for a *cerebral angiogram.
[From Greek *arteria* an artery + *gramme* a line]

cerebral arteriography *n.* Another name for *cerebral angiography.

cerebral arteriosclerosis *n.* An *organic disorder involving *arteriosclerosis of the brain, the signs and symptoms of which may be neurological (such as *aphasia, *athetosis, *chorea, *dementia, *parkinsonism), or cognitive and affective (such as *amnesia, *delusions, *affective flattening), or both.
[From Latin *cerebrum* the brain + Greek *arteria* an artery + *sklerosis* a hardening, from *skleros* hard + *-osis* indicating a process or state]

cerebral blood flow *n.* The flow of blood to specific parts of the brain to fuel the functions being performed there, generally accepted as an index of *synaptic activity. Studies of *regional cerebral blood flow are used to localize brain functions. **CBF** *abbrev.*

cerebral cortex *n.* The outer layer of *grey matter covering the *cerebrum, largely responsible for sensory, motor, emotional, and integrative functions, divided into two *cerebral hemispheres each subdivided into the *frontal lobe, *parietal lobe, *temporal lobe, and *occipital lobe. It varies in thickness from 2 millimetres to 4 millimetres, covers a surface area of approximately 1.4 square metres (roughly equivalent to 15 square feet, the upper surface area of a large umbrella), mostly hidden within the walls of the *sulci, and it contains approximately 50 billion *neurons and 500 billion *neuroglial cells. *See also* allocortex, angular gyrus, archaeocortex, association area, auditory cortex, Broca's area, Brodmann area, caudate nucleus, cingulate gyrus, fasciculus, Heschl's gyrus, longitudinal fissure, mesocortex, motor cortex, neocortex, nigrostriatal bundle, olfactory cortex, palaeocortex, parahippocampal gyrus, piriform cortex, planum temporale, postcentral gyrus, precentral gyrus, rhinencephalon, somatosensory cortex, striatum, sulcus, superior temporal gyrus, telencephalon, visual cortex, Wernicke's area.
[From Latin *cerebrum* a brain + *cortex* bark]

cerebral dominance *n.* The tendency for one of the *cerebral hemispheres of the brain to dominate certain functions, as when the left hemisphere predominates for language functions, or when it predominates for voluntary motor control in a person who is right-handed, or when the right hemisphere predominates, perhaps in the same person, for spatial and musical functions. *See also* handedness (1), laterality, Wada test.
[From Latin *cerebrum* brain + *dominari* to master]

cerebral gigantism *n.* A congenital disorder characterized by large size and weight at birth, accelerated growth in infancy and childhood, *acromegalic features, and neurological disorder usually accompanied by *moderate mental retardation. Also called *Sotos syndrome*, after the US paediatrician Juan Fernandez Sotos (born 1927) who, with four colleagues, first described it in 1964.

cerebral hemisphere *n.* Either of the two halves of the *cerebrum, separated by the *longitudinal fissure, having slightly different functions in humans. Also called simply a *hemisphere*. *See also* cerebral dominance, laterality.
[From Latin *cerebrum* brain + *hemi-* half + *sphaira* a sphere or globe]

cerebral palsy *n.* A form of congenital *paralysis with muscular discoordination, caused by brain injury during birth, viral infection, or lack of oxygen in the brain before, during, or immediately after birth, often associated with some degree of *mental retardation.
[Corruption of *cerebral paralysis*]

cerebral peduncle *n.* Either of two large bundles of white nerve fibres in front of the brainstem, connected to the sides of the *pons, arising from the cerebral hemispheres and

carrying descending fibres of the *corticospinal tract. *Compare* cerebellar peduncle.
[From Latin *cerebrum* the brain + *pedunculus*, a corruption of *pediculus* a little foot, from *pes, pedis* a foot]

cerebral ventricle *See under* ventricle.

cerebrospinal *adj*. Of or relating to the brain and spinal cord.

cerebrospinal fluid *n*. The clear colourless fluid that fills the *subarachnoid space, thereby immersing the entire *central nervous system, and that circulates through the *ventricles of the brain, within which it is secreted, before flowing passively into the venous bloodstream, the total volume of fluid (about 150 millilitres) being replaced in an adult human being every three or four hours. Also called *neurolymph*. *See also* choroid plexus, ependyma, ependymal cell, hydrocephalus. **CSF** *abbrev*.

cerebrovascular *adj*. Of or relating to the blood vessels of the *cerebrum.
[From *cerebrum* + Latin *vasculum* a little vessel, diminutive of *vas* a vessel]

cerebrovascular accident *n*. Another name for a *stroke. **CVA** *abbrev*.

cerebrum *n*. The largest brain structure, comprising the *diencephalon and the *cerebral hemispheres, the outer layer or *cerebral cortex of which controls most sensory, motor, and cognitive processes in humans.
[Latin *cerebrum* a brain]

certainty effect *n*. The tendency of human judges to overweight outcomes that are certain relative to outcomes that are merely probable. Thus, if given a choice between $1,000 and gamble in which a fair coin is tossed and the prize is $2,010 if the coin falls heads and nothing if it falls tails, most people prefer the certainty of $1,000, although the *expected value of the gamble is $1,005. This phenomenon arises from *risk aversion.

ceruminous deafness *n*. Loss of hearing caused by the build-up of earwax in the *external auditory canal of the outer ear. *See also* conductive deafness.
[From *cerumen* earwax, from Latin *cer(a)* wax + *(alb)umen* egg white, from *albus* white]

cerveau isolé *n*. A surgical preparation in which the brainstem is severed between the diencephalon and the hindbrain, or between the superior colliculi and the inferior colliculi. Because it separates the brain from the *ascending reticular activating system, cats operated on in this way show chronic somnolence, with only *delta wave activity in their *EEGs, their *pupils are constricted, and no eye movements occur. *See also* decerebrate rigidity. *Compare* encéphale isolé.
[From French *cerveau* the cerebrum + *isolé* isolated]

C fibre *n*. A very small unmyelinated type of *afferent nerve fibre with low conduction velocity (1 to 2 metres per second), found especially in the *autonomic nervous system and in receptors for dull pain and temperature. US *C fiber*. *See also* axon reflex. *Compare* alpha fibre, delta fibre, gamma fibre, Ia fibre, Ib fibre, II fibre.

chained reinforcement schedule *n*. A *compound reinforcement schedule in which *reinforcement (1) is delivered after an organism has completed two or more *simple reinforcement schedules in succession, a signal being given to indicate to the organism which schedule is operating at any particular time. Also called a *chained schedule*. *See also* reinforcement schedule. *Compare* tandem reinforcement schedule.

chain ganglia *n*. Another name for a *sympathetic ganglionic chain.

chairwork *n*. Another name for the *empty-chair technique.

chandelier cell *n*. A type of inhibitory neuron found in the cerebral cortex, the axons of which form synapses with numerous pyramidal cells.
[So called because of its appearance]

change of life *n*. A euphemism or non-technical name for the *climacteric or *menopause.

channel of communication *See* communication channel (1, 2).

character *n*. **1**. The aggregate or combination of psychological *traits that distinguish a person from others. **2**. Any genetically determined structure, function, or phenotypic characteristic of an organism. **3.** A symbol, such as a letter of the alphabet, used in a system of writing; or in computer technology, any unit of information in the form of a symbol that can be represented by a unique binary code.

[From Latin *character* a distinguishing mark, from Greek *charakter* an engraver's tool, from *charassein* to cut or engrave]

character convergence *n.* A form of interaction between the evolution of two species in which they come to resemble each other more closely in one or more characters or traits. *Compare* character displacement.

character disorders *n.* Another name for *personality disorders. Also called *character neuroses*, misleadingly in view of the fact that symptoms of personality disorders are not typically *ego-dystonic.

character displacement *n.* A form of interaction between the evolution of two species in which they diverge from each other in one or more characters or traits. *Compare* character convergence.

characteristic features *n.* In *prototype theory, the *features (1) or *attributes of a prototypical instance of a concept or of a prototypical member of a category, shared by many or most but not all instances or members, and providing a basis for assigning meaning to the concept or category. *Compare* defining properties.

characteristic frequency *n.* The frequency of a sound at which the threshold of a single fibre of an auditory nerve is lowest and to which it is therefore most responsive. *See also* tuning curve. **CF** *abbrev.*

character neurosis *n.* In *psychoanalysis, a type of *neurosis in which psychological conflict manifests itself in the form of character traits or patterns of behaviour rather than clearly identifiable *signs (1) or *symptoms. It is exemplified in articles by Sigmund Freud (1856–1939) in 1908 on 'Character and Anal Erotism' (*Standard Edition*, IX, pp. 169–75), in 1916 on 'Some Character Types Met With in Psycho-Analytic Work' (*Standard Edition*, XIV, pp. 311–33), and in 1931 on 'Libidinal Types' (*Standard Edition*, XXI, pp. 215–20). It was used

extensively in the theories of the Austrian-born (later US-based) psychiatrist Wilhelm Reich (1897–1957), especially in his book *Charakteranalyse* (Character Analysis) published in 1933.

Charlie *n.* A street name for *cocaine.

Charpentier bands *n.* Illusory black spokes that are seen when a black disc with a white sector is rotated slowly.

[Named after the French physician (Pierre Marie) Augustin Charpentier (1852–1916) who discussed them]

Charpentier's illusion *n.* Another name for the *size–weight illusion.

[Named after the French physician (Pierre Marie) Augustin Charpentier (1852–1916) who published an article on it in 1891, although the German psychologists Georg Elias Müller (1850–1934) and Friedrich Schumann (1863–1940) had already discovered and reported the illusion in 1889]

cheating husbands problem *See* muddy children problem.

cheese effect *n.* An acute attack of hypertension that can occur in a person taking a *monoamine oxidase inhibitor (MAOI) drug who eats cheese, caused by an interaction of the MAOI with *tyramine, formed in ripe cheese when bacteria provide an enzyme that reacts with the amino acid *tyrosine in the cheese. Other foods and drinks that produce the same effect include pickled herring, yeast extract, and certain red wines. Also called the *cheese reaction*.

chemically gated ion channel *n.* An *ion channel, the permeability of which is regulated by a *neurotransmitter; different neurotransmitters sometimes opening and closing different ion channels in the cell membrane. *Compare* voltage-gated ion channel.

chemical sense *n.* A sensory system that responds to chemical stimuli, especially the sense of *taste or *smell mediated by *chemoreceptors. *See also* common chemical sense, redintegration.

chemoaffinity hypothesis *n.* The proposition that molecules of specific chemical substances guide neurons in the formation of

appropriate *synapses (1) during development and regeneration.
[From chem(ical) + affinity]

chemoreceptor n. A *sensory receptor in a biological cell membrane specialized to allow the binding of molecules from external chemical stimuli, leading to the generation of sensations of *taste or *smell. Also called a chemoceptor.

chemorepellant n. Any chemical substance that causes organisms to move away from it or to avoid it.

chemotaxis n. Responses of a micro-organism or a cell to a chemical stimulus by moving towards or away from it. **chemotactic** adj.
[From Greek taxis order]

cherology n. A term coined in the 1960s, by analogy with *phonology, to denote the study of *sign language. See also American Sign Language, British Sign Language.
[From chereme a basic contrastive unit in a sign language + Greek logos word, discourse, or reason]

Cheshire Cat effect n. A form of *binocular rivalry in which a moving object seen by one eye renders invisible a stationary object in the same region of the visual field seen by the other eye. The effect can be demonstrated vividly by dividing the visual field with a mirror held edge-on in front of the nose at a slight angle, so that one eye looks straight at a stationary object, such as a sleeping cat, while the other sees a reflection of stationary objects in another part of the environment. If a hand is then waved about on the mirror side, in the region of the visual field where the cat is seen with the other eye, then part or the whole of the cat disappears.
[Named after an episode at the end of Chapter 6 of Alice's Adventures in Wonderland by Lewis Carroll, the pen name of Charles Lutwidge Dodgson (1832–98), in which the Cheshire Cat 'vanished quite slowly, beginning with the end of the tail, and ending with the grin, which remained some time after the rest of it had gone']

chiaroscuro n. The disposition of areas of light and shade in an image; specifically one of the monocular cues of visual *depth perception, patterns of shadow and highlight providing information about depth (see illustration). The human visual system usually interprets such information on the unconscious assumption that the light source is above. Also called shading. See also anaglyptoscope.
[From Italian chiaro clear + oscuro obscure or dark]

Chiaroscuro. The shapes on the left appear convex and those on the right concave, because the visual system assumes by default that the light source is above. If the page is turned upside down, the appearance of depth reverses.

chiasm n. A crossing over or *decussation of two structures, as in the fibres of the nerves in the *optic chiasm, which in humans and other animals with forward-pointing eyes and therefore overlapping visual fields are only partly crossed or decussated. Also called a chiasma. **chiasms, chiasmata, or chiasmas** pl. **chiasmic or chiasmal** adj.
[From Greek chiasma a cross, named after the shape of the upper-case letter chi (X)]

chiasmus n. A *figure of speech in which the main elements are repeated in a reversed order to create a symmetrically balanced structure, as in Ask not what your country can do for you; ask what you can do for your country (The inaugural address of John F. Kennedy, 1917–63, 35th US president, 15 July 1960).
[From Greek chiasmos a crisscross arrangement, from chiasma a cross, named after the shape of the upper-case letter chi (X)]

Chicken game n. A two-person strategic *game (1), generally considered to be the prototype of a dangerous game. In its canonical interpretation, two motorists speed towards each other. Each has the option of swerving to avoid a head-on collision or driving straight ahead. If both swerve, the outcome is a draw with second-best payoffs to each; if both drive straight ahead, they risk annihilation and each receives the worst (fourth-best) payoff; but if one chickens out by swerving while the other exploits the co-player's caution by driving straight on, then the swerver loses face and earns the third-best payoff, and the 'exploiter' wins a prestige victory and earns the best payoff. The game provides a strategic model of brinkmanship. Written accounts of Chicken can be traced at least as far as far back as the 8th century BC when the Greek epic poet Homer described in *The Iliad* (p. 273 of Rouse's translation) a version played with chariots that Antilochos won against Menelaos, but the game was first analysed and studied empirically in the early 1960s. *See also* Hawk–Dove game.

[Named and first described in its canonical interpretation in 1959 by the Welsh philosopher Bertrand (Arthur William) Russell (1872–1970) in *Common Sense and Nuclear Warfare* (p. 30), from a slang sense of *chicken*, a cowardly person, which became popular after the release in 1955 of Nicholas Ray's film *Rebel Without a Cause* starring James Dean, in which teenagers played a slightly different version of the game involving driving cars over a cliff and jumping out at the last moment]

child abuse *n.* Any form of physical, mental, or sexual exploitation of or cruelty towards a child by a parent or other adult, causing significant harm to its victim. *See also* battered baby syndrome, battered child syndrome, factitious disorder by proxy, sexual abuse.

child-directed speech *n.* Another name for *caretaker speech.

childhood amnesia *n.* Another name for *infantile amnesia.

childhood autism *n.* An alternative name for *autistic disorder manifested during childhood. *Compare* infantile autism.

childhood disintegrative disorder *n.* A *pervasive developmental disorder characterized by at least two years of apparently normal development followed by significant loss of language abilities, social skills, bowel or bladder control, motor skills, or play, together with impairment in social interaction and communication, or restricted, repetitive, or stereotyped mannerisms, interests, or activities. Also called *dementia infantalis*, *disintegrative disorder*, or *Heller's syndrome*, after the Austrian neuropsychiatrist Theodor O. Heller (1869–

1938) who first described it in 1908. *Compare* autistic disorder.

Children's Apperception Test *n.* A version of the *TAT designed specifically for children, consisting of 10 pictures in which animals take the place of human beings in the pictures on the assumption that children are likely to empathize more easily with animal figures. The test was constructed by the Austrian-born US psychiatrist Leopold Bellak (1916–2000) and Sonia Bellak and published in 1949; Leopold Bellak described it in his book *The Thematic Apperception Test and the Children's Apperception Test in Clinical Use* (1954). *Compare* Blacky pictures. **CAT** *abbrev.*

chimera *n.* **1.** An organism composed of two or more genetically distinct tissue types or created by combining genes from two or more different individuals or species. Also called a *mosaic*. Also spelt *chimaera*. **2.** In Greek mythology, a fire-breathing monster with a lion's head, a goat's body, a serpent's tail. **chimeric** or **chimaeric** *adj.*
[From Greek *chimaira* a she-goat]

chimeric face *n.* A facial portrait made by combining the left and right halves of the faces of two different people, used to study the functions of the cerebral hemispheres, especially in *split-brain preparations, because *fixation (1) on the midpoint leads to each half of the image being represented in the opposite cerebral hemisphere.

China white *n.* A street name for the drug *fentanyl.

Chinese room *n.* A *Gedankenexperiment first proposed by the US philosopher John Searle (born 1932) in the journal *Behavioral and Brain Sciences* in 1980 as a refutation of the *strong AI proposition that a computer capable of passing the *Turing test by responding to inputs in a manner indistinguishable from a human being would necessarily have a mind and be capable of thought. Searle's Chinese room contains a person who understands no Chinese but has detailed and comprehensive instructions for the mechanical processing (without translation) of Chinese symbols to generate meaningful responses to written messages. Anyone who delivers a message in Chinese to the room receives a reply in Chinese and has no way of knowing that the person in the room does not understand a word (or a *logograph) of Chinese. Searle argued that an *artificial intelligence machine or program is analogous to the Chinese room, and that passing the Turing test would not prove that it had a mind or that it could think, because a computational simulation of a phenomenon is very different from the phenomenon itself. If valid, the argument undermines *weak AI as well as strong AI. Compare Gödel's theorem.

chi-square distribution n. In statistics, a *probability distribution used to obtain an approximate measure of the discrepancy between sets of observed and expected scores and to perform a *chi-square test. If a set of values distributed according to the *normal distribution are squared and then summed, the resulting scores are distributed according to the chi-square distribution. Symbol: χ^2.
[Named after the square of chi the 22nd letter of the Greek alphabet]

chi-square test n. In statistics, a test based on the *chi-square distribution to test for a possible association between two variables measured on *nominal scales (called the chi-square test of association) or to determine the *goodness of fit (1) of observed frequencies to a theoretical *frequency distribution (called the chi-square goodness of fit test), the same formula being used for both types of test. In both cases, researchers most commonly use the Pearson chi-square test, the formula for calculating the test statistic being $\chi^2 = \Sigma(O - E)^2/E$, where O represents an observed frequency, E an expected frequency under the *null hypothesis, and the summation is over all pairs of observed and expected frequencies. The main alternative is the *likelihood ratio chi-square test. See also non-parametric statistics. Compare log-linear analysis. Symbol: χ^2.

chloral hydrate n. A colourless crystalline compound that acts as a central nervous system *depressant and is used as a sedative–hypnotic drug. Also called Noctec (trademark). [So called because it is produced by mixing the aldehyde chloral with water]

chlordiazepoxide n. A member of the *benzodiazepine group of drugs, used as an anxiolytic, sedative, and muscle relaxant, and in the treatment of *alcohol-related disorders. In its hydrochloride form it is usually called

Librium (trademark). See also sedative-, hypnotic-, or anxiolytic-related disorders. **CDP** abbrev.
[From chlor- denoting chlorine + di- two, from Greek dis twice + az- denoting nitrogen, from Greek a- not + zaein to live + ep(oxide) a compound containing oxygen joined to other atoms, from Greek epi on or above + oxide a compound of oxygen and another element, from French oxy(gène) + (ac)ide]

chloride n. Any of the salts of hydrochloric acid or any compound containing a chlorine atom.

chloroacetophenone See CN gas.

chlorpromazine n. Chlorpromazine hydrochloride, a *neuroleptic (1) drug that stabilizes the autonomic nervous system during stress by blocking *dopamine neuroreceptors and is effective in reducing psychotic symptoms, originally developed in 1950 as the first of the *phenothiazines. Also called Largactil or Thorazine (trademark). See also dopamine antagonist.
[From chlor- denoting chlorine + pro(pyl) containing the monovalent group C_3H_7 + (a)m(ine) + azine denoting an organic compound with a six-member ring and at least one nitrogen atom]

choice of neurosis n. In *psychoanalysis, the combination of processes that determine which particular *neurosis a patient develops. The notion that a patient in some sense chooses a neurosis was first mentioned by Sigmund Freud (1856–1939) in a letter to his friend, the German physician Wilhelm Fliess (1858–1928) in 1896 (Standard Edition, I, pp. 220–1) and was developed fully in 1913 in an article on 'The Disposition to Obsessional Neurosis' (Standard Edition, XII, pp. 317–26). See also compromise formation, return of the repressed, symptom formation.

choice reaction time n. *Reaction time in a situation in which there are two or more possible stimuli requiring different responses. The usual measure involves a home button surrounded by eight other buttons, arranged in a semicircle around it, each accompanied by a small light. The person being tested places a finger or a stylus on the home button and then attempts to move it as quickly as possible to press whichever of the other buttons is lit up on each trial. It is negatively correlated with psychometric measures of intelligence. Also called *complex reaction time* or *compound reaction time*. *See also* Hick's law, processing speed. *Compare* discrimination reaction time, simple reaction time. **CRT** *abbrev.*

choice shift *n.* Another name for the *risky shift phenomenon or, more generally the *group polarization phenomenon.

cholecystokinin *n.* A hormone secreted in the *duodenum that causes the *gall bladder to contract and that stimulates the secretion of enzymes by the *pancreas, also present in the central nervous system, where it acts as a *neurotransmitter, amplifying the effects of *dopamine in the brain. *See also* kinin. **CCK** *abbrev.*
[From Greek *chole* bile + *kystis* a bladder + English *kinin*]

cholesterol *n.* A *sterol present in all animal tissues, blood, bile, and fat, involved in the transport of lipids in the bloodstream and in the formation of *steroid hormones. High levels of cholesterol in the blood may sometimes cause *atherosclerosis, leading to coronary heart disease, and may be implicated in neurological impairments such as *vascular dementia (multi-infarct dementia).
[From Greek *chole* bile + *stereos* solid]

choline *n.* An alcohol present in *bile, synthesized from *lecithin, and a precursor in the synthesis of *acetylcholine in the body. *See also* muscarine.
[From Greek *chole* bile + *-ine* indicating an organic compound]

cholinergic *adj.* Releasing *acetylcholine; also activated by or responding to acetylcholine, this extended usage being widespread but consistently rejected by the English physiologist Sir Henry Hallet Dale (1875–1968), who coined the suffix *-ergic*, and by many other authorities. The term applies especially to nerve fibres such as those in the *parasympathetic nervous system or in the *nucleus basalis of Meynert that use acetylcholine as their *neurotransmitter, or any drug that stimulates the activity of the parasympathetic nervous system, causing such effects as constriction of the pupils of the eyes and preparation for close-up vision, sali-vation, slowing of the heart, secretion of gastric juices, and voiding of urine. *See also* muscarinic receptor, nicotinic receptor. *Compare* adrenergic, anticholinergic, dopaminergic, GABAergic, noradrenergic, serotonergic.
[From *(acetyl)cholin(e)* + Greek *ergon* work + *-ikos* of, relating to, or resembling]

cholinesterase *n.* Another name for *acetyl-cholinesterase.
[From *choline* + *ester* + Greek *-ase* denoting an enzyme, from *diastasis* separation]

cholinoceptor *n.* A *neuroreceptor for *acetylcholine. *See also* muscarinic receptor, nicotinic receptor.

cholinomimetic *adj. n.* (Of or relating to) any substance, such as *carbachol or *metha-choline, that mimics the action of *acetyl-choline in the nervous system. *See also* muscarine, nicotine.
[From *(acetyl)choline* + Greek *mimesis* imitation, from *mimeisthai* to imitate]

Chomskyan *adj.* Of, relating to, or resembling the theory of language of the US linguist and philosopher (Avram) Noam Chomsky (born 1928). *See* anomalous sentence, competence (2), deep structure, generative grammar, language acquisition device, performance (2), surface structure, transformational grammar, universal grammar.

chorda tympani *n.* One of the branches of the *facial nerve, running through the cavity of the middle ear, supplying efferent impulses to two of the salivary glands and receiving afferent impulses from the anterior (front) two-thirds of the tongue, responsible for all of the sweet and some of the sour and salty taste sensations. In spite of its name, it is not involved in hearing.
[From Latin *chorda* a string + *tympanum* a drum, so called because it crosses the eardrum in the middle ear]

chorea *n.* Involuntary, rapid, jerky, non-repetitive, purposeless movements, such as flexing and extending the fingers, raising and lowering the shoulders, or grimacing, characteristic especially of *Huntington's disease.
[From Greek *choreia* a dance]

chorea minor *n.* Another name for *Sydenham's chorea.

choreiform *adj*. Resembling the rapid, jerky movements of *chorea.

chorionic gonadotrophin *n*. A *gonadotrophin secreted by the placenta in humans and other mammals, stimulating the release of *progesterone by the *corpus luteum. A measure of its presence in the urine is used as a pregnancy test. Also spelt *chorionic gonadotropin*.
[From Greek *chorion* an afterbirth]

choroid *n*. The vascular *membrane between the outer *sclera and the *retina of the eye.
[From Greek *chorion* the membrane surrounding an embryo or foetus]

choroid plexus *n*. A collection of small, reddish tufts of vascular membrane that project into the cerebral *ventricles, secrete *cerebrospinal fluid, and act like a 'kidney' for the brain, maintaining the chemical stability of the fluid as the kidneys do the blood. *See also* ependyma, ependymal cell, plexus.
[From Greek *chorioeides* resembling a placenta, from *chorion* an afterbirth]

chroma *n*. The quality or hue of a colour irrespective of the *achromatic (1) black/grey/white colour present. *See also* Munsell colour system, saturation (1).
[From Greek *chroma* colour]

chromaesthesia *n*. A form of *synaesthesia (1) in which stimuli not normally associated with colour, such as musical tones or numbers, elicit sensations of colour. When the stimuli are auditory it is also called *chromatic audition, colour audition, coloured audition, colour hearing*, or *coloured hearing*. US *chromesthesia*.
[From Greek *chroma* colour + *aisthesis* feeling + -*ia* indicating a condition or quality]

chromaffin cell *n*. A type of cell that is abundantly present in the *adrenal medulla and that synthesizes *adrenalin (epinephrine) from tyrosine in the presence of the cofactor vitamin C, stores it in vesicles, and secretes it into the bloodstream together with various other proteins and peptides in response to fear, anxiety, or stress. About ten per cent of chromaffin cells synthesize and secrete the closely related substance *noradrenalin (norepinephrine).
[From *chromium* + Latin *affinis* related to, alluding to the propensity of adrenalin to stain brown when exposed to chromium salts]

chromatic *adj*. **1.** Of, relating to, or having colour. A *chromatic colour* is a colour having *chroma, in contradistinction to an *achromatic colour without chroma. **2.** Pertaining to musical tones that are sharpened or flattened without changing the key of the passage, or the musical scale containing all twelve *semitones of the octave, also called the *chromatic scale*. *Compare* diatonic.
[From Greek *chromatikos* of or relating to colour, from *chroma, -atos* colour + -*ikos* of, relating to, or resembling]

chromatic aberration *See under* aberration (3).

chromatic adaptation *n*. **1.** A form of *adaptation (2) resulting from continuous exposure to light of a particular colour or hue and consequent bleaching of the associated *visual pigment, causing a gradual loss of *saturation (1) of the perceived colour and the appearance of its *complementary colour if a white surface is viewed. *See also* xanthopsia. **2.** More generally, an alteration of the balance of pigments in a biological membrane in response to the colour and intensity of the ambient light. Also called *colour adaptation*.

chromatic audition *n*. Another name for *colour hearing.

chromaticity *n*. The quality of colour or light in terms of the purity of its dominant wavelength, involving both *hue and *saturation (1). The *chromaticity coordinates* of a colour are the three *tristimulus values, symbolized by x, y, and z, representing the proportions of the three *additive primaries that when mixed match the given colour. Also called *chromaticness*. *See also* primary colour (1, 2, 3).

chromaticness *n*. Another name for *chromaticity.

chromatic system *n*. In the *opponent-process theory of colour vision, the pathway that carries information about an object's *hue. *Compare* achromatic system.

chromatic threshold *n*. The minimal stimulus, depending on the wavelength of the light, that induces a sensation of colour or hue.

chromatic vision n. Normal vision in which colours are perceived and distinguished, in contradistinction to *colour-blindness.

chromatid n. Either of the two threadlike strands formed when a *chromosome divides longitudinally during *mitosis.
[From *chromatin*]

chromatin n. The part of a cell nucleus that contains *DNA, *RNA, and *proteins and is readily stained with *basic (1) dyes.
[From Greek *chroma, chromatos* colour]

chromatopsia n. A form of partial blindness characterized by loss or serious impairment of all aspects of vision except colour perception, resulting in a form of misidentification exemplified by guessing that a blue vehicle in a television picture is sky in spite of its different form, relative size, and movement. The condition is occasionally found in people who suffer the effects of smoke inhalation during fires, resulting in carbon monoxide poisoning and oxygen deprivation, causing widespread damage to most areas of the *visual cortex apart from *blobs in Area V1 and the associated thin stripes in Area V2, both of which mediate colour perception and are more richly supplied with blood vessels than other areas of the visual cortex and therefore more likely to survive such conditions. *Compare* achromatopsia. **chromatopsic** *adj.*
[From Greek *chroma, chromatos* colour + *opsis* sight, from *ops* an eye + -*ia* indicating a condition or quality]

chromesthesia *See* chromaesthesia.

chromophore n. The group of atoms in a chemical compound that are responsible for its colour, including the atoms in the *visual pigments of the eye's photoreceptors.
[From Greek *chroma* colour + *phoros* bearing, from *pherein* to bear]

chromosomal aberration n. Any visible or gross abnormality in the number or structure of a set of *chromosomes. *See* Klinefelter's syndrome, trisomy, Turner's syndrome, XXX syndrome, XYY syndrome. *Compare* Williams syndrome.

chromosome n. A microscopic rod-shaped structure in the nucleus of every *cell, containing *DNA that encodes the *genes and determines hereditary characteristics. There are 46 chromosomes in every human *somatic cell, 22 pairs of *autosomes and one pair of *sex chromosomes, whereas each of the sex cells or *gametes carries only 23 chromosomes—one member of every pair. **chromosomal** *adj.*
[From Greek *chroma* colour + *soma* a body, so called because they stain deeply with basic dyes]

chromosome 21 n. The name of the *chromosome implicated in a genetic defect leading to the *amyloid plaques in the brains of people with *Alzheimer's disease. It is also responsible for *Down's syndrome, which develops when it is present in three rather than two copies (*see* trisomy), and it may play a part in other disorders.

chronic *adj.* Lasting a long time; of or relating to a disorder or a symptom that develops slowly and either persists or recurs frequently. *Compare* acute.
[From Greek *chronikos* of or relating to time, from *chronos* time + -*ikos* of, relating to, or resembling]

chronic fatigue syndrome n. A controversial disorder, first described and named in the *Annals of Internal Medicine* in 1988 and redefined in an influential article in the same journal in 1994, characterized by persistent or recurrent *fatigue (1) experienced for at least six months, not resulting from unusual exertion or any apparent medical cause and not significantly relieved by rest, resulting in a marked decline in occupational, educational, social, and personal activities. Four or more of the following symptoms must then also occur persistently or recurrently for at least six months after (and not before) the onset of the disorder: severe impairment of short-term memory or concentration, sore throat, tender lymph nodes, muscle pain, multiple joint pain without swelling or redness, unfamiliar types of headaches, unrefreshing sleep, and discomfort lasting more than 24 hours following physical exertion. Some authorities believe that it often follows and is perhaps caused by a viral infection. Also called *myalgic encephalomyelitis* (ME) or *postviral syndrome*. **CFS** *abbrev.*

chronic motor or vocal tic disorder n. A *tic disorder characterized by the presence of either motor tics or vocal tics, but not both, and apart from that sharing the features of *Tourette's disorder.

chronic pain n. Prolonged or lasting *pain, defined in the *Classification of Nursing Diagnoses* (1994) of the North American Nursing Diagnosis Association as a condition in which an individual experiences pain that continues for more than six months. *Compare* acute pain.

chronobiology n. The branch of biology concerned with *biological rhythms. *See* biological clock, biological rhythm. *See also* alpha wave, basic rest–activity cycle, beta wave, circadian rhythm, circannual rhythm, delta wave, gamma wave, infradian rhythm, menstrual cycle, sensorimotor rhythm, sleep–wake cycle, suprachiasmatic nucleus, telomere, theta wave, ultradian rhythm, *Zeitgeber*.
[From Greek *chronos* time + English *biology*]

chronological age n. A person's actual age, in terms of time elapsed since birth, in contrast to *mental age. *See also* developmental quotient, IQ. *Compare* social age. **CA** *abbrev.*
[From Greek *chronos* time + *logos* word, discourse, or reason + Latin *-icalis* of, relating to, or resembling]

chunking n. The grouping together of a number of items of information so that they are processed cognitively as a single entity called a *chunk*, as when the letters *c, h, u, n, k, i, n,* and *g* are perceived, interpreted, and easily remembered as a single word, whereas without the key the same letters presented alphabetically as *c, g, h, i, k, n, n, u* would be difficult to memorize for more than a few seconds. The limitation of *short-term memory to about seven items of information can be overcome by chunking because, as first pointed out in 1956 by the US psychologist George A(rmitage) Miller (born 1920), the limitation applies to chunks. In 1974 the US economist and decision theorist Herbert A(lexander) Simon (1916–2001) suggested that the capacity of short-term memory is about five chunks, but that as the number of elements per chunk increases, the number of chunks that can be remembered decreases slightly. Simon found that he could not recall the following nine words after one

quick reading: *Lincoln, milky, criminal, differential, address, way, lawyer, calculus, Gettysburg;* but when they were arranged into the following four chunks, he could remember them easily: *Lincoln's Gettysburg address, milky way, criminal lawyer, differential calculus. See also* magical number seven, span of apprehension, subitize.

CIE colour system n. An internationally accepted system put forward in 1931 by the Commission Internationale de l'Éclairage (the French International Lighting Commission) for specifying any spectral colour precisely in terms of the proportions (*tristimulus values) of three *additive primary colours *x, y,* and *z* required by a standard observer to match it. Also called the *XYZ system.* The *CIE colour diagram* (see illustration) shows the colour that results from mixing any pair of spectral colours with each other or with purple or white.

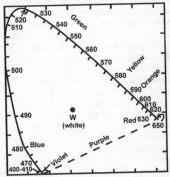

CIE colour diagram. The spectral locus (curve) is shown, together with purple and white. To predict the appearance of a mixture of two colours, draw a straight line connecting them and locate the point on the line corresponding to the proportion of each. Thus an equal mixture of green at 550 nm with red at 630 nm is equidistant between these two points, matching yellow at 580 nm; and an equal mixture of blue-green at 505 nm with yellow-green at 550 nm yields a point in the interior matching a mixture of three parts green at 520 nm with one part white.

cilia n. pl. The hairlike structures projecting from the surface of a cell or membrane, the rhythmic beating of which causes the surrounding liquid to move or, in certain organisms, including protozoans such as

*paramecia and flatworms, causes the organism itself to move. *See also* kinocilium, microtubule, stereocilium. **cilium** *sing.*
[From Latin *cilium* an eyelash]

ciliaris *n.* Another name for the *ciliary muscle.

ciliary body *n.* The thickened vascular tunic of the eye between the *choroid and the *iris, including the *ciliary muscle.
[From Latin *cilium* an eyelash]

ciliary muscle *n.* The circular ring of smooth muscle fibres that is attached to the *choroid and *crystalline lens of the eye and that reduces the convexity of the lens when it contracts. Also called the *ciliaris*. *See also* cycloplegia.

ciliary reflex *n.* A reflex relaxation of the *ciliary muscles of the eyes in response to an object appearing suddenly in front of the face. It causes the convexity of the lenses to increase, preparing the eyes for *near vision, and it is part of the *accommodation reflex.

ciliary zonule *n.* Another name for the *zonule of Zinn.

cingulate gyrus *n.* A gyrus within the *longitudinal fissure above and almost surrounding the *corpus callosum. It is part of the *limbic system and is involved in *pain sensations, control of visceral responses associated with emotions, and the planning of motor actions.
[From Latin *cingere* to gird + Greek *gyros* a circle or ring, alluding to the way it partly encircles the corpus callosum]

cingulum *n.* The *white matter within the *cingulate gyrus.

circadian rhythm *n.* Any *biological rhythm or cycle, such as the *sleep–wake cycle in humans, that occurs or fluctuates at intervals of approximately 25 hours in controlled environments from which day/night cues have been eliminated. Also called a *diurnal rhythm*. *See also* biological clock, chronobiology, circadian rhythm sleep disorder, pineal gland, suprachiasmatic nucleus, *Zeitgeber*. *Compare* circannual rhythm, infradian rhythm, ultradian rhythm.
[From Latin *circa* about + *dies* a day]

circadian rhythm sleep disorder *n.* One of the *dyssomnias, characterized by persistent or recurrent disruption of sleep, resulting in *hypersomnia or *insomnia, caused by a mismatch between the exogenous environmental sleep–wake schedule and the person's endogenous *circadian rhythm. The disorder may arise from a persistent pattern of late sleeping, *jet lag, or shift working. Also called *desynchronized sleep rhythm*. *Compare* delayed sleep-phase syndrome.

circannual rhythm *n.* Any *biological rhythm involving a biological or psychological process that occurs or fluctuates at intervals of approximately one year, even in controlled environments from which seasonal cues have been eliminated, such as the seasonal changes in behaviour of some migratory birds, which persist even under constant laboratory conditions from which fluctuations in temperature, daylight, and other seasonal cues have been excluded. *See also* biological clock, chronobiology, *Zeitgeber*. *Compare* circadian rhythm, infradian rhythm, ultradian rhythm.
[From Latin *circa* about + *annus* a year]

circaseptan rhythm *n.* Any *biological rhythm with a period of approximately seven days.
[From Latin *circa* about + *septem* seven]

circling dance *n.* Another name for the honey-bee's *round dance.

circular pitch illusion *n.* Another name for the *auditory staircase illusion.

circumstantiality *n.* A speech style that is logical and does not involve *loosening of associations but is difficult to follow because it dwells on irrelevant details and takes an inordinate length of time coming to the point. *Compare* Ganser syndrome, tangentiality.
[So called because it is circumstantial in the sense of being filled with minute details]

circumvallate papilla *n.* Any of the dozen or so large *papillae arranged in an inverted V formation near the back of the *tongue, each surrounded by a ridge on its upper margin and studded near its base with *taste buds, mainly responsive to bitter tastes. *Compare* filiform papilla, foliate papilla, fungiform papilla. **circumvallate papillae** *pl.*

[From Latin *circumvallatus* surrounded with a wall, from *circumvallare* to surround with a wall, from *circum* around + *vallum* a rampart]

circumventricular organ *n.* Any of a small number of brain structures, most importantly the *subfornical organ, *posterior pituitary, and *pineal gland, that lie adjacent to the ventricular system of the brain and outside the *blood–brain barrier and are therefore able to monitor substances in the bloodstream that are inaccessible in other areas of the brain.

Cirpam(il) *n.* A proprietary name for the antidepressant drug *citalopram.
[Trademark]

cisterna *n.* A hollow space containing a bodily fluid such as *cerebrospinal fluid or *lymph, especially several *subarachnoid pockets or pools of cerebrospinal fluid at the base of the brain, the most prominent of which are the *cisterna magna* between the *cerebellum and the bottom of the *medulla oblongata, the *superior cisterna* above the *midbrain, and the *lumbar cisterna* in the lower spinal area. Also called a *cistern*.
[From Latin *cisterna* an underground tank, from *cista* a box]

cis–trans complementation test *n.* A test to determine the unit of genetic function and to provide a criterion for defining a *cistron by examining whether two independent recessive mutations giving the same abnormal *phenotype are located on the same or different genes. A cross is made between *homozygotes of each mutation, and the *heterozygous offspring are examined. If the mutations are in different genes, then neither mutation will be expressed in the heterozygous offspring because of *complementation (each mutant *allele being compensated for by the normal allele received from the other parent), whether the mutations are on the same chromosome (in *cis* position) or on different chromosomes (in *trans* position); but if the mutations are in the same gene, then the mutation will be expressed in the offspring, but only if the mutations lie in *trans* position, because in that case both alleles at the specified locus will be mutants. Also called the *cis–trans test* or *complementation test*.
[From Latin *cis* in this side + *trans* across, over, or beyond]

cistron *n.* A sequence of DNA constituting a single functional gene or coding for a single *polypeptide; defined more rigorously by the *cis–trans complementation test, two recessive mutations within a single cistron failing to complement each other in a *heterozygous phenotype when on different chromosomes but showing complementation when on the same chromosome. *See also* operon.
[From *cis–trans*, on the model of *codon*]

citalopram *n.* An *antidepressant drug belonging to the group of *selective serotonin reuptake inhibitor (SSRI) agents. Also called *Cipram*, *Cipramil*, *Elopram*, or *Seropram* (trademarks).

citation form *n.* The pronunciation of a word in isolation, often quite different from the way it is pronounced in any linguistic context.

citric acid cycle *n.* Another name for the *Krebs cycle.
[So called because citric acid is formed during the process]

clairaudience *n.* A conjectural *paranormal ability to sense sounds that are beyond the range of normal hearing. *See also* extra-sensory perception (ESP). *Compare* clairvoyance.
[From French *clair* clear, from Latin *clarus* clear + *audientia* hearing, from *audire* to hear]

clairvoyance *n.* *Extra-sensory visual perception of objects or events, a conjectural *paranormal phenomenon. When the objects or events are far away it is also called *remote viewing*. *Compare* clairaudience, precognition, telaesthesia, telegnosis, telepathy. **clairvoyant** *adj.*
[From French *clair* clear, from Latin *clarus* clear + French *voir* to see, from Latin *videre* to see]

clamon *n.* Any secret behavioural strategy or device for the entrapment of wrongdoers or miscreants, such as the use of an ultraviolet security marker to label personal property with an inscription that is invisible under ordinary light, or the insertion of a *digital signature into text to deter plagiarism.
[From *cla(ndestine) mon(ition)*, a furtive or concealed warning, from Latin *clandestinus* concealed or hidden, from *clam* secretly + *monere*, *monitum* to warn or advise]

clang association n. An association made between words or phrases based on their similar sound rather than their associated meaning, as between *claustrophobia* and *close to February*.
clanging n. Speaking or thinking according to *clang associations rather than meaningful associations.

clasp-knife rigidity n. A form of muscular spasm or exaggerated muscle *tonus in a limb or body part that resists passive movement and then suddenly gives way, in the manner of a jackknife. It is indicative of a lesion in the *corticospinal tract. *See also* decerebrate rigidity. *Compare* catalepsy, cerea flexibilitas, cogwheel rigidity.

class n. **1.** Members of a society sharing a similar social rank and certain economic and cultural characteristics in common, also called a *social class* or a *socio-economic class*; in Marxist theory, members of a society sharing a common relationship to the means of production, the three major classes being capitalists, landlords, and workers or proletarians. **2.** In biology, any *taxonomic group into which a *phylum is divided, containing one or more *orders (3). Examples are the classes of Amphibia, Mammalia, and Reptilia within the phylum Chordata.
[From Latin *classis* a class or rank]

classical conditioning n. One of the two major forms of *conditioning (1), being the process of *learning (1) through which an initially neutral *stimulus (1), such as the ticking of a metronome, comes to elicit a particular *response, such as salivation, as a consequence of being paired repeatedly with an *unconditioned stimulus, such as food. Also called *Pavlovian conditioning*. *See also* backward conditioning, delayed conditioning, feature negative learning, feature positive learning, forward conditioning, higher-order conditioning, latent inhibition. *Compare* operant conditioning.

classical receptive field *See under* receptive field.

classical test theory n. A statistical approach to the theory of psychological testing in which an individual's measured score is assumed to be equal to the true score plus random measurement error. The measurement error is usually assumed to have a *mean of zero and to be uncorrelated with the true score. Within this theoretical framework, the *reliability of a test item is defined as the proportion of the total *variance in scores that is due to variance in the true scores. Also called *classical measurement theory*. The principal alternative is *item response theory.

claustrum n. Either of two thin sheets of grey matter, composed chiefly of spindle cells, separating the internal capsule from the insula, situated on either side of the *lenticular nucleus at the base of the brain.
[From Latin *claustrum* a bar]

Clérambault's syndrome n. A name sometimes applied to *erotomanic delusional disorder, especially in women.
[Named after the French psychiatrist Gaétan G. de Clérambault (1872–1934), who studied it]

Clever Hans n. The most famous of the *Elberfeld horses, trained by von Osten in 1901 and displayed in Berlin for several years, appearing to have a good knowledge of spoken and written German and an ability to tell the time and carry out mental arithmetic, among other equally unlikely capabilities. Clever Hans (*der kluge Hans*) answered yes/no questions by tapping its hoof on the ground according to a prearranged code, and fraud seemed unlikely, because von Osten allowed anyone to watch the horse perform and even to put questions to the horse in his absence, but the psychologist Oskar Pfungst (1874–1932) studied the horse experimentally and discovered that its abilities were illusory. Clever Hans could not respond intelligently when no one within its visual field knew the right answer to the question being asked: for example, if one person whispered a number into its left ear and another person a different number into its right ear, then if Clever Hans was asked to add the two numbers, it was stumped. Pfungst concluded that Clever Hans had learnt to respond to *non-verbal communication: it began tapping whenever people standing nearby adopted expectant postures and turned their attention to its hoof, and it stopped as soon as the onlookers (probably unwittingly) gave anticipatory head and eye movements when the correct number of taps was reached. Von Osten usually wore a wide-brimmed hat, which had the effect of amplifying small head movements and making the horse's task easier, but he was probably unaware of this. In 1907 Pfungst published an account, the English translation of which was entitled *Clever Hans (the Horse of Mr von Osten): A Contribution to Experimental and Animal Psychology* (1911). *See also* facilitated communication.

client *n.* A person in receipt of a professional service, including a person being treated by a professional psychologist, psychiatrist, psychoanalyst, or counsellor. Also called a *patient*.

client-centred therapy *n.* A technique of *counselling or *psychotherapy developed by the US psychologist Carl Rogers (1902–87) from the 1940s onwards, in which therapists or counsellors deliberately refrain from interpreting what their clients say but try instead to convey an attitude of *unconditional positive regard* in the context of a permissive, accepting, non-threatening relationship, and to help by clarifying, rephrasing, and *reflecting back the feelings or emotions that lie behind the clients' words and behaviour, the assumption being that people are capable of identifying the sources of their own emotional problems and of working out solutions for themselves once they are freed from feelings of anxiety and insecurity. US *client-centered therapy*. Also called *client-centred counselling, person-centred therapy* or *counselling, non-directive therapy* or *counselling*.

climacteric *n.* Another name for the *menopause; by analogy, a supposed period in a man's life corresponding to the female menopause, characterized by diminished sexual activity and energy, also called a *male menopause*; more generally, any critical phase of development when major bodily changes occur.
[From Greek *klimakterikos* a critical event or period, from *klimakter* a rung of a ladder, from *klimax* a ladder + *-ikos* of, relating to, or resembling]

climbing fibre *n.* One of the two types of afferent neurons conveying signals to the *cerebellum, projecting from the contralateral *inferior olivary nucleus and forming multiple synapses with single *Purkinje cells of the cerebellar cortex. US *climbing fiber*. *Compare* mossy fibre.

Clinical History Schedule *n.* A semi-structured clinical interview, designed for the objective evaluation of patients with mental disorders, forming part of the *SCAN system. **CHS** *abbrev.*

clinical prediction *n.* Prediction based on subjective judgement or intuition, as when a psychologist uses clinical experience to formulate a prediction informally, on the basis of interview impressions, other life-history data, and possibly psychometric test data, about how an individual is likely to behave or respond to treatment. The first systematic analysis and comparison of clinical prediction and *actuarial prediction was made by the US psychologist Paul Everett Meehl (born 1920) in his book *Clinical and Statistical Prediction: A Theoretical Analysis and a Review of the Evidence* in 1954.

clinical psychology *n.* One of the major professions of psychology, concerned with the nature, diagnosis, classification, treatment, and prevention of *mental disorders and disabilities, to be distinguished in careful usage from *abnormal psychology, which is the scientific study of mental disorders. *See also* psychiatry. **clinical psychologist** *n.* One who practises clinical psychology.

clinical trial *n.* A research investigation designed to provide objective information on the therapeutic efficacy of a drug or other form of treatment, the most important type of clinical trial being the *randomized controlled trial (RCT).

clipping *n.* Pronouncing a *vowel more quickly than normal, without changing its sound quality, as in the pronunciation of the vowel in the word *rice* compared with the same vowel in the word *rise*. In English, a vowel is clipped when followed by a *fortis consonant rather than a *lenis consonant within the same syllable, and this phenomenon is called pre-fortis clipping: compare *beat/bead, loose/lose, rate/raid*.

clitic *n.* A linguistic item that resembles a word but cannot function independently because of its dependence on an adjoining word and can never be stressed. A clitic is thus intermediate between a word and an affix (prefix or suffix). The usual examples are the French pronouns *je* and *tu*, but the English negative *-n't* (in words like *shouldn't*) is another example. *See also* enclitic, proclitic.

[Back formation from *enclitic* and *proclitic*]

clitoris *n*. An elongated erotically sensitive erectile organ visible near the front of a woman's *vulva and extending far into her body. It is much larger than is generally realized and as is shown in standard diagrams, and it is homologous with the male *penis. **clitoral** *adj*. **clitoridectomy** *n*. Surgical removal of the external tip of the *clitoris in female circumcision.

[From Greek *kleitoris* a clitoris]

cloacal theory *n*. In *psychoanalysis, a sexual theory, often adopted by children, that confuses the female vagina and the anus, recognizing only one orifice that is believed to function as a birth canal and also for defecation and coitus. Sigmund Freud (1856–1939) first referred to it in 1908 in an article 'On the Sexual Theories of Children' (*Standard Edition*, IX, pp. 209–26). According to Freud, children of both sexes tend to believe that 'the baby must be evacuated, like a piece of excrement, like a stool' (p. 219). Also called *cloaca theory*.

[From *cloaca* the pelvic cavity of most vertebrates, apart from higher mammals, into which both the alimentary canal and the genital ducts open, from Latin *cloaca* a sewer, from Greek *klyzein* to wash out]

clomipramine *n*. Clomipramine hydrochloride, a *tricyclic antidepressant drug, closely related to *imipramine, that is a potent *selective serotonin reuptake inhibitor, and is used chiefly in the treatment of obsessive–compulsive disorder. Also called *Anafranil* (trademark).

[From *c(h)lo(ro)-* denoting chlorine + *(i)mipramine*]

clone *n*. **1.** An organism with identical genetic constitution to one or more others, descended from a common parent or ancestor by a form of asexual reproduction or created artificially. **2.** A segment of *DNA that has been isolated and copied by *genetic engineering. *vb*. **3.** To replicate as a *clone (1, 2) or clones. **cloning** *n*. Producing *clones (1, 2).

[From Greek *klon* a shoot or bud]

clonic convulsion *n*. An involuntary rhythmic alternation between contraction and relaxation of skeletal muscles. Also called a *clonic spasm*. *Compare* tonic–clonic, tonic convulsion.

[From Greek *klonos* contraction]

closed head injury *n*. A blow to the head causing brain damage without penetrating the skull.

closed-loop control *n*. In *cybernetics, a control process in which a system's output is returned to its input as *feedback, this being characteristic of *controlled processing and all *homeostatic processes. *Compare* open-loop control.

closed node *n*. A *node (2) that has been processed. *Compare* open node.

closed question *n*. A question to which an answer must be selected from a limited set. Questionnaire items with fixed *response categories are closed questions, and questions in interviews or informal conversations can be open or closed. *Are you angry about that?* is a closed question, because it implies a yes/no answer, whereas *How do you feel about that?* is an *open-ended question, because the range of possible answers is unlimited. Open-ended questions are more effective in breaking the ice or drawing out responses in tense or awkward social situations. Also called a *close-ended question*.

close-ended question *n*. Another name for a *closed question.

close vowel *n*. A *vowel (see the diagram accompanying that entry) produced at a high position in the mouth with the body of the tongue raised towards the roof of the mouth, such as the vowels in *seen* and *soon*. Also called a *high vowel*. *Compare* mid vowel, open vowel.

closure grouping law *n*. One of the four original *grouping laws of *Gestalt psychology, formulated in 1923 by the German psychologist Max Wertheimer (1880–1943) to explain the organization of parts into wholes by the visual system. According to the law, elements that are perceived to form a closed contour tend to be grouped together, so that the array [ ] [ ] [ ] [ ] tends to be perceived as four rectangular units rather than eight separate elements. *See also* cloze procedure, common fate, common region, connectedness grouping law, Landolt circle, *Prägnanz*. *Compare* good continuation, proximity grouping law, similarity grouping law.

clouding of consciousness *n*. A state of consciousness affecting *thinking, *attention, and *perception, in which one is confused about, or not fully aware of, one's immediate surroundings.

Cloud nine *n*. A street name for *ephedrine.

clozapine *n*. A *dibenzodiazepine drug that belongs to the group of *atypical antipsychotics and that acts as a receptor antagonist of both *serotonin and *dopamine and is used in the treatment of schizophrenia, having fewer *neuroleptic-induced side-effects than are associated with conventional *neuroleptic (1) drugs. Also called *Clozaril* (trademark). *See also* dopamine antagonist.
[From *c(h)lo(ro)-* denoting chlorine + *(ben)z(odi)a(ze)pine*]

cloze procedure *n*. A method for testing a person's ability to comprehend written text by guessing missing words that have been deleted at regular intervals from the text.
[From to *close* in the sense of to complete, alluding to the *closure grouping law of Gestalt psychology]

cluster analysis *n*. A statistical technique, introduced in 1935 by the US psychologist Robert Choate Tryon (1901–67) for assigning a set of individual people or other items to groups called *clusters* on the basis of one or more measurements of the individuals, so that individuals within the same cluster are in some sense closer or more similar to one another than to individuals in another cluster. For example, measurements of a cross-section of the population on variables such as age, income, and number of books in the home, if subjected to cluster analysis, may reveal distinct and recognizable clusters such as students, pensioners, and unemployed people. There are many different methods of cluster analysis, including *agglomerative hierarchical clustering, *average linkage between groups method, *average linkage within groups method, *complete linkage clustering, *divisive hierarchical clustering, *nearest neighbour method, *single-linkage clustering, and (perhaps most

popular) *Ward's method. *See also* dendrogram, horizontal icicle plot. *Compare* factor analysis, principal-components analysis. **cluster-analytic** *adj*.

clustering *n*. In *free recall, a tendency for items that are conceptually related to be remembered consecutively whether or not they were grouped together during the learning phase. For example, if the names of cities, trees, and animals are learnt in random order, the cities will tend to be recalled together in one group, the trees in another group, and the animals in a third group.

cluster sample *n*. A *probability sample used when there is no suitable *sampling frame of the population but a sampling frame for subgroups is available. Thus, to survey hospital patients throughout an entire country, an investigator may be able to select a random sample of hospitals from a list of all hospitals in the country and could then apply a questionnaire to all patients in the selected hospitals. *See also* multistage cluster sampling, random digit dialling, simple random sample, stratified random sample. *Compare* accidental sample, convenience sample, non-probability sample, opportunity sample, quota sample, self-selected sample, snowball sample.

cluster suicides *n*. Multiple suicides occurring in the same area at about the same time, usually assumed to involve *social contagion.

clysmaphilia *n*. An alternative spelling of *klysmaphilia.

CN gas *abbrev*. Chloroacetophenone gas, a chlorine compound used as a *tear gas.
[So called because it is a chlorine derivative of acetophenone]

coaction effect *n*. The effect on an individual's task performance of the presence of other individuals engaged in the same activity. Depending on the nature of the task, the effect on performance may be positive or negative. *See also* drive theory of social facilitation, social facilitation. *Compare* audience effect, social loafing.
[From Latin *co-* together + *agere, actum* to do]

coactor *n*. Any organism engaging in joint action with another or engaging in the same behaviour in the same place as another.

cocaine n. A highly addictive *sympatho-mimetic *alkaloid substance obtained from the Andean coca shrubs *Erythroxylon coca* and *E. truxillense*, consumed as a drug in various forms, including coca leaves, which are chewed by native populations in parts of Central and South America, coca paste (*basulca), which may be smoked, and cocaine hydrochloride, which is either snorted through the nostrils in powder form or dissolved in water and injected intravenously. It is the prototypic local anaesthetic drug, though no longer used for that purpose owing to the risk of its being abused if readily available in medicine cabinets. It also blocks the amine reuptake mechanism of noradrenergic and dopaminergic neurons, thereby causing *noradrenalin (norepinephrine) and *dopamine to accumulate at *synapses (1) in the central nervous system, resulting in mood elevation, and it acts as a central nervous system *stimulant by increasing the release of *catecholamines, high doses producing visual, auditory, and sometimes tactile hallucinations, together with paranoia and disruption of thought processes. Until 1904 it was one of the ingredients of Coca Cola. Its street names include *Charlie*, *coke*, and *snow*. Formula $C_{17}H_{21}NO_4$. *See also* addiction, cocaine-related disorders, crack, dependence (2), speedball, substance dependence, substance-induced disorders, substance-related disorders, substance use disorders. *Compare* amphetamine, tricyclic antidepressant.
[From *coca* + *-ine* indicating resemblance, from Latin *-inus* resembling or consisting of]

cocaine bug n. A name given to *formication when it occurs as a *withdrawal symptom in cocaine users. Also called the *Magnan sign*.

cocaine-related disorders n. *Substance-related disorders associated specifically with the consumption of *cocaine or *crack. *See* substance abuse, substance dependence, substance-induced disorders, substance use disorders.

coccygeal nerve n. Either of a pair of *spinal nerves attached to the bottom of the spinal cord, serving the *striped muscles, the skin, and the *autonomic nervous system.
[From Greek *kokkyx* the cuckoo, from the resemblance of the coccyx to a cuckoo's beak]

cochlea n. The spiral bony tube in the inner ear containing the *organ of Corti with its *basilar membrane on which are situated *hair cells that respond to sound waves by converting them into nerve impulses. *See also* scala. **cochleae** *pl.* **cochlear** *adj.*
[From Latin *cochlea* a snail or spiral, from Greek *kochlias* a snail]

cochlear canal n. A spiral tunnel within the *cochlea of the inner ear, narrowing gradually in diameter towards the apex of the cochlea, communicating through one opening with the *middle ear, through a second with the *vestibular system, and through a third with a tiny canal on the inner surface of the temporal bone. *See also* oval window, round window, scala. Also called the *cochlear duct*.

cochlear duct n. Another name for the *cochlear canal.

cochlear emissions n. Sounds generated by vibrations originating within the *cochlea.

cochlear implant n. An electronic device surgically inserted into the *cochlea of a deaf person, feeding electrical signals from a transmitter outside the scalp into the *vestibulocochlear nerve. It does not transmit speech clearly but restores some awareness of sound in a totally deaf person.

cochlear microphonic n. The summated electrical activity of large numbers of neurons in the *cochlea, recorded from flat metal electrodes attached to the skin in the vicinity of the ear, analogous to the *EEG or the *electroretinogram. Also called a *cochleogram*. **CM** *abbrev.*

cochlear nerve n. One of the two major branches of the *vestibulocochlear nerve, transmitting auditory information from the *organ of Corti in the cochlea of the inner ear to the brain. *See also* vestibular nerve.

cochlear nucleus n. Either of the nuclei of the *cochlear nerves in the floor of the fourth ventricle of the brain, the first relay station for auditory nerve fibres.

cochlear window n. Another name for the *round window.

cochleogram *n.* Another name for the *cochlear microphonic.

cochleotopic map *n.* Another name for a *tonotopic map.

Cochran's C *n.* In statistics, a test of the assumption of *homogeneity of variance required by procedures such as *analysis of variance (ANOVA), namely that several groups come from populations with the same variance. Cochran's C test is based on the ratio of the largest group variance to the sum of all the group variances.
[Named after the Scottish statistician William Gemmell Cochran (1909–80) who developed the test in 1947]

Cochran's Q *n.* In statistics, a test of the null hypothesis that several related dichotomous variables, measured on the same individual or on matched individuals, have the same mean. Cochran's Q is an extension of the *McNemar test to the k-sample case.
[Named after the Scottish statistician William Gemmell Cochran (1909–80) who developed the test in 1950]

cockney *n.* A working-class native of the East End of London, traditionally within earshot of the bells of St Mary-le-Bow church, and the associated *dialect of English, incorporating the *glottal stop and *rhyming slang.
[From Middle English *coken-ey* a cock's egg, hence an oddity, or perhaps from French *co-quin* a rogue]

cocktail party phenomenon *n.* A phenomenon of selective *attention in speech perception that enables a listener to attend to one among several equally loud conversations occurring simultaneously, factors such as voice quality and directional cues facilitating the task. Conversations recorded on audiotape under similar circumstances are very much harder to understand. The term was introduced in 1957 by the British telecommunications engineer Colin Cherry (1914–79). *See also* attenuation theory, bottleneck theory, filter theory, selective attention.

co-counselling *n.* A technique of do-it-yourself *counselling or *psychotherapy in which people work in pairs, taking turns at playing the role of counsellor and client. It was developed in the 1950s by the US counsel-lor (Carl) Harvey Jackins (1916–99). US *co-counseling.* Also called *re-evaluation counsel(l)ing. Compare* co-facilitator.

coda *n.* The *consonant at the end of a syllable, if one exists. The main part of a syllable is almost invariably a *vowel, and if nothing follows it, as in all Japanese syllables, then the vowel is said to have zero coda. In English up to four consonants can be present in a coda, as in the word *sixths.*
[From Latin *cauda* a tail]

codeine *n.* A white crystalline *alkaloid and *narcotic analgesic drug, synthesized partly from *morphine and having similar, though much milder, effects. *See also* opioid-related disorders.
[From Greek *kodeia* the head of a poppy + *-ine* indicating resemblance, from Latin *-inus* resembling or consisting of]

co-dependency *n.* A relationship or partnership in which two or more people support or encourage each other's unhealthy habits, especially substance dependencies.

coding test *n.* Any *intelligence test item or subtest in which the respondent has to encode information according to a specified rule. Also called a *recoding test,* a *symbol-substitution test,* or a *substitution test. See* digit-symbol test.

codon *n.* A triplet of *bases (1) in a *DNA molecule, or a corresponding triplet in an *RNA molecule, that either codes for a single *amino acid during *protein synthesis or is interpreted as a marker for the beginning or end of a segment of nucleic acid to be translated. *See also* exon, genetic code, intron, start codon, stop codon.
[A blend of *cod(ing)* and *(regi)on*]

codon family *n.* A set of *codons all coding for the same *amino acid or signalling the end of a genetic message, such as the set of *RNA codons GGU, GGC, GGA, and GGG, all coding for the amino acid *glycine, or the set UAA, UAG, and UGA, all reserved as *stop codons. With only 20 amino acids involved in the synthesis of proteins and four bases to encode them, there is redundancy in the genetic code, because there are 64 possible triplets of four bases; consequently, every amino acid apart from *tryptophan (UGG) is encoded by at least two different codons.

coefficient alpha *n*. Another name for *Cronbach's alpha.

coefficient of consanguinity *n*. The probability, symbolized by F_{ij} or f_{ij}, that a pair of *alleles belonging to different individuals are the same, given their degree of common ancestry. Also called the *coefficient of kinship*. *Compare* coefficient of relationship.

coefficient of determination *n*. In statistics, a measure of the *goodness of fit (1) of a set of scores to a *linear model. It is defined as the proportion of the variance in the *dependent variable that is explained by the model. It can range in value from 0 to 1, with 1 indicating perfect fit. Symbol: R^2.

coefficient of kinship *n*. Another name for the *coefficient of consanguinity.

coefficient of relationship *n*. The proportion of *alleles that are the same in two related individuals, symbolized by *r*. *Compare* coefficient of consanguinity.

coefficient of reliability *See* reliability coefficient.

coefficient of validity *See* validity coefficient.

coenaesthesis *n*. The general feeling of bodily existence arising from the sum of bodily sensations as distinct from the particular sensations themselves; the vital sense. Also called *coenesthesia*. US *cenesthesis*, *cenesthesia*.
[From Greek *koinos* common + *aisthesis* feeling]

co-evolution *n*. A process in which the simultaneous evolution of two or more organisms, such as a *predator and its *prey, is dependent on or influenced by their mutual interaction or relationship.

co-facilitator *n*. A counsellor or therapist who works in conjunction with another, especially in leading a *group therapy session. Also called a *co-therapist*.

cognate languages *n*. Languages sharing a common source, such as Italian and Spanish, which both come from Latin.

cognition *n*. The mental activities involved in acquiring and processing *information (1). Its study includes *cognitive psychology, *psycholinguistics, *artificial intelligence, and *cognitive neuropsychology. A cognition is an item of knowledge or belief. *See also* information processing.
[From Latin *cognoscere* to get to know, from *com-* together + *noscere* to know]

cognitive *adj*. Of, relating to, or involving *cognition.

cognitive ability *n*. An ability to perform any of the functions involved in *cognition; more generally, another name for *intelligence.

cognitive–analytic therapy *n*. A form of *brief psychotherapy based on *object relations theory, *personal construct theory, and aspects of *behaviour therapy and *cognitive therapy.

cognitive–appraisal theory *n*. A theory of *emotions according to which *arousal provides the basis for any emotion, but the quality of the emotion is provided by the person's interpretation of its cause, the specific emotion that is felt depending on the person's interpretation and explanation of the felt arousal. The theory, proposed in 1964 by the US psychologist Stanley Schachter (1922–97), is a type of *attribution theory based on the *James–Lange theory but taking into account the main criticism of it—that different emotions tend to share the same bodily responses. In a famous experiment in 1962 by Schachter and the US psychologist Jerome E(verett) Singer (born 1929), participants were injected with adrenalin, and some of them were led to interpret the resulting arousal as a purely physiological side-effect of the injection. The participants were then placed in situations designed to elicit either euphoria or anger, and those who had been led to attribute the arousal to the injection expressed less emotion than those who attributed it to the situations they were placed in, although the results were not entirely clear-cut. Also called the *cognitive–evaluation theory*. *Compare* Cannon–Bard theory.

cognitive behaviour modification *n*. A form of *psychotherapy based on *cognitive therapy and *behaviour modification, in which the client or patient learns to replace dysfunctional self-speech (such as *I knew I'd never be able to cope with this job*) with adaptive alternatives

(*The job's not going well, but I am capable of working out a plan to overcome the problems*). Its applications include anger control, stress management, coping with anxiety, and developing social skills. US *cognitive behavior modification*. Also called *cognitive behaviour therapy (CBT)* or *cognitive behavioural therapy*. *See also* thought stopping. *Compare* behaviour therapy. **CBM** *abbrev*.

cognitive consistency theory *n*. Any of a number of theories of *attitude (1) and *attitude change according to which people strive to maintain consistency between their cognitions. The most prominent are *balance theory, *congruity theory, and *cognitive dissonance theory.

cognitive derailment *n*. A pattern of *thinking, closely related to *loosening of associations, in which ideas tend to slide from one track on to an unrelated or only indirectly related track. It is manifested in speech by idiosyncratic shifts between meaningful sentences or clauses, rather than within them. *See also* disorganized speech. *Compare* incoherence.

cognitive development *n*. The growth of cognitive abilities and capacities from birth to old age.

cognitive disorders *n*. A group of *mental disorders, the predominant symptoms of which are clinically significant deficits in an aspect or aspects of *cognition. *See* amnestic disorder, delirium, dementia.

cognitive dissonance *n*. A deceptively simple *cognitive consistency theory, first proposed in 1957 by the US psychologist Leon Festinger (1919–89), concerned with the effects of inconsistent cognitions—interpreted as items of knowledge or belief. If one of a pair of cognitions follows from the other, then the two are consonant; if one follows from the converse of the other, then they are dissonant; and if neither follows from the other or from its converse, then they are irrelevant to each other. The 'follows from' criterion is psychological rather than logical, consonance being said to exist if an outside observer would consider it more likely that a person who held one of the cognitions would also hold the other, rather than its converse. The dissonance relation is a motivating state of tension that tends to generate three kinds of dissonance-reducing behaviour: changing one of the cognitions, decreasing the perceived importance of dissonant cognitions, and/or adding further (justifying) cognitions. The standard example of a dissonance relation is the pair of cognitions *I smoke cigarettes* and *cigarette smoking damages my health*. People who hold both cognitions can reduce the dissonance in three ways: changing the first cognition by giving up smoking or convincing themselves that they have given up, but this is difficult because this cognition is behaviourally anchored; changing the second cognition by rejecting, ignoring, or playing down the evidence linking cigarette smoking to ill health, but it is difficult in this case because of the overwhelming evidence; or adding justifying cognitions such as *But I smoke only low-tar brands, But I'm more likely to die in a car accident than from the effects of smoking*, and so on, which is the easiest and commonest method of dissonance reduction. The theory generates counter-intuitive predictions relating to the effects of free choices, resisting temptations, and telling lies. Also called *dissonance theory*. *See also* endowment effect, equity theory, forced compliance, self-perception theory.

cognitive economy *n*. The tendency for cognitive processes to minimize processing effort and resources. For example, we do not squander memory capacity on storing the information *has two legs* for every individual we know; instead, we store this fact as a general *default assumption* for people in general and add a separate memory *has one leg* or *has no legs* only in exceptional cases in which the default does not apply. *See also* cognitive miser, default reasoning, principle of least effort.

cognitive enhancer *n*. Another name for a *smart drug.

cognitive–evaluation theory *n*. Another name for the *cognitive-appraisal theory.

Cognitive Failures Questionnaire *n*. A questionnaire first published in 1982 by the English psychologist Donald E(ric) Broadbent (1926–93) and several colleagues, in which respondents answer questions about lapses such as forgetting to buy certain items when shopping. It is designed to measure forgetfulness and *absent-mindedness in everyday life. **CFQ** *abbrev*.

cognitive heuristic *n*. Another name for a *heuristic.

cognitive illusion *n*. An *illusion in the cognitive domain, one of the best known examples being the *size–weight illusion, although it is also a tactile illusion. *See also* experimentally induced false memory, filled-duration illusion, illusory correlation, Rumpelstiltskin phenomenon, Tycho's illusion.

cognitive interview *n*. A structured form of interviewing developed in 1984 by the US psychologist R(alph) Edward Geiselman (born 1949) and colleagues as an investigative tool in *forensic psychology to maximize the amount of reliable information that witnesses can recall. It incorporates several memory-enhancing features, such as reinstating the context of the episode to be recalled (*see* state-dependent memory) and encouraging the interviewee to think about the events in different sequences and from different perspectives.

cognitive invention *n*. A term introduced by the US psychologist Irvin Rock (1922–95) to denote the process by which *illusory contours arise.

cognitive map *n*. A mental representation of a portion of the physical environment and the relative locations of points within it. Cognitive maps are generally distorted by simplifying assumptions and preconceptions: in people's cognitive maps roads tend to join at right angles even when they do not in reality, and in the cognitive maps of most British people, Bristol lies to the west of Edinburgh, presumably because of knowledge that Bristol is on the west coast and Edinburgh on the east coast, whereas on a cartographer's map the reverse is true. Humans and animals, including birds, navigate partly by cognitive maps and partly by heading vectors (travelling in a fixed direction towards the goal), the former but not the latter being controlled by the *hippocampus. The term was introduced in an article in the journal *Psychological Review* in 1948 by the US psychologist Edward C(hace) Tolman (1886–1959), who described an experiment in which he trained a group of rats to run through a maze to a goal box, then blocked off the path that the rats were using and observed that most of the rats unhesitatingly chose alternative paths heading in the right general direction. Also called a *conceptual map* or a *mental map*.

cognitive miser *n*. An interpretation of *stereotypes as psychological mechanisms that economize on the time and effort spent on *information processing by simplifying social reality, which would otherwise overwhelm our cognitive capacities with its complexity. The concept was introduced by the US journalist Walter Lippmann (1899–1974) in his book *Public Opinion* in 1922. A more general term for essentially the same phenomenon is *cognitive economy. *See also* dual-process model, principle of least effort.

cognitive neuropsychology *n*. The study of *deficits or *impairments in human *cognitive function resulting from brain damage. Alongside *cognitive psychology and *artificial intelligence, it is one of the three main approaches to cognition and has been especially fruitful in research into processes such as reading and writing. For example, it has established that different routes exist for translating written words into speech, because some brain-damaged patients with *surface dyslexia are able to read only by translating each letter into its corresponding sound and have great difficulty with orthographically irregular words like *yacht*, whereas others with *deep dyslexia or *phonological dyslexia can read only by whole-word recognition and have difficulty with simple non-words like *bink*, because they cannot translate letters into sounds. *See also* neurolinguistics.

cognitive penetrability *n*. The degree to which a cognitive process is unconsciously influenced by assumptions and expectations. For example, research has shown that if one imagines shifting one's gaze from a lighthouse to a bridge, then the time taken is not related to the imagined distance, whereas if one imagines walking or running from the lighthouse to the bridge, or imagines an object moving between these locations, then the time taken is proportional to the imagined distance, suggesting that these cognitive processes are unconsciously influenced by assumptions and expectations about physical movement and are therefore cognitively penetrable. The concept was introduced and named in articles in 1978 and 1979 by the Canadian psychologist Zenon Walter

Pylyshyn (born 1937), who carried out the lighthouse–bridge experiment and who also argued that the reason why the time taken for *mental rotation increases in direct proportion to the angle through which the image is rotated, is that mental rotation is cognitively penetrable inasmuch as it is influenced by the assumption that the object rotates smoothly through intermediate positions.

cognitive psychology n. The branch of psychology concerned with all forms of *cognition, including *attention, *perception, *learning (1, 2), *memory, *thinking, *problem solving, *decision making, and *language (1). See also information processing.

cognitive restructuring n. Any form of *cognitive therapy, especially *rational emotive behaviour therapy, in which clients are encouraged and helped to adopt more rational or constructive ways of thinking about their problems.

cognitive schema See schema.

cognitive science n. An umbrella term for an interdisciplinary enterprise, embracing cognitive psychology, psychobiology, anthropology, computer science, artificial intelligence, linguistics, and philosophy, concerned with information acquisition and processing. It includes research into language, learning, perception, thinking and problem solving, and knowledge representation.

cognitive set n. A temporary readiness to think or to interpret information in a particular way. See also Aufgabe, set (2).

cognitive style n. A characteristic and self-consistent mode of intellectual and perceptual functioning. The earliest classification of cognitive styles was suggested in 1923 by the Swiss psychologist Carl Gustav Jung (1875–1961), and a modified form of it is assessed through the *Myers–Briggs Type Indicator (MBTI). See also convergence–divergence, field dependence–independence, intolerance of ambiguity, locus of control, reflection–impulsivity.

cognitive therapy n. A form of *psychotherapy aimed at modifying people's beliefs, expectancies, assumptions, and styles of thinking, based on the assumption that psychological problems often stem from erroneous patterns of thinking and distorted perceptions of reality (such as overgeneralizations of the type, People are always letting me down) that can be identified and corrected. It has been applied especially to the treatment of depression. The first widely used form of cognitive therapy, not labelled as such, was *rational emotive therapy (RET), and the most influential proponent of a later and more complex form of cognitive therapy was the US psychiatrist Aaron (Temkin) Beck (born 1921). Beck was the first to suggest in his book Depression: Clinical, Experimental, and Theoretical Aspects (1967) that depression-prone people tend to have negative *self-schemas revolving around assumptions of inadequacy, failure, loss, and worthlessness; Beck assumed that these beliefs are unrealistic and biased, but research into *depressive realism suggests the opposite. See also cognitive restructuring, depressive realism.

cognitivism n. A psychological perspective according to which the study of cognition is likely to lead to a broad understanding of human psychology.

cogwheel rigidity n. A form of myotonia or muscular rigidity characteristic of *Parkinson's disease, in which pushing on an arm causes it to move in jerky increments rather than smoothly. Compare catalepsy, cerea flexibilitas, clasp-knife rigidity.

cohesive self n. In *self-psychology, a coherent structure representing the normally functioning self.

cohoba n. A psychotropic snuff containing *bufotenin, derived from the seeds of the South American tree Piptadenia peregrina. Compare Amanita muscaria, fly agaric. [From Latin American Spanish cojoba cohoba, derived from native Arawakan]

cohort n. A group of people who share some experience or demographic *trait in common, especially that of being the same age (an age cohort). A cohort study is a type of research design in which a cohort of individuals is investigated repeatedly over an extended period. A cohort effect is a potentially misleading conclusion about developmental changes derived from a *cross-sectional study, such as the conclusion that individual IQs decline

precipitately from about 20 years of age, a finding that is in fact due to younger cohorts having higher average IQs than older ones (*see* Flynn effect).
[From Latin *cohors* company of soldiers]

coitus *n.* Sexual intercourse. Also called *coition*.
[From Latin *coitus* uniting, from *coire* to meet, from *co-* together + *ire* to go]

coitus interruptus *n.* Sexual intercourse deliberately interrupted by withdrawing the penis before ejaculation.

coitus reservatus *n.* Sexual intercourse in which ejaculation is deliberately delayed or avoided altogether.

coke *n.* A common street name for *cocaine.

cold pressor pain *n.* Pain induced by immersing a hand and forearm in circulating ice water close to freezing point, used in experimental studies of pain because it causes no permanent tissue damage. Pain begins to mount immediately and typically becomes unbearable after approximately 40 seconds. *See also* algesimeter, dolorimeter, hidden observer, ischaemic pain.

cold spot *n.* A small area of the skin supplied by *free nerve endings that transmit sensations of coldness when touched by cold stimuli. *See also* paradoxical cold, paradoxical heat. *Compare* warm spot.

cold turkey *n.* A slang term for the signs and symptoms, often including shivering and goose pimples, that are brought about by abrupt drug *withdrawal.

colera *n.* Another name for *bilis.
[Spanish *colera* bile]

collective unconscious *n.* In *analytical psychology, a part of the *unconscious (2) additional to the *personal unconscious, containing memories, instincts, and experiences that are shared by all people. According to Carl Gustav Jung (1875–1961), these mental elements are inherited and often organized into *archetypes (2), and they become manifest in dreams and in fairy tales, myths, religions, and other cultural phenomena. Also called the *objective psyche*, *racial memory*, or

racial unconscious. *See also* anima, animus (3), archetypal form, psychoid.

colliculus *n.* A small elevation or prominence, especially any one of the four prominences on the *tectum of the midbrain, which are collectively called the *corpora quadrigemina*. *See* inferior colliculus, superior colliculus. **colliculi** *pl.*
[From Latin *colliculus* a small hill, from *collis* a hill]

colorimeter *n.* An instrument for determining or specifying the quality of colours by comparing them with standard colours or combinations of colours. **colorimetric** *adj.* Of or relating to *colorimetry. **colorimetry** *n.* The science of determining and specifying colours by using a *colorimeter.
[From Latin *color* a colour or hue + Greek *metron* a measure]

colour *n.* The distinctive visual sensation induced by light in the *visible spectrum having a particular wavelength, not in absolute value but relative to the wavelengths emitted by or reflected from objects or surfaces in other parts of the visual field. Its dimensions are *hue, *saturation (1), and *lightness. US *color*. *See* colour-blindness, cone, Land effect, Munsell colour system, primary colour (1, 2, 3), spectrum. *See also* Benham's top, Bezold–Brücke phenomenon, categorical perception, chroma, chromaesthesia, chromatic (1), chromatic adaptation (1), chromaticity, chromatopsia, CIE colour system, colorimeter, colour assimilation, colour circle, colour constancy, colour contrast, colour induction, colour solid, colour triangle, colour zone, complementary colours, cone pigment, film colour, flight of colours, Grassmann's laws (perception), isoluminant, Ladd-Franklin theory, Maxwell disc, McCollough effect, metamer, opponent-process theory, pattern-induced flicker colour, Rayleigh equation, retinex theory, Stroop effect, surface colour, Talbot's law, trichromacy, trichromatic theory, tristimulus values, Young–Helmholtz theory.
[From Old French *colour* colour, from Latin *color* a colour or hue, cognate with *celare* to cover or conceal]

colour adaptation *n.* Another name for *chromatic adaptation (1, 2). US *color adaptation*.

colour anomaly n. A defect in colour vision, the term usually being reserved for relatively mild forms of *colour-blindness. US *color anomaly*. Also called *colour weakness*.

colour assimilation n. A tendency for a colour to become tinged with a different colour that is juxtaposed with it, as when an area of colour such as grey is surrounded by an area of another colour such as red that is not its *complementary colour. US *color assimilation*. See also assimilation (6). Compare colour contrast.

colour audition n. Another name for *colour hearing. US *color audition*. Also called *coloured audition* or *colored audition*.

colour-blindness n. Inability to distinguish some colours from others under bright illumination, a condition affecting between 7 and 8 per cent of men and 0.4 per cent of women, the major form being *daltonism, characterized by a defective ability to distinguish reds from greens, rather than *achromatopsia (total colour-blindness) or *monochromatism. Everyone is totally colour-blind in dim light when *scotopic vision depends on *rods, and mammals with poor or absent colour vision in bright light include rats, mice, rabbits, dogs, and nocturnal owl monkeys; cats have colour vision but use it only when there is no other way of distinguishing between objects. US *color-blindness*. See also achromatopsia, anomalous dichromacy, anomalous trichromacy, colour anomaly, colour deficiency, cone pigment, daltonism, deuteranomaly, deuteranopia, dyschromatopsia, Holmgren test, Horner's law, Ishihara test, parachromatopsia, protanomaly, protanopia, pseudo-isochromatic, Rayleigh equation, Stilling test, tritanomaly, tritanopia. Compare chromatic vision, chromatopsia, colour dysnomia. **colour-blind** adj. US *color-blind*.

colour circle n. A diagram showing the relationship between the *hue and *saturation (1) dimensions of colours, differences in hue being represented by different positions around the circumference of the circle in their natural *spectrum order, with similar hues close together and *complementary colours opposite one another, and saturation represented by the distance from the centre, white light being situated at the centre and saturation increasing radially towards the circumference, a special segment of which is occupied by the *non-spectral colour purple linking spectral blue with spectral red and completing the circle. *Achromatic (1) colour is not represented, and therefore neither is the *lightness dimension of colour. US *color circle*. See also metamer. Compare colour solid, colour triangle.

colour constancy n. The tendency for an object or a surface to retain approximately the same apparent colour as the amount and wavelength of light reflected from it changes under varying conditions of illumination, as when the intensity of daylight decreases and its wavelength increases at sunset. The computations required to achieve this result occur in Area V4 of the *visual cortex, situated on the *fusiform gyrus. US *color constancy*. See also Land effect, perceptual constancy, retinex theory.

colour contrast n. The change in perceived colour resulting from its juxtaposition with a different colour, as occurs when *complementary colours such as blue and yellow are juxtaposed, making the blue look bluer and the yellow yellower, or when red and cyan (blue-green) are juxtaposed, making the red look redder and the cyan more intensely cyan, *simultaneous contrast occurring when a colour is viewed alongside another and tends to shift towards the complementary colour of the other colour, and *successive contrast occurring when one colour and then another is viewed, the second tending to shift towards the complementary colour of the first. US *color contrast*. See also appurtenance, contrast (2), visual induction. Compare colour assimilation.

colour deficiency n. Any defect in the capacity to perceive colours. US *color deficiency*. See colour-blindness.

colour dysnomia n. A defective ability to name colours in spite of an intact ability to match and distinguish them, usually interpreted as a form of nominal aphasia (see under aphasia). US *color dysnomia*. Compare agnosia, colour-blindness.
[From Greek *dys*- bad or abnormal + *onoma* a name + *-ia* indicating a condition or quality]

coloured noise n. Any *noise (2) apart from *white noise. US *colored noise*.

colour equation n. A formula showing the proportions of three *additive primary colours required by a viewer to match a specified stimulus colour, especially a formula based on the *CIE colour system. US *color equation*. *See also* Grassmann's laws (perception), primary colour (1), Rayleigh equation, tristimulus values.

colour flight *See* flight of colours.

colour hearing n. Any form of *chromaesthesia in which the stimuli that elicit sensations of colour are auditory. US *color hearing*. Also called *coloured audition* or *coloured hearing*.

colour induction n. The generation of illusory sensations of colour without direct stimulation of the corresponding *cones in the retina, by any of a number of different devices. US *color induction*. *See also* afterimage, Benham's top, Bidwell's ghost, chromaesthesia, colour assimilation, colour contrast, flight of colours, Land effect, pattern-induced flicker colour, Purkinje image.

colour mixing n. Producing a colour by combining light of two or more different wavelengths. US *color mixing*. *See* additive colour mixture, subtractive colour mixture. *See also* Maxwell disc.

colour solid n. A three-dimensional onion-shaped or spindle-shaped representation of the relationship between the *hue, *saturation (1), and *lightness dimensions of colours, the vertical dimension representing *achromatic (1) colour or lightness, with white at the pointed top and black at the pointed bottom, and the horizontal cross-section consisting of a *colour circle or ellipse of variable diameter representing hue and saturation. US *color solid*. *Compare* colour triangle.

colour spindle n. A spindle-shaped *colour solid. US *color spindle*.

colour surface n. Any two-dimensional representation of the relationships between *hue and *saturation (1), notably a *colour circle or a *colour triangle. US *color surface*. *Compare* colour solid.

colour triangle n. A triangular representation of the relationship between the *hue and *saturation (1) dimensions of colours, having hues arranged in their natural *spectrum order around its perimeter, with similar hues close together and *complementary colours opposite one another, the centre representing white light and saturation increasing towards the perimeter, a part of which is occupied by the *non-spectral colour purple linking spectral blue with spectral red. *Achromatic (1) colour is not represented, and therefore neither is the *lightness dimension of colour. US *color triangle*. *Compare* colour circle, colour solid.

colour weakness n. Any deficiency in colour vision falling short of *achromatopsia. US *color weakness*. Also called *colour anomaly*. *See also* colour-blindness.

colour wheel n. Another name for a *Maxwell disc. US *color wheel*.

colour zone n. Any of the three concentric areas of the *retina in which *hues are perceived in particular ways, namely the *macula lutea in which all hues are visible to a person with normal vision; the intermediate zone in which blues, yellows, and *achromatic (1) colours appear normally but reds and greens are perceived as shades of grey, yellow, or blue; and the peripheral zone in which all hues appear as achromatic colours. US *color zone*.

coma n. A state of deep unconsciousness and absence of responses to external and internal stimuli caused by severe head injury, brain tumour, loss of blood supply to the brain, acute infection, stroke, drug overdose, or poisoning. **comatose** adj. In a state of *coma. [From Greek *koma* heavy sleep]

combat fatigue n. An obsolescent and misleading term (because fatigue is not necessarily a symptom) for *post-traumatic stress disorder, especially when caused by traumatic experiences during military actions. Also called *shell shock*.

combination tone n. A musical tone such as a *difference tone or a *summation tone that is heard in a *complex tone but is not present in the sensations produced by the constituent components of the stimulus when they are presented singly. When there are two components, the lower having a frequency of f_1 and the higher a frequency of f_2, then the most easily audible combination tone is generally

$2f_1 - f_2$, thus if tones with frequencies of 1,800 hertz and 2,000 hertz are presented, then a combination tone with frequency 1,600 hertz is heard, because $(2 \times 1,800) - 2,000 = 1,600$. *See also* cancellation method, missing fundamental illusion, otogenic tone.

combined parent-figure *n.* A concept introduced into *psychoanalysis by the British-based Austrian psychoanalyst Melanie Klein (1882–1960) to denote an infantile fantasy in which the parents are united in a permanent sexual act, the mother containing the father's penis or the whole father, or the father containing the mother's breast or the whole mother. Klein developed the concept fully in her book *The Psycho-Analysis of Children* (1932, at pp. 103–4). Also called a *combined parent. See also* phallic woman.

commensal *adj.* Of or relating to two distinct species that live in close proximity to each other without being interdependent.
[From Latin *com-* together + *mensa* a table, alluding to eating from the same table]

commissure *n.* A band of fibres or tissue linking two homologous organs, structures, or parts, especially the great cerebral commissure called the *corpus callosum connecting the two cerebral hemispheres, and other minor inter-hemisphere bundles of nerve fibres, such as the *anterior commissure, *hippocampal commissure, *massa intermedia, *middle commissure, and *posterior cerebral commissure.
[From Latin *commissura* a joining together, from *com-* together + *mittere* to send]

commissurotomy *n.* Surgical severing of a cerebral *commissure linking the two hemispheres of the brain, usually the *corpus callosum, performed on humans as a treatment for chronic, generalized *epilepsy. Also called *commissurectomy. See* split-brain preparation. *See also* disconnection syndrome.
[From Latin *commissura* a connection + Greek *tome* a cut]

common chemical sense *n.* A *chemical sense that is stimulated by substances such as irritant solutions or vapours capable of exciting receptors in mucous membranes of the nose, mouth, eyes, and respiratory tract. It is mediated by the *trigeminal nerve, and it accounts for the burning sensation caused by *capsaicin, the active ingredient in chilli pepper. Also called *trigeminal chemoreception.*

common fate *n.* A special case of the *good continuation grouping law of *Gestalt psychology, applying to elements that are moving in time in the same direction and at the same speed and tending to cause them to be grouped together perceptually. *See also* Prägnanz. *Compare* closure grouping law, common region, connectedness grouping law, proximity grouping law, similarity grouping law.

common knowledge *n.* Any *proposition (1) that every member of a specified group knows to be true, knows that every other member knows to be true, knows that every other member knows that every other member knows to be true, and so on. It is not the same as all members of the group merely knowing the proposition to be true, as shown in the *muddy children problem. The concept was introduced in 1969 by the US philosopher David K(ellogg) Lewis (born 1941) in his book *Convention: A Philosophical Study* (pp. 52–68).

common ratio effect *n.* A famous violation of *expected utility theory that seems intuitively appealing to many human decision makers, a typical example being as follows. An urn contains 100 chips numbered 1 to 100. First, you are given a choice between the following pair of options:

> Option *A*: A chip is drawn at random from the urn. If it is numbered 1–20, you receive nothing; if it is numbered 21–100, you receive £16.
> Option *B*: You receive £10 with certainty.

Now you face a choice between a second pair of options:

> Option *C*: A chip is drawn at random from the urn. If it is numbered 1–80, you receive nothing; if it is numbered 81–100, you receive £16.
> Option *D*: A chip is drawn at random from the urn. If it is numbered 1–75, you receive nothing; if it is numbered 76–100, you receive £10.

Many people prefer *B* to *A*, because it guarantees a substantial payoff without the risk associated with *A*, and many of the same people also prefer C to D, because it offers the prospect of a higher payoff than D with only slightly greater risk. But it is easy to show that this pattern of preferences violates expected utility theory. Writing $u(16)$ for the utility of £16 and $u(10)$ for the utility of £10, the preference of B over A implies that $0.80 \times u(16) < u(10)$, which means that $u(16) < 1.25 \times u(10)$. But the preference of C over D implies that $0.20 \times u(16) > 0.25 \times u(10)$, which simplifies to $u(16) > 1.25 \times u(10)$, a contradiction. In general, if $x > y > z$ are sums of money, and p and q are non-zero probabilities, then the common ratio effect occurs if a decision maker prefers the prospect $py + (1 − p)y$ to $px + (1 − p)z$, and also prefers $p(1 − q)x + (1 − p)(1 − q)z + qz$ to $p(1 − q)y + (1 − p)(1 − q)y + qz$. *Compare* Allais paradox, Ellsberg paradox, modified Ellsberg paradox, St Petersburg paradox. **CRE** *abbrev.*

common region *n.* A *grouping law formulated in 1990 by the US psychologist Stephen E. Palmer (born 1948) to explain the organization of parts into wholes by the visual system. According to the law, elements that are located within the same perceived region tend to be grouped perceptually, so that the array

[O O] [O O] [O O] [O O]

tends to be perceived as being composed of four pairs rather than eight separate elements. Also called the *enclosure grouping law*. *See also* Prägnanz. *Compare* closure grouping law, common fate, connectedness grouping law, good continuation, proximity grouping law, similarity grouping law.

commons dilemma *n.* A type of *resource dilemma interpreted as a problem of overgrazing on a common pasture, illustrated by the following simple example. Three farmers each own a single cow weighing 1,000 kg and have access to a common that can sustain a maximum of three cows without deterioration. They all want to increase their wealth by adding a further cow to the common, but for each additional cow on the common the weight of every cow decreases by 200 kg. If one farmer adds a cow, then that farmer's personal wealth increases from 1,000 kg (one 1,000 kg cow) to 1,600 kg (two 800 kg cows); if two farmers add a cow each, then the wealth of each increases from 1,000 kg to 1,200 kg (two 600 kg cows); and if all three add a cow each, then the wealth of each *decreases* from 1,000 kg to 800 kg (two 400 kg cows), and each

farmer is poorer than if each had acted co-operatively by not adding a further cow to the common. It is always in a farmer's individual self-interest to acquire an additional cow, whether or not one or more of the others does so, but if they all pursue individual self-interest in this way, then each ends up poorer than if they all cooperate, which means that the problem is a *social dilemma.
[So called because of a reference in 1833 in an essay on population growth by the English economist William Forster Lloyd (1795–1852) to the 'tragedy of the commons'—the overgrazing of the commons in 14th-century England, which led to the enclosures and the eventual disappearance of many of the commons]

communality *n.* In *factor analysis, the proportion of the total *variance in the scores of one variable accounted for by the factors that the variable has in common with other variables.

communication channel *n.* **1.** The medium or route through which a message is communicated to its recipients, the most common channels being face-to-face communication, telephone, films, Internet, television, radio, and the printed media, including newspapers, books, and magazines. **2.** Another name for *sensory modality.

communication disorders *n.* A group of *mental disorders characterized by impairment in communication skills, including *expressive language disorder, *mixed receptive–expressive language disorder, *phonological disorder, *receptive language disorder, and *stuttering. *Compare* aphasia, language disorders.

community psychiatry *n.* A branch of *psychiatry devoted to the prevention and treatment of mental disorders and the provision of mental health care to people in local communities.

community psychology *n.* A branch of *applied psychology involving work at a community level, often including *counselling and *health psychology.

companionate love *n.* A type of love characterized by intimacy and commitment but lacking erotic passion. *See under* love.

comparable forms n. In psychometrics, *alternative forms of a test that are similar in content but have not been shown to have similar psychometric properties.

comparative judgement n. Any judgement of something in relation to something else; more specifically, a sensory judgement elicited by the *method of comparative judgement. See also law of comparative judgement.

comparative psychology n. The study of behaviour in different species, seeking to throw light on the underlying mechanisms and evolution of behaviour. The term is often applied loosely to any form of *animal psychology.

comparative reference group See under reference group.

comparison stimulus n. Another name for a *variable stimulus. **Co** abbrev.

compensation n. The act or process of making amends, or something done or given to make up for a loss. In *psychoanalysis, a *defence mechanism in which one attempts to redress a perceived deficiency that cannot be eliminated, such as a physical defect, by excelling in some other way. The Austrian psychiatrist Alfred Adler (1870–1937) attached great importance to it in his *individual psychology, especially in his concept of the *inferiority complex.

compensation neurosis n. A collection of symptoms presented by a person who has the prospect of receiving financial compensation for an industrial injury, failed surgical operation, car accident, or the like, susceptible to being interpreted as an attempt to profit from the incident. Compare factitious disorder, malingering.

compensatory eye movement n. A normally involuntary *smooth eye movement that occurs in response to a movement of the head to keep the *gaze fixated on the same point in the visual field.

competence n. **1.** The capacity, skill, or ability to do something correctly or efficiently, or the scope of a person's or a group's ability or knowledge. **2.** In linguistics, a term introduced by the US linguist and philosopher (Avram) Noam Chomsky (born 1928) to denote a person's unconscious knowledge of the grammatical rules of a language, especially those of *generative grammar and *transformational grammar. Also called linguistic competence. Compare performance (2). **3.** The legal authority of a court or other body to deal with a particular matter.
[From Latin competens competent, from competere to be fit and proper, from com together + petere to aim at or seek]

competency test n. An *achievement test used to determine whether a person has attained a predetermined level of skill or knowledge in some specified *content domain.

competitive antagonist n. An *antagonist (3) drug that interacts with a class of *neuroreceptors, without itself eliciting any response, by producing a change in the neuroreceptors that prevents the *agonist (3) from acting on them. Also called a receptor blocker. Compare non-competitive antagonist.

competitive exclusion principle n. The proposition that two distinct but similar species cannot occupy the same *ecological niche indefinitely. Also called Gause's principle.

complemental series n. In *psychoanalysis, an arrangement or distribution of a group of cases, from one extreme where hereditary causes predominate, to the other extreme where environmental causes predominate, enabling any specific case to be assigned to a position on a scale according to the relative contributions of nature and nurture. Sigmund Freud (1856–1939) expounded this concept most clearly in 1916–17 in his Introductory Lectures on Psycho-Analysis (Standard Edition, XV–XVI, especially at pp. 346–7, 362).

complementarity hypothesis See need complementarity hypothesis.

complementary afterimage n. An *afterimage in which colours appear approximately as the *complementary colours of the original stimulus. See also negative afterimage (1, 2), positive afterimage.

complementary base pairing n. Bonding between the bases adenine and thymine in DNA, between adenine and uracil in RNA, and between cytosine and guanine in both DNA and

RNA. Also called *base pairing. See also* purine, pyrimidine.

complementary colours *n.* Any pair of colours that produce white or grey when mixed in the correct proportions. There is an infinite number of such complementary pairs, but the following typical examples can be read off the *CIE colour system diagram: red (650 nanometres) and blue-green or cyan (495 nm); yellow (580 nm) and blue (480 nm); green (535 nm) and deep bluish purple or magenta (a 2:5 mixture of blue and red). US *complementary colors. See also* colour assimilation, colour circle, colour contrast, Purkinje image.

complementary DNA *n.* A form of *DNA synthesized artificially from a *messenger RNA template for producing clones by *genetic engineering. **cDNA** *abbrev.*

complementation *n.* In genetics, the combination of a pair of *homologous chromosomes, with a *recessive mutant gene in one and a normal dominant *allele at the same locus in the other, resulting in a normal *phenotype, the deficiency being corrected by the normal allele of the other chromosome. *See also cis–trans* complementation test, sex-linked.

complementation test *n.* Another name for the *cis–trans* complementation test.

complete linkage clustering *n.* In statistics, a technique of *cluster analysis in which the distance between two clusters is calculated as the distance between their two furthest members, also called the *furthest neighbour method.*

complete Oedipus complex *See under* Oedipus complex.

completion test *n.* A type of *intelligence test item in which an incomplete series of items is shown and the respondent tries to select or supply the missing item. The most common form of completion test is a *number-completion test. Also called a *continuation problem.*

complex *n.* **1.** An organized structure made up of interconnected units. **2.** In *psychoanalysis, an organized collection of ideas, emotions, impulses, and memories that share a common emotional tone and that have been excluded either partly or entirely from consciousness but continue to influence a person's thoughts, emotions, and behaviour. This concept was introduced in 1895 by the Austrian physician Josef Breuer (1842–1925) in *Studies on Hysteria (Standard Edition*, II, at p. 231) and later adapted by Sigmund Freud (1856–1939) and Carl Gustav Jung (1875–1961). The word *complex* is derived from *complexion (2) in the transitional sense already established by the time of Shakespeare's *Hamlet*: 'So oft it chances in particular men, / That for some vicious mole of nature in them, / As in their birth, wherein they are not guilty / (Since nature cannot choose his origin), / By the o'ergrowth of some complexion, / Oft breaking down the pales and forts of reason . . .' (I.iv.23–8). *See* castration complex, complex indicator, Diana complex, Electra complex, father complex, inferiority complex, inverted Oedipus complex, Jocasta complex, mother complex, Oedipus complex, Orestes complex, particular complex, Phaedra complex, word-association test. **3.** In informal usage, an *obsession or a *phobia. *Compare* complexion (2).
[From Latin *com-* together + *plexus* plaited or twined, from *plectere* to braid]

complex cell *n.* Any of a number of different types of neurons in the *primary visual cortex (Area V1) in the occipital lobe of the brain, being the most common cell types in that region, responding maximally to stimuli in the form of lines, edges, and/or bars oriented at particular angles and moving at right-angles to their longitudinal axes or stationary anywhere in their *receptive fields, their behaviour being impossible to explain by a straightforward subdivision of the receptive field into excitatory and inhibitory regions. The first complex cell was discovered in a cat's cerebral cortex in 1958 by the Canadian-born US neurophysiologist David H(unter) Hubel (born 1926) and his Swedish-born collaborator Torsten N(ils) Wiesel (born 1924). *See also* bar detector, edge detector, end-stopped receptive field, feature detector, hypercomplex cell, orientation-specific cell. *Compare* simple cell.

complex indicator *n.* In *analytical psychology, an aspect of a person's response to a *word-association test that is suggestive of a *complex (2). Carl Gustav Jung (1875–1961), who popularized the test, listed the main complex indicators in an article entitled 'The Association Method' in the *American Journal of Psychology* in 1910: an unusual reaction to a word, such as laughing or blushing, an abnormally long reaction time, a repetition of the stimulus word, an absurd or far-fetched association, and a failure to respond to a stimulus word.

complexion *n*. **1.** The colour or appearance of the skin, originally believed to be indicative of a person's temperament. *See* complexion (2). **2.** In medieval physiology, the combination of qualities or *humours (3) believed to determine a person's temperament or personality, as in the Prologue to Chaucer's *Canterbury Tales*: 'Of his complexion he was sangwyn' (line 333). *See also* complex (2).
[From Latin *complexio, complexionis* a combination, from *com-* together + *plectere* to plait]

complex reaction time *n*. Another name for *choice reaction time.

complex receptive field *n*. The *receptive field of a *complex cell.

complex tone *n*. A sound wave composed of a number of *pure tones of different *frequencies (1). *See also* Fourier analysis, harmonic, overtone, partial tone, tone (1).

compliance *n*. A form of *social influence in which a person yields to explicit requests from another person or other people. Also called *social compliance*. *See* door-in-the-face technique, foot-in-the-door technique, lowball technique. *See also* forced compliance, law of social impact. *Compare* conformity, obedience.

compliance, somatic *See* somatic compliance.

componential theory *n*. A theory of *concepts, *concept formation, and *semantics according to which the meaning of a concept or a word can be understood by analysing it into its set of *defining properties. The standard example is the concept *even number*, which is completely specified by the defining property *evenly divisible by two*; the theory amounts to an assumption that all concepts can be reduced to their defining properties or essences in this way. It is a form of essentialism that can be

traced to the writings of the Greek philosophers Plato (?427–?347 BC), in *Laws* (859d–e), and especially Aristotle (384–322 BC), in *Metaphysics* (Bekker edition, pp. 1030–1). It is still hugely influential and is often encountered in the form of a belief that every concept has a defining *attribute or essence that determines its identity, or that one ought always to define one's terms in any argument or discussion, but it was severely attacked by the Austrian-born British philosopher Karl R(aimund) Popper (1902–94) in *The Open Society and its Enemies* (1945) and has serious weaknesses in psychology—*see under* prototype theory. Also called a *definitional theory* or a *feature list theory*.

component instinct *n*. In *psychoanalysis, any of the basic elements of the *sexual instinct as defined by its *instinctual source (oral, anal, and so on) and to a lesser extent by its *instinctual aim and *instinctual object. Sigmund Freud (1856–1939) introduced the concept in 1905 in his book *Three Essays on the Theory of Sexuality* (*Standard Edition*, VII, pp. 130–243). In one of his encyclopedia articles published in 1923, he explained: 'The sexual instinct, the dynamic manifestation of which in mental life we shall call "*libido*", is made up of component instincts into which it may once more break up and which are only gradually united into well-defined organizations. . . . The first (pregenital) stage of organization to be discerned is the *oral* one' (*Standard Edition*, XVIII, pp. 235–59, at p. 244). Also called an *instinctual component*, a *partial instinct*, or a *part instinct*.

composite light *n*. In the terminology introduced by the English physicist and mathematician Sir Isaac Newton (1642–1727) in a paper to the Royal Society in 1675, and elaborated in his book *Opticks* in 1704, any light that can be broken down into constituent colours. *Compare* pure light.

compound eye *n*. The type of eye found in insects and some crustaceans, composed of a cluster of separate simple eyes, called *ommatidia, closely packed together but separated by darkly pigmented cells, arranged on a convex membrane and covered by a transparent *cornea.

compound reaction time *n*. Another name for *choice reaction time.

compound reinforcement schedule n. In *operant conditioning, any *reinforcement schedule that incorporates two or more simple schedules. Also called a *compound schedule* or a *higher-order reinforcement schedule*. *See* chained reinforcement schedule, tandem reinforcement schedule. *Compare* simple reinforcement schedule.

compromise formation n. In *psychoanalysis, a form assumed by a repressed wish, idea, or memory to gain admission to consciousness as a *symptom, usually *neurotic (1), a *dream (1), a *parapraxis, or some other manifestation of unconscious activity, the original idea being distorted beyond recognition so that the unconscious element that needs to be repressed and consciousness that needs to be protected from it are both partially satisfied by the compromise. The idea was introduced by Sigmund Freud (1856–1939) in 1896 in his article 'Further Remarks on the Neuro-Psychoses of Defence' (*Standard Edition*, III, pp. 162–85, at p. 170) and developed further in his book *Introductory Lectures on Psycho-Analysis* (1916–17): 'The two forces which have fallen out meet once again in the symptom and are reconciled. It is for that reason, too, that the symptom is so resistant: it is supported from both sides' (*Standard Edition*, XV–XVI, at pp. 358–9). *See also* choice of neurosis, return of the repressed, substitute formation, symptom formation.

compulsion n. A repetitive pattern of behaviour (such as hand-washing, tidying, or checking) or mental activity (such as praying, counting, reciting words or phrases silently) that a person feels compelled to perform, following strict rules or rituals, with the aim of relieving anxiety or avoiding some dreaded outcome, the behaviour or mental activity being either clearly excessive or not realistically capable of achieving its desired objective, and being recognized as such by the person concerned. *See also* functional autonomy, obsessive–compulsive disorder, obsessive–compulsive personality disorder, repetition compulsion. *Compare* obsession. **compulsive** adj.
[From Latin *compulsare* to compel habitually, from *compellere* to compel + *-ion* indicating an action, process, or state]

compulsion to repeat n. Another name for a *repetition compulsion.

compulsive personality *See* obsessive–compulsive personality disorder.

computational theory n. A formal analysis of perception, especially one based on the theory of vision pioneered in the late 1970s by the English psychologist David Courtenay Marr (1945–80), which seeks to explain how the pattern of light falling on the retinas of the eyes is transformed into an internal *representation (2) of the shapes, colours, and movements of what is observed, the three stages in the process being the *primal sketch, the *2½-D sketch, and the *3-D model description. *See also* eye–head movement system, generalized cone, image–retinal system, zero-crossing.

computed (axial) tomography *See under* CT scan.

computer vision n. A branch of *artificial intelligence concerned with designing or programming computers to process visual stimuli in order to perform such functions as recognizing objects or faces, analysing X-ray images or breast scans, or searching for comets in images from optical telescopes. *See also* optical character recognition, pattern recognition, perceptron, template matching.

conation n. The psychological processes involved in purposeful action. **conative** adj.
[From Latin *conatus* attempt, undertaking, or effort]

concept n. A mental representation, idea, or thought corresponding to a specific entity or class of entities, or the defining or prototypical *features (1) of the entity or class, which may be either concrete or abstract. The traditional psychological definition is a category that divides some domain into positive and negative instances. According to some authorities, to qualify as a concept the mental process must be conscious: young children do not have concepts of *noun* or *verb* although their linguistic behaviour shows that they understand these concepts and can discriminate between them. According to evidence, people can form concepts without awareness: in 1920 the US psychologist Clark L(eonard) Hull (1884–1952) reported one of the earliest experiments on *concept formation in which participants or subjects sorted Chinese characters into two categories with the help of simple right/wrong feedback, the concept being based on the presence or absence of a certain radical element, but even after learning to sort the elements more or less correctly, some people were unable to describe or draw the defining *attribute. *See also* basic-level category, componential theory, conjunctive concept, construct, disjunctive concept, exemplar, intension, intuition, prototype theory. **conceptual** *adj.* Of, relating to, or based on a *concept or concepts.

[From Latin *conceptum* something received or conceived, from *concipere* to take in or conceive, from *con-* with + *capere, ceptum* to take]

concept formation *n.* The process by which a *concept is acquired or learnt, usually from exposure to examples of items that belong to the concept category and items that do not belong to it. In general, it involves learning to distinguish and recognize the relevant *attributes according to which items are classified and the rules governing the combination of relevant attributes, which may be disjunctive, as in the concept of a coin, which may be circular, polygonal, or annular. Also called *concept identification* or *concept learning*. *See also* componential theory, feature comparison model, intuition, mismatch, overextension, prototype theory, semantics, 2-4-6 problem, underextension, Vygotsky blocks.

concept identification *n.* Another name for *concept formation.

concept learning *n.* Another name for *concept formation.

conceptual dependency theory *n.* In the field of *knowledge representation, a theory of how meaning is represented. According to the theory, propositions are reduced to a small number of *semantic primitives, such as agents, actions, and objects, and are interpreted according to knowledge stored as *scripts (3). The theory was introduced in the 1970s by the US linguist and cognitive scientist Roger C. Schank (born 1946).

conceptually driven processing *n.* Any *cognitive or *perceptual process that is controlled by higher-level processing or *top-down processing. *See also* constructivism.

conceptual map *n.* Another name for a *cognitive map.

conceptual tempo *n.* Another name for *reflection–impulsivity.

concomitant variable *n.* Another name for a *covariate.

concordance *n.* **1.** In genetics, the proportion of *monozygotic twins, or relatives of other known degrees of genetic relatedness, who share the same characteristic or *phenotype. *See also* map distance, twin study. *Compare* discordance (1). **2.** In statistics, the degree of agreement between *ranks. *See* gamma statistic, Kendall coefficient of concordance, Kendall's tau, Somers' *D. Compare* discordance (2). **concordant** *adj.*

Concorde fallacy *n.* Continuing to invest in a project merely to justify past investment in it, rather than assessing the current rationality of investing, irrespective of what has gone before. Thus gamblers often throw good money after bad in an attempt to escape from escalating debts, marriage partners often become trapped in escalating spirals of hostility and counter-hostility from which they feel increasingly incapable of extricating themselves on account of past emotional investments, and the length of time a female great golden digger wasp *Sphex ichneumoneus* is prepared to fight over a disputed burrow depends not on how much food there is in the burrow but on how much she herself has put there, the wasp that has carried the largest amount of prey into the burrow being generally least willing to give up fighting. The phenomenon was first identified and named in an article in the journal *Nature* in 1976 by the British ethologist Richard Dawkins (born 1941) and his undergraduate student Tamsin R. Carlisle (born 1954). Also called the *sunk cost fallacy*, especially in decision theory and economics. *See also* Dollar Auction game.

[Named after the Anglo-French supersonic airliner, the Concorde, whose cost rose steeply during its development phase in the 1970s so that it soon became uneconomical, but British and French governments continued to support it to justify past investment]

concrete operations *n.* According to the theory of cognitive development of the Swiss psychologist Jean Piaget (1896–1980), the stage of cognitive development between the ages of approximately 7 and 12 years during which a child becomes proficient at manipulating internal representations of physical objects and acquires mastery of the various forms of *conservation. *See also* mental operation. *Compare* formal operations, pre-operational stage, sensorimotor stage.

concurrent validity *n*. In psychometrics, a form of *criterion validity based on predictor and criterion scores obtained at approximately the same time, as when a test of depression is validated against clinical diagnoses made at about the same time. *Compare* predictive validity.

concussion *n*. Jarring of the brain caused by a blow to the head, a fall, or an explosion, causing a temporary loss of consciousness or disturbance of normal brain function. **concuss** *vb*.
[From Latin *concussus* violently shaken, from *concutere* to shake violently, from *quatere* to shake + *-ion* indicating an action, process, or state]

condensation *n*. Compressing or making more compact. In *psychoanalysis, the representation of several chains of mental associations by a single idea. This phenomenon is manifested in *dreams (1), *neurotic (1) or other *symptoms, jokes, and other manifestations of unconscious activity, and it is characteristic of the *primary process. Sigmund Freud (1856–1939) first referred to it in 1900 in his book *The Interpretation of Dreams* (*Standard Edition*, IV–V, at pp. 293–5). By 1916–17, when his *Introductory Lectures on Psychoanalysis* was published, Freud had come to the view that condensation is probably not caused directly by *censorship but that it serves the interests of censorship none the less (*Standard Edition*, XV, at p. 191). In an article in the journal *La Psychoanalyse* in 1957, the French psychoanalyst Jacques Lacan (1901–81) related condensation to *metaphor and the defence mechanism of *displacement to *metonymy. *See also* dreamwork, overdetermination.

conditional probability *n*. Another name for *posterior probability: the probability assigned to an event in accordance with *Bayes' theorem in the light of empirical evidence as to its observed relative frequency. *See also* conditional reasoning. *Compare* prior probability (2).

conditional reasoning *n*. A form of logical reasoning based on *conditional statements* or *conditional propositions* having the form *If p, then q*, in which *p* is the *antecedent and *q* is the *consequent. An example is *If this substance is glass, then a diamond will scratch it*. The conditional statement is logically equivalent to *Not-(p and not-q)*, and it is true, by definition, if and only if *p* and *q* are both true or *p* is false (whether *q* is true or false). A *subjunctive conditional* is a conditional statement or *proposition (1) in which the antecedent and consequent are both hypothetical or contingent: *If the polar ice cap were to melt, then many people would drown*. A *counterfactual conditional* is a subjunctive conditional in which the antecedent is not merely hypothetical but false: *If she had pulled the trigger, then I would have been killed*; and in logic it is necessarily true because its antecedent is false. *See also* affirming the antecedent, affirming the consequent, biconditional, denying the antecedent, denying the consequent, simulation heuristic.

conditional response *n*. An uncommon but more accurate name for a *conditioned response. Also called a *conditional reflex*.

conditional stimulus *n*. An uncommon but more accurate name for a *conditioned stimulus.

conditioned emotional response *n*. A phenomenon of *conditioning (1) that occurs when a baseline behaviour such as lever pressing for food reward is established at a stable rate of responding, then a long-lasting *conditioned stimulus (such as a 90-second tone) is presented and terminates with the presentation of an aversive *unconditioned stimulus (such as a brief electric shock). After several such pairings of conditioned and unconditioned stimulus, the organism suppresses responding during the conditioned stimulus presentation, even though the food reward is still available in response to lever pressing and is completely independent of the tone–shock pairing, the usual interpretation being that the conditioned stimulus (tone) elicits a *conditioned response (fear) that is incompatible with the suppressed behaviour (feeding). Also called *conditioned suppression*. **CER** *abbrev*.

conditioned food aversion *n*. Another name for *food aversion learning.

conditioned reflex n. Another name for a *conditioned response, presupposing that such a response arises from modification of a *reflex arc. Also called a *conditional reflex*.

conditioned response n. In *classical conditioning, a learned response that follows a *conditioned stimulus as a consequence of a process of classical conditioning. *Conditioned* is a slight mistranslation of *conditional*, the term originally used by the Russian physiologist Ivan Petrovich Pavlov (1849–1936), referring to a response occurring only conditionally (after a process of conditioning). Also called a *conditioned reflex* or a *conditional reflex*, presupposing that it arises from modification of a *reflex arc. *Compare* unconditioned response. **CR** *abbrev.*

conditioned stimulus n. In *classical conditioning, a *stimulus (1) such as the ticking of a metronome that is initially neutral but that comes to elicit a particular *response such as salivation only as a consequence of being paired with an *unconditioned stimulus such as food during a process of classical conditioning. It is a slight mistranslation of *conditional stimulus*, the term originally used by the Russian physiologist Ivan Petrovich Pavlov (1849–1936), meaning a stimulus that elicits a particular response only conditionally (after a process of conditioning). *Compare* unconditioned response. **CS** *abbrev.*

conditioned suppression n. Another name for a *conditioned emotional response. More generally, a reduction in the frequency of a *conditioned response resulting from the presence of a stimulus previously associated with pain.

conditioned taste aversion n. Another name for *food aversion learning.

conditioning n. **1.** The process of *learning (1) through which the behaviour of organisms becomes dependent on environmental *stimuli (1). Its two major forms are *classical conditioning (Pavlovian conditioning) and *operant conditioning (instrumental conditioning). *See also* associative learning, autoshaping, behaviourism, shaping (1). **2.** In linguistics, the influence of linguistic context on a linguistic unit or form. The *allophone of a *phoneme may be determined by

phonological context (for an example, *see under* aspiration); or the *allomorph of a *morpheme may be determined by grammatical context, as when the morpheme *a* becomes *an* before a *vowel. **3.** Another name for *Bayesian inference.
[Sense 1 is a back formation from *conditioned* (originally *conditional*) *response*]

Condorcet's paradox n. A *paradox of *intransitive preferences arising from the aggregation of individual *transitive preferences under majority rule. Its simplest manifestation is in a group of three voters choosing among three alternatives x, y, and z, the first voter preferring the three alternatives in the order xyz, the second yzx, and the third zxy. In a majority vote, x is preferred to y by a majority of two to one (the first and third voters preferring the alternatives in that order), and similarly y is preferred to z by a majority, and z is preferred to x by a majority. Also called a *cyclic majority* or the *paradox of voting*. *See also* Arrow's impossibility theorem.
[Named after the French philosopher and mathematician Marie Jean Antoine Nicolas de Caritat Condorcet (1743–94) who discovered it in 1785]

conduct disorder n. A *mental disorder of childhood or adolescence characterized by repetitive and persistent violations of the rights of others and of social norms and rules, including bullying, aggressive or threatening behaviour towards people or animals, deliberate destruction of property, deceitfulness, or theft, with the behaviour causing significant impairment in social, academic, or occupational functioning. *See* oppositional defiant disorder. *Compare* antisocial personality disorder.

conduction aphasia *See under* aphasia.

conductive deafness n. Any form of *deafness resulting from disease, damage, or obstruction in the *outer ear canal or the *middle ear. Common causes are accumulation of wax in the outer ear (*ceruminous deafness), *otitis media, and otosclerosis, a disorder of the *oval window in which the *stapes becomes fused with the vestibule of the *bony labyrinth. Also called *conduction deafness* or *transmission deafness*. *Compare* central auditory processing disorder, sensorineural deafness.

cone *n*. One of the two classes of *photoreceptors at the back of the *retina, mediating *photopic vision, responsive to bright light, colour-sensitive and found especially abundantly in the *fovea, with an outer segment at its back end containing photosensitive membranes stacked like an orderly pile of discs decreasing in diameter towards the tip, studded with light-absorbing molecules of *visual pigment, and a *synapse (1) at the other end transmitting nerve impulses to *bipolar cells and *horizontal cells in the retina. Cones are divided into three types containing different visual pigments having broad and overlapping sensitivity curves with peak absorption at about 430, 530, and 560 nanometres, loosely called blue, green, and red cones, respectively. Because of the overlap, signals from one type of cone are not sufficient to give rise to a specific sensation of colour, light of any wavelength invariably causing two or more types to respond in different degrees, and the relative strengths of the signals from all three types providing the necessary information for sensations of colour, as when weak signals from red and green cones accompanied by strong signals from blue cones evoke the sensation of blue, or when equal signals from red and green cones accompanied by weak signals from blue cones evoke the sensation of yellow. The human retina contains approximately 6 million cones, far outnumbered by the 120 million rods. Also called a *retinal cone*. *See also* dominator, ganglion cell, modulator, pigment, trichromatic theory. *Compare* rod.
[So called because it is cone-shaped, with a tapering outer segment]

cone of confusion *n*. A cone-shaped set of points, radiating outwards from a location midway between an organism's ears, from which a sound source produces identical *phase delays and *transient disparities, making the use of such binaural cues useless for *sound localization. Any cross-section of the cone represents a set of points that are equidistant from the left ear and equidistant from the right ear.

cone pigment *n*. Any of three distinct *visual pigments in the normal (non-colour-blind) human retina that are responsible for colour vision and that have peak sensitivities at approximately 430 nanometres, 530 nm, and 560 nm, usually called blue, green, and red pigments, respectively, although light of these wavelengths actually looks violet, blue-green, and yellowish-green. *See also* iodopsin. *Compare* rhodopsin.

confabulation *n*. A memory disorder related to *amnesia but involving the generation of fabricated accounts of events, experiences, or facts, either deliberately or without conscious intent, to compensate for memory loss. Some authorities think of it as 'honest lying'. It is a common sign of *Korsakoff's psychosis.
[From Latin *con-* with + *fabula* a story + *-(a)tion* indicating a process or condition]

confederate *n*. A person taking part in a conspiracy. In research methodology, an accomplice of the experimenter in research involving deception, pretending to be an experimental participant or subject, along with the real participants, but actually playing out an assigned role. Also called a *stooge*. *Compare* naive participant.

confidence interval *n*. In statistics, a range of values bounded by *confidence limits* within which there is a specified probability that the true value of a population *parameter is expected, with a specified level of confidence, to lie. By convention, the 95 and 99 per cent confidence intervals are most often used. For example, in a population of 8,000, a sample of 950 respondents is required to achieve a 95 per cent confidence interval of ±3 per cent. This means that if a survey found that 25 per cent of a random sample were in favour of capital punishment, then if 100 different random samples of that size were drawn from the population, 95 per cent of them would give results between 22 and 28 per cent. In large populations, over about 5,000, the necessary sample size for a given confidence interval is surprisingly insensitive to the population size: for a population of 40,000, a sample of 1,050 is required to achieve the same 95 per cent confidence interval of ±3 per cent, and the required sample size increases only very slowly for larger samples than that, hence opinion polls in the UK (population 56 m), the US (population 250 m), and Ireland (population $3\frac{1}{2}$ m) all use sample sizes slightly over 1,000 to achieve 95 per cent confidence intervals of ±3 per cent, which is the conventional confidence interval for public opinion polls. *See also* probable error.

confidence limits n. The bounds of a *confidence interval.

configural scoring rule n. In psychometrics, any rule for assigning weights to predictor variables so that the interpretation of one predictor score depends on the level of one or more others, as for example in a *lexicographic semiorder. See also scoring formula.

configural superiority effect n. The tendency for some complex visual stimuli, such as faces or printed words, to be more easily recognizable than any of their constituent parts presented in isolation. Also called the *object superiority effect. See also word superiority effect.

configuration law n. Another name for the principle of *Prägnanz in Gestalt psychology.

confirmation bias n. The tendency to test one's beliefs or conjectures by seeking evidence that might confirm or verify them and to ignore evidence that might disconfirm or refute them. This bias, which helps to maintain *prejudices and *stereotypes, is clearly manifested in problem-solvers' behaviour in the *Wason selection task and the *2-4-6 problem. See also falsifiability, Hempel's paradox, logical positivism. Compare matching bias.

confirmation paradox n. Another name for *Hempel's paradox.

confirmatory factor analysis n. The use of *factor analysis to test *hypotheses about the factors underlying a set of correlations. Compare exploratory factor analysis.

conflict, psychical See psychical conflict.

conformity n. A form of *social influence in which a person yields to group pressure in the absence of any explicit order or request from another person to comply, as in the *Asch experiment. See also anticonformity, law of social impact. Compare compliance, obedience.

confounding n. In research design, the problem that arises when two or more *causal variables, often an *independent variable and an *extraneous variable, are not properly controlled, so that their separate effects on the *dependent variable cannot be disentangled.

[From Latin confundere to mingle or pour together, from fundere to pour]

confusion matrix n. A *matrix representing the relative frequencies with which each of a number of stimuli is mistaken for each of the others by a person in a task requiring recognition or identification of stimuli. Analysis of these data allows a researcher to extract *factors (2) indicating the underlying dimensions of similarity in the perception of the respondent. For example, in colour-identification tasks, relatively frequent confusion of reds with greens would tend to suggest *daltonism.

congener n. **1.** A member of the same *genus as another organism. **2.** A drug that belongs to the same category, class, or group as its parent compound. **3.** Any additional substance apart from alcohol that is present in an alcoholic beverage and that is partly responsible for its effects.
[From Latin con with + genus birth]

congenital facial diplegia n. Another name for *Möbius syndrome.

congenital oculofacial paralysis n. Another name for *Möbius syndrome.

congruent validity n. The *validity of a test determined by its *correlation with existing tests designed to measure the same *construct.

congruity theory n. A *cognitive consistency theory of *attitude change, based on *balance theory but formulated as a quantitative model, according to which if a source S and attitude object O are linked by an associative assertion (such as S is an O, S likes O, S shakes hands with O, or S goes with O) or a dissociative assertion (such as S is not an O, S dislikes O, S avoids O, or S criticizes O), then the attitudes to both S and O of the person receiving this message will shift towards a point of equilibrium, the less polarized of the two elements moving proportionately more than the more polarized one. Attitudes towards S and O are measured on a seven-point *semantic differential scale from -3 to $+3$, and the change equation for the source is $Change(S) = [|O|/(|O| + |S|)]P$, where $|O|$ and $|S|$ are the absolute values (ignoring any negative signs) of the two initial attitudes and P is the pressure towards change—the total amount of change required to produce congruity. Similarly, the change equation for the attitude object is Change(O) = $[|S|/(|S| + |O|)]P$. For example, if a person has a positive attitude towards the composer Tchaikovsky (+2) and a very negative attitude towards homosexuality (−3), and if the person discovers that Tchaikovsky was gay, then the distance between the two and hence the value of P is 5, and Change(S) = $[3/(3 + 2)]5 = 3$, which means that the attitude towards Tchaikovsky moves three units in the direction of the attitude towards homosexuality; and by a similar calculation, the attitude towards homosexuality moves two units in the direction of the attitude towards Tchaikovsky; so that the person's attitudes to Tchaikovsky and homosexuality both end up at −1. For a dissociative assertion, the two move away from each other. In the light of empirical findings two correction factors were added to the theory: an *assertion constant* to account for the fact that the attitude towards the attitude object tends to change more than the attitude towards the source, and a *correction for incredulity* that reduces the amount of change in both S and O in proportion to their distance apart (for an associative assertion) or their closeness (for a dissociative assertion). The theory was formulated in 1955 by the US psychologist Charles E(gerton) Osgood (1916–91) and the Canadian-born US psychologist Percy (Hyman) Tannenbaum (born 1927).

conjoint measurement theory *n.* A mathematical method for constructing measurement *scales (1) for objects with multiple *attributes in such a way that attributes are traded off against one another and the scale value of each object is a function of the scale values of its component attributes. The method determines whether apparent *interaction effects arise from actual interactions between the underlying attributes or as *artefacts (2) of the particular *measurement model adopted. *Axiomatic conjoint measurement* investigates qualitative aspects of the data to determine how best to scale the data to provide the optimal composition rule. In *numerical conjoint measurement*, also called *conjoint analysis*, a particular composition rule is assumed and then the data are scaled, if possible, to yield an *additive model solution. The theory was introduced in 1964 by the US mathematical psychologist Robert Duncan Luce (born 1925) and the US statisti-

cian John Wilder Tukey (1915–2000). *See also* axiomatic measurement theory, unfolding technique.

[From Latin *coniungere* to link together, from *com* together + *iungere* to join]

conjoint therapy *n.* Any form of *psychotherapy or *counselling in which two or more clients or patients are treated simultaneously. *See also* group therapy.

conjugate movement *n.* A coordinated movement, as of the two eyes turning together in the same direction or the pupils of both eyes constricting at the same time (a *conjugate eye movement*). Also called a *consensual movement*. *See also* Deiters' nucleus, pupillary light reflex. *Compare* disjunctive eye movement.

[From Latin *coniugare* to join together, from *con-* together + *iugare* to marry or join, from *iugum* a yoke]

conjunction *n.* **1.** The act or process of joining together, or the state of being joined. **2.** In logic, two *propositions (1) connected by an operator denoting *and* to form a single compound proposition, usually written $p \wedge q$, where p and q represent the component propositions or conjuncts, the compound proposition being true only if both of its conjuncts are true. *See also* conjunction fallacy. *Compare* disjunction (2).

[From Latin *con-* with + *iunctio* joining + *-ion* indicating an action, process, or state]

conjunction fallacy *n.* A widespread error of judgement according to which a combination of two or more *attributes is judged to be more probable or likely than either attribute on its own. It was identified and named in 1982 by the Israeli psychologists Amos Tversky (1937–96) and Daniel Kahneman (born 1934) who presented undergraduate students with personality sketches of a hypothetical person called Linda (young, single, deeply concerned about social issues, and involved in anti-nuclear activity) and asked them whether it was more probable that (a) Linda is a bank teller, or (b) Linda is a bank teller who is active in the feminist movement; 86 per cent of the students judged (b) to be more probable than (a). This is a fallacy, because it is an elementary principle of probability theory that the probability of the *conjunction (2) A and B can never exceed the probability of *A* or the probability of *B*. The fallacy arises from the use of the *representativeness heuristic, because Linda seems more typical of a feminist bank teller than of a bank teller. *See also* Kolmogorov's axioms.

conjunction search *n.* A search for a target stimulus representing a *conjunctive concept among a number of distractor stimuli. *Compare* disjunction search, feature search.

conjunctive concept *n.* A concept defined by the simultaneous possession or *conjunction (2) of two or more *attributes, for example, a red square. *Compare* disjunctive concept.

conjunctive eye movement *n.* Another name for a *conjugate movement.
[From Latin *coniunctivus* joined, from *coniungere* to conjoin, from *iungere* to join]

connectedness grouping law *n.* A perceptual *grouping law formulated in 1990 by the US psychologists Irvin Rock (1922–95) and Stephen E. Palmer (born 1948) to explain the organization of parts into wholes by the visual system. According to the law, the perceptual system has a tendency to perceive any uniform, connected line or area as a single unit, so that the array

O–O O–O O–O O–O

tends to be perceived as being composed of four rather than eight or twelve elements. *See also* Prägnanz. *Compare* closure grouping law, common fate, common region, good continuation, proximity grouping law, similarity grouping law.

connectionism *n.* **1.** An approach to *artificial intelligence involving the design of intelligent systems composed of *neural networks in which items of knowledge are represented not by single locations or units but by patterns of activation over collections of units, these patterns being adaptive inasmuch as they are capable of learning from experience. It was first introduced in 1948 in an article on 'Intelligent Machinery' by the English mathematician Alan Mathison Turing (1912–54) but became popular only after the publication in 1981 of a connectionist model of human memory developed by the US cognitive scientist James L(loyd) McClelland (born 1948). Turing's article was partly anticipated by an article in 1943 by the US neurophysiologist Warren S(turgis) McCulloch (1898–1968) and the self-taught US logician Walter Pitts (1923–69), but that early version crucially lacked the ability to learn. Also called *parallel distributed processing*. *See also* back-propagation algorithm, cascade processing, delta rule, distributed network model, gradient descent, Hebbian rule, hill climbing, knowledge representation, teacher unit. *Compare* distributed cognition. **2.** A term used by the US psychologist Edward Lee Thorndike (1874–1949) to refer to his interpretation of trial-and-error learning as the formation of associations between situations (not ideas) and responses. *See also* law of effect. *Compare* associationism. **connectionist** *n.* **1.** One who practises or advocates *connectionism (1, 2). *adj.* **2.** Of or relating to *connectionism (1, 2).

connectionist model *n.* Any model of *information processing based on the conceptual framework of *connectionism (1). Also called a *connectionist network*.

connotation *n.* **1.** An association or idea suggested or implied by a word or expression; for example, the word *mother* has connotations of home, family, maternal love, and so on. This meaning should be carefully distinguished from sense 2. *See also* semantic differential. *Compare* denotation (1). **2.** In philosophy, the set of *attributes or properties that determine the thing or things to which a word or expression refers; hence the connotation of the word *mother* is the following set of attributes or properties: {female, human or animal, parent}. *See also* intension. *Compare* denotation (2). **connotative** *adj.* **connote** *vb.*
[From Latin *connotare* to connote, from *con-* with + *notare* to mark, from *nota* a mark or sign + *-ation* indicating a process or condition]

consanguinity, coefficient of *See* coefficient of consanguinity.

consanguinity study *n.* Another name for a *kinship study.

conscientiousness *n.* One of the *Big Five personality factors, characterized by *traits such as organization, thoroughness, reliability, and practicality, and the relative absence of carelessness, negligence, and unreliability. Also called *dependability*. **conscientious** *adj.*
[From Latin *con* with + *scire* to know]

conscious *adj.* **1.** Of or relating to the function of the mind through which one is aware of mental experiences such as perceptions, thoughts, emotions, and wishes. In *psychoanalysis, functioning as a noun (*the conscious*), denoting the conscious mind. *See also* consciousness. *Compare* unconscious (1). **2.** Awake, alert, and aware of what is happening in the immediate vicinity; not in a state of sleep, trance, or coma. **3.** Aware of and giving due weight to something, as in *Are you conscious of the need for action?* or *I am not at all clothes-conscious.*
[From Latin *conscius* sharing knowledge, from *con* with + *scire* to know]

consciousness *n.* The state of being *conscious (1, 2); the normal mental condition of the waking state of humans, characterized by the experience of perceptions, thoughts, feelings, awareness of the external world, and often in humans (but not necessarily in other animals) self-awareness. *See also* altered state of consciousness, astonishing hypothesis, attention, functionalism, marginal consciousness, perception–consciousness system, stream of consciousness, thing-presentation, topography, word-presentation. *Compare* preconscious, unconscious (1, 2). **Cs** *abbrev.*

consensual pupillary reflex *n.* Another name for the *pupillary light reflex. Also called the *consensual light reflex.*
[From Latin *consensus* agreement, from *consentire* to agree or feel together, from *com* with + *sentire* to feel]

consensual validity *n.* The *validity of a test determined by its general acceptance in the community of test administrators or by the number of users who judge it to be valid. *See also* face validity, intrinsic validity.

consensus sequence *n.* A sequence of *DNA such as the *telomere sequence TTAGGG that is found in widely divergent organisms and has a similar function in each. Also called a *canonical sequence.*

consequent *See under* conditional reasoning.

conservation *n.* A term introduced by the Swiss psychologist Jean Piaget (1896–1980) to denote the understanding that material quantity is unaffected by certain transformations that change its appearance. *Conservation of number* is exemplified by understanding the invariance of the number of objects when their spatial arrangement is changed, *conservation of substance* the invariance of the quantity of a liquid when it is poured into a differently shaped container, and *conservation of mass* and *conservation of volume* the invariance of the mass and the volume of a lump of plasticine, play dough, or similar material when it is moulded into a different shape. The various types of conservation generally appear at different stages of a child's development, first number and substance, then mass, then volume; conservation of number and substance typically appearing by age 7 or 8 and the others soon after. The lack of mastery of conservation of number in a younger child at the *pre-operational stage of development can be demonstrated by setting up a row of egg-cups, each containing an egg, asking the child to confirm that the number of egg-cups is the same as the number of eggs, then removing the eggs and moving them close together to make a row that is much shorter than the row of egg-cups, and asking the child whether there are more eggs than egg-cups, more egg-cups than eggs, or the same number of egg-cups and eggs. A child who has not yet mastered the conservation of number usually believes that there are more egg-cups, because the row is longer. Variations of this experiment were first described by Piaget in 1941 in his book *La Genèse du Nombre chez l'Enfant* (*The Child's Conception of Number*, English translation published in 1952). *See also* centration, concrete operations, décalage.

conservation of energy law *n.* The first law of *thermodynamics, stating that when a system changes from one state to another, energy is converted to a different form but the total energy remains unchanged or is conserved, making a perpetual-motion machine impossible. It was discovered by the German physician and physicist Julius Mayer (1814–1878), who submitted it to the leading physics journal *Annalen der Physik*, but it was rejected, and Mayer was forced to publish it in an obscure chemistry journal where it had little impact; then it was independently rediscovered by the Scottish physicist and mathematician William Thomson (later Lord Kelvin, 1824–1907), who presented it to the Royal Society in 1851 and was credited with its discovery. *See also* principle of constancy.

consistency theory *See* cognitive consistency theory.

consolidation *n*. The process whereby new information is fixed in *long-term memory, where it is integrated with existing stored information. The process continues for some time after exposure to the new information. *See also* calpain, Hebb synapse, hippocampus, long-term potentiation, phase sequence.

consonant *n*. Any speech sound that involves a significant obstruction of the airstream in the vocal tract and that functions at the beginning or end of a syllable, either singly or in a cluster, or a letter of the alphabet representing such a speech sound. *Plosive consonants involve complete stoppage of the airstream and are maximally consonantal; *nasal (2) consonants complete blockage of the airstream through the mouth but not the nose; *fricatives considerable obstruction but not stoppage; *lateral consonants obstruction in the centre of the mouth only; and *approximants relatively little obstruction of the airflow. *Compare* semivowel, vowel. **consonantal** *adj*.
[From Latin *consonare* to sound at the same time]

consonant trigram *n*. A string of three consonants, such as *CBT*, sometimes used in experiments on memory instead of *CVC trigrams. Also called a *CCC trigram*.

consonant–vowel–consonant trigram *n*. A string of three letters, beginning and ending with a consonant, with a vowel in the middle, such as *KUG*. *See also* CVC, nonsense syllable.

conspecific *n*. **1.** An organism of the same species as another. *adj*. **2.** Belonging to the same species.
[From Latin *con* with + *specificus* of or relating to a species, from *species* appearance, from *specere* to look + -*ikos* of, relating to, or resembling]

constancy *See* perceptual constancy.

constancy, principle of *See* principle of constancy.

constant error *n*. In *psychophysics, any systematic error of judgement or perception involving either overestimation or underestimation of a variable magnitude. It is used as a measure of the magnitude of certain perceptual illusions. *Compare* variable error. **CE** *abbrev*.

constant stimuli method *See* method of constant stimuli.

constituent *n*. A component part of a larger whole; in linguistics, a word, phrase, or clause forming part of a larger linguistic structure. For example, a sentence can be analysed into its constituent subject and predicate, and each of these units can be analysed further into their constituent parts. The results of such an analysis into constituents at different levels may be depicted by a *phrase marker.
[From Latin *constituens* setting up, from *constituere* to establish, from *con* together + *statuere* to place]

constitutional psychology *n*. A theory, especially that of the US psychologist William H. Sheldon (1899–1977), postulating that *personality is dependent on physique or *somatotype. *See* ectomorph, endomorph, mesomorph. *Compare* Kretschmer constitutional type.

construct *n*. A *model based on observation guided by a theoretical framework. In *psychometrics, a psychological attribute, such as *intelligence or *extraversion, on which people differ from one another; more generally any complex *concept synthesized from simpler concepts. Also called a *latent variable*. *See also* hypothetical construct, psychoanalytic construction, theory (2).
[From Latin *constructus* piled up or built, from *construere* to pile up or build, from *con-* together + *struere* to arrange or erect]

constructional apraxia *See under* apraxia.

construction in analysis *n*. Another name for *psychoanalytic construction.

constructive memory *n*. The production of memories under the influence of prior experience and expectations in such a way that existing *schemas or new information affect how the information is stored in memory. *See also* constructivism, Piaget kidnapping memory, reality monitoring. *Compare* reconstructive memory.

constructivism n. A doctrine according to which perceptions, memories, and other complex mental structures are actively assembled or built by the mind, rather than being passively acquired. The idea was introduced in 1932 by the English psychologist Sir Frederic Charles Bartlett (1886–1969) to explain phenomena that he observed in his study of memory. An influential example of constructivism in perception is the concept of the *perceptual cycle introduced by the US psychologist Ulrich (Richard Gustav) Neisser (born 1928), and it has been used by the English psychologist Richard L(angton) Gregory (born 1923) and others to explain a number of visual illusions. Radical constructivism, deriving from writings in the 1950s of the Swiss psychologist Jean Piaget (1896–1980), is based on the assumption that children construct mental structures by observing the effects of their own actions on the environment. Social constructivism, first popularized by the Austrian-born US sociologist Peter Ludwig Berger (born 1929) and the Yugoslav-born US sociologist Thomas Luckmann (born 1927) in their influential book *The Social Construction of Reality* (1966), focuses on the way people come to share interpretations of their social environment. *See also* constructive memory, reconstructive memory, schema, top-down processing.

construct validity n. In psychometrics, the extent to which a test measures a specified *construct or *hypothetical construct, determined by interpreting the psychological meaning of test scores and testing implications of this interpretation. For example, according to the construct of *extraversion proposed by the German-born British psychologist Hans J(ürgen) Eysenck (1916–97), extraverts form *conditioned responses more slowly than introverts; therefore, if a scale designed to measure extraversion is administered to a group of respondents, and high scorers are shown in a conditioning procedure to condition more slowly than low scorers, then these data constitute evidence for the construct validity of the scale relative to Eysenck's concept of extraversion. More specific interpretations of construct validity have been suggested in terms of *convergent validity and *discriminant validity in relation to the *multitrait–multimethod matrix, and in terms of the *nomological network.

consumer psychology n. A branch of psychology devoted to the study of the delivery of goods and services and the effects of advertising, marketing, packaging, and display on the behaviour of purchasers.

consummate love n. A type of love characterized by erotic passion, commitment, and intimacy. *See under* love.
[From Latin *consummare, consummatum* to perfect, from *con* with + *summus* the highest, from *summa* a sum]

contact hypothesis n. The proposition that sheer social contact between hostile groups is sufficient to reduce intergroup hostility. Empirical evidence suggests that this is so only in certain circumstances.

contact receptor n. A *sensory receptor such as a *touch receptor or a *taste receptor that is stimulated by an object or substance touching it. *Compare* distance receptor.

contagion, behavioural/social *See* behavioural contagion, social contagion.

content-addressable memory n. In computer technology, a memory store that can be accessed by specifying the information that it contains, so that an instruction to find a particular item of information can be automatically converted into an instruction to go to the physical location where that information is stored. Human memory is evidently content addressable, and so are the memory systems of *connectionism (1) and *parallel distributed processing. Also called a *content-addressable store*.

content analysis n. A collection of techniques often used in *qualitative research for the systematic and objective description and classification of the manifest or latent subject matter of written or spoken verbal communications, usually by counting the incidence or coincidence of utterances falling into several (usually predetermined) categories.

content domain n. In psychometrics, a clearly defined body of knowledge, skills, abilities, aptitudes, or tasks that may be measured with an appropriately constructed test. *See also* content validity, domain-referenced test, domain sampling.

contentive *n*. Another name for a *content word.

content psychology *n*. The psychological study of the components of consciousness as practised in *structuralism (2), rather than of individual acts. *Compare* act psychology.

content validity *n*. In psychometrics, the extent to which the items of a test are appropriate to the *content domain of the test. For example, a test used for employment selection has high content validity if the test items cover the abilities, skills, or competencies required to perform the job and do not cover other irrelevant attributes. *See also* domain-referenced test, domain sampling.

content word *n*. Any word with an independent meaning that can be stated, such as *flower*, *write*, and the great majority of words in any natural language. Also called a *contentive* or a *lexical word*. *Compare* function word.

context-dependent grammar *n*. A type of *generative grammar in which a rule can be conditional on the linguistic context—the linguistic units adjacent or nearby those to which the rule applies directly. For example, *Rewrite X as X + Y in the context of Z* is a typical *context-dependent rule* in such a grammar. Also called a *context-sensitive grammar*. *Compare* context-free grammar.

context-dependent memory *n*. A form of *state-dependent memory associated with the context in which information is learned and recalled.

context effect *n*. Any influence of surrounding objects, events, or information on an organism's response to a *stimulus (1), especially on perception and cognition. *See also* adaptation-level theory, associative illusion, dialectical montage, field effect, Gelb effect, induced motion, Kardos effect, word superiority effect. *Compare* framing effect.

context-free grammar *n*. A type of *generative grammar in which the rules apply regardless of the linguistic context—the linguistic units adjacent or nearby those to which the rule applies directly. For example, *Rewrite X as X + Y* is a possible *context-free rule* in such a grammar, and it would apply irrespec-

tive of linguistic context. *Compare* context-dependent grammar.

context-sensitive grammar *n*. Another name for a *context-dependent grammar.

contiguity law *n*. In the doctrine of *associationism, the most basic law, introduced by the Scottish philosopher James Mill (1773–1836), according to which mental elements or ideas become associated when they are close to one another in time or space. Thus redness is associated with warmth because the two are often contiguous in everyday experience, as when one encounters a hearth full of glowing coals. *See also* grouping law. *Compare* frequency law, similarity law.
[From Latin *contigere* to touch on all sides, from *con-* wholly + *tangere* to touch]

contiguity theory *n*. The learning theory of the US psychologist Edwin R. Guthrie (1886–1959), according to which an organism invariably gives the same response to a *stimulus (1) pattern that it gave when it last encountered the pattern (including internal stimuli), the function of *reinforcement being to create a new stimulus pattern to which the organism responds similarly in the future.

contingency coefficient *n*. In statistics, a measure of association between two categorical variables, applicable to a *contingency table of any size. It is based on the *chi-square distribution and ranges from 0 (no association) to 1 (perfect association) and is calculated by dividing the chi-square value for the table by the chi-square value plus the number of observations and then extracting the square root. *Compare* Cramér's *C*, phi coefficient.

contingency management *n*. A technique of *behaviour therapy in which therapists and family members ignore behaviour that is symptomatic of the disorder being treated and actively reward behaviours that are incompatible with the disorder.

contingency table *n*. A rectangular array of numbers formed by the intersection of two classification variables, showing frequencies of observations in each of its cells. For example, if the two variables are male/female and left-handed/right-handed, then the frequencies of cases in each of the four categories could be displayed in a 2 × 2 contingency table, that is, a contingency table with two rows and two columns.

contingency theory of leadership effectiveness *n*. A model of leadership style and leadership effectiveness proposed by the US-based Austrian psychologist Fred Fiedler (born 1922) in his book *A Theory of Leadership Effectiveness* (1967), according to which a directive, authoritarian leadership style is most effective when circumstances are either very unfavourable or very favourable for the leader, and non-directive leadership is most effective in intermediate circumstances. The three key factors determining the favourableness of the circumstances for the leader are leader–member relations (how much the leader is liked and respected by the group members), position power (how much authority the leader has over the group members), and task structure (how structured the group task is).

contingent aftereffect *n*. A type of *aftereffect that results from selective adaptation to specific stimulus features, the resultant effect being contingent on the presence in the visual field of one of these features, the classic example being the *McCollough effect in which illusory colours are contingent on the presence of particular grating patterns. *See also* tilt aftereffect.

contingent negative variation *n*. A type of *event-related potential, believed to indicate attention, consisting of a large negative change in potential voltage across the cerebral cortex, especially in the frontal lobe, that develops slowly in a person who is actively expecting the occurrence of some significant stimulus requiring a response. It is observable as an *evoked potential occurring typically during the 1–2 seconds after a warning signal is given. *See also* P300. *Compare* readiness potential. **CNV** *abbrev*.

continuant *n*. Any speech sound such as /l/, /f/, /r/, or /s/ whose *articulation involves incomplete blockage of the airstream through the vocal tract. *Compare* plosive.

continuation problem *n*. Another name for a *completion test.

continuity (Gestalt) *See* good continuation.

continuity theory *n*. A theory of learning espoused by the US psychologist Clark L. Hull (1884–1952), among others, according to which an organism learns a small amount about all *stimuli (1) that it encounters, and learning is therefore gradual and continuous. *Compare* discontinuity theory.

continuous reinforcement *n*. In *operant conditioning, a *reinforcement schedule in which the organism is rewarded after every response. *Compare* partial reinforcement.

continuous variable *n*. In statistics, any *variable that has a *continuum of possible values, so that integration rather than simple addition is required to determine cumulative probabilities of its *probability distribution. *See also* metathetic stimulus dimension, prothetic stimulus dimension. *Compare* discrete variable.

continuum *n*. A continuous sequence or dimension in which adjacent points are not noticeably different but the extremes are clearly distinct.
[From Latin *continuus* uninterrupted, from *continere* to hang together, from *com* together + *tenere* to hold]

contour *n*. A visual line, edge, or border outlining a part of the visual field, usually determined by abrupt *lightness, *colour, or *texture gradients but sometimes induced as a subjective or *illusory contour without any corresponding retinal image gradient. *See also* Ehrenstein's brightness illusion, illusory contour, Kanizsa triangle, zero-crossing.

contrafreeloading *n*. Working for *reinforcement (1) even though the identical reinforcement is freely available, as when a rat repeatedly presses a lever for food (earned food) that is available to be taken with less effort from a dish (free food). This phenomenon has been shown to occur in a wide variety of vertebrate species, including fish, birds, gerbils, mice, rats, monkeys, chimpanzees, and human children and adults, a rare and possibly unique exception being the domestic cat *Felis domesticus*, and it apparently contradicts conventional theories of learning and motivation because, if reinforcement or reward is equated with food eaten, then organisms seem not to be maximizing the reinforcement/effort or reward/cost ratio.

[From Latin *contra* against + US English *free-loading* obtaining goods or services at someone else's expense]

contralateral *adj.* On, pertaining to, or affecting the opposite side of the body. *Compare* ipsilateral.
[From Latin *contra* against + *lateralis* of or relating to a side, from *lateris* a side]

contrast *n.* **1.** A distinction between things being compared, or an emphasis on the distinction between things that are juxtaposed. **2.** In perception, an enhancement of the perceived differences between stimuli resulting from juxtaposing them. In *simultaneous contrast the stimuli are presented together; in *successive contrast they are presented sequentially. *See* colour contrast, lightness contrast, warmth contrast. *See also* contrast ratio. **3.** In statistics, a comparison of two or more *means calculated by forming a weighted linear combination of means. For example, the contrast $\frac{1}{2}$(Mean 1) + $\frac{1}{2}$(Mean 2) – (Mean 3) could be used to test the *null hypothesis that the average of Mean 1 and Mean 2 is equal to Mean 3 in the population. In most cases it is necessary for statistical reasons for the contrast to be *orthogonal (3), as are the coefficients of $\frac{1}{2}$, $\frac{1}{2}$, and –1 in this example. **4.** The degree to which areas of an optical image, such as those in television or photographic pictures, differ in *luminance, often indexed by $(Lmax - Lmin)/(Lmax + Lmin)$, where $Lmax$ is a measure of the luminance of the brightest area and $Lmin$ the luminance of the darkest area. *See also* contrast ratio, contrast threshold. **5.** Exaggerating or increasing the discrepancy between one's own attitude and that of a source of a persuasive communication or message. *See also* assimilation–contrast theory. *Compare* assimilation (4).
[From Latin *contra* opposite to + *stare* to stand]

contrast ratio *n.* An index of the difference between the *luminance of an image (L_i) and the luminance of its background (L_b) usually expressed as a percentage of the background luminance: $100 \times (L_i - L_b)/L_b$. *Compare* contrast (4).

contrast sensitivity function *n.* A graph depicting the relationship between the *spatial frequencies of simple visual images such as *gratings with variable distances between their bars and a viewer's ability to perceive the fluctuations in luminance across the images, the horizontal axis showing different spatial frequencies and the vertical axis sensitivity, the reciprocal of the *absolute threshold. Also called a *modulation transfer function* (MTF). **CSF** *abbrev.*

contrast threshold *n.* An *absolute threshold for *contrast (4), being the minimum contrast required for an observer to detect a target image reliably.

control analysis *n.* A *psychoanalysis carried out by a student training to become an analyst, under the supervision of a qualified analyst. Also called a *supervised analysis*. *Compare* training analysis.

control, delusion of *See* delusion of control.

control group *n.* In experimental design, a comparison group of research participants or subjects who, when the *independent variable is manipulated, are not exposed to the treatment that subjects in the *experimental group are exposed to, but who in other respects are treated identically to the experimental group, to provide a baseline against which to evaluate the effects of the treatment. *Compare* experimental group.

controlled association *n.* Another name for *directed association.

controlled experiment *n.* Another name for a true *experiment.

controlled processing *n.* Any form of *information processing requiring conscious *attention or control, as in the performance of a novel or difficult task. Compared to *automatic processing, controlled processing is generally much slower, requires more effort, is more easily impaired by fatigue or alcohol, and does not normally involve parallel processing of information from more than one sensory channel, but it can be developed faster and with less practice than automatic processing, often in a few trials, and it leaves the learner with greater control of the behaviour. *See also* dual-process model, principle of least effort.

control variable *n.* **1.** In experimental design, any variable apart from the *independent variable that is controlled by the experimenter by being randomized, held constant, statistically controlled, or suppressed in some other way (also called a *controlled variable*). **2.** Any variable whose values are used to separate cases into subgroups in a cross-tabulation.

convenience sample *n.* A *non-probability sample of research participants or subjects selected not for their representativeness but for their accessibility or handiness, as when university researchers use their own students. *See also* accidental sample, opportunity sample, quota sample, self-selected sample, snowball sample. *Compare* cluster sample, probability sample, random digit dialling, simple random sample, stratified random sample.

conventional fighting *n.* The relatively harmless forms of combat used by many species to settle conflicts over scarce resources, as when bighorn rams leap at each other head-on, although they could inflict more damage by charging each other in the flank; many species of fish seize each other's leathery jaws, rather than biting where more injury would be inflicted; male fiddler crabs never injure each other, although their enlarged claws are powerful enough to crush their opponents; rattlesnakes wrestle but never bite; male deer lock antlers but seldom use them to pierce each other's bodies; and some antelopes actually kneel down to fight. Also called *ritualized fighting*. *See also* display (1, 2), dominance hierarchy, Hawk–Dove game, Hawk–Dove–Retaliator game, resource-holding potential, submissive behaviour. *Compare* escalated fighting.

conventional morality *n.* The second *Kohlberg stage of moral development, in which right and wrong are defined in terms of convention and 'what people would say'. It is divided into two levels: at Level 3 the child's moral behaviour is guided by the goal of gaining approval and avoiding disapproval of others (*I should not tell lies because then people will respect me*), and at Level 2 by rigid codes of 'law and order' (*I should not tell lies because it is forbidden*). *Compare* postconventional morality, preconventional morality.

convergence *n.* Any process of coming together, specifically *ocular convergence. *Compare* divergence.

[From Latin *convergere* to bend together, from *con-* together + *vergere* to incline]

convergence–divergence *n.* A *cognitive style defined by two radically different modes of *thinking. At one extreme is *convergent thinking*, characterized by a tendency to home in on a unique solution to a problem, usually involving the synthesis of information, typified by analytical, deductive thinking in which formal rules are followed, as in arithmetic. It is logical, consciously controlled, reality-oriented, and largely dependent on previously learnt knowledge and skills, and it is measured by conventional IQ tests. At the opposite extreme is *divergent thinking*, characterized by the fluent production of a variety of novel ideas relevant to the problem in hand. Divergent thinkers prefer, and perform better at, open-ended problems that do not have unique solutions. Tests of divergent thinking, which tap more creative types of thinking, include items such as the following: 'How many uses can you think of for a brick?' In a study of schoolboys, the English psychologist Liam Hudson (born 1933) found that most of the boys could think of only three or four answers in about three minutes, but most of those whom he identified as divergent thinkers gave ten or more answers. Some psychologists equate divergent thinking with creativity. The concept was introduced in 1946 by the US psychologist J(oy) P(aul) Guilford (1897–1987), and convergent production and divergent production are two of the five different types of mental operations in *Guilford's cube.

convergence insufficiency *n.* Diminished or impaired *ocular convergence.

convergent validity *n.* A form of *validity that, together with *discriminant validity, provides evidence of *construct validity. It is based on the assumption that different measures of the same *hypothetical construct ought to correlate highly with one another if the measures are valid. The concept was introduced in an article by the US psychologists Donald T(homas) Campbell (1916–96) and Donald W(inslow) Fiske (born 1916) in the journal *Psychological Bulletin* in 1959. *See also* multitrait–multimethod matrix.

conversational maxims *n.* Four assumptions about the quality, quantity, relevance, and manner of utterances in ordinary conversations suggested in 1975 by the English philosopher H(erbert) P(aul) Grice (1913–88) and generally assumed to underpin the *cooperative principle. Also called *Gricean maxims*.

conversation analysis *n*. A collection of techniques used in *ethnomethodology and other forms of *qualitative research for analysing naturally occurring verbal dialogues. It studies the structure and coherence of conversations using empirical and inductive techniques in contrast to the theoretical and deductive approach characteristic of *discourse analysis. **CA** *abbrev*.

conversion *n*. A qualitative alteration in form, character, or function. In *psychoanalysis, a *defence mechanism in which an unconscious conflict that would otherwise arouse *anxiety is expressed symbolically, the repressed wish or idea being transformed into a physical *symptom, such as a pain, paralysis, or loss of sensory function. Sigmund Freud (1856–1939) introduced the concept in 1894 in an article on 'The Neuro-Psychoses of Defence' (*Standard Edition*, III, pp. 45–61, at p. 49) and developed it further in 1908/9 in an article entitled 'Some General Remarks on Hysterical Attacks' (*Standard Edition*, IX, pp. 229–33). *See also* conversion disorder, conversion hysteria.

conversion disorder *n*. A *somatoform disorder characterized by *conversion symptoms, not limited to pain or sexual dysfunction and not occurring exclusively during the course of *somatization disorder or any other mental disorder, but associated with a variety of *psychosocial stressors or conflicts. In some taxonomies of mental disorders, such as *ICD-10, but not *DSM-IV, it is classified as a *dissociative disorder. *See also* conversion, conversion hysteria, conversion symptom, *la belle indifférence*. *Compare* factitious disorder, malingering.

conversion hypothesis *n*. A conjecture that some errors in judging the validity of *syllogisms arise because people mentally translate a premise into one that appears equivalent but actually has a different logical meaning, for example *If p, then q* may be translated mentally to *If and only if p, then q*, which could lead to the incorrect inference, *If not-p, then not-q*. *Compare* atmosphere hypothesis.

conversion hysteria *n*. An obsolescent term for *dissociative disorder. In *psychoanalysis, Sigmund Freud (1856–1939) introduced the term in his celebrated analysis of *Little Hans in an article in 1909 entitled 'Analysis of a Phobia in a Five-Year-Old Boy' (*Standard Edition*, X, pp. 5–149, at p. 116) to denote a form of hysteria characterized by physical symptoms (paralyses, anaesthesias, blindness, deafness, and the like) and to distinguish it from forms of hysteria characterized by anxiety and phobias without physical symptoms. *See also* conversion, conversion disorder, conversion symptom, transference neurosis (1).

conversion symptom *n*. A loss or change of sensory or voluntary motor functioning, such as blindness, deafness, numbness, or paralysis, not fully explained by any neurological or *general medical condition or drug, and not intentionally produced, but judged to be of psychological origin. Also called a *conversion reaction*. *See also* conversion, conversion disorder, conversion hysteria, glove anaesthesia.

convolution *n*. Any of the convex folds or ridges on the surface of the brain, also called a *gyrus*; more generally, anything coiled or twisted together or, by analogy, any confused or intricate issue or condition. **convolute** *vb*. **convoluted** *adj*.
[From Latin *convolutus* rolled up, from *con* with + *volvere*, *volutus* to turn + -*ion* indicating an action, process, or state]

convulsant *adj*. *n*. (Of or pertaining to) a drug such as *picrotoxin, *strychnine, or *tetanus toxin that produces *convulsions by blocking the *inhibitory action of neurotransmitters such as *GABA or *acetylcholine in the nervous system. *Compare* anticonvulsant.

convulsion *n*. An episode, which may be recurrent and episodic, of violent involuntary contractions of a group of muscles of the body, as in a *convulsive disorder, or acute, as in a convulsion following a head injury and concussion. *See* clonic convulsion, seizure, tonic–clonic, tonic convulsion. *See also* anticonvulsant, audiogenic seizure.
[From Latin *convulsio* cramp + -*ion* indicating an action, process, or state]

convulsive disorders *n*. Disorders such as *epilepsy that are characterized by recurrent *convulsions.

convulsive therapy *See* electroconvulsive therapy.

cooing *n.* The earliest identifiable stage in the development of infant vocalization, usually beginning at about three months and characterized by indeterminate *vowel-like sounds, including *phonemes not found in the language that the infant will eventually acquire. Cooing is eventually supplanted by *babbling.

Cook's D *n.* In *regression analysis, a measure of the influence of a particular case on the overall results. A large value of Cook's D indicates that exclusion of the case would cause the regression coefficients to change substantially.
[Named after M. B. Cook, who published the statistic in 1951]

Coolidge effect *n.* An increase in sexual responsiveness and reduction in the sexual *refractory period (1) resulting from the arrival of a new mating partner.
[Named after US President Calvin Coolidge (1872–1933) and the following apocryphal story, which is seldom recounted in print. During a visit to an egg farm with her husband in the 1920s, Mrs Coolidge, the First Lady, was impressed by the frequency with which the roosters were mating with the hens, and she pointedly asked an aide to draw this to the attention of her husband. President Coolidge enquired whether each rooster always mated with the same hen, and the reply came that, to maintain the high frequency of mating, each rooster had to be paired with a new hen every few days. The President asked the aide to draw this to the attention of his wife.]

Coombs unfolding technique *n.* Another name for the *unfolding technique.

cooperative principle *n.* A precept derived from the writings of the English philosopher H(erbert) P(aul) Grice (1913–88) according to which speakers normally try to cooperate when communicating, and in particular they usually attempt to be truthful, informative, relevant, and clear—following Grice's conversational maxims of quality, quantity, relevance, and manner, respectively. Speakers may flout any of these maxims, for example by lying or being sarcastic, but conversation normally proceeds on the assumption that the maxims are being followed. Thus if Person *A* says *I'm thirsty*, and Person *B* replies *I can recommend the Queen's Head*, then, in the UK at least, if the cooperative principle is being followed, *A* will normally assume that *B* is referring to a pub rather than, for example, to the upper part of the sovereign's body or to a coin or a banknote carrying her effigy. Some linguists believe that the maxim of relevance is the fundamental explanatory principle of human communication. *See also* distributed cognition, pragmatics, theory of mind.

Coopersmith Self-Esteem Inventories *n.* An instrument comprising three forms designed to measure self-esteem: two forms for school-children and an adult form, all items having dichotomous response categories (*Like me* or *Unlike me*). Each scale yields scores for self-esteem in relation to social self and peers, home and parents, school and academic, total self, and a *lie scale score. The scales were constructed by the US psychologist Stanley Coopersmith (1926–79), and the original version was published in Coopersmith's book *Antecedents of Self-Esteem* (1967). **CSEI** *abbrev.*

coprolagnia *n.* An alternative name for *coprophilia.
[From Greek *kopros* excrement + *lagneia* lust + -*ia* indicating a condition or quality]

coprolalia *n.* Repetitive or obsessive obscene utterances, such as sometimes occurs in *Tourette's disorder.
[From Greek *kopros* excrement + *lalia* speech + -*ia* indicating a condition or quality]

coprophagia *n.* Eating of excrement or faeces. *See also* pica.
[From Greek *kopros* excrement + *phagein* to consume + -*ia* indicating a condition or quality]

coprophilia *n.* A *paraphilia characterized by recurrent sexually arousing fantasies, sexual urges, or behaviour involving excrement or faeces; more generally, an exaggerated interest in or preoccupation with faeces and their excretion.
[From Greek *kopros* excrement + *philos* loving, from *phileein* to love + -*ia* indicating a condition or quality]

copropraxia *n.* Compulsive or repetitive obscene *gestures (1), such as sometimes occur in *Tourette's disorder.

[From Greek *kopros* excrement + *praxis* a deed or action, from *prassein* to do + *-ia* indicating a condition or quality]

copulation *n*. Sexual intercourse or coitus. **copulate** *vb*.
[From Latin *copula* a bond or connection, from *co-* together + *apere* to fasten + *-ation* indicating a process or condition]

corium *n*. Another name for the *dermis.
[From Latin *corium* skin, rind, or leather]

cornea *n*. The convex, transparent, five-layered fibrous membrane that forms the outer covering of the eyeball and that is responsible for about two-thirds of the *refraction of light required for focusing visual images on the retina, the remaining one-third being supplied by the *crystalline lens of the eye. *See also* eye. **corneal** *adj*.
[From Latin *corneus* horny, from *cornu* a horn]

corneal reflex *n*. A *reflex closing of the eyelids when the cornea is touched or a puff of air is blown on to it, mediated by the fifth cranial *trigeminal nerve (sensory) and the seventh cranial *facial nerve (motor), often diminished or absent in people who wear contact lenses.

Cornsweet illusion *n*. Another name for the *Craik–O'Brien effect.
[Named after the US cognitive scientist Tom Norman Cornsweet (born 1929) who studied it]

cornu ammonis *n*. Another name for *Ammon's horn.
[From Latin *cornu* a horn + *Ammonis* of Ammon]

coronal plane *n*. A vertical plane dividing the brain or any other organ or organism into front and back parts. Also called a *frontal plane*. *Compare* horizontal plane, sagittal plane, transverse plane.
[From Latin *corona* a crown, alluding to the position in which a tiara is normally worn]

coronal section *n*. A cutting through a *coronal plane. Also called a *frontal section*. *Compare* horizontal section, sagittal section, transverse section.

coronal suture *n*. The serrated line down each side of the skull towards the temple where the frontal and parietal bones join together.

corpora cavernosa *n. pl*. Masses of tissue situated along the *penis and *clitoris that, together with the *corpus spongiosum, form the erectile tissue capable of responding to sexual excitement. *See also* cyclic GMP, nitric oxide, Viagra. **corpus cavernosum** *sing*.
[From Latin *corpus* body + *cavernosus* hollow]

corpora quadrigemina *n*. A generic name for the *inferior colliculi and *superior colliculi.
[From Latin *corpora* bodies, from *corpus* a body + *quadrigemina* fourfold]

corpus callosum *n*. The largest bundle of nerve fibres in the nervous system, consisting of a broad curved band of more than 200 million white fibres (axons) connecting matching areas of the left and right cerebral hemispheres. The main central part is called the trunk of the corpus callosum, and the other parts are its *splenium, *genu, and *rostrum (1). *See also* alien hand sign, disconnection syndrome, left-sided apraxia, split-brain preparation, tapetum (2). *Compare* anterior commissure, hippocampal commissure, massa intermedia, middle commissure, posterior cerebral commissure.
[From Latin *corpus* a body + *callosum* callous]

corpus luteum *n*. A mass of yellow glandular tissue that forms in a *Graafian follicle when an *ovum is released and that secretes *progesterone in preparation for the implantation of the ovum in the uterus. *See also* relaxin. **corpora lutea** *pl*.
[From Latin *corpus* body + *luteus* yellow]

corpus spongiosum *n*. The spongy blood-carrying tissue of the *penis or *clitoris that, together with the *corpora cavernosa, forms the erectile tissue capable of responding to sexual excitement. *See also* cyclic GMP, nitric oxide.
[From Latin *corpus* body + *spongiosum* spongy]

corpus striatum *n*. A term used confusingly for the *caudate nucleus and *lenticular nucleus taken together, because of their striped appearance in stained sections, leading to frequent confusion with the *striate cortex (to which it is unrelated) and the *striatum. It includes the striatum, also called the

neostriatum, and the palaeostriatum, usually called the *globus pallidus*.
[From Latin *striatus* streaked, from *stria* a furrow or a flute of a column]

correction for attenuation *See* attenuation.

correct rejection *n*. In *signal detection theory, an instance of failing to detect a signal when the signal is in fact absent. Also called a *correct reject*. *Compare* false alarm (2), hit, miss.

correlation *n*. In statistics, the degree of (usually) linear relationship between two variables such that high scores on one tend to go with high scores on the other and low scores on one with low scores on the other (positive correlation), or such that high scores on one tend to go with low scores on the other (negative correlation). The most commonly used index of correlation, the *product–moment correlation coefficient, symbolized by *r*, ranges from 1.00 for perfect positive correlation, through zero for uncorrelated variables, to −1.00 for perfect negative correlation. The concept of the correlation coefficient was first suggested by the English explorer, amateur scientist, and psychologist Sir Francis Galton (1822–1911) at a meeting of the Royal Institution in London in 1877. *See also* autocorrelation, Kendall's tau, partial correlation, Spearman rank correlation coefficient. **correlate** *vb*. **correlational** *adj*.
[From Latin *com* together + *relatio* a relation + *-ion* indicating an action, process, or state]

correlational study *n*. A non-experimental type of research design, without manipulation of an *independent variable or control of *extraneous variables, in which patterns of *correlations between two or more variables are analysed. *See* analysis of covariance structures, multiple regression, path diagram.

correlation centre *n*. Any of a large number of regions in the brain where information from disparate sense organs is integrated. US *correlation center*.

correlation coefficient *n*. A numerical index of *correlation, usually the *product–moment correlation coefficient, but sometimes another index, such as *Kendall's tau or *Spearman rank correlation coefficient.

correlation ratio *n*. In statistics, a correlation coefficient that provides an index of the degree of non-linear relationship between two variables. The correlation ratio is symbolized by η and is also called *eta*, the seventh letter of the Greek alphabet. *Compare* product–moment correlation coefficient.

correlogram *n*. A plot of the *autocorrelation of a *time series at lags 1, 2, and so on. The shape or form of the correlogram reveals information about trends and cycles in the time series.
[From *correlation* + Greek *gramme* a line]

correspondence analysis *n*. A technique of data analysis applicable to categorical scores in two-way *contingency tables, usually involving the depiction of the interrelationships between categories of row and column variables in two-dimensional maps. It is sometimes considered a form of *factor analysis and sometimes as *principal-components analysis of qualitative data.

correspondence problem *n*. In visual depth perception based on *binocular disparity, the matching up in the retinal images of points that are projections of *corresponding retinal points in the object or image being perceived, a computational problem that is carried out unconsciously by the visual system. *See also* corresponding retinal points.

correspondent inference *n*. Another name for the *fundamental attribution error. The term was introduced in 1965 by the US psychologists Edward Ellsworth Jones (1926–93) and Keith Eugene Davis (born 1936). Also called *correspondence bias*, although this is avoided in careful usage.

corresponding retinal points *n*. For a given degree of *ocular convergence, any pair of points, one on each retina, on to which a point in the visual field is projected. If the left retina and its image were to be superimposed on the right retina and its image, with the two foveas overlapping, then the corresponding retinal points and all other points on the *horopter would coincide. *See also* correspondence problem.

corridor illusion *n*. A visual illusion that causes images of equal size in a perspective

Corridor illusion. The three human figures are the same size.

picture of a corridor to appear larger the further away they seem to be (see illustration). *See also* perspective, Ponzo illusion, size constancy.

cortex *n.* The outer layer of any organ or part, such as the *cerebrum, the *cerebellum, or *adrenal gland. Often used as a shorthand for the *cerebral cortex. **cortical** *adj.*
[From Latin *cortex* bark or outer layer]

cortical blindness *n.* Any form of *blindness, such as *achromatopsia, caused by damage to the *visual cortex.

cortical deafness *n.* Any form of *deafness caused by damage to the *auditory cortex, another name for *central auditory processing disorder.

cortical spreading depression *n.* Another name for *spreading depression.

corticobulbar pathway *n.* A bundle of nerve fibres belonging to the *trigeminal nerve, *facial nerve, and *hypoglossal nerve, leading from the primary *motor cortex to nuclei in the medulla oblongata. A lesion in this pathway can lead to *pseudobulbar palsy.
[From *cortex* + Greek *bolbos* an onion, alluding to the onion-shaped medulla oblongata]

corticopontine *adj.* Pertaining to a tract of nerve fibres connecting the *cerebral cortex and the *pons.

corticospinal tract *n.* The bundle of nerve fibres that originate mainly from the *motor cortex and descend through the *internal capsule, *brainstem, and *spinal cord, most of the fibres crossing the midline of the body at the *pyramidal decussation. It mediates voluntary movements of all kinds, and damage to it causes *paresis or *paralysis. Also called the *pyramidal tract.* **CST** *abbrev.*

corticosteroid *n.* Any *steroid hormone that is synthesized in and secreted by the *adrenal cortex, including the *glucocorticoids and *mineralocorticoids, or any of a group of synthetic drugs with a similar pharmacological action used to treat inflammatory or allergic conditions. *See* aldosterone, cortisol, cortisone, corticosterone, prednisone, prednisolone.

corticosterone *n.* A *corticosteroid hormone belonging to the *glucocorticoid group, secreted by the *adrenal cortex in response to serious injury or stress, shifting the body from carbohydrate to fat metabolism, regulating blood pressure, having anti-inflammatory effects, and sometimes suppressing immune responses.

corticotrophin *n.* Another name for *adrenocorticotrophic hormone (ACTH). Also spelt *corticotropin.*

corticotrophin-releasing hormone *n.* A *releasing hormone that is secreted by the hypothalamus and that controls the secretion of *adrenocorticotrophic hormone (ACTH) from the anterior pituitary. Also spelt *corticotropin releasing hormone.* Also called *corticotrop(h)in-releasing factor (CRF).* **CRH** *abbrev.*

Corti's membrane *n.* Another name for the *tectorial membrane.

cortisol *n.* A *corticosteroid hormone belonging to the *glucocorticoid group secreted into the bloodstream by the adrenal cortex in response to *adrenocorticotrophic hormone (ACTH) secreted by the anterior pituitary, especially in response to stress or injury, switching the body from carbohydrate to fat metabolism, regulating blood pressure, and having powerful anti-inflammatory effects. The amount of cortisol (and also adrenalin or epinephrine and noradrenalin or norepinephrine) in the blood or urine is sometimes used as a measure of stress. Also called *hydrocortisone.*
[From *cortis(one)* + Latin *ol(eum)* oil]

cortisone n. A *corticosteroid hormone secreted by the adrenal cortex that suppresses inflammation and promotes carbohydrate formation. See also DHEA.
[From corti(co)s(ter)one]

Corti's organ See organ of Corti.

cost–benefit analysis n. A method of assigning a numerical value to the cost-effectiveness of a proposed operation, procedure, or undertaking. It is based on techniques of forecasting that are used to judge the value of each option in relation to its cost, to choose the option or options with the greatest net benefit, and sometimes to determine the optimal scale of the chosen operation(s), for example in terms of the amount to be invested. The basic decision criterion is maximization of the *difference* between total present benefits and total present costs (maximization of benefits minus costs), not the *benefit–cost ratio (benefits divided by costs), contrary to common belief and practice in some agencies, including the US Army Corps of Engineers. Also called *benefit–cost analysis* or *C–B analysis*. **CBA** abbrev.

Cotard's syndrome n. A pessimistic and distrustful *delusional condition characterized by a tendency to deny everything, even to the point of believing that one's body has disintegrated and that one's family no longer exists. Also called *délire de négation* or *insanity of negation*.
[Named after the French neurologist Jules Cotard (1840–87), who first described it in 1880]

co-therapist n. A therapist who works in conjunction with another, especially in leading a *group therapy session. Also called a *co-facilitator*.

counselling n. The practice or profession of applying psychological theories and communication skills to clients' personal problems, concerns, or aspirations. Some forms of counselling also include advice-giving, but the dominant ethos is one of providing facilitation without directive guidance. Counselling psychologists work with individuals, couples, and families in a variety of settings, including counselling agencies, general practitioners' surgeries, educational establishments, business organizations, and private practice. US *counseling*. See assertiveness training, client-centred therapy, co-counselling, disaster counselling, educational psychology, genetic counselling, Gestalt therapy, marriage counselling, offender counselling, outplacement counselling, pastoral counselling. See also counselling psychology, distress relief quotient. Compare psychotherapy.
[From Latin *consilium* advice, from *consulere* to consult]

counselling psychology n. A branch of *applied psychology concerned with the application of psychological principles and research to *counselling. US *counseling psychology*.

counteracting selection n. Pressures of *natural selection that favour certain genes at one level (individual, family, or population) but disfavour them at another. Compare reinforcing selection.

counterbalancing n. **1.** In experimental design, a method of controlling for the effects of an *extraneous variable by ensuring that its effects are equal in all *treatment conditions. For example, *order effects can be counterbalanced by administering the various procedures in different sequences. **2.** In questionnaire design, a method of controlling for *acquiescence response set by wording a test so that an affirmative answer is scored in the direction of the *attribute being measured in half of the questions and in the opposite direction in the rest. See also balanced scale.

countercathexis n. In *psychoanalysis, the process by which ideas that have undergone *repression and are constantly striving to break through into consciousness are prevented from doing so by an equal force operating in the opposite direction. It was first postulated in 1900 by Sigmund Freud (1856–1939) in his book The Interpretation of Dreams (Standard Edition, IV–V, at pp. 604–5), and it was subsequently used to explain the operation of *defence mechanisms. Also called anticathexis. See also reaction formation. Compare cathexis.

counterexample set n. In *logic, the premises of an argument, followed by the conclusion with 'It is not true that' in place of 'Therefore'. For example, this is an argument: Pensioners who live in rented accommodation are eligible for the maximum tax rebate. I am a pensioner. *I live in rented accommodation. Therefore I am eligible for the maximum tax rebate.* The counterexample set of this argument is: *Pensioners who live in rented accommodation are eligible for the maximum tax rebate. I am a pensioner. I live in rented accommodation. It is not true that I am eligible for the maximum tax rebate.* An argument is valid precisely if its counterexample set is inconsistent, as this counterexample set obviously is.

counterfactual conditional *n.* A conditional statement or proposition (of the form *If p, then q*) in which *p* is assumed to be false and *q* hypothetical. Such a statement or proposition is invariably and necessarily true: for example *If 2 + 2 = 5, then I'm a monkey's uncle* is true. *See* conditional reasoning.

counterfactual reasoning *n.* Reasoning based on *counterfactual conditionals.

counter-transference *n.* In *psychoanalysis, the analyst's emotional reactions to the patient and to the patient's *transference, influenced by the analyst's unconscious needs and conflicts. It should be carefully distinguished from the analyst's conscious reactions to the patient. It was first mentioned by Sigmund Freud (1856–1939) in 1910 in an article on 'The Future Prospects of Psycho-Analytic Therapy' (*Standard Edition*, XI, pp. 141–51). Since the 1970s there has been an increasing tendency in psychoanalysis to exploit the counter-transference in a controlled manner as part of the technique of psychoanalysis, support for this approach being drawn from Freud's comment in 1913 in an article on 'The Disposition to Obsessional Neurosis' that 'everyone possesses in his own unconscious an instrument with which he can interpret the utterances of the unconscious in other people' (*Standard Edition*, XII, pp. 317–26, at p. 320).

couples therapy *n.* Any form of *psychotherapy aimed at treating problems of couples, whether married or not. *Compare* marital therapy.

courtship *n.* **1.** A pattern of behaviour, often involving a form of *display (1), shown by members of one or both sexes as a prelude to copulation, ensuring that mating occurs between members of the same species, between opposite sexes, and with females that are re-

ceptive. **2.** The art or process of wooing someone with the intention of marriage.
[From Latin *cortis* a courtyard, related to *hortus* a garden]

covariance *n.* In descriptive statistics, an index of the degree of association between two variables, defined as the expected (average) value of the product of the deviations of the two variables from their means, calculated in samples by transforming the scores in both groups to deviations from their respective group means, multiplying pairs of scores from each group together, and calculating the *mean of these products. The covariance of variables X and Y is written $Cov(X, Y)$. *See also* product–moment correlation coefficient. *Compare* variance.

covariance structures, analysis of *See* analysis of covariance structures.

covariate *n.* In *analysis of variance (ANOVA), a variable that is measured in addition to a dependent variable and that represents a source of variance in the dependent variable not controlled for in the experiment. For example, in an experiment on reading comprehension, the covariate might be the research participants' or subjects' ages. In *analysis of covariance (ANCOVA) such a covariate can be controlled for statistically. Also called a *concomitant variable*.
[From *covariance*]

covariation principle *n.* In *attribution theory, the tendency to ascribe behaviour to a cause that is present only when the behaviour occurs, or that is observed to vary over time with the behaviour. A typical example is the tendency to attribute competitive behaviour to external causes in people who are observed to behave competitively in interactions with competitive partners but to attribute the competitiveness to internal dispositional causes in people who appear to behave competitively independently of their partners' actions. *See also* causal schema, Kelley's cube.
[From Latin *com* together + *variare* to vary + *-ation* indicating a process or condition]

cover memory *n.* Another name for a *screen memory.

crack *n.* A street name for an *alkaloid extracted from *cocaine hydrochloride salt, mixed with sodium bicarbonate, and dried into so-called rocks. It differs from other forms of cocaine inasmuch as it is easily vaporized by heat and can be inhaled to produce an extremely rapid effect. Also called *free base*. *See also* cocaine-related disorders, freebasing. [So called because it makes a crackling sound when it is heated]

Craik–O'Brien effect *n*. A powerful visual illusion produced by separating two identical grey areas with a blurred contour flanked by a narrow light strip merging into a narrow dark strip, resembling the appearance of *Mach bands, causing the whole grey area adjacent to the light strip to appear much lighter than the grey area adjacent to the dark strip, the illusion being eliminated if the contour and flanking strips are covered with a narrow object such as a pencil or (if the contour is curved) a piece of string or cord (see illustration). Also called the *Cornsweet illusion* or the *Craik–O'Brien-Cornsweet illusion*.
[Named after the Scottish philosopher and psychologist Kenneth John William Craik (1914–45) who was the first to describe it in his doctoral thesis in 1940, and who died following a car accident before publishing it, and the US physicist Vivian O'Brien (born 1924) who rediscovered and published it in 1958]

Craik–O'Brien effect. The shading of the inner region is identical to that of the outer region, as can be confirmed by covering up the contour between the two regions with a ring of suitable size or a piece of string or cord, or by viewing the inner and outer regions through two small holes in a piece of thick paper or cardboard.

Cramér's C *n*. In statistics, a measure of association between two categorical variables, applicable to a *contingency table of any dimensions, based on the *chi-square distribution. The value of C is calculated by taking the square root of $\chi^2/N(k-1)$, where N is the total number of scores and k is either the number of rows or the number of columns, whichever is smaller. Unlike the *contingency coefficient, the value of C is relatively independent of the number of rows and columns. Also called *Cramér's V. See also* phi coefficient.
[Named after the Swedish mathematician and statistician Harald Cramér (1893–1985) who introduced it]

cranial accessory nerve *n*. Another name for either of the pair of *accessory nerves that are distributed by the *vagus nerve to the muscles of the larynx and pharynx.

cranial index *n*. A numerical indication of the narrowness of a *cranium or head, given by its maximum length divided by its maximum breadth multiplied by 100. *Compare* cephalic index.

cranial nerve *n*. Any of the 12 pairs of nerves attached directly to the brain and projecting through natural openings in the skull, supplying the sense organs and the muscles of the head, neck, shoulders, heart, viscera, and vocal tract. They are referred to by either their names or their numbers, which are: *olfactory nerve (I), *optic nerve (II), *oculomotor nerve (III), *trochlear nerve (IV), *trigeminal nerve (V), *abducens nerve (VI), *facial nerve (VII), *vestibulocochlear nerve (VIII), *glossopharyngeal nerve (IX), *vagus nerve (X), *accessory nerve (XI), and *hypoglossal nerve (XII). *Compare* spinal nerve.

cranium *n*. The skull. **cranial** *adj*.
[From Latin *cranium* a skull, from Greek *kranion* a skull]

creatine *n*. A product of protein metabolism produced by the liver and kidneys and found in *striped muscle, where it helps to replenish energy and reduce muscle fatigue. It is sometimes taken by athletes and sports competitors as a *performance enhancer, and is liable to cause liver and kidney damage if taken in excess, but it is difficult to legislate against because it is a naturally occurring amino acid and is also found in dietary meat. *See* creatine phosphate.
[From Greek *kreas, kreatos* flesh + *-ine* indicating an organic compound]

creatine phosphate n. The *phosphate of *creatine through which phosphate is stored in muscles to enable adequate quantities of *ATP to be produced. Also called *phosphocreatine*.

creationism n. The doctrine that all things, including organisms, owe their existence to God's creation and not to *evolution. **creationist** n. One who believes in or promotes *creationism.

creativity n. The production of ideas and objects that are both novel or original and worthwhile or appropriate, that is, useful, attractive, meaningful, or correct. According to some researchers, in order to qualify as creative, a process of production must in addition be *heuristic or open-ended rather than *algorithmic (having a definite path to a unique solution). *See also* convergence–divergence, multiple intelligences, triarchic theory of intelligence. **creative** adj.

credibility n. The quality of meriting belief or confidence. In social psychology, the persuasiveness of a person or message source, generally associated with prestige. Research has shown that it consists of two major components, namely perceived trustworthiness and perceived competence or expertness, and a *multiplicative model is required to represent the way they combine: if either approaches zero, then so does credibility, irrespective of the value of the other. The first serious discussion of it was by the Greek philosopher Aristotle (384–322 BC) in his *Rhetoric*, the key passage being: 'Persuasion is achieved by the speaker's personal character when the speech is also spoken as to make us think him credible. We believe good men more fully and more readily than others; this is true generally whatever the question is, and absolutely true where exact certainty is impossible and opinions are divided' (Book I, Chapter 2, Bekker edition, p. 1356a). *See also* prestige suggestion, sleeper effect.

creole n. A form of language, originally a *pidgin, that has become the mother tongue of a speech community through a process of creolization. Striking similarities, such as similar rules for conjugating verbs, have been noted in the structure of all creole languages and cannot be explained by a common ancestor language or exposure to other languages, which suggests that what is common to creole languages in widely scattered communities may be the basis of language acquisition everywhere, or that children learn languages by first constructing an abstract form of a creole.
[From Portuguese *crioulo*, which originally meant a person of European descent born and brought up in a colonial territory]

Crespi effect n. Another name for *behaviour contrast in its positive form, when increased reward leads to increased response rate.
[Named after the US psychologist Leo P. Crespi (born 1916) who first reported it in an article in the *American Journal of Psychology* in 1942]

cretinism n. A congenital deficiency of *thyroxine, the thyroid hormone, resulting in arrested physical development and *mental retardation if untreated. **cretin** n. A person with congenital thyroid deficiency; colloquially (and offensively) a stupid person.
[French *crétin* from Latin *Christianus* Christian, here meaning human, referring to the fact that such afflicted people are not animals]

Creutzfeldt–Jakob disease n. A progressive and degenerative human *prion disease that attacks the central nervous system, causing *dementia, with loss of virtually all cognitive functions, *ataxia, and death within 1–2 years. One form of it, called *new-variant Creutzfeldt-Jakob disease (nvCJD* or *vCJD)* may be caused by eating beef products from cattle infected with *BSE. **CJD** abbrev.
[Named after the German neurologists Hans G. Creutzfeldt (1885–1964) and Alfons M. Jakob (1882–1927) who first described its signs and symptoms; Creutzfeldt described one case, now considered atypical, in 1920, and Jakob described four more in 1921]

crib, air *See* air crib.

cri du chat n. A rare congenital condition caused by a partial deletion of chromosome 5, resulting in *mental retardation.
[French *cri du chat* cat's cry, referring to the cat-like cries emitted by a child with the condition as a result of underdevelopment of the larynx]

criminal profiling n. In *investigative psychology, the analysis of the behaviour and circumstances associated with serious crimes in an effort to identify the probable characteristics of the perpetrator. It is used especially in cases of serial murder or rape.

criminological psychology n. A field of *applied psychology devoted to psychological problems associated with criminal behaviour, criminal investigation, and the treatment of criminals. The term is sometimes used synonymously with *forensic psychology, but this is avoided in careful usage. See also criminal profiling, investigative psychology.

crisis intervention n. A form of *brief psychotherapy applied to problems arising from medical or other emergencies, often in hospitals.

crista n. A ridge or crest-like biological structure, especially (a) one of the folds in the inner membrane of a *mitochondrion, or (b) the *crista acoustica. **cristae** pl.
[From Latin crista a ridge or crest]

crista acoustica n. A crest-shaped structure on the inner surface of the bulge or ampulla of each *semicircular canal, containing *hair cells that project into the gelatinous membrane of the canals, functioning as sensory receptors for the labyrinthine sense and responding only to accelerations of the head, which cause them to bend. Also called simply a crista. **cristae acousticae** pl.
[From Latin crista a ridge or crest + Greek akoustikos of or relating to sound, from akouein to hear + -ikos of, relating to, or resembling]

criterion-referenced test n. A test that measures an *attribute of a respondent against a predefined absolute standard (the criterion) without reference to the scores of other respondents. See also criterion validity. Compare domain-referenced test, norm-referenced test.

criterion validity n. In psychometrics, any measure of *validity based on determining the strength of the relationship between scores on the test and an independent criterion that is accepted as a standard against which the test may be judged. For example, in validating a test to measure depression, the criterion might be diagnosis of depression by clinical psychologists or psychiatrists, or in validating a test to measure scholastic aptitude, the criterion might be scores on tests of school performance. See also concurrent validity, criterion-referenced test, predictive validity.

criterion variable n. Another name for a *dependent variable in *canonical correlation, *discriminant function analysis, and *multiple regression.

critical band n. For any specified *tone (1), the range of frequencies of sounds that are capable of *masking the tone, sounds outside this range having little or no masking effect. The critical bandwidth increases from a minimum of about 100 hertz for a tone of 500 hertz to over 1,000 hertz for tones above 5,000 hertz. See also auditory masking.

critical flicker frequency n. The threshold rate at which light from an intermittent or fluctuating source begins to be seen as continuous or fused, the usual criterion being the viewer's report of seeing it as continuous 50 per cent of the time. It depends on the *luminance of the image, its *angular size, and the level of adaptation of the eyes, but it is often taken as approximately 30 hertz or cycles per second. Television presents 25 still images per second (British standard) or 30 per second (US standard), but each image is given twice to raise the flicker rate to 50 or 60 per second, comfortably above the critical flicker frequency. Also called critical fusion frequency (cff) or flicker fusion frequency (fff). See also brightness enhancement, episcotister, Ferry–Porter law, flicker. Compare auditory flutter fusion. **cff** abbrev.

critical period n. A biologically determined stage of development at which a person or animal is optimally ready to acquire some pattern of behaviour. See also imprinting.

critical theory n. A philosophical analysis of culture in general and literature in particular, associated especially with the *Frankfurt school, that rejects the possibility of a value-free social science and attempts to address the historical and ideological factors that influence culture and human behaviour. Its proponents conceive it as a practical and *normative (1) theory, rather than as a positive or descriptive theory, and one that seeks to expose the contradictions in people's belief systems and social practices with a view to changing them.

Crocker–Henderson system n. A system for classifying *odours based on four primary odours: fragrant, acid, burnt, and caprylic (goat-like or putrid), with each component being given a score from 0 to 8; thus acetic acid, for example, is characterized as 3803—moderately fragrant, very acid, not at all burnt, and moderately caprylic. Also called the *odour square* or *smell square*. *Compare* Henning's prism, Zwaardemaker smell system.
[Named after the US chemists Ernest Charlton Crocker (1888–1964) and Lloyd F. Henderson, who put it forward in 1927]

Cronbach's alpha n. In psychometrics, a reliability coefficient indicating the degree of *internal consistency of items within a test. Mathematically, it is the equivalent of the average of all possible *split-half reliability coefficients of the test. If certain assumptions are met, it ranges from 0 (zero internal consistency) to 1 (perfect internal consistency); a negative alpha coefficient indicates that items of the scale are negatively correlated and that an inappropriate reliability model is being used. Also called *alpha reliability coefficient* and *coefficient alpha*. *See also* Kuder–Richardson coefficient.
[Named after the US psychologist Lee J(oseph) Cronbach (1916–2001) who introduced it in *Psychometrika* in 1951, and *alpha* (α) the first letter of the Greek alphabet, which symbolizes it]

cross-adaptation n. A temporary loss of sensitivity to a stimulus, especially an odour or a taste, following exposure to a different stimulus, as when exposure to sodium chloride (table salt) reduces sensitivity to other salts, or exposure to sucrose (table sugar) reduces sensitivity to fructose and other sweet substances. *See also* adaptation (2).

cross-cultural survey n. Any investigation using *survey research methods to compare different cultural or subcultural groups.

cross-dependence n. Transferral of *dependence (2) on a drug to a different drug, enabling addiction to a dangerous drug such as *heroin to be treated by replacing it with a supposedly less dangerous substitute such as *methadone. *Compare* cross-tolerance.

cross-dressing n. Another name for *transvestism.

crossing over n. The interchange or swapping of *homologous sections of paired *chromosomes during *meiosis (1), producing variability in the hereditary characteristics of the offspring. Also called *crossover* or *breakage and reunion*. *See also* DNA recombination, linkage.

cross-modal matching n. A scaling method used in *psychophysics in which an observer matches the apparent intensities of stimuli across two *sensory modalities, as when an observer adjusts the brightness of a light to indicate the loudness of a variable stimulus sound. Some authorities consider *magnitude estimation and *magnitude production to be forms of cross-modal matching in which one modality is the observer's perception of the number system. Also called *cross-modality matching*.

cross-modal transfer n. The use of information gained through one *sensory modality to interpret information gained from another, as when a person born blind acquires the power of vision late in life, usually through a surgical operation, and immediately recognizes familiar objects by sight alone. In 1690 the English empiricist philosopher John Locke (1632–1704) expressed the opinion in his *Essay Concerning Human Understanding* (Book 2, Chapter 9, section 8) that such a person would not at first recognize any objects by sight alone, but in 1963 the case of SB reported by the English psychologists Richard L(angton) Gregory (born 1923) and his research assistant Jean G. Wallace clearly refuted Locke's view and showed that cross-modal transfer had occurred, SB being able, immediately after his eye operation in middle age, to read upper-case letters and numerals that he had learnt only through touch. Also called *cross-modality transfer*. *See also* Molyneux's question.

cross-sectional study n. A research design commonly used in developmental psychology and other branches of the discipline in which samples of research participants or subjects of different ages or from different groups are studied simultaneously and their behaviour compared. In contrast to a *longitudinal study, this design does not control for *cohort effects.

cross-tabulation n. In statistics, a table with a cell for each combination of values of two or more variables in which the entries represent the number of cases having each specific combination of values.

cross-tolerance n. *Tolerance (3) to a drug resulting indirectly from tolerance to a different but chemically related drug. Compare cross-dependence.

cross-validation n. 1. In psychometrics, evaluating the *validity of a test by administering it to an independent sample drawn from the same population as the sample on which it was originally validated, in order to determine the stability of the scores. 2. In *regression analysis and *multiple regression, measurement of *predictor variables, and comparison of predicted and observed values of the *dependent variable, in a fresh sample drawn from the same population as the sample from which the regression equation was derived, in order to determine the stability of the predictions.

crowd psychology n. The study of collective behaviour in crowds and mobs, including phenomena such as *deindividuation, *diffusion of responsibility, *personal space.

cryptaesthesia n. In *parapsychology, a putative hidden sense underlying extra-sensory perception. US cryptesthesia.
[From Greek kryptos hidden + aisthesis feeling + -ia indicating a condition or quality]

cryptomnesia n. An apparently creative or original idea that is in fact derived from a latent or subconscious memory.
[From Greek kryptos hidden + mneme memory, from mnasthai to remember + -ia indicating a condition or quality]

cryptophasia n. Another name for *autonomous speech.

crystalline lens n. The biconvex, transparent, elastic structure immediately behind the iris of the vertebrate *eye that helps to focus light rays on to the retina, although most (about

two-thirds) of the refraction of light entering the eye occurs at the *cornea. The degree of convexity of the crystalline lens can be altered by radial *ciliary muscles up to about age 45, after which the lens becomes hard and its focus cannot be altered. See also aberration (3), accommodation (1), ametropia, aphakia, astigmatism, cataract, cycloplegia, lens, refraction. Compare compound eye, ommatidium.
[So called because of its internal crystalline structure]

crystallized intelligence n. A fundamental *factor (2) of human intelligence, derived from *factor analysis, corresponding roughly to *verbal intelligence, consisting of the knowledge and expertise accumulated over a lifetime of experience, and measured by vocabulary and comprehension subtests of IQ tests. The concept was introduced in 1971 by the English-born US psychologist Raymond B(ernard) Cattell (1905–98). Also called crystallized ability. Compare fluid intelligence. **Gc** abbrev.

CS gas abbrev. A gas that irritates the mucous membranes of the eyes, nose, throat, and lungs, causing pain, temporary blindness, and breathing difficulty, used as an *incapacitant primarily for crowd control. Formula: $C_6H_4ClCH:C(CN)_2$. Compare BZ gas, CN gas, Mace, pepper spray, tear gas.
[From the surname initials of the US chemists Ben B. Corson (1896–1987) and Roger W. Staughton (1906–57) who first developed it in 1928, not (as widely believed) an abbreviation of Civilian Security gas]

CT scan abbrev. Computed (or computerized) tomography scan, a non-invasive method of *brain imaging or of visualizing other organs of the body, in which a computer builds up a three-dimensional picture from a series of plane cross-sectional X-ray images made at evenly spaced intervals along an axis. Formerly called a CAT (computed axial tomography) scan.

cue n. 1. An *attribute of an object or event to which an organism responds, typical examples being the size or shape of a visual *stimulus (1) to which a response may be conditioned. 2. A dimension or aspect of a proximal *stimulus (3) on the basis of which an organism makes inferences about a distal

*stimulus (2), typical examples being the monocular and binocular depth cues on the basis of which *depth perception occurs. **3.** In research into memory, a stimulus that aids the recall of information not recalled spontaneously. *See also* acoustic cue (2), cued recall, priming (1), probe. **4.** A signal to an actor or performer to begin performing, or more generally a hint about how to behave in a certain situation. *vb.* **5.** To supply someone with a *cue (3, 4).
[Perhaps from French *queue* a tail, from Latin *cauda* a tail; in the 17th century written *Q*, standing for Latin *quando* when (the actor should begin)]

cued recall *n*. Retrieval of information from memory with the help of *cues (3), typical examples of such cues being the first letter of a word or name to be remembered, or the category to which the item of information belongs (such as, *a kind of food*). It is often contrasted with *free recall. *See also* priming (3), recall.

cultural anthropology *n*. The branch of anthropology devoted to the study of cultural as opposed to physical or biological aspects of humans, especially (though not exclusively) in non-literate societies. *Compare* physical anthropology, social anthropology.

cultural truism *n*. A proposition that most members of a cultural group accept without question and have never heard questioned, such as (in Western industrial cultures) *It is a good idea to brush your teeth three times a day if possible*. *See* inoculation theory.

culture *n*. The sum total of the ideas, beliefs, customs, values, knowledge, and material artefacts that are handed down from one generation to the next in a society.
[From Latin *cultus* cultivation, from *colere* to till]

culture-bound syndromes *n*. Patterns of aberrant behaviour that do not fit easily into standard classifications of mental disorders and are entirely or mainly restricted to particular cultural groups, usually (ethnocentrically) excluding disorders such as *anorexia nervosa that are restricted to Western industrial cultures. Also called *culture-specific disorders* or *syndromes*. *See* amok, ataque de nervios, bilis, bouffée délirante, brain fag, brujeria, ca-

fard, colera, dhat, espanto, falling out, ghost sickness, hwa-byung, iich'aa, koro, latah, locura, mal de ojo, mal de pelea, mal puesto, nervios, pa-leng, perdida del alma, pibloktoq, qi-gong psychotic reaction, rootwork, saka, sangue dormido, shenjing shuairuo, shen-k'uei, shin-byung, shinkei-shitsu, spell, susto, taijin kyofusho, tripa ida, ufufunyane, uqamairineq, windigo, zar.

culture-fair *adj*. Of or relating to a psychometric test that is fair and appropriate for respondents of all cultures or subcultures. *Non-verbal tests of *intelligence, such as *Raven's Progressive Matrices, the *Cattell Culture-Fair Test, the *Peabody Picture Vocabulary Test, or the *Porteus Maze Test, are generally considered more culture-fair than verbal and information-based tests and subtests, but culture-fairness is a matter of degree, and no *IQ test could be entirely *culture-free unless it were based on purely biological measures such as properties of *event-related potentials. *See also* choice reaction time, inspection time, nerve conduction velocity, N140, processing speed, P200, string length. **culture-fairness** *n*.

culture-free *adj*. Of or relating to a psychometric test yielding scores that are completely independent of all cultural influences. *See* culture-fair.

culture shock *n*. Disorientation, often accompanied by feelings of isolation and rejection, resulting from a radical change in culture, through migration to a different country, or when a person's culture is confronted by another, alien culture. In severe cases, it may lead to *adjustment disorder.

culture-specific disorders *See* culture-bound syndromes.

cumulative record *n*. A *learning curve drawn by a pen that moves across a roll of paper at a steady rate, increasing its vertical height by a fixed amount for every response of an organism, such as a lever press by a rat in a *Skinner box or a peck by a pigeon of an illuminated plastic key. To prevent the curve rising off the top of the paper, the pen resets instantly to the bottom of the paper whenever it approaches the top. The slope of the curve within a specified region indicates the rate of responding at that time. It was invented by the US psychologist B(urrhus) F(rederic) Skinner (1904–90) while he was a postgraduate student at Harvard University in the late 1920s. *See also* learning curve, operant conditioning, reinforcement (1). **cumulative recorder** *n.* A device for producing a *cumulative record.

[So called because it represents a cumulative distribution of responses]

cuneate nucleus *n.* Either of two areas of the *medulla oblongata where the left or right *fasciculus cuneatus terminates, functioning as a relay station for somatosensory information. Also called the *nucleus cuneatus*.

[From Latin *cuneatus* wedge-shaped, from *cuneus* a wedge]

cunnilingus *n.* Sexual activity in which a woman's genitalia are stimulated by her partner's tongue and lips. Also called *cunnilinctus* or *cunnilinctio*. *Compare* fellatio.

[From Latin *cunnus* a vulva + *lingere* to lick, from *lingua* a tongue]

cupula *n.* A dome-shaped gelatinous membrane within the *semicircular canals of the inner ears into which the *hair cells of the *crista project. **cupulae** *pl.*

[From Latin *cupula* a small cask, from *cupa* a tub]

curare *n.* A black resin that is present in the bark of certain trees indigenous to tropical South America and is used as an arrow poison by South American Indians and as a muscle relaxant in modern medicine. It blocks the action of *acetylcholine in the somatic nervous system, paralysing skeletal muscles. **curarize** *vb.* To paralyse the skeletal muscles with *curare, as in experiments in which visceral or autonomic responses are being studied and indirect effects via voluntary responses need to be ruled out. *See also* nicotinic receptor. *Compare* atropine, strychnine.

[From Portuguese *curare*, from Carib *kurari* curare]

curvature illusion *n.* A visual illusion in which a semicircle appears more curved than a shorter circular arc with the same radius of curvature (see illustration).

cutaneous sense *n.* Any of a number of sensory systems having receptors located in

Curvature illusion. The two arcs have the same radius of curvature and are parallel.

the *skin, including the four basic senses of heat, cold, pain, and pressure first identified in 1904 by the Austrian physiologist Max von Frey (1852–1932), pressure now being known to include sensations of texture and vibration. Also called a *dermal sense* or *skin sense*. *See also* delta fibre, dorsal column, fasciculus cuneatus, fasciculus gracilis, Merkel cell, pallaesthesia, somatosensory cortex, somatosensory homunculus, spinothalamic tract, tactile acuity, temperature sense, touch receptor. *Compare* dynamic touch, haptic touch.

[From Latin *cutaneus* of or relating to the skin, from *cutis* skin]

cut score *n.* In psychometrics, in a scale used for selection, a predetermined score at or above which respondents are deemed to have passed or are accepted and below which they are deemed to have failed or are rejected.

CVC *abbrev.* Consonant–vowel–consonant, the type of *nonsense syllable most often used in research into memory, typical examples being *WUD* and *KEB*, the initials C and V standing for phonetic consonants and vowels—speech sounds rather than letters—so that strictly speaking *DAX* is not CVC but CVCC, because the *X* represents two *phonemes /ks/. The various types of syllable that can exist within a language are denoted analogously; thus in English it is possible to have clusters of up to three consonants at the beginning of a syllable (as in *splash*, which is CCCVC) and up to four at the end of a syllable (as in *sixths*, which is CVCCCC). *See also* CVC trigram.

CVC trigram *abbrev.* A three-letter word or non-word composed of a consonant, vowel, and consonant in that order, for example *DOG* or *KEB*. *See also* CVC, nonsense syllable.

[From Greek *treis* three + *gramma* a letter]

CV digram *abbrev.* A two-letter word or non-word composed of a consonant followed by a vowel, for example *PA* or *BU*.
[From Greek *dis* twice + *gramma* a letter]

cyanocabalamin *See* vitamin B$_{12}$.

cybernetics *n.* The comparative study of automatic *feedback and control processes in mechanical, electronic, and biological systems, especially processes in which negative feedback keeps the system in a particular state or on course towards a particular goal. The term was coined in 1947 by the US mathematician Norbert Wiener (1894–1964) and the Mexican neurophysiologist Arturo Rosenblueth (1900–70). *See also* closed-loop control, homeostasis, open-loop control, TOTE. **cybernetic** *adj.*
[From Greek *kybernetes* a steersman + *-ikos* of, relating to, or resembling, chosen in recognition of the fact that the first significant publication on feedback mechanisms was an article in 1868 on mechanical governors by the Scottish physicist James Clerk Maxwell (1831–79)]

cyberspace *n.* A notional electronic environment created by computer networks, such as the Internet, in which people communicate and interact.
[From *cyber(netics)* + *space*]

cyclic AMP *n.* Cyclic adenosine monophosphate, a compound widely distributed in biological cells that regulates reactions dependent on *hormones and *neurotransmitters and functions as a universal *second messenger. **cAMP** *abbrev. See also* AMP.

cyclic GMP *n.* Cyclic guanosine monophosphate, a compound that is analogous to *cyclic AMP and that keeps *sodium channels open in the outer membranes of rods and cones in the retina when its ring structure is intact, but is inactivated by *transducin if stimulated by light, closing the sodium channels and triggering *action potentials. It also relaxes the smooth muscles in the walls of arteries in the penis, causing the arteries to dilate and tending to constrict veins, its secretion increasing in response to sexual excitement and affecting the *corpora cavernosa and the *corpus spongiosum of the penis or clitoris, facilitating the inflow and reducing the outflow of blood into the erectile tissue.

See also phosphodiesterase type 5, Viagra. **cGMP** *abbrev.*

cyclic guanosine monophosphate *See* cyclic GMP.

cyclic majority *n.* An *intransitive preference order arising from majority voting in a group of individuals with transitive individual preferences. *See* Condorcet's paradox.

cyclic model of perception *n.* Another name for the *perceptual cycle.

cyclic preferences *n.* Another name for *intransitive preferences, especially when cyclicity exists among more than three alternatives, as in the following example. A die is rolled, and the outcomes I, II, . . . , VI, denoting the number of dots on the face that comes up, are equiprobable. Before the die is rolled, you are given a choice between two gambles as follows, with payoffs in pounds, dollars, or any other currency:

Die shows:	I	II	III	IV	V	VI
Gamble *A* payoffs:	1	2	3	4	5	6
Gamble *B* payoffs:	2	3	4	5	6	1

This means that if you choose Gamble *A*, then if I comes up you win 1 unit, if II comes up you win 2 units, and so on, whereas if you choose Gamble *B*, then if I comes up you win 2 units, if II comes up you win 3 units, and so on. If you are like most people, you probably prefer Gamble *B* to Gamble *A*, because it offers a higher payoff in five cases out of six, despite the fact that the payoff from Gamble *A* is much greater in the sixth case. Next, you choose between the following pair of gambles:

Die shows:	I	II	III	IV	V	VI
Gamble *B* payoffs:	2	3	4	5	6	1
Gamble *C* payoffs:	3	4	5	6	1	2

You probably prefer *C* to *B* for the same reason as before. Continuing in the same way, you eventually choose between the following gambles:

Die shows:	I	II	III	IV	V	VI
Gamble *F* payoffs:	6	1	2	3	4	5
Gamble *G* payoffs:	1	2	3	4	5	6

You probably prefer *G* to *F* for the usual reason. Taking all your preferences into account, your preference order, from most preferred on the left to least preferred on the right, is *GFEDCBA*. But *G* is identical to *A*, which means that your preferences are cyclic: *GFEDCBG*. . . . *See also* decision theory, money pump. *Compare* transitive preferences.

Cyclopean eye *n*. A hypothetical brain structure where the images from both eyes are brought together, believed by the French philosopher René Descartes (1596–1650) to be the pineal gland, by virtue of its location in the centre of the head, but eventually, in 1959, located by the Canadian-born US neurophysiologist David H(unter) Hubel (born 1926) and his Swedish-born collaborator Torsten N(ils) Wiesel (born 1924) in the *binocular cells of the *visual cortex, approximately half the neurons in the *primary visual cortex being binocular. *See also* disparity-selective cell.
[Named by the German physiologist, physicist, and mathematician Hermann Ludwig Ferdinand von Helmholtz (1821–94) after the Cyclops in Greek mythology with an eye in the middle of its forehead]

Cyclopean perception *n*. A term introduced by the Hungarian-born US radar engineer and psychologist Bela Julesz (born 1928) to refer to *stereopsis, especially of *random-dot stereograms or *anaglyphs.

Cyclopean stimulus *n*. Any stimulus, such as a *random-dot stereogram, that requires binocular vision in order to be perceived.

cyclophoria *n*. A form of *heterophoria in which the vertical axis of one eye rotates to the left or right because of a weakness of one of the *oblique muscles of the eye. *Compare* esotropia, exophoria, heterophoria, hyperphoria, hypophoria.
[From Greek *kyklos* a circle, ring, or wheel + *-phoros* carrying, from *pherein* to bear]

cycloplegia *n*. Paralysis of the *ciliary muscles that alter the shape of the *crystalline lens of the eye, resulting in loss of ability to focus, often induced by *anticholinergic drugs. **cycloplegic** *adj*.

cyclothymia *n*. A chronic instability of mood characterized by recurrent periods of *depression and elation, below the threshold of severity of *cyclothymic disorder.

cyclothymic disorder *n*. A *mood disorder within the category of *bipolar disorders characterized by chronic instability of moods, with recurrent *hypomanic episodes and *depressive episodes falling short of *major depressive episodes. Its sub-clinical form is called *cyclothymia*.
[From Greek *kyklos* a circle + *thymos* spirit]

cyclotron *n*. A device used to accelerate particles in a strong electromagnetic field, used in a *PET scan.
[From Greek *kyklos* a circle, ring, or wheel + *(elek)tron* amber (in which electricity was first observed)]

cyproterone *n*. A synthetic steroid whose acetate is used as an *antagonist (3) to *androgens.
[Probably from *cy(cle)* + *pro(ges)terone*]

cytoarchitectonic map *n*. A chart, especially of the brain, based on variations in the cellular structure of tissues, the most widely used being the map of *Brodmann areas.
[From Greek *kytos* a vessel + *architekton* a master builder, from *archi-* chief + *tekton* a builder]

cytology *n*. The study of the structure and function of biological cells.
[From Greek *kytos* a vessel + *logos* word, discourse, or reason]

cytomegalovirus *n*. A virus, belonging to the group of *herpes viruses, that causes the cells that it infects to enlarge and can result in birth defects when pregnant women are infected with it.
[From Greek *kytos* a vessel + *megale* big + English *virus*]

cytoplasm *n*. The *protoplasm surrounding the *nucleus (1) of a *cell. Also called the *perikaryon* or (now rarely) *plasma*. *See also* ectoplasm (1), maternal inheritance, mitochondrial DNA.
[From Greek *kytos* a vessel + *plasma* a form]

cytosine *n*. One of the constituent *bases (1) of the nucleic acids *DNA and *RNA, having an affinity for *guanine. **C** *abbrev*.
[From Greek *kytos* a vessel + *-ine* indicating an organic compound]

cytoskeleton *n*. The network of fibrous proteins that provides the framework for the shape of a *neuron or other cell, containing *mictrotubules that act as transport routes for molecules within the cell and a poorly understood control mechanism analogous to the nervous system of an organism, in some circumstances enabling the cell to make purposeful movements. *See also* mitosis, paramecium.

cytotoxic *adj.* Poisonous to living cells. *See also* neurotoxin. **cytotoxin** *n.* Any *cytotoxic substance.

[From Greek *kytos* a vessel + *toxikon* arrow-poison, from *toxon* a bow + *-ikos* of, relating to, or resembling]

dactylology *n*. A type of *sign language in which each letter of the alphabet has its own special sign. Also called *finger spelling*.
[From Greek *daktylos* a finger + *logos* word or discourse]

Dale's law *n*. The principle according to which a *neuron can release only one *neurotransmitter substance from its *synaptic endings. This law has been repealed in the light of research findings.
[Named after the English physiologist Sir Henry Hallet Dale (1875–1968) who propounded it]

daltonism *n*. The most common type of *colour-blindness, occurring in about 7 or 8 per cent of males and 0.4 per cent of females, usually a form of *deuteranomaly or *deuteranopia resulting in a defective ability to distinguish reds from greens, caused by a *recessive *X-linked gene and expressed predominantly in males, because they have only one X chromosome and therefore *complementation cannot occur. Also called *red–green colour-blindness*. *See also* Horner's law.
[Named after the English chemist and physicist John Dalton (1766–1844) who was red–green colour-blind and gave the first account of his condition in 1794, describing blood as appearing similar in colour to objects usually described as bottle-green]

dance of the bees *See* round dance, waggle dance.

dance therapy *n*. A form of *psychotherapy in which clients or patients are encouraged to express their feelings and inner conflicts through dance.

dancing mania *n*. Another name for *tarantism.

dantrolene *n*. Dantrolene sodium, a skeletal muscle relaxant drug that acts by limiting the release of calcium ions in muscle fibres and that is used in the treatment of muscle spasticity resulting from spinal cord injury.

dark adaptation *n*. A form of *adaptation (2) in which the visual system is adjusted for efficient response in dim illumination, the *pupil dilating and the *absolute threshold for vision gradually decreasing with time spent in the dark, the threshold for red, orange, and yellow objects or images attaining its minimum after about 5 minutes, and the threshold for green, blue, and violet also decreasing to a plateau after about 5 minutes but then declining again from about 10 minutes and approaching its minimum after about 25 minutes, this dual or *duplexity function being due to the different adaptation rates of the *photopic and *scotopic systems. *See also* field adaptation, photochromatic interval, Purkinje shift. *Compare* light adaptation. **dark-adapted** *adj*. Of or relating to the eye or the visual system after it has undergone *dark adaptation.

dark focus *n*. A stable resting *accommodation (1) of the eye's *crystalline lens, usually corresponding to a focal distance of about one metre, that the eye assumes when confronted with a stimulus lacking any features on which to focus, such as a completely enveloping blank screen resembling the inside of a giant ping-pong ball, or a blank screen viewed through a lens that makes it appear too close to focus on, or an *isoluminant stimulus, or complete darkness. It produces a temporary condition of *anomalous myopia.

dark light *n*. The dim cloud of light that is experienced in complete darkness owing to the spontaneous activity of neurons in the visual system. Also called *intrinsic light* or *idioretinal light*, either of which is less of an *oxymoron.

Darvon n. A proprietary name for the narcotic analgesic drug *propoxyphene hydrochloride.
[Trademark]

Darwinian evolution n. The theory according to which species evolve by *natural selection. *See also* neo-Darwinism. *Compare* Lamarckism, Lysenkoism, neo-Lamarckism, non-Darwinian evolution.
[Named after the English naturalist Charles (Robert) Darwin (1809–82) who expounded the theory in 1859 in his book *The Origin of Species by Means of Natural Selection or the Preservation of Favoured Races in the Struggle for Life*]

Darwinian fitness n. The lifetime reproductive success of an organism or *genotype, indexed by the average number of offspring that it produces, relative to other organisms or genotypes, and hence the relative number of copies of its *genes that it passes on to future generations. *See also* fitness. *Compare* inclusive fitness.

Darwinian reflex n. Another name for the *grasp reflex.

Darwinism n. Another name for *Darwinian evolution. **Darwinist** n. One who promotes or believes in *Darwinian evolution.

Dasein n. In the philosophy of the German philosopher Georg Wilhelm Friedrich Hegel (1770–1831), existence. In *existentialism, it is usually translated as being-in-the-world.
[From German *dasein* to be there, from *da* there + *sein* to be]

Daseinsanalyse n. Another name for *existential analysis, focusing on *Dasein. *See also* existential therapy.

data n. pl. Facts or information collected for reference or analysis. In statistics and measurement theory, results of any empirical investigation, usually but not necessarily in the form of numerical scores, that may be interpreted to provide information about the outcome of the investigation. According to the US psychologist Clyde Hamilton Coombs (1912–88), data are what are derived from observations or *raw scores by the application of a *measurement model that may or may not be explicitly described. Often treated as singular (*We have not finished analysing this data*) but this is avoided in careful usage. **datum** *sing.*
[From Latin *data* things given, from *dare* to give]

data-driven processing n. Another name for *bottom-up processing.

dataholic n. An informal term for a person addicted to information, especially a person who spends an excessive amount of time gathering information from the Internet and suffers from *withdrawal symptoms when deprived of access to information. *See* Internet addiction syndrome.
[Formed on the model of *alcoholic*, from *data* + *(alco)holic*]

data set n. A collection of *data relevant to a single research problem.

data snooping n. In statistics, laboratory jargon for the haphazard and unplanned inspection of the results of an investigation in the hope of finding significant effects when the results that had been expected or hoped for have not emerged. Not to be confused with *exploratory data analysis.

date rape n. Rape committed by someone with whom the victim has gone on a date, or by someone whom the victim is dating.

date rape drug n. A drug that is used to facilitate *date rape, especially *Rohypnol.

day blindness n. A non-technical name for *hemeralopia.

daydream n. A pleasant dreamlike *fantasy (2), such as the *Madame Butterfly fantasy, that distracts one's attention from the present.

daylight vision n. A non-technical name for *photopia.

deadly nightshade n. The plant *Atropa belladonna*, from which the poisonous *alkaloids *atropine and *hyoscyamine are extracted. Also called *belladonna*.

deaf mute *n*. An obsolescent term for a person who is unable to hear or to speak.

deafness *n*. Complete or partial loss of hearing, congenital or acquired, affecting about 10 per cent of adults and more than 50 per cent of people over 65 years old in the UK, the US, and other advanced industrial countries; divided into *conductive deafness, *sensorineural deafness, and *central auditory processing disorder. Also called *hearing impairment* or *hearing loss*, especially when there is some residual hearing. *See also* amblyacusia, anacusia, asonia, ceruminous deafness, cochlear implant, conversion symptom, cortical deafness, decibel, hypacusia, otitis, otosclerosis, ototoxic, paracusia, postencephalitic syndrome, presbyacusis, Tadoma method, teletactor, vestibulitis, word deafness. *Compare* diplacusis, dysacusia, hyperacusis. **deaf** *adj*.

death instinct *n*. Another name for *Thanatos.

debriefing *n*. Providing research participants or subjects with a retrospective explanation of the purpose of the investigation, including any deception that may have been involved. The ethical codes of the American Psychological Association, the British Psychological Society, and other professional bodies encourage debriefing wherever possible, although there are research studies in which it is not feasible, in some *naturalistic observation studies, for example, in which the research participants are not even aware of having participated. *See also* dehoaxing.

décalage *n*. A term introduced by the Swiss psychologist Jean Piaget (1896–1980) for the non-simultaneous attainment of different but closely related operational abilities. *Horizontal décalage* is the non-simultaneous attainment of different aspects of a cognitive operation during the same developmental stage, as when conservation of volume is preceded by conservation of mass, which in turn is preceded by conservation of number and substance, all of these attainments occurring during the stage of concrete operations; *vertical décalage* refers to changes that occur as a child progresses from one developmental stage to another; and *oblique décalage* refers to refinements of abilities at one developmental stage that prepare the way for attainments at a later stage.
[From French *décalage* a gap or lag, from *décaler* to bring forward]

decathexis *n*. In *psychoanalysis, the withdrawal of *cathexis from an idea or *instinctual object, as occurs in *narcissistic neurosis, when cathexis is withdrawn from external instinctual objects and turned on the *ego. Also called *withdrawal of cathexis. See also* isolation of affect.

decay theory *n*. The proposition that forgetting is caused by passive degeneration or deterioration of *memory traces. *Compare* proactive interference, retroactive interference.

decentration *n*. The process of cognitive development by which a child progresses from *centration to a more objective way of perceiving the world. Also called *decentering*.

decerebrate rigidity *n*. A postural syndrome of continuous muscular spasm, exaggerated *tonus, and *clasp-knife rigidity resulting from a lesion in the *brainstem or *cerebellum.
[From Latin *de* away + *cerebrum* a brain]

decibel *n*. A unit equal to one-tenth of a *bel for expressing the intensity of a sound or any other power level relative to a reference level. When it is used to specify absolute rather than relative sound intensity, the reference level is conventionally fixed at $10^{-16}\,W/cm^2$ (watts per square centimetre), slightly below the average human *absolute threshold for a sound of 1,000 hertz (about two octaves above Middle C), and the intensity so defined is referred to as *decibel sound pressure level (dB SPL)* or simply *sound pressure level (SPL)*. A sound of 60 dB SPL, the approximate level of ordinary conversational speech, is 60 dB higher than the reference level and has an intensity of $10^{-10}\,W/cm^2$, and a doubling or halving of absolute sound pressure level always corresponds to a change of 3 dB SPL. If two people speak at once, the sound level rises from 60 to 63 dB SPL, if four people speak at once it rises to approximately 66 dB SPL, and so on. In units of dB SPL, a sound that is loud enough to reach the pain threshold is about 130, a loud rock group reaches about 120, a person shouting at close range 100, a busy street 80, a loud conversation 70, a normal conversation 60, a quiet conversation 50, a soft whisper 30, and for a sound at 1,000 hertz the average human absolute threshold is 6.5 dB SPL. Exposure to sound above 85 dB SPL entails a risk of damage to the outer hair cells and permanent hearing loss. *See also* equal-loudness contour, phon, sensation level. **dB** *abbrev.*

[From Latin *deci(mus)* tenth + English *bel*, named after the Scottish-born US scientist Alexander Graham Bell (1847–1922), inventor of the telephone]

decile *n.* Any of the ten equal groups into which a distribution of scores can be divided, or the value of a variable such that a specified proportion of scores arranged in order of magnitude, divided into tenths, falls below that value, the sixth decile, for example, being the value of the variable such that 60 per cent of the other scores fall below that value. The fifth decile is the *median. See also* partile. *Compare* percentile, quartile.

[From Latin *decem* ten]

decision analysis *n.* Applied *decision theory.

decision frame *See under* framing effect.

decision making *n.* The act or process of choosing a preferred option or course of action from a set of alternatives. It precedes and underpins almost all deliberate or voluntary behaviour. Three major classes of theories have guided research into decision making: normative, descriptive (or positive), and prescriptive theories. *See* dual-process model, normative (1). *See also* Allais paradox, behavioural decision theory, bounded rationality, Buridan's ass, certainty effect, common ratio effect, cost–benefit analysis, cyclic preferences, decision theory, dominant alternative/strategy, elimination by aspects, Ellsberg paradox, expected utility, expected utility theory, expected value, framing effect, game theory, heuristic, lexicographic choice, maximin, minimal social situation, modified Ellsberg paradox, Monty Hall problem, multi-attribute decision making, Newcomb's problem, portfolio theory, preference reversal (1, 2), prospect theory, psychological decision theory, rational choice theory, revealed preference, risk aversion, risk seeking, risky shift, satisficing, social dilemma, St Petersburg paradox, subjective expected utility theory, sure-thing principle, utility theory.

decision rule *n.* A formal or mechanical principle or formula for choosing a course of action in response to any given input data. A typical example is a formula for deciding whether a student passes or fails a course on the basis of a set of marks; another is a *significance test for deciding whether or not to reject a *null hypothesis.

decision theory *n.* A *normative (1) approach to decision making based on *expected utility theory, some versions also incorporating *Bayesian inference. It starts from the assumption that, for any pair of alternatives, the decision maker can express a preference, and that the preferences satisfy the following axioms, which accord with our intuitions about preferences. (1) *Completeness*: for every pair of alternatives x and y, either x is preferred to y, y is preferred to x, or the decision maker is indifferent between x and y; (2) *Reflexivity*: every alternative x is at least as preferable as itself; (3) *Transitivity*: if x is at least as preferable as y, and y is at least as preferable as z, then x is at least as preferable as z. The theory then requires a decision maker always to choose a maximally preferable alternative (which may not be unique). Many writers use the term synonymously with *rational choice theory. Applied decision theory, taking into account the decision makers' *utility functions, is called *decision analysis. See also* expected utility theory, intransitive preferences, money pump. *Compare* behavioural decision theory, psychological decision theory. **DT** *abbrev.*

declarative knowledge *n.* Awareness and understanding of factual information about the world—*knowing that* in contrast to *knowing how*. Its necessary and sufficient conditions are that the information must be true, that the person must believe it to be true, and that the person must be in a position to know it. Typical items of declarative knowledge might include: that Princess Diana died in 1997; that Goethe was 83 when he finished writing *Faust*; that there is a village in Hertfordshire, England, called Ugley. *See also* ACT*, declarative memory, knowledge. *Compare* acquaintanceship knowledge, non-declarative knowledge, procedural knowledge.

declarative memory *n.* A storage system for *declarative knowledge, involving structures in the *temporal lobes, especially the *hippocampus. Information contained in it is acquired by a form of learning that requires conscious awareness and that occurs quickly, often in a single trial, generally involving the formation of associations among multiple stimuli. Also called *explicit memory*. *See also* ACT*, episodic memory, mirror drawing, semantic memory. *Compare* procedural memory.

deconstruction *n*. A method of critical analysis, associated prominently with the writings of the Algerian-born French philosopher and literary critic Jacques Derrida (born 1930), in which the meaning of a word or other form of expression is considered to be volatile and unstable and not anchored in the relationship between words and the things that they are supposed to designate, but permanently deferred and always subject to and produced by its difference from other meanings. Deconstruction arose primarily as an attack on *structuralism (1), aiming to show inherent contradictions in the rules governing the structure of texts, especially binary oppositions. It suggests that there is no firm or fixed presence that can guarantee or underwrite the meaning of a term. *Compare* psychoanalytic construction. **deconstruct** *vb*. To perform *deconstruction on a text or other verbal product, especially by questioning the basis of the opposition between speech and writing. This usage, though common in popular discourse, is regarded as spurious by some deconstructionists who believe that there is no verb associated with *deconstruction*.

decreolization *n*. The process by which a *creole becomes a standard language in a particular area.

decussation *n*. A *chiasm, crossing over, or intersection in the form of the letter X, as in the nerve fibres in the *optic chiasm or the *pyramidal decussation, both of which are partly rather than fully decussated in the human brain. The partial decussation of the visual pathways was discovered in 1704 by the English mathematician and physicist Isaac Newton (1642–1727). In most fishes and birds the visual pathways are completely crossed, but as animals evolved with eyes more towards the front of the head than the side, the percentage of uncrossed fibres increased. In mammals, the percentage of uncrossed fibres is related to the amount of overlap between the visual fields of the two eyes, overlapping

visual fields providing an accurate depth perception through *stereopsis. In human beings there is almost complete overlap of visual fields and almost half the fibres are uncrossed. Most other sensory and motor information is fully crossed, except in the *cerebellum. *See also* divided visual field, ventromedial tract. **decussate** *vb*.
[From Latin *decussis* the numeral 10, written X, from *decem assi* a coin worth ten asses, from *decem* ten + *as, assis* a Roman copper coin + *-ation* indicating a process or condition]

deduction *n*. The form of reasoning characteristic of logic and mathematics in which a conclusion is inferred from a set of premises that logically imply it. The term also denotes a conclusion drawn by this process. *See also* deductive reasoning, inference, logic. *Compare* induction (1, 2). **deduce** *vb*. **deductive** *adj*.
[From Latin *deducere* to lead away or deduce, from *de-* from + *ducere* to lead + *-ion* indicating an action, process, or state]

deductive reasoning *n*. A form of logical reasoning based on *deduction in which a conclusion is derived from premises using rules of inference, a valid deduction being one in which it is impossible to assert the premises and deny the conclusion without contradiction. One form, though by no means the only form, of deductive reasoning is the *syllogism. *See also* conditional reasoning, modal logic.

deep dyslexia *n*. A form of *dyslexia characterized by inability to read non-words (such as *kebby*), semantic errors, and impairment in reading abstract rather than concrete words; reading by relying on an established vocabulary of words that are recognized by sight. A person with deep dyslexia may misread *drink* as *beer* or *country* as *nation* and may also make visual errors such as reading *single* as *signal*. *See also* cognitive neuropsychology. *Compare* surface dyslexia.

deep structure *n*. A representation of a sentence at a fundamental level, with the grammatical relations between its parts explicitly shown, before any of the transformational rules have been applied to produce the *surface structure. In a famous example suggested by the US linguist and philosopher (Avram) Noam Chomsky (born 1928), the sentences *John is eager to please* and *John is easy to please* have similar surface structures but completely different deep structures, because the first involves John pleasing someone and the second John being pleased by someone. *See also* case grammar, generative grammar, transformational grammar.

deep tendon reflex *n*. The simplest type of reflex, involving only two neurons, characterized by a quick contraction of a muscle (with a normal latency of 15–25 milliseconds), triggered by a signal from a *muscle spindle in response to a sudden stretch induced by a sharp tap on the muscle tendon. Absence of the reflex indicates damage to the muscle, nerves, or spinal cord, and a hyperactive reflex suggests *hyperthyroidism or a lesion in the *pyramidal tract. The most important deep tendon reflexes are the *Achilles tendon reflex, *biceps reflex, *patellar reflex, and *triceps reflex. Also called a *myostatic reflex*, or *tendon reflex*. *See also* monosynaptic reflex, reflex, stretch reflex. **DTR** *abbrev*.

Deese–Roediger–McDermott paradigm *See under* experimentally induced false memory.

default reasoning *n*. A form of *nonmonotonic reasoning in which a *premise is assumed to be true by default but can be rejected if a further premise is added. For example, in the argument *Birds fly; Tweety is a bird; Therefore Tweety can fly*, the default premise *Birds fly* may be defeasible in the light of a further premise, such as *Tweety is a penguin*. *See also* frame problem. Also called *default logic*, but this is avoided in careful usage, because default reasoning violates the *extension theorem and is therefore not strictly logical. *See also* cognitive economy.

defence, ego *See* ego defence mechanism.

defence hysteria *n*. In *psychoanalysis, one of three types of *hysteria distinguished by Sigmund Freud (1856–1939) in 1894 in his article 'The Neuro-Psychoses of Defence' (*Standard Edition*, III, pp. 45–61), and by the Austrian physician Josef Breuer (1842–1925) and Freud in 1895 in their book *Studies on Hysteria* (*Standard Edition*, II), characterized by prolific use of *defence mechanisms. After 1895 Freud came to believe that defence plays a part in all hysteria, and he abandoned the tripartite distinction, but others continued to use it. US *defense hysteria*. *Compare* hypnoid hysteria, retention hysteria.

defence mechanism *n*. A term used originally in *psychoanalysis and later more widely in psychology and psychiatry to refer to a process whereby the *ego protects itself against demands of the *id. More generally, it is a pattern of feeling, thought, or behaviour arising in response to a perception of psychic danger, enabling a person to avoid conscious awareness of conflicts or anxiety-arousing ideas or wishes. In his book *The Ego and the Id* (1923), Sigmund Freud (1856–1939) made it clear that it is an unconscious function of the ego: 'We have come upon something in the ego itself which is also unconscious, which behaves exactly like the repressed—that is, which produces powerful effects without itself being conscious and which requires special work before it can be made conscious' (*Standard Edition*, XIX, pp. 12–66, at p. 17). The most influential survey and discussion of defence mechanisms was provided by Freud's daughter, the Austrian-born British psychoanalyst Anna Freud (1895–1982), in her book *The Ego and the Mechanisms of Defence* (1936/7). US *defense mechanism*. Also called an *ego defence mechanism*. *See* acting out (2), compensation, conversion, denial, displacement, dissociation, externalization, foreclosure, idealization, identification (2), identification with the aggressor, incorporation, intellectualization, introjection, isolation of affect, negation (2), projection (1), rationalization, reaction formation, regression (2), repression, reversal (1), splitting of the object, sublimation, substitution, suppression, symbolization, and undoing. *See also* cathexis, countercathexis, defence hysteria, word-association test.

defence, perceptual *See* perceptual defence.

defensive technique *n*. In *psychoanalysis, a concept introduced by the Scottish psychoanalyst W. Ronald D. Fairbairn (1889–1964) to denote any of four different processes that occur during normal development, in the transition to quasi-independence, as a result of *splitting of the object (the mother or breast) into a *good object that satisfies and a bad object that frustrates. The particular technique adopted depends on where (internally or externally) the good object and the bad object are located, and this also explains the form that a mental disorder is likely to take if development does not proceed normally. *See* hysterical technique, obsessional technique, paranoid technique, phobic technique.

deferred action *n.* In *psychoanalysis, a term used frequently by Sigmund Freud (1856–1939), though never defined by him, apparently to denote the revision of memories to fit in with new experiences or the attainment of later stages of development. Freud used the German word *Nachträglichkeit*, meaning the state or condition of being after the event or having hindsight, and the usual translation as *deferred action* may be slightly misleading. The French psychoanalyst Jacques Lacan (1901–81) was the first to draw attention to the importance of the concept in Freud's writings. *See also* false memory, reconstructive memory.

deficit *n.* A shortfall; more specifically, any deficiency in functioning owing to a disorder or *impairment.
[From Latin *deficit* it lacks, from *deficere* to lack]

defining properties *n.* In *componential theory, a set of *attributes or *features (1) that specify the meaning of a particular concept, each a necessary or essential attribute of any instance of the concept, the entire set constituting a sufficient definition of the concept. This classical interpretation of concepts was undermined by the Austrian-born British philosopher Ludwig (Josef Johann) Wittgenstein (1889–1951), who showed in his *Philosophical Investigations* (1953, paragraph 66) that concepts such as *game* or *chair* lack defining properties. *See* feature theory, prototype theory. *Compare* characteristic features.

definitional theory *n.* Another name for the *componential theory of concept formation.

defusion of instincts *n.* In *psychoanalysis, the separation of *Eros and *Thanatos, so that they pursue independent *instinctual aims. Sigmund Freud (1856–1939), in his book *The Ego and the Id* (1923), cited the *ambivalence of obsessional neurosis (*obsessive–compulsive disorder) as one of the clearest examples of this phenomenon (*Standard Edition*, XIX, pp. 12–66, at p. 42). *Compare* fusion of instincts.

degraded stimulus *n.* A stimulus whose detectability or discriminability has been reduced by decreasing its signal-to-noise ratio. Also called an *impoverished stimulus*. *See also* Abraham Lincoln effect, block portrait.

degrees of freedom *n.* In statistics, a quantity associated with many *significance tests and with estimates of variability such as the sample *variance, defined as the number of observations minus the number of restrictions on the freedom of the observations to vary. For example, in estimating the variance in a sample of n scores with a known mean, there are $n - 1$ degrees of freedom, because having calculated $n - 1$ deviations from the mean, the last deviation is not free to vary but can assume only one value. Similarly, in a 2×2 contingency table with fixed row and column totals (marginals), there is only 1 degree of freedom, because if a value is assigned to any of the four cells, then the other three are determined by the constraints and have no freedom to vary. *df* *abbrev.*

dehoaxing *n.* A form of *debriefing following research involving deception, in which research participants or subjects are told the true nature of the research, both for ethical reasons and to eliminate any undesirable effects of the deception.

dehydroepiandrosterone *See* DHEA.

deimatic *adj.* Frightening or threatening, of or relating to a posture adopted by an animal to intimidate another.
[From Greek *deimatos* frightening, from *deimos* fright]

deindividuation *n.* A psychological state characterized by loss of the sense of individuality and a submerging of personal identity and accountability in a group. In some circumstances it can lead to a relaxation of inhibitions and the release of antisocial behaviour, and it has been used to explain certain forms of mob behaviour. *See also* bystander effect, diffusion of responsibility. *Compare* individuation.

Deiters' cell *n.* A modified cell with an elongated ending and a terminal plate, such cells alternating with and supporting the outer *hair cells of the *organ of Corti.
[Named after the German anatomist Otto F. K. Deiters (1834–63)]

Deiters' nucleus *n.* A cluster of nerve cell bodies in the *medulla oblongata, with neural connections to the *flocculonodular lobe of the cerebellum, receiving afferent impulses

from the *semicircular canals via the *vestibular nerve, and sending efferent motor impulses to the spinal cord and cerebral cortex. It controls equilibrium, muscular tonus, and conjugate eye movements. Often misspelt *Deiter's nucleus*.
[Named after the German anatomist Otto F. K. Deiters (1834–63) who discovered it]

deixis *n*. Features of language that refer to personal, locational, or temporal characteristics of the situation in which an utterance occurs and whose meaning is therefore relative to the situation, such as *this/that*, *here/there*, *now/then*, *I/you*. The term is also sometimes applied to words that refer backwards or forwards in discourse, namely *anaphora and *cataphora. **deictic** *n*. A verbal expression exhibiting *deixis.
[From Greek *deiknynai* to show]

déjà vu *n*. A form of *paramnesia (1) distinguished by a delusion of having already seen or experienced before something that is in reality being encountered for the first time. Less common variants include *déjà entendu* (already heard), *déjà éprouvé* (already experienced or tested), *déjà fait* (already done), *déjà pensé* (already thought), *déjà raconté* (already told or recounted), *déjà voulu* (already desired). *See also* promnesia. *Compare* jamais vu.
[From French *déjà* already + *vu* seen]

de la Tourette's syndrome *See* Tourette's disorder.

delay conditioning *n*. A type of *conditioning (1) in which the *conditioned stimulus is presented repeatedly for longer and longer periods of time until there is eventually a very long delay between the onset of the conditioned stimulus and the occurrence of the *unconditioned stimulus. The Russian physiologist Ivan Petrovich Pavlov (1849–1936) found that animals were not only able to bridge this gap in time but were ultimately able to delay the occurrence of the *conditioned response until it just preceded the arrival of the unconditioned stimulus. *Compare* trace conditioning.

delayed auditory feedback *n*. A procedure in which a person speaks into a microphone attached to a tape recorder, and the speech is played back to the speaker through headphones after a brief delay. With a delay of about 200 milliseconds (one-fifth of a second), the effect on most speakers is a severe disruption of speech, with stuttering, slurring, and often complete inability to produce intelligible words. **DAF** *abbrev*.

delayed conditioning *n*. A form of *classical conditioning in which the *conditioned stimulus precedes the *unconditioned stimulus by a significant time period and the organism learns to withhold its *conditioned response. *See* delay conditioning.

delayed gratification *n*. Renouncing immediate reward or satisfaction in order to obtain a larger reward in the future, as when a person invests money instead of spending it immediately.

delayed matching to sample *See* matching to sample.

delayed-response task *n*. A test of *working memory in which the human or non-human organism responds on the basis of stored internal representations rather than information currently present in the environment. Typically, the organism receives a brief visual or auditory stimulus that is then withdrawn, and after a delay of several seconds attempts to identify the location where the stimulus appeared, and is rewarded if correct.

delayed sleep-phase syndrome *n*. One of the *dyssomnias, characterized by falling asleep very late, sleep-onset *insomnia, and difficulty waking up in time to meet work, school, or social demands. *Compare* circadian rhythm sleep disorder. **DSPS** *abbrev*.

delay-line timing circuit *n*. A series of neuronal connections or circuits that are capable of sustaining activity for an extended period of time.

Delboeuf illusion *n*. A visual illusion in which a circle surrounded by a concentric circle of slightly greater diameter appears larger than another circle of the same size surrounded by a concentric circle of much greater diameter.
[Named after the Belgian physicist and psychologist Joseph Rémy Léopold Delboeuf (1831–96) who published it in 1893]

deletion *n*. An erasure or blotting out. In genetics, the loss or absence of part of a *chromosome. **deletion mutation** n. A type of *mutation in which one or more *bases (1) are lost from a segment of *DNA.

Delilah syndrome n. Promiscuity in a woman motivated by a desire to render men weak and helpless.
[Named after the Philistine mistress of Samson (in Judges 16:4–22), who deprived him of his strength by cutting off his hair]

deliriant adj. n. (Of or relating to) a substance such as an *inhalant that produces a state of *delirium or a degree of general *anaesthesia. See also inhalant-related disorders, nitrite inhalant, solvent abuse.

delirium n. A *mental disorder involving *clouding of consciousness and impairment of cognition, involving such symptoms as memory loss, disorientation, language disturbance, perceptual change, and often sleep disturbances (insomnia or nightmares), the disorder developing quickly (usually in a matter of hours or days) and not being explicable by *dementia, but accompanied by evidence that it is caused by a *general medical condition, *substance intoxication or *withdrawal, medication, or exposure to a *toxin. See also cognitive disorders, substance intoxication delirium, substance withdrawal delirium.
[From Latin delirium insanity, from delirus insane, from delirare to turn aside, from de from + lira a furrow]

delirium tremens n. An acute and sometimes fatal *rebound effect occurring as a reaction to alcohol withdrawal following prolonged alcohol abuse, characterized by *anorexia and *insomnia followed by *psychomotor agitation, *anxiety, *hallucinations, *delusions, coarse *intention tremor of the hands, feet, legs, and tongue, fever, *tachycardia, and profuse sweating. Compare alcohol hallucinosis. **DTs** abbrev.
[From Latin tremens trembling, from tremere to shake]

Delphi method n. A method of research, analysis, decision making, and often forecasting, developed in the early 1950s by the RAND Corporation in the US, involving the repeated collection and distribution of the judgements and opinions of individual experts through the exchange of written documents or electronic mail. Proponents claim that it avoids domination of the decision process by forceful personalities and the disrupting effects of interpersonal dynamics in face-to-face groups. Also called the Delphi technique.
[Named after the oracle of Delphi in ancient Greece]

delta fibre n. A small-diameter, thinly myelinated type of *afferent nerve fibre with low conduction velocity, such as any of the afferent fibres from certain pain, temperature, and touch receptors. US delta fiber. Also written δ fibre. Compare alpha fibre, Ia fibre, Ib fibre, II fibre, C fibre, gamma fibre.
[From delta (δ) the fourth letter of the Greek alphabet]

delta movement n. A form of *apparent movement, first described in 1915 by the German Gestalt psychologist Adolf Korte, that occurs when two stimuli quite close together are presented in an alternating pattern, the second being much brighter than the first. Under certain conditions relating to sizes of the stimuli and interstimulus interval, the visual illusion is created of the second stimulus moving in a reverse direction from its position towards the first stimulus. Also called delta motion. Compare alpha movement, beta movement, gamma movement.

delta-9-tetrahydrocannabinol n. The chemical name for the primary psychotropic substance in *cannabis. **THC** or **delta-9-THC** abbrev.

delta rule n. In the *back-propagation algorithm, adjustment of the weights of connections between units as a function of the discrepancies between actual output and target output as determined by a *teacher unit. Also called the Widrow–Hoff rule. See also connectionism (1), Hebbian rule.

delta sleep-inducing peptide n. A *peptide consisting of nine amino acids, extracted from the venous blood of rabbits after putting them to sleep through electrical stimulation of the thalamus. When injected into other rabbits, it induces *slow-wave sleep, and when injected into human subjects it has a similar effect.
[So called because it induces deep sleep with associated *delta waves]

delta wave n. A very low-frequency (1–3 hertz), high amplitude (approximately 150 microvolts) *EEG wave characteristic of deep, dreamless, *slow-wave sleep. Also called a *delta rhythm*. See also delta sleep-inducing peptide.

delusion n. A false belief maintained in the face of overwhelming contradictory evidence, apart from beliefs that are articles of religious faith or are widely accepted in the person's culture. *See* delusional jealousy, delusional misidentification, delusion of control, delusion of depersonalization, delusion of reference, erotomania (1), grandiose delusion, lycanthropy (2), nihilistic delusion, persecutory delusion, somatic delusion, systematized delusion, thought broadcasting delusion, thought insertion delusion. *See also* delusional disorder. *Compare* hallucination, illusion. **delusional** *adj*.
[From Latin *deludere* to mock or play false, from *de* away from + *ludere* to play + *-ion* indicating an action, process, or state]

delusional disorder n. A *mental disorder characterized by one or more *delusions that are prominent but not bizarre, such as being stalked, poisoned, loved from afar, deceived by a sexual partner, or having a physical abnormality. *See* erotomanic delusional disorder, grandiose delusional disorder, jealous delusional disorder, persecutory delusional disorder, somatic delusional disorder. *See also* Schreber case. *Compare* paranoid personality disorder, paranoid schizophrenia.

delusional jealousy n. A *delusion that one's sexual partner is being unfaithful.

delusional misidentification n. Any *delusion involving the identity of another person or people, the best known examples occurring in *Capgras syndrome, *Frégoli syndrome, and *intermetamorphosis.

delusion, nihilistic *See* nihilistic delusion.

delusion of control n. A *delusion that one's actions or thoughts are being controlled by an external agent.

delusion of depersonalization n. A *delusion, the main content of which is a belief of *depersonalization.

delusion of grandeur n. Another name for a *grandiose delusion.

delusion of influence n. Another name for a *delusion of control.

delusion of persecution *See* persecutory delusion.

delusion of reference n. A *delusion that certain people, events, or things in one's environment have a special (usually baleful) significance, such as a belief that people are talking about one or plotting behind one's back. *Compare* ideas of reference, paranoia.

demand characteristics n. Features of an experimental situation that encourage certain types of behaviour from the research participants or subjects and can contaminate the results, especially when this behaviour arises from research participants' expectations or preconceptions or from their interpretations of the experimenter's expectations. *See also* experimenter effect, experimenter expectancy effect, reactivity.

deme n. A group of closely related organisms living in the same locality. A deme of organisms related genetically is called a *genodeme*, and a deme of organisms related through mating is called a *gamodeme*.
[From Greek *demos* a district in local government]

dementia n. Impairment or loss of memory, especially evident in the learning of new information, and of thinking, language, judgement, and other cognitive faculties, without *clouding of consciousness; any of a family of *mental disorders characterized by memory impairment, especially for newly acquired information, and one or more cognitive disturbances (notably *aphasia, *apraxia, or *agnosia) causing significant difficulties in social or occupational functioning. It is characteristic of old age, occurring in about 10 per cent of people in their early 80s and rising to 20 per cent of those in their late 80s. The most important types are dementia of the Alzheimer type (*see* Alzheimer's disease), *vascular dementia or *multi-infarct dementia, dementia resulting from *HIV infection, head trauma, *Parkinson's disease, *Huntington's disease, *Pick's disease, *Creutzfeldt–Jakob disease, and substance-induced persisting dementia resulting from *alcohol, *inhalants, *sedatives, *hypnotics, or *anxiolytics. *See also* childhood disintegrative disorder, cognitive disorders, presenile dementia, progressive supranuclear palsy, senile dementia. *Compare* amentia.

[From Latin *dementare* to drive mad, from *de* from + *mens* mind + *-ia* indicating a condition or quality]

dementia infantalis *n.* Another name for *childhood disintegrative disorder.

dementia praecox *n.* An obsolete name for *schizophrenia.

[From Latin *dementia* insanity + *praecox* premature]

Demerol *n.* A proprietary name for *pethidine (meperidine).

[Trademark]

demography *n.* The study of human populations, especially as regards size, structure, density, and distribution. **demographic** *adj.*

[From Greek *demos* the people + *graphein* to write]

dendrite *n.* A collection of branched, threadlike extensions of a *neuron specialized to receive impulses via *synapses (1) from other neurons or from *sensory receptors and to conduct them towards the cell body or soma. Also called a *dendron. See also* microtubule. *Compare* axon. **dendritic** *adj.*

[From Greek *dendron* a tree]

dendrodendritic *adj.* Of or relating to a relatively uncommon type of *synapse (1) between the *dendrite of one neuron and the dendrite of another. It does not generate nerve impulses but alters the receptivity of the target neuron. *Compare* axoaxonic, axodendritic, axosomatic. **D-D** *abbrev.*

dendrogram *n.* In statistics, a branching diagram showing the clusters formed at each step of a hierarchical *cluster analysis.

[From Greek *dendrites* of or relating to a tree, from *dendron* a tree + *gramme* a line]

dendron *n.* Another name for a *dendrite.

denial *n.* In *psychoanalysis, a *defence mechanism involving a disavowal or failure consciously to acknowledge thoughts, feelings, desires, or aspects of reality that would be painful or unacceptable, as when a person with a terminal illness refuses to acknowl-

edge the imminence of death. Sigmund Freud (1856–1939) introduced it into psychoanalysis in 1923 in an article on 'The Infantile Genital Organization' (*Standard Edition*, XIX, pp. 141–5), where he discusses it in relation to children denying that girls do not have penises although they can see that to be the case, and he developed the concept further in 1938/40 in his book *An Outline of Psycho-Analysis* (*Standard Edition*, XXIII, pp. 144–207, at pp. 203–4). Also called *disavowal*.

denotation *n.* **1.** The explicit dictionary meaning of a word or expression, with reference to the entity or thing that the word designates. This meaning should be carefully distinguished from sense 2. *See also* semantic feature, semantic-feature hypothesis. *Compare* connotation (1). **2.** In philosophy, the particular entities to which a word or expression can correctly be applied; hence the denotation of the word *mother* is the set of all particular mothers in the world, including the mother of anyone who reads these words, the Queen Mother (mother of Queen Elizabeth II, Queen of Great Britain and Northern Ireland), Mary mother of Christ, and so on. Some words and expressions have no denotation in this sense, a familiar example being *unicorn*, although it does have a *connotation (2), namely *horse-like one-horned animal. See also* intension. *Compare* connotation (2). **denotative** *adj.* **denote** *vb.*

[From Latin *denotare* to mark, from *de* from + *notare* to mark, from *nota* a mark or sign + *-ation* indicating a process or condition]

density, tonal *See* tonal density.

dental *adj.* Of, relating to, or denoting a speech sound articulated with the tongue tip against upper teeth, as in the initial *phonemes in *thin* and *this. See also* articulation, place of articulation.

[From Latin *dens, dentis* a tooth + *-alis* of or relating to]

dentate gyrus *n.* A small crescent-shaped structure in the hippocampal formation (*see* hippocampus), separated from the narrow tip of *Ammon's horn. Often confused with the *dentate nucleus.

[From Latin *dens, dentis* a tooth + Greek *gyros* a circle or ring]

dentate nucleus *n.* A large wrinkled horseshoe-shaped strip of nerve cell bodies deep within each hemisphere of the *cerebellum, involved in the control of rapid skilled movements. Often confused with the *dentate gyrus.

[From Latin *dens, dentis* a tooth + *nucleus* a kernel, from *nux, nucis* a nut, alluding to its toothed appearance]

denying the antecedent *n*. In *conditional reasoning, arguing invalidly from a hypothetical proposition of the form *If p then q* that, because *p* is false, therefore *q* is false. For example, given the proposition *If the burglars entered by the front door, then they forced the lock*, it is invalid to deduce from the fact that the burglars did not enter by the front door that they did not force the lock. *Compare* affirming the antecedent, affirming the consequent, denying the consequent.

denying the consequent *n*. In *conditional reasoning, arguing validly from a hypothetical proposition of the form *If p then q* that, because *q* is false, therefore *p* is false. For example, given the proposition *If the burglars entered by the front door, then they forced the lock*, it is valid to deduce from the fact that the burglars did not force the lock that they did not enter by the front door. Also called *modus tollens*. *Compare* affirming the antecedent, affirming the consequent, denying the antecedent.

deoxyribonucleic acid *See* DNA.

deoxyribose *n*. Any of a group of sugars similar to *ribose but having one of its alcoholic hydroxyl groups replaced by hydrogen, especially the sugar that forms part of the backbone of *DNA and emerges as a product of the hydrolysis of DNA.

[From *deoxy-* indicating less oxygen + *ribose*]

dependability *n*. Another name for *conscientiousness.

dependence *n*. **1.** Reliance on another person for financial, emotional, or some other form of support. **2.** A psychological and sometimes physical state of reliance on a substance, especially on a narcotic drug such as cocaine or heroin, but also on everyday drugs such as nicotine, caffeine, or alcohol, characterized by a compulsion to take the drug in order to experience its effects and generally also *withdrawal and *tolerance (3). *See also*

addiction, cross-dependence, nucleus accumbens, substance dependence. **3.** In probability theory and statistics, a relation between variables that are correlated with one another.

dependent personality disorder *n*. A *personality disorder characterized by a pervasive and excessive need to be taken care of, leading to submissive, clinging behaviour and *separation anxiety, beginning by early adulthood and indicated by such signs and symptoms as difficulty making everyday decisions without advice and reassurance from others; a need for others to assume responsibility for major areas of life; difficulty expressing disagreement with others for fear of disapproval or loss of support; difficulty initiating projects or doing things alone; tendency to go to excessive lengths to gain nurturance or support; fear of being unable to cope when alone; urgent seeking of a new relationship as a source of care and support as soon as one ends; and unrealistic preoccupation with fears of being left to cope alone.

dependent variable *n*. In research methods and statistics, a variable that is potentially liable to be influenced by one or more *independent variables. The purpose of an *experiment is typically to determine whether one or more independent variables influence one or more dependent variables in a predicted manner. In *multiple regression, a set of independent or *predictor variables are combined in a *linear model to provide a best prediction of a dependent variable, which is sometimes called a *criterion variable. *See also* intervening variable. **DV** *abbrev*.

depersonalization *n*. A feeling of emotional detachment or estrangement from the perception of self, as if one were acting in a play or observing one's physical and mental activities from without. If it causes clinically significant distress or impairment in social, occupational, or other important areas of functioning, then it may be diagnosed as *depersonalization disorder. *See also* alienation (3), delusion of depersonalization, out-of-body experience, self-estrangement. *Compare* derealization.

depersonalization–derealization syndrome *n*. A generic term for disorders characterized by either *depersonalization or *derealization.

depersonalization disorder n. A *dissociative disorder characterized by persistent and recurrent feelings of *depersonalization causing clinically significant distress or impairment in social, occupational, or other important areas of functioning. Also called *depersonalization neurosis*.

depolarization n. A reduction in the voltage across a neuron's *cell membrane from its normal *resting potential of −70 millivolts or mV (negative on the inside). The reduction tends to excite the neuron and increase its propensity to transmit a nerve impulse, the momentary collapse and reversal of the resting potential constituting an *action potential. *See also* excitatory postsynaptic potential. *Compare* hyperpolarization.

deprenyl n. A drug that controls the symptoms and slows the progression of *Parkinson's disease by inhibiting the action of a *monoamine oxidase enzyme that destroys *dopaminergic cells in the *substantia nigra. It has more general anti-oxidant effects, in low doses it increases the life expectancy of experimental animals by more than twenty per cent, and it is sometimes considered to be a *smart drug. *See also* antiparkinsonian.

depressant drug n. Any drug that reduces or tends to reduce the function of a system or organ of the body, especially a drug that reduces or slows down the activity of the *central nervous system and that in high dosages can lead to slurred speech, behaviour resembling drunkenness, coma, and death. Among the most frequently used depressants are *alcohol, the *barbiturates, the *benzodiazepines, *chloral hydrate, *glutethimide, *haloperidol, *methaqualone, *paraldehyde, *phencyclidine, and *scopolamine. A common street name for depressant drugs in general is *downers*. Also called a *psychomotor depressant*. *See also* sedative–hypnotic, sedative-, hypnotic-, or anxiolytic-related disorders, substance abuse, substance-related disorders. *Compare* stimulant drug.
[From Latin *depressum* pressed down, from *de* down + *premere*, *pressum* to press]

depressed mood n. A *mood (1) state characterized by *depression.

depression n. A *mood (1) state of sadness, gloom, and pessimistic ideation, with loss of interest or pleasure in normally enjoyable activities, accompanied in severe cases by *anorexia and consequent weight loss, *insomnia (especially middle or terminal insomnia) or *hypersomnia, *asthenia, feelings of worthlessness or guilt, diminished ability to think or concentrate, or recurrent thoughts of death or suicide. It appears as a symptom of many mental disorders. *See* dysthymic disorder, major depressive episode. *See also* agitated depression, anaclitic depression, antidepressant, cognitive therapy, depressive episode, depressive mood, depressive realism, dysthymia (1), endogenous depression, exogenous depression, inositol, involutional depression, involutional psychosis, learned helplessness, major depressive disorder, masked depression, melancholia, MHPG, neurotic depression, nervous breakdown, noradrenalin, postpartum blues, postpartum depression, premenstrual syndrome, pseudodementia, psychomotor retardation, psychotic depression, reactive depression, reserpine, retarded depression, schizoaffective disorder, seasonal affective disorder (SAD), serotonin, unipolar depression. *Compare* pseudodepression. **depress** vb. **depressive** adj.
[From Old French *depresser* to depress, from Latin *depressum* pressed down, from *de-* down + *premere* to press + *-ion* indicating an action, process, or state]

depression, anaclitic *See* anaclitic depression.

depression scale n. Any scale to measure *depression, including the Depression scale of the *MMPI and the *Beck Depression Inventory.

depressive disorders n. A class of *mood disorders. *See* dysthymic disorder, major depressive disorder.

depressive episode n. A period of *depression. *See also* major depressive episode.

depressive neurosis n. Another name for *dysthymic disorder.

depressive position n. In *Kleinian analysis, a modality of *object relations occurring after the *paranoid–schizoid position, from about the fourth month until the end of the first year of life, and sometimes reappearing during childhood and adulthood, especially during states of mourning and depression. During the depressive position, the infant for the first time recognizes the mother as a *whole object, the splitting into *good object and bad object is reduced, with both libido and aggressive drives tending to focus on the same *instinctual object, resulting in *ambivalence, and anxiety is aroused by fear of losing the mother. The concept was introduced in 1934 by the British-based Austrian psychoanalyst Melanie Klein (1882–1960), who explained her preference for the word *position* to *stage* or *phase* in a co-authored book in 1952: 'these groupings of anxieties and defences, although arising first during the earliest stages, are not restricted to them but occur and recur during the first years of childhood and under certain circumstances in later life' (*Developments in Psycho-Analysis*, p. 236). *See also* reparation, splitting of the object.

depressive realism *n*. A reduction or absence of *unrealistic optimism and the *overconfidence effect in a person with *depression, depressed people being characteristically (across situations and domains) more accurate in their processing of information related to themselves and non-depressed people being characteristically positively biased. The concept was introduced in 1979 in an article by the US psychologists Lauren B(ersh) Alloy (born 1953) and Lyn Y(vonne) Abramson (born 1950) in the *Journal of Experimental Psychology: General*. *See also* illusion of control.

deprivation, maternal *See* maternal deprivation.

depth cue *n*. Any *cue (2), indication, or hint of distance that contributes towards visual *depth perception. *See* binocular cue, monocular cue.

depth from motion *n*. Another name for *structure from motion (SFM).

depth interview *n*. A type of *interview used in *qualitative research, and especially in *motivational research and *dynamic psychology generally, typically lasting at least an hour and attempting to uncover unconscious motives and wishes, sometimes supplemented with *projective tests. *See also* depth psychology.

depth of field *n*. The range of distance from a point behind to a point in front of an object being focused by the eye's lens, or by any lens, within which the image is in focus, the range being relatively great when the *pupil or aperture is constricted, which is usually the case in bright light, and relatively small when the pupil or aperture is dilated in dim light. Also called *depth of focus*.

depth of processing *n*. The cognitive level at which a stimulus is analysed. For example, the word *clock*, presented as a visual stimulus, may be perceived as a collection of black marks on white paper, or as a string of five letters, or as a word with a corresponding pronunciation, or it may evoke a mental representation of a complicated mechanism capable of keeping time, each of these responses representing a greater depth of processing than its predecessor. *See* levels of processing.

depth perception *n*. The visual perception of three-dimensional space through *monocular cues and *binocular cues that are present in the two-dimensional images projected on to the retinas of the eyes. It is served by the *magnocellular system, which is colour-blind (*see* isoluminant). The monocular depth cues are *accommodation (1), *aerial perspective, *chiaroscuro, *elevation in the visual field, *interposition, *linear perspective, *monocular parallax, *relative size, and *texture gradient. The binocular depth cues are *ocular convergence and *stereopsis. *See also* kinetic depth effect, pictorial depth, reduction screen.

depth psychology *n*. A term introduced by the Swiss psychiatrist Eugen Bleuler (1857–1939) to denote psychological approaches that take account of *unconscious (2) forces, especially *psychoanalysis in its various forms and varieties. *See also* depth interview, dynamic psychology, metapsychology.

derailment *See* cognitive derailment.

derealization *n*. An experience or perception of the external world as unreal, strange, or alien, as if it were a stage on which people were acting. *See also* alienation (3). *Compare* depersonalization.

de-reflection n. A technique of *logotherapy designed to counter *hyper-reflection by turning the clients' attention away from themselves and their own activity. It is used chiefly for the treatment of *male erectile disorder, *male orgasmic disorder, and impotence. See also centipede effect, Humphrey's law.

dereism n. Thinking that deviates from reality or logic. **dereistic** adj.
[From Latin de from + res a thing + Greek -ismos indicating a state or condition]

derived score n. In psychometrics, a score obtained by applying a mathematical *transformation to a *raw score. Common forms of derived scores are *IQ scores, *stanine scores, *sten scores, *T scores, and *z scores.

dermal sense n. Another name for a *cutaneous sense.
[From Greek derma skin]

dermis n. The inner layer of the *skin, below the *epidermis, containing connective tissue, blood vessels, fat, and most of the skin's *free nerve endings. Also called the corium, derm, or derma.
[From Greek derma skin]

dermo-optical perception n. A *paranormal ability claimed by some people to see with the skin, often demonstrated by reading print or perceiving pictorial images or colours with the tips of the fingers shielded from vision.

descending reticular formation n. The part of the *corticospinal tract that descends through the *reticular formation in the brainstem and controls spinal reflexes and motor behaviour. Compare ascending reticular activating system.

descriptive research n. Research that has no other purpose than to describe phenomena and is not intended to explain, predict, or control them. Compare action research, applied research, basic research, evaluation research, exploratory research.

descriptive statistics n. Summaries of numerical data that make them more easily interpretable, including especially the *mean, *variance, *standard deviation, *range, *standard error of the mean, *kurtosis, and *skewness of a set of scores. The *correlations between variables are also considered to be descriptive statistics by most statisticians. Compare inferential statistics.

descriptive theory See under normative (1).

desensitization See systematic desensitization.

designer drug n. A drug synthesized specifically to mimic the *psychotropic effect of an existing (usually illegal) substance, with a slightly modified molecular structure to avoid classification as an illicit drug, typical examples being *ecstasy (2), *MDA, and *MPPP.

desipramine n. A *tricyclic antidepressant used in the treatment of *mood disorders, especially *bipolar disorders.
[From des(methyl) (im)ipramine demethylated imipramine, from Latin de from or away from + methyl the alkyl radical CH_3 derived from methane by removal of one hydrogen atom, from Greek methy wine + hyle wood]

destructive instinct n. In *psychoanalysis, a term denoting *Thanatos or the death instinct in so far as it is directed outwards.

destrudo n. In *psychoanalysis, a term coined by the Italian psychoanalyst Edoardo Weiss (1889–1971) to denote the form of energy associated with *Thanatos, intended as a counterpart to *libido. See also mortido.
[A blend of destru(ctive) + (libi)do]

desynchronized EEG n. An *EEG pattern lacking regular periodicity in its waveform as a result of blocking of *alpha wave activity through arousal or focused attention in the waking state, or blocking of *delta wave activity through dreaming during sleep.

desynchronized sleep n. Another name for *REM sleep. **D sleep** abbrev.
[So called because it is characterized by desynchronized EEG patterns]

desynchronized sleep rhythm n. Another name for *circadian rhythm sleep disorder.

detection task n. Any task in which an observer tries to perceive a signal or a stimulus. See also receiver operating characteristic, signal detection theory. Compare identification task.

determinant *n.* A number associated with any square *matrix showing whether the matrix is *singular*, that is, whether two or more rows or columns of the matrix are linearly dependent in the sense of being linear combinations of each other. If the determinant is equal to zero, then the matrix is singular, and many statistical techniques require matrices that are assumed to be non-singular.
[From Latin *determinare* to set boundaries, from *terminus* a boundary]

determination, coefficient of *See* coefficient of determination.

determiner *n.* A word such as a definite or indefinite article (*the*, *a*), a *quantifier (2) (*all*, *some*, *every*, *many*, *any*), or a demonstrative or possessive adjective or pronoun (*this*, *that*, *my*, *our*, *your*, *his*, *her*, *their*) that limits or determines the meaning of a noun or noun phrase, as in the sentence *I received your letter*, in which *your* determines the meaning of *letter*.

determinism, psychic *See* psychical determinism.

deterministic *adj.* Of, relating to, or consisting of a non-random process or variable whose past completely determines its future forever, so that it can be equally well predicted from its remote past as from its recent past. *Compare* stochastic.

detour problem *n.* Any problem in which a goal can be reached only by moving away from it at some stage, often because an obstacle blocks the direct route to the goal. Also called an *Umweg* problem.

detoxification *n.* The process of freeing a drug user or an alcoholic from dependence on or addiction to a substance. **detoxification centre** *n.* A unit or facility that specializes in *detoxification. US *detoxification center*. **detoxify** *vb.* To carry out a process of *detoxification, or more generally to remove the poison from someone or something.
[From Latin *de* indicating a deprivation + *toxicum* a poison + *-ation* indicating a process or condition]

detrended normal plot *n.* In statistics, a graph of the differences between observed and expected values, the expected values being based on the assumption of a *normal distribution. If the observed scores are normally distributed, then the points should cluster in a horizontal band close to zero without any discernible pattern. *See also* normal probability plot.

detumescence *n.* Subsidence of a swelling or enlargement, especially of the penis during the resolution phase of the *sexual response cycle. *Compare* tumescence.
[From Latin *detumescere* to cease swelling, from *de* away from + *tumescere* to begin to swell, from *tumere* to swell]

deuteranomaly *n.* A form of partial *colour-blindness in which the proportion of green light required to be mixed with red to match yellow is abnormally high according to the normal *Rayleigh equation, owing to a deficiency in the *visual pigment that absorbs light in the middle part of the visible spectrum. *Compare* deuteranopia, protanomaly, tritanomaly.
[From Greek *deuteron* second, alluding to the second of the three *primary colours (1) red, green, and blue + *anomalos* uneven or inconsistent, from *an-* without + *homalos* even, from *homos* the same]

deuteranopia *n.* The most common form of *anomalous dichromacy in which the *visual pigment that absorbs medium-wavelength (green) light is non-functional, resulting in poor hue discrimination in the red and green regions of the spectrum and a tendency to confuse reds with greens and greens with blues. *Compare* deuteranomaly, protanopia, tritanopia.
[From Greek *deuteros* second, alluding to the second of the three *primary colours (1) red, green, and blue + *anopia* blindness, from *an-* without + *ops* an eye + *-ia* indicating a condition or quality]

developmental age *n.* In psychometrics, a score on a test of ability or intelligence expressed in terms of the average age in years at which the score is attained by children according to the standardization data. *See also* developmental quotient.

developmental coordination disorder *n.* A *motor skills disorder characterized by substantially below-average motor coordination (crawling, sitting, walking, playing games, and the like) for the given age, intelligence, and education; the *deficit interfering significantly with scholastic or academic achievement or everyday life and not being due merely to a sensory deficit.

developmental crises n. A concept introduced in 1959 by the German-born *ego psychologist Erik H. Erikson (1902–94), and popularized in his book *Childhood and Society* (1963), denoting eight stages in life, each presenting a fundamental opposition that needs to be resolved. They are *early infancy*: basic trust versus basic mistrust; *later infancy* (during toilet training): autonomy versus shame and doubt; *early childhood* (while learning to walk): initiative versus guilt; *middle childhood* (during the *latency period of the early school years): industry versus inferiority; *puberty and adolescence*: identity versus role confusion; *young adulthood*: intimacy versus isolation; *mature adulthood*: generativity versus stagnation; *late adulthood*: ego integrity versus despair. Erikson regarded particular ego 'virtues' as emerging through the resolution of each phase, namely hope, will, purpose, competence, fidelity, love, care, and wisdom respectively. *See also* ego identity, identity crisis.

developmental disorder *See* pervasive developmental disorders, specific developmental disorder.

developmental dyslexia n. One of the two major categories of *dyslexia, forms of the disorder that develop during childhood from unknown causes, also called *reading disorder*. *Compare* acquired dyslexia.

developmental psychology n. The branch of psychology concerned with psychological phenomena of all kinds in infants, children, adolescents, adults, and old people, and all the psychological changes that occur across the lifespan. It includes research into the development of perception, cognition, language, skills, moral attitudes, and social relationships.

developmental quotient n. In psychometrics, *developmental age divided by *chronological age, sometimes multiplied by 100. *See* IQ. **DQ** *abbrev*.

deviation IQ n. The modern, statistical conception of *IQ, introduced in 1939 by the Romanian-born US psychologist David Wechsler (1896–1981), according to which IQ is a normally distributed variable with a mean of 100 and a *standard deviation of 15 (usually). By definition, an IQ of 100 is average, approximately 68 per cent of IQ scores fall between 85 and 115, approximately 95 per cent fall between 70 and 130, approximately 99.74 fall between 55 and 145, and so on. *See also* normal distribution. *Compare* ratio IQ.
[So called because it is based on standard deviations]

deviation score n. In statistics, a score representing the difference between the *raw score and the *arithmetic mean of the raw scores in the group to which it belongs. For example, in the group of raw scores 1, 4, 10, the mean is 5, so the corresponding deviation scores are (1 − 5), (4 − 5), and (10 − 5), that is, −4, −1, and 5. The term is also used to refer to a score expressed in units of *standard deviations, also called a *z score.

devotee n. **1.** A person who is ardently enthusiastic about something. **2.** A colloquial name for a person with *acrotomorphilia.

dexamethasone n. A potent synthetic *glucocorticoid hormone, used as an anti-inflammatory and anti-allergic drug, that inhibits the secretion of *adrenocorticotrophic hormone (ACTH) by the pituitary gland, and consequently also the secretion of *cortisol (hydrocortisone) by the adrenal glands. *See also* dexamethasone suppression test.
[From d(ecah)exameth(yl) (corti)sone, from Greek *deka* ten + *hex* six + *methyl* the alkyl radical CH$_3$ derived from methane by removal of one hydrogen atom, from Greek *methy* wine + *hyle* wood + English *cortisone*]

dexamethasone suppression test n. A diagnostic procedure involving the injection of *dexamethasone, followed by a measure of the extent to which *cortisol secretion into the bloodstream has been suppressed. Patients with Cushing's syndrome (overactivity of the adrenal glands) fail to suppress cortisol secretion, and so do some patients with severe *depression, *melancholia, *anorexia nervosa, and *bulimia nervosa. **DST** *abbrev*.

dextroamphetamine n. Dextroamphetamine hydrochloride or sulphate (US *sulfate*), a dextrorotatory (right-handed) form of *amphetamine, used as a central nervous system *stimulant.

[From Latin *dexter* right + English *amphetamine*]

DF extremes analysis *n*. In behaviour genetics, a method for estimating the *heritability of a disorder such as dyslexia that is defined qualitatively, people being diagnosed as either having the disorder or not having it, but that depends on an underlying *trait that varies quantitatively along a *continuum. The method involves testing a random selection of people who have twins, isolating those that have the disorder, then testing the *monozygotic and *dizygotic twins of those individuals, the assumption being that if the disorder is influenced by genes that also affect variability within the normal range, then the mean scores of the monozygotic and dizygotic twins of the disordered individuals should both be closer to the mean of the disordered group than to the mean of the random group of twins, and the mean of the monozygotic twins should be closer to the mean of the disordered group than should the mean of the dizygotic twins.

[Named after the behavioural geneticists John C. DeFries (born 1934) and David W. Fulker (1937–98) who developed it in the 1990s at the University of Colorado]

dhat *n*. A *culture-bound syndrome found in India, where there is another similar syndrome called *jiryan*, and Sri Lanka, where a syndrome resembling dhat is called *sukra prameha*, characterized by severe *anxiety, together with *hypochondria focused on concerns about weakness and exhaustion, attributed to excessive discharge of semen by both men and women (also believed to secrete semen), and whitish discolouration of urine interpreted as semen loss. Also written *dhatu*. *Compare* shen-k'uei.

[From Hindi *dhatura* a plant with strongly narcotic properties]

DHEA *abbrev*. Dehydroepiandrosterone, a *steroid hormone that is produced by the *adrenal cortex and is often called the mother (or grandmother) of hormones because it functions as a precursor of many other hormones, including *cortisone, *oestrogen, *progesterone, and *testosterone. It plays a part in weight control, and its decline

with age is believed to account for some of the diseases of old age. Formula: $C_{19}H_{28}O_2$.

diabetes *n*. Any of several diseases characterized by the excretion of abnormally large quantities of urine. **diabetes insipidus** *n*. A form of *diabetes caused by a disorder of the pituitary gland and malfunction of the kidneys. **diabetes mellitus** *n*. A form of *diabetes caused by a loss of *insulin secretion from the *islets of Langerhans, leading to a failure of carbohydrate metabolism and excess sugar in the urine. *See also* blindness, hypoglycaemia. **diabetic** *adj*. Of, relating to, or for *diabetes or people with diabetes.

[From Greek *diabetes* a siphon, from *dia* through + *banein* to go + Latin *insipidus* insipid, or *mellitus* honied, from *mel* honey]

diagnosis *n*. The process of identifying a disorder by examining its *signs (1) and *symptoms; an identification of a disorder reached by such a process. *See also* differential diagnosis.

[From Greek *dia* between + *gnosis* knowing]

Diagnostic and Statistical Manual of Mental Disorders *See* DSM-IV.

diagnostic checking *n*. In statistics and mathematical modelling, the process of carrying out visual and statistical checks to see how well the estimated model fits the data and whether the necessary assumptions of the model have been satisfied.

dialect *n*. A variety of a language, identifiable by its vocabulary and grammar, spoken by people in a particular geographical area or by members of a particular social class or group, to be distinguished from an *accent (1), which is distinguished by pronunciation only. *Compare* acrolect, basilect, idiolect, lect, mesolect. *See also* eye dialect. **dialectology** *n*. The study of *dialects, especially regional dialects.

[From Greek *dialektos* speech or dialect]

dialectical montage *n*. A term introduced by the Russian film-maker and editing theorist Lev Kuleshov (1899–1970) for a type of *context effect that enables an actor in a film or motion picture in certain circumstances to convey emotion without expressing it. In 1922 Kuleshov carried out an experiment in which the famous Russian actor Ivan

Mozhukhin (1889–1939) posed with a neutral *facial expression for several seconds, and a close-up shot of his face was intercut with shots of a bowl of soup, a woman in a coffin, and a child playing with a toy. Viewers of the resulting montage thought they could see faint expressions of satisfaction, sadness, and happiness on Mozhukin's face as he appeared to respond to each of the cutaway vignettes in turn.

[From Greek *dialektikos* pertaining to argument, from *dia* between + *legein* to speak + *-ikos* of, relating to, or resembling + French *montage* an assemblage or superimposition of images, from *monter* to mount]

dialinguistics *n*. The study of the full range of dialects and languages in a speech community.

[A blend of *dialect* + *linguistics*]

dialysis *n*. The diffusion of small particles in a solution across a *semipermeable membrane from the side where the solution is more concentrated to the side where it is less concentrated. *Compare* osmosis.

[From Greek *dialysis* a dissolution, from *dia* through or across + *lysis* a loosening]

Diana complex *n*. In the *individual psychology of the Austrian psychiatrist Alfred Adler (1870–1937) and his followers, the repressed wish of a woman to be a man. *See also* complex (2), gender identity disorder, masculine protest.

[Named after Diana, the virginal Roman goddess of the moon]

diary study *n*. A research methodology in which the research participants or subjects record their own behaviour or experiences for subsequent analysis and interpretation by the investigator.

diaschisis *n*. A temporary disruption of brain activity caused by a localized injury, resulting in a generalized breaking up of a pattern of functioning, not caused directly by the lesion itself but arising from indirect or secondary effects in other areas of the central nervous system.

[From Greek *dia* through + *schizein* to split]

diathesis *n*. A hereditary predisposition to a disorder.

[From Greek *diathesis* arrangement, from *dia* asunder + *tithenai* to place]

diathesis-stress hypothesis *n*. The conjecture that many disorders are caused by the interaction of predisposing *diathesis and precipitating environmental *stress (1) factors.

diatonic *adj*. Pertaining to any musical scale that contains seven notes or tones, separated by five intervals of a *tone (2) and two intervals of a *semitone, the most familiar examples being the major and minor scales of Western music. *Compare* chromatic (2).

[From Latin *diatonicus* diatonic, from Greek *diatonikos* diatonic, from *dia* between + *tonos* a tone + *-ikos* of, relating to, or resembling]

diazepam *n*. A member of the *benzodiazepine group of drugs, used as a sedative and muscle relaxant. Often referred to as *Valium* (trademark). *See also* sedative-, hypnotic-, or anxiolytic-related disorders. **DZP** *abbrev*.

[From *di-* two, from Greek *dis* twice + *az-* denoting nitrogen, from Greek *a-* not + *zaein* to live + *ep(oxide)* a compound containing oxygen joined to other atoms, from Greek *epi* on or above + *oxide* a compound of oxygen and another element, from French *oxy(gène)* + *(ac)ide*]

dibenzodiazepine *n*. Any drug having a dibenzodiazepine nucleus in its chemical structure, including *carbamazepine, various *tricyclic antidepressant drugs, and a class of *atypical antipsychotic drugs such as *clozapine or *risperidone that block both *serotonin and *dopamine receptors and cause fewer *neuroleptic-induced side-effects than are associated with conventional neuroleptic drugs. *See also* dopamine antagonist.

[From Greek *dis* twice + English *benzodiazepine*]

dichhaptic technique *n*. Simultaneous presentation of a different tactile stimulus (such as letter shapes or novel shapes without names) to each of the two hands, shielded from vision, in order to study *laterality of functions, based on the fact that the touch receptors in each hand are projected predominantly to the opposite or contralateral *somatosensory cortex, the results generally confirming a left hemisphere dominance for linguistic or sequential functions and a right hemisphere dominance for spatial functions. Also spelt *dichaptic. Compare* dichoptic, dichotic.

[From Greek *dicha* in two, from *dis* twice + *haptein* to touch]

dichoptic adj. Of or relating to the presentation of different stimuli to each eye. Compare binocular, monoptic (2).
[From Greek dicha in two, from dis twice + optikos of or relating to vision, from optos visible, from ops an eye]

dichoptic masking n. A form of *visual masking in which a test stimulus is presented to one eye and a masking stimulus to the other. When masking is found, it can be inferred that it must occur at a higher level of the visual system than the eyes. See also central masking.

dichotic adj. Of or relating to the simultaneous presentation of a different auditory message to each ear via earphones, a task used to study *attention and *laterality of functions, based on the fact that the nerve fibres that carry auditory signals from each ear are almost entirely crossed to the *auditory cortex of the opposite *cerebral hemisphere. Often confused with *binaural. See also shadowing. Compare dichhaptic technique, diotic.
[From Greek dicha in two, from dis twice + ous, otos an ear]

dichromacy See anomalous dichromacy. Also called dichromasy, dichromatism, dichromatopsia, dichromopsia.

dictyosome n. Another name for a Golgi body. See Golgi apparatus.
[From Greek diktyon a net + soma a body, alluding to the common appearance of a Golgi body when stained]

diencephalic amnesia n. A form of amnesia resulting from loss of neurons in the *diencephalon, especially the midline *thalamus and the *mammillary bodies of the *hypothalamus. This pattern of pathology is often associated with *Korsakoff's psychosis or syndrome as a consequence of alcohol abuse and thiamine deficiency.

diencephalon n. The bottom part of the forebrain or prosencephalon, linking the cerebral hemispheres with the midbrain, including the *basal ganglia, *thalamus, *hypothalamus, and *epithalamus. See also global amnesia. Compare telencephalon.
[From Greek dia between + en in + kephale head, alluding to its position between the cerebral hemispheres and the brainstem]

diethylstilboestrol n. Another name for *stilboestrol. US diethylstilbestrol.
[From Greek dis twice + English eth(er), from Greek aithein to burn + English stilboestrol]

difference limen n. Another name for a *difference threshold or just noticeable difference. **DL** abbrev.
[From Latin limen a threshold]

difference threshold n. In *psychophysics, the smallest detectable change in a stimulus or difference between two stimuli that can be reliably detected, often defined as the difference for which the percentage of correct discriminations is 75 per cent, though other percentages are sometimes used. Also called the difference limen (DL), discrimination threshold, or just noticeable difference (jnd). See also acuity, ABX paradigm, Bunsen–Roscoe law, differential acuity, discrimination function, Fullerton–Cattell law, Piper's law, Ricco's law, Weber fraction, Weber's law. Compare absolute threshold.

difference tone n. A *combination tone whose frequency is equal to the difference between the frequencies of the two tones generating it. Compare summation tone.

differential acuity n. The maximum keenness or sharpness of a sense organ in detecting differences or discriminating between stimuli, usually expressed in terms of the *difference threshold. See also acuity. Compare absolute acuity.

Differential Aptitude Tests n. An integrated battery of psychometric tests designed for educational and vocational guidance of schoolchildren. The tests measure the following eight aptitudes: verbal reasoning, numerical ability, abstract reasoning, clerical speed and accuracy, mechanical reasoning, spatial relations, spelling, and language usage. **DAT** abbrev.

differential diagnosis n. The process of distinguishing between two or more disorders with similar or overlapping signs and symptoms. See also diagnosis.

differential inversion effect n. The relatively greater decrease in recognizability resulting from inverting images of human faces compared to images of other objects. The effect is not peculiar to faces, as was initially believed when it was discovered in 1969 by the US psychologist Robert Kuo-Zuir Yin (born 1931), but is found with other classes of stimuli that are recognizably different only to viewers who have expert knowledge of them, as when experts on sporting dogs view inverted profiles of dogs. *See also* Margaret Thatcher illusion. *Compare* caricature advantage.

differential reinforcement *n.* In *operant conditioning, *reinforcement (1) that is contingent on more than a single response, as when a rat is reinforced for pressing a lever when one type of signal is given but not another. It is useful for determining what kinds of discriminations the organism is capable of making. *See also* differential reinforcement of high response rates, differential reinforcement of low response rates, differential reinforcement of other behaviour, differential reinforcement of paced responses.

differential reinforcement of high response rates *n.* In *operant conditioning, a *reinforcement schedule in which an organism is rewarded only when it responds within a specified interval after its previous response. *See also* differential reinforcement. *Compare* differential reinforcement of low response rates. **DRH** *abbrev.*

differential reinforcement of low response rates *n.* In *operant conditioning, a *reinforcement schedule in which an organism is rewarded only for a response made after a specified interval has elapsed since its previous response. *See also* differential reinforcement. *Compare* differential reinforcement of high response rates. **DRL** *abbrev.*

differential reinforcement of other responses *n.* In *operant conditioning, a *reinforcement schedule in which an organism is rewarded for abstaining from making a specified response for a predetermined period of time, any other response being reinforced. *See also* differential reinforcement. **DRO** *abbrev.*

differential reinforcement of paced responses *n.* In *operant conditioning, a *reinforcement schedule in which an organism is rewarded for responding at a particular rate, both slower and faster rates of responding

leading to withdrawal of reinforcement. *See also* differential reinforcement. **DRP** *abbrev.*

diffraction grating *n.* A plate of glass or a mirror that has equidistant parallel grooves engraved on its surface and that diffracts light, often more strongly than a *prism. *See also* spectrum.
[From Latin *diffractio* a breaking into pieces, from *diffringere* to shatter, from *dis-* apart + *frangere* to break]

diffuse fibres *n.* Touch receptors with large *receptive fields that have ill-defined borders.

diffusion of responsibility *n.* A reduced sense of personal responsibility and individual accountability experienced by members of a group, often leading to behaviour untypical of any of the group members when alone. *See* bystander effect, deindividuation, social loafing.

digestive tract *n.* Another name for the *alimentary canal.

digital *adj.* Of, relating to, consisting of, or containing digits or numerals; representing measurements in the form of discrete numbers rather than continuously varying quantities such as points on a dial. The term is descriptive of the form in which electronic data are stored and handled by computers. *See also* bit. *Compare* analogue (2).
[From Latin *digitus* a toe or finger + *-alis* of or related to]

digitalis *n.* Any plant of the genus *Digitalis*, including the foxglove, or a drug prepared from its dried leaves and seeds, functioning as a sympathetic nervous system *stimulant, used in the treatment of various forms of heart failure. *See also* xanthopsia. **digitalin** or **digitoxin** *n.* The poisonous bitter-tasting white substance extracted from foxglove leaves in the preparation of *digitalis.
[From Latin *digitalis* of or relating to a finger or toe, from *digitus* a finger or toe, referring to the purple foxglove flowers, which children like to attach to their fingers like thimbles]

digital signature *n.* A technical device for producing an electronic fingerprint, usually a *hash function*, created and verified by public-key cryptography, applied to electronic data for authentication of documents, especially those transmitted via the Internet, and for legal identification of signers with documents.

digit span *n*. A type of *intelligence test item or subtest in which the respondent tries to repeat back a string of numbers that are read out. Sometimes the numbers have to be repeated in reverse order.

digit–symbol test *n*. A type of *intelligence test item or subtest in which the respondent learns a code in which each digit is represented by a symbol—for example, 1 might be represented by a star, 2 by a square, 3 by a triangle, and so on—and then tries to substitute the correct symbols for a series of digits as quickly and accurately as possible. Also called a *symbol–digit test* or a *coding test*.

digram *n*. A combination of two letters, which may be a word (*do*) or a non-word (*kd*). *See also* CV digram. *Compare* digraph.
[From Greek *dis* twice + *gramma* a letter or character]

digraph *n*. A two-letter combination representing a single speech sound, such as *sh* in *sheet* or *ph* in *digraph*. *Compare* digram, diphthong.

dihybrid *n*. A cross between parents differing in two pairs of genes or two independently heritable characters. Also called a *dihybrid cross*. *Compare* hybrid (1).
[From Greek *dis* twice + English *hybrid*]

dilator pupillae *n*. The muscle that contracts the *iris and thereby dilates the pupil of the eye. *Compare* sphincter pupillae.
[From Latin *dilatare* to spread out + *pupilla* a pupil, diminutive of *pupa* a girl or a doll, alluding to the tiny reflection in the eye]

dimension-abstracted oddity *n*. A type of *oddity problem in which the set of stimuli contains an odd one out, distinguishable from the others on an oddity-defining dimension, and the other alternatives are indistinguishable from one another on the oddity-defining dimension but distinguishable from one another on other dimensions, often called *ambiguous dimensions*. Such a problem differs from a conventional oddity problem, in which, apart from the odd one out, the stimuli are indistinguishable from one

another on any dimension. A typical example might involve a set of objects differing perceptibly in size, colour, and shape, including an odd one out that is a different size from the other stimuli, which in turn are indistinguishable in size but differ from one another in colour and shape.

dimethyltryptamine *n*. The chemical name of *DMT.
[From Greek *dis* twice + *methyl* the alkyl radical CH_3 derived from methane by removal of one hydrogen atom, from Greek *methy* wine + *hyle* wood + English *tryptamine*]

dimorphic *adj*. Of or relating to a species with two distinct *phenotypic forms, such as physically distinct male and female forms. Also written *dimorphous*. **dimorphism** *n*. *See also* sexual dimorphism.
[From Greek *dis* twice + *morphe* a form or shape + *-ikos* of, relating to, or resembling]

ding-dong theory *n*. A dismissive name for the *onomatopoeic theory of the origins of language. Also called the *bow-wow theory*.
[From the sound of bells ringing]

Dionysian *adj*. Spontaneous and uncontrolled; in the philosophy of the German philosopher Friedrich Wilhelm Nietzsche (1844–1900), of or relating to creative qualities of spontaneity, irrationality, and rejection of discipline. *Compare* Apollonian.
[Named after Dionysus, the Greek god of wine and bestower of ecstasy]

dioptre *n*. A unit of measurement for the refractive power of a lens, being the reciprocal of the lens's *focal length in metres. US *diopter*.
[From Greek *dioptron* a spyglass from *dia* through + *opsesthai* to see]

dioptric aberration *n*. Another name for *aberration (3).

diotic *adj*. Of or relating to an auditory signal that is identical in both ears. *Compare* dichotic.
[From Greek *dis* twice + *ous, otos* an ear]

diphthong *n*. Any complex *vowel sound comprising a *glide from one vowel sound to another within a single syllable, with movement of the tongue between the two sounds. In *Received Pronunciation there are three

diphthongs in which the final sound is similar to the vowel in *tip* (as in the words *day*, *tie*, *boy*); two in which the final vowel sound is similar to the vowel in *put* (as in *go* and *how*); and three in which the final vowel sound is similar to the vowel in *the* (as in *veer*, *care*, and *poor*). *Compare* digraph, monophthong, triphthong.
[From Greek *di-* two + *phthongos* sound]

diplacusis *n.* A hearing impairment arising from a difference between the two ears, resulting in hearing a single tone as two tones of different pitch. Also spelt *diplacousis*. Also called *diplacusia* or *diplacousia*.
[From Greek *diploos* double + *akusis* hearing, from *akouein* to hear + *-sis* indicating a condition or state]

diplaesthesia *n.* An illusory experience of touching two objects when actually touching only one, occurring occasionally as a neurological sign. US *diplesthesia*. *See also* Aristotle's illusion.
[From Greek *diploos* double + *aisthesis* feeling + *-ia* indicating a condition or quality]

diplegia *n.* Bilateral paralysis of corresponding parts on both sides of the body. *Compare* hemiplegia, monoplegia, ophthalmoplegia, paraplegia, quadriplegia, triplegia. **diplegic** *adj.*
[From Greek *dis* twice + *plege* a blow + *-ia* indicating a condition or quality]

diploid *adj.* Of or relating to a cell that has a full complement of paired *chromosomes, such as a body or somatic cell of humans and most sexually reproducing animals, rather than half the normal number, as in sex cells or gametes; also of or relating to an organism whose body cells contain paired chromosomes. *Compare* haplodiploid, haploid. **diploidy** *n.* The state or condition of being *diploid.
[From Greek *diploos* double + *-oeides* denoting resemblance of form, from *eidos* shape]

diplopia *n.* Double vision resulting from incorrect fixation or defective functioning of the *extra-ocular muscles or the nerves that control the muscles, sometimes resulting from fatigue, stress, or intoxication by alcohol or other depressant drugs. Diplopia when looking down, as when descending stairs, is a cardinal symptom of malfunction of the *trochlear nerve. *See also* binocular disparity.

[From Greek *diploos* double + *ops* an eye + *-ia* indicating a condition or quality]

dipsomania *n.* Intermittent pathological craving for alcohol. *Compare* alcohol dependence.
[From Greek *dipsa* thirst + *mania* madness + *-ia* indicating a condition or quality]

Dircks's ghost *n.* A fairer name for what is usually called *Pepper's ghost.
[Named after the retired English civil engineer and patent agent Henry Dircks (1806–73) who invented it in 1862]

direct analysis *n.* A technique of *psychoanalysis in which the analyst presents *interpretations (2) to the patient bluntly, attempting to communicate directly with the patient's *unconscious (2). For example, the analyst might interpret a male patient's *Oedipus complex by telling him: `You want to fuck your mother and cut your father's balls off'. It was introduced in 1946 by the US psychoanalyst John N(athaniel) Rosen (born 1902), who claimed that it was especially effective in treating *schizophrenia, in which the unconscious overwhelms the patient's defences, but in the early 1980s it became enveloped in controversy and Rosen stopped practising it. The technique is discussed in detail in Rosen's book *Direct Analysis: Selected Papers* (1953).

directed association *n.* In *analytical psychology, spontaneously produced chains of related ideas proceeding from the recollection of a dream. In contrast to *free association, the associated ideas are required constantly to relate to the original dream memory. Also called *controlled association*.

directed thinking *n.* In *analytical psychology, conscious use of language and concepts, closely tied to reality, characteristic of intellectual communication, scientific exposition, and common sense. It is closely related to the *secondary process of *psychoanalysis. Carl Gustav Jung (1875–1961) discussed it at length, contrasting it with *fantasy thinking (*Collected Works*, 5, paragraphs 4–46).

directional selection *n.* A form of *natural selection operating against one extreme of the range of variation of a characteristic and shifting the entire population towards the opposite extreme by either increasing or reducing the frequency of an *allele.

directional test n. In *inferential statistics, a test of the significance of a departure from the *null hypothesis in one direction only, so that a departure in the opposite direction, no matter how large, is attributed to chance. In a *non-directional test*, a departure from the null hypothesis in either direction results in its rejection. See also 1-tailed probability. Also called a *1-tailed test*.

direction-sensitive neuron n. A *ganglion cell in the *retina that is specialized to respond to movement in just one direction in the visual field and that underlies the *image–retinal system. It is believed to receive excitatory signals from one or more *photoreceptor cells and inhibitory signals from one or more others, the excitatory cells being positioned on the retina in front of the inhibitory cells, relative to the direction of movement that the direction-sensitive neuron is tuned to detect, so that when an image crosses the retina in that direction excitatory signals reach the direction-sensitive ganglion cell before inhibitory signals, and consequently the inhibitory signals fail to suppress the responses of the ganglion cells and the ganglion cells therefore fire, eliciting a perception of movement. Also called a *direction-selective cell* or a *motion detector*.

directory plus one sampling n. A variation of *random digit dialling (RDD) in which a *probability sample of telephone subscribers is drawn by selecting telephone numbers randomly from directories and adding one to the final digit of each number before dialling it, the purpose being to ensure that ex-directory subscribers are adequately represented in the sample.

direct perception n. A theory of (mainly visual) perception, developed by the US psychologist James Jerome Gibson (1904–79) over a period of more than three decades, according to which the flux of light (called the *ambient optic array*) reaching the visual *receptors (1) of a perceiving organism is richly structured; movements of the organism or of surrounding objects cause some aspects of the array to change while others remain constant, hence the array is composed of *variants* and *invariants*, and the invariants are sufficient to provide perception of aspects of the environment

such as spatial arrangements and surfaces directly, that is, without recourse to inference or memory. See also affordance, air theory, Gibsonian, global psychophysics, motion perspective.

direct scaling n. In *psychophysics, any method of scaling such as *magnitude estimation or *cross-modal matching in which an observer specifically estimates the magnitude of the variable stimulus. Compare indirect scaling.

dirhinic adj. Of or relating to any olfactory stimulus that affects both nostrils alike. [From Greek *dis* twice + *rhis, rhinos* the nose + *-ikos* of, relating to, or resembling]

disabling agent See incapacitant.

disassortative mating n. Preference for mating partners with dissimilar *phenotypes, observed in some species but much less common than *assortative mating. See also population genetics.

disaster counselling n. A form of *counselling offered to the victims of major disasters, including accidents such as aircraft crashes, criminal acts such as terrorist bombs, and natural catastrophes such as earthquakes. The survivors of such disasters often experience *post-traumatic stress disorder and other psychological problems. US *disaster counseling*.

disavowal n. In *psychoanalysis, another name for *denial.

disconnection syndrome n. A term coined in 1965 by the US neurologist Norman Geschwind (1926–84) for a condition in which information transfer between parts of the brain is interrupted or blocked. See also aphasia, arcuate fasciculus, commissurotomy, left-sided apraxia, split-brain preparation, tactile aphasia.

discontinuity theory n. A theory of learning propounded by the US physiological psychologist Karl Spencer Lashley (1890–1958) according to which an organism does not learn gradually about *stimuli (1) that it encounters but forms hypotheses, such as *always turn left*, and learns about a stimulus only in relation to its current hypotheses, so that a process of learning can include sudden jumps, as one hypothesis is replaced by another. *Compare* continuity theory.

discordance *n.* **1.** In genetics, the proportion of *monozygotic twins (or relatives of other known degrees of genetic relatedness) who display different forms of a particular characteristic or different *phenotypes. *See also* map distance, twin study. *Compare* concordance (1). **2.** In statistics, the degree of disagreement between *ranks. *See* gamma statistic, Kendall coefficient of concordance, Kendall's tau, Somers' *D*. *Compare* concordance (2). **concordant** *adj.*

discourse *n.* A continuous stream of spoken (and sometimes written) language longer than a sentence.
[From Latin *discursus* argument, from *discurrere* to run to and fro, from *dis-* apart + *currere* to run]

discourse analysis *n.* A method of *qualitative research and a field of study devoted to understanding all forms of spoken interaction and written texts. It views language critically as an activity that constructs reality rather than merely describing or referring to it, and its theoretical approach is influenced by *deconstruction, *semiology, and *speech act theory and tends to be critical of traditional theories and research methodologies in psychology. Research focuses on well-formed rules governing the sequence of permissible linguistic units and on such aspects of language as *discourse markers*—verbal expressions such as *anyway, oh well,* or *I mean* that demarcate units of speech. *See also* conversation analysis, psychoanalytic construction. **DA** *abbrev.*

discrepancy effects *n.* The effects on *attitude change resulting from the distance of persuasive communications or messages from the recipients' initial attitude positions. *See* assimilation (4), assimilation–contrast theory, boomerang effect, contrast (5).

discrete processing *n.* The implementation of later stages of *information processing only after the completion of earlier stages, so that information is not passed on to the next stage until processing at the current stage is complete. *See also* serial processing. *Compare* cascade processing, parallel processing.

discrete variable *n.* In statistics, any *variable whose adjacent values are not infinitesimally close, so that cumulative values of its *probability distribution require simple addition rather than integration. *See also* metathetic stimulus dimension, prothetic stimulus dimension. *Compare* continuous variable.

discriminability *n.* The extent to which stimuli can be distinguished from one another or discriminated. In *signal detection theory, it is more specifically an index of the extent to which a signal can be detected or distinguished from noise, and it is also called *d* prime or *d′*. **discriminable** *adj.*
[From Latin *discriminare* to divide, from *discrimen* a division, from *discernere* to divide, from *dis* apart + *cernere* to separate + *-abilitas* capacity, from *habilis* able]

discriminanda *n.* Any set of stimuli among which an organism has to discriminate before making a response.

discriminant function analysis *n.* In statistics, a procedure for optimal classification of individuals into groups or classes on the basis of a number of discriminating variables on which each of the individuals has been measured. For example, a researcher might use the discriminating variables age, sex, level of education, and income in order to discriminate optimally between people who support capital punishment and those who oppose it. This is achieved by weighting the variables and combining them into discriminant functions that separate the two groups maximally. This procedure is mathematically equivalent to *canonical correlation with the discriminating variables considered as predictor variables and the group membership variable considered as a dummy criterion variable taking on arbitrary values (0 and 1 in the case of two groups). Alternatively, it may be thought of as *multiple regression with a categorical dependent variable. Also called *discriminant analysis*. **DFA** *abbrev.*

discriminant validity *n.* A form of *validity that, together with *convergent validity, provides evidence of *construct validity. It is based on the assumption that measures of unrelated *hypothetical constructs ought not to correlate highly with one another if the measures are valid: they ought to discriminate between dissimilar constructs. The concept was introduced in an article by the US psychologists Donald T(homas) Campbell (1916–96) and Donald W(inslow) Fiske (born 1916) in the journal *Psychological Bulletin* in 1959. *See also* multitrait–multimethod matrix.

discriminating power *n.* In psychometrics, the degree to which a test yields different scores when applied to different criterion groups; specifically, the degree to which an item in an *attitude scale, or the scale as a whole, yields different scores when it is applied to people holding different attitudes towards the attitude object in question. *See also* item discrimination index.

discrimination *n.* **1.** The act or process of distinguishing between stimuli or of recognizing or understanding the differences between things. *See also* discriminability, discrimination learning. **2.** The unfair or prejudiced treatment of a person or group, as in *racial discrimination* or *sexual discrimination*. **discriminate** *vb.*

discrimination function *n.* The *difference threshold expressed as a function of the physical intensity of the stimuli, as when the difference threshold for loudness is plotted against sound pressure level to yield a loudness discrimination function, showing the lowest thresholds for intermediate sound pressure levels.

discrimination learning *n.* Any form of *learning (1) in which the organism has to discriminate between two or more *stimuli (1) in order to respond correctly, studies of such learning often being used to establish the capacity of the organism to make certain discriminations. *See also* peak shift, probability learning.

discrimination reaction time *n.* *Reaction time to differences in an objectively measurable perceptual dimension such as brightness, length, or weight. A common procedure for measuring it involves an observer comparing pairs of visual displays, presented simultaneously, and responding by pressing one of two buttons according to which display appears brighter, longer, heavier, or greater in magnitude on whatever dimension is being examined, the time elapsing between stimulus presentation and key-pressing response being the discrimination reaction time. The

three main dependent variables in research using this technique are reaction time, degree of confidence, and relative frequency of each available response. *Compare* choice reaction time, simple reaction time. **DRT** *abbrev.*

discrimination threshold *n.* Another name for the *difference threshold.

discriminative response *n.* A *response made by an organism to one of two or more different stimuli that it has to distinguish from the other(s) in order to obtain a reward.

dishabituation *n.* The restoration of the prior strength of an *unconditioned response that has been weakened by *habituation (2), such restoration usually being induced by a strong stimulus of a different type. *See also* disinhibition. **dishabituate** *vb.*

disinhibition *n.* The reappearance of a *conditioned response that has been inhibited, usually by *extinction (2), following the presentation of a novel or strong stimulus. Also called *inhibition of inhibition*. *Compare* inhibition (3).

disintegrative disorder *n.* An alternative name for *childhood disintegrative disorder.

disjunction *n.* **1.** The act or process of disconnecting, or the state of being disconnected, especially the separation during *meiosis or *mitosis of the members of each pair of *homologous chromosomes. **2.** In logic, two *propositions (1) connected by an operator denoting *or* to form a single compound proposition, usually written *p* ∨ *q*, where *p* and *q* represent the component propositions or disjuncts, the compound proposition being true if one or both of its disjuncts are true. Also called an *inclusive disjunction* to distinguish it from the less common *exclusive disjunction*, which is true if either of its disjuncts is true but not if both are true. *See also* disjunctive concept. *Compare* conjunction (2). [From Latin *dis-* indicating reversal + *iunctio* joining + *-ion* indicating an action, process, or state]

disjunction search *n.* A search for a target stimulus representing a *disjunctive concept among a number of distractor stimuli. *Compare* conjunction search, feature search.

disjunctive concept *n.* A concept defined by a *disjunction (2) specifying the possession of either one *attribute or another, for example, a figure that is either red or is a square. *Compare* conjunctive concept.

disjunctive eye movement *n.* Any turning of the eyes in different directions. *Compare* conjugate movement.
[From Latin *dis-* apart + *iungere* to join]

disorder of excessive somnolence *n.* Another name for *primary hypersomnia. **DOES** *abbrev.*

disorder of initiating and maintaining sleep *n.* Any of the *dyssomnias. **DIMS** *abbrev.*

disorder of written expression *See* written expression, disorder of.

disorganized schizophrenia *n.* One of the major types of *schizophrenia, the essential features of which are *disorganized speech and behaviour and *affective flattening or inappropriate *affect.

disorganized speech *n.* In certain mental disorders, notably forms of *disorganized schizophrenia, speech suggestive of *thought disorder, manifested by *cognitive derailment, *loosening of associations, *incoherence, or replies that are unrelated or only obliquely related to the questions posed (*see* Ganser syndrome).

disorientation *n.* **1.** Generally, a loss of one's bearings. **2.** In relation to a mental disorder, confusion about who or where one is or such matters as the day of the week, time of day, or season of the year.

disparate retinal points *n.* Any pair of points, one on each retina, that are not *corresponding retinal points.
[From Latin *disparatus* unequal, from *dis-* indicating reversal + *parare* to make ready, influenced by *dispar* unequal, from *par* equal]

disparity, binocular *See* binocular disparity.

disparity, retinal *n.* Another name for *binocular disparity.

disparity-selective cell *n.* A *binocular cell in the *visual cortex that receives inputs from both eyes and responds only when the *bin-ocular disparity is within certain predetermined limits, thus providing a basis for *stereopsis. Also called a *disparity-selective neuron*, a *disparity-tuned cell*, or a *disparity-tuned neuron*. *See also* stereoblindness.

dispersion *n.* In descriptive statistics, the degree of scatter or variability in a group of scores, usually measured by the *variance or *standard deviation. *See also* interquartile range, probable error, range, semi-interquartile range.

displaced aggression *n.* In *psychoanalysis, aggression that has undergone *displacement and has been redirected from its original target, usually a source of frustration, on to a substitute target.

displacement *n.* Moving something from its current position. In *psychoanalysis, a *defence mechanism involving redirection of emotional feelings from their original object to a substitute object related to the original one by a chain of associations. Although not essential to the concept as originally conceived by Sigmund Freud (1856–1939), and expounded further in 1900 in his book *The Interpretation of Dreams* (Standard Edition, IV–V, at pp. 180–1, 306–8) and in other writings, the substitute object may be less threatening than the original one, and the displacement may therefore have the effect of avoiding or reducing anxiety. Displacement is a characteristic mechanism of the *primary process. In an article in the journal *La Psychoanalyse* in 1957, the French psychoanalyst Jacques Lacan (1901–81) related displacement to *metonymy and the defence mechanism of *condensation to *metaphor. *See also* displaced aggression, dreamwork, quota of affect, transference.

displacement activity *n.* In ethology, the substitution of an irrelevant pattern of behaviour for behaviour that is appropriate to a particular situation, especially as a reaction to a conflict of motives. Male stickleback fish stand on their heads and dig into the sand as if building a nest when the impulses of attack and retreat are evenly balanced; fighting roosters often peck at the ground between bouts as though feeding; and humans often scratch their heads or perform self-grooming *gestures (1) when in a state of conflict, embarrassment, or stress. Also called *displacement behaviour*. *See also* adaptor.

display *n.* **1.** An exhibition or show; especially an ostentatious pattern of behaviour by an animal as part of a *courtship (1) ritual or when defending territory, establishing a position in a *dominance hierarchy or *pecking order, or engaging in some other form of social behaviour. *See also* conventional fighting. *vb.* **2.** To engage in a display.
[From Latin *displicare* to unfold, from *dis-* indicating reversal + *plicare* to fold]

display rule *n.* A cultural *norm (1) or convention governing the circumstances in which *facial expressions and other *affect displays are allowed, suppressed, or exaggerated. For example, in European and North American cultures, it is considered bad etiquette to smile broadly if a person slips on a banana peel and falls face-down, whereas one is expected to smile when greeting an acquaintance even if not genuinely happy. Japanese culture prescribes suppression of affect displays in many situations in which they are allowed or encouraged elsewhere, this no doubt being the origin of the notion of the inscrutable East.

dispositionist bias *n.* Another name for the *fundamental attribution error, considered more apt by some social psychologists.

disruptive behaviour disorders *n.* A generic name for *attention-deficit/hyperactivity disorder, *conduct disorder, and *oppositional defiant disorder. US *disruptive behavior disorders*.

disruptive selection *n.* A form of *natural selection operating against the middle range of variation of a characteristic and tending to split the population into two extreme types. *See also* apostatic selection. *Compare* stabilizing selection.

dissocial personality disorder *n.* Another name (used in *ICD-10) for *antisocial personality disorder. The diagnostic criteria are similar, with the addition of incapacity to maintain enduring relationships, though with no difficulty in establishing them, and incapacity to experience guilt or to profit from adverse experience, particularly punishment.

dissociation *n.* Partial or total disconnection between memories of the past, awareness of

identity and of immediate sensations, and control of bodily movements, often resulting from traumatic experiences, intolerable problems, or disturbed relationships. *See also* dissociative disorders, dissociation theory, neodissociation theory.
[From Latin *dissociare* to separate, from *dis*-apart + *sociare* to associate + *-ation* indicating a process or condition]

dissociation theory *n.* A theory proposed in 1899 by the French psychologist and neurologist Pierre Janet (1859–1947) to explain *automatism and in 1907 to explain *hysteria. According to the theory, these disorders are the result of *dissociation. *See also* neodissociation theory.

dissociative amnesia *n.* A *dissociative disorder characterized by loss of memory, usually for important recent events associated with serious problems, *stress (1), or unexpected *bereavement. It is not diagnosed if it is attributable to ordinary forgetfulness, fatigue, drugs, or a *general medical condition. *See also* amnesia, dissociation.

dissociative convulsions *n.* A *dissociative disorder characterized by sudden spasmodic *convulsions resembling those of *epilepsy but not associated with loss of consciousness.

dissociative disorders *n.* A category of *mental disorders with *dissociation as a prominent feature. *See* depersonalization disorder, dissociative amnesia, dissociative convulsions, dissociative fugue, dissociative identity disorder, dissociative movement disorders, dissociative stupor, dissociative trance disorder, Ganser syndrome. In some taxonomies of mental disorders, including *ICD-10, but not in *DSM-IV, *conversion disorder is also classified as a dissociative disorder. **DD** *abbrev.*

dissociative fugue *n.* A *dissociative disorder characterized by sudden unexpected travel away from home, *amnesia for some or all of the past, confusion about personal identity or (occasionally) the assumption of a new identity. It is not diagnosed if it is caused by drugs or a *general medical condition. *Compare* fugue.
[From Latin *fuga* a flight]

dissociative identity disorder *n.* A *dissociative disorder characterized by the presence of two or more (sometimes many) separate personalities, each with its own memories and patterns of behaviour, at least two of which take turns in recurrently taking control of behaviour, the disorder also being characterized by *amnesia for personal information that is too great to be attributable to ordinary forgetfulness. It is sometimes interpreted as a form or variant of *post-traumatic stress disorder, and some researchers and practitioners believe that it is usually a consequence of childhood abuse or other traumatic experiences, but the disorder is the subject of considerable controversy and is not universally recognized. Also called *multiple personality disorder* (MPD) or *split personality*. Often confused with (but in fact unrelated to) *schizophrenia. **DID** *abbrev.*

dissociative movement disorders *n.* Forms of *dissociative disorders in which there is a partial or complete loss of ability to perform bodily movements that are normally under voluntary control, without any apparent *organic disorder, including dissociative forms of *akinesia, *aphonia, *apraxia, *ataxia, *convulsions, *dysarthria, *dyskinesia, and *dysstasia. Also called *dissociative motor disorders* or *motor dissociative disorders*.

dissociative stupor *n.* Profound diminution or absence of voluntary movement and responsiveness to external stimuli apparently resulting from *stress (1). *See also* dissociation.

dissociative trance disorder *n.* A condition (included in the *DSM-IV appendix of conditions meriting further study, but not in the *ICD-10 classification) characterized by behaviour and experience associated with a *trance or a *possession trance. Also called *trance and possession disorder*. *See also* dissociation, dissociative disorder.

dissonance theory *n.* Another name for *cognitive dissonance theory.

distal *adj.* Farther or farthest from the centre, point of attachment, or origin. *Compare* proximal.
[From *distant* + *-al* from Latin *-alis* of or relating to, by analogy with *central*]

distal criterion *n.* Another name for an *ecological criterion.

distal stimulus *n.* An object, event, or agent in the external environment producing a pattern of physical energy called the *proximal stimulus that in turn excites a *sensory receptor.

distance receptor *n.* A *sensory receptor for stimuli such as light and sound that are produced by distant stimuli. *Compare* contact receptor.

distance sense *n.* Another name for a *far sense.

distinctive feature *n.* Any *feature (1) or *attribute of speech or writing that is relevant or significant inasmuch as it enables a contrast to be made between phonological, syntactic, or semantic units of a language, especially the phonological attributes that distinguish *minimal pairs and that therefore underlie the definition of a *phoneme. *See also* acoustic cue (1).

distorted-room illusion *n.* Another name for the *Ames room.

distractibility *n.* Diminished ability to maintain attention, usually manifested as excessive shifting of attention from one topic to another or a tendency to be captivated by unimportant details or stimuli.

distractor *n.* A stimulus that diverts attention from a *target item that a research participant is searching for or trying to concentrate on, frequently used in studies of perception and memory. A *token distractor* resembles the target item closely, differing from it in detail only, whereas a *type distractor* differs substantially from the target item. Also called a *foil*.

distress relief quotient *n.* The ratio of verbal expressions of distress to verbal expressions of relief in a sequence of discourse, sometimes used as an index to track the process of improvement in *psychotherapy or *counselling.

distributed cognition *n.* *Information processing that is shared among several separate agents. The classic example, due to the US cognitive scientist Edwin Hutchins (born 1948), is that of a group of crew members cooperating to navigate a large ship: one crew member plots the ship's position on a chart, another takes compass bearings on landmarks, another keeps time and communicates with the bearing-takers, another maintains a deck log in which changes in heading and speed are recorded, another monitors water depth, and another operates the steering mechanism. It should be distinguished from *parallel distributed processing or *connectionism (1), in which separate sub-processes are distributed within a single agent. The *cooperative principle is often cited as an example of distributed cognition, making purposeful communication possible as a cooperative endeavour.

distributed network model *n*. A representation of anything by a pattern of activation over a number of connected units, characteristic of *connectionism (1). Also called *distributed representation*.

distributed practice *n*. Learning that is divided up into sessions, leaving gaps either between trials or between blocks of trials, generally leading to superior recall after a delay relative to *massed practice.

distributed representation *n*. Another name for a *distributed network model.

distribution-free test *n*. In inferential statistics, any significance test that makes no assumptions about the precise distribution or form of the sampled *population. Although the term *distribution-free* is often used interchangeably with *non-parametric*, strictly speaking it is possible for a test to be distribution-free without being non-parametric; for example the *sign test makes no assumptions about the distribution of the sampled population but tests the hypothesis that a certain parameter of the binomial distribution (the proportion of successes) is 1/2, so it is not really non-parametric. *See also* non-parametric statistics, probability distribution.

distribution (probability) *See* probability distribution.

disulfiram *n*. A drug that induces nausea when taken with *alcohol and is used in the treatment of *alcoholism. *See* Antabuse.

diurnal *adj*. Occurring during the day or daily. *Compare* nocturnal.

[From Latin *diurnalis* of or relating to a day, from *dies* a day]

diurnal rhythm *n*. Another name for a *circadian rhythm. *See also* biological clock, chronobiology, *Zeitgeber*.

divergence *n*. The act, process, or condition of separation or of going in different directions, especially *ocular divergence, the turning outwards of the eyes in order to fixate an object or image further away than the previous fixation point. *See also* horopter, vergence. *Compare* convergence.

[From Latin *divergere* to move apart, from *di*- apart + *vergere* to incline]

divergent thinking *n*. Imaginative thinking, characterized by the generation of multiple possible solutions to a problem, often associated with *creativity. The concept was introduced in 1946 by the US psychologist J(oy) P(aul) Guilford (1897–1987) and is one of the five different types of mental operations in *Guilford's cube. *See* convergence–divergence.

divided visual field *n*. A generic name for a variety of experimental techniques in which a viewer *fixates (1) on a point while visual stimuli are flashed briefly in the left or right *visual field, and measures of response accuracy and *reaction time are taken, in order to study lateralization of brain functions. It is based on the fact that the partial *decussation of nerve fibres at the *optic chiasm results in each half of the visual field being projected to the opposite-hemisphere *primary visual cortex (Area V1). *See also* homonymous hemianopia, laterality.

divisive hierarchical clustering *n*. In statistics, any technique of *cluster analysis that begins with all individuals or cases grouped into a single cluster and then splits individuals into separate clusters until there are as many clusters as individuals.

dizygotic *adj*. Developed from two *zygotes. *Compare* monozygotic. **DZ** *abbrev*.

[From Greek *dis* double + *zygotos* yoked, from *zygon* a yoke + *-itikos* resembling or marked by]

dizygotic twins *n*. Twins that are *dizygotic, arising from the fertilization of two separate ova or eggs by two separate spermatozoa at about the same time, leading to the development of individuals usually (if they have the same father) sharing about half their genes in common like ordinary siblings. Their relative frequency is affected by many environmental factors and is greatly increased by the use of fertility drugs. Also called *fraternal twins* or *non-identical twins*. *See also* twin study. *Compare* monozygotic twins. **DZ twins** *abbrev.*

DMT *abbrev.* The usual name for dimethyltryptamine, a *hallucinogenic and *psychedelic drug belonging to the group of *indole alkaloids, found in many South American snuffs. *See also* phantasticant.

DNA *abbrev.* Deoxyribonucleic acid (also written *desoxyribonucleic acid*), a self-replicating molecule that is the major functional constituent of *chromosomes and is also found inside *mitochondria in the cytoplasm of cells, containing the *genes transmitted from parents to offspring in most organisms, and consisting of two strands of complementary chemical *base (1) pairs (adenine paired with thymine and cytosine with guanine) incorporating the genetic information, the strands

being linked to a backbone composed of the sugar *deoxyribose alternating with a *phosphate and coiled into a double helix (spiral) (see illustration). Human DNA contains approximately 32,000 genes, each gene consisting of a sequence of base pairs encoding a corresponding sequence of *amino acids that constitute a specific *protein. *See also* cistron, codon, complementary base pairing, double helix, genetic code, intron, mitochondrial DNA, nucleotide, plasmid, polymerase chain reaction, purine, pyrimidine, recombinant DNA, restriction mapping, telomere, transposon.

DNA cloning *n.* Producing *clones (2) of *genes. Also called *gene cloning*.

DNA fingerprinting *n.* Another name for *genetic fingerprinting.

DNA hybridization *n.* A technique for determining the similarity of two strands of DNA, or of DNA and RNA, by bringing single strands of each molecule together and examining the degree of double helix formation, which is in-

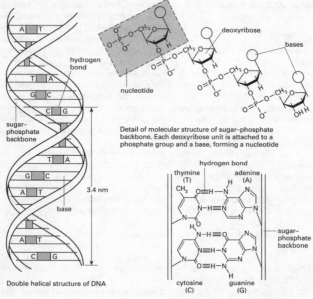

Detail of molecular structure of sugar–phosphate backbone. Each deoxyribose unit is attached to a phosphate group and a base, forming a nucleotide

Double helical structure of DNA

The four bases of DNA, showing the hydrogen bonding between base pairs

DNA. Molecular structure.

dicative of corresponding base sequences. It is also used to isolate specific DNA or RNA molecules from a mixture by causing complementary strands to reassociate. The technique is based on the fact that if DNA (or a mixture of DNA and RNA) is heated to the point at which it dissociates into single strands and is then cooled, double helixes re-form at regions of base-sequence complementarity. *See also* annealing (2), hybridization.

DNA ligase *n.* An *enzyme that is capable of uniting two strands of *DNA and is used in *recombinant DNA techniques and in *genetic engineering.
[From Latin *ligare* to bind + Greek *-ase* denoting an enzyme, from *diastasis* separation]

DNA polymerase *n.* Any of several *enzymes that catalyse the synthesis of additional units of *DNA by a process of *transcription (2), using single-stranded DNA as a template. *See also* DNA replication, polymerase chain reaction. *Compare* RNA polymerase.
[From *DNA* + *polymer* + Greek *-ase* denoting an enzyme, from *diastasis* separation]

DNA profiling *n.* Another name for *genetic fingerprinting.

DNA recombination *n.* Any process of *DNA exchange in a sexually reproducing organism that produces chromosomes containing new combinations of *genes not found in the cells of either of its parents, especially the rearrangement of genes resulting from *independent assortment and *crossing over. Also called *genetic recombination* or simply *recombination*. Often confused with *recombinant DNA.

DNA replication *n.* The process, catalysed by *DNA polymerase, whereby the two complementary strands of a *DNA double helix molecule separate, each strand then functioning as a template for the synthesis of a new complementary strand, resulting in the formation of two double-stranded DNA molecules identical to the original.

DNA sequence *n.* The order in which *base (1) pairs appear in a *DNA molecule, determining within the protein-coding sections of DNA the order of the *amino acids to be synthesized. Also called a *base sequence* or a *nucleotide*

sequence. **DNA sequencing** *n.* Determining the *DNA sequence in a sample of nucleic acid.

DNA splicing *n.* In *genetic engineering, artificial rearrangement of sections of *DNA using *restriction enzymes and *DNA ligase.

doing gender *n.* The study of the interpersonal aspects of *gender (1), focusing on the ways in which cognitive categories based on *sex (1) act as social cues that influence people's behaviour and elicit gender-specific patterns of interaction, thereby creating, maintaining, and reinforcing social inequalities.

Dollar Auction game *n.* A strategic *game (1) devised by the US economist Martin Shubik (born 1926) and published in the *Journal of Conflict Resolution* in 1971, designed to model strategic escalation and entrapment. A dollar bill (or other currency note) is auctioned to the highest bidder in a group. The highest bidder gets the dollar bill, and the second-highest bidder receives nothing, but *both* bidders must pay the auctioneer amounts corresponding to their last bids. Suppose the bidding stops at 40c and the previous (second-highest) bid was 35c, then the 40c bidder gets the dollar, and the auctioneer collects 40c from that bidder and 35c from the second-highest bidder (who receives nothing in return). The first moment of truth occurs after two bids have been made—say 10c and 20c. If no other bids are made, then the first bidder will simply lose 10c, but putting in a further bid for 30c opens up the possibility of winning 70c provided that the auction ends there. The most disturbing moment of truth occurs if the bidding reaches the one-dollar mark, and the second-highest bidder must decide whether to bid more than a dollar for the one-dollar payoff in the hope of minimizing what is by then an inevitable loss: for example, a bid of 105c will result in a loss of only 5 cents if the bidding stops there, but the other bidder may bid even higher for the same reason. Once the bidding passes the one-dollar threshold, the bidders are motivated to minimize losses rather than to maximize gains. When played with real bidders, the game is usually highly profitable for the auctioneer, and controlled experiments have shown that bidding almost invariably exceeds the value of the prize and sometimes goes as high as 20 dollars, causing much distress to the participants. *See also* Concorde fallacy.

Dollo's law *n*. The proposition that a structure or function lost in the course of evolution is never regained in its original form, and that in this sense evolution is irreversible.
[Named after the Belgian palaeontologist Louis Antoine Marie Joseph Dollo (1857–1931) who propounded it in 1893]

dolls *n*. A street name for *barbiturate drugs in general.

Dolophine *n*. A proprietary name for the narcotic drug *methadone.
[Trademark]

dolorimeter *n*. A device for measuring *pain on a scale from mildly unpleasant to unbearable by means of heat applied to the skin. *See also* algesimeter, cold pressor pain, ischaemic pain. **dolorimetry** *n*. The measurement of pain sensations using a *dolorimeter. **dolorimetric** *adj*. Of or relating to *dolorimetry.
[From Latin *dolor* pain, from *dolere* to grieve + *metron* a measure]

dolorology *n*. The study of the origins, nature, and management of pain.
[From Latin *dolor* pain, from *dolere* to grieve + *logos* word, discourse, or reason]

domain-referenced test *n*. A test that measures an *attribute by estimating the proportion of a specified *content domain of knowledge, skills, or abilities the respondent has acquired. *See also* content validity, domain sampling. *Compare* criterion-referenced test, norm-referenced test.

domain sampling *n*. In psychometrics, the process of choosing test items that are appropriate to the *content domain of the test. *See also* content validity, domain-referenced test.

domains of processing theory *n*. The proposition that the more *elaboration is involved in information processing at a given level of processing, the better it will be remembered. *See also* elaboration, levels of processing.

dominance *See* dominance (genetic), dominant alternative/strategy.

dominance, eye *See* eye dominance.

dominance (genetic) *n*. The property of being a *dominant gene. If a *hybrid (1) between two strains is on average exactly intermediate between the two on some measured *trait, then there is zero dominance and complete *additivity; if the average hybrid is somewhat more similar to one of the strains, then there is partial dominance by the corresponding *allele; and if the average hybrid is exactly like one of the strains, then there is complete dominance by the corresponding allele. Also called *genetic dominance*. *See also* heterozygous, overdominance, penetrance. *Compare* epistasis. **dominant** *adj*.

dominance hierarchy *n*. A more or less stable rank order of animals competing for resources such as food, territory, or mates, in which each individual is more likely than not to lose a fight or competition against any individual above it in the rank order and to win against any individual below it. Such hierarchies, usually established and maintained by aggressive *displays (1) or *conventional fighting rather than *escalated fighting, have been found in both captive and wild populations of many species, though they are not always perfectly linear (they tend to include non-linearities in which A dominates B, B dominates C, C dominates A), and the middle position of a hierarchy tends to be less stable and less linear than the top and bottom. *See also* hook order, pecking order.

dominant alternative/strategy *n*. In decision theory and game theory, an alternative or *strategy (2) that, in every contingency that might arise, yields a *payoff at least as good as the payoff from any other available alternative or strategy and a strictly better payoff in at least one. A dominant strategy is *strongly dominant* if it yields a strictly better payoff than any other alternative or strategy in every possible contingency, otherwise it is *weakly dominant*. An alternative or strategy that is not dominated by any other is an *admissible alternative/strategy*, and in a decision problem in which a dominant strategy exists, another alternative or strategy that is not dominant is a *dominated alternative/strategy* or an *inadmissible alternative/strategy*. It is generally agreed that a *rational decision maker or player will never deliberately choose a dominated alternative or strategy, but this principle appears counter-intuitive to some people in puzzles such as *Newcomb's problem and the

*Prisoner's Dilemma game. Also called a *dominating alternative/strategy*. *See also* prospect theory, sure-thing principle.

dominant gene *n*. A *gene displaying *dominance (genetic) in the sense that if it is inherited from one parent it tends to produce the same *phenotype in the organism whether the corresponding *allele inherited from the other parent is the same or different. For example, the gene for brown eyes is dominant and the allele for blue eyes is recessive, so an individual who is heterozygous at this locus will have brown eyes, and only an individual with two blue-eyed alleles will be phenotypically blue-eyed. Also (less commonly but more accurately) called a *dominant allele*. *See also* sex-influenced trait. *Compare* recessive gene.

dominator *n*. Anyone or anything that dominates; in visual perception a hypothetical *ganglion cell receiving inputs from a group of retinal *cones that respond to brightness, its responses being regulated by *modulator cells.

Donders' law *n*. The proposition that for any head position and any direction of *gaze the eye always assumes the same position, resulting in the fixation point being focused on the *fovea.
[Named after the Dutch ophthalmologist Franciscus Cornelius Donders (1818–89) who formulated it in 1846]

Donders' method *n*. Another name for the *subtraction method.
[Named after the Dutch ophthalmologist Franciscus Cornelius Donders (1818–89) who introduced it in 1868]

Don Juanism *n*. A non-technical name for *satyriasis.
[Named after the legendary Spanish nobleman Don Juan, noted for his insatiable sexual appetite]

door-in-the-face technique *n*. A technique for eliciting *compliance by making a very large initial request, which the recipient is sure to turn down, followed by a smaller request. It was introduced in 1975 by the US social psychologist Robert B(eno) Cialdini (born 1945) and several colleagues who performed a field experiment in which students were ap-

proached on campus and requested to volunteer to spend two hours a week, for two or more years, as unpaid counsellors at a local juvenile detention centre. No one agreed to this, but when they were then asked whether they would be willing on just one occasion to escort a group of juveniles from the detention centre on a two-hour trip to the zoo, 50 per cent agreed, compared with 17 per cent in the control group who received only the second, smaller request. Also called the *rejection-then-retreat technique*. *See also* foot-in-the-door technique, lowball technique.

dopa *n*. An *amino acid found in certain fruits and vegetables, especially broad beans, derived by oxidation from *tyrosine, and abundantly present in the adrenal glands. It is a precursor of *dopamine, *adrenalin (epinephrine), and *noradrenalin (norepinephrine). The laevorotatory (left-handed) isomer *L-dopa is used to treat *Parkinson's disease.
[A contraction of its chemical name *d(ihydr)o(xy)p(henyl)a(lanine)*]

dopamine *n*. A *biogenic amine and *catecholamine that is one of the *neurotransmitter substances significantly involved in central nervous system functioning, and that also functions as a *hormone. Its three main pathways within the brain are from the *midbrain to the *basal ganglia (*see also* Parkinson's disease), from the midbrain to the *frontal lobes, and from the midbrain to the *limbic system, the mesolimbic dopamine pathway being strongly implicated in experiences of pleasure or reward and also responses to salient stimuli in general. Formula: $C_8H_{11}NO_2$. Also called *3-hydroxytyramine*. *See also* dopaminergic, L-dopa, mesolimbic system, mesotelencephalic pathway, nucleus accumbens, 6-hydroxydopamine, ventral tegmental area. **DA** *abbrev*.
[From *dopa* + *amine*]

dopamine antagonist *n*. Any drug such as *olanzapine or one of the *phenothiazines, *butyrophenones, or *dibenzodiazepines that inhibits the action of *dopamine by blocking the dopamine receptors. *See also* antagonist (3), neuroleptic (1). *Compare* dopaminomimetic.

dopaminergic *adj*. Releasing *dopamine; also activated by or responding to dopamine, this extended usage being widespread but

consistently rejected by the English physiologist Sir Henry Hallet Dale (1875–1968), who coined the suffix *-ergic*, and by many other authorities. The term applies especially to nerve fibres, such as those of the *mesotelencephalic pathway and the *mesolimbic system, that use dopamine as their main or only *neurotransmitter. *Compare* adrenergic, cholinergic, GABAergic, noradrenergic, serotonergic.
[From *dopamine* + Greek *ergon* work + *-ikos* of, relating to, or resembling]

dopaminomimetic *adj. n.* (Of or relating to) a drug such as *apomorphine or *bromocriptine that reproduces some or all of the effects of *dopamine by acting on dopamine receptors as an *agonist (3). *Compare* dopamine antagonist.
[From *dopamine* + Greek *mimesis* imitation, from *mimeisthai* to imitate]

dope *n.* A term used for a variety of substances; more specifically, a street name for *cannabis, *heroin, or occasionally other drugs.
[From Dutch *doop* a sauce, from *doopen* to dip]

Doppelgänger *n.* A *reduplicative paramnesia in which a person believes that he or she has a double or replica. *Compare* Capgras syndrome.
[German: literally double-goer]

Doppler effect *n.* An increase in the *frequency (1) of a sound wave, or of an electromagnetic wave such as light, emitted by a source moving towards the observer, or a decrease in frequency from a source moving away from the observer, a familiar example being the rise and fall in the pitch of an ambulance siren as it approaches and then recedes, the effect being the result of a compression or stretching out of waves due to the motion of the source relative to the observer. Also called the *Doppler shift. See also* biosonar.
[Named after the Austrian physicist Christian Johann Doppler (1803–53) who formulated it in 1842]

Dora *n.* In *psychoanalysis, the pseudonym of an 18-year-old woman treated by Sigmund Freud (1856–1939) in 1900 for *hysteria and discussed in his famous case study in 1901/5 entitled 'Fragment of an Analysis of a Case of

Hysteria' (*Standard Edition*, VII, pp. 7–122). *See also* urethral erotism.

Doriden *n.* A proprietary name for the depressant drug *glutethimide.
[Trademark]

dorsal *adj.* Of, relating to, or situated towards the spine, except in the human forebrain, where *dorsal* is synonymous with *superior* or *top*, as if humans walked on all fours and the cerebrum were not bent forwards 80 degrees relative to the brainstem to keep it horizontally oriented when standing upright. *Compare* ventral.
[From Latin *dorsum* the back]

dorsal column *n.* A column of nerve fibres, including the *fasciculus cuneatus and *fasciculus gracilis, lying dorsally in the posterior *funiculus of each lateral half of the spinal cord, conveying sensations of touch and proprioception. It is one of two major routes by which afferent spinal nerve fibres carrying sensations of *somaesthesis are transmitted to the thalamus. *Compare* spinothalamic tract.

dorsal root *n.* The short pathways into which a spinal nerve divides near its point of attachment to the back of the spinal cord, containing afferent or sensory fibres transmitting nerve impulses to the spinal cord. *See also* Bell–Magendie law, dorsal root ganglion. *Compare* ventral root.

dorsal root ganglion *n.* Any of a number of swellings containing sensory neuron cell bodies located outside the spinal cord close to the dorsal roots of the spinal nerves. **dorsal root ganglia** *pl.*
[From Greek *ganglion* a cystic tumour]

dorsomedial thalamus *n.* A nucleus in the *thalamus that transmits afferent nerve impulses to the *prefrontal cortex. It usually degenerates in cases of *Korsakoff's psychosis associated with dense *amnesia.

dose–response curve *n.* The functional relationship between the dosage of a drug and the size or strength of a physiological or behavioural response to it. It is almost invariably monotonically increasing, with larger dosages of the drug producing larger responses, at least within a certain range, but very low and/or very high dosages may not

doves

follow this pattern. For example, a low dosage of adrenalin (epinephrine) or acetylcholine produces a slight drop in blood pressure, whereas a high dosage produces a large increase in blood pressure, and a low dosage of caffeine may enhance typing skill whereas a larger dosage impairs it. Also called the *dose–response relation(ship)*. *See also* initial values law.

Dostoevsky syndrome *n.* Another name for *interictal syndrome.
[Named after the Russian novelist Fyodor (Mikhailovich) Dostoevsky (1821–81) who is believed to have manifested the syndrome]

double-aspect theory *n.* A response to the *mind–body problem according to which mental and physical phenomena and processes are not two different kinds of things but rather different aspects of the same thing, just as a cloud and a mist are the same thing seen from different vantage points, or the morning star and the evening star are the same thing (the planet Venus). *See also* identity theory, materialism, monism.

double bind *n.* An inescapable dilemma involving conflicting demands that allow no right or satisfactory response. An influential theory of the aetiology of *schizophrenia was put forward by the English-born US anthropologist Gregory Bateson (1904–80) and several co-authors in an article in the journal *Behavioral Science* in 1956, according to which schizophrenia is caused by parenting styles that create double binds for children, as when a mother complains to her son for not giving her a kiss but recoils physically whenever the child does kiss her. This theory was enthusiastically adopted by the Scottish psychiatrist Ronald D(avid) Laing (1927–89) and others during the 1970s and 1980s, but empirical evidence has not been forthcoming in support of the theory, despite its attractiveness. *See also* avoidance–avoidance conflict, schizophrenogenic.

double-blind study *n.* A research design planned in such a way that, in order to control for *experimenter effects and the influence of *demand characteristics, neither the experimenter nor the research participants or subjects know, until after the data have been collected, which experimental treatment has been applied to which individuals. This type of design is used, for example, in drug trials,

often with the use of a *placebo (1), to avoid contamination of the results from biases and preconceptions on the part of the experimenter or the subjects. *See also* randomized controlled trial, randomized double-blind experiment. *Compare* open study, single-blind study.

double helix *n.* The molecular structure of *DNA: two spirals or helixes coiled round a single axis with *complementary base pairing between the strands. It is also displayed by double-stranded *RNA. It was discovered in 1953 by the US biologist James D(ewey) Watson (born 1928) and the English molecular biologist Francis H(arry) C(ompton) Crick (born 1916), working with X-ray diffraction images produced by the biophysicist Rosalind E. Franklin (1920–58), although the Nobel prize awarded for this work in 1962 went to Watson, Crick, and Franklin's research supervisor at King's College London, the New Zealand-born biophysicist Maurice H(ugh) F(rederick) Wilkins (born 1916).
[From Greek *helix* a spiral]

double-opponent receptive field *n.* A type of *centre-surround receptive field characteristic of neurons belonging to *blobs in the *primary visual cortex in which stimulation of the centre with light of a particular range of wavelengths elicits neural responses and stimulation with the complementary-colour wavelength inhibits responses, whereas stimulation of the immediately surrounding area elicits the reverse responses, the commonest type, involving red (r) and green (g), being a r^+g^- centre surrounded by a r^-g^+ ring.

double recessive *n.* Carrying two copies of a *recessive gene and therefore manifesting the recessive *phenotype.

double vision *n.* A non-technical name for *diplopia.

Dover's powder *n.* A preparation containing *opium that was formerly used as an *analgesic (1), to induce sweating, and to control muscular spasms.
[Named after the English physician Thomas Dover (1660–1742) who popularized its medicinal use]

doves *n.* A branded version of the stimulant designer drug *ecstasy (2).
[Identified by a symbol of a dove]

downers n. A common street name for central nervous system *depressant drugs in general. Compare uppers.

Down's syndrome n. A disorder linked to a *chromosomal abnormality resulting in a broadened and flattened face and nose, short, stubby fingers, skin folds at the edges of the eyes, *mental retardation, and the premature development of *Alzheimer's disease, usually in middle age. Formerly called mongolism. See also chromosome 21, trisomy. Compare Williams syndrome. **DS** abbrev.
[Named after the English psychiatrist John Langdon Haydon Down (1828–96) who first described it]

d prime n. In *signal detection theory, an index of the detectability or discriminability of a signal, given by the difference between the means (or separation between the peaks) of the signal-plus-noise and the noise-only probability distributions, divided by the *standard deviation of the noise-only distribution. See also noise (2), receiver operating characteristic, two-alternative forced-choice task. Symbol: **d'**.

Dracula hormone n. Another name for *melatonin.
[Named after the exclusively nocturnal vampire in Bram Stoker's novel Dracula (1897)]

drama therapy n. A form of *psychotherapy, including *psychodrama, in which clients or patients are encouraged to express their feelings and inner conflicts through acting them out in front of others. Sometimes written dramatherapy. See also sociodrama.

drapetomania n. A form of mania supposedly affecting slaves in the nineteenth century, manifested by an uncontrollable impulse to wander or run away from their white masters, preventable by regular whipping. The disorder was first identified in a medical report that is often cited as a fanciful case of *psychologism. Compare dysaesthesia aethiopis.
[Coined by the US physician Samuel Adolphus Cartwright (1793–1863) in the New Orleans Medical and Surgical Journal in 1851, from Greek drapeteusis an escape + mania madness]

Draw-a-Man test n. A test of a child's intellectual ability based on a method of scoring the child's drawing of a human figure. It was introduced in 1926 by the US psychologist Florence Laura Goodenough (1886–1959). Also called the Goodenough Draw-a-Man test or the Goodenough test. **DAM** abbrev.

Draw-a-Person test n. A *projective test developed by the US psychologist Karen Alper Machover (1902–96) and discussed in her book Personality Projection in the Drawing of the Human Figure (1949). The respondent is handed a blank sheet of paper and a pencil and is asked simply to draw a person, then, on a separate sheet, to draw a person of opposite sex to the first, then finally to indicate the age, educational level, occupation, fears, and ambitions of each person drawn. The drawings are interpreted in terms of feature placement (size, body details, positioning, clothing, and so on), the assumptions being that people tend to project acceptable impulses on to the same-sex figure and unacceptable impulses on to the opposite-sex figure, and that various features have special significance: large eyelashes indicate hysteria; prominent eyes or ears indicate suspiciousness; large figures suggest *acting out; small figures, lack of facial features, or dejected facial expressions indicate depression; lack of body periphery details indicate suicidal tendencies; dark shading indicates aggressive impulses; lack of physical details suggests psychosis or brain damage; and so on. Also called the Machover Draw-a-Person Test. **DAP** abbrev.

dream n. **1.** The mental experiences, usually in the form of a sequence of ideas, images, and imagined events, often accompanied by emotions, occurring during *REM sleep. See also dream analysis, dreamwork, interpretation (2), lucid dream, nightmare, sleep terror disorder. vb. **2.** To experience a dream or dreams; hence, figuratively, to imagine or fantasize.
[From Old English dream a song]

dream analysis n. A technique of *psychoanalysis in which *interpretation (2), aided by *free association, is applied to the *manifest content of *dreams (1) in an effort to reveal their *latent content which, according to psychoanalytic theory, invariably consists of unconscious *wish fulfilments that are potentially disturbing to the dreamer and would interrupt sleep if they were not disguised through symbolism. Sigmund Freud (1856–1939) propounded this theory in his book The Interpretation of Dreams (1900, Standard

Edition, IV–V). However, in his later book *Beyond the Pleasure Principle* (1920), he raised doubts about the assumption that dreams are wish fulfilments and suggested that they may serve a more primitive function (*Standard Edition*, XVIII, pp. 31–3). *See also* dreamwork, overdetermination, Wolf Man.

dream interpretation *See* dream analysis.

dreamwork *n.* In *psychoanalysis, a collective name for all the processes that transform the *latent content of a *dream (1) into its *manifest content, concealing its meaning from the dreamer and thus allowing undisturbed sleep to occur. Sigmund Freud (1856–1939) identified the processes in his book *The Interpretation of Dreams* (1900, *Standard Edition*, IV–V) as *condensation, *displacement, *secondary revision, and *representability. *See* dream analysis. *See also* overdetermination.

dressing apraxia *See under* apraxia.

drink–driving *n.* The crime of driving with excess alcohol in the blood. In the UK and many other jurisdictions, the drink–drive limit is 80 mg/dl (0.08 g/dl), often rather misleadingly referred to as 0.08 per cent blood alcohol concentration. It equates to roughly four units of alcohol (half pints of beer, glasses of wine, or measures of spirits) taken by an average 150 lb (68 kg) person in quick succession, and this is also the figure recommended by the American College of Emergency Physicians (ACEP) as *per se* evidence of driving while impaired. In some countries, including several members of the European Union, the drink-drive limit is 50 mg/dl, and in Sweden it is 20 mg/dl. *See also* alcohol, blood alcohol concentration.

drive *n.* Any internal source of *motivation that impels an organism to pursue a goal or to satisfy a need, such as sex, hunger, or self-preservation. A *primary drive* is an innate physiological urge or need, such as hunger, thirst, or the need for sex; a *secondary drive* is an acquired non-physiological urge, such as the *need for achievement or the *need for affiliation. More generally, a person's energy and determination to achieve something (*We're looking for a salesman with a lot of drive*). In *psychoanalysis, another name for *instinct (3). *See also* need (2).

drive strength *n.* In *Hullian learning theory, the strength of a primary *drive operative during the formation of a habit. *D* abbrev.

drive theory of social facilitation *n.* A theory formulated in 1965 by the US-based Polish psychologist Robert B(oleslaw) Zajonc (born 1923) to explain what had until then appeared to be contradictory findings on *audience effects and *coaction effects. According to the theory, when an individual performs a task, the effect of an audience or coactors is to increase the individual's *arousal level, which in turn increases the emission of dominant responses in the individual's response repertoire. If the task is simple or well learned, then the dominant responses are likely to be mostly correct, and the audience or coaction effect results in an improvement or enhancement of performance; but if the task is difficult or inadequately learned, then wrong responses are likely to predominate and the effect is an impairment of performance. *See also* evaluation apprehension, social facilitation.

droperidol *n.* A *neuroleptic (1) and *sedative drug belonging to the group of *butyrophenones, often prescribed in combination with a narcotic drug such as *fentanyl. *Compare* haloperidol.

drosophila *n.* Any fruit fly of the genus *Drosophila*, especially *D. melanogaster*, widely used in research in genetics because it breeds quickly and prolifically, is easy to maintain, displays scores of hereditary characteristics that can be observed without difficulty, and has relatively simple genetic material comprising only four pairs of chromosomes per cell.
[From Greek *drosos* dew or moisture + *phileein* to love]

drug *n.* Any chemical substance that can affect the structure or function of a living body, often used as a medicine, or in making a medicine, or taken for its pleasurable or satisfying effects. *See also* drug action, drug effect, psychotropic, substance abuse.
[From French *drogue* a drug, perhaps from Middle Dutch *droge* a dry barrel]

drug abuse *n.* Another name for *substance abuse. Preferred usage *drug misuse*. *See also* addiction, dependence (2), substance dependence, substance-induced disorders, substance-related disorders, substance use disorders.

drug action n. The interaction of a *drug with components of living tissues, such as *neuroreceptors, and the biochemical consequences of this interaction, distinguished in careful usage from the *drug effect—the physiological and psychological consequences of the drug's action. See also psychopharmacology. Compare pharmacodynamics.

drug addiction See addiction.

drug-dependent memory n. A form of *state-dependent memory associated with states induced by *psychotropic drugs during learning and recall.

drug effect n. The physiological and psychological effects of a *drug, distinguished in careful usage from the biochemical *drug action. See also psychotropic. **drug tolerance** See tolerance (3).

DSM-IV abbrev. The Diagnostic and Statistical Manual of Mental Disorders (4th edition) of the American Psychiatric Association, widely regarded as one of the most authoritative reference works on matters of definition and classification of mental disorders. The first edition appeared in 1952, the second in 1968, the third in 1980, a revision of the third in 1987, and the fourth in 1994. Compare ICD-10.

dual-code theory n. **1.** A theory of *imagery according to which imaginative cognition involves the activity of two functionally independent subsystems: a non-verbal imagery system specialized to handle objects and events, and a verbal imagery system specialized to perceive and generate language. See also dual-process model. **2.** A theory according to which physical objects and events are stored in memory in the form of both visual images and verbal representations, whereas abstract information is represented only verbally. **DCT** abbrev.

dualism n. The state of being twofold or double, especially a philosophical doctrine regarding the *mind–body problem according to which reality comprises two realms of existence, usually identified as mind and matter, or two types of entities, mental and

physical. See also Cartesian dualism, category mistake, epiphenomenalism, interactionism (1), psychophysical parallelism. Compare double-aspect theory, identity theory, monism. [From Latin dualis twofold, from duo two]

dual personality n. Multiple personality disorder involving two separate personalities. See dissociative identity disorder.

dual-process model n. Any of a number of theories of social information processing that emerged in the 1980s and 1990s to explain social *attitudes (1), *stereotypes, *person perception, *memory, and *decision making, although the roots of the idea can be traced at least as far back as the Principles of Psychology (1890, p. 451) of the US psychologist William James (1842–1910). According to these theories, two qualitatively different mechanisms of information processing operate in forming judgements, solving problems, or making decisions, the first being a quick and easy processing mode based on effort-conserving *heuristics, and the second being a slow and more difficult rule-based processing mode based on effort-consuming systematic reasoning. The first type of process is often unconscious and tends to involve *automatic processing, whereas the second is invariably conscious and usually involves *controlled processing, and in some domains of application the first is affective and the second cognitive. The most influential dual-process theory is the *elaboration likelihood model. See also cognitive economy, cognitive miser, hodological space, principle of least effort.

dual-task performance n. An experimental paradigm in which participants or subjects perform two tasks simultaneously under different instructions, such as counting backwards from 100 while responding with key-presses to signals presented through headphones. It is widely used in research into *attention.

Duchenne muscular dystrophy n. The commonest form of *muscular dystrophy, characterized by progressive wasting of leg and pelvis muscles, usually in boys under 10 years old, caused by an *X-linked *recessive gene. Also called Duchenne dystrophy. **DMD** abbrev.
[Named after the French neurologist Guillaume Benjamin Amand Duchenne

(1806–75) who was the first to describe it in 1858]

ductless gland n. Another name for an *endocrine gland.

duetting n. A series of bird calls each followed by a rapid antiphonal response from a mating partner, functioning as a recognition and bonding signal. It is often mistaken for the song of a single bird, as by William Shakespeare (1564–1616) in *Love's Labour Lost* (V.ii) when he attributed *tu-whit*, *tu-who* to a single staring owl.

dulosis n. A practice in some species of ants of forcing members of a different species to work for the colony as slaves.
[From Greek *doulosis* enslavement, from *doulos* a slave + -*osis* indicating a process or state]

Duncan's multiple range test n. In statistics, a method of *multiple comparisons in which the group means are ranked from smallest to largest, and then the number of steps that two means are apart in this ranking is used to compute a range statistic for each comparison. *Compare* Bonferroni correction, least-significant difference test, Newman–Keuls test, Scheffé test, Tukey-HSD test.
[Named after the Australian-born US statistician David Beattie Duncan (born 1916) who developed it in 1957]

duodenum n. The first section of the small intestine, into which the pancreas and gall bladder secrete digestive enzymes.
[Shortened from Latin *intestinum duodenum digitorum* intestine of twelve fingers' length]

duplexity function n. The dual curve of *dark adaptation resulting from the different adaptation rates of *photopic and *scotopic vision. Also called the *duplicity function*.

duplexity theory n. The conceptualization of the *retina as containing two different types of photoreceptors, now identified as *rods and *cones, mediating *scotopic and *photopic vision respectively. Also called *duplicity theory*.

duplicity function n. Another name for the *duplexity function.

duplicity theory n. Another name for the *duplexity theory.

dura mater n. The outermost and toughest of the three *meninges covering the brain and spinal cord, attached tightly to the arachnoid membrane. Often shortened to *dura*. Also called the *pachymeninx*. *Compare* arachnoid membrane, pia mater.
[From Latin *dura mater* hard mother, a literal translation of its Arabic name *umm al-jafiyah* in accordance with the Arabic usage of *mother* to indicate a relation between things]

duration estimation paradox n. A tendency for people to make more accurate prospective time estimations, that is, signalling when they believe that a specified period has elapsed, than retrospective time estimations, that is, estimating at the end of a period how long they believe it to have lasted.

Dutch book n. A *money pump in which a person holds intransitive or *cyclic preferences, for example, preferring x to y, y to z, and z to x. Such a person is therefore willing to pay to have any of them exchanged for one that is preferred to it, and is then willing to pay to have that one exchanged for another, and so on indefinitely. The property that differentiates a Dutch book from any other money pump is that the price for each exchange is lowered until the person is willing to pay for it, although the term is often used as a synonym for a money pump.
[Probably named after a Dutch auction in which the price of a lot is reduced by steps until a buyer comes forward]

dyad n. A two-person group; more generally, an entity consisting of two elements or parts.
dyadic n. Of or relating to a dyad or dyads.
[From Latin *dyas* a dyad, from Greek *duo* two]

dynamic adj. Of, relating to, or consisting of forces that produce movement or change. In *psychoanalysis, of or relating to *dynamic psychology.
[From Greek *dynamikos* powerful, from *dynamis* power, from *dynasthai* to be able]

dynamic aphasia n. A name given by the Russian neuropsychologist Alexandr Romanovich Luria (1902–77) to a variant of non-fluent aphasia (*see under* aphasia) characterized by almost total failure to initiate speech, and responses to questions that are sparse and laconic and given only after long pauses, but no impairment in ability to name objects, to read, and to repeat sentences.

dynamic assessment *n.* An approach to assessment following the same basic principles as *dynamic testing, including not only tests but also other forms of assessment, such as projects, essays, and performances.

dynamic labyrinth *n.* The *semicircular canals and their *cristae, operating the *vestibulo-ocular reflex to keep *gaze fixated on target when the head is moved.

dynamic memory span *n.* The number of items that a person can remember when presented with a continuous sequence of items, such as words, numbers, or letters, the sequence being halted without warning and the person asked to recall as many items as possible, working back from the most recent items. The usual span is only approximately three items, compared to a *memory span of approximately seven items when the sequence is confined to that length. *See also* short-term memory.

dynamic psychology *n.* A term loosely applied to all forms of *psychoanalysis, alluding to the *dynamic interplay of psychological process and phenomena arising from *instincts (3) that facilitate, inhibit, and combine with one another, or produce *compromise formations. In 1909/10, Sigmund Freud (1856–1939) distinguished his theory of the split between *consciousness and the *unconscious (2) from static theories that had gone before: 'We explain it dynamically, from the conflict of opposing mental forces, and recognize it as the outcome of an active struggling on the part of the two psychical groupings against each other' ('Five Lectures on Psycho-Analysis', *Standard Edition*, XI, pp. 9–55, at pp. 25–6). *See also* depth interview, depth psychology, metapsychology, motivational research.

dynamic testing *n.* An approach to *psychometrics that attempts to measure not only the products or processes of learning but also the potential to learn. It focuses on the difference between latent capacity and developed abilities, or the extent to which developed abilities reflect latent capacity, and it seeks to quantify the psychological processes involved in learning and change, rather than the products of such processes, by presenting sequences of progressively more challenging tasks and providing continuous feedback on performance in an atmosphere of teaching and helping that guides the testee towards the right answer. Credit for introducing the concept is usually assigned to the Russian psychologist Lev Semyonovich Vygotsky (1896–1934) who discussed it in *Thought and Language* (1934). Also called *dynamic assessment. See also* Learning Potential Assessment Device, *Lerntest*, zone of proximal development. *Compare* static assessment environment.

dynamic touch *n.* The ability to discern certain physical properties of an object by moving it around, an example being the ability of people to judge the length of a rod quite accurately by grasping one end of it and swinging it around, even in the dark or with the hand and the rod screened from vision. *See also* touch. *Compare* cutaneous sense, haptic touch.

dynamic visual acuity *n.* The keenness or sharpness of perception of a moving target, related to skills such as driving. *See also* acuity, visual acuity.

dynamometer *n.* Any of a number of different devices for measuring muscular strength or effort. **dynamometry** *n.* The measurement of power or force.
[From Greek *dynamis* power + *metron* measure]

dyne *n.* The unit of force required to accelerate a mass of 1 gram by 1 centimetre per second per second, equivalent to 1/100,000 *newton, sometimes used to express the pressure of sound waves.
[From Greek *dynamis* power or force]

dynorphin *n.* One of a number of *endogenous opioid peptides that are found in the central nervous system and that have a strong affinity for *opiate receptors. *Compare* beta-endorphin, endorphin, enkephalin.
[From Greek *dyn(amis)* power + English *(end)orphin*]

dysacusia *n.* A condition characterized by pain or discomfort from sounds or noises, usually resulting from damage to the *cochlea. Also spelt *dysacusia. Also called *dysacusis, dysacusmia,* or *dysacousis.* **dysacusic** *adj.*
[From Greek *dys-* bad or abnormal + *akousis* hearing, from *akouein* to hear + *-ia* indicating a condition or quality]

dysaesthesia *n*. A loss of feeling, usually experienced as numbness or *paraesthesia, often resulting from spinal injury and experienced below the level of the lesion. US *dysesthesia*.
[From Greek *dys-* bad or abnormal + *aisthesis* sensation + *-ia* indicating a condition or quality]

dysaesthesia aethiopis *n*. A mental disorder supposedly peculiar to black slaves and endemic among them in North America in the mid nineteenth century, manifested by laziness and insensibility to pain when whipped. The article in which it was first reported is often cited as a fanciful example of *psychologism. US *dysesthesia aethiopis*. *Compare* drapetomania.
[Coined by the US physician Samuel Adolphus Cartwright (1793–1863) in the *New Orleans Medical and Surgical Journal* in 1851, from *Aethiop* an archaic word for a black person]

dysarthria *n*. Imperfect articulation of speech caused by paralysis, weakness, or involuntary movements of the muscles involved in speech production.
[From Greek *dys-* bad or abnormal + *arthron* articulation + *-ia* indicating a condition or quality]

dysbasia *n*. Partial *abasia; impairment in the ability to walk.
[From Greek *dys-* bad or abnormal + *basis* a step, from *bainein* to step or go + *-ia* indicating a condition or quality]

dysbulia *n*. Mild *aboulia. Also spelt *dysboulia*.

dyscalculia *n*. Impairment in ability to do arithmetic. *See also* specific disorder of arithmetic skills. *Compare* acalculia.
[From Greek *dys-* bad or abnormal + Latin *calculare* to count, from *calculus* diminutive of *calx* a stone + *-ia* indicating a condition or quality]

dyschiria *n*. Difficulty in distinguishing left from right.
[From Greek *dys-* bad or abnormal + *cheir* a hand + *-ia* indicating a condition or quality]

dyschromatopsia *n*. Any acquired loss of colour vision. *See* colour-blindness. *See also* achromatopsia, parachromatopsia.
[From Greek *dys-* bad or abnormal + *chroma* colour + *ops* an eye + *-ia* indicating a condition or quality]

dysdiadochokinesia *n*. Impaired ability to perform rapidly alternating movements, such as rapid rhythmic tapping of the fingers. Also called *dysdiadochokinesis*. *Compare* adiadochokinesia.
[From Greek *dys-* bad or abnormal + *diadochos* working in turn + *kinesis* movement + *-ia* indicating a condition or quality]

dysesthesia *See* dysaesthesia.

dysexecutive syndrome *n*. An impairment in ability to plan and organize purposive behaviour, caused by lesions in the *frontal lobes of the brain.

dysfunction *n*. Abnormality or disturbance of function. **dysfunctional** *adj*.
[From Greek *dys-* bad or abnormal + Latin *functio* to perform + *-ion* indicating an action, process, or state]

dysgenic *adj*. Liable to lead to a degeneration or diminution in the quality or fitness of a group of interbreeding organisms. *Compare* eugenic.
[From Greek *dys-* bad or abnormal + *genein* to produce + *-ikos* of, relating to, or resembling]

dysgeusia *n*. Impaired or abnormal sense of taste. *See* ageusia, cacogeusia, hypergeusia, hypogeusia, parageusia, taste blindness.
[From Greek *dys-* bad or abnormal + *geusis* taste + *-ia* indicating a condition or quality]

dysgraphia *n*. Inability to write correctly, resulting from a neurological or other disorder. *See also* agraphia.
[From Greek *dys-* bad or abnormal + *graphein* to write + *-ia* indicating a condition or quality]

dyskinesia *n*. Involuntary repetitive bodily movements. *See also* tardive dyskinesia. **dyskinetic** *adj*.
[From Greek *dys-* bad or abnormal + *kinesis* movement + *-ia* indicating a condition or quality]

dyskinesia, tardive *See* tardive dyskinesia.

dyslalia *n*. Defective speech, characteristic of people with *aphasia.
[From Greek *dys-* bad or abnormal + *lalia* speech]

dyslexia *n.* Impairment in ability to read, not resulting from low *intelligence. It was first described in 1877 by the German physician Adolf Kussmaul (1822–1902), who coined the term *word blindness* to refer to it. *See also* acquired dyslexia, alexia, attentional dyslexia, catalexia, central dyslexias, cognitive neuropsychology, deep dyslexia, developmental dyslexia, neglect dyslexia, phonological dyslexia, spelling dyslexia, surface dyslexia, visual word-form dyslexia. Also called *alexia*, *hypolexia*, and *word blindness*. *See also* reading disorder, strephosymbolia. *Compare* hyperlexia. **dyslexic** *adj.*
[From Greek *dys-* bad or abnormal + *lexis* a word + *-ia* indicating a condition or quality]

dysmenorrhoea *n.* Painful or difficult menstruation. US *dysmenorrhea*.
[From Greek *dys-* bad or abnormal + *men* a month + *rhoia* a flow]

dysmetria *n.* Impaired ability to judge distances associated with body movements, typically underestimating or overestimating the amount of muscular effort required to make a voluntary movement, usually caused by a lesion in the *cerebellum.
[From Greek *dys-* bad or abnormal + *metron* a measure + *-ia* indicating a condition or quality]

dysmnesia *n.* A memory disorder characterized by an inability to learn simple new skills in spite of an ability to perform complex skills learnt before the onset of the disorder. Also called *dysmnesic syndrome*.
[From Greek *dys-* bad or abnormal + *mnasthai* to remember + *-ia* indicating a condition or quality]

dysmorphophobia *n.* **1.** A pathological fear of a personal physical defect or deformity. **2.** Another name for *body dysmorphic disorder.
[From Greek *dys-* bad or abnormal + *morphe* form + *phobos* fear + *-ia* indicating a condition or quality]

dysorexia *n.* Any abnormality or disorder of appetite.
[From Greek *dys-* bad or abnormal + *orexis* appetite + *-ia* indicating a condition or quality]

dysosmia *n.* Impaired or abnormal sense of smell. *See* anosmia, cacosmia, hyperosmia, hyposmia, parosmia, specific anosmia.

[From Greek *dys-* bad or abnormal + *osme* a smell + *-ia* indicating a condition or quality]

dyspareunia *n.* A *sexual dysfunction in both women and men, characterized by recurrent or persistent genital pain associated with sexual intercourse, causing significant distress or problems of interpersonal interaction. It is not diagnosed as such if it is attributable to a drug or a *general medical condition. *Compare* vaginismus.
[From Greek *dys-* bad or abnormal + *para* beside + *eune* a bed + *-ia* indicating a condition or quality]

dysphagia *n.* Difficulty in swallowing. *Compare* anorexia, aphagia.
[From Greek *dys-* bad or abnormal + *phagein* to consume + *-ia* indicating a condition or quality]

dysphasia *n.* Another name for *aphasia.
[From Greek *dys-* bad or abnormal + *pheme* speech + *-ia* indicating a condition or quality]

dysphemia *n.* Impaired ability to speak; Broca's aphasia (*see under* aphasia).
[From Greek *dys-* bad or abnormal + *pheme* speech + *-ia* indicating a condition or quality]

dysphemism *n.* A usage of language in which an unpleasant or derogatory word or expression is substituted for a neutral one, as in *jackals and hyenas of the press* for *journalists*, or *self-abuse* for *masturbation*. *Compare* euphemism.
[From Greek *dys-* ill, bad, or abnormal + *pheme* speech, from *phanai* to speak]

dysphonia *n.* Inability to speak normally, resulting from impairment of voice quality, such as hoarseness or strain of the vocal cords. *Compare* aphasia.
[From Greek *dys-* bad or abnormal + *phone* voice or sound + *-ia* indicating a condition or quality]

dysphoria *n.* A feeling of uneasiness, discomfort, anxiety, or anguish.
[From Greek *dys-* bad or abnormal + *pherein* to bear + *-ia* indicating a condition or quality]

dysphoric mood *n.* Any disagreeable or unpleasant *mood (1), such as sadness or anxiety.

dysplastic body type *n*. A misshapen and ugly *somatotype believed by the German psychiatrist Ernst Kretschmer (1888–1964) and his followers to be prone to *schizophrenia. *See also* Kretschmer constitutional type. *Compare* asthenic body type, athletic body type, pyknic body type.
[From Greek *dys-* bad or abnormal + *plastikos* mouldable, from *plassein* to form + *-itikos* resembling or marked by]

dyspnoea *n*. Difficult or abnormal breathing. US *dyspnea*.
[From Greek *dys-* bad or abnormal + *pnoe* breathing]

dyspraxia *n*. An impairment in ability to perform deliberate movements, not caused by any defect in sensory or motor functions. *Compare* apraxia.
[From Greek *dys-* bad or abnormal, *praxis* a deed or action, from *prassein* to do + *-ia* indicating a condition or quality]

dysprosody *n*. A pathological deficit in the ability to generate appropriate *prosody in speech. Also called *expressive dysprosody*. *Compare* aprosodia. **dysprosodic** *adj*.
[From Greek *dys-* bad or abnormal, *prosoidia* a song set to music, from *pros* towards, *oide* a song]

dyssocial personality *See* dissocial personality disorder.

dyssomnias *n*. Disorders of *sleep with *insomnia or *hypersomnia as the major symptom, causing clinically significant distress or impairment in social, occupational, or other important areas of functioning. *See* breathing-related sleep disorder, central alveolar hypoventilation syndrome, circadian rhythm sleep disorder, delayed sleep-phase syndrome, hypersomnia, insomnia, narcolepsy, primary hypersomnia, primary insomnia, sleep apnoea. Also called *disorders of initiating and maintaining sleep (DIMS)*. *See also* cataplexy (1). *Compare* parasomnias, pseudoinsomnia.
[From Greek *dys-* bad or abnormal + *somnus* sleep]

dysstasia *n*. Impairment in ability to stand upright.
[From Greek *dys-* bad or abnormal + *stasis* a standing + *-ia* indicating a condition or quality]

dyssymbiosis *n*. A pathological mother–child relationship in which the child manipulates the mother with neurotic or psychotic mechanisms.
[From Greek *dys-* bad or abnormal + *syn-* together + *bios* life + *-osis* indicating a process or state]

dyssynergia *n*. Impaired muscular coordination resulting from a *neurological disorder.
[From Greek *dys-* bad or abnormal + *synergia* co-operation, from *syn-* together + *ergein* to work + *-ia* indicating a condition or quality]

dystaxia *n*. Partial *ataxia.
[From Greek *dys-* bad or abnormal + *taxis* order + *-ia* indicating a condition or quality]

dysthymia *n*. **1.** A mild but chronic depressive *mood (1) state, not severe enough to lead to a diagnosis of *depression or *dysthymic disorder. **2.** A term used by the German-born British psychologist Hans J(ürgen) Eysenck (1916–97) for people scoring high on measures of neuroticism and introversion and manifesting traits of *anxiety, *depression, and *compulsions.
[From Greek *dys-* bad or abnormal + *thymos* spirit + *-ia* indicating a condition or quality]

dysthymic disorder *n*. A form of *depression (not included in the *DSM-IV or *ICD-10 classifications) with similar signs and symptoms to *major depressive disorder but considered less severe and more chronic, with the *major depressive episodes being less discrete and the depression less severe and more persistent than in major depressive disorder. Also called *depressive neurosis*, *minor depressive disorder*, or *neurotic depression*. *See also* antidepressant, cognitive therapy, inositol.
[From Greek *dys-* bad or abnormal + *thymos* spirit]

dystonia *n*. A neurological condition associated with *neuroleptic (1) medication or damage to the *basal ganglia, characterized by disordered muscle *tonus and usually spasm of the muscles of the trunk, shoulders, and neck, causing unnatural body postures. *See also* yips. **dystonic** *adj*.
[From Greek *dys-* bad or abnormal + *tonos* tension, from *teinein* to stretch + *-ia* indicating a condition or quality]

dystopia *n*. An imaginary world or place where everything is as bad as possible.

[Coined by the English philosopher John Stuart Mill (1806–73) from Greek *dys-* bad or abnormal + English *utopia*]

dystrophy *n*. **1.** Any abnormality caused by deficient nutrition; a term often applied to muscle wasting. **2.** A shortened name for *muscular dystrophy.

[From Greek *dys-* bad or abnormal + *trophe* nourishment]

dysuria *n*. Painful or difficult urination. [From Greek *dys-* bad or abnormal + *ouron* urine + *-ia* indicating a condition or quality]

ear *n.* The organ of hearing and equilibrium, which in vertebrates is usually divided into the sound-collecting *outer ear separated by a *tympanic membrane from the sound-transmitting *middle ear, separated in turn by a *round window and an *oval window from the *inner ear in which are situated the *vestibular system and its *semicircular canals containing sensory receptors that govern sensations of balance, orientation, and acceleration, and the *cochlea with its auditory *organ of Corti (see illustration).

eardrum *n.* A non-technical name for the *tympanic membrane.

early oral phase *n.* The first of the two phases of the *oral stage, according to a subdivision suggested in 1924 by the German psychoanalyst Karl Abraham (1877–1925) in his book *Versuch einer Entwicklungsgeschichte der Libido* (A Study of the Developmental History of the Libido). It is characterized by sucking, in contrast to the second *oral sadistic phase, which is characterized by biting. Also called the *oral-incorporative phase*.

ear-minded *adj.* Having a marked preference or ability to think in sounds or to carry out mental operations by auditory images. **ear-mindedness** *n.*

eating disorders *n.* A class of *mental disorders characterized by disturbances or problems associated with feeding or eating. *See* anorexia nervosa, bulimia nervosa, feeding disorder of infancy or early childhood, pica, rumination disorder.

Ebbinghaus curve *n.* A graph depicting the rate of forgetting of information. The amount of learned material—originally the number of *nonsense syllables—remembered is plotted

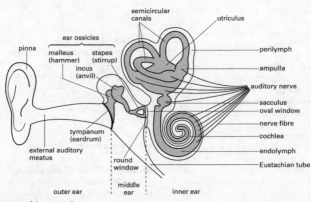

Ear. Main structures of the mammalian ear.

on the vertical axis against time on the horizontal axis.
[Named after the German psychologist Hermann von Ebbinghaus (1850–1909) who introduced it in his book *Über das Gedächtnis* (On Memory) in 1885]

Ebbinghaus illusion *n*. A visual illusion in which a circle appears larger when surrounded by smaller circles than when surrounded by larger circles (see illustration). Also called the *Titchener circles* or *Titchener illusion*.
[Named after the German psychologist Hermann von Ebbinghaus (1850–1909) who published a version of it in 1902, although the English psychologist Edward Bradford Titchener (1867–1927) had already discovered and published it in 1898]

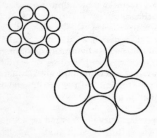

Ebbinghaus illusion. The circles at the centre of each cluster are identical.

Ebonics *n*. Another name for *Black English Vernacular.
[A *blend of *ebony*, from Latin *ebenus* ebony, from Greek *ebenos* ebony, + *phonics* the science of spoken sounds, from Greek *phonikos* of or relating to speech, from *phone* a voice or sound + *-ikos* of, relating to, or resembling]

eccentric *adj*. **1.** Positioned off centre. **2.** Of or relating to a retinal image cast by a visual stimulus off the centre of the *fovea. **3.** Odd or unconventional. **eccentricity** *n*.
[From Greek *ek* out of + *kentron* centre]

eccentric chessboard figure *n*. Another name for the *Münsterberg illusion.
[From German *verschrobene Schachbrettfigur*, Münsterberg's own name for it]

eccentric projection *n*. The *eccentric (1) localization of a sensation at the position in space of the stimulus object rather than at the point where the sense organ is stimulated, so that the greenness of a leaf is perceived as being on the tree rather than on the retina. Visual sensations are projected eccentrically in most cases, but touch sensations are projected only with *haptic touch when objects are held in the hand, smells have indefinite spatial location, and eccentric projection is not possible for tastes. Also called *extradition*.

echoic store *n*. One of the *sensory registers, supposedly allowing an auditory image to persist for up to two seconds after its stimulus has ceased, making speech intelligible and enabling *sound localization with the use of *binaural time differences between the arrival of the sound at the two ears, although there is controversy regarding its existence. Also called *echoic memory*. *See also* precategorical acoustic store, sensory memory. *Compare* iconic store.
[From Greek *echo* a sound + *-ikos* of, relating to, or resembling]

echolalia *n*. A pathological parrot-like repetition of overheard words or speech fragments, often with a mocking intonation, symptomatic of some mental disorders, including *catatonic schizophrenia, *latah, *pibloktoq, and some *tic disorders. *Compare* echopraxia.
[From Greek *echo* a sound + *lalia* speech]

echolocation *n*. A method of determining the position of objects by emitting sound or *ultrasound and analysing the returning echoes. Also written *echo location*. *See* biosonar. **echolocate** *vb*.

echopraxia *n*. Automatic or uncontrollable imitation of other people's movements, *gestures (1), or postures, symptomatic of some mental disorders, including *catatonic schizophrenia, *latah, and *pibloktoq. *Compare* echolalia.
[From Greek *echo* a sound + *praxis* a deed or action + *-ia* indicating a condition or quality]

eclipse scotoma *See under* scotoma.

ecmnesia *n*. Loss of memory for events of a particular period.
[From Greek *ek* from + *mneme* memory + *-ia* indicating a condition or quality]

ecological criterion *n*. In the writings of the Hungarian-born US psychologist Egon Brunswik (1903–55) and his followers, an aspect of an *ecology (2) that an organism cannot perceive directly but judges from a sensory *cue (2) to the best of its ability, the correlation between the sensory cue and the ecological criterion being the *ecological validity (2) of the cue. Also called a *distal criterion*. *See also* Brunswikian, lens model, probabilistic functionalism.

ecological fallacy *n*. The inference of individual characteristics from aggregate data. The difficulty that most people have in understanding the following story illustrates the fallacy. *A man was attacked by a mugger while he was walking home from a football match with his young son Peter. Peter left his father lying unconscious in the street and ran into a nearby police station to report the mugging. When Peter arrived at the police station, one of the officers on duty greeted him warmly, because Peter was that police officer's son*. This story sounds impossible or illogical to most people when they read it or hear it for the first time, because they tend to commit the ecological fallacy in interpreting it. In fact, there is nothing illogical about the story. *See also* Brunswikian, ecology (2), lens model, nomothetic, probabilistic functionalism.

ecological niche *n*. The position or role of an organism in its environment, defined by such factors as its food, predators, and temperature tolerances.

ecological validity *n*. **1.** The confidence with which the conclusions of an empirical investigation can be generalized to naturally occurring situations in which the phenomenon under investigation occurs. *See also* validity, validity generalization. *Compare* external validity, internal validity. **2.** In the writings of the Hungarian-born US psychologist Egon Brunswik (1903–55) and his followers, the correlation between a sensory *cue (2) that an organism uses to judge an *ecological criterion and the actual though imperceptible ecological criterion itself. *See also* Brunswikian, ecology (2), lens model, probabilistic functionalism.

ecology *n*. **1.** The study of the relationship of living organisms to their natural environments. *See also* ecosystem. **2.** In the writings of the Hungarian-born US psychologist Egon

Brunswik (1903–55) and his followers, the environmental context to which an organism must adapt functionally. *See also* ecological criterion, ecological fallacy, ecological validity (2), lens model. **ecological** *adj*.
[From German *Ökologie*, from Greek *oikos* a house + *logos* word, discourse, or reason]

economic *adj*. Of or relating to the management of resources or the production, distribution, and consumption of goods and services. In *psychoanalysis, of or relating to the circulation and distribution of *cathexis or *instinctual energy within the mental apparatus. *See also* hydraulic theory, metapsychology, principle of constancy, quota of affect.
[From Greek *oikonomia* household management, from *oikos* a house + *nemein* to manage]

ecosystem *n*. A relatively self-contained biological community and its physical environment considered as a functioning unit. *See also* ecology (1). *Compare* habitat.
[From Greek *oikos* a house + English *system*]

écouteur *n*. A person who derives sexual gratification from eavesdropping on sexual encounters between others or listening to other people speaking about sex. *Compare* voyeur.
[From French *écouter* to listen]

ecstasy *n*. **1.** A state of exalted pleasure or euphoria. **2.** The common name for the central nervous system *stimulant and *designer drug 3,4-methylene-dioxy-methamphetamine (MDMA), a *phenylalkylamine originally synthesized by the pharmaceutical company Merck in 1912 and patented two years later as an appetite suppressant, then rediscovered as a street drug in the late 1970s. It is an *amphetamine analogue, sharing many of the characteristics of *speed (amphetamine sulphate) but also increasing *serotonin and *dopamine activity in the brain and inducing feelings of euphoria, empathy, and benevolence. It often causes hyperthermia (overheating) and extreme thirst, especially when accompanied by prolonged and energetic dancing. It sometimes has *hallucinogenic effects, though a typical 75–100 mg dosage is not normally hallucinogenic, and prolonged use often results in damage to *serotonergic nerve fibres. It is sometimes called the *hug drug* or *XTC* and has many branded versions and street names, including *Adam*, *apples*, doves, *E*, and *Einsteins*, and other constantly changing names depending on colour and appearance, such as *custards*, *diamonds*, *rhubarb*, and *strawberries*. *See also* amphetamine-related disorders, empathogen, substance-related disorders.

[From Greek *ekstasis* trance, from *ex* out + *histanai* to cause to stand]

ectoderm *n*. The outer germ layer of a human or animal embryo, or the epidermis and nervous tissue that develops from it. *Compare* endoderm, mesoderm. **ectodermal** or **ectodermic** *adj*.

[From Greek *ektos* outside + *derma* skin]

ectomorph *n*. A light and delicate physique or body build, believed by the US psychologist William H. Sheldon (1899–1977) and followers of his *constitutional psychology to be associated with such personality characteristics as alertness, intellectualism, and inhibition. *Compare* endomorph, mesomorph. **ectomorphic** *adj*. **ectomorphy** *n*. The state or condition of being an *ectomorph.

[From Greek *ektos* outside + *morphe* a form or shape]

ectopic *adj*. Abnormally displaced.

[From Greek *ek* outside + *topos* a place + *-ikos* of, relating to, or resembling]

ectopic pregnancy *n*. The abnormal development of a fertilized ovum outside the uterus, usually within a Fallopian tube. *Compare* entopic.

ectoplasm *n*. **1.** The outer layer of *cytoplasm that differs in many cells from the inner cytoplasm in being a clear gel. **2.** In parapsychology, a substance supposedly exuded by a spirit medium during a trance.

[From Greek *ek* outside + *topos* a place + *plasma* a form]

ectotherm *n*. Any animal that does not generate its own body heat but derives it externally, specifically a fish, amphibian, or reptile. *Compare* endotherm. **ectothermic** *adj*. Coldblooded.

[From Greek *ektos* outside + *therme* heat]

edge detector *n*. A cell in the *primary visual cortex (Area V1) that responds maximally to a straight edge that is darker on one side than the other and has a particular position and

orientation on the retina, the response being strongest when the stimulus is moving. *See also* complex cell, end-stopped receptive field, feature detector, hypercomplex cell, simple cell. *Compare* bar detector.

edge effect *n*. Another name for the *serial position effect.

educable mentally retarded *adj*. An educational category equivalent to *mild mental retardation. **EMR** *abbrev*.

educationally subnormal *adj*. Of or pertaining to someone with a *learning disability. **ESN** *abbrev*.

educational psychology *n*. A field of *applied psychology devoted to education. In the US, educational psychologists are trained in education rather than psychology, and they work mainly as counsellors in universities and colleges. In the UK they are trained in both psychology and education and are employed mainly in child guidance clinics and school psychological services or as independent or private consultants. This is called *school psychology* in the US. The work of educational or school psychologists involves the diagnosis and treatment of educational, emotional, and behavioural problems in children of all ages up to the late teens.

Edwards Personal Preference Schedule *n*. A personality inventory comprising 225 pairs of statements relating to likes and preferences (*A: I like to do things by myself. B: I like to help others do things*), the respondent being required to choose the preferred alternative in each case. The scale is *ipsative, and it yields scores on 15 needs based on the theory of personality introduced by the US psychologist Henry Alexander Murray (1893–1988) in his book *Explorations in Personality* (1938), namely needs for achievement, deference, order, exhibition, autonomy, affiliation, intraception, succourance, dominance, abasement, nurturance, change, endurance, homosexuality, and aggression. **EPPS** *abbrev*.

[Named after the US psychologist and statistician Alan L. Edwards (1914–94) who introduced it in 1953]

EEG *abbrev*. Electroencephalogram, a graphical representation of the gross electrical activity of the brain, recorded via electrodes

attached to the scalp by an instrument called an *electroencephalograph*, first demonstrated in 1924 and examples published in 1929 by the German psychiatrist Hans Berger (1873–1941). EEGs manifest approximately periodic oscillating waves because of a form of *feedback in which groups of excitatory neurons stimulate inhibitory neurons, which in turn stimulate excitatory neurons, creating negative-feedback circuits that cycle indefinitely. *See also* alpha blocking, alpha wave, beta wave, brain imaging, delta wave, desynchronized EEG, gamma wave, sensorimotor rhythm, theta wave. *Compare* electrocorticogram, encephalogram.
[From Greek *elektron* amber (in which electricity was first observed) + *en* in + *kephale* the head + *gramme* a line]

EEG spindle *n*. Another name for a *sleep spindle.

effective dosage *n*. The minimum dosage of a drug that is required to produce a specified effect in an organism. **ED** *abbrev*.

effective dosage 50 *n*. Another name for the *median effective dosage. *See also* therapeutic index, therapeutic ratio. *Compare* lethal dosage, toxic dosage. **ED-50** or **ED$_{50}$** *abbrev*.

effector *n*. A cell or organ that is specialized to perform a specific function in response to a signal from the nervous system, the most important examples being a *muscle, *gland, *cilium, or *electric organ.

efferent *adj*. Away from the central nervous system; of or relating to a *motor neuron or a *motor nerve that transmits impulses away from the central nervous system to a muscle, gland, or other *effector. *Compare* afferent.
[From Latin *efferre* to carry off, from *e* from + *ferre* to carry]

ego *n*. In *psychoanalysis, one of the three components of the human mental apparatus in the second formulation of the theory by Sigmund Freud (1856–1939), after he replaced the *topography of unconscious–preconscious–conscious with the structural model of id–ego–superego in 1920. It is a largely *conscious (1) part of the mind, governed mainly (though not exclusively) by the *reality principle, mediating between external reality, the *id, and the *superego. In his book

The Ego and the Id (1923) Freud described its role as follows: 'it owes service to three masters and is consequently menaced by three dangers: from the external world, from the libido of the id and from the severity of the superego' (*Standard Edition*, XIX, pp. 12–66, at p. 56). The ego is not simply the conscious mind, as is often stated in popularized accounts of Freud's theory: in a neurosis, the ego generates *defence mechanisms, and this ego function is largely unconscious. Freud introduced the concept of the ego in his earliest writings, using the German word *Ich*, a noun that he coined from the ordinary everyday pronoun *ich* (I), and the translator James Strachey (1887–1967) rendered it as *ego*, adding a veneer of obscurity and technicality that the original German lacks. In colloquial usage, the word is used to denote a person's sense of self-esteem (*Getting the job boosted her ego*) or self-importance (*The managing director has a big ego*). *See also* ego-dystonic, ego ideal, ego instinct, ego interest, ego involvement, ego libido, ego psychology, ego strength, ego-syntonic, mirror phase, pleasure-ego, reality-ego, regression in the service of the ego, splitting of the ego.
[From Latin *ego* I]

ego-alien *adj*. A synonym for *ego-dystonic.

egocentre *n*. A point in the body where sensations from a particular *sensory modality are perceived or felt to converge. US *egocenter*. *See* auditory egocentre, tactile egocentre, visual egocentre.
[From Latin *ego* I + *centrum* the centre]

egocentric *adj*. Self-centred. *See also* egocentrism. *Compare* egomania.
[From Latin *ego* I + *centrum* the centre + *-icus* of, relating to, or resembling]

egocentric localization *n*. Awareness of the spatial positions of objects in the immediate environment relative to one's body.

egocentrism *n*. Self-centredness, a term given a technical meaning in 1926 by the Swiss psychologist Jean Piaget (1896–1980) to denote a cognitive state in which a child in the *preoperational stage of development comprehends the world only from its own point of view and is unaware that other people's points of view differ from its own. It implies a failure to differentiate subjective from objective aspects of experience, and it therefore imposes an unconscious personal bias on cognition. The classic demonstration of it is Piaget's three mountains task, in which a child sits in front of a table-top model of three mountains and is asked how the scene would look to a doll viewing it from a different angle; most children in the pre-operational stage (children about 5 years old, for example) consistently describe the doll's viewpoint as being the same as their own. *See also* automorphic perception, false-consensus effect. **egocentric** *adj.*

[From Latin *ego* I + *centrum* the middle + Greek *-ismos* indicating a state or condition]

ego defence mechanism *n.* Another name for a *defence mechanism. US *ego defense mechanism.*

ego-dystonic *adj.* Experienced as self-repugnant, alien, discordant, or inconsistent with the total personality, as *obsessions are generally experienced to be, and as *homosexuality may sometimes be. The term was introduced by Sigmund Freud (1856–1939) in 1914 in an article 'On Narcissism: An Introduction' (*Standard Edition*, XIV, pp. 73–102, at p. 99), and he discussed it again in 1923 in an encyclopedia article (*Standard Edition*, XVIII, pp. 235–59, at p. 246). *See also* ego-dystonic sexual orientation. *Compare* ego-syntonic. **ego dystonia** *n.*

[From Latin *ego* I + Greek *dys-* bad or abnormal + *tonos* tone + *-ikos* of, relating to, or resembling]

ego-dystonic sexual orientation *n.* A controversial term for a sexual preference that is experienced as *ego-dystonic. Hence *ego-dystonic bisexuality, ego-dystonic homosexuality.* In 1973 the American Psychiatric Association removed the mental disorder of *homosexuality from the *Diagnostic and Statistical Manual of Mental Disorders*, resulting in a furious reaction from dissident psychiatrists, who accused the leadership of the Association of capitulation to gay liberationists, and after an acrimonious debate and a referendum of the entire membership of the Association, the third edition (*DSM-III*) included homosexuality only under *ego-dystonic homosexuality.* Also called *sexual orientation disturbance* (*SOD*).

ego ideal *n.* In *psychoanalysis, an internal notion of personal perfection serving as a model to which one strives to conform, derived from the fusion of *narcissism and early *identification (2) with parents.

Sigmund Freud (1856–1939) introduced the concept in 1914 in an article 'On Narcissism: An Introduction', where its origins in narcissism were clearly stated: 'What man projects before him as his ideal is the substitute for the lost narcissism of his childhood in which he was his own ideal' (*Standard Edition*, XIV, pp. 73–102, at p. 94), and he used it as a central role to explain social phenomena in his book *Group Psychology and the Analysis of the Ego* (1921, *Standard Edition*, XVIII, pp. 69–143). In his later book *New Introductory Lectures on Psycho-Analysis* (1932/3), he described it as one of the three functions of the *superego, the other two being self-observation and conscience (1933, *Standard Edition*, XXII, pp. 5–182, at p. 66).

ego identity *n.* In *ego psychology, a term introduced by the German-born psychoanalyst Erik H. Erikson (1902–94) in 1946 to denote a psychological state that an individual achieves at the end of adolescence if earlier *developmental crises have been successfully negotiated.

ego instinct *n.* In *psychoanalysis, a *self-preservation instinct that supplies energy to the *ego in a defensive conflict, distinguished by Sigmund Freud (1856–1939) in his early (1910–15) classification from an *object instinct, which is concerned with sexual or destructive relations to an external object. Freud introduced the concept in 1910 in an article on 'The Psycho-Analytic View of Psychogenic Disturbance of Vision' (*Standard Edition*, XI, pp. 211–18), the key passage being: 'A quite specially important part is played by the undeniable opposition between the instincts which subserve sexuality, the attainment of sexual pleasure, and those other instincts which have as their aim the self-preservation of the individual—the ego-instincts' (pp. 214–15). In his later classification from 1920 onwards, he recognized as ego instincts not merely sexual instincts subserved by *Eros (the life instincts), but also destructive instincts subserved by *Thanatos (the death instinct). *See also* ego interest.

ego integrity versus despair *n.* One of the crises in the developmental theory of the German-born *ego psychologist Erik H. Erikson (1902–94). *See* developmental crises.

ego interest *n.* In *psychoanalysis, *cathexis of the ego by *ego instincts, in contrast to *narcissism, which is cathexis of the ego by *sexual instincts. Sigmund Freud (1856–1939) drew this distinction in 1915/17 in 'A Metapsychological Supplement to the Theory of Dreams' (*Standard Edition*, XIV, pp. 217–36, at p. 223).

ego involvement *n.* The involvement of one's *self-esteem in an activity or task. **ego-involving** *adj.*

egoistic suicide *See under* suicide.

ego libido *n.* In *psychoanalysis, *libido involved in the *cathexis of oneself, in contradistinction to *object libido, which is libido involved in the cathexis of an external *instinctual object. Sigmund Freud (1856–1939) discussed this distinction in 1914 in his article 'On Narcissism: An Introduction' (*Standard Edition*, XIV, pp. 73–102, at pp. 77–81), where he theorized that an energy balance exists, ego libido decreasing as object libido increases, and vice versa. Also called *narcissistic libido*. *See also* narcissism.

egomania *n.* Pathological love for or preoccupation with oneself. *Compare* egocentric. **egomaniac** *n.* A person with *egomania. **egomaniacal** *adj.*
[From Latin *ego* I + *mania* madness]

ego psychology *n.* A school of *psychoanalysis based on the analysis of the *ego, founded in 1939 by the Austrian-born US psychoanalyst Heinz Hartmann (1894–1970), including the US-based German psychologist Ernst Kris (1901–57), the Hungarian-born US psychologist David Rapaport (1911–60), and the German-born (of Danish parentage) psychoanalyst Erik H. Erikson (1902–94). The essential theme is that the ego is capable of functioning autonomously and is not confined to internal conflicts with the *id and *superego. Hartmann argued that gratification is gained from the sheer exercise of one's functions, as when a child is delighted by learning to walk or to draw, and Rapaport identified novelty-seeking as a self-rewarding activity. Ego psychologists reject the classical psychoanalytic theory of motivation in terms of tension reduction only. *See also* developmental crises, ego identity, identity crisis, psychosocial moratorium, regression in the service of the ego.

ego regression *See under* regression (2).

ego-splitting *See* splitting of the ego.

ego strength *n.* In *psychoanalysis, the degree to which the *ego is capable of handling the demands of the *id and the *superego without disruption, a person with high ego strength being self-confident, strong-willed, and robust in response to frustration.

ego-syntonic *adj.* Experienced as consistent or harmonious with the total *personality. The term was introduced by Sigmund Freud (1856–1939) in 1914 in an article 'On Narcissism: An Introduction' (*Standard Edition*, XIV, pp. 73–102, at p. 99), and discussed again in 1923 in an encyclopedia article (*Standard Edition*, XVIII, pp. 235–59, at p. 246). *Compare* ego-dystonic. **ego syntony** *n.*
[From Latin *ego* I + Greek *syn-* together + *tonos* tone + -*ikos* of, relating to, or resembling]

Ehrenstein's brightness illusion *n.* A visual illusion in which a lattice of black lines with the regions around their intersections erased appears to have white discs with *illusory contours at the intersections, seemingly occluding the lines and appearing lighter than the background (see illustration). If the colours are reversed, then illusory dark discs appear at the erased intersections. Also (ambiguously) called the *Ehrenstein illusion*. *Compare* Ehrenstein's square illusion, Hermann grid.
[Named after the German Gestalt psychologist Walter Ehrenstein (1899–1961) who discovered it in 1939/40 and published it in 1941]

Ehrenstein's brightness illusion. The white patches at the intersections of the lines are illusory.

Ehrenstein's square illusion *n.* A visual illusion in which a square superimposed on a fan-like pattern of diverging lines appears distorted into a trapezium (US trapezoid). It is closely related to the *Ponzo illusion and the *Orbison illusion. Also (ambiguously) called the *Ehrenstein illusion*. *Compare* Ehrenstein's brightness illusion.

[Named after the German Gestalt psychologist Walter Ehrenstein (1899–1961) who first reported it in his doctoral dissertation in 1921 and published it in 1925]

eidetic image *n.* A mental image or memory that is extraordinarily clear and vivid, as though actually being perceived, a significant minority of children and a much smaller proportion of adults being capable of such imagery, according to some authorities. More specifically, it is a clear and vivid visual image representing a previously perceived stimulus, persisting for more than a few seconds and often for several or many minutes, appearing to be located in front of the eyes. It is distinguished from an *afterimage, which does not have these properties.
[From Greek *eidetikos* belonging to a (visual) image, from *eidos* form + *-ikos* of, relating to, or resembling]

eidetiker *n.* A person who perceives *eidetic images.

Eigengrau *n.* A nondescript grey fog that is perceived by a viewer experiencing *stabilized retinal images.
[From German *eigen* own or one's own + *grau* grey]

eigenvalue *n.* In statistics, a quantity often used in *multivariate statistics to indicate the relative contribution of a *factor (2) or *independent variable to the *variance in a *dependent variable.
[From German *eigen* own + English *value*]

Eigenwelt *n.* In *phenomenology and *existentialism, the personal world as it is experienced, including one's awareness of mind and body and the sense of who one is. *See also* existential analysis, existential therapy. *Compare* Mitwelt, Umwelt.
[From German *eigen* own or one's own + *Welt* world]

eight-month anxiety *n.* Another name for *stranger anxiety.

Einfühlung *n.* Another name for *empathy.
[German]

Einsteins *n.* A street name for the stimulant designer drug *ecstasy (2).

Einstellung *n.* A temporary attitude, expectation, or state of readiness, especially in relation to a stimulus that is about to be experienced. Nowadays more often called a *set*. *See also Aufgabe*, functional fixedness, set (2), water-jar problem.
[From German *Einstellung* adjustment or setting, from *ein* in + *Stellung* placement, from *stellen* to place]

ejaculation *n.* **1.** The emission of semen by a male during *orgasm. **2.** A sudden utterance or exclamation. **ejaculate** *vb.* **ejaculatory** *adj.*
[From Latin *eiaculatio* ejaculation, from *e* from + *iaculatus* thrown, from *iacere* to throw + *-ation* indicating a process or condition]

ejaculatio praecox *n.* Another name for *premature ejaculation. *See also* male orgasmic disorder.
[From Latin *eiaculatio* ejaculation + *praecox* premature]

ejaculatio retardata *n.* Delayed ejaculation. *See* ejaculatory incompetence.
[From Latin *eiaculatio* ejaculation + *retardata* retarded or delayed]

ejaculatory incompetence *n.* Inability or delay in reaching orgasm and ejaculating. *See* impotence (2), male orgasmic disorder.

elaborated code *n.* A concept introduced by the British sociologist Basil Bernstein (1924–2000) in an article in the *British Journal of Sociology* in 1958 to denote a comparatively complex and formal use of language, not restricted to immediate situations (context free), with a wide semantic and syntactic range, characteristic of middle-class speakers. *Compare* restricted code.

elaboration *n.* The depth or level at which information is processed, or the extent to which a person processes information or arguments in relation to existing knowledge or beliefs. *See also* elaborative rehearsal. **elaborate** *vb.*

elaboration likelihood model *n.* A model of *persuasion and *attitude change according to which recipients of a persuasive message who are highly motivated and able to process the content of the message with care tend to elaborate or think about issue-relevant arguments, and if they find the arguments in the message compelling, then they may show lasting *attitude change, whereas recipients whose motivation and processing ability are low are likely to be influenced by peripheral factors such as the attractiveness of the source, and any attitude change achieved by this peripheral route will tend to be short-lived and poorly predictive of behaviour. The model was formulated in 1981 and revised in 1986 by the US psychologists Richard E(dward) Petty (born 1951) and John T(errance) Cacioppo (born 1951). *See also* dual-process model, elaboration, elaborative rehearsal. **ELM** *abbrev.*

elaboration, secondary *n.* Another name for *secondary revision.

elaborative rehearsal *n.* Deep processing of material that needs to be remembered, involving formation of associations, organization (grouping of material into categories), use of mnemonic strategies, or other forms of cognitive processing. *See also* elaboration, elaboration likelihood model, rehearse (2). *Compare* maintenance rehearsal.

elation effect *n.* Another name for *behaviour contrast in its positive form, when increased reward leads to increased response rate.

Elavil *n.* A proprietary name for the tricyclic antidepressant drug *amitriptyline. [Trademark]

Elberfeld horses *n.* Trained horses in Germany in the early years of the 20th century that appeared to possess remarkable human-like intellectual abilities, including especially *Clever Hans. [Named after the German city of Elberfeld, later merged into Wuppertal, where they were trained]

elder abuse *n.* Any form of physical, mental, sexual, or economic exploitation or cruelty by a carer towards an old person, causing significant harm to its victim. *See also* sexual abuse, spouse abuse.

elective mutism *n.* An alternative name for *selective mutism.

Electra complex *n.* In *analytical psychology, the female *Oedipus complex. Carl Gustav Jung (1875–1961) introduced the term in an article in 1913 in the *Jahrbuch für psychoanalytische und psychopathologische Forschungen*, although Sigmund Freud (1856–1939) stated in 1920 that he did not consider the term useful (*Standard Edition*, XVIII, p. 155n), and in an article on 'Female Sexuality' in 1931, he went further in denying the existence of such a complex: 'It is only in the male child that we find the fateful combination of love for one parent and simultaneous hatred for the other as a rival' (*Standard Edition*, XXI, pp. 225–43, at p. 229). *See also* complex (2). [Named after Electra in Greek mythology who arranged for the murder of her mother Clytemnestra, who in turn had murdered Electra's father Agamemnon]

electrical brain stimulation *n.* Stimulation of specific areas of the brain with weak electrical currents in order to determine their functions. *See also* electrical self-stimulation of the brain. **EBS** *abbrev.*

electrical self-stimulation of the brain *n.* Performance by an experimental animal of a response, such as pressing a lever, to deliver a weak electrical current to an area of the brain into which an electrode is permanently implanted. *See* pleasure centre. **ESSB** *abbrev.*

electrical synapse *n.* Another name for a *gap junction.

electric organ *n.* A specialized area of modified muscle tissue in certain fishes such as the electric eel (*Electrophorus electricus*), the electric catfish (*Malapterurus electricus*), or the electric ray (*Tetranarce occidentalis*), such tissue being capable of discharging an electric shock to any animal that touches it. *See also* electroreceptor.

electric receptor *n.* Another name for an *electroreceptor.

electroconvulsive therapy *n.* A treatment for some forms of *depression and other mental disorders by administering an anaesthetic and a muscle relaxant drug and then passing an electric current through the brain to induce *convulsions or *coma. Also called *electric shock therapy (EST)*, *electroconvulsive shock (ECS)*, *shock therapy*. **ECT** *abbrev.*

electrocorticogram *n.* A form of *EEG in which the electrodes are placed in direct contact with brain tissue.

[From Greek *elektron* amber (in which electricity was first observed) + Latin *cortex* bark or outer layer + Greek *gramme* a line]

electrodermal response *n.* Another name for *galvanic skin response (GSR). **EDR** *abbrev.*

electroencephalogram *See* EEG.

electrokymograph *n.* An instrument for recording the flow of air from the mouth and nose during speech.
[From *electro-* electric, from Greek *elektron* amber (in which electricity was first observed) + Greek *kyma* a wave + *graphein* to write]

electrolaryngograph *n.* An instrument for recording the vibration of the *vocal folds during speech.
[From *electro-* electric, from Greek *elektron* amber (in which electricity was first observed) + Greek *larynx* the larynx + *graphein* to write]

electrolyte *n.* A liquid or gel solution that contains free *ions and can therefore conduct electricity, or a chemical compound such as an acid, base, or salt that releases free ions when it is dissolved. The main electrolytes required for human physiology are solutions of the salts of *calcium for relaxation of skeletal muscles and contraction of cardiac muscle, *potassium for contraction of skeletal muscles and relaxation of cardiac muscle, and *sodium for maintaining fluid balance. **electrolysis** *n.* The process of passing an electrical current through an *electrolyte.
[From Greek *elektron* amber (in which electricity was first observed) + *lysis* loosening]

electromagnetic sense *n.* Another name for the *magnetic sense.

electromyogram *n.* A recording of the electrical activity of a muscle with an instrument called an *electromyograph. **EMG** *abbrev.*
[From Greek *elektron* amber (in which electricity was first observed) + *mys*, *myos* a muscle + *gramme* a line]

electromyograph *n.* An instrument for measuring the electrical activity of muscles and producing an *electromyogram.
[From *electro-* electric, from Greek *elektron* amber (in which electricity was first observed) + Greek *mys*, *myos* a muscle + *graphein* to write]

electro-oculogram *n.* A recording of eye movements, even behind the closed lids of a person who is asleep, obtained from an instrument called an electro-oculograph that measures electrical potentials in the *extra-ocular muscles. **EOG** *abbrev.*
[From Greek *elektron* amber (in which electricity was first observed) + Latin *oculus* the eye + Greek *gramme* a line]

electropalatograph *n.* An instrument for recording the contacts between the tongue and palate during speech.
[From *electro-* electric, from Greek *elektron* amber (in which electricity was first observed) + English *palate* + Greek *graphein* to write]

electrophoresis *n.* The migration of suspended particles, such as segments of *DNA, usually through a gel or colloid under the influence of an applied electrical field, the lightest particles tending to move furthest. Also called *gel electrophoresis. See also* genetic fingerprinting, restriction mapping.
[From Greek *elektron* amber (in which electricity was first observed) + *phoreein* to bear]

electroreceptor *n.* A *sensory receptor possessed by some species of fish that is specialized for detecting electrical discharges. *See also* electric organ. *Compare* magnetic sense.
[From Greek *elektron* amber + English *receptor*]

electroretinogram *n.* The summated electrical activity of large numbers of neurons in the *retina, recorded from the front of the eyes, analogous to the *cochlear microphonic or the *EEG. **ERG** *abbrev.*

electroshock therapy (EST) *n.* Another name for *electroconvulsive therapy.

element movement *n.* A form of apparent movement that occurs in the *Ternus phenomenon when a short interstimulus interval is used, one element appearing to hop back and forth across the others.

elevated mood *n.* A heightened mood characterized by feelings of euphoria, elation, and well-being. A person in such a mood may describe the feeling as *high* or *ecstatic*.

elevation in the visual field *n.* The relative height of an object relative to the rest of the visual field, suggestive of distance because the horizon is generally higher than the foreground, hence one of the monocular cues of visual *depth perception. Also called *height in the visual field*.

elimination by aspects *n*. A theory of *multi-attribute decision making, introduced in 1972 by the Israeli psychologist Amos Tversky (1937–96), according to which a choice is reached through an iterated series of eliminations. At each iteration, the decision maker selects an *attribute (aspect), the probability of selection being proportional to the attribute's perceived importance, and eliminates all alternatives lacking that attribute, then selects the next most important attribute and proceeds in the same way, and so on until all but one of the alternatives have been eliminated. It is a *stochastic version of *lexicographic choice, and although it is not guaranteed to produce an optimal choice it appears from experimental tests to be characteristic of human multi-attribute decision making. *See also* bounded rationality. **EBA** *abbrev*.

elimination disorders *n*. A group of *mental disorders associated with defecation or urination. *See* encopresis, enuresis.

elision *n*. The omission of a speech sound that would normally be present, especially in *allegro speech, as when the second /t/ sound in the phrase *next time* is omitted, or when *terrific* is pronounced as a two-syllable rather than a three-syllable word. *Compare* haplology.
[From Latin *elidere* to knock + *-ion* indicating an action, process, or state]

Ellen West *n*. The pseudonym of a young woman with *anorexia nervosa who became the subject of the most famous case study of *existential analysis, a long and disturbing account by the Swiss psychiatrist Ludwig Binswanger (1881–1966), published in the *Schweizer Archiv für Neurologie und Psychiatrie* in three instalments in 1944. Quotations from the patient's own diary and letters, in which she recorded her most intimate thoughts and feelings during her psychological decline, were used by Binswanger to draw the reader into her distressing mental state, which ended in tragic death.

Ellsberg paradox *n*. A *paradox of choice that usually elicits responses inconsistent with *expected utility theory. Two urns are filled with red and green balls. Urn *A* contains 50 red balls and 50 green balls randomly mixed; Urn *B* contains 100 red and green balls randomly mixed in an unknown ratio. You choose an urn and a colour, and you then draw a ball at random from your chosen urn. If the ball is your chosen colour, you win a prize. Most people strongly prefer to draw a ball of either colour from Urn *A*, although this violates the axioms of expected utility theory. According to expected utility theory, if a decision maker prefers to draw a red ball from Urn *A* than to draw a red ball from Urn *B*, then the (subjective) probability of drawing a red ball from Urn *B* must be less than 1/2; but that means that the (subjective) probability of drawing a green ball from Urn *B* must be greater than 1/2, and the decision maker should therefore prefer it to drawing a red ball from Urn *A*, which carries a 1/2 probability of winning. According to Ellsberg, human decision makers tend to maximize expected utility (or subjective expected utility) in judgements involving *risk (2), such as exists in Urn *A*, to use *maximin strategies (to maximize minimum utility) in judgements involving *uncertainty (2), as in Urn *B*, and to use compromise strategies when the degree of confidence in their probability estimates is intermediate between risk (high confidence) and uncertainty (low confidence), confidence being derived from the amount, type, reliability, and unanimity of information. This implies that expected utility theory, subjective expected utility theory, and the concept of *revealed preferences apply to situations of risk but not to situations involving uncertainty. Also called the *Ellsberg–Fellner* paradox, in recognition of an article by the US economist William Fellner (1905–83), drawing attention to the same phenomenon, published in 1961 in the same volume of the *Quarterly Journal of Economics* in which Ellsberg's article appeared. *See also* modified Ellsberg paradox. *Compare* Allais paradox, common ratio effect, St Petersburg paradox.
[Named after the US political analyst Daniel Ellsberg (born 1931) who published it in 1961]

Elopram *n*. A proprietary name for the antidepressant drug *citalopram.
[Trademark]

elusion *n*. The act or process of eluding or evading. In *psychoanalysis, a term first used by the Scottish psychiatrist Ronald D(avid)

Laing (1927–89) in his book *The Self and Others* (1961) to denote a mechanism whereby people avoid confrontation with themselves and others by self-impersonation, that is, by deliberately playing out the roles that are assigned to them. Laing cited *Madame Bovary* (1857) by the French novelist Gustave Flaubert (1821–80) as an example of this mechanism.

emasculation *n*. Another name for *castration.
[From Latin *emasculare* to castrate, from *masculus* manly or virile, from *mas* male or masculine + *-ation* indicating a process or condition]

embedded-figures test *n*. A test designed by the German Gestalt psychologist Kurt Gottschaldt (1902–91), and first published in the journal *Psychologische Forschung* in 1926, in which the respondent tries to locate simple geometrical shapes that are hidden in more complex diagrams. It is most often used to measure *field dependence–independence, people who are field independent performing the task significantly better than those who are field dependent. Also called the *Gottschaldt figures test*. **EFT** *abbrev*.

emblem *n*. A visible object, symbol, or representation of something else, especially (in social psychology) a *gesture (1) that functions as a substitute for a verbal expression. Many non-verbal emblems, including waving the hand for *goodbye*, putting a forefinger to the lips for *silence*, or crossing two fingers for *good luck*, have wide cross-cultural consistency, whereas others are regionally specific: making a ring with the thumb and forefinger indicates *OK* in the US and northern Europe, whereas in southern Europe it conveys *nothing* or *zero*, and in Japan *money*; and the chin-flick emblem (tapping the back of the fingers against the underside of the chin) means *get lost* in France and northern Italy but is largely unknown in the UK and the US. *See also* kinesics, submissive behaviour. **emblematic** or **emblematical** *adj*.
[From Latin *emblema* a raised decoration or mosaic, from Greek *emblema* something inserted, from *en* in + *ballein* to throw]

embrace reflex *n*. Another name for the *Moro reflex.
[So called because of its resemblance to a gesture of embrace]

embryo *n*. An *organism in the earliest phase of its development after the first cleaving of the *zygote; in humans, up to about the end of the second month after conception, before the main internal organs have begun to take shape, thereby being distinguished from a *foetus, or more loosely up to birth. *See also* blastocyst, morula. **embryonic** *adj*.
[From Greek *embryon* an embryo, from *bryein* to swell]

embryology *n*. The study of the formation and development of *embryos.

emic *adj*. In linguistics, of or relating to speech characteristics that are considered in terms of their function within a particular language. For example, an emic approach to *intonation focuses on those features of pitch pattern that signal differences in meaning, whereas an *etic approach analyses pitch movements regardless of meaning. In sociology and social psychology, of or relating to an account of a social phenomenon made from the perspective or viewpoint of a participant in the social situation, in contrast to an *etic account given by an outside observer such as a researcher.
[Coined in 1967 by the US linguist Kenneth Lee Pike (1912–2000), from *(phon)emic*]

emitted behaviour *n*. In the theory of *operant conditioning, responses made spontaneously by an organsim as a result of internal factors rather than external *reinforcement. *See also* operant. US *emitted behavior*.

Emmert's law *n*. The apparent increase in the size of a visual *afterimage when viewed against a relatively nearby surface and then against a more distant surface. Formally, the law asserts that $h/H = d/D$, where h is the linear size (height, width, or diameter) of the object, H is the apparent linear size of its image, d is the object's distance from the observer, and D is the distance between the observer and the surface on which the afterimage is perceived. The relation is one of proportionality, a doubling of distance producing a doubling in apparent size, because it follows from the law that $H = hD/d$, and the explanation lies in the fact that the visual angle remains constant but the apparent distance increases, which would normally indicate an increase in size (*see under* visual angle). The law can be demonstrated by staring at a brightly lit image with a steady gaze for a minute and then shifting one's gaze first to a blank sheet of paper and then to a distant wall: the afterimage will appear to grow much larger.

[Named after the Swiss ophthalmologist and psychologist Emil Emmert (1844–1911) who formulated it in 1881, although it had been discovered more than two centuries earlier by the Italian physicist Benedetto Castelli (1578–1643)]

emmetropia *n*. The condition of perfect vision in which light rays from distant objects, which are approximately parallel, are focused on the retina without *accommodation (1). *Compare* hyperopia, myopia. **emmetrope** *n*. A person with *emmetropia. **emmetropic** *adj*. [From Greek *emmetros* in due measure, from *en* in + *metron* a measure + *ops* an eye + *-ia* indicating a condition or quality]

emotion *n*. Any short-term evaluative, affective, intentional, psychological state, including happiness, sadness, disgust, and other inner feelings. *See also* affect, Cannon–Bard theory, cognitive-appraisal theory, James–Lange theory, personal construct theory, primary emotions. *Compare* mood. **emotional** *adj*. [From Latin *e-* away + *movere*, *motum* to move + *-ion* indicating an action, process, or state]

emotional intelligence *n*. Ability to monitor one's own and other people's emotions, to discriminate between different emotions and label them appropriately, and to use emotional information to guide thinking and behaviour. The term appeared sporadically in the psychological literature during the 1970s and 1980s, but the concept was first formally defined in 1990 by the US psychologists Peter Salovey (born 1958) and John D. Mayer (born 1953), who later specified four groups of competencies that it encompasses: (a) the ability to perceive, appraise, and express emotions accurately; (b) the ability to access and evoke emotions when they facilitate cognition; (c) the ability to comprehend emotional messages and to make use of emotional information; and (d) the ability to regulate one's own emotions to promote growth and well-being. The following passage from *The Nicomachean Ethics* by the Greek philosopher Aristotle (384–322 BC) is often quoted as an illustration of emotional intelligence: 'Those who are not angry at the things they should be angry at are thought to be fools, and so are those who are not angry in the right way at the right time, or with the right persons; for such a man is thought not to feel things nor to be pained by them, and, since he does not get angry, he is thought unlikely to defend himself' (Book 4, Chapter 5, Bekker edition, p. 1126a). Popularized interpretations of emotional intelligence include various other factors such as interpersonal skills and adaptability. Also called *social intelligence*, especially when focusing on competencies belonging to (a) and (c). *See also* emotional quotient, intelligence, multiple intelligences, PONS.

emotional quotient *n*. An index of *emotional intelligence analogous to the *IQ index of conventional intelligence. A number of scales to measure the emotional quotient were developed following the publication in 1995 of a best-selling book *Emotional Intelligence* by the US psychologist and journalist Daniel Goleman (born 1946). Early measures of this variable were based on self-report measures of individuals' perceptions or appraisals of their own competencies and experiences in areas of functioning associated with emotional intelligence; development of more valid measures focusing on the key competencies began in the late 1990s. **EQ** *abbrev*.

empathogen *n*. Any drug such as *ecstasy (2) or *GHB that induces a feeling of *empathy and benevolence towards others. *See also* sociabilizer. [From *empathy* + Greek *genein* to produce]

empathy *n*. The capacity to understand and enter into another person's feelings and emotions or to experience something from the other person's point of view. Also called *Einfühlung. See also* empathogen. [From Greek *empatheia* affection or passion, from *en-* in + *pathos* suffering]

empirical *adj*. Derived from observation or experiment rather than speculation or theory. *See also* a posteriori, a priori, empiricism. [From Greek *en* in + *peira* a trial + *-ikos* of or relating to]

empirical induction *n*. Another name for *induction (1).

empiricism n. The doctrine associated especially with the English philosopher John Locke (1632–1704), the Irish philosopher Bishop George Berkeley (1685–1753), and the Scottish philosopher David Hume (1711–76), collectively known as British empiricists, that all elements of knowledge—or, in a less extreme version, all factual knowledge as distinct from logically deduced inferences—is derived from experience, adherents to this view often taking the experimental method as a prototype of knowledge acquisition in general. *See also* a priori, a posteriori, Hume's fork, inference, logical empiricism, logical positivism, Molyneux's question, positivism (1), tabula rasa, transactionalism. *Compare* nativism, rationalism (1, 2). **empiricist** *adj. n.*

empty-chair technique n. In *Gestalt therapy, a technique in which the client switches between two chairs, acting out both sides of a conversation or argument with a spouse, relative, or other significant person. Also called *chairwork*.

enantiodromia n. The principle attributed to the Greek philosopher Heraclitus (?535–?475 BC) according to which everything eventually changes into its opposite. In *analytical psychology, Carl Gustav Jung (1875–1961) described it as 'the principle which governs all cycles of natural life, from the smallest to the greatest' (*Collected Works*, 7, paragraph 112).
[From Greek *enantios* opposite + *dromos* course + *-ia* indicating a condition or quality]

enantiomorph n. A structure that is a mirror image of another, being exactly the same shape as the other except for the reversal of left and right. Some pairs of molecules have this relational property. *See also* handedness (2), mental rotation, mirror reversal problem. **enantiomorphic** *adj.*
[From Greek *enantios* opposite + *morphe* a form or shape]

encéphale isolé n. A surgical preparation in which the central nervous system is severed between the bottom of the medulla oblongata and the top of the spinal cord. In cats operated on in this way, a normal sleep–wake cycle has been observed in their *EEGs. *Compare cerveau isolé*.
[From French *encéphale* the brain + *isolé* isolated]

encephalic *adj.* Of or relating to the brain.
[From Greek *en* in + *kephale* the head + *-ikos* of, relating to, or resembling]

encephalitis n. Inflammation of the brain, causing signs and symptoms such as headache, neck pain, fever, nausea, vomiting, and sometimes neurological disturbances such as *convulsions, *paralysis, *asthenia, or *coma, sometimes leading to death. *Compare* encephalomyelitis, encephalopathy.
[From Greek *enkephalos* brain, from *en* in + *kephale* head + *-itis* inflammation]

encephalitis lethargica n. A form of *encephalitis, characterized by extreme lethargy and sleepiness, that emerged at the end of the First World War, developed into a worldwide epidemic in the 1920s, claiming the lives of more than a million people, and ended abruptly in 1928 without its cause ever having been determined, and that may have reappeared sporadically in subsequent decades. Also (colloquially) called *sleepy sickness*.

encephalization n. The increasing anatomical sophistication of the developing brain, beginning with the spinal cord and brainstem, followed by midbrain and forebrain regions, with the cerebral cortex, and particularly the frontal lobes, the last to show fully developed anatomical complexity.
[From Greek *en* in + *kephale* the head + *-izein* to cause to become + *-ation* indicating a process or condition]

encephalization quotient n. An index of the comparative *intelligence of animal species formulated by the Polish-born US psychologist Harry Jacob Jerison (born 1925): brain volume of the animal in question divided by brain volume of a standard comparison animal belonging to the same class, correcting for body size. If a cat is arbitrarily assigned a standard mammalian encephalization quotient of 1.0, then a rat scores 0.4, a chimpanzee 2.5, a dolphin 6.0, and a human 6.3. *Compare* A/S ratio, progression index. **EQ** *abbrev.*
[From Greek *en* in + *kephale* the head + Latin *quotiens* how many]

encephalogram n. An X-ray image of the brain, often taken after first replacing the *cerebrospinal fluid with air or dye to show the *ventricles clearly. Also called an *encephalograph*. *See also* pneumoencephalogram.

Compare EEG. **encephalography** *n*. The production and interpretation of *encephalograms.
[From Greek *en* in + *kephale* the head + *gramme* a line]

encephalomalacia *n*. Softening of the brain caused by a vascular disorder associated with inadequate cerebral blood flow.
[From Greek *en* in + *kephale* the head + *malakia* softness, from *malakos* soft + *-ia* indicating a condition or quality]

encephalomyelitis *n*. Inflammation of the brain and spinal cord, causing fever, headache, stiff neck, back pain, vomiting, and possibly *convulsions, *coma, and death. A person who recovers from this condition may be left with a *convulsive disorder or impairment in intellectual ability. *Compare* encephalitis, encephalopathy, myalgic encephalomyelitis.
[From Greek *enkephalos* brain, from *en* in + *kephale* head + *myelos* marrow + *-itis* inflammation]

encephalon *n*. A technical name for the brain.
[From Greek *enkephalos* the brain, from *en* in + *kephale* the head]

encephalopathy *n*. Any pathological abnormality in the structure or function of the brain, especially a chronic and degenerative condition such as *BSE, *Creutzfeldt–Jakob disease (CJD), *Gerstmann–Sträussler–Scheinker syndrome (GSS), *fatal familial insomnia (FFI), or *Wernicke's encephalopathy. *Compare* encephalitis, encephalomyelitis.
[From Greek *enkephalos* brain, from *en* in + *kephale* head + *pathos* suffering]

enclitic *n*. A monosyllabic *clitic that follows the word on which it depends. *Compare* proclitic.
[From Greek *enklitikos* something leaning, from *enklinein* to cause to lean + *-itikos* resembling or marked by]

enclosure grouping law *n*. Another name for the *common region grouping law of Gestalt psychology.

encoding *n*. Converting information into a different form or representation, especially (in psychology) the process whereby physical sensory information is transformed into a representation suitable for *storage in *memory and subsequent *retrieval. *See also* levels of processing. **encode** *vb*.

encoding specificity *n*. The effect on *recall from memory of the relation between *encoding operations at the time of learning and the *cues (3) available at the time of recall, the effectiveness of the encoding operation being dependent on the nature of the cues at recall, and the effectiveness of particular cues at recall being dependent on the nature of the earlier encoding operations. For example, research has shown that if a person reads the sentence *The man tuned the piano*, together with many other sentences, and later tries to recall the objects mentioned in all the sentences, then the cue *nice sound* facilitates the recall of *piano*, whereas the cue *something heavy* does not; but if the original sentence is *The man lifted the piano*, then *something heavy* is an effective cue but *nice sound* is not. References to this phenomenon can be traced to a book by the US psychologist Harry L. Hollingworth (1880–1956) published in 1928, where it was called the *principle of reinstatement of stimulating conditions*. Also called *encoding–retrieval interaction* or *transfer-appropriate processing*. *See also* state-dependent memory.

encopresis *n*. An elimination disorder of children at least 4 years old (or of equivalent *mental age), characterized by repeated defecation in inappropriate places, such as in clothing or on the floor, whether unintentionally or (less commonly) intentionally, the behaviour not being attributable to laxatives or other substances or to a *general medical condition.
[From Greek *en* in + *kopros* excrement + *-esis* on the model of *enuresis*]

encounter group *n*. A form of *experiential therapy or *group therapy that aims to increase self-awareness and to encourage greater understanding of others through open and uninhibited expression of feelings along with verbal and physical confrontation and contact. *Compare* T-group.
[From Old French *encontrer* to meet face to face, from Latin *en* in + *contra* against]

end bulb *n*. Another name for an *axon's *bouton.

end effect *n*. Another name for the *serial position effect.

endemic *adj*. In *epidemiology, of or relating to a disorder commonly found in a particular place or population. *Compare* epidemic (2), pandemic (2).
[From Greek *endemos* native, from *en* in + *demos* the people + *-ikos* of, relating to, or resembling]

Endep *n*. A proprietary name for the tricyclic antidepressant drug *amitriptyline.
[Trademark]

end foot *n*. Another name for a *bouton, or more generally a structure at the end of either an *axon or a *dendrite.

endocannabinoid *n*. A substance manufactured within the body, closely related to the active *psychotropic ingredient of *cannabis, functioning as an important regulator to control pain, to govern the flow of blood, and to influence the operation of the *immune system in ways that are not well understood. The existence of endocannabinoids, suspected for decades, was established in the late 1990s.
[From Greek *endon* within + English *cannabis* + *-oid* indicating likeness or resemblance, from Greek *eidos* shape or form]

endocrine disorder *n*. Any disorder of the *endocrine glands or their functions, including disorders of the *HPA axis, which often have psychological effects.

endocrine gland *n*. Any of the ductless glands, including the *adrenal glands, *islets of Langerhans, *ovaries, *parathyroid glands, *pineal gland, *pituitary gland, *testes, *thymus gland, and *thyroid glands, that secrete *hormones directly into the bloodstream, where they come into contact with specific receptors on target cells, allowing the endocrine system to function as an extensive signalling system within the body, alongside but independently of the nervous system. Secretions from the *hypothalamus control those of the pituitary gland, the master endocrine gland, and secretions from the pituitary in turn control those of the other endocrine glands. Also called a *ductless gland*. *Compare* exocrine gland. *See also* neuroendocrine.
[From Greek *endon* within + *krinein* to separate]

endocrine system *n*. The complete set of *endocrine glands and associated structures in an organism considered as a functional unit.

endocrinology *n*. The study of the *endocrine glands and their secretions.

endoderm *n*. The innermost germ layer of a human or animal *embryo, from which the lining of the digestive and respiratory tracts are formed. *Compare* ectoderm, mesoderm.
[From Greek *endon* within + *derma* skin]

endogamy *n*. The cultural practice or custom of marriage between people within the same clan, tribe, or other group of related individuals; more generally, the fusion of *gametes from closely related parents. *Compare* exogamy.
[From Greek *endon* within + *gameein* to marry]

endogenous depression *n*. A form of *depression that is not a reaction to an upsetting event or experience. *Compare* reactive depression.
[From Greek *endon* within + *genes* born]

endogenous opioid *n*. Any *opiate that is produced naturally in the brain and that binds to opiate receptors and blocks pain sensations. *See* beta-endorphin, dynorphin, endorphin, enkephalin.
[From Greek *endon* within + *genes* born]

endolymph *n*. A fluid contained within the *scala media and the *semicircular canals of the inner ears, functioning as an inertial mass resisting angular acceleration of the head, so that when the head is rotated, the *hair cells that extend from the crista into the gelatinous membrane or cupula bend in the opposite direction, triggering nerve impulses. *See also* otolith. *Compare* perilymph.
[From Greek *endon* within + Latin *lympha* water, influenced by Greek *nymphe* a nymph, alluding to the fact that it is a fluid within the membranous labyrinth, unlike perilymph]

endomorph *n*. A heavy and rounded physique or body build, believed by the US psychologist William H. Sheldon (1899–1977) and followers of his *constitutional psychology to be associated with such personality characteristics as placidity, lack of anxiety, and pursuit of pleasure. *Compare* ectomorph, mesomorph. **endomorphic** *adj*. **endomorphy** *n*. The state or condition of being an *endomorph.
[From Greek *endon* within + *morphe* a form or shape]

endoplasmic reticulum n. An extensive convoluted *membrane inside cells, occurring in clumps called Nissl bodies, in which certain proteins are synthesized by *ribosomes and are transported through or secreted from the cell. Areas of endoplasmic reticulum that are studded with protein-synthesizing ribosomes are called *rough endoplasmic reticulum (RER)*, and areas that are not are called *smooth endoplasmic reticulum (SER)*. *See also* aspirin, microsome, prostaglandin. **ER** *abbrev*.
[From Greek *endon* within + *plasma* a form + Latin *reticulum* a little net, diminutive of *rete* a net]

endopsychic *adj*. Of, relating to, or consisting of the contents of the mind.
[From Greek *endon* within + *psyche* the mind + *-ikos* of, relating to, or resembling]

end organ n. The structure at the end of a peripheral neuron or nerve, such as a *bouton at the end of a *motor nerve or a *sensory receptor at the end of a *sensory nerve.

endorphin n. Any member of the group of *endogenous opioid peptides that occur naturally in the brain and that bind to *opiate receptors and block *pain sensations, the other major families of brain opiates being *dynorphin and *enkephalin. The most important type of endorphin is *beta-endorphin (β-endorphin).
[From Greek *endon* within + *Morpheus* the god of sleep and dreams]

endothelium n. A single layer of cells that is derived from the embryonic *mesoderm and that lines the internal cavities of the blood vessels and other fluid-filled internal cavities and glands of the body. *Compare* epithelium. **endothelial** *adj*.
[From Greek *endon* within + *thele* a nipple]

endotherm n. Any animal that generates its own body heat, specifically a bird or a mammal. *Compare* ectotherm. **endothermic** *adj*. Warm-blooded.
[From Greek *endon* within + *therme* heat]

endowment effect n. The tendency to demand much more to give up an object than one is willing to pay to acquire it. The phenomenon was identified and named in 1980 by the US economist Richard H. Thaler (born 1945) and subsequently investigated experimentally by Thaler and others. In a typical experiment, participants were given either a lottery ticket or $2.00. Some time later, each participant was offered the opportunity to trade the lottery ticket for money, or vice versa, but very few chose to switch, most preferring what they were endowed with. The phenomenon is closely related to *loss aversion, and it shows that preferences must be understood in relation to status quo reference points, as in *prospect theory. Also called *status quo bias*. *See also* cognitive dissonance.

end plate n. A shortened name for a *motor end plate.

end-plate potential n. The *depolarization of a *postsynaptic cell membrane of a muscle fibre when it is stimulated at the *motor end plate by a *motor neuron, causing the muscle fibre to contract. *Compare* miniature end-plate potential. **EPP** *abbrev*.

end-stopped receptive field n. An area of the retina that when stimulated by a bar or an edge oriented at a particular angle causes a neuron in the *primary visual cortex (Area V1) to discharge a nerve impulse, but that elicits a weaker response or no response from the neuron if the length of the stimulus exceeds a certain limit. A cortical neuron that responds in this way is called an *end-stopped neuron* or *end-stopped cell*. *See also* hypercomplex cell, receptive field.

engineering psychology n. Another name for *ergonomics.

engram n. A physical representation of a memory in the brain; a memory trace. Also called a *memory trace* or a *neurogram*.
[From German *Engramm* an engram, from Greek *en* in + *gramme* a line]

enkephalin n. Either of two major *endogenous opioid peptides, met-enkephalin and leu-enkephalin, occurring naturally in the brain in small quantities and functioning as both *hormones and *neurotransmitters, binding to opiate receptors and blocking *pain sensations, the other major families of brain opiates being *dynorphin and *endorphin.
[From Greek *en* in + *kephale* head + *-in(e)* indicating an organic compound]

entelechy *n.* According to the ancient Greek philosopher Plato (?427–347 BC), actuality as opposed to potential; according to the German rationalist philosopher and mathematician Gottfried Wilhelm von Leibniz (1646–1716), either the soul or a fundamental constituent element of reality called a *monad; according to the vitalist philosophers, a life force directing an organism towards a final end.
[From Greek *en* in + *telos* an end + *echein* to have]

entopic *adj.* Situated normally. *Compare* ectopic.
[From Greek *endon* in + *topos* a place + *-ikos* of, relating to, or resembling]

entorhinal cortex *n.* A thin strip of cortex in the *limbic system, at the front of the parahippocampal gyrus, adjacent to and closely connected with the hippocampus, involved in integrating information from disparate sensory systems and in certain memory functions. *See also* Papez circuit, perforant pathway.
[From Greek *entos* within + *rhis, rhinos* the nose, alluding to the *rhinencephalon]

entrainment *n.* The adjustment of a *biological clock to synchronize with an external *Zeitgeber* such as the *diurnal cycle of light and dark. **entrain** *vb.*

entropy *n.* A measure of the degree of disorder of a closed system, originally applied to a contained gas, expressed by $S = \Sigma p_i \log_2 p_i$ where p_i is the probability of a particular state of the system, the value of S in a closed system never decreasing over time according to the second law of *thermodynamics. In work on *information theory, the US mathematicians Norbert Wiener (1894–1964) and Claude E(lwood) Shannon (1916–2001) interpreted information as negative entropy, but this was deprecated by the British telecommunications engineer Colin Cherry (1914–79) and others. *See also* Nernst heat theorem.
[Coined in 1865 by the German physicist and mathematician Rudolf Julius Clausius (1822–88) from Greek *en* in or into + *tropos* a turn, from *trapein* to turn, alluding to transformation of energy]

enuresis *n.* An elimination disorder of children at least 5 years old (or of equivalent *mental age), characterized by repeated urination into clothes or bedding, whether unintentional or (less commonly) intentional, occurring frequently or causing clinically significant distress or impairment of social, academic, or occupational functioning, the behaviour not being attributable to diuretics or other substances or to a *general medical condition.
[From Greek *en* in + *ouresis* urination]

environment *n.* The external surroundings within which an organism lives; or any external factors that affect the organism's development or behaviour, as distinct from intrinsic *genetic factors. **environmental** *adj.*
[From Old French *environner* to surround, from *environ* around]

environmentability *n.* The proportion of the *variance in a *phenotypic trait explained by, attributable to, or shared with environmental variance in a specified population at a particular time, and symbolized by e^2. If environmental variance is V_E and total phenotypic variance is V_P, then $e^2 = V_E/V_P$. *Compare* heritability.
[Formed from *environment* by analogy with *heritability*]

environmental psychology *n.* The study of psychological aspects and effects of the physical surroundings, including especially the built environment, in which people live and work.

envy, penis *See* penis envy.

enzyme *n.* Any of a large group of *protein substances that are produced in living cells and that function as catalysts in biochemical reactions. An enzyme usually has an affinity for a particular chemical structure (the substrate), and the enzyme-substrate complex proceeds through the chemical reaction faster than the substrate alone. Chemical names ending in *-ase* are generally enzymes. *See* acetylcholinesterase, adenylate cyclase, ATPase, catechol-o-methyl-transferase, DNA ligase, DNA polymerase, esterase, luciferase, monoamine oxidase, pepsin, phosphodiesterase type 5, polymerase chain reaction, restriction enzyme, reverse transcriptase, RNA polymerase, tyrosine hydroxylase, tryptophan hydroxylase.
[From Greek *en* in + *zyme* leaven]

enzyme induction n. The synthesis, usually by the liver, of an *enzyme specifically adapted to metabolize a food or drug newly introduced to the body. It is one of the mechanisms of drug *tolerance (3).

eonism n. The wearing of female clothing by a male. See transvestism.
[Named after Charles Eon de Beaumont (1728–1810), a celebrated French transvestite in the court of Catherine the Great]

ependyma n. An epithelial *membrane that lines the *ventricles of the brain and the central canal of the spinal cord. **ependymal** adj. Of or relating to the *ependyma. See also ependymal cell.
[From Greek ependyma an outer garment, from epi on + endyma a dress or garment, from endyein to put on]

ependymal cell n. Any of the *neuroglial cells of the *ependyma in the ventricles of the brain, with *cilia on their surfaces helping to propel cerebrospinal fluid through the ventricular system. Specialized ependymal cells form the *choroid plexus.

ephedrine n. A central nervous system *stimulant drug and *sympathomimetic, extracted mainly from the Chinese mahuang plant or manufactured synthetically, that acts indirectly by increasing the release of *noradrenalin (norepinephrine) from presynaptic neurons in the central nervous system and is used mainly for treating hay fever and asthma. It manifests *tachyphylaxis, a standard dosage producing a rapid and short-lived increase in blood pressure, but the same dosage repeated at 10-minute intervals resulting in smaller and smaller effects until, after several dosages, there is virtually no change in blood pressure. Also spelt ephedrin. Its street names include Cloud nine and herbal ecstasy. Formula: $C_6H_5CHOHCH(CH_3)-NHCH_3$.
[From Latin Ephedra sinica the biological name of the mahuang plant from which it was originally extracted + -ine indicating a chemical compound]

epicene adj. **1.** Having characteristics of both *sexes (1) or neither sex. Compare androgynous, hermaphrodite (2). **2.** Of or relating to a noun that may refer to either *sex (1) without changing its form, such as flight attendant as opposed to air stewardess or firefighter as opposed to fireman. See also political correctness.

[From Greek epikoinos common (to both), from epi on + koinos common (to both)]

epicritic adj. Of or relating to certain *sensory nerve fibres in the skin that are capable of fine discrimination between small degrees of variation.
[From Greek epikritikos decisive, from epi on + krinein to separate or judge + -itikos resembling or marked by]

epidemic n. **1.** In *epidemiology, an outbreak of a disorder afflicting large numbers of people in a particular place or population before moving to a different area. adj. **2.** Of, relating to, or taking the form of an *epidemic (1). Compare endemic, pandemic (2).
[From Greek epidemos general, from epi among + demos the people + -ikos of, relating to, or resembling]

epidemiology n. The study of the *incidence, *prevalence, distribution, and control of disorders.
[From Greek epi among + demos the people + logos word, discourse, or reason]

epidermis n. The thin outer *epithelial layer of the *skin, with a total surface area of approximately 1.67 square metres (18 square feet) in a human adult, containing some of the *touch receptors and *pain receptors. Compare dermis. **epidermal** or **epidermic** adj.
[From Greek epi on + derma the skin]

epidural adj. On or outside the *dura mater.
[From Greek epi on + Latin *dura mater]

epidural anaesthetic n. An injection of an anaesthetic into the space outside the dura mater at the bottom of the spinal cord, especially during childbirth.

epigenesis n. **1.** The theory, now universally accepted, that the development of an *embryo consists of the gradual differentiation of the fertilized *ovum and the piecemeal production and organization of structures, organs, and parts, in opposition to the theory of *preformationism, according to which an embryo is fully differentiated in the ovum or a spermatozoon and merely increases in size during development. **2.** More generally, changes in an organism that are due to environmental factors or to gene–environment

interaction rather than to purely genetic factors. **3.** The appearance of specific characteristics at certain stages of development.
[From Greek *epi* on + *genesis* birth]

epilepsy *n.* A *neurological disorder, generally of unknown *aetiology though sometimes associated with brain damage, especially to the *hippocampus or *temporal lobes, characterized by recurrent *convulsions, sensory disturbances, *absences, or all of these, sometimes preceded by *auras (2), often associated with abnormal *EEG patterns during and also between attacks. *See also* amygdalohippocampectomy, clonic convulsion, commissurotomy, hemispherectomy, idiopathic epilepsy, Jacksonian epilepsy, major epilepsy, minor epilepsy, phosphene, photosensitive epilepsy, scotoma, status epilepticus, temporal lobe epilepsy, tonic–clonic, tonic convulsion.
[From Greek *epi* on + *lepsis* a seizure, from *lambanein* to seize]

epinephrine *n.* Another name for *adrenalin, especially in US usage. **E** *abbrev.*
[From Greek *epi* on + *nephros* a kidney + *-ine* indicating an organic compound]

epinosic gain *n.* Another name for *secondary gain. Also called *epinosic advantage*.
[From Greek *epi* on + *nosos* a disorder]

epiphenomenalism *n.* An approach to the *mind–body problem that is a form of *dualism and one-way *interactionism (1), assuming as it does that mental experiences are real but are merely trivial by-products or *epiphenomena of one particular class of physical brain processes, real but incidental, like the smoke rising above a factory, so that physical processes can cause mental experiences but not vice versa. *Compare* psychophysical parallelism.
[From Greek *epi* on + *phainein* to show + *-ismos* indicating a state or condition]

epiphenomenon *n.* A by-product or any fortuitous or extraneous side-effect of a *phenomenon.
[From Greek *epi* after + *phainomenon* a thing shown, from *phainein* to show]

epiphysis *n.* Short for epiphysis cerebri, literally a growth on the brain, the rarely used technical name of the *pineal gland.

[From Greek *epi* on + *physis* growth, from *phyein* to produce, alluding to its appearance as a pimple on the base of the brain]

episcotister *n.* A device consisting of a rapidly rotating disc with opaque and transparent sectors of adjustable relative sizes, used for reducing the intensity of light by a known proportion and to determine *critical flicker frequency thresholds.
[From Greek *episkotizein* to shadow or darken, from *epi* on + *skotizein* to darken, from *skotos* dark]

episodic amnesia *n.* Inability to recall certain (usually emotionally laden) experiences, with the rest of the memory functions intact. Also called *catathymic amnesia* or *lacunar amnesia*. *Compare* episodic memory.

episodic memory *n.* A type of *long-term memory for personal experiences and events, such as being stung by a bee many years ago, getting married a few months ago, reading a particular book yesterday, or having an egg for breakfast a few minutes ago. Such knowledge is characteristically stored as information about specific experiences and events occurring at particular times and places, and it affords a sense of personal continuity and familiarity with the past. It accounts for only a small proportion of human memory, most of our memories having no basis in personal experience. The concept was introduced in 1972 by the Estonian-born Canadian psychologist Endel Tulving (born 1927), who distinguished it from *semantic memory and from *procedural memory. *Compare* episodic amnesia.
[So called because it relates to episodes in one's life]

episodic paroxysmal anxiety *n.* Another name for *panic disorder.

epistasis *n.* In genetics, the suppression or masking of a gene by another gene that is not its *allele. *See also* penetrance. *Compare* dominance (genetic), dominant gene. **epistatic** *adj.*
[From Greek *epistasis* a stoppage, from *epi* on + *stasis* a standing]

epistemic *adj.* **1.** Of or relating to knowledge or *epistemology. **2.** Of or relating to the use of a modal verb, such as *can*, *may*, *shall*, or *will* in a context in which the truth or falsity of a

*proposition (1) is at issue, as in *Can she drive a car?*
[From Greek *episteme* knowledge + *-ikos* of, relating to, or resembling]

epistemic reasoning *n.* *Reasoning about knowledge, especially reasoning that involves *modal logic. The *muddy children problem is a classic illustration of epistemic reasoning, and the *unexpected hanging is its most famous paradox.

epistemology *n.* The theory of *knowledge, especially the enquiry into what is to count as knowledge, the validity of knowledge, what distinguishes mere belief from knowledge, what kinds of things are knowable, and whether anything can be known for certain. *See also* genetic epistemology, sociology of knowledge.
[From Greek *episteme* knowledge + *logos* word, discourse, or reason]

epithalamus *n.* The part of the diencephalon immediately above the thalamus, comprising the *habenula, *pineal gland, and *posterior cerebral commissure.
[From Greek *epi* on + English *thalamus*]

epithelium *n.* A sheet of tissue of tightly bound cells only a few cells thick that is derived from the embryonic *ectoderm and *endoderm and that covers the outer surface of the body, the *mucous membranes, and the lining of the gut, the retinas, and the glands. *See also* epidermis, nasal epithelium *Compare* endothelium. **epithelia** *pl.* **epithelial** *adj.*
[From Greek *epi* on + *thele* a nipple]

epoche *n.* In *phenomenology, suspension of preconceptions, interpretations, and explanations as a precondition for the experience and description of uninterpreted sense experiences and ideas. Also called *bracketing*.
[From Greek *epoche* stoppage or cessation, from *epechein* to hold back or pause, from *epi* on + *echein* to hold or have]

equal and unequal cases *See* method of equal and unequal cases.

equal-appearing intervals *See* method of equal-appearing intervals, Thurstone scale.

equality grouping law *n.* Another name for the *similarity grouping law of Gestalt psychology.

equal-loudness contour *n.* A plot determined by *loudness matching of tones, varying in frequency across the audible range, with the intensity levels in *decibel sound pressure level (dB SPL) that cause them to sound equally as loud to a listener as a standard comparison tone. For a standard comparison tone with a frequency of 1,000 hertz presented at an intensity of 60 dB SPL, a tone with a frequency of 100 hertz may sound equally loud and therefore attain a loudness level of 60 *phons at about 80 dB SPL, and so on. It was introduced in 1933 by the US acoustical scientist Harvey Fletcher (1884–1981) and the US engineer Wilden A. Munson (1902–82) and is also called a *Fletcher–Munson contour* or an *isophonic contour*.

equated forms *n.* Another name for *parallel forms.

equilibration *n.* In the theories of the Swiss psychologist Jean Piaget (1896–1980) and his followers, a process of *adaptation (3) to the environment that occurs mainly through *assimilation (2) and *accommodation (2) and that tends to maintain a state of cognitive equilibrium or balance when an individual acquires new information.

equilibrium hypothesis *n.* The proposition that participants in a social interaction who feel that the degree of intimacy conveyed by certain channels of *non-verbal communication is inappropriate to the level of intimacy of the relationship, will tend to compensate by reducing the intimacy conveyed through other channels. For example, when crowded situations such as underground trains force people to stand closer together than is ordinarily appropriate with strangers, they tend to reduce the level of intimacy by engaging in less *eye contact. The hypothesis was formulated by the English psychologist Michael Argyle (1925–2002) and his undergraduate student Janet Dean (now Janet Dean Fodor, born 1942) and first published in the journal *Sociometry* in 1965, together with experimental evidence that increased proximity tends to result in decreased eye contact.

equilibrium point (in game theory) *n.* Another name for a *Nash equilibrium. Often called simply an *equilibrium*.

equilibrium potential *n.* Another name for the *resting potential.

equiluminant *adj.* Another word for *isoluminant.

equipotentiality *n.* The principle formulated by the US physiological psychologist Karl Spencer Lashley (1890–1958) that different regions of the *cerebral cortex are equally involved in performing specific functions and have the capacity to take over functions from other regions that are damaged. This principle is now known to be true only within limits, there being a great deal of *localization of function in the brain. *See also* mass action.

equity theory *n.* A theory of social justice according to which people perceive a situation as fair when their own ratio of outcomes to inputs is the same as those of others with whom they compare themselves. Outcomes are the perceived receipts from a social interaction or exchange, including material benefits, social status, and intrinsic rewards, and inputs are the perceived contributions, including material contributions, seniority, education, skills, and effort. In terms of the theory, inequity is felt as uncomfortable even when it is in an individual's favour, and it tends to generate behaviour aimed at restoring equity, such as altering inputs or outcomes or cognitively distorting them, leaving the field, attempting to distort the other person's perceptions of inputs or outcomes, or changing the person used as a point of comparison. It was formulated by the US sociologist George Caspar Homans (1910–89) in his books *The Human Group* (1950) and *Social Behavior: Its Elementary Forms* (1961) and introduced into psychology in 1965 by the Belgian-born US psychologist J. Stacy Adams (born 1925). *See also* cognitive dissonance, relative deprivation.

equivalent-form reliability *n.* A measure of the *reliability of a test based on the correlation between *equivalent forms of a test. Also called *parallel-form reliability*.

equivalent forms *n.* In psychometrics, *alternative forms of a test that are similar in all important properties.

equivocal sign *n.* Another name for a *soft sign.

erectile dysfunction/disorder *See* impotence (2), male erectile disorder.

erectile impotence *See under* impotence (2).

ergonomics *n.* A branch of *industrial/organizational psychology or *occupational psychology concerned with fitting jobs to people rather than people to jobs. Ergonomists design jobs, equipment, and work places to maximize performance and well-being and to minimize accidents, fatigue, boredom, and energy expenditure. Also (especially in the US) called *biotechnology, human factors psychology*, or *engineering psychology*. *See also* knobs-and-dials psychology, personnel psychology. **ergonomic** *adj.* **ergonomist** *n.* One who practises *ergonomics.
[From Greek *ergon* work + *nomos* management, from *nemein* to manage]

ergot *n.* A fungus that grows on wheat or rye, or an *alkaloid drug derived from it that induces contractions of the womb in women and is a powerful vasoconstrictor, useful in the treatment of *migraine headaches and haemorrhage.
[From French *ergot* a cock's spur, which the fungal projections on the ears of wheat or rye resemble in shape]

ergotism *n.* Poisoning resulting from eating grain affected by *ergot or from an overdose of ergot alkaloid drugs (often in medicines prescribed for migraine headaches), characterized by cerebrospinal symptoms, spasms, cramps, and dry gangrene caused by vasoconstriction. *See also* bromocriptine.

Erhard Seminars Training *See* est.

Eriksonian *adj.* Of or relating to the theories of the German-born psychoanalyst of Danish extraction Erik H. Erikson (1902–94), or to the work of the US physician Milton H. Erikson (1901–80), who developed a form of therapy based on hypnosis. *See* developmental crises, ego identity, ego psychology, identity crisis.

Erklärung *See under* Verstehen.

erogenous zone *n.* Any area of the body that is capable of causing or increasing sexual arousal when stimulated. *See also* erotogenic zone.
[From Greek *eros* love or desire + *genes* born]

Eros *n.* In *psychoanalysis, the life instincts, usually including both *the sexual instinct

and the *ego instinct (the *self-preservation instinct), the aim of which are to create and maintain the integrity of things. Sigmund Freud (1856–1939) was not entirely consistent in his usage of the term: in his book *Beyond the Pleasure Principle* (1920), he used it as a synonym for *libido: 'the libido of our sexual instincts would coincide with the Eros of the poets and philosophers' (*Standard Edition*, XVIII, p. 50), but in other publications he included self-preservation within its scope. In his last discussion of this issue in his book *An Outline of Psycho-Analysis* (1938/40) he defined libido as the energy associated with Eros: 'the total available energy of Eros, which henceforward we shall speak of as "libido" ' (*Standard Edition*, XXIII, p. 149), and he also identified the underlying principle of Eros to be *binding: 'to establish ever greater unities and to preserve them', whereas the principle underlying *Thanatos is 'to undo connections and so to destroy things' (p. 148). *See also* horme, object instinct.
[Named after Eros in Greek mythology, the god of love and daughter of Aphrodite, from Greek *eros* love or sexual desire]

erotic *adj*. Of or relating to sexual desire.
[From Greek *eros* love + *-ikos* of, relating to, or resembling]

erotic love *n*. A primary type of *love that is passionate and *erotic, being rooted in sexual attraction. *Compare* agapic love, ludic love, manic love, pragmatic love, storgic love.

erotism *See* allo-erotism, anal erotism, auto-erotism, organ erotism, phallic erotism, urethral erotism.

erotogenic zone *n*. In *psychoanalysis, another name for an *erogenous zone, specifically the oral, anal, and genital areas of the body. Sigmund Freud (1856–1939) first outlined his ideas about erotogenic zones in 1896 and 1897 in letters to his friend, the German physician Wilhelm Fliess (1858–1928), and then published his theory in 1905 in his book *Three Essays on the Theory of Sexuality* (*Standard Edition*, VII, pp. 130–243, at pp. 183–4). By 1938, when he published *An Outline of Psycho-Analysis*, he had decided that 'in fact the whole body is an erotogenic zone' (*Standard Edition*, XXIII, pp. 144–207, at p. 151). Also called a *primary zone*. *See also* anal erotism, instinctual source, libidinal stage, oral

erotism, phallic erotism, urethral erotism. *Compare* hysterogenic zone.
[From Greek *eros* love or sexual desire + *genes* born + *-ikos* of, relating to, or resembling]

erotomania *n*. **1.** A *delusion of being loved by another person, often a famous person or someone of higher status in the workplace. *See also* erotomanic delusional disorder. **2.** Abnormally strong sexual desire.
[From Greek *erotikos* of or relating to love, from *eros* love + *-ikos* of, relating to, or resembling + *mania* madness]

erotomanic delusional disorder *n*. A type of *delusional disorder in which the central delusion is *erotomania (1); also called *Clérambault's syndrome*, *psychose passionelle*, or *pure erotomania*.

error variable *n*. In statistics, any variable defined by the difference between observed scores and values predicted by a *model.

error variance *n*. In statistics, the portion of the *variance in a set of scores that is due to *extraneous variables and measurement error.

erythrocyte *n*. A red button-shaped blood corpuscle containing *haemoglobin and transporting oxygen to and carbon dioxide from body tissues. Also called a *red blood cell* or *red blood corpuscle*. *See also* erythropoietin, stem cell. *Compare* leucocyte.
[From Greek *erythros* red + *kytos* a vessel]

erythropoietin *n*. A protein that is secreted by the kidney in response to low levels of oxygen in the blood and that increases the rate of formation of *erythrocytes in the *blood. Sometimes injected by competitive cyclists and other athletes as a virtually undetectable *performance enhancer that allows more oxygen to be transported to the muscles, thereby raising the level of *aerobic energy production. **EPO** *abbrev*.
[From Greek *erythro(s)* red + *poiet(ikos)* capable of making, from *poiein* to make + *-itikos* resembling or marked by + *-in(e)* indicating an organic compound]

erythropsia *n*. A visual defect in which everything appears reddish, often caused by overexposure to bright light. Also spelt *erythropia*.

[From Greek *erythr(os)* red + *ops* an eye + *-ia* indicating a condition or quality]

escalated fighting *n*. Physical aggression or conflict involving actual or potential bodily injury to the participants, comparatively rare among animals and humans. *See also* Hawk–Dove game, Hawk–Dove–Retaliator game, resource-holding potential. *Compare* conventional fighting.

E scale *abbrev*. A scale to measure *ethnocentrism, especially the scale first published by the German philosopher, sociologist, and psychologist Theodor W(iesengrund) Adorno (1903–69) and several colleagues in the book *The Authoritarian Personality* (1950). *See also* authoritarianism.

escape conditioning *n*. A form of *operant conditioning in which an organism learns to avoid an aversive stimulus. Typically, a rat is placed in a long, narrow alleyway with an electrified grid floor and can escape painful stimulation by running to the end of the alley and stepping into a non-electrified goal box, learning being evidenced by progressively faster running speeds. Also called *escape learning*. *Compare* avoidance conditioning.

escape learning *n*. Another name for *escape conditioning.

Escher figure *n*. Another name for an *impossible figure.
[Named after the Dutch graphic artist Maurits C(ornelis) Escher (1898–1972) who included many impossible figures in his etchings]

eserine *n*. Another name for *physostigmine.
[From *éséré* West African name for the *Calabar bean + *-ine* indicating an organic compound]

esophagus *See* oesophagus.

esotropia *n*. A form of *strabismus in which one or both eyes turn inwards towards the nose, referred to non-technically as *cross-eye squint*. **esotropic** *adj*.
[From Greek *eso* inner + *tropos* a turn + *ops* an eye + *-ia* indicating a condition or quality]

espanto *n*. Another name for *susto.
[Spanish *espanto* fright or terror, from *espantar* to scare or frighten]

ESP cards *n*. Another name for *Zener cards.

essential amino acid *See under* amino acid.

est *abbrev*. Erhard Seminars Training, a technique of *group therapy, designed to raise self-awareness and foster psychological growth, in which people spend sessions lasting many hours deprived of food, drink, and toilet facilities during which they are hectored, abused, and demeaned by stewards. In 1984 the name was changed to Landmark Forum, but it continued to be called est by many people.
[Named after the US businessman Werner Erhard (born 1935), who developed the technique in 1971 after dropping his original name Jack Rosenberg and styling himself after the German theoretical physicist Werner Heisenberg and the German economics minister Ludwig Erhard]

ester *n*. A compound formed by a reaction between an alcohol and an acid with the elimination of water, usually resulting in the formation of a volatile aromatic oil or fat that is *psychotropic when inhaled. *See also* inhalant-related disorders.
[Named in 1822 by the German chemist and physician Leopold Gmelin (1788–1853), from German *Es(sig)* vinegar + *(Ä)t(h)er* ether]

esterase *n*. Any *enzyme that *hydrolyses an *ester into an alcohol and an acid.
[From *ester* + *-ase* denoting an enzyme, from *diastasis* separation]

esthesiometer *See* aesthesiometer.

estimation *n*. The branch of statistics devoted to estimating *parameters on the basis of data from samples and analysing the properties of estimators such as unbiasedness and efficiency.

estradiol *See* oestradiol.

estrogen *See* oestrogen.

estrone *See* oestrone.

estrous cycle *See* oestrous cycle.

estrus *See* oestrus.

eta coefficient *See* correlation ratio.
[From the name of η, the seventh letter of the Greek alphabet]

ethanol n. Another name for *ethyl alcohol. See alcohol.

ethereal odour n. One of the six primary odours in *Henning's prism, one of the nine in *Zwaardemaker smell system, and one of the seven in the *stereochemical theory, resembling the odour of ether or cleaning fluid. US *ethereal odor*.
[From Greek *aither* ether]

ethnic adj. Of, relating to, or characteristic of a human community or group with shared historical roots and a common language, religion, and culture. Ethnic groups are often, though not always, distinguished also by shared territory and/or common *race (2). **ethnicity** n. Shared historical, linguistic, religious, and cultural identity of a social community, group, nation, or race.
[From Greek *ethnos* a nation + -*ikos* of, relating to, or resembling]

ethnic marker n. Any of the signs by which *ethnic boundaries are defined or maintained, including language, religious and cultural symbols, or territory.

ethnocentrism n. A tendency or disposition to judge other *ethnic groups, cultures, nations, or societies by the standards and customs of one's own, often accompanied by a dislike or misunderstanding of other such groups and a belief in the intrinsic superiority of one's own. *See also* authoritarianism. *Compare* ableism, ageism, fattism, heterosexism, racism, sexism, speciesism. **ethnocentrist** n. **1.** One who practises or advocates *ethnocentrism. adj. **2.** Of or relating to *ethnocentrism.
[From Greek *ethnos* a nation + *kentron* a sharp point]

ethnography n. **1.** The branch of anthropology devoted to the scientific study of individual human societies. **2.** A scientific study of an individual human society. **ethnographer** n. One who practises *ethnography. **ethnographic** or **ethnographical** adj.
[From Greek *ethnos* a nation + *graphein* to write]

ethnology n. The branch of anthropology concerned with the comparative study of cultures; formerly, the historical and comparative study of *races (2). **ethnological** adj. **ethnologist** n. One who practises *ethnology.

[From Greek *ethnos* a nation + *logos* word, discourse, or reason]

ethnomethodology n. A term coined in 1967 by the US sociologist Harold Garfinkel (1917–87) to denote an approach to the study of human communication emphasizing common-sense language and interpretations of the world and making considerable use of *participant observation. *See also* conversation analysis. **ethnomethodological** adj.
[From Greek *ethnos* a nation or race + English *methodology* denoting people's method]

ethology n. The study of behaviour in natural habitats, especially but not exclusively animal behaviour. *Compare* animal psychology, comparative psychology. **ethological** adj. **ethologist** n. One who practises *ethology.
[From Greek *ethos* character + *logos* word, discourse, or reason]

ethyl alcohol n. The main psychotropic constituent of intoxicating liquors. Also called *ethanol*. Formula C_2H_5OH. *See* alcohol.
[From *eth(er)*, from Greek *aithein* to burn + *(h)yl(e)* wood or matter + English *alcohol*]

etic adj. In linguistics, of or relating to speech characteristics that are considered without regard to their function within the language. In sociology and social psychology, of or relating to an account of a social phenomenon made from the perspective or viewpoint of an outside observer, such as a researcher, rather than that of a participant in the social situation. *Compare* emic.
[From *(phon)etic*]

etiology *See* aetiology.

etymological fallacy n. The belief that an earlier or the earliest meaning of a word is necessarily the right one. That it is fallacious is illustrated by the fact that *orchard* once meant a treeless garden, *treacle* a wild beast, and *villain* a farm labourer.

etymology n. The study of the origins and development of words and their meanings.
[From Greek *etymos* true + *logos* a word]

eugenic adj. Tending to lead to an increase in the quality or fitness of a group of interbreeding organisms. *Compare* dysgenic. **eugenicist** n. One who practises or advocates *eugenics.

[From Greek *eu* well or good + *genein* to produce + *-ikos* of, relating to, or resembling]

eugenics *n*. The science or pseudoscience concerned with the genetic improvement of the human species, or of selected *races (2), especially by selective breeding.

eukaryote *n*. An organism composed of cells with well-defined *nuclei (1) containing genetic material. All organisms except bacteria, cyanobacteria (blue-green algae), and viruses are eukaryotes. Also spelt *eucaryote*. *Compare* prokaryote.
[From Greek *eu* well or good + *karyon* a kernel]

eukaryotic cell *n*. A biological cell with a *nucleus (1) containing genetic information. Also spelt *eucaryotic cell*.

Euler diagram *n*. A pictorial representation of *propositions (1) or *sets (1) by means of overlapping circles. A *Venn diagram is a refined and improved version of it. Also called *Euler's circles*.
[Named after the Swiss mathematician Leonhard Euler (1707–83) who introduced them and used them extensively]

euphemism *n*. A usage of language in which an inoffensive word or expression is substituted for one that is considered unpleasant or derogatory, as in *pass away* for *die* or *sleep with* for *have sexual intercourse with*. *Compare* dysphemism.
[From Greek *eu* good + *pheme* speech, from *phanai* to speak]

euphoria *n*. An *affective state of exaggerated well-being or elation.
[From Greek *eu* good + *pherein* to bear + *-ia* indicating a condition or quality]

euphoriant *adj. n*. (Of or relating to) anything, especially a *psychotropic drug, that induces or tends to induce euphoria. *See* anabolic steroid, antidepressant, anxiolytic, aphrodisiac, betel, cannabis, catnip, empathogen, hallucinogen, kava, mescaline, narcotic, opium, phantasticant, psychedelic, stimulant drug.
[From Greek *euphoria* good ability to endure, from *eu* good + *pherein* to bear]

eusocial *adj*. Of or relating to certain species of *social insects that cooperate in caring for their young, show reproductive division of labour, with sterile organisms working for others that are reproductive, and contribute simultaneously to the work of the colony with an overlap of at least two generations. The eusocial insects include all ants and termites and some bees and wasps. **eusociality** *n*.
[From Greek *eu* well or good + Latin *socius* a companion]

Eustachian tube *n*. A passageway lined with a mucous membrane that joins the *pharynx and the *middle ear cavity, allowing equalization of the air pressure in the middle ear when atmospheric pressure changes, as when travelling by aircraft. Also (non-technically) called an *auditory tube*. *Compare* auditory canal.
[Named after the Italian physician Bartolomeo Eustachio (1520–74) who was the first to describe it in his *De Auditu Organis* in 1562]

eustress *n*. Any form of *stress (1) that is beneficial, usually associated with a feeling of fulfilment and achievement rather than anxiety.
[Formed from Greek *eu* well or good + English *stress*, on the model of *distress*]

euthymic mood *n*. A *mood (1) within the temperate range, without the characteristics of *depressed mood, *dysphoric mood, *elevated mood, *irritable mood, or any other strongly affective mood.
[From Greek *eu-* well + *thymos* spirit]

evaluation apprehension *n*. Anxiety induced in a person performing some task while being observed by others and feeling anxious about being judged or appraised by them. One of its effects is to increase the person's level of *arousal, which may improve or impair performance, depending on the nature of the task. *See also* audience effect, coaction effect, drive theory of social facilitation.

evaluation research *n*. A form of *applied research undertaken to test the effectiveness of some programme or intervention, such as a new teaching method in a school system or a new crime prevention policy in a city. *See also* basic research, descriptive research, exploratory research. *Compare* action research.

Eve *n*. In the Old Testament (Genesis 2:18–25), the first woman, fashioned from Adam's rib.

By analogy, the name given by the US biochemist Allan C. Wilson (1935–91) to a woman living in Africa 150,000–200,000 years ago from whom the *mitochondrial DNA of the entire population of the world evolved, according to research using the technique of the *evolutionary clock.

[Named after the Old Testament Eve, influenced by the fact that the name echoes the first syllable of *evolution*]

event-related potential n. Another name for an *evoked potential, especially an *EEG response originating outside the primary sensory areas of the brain, initiated by cognitive activity, associated with the sequential processing of information. Also called an *endogenous evoked potential*. See also contingent negative variation, N140, P200, P300, string length. **ERP** abbrev.

evil eye n. An English name for *mal de ojo.

eviration n. A delusion of a man that he has been transformed into a woman.
[From Latin *e-* away + *vir* a man + *-ation* indicating a process or condition]

evoked potential n. A type of *EEG response, either generated in the primary sensory areas of the brain, initiated by a sensory stimulus, and called a sensory or exogenous potential, or generated elsewhere in the brain, initiated by cognitive activity, and called an event-related or endogenous potential. It is conventionally plotted as an amplitude change over time and symbolized by a letter followed by a number, thus the second positive evoked potential occurring 150 milliseconds after the initiating event is written either P2 (because it is the second positive potential) or P150. Also called an *evoked response*. See also average evoked potential, contingent negative variation, event-related potential, nerve conduction velocity, N140, P200, P300, string length. **EP** abbrev.

evolution n. The gradual changes in populations of organisms over successive generations, producing new species that are quite distinct from their remote ancestors. See also Darwinian evolution, natural selection.
[From Latin *evolutio* an unrolling, from *evolvere* to unroll, from *e-* from + *volvere*, *volutum* to roll + *-ion* indicating an action, process, or state]

evolutionarily stable strategy n. Any hereditary pattern of behaviour that is fixed in the sense that, in a population in which most individuals adopt it, no alternative behaviour pattern has a greater *Darwinian fitness, and therefore none is favoured over it by *natural selection. The concept was introduced in 1973 by the English biologist John Maynard Smith (born 1920) and the US physicist and chemist George R. Price (1922–75). Often mistakenly written *evolutionary stable strategy*. See also Hawk–Dove game, Hawk–Dove–Retaliator game, strategy (2). **ESS** abbrev.

evolutionary bottleneck n. A sudden decrease in the size of a population, usually because of an environmental catastrophe, resulting in a loss of genetic variability and therefore adaptability even if the population recovers to its original size. See also average heterozygosity.

evolutionary clock n. The accumulation of changes in non-genetic stretches or *introns of (especially) *mitochondrial DNA that occur at a fairly constant rate and can be calibrated with real time to enable estimates to be made of how long ago present-day organisms diverged from their common ancestors. See also Eve, maternal inheritance, parsimony principle. *Compare* glottochronology, lexicostatistics.

examination anxiety n. Another name for *test anxiety. Also called *exam anxiety*.

excitation n. The action of a *stimulus (1, 5) in evoking a *response from an organism, or from a cell, tissue, or organ, or the disturbed or altered state resulting from such arousal. See also excitatory, excitatory postsynaptic potential. *Compare* inhibition (2, 3). **excite** vb.
[From Latin *ex-* out + *ciere* to set in motion + *-ation* indicating a process or condition]

excitatory adj. Tending to cause *excitation. In neurophysiology, characteristic of *neurons that cause other neurons to fire, or neurotransmitters, the action of which tends to cause neurons to fire, or *synapses (1) at which the transmission of nerve impulses tends to cause postsynaptic neurons to fire. See also excitatory postsynaptic potential. *Compare* inhibitory.

excitatory postsynaptic potential *n*. A graded depolarization or decrease in electrical potential across the membrane of a *post-synaptic neuron, occurring in response to a signal transmitted across a synapse by a *presynaptic neuron, increasing the propensity of the postsynaptic neuron to initiate a nerve impulse. Also called *postsynaptic excitation*. *See also* action potential, depolarization, postsynaptic potential, resting potential. *Compare* inhibitory postsynaptic potential. **EPSP** *abbrev*.

excluded middle law *n*. The principle or law according to which for any proposition *p*, the proposition *p or not-p* is true by logical necessity. Also called the *principle of the excluded middle*.

exclusive disjunction *See under* disjunction (2).

executive *See* central executive.

exemplar *n*. An instance or representative of a *concept; more generally something to be copied or imitated. *Compare* prototype (2).
[From Latin *exemplarium* a model, from *exemplum* an example]

exhaustion stage *n*. The third and final stage of the *general adaptation syndrome to stress, reached by an organism that has failed to adapt to a stressor, characterized by physical and/or mental disorder or disease. *See also* alarm reaction, resistance stage.

exhibitionism *n*. **1.** A *paraphilia characterized by recurrent, intense sexual fantasies, urges, or behaviour involving exposure of one's sexual organs to unsuspecting strangers. **2.** Extravagant, theatrical, or boasting behaviour designed to draw attention to oneself.
[From Latin *exhibere* to display, from *ex-* out + *habere* to have]

existential analysis *n*. A form of *psychoanalysis based on *existentialism, introduced in the early 1930s by the Swiss psychiatrist Ludwig Binswanger (1881–1966) and described in his 726-page book *Grundformen und Erkenntnis menschlichen Daseins* (1942, Basic Forms and Knowledge of Human Existence), the aim of which is not to cure symptoms but to reconstruct the inner experience of patients, even severely *psychotic (1) patients, and to get them to confront their existence and exercise their autonomy. The most famous case study in existential analysis, and one of the most disturbing in the annals of psychiatry, is Binswanger's case of *Ellen West. Also called *Daseinsanalyse*. *See also* bad faith, *Eigenwelt*, existential therapy, *Mitwelt*, *Umwelt*. **existential analyst** *n*. One who practises *existential analysis.

existentialism *n*. A philosophical movement, inspired by *phenomenology, that developed in the second quarter of the 20th century under the influence of the Danish philosopher and religious thinker Søren Aabye Kierkegaard (1813–55), the German philosopher Martin Heidegger (1889–1976), and the French philosophers and writers Jean-Paul Sartre (1905–80), Simone de Beauvoir (1908–86), and Albert Camus (1913–60). It stresses the existence of the individual person as a free agent who is burdened with personal responsibility and whose existence cannot be investigated objectively, being revealed by reflection on existence in time and space. It tends to disparage scientific methodology and knowledge and to reject objective values. *See also* angst (2), antipsychiatry, bad faith, *Dasein*, *Daseinsanalyse*, *Eigenwelt*, existential analysis, existential therapy, hermeneutics (3), *Mitwelt*, *Umwelt*. **existential** *adj*. Of or relating to existence or to *existentialism. **existentialist** *adj*. Of or relating to *existentialism.

existential quantifier *See* quantifier.

existential therapy *n*. A diverse and fragmented group of techniques of *psychotherapy, including both *existential analysis and various other techniques based loosely on the philosophies of *phenomenology and *existentialism, in which clients are encouraged to confront their inner emotions and values, stripping away preconceptions and assumptions, and to take responsibility for their lives. *See also* angst (2), antipsychiatry, bad faith, intentionality (2).

exocrine gland *n*. A gland that originates in *epithelial tissue and secretes through a duct on to the *skin or a *mucous membrane rather than directly into the bloodstream. *See* Bartholin's gland, gastric gland, mammary gland, salivary gland, sweat gland. *Compare* endocrine gland.
[From Greek *exo* outside + *krinein* to separate]

exogamy *n.* The cultural practice or custom of marriage between people of different clans, tribes, or other groups of related individuals; more generally, outbreeding, or the fusion of *gametes from parents that are not closely related. *Compare* endogamy.
[From Greek *exo* outside + *gameein* to marry]

exogenous depression *n.* Another name for *reactive depression. *Compare* endogenous depression.
[From Greek *exo* outside + *genes* born]

exon *n.* Any segment of a gene consisting of *codons representing instructions for synthesizing a protein. *Compare* intron.
[From Greek *exo* outside, on the model of *codon*]

exophoria *n.* A form of latent *strabismus in which the eyes tend to turn outward towards the temples. *Compare* cyclophoria, esotropia, heterophoria, hyperphoria, hypophoria.
[From Greek *ex* out + *-phoros* carrying, from *pherein* to bear]

expansive mood *n.* A *mood (1) characterized by unrestrained emotional expression, often accompanied by an overvaluation of one's importance or significance to others; sometimes merely another name for *elevated mood.

expectancy-value theory *n.* A theory according to which behaviour is affected by the values of the possible outcomes weighted by the estimated probabilities of those outcomes. The earliest version of it was put forward in 1944 by the Polish/German-born US psychologist Kurt Lewin (1890–1947) and several colleagues. In relation to *attitudes (1) it is the theory according to which an attitude reflects the subjective probability (expectancy) that the object of the attitude has certain *attributes, weighted by the subjective feelings (values) evoked by those attributes. For example, a person may have an expectancy (high subjective probability) that *a united Ireland* (the attitude object) would lead to *peace between Irish Catholics and Protestants* (a positively valued attribute). To predict a person's attitude to a united Ireland, the expectancy and value terms for each attribute are multiplied together, and these products are then added: Attitude = Σ Expectancy × Value. This approach to attitudes was formulated in 1975 by the US psychologist Martin Fishbein (born

1936) and the Polish-born US psychologist Icek Ajzen (born 1942). *See also* theory of reasoned action.

expectation-dependent priming *See under* priming (1).

expected utility *n.* The average *utility (1) associated with a decision, calculated by multiplying each of the possible outcomes of the decision by its probability and then summing the resulting products. If the probabilities are subjective, rather than objective measures of relative frequency, then it is called *subjective expected utility*. *Compare* expected value. **EU** *abbrev.*

expected utility theory *n.* A theory of decision making, formalized in 1947 by the Hungarian-born US mathematician John von Neumann (1903–57) and the German-born US economist Oskar Morgenstern (1902–77), according to which a decision maker chooses actions or strategies that maximize *expected utility, and utilities are determined by *revealed preferences. If the probabilities are subjective, then it is called *subjective expected utility theory*. *See also* Allais paradox, cancellation heuristic, common ratio effect, Ellsberg paradox, modified Ellsberg paradox, Newcomb's problem, Pascal's wager, preference reversal (1, 2), prospect theory, rational choice theory, Ultimatum game, utility theory. **EU theory** *abbrev.*

expected value *n.* The average value associated with a decision, calculated in the same way as an *expected utility but using the monetary value of the outcomes rather than their *utility (1) in the calculation. *See also* prospect theory, risk aversion, St Petersburg paradox. **EV** *abbrev.*

experiential therapy *n.* Any of a group of techniques of *psychotherapy that focus on emotional release, inner growth, and *self-actualization, including *encounter groups, *Gestalt therapy, *primal therapy, and *transcendental meditation (TM).

experiment *n.* A research method whose defining features are manipulation of an *independent variable or variables and control of *extraneous variables that might influence the *dependent variable. Control of extraneous variables is often, though not necessarily, achieved through *randomization. Experimental methods are uniquely powerful in allowing rigorous examination of *causal effects without the uncertainties of other research methods. *See also* control group, experimental group, hypothetico-deductive method, randomized controlled trial, randomized double-blind experiment. *Compare* case study, correlational study, observational study, quasi-experiment, survey research. [From Latin *experimentum* proof or trial]

experimental analysis of behaviour *n.* The application of the theory of *operant conditioning to behaviour, especially in animals, focusing almost exclusively on the effects of *reinforcement on rate of *response. The term can also be applied to the study of behaviour through experiments generally, but in practice it has tended to become confined to the meaning defined above. US *experimental analysis of behavior*.

experimental design *n.* The general plan of an *experiment, including the method of assigning research participants or subjects to *treatment conditions, controlling *extraneous variables, manipulating the *independent variable, and measuring the *dependent variable.

experimental group *n.* In *experimental design, a group of research participants or subjects exposed to an *independent variable in order to examine the *causal effect of that treatment on a *dependent variable. *Compare* control group.

experimental hypothesis *n.* Another name for an *alternative hypothesis.

experimentally induced false memory *n.* Any repeatable technique for generating *false memories, especially a procedure first reported in 1959 by the US psychologist James Deese (1921–99) in an article in the *Journal of Experimental Psychology*. Deese constructed several lists of 12 words, each list consisting of the most common *word-association test responses to a critical word that was not included in the list, a typical example being the critical word *needle*, from which Deese constructed the list *thread, pin, eye, sewing, sharp, point, pricked, thimble, haystack, pain, hurt, injection*. Experimental participants studied each list, and then tried to recall the words contained in it, and on some of the lists (including the *needle* list) many participants falsely recalled the critical word as having been included in the list, though on other lists they did not—for example, on the *butterfly* list (*moth, cocoon*, and so on), not a single participant falsely recalled the critical word. In an article in the *Journal of Experimental Psychology: Learning, Memory, and Cognition* in 1995, the US psychologists Henry L(ederer) Roediger III (born 1947) and Kathleen B(lyth) McDermott (born 1968) replicated and extended Deese's neglected experiment using published word-association norms. Their results revealed that on immediate *free recall tests, the missing critical words were falsely recalled by 40 per cent of participants, and in a subsequent experiment with 15-word lists, the rate of false recall rose to 55 per cent. This experimental procedure creates a powerful *cognitive illusion, causing people to believe that they can remember experiences that did not occur. *See also* eyewitness misinformation effect.

experimental neurosis *n.* An abnormal pattern of behaviour in an animal usually induced by presenting it with an insoluble learning problem or subjecting it to inescapable electric shocks. *See also* learned helplessness.

experimental psychology *n.* The study of psychological processes such as cognition (including perception, memory, thinking, and language), learning, and skills through controlled experiments. The term was originally applied to any psychological research using experimental methods, but it has acquired specialized connotations, and in practice experimental research in social psychology, for example, is not normally published in the major journals of experimental psychology.

experimental variable *n.* Another name for an *independent variable.

experimenter bias *See* experimenter effect, experimenter expectancy effect.

experimenter effect *n.* A biasing effect on the results of an experiment caused by expectations or preconceptions on the part of the experimenter. Also called *experimenter bias. See also* demand characteristics, experimenter expectancy effect.

experimenter expectancy effect n. A particular type of *experimenter effect in which the expectations of the experimenter as to the likely outcome of the experiment acts as a *self-fulfilling prophecy, biasing the results in the direction of the expectation. In a series of classic experiments carried out by the German-born US psychologist Robert Rosenthal (born 1933) in the early 1960s, the effect was induced by telling experimenters what kind of behaviour to expect from laboratory animals. In one experiment published in 1963, 12 psychology students were each given five laboratory rats of the same strain, but six were told that the rats had been bred for maze brightness and the other six that they had been bred for maze dullness. The students were given the assignment of running the rats in a maze-learning experiment, and the rats believed to be bright performed significantly better than those believed to be dull. Later research suggested that in such experiments the effect is due to subtle differences in the way experimenters handle the animals. Also called the *Rosenthal effect. See also* demand characteristics, Oedipus effect, Pygmalion effect.

expert system n. In *artificial intelligence, a computer program based on a database of expert knowledge in a specified field, such as medical diagnosis, designed to offer advice or make decisions requiring a high level of expertise.

explicit memory n. Memory that is revealed when performance on a task requires conscious recollection of information previously learnt. The term was introduced by the Canadian psychologist Peter Graf (born 1951) and the US psychologist Daniel L. Schacter (born 1952) in an article in the *Journal of Experimental Psychology: Learning, Memory, and Cognition* in 1985. *Compare* implicit memory.

exploitative orientation n. In *neo-Freudian theory, a term used by the German-born US psychoanalyst Erich Fromm (1900–80) to denote a character type who tries to take things from others by force and cunning, an extreme example being a person with *kleptomania. *Compare* hoarding orientation, marketing orientation, productive orientation, receptive orientation.

exploratory data analysis n. A general term introduced in 1977 by the US statistician John

Wilder Tukey (1915–2000) to refer to techniques of summarizing, organizing, and displaying data in ways that help to show what the data mean. Typical examples are *box-and-whisker plots and *stem-and-leaf displays. Not to be confused with *data snooping. **EDA** *abbrev.*

exploratory factor analysis n. The use of *factor analysis to discover the latent factors lying behind a set of correlated variables. *Compare* confirmatory factor analysis.

exploratory research n. Research that is not explicitly intended to test hypotheses (as in *basic research) nor to solve practical problems (as in *applied research) but is used to make initial forays into unfamiliar territory when studying new or poorly understood phenomena. *Compare* action research, descriptive research, evaluation research.

explosive disorder *See* intermittent explosive disorder.

exposure therapy n. Another name for *flooding.

expression n. **1.** The transformation of ideas into words. **2.** Any non-verbal manifestation of *emotion. **3.** In genetics, the effect of a *gene on a *phenotype (also called *gene expression*). **express** *vb.* **expressive** *adj.*
[From Latin *expressus* squeezed out, from *ex-* out + *premere*, *pressum* to press + *-ion* indicating an action, process, or state]

expressive aphasia *See under* aphasia.

expressive behaviour n. Behaviour that communicates emotions or personality. In human beings this occurs especially through *facial expression, though it can also occur through other types of *affect displays, dress styles, handwriting, and so on.

expressive dysprosody *See* dysprosody.

expressive language disorder n. A *communication disorder characterized by a measured level of expressive *language (1) development substantially below the person's non-verbal intelligence and language comprehension, the deficit interfering substantially with scholastic, academic, or occupational achievement or social interaction and not being due solely to mental retardation, speech or sensory deficit, or environmental deprivation. *See also* aphasia. *Compare* receptive language disorder.

expressivity *n.* In genetics, the strength of a gene's effect on a *phenotype.

extended family *n.* A family unit comprising not only a mother, father, and their children, but also other relatives, such as grandparents, uncles, and aunts. *Compare* nuclear family.

extended phenotype *n.* All effects that a *gene has on the external world in comparison with the effects of its *alleles, including effects associated with such phenomena as *co-evolution, *inclusive fitness, evolutionary *arms races, and *reciprocal altruism, all of which have a bearing on the number of copies of the gene that are likely to be transmitted to the next generation. It is distinguished from the conventional *phenotype, which is restricted to the gene's effects on the individual organism in which it resides and which excludes extra-organismic effects associated with such phenomena. *See also* selfish gene. [Coined in 1982 by the British ethologist Richard Dawkins (born 1941) in the title of his book *The Extended Phenotype*]

extension/intension *See* intension.

extension theorem *n.* In *logic, a theorem of semantic entailment in propositional calculus according to which if a set of premises *P* entails a conclusion *q*, then the addition of further premises from a larger set *S* that includes *P* cannot affect the truth of the conclusion *q*. The theorem underpins the *monotonicity of logic. *See also* default reasoning, non-monotonic reasoning.

external auditory canal *n.* The passageway leading from the *outer ear to the *tympanic membrane. Also called the *external meatus*. *Compare* internal auditory canal.

external control of reinforcement *See under* locus of control.

external ear *n.* Another name for the *outer ear.

external eye muscle *n.* Another name for an *extra-ocular muscle.

externalization *n.* In *psychoanalysis, a *defence mechanism whereby a person unconsciously attributes inner impulses to the external world, as when a child converts unconscious angry or aggressive impulses into a fear of monsters or demons in the dark. A common form of externalization is *projection (1). *See also* defensive technique. **externalize** *vb.*

external meatus *n.* Another name for the *external auditory canal. [From Latin *meatus* a course]

external rectus *n.* Another name for either of the lateral *rectus muscles attached externally to the eyeball.

external validity *n.* The extent to which the conclusions of an empirical investigation remain true when different research methods and research participants or subjects are used. The term is also used to denote *concurrent validity or *predictive validity established by reference to an external criterion, in other words *criterion validity. *See also* replication (2), validity, validity generalization. *Compare* ecological validity (1), internal validity.

exteroception *n.* Any form of sensation that results from stimuli located outside the body and is detected by *exteroceptors, including vision, hearing, touch or pressure, heat, cold, pain, smell, and taste. *Compare* interoception, kinaesthesis, proprioception. **exteroceptive** *adj.* [From Latin *exterus* exterior + English *receptor* + -*ion* indicating an action, process, or state]

exteroceptor *n.* Any of several *sensory receptors specialized for *exteroception, whether a *somatic receptor or a *telereceptor. *Compare* interoceptor, proprioceptor.

extinction *n.* **1.** The wiping out or elimination of something, including a species or life form. **2.** The diminution in the strength or frequency of a *conditioned response as a result of its having been elicited repeatedly without *reinforcement (1, 2). *Compare* habituation (2). **extinct** *adj.*

extracellular *adj.* Outside cells. [From Latin *extra* outside + *cella* a room, from *celare* to hide]

extracellular fluid n. Fluid that circulates around and between the cells of the body and is separated from the *intracellular fluid by semipermeable cell membranes. See also osmosis, sodium pump. Compare intracellular fluid. **ECF** abbrev.

extracellular thirst n. Another name for *hypovolaemic thirst.

extradite vb. **1.** To hand a person over to a foreign government for trial or punishment. **2.** To localize a sensation away from the centre of the sensation. See eccentric projection. **extradition** n. The act or process of *extraditing.
[From Latin ex from + traditio a handing over, from tradere to give up, from trans across + dare to give]

extrafusal adj. Of or relating to ordinary contractile muscle fibres outside *muscle spindles. When an extrafusal fibre is stimulated by a *motor neuron, *actin filaments slide to overlap with *myosin filaments, causing the muscle to contract. Compare intrafusal.
[From Latin extra outside + fusus a spindle]

extraneous variable n. In statistics and research design, a variable that is of no immediate interest to a researcher but is capable of influencing variables that are of interest. In experimental design, such an extraneous variable is capable of influencing the *dependent variable, and it is normally controlled by *randomization; when it cannot be controlled, efforts are often made to measure and allow for it. Also called a nuisance variable.

extra-ocular muscle n. A generic name for either of the *oblique muscles or any of the *rectus muscles that control the rotation of the eyeball within its socket. Also called an extrinsic eye muscle. See also electro-oculogram.
[From Latin extra outside + oculus an eye]

extrapyramidal adj. Of or relating to structures outside the pyramidal tract or *corticospinal tract of the central nervous system, the pathway responsible for coordinating and integrating motor behaviour.
[From Latin extra outside + English pyramidal]

extrapyramidal syndrome n. A condition arising from a lesion in the *extrapyramidal system or as a side-effect of medication with psychotropic drugs, including such signs and symptoms as *tremor, *parkinsonism, *akathisia, *dystonia, *akinesia, *myotonia, drooling, and absence of facial expression.

extra-sensory perception n. A generic term for various conjectural *paranormal phenomena that are defined by the Journal of Parapsychology to involve experience of, or response to, a target object, state, event, or influence without sensory contact, hence perception without the use of sense organs, usually divided into *clairvoyance, *telepathy, and *precognition. It is often defined as perception by means as yet unexplained by science, but this debilitating interpretation is avoided in careful usage, because it encompasses types of perception that are not necessarily extra-sensory or paranormal and therefore implies (for example) that the *infra-red vision of rattlesnakes was a form of extra-sensory perception before it was explained in the 1930s, that the use of *biosonar by bats was a form of extra-sensory perception before it was explained in 1941, and that the use of the stars as a navigational aid by nocturnally migrant birds such as European warblers was a form of extra-sensory perception before it was explained in the mid 1950s; and there are numerous phenomena in human and animal perception that are still unexplained but do not necessarily involve extra-sensory perception. See also cryptaesthesia, psi, psi-missing, Zener cards. Compare psychokinesis. **ESP** abbrev.
[From Latin extra outside + sensorius of the senses, from sensus felt, from sentire to sense. The US parapsychologist Joseph Banks Rhine (1895–1980) claimed in 1934 to have coined the term, but a book by the Haitian-born German physician Gustav Pagenstecher (1855–1942) entitled Aussersinnlicher Wahrnehmung, which means extra-sensory perception in German, had already been published in 1924]

extra-spectral colour n. Another name for a *non-spectral colour. US extra-spectral color.
[From Latin extra outside + spectrum a spectacle, from spectare to watch, from specere to look at + -alis of or relating to]

extrastriate cortex n. Areas of the cerebral cortex near and functionally related to the *primary visual cortex (Area V1).

[So called because they are outside the *striate cortex]

extraversion n. One of the *Big Five personality factors, ranging from extreme extraversion, characterized by *traits such as sociability and assertiveness, to extreme *introversion, characterized by reserve and passivity. The concept of introversion/extraversion was introduced in 1910 by Carl Gustav Jung (1875–1961). Also called *surgency*. Often spelt *extroversion*, but this is an unnecessary deviation from the Latin root. See also little thirty. **extravert** n. A person who manifests *extraversion. **extraverted** adj.
[From Latin *extra* outside + *vertere* to turn]

extrinsic eye muscle n. Another name for an *extra-ocular muscle.
[From Latin *extrinsecus* on the outside, from *exter* outward + *secus* alongside]

eye n. The organ of vision in animals, each of the human eyeballs being protected by an upper and a lower eyelid and rotating within its bony orbit under the control of four *rectus muscles and two *oblique muscles, its structure allowing light to enter through the transparent external *cornea and to pass through the *aqueous humour, the dark central adjustable *pupil in the iris, the *crystalline lens, and the *vitreous humour, to be projected on to the *retina where light-sensitive *photoreceptors specialized to convert the light into nerve impulses transmit visual information along the *optic nerve via the *lateral geniculate nuclei to the *visual cortex (see illustration). *Compare* compound eye, ommatidium.

eye contact n. The event of two people simultaneously *gazing at each other in the vicinity of each other's eyes. Also called *mutual gaze. See also* equilibrium hypothesis, gaze aversion, non-verbal communication, regulator.

eye dialect n. An alteration to the spelling of words to indicate a regional or social *dialect, as in the following: *Aw knaow you. Youre the one that took way may girl. Youre the one that set er agen me. Well, I'm gowin to ev er aht* (Bill Walker, 'a rough customer of about 25', in Act II of George Bernard Shaw's play *Major Barbara*).

eye dominance n. An unconscious preference for the use of one eye rather than the other, analogous to hand preference, though there is no simple relation between the two.

eye-dominance column n. Another name for an *ocular-dominance column.

eye–head movement system n. A subsystem of the visual system that enables the movement of objects in the environment to be computed from the *image–retinal system, discounting movements of the eyes and head, necessary because movements of images across the retinas provide insufficient information for determining movement of objects in the environment, given that eye and head movements cause retinal images to move even when the objects themselves are stationary. *See also* reafference.

eye-movement desensitization and reprocessing n. A form of *psychotherapy designed originally for treating *post-traumatic stress disorder (PTSD) and sometimes applied to

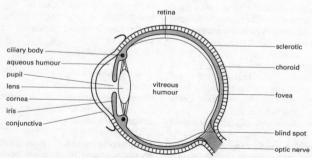

Eye. Main structures of the vertebrate eye.

other anxiety disorders. When it is applied to PTSD, the client or patient is first asked to visualize or recall the traumatic experience as vividly as possible and to provide a verbal statement, such as *I feel as if I'm about to die*, epitomizing its psychological impact. The client then rates the experienced level of anxiety on a 0–10 scale of Subjective Units of Distress (SUDs) and provides a competing positive statement epitomizing a desired response to the imagined situation, such as *I can survive*, and a rating of degree of belief in this statement, on a 0–8 scale of Validity of Cognition. Following these preparatory steps, the client focuses visual attention on an object and tracks its movements as the therapist sweeps it rhythmically back and forth in groups of 12 to 24 side-to-side movements in front of the client's face, at a rate of approximately two strokes per second. After each group of strokes, the client is asked to blank out the visual image or memory, to inhale deeply, and to revise the SUD and Validity of Cognition ratings, and this process continues until the SUD rating falls below 2 and the Validity of Cognition rating rises above 6. The technique was developed in 1987 and introduced in 1989 by the US psychologist Francine Shapiro (born 1948), who discovered fortuitously that back-and-forth eye movements reduced her own anxiety. **EMDR** *abbrev.*

eye-movement potential *n.* A brief, high-amplitude *EEG spike, identical in appearance to a *PGO spike and originating in the same brain structures, but occurring in the waking state as an alerting response to unexpected sensory stimuli.

eye-placement principle *n.* A principle of composition in portrait painting that involves the placement of one of the subject's eyes somewhere on the vertical axis running down the centre of the frame. It was discovered by the British-born US psychologist Christopher W(illiam) Tyler (born 1943) and published in the journal *Nature* in 1997. Tyler found that it has governed portrait painting throughout the modern period, 68 per cent of portraits showing one of the sitter's eyes within a narrow strip centred on the vertical axis occupying 10 per cent of the frame width, but that it had not been mentioned in manuals of composition, suggesting that it operates unconsciously.

eye rhyme *n.* Words that have similar endings in their written form but are pronounced differently, such as *love* and *move*.

eye–voice span *n.* In relation to a person who is reading aloud, the average number of units (either words or syllables) by which the speech is ahead of the written text, used as a measure of reading proficiency.

eyewitness misinformation effect *n.* A phenomenon whereby misleading post-event information distorts an eyewitness's recall of an event, as when a victim of a sexual assault who is subsequently told that an arrested suspect has a tattoo on his left arm comes to believe that she can recall seeing a tattoo on the perpetrator's arm. The effect may be caused by the post-event information overwriting the original memory, or by the eyewitness becoming confused about the sources of different items of information, without the original memory necessarily being impaired. These processes were first studied systematically by the US psychologists Elizabeth F. Loftus (born 1944) and John Palmer (born 1954), who reported their findings in the *Journal of Verbal Learning and Verbal Behavior* in 1974, and the effect was discussed at length by Loftus in her book *Eyewitness Testimony* (1979). In the original experiment, participants viewed a video recording of two cars colliding, and they were then asked how fast the cars were going when they *hit* or when they *smashed* into each other; when the word *smashed* was used in the question, the participants estimated the speed as 7 miles per hour faster, on average, than when the word *hit* was used, and a week later, 32 per cent of those exposed to the word *smashed* falsely recalled broken glass in the video, compared to only 14 per cent of those exposed to the word *hit*. Also called the *misinformation effect*. *See also* experimentally induced false memory, false memory, false memory syndrome, paramnesia (1), Piaget kidnapping memory, reality monitoring, recovered memory.

eyewitness testimony *n.* Evidence of events that occurred, actions that were performed, or words that were spoken, given in court by a person who observed the events or actions at first hand or heard the words being spoken. *See also* eyewitness misinformation effect, false memory, weapon focus.

Eysenck Personality Inventory *n.* A questionnaire designed to measure two major dimensions of personality, namely *extraversion and *neuroticism, according to the theory of personality propounded by the German-born British psychologist Hans J(ürgen) Eysenck (1916–97). It was published in 1963 as a commercial test by Hans and Sybil B. G. Eysenck (born 1927), as a revision of the *Maudsley Personality Inventory. *See also* Eysenck Personality Questionnaire. **EPI** *abbrev.*

Eysenck Personality Questionnaire *n.* A revised version of the *Eysenck Personality Inventory (EPI), measuring three major dimensions of personality, namely *extraversion, *neuroticism, and *psychoticism, and including a *lie scale. It was published as a commercial test in 1975. **EPQ** *abbrev.*

F₁ *abbrev.* The first *filial generation. F_2 represents the second filial generation, and so on.

face–goblet illusion *n.* Another name for the *reversible goblet.

face recognition *n.* The sum total of the processes involved in the recognition and identification of faces. *See also* fusiform gyrus, prosopagnosia, superior temporal sulcus.

face validity *n.* The *validity of a test estimated or judged intuitively, without recourse to any objective evidence. Also called *a priori validity*. *See also* consensual validity, intrinsic validity.

facial expression *n.* A form of *non-verbal communication in which an *affect display is communicated via the face, the musculature of which is sufficiently complex to enable a vast range of expressions to be conveyed. *See also* dialectical montage, display rule, expressive behaviour, facial nerve, Möbius syndrome, primary emotion.

facial nerve *n.* Either of the seventh pair of *cranial nerves, supplying the muscles involved in *facial expression, the salivary and nasal glands, the taste buds towards the front two-thirds of the tongue, and the stapedius muscle of the inner ear. It is the most frequently paralysed of all peripheral nerves, as in *Bell's palsy. *See also* chorda tympani, corneal reflex, glossopalatine nerve.

facial vision *n.* An awareness of obstacles without vision, experienced by people who are blindfolded and often highly developed in people who are blind, usually felt as a tactile sensation in the facial area but shown by experiments to be explained by reflected sound waves and mediated entirely by hearing. Also called *obstacle sense*. *See also* biosonar.

facilitated communication *n.* A teaching method and therapeutic technique in which facilitators or partners help people with severe developmental disabilities to communicate by providing sufficient manual guidance to enable them to convey messages through a keyboard, a picture board, or a speech synthesizer. When applied to a person with *autistic disorder, *cerebral palsy, *Down's syndrome, or severe *mental retardation, it often appears to reveal unexpected literacy and a far higher level of intellectual functioning than the person was believed to possess, but *single-blind studies and *double-blind studies have revealed that disabled people are unable to respond intelligently to stimuli that are unseen by their facilitators and that the facilitators unwittingly control the responses in a manner reminiscent of *Clever Hans. It was pioneered by the Australian special needs educator Rosemary Crossley (born 1945), who applied it to 12 children with physical and mental handicaps in the early 1970s, and in 1989 it was adopted enthusiastically by a number of speech therapists and special educators in the United States. Also called *facilitated communication training*. **FC** or **FCT** *abbrev.*

facilitation *n.* The act or process of assisting the progress of something or making it easier; more specifically, the increased ease with which *neurons transmit impulses as a result of prior excitation. *See also* cell assembly, long-term potentiation, phase sequence.
[From Latin *facilis* easy, from *facere* to do + *-ation* indicating a process or condition]

facilitative priming *See under* priming (1).

factitious disorder *n.* A persistent pattern of feigned symptoms and/or self-inflicted injuries to simulate disorder, in the absence of a confirmed physical or mental condition, and without any economic or other external incentive for the behaviour, the motive being to receive medical treatment, to gain admission to hospital, or to assume the sick role, multiple surgical operations often being eagerly sought. Also called *Munchausen syndrome*, *pathomimicry*, or (colloquially) *hospital hopper syndrome. See also* factitious disorder by proxy, Ganser syndrome. *Compare* compensation neurosis, malingering, pseudologia fantastica, somatoform disorders.

[From Latin *facticius* artificial or made, from *facere* to make]

factitious disorder by proxy *n.* A pattern of behaviour included in the *DSM-IV appendix of conditions meriting further study, but not in the *ICD-10 classification, characterized by intentional feigning of physical or psychological signs or symptoms in another person who is being cared for, without any economic or other external incentive for the behaviour, the motive being to procure medical treatment for the person being cared for and thereby to assume a sick role by proxy. According to the British paediatrician (Samuel) Roy (later Sir Roy) Meadow (born 1933), who was the first to identify the phenomenon and who coined the alternative term *Munchausen by proxy syndrome* (*MBPS*) in 1977, it is not a psychological disorder but a form of physical or psychological abuse of children or others being cared for. *See also* factitious disorder.

factor *n.* **1.** In experimental design, another name for an *independent variable. **2.** In *factor analysis, one of the underlying dimensions derived from the larger number of original variables. It is a derived, hypothetical dimension that accounts, in part, for the correlations between a number of variables. The term is also commonly applied to the psychological *construct associated with the dimension derived from factor analysis, as when the common factor *g is interpreted as general intelligence. *See also* group factor. **3.** More generally, anything that contributes to an outcome or result. **factorial** *adj.*

[From Latin *factor* something that acts, from *facere* to do]

factor analysis *n.* A statistical technique for analysing the correlations between a large number of variables in order to reduce them to a smaller number of underlying dimensions, called *factors*, in a manner analogous to

the way in which all spectral colours can be reduced to combinations of just three primary colours, and to determine how much of the *variance in each of the original variables is explained by each factor. *See also* analysis of covariance structures, cluster analysis, communality, confirmatory factor analysis, correspondence analysis, exploratory factor analysis, g, primary mental abilities, principal-components analysis, Q-methodology, R-methodology, rotation, simple structure. **factor-analytic** *adj.*

factorial analysis of variance *n.* Another name for *multifactorial analysis of variance.

factorial design *n.* Any experimental design in which there are two or more *independent variables or factors, and every level of each factor is combined with every level of each other factor. For example, if there are two factors, and if one of the factors has two levels, the other has three levels, and all six combinations are represented, then the design is called a 2×3 factorial design.

factorial validity *n.* The *validity of a test determined by its *correlation with a *factor (2) determined by *factor analysis. The idea behind this form of validity was introduced by the English statistician and psychologist Charles Spearman (1863–1945) in an article in the *American Journal of Psychology* in 1904, where he interpreted intelligence as the factor g that underlies all test items and subtests with good *content validity (that is, items and subtests that appear to require intelligence) and argued that the most valid tests are those with highest loadings on the factor g.

faculty psychology *n.* An obsolete school of psychology based on arbitrarily posited powers or capacities (called *faculties*) into which the mind was divided, such as will, reason, and instinct, through whose interaction all mental functions and phenomena were supposed to occur. The most influential figure in the development of this approach was the German philosopher and mathematician Christian Wolff (1679–1754), whose *Psychologia Empirica* (1732) and *Psychologia Rationalis* (1734) popularized a version of faculty psychology that formed the foundation for the later development of *phrenology.

[From Latin *facultas* a capacity]

failure neurosis *n*. A term introduced in 1939 by the French psychoanalyst René Laforgue (1894–1962) for a class of disorders characterized by behaviour that appears calculated to bring misfortunes on oneself and an inability to accept the things that one most ardently desires. This syndrome is an extension and elaboration of ideas first set forth in 1916 by Sigmund Freud (1856–1939) in an article entitled 'Some Character-Types Met With in Psycho-Analytic Work' (*Standard Edition*, XIV, pp. 311–33, at pp. 317–18). Also called *failure syndrome*. Compare fate neurosis.

Fairbairn's revised psychopathology *n*. In *psychoanalysis, a term used to denote the theory of mental disorder proposed by the Scottish psychoanalyst W. Ronald D. Fairbairn (1889–1964), especially his theory of the *defensive technique. He published an early version of it in 1941 in an article entitled 'A Revised Psychopathology of the Psychoses and Psychoneuroses', reprinted in his book *Psychoanalytic Studies of the Personality* (1952). *See* hysterical technique, obsessional technique, paranoid technique, phobic technique.

falling out *n*. A *culture-bound syndrome found among communities in the southern United States and the Caribbean, characterized by a sudden collapse, occurring either without warning or after a brief spell of dizziness, followed by a sensation of blindness, although the eyes are open, and an inability to speak or move although the person is aware of what is happening in the immediate vicinity. It is sometimes interpreted as a *conversion disorder or a *dissociative disorder. Also called *blacking out*.

false alarm *n*. **1.** A warning signal that turns out to have been unnecessary. **2.** In *signal detection theory, an incorrect detection of a signal when it is absent. Also called a *false positive*. *See also* memory operating characteristic, receiver operating characteristic. *Compare* correct rejection, hit, miss.

false anorexia *n*. Another name for *pseudoanorexia.

false-consensus effect *n*. A form of *assimilation (4) characterized by a tendency to overestimate the extent to which other people share one's beliefs, attitudes, and behaviours.

In *social perception and *attribution, people tend to assume that their own responses are more common than they really are and to consider alternative responses as uncommon, deviant, or inappropriate. The concept was introduced and named by the Canadian psychologist Lee D(avid) Ross (born 1942) and two colleagues in an article in the *Journal of Experimental Social Psychology* in 1977 in which they reported four experiments, including a typical one in which Stanford University students were asked whether they would be willing to walk around the campus for 30 minutes wearing a sandwich board inscribed with the message REPENT; those who agreed to do this estimated, on average, that 63.50 per cent of their fellow students would also agree, and those who refused estimated that 76.67 per cent of their fellow students would also refuse. *See also* assimilation–contrast theory, automorphic perception, egocentrism.

false friends *n*. Words in different languages that resemble each other but have different meanings. For example, in French *magasin* means shop or store, not magazine, and *sensible* means sensitive, not sensible; and in German *Mist* means excrement, not mist, and *Gift* means poison, not gift.

false memory *n*. An apparent recollection of something that one did not actually experience, especially sexual abuse during infancy or childhood, often arising from suggestion implanted during counselling or psychotherapy. A classic example, though one unrelated to counselling and psychotherapy, is the *Piaget kidnapping memory. Also called a *pseudomemory* or *pseudomnesia*. *See also* deferred action, déjà vu, experimentally induced false memory, eyewitness misinformation effect, false memory syndrome, infantile amnesia, paramnesia (1), recovered memory.

false memory syndrome *n*. A condition in which a person's identity and personal relationships are strongly influenced by an objectively false but strongly believed memory of a traumatic experience, such as an objectively false recollection of sexual abuse by a parent or other relative or abduction by alien beings. *See* false memory. *See also* constructive memory, eyewitness misinformation effect, infantile amnesia, paramnesia (1), Piaget kidnapping memory, reconstructive memory, recovered memory. **FMS** *abbrev*.

false negative *n*. An incorrect classification of an element as not belonging to a class to which it does in fact belong or, especially in *signal detection theory, a failure to detect a signal when it is in fact present. Also called a *miss*. *Compare* correct rejection, false alarm (2), hit.

false neurotransmitter *n*. Any substance that is not a neuron's normal *neurotransmitter but that can be taken up by the neuron, stored in its vesicles, and released along with the neuron's normal neurotransmitter when the neuron is stimulated. It may inhibit the function of the neuron if it is less effective than the normal neurotransmitter or enhance the neuron's function if it is more effective.

false positive *n*. An incorrect classification of an element as a member of a class to which it does not in fact belong, as when a decision procedure results in a person being wrongly diagnosed as having a disorder. In *signal detection theory it is often called a *false alarm*. *Compare* correct rejection, hit, miss.

false pregnancy *n*. Another name for *pseudocyesis.

falsifiability *n*. In the philosophy of science, the property of a *hypothesis or theory of being capable of refutation by *empirical evidence, with the implication that a hypothesis lacking this property does not belong to science. The concept was introduced by the Austrian-born British philosopher Karl R(aimund) Popper (1902–94) as a solution to the problem of *induction (1) and as a criterion of demarcation between science, which deals with falsifiable hypotheses, and metaphysics, which admits unfalsifiable propositions. *See also* confirmation bias, hypothetico-deductive method. *Compare* logical empiricism, logical positivism.

family *n*. **1.** The primary social group, comprising parents, their offspring, and in some societies other relatives sharing the same household (the extended family); or more generally any group of individuals related by blood or descended from an identifiable common ancestor. **2.** In biology, a *taxonomic group into which an *order (3) is divided, containing one or more *genera. For example, Felidae, the cat family, and Canidae, the dog

family, together with the other meat-eating families of bears, raccoons, hyenas, civets, and weasels are all members of the order Carnivora.
[From Latin *familia* a household]

family neurosis *n*. A term used mainly in French *psychoanalysis, not to denote any specific disorder, but to refer to the tendency for individual neuroses of family members to complement and reinforce one another. The concept was introduced in the title of an article published in a French psychoanalytic journal in 1936: 'La névrose familiale'.

family study *n*. In behaviour genetics, another name for a *kinship study.

family therapy *n*. A form of *psychotherapy, based on the assumption that psychological problems are often rooted in and sustained by family relationships, in which two or more members of a family participate simultaneously with the aim of improving communication and modes of interaction between them. *See also* systems theory.

famous names test *n*. A technique for measuring *long-term memory and providing evidence for *amnesia. Respondents are presented with the names of people who were famous for limited periods up to several decades previously and are asked to try to identify them and recall what they were famous for. The names that are chosen are usually of people such as Winston Churchill, John F. Kennedy, and Elvis Presley, who were so famous that respondents with intact memories are expected to remember all of them.

fan effect *n*. A tendency for the amount of time required to retrieve a particular fact about a concept to increase with the number of facts that are known about that concept. The effect has been found in retrieval of various categories of knowledge, and also in face recognition, and it may in part be responsible for the slowing of memory retrieval with age. The concept was first reported in 1974 by the Canadian-born US psychologist John R(obert) Anderson (born 1947), who performed an experiment in which participants tried to memorize a list of 26 sentences about people in locations, such as *A hippie is in the park*, *A hippie is in the church*, and *A lawyer is in the cave*. In the list, each person (concept) was associated with

either one, two, or three locations (facts); for example, *hippie* was associated with *park*, *church*, and *bank*, and in addition each location was associated with either one, two, or three persons, for example, *cave* was associated with *lawyer* only. Recall was tested by asking the participants to pick out the target sentences from a list in which the sentences that they had learnt were mixed up with *foils constructed from the same people and locations in novel combinations. The average time required to accept target sentences and reject foils was 1.19 seconds for concepts with one associated fact, 1.28 seconds for concepts with two associated facts, and 1.30 for concepts with three associated facts, and this effect has been replicated many times. *See also* ACT*.
[An acronym, from *f*acts *a*ssociated with *n*ode, a concept being represented by a *node (2) in Anderson's network model. Anderson did not use the word *fan* in his original 1974 article but began using it immediately after]

fantasize *vb.* To engage in *fantasy (1) or to produce *fantasies (1, 2).

fantasticant *See* phantasticant.

fantasy *n.* **1.** Imagination or mental *imagery. *See also* alexithymia, fantasy thinking, hypoactive sexual desire disorder. **2.** A product of the imagination, especially one detached from reality, or a *daydream such as the *Madame Butterfly fantasy. *See also* primal fantasy. **3.** A whimsical or unrealistic plan or idea. Also spelt *phantasy*.
[From Latin *phantasia* a fantasy, from Greek *phantazein* to make visible, from *phainein* to show, from *phaein* to shine]

fantasy thinking *n.* In *analytical psychology, a form of thinking based on *fantasy (1) that relies on *imagery, *emotion, and *intuition, without logical or moral constraints. It is closely related to the *primary process of *psychoanalysis, and it occurs in dreams and mythology; it is debatable whether it should be called thinking. Carl Gustav Jung (1875–1961) contrasted it with *directed thinking (*Collected Works*, 5, paragraphs 4–46).

far point *n.* The most distant point from the eye at which an object is focused on the retina without *accommodation (1) of the crystalline lens, theoretically located at infinity for a normal eye but in practice usually set as 6 metres or 20 feet. *See also* range of accommodation. *Compare* near point.

far sense *n.* Any of the senses, such as vision or hearing, that are mediated by *telereceptors and that enable an organism to perceive objects or events at a distance. Also called a *distance sense*. *Compare* near sense.

far-sighted *adj.* **1.** Having the ability to see at great distances. **2.** Exhibiting foresight and shrewd judgement. **3.** A non-technical word for *hyperopic. **far-sightedness** *n.*

far vision *n.* Distance viewing, usually defined for objects more than 2 feet or about 60 centimetres from the eyes. *See also* accommodation (1), accommodation reflex, ciliary reflex, myopia, sympathetic nervous system. *Compare* near vision.

fascicle *n.* Another name for a *fasciculus.
[From Latin *fascis* a bundle]

fasciculus *n.* A small bundle or bunch, especially a bundle of nerve fibres such as the *arcuate fasciculus, *fasciculus cuneatus, *fasciculus gracilis, *inferior longitudinal fasciculus, *superior longitudinal fasciculus, *subthalamic fasciculus, or *uncinate fasciculus. Also called a *fascicle*.
[From Latin *fasciculus* a small bundle, diminutive of *fascis* a bundle]

fasciculus cuneatus *n.* A subdivision of the bundle of ascending nerve fibres in the posterior funiculus of the spinal cord, the part towards either side that carries information about touch and position from the arm on the same side of the body and that terminates in the *cuneate nucleus. *See also* dorsal column. *Compare* fasciculus gracilis.
[From Latin *cuneatus* wedge-shaped, from *cuneus* a wedge]

fasciculus gracilis *n.* A subdivision of the bundle of ascending nerve fibres in the posterior funiculus of the spinal cord, the part towards the centre that carries information about touch and position of the leg on the same side of the body and that terminates in the *gracile nucleus. *Compare* fasciculus cuneatus.
[From Latin *gracilis* slender]

fast glycolytic fibre *n.* A type of *fast-twitch fibre that is light-coloured and is adapted for

*anaerobic metabolism. US *fast glycolytic fiber.* *Compare* fast oxidative glycolytic fibre. **FG fibre** *abbrev.*
[So called because it is adapted for metabolism by *glycolysis]

fast oxidative glycolytic fibre *n.* A type of *fast-twitch fibre that is red and is adapted for oxidative metabolism. US *fast oxidative glycolytic fiber.* *Compare* fast glycolytic fibre. **FOG fibre** *abbrev.*
[So called because it is adapted for oxidative or aerobic metabolism by *glycolysis]

fast-twitch fibre *n.* A *striped muscle fibre that responds quickly and powerfully but is more prone to fatigue than *slow-twitch fibre. US *fast-twitch fiber.* *See* fast glycolytic fibre, fast oxidative glycolytic fibre.

fatal familial insomnia *n.* A human *prion disease characterized by *insomnia, disorders of the *autonomic nervous system, *ataxia, *dementia, and death within three years. **FFI** *abbrev.*

fate neurosis *n.* In *psychoanalysis, a syndrome of repeating patterns of unpleasant life events, the recurrences appearing to be misfortunes but bearing an uncanny similarity to one another. It was discussed by Sigmund Freud (1856–1939) in 1920 in his book *Beyond the Pleasure Principle* (*Standard Edition*, XVIII, 7–64, at pp. 21–2), where he gave examples of people whose good deeds are constantly repaid by ingratitude or bad luck, people who are repeatedly betrayed by friends, and similar cases, and he explained it as a manifestation of a *repetition compulsion. The word that Freud coined was *Schicksalzwang* (fate compulsion) rather than *Schicksalneurose* (fate neurosis), but the latter term became conventional in both German and English. *Compare* failure neurosis.

father complex *n.* In *psychoanalysis, *ambivalence in a boy's feelings towards his father, being one of the elements of the *Oedipus complex. *See also* complex (2).

fatigue *n.* **1.** Weariness or exhaustion, normally resulting from physical or mental work or lack of sleep. **2.** In physiology, a temporary diminution in the response of an organ or part to a stimulus resulting from overactivity.

[From French *fatiguer* to tire, from Latin *fatigare* to tire]

fatigue syndrome *See* chronic fatigue syndrome.

fattism *n.* Discrimination against people who are overweight, or the tendency to poke fun at them. The word was coined by the US psychologist Rita (Jackaway) Freedman in her book *Bodylove* (1988). Also spelt *fatism.* *Compare* ableism, ageism, ethnocentrism, heterosexism, racism, sexism, speciesism.
fattist or **fatist** *n.* **1.** One who practises or advocates *fattism. *adj.* **2.** Of or relating to *fattism.
[From *fat* + Greek *-ismos* indicating a state or condition, on the model of words such as *racism*]

fatuous love *n.* A type of love characterized by erotic passion and commitment but lacking intimacy. *See also under* love.
[From Latin *fatuus* foolish]

fear of success *n.* Anxiety about accomplishing goals and achieving ambitions, especially among women because of cultural associations of ambition and success with lack of femininity, as a consequence of which success can lead to social rejection and disapproval. The concept was introduced in 1968 in a doctoral dissertation by the US psychologist Matina S(ouretis) Horner (born 1929) and became well known after an article by her in the *Journal of Social Issues* in 1972. Horner presented men and women with the following brief statement and asked them to write stories based on it: 'After first-term finals, (Anne/John) finds (herself/himself) at the top of (his/her) medical class.' The stories written by women responding to the version with the female character called Anne often expressed ambivalence and conflict over Anne's success—they described Anne living a lonely and miserable life, being ugly and horrid, having no love life, and so on. Evidence of fear of success was found in only 10 per cent of stories written by men but in 65 per cent of stories written by women. Later research reported some decline in fear of success among women as gender inequality declined after the early 1970s, and evidence emerged that both men and women fear success in various circumstances, including occupations that are not traditional for their gender. *See also* success neurosis.

feature *n*. **1.** Any attribute of a sensory *stimulus (1, 2, 3). A *local feature is an attribute of part of the stimulus, and a *global feature is an attribute of the stimulus as a whole. *See also* acoustic feature, characteristic features, concept, defining properties, distinctive feature, feature comparison model, feature detection theory, feature detector, feature integration theory, feature search, levels of processing, prototype theory. **2.** More specifically, any of the distinctive parts of the face, such as the eyes, nose, mouth, ears, or chin.
[From Old French *faiture* a feature, from Latin *factura* a making, from *facere* to make]

feature abstraction theory *n*. Another name for *feature detection theory.

feature comparison model *n*. Any theory of *concept formation according to which a decision as to whether a particular item or element belongs to a class proceeds by comparing the *features (1) of the item with those of the class. For example, the theory posits that a person decides whether a particular animal is a cat by checking it for various features associated with cats, such as whiskers, a tail, a propensity to mew, and so on. **FCM** *abbrev*.

feature contrast *n*. In perceptual learning, the isolation of distinctive *features (1) of stimuli by first examining a pair of stimuli that are clearly or obviously differentiated on the feature in question and then responding to a sequence of pairs in which discrimination becomes progressively more difficult.

feature detection theory *n*. Any of a number of theories according to which the perception of objects proceeds by recognizing individual *features (1), such as a pair of wheels, a pair of pedals, a handlebar, a saddle, and an M-shaped metal frame, and assembling them to form a coherent pattern, in this example a bicycle, which is then identified as such. Also called *feature abstraction theory*. *Compare* feature integration theory, top-down processing.

feature detector *n*. A neuron that responds selectively to a specific *feature (1) of its input, such as an *edge detector, a *bar detector, or a cell specified for facial recognition in the visual association cortex (*see under* visual cortex). *See also* complex cell, grandmother cell, hypercomplex cell, simple cell.

feature integration theory *n*. A theory first presented in 1977 and 1980 by the US-based English psychologist Anne (Marie) Treisman (born 1935) and colleagues according to which *features (1) of a stimulus such as colour and shape are analysed separately and only later integrated in the process of perception. Indirect evidence for this comes from experiments showing that, without attention, features are often incorrectly bound, giving rise to illusory conjunctions, and that a red square hidden among blue squares can be detected just as quickly if it is hidden among 20 blue squares as among 10 blue squares, but the time taken to detect a red square hidden among blue squares and red triangles increases with the number of distractor items. *See also* binding problem, conjunction search, conjunctive concept. *Compare* feature detection theory.

feature list theory *n*. Another name for the *componential theory of concept formation.

feature negative learning *n*. A form of *classical conditioning in which an animal is given *reinforcement (2) in the presence of a *conditioned stimulus that has feature *B* but not a stimulus that has features *A* and *B*. *Compare* feature positive learning.

feature positive learning *n*. A form of *classical conditioning in which an animal is given *reinforcement (2) in the presence of a *conditioned stimulus with two features *A* and *B* but not a stimulus that has only feature *B*. *Compare* feature negative learning.

feature search *n*. A search for a particular *feature (1) or *attribute, as when a person scans a page in a telephone directory searching for telephone numbers ending with the digit 9. *Compare* conjunction search, disjunction search.

feature theory *n*. Any theory according to which objects or concepts are recognized by examining their individual features and comparing them to a stored list of *defining properties for the object or concept concerned. One of the problems with any such theory is that it takes no account of relations between features.

Fechner–Benham colours n. Another name for *pattern-induced flicker colours induced by *Benham's top. US *Fechner–Benham colors*. Also called *Fechner colours* or *subjective colours*. [Named after the German philosopher, physician, psychologist, and mystic Gustav Theodor Fechner (1801–87) who discovered the phenomenon in 1838 using a disc with 18 progressively longer arcs and the English amateur scientist and polymath Charles Edwin Benham (1860–1929) who rediscovered the phenomenon in its more familiar form in 1894]

Fechner's law n. In *psychophysics, the proposition that the magnitude of a sensation is proportional to the logarithm of the intensity of the stimulus causing it, usually expressed by the equation $\psi = k \log \phi$, where ψ is the magnitude of the sensation, ϕ is the physical intensity of the stimulus, and k is a constant scaling factor that varies from one kind of sensation to another. It has been largely supplanted by a *power law, which Fechner's law approximates for many sensory modalities. Also called the *Weber–Fechner law*, Fechner himself having called it *Weber's law*. See also psychophysical function. [Named after the German philosopher, physician, psychologist, and mystic Gustav Theodor Fechner (1801–87) to whom it came as a revelation as he lay in bed on 22 October 1850 contemplating the *mind–body problem, although its influence was felt mainly after the publication of his *Elemente der Psychophysik* in 1860]

Fechner's paradox n. An increase in the perceived *lightness of an image or scene that is viewed first with both eyes, but with an achromatic light-reducing filter over one eye, and then with the other eye alone and without a filter, despite the fact that less light enters the visual system in the second viewing. It arises as a direct consequence of *binocular summation, according to which the perceived lightness of an image or scene viewed binocularly is approximately the average of the brightness of the two stimuli perceived monocularly. It is a surprising phenomenon rather than a true *paradox. [Named after the German philosopher, physician, psychologist, and mystic Gustav

Theodor Fechner (1801–87) who first pointed it out]

feeble-mindedness n. An obsolescent term for *mild mental retardation.

feedback n. The return of part of a system's output to its input, usually as a means of achieving self-correction or modification of performance. In *negative feedback* an increase in output causes a decrease in input, as in a thermostat or other self-regulating mechanism and many *homeostatic biological processes including *EEG waves. In *positive feedback* an increase in output causes an increase in input, as in the howling of a public address system when a microphone is held too close to its loudspeaker. The term is also used informally for information given to research participants about their own performance or behaviour. See also closed-loop control, cybernetics, delayed auditory feedback, open-loop control, TOTE. Compare feedforward.

feedforward n. The effect of a signal preempting a subsequent error, such as the efferent output of the extra-ocular muscles during a *saccade, suppressing the sensation of movement that would otherwise be created by the motion of images across the retinas during the saccade. See also visual suppression. Compare feedback.

feeding centre n. One of the two structures of the *appestat, situated in both halves of the lateral *hypothalamus, stimulation of which increases eating and destruction inhibits eating. US *feeding center*. See also lateral hypothalamic feeding centre. Compare satiety centre.

feeding disorder of infancy or early childhood n. An *eating disorder with onset before 6 years of age characterized by a persistent failure to eat adequately, leading to significant weight loss over an extended period, the behaviour not being attributable to a gastrointestinal or other medical condition or lack of available food.

feeling type n. One of the subsidiary personality types in *analytical psychology. See function type.

fellatio n. Sexual activity in which a man's genitalia are stimulated by his partner's tongue and lips. Also called *fellation*. *Compare* cunnilingus. **fellate** *vb*. To perform *fellatio. [From Latin *fellare* to suck]

female orgasmic disorder *n*. A *sexual dysfunction characterized by a persistent or recurrent delay or absence of orgasm following the excitement phase of the female *sexual response cycle, causing significant distress or interpersonal problems, and not being attributable to a drug or a *general medical condition.

female sexual arousal disorder *n*. A *sexual dysfunction characterized by persistent or recurrent inability to attain or maintain adequate lubrication and swelling of the external sexual organs until completion of sexual activity, causing significant distress or interpersonal problems, not attributable to a drug or a *general medical condition.

fenestra *n*. A window, or a window-like opening in an anatomical structure. **fenestrae** *pl*.
[From Latin *fenestra* a window]

fenestra ovalis *n*. The *oval window. Also called the *fenestra vestibuli*.

fenestra rotunda *n*. The *round window. Also called the *fenestra cochleae* or *fenestra tympani*.

fentanyl *n*. A *narcotic analgesic drug that has a pharmacological action similar to that of morphine and is used as an adjunct to general anaesthesia, as a sedative or *neuroleptic (1) drug, and sometimes as a street drug. Its most common street name is *China white*. *See also* droperidol.
[A corruption of *phenethyl*]

feral *adj*. Wild or untamed, especially after having previously been domesticated.
[From Latin *feralis* wild, from *fera* a wild beast]

feral child *n*. A child supposedly raised by wild animals with little or no involvement of other humans. *See also* Kaspar Hauser experiment, Wild Boy of Aveyron.

Ferberize *vb*. To train an infant to be self-reliant and to sleep on its own by placing it in its crib, leaving the room, and ignoring its crying for at least 20 minutes, then returning, patting it but not picking it up, and leaving

quickly. When this influential but controversial child-care practice is followed, the procedure is repeated every night, increasing by five minutes per night the waiting period before responding to the infant's crying with patting. **Ferberization** *n*. The practice of *Ferberizing.
[Named after the US paediatric sleep researcher Richard Ferber (born 1944) who developed it in 1986]

Ferry–Porter law *n*. The proposition that the *critical flicker frequency increases in proportion to the logarithm of light intensity. Also called *Porter's law*.
[Named after Edwin Sidney Ferry (1868–1956), US physicist, and Thomas Cunningham Porter (1860–1933), assistant science and mathematics master at Eton College, England, who discovered it independently]

fertility *n*. The reproductive activity of an organism or of a population, species, or other taxonomic group, indexed by the number of viable offspring that it produces in a specified time period.
[From Latin *fertilis* fruitful, from *ferre* to bear]

fertilization *n*. The union of a male and a female *gamete, such as an ovum and a spermatozoon in humans, to produce a *zygote.

festination *n*. A manner of walking with an involuntary acceleration of gait, as if trying to catch up with one's displaced centre of gravity, often shown by people with *Parkinson's disease.
[From Latin *festinare* to hurry + *-ation* indicating a process or condition]

fetal alcohol syndrome *See* foetal alcohol syndrome.

fetal brain transplantation *See* foetal brain transplantation.

fetish *n*. **1.** An inanimate object to which a pathological sexual attachment is formed, or by extension a person who is the object of an obsessive *fixation (3). **2.** An object, the possession of which is believed to procure the services of a spirit lodged within it. *See also* fetishism.
[From Portuguese *fetiço* magic, from *fetiço* artificial, from Latin *facticius* artificial or made, from *facere* to make]

fetishism *n.* A *paraphilia characterized by recurrent, intense sexual fantasies, urges, or behaviour involving inanimate objects such as women's undergarments, stockings, or shoes that are treated as *fetishes (1). *See also* splitting of the ego. **fetishistic** *adj.*

fetishistic transvestism *n.* A *paraphilia characterized by recurrent sexually arousing fantasies, sexual urges, or behaviour involving the wearing of clothes of the opposite sex and appearing as a member of the opposite sex. Also called *transvestic fetishism*. *Compare* transsexualism, transvestism.
[From Latin *trans* across + *vestire* to dress]

fetus *n.* An alternative (etymologically more correct) spelling of *foetus.
[From Latin *fetus* offspring]

fibril *n.* A small fibre or threadlike structure such as one of the contractile strands of muscle tissue.
[From Latin *fibrilla* a little fibre, diminutive of *fibra* a fibre]

fibrillation *n.* A localized and involuntary twitching of muscle fibres; also, a chaotic twitching of muscle fibres of the heart.
[So called because it arises from the discoordinated actions of muscle *fibrils]

fictional finalism *n.* In the *individual psychology of the Austrian psychiatrist Alfred Adler (1870–1937) and his followers, a term used to denote the characteristic form of human motivation, being driven by striving after unattainable ultimate goals. Except in cases of neurosis, however, people are normally able to suspend such fantasies and adopt more realistic judgements of the future.

fiction, guiding *See* guiding fiction.

field *n.* A bounded area, especially a region within which a body experiences forces resulting from the presence of other bodies not in contact with it (as in a gravitational or a magnetic field), or more generally any region within which certain specified phenomena occur. *See also* field dependence–independence, field effect, field theory, life space, receptive field, topological psychology, visual field.

field adaptation *n.* The component of *visual adaptation during *dark adaptation or *light adaptation that occurs relatively quickly through neural processes rather than as a result of pigment bleaching. Also called *neural adaptation*.

field dependence–independence *n.* A *cognitive style characterized by the propensity to differentiate perceptual and other experiences from their backgrounds or contexts, a person with a weak propensity of this kind being field dependent and a person with a strong propensity field independent. Men tend on average to be more field independent than women, adults than children, and people who score high on abstract reasoning subtests of IQ tests (as opposed to vocabulary, information, and comprehension subtests) than those who score low on such subtests. It was discovered in 1950 by the US psychologist Herman A. Witkin (1916–79) and is usually measured by the *rod-and-frame test, the *embedded-figures test, or the *tilting-room test. Field independence is also called *psychological differentiation*. **FD-I** *abbrev.*

field effect *n.* A term used by *Gestalt psychologists to denote a *context effect in which the appearance of an image or part of an image is affected by its spatial or temporal setting, as in *associative illusions. *See also* Prägnanz.

field experiment *n.* Any *experiment carried out in a natural setting rather than in the artificial environment of a laboratory. *Compare* field study.

field of vision *n.* Another name for the *visual field.

field study *n.* A research investigation, possibly but not necessarily a *field experiment, carried out in a natural setting rather than in the artificial environment of a research laboratory.

field theory *n.* Any theory in which phenomena are interpreted as resulting from the dynamic interplay of elements within a *field, especially (in psychology) the theory introduced in 1935 by the Polish/German-born US psychologist Kurt Lewin (1890–1947). According to Lewin's field theory, psychological events occur within a type of field called a *life space, within which the important relations are qualitative aspects of connection and position, such as belongingness, membership, and part–whole relationships. Behaviour is interpreted as a function of the person and the life space, this relation being expressed by the equation $B = f(LS)$, and the life space is interpreted as the person and the environment, so that $B = f(P, E)$, meaning that behaviour is a joint function of the person and the environment, behaviour being represented as *locomotion* from one region of the life space to another, regions that attract or repel having *valence*. *See also* hodological space, Lewinian, topological psychology.

fight-or-flight response *n.* A term introduced by the US physiologist Walter Bradford Cannon (1871–1945), and popularized in his book *Bodily Changes in Pain, Hunger, Fear and Rage* (1929), for the syndrome of physiological *responses of an organism confronted with a situation that evokes fear, pain, or anger, such responses being mobilized by the secretion of *adrenalin (epinephrine) from the adrenal medulla, preparing the organism to fight or to flee. It includes increased blood pressure, accelerated heart rate, deepened respiration, increased sweating, dilation of the pupils, diversion of blood flow from the digestive tract to the skeletal muscles and cessation of digestive processes, release of sugar from reserves in the liver, and closure of the sphincter of the bladder, leading to retention of urine.

figural aftereffect *n.* A change in perception of a visual stimulus resulting from prolonged (usually 30 seconds or more) exposure to a different visual stimulus, as when the contour of the second stimulus falling on the retina near the contour of the original stimulus appears displaced away from the position occupied by the original contour, or more generally any distortion in visual perception resulting from a prior visual stimulus, as occurs in *successive contrast. *See also* aftereffect, contingent aftereffect, motion aftereffect, spiral aftereffect, tilt aftereffect, visual aftereffect. **FAE** *abbrev.*

figure–ground reversal *n.* A phenomenon underlying many *ambiguous figures, the alternating perceptions of which depend on shifting interpretations of which parts of the image represent the figure and which represent the (back)ground. The Dutch graphic artist Maurits C(ornelis) Escher (1898–1970) often exploited this phenomenon, together with visual puzzles in the form of *impossible figures (Escher figures). *See* reversible goblet.

figure of speech *n.* A linguistic expression or device in which words are used to create special effects or to express ideas different from their usual or literal meaning. Also called an *image. *See* apostrophe (1), chiasmus, metaphor, metonymy, oxymoron, personification, simile, synecdoche.

filament *n.* Any slender, threadlike structure, such as the tail of a *spermatozoon.
[From Latin *filum* a thread, from *filare* to spin]

file drawer problem *n.* A bias in the body of published research in any field resulting from the fact that studies reporting positive results are more likely to be published than those reporting negative or non-significant results. It is especially problematical in research areas such as *parapsychology, and in any area it makes difficulties for the interpretation of *meta-analyses.
[So called because researchers relegate unpublished findings to file drawers]

filial generation *n.* In genetics, any generation following a parental generation that has been designated arbitrarily as the first in a hereditary line. By convention, F_1 designates the first filial generation, F_2 the second filial generation, and so on.
[From Latin *filialis* pertaining to a son or daughter, from *filius* a son]

filial imprinting *See* imprinting.

filial regression *n.* The tendency for a child of a parent who scores extremely high or extremely low on some heritable characteristic, such as IQ or physical stature, to score closer to the population *mean than the parent. This phenomenon is explained by *regression towards the mean. Also called *Galton's law of filial regression*. *See also* overdominance.
[From Latin *filius* a son + *regressus* a retreat + *-ion* indicating an action, process, or state]

filled-duration illusion *n.* A *cognitive illusion that causes a specified period of time to be experienced as longer when many events are experienced during it than when it is relatively empty. For example, if two clicks mark the beginning and end of a period of silence (an unfilled interval), it tends to be perceived as shorter than the same objective interval filled with a sequence of clicks (a filled interval). *Compare* filled-space illusion.

filled pause *n.* A vocal hesitation into which the speaker inserts a meaningless vocalization such as *um* or *er*.

filled-space illusion *n.* A visual illusion in which a line, area, or volume appears larger if it is occupied by a number of distinct elements than if it is empty (see illustration). The first written reference to it is to be found in Book 16, Chapter 7 of *Problems*, a work often spuriously attributed to the Greek philosopher Aristotle (384–322 BC), probably written by one of his followers. The illusion is there presented the wrong way round, and the explanation that is offered to explain it is therefore beside the point: 'Why is it that magnitudes always appear less when divided than when taken as a whole? Is it because, though things which are divided always possess number, in size they are smaller than that which is single and undivided?' The first systematic investigation of the illusion was reported in 1860–1 (not 1854–5 as often stated) by the German physicist Johann Joseph Oppel (1815–94). Also called the *filled and unfilled extent illusion*, the *Oppel illusion*, or the *Oppel–Kundt illusion*. *See also* Kundt's rules. *Compare* filled-duration illusion.

Filled-space illusion. The distance between A and B is the same as that between B and C.

fillet *n.* A narrow strip of meat or other material; also, a non-technical name for the *lemniscus.
[Via Old French from Latin *filum* a cord or thread]

filling-in *n.* The action of the visual system or other perceptual system, when responding to a stimulus with gaps or missing information, of guessing the missing information by assuming that it is the same as the information presented and generating perception without

gaps. *See also* blind spot (1), filling-in illusion, phonemic restoration.

filling-in illusion *n.* A visual illusion of *filling-in consisting of a central black dot surrounded by a dark region that fades very gradually into a lighter background. Steady, unmoving fixation on the dot with one eye (keeping the other eye closed or covered) causes the dark region to vanish after a few seconds by a process of *filling-in, but the effect is eliminated if the dark region is surrounded by a clearly defined ring or boundary (see illustration). The illusion arises from an approximation to a *stabilized retinal image: the eye movements resulting from *physiological nystagmus during fixation do not produce any noticeable changes in the peripheral areas of the retinal image because of its smoothly graded contour, and the visual system therefore allows the image to fade as if it were fixed, but the addition of a sharply defined ring or boundary makes movements in the peripheral image detectable and causes the visual system to refresh that part of the image.

Filling-in illusion. In the left-hand figure, steady fixation on the black dot with one eye, keeping the other eye covered or closed, causes the dark region surrounding the dot to disappear, whereas in the right-hand figure the ring prevents fading.

film colour *n.* A misty appearance of colour without any fixed distance that is experienced when there are no lines or edges present in the visual field. US *film color*. Also called *volume colour*. *See also* Ganzfeld. *Compare* surface colour.

filiform papilla *n.* Any of the numerous threadlike *papillae that are situated on the upper surface of the *tongue and that conspicuously lack *taste buds. *Compare* circumvallate papilla, foliate papilla, fungiform papilla. **filiform papillae** *pl.*
[From Latin *filum* a thread + *forma* a shape]

filter *n*. **1.** A porous substance or device that removes suspended particles while allowing fluid to pass through it. **2.** Any electronic, acoustic, optical, or purely mathematical device that blocks signals of certain frequencies while allowing others to pass. *See also* band-pass filter. *vb*. **3.** To remove or separate suspended particles from a fluid or certain wavelengths from a signal, or more generally to exclude certain types of stimuli from attention. *See also* filter theory.

filter theory *n*. A theory of *attention proposed in 1958 by the English psychologist Donald E(ric) Broadbent (1926–93) according to which there exists a *central processor (2) with a limited capacity that can select only one sensory input channel at a time and can switch between input channels no more than about twice per second, information in an unattended channel being held in *short-term memory for a few seconds. Evidence for the theory was provided by *split-span* experiments in which pairs of digits were presented simultaneously to both ears at a rate of up to two per second, and listeners invariably recalled them ear by ear rather than pair by pair, evidently switching attention from one ear to the other, but later findings necessitated refinements of the theory. *See also* attenuation theory, cocktail party phenomenon, bottleneck theory, selective attention.

fimbria *n*. The fringe of white nerve fibres along the edge of the *hippocampus, meeting in the *fornix.
[From Latin *fimbriae* fibres or a fringe]

finger agnosia *n*. A form of *autotopagnosia, usually associated with a lesion in the posterior region of the dominant hemisphere, characterized by a primary inability to recognize, identify, differentiate, name, select, or indicate individual fingers of either hand. If a person with finger agnosia is touched on either one or two fingers, each finger being touched in either one or two places, such a person is unable to state how many fingers are being touched. *See also* agnosia, Gerstmann syndrome.

fingerprint, genetic *See* genetic fingerprinting.

finger spelling *n*. Another name for *dactylology.

finite-state grammar *n*. A simplified form of *generative grammar capable of yielding only a limited number of sentences.

fire-setting, pathological *n*. Another name for *pyromania.

first censorship *See under* censorship.

first-order approximation to language *See* approximation to language.

fishberry *n*. The climbing plant *Cocculus indicus* that contains *picrotoxin.
[So called because its berries are sometimes fed to fish so that they die and float to the surface]

Fisher's exact test *n*. A statistical test that can be applied to data in a 2×2 contingency table and is especially useful when the total sample size or some of the expected values are small so that the *chi-square test cannot be used. This *distribution-free test establishes the exact probability, under the *null hypothesis that the row and column variables are independent, of obtaining a result as extreme or more extreme than the observed result assuming that the marginals (the row and column totals) are fixed. It is the prototypical *randomization test. Also called *Fisher's exact probability test*, *Fisher–Yates test*.
[Named after the English statistician and geneticist Ronald Aylmer Fisher (1890–1962) who in 1934 encouraged Frank Yates (1902–94) to develop it]

Fisher's r to z transformation *n*. In statistics, a method of transforming *product–moment correlation coefficients into *standard scores or *z* scores to facilitate interpretation and to enable tests such as those for the significance of the difference between two correlation coefficients to be carried out.
[Named after the English statistician and geneticist Ronald Aylmer Fisher (1890–1962)]

Fisher–Yates test *n*. Another name for *Fisher's exact test.

***fis* phenomenon** *n*. A child's refusal to accept an adult's rendering of what the child has just said. The phenomenon was first reported in 1960 by the US psychologists Jean Berko (born 1931, later called Jean Berko Gleason) and Roger William Brown (1925–97) in an account of a child who called his plastic fish a *fis* but refused to accept this pronunciation from adults and was satisfied only when they called it a *fish*. This is often taken to illustrate that young children can hear more than they can say.

fission *n.* **1.** The process of splitting something into parts. **2.** A form of *asexual reproduction in which a single-celled organism such as a *bacterium divides into two or more equal parts, each of which then develops into a new cell.
[From Latin *fissio* a cleaving + *-ion* indicating an action, process, or state]

fissure *n.* A narrow cleft or crack; any of the longer and deeper grooves or furrows between the *gyri or convolutions of the brain. Also called a *sulcus*.
[From Latin *fissus* split, from *findere* to split]

fissure of Rolando *n.* Another name for the *central sulcus.
[Named after the Italian physician Luigi Rolando (1773–1831)]

fissure of Sylvius *n.* Another name for the *lateral sulcus.
[Named after the Flemish anatomist Franciscus Sylvius (1614–72), also called Franz de le Boë, who apparently discovered it]

fitness *n.* The condition of being fit and healthy, or of being suitable for a particular function. More specifically, the degree of *adaptation (1) of an organism to its environment, usually measured in terms of the average contribution of its *genotype to the next generation, relative to that of other genotypes. Also called *genetic fitness*. *See also* Darwinian fitness. *Compare* inclusive fitness.

Fitts' law *n.* In *reaction time experiments in which a subject or participant moves a stylus as quickly as possible from a starting position to a target, a relation observed between movement time (*MT*) on the one hand and target width (*W*) and movement amplitude (*A*) on the other, expressed by the equation $MT = a + b\log_2(2A/W)$, where *a* and *b* are constants representing the intercept and slope of the function respectively. Thus movement time decreases with the size of the target and increases with the amplitude of the movement.

Often incorrectly spelt *Fitt's law*. *Compare* Hick's law.
[Named after the US psychologist Paul Morris Fitts (1912–65) who formulated it in 1954]

5-hydroxyindoleacetic acid *n.* A substance that is produced by the *metabolism of *serotonin and whose concentration in *cerebrospinal fluid has been found to be negatively correlated with suicidal depression. *See also* bufotenin. **5-HIAA** *abbrev.*

5-hydroxytryptamine *n.* The chemical name for *serotonin. **5-HT** *abbrev.*

5-hydroxytryptophan *n.* A precursor of *serotonin (5-hydroxytryptamine), synthesized in the brain from dietary *tryptophan, an amino acid that, unlike serotonin itself, is able to cross the *blood–brain barrier. **5-HTP** *abbrev.*

5 per cent trim *n.* In statistics, the *arithmetic mean calculated after eliminating the largest five per cent and smallest five per cent of the cases. It is used occasionally when a set of scores contains values that are much smaller or much larger than the rest, because in such cases it may yield a more useful indication of *central tendency than the untrimmed mean. *See also* trimmed mean.

fixate *vb.* **1.** To train one's eyes on an object or point in the visual field so that its image falls on the *foveas of the eyes. *See also* Donders' law, reading span. **2.** To engage or indulge in *fixation (3); to become preoccupied or obsessed with something.
[From Latin *fixus* fixed]

fixation *n.* **1.** The act or process of *fixating (1). Also called *visual fixation*. *See also* Donders' law, reading span. **2.** In *psychoanalysis, the persistence of a mode of *libidinal satisfaction characteristic of an earlier stage of *psychosexual development, as when *libido remains attached to a particular *instinctual object or an *erotogenic zone associated with a pre-genital *libidinal stage, such as the *oral stage, *anal stage, or *phallic stage. The concept rests on the insight that people retain throughout life latent attachments to earlier modes of satisfaction and *object-relationships, and that these are reactivated by *regression (2). Sigmund Freud (1856–1939) referred to it in 1905 in his book *Three Essays on the Theory of Sexuality* (*Standard Edition*, VII, pp.

130–243) and repeatedly in his later writings. *See also* anal character, genital character, oral character, phallic character, urethral character. **3.** The act or process of becoming preoccupied or obsessed with something.

fixed-action pattern *n.* In ethology, a *response to a *sign stimulus or *releaser, taking the form of a stereotyped pattern of innate behaviour, such as the aggressive attack of a male European robin elicited by the red feathers on the breast of a rival. It is relatively uninfluenced by learning and is assumed to be governed by an *innate releasing mechanism. *See also* vacuum activity. **FAP** *abbrev.*

fixed idea *See idée fixe.*

fixed image *n.* Another name for a *stabilized retinal image.

fixed-interval schedule *n.* In *operant conditioning, a simple *reinforcement schedule in which reward follows the first response that the organism makes after a predetermined time interval, and then the first response that it makes after the same interval, and so on, the duration of the interval being specified in seconds as an affix to the abbreviation, hence *FI20* indicates a fixed-interval schedule with a 20-second interval. Also called a *fixed-interval reinforcement schedule. See also* simple reinforcement schedule. *Compare* fixed-ratio schedule, variable-interval schedule, variable-ratio schedule. **FI** *abbrev.*

fixedness, functional *See* functional fixedness.

fixed-ratio schedule *n.* In *operant conditioning, a simple *reinforcement schedule in which reward is delivered after the organism has made a fixed number of responses, and is delivered again after the same number of responses, and so on, the number of responses required before each reinforcement being specified as an affix to the abbreviation, hence *FR10* indicates a fixed-ratio schedule with reinforcement after every 10 responses. Also called a *fixed-ratio reinforcement schedule. See also* simple reinforcement schedule. *Compare* fixed-interval schedule, variable-interval schedule, variable-ratio schedule. **FR** *abbrev.*

fixed-role therapy *n.* A form of *psychotherapy based on the *personal construct theory of the US psychologist George A(lexander) Kelly (1905–66), first explored by Kelly and his colleagues in 1939 and described in his book *The Psychology of Personal Constructs* (1955, Volume 1, pp. 360–451), in which the client begins with a self-characterization then modifies it in the direction of a desired alternative. *See also* personal constructs therapy. **FRT** *abbrev.*

flashback *n.* **1.** In a novel, film, or other fictional work, a sudden transition to an earlier episode in the narrative. **2.** A recurrence of a memory, or the experience of reliving an episode from the past. *See also* posttraumatic stress disorder. **3.** After consumption of a *hallucinogen, the re-experiencing of some of the perceptual effects of the intoxication, such as geometric illusions, false perceptions of motion in the periphery of the visual field, flashes of light or colour, *afterimages, *micropsia, and *macropsia. Also called *posthallucinogen perception disorder*.

flashbulb memory *n.* An unusually vivid, richly detailed, and long-lasting memory for the circumstances surrounding a dramatic event. The standard example is the assassination of the US president John F. Kennedy in 1963: most people who were adults at the time have flashbulb memories of where they were and what they were doing when they first heard about this event.
[So called because is has the subjective quality of something indelibly recorded as by a flash camera, although research has shown that in reality it is often less than perfectly accurate]

flattening of affect *See* affective flattening.

flavour *n.* The quality of a food or drink perceived in the mouth, determined by a combination of sensory effects including its taste, odour, texture, temperature, colour, irritability, and sound (when chewed). US *flavor. See also* taste.
[From Old French *flaour* flavour, probably influenced by *savour* taste, from Latin *sapor* taste, from *sapere* to taste]

flavour aversion learning/conditioning *See* food aversion learning.

Flesch indices *n.* Indices designed to measure two aspects of the readability of text: the *reading ease score, which measures how easy the text is to read, and the *human interest score, which measures how interesting it is to read.

[Named after the Austrian-born US researcher Rudolf (Franz) Flesch (1911–86), who devised the indices in 1946 and revised them in 1949]

Fletcher–Munson contour n. Another name for an *equal-loudness contour. Also called a *Fletcher–Munson curve*.

[Named after the US acoustical scientist Harvey Fletcher (1884–1981) and the US engineer Wilden A. Munson (1902–82) who introduced it in 1933]

flexibilitas cerea See cerea flexibilitas.

flexion reflex n. A type of *reflex (1) consisting of a quick, involuntary bending of a joint to withdraw a limb, hand, finger, or other part in response to a strong painful *stimulus (1) applied to it.

[From Latin *flectere, flexum* to bend]

flicker n. Intermittent or rapidly fluctuating light, or the visual sensation resulting from a light stimulus fluctuating periodically in brightness below the *critical flicker frequency. Compare auditory flutter.

flicker fusion frequency n. Another name for *critical flicker frequency. **fff** abbrev.

flight into health n. In *psychoanalysis, a sudden claim by a patient to be fully recovered and in no further need of help, interpreted as a defensive reaction to *psychotherapy. The term is based on the original concept of the *flight into illness.

flight into history n. In *counselling and *psychotherapy, a tendency to dwell excessively on the past, interpreted as a defensive reaction to pain or embarrassment evoked by the present. The term was coined on the model of *flight into illness.

flight into illness n. An attempt to escape from unacceptable feelings or conflicts by developing *neurotic (1), *psychotic (1), or *psychosomatic symptoms. The term originated in *psychoanalysis: Sigmund Freud (1856–1939) referred in 1894 to the 'flight into psychosis' (Standard Edition, III, p. 59), then in 1908 to the 'flight into neurotic illness' (Standard Edition, IX, p. 192), and then finally in 1909 to the 'flight into illness' (Standard Edition, IX, p. 231). See also primary gain. Compare flight into health, flight into history.

flight of colours n. The sequence of *afterimages of different colours that follow brief exposure to a bright stimulus, especially in dark-adapted eyes. It can be demonstrated by adapting one's eyes in the dark for 25 minutes, then switching on a light, fixating it with a steady gaze for several seconds, turning the light off, and keeping the eyes as steady as possible—the phenomenon tends to vanish when the eyes are moved. US *flight of colors*. Also called *colour flight* or *color flight*.

flight of ideas n. A form of *thought disorder in which a rapid flow of thoughts occur, flitting from one topic to another, usually with transitions based on arbitrary conceptual or verbal links. It is often seen in a *manic episode and occasionally in certain forms of *schizophrenia.

floater n. A dark speck that appears to float in front of one's eyes and appears to follow their movements, caused by dead cells and fragments of cells suspended in the vitreous humour and crystalline lens of the eye.

floating-finger illusion n. A visual illusion that is seen when the forefingers of each hand are held horizontally about 30 centimetres in front of the eyes, with the fingertips touching and the gaze focused on a point in the distance, and the fingertips are then drawn apart about one centimetre. A disembodied finger, with two tips, appears floating in mid-air, and it can be lengthened or shortened by varying the distance between the fingertips (see illustration). The illusion was discovered in 1928 and described in the journal Psychological Review by the US psychologist Winford Lee Sharp (1890–1975).

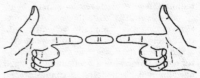

Floating-finger illusion

flocculonodular lobe n. The evolutionarily oldest part of the *cerebellum, present even in fishes, consisting of a pair of small irregular structures (flocculi) joined in the middle by a *node (1) or nodulus and separated by a deep fissure from the back of the cerebellum, connected to the vestibular system and concerned chiefly with posture, balance, and ballistic movements.

[From Latin *flocculus* a small tuft of wool, diminutive of *floccus* a tuft of wool + *nodulus* a small knot, diminutive of *nodus* a knot, alluding to its appearance as two small tufts of wool with a small knot in the middle]

flooding *n*. A technique of *behaviour therapy used to treat *post-traumatic stress disorder, *phobias, and other *anxiety disorders by exposing the anxious person intensively to the anxiety-producing situation until the anxiety subsides. Also called *exposure therapy*, *implosion therapy*.

floor effect *n*. In statistics and measurement theory, an artificial lower limit on the value that a *variable can attain, causing the distribution of scores to be skewed. For example, the distribution of scores on an ability test will be skewed by a floor effect if the test is much too difficult for many of the respondents and many of them obtain zero scores. Also called a *basement effect*. *Compare* ceiling effect.

floral odour *See* fragrant odour.

flow chart *n*. A diagram consisting of a series of boxes, each representing a particular process or operation, joined by arrows indicating the output of one process or operation to another. There is usually one particular box from which the sequence begins, and some boxes, often distinguished by a distinctive shape, may represent decision or choice points from which two or more arrows emerge, each indicating a different decision or choice. Also called a *block diagram*.

flowery odour *See* fragrant odour.

fluent aphasia *See under* aphasia.

fluid intelligence *n*. A fundamental *factor (2) of human intelligence, derived from *factor analysis, corresponding roughly to non-verbal reasoning, requiring rapid understanding of novel relationships, measured by tests such as *Raven's Progressive Matrices. The concept was introduced in 1971 by the English-born US psychologist Raymond B(ernard) Cattell (1905–98). Also called *fluid ability*. *Compare* crystallized intelligence. **Gf** *abbrev*.

flunitrazepam *n*. The chemical name of the benzodiazepine drug *Rohypnol, sometimes called the *date rape drug*.

fluoxetine *n*. Fluoxetine hydrochloride, the chemical name of the antidepressant drug *Prozac. **FXT** *abbrev*.

fluphenazine *n*. Fluphenazine hydrochloride, or fluphenazine decanoate, or fluphenazine enanthate, different forms of a *neuroleptic (1) drug belonging to the group of *phenothiazines, frequently used in the treatment of schizophrenia. Also called *Prolixin* (trademark).

flutter, auditory *See* auditory flutter.

fluvoxamine *n*. An antidepressant drug belonging to the group of *selective serotonin reuptake inhibitors (SSRIs). Also called *Luvox* (trademark).

fly agaric *n*. The slightly poisonous woodland mushroom *Amanita muscaria*, with a scarlet cap, white warts, and gills, made famous by *Alice's Adventures in Wonderland* by Lewis Carroll, the pen name of Charles Lutwidge Dodgson (1832–98). It contains the drugs *muscimol, *muscarine, *ibotenic acid, and *bufotenin, sometimes eaten for its *hallucinogenic effects and used for ritual purposes by shamans of eastern Siberia. Also called *magic mushroom*. *See also* liberty cap, teonanactyl. *Compare* cohoba.

[From Greek *agarikon* a mushroom, called *fly agaric* because of its use as a poison on flypaper]

Flynn effect *n*. A secular increase in average IQ scores, typically averaging about three IQ points per decade, that has been occurring since the introduction of IQ tests in many industrialized societies, including the United States, the United Kingdom, Belgium, France, The Netherlands, Norway, Israel, Canada, New Zealand, Australia, and Japan, the effect being most pronounced on measures of *fluid intelligence such as *Raven's Progressive Matrices. Because IQ tests are periodically re-

standardized to a mean of 100, the increase is not apparent in continuously rising average IQ scores, but people who score 100 on a newly standardized test tend to score more than 100 on older ones. The effect has been attributed to various causes, including improved nutrition and parenting, better schooling, increased test-taking sophistication, and various effects of growing up with television and video games in an increasingly complex environment, but it is generally acknowledged to be poorly understood and largely mysterious. *See also* cohort.
[Named after the US-born New Zealand political scientist James R(obert) Flynn (born 1934) who was the first to draw attention to it in two influential articles in the journal *Psychological Bulletin* in 1984 and 1987]

***F* max** *n*. Another name for *Hartley's *F* max.

focal colour *n*. A colour that is a *prototypical instance of a particular colour name, such as a shade of red that a majority of viewers consider to be the best example of a red colour. US *focal color*.

focal epilepsy *n*. Another name for *Jacksonian epilepsy.

focal length *n*. The distance between the centre of a lens or curved mirror and its *focal point. *See also* dioptre.

focal point *n*. The point at which parallel light rays passing through a lens or reflected from a curved mirror converge, or the point from which they appear to diverge after refraction or reflection by the lens or mirror. Also called the *focus* or the *principal focus*. *See also* focal length.

focal system *n*. The aspect of vision that governs object identification and discrimination, using predominantly *central vision without *peripheral vision. *Compare* ambient system.

focal therapy *n*. A form of *brief psychotherapy that concentrates solely on a single core problem.

focus *See* focal point.

focus group *n*. A small group of people selected and assembled for research purposes, to participate in an organized discussion, under the guidance of a moderator, of an issue or topic of which they have personal experience. Focus groups were first proposed by the US sociologist Robert K(ing) Merton (born 1910) and co-authors in *The Focused Interview: A Manual of Problems and Procedures* (1956), and they have had a long history in *market research, where they have been used to sample the range of opinions and attitudes that might be expected in the wider population. They have been used to a lesser extent in psychology, generally in the tradition of *qualitative research, when interaction between group members is felt to add an important element that is lacking in other types of *interviews.

foetal alcohol syndrome *n*. A highly variable pattern of congenital defects, including small stature, mental retardation, pixie-like facial features, and malformations of the skull and brain, that tend to occur in infants of mothers who drink large quantities of alcohol during pregnancy. Also spelt *fetal alcohol syndrome*. **FAS** *abbrev*.

foetal brain transplantation *n*. The surgical grafting of brain tissue from an aborted foetus into the brain of an adult to repair damage caused by disease or injury, as in the replacement of dopamine-secreting brain tissue in the *substantia nigra or *striatum of patients with *Parkinson's disease. Also spelt *fetal brain transplantation*.

foetus *n*. An unborn animal at an early stage of development, after its main internal organs have begun to become distinctly formed, especially an unborn human baby from the end of the eighth week of pregnancy (to distinguish it from an *embryo) until birth. US *fetus*, this spelling being more correct etymologically but unusual in British orthography. *See also* blastocyst, morula, zygote. **foetal** or **fetal** *adj*.
[From Latin *fetus* offspring]

foil *n*. In research methodology, another name for a *distractor.

foliate papilla *n*. Any of a large number of paired oval *papillae on the sides of the back part of the *tongue with *taste buds at their bases that respond mainly to sour tastes. *Compare* circumvallate papilla, filiform

papilla, fungiform papilla. **foliate papillae** *pl*.
[From Latin *folium* a leaf + *forma* a shape]

folie à deux *n*. Another name for *shared psychotic disorder. Also *folie à trois* (a delusion shared by three people living together), *folie à quatre* (a delusion shared by four people living together), and so on.
[French *folie* insanity + *à* of + *deux* two]

folium *n*. One of the flattened structures of the *cerebellum that expand sideways to form its superior lobes.
[From Latin *folium* a leaf]

folk etymology *n*. **1**. An alteration in the form of a word through the influence of a more familiar word or words that people associate with it, as in *sparrow-grass* for *asparagus*. **2**. A popular misconception about the origin of a word. Thus *belfry*, the part of a tower in which bells are hung, comes from Medieval Latin *berfredus* a tower, not from the English word *bell*; *crap*, excrement or faeces, comes from Middle Dutch *krappe* chaff and is not named after Thomas Crapper (1836–1910), the Victorian English sanitary engineer who contributed to the development of the siphonic flush toilet and whose *aptronym is inscribed on a manhole cover, popular with brass-rubbers, in the cloisters of Westminster Abbey; *penthouse*, a top-floor flat, comes via Middle English *pentis* from Latin *appendicium* an appendage, not from English *pent* or *house*; and *pickaxe*, a large double-pointed garden tool, comes from Old French *picois* a mattock, not from English *pick* or *axe*. *See also* back formation, metanalysis.

folk psychology *n*. The assumptions, hypotheses, and beliefs of ordinary people about behaviour and mental experience. *See also* basic-level category, grounded theory, implicit personality theory.

follicle *n*. Any small sac or cavity, such as the pit in which a hair-root is embedded.
[From Latin *folliculus* a small bag, diminutive of *folis* a bellows or money-bag]

follicle-stimulating hormone *n*. A *gonadotrophic hormone that is secreted by the anterior pituitary and that stimulates the growth of *Graafian follicles in females and production of *spermatozoa in males. *See also*

oestrous cycle. *Compare* luteinizing hormone. **FSH** *abbrev*.

follicular phase *n*. The first phase of the *oestrous cycle or *menstrual cycle, initiated by the secretion of *follicle-stimulating hormone and ending with *ovulation. Also called the *proliferative phase*. *Compare* luteal phase, menstrual phase.
[Named after the *Graafian follicles]

following behaviour *n*. In *ethology, the trailing of a young bird or animal behind its parent or another organism or object, especially as a consequence of *imprinting.

fontanelle *n*. A soft membranous gap between the immature skull bones of an infant or foetus. Also spelt *fontanel*. *See also* bregma.
[From Old French *fontanele* a little fountain, from Latin *fons, fontis* a fountain]

food aversion learning *n*. Avoidance of food with a distinctive taste by an organism that has felt ill after eating food with that taste, the aversion often being learned after a single trial, even if the ill feeling arises many hours after eating the food and is not caused by the food. In the original experiment carried out by the US psychologists Sam Revusky (born 1933) and John Garcia (born 1917) and published in 1970, rats were fed a sweet-tasting sucrose solution and were then injected with lithium chloride, which made them mildly ill, and they refused to touch the sucrose solution the next day. Also called *conditioned food/taste aversion, flavour aversion learning/conditioning, food aversion conditioning, food avoidance learning/conditioning, Garcia effect, learned flavour aversion, learned taste aversion, taste aversion learning/conditioning, toxicosis*.

food chain *n*. In *ecology (1), a hierarchy of organisms in which each is consumed as food by one or more of the ones above it. *See also* pyramid of numbers.

foot-candle *n*. An obsolescent unit of *illuminance, equal to one lumen per square foot. *See also* foot-lambert. **fc** *abbrev*.

foot-in-the-door technique *n*. A technique for eliciting *compliance by preceding a request for a large commitment with a request for a small one, the initial small request serving the function of softening up the target person. It was introduced and named in 1966 by the US social psychologists Jonathan L. Freedman (born 1937) and Scott C(ameron) Fraser (born 1943), who reported a field experiment in which householders were visited in their homes where some were asked whether they would be willing to put a very small sticker in their house or car windows about road safety or keeping California beautiful and others were asked to sign a petition on one of these issues; two weeks later, a different person, supposedly from a different organization, arrived and asked the same householders whether they would be willing to have a hole dug in their front gardens and a large, ugly *Drive Carefully* sign planted there. Among a control group who had not received the earlier small request, only 17 per cent agreed to have the safe driving sign planted in their gardens, but 55 per cent of the participants in the foot-in-the-door condition agreed. *See also* door-in-the-face technique, lowball technique.

foot-lambert *n.* An obsolescent unit of *luminance equal to that of a surface emitting or reflecting one *lumen per square foot, a completely reflecting surface illuminated by 1 foot-candle having a luminance of 1 foot-lambert. *See also* lambert. **ft-L** *abbrev.*

foramen magnum *n.* The large hole at the base of the skull through which the *spinal cord passes.
[From Latin *foramen* a hole, from *forare* to bore or pierce + *magnum* large]

foramen of Monro *n.* Either of the openings of the two lateral *ventricles of the brain into the third ventricle. Also called the *interventricular foramen.*
[Named after the Scottish anatomist Alexander Monro (1733–1817) who first drew attention to it in 1783]

forced-choice *adj.* Of or relating to a test, experiment, procedure, or questionnaire in which the respondent has to select a response from a set of alternatives such as *Yes/No* or *Strongly Disagree/Disagree/Neutral/Agree/Strongly Agree. See also* response category. *Compare* free response.

forced compliance *n.* Yielding to social pressure to make a statement or behave in a way that conflicts with one's attitudes, as when an experimenter induces a research participant to tell a lie to another research participant. According to the theory of *cognitive dissonance, such behaviour tends to result in an *attitude change to reduce the dissonance between the two cognitions *My attitude is X* and *My statement (or behaviour) was anti-X.* The second cognition is behaviourally anchored and cannot easily be changed once the statement has been made or the action performed, but the first cognition can and often does change. The theory predicts, and experimental research confirms, that the attitude tends to be greatest when the justification for the counterattitudinal behaviour is least—for example, when the person was offered a small rather than a large financial incentive for it.

forebrain *n.* The front part of the brain, divided into the *telencephalon and *diencephalon. It includes the *cerebral hemispheres, *thalamus, *hypothalamus, and associated structures. Also called the *prosencephalon*, especially in a developing embryo. *Compare* midbrain, hindbrain.

foreclosure *n.* In *psychoanalysis, a *defence mechanism, first identified in 1956 by the French psychoanalyst Jacques Lacan (1901–81), involving the expulsion of a fundamental signifier, such as the *phallus as a fundamental signifier of the *castration complex, from a person's symbolic universe. It may be a defence mechanism specific to *psychosis (1), and it differs from *repression inasmuch as the foreclosed signifier is not integrated into the person's unconscious and does not re-emerge from within as a *neurotic (1) *symptom but may return in the form of a *psychotic (1) *hallucination. The idea is traceable to an article in 1894 by Sigmund Freud (1856–1939) on 'The Neuro-Psychoses of Defence' (*Standard Edition,* III, pp. 45–61): 'There is, however, a much more energetic and successful kind of defence. Here, the ego rejects the incompatible idea together with its affect and behaves as if the idea had never occurred to the ego at all' (p. 58).

forensic linguistics *n.* The application of linguistic techniques in the investigation of crimes to show, for example, that an incriminating utterance recorded on tape is unlikely to have been spoken by the defendant in a criminal trial, or that different passages in an alleged confession were probably written by different people. *See also* stylostatistics.

forensic psychiatry *n.* Applications of *psychiatry to legal questions, such as diminished responsibility and fitness to stand trial. *Compare* forensic psychology.
[From Latin *forensis* public, from *forum* a public place]

forensic psychology *n.* A field of *applied psychology devoted to psychological aspects of legal processes in court. The term is increasingly often applied to *criminological psychology as well, although the derivation of the word suggests a more limited meaning. *Compare* forensic psychiatry.

foreplay *n.* Sexual activity, such as kissing and stroking, preceding sexual intercourse.

forgetting *n.* The process by which memories are lost. *See* decay theory, memory, proactive interference, retroactive interference.

forgetting law *n.* The proposition that the amount of information forgotten increases linearly with the logarithm of the time elapsed since learning.

formal operations *n.* In the theory of cognitive development of the Swiss psychologist Jean Piaget (1896–1980), the developmental stage beginning at about 12 years when children become proficient in manipulating their internal representations of abstract concepts as well as concrete objects. *See also* mental operation. *Compare* concrete operations, pre-operational stage, sensorimotor stage.

formal universals *n.* One of the classes of *linguistic universals, consisting of the abstract rules that govern the grammars of languages, such as the transformational rules that all languages appear to have for converting a statement such as *This job is easy* into a question such as *Is this job easy?* In this case the transformational rule is simply to move the verb to the beginning of the sentence. *See also* transformational grammar, universal grammar.

formant *n.* A peak in the spectrum of frequencies of a specific speech sound, analogous to the *fundamental frequency or one of the *overtones of a musical tone, which helps to give the speech sound its distinctive sound quality or *timbre. For example, in a typical female voice, the first two formants F1 and F2 of the *schwa vowel in the word *bird* or *fern* are about 650 hertz and 1,593 hertz; in a typical male voice F1 is about 513 hertz and F2 about 1,377 hertz.

form constancy *n.* Another name for *shape constancy. *See also* perceptual constancy.

formication *n.* The sensation of insects crawling over or under one's skin, most commonly experienced as a symptom of *withdrawal from alcohol or cocaine. Also called *parasitosis*. *See also* cocaine bug, tactile hallucination.
[From Latin *formicare* to crawl around, from *formica* an ant + -*ation* indicating a process or condition]

fornix *n.* Any structure resembling an arch, especially the archlike band of white fibres in the limbic system at the base of the brain, projecting from the *hippocampus to the *mammillary bodies, involved in memory and the control of eating. Also called the *vault*. **fornical** *adj.*
[From Latin *fornix* a vault]

Förster phenomenon *n.* Another name for the *Aubert–Förster phenomenon.

fortis *adj.* Of or relating to a *consonant speech sound articulated with considerable muscular tension of the organs of speech and strong breath pressure, such as the initial phonemes in *pie*, *tea*, *key*, *chew*, *jaw*, *fee*, *thigh*, *see*, and *shoe*. In English, a *vowel is shortened when it occurs immediately before a fortis consonant, and this is called pre-fortis *clipping. *Compare* lenis.
[From Latin *fortis* strong]

Fortral *n.* A proprietary name for the narcotic analgesic drug *pentazocine.
[Trademark]

40-hertz oscillations *n.* Another (inaccurate) name for *gamma waves.

forward association *n.* A learned association between a *stimulus (1) and either another stimulus or a *response occurring later in time. *Compare* backward association.

forward conditioning *n*. The usual method of *classical conditioning, in which the *conditioned stimulus precedes the *unconditioned stimulus. *Compare* backward conditioning.

forward masking *n*. A form of *masking that occurs when the perception of a stimulus called the *test stimulus* is diminished or eliminated by the presentation of a different stimulus called the *masking stimulus* that precedes it. In the case of *visual masking, when the test stimulus and masking stimulus do not overlap spatially, the phenomenon is called *paracontrast. *See also* auditory masking. *Compare* backward masking, simultaneous masking.

founded content *n*. Another name for *Gestaltqualität*.
[From *found* to cast metal or some other substance by melting and pouring it into a mould]

founder effect *n*. The tendency for an isolated offshoot of a population to develop genetic differences from the parent population owing to the distribution of *alleles in its founder members not being perfectly representative of the distribution in the parent population. *Compare* genetic drift.

four-card problem *n*. Another name for the *Wason selection task.

Fourier analysis *n*. The decomposition of a *time series or a periodic phenomenon such as a sound wave or the variation in luminance across a visual image into its component *sinusoidal components of different frequencies and amplitudes by fitting terms of a *Fourier series to it. *See also* Fourier series, Fourier theorem, Fourier transform, Ohm's acoustic law.
[Named after the French mathematician Baron Jean Baptiste Joseph Fourier (1768–1830) who published the fundamental mathematical results underlying it in 1822]

Fourier series *n*. An infinite series of the form
$\frac{1}{2}a_0 + a_1 \cos x + b_1 \sin x + a_2 \cos 2x + b_2 \sin 2x + \ldots$
that can be used to decompose or to approximate a *time series or periodic function in *Fourier analysis.

Fourier theorem *n*. A mathematical proof that any periodic function can be decomposed by *Fourier analysis into a *Fourier series that is a sum of sine and cosine terms with suitable constants.

Fourier transform *n*. A function of the form $f(t)$ that can be obtained from another function $f(x)$ by multiplying by e^{itx} and integrating over all values of x. It plays a crucial part in *Fourier analysis.

fourth ventricle *See under* ventricle.

fovea *n*. Any small pit or depression on or in the body, especially the *fovea centralis*, the small pit in the centre of the *macula lutea of the *retina, about half a millimetre in diameter, densely packed with *cones but lacking rods, where the image of an object in the direct line of vision falls and where vision is sharpest. *See also* Arago phenomenon, Donders' law, parafovea. **foveae** *pl*. **foveal** *adj*.
[From Latin *fovea* a pit]

fractionation *n*. A technique of scaling used in *psychophysics in which an observer is presented with a stimulus that is assigned an arbitrary value or number, then the observer is asked to select a stimulus whose magnitude is exactly half, that stimulus being assigned a number half the size of the first one, and so on. *See also* mel.

fragile X syndrome *n*. The most common inherited cause of *mental retardation, involving an easily damaged X chromosome with a tip hanging by a narrow thread; the syndrome is often accompanied by *attention-deficit/ hyperactivity disorder, with additional characteristics such as enlarged head, long face, prominent ears and (in males) enlarged testicles.

fragrant odour *n*. One of the six primary odours in *Henning's prism, one of the four in the *Crocker–Henderson system, and one of the seven in the *stereochemical theory, resembling the odour of lavender or rose petals. US *fragrant odor*. Also called *flowery odour* or *floral odour*.

frame *n*. **1.** A rigid structure surrounding or enclosing an object such as a picture or a window. **2.** An underlying assumption or set of assumptions that supports an interpretation or a concept and that functions as an interpretive frame of reference for thinking about the concept. In the branch of *artificial intelligence devoted to *knowledge representation, a frame is a knowledge structure of an everyday aspect of the world such as a house, containing fixed structural information (all houses are assumed to have walls, a roof, and various other fixed attributes) and slots capable of accepting one of two or more values representing variable information (a house may be built from brick, concrete, or wood, and it may or may not have a garden, a garage, a swimming pool, and so on). This sense, close to the concept of a *schema, was formulated in 1975 by the US cognitive scientist Marvin (Lee) Minsky (born 1927). *See* frame problem, framing effect. **3.** A single image in a sequence forming a cinema, television, or video film; hence, figuratively, a part of a *script (3) representing a single event, action, or scene. *See also* schema.

frame problem *n.* In *artificial intelligence and especially *knowledge representation, the problem of specifying formally what is left unchanged when an action is performed. A simple example might involve moving a block from a table on to the floor: this obviously leaves the colour of the block unchanged, and in a formal representation of the action this needs to be made explicit, because some actions do have side-effects, but a difficulty arises from the fact that an infinity of potential changes have to be accounted for. This problem is often solved with the help of some form of *non-monotonic reasoning, especially *default reasoning.

frameshift mutation *n.* A *mutation resulting from the insertion or deletion of a base pair, or a number of base pairs that is not a multiple of three, causing subsequent base pairs to be grouped wrongly into triplets at the stage of translation into *amino acids. *See also* frameshift suppression.
[So called because the genetic code is in effect read through a moving window or frame displaying three bases at a time]

frameshift suppression *n.* The process whereby the effects of a *frameshift mutation are overcome, either by the reinsertion of the original gene or by the action of a specialized form of *transfer RNA, called an extragenic frameshift suppressor, that can recognize four-base sequences.

framing effect *n.* An effect of the description, labelling, or presentation of a problem on responses to it. A classic example was provided in 1981 by the US-based Israeli psychologists Amos Tversky (1937–96) and Daniel Kahneman (born 1934), who invited participants to choose between two programmes for combating an unusual disease that was expected to kill 600 people. Participants in one group were told that programme A would save 200 lives, whereas programme B had a 1/3 probability of saving 600 lives and a 2/3 probability of saving no one, and in this *frame (2), focusing on gains, 72 per cent preferred A to B. Participants in a second group were told that under programme C 400 people would die, whereas under programme D there was a 1/3 probability that no one would die and a 2/3 probability that 600 would die, and in this frame, focusing on losses, 78 per cent preferred D to C. The majority of participants were *risk-averse in their preference of A over B in the gain frame but *risk-seeking in their preference of D over C in the loss frame, although the two frames are merely different ways of describing the same problem. This effect occurs even if both problems are presented to the same group of participants. A framing effect on a decision is called a *decision frame*. *See also* cancellation heuristic, prospect theory, risk aversion, Wason selection task. *Compare* context effect.

Frankfurt school *n.* A movement involving political philosophy and psychology founded at the Institute for Social Research at the University of Frankfurt in Germany, closed by the Nazis in 1933, and re-established in 1934 at Columbia University in New York. Its leading figures included Max Horkheimer (1895–1973), Theodor W(iesengrund) Adorno (1903–69), and Herbert Marcuse (1898–1979), who were united by a belief in the possibility and desirability of a Marxist *critical theory and a rejection of *positivism (1, 2).

Fraser illusion *n.* Another name for any of the forms of the *twisted-cord illusion, which Fraser himself called the 'twisted cord with a chequer-work background illusion'. *See also* Fraser spiral.
[Named after the Scottish physician and psychologist James Fraser (1863–1936) who published it as a new illusion in the *British Journal of Psychology* in 1908]

Fraser spiral *n.* A *twisted-cord illusion in which a series of concentric circles composed of cord made by twisting dark and light strands together, or of thin strips of diagonal stripes resembling such a twisted cord, appear as a spiral when presented against a chequered background composed of radiating curved bands (see illustration). The term is a misnomer, given that it is not actually a spiral.

[Named after the Scottish physician and psychologist James Fraser (1863–1936) who published it together with other twisted-cord illusions in the *British Journal of Psychology* in 1908]

Fraser spiral. What appears to be a spiral is in fact a series of concentric circles, as can be confirmed by tracing all the way round any of them.

fraternal twins *n.* A non-technical name for *dizygotic twins.
[From Latin *frater* a brother]

free association *n.* A technique of *psychoanalysis in which the patient is encouraged to relate to the analyst all thoughts, feelings, wishes, sensations, memories, and images that come to mind, however embarrassing or trivial they might seem. It is designed to incapacitate the *second censorship* between the *preconscious and *consciousness, thereby exposing the unconscious defences operating through the *first censorship* between the *unconscious (2) and preconscious. Sigmund Freud (1856–1939) revealed in 'A Note on the Prehistory of the Technique of Analysis' in 1920 that he was influenced by the German political writer and satirist Ludwig Börne (originally called Löb Baruch, 1786–1838), who recommended a form of generative writing that begins by putting on paper everything that comes to mind, in order to avoid self-censorship and to increase originality (*Standard Edition*, XVIII, pp. 263–5, at p. 265). Some credit for developing the technique should be given to Frau Emmy von N, one of Freud's earliest patients who, as Freud recounted in 1895 in his co-authored book *Studies on Hysteria* (*Standard Edition*, II), asked him 'not to keep on asking her where this or that came from, but to let her tell me what she had to say' (p. 63), and when she followed this procedure, her verbal accounts turned out to contain 'a fairly complete reproduction of the memories and new impressions which have affected her since our last talk, and it often leads on, in a quite unexpected way, to pathogenic reminiscences of which she unburdens herself without being asked to' (p. 56). At about the same time (in 1904) and independently of Freud, Carl Gustav Jung (1875–1961) introduced his *word-association test, and this also influenced the development of the technique of free association. *See also* dream analysis, fundamental rule of psychoanalysis. *Compare* directed association, introspection.

freebasing *n.* Increasing the potency of *cocaine by extracting its active alkaloid (the free base), heating it, and inhaling the vapours through a cigarette or water pipe (*bong). *See also* crack.

free energy *n.* In *psychoanalysis, psychic energy in the *primary process, which seeks immediate and total discharge through the most direct route available. Sigmund Freud (1856–1939) published his theory of free energy and *bound energy in 1895, in his 'Project for a Scientific Psychology' (*Standard Edition*, I, pp. 177–397), basing it on the *principle of constancy. *See also* nirvana principle, pleasure principle.

free-floating anxiety *n.* Another name for *generalized anxiety disorder.

Freemish crate *n.* A popular *impossible figure depicting the frame of a box-like object that can be drawn but could not exist in actual space (see illustration).
[Origin obscure, named in a letter to the *Scientific American* in June 1966 containing the earliest published version of the object]

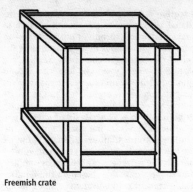

Freemish crate

free morpheme *n.* A *morpheme that can occur on its own as a word, such as *tree*. *Compare* bound form.

free nerve ending *n.* A *sensory receptor consisting of finely myelinated or unmyelinated ends of the axons of nerve fibres, located throughout the body but concentrated mainly in the *dermis or *epidermis of the skin, in certain *mucous membranes, in the *corneas of the eyes, adjacent to the roots of hairs, and around the bodies of *sweat glands. Some free nerve endings are *pain receptors (nocireceptors); others function as *temperature receptors supplying *warm spots and *cold spots on the skin.

free operant avoidance conditioning *n.* Another name for *Sidman avoidance conditioning.

free radical *n.* Any of a number of highly reactive *radical (2) molecules having an unpaired electron occupying the outer orbital and therefore being prone to snatch electrons from other molecules in processes such as oxidation, which rusts metals, spoils butter, and injures cells in the body, probably including neurons in the basal ganglia in Parkinson's disease. *See also* mitochondrial DNA.

free recall *n.* Retrieval of information from memory without the help of *cues (3), and hence often contrasted with *cued recall. The term is also used for retrieval of a number of items of information in any order, in contradistinction to *serial recall. *See also* clustering, recall.

free response *n.* In psychometrics, a response to a test item that the respondent supplies without constraints, in contradistinction to a response that the respondent chooses from a set of alternatives. *Compare* forced-choice, multiple-choice, response category.

free-rider problem *n.* Another name for a *public goods dilemma.
[From the colloquial term *free-rider*, a person who enjoys benefits obtained for workers by a trade union without joining the union]

Frégoli syndrome *n.* A *delusional misidentification of strangers as familiar people in disguise; thus a delusion of overidentification, in contrast to *Capgras syndrome, which involves underidentification. *Compare* intermetamorphosis.
[Named after Leopoldo Frégoli (1867–1936), an Italian actor of the *belle époque* who was famous for his ability as a mimic]

frequency *n.* **1.** The number of times that an event occurs in a specified time period; more specifically the number of times that a wave repeats itself in one second, generally expressed in *hertz (Hz) or cycles per second. Frequency (*f*) is equivalent to the velocity of propagation (*v*) divided by wavelength (*λ*): $f = v/\lambda$. The *audibility range of sound waves extends from about 16 Hz at the low end to about 20,000 Hz at the high end for a person with normal hearing, and the *visible spectrum of light from about 405,405 billion Hz at the red end to about 769,231 billion Hz at the violet end. *See also* spatial frequency. **2.** In statistics and measurement theory, the number of items or scores falling into a particular class. *Frequency data* are scores representing counts rather than other kinds of measurements.

frequency-dependent *adj.* Of or relating to a *gene or *allele whose *Darwinian fitness is dependent on the frequency of the gene or allele in the population, as when a phenotypic characteristic is advantageous only if it is unusual in the population or only if it is common.

frequency-dependent selection *n.* A form of *natural selection in which the *fitness of a particular *genotype depends on its frequency in the population. *See also* apostatic selection, stabilizing selection.

frequency distribution *n*. In statistics, a table or graph showing classes into which the data have been grouped, together with their corresponding frequencies, that is, the number of scores falling into each class.

frequency law *n*. In the doctrine of *associationism, a law introduced by the English philosopher John Stuart Mill (1806–73), according to which mental elements that frequently occur together tend to become associated. It was influential in the early development of *behaviourism. *See also* grouping law. *Compare* contiguity law, similarity law.

frequency polygon *n*. In descriptive statistics, a line graph showing the relationship between the values of scores, usually on the horizontal axis, and their frequencies of occurrence, usually on the vertical axis.

frequency theory *n*. A theory of pitch perception first proposed in 1886 by the British physiologist William Rutherford (1839–99) according to which the ear converts acoustic vibrations into nerve impulses by emitting one impulse for each cycle of the sound wave in the manner of a telephone. This mechanism is believed to operate for low-frequency sounds, but because an auditory neuron can respond up to only about 500 hertz, this theory cannot explain the perception of higher-pitched sounds within the *audibility range. Also called the *telephone theory*. *Compare* place theory, volley theory.

frequency threshold curve *n*. Another name for the *tuning curve. **FTC** *abbrev*.

frequency tuning curve *n*. Another name for the *tuning curve. **FTC** *abbrev*.

Freudian *adj*. Of or relating to the *psychoanalytic ideas and practices of the Austrian neurologist Sigmund Freud (1856–1939) or of his daughter, the Austrian-born British psychoanalyst Anna Freud (1895–1982). The term *Freudian analysis* generally refers to the classical approach of Anna Freud and is used in contradistinction to *Adlerian, *Eriksonian, *Jungian, *Kleinian, *Kohutian, *Lacanian, *Winnicottian, and other schools of analysis.

Freudian slip *n*. A colloquial name for a *parapraxis.

fricative *n*. A *consonant speech sound articulated by narrowing the mouth passage to make the airflow turbulent but to allow it to pass through without interruption, as in the initial *phonemes in the words *fire*, *high*, *see*, *shoe*, *thee*, *thigh*, *vow*, *zoo*, and the second phoneme in *azure*. *See also* manner of articulation.

Friedman two-way analysis of variance *n*. A distribution-free statistical test of the *null hypothesis that several related samples are distributed similarly. For each subject or case, the scores are ranked across samples, and the test statistic is based on these ranks. The standard equivalent distribution-dependent test is one-way *analysis of variance (ANOVA). Also called *Friedman two-way ANOVA*.
[Named after the prominent US economist Milton Friedman (born 1912) who developed it in 1937]

fright *n*. Sudden fear or alarm. Sigmund Freud (1856–1939) distinguished in 1920 between fright (German *Schreck*), anxiety (*Angst*), and fear (*Furcht*): fright 'is the name we give to the state a person gets into when he has run into danger without being prepared for it'; anxiety 'describes a particular state of expecting the danger or preparing for it, even though it may be an unknown one'; and fear 'requires a definite object of which to be afraid' (*Beyond the Pleasure Principle*, *Standard Edition*, XVIII, pp. 7–64, at pp. 12–13).

frigidity *n*. **1.** A lack of warmth, passion, or emotional responsiveness. **2.** More specifically in relation to females, sexual unresponsiveness. *See also* dyspareunia, female orgasmic disorder, female sexual arousal disorder, vaginismus. **frigid** *adj*.
[From Latin *frigidus* frozen, from *frigus* cold]

Fromm's typology *n*. In *neo-Freudian theory, a classification of character types suggested by the German-born US psychoanalyst Erich Fromm (1900–80) in his book *Man for Himself* (1947), comprising: *exploitative orientation, *hoarding orientation, *marketing orientation, *productive orientation, *receptive orientation.

frontal eye field *See under* motor cortex. **FEF** *abbrev*.

frontal leucotomy *n*. Surgical severing of the neural connections between the *thalamus and the *frontal lobes of the brain to relieve severe cases of *schizophrenia and *bipolar disorders. Also called *prefrontal leucotomy* or simply *leucotomy*. *Compare* frontal lobotomy. Also spelt *frontal leukotomy*.
[From Greek *leukos* white + *tome* a cut, alluding to white matter in the brain]

frontal lobe *n*. The anterior *lobe of each *cerebral hemisphere, separated on its lateral or outer surface from the parietal lobe by the *central sulcus and from the temporal lobe by the *lateral sulcus, involved in attention, short-term memory, and activities requiring planning and organization. Lesions in this area are associated with *frontal lobe syndrome. *See also* aprosodia, dysexecutive syndrome, frontal leucotomy, frontal lobe syndrome, frontal lobotomy, lobe, prefrontal cortex, pseudodepression, Wisconsin Card Sorting test, *Witzelsucht*.

frontal lobe syndrome *n*. A pattern of signs and symptoms associated with damage to the *frontal lobe of the brain, typically including general impairment of planning functions, and either boastfulness, lack of inhibition, *hypomanic episodes, impulsiveness, and antisocial behaviour, or *depression, apathy, negligence about personal appearance, and *perseveration (2). *See also* dysexecutive syndrome.

frontal lobotomy *n*. Surgical removal of portions of the *frontal lobes of the brain, usually in the *prefrontal cortex, and severing of the neural connections between the *thalamus and the *frontal lobes, as a method of treating intractable *depression or pain. Also called *prefrontal lobotomy* or simply *lobotomy*. *Compare* frontal leucotomy.
[From Greek *lobos* a lobe + *tome* a cut]

frontal plane *n*. Another name for a *coronal plane.

frontal section *n*. Another name for a *coronal section.

front vowel *n*. A *vowel (see the diagram accompanying that entry) produced in the front of the mouth with the front part of the tongue raised, such as the vowels in *see*, French *thé*,

red, *trap*, and German *Mann*. *Compare* back vowel, central vowel.

frotteurism *n*. A *paraphilia characterized by recurrent, intense sexual fantasies, urges, or behaviour involving touching or rubbing up against non-consenting people, often in crowded public places. Also called *frottage*.
frotteur *n*. One who practises *frotteurism.
[From French *frotter* to rub]

frozen noise *n*. A burst of *white noise that has been recorded and is repeated over and over again. *Compare* pink noise, coloured noise.

frustration *n*. The blocking or prevention of a potentially rewarding or satisfying act or sequence of behaviour; or the emotional response to such hindrance. *See also* frustration–aggression hypothesis.
[From Latin *frustrare* to cheat + *-ation* indicating a process or condition]

frustration–aggression hypothesis *n*. A conjecture, originally put forward by the US psychologist John Dollard (1900–80) and four colleagues in their book *Frustration and Aggression* in 1939, the strongest form of which states that the instigation to aggressive behaviour always presupposes frustration and that frustration always leads to aggression.

F scale *n*. A questionnaire to measure *authoritarianism, first published by the German philosopher, sociologist, and psychologist Theodor W(iesengrund) Adorno (1903–69) and several colleagues in the book *The Authoritarian Personality* (1950). It is composed of the following nine aspects, typical items being shown in italics, and a Yes answer always indicating a tendency to authoritarianism. Conventionalism (rigid adherence to conventional middle-class values): *Obedience and respect for authority are the most important virtues children should learn*; Authoritarian Submission (a submissive and uncritical attitude towards authority figures): *Young people sometimes get rebellious ideas, but as they grow up they ought to get over them and settle down*; Authoritarian Aggression (a punishing attitude towards violations of conventional values): *Sex crimes, such as rape and attacks on children, deserve more than mere imprisonment; such criminals ought to be publicly whipped, or* *worse*; Anti-Intraception (a dislike of subjectivity and imagination): *When a person has a problem or worry, it is best for him not to think about it, but to keep busy with more cheerful things*; Superstition and Stereotypy (a belief in supernatural determinants of human fate and a tendency to think in rigid categories): *Some day it will probably be shown that astrology can explain a lot of things*; Power and Toughness (a preoccupation with strong/weak, leader/follower relationships): *People can be divided into two distinct classes: the weak and the strong*; Destructiveness and Cynicism (a distrustful and misanthropic attitude towards people in general): *Human nature being what it is, there will always be war and conflict*; Projectivity (a tendency to project one's own unconscious impulses on to others): *Homosexuals are hardly better than criminals and ought to be severely punished*; Sex (exaggerated concern with people's sexual activities): *The wild sex life of the old Greeks and Romans was tame compared to some of the goings-on in this country, even in places where people might least expect it*. Also called the *California F scale*.

[From *(Potentiality for) F(ascism) scale*]

F statistic *n*. An important statistic that underlies the *analysis of variance (ANOVA). For a set of scores divided into groups, it is defined as the total *variance or *mean square between groups divided by the total variance or mean square within groups. Also called the *F ratio*.

fugue *n*. A form of *dissociation characterized by apparently purposeful travel outside one's normal range of movement, with *amnesia during the period of travel. If it causes significant distress or impairment in social, occupational, or other areas of functioning, it may be diagnosed as the mental disorder *dissociative fugue.

[From Latin *fuga* a flight]

Fullerton–Cattell law *n*. In *psychophysics, the proposition that for any stimulus intensity I, the *difference threshold ΔI is proportional to the square root of I, hence $\Delta I = k\sqrt{I}$, where k is a constant, rather than being proportional to I itself, as in *Weber's law, which is both simpler and generally more accurate.

[Named after the US psychologists George Stuart Fullerton (1859–1925) and James McKeen Cattell (1860–1944) who formulated it in 1892]

full primal sketch *See under* primal sketch.

functional *adj*. In relation to a disorder, referring to changes in behaviour or action, without any observable change in physical structure in the person or any organ or body part.

functional analysis of behaviour *n*. The application of the laws of *operant conditioning, or less commonly those of another learning theory, to establish the relationships between *stimuli (1) and *responses. US *functional analysis of behavior*.

functional autonomy *n*. The property of a drive or habit that has become detached from the goal that originally motivated it and operates independently. A classic example is the drive or habit associated with making money, initially to buy goods and services that improve the quality of one's life, but often becoming an end in itself. Many *compulsions such as hand-washing manifest functional autonomy.

functional equivalence hypothesis *n*. The proposition that *imagery, although it does not result from stimulation of sense organs, is essentially the same as perception in the way that it functions.

functional fixedness *n*. An impaired ability to solve a problem requiring the use of a particular object, the impairment being caused by recent use of the object for a different function, or by recent perception of the object performing a different function. The phenomenon was first reported in 1935 by the German-born US psychologist Karl Duncker (1903–40), who experimented with five problems, including what he called the *box problem*: Three small lighted candles are to be attached to a wooden door at eye level. The participants or subjects were presented with many objects, including a matchbox containing matches, a similar-sized cardboard box containing small candles, and a third similar box containing thumbtacks (drawing pins). The solution was to empty the three boxes, to fix them to the door with thumbtacks, and to stand a lighted candle in each box. Only 43 per cent of Duncker's subjects solved the box problem in that form, but 100 per cent of a control group solved it when presented with the same objects but with the three boxes empty, thus avoiding functional fixedness arising from perceiving the boxes as containers of other objects. Across all five problems, Duncker found that functional fixedness of the crucial objects reduced the number of solutions by almost a half. Duncker pointed out that the phenomenon applies not only to physical objects or tools, but also to mental objects or concepts. A translation from the original German into English of Duncker's classic article was published in the journal *Psychological Monographs* in 1945. Also called *functional fixity* or *functional embeddedness*. *See also Einstellung*, set (2).

functionalism *n*. Any doctrine that emphasizes utility or purpose, especially the school of psychology that was launched in 1896 by the US pragmatist philosopher and psychologist John Dewey (1859–1952) and that flourished for many years at the University of Chicago under the influence of Dewey, George Herbert Mead (1863–1931), and James Rowland Angell (1869–1949), at Columbia University under the influence of Edward Thorndike (1874–1949) and Robert S(essions) Woodworth (1869–1962), and at Harvard University under the influence of William James (1842–1910). Instead of analysing the structure of mental experience, as was conventional in *structuralism (2), functionalism examined both mental experience and behaviour from the standpoint of their functional value in adapting the organism to its environment, in a deliberate attempt to introduce evolutionary ideas into psychology. Conscious experiences were interpreted as phenomena that arise when automatic, reflex behaviour is inadequate to meet the needs of an organism, as when a person who is learning to ride a bicycle eventually ceases to be conscious of every movement when conscious awareness is no longer needed. The early practitioners of functionalism were the first to use non-human animals in psychological experiments. During the 1920s and 1930s, functionalism was gradually swallowed up by *behaviourism.

[From Latin *functio* a performance, from *fungi* to perform + Greek *-ismos* indicating a state or condition]

functionalist *n*. A member or follower of the school of *functionalism, or one who advocates or practises functionalism.

functional MRI *See under* MRI.

function type *n*. In *analytical psychology, any of the personality types identified by Carl Gustav Jung (1875–1961). According to Jung, people fall into the *rational type* (subdivided into *feeling type* or *thinking type*) or *irrational type* (subdivided into *sensing type* or *intuitive type*). Jung also distinguished between *extraverts* and *introverts*. *See also* Myers–Briggs Type Indicator.

function word *n*. Any word that fulfils a specific grammatical role but has little or no independent meaning outside of its linguistic context, typical examples being articles such as *the*, pronouns such as *she*, and conjunctions such as *and*. *See also* telegraphic speech. *Compare* content word.

fundamental attribution error *n*. A pervasive tendency to underestimate the importance of external situational pressures and to overestimate the importance of internal motives and dispositions in interpreting the behaviour of others. In a typical experiment, participants filled in questionnaires indicating their attitudes towards the Cuban leader Fidel Castro and towards the legalization of cannabis, then half of them were instructed to write essays in favour of Castro and the rest to write essays in favour of legalizing cannabis. The pro-Castro essays were then shown to the writers of the pro-cannabis essays and vice versa, and the readers estimated the writers' true attitudes towards the issues discussed in their essays. Although the readers knew the constraints under which the essays had been written, they failed to take these external situational factors sufficiently into account and persistently misjudged the writers' attitudes in the direction of the views expressed in the essays. The phenomenon was first identified in 1929 in an article in the journal *Zeitschrift für angewandte Psychologie* by the Polish-born Austrian psychologist Gustav Ichheiser (1897–1969) and was subsequently observed and described in 1944 by the Austrian-born US psychologist Fritz Heider (1896–1988), and in 1965 by the US psychologist Edward Ellsworth Jones (1926–93), who called it *correspondent inference*, but it was not until 1977 that it was named and given prominence by the Canadian psychologist Lee D(avid) Ross (born 1942), to whom it is often (mis)attributed. Ross later came to believe that it could more aptly be called the *dispositionist bias*, and many other social psychologists call it the *overattribution bias*. Cross-cultural research suggests that it is far less pervasive in more collectivist (less individualist) cultures than in the US and northern Europe. *See also* attribution, attributional bias, attribution theory, Kelley's cube.

fundamental colour *n*. Another name for a *primary colour (1, 2, or 3). US *fundamental color*.

fundamental frequency *n*. The *pure tone with the lowest frequency forming a component of a *complex tone, or the analogous sine wave in some other complex oscillatory vibration. Also called a *fundamental*. *See also* missing fundamental illusion. *Compare* harmonic.

fundamental rule of psychoanalysis *n*. The principle according to which a patient undergoing *psychoanalysis should engage wholeheartedly in *free association. Also called the *basic rule of psychoanalysis*. *See also* intellectualization, therapeutic alliance.

fungiform papilla *n*. Any of a large number of flat-topped, mushroom-shaped, reddish-coloured *papillae on the upper surface of the *tongue, most of which are studded with *taste buds around their bases. *Compare* circumvallate papilla, filiform papilla, foliate papilla. **fungiform papillae** *pl*.
[From Latin *fungus* a mushroom + *forma* a shape]

funiculus *n*. Any of the three bundles of nerve fibres into which the H-shaped column of *grey matter running through the length of the *spinal cord divides the *white matter: the lateral funiculus on either side of the H, the posterior funiculus between the dorsal uprights of the H, and the anterior funiculus between the ventral uprights of the H. **funiculi** *pl*.
[From Latin *funiculus* a string, diminutive of *funis* a rope]

furthest neighbour method *n*. Another name for *complete linkage clustering.

fusiform cell *n*. Another name for a *spindle cell.
[From Latin *fusus* a spindle + *forma* a shape]

fusiform gyrus *n*. A spindle-shaped *gyrus on the medial (inside) surface of each *temporal lobe, at the junction with the occipital lobe, occupied by Area V4 of the *visual cortex, largely responsible for colour perception and also implicated in face recognition. It is sometimes taken to include a region that is adjacent and anterior to this and is involved in object perception.
[From Latin *fusus* a spindle + *forma* a shape + Greek *gyros* a circle or ring]

fusion *See* binocular fusion.

fusional language *n*. Another name for an *inflecting language.

fusion of instincts *n*. In *psychoanalysis, the mixing of *Eros and *Thanatos so that they operate jointly, in contrast to the *defusion of instincts in which they operate independently, each pursuing its own *instinctual aim. In a key passage on this phenomenon, Sigmund Freud (1856–1939) wrote in his book *New Introductory Lectures on Psycho-Analysis* (1933, *Standard Edition*, XXII, pp. 5–182): 'In sadism and masochism we have before us two excellent examples of a mixture of two classes of instinct, of Eros and aggressiveness; and we proceed to the hypothesis that this relation is a model of one—the very instinctual impulse that we can examine consists of similar fusions or alloys of the two classes of instinct. These fusions, of course, would be in the most varied ratios' (pp. 104–5).

fuzzy logic *n*. A form of logic based on *fuzzy set theory in which *propositions (1) have continuously graded truth values ranging from 0 to 1, rather than being either false (0) or true (1) as in conventional *Boolean logic. It is influential mainly in the field of *knowledge representation and *neural networks.

fuzzy set *n*. A generalized concept of a set in which elements have continuously graded degrees of set membership ranging from 0 to 1, rather than either not belonging (0) or belonging (1) as in conventional *set theory. It was developed in 1965 by the Azerbaijani-born US engineer and systems theorist Lotfi A. Zadeh (born 1921) to reflect the fact that many natural categories, such as baldness, tallness, and beauty, have intrinsically indistinct boundaries. *See also* fuzzy logic, guppy effect, prototype theory.

g *abbrev.* General factor of ability or intelligence, a concept first proposed in an article by the English psychologist Charles Edward Spearman (1863–1945) in the *American Journal of Psychology* in 1904 on the basis of *factor analysis to explain the correlations between scores on diverse intelligence tests and subtests. Spearman interpreted it as mental energy, but others reinterpreted it as abstract reasoning ability or as neural processing speed, and some, starting in 1916 with the English psychologist Godfrey H(ilton) (later Sir Godfrey) Thomson (1881–1955), viewed it as a mere statistical abstraction devoid of psychological meaning. Also called *general ability*. *See also* factorial validity. *Compare* primary mental abilities.

GABA *abbrev.* Gamma-aminobutyric acid, the commonest inhibitory *neurotransmitter in the central nervous system. When it is released into a synapse, it tends to prevent the postsynaptic neuron from firing. *See also* picrotoxin, Purkinje cell.
[From *g(amma)* (γ) the third letter of the Greek alphabet + *a(mine)* + Greek *b(outyron)* butter, from *bous* ox + *tyros* cheese + *-ikos* of, relating to, or resembling]

GABAergic *adj.* Releasing *GABA; also activated by or responding to GABA, this extended usage being widespread but consistently rejected by the English physiologist Sir Henry Hallet Dale (1875–1968), who coined the suffix *-ergic*, and by many other authorities. *Compare* adrenergic, cholinergic, dopaminergic, noradrenergic, serotonergic.

GABA receptor complex *n.* A structure that is present in certain cells of the central nervous system and that comprises three interacting neuroreceptors, the first being a receptor that is stimulated by sedative or hypnotic drugs such as *barbiturates and is inhibited by *convulsant drugs; the second a receptor that is stimulated by *benzodiazepines; and the third the primary *GABA receptor, stimulation of which inhibits neuronal activity by enlarging chloride channels, this effect being augmented by the presence of either barbiturates or benzodiazepines and blocked by convulsants.

gag reflex *n.* A reflex contraction of muscles in the *pharynx and retraction of the tongue in response to stroking of the *velar or *pharyngeal surfaces. Its absence is a sign of a lesion in the vagus nerve or the glossopharyngeal nerve. Also called the *pharyngeal reflex*.
[From *gag* to retch]

gain from illness *n.* An umbrella term for *primary gain and *secondary gain.

gain–loss effect *n.* The finding that people tend to be most attracted to others whose liking for them appears to have increased, and least attracted to others whose liking for them appears to have decreased, such increases and decreases in the perceived estimation of others having more impact on their attraction towards those others than constant levels of liking or rewarding behaviour from them. The phenomenon was first remarked on by the Dutch philosopher Baruch Spinoza (1632–77) in his *Ethics*, published posthumously in 1677: 'Hatred which is completely vanquished by love passes into love; and love is thereupon greater than if hatred had not preceded it. For he who begins to love a thing, which he had wont to hate or regard with pain, from the very fact of loving feels pleasure' (proposition 44). The phenomenon was first studied empirically by the US psychologists Elliot Aronson (born 1932) and Darwyn E. Linder (born 1939) who reported in the *Journal of Experimental Social Psychology* in

1965 the results of an experiment in which students overheard conversations in which they were being discussed by a fellow student either entirely positively, entirely negatively, beginning with negative comments and becoming more positive (gain), or beginning with positive comments and becoming more negative (loss). The students were later asked how much they liked the fellow student whose conversation they had overheard, and the results showed that their liking was greatest in the gain condition and least in the loss condition.

gain, primary/secondary *See* primary gain, secondary gain.

gain score *n.* In psychometrics, the difference between a person's score on a test and the same person's score on the same test, or an *equivalent form or *parallel form, administered earlier.

gait apraxia *n.* A form of *apraxia characterized by difficulty in walking, and often in making other voluntary movements with the feet or legs such as kicking a ball, sometimes sufficiently severe to require confinement to a wheelchair.
[From Old Norse *gata* a path, way, street, or manner of behaviour]

gait ataxia *n.* A form of *ataxia caused by a lesion in the *anterior lobe of the *cerebellum, usually as a consequence of *alcohol dependence, characterized by staggering movement even when sober and inability to stand still with feet together. *See also* Romberg's sign. *Compare* locomotor ataxia.

gall bladder *n.* A muscular sac attached to the right side of the liver that releases *bile into the duodenum.
[From Greek *chole* bile]

Galton bar *n.* A device consisting of a horizontal rod that can be bisected by an adjustable vertical pointer, used to test the accuracy of visual estimates of length.
[Named after the English explorer, amateur scientist, and psychologist Sir Francis Galton (1822–1911) who invented it]

Galton's law of filial regression *n.* Another name for *filial regression.
[Named after the English explorer and scientist Sir Francis Galton (1822–1911) who first drew attention to it]

Galton whistle *n.* An instrument for emitting high-pitched tones and *ultrasound for determining the upper limits of the *audibility range in humans and other animals. The original version, which the English explorer, amateur scientist, and psychologist Sir Francis Galton (1822–1911) first described in 1876, was a whistle attached to a hollow walking-stick, with a rubber bulb for its operation in the handle, which he used to experiment on animals at London Zoo and elsewhere.

galvanic skin response *n.* A fall in the resistance of the *skin to the passage of a weak electric current, usually measured in the palm of the hand in units of ohms, indicative of emotion or physiological arousal, also called a *psychogalvanic response (PGR)* or an *electrodermal response (EDR)*. *See also* polygraph. *Compare* skin conductance response. **GSR** *abbrev.*
[From *galvanic* of or relating to current electricity, named after the Italian physiologist Luigi Galvani (1737–98) who first showed that muscles contract when electricity is passed through them]

gambler's fallacy *n.* The false belief that the probability of an event in a random sequence is dependent on preceding events, its probability increasing with each successive occasion on which it fails to occur. Thus if black has come up many times in succession at a roulette table, a false belief may develop that red is increasingly likely on each subsequent spin of the wheel, to even out the sequence in the long run; or if a fair coin is tossed repeatedly and tails comes up many times in a row, a gambler may believe that heads is more likely on the following toss; or if a mother gives birth to several girls in succession, she may come to believe that the probability of a boy is greater than $\frac{1}{2}$ for her next baby. *See also* sample size fallacy.

gambling, pathological *See* pathological gambling.

game *n.* **1.** An interactive decision modelled in *game theory. Also called a *strategic game* or a *game of strategy*. *See* Chicken game, Dollar Auction game, give-some game, Newcomb's problem, *N*-person Prisoner's Dilemma,

Prisoner's Dilemma game, public goods dilemma, resource dilemma, social dilemma, take-some game, Ultimatum game. **2.** More generally, any sport, recreational contest, amusement, or pastime conducted according to a code or system of rules.

gamete *n.* A sexual reproductive cell, such as an *ovum or a *spermatozoon, that fuses with another during fertilization. Also called a *germ cell*.
[From Greek *gamete* a wife and *gametes* a husband, from *gameein* to marry]

game theory *n.* A branch of mathematics devoted to the logic of interactive decision making, applicable to any social interaction in which there are two or more decision makers, called *players, each having two or more ways of acting, called *strategies (2), such that the outcome depends on the strategy choices of all the players, and the players have well-defined preferences among the possible outcomes so that numerical *payoffs reflecting these preferences can be assigned to all players for all outcomes. Many social, economic, political, military, and interpersonal conflicts are games in the technical sense, and experimental games based on game theory have been used to study such phenomena as individual and collective rationality, cooperation and competition, trust and suspicion, threats and commitments. Also called the *theory of games* or *games theory*, though the latter phrase is avoided in careful usage. *See* game (1). *See also* admissible alternative/strategy, dominant alternative/strategy, evolutionarily stable strategy, maximin, minimal social situation, minimax, mixed-motive game, mixed strategy, Nash equilibrium, normative (1), payoff, player (1), programmed strategy, social dilemma, strategy (2), sure-thing principle, tit for tat strategy, utility (1), win-stay, lose-change strategy, zero-sum game.

gamma-aminobutyric acid *n.* The full name of what is usually called *GABA.
[From *gamma* (γ) the third letter of the Greek alphabet + *amine* + Greek *boutyron* butter, from *bous* ox + *tyros* cheese + -*ikos* of, relating to, or resembling]

gamma fibre *n.* A medium-diameter partly myelinated type of *efferent somatic nerve fibre, composed of *gamma motor neurons and having intermediate conduction velocity. A typical example is a fibre supplying a muscle spindle. US *gamma fiber*. Also written *γ fibre*. *Compare* alpha fibre, Ia fibre, Ib fibre, II fibre, C fibre.
[From *gamma* (γ) the third letter of the Greek alphabet]

Gamma-hydroxybutyrate *See* GHB.

gamma motor neuron *n.* A type of spinal *motor neuron that supplies *intrafusal muscles and forms part of a *gamma fibre. Also called a *gamma motoneuron*. *Compare* alpha motor neuron, Renshaw cell.

gamma movement *n.* A form of *apparent movement that is elicited when a stimulus is presented in an alternating pattern of high and low illumination or *brightness, with an interstimulus interval of about 60 milliseconds, the visual illusion being created of a single object expanding and shrinking in all dimensions. Also called *gamma motion*. *See also* Korte's laws. *Compare* alpha movement, beta movement, delta movement.

gamma-OH *n.* A proprietary name for gamma-hydroxybutyrate. *See* GHB.

gamma statistic *n.* In descriptive statistics, an index of association between two variables measured on *ordinal scales. If two pairs of scores are examined, they must either be concordant, in the sense that the one ranked higher than the other on the first variable is also ranked higher than the other on the second variable, or discordant. Gamma is defined as the difference between the number of concordant pairs and the number of discordant pairs divided by the total number of concordant and discordant pairs, and it ranges from 0 to 1. Also called *Goodman–Kruskall gamma*, and closely related to *Somers' D and to *Kendall's tau.
[From *gamma* the name of γ, the third letter of the Greek alphabet]

gamma wave *n.* A high-frequency (35–75 hertz) *EEG wave that occurs during thinking. Also called a *40-hertz oscillation*, but this inaccurate term is avoided in careful usage.
[From *gamma* (γ) the third letter of the Greek alphabet]

gamodeme *See under* deme.

ganglion n. A nerve-centre or collection of neuron cell bodies usually (apart from the *basal ganglia and adjacent structures) located in the *peripheral nervous system. See dorsal root ganglion, postganglionic, preganglionic, sympathetic ganglionic chain. **ganglia** or **ganglions** pl.
[From Greek ganglion a cystic tumour]

ganglion cell n. A type of *neuron found in the inner layer of the *retina, nearest the front of the eye, receiving inputs from retinal *bipolar cells, which in turn receive inputs from *rods and *cones. An ON ganglion cell is excited by a spot of light and inhibited by light in a ring surrounding the spot, the inhibition being effected by *horizontal cells; an OFF ganglion cell behaves in the opposite way. Two types of ganglion cells are intermixed in the inner layer: large ganglion cells, which form the first stage of the *magnocellular system and that do not distinguish between signals from different types of photoreceptors and simply add the signals from all three types of cones together, and small ganglion cells that form the first stage of the *parvocellular system and that distinguish between different cone types, from which they add and subtract information, as when a red-minus-green ganglion cell responds only to red light. See also centre-surround receptive field, direction-sensitive neuron, dominator, midget cell, parasol cell, modulator, off-centre cell, on-centre cell, spiral ganglion cell.

ganja n. A common street name for *cannabis.
[From Hindi gaja, from Sanskrit grñja]

Ganser syndrome n. A condition sometimes classified as a *dissociative disorder and sometimes as a *factitious disorder, characterized by the giving of approximate answers to questions, the answers being suggestive of a knowledge of the right answers. Thus, on being asked how many legs a dog has, a person with Ganser syndrome may reply either three or five, and Sigbert Ganser labelled this Vorbeireden, literally talking past. Also called nonsense syndrome. See also prison psychosis. Compare circumstantiality, tangentiality.
[Named after the German psychiatrist Sigbert J. M. Ganser (1853–1931) who first described it in 1897]

Ganzfeld n. A uniform and featureless *visual field, usually created by taping halved ping-pong balls over both eyes and shining a dim red light on to them, perceived as *film colour.
[From German ganz whole + Feld field]

gap junction n. A rare type of synapse in which a signal is transmitted from one neuron to another by electrical induction across a very narrow gap between them without the involvement of any chemical neurotransmitter. Also called an electrical synapse.

Garcia effect n. Another name for *food aversion learning.
[Named after the US psychologist John Garcia (born 1917) who did much of the early work on it]

gargoylism n. A term sometimes used to describe the grotesque facial features associated with some forms of *mental retardation, especially *Hurler's syndrome.

gastric gland n. A tubular *exocrine gland in the stomach wall that secretes gastric juice containing pepsin, hydrochloric acid, and mucus.
[From Greek gaster the stomach]

gastrointestinal adj. Of or relating to the *stomach and the *intestinal tract. **GI** abbrev.
[From Greek gaster the stomach + Latin intestinum gut, from intestinus internal]

gastrointestinal tract n. Another name for the *alimentary canal.

gate-control theory n. A theory of *pain, put forward by the US psychologist Ronald Melzack (born 1929) and the US-based English anatomist Patrick D(avid) Wall (1925–2001) in an article in the journal Science in 1965, according to which pain signals transmitted by small-diameter nerve fibres may be blocked at the level of the *spinal cord and prevented from reaching the brain by the firing of larger sensory nerve fibres, which act as a gate without normally transmitting pain signals themselves. Chronic pain occurs when disease, injury, or infection damage the large fibres that normally close the gate so that pain messages are not blocked on their path to the brain. According to this theory, *acupuncture anaesthesia may work by stimulating large-diameter sensory nerves to close the spinal gates.

gateway drug *n*. A generic name for *alcohol, *cocaine, or *cannabis, referring to their supposed roles as avenues leading people on to harder drugs. *See also* soft drug.

gating *n*. The exclusion from attention of certain stimuli while attending to other stimuli.

Gause's principle *n*. In *ecology (1), the proposition that two or more similar species cannot share the same *ecological niche indefinitely. Also called the *competitive exclusion principle*. [Named after the Soviet biologist Georgyi Frantsevich Gause (1910–86) who propounded it in 1934]

Gaussian distribution *n*. Another name for the *normal distribution. [Named after the mathematician Johann Karl Friedrich Gauss (1777–1855), born in the Duchy of Brunswick in what is now Germany, who investigated its basic properties]

gaze *vb*. *n*. To look steadily at something or someone, or a prolonged and steady look. In social psychology, it refers to steady looking at other people in the region of their eyes, and it is a form of *non-verbal communication. It tends to increase with interpersonal liking, but also when a person is attempting to dominate another, and one of its important functions is to regulate turn-taking in conversations: speakers tend to gaze at the beginning and end of a speaking turn. *Mutual gaze* or *eye contact* occurs when two people simultaneously gaze in the direction of each other's eyes, as tends to occur at points in a conversation when the floor is handed over smoothly to another speaker. *See also* Bálint's syndrome, compensatory eye movement, Donders' law, dynamic labyrinth, regulator, rotating head illusion. [From Swedish dialect *gasa* to stare or gape at]

gaze aversion *n*. Active avoidance of *eye contact, such as occurs as a result of embarrassment or a feeling of being socially dominated and is often observed in people with *autistic disorder. Also called *gaze avoidance*. *See also* equilibrium hypothesis.

GBH *abbrev*. **1.** Grievous bodily harm, a technical term in English law denoting the crime of causing serious physical injury to another person, contrasted with *actual bodily harm*

(ABH), the crime of causing minor physical injury to another person. **2.** A common jocular reference to *GHB.

gear *n*. A common street name for *heroin.

Gedankenexperiment *n*. An imaginary experiment, such as the *Chinese room or the *Turing test. As an example of how such an experiment can be highly illuminating, imagine walking into a dark room and switching on a 60-watt light, and then another 60-watt light. It is obvious from experience, without actually performing the experiment, that the room will not seem twice as brightly lit after the second light it turned on, which shows that the sensation of brightness does not double when the physical intensity of the light doubles (*see* Fechner's law, power law). Also called a *thought experiment* or an *armchair experiment*. [From German *Gedanke* a thought + *Experiment* an experiment]

Gelb effect *n*. The appearance of a black surface as white when it is brightly illuminated by a narrowly focused spotlight and viewed in front of a dimly illuminated background. If a white object is held in the beam of the spotlight in front of the black surface, the black surface immediately appears black, but as soon as the white object is removed it reverts to looking white. This phenomenon can be demonstrated using a slide projector or electric torch (flashlight) to produce a narrow beam of light. Together with its counterpart, the *Kardos effect, it demonstrates that the lightness dimension of colour is not determined straightforwardly by physical light intensity but is subject to *context effects, as are other dimensions of colour. *See also* lightness, luminance. *Compare* Land effect. [Named after the Russian-born German psychologist Adhémar Maximillian Maurice Gelb (1887–1936) who published his discovery of it in a book chapter in 1929]

gel electrophoresis *See* electrophoresis.

gender *n*. **1.** Non-technically, a synonym for *sex (1). More specifically, especially in feminist psychology, the behavioural, social, and cultural attributes associated with sex. *See also* doing gender. **2.** The categories into which nouns of a language are divided (such as masculine, feminine, and neuter).

[From Old French *gendre* gender, from Latin *genus* a kind]

gender dysphoria *n.* A chronic aversion to physical or social attributes of one's own biological *sex (1) or *gender (1). *See also* gender identity disorder.

gender identity *n.* A sense of awareness, usually beginning in infancy, continuing throughout childhood, and reaching maturity in adolescence, of being male or female, or of the *gender (1) associated with one's biological *sex (1). *See also* gender identity disorder.

gender identity disorder *n.* A *mental disorder characterized by a strong and persistent identification with the opposite sex, coupled with persistent discomfort with one's own *sex (1) or *gender (1) role, causing significant distress or impairment in social, occupational, or other important areas of functioning. A common manifestation is *transvestism. *See also* Diana complex, masculine protest.

gender role *n.* A set of behaviour patterns, attitudes, and personality characteristics stereotypically perceived as masculine or feminine within a culture. *See also* gender (1).

gene *n.* The unit of hereditary transmission encoded in *DNA, occupying a fixed *locus on a *chromosome and transmitted from a parent to its offspring, consisting of a sequence of *base (1) pairs corresponding to a specific sequence of *amino acids making up a *protein, functioning either to build body cells (if it is a *structural gene) or else to regulate the expression of other genes (if it is a *regulator gene). The human *genome, present in every body cell, contains approximately 32,000 genes encoded in about 4 billion base pairs. *See also* cistron, codon, gene activator, gene locus, gene mapping, gene operator, gene repressor, gene splicing, operon, supergene. **genetic** *adj.* Of or pertaining to *genes.
[From German *Gen* a gene, from Greek *genes* born]

gene activator *n.* A protein that increases the expression of a *structural gene by binding to a *gene operator in a segment of *DNA. *See also* activator gene. *Compare* gene repressor.

gene amplification *n.* The duplication of a gene to produce multiple copies of it within a cell nucleus.

gene cloning *n.* Producing *clones (2) of genes. Also called *DNA cloning*.

gene complex *n.* A group of genes that combine to produce a distinct characteristic of a *phenotype.

gene expression *n.* The transcription of a gene into an *RNA sequence or a *protein, or more generally its effects on a *phenotype. Also called *expression*.

gene frequency *n.* The relative frequency of a specific *allele of a gene in a population relative to the frequency of its other alleles.

gene locus *n.* The site occupied by a particular gene on a *chromosome. If the gene has two or more *alleles, then they occupy the same gene locus. Also called simply a *locus*. **gene loci** *pl.*
[From Latin *locus* a place]

gene mapping *n.* The determination of the positions of genes on chromosomes (*gene loci) by such means as studying *linkages that emerge when genes that are close to one another tend to be inherited together. Also called *genetic mapping*.

gene operator *n.* A binding site in a region of *DNA to which a *gene regulator can become attached, thereby affecting the expression of a *structural gene by increasing or repressing the synthesis of its protein product. Also called an *operator*. *See* gene activator, gene repressor. *See also* operon.

gene pool *n.* The sum total of all genes present in an interbreeding population. *Compare* meme pool.

genera *n. pl.* Plural of *genus.

general ability *See* g.

general adaptation syndrome *n.* The three-stage biological response of an organism to *stress (1) according to the Austrian-born Canadian physician and endocrinologist Hans Selye (1907–82), comprising an *alarm reaction, a *resistance stage, and an *exhaustion stage. Also called the *adaptation syndrome*. **GAS** *abbrev.*

General Health Questionnaire *n.* A self-rating questionnaire that takes between six and eight minutes to fill in and is designed to provide a rough-and-ready screening device for a wide range of mental disorders excluding *psychoses (1). It comprises 60 items, each describing a symptom and being accompanied by four response categories indicating personal experience of the symptom (*less than usual, no more than usual, rather more than usual, much more than usual*) from which the respondent chooses one. Shorter versions containing 20, 28, and 30 items have also been constructed. It was developed by the English psychiatrist David (Paul Brandes) Goldberg (born 1934) and published initially in monograph form in 1972; this was followed by a co-authored article in the journal *Psychological Medicine* in 1979 describing a scaled version of the questionnaire. **GHQ** *abbrev.*

generalizability theory *n.* In psychometrics, the use of *analysis of variance to estimate the extent to which the scores derived from a test are applicable beyond the specific test items, respondents, and testing conditions from which they were obtained. It is an extension of the theory of *reliability.

generalization, acoustic *See* acoustic generalization.

generalization gradient *n.* In *stimulus generalization, a change in the strength or frequency of a response to a variable stimulus as a function of the degree to which it resembles a particular stimulus to which the response has been learned or conditioned. It is sometimes used to examine perceptual similarity and discrimination in infants and non-human organisms that cannot give verbal judgements.

generalization, semantic *See* semantic generalization.

generalized anxiety disorder *n.* An *anxiety disorder characterized by excessive and largely uncontrollable *anxiety not focused on any specific circumstances but related to everyday events or activities such as problems at work or school, with symptoms of restlessness, tiredness, difficulty concentrating, irritability, muscle tension, or sleep disturbance (insomnia or restless sleep), causing significant impairment in everyday functioning. Also called *anxiety neurosis, free-floating anxiety*. *See also* actual neurosis, overanxious disorder. **GAD** *abbrev.*

generalized cone *n.* In the *computational theory of vision pioneered in the late 1970s by the English psychologist David Courtenay Marr (1945–80), a basic element that is used in the perceptual *representation (2) of a three-dimensional object and that consists of a surface formed by moving a cross-section of constant shape but continuously variable size along an axis. For example, with a circular cross-section and a vertical axis of movement, a generalized cone can generate a three-dimensional outline of a wine glass, the diameter of the circle changing as it moves down the glass, and multiple generalized cones with differently shaped cross-sections and axes of movement can be used to generate images of more complex objects such as people. *Compare* geon.

generalized habit strength *n.* In *Hullian learning theory, the *habit strength after taking into account the reduction resulting from a difference between the current *stimulus (1) and the stimulus present during the learning process. $_s\bar{H}_R$ *abbrev.*

generalized matching to sample *See* matching to sample.

generalized oddity problem *n.* A form of *serial learning (2) in which, in order to solve an *oddity problem, an organism has to generalize a principle established in a series of earlier oddity problems with different sets of stimuli, as when the general principle is that the reward is always in the smallest container.

generalized reaction potential *n.* In *Hullian learning theory, the strength of an organism's propensity to respond to a stimulus after taking into account *generalized habit strength and several other intervening variables. *See also* net reaction potential. $_s E_R$ *abbrev.*

general medical condition *n.* Any disorder not considered to be a *mental disorder, specifically any disorder not included in the section devoted to mental and behavioural disorders in *ICD-10 and used in *DSM-IV as a term of convenience, without any implication of a fundamental or sharp distinction between mental disorders and general medical conditions.

general paralysis (paresis) of the insane *n.* An obsolete term for *neurological impairments arising from tertiary syphilis. *See also* paresis. **GPI** *abbrev.*

General Problem Solver *n.* A computer program designed to simulate human *problem solving, introduced in 1958 by the US cognitive scientist Allen Newell (1927–92) and the US economists and decision theorists John Clark Shaw (born 1933) and Herbert A(lexander) Simon (1916–2001), and developed further in 1972 by Newell and Simon. In this program, a problem is represented as a table of connections showing the distances between all pairs of states (initial, intervening, and final), and problem solving is modelled as a search through the problem space using permissible operators (actions), the task being to find a path of operators from an initial state to a goal state. A typical initial state is the starting position in a game of chess, and the corresponding goal state is checkmating the opponent; a more commonplace initial state is being at home with a child and a car that has a flat battery, and the corresponding goal state in this case might be delivering the child to nursery school. In general, the problem space is too large for exhaustive search to be feasible, and therefore the cognitive *heuristic of *means–end analysis is implemented. The program is able to solve *water-jar problems, the *Tower of Hanoi problem, and many logic problems and chess problems. It represents one of the first major landmarks in the history of *artificial intelligence. **GPS** *abbrev.*

general systems theory *n.* A theory of organization and wholeness, introduced by the Austrian biologist Ludwig von Bertalanffy (1901–72) in 1940 and expounded at length in his book *General Systems Theory* (1968), after he had moved to the US. It seeks to incorporate ideas of hierarchical organization, multivariable interaction, and goal-directed processes that are absent from physics and, according to general systems theorists, are therefore bypassed, denied, or overlooked in psychology and other areas where they occur. **GST** *abbrev.*

generative grammar *n.* A term introduced by the US linguist and philosopher (Avram) Noam Chomsky (born 1928) in his book *Syntactic Structures* (1957) to refer to a description of a language in terms of a finite set of explicitly specified rules capable of generating the potentially infinite set of all grammatical sentences in the language, and only those sentences. *See also* case grammar, context-dependent grammar, context-free grammar, kernel, competence (2), performance (2), phrase-structure grammar, rewrite rule. *Compare* finite-state grammar, transformational grammar.

generativity versus stagnation *n.* One of the crises in the developmental theory of the German-born *ego psychologist Erik H. Erikson (1902–94). *See* developmental crises.

generator potential *n.* A graded change in the voltage difference across the membrane of a *sensory receptor that results from an appropriate stimulus and that tends either to excite or to inhibit an *action potential in the associated sensory neuron. Also called *receptor potential*.

gene repressor *n.* A protein that prevents the expression of a *structural gene by binding to a *gene operator in a segment of *DNA. *See also* repressor gene. *Compare* gene activator.

generic knowledge *n.* Knowledge of facts other than personal experiences or episodes from one's life. It is the type of information that is stored in *semantic knowledge.

gene splicing *n.* A technique of genetic engineering in which a phenotypic characteristic is produced in an organism by introducing DNA from another organism into its genetic material.

gene therapy *n.* The prevention and treatment of genetic defects by replacing or supplementing affected cells with genetically corrected cells.

genetic activation *n.* The process whereby the expression of a *structural gene is enhanced by a *gene activator. Also called *gene activation* or simply *activation*. *Compare* genetic repression.

genetically modified *adj*. Of or relating to a plant or animal that has been altered by *genetic engineering. **GM** *abbrev*.

genetic code *n*. The system by which genetic information is represented in the arrangement of the *bases (1) of the *DNA molecule, thereby determining the proteins to be synthesized by the cell. The four bases are arranged in triplets, each specifying a particular *amino acid, and the amino acids combine to form *proteins (see illustration). *Mitochondrial DNA has its own genetic code, slightly different from the universal code of nuclear DNA and subject to variation between species. The idea of a genetic code in the sequence of bases was first suggested in 1954 (the year after the discovery of the *double helix) by the Russian-born US physicist George Gamow (1904–68), but the dictionary of *codons was worked out in detail between 1961 and 1967 by the US biochemist Marshall Warren Nirenberg (born 1927), the Indian-born US molecular chemist Har Gobind Khorana (born 1922), and the US biochemist Robert William Holley (1922–93), for which they shared a Nobel prize in 1968. *See also* codon family, exon, intron.

genetic counselling *n*. Information given to prospective parents on the basis of *chromosomal investigation and (with pregnant women) *amniocentesis, including the odds that their own child would have genetic abnormalities and the course and management of such conditions, especially when there is a family history of genetic disorders. US *genetic counseling*.

genetic dominance *See* dominance (genetic).

genetic drift *n*. Change in the relative frequencies of genes in a population resulting not from natural selection but from *neutral mutation. Also called *non-Darwinian evolution* or *random drift*. *See also* Darwinian evolution, natural selection. *Compare* founder effect.

genetic engineering *n*. The artificial manipulation and alteration of *DNA, using techniques such as *gene cloning and *gene splicing, in the course of research, to modify

First base in codon	Second base in codon				Third base in codon
	U	C	A	G	
U	UUU Phe	UCU Ser	UAU Tyr	UGU Cys	U
	UUC Phe	UCC Ser	UAC Tyr	UGC Cys	C
	UUA Leu	UCA Ser	UAA (stop codon)	UGA (stop codon)	A
	UUG Leu	UCG Ser	UAG (stop codon)	UGG Trp	G
C	CUU Leu	CCU Pro	CAU His	CGU Arg	U
	CUC Leu	CCC Pro	CAC His	CGC Arg	C
	CUA Leu	CCA Pro	CAA Gln	CGA Arg	A
	CUG Leu	CCG Pro	CAG Gln	CGG Arg	G
A	AUU Ile	ACU Thr	AAU Asn	AGU Ser	U
	AUC Ile	ACC Thr	AAC Asn	AGC Ser	C
	AUA Ile	ACA Thr	AAA Lys	AGA Arg	A
	AUG Met (start codon)	ACG Thr	AAG Lys	AGG Arg	G
G	GUU Val	GCU Ala	GAU Asp	GGU Gly	U
	GUC Val	GCC Ala	GAC Asp	GGC Gly	C
	GUA Val	GCA Ala	GAA Glu	GGA Gly	A
	GUG Val	GCG Ala	GAG Glu	GGG Gly	G

Genetic code. The bases uracil, cytosine, adenine, and guanine are represented by the letters U, C, A, and G respectively, and the amino acids for which they code by Phe (phenylalanine), Leu(leucine), and so on.

plants and animals that are being bred, to manufacture proteins such as insulin, or to find treatments for genetic disorders. *See also* clone (1, 2), complementary DNA, DNA cloning, DNA hybridization, DNA ligase, DNA splicing, gene splicing, gene therapy, genetically modified, heteroduplex DNA, hybridization, monoclonal antibody, plasmid, recombinant DNA, restriction enzyme, transgenic. *Compare* memetic engineering, polymerase chain reaction.

genetic epistemology *n.* The term used by the Swiss psychologist Jean Piaget (1896–1980) to describe the nature of his own research. He began his research career with the ambition of contributing to *epistemology, believing that many epistemological problems were in fact empirical questions and that a genetic (by which he meant developmental) approach would be most fruitful. His three-volume series specifically devoted to genetic epistemology, *Introduction à l'Épistémologie Génétique* (1950) covers various branches of knowledge, including mathematics, logic, physics, biology, psychology, and sociology, all from an epistemological point of view. *See also* Piagetian.

genetic equilibrium *n.* A state or condition of a population in which the relative frequencies of genes stay constant from generation to generation. *See* Hardy–Weinberg law.

genetic fingerprint *n.* A unique pattern of repeated DNA sequences discovered by *restriction mapping and used in *genetic fingerprinting.

genetic fingerprinting *n.* A technique for establishing an individual's identity, for determining possible genetic relationships with other individuals, or for linking a suspected criminal to a crime scene where a sample of blood, saliva, semen, or tissue was found, by examining certain highly variable sequences of DNA fragments found by *restriction mapping, the DNA on which attention is focused being *introns, *junk DNA, and especially *repetitive DNA that are virtually unique to each individual. When only a very small sample of nuclear DNA is available, the *polymerase chain reaction is used to amplify it, or *mitochondrial DNA is used instead, because it is generally more plentiful in samples of bone, teeth, hair, and faeces. The technique

was developed in the early 1980s by the English geneticist Alec (John) Jeffreys (born 1950) and first used as evidence in a murder trial in 1987. Also called *DNA fingerprinting* or *DNA profiling*.

genetic fitness *See* fitness.

genetic mapping *n.* Another name for *gene mapping.

genetic polymorphism *n.* The existence in a population of variable *alleles coding for differences in *phenotypic characteristics, such as the alleles coding for different eye colours or different ABO blood types in humans, a gene locus being defined as polymorphic if the most frequent *homozygote constitutes less than 90 per cent of the population. It has been estimated that between 20 and 50 per cent of all *structural gene loci in humans occur in two or more allelic forms. *See also* balanced polymorphism, neutral mutation, polymorphic gene, transient polymorphism.
[From Greek *polys* many + *morphe* a form or shape]

genetic recombination *See* DNA recombination.

genetic repression *n.* The process whereby the expression of a *structural gene is inactivated by a *gene repressor. Also called *gene repression* or simply *repression*. *Compare* genetic activation.

genetics *n.* The branch of biology devoted to the study of heredity and variation, including their physical basis in *DNA. **geneticist** *n.* One who practises *genetics.
[From Greek *genesis* birth + *-itikos* resembling or marked by]

genetic variance *n.* A statistical measure of *genetic variation used in calculations of *heritability. Also called *genotypic variance*. *See also* variance.

genetic variation *n.* Variability in hereditary characteristics within a population resulting from the existence of variant forms of genes, called *alleles, and from genetic recombination resulting from *independent assortment and *crossing over. *See also* genetic variance.

genital character n. In *psychoanalysis, a personality pattern associated with successful negotiation of *libidinal stages up to the *genital stage, characterized by the capacity for *genital love. Also called the *genital personality*.

genital love n. In *psychoanalysis, the sensual and affectionate form of *love that a person is capable of after successfully negotiating the various *libidinal stages preceding the *genital stage and overcoming the *Oedipus complex. The term does not occur in the writings of Sigmund Freud (1856–1939), but the concept is implicit in his book *Three Essays on the Theory of Sexuality* (1905) and in his article in 1912 'On the Universal Tendency to Debasement in the Sphere of Love' (*Standard Edition*, XI, pp. 179–90). *See also* genital character.

genital stage n. In *psychoanalysis, the final *libidinal stage of *psychosexual development coming after the *oral stage, *anal stage, *phallic stage, and *latency period. The genital stage is characterized by a focus of *libido on the genital area, and it emerges during puberty, when the *Oedipus complex reappears and is overcome with greater or lesser success through mature *object-choices. The concept was developed by Sigmund Freud (1856–1939) in a section added in 1915 to his book *Three Essays on the Theory of Sexuality* (1905), where he suggested that its roots lie in childhood: 'The only difference lies in the fact that in childhood the combination of the component instincts and their subordination under the primacy of the genitals have been effected only very incompletely or not at all. Thus the establishment of that primacy in the service of reproduction is the last phase through which the organization of sexuality passes' (*Standard Edition*, VII, pp. 130–243, at p. 199). Also called the *genital phase*. *See also* genital character, genital love, pregenital.

genius n. A person of exceptional intelligence or ability; also such exceptional intelligence or ability itself (*Michelangelo's artistic genius*). It was first investigated in psychology by the English explorer, amateur scientist, and psychologist Sir Francis Galton (1822–1911), who used eminence as the main criterion of genius in his book *Hereditary Genius* (1869). In later research in psychology, a permissive criterion such as an *IQ score of 140 or above

has often been used to define it, and in the influential *Genetic Studies of Genius* carried out from 1921 onwards by the US psychometrician Lewis M(adison) Terman (1877–1956) and his colleagues, the 'geniuses' were children with IQs above 135. Also called *giftedness*. **geniuses** pl.
[From Latin *genius* attendant spirit present from one's birth, innate ability or talent, from *gignere, genitum* to beget]

genodeme *See under* deme.

genogram n. In counselling and psychotherapy, a client's diagrammatic representation of past and present family members and their interrelationships.
[From Greek *genos* begetting + *gramme* a line]

genome n. The full genetic complement of an organism; the *haploid complement of a *diploid organism such as the human species. *Compare* phenome.
[A blend of *gen(e)* + *(chromos)ome*]

genotropism n. The doctrine first proposed by the Hungarian geneticist Leopold (Lipot) Szondi in the journal *Acta Psychologica* in 1938, and developed further in 1944 in his book entitled *Schicksalsanalyse* (Analysis of Destiny), that latent *recessive genes determine instinctive or spontaneous choices (in love, friendship, occupation, illness, and even manner of death) and underlie attraction between people sharing the same genes. *See also* Szondi test. **genotropic** adj.
[From *gene* + Greek *tropos* a turn, from *trapein* to turn + *-ismos* indicating a state or condition]

genotype n. The genetic constitution of a single organism at a particular *locus or set of loci; or more loosely the entire genetic constitution or *genome of a single organism. *Compare* phenotype. **genotypic** adj.
[From *gene* + *type*]

genotypic variance n. Another name for *genetic variance. *See* heritability.

genu n. Any knee-shaped structure, especially the bend at the front of the *corpus callosum.
[From Latin *genu* a knee]

genus n. One of the *taxonomic groups into which a *family (2) is divided, containing one or more *species. By convention, a species is

denoted by the name of the genus, the initial letter of which is written in upper case, or by its upper-case initial alone, followed by the specific name in lower case. Thus the genus *Felis* of cats includes the species *Felis domesticus* (the domestic cat), *F. leo* (the lion), *F. tigris* (the tiger), *F. pardus* (the leopard), and so on. **genera** *pl.* **generic** *adj.*
[From Latin *genus* birth]

geometric illusion *n.* Another name for an *associative illusion. The term is also used as a synonym for a *visual illusion of any type, but this over-extended interpretation is avoided in careful usage. Also called a *geometrical illusion*.

geometric mean *n.* In descriptive statistics, the average value of a set of *n* scores calculated by multiplying the scores together and then extracting the *n*th root of the resulting product. The geometric mean of two scores is the square root of their product. *Compare* arithmetic mean, harmonic mean.

geon *n.* Any of a hypothetical set of three-dimensional geometric elements, such as spheres, cubes, and cylinders, into which a complex figure may be decomposed in the process of perception. Geons are easily distinguishable from all vantage points and are highly resistant to visual distortion. They are central to the recognition-by-component theory of the US psychologist Irving Biederman (born 1939). *Compare* generalized cone.
[A blend of *geo(metrical)* and *(ic)on*]

geophagia *n.* A form of *pica characterized by the eating of earth or dirt.
[From Greek *ge* earth + *phagein* to consume + *-ia* indicating a condition or quality]

geriatrics *n.* The branch of medicine devoted to the prevention, diagnosis, and treatment of disorders affecting old people. *See also* psychogeriatrics. *Compare* gerontology. **geriatric** *adj.*
[From Greek *geras* old age + *iatros* a doctor + *-ikos* of, relating to, or resembling]

germ cell *n.* Another name for a *gamete or sexual reproductive cell.
[From Latin *germen* a seed]

germ line *n.* The cells that give rise to germ cells or *gametes, being the part of a body that is potentially immortal and can be passed on indefinitely from parents to offspring, in contradistinction to the *somatic cells.

germ plasm *n.* The part of a *gamete containing the *chromosomes.
[From Latin *germen* a seed + *plasma* a form]

gerontology *n.* The study of ageing. *Compare* geriatrics.
[From Greek *geron, gerontos* an old man + *logos* word, discourse, or reason]

Gerstmann–Sträussler–Scheinker syndrome *n.* A human *prion disease usually regarded as a variant of *Creutzfeldt-Jakob disease with pathology mainly in the *cerebellum, leading to *cerebellar syndrome. **GSS** *abbrev.*
[Named after the Austrian neurologist Josef Gerstmann (1887–1969) and his colleagues E. Sträussler, and Ilya Mark Scheinker who first described its signs and symptoms in 1936]

Gerstmann syndrome *n.* A neurological disorder characterized by left–right disorientation, *agraphia, *acalculia, and *finger agnosia, generally associated with lesions in the *parietal lobe of the dominant cerebral hemisphere.
[Named after the Austrian neurologist Josef Gerstmann (1887–1969) who first noticed in 1930 the tendency for the four components of the syndrome to occur together]

Gesell Developmental Schedules *n.* A set of norms based on 27 observations of behaviour of infants and young children in standardized situations, providing an assessment of gross motor, fine motor, language, personal–social, and adaptive development. Also called the *Gesell Developmental Scales*.
[Named after the US psychologist and paediatrician Arnold (Lucius) Gesell (1880–1961) who, in collaboration with several colleagues, published them in a book entitled *The First Five Years of Life* in 1940]

Gestalt *n.* A perceptual configuration or structure that possesses qualities transcending the sum of its constituent elements or parts and that cannot be described simply in terms of its parts. A classic example underlies *melodic constancy: the sequence of notes C, D, E, C, C, D, E, C played evenly on any musical instrument is instantly recognizable as the

well-known folk tune *Frère Jacques*; and the sequence F, G, A, F, F, G, A, F, which does not contain a single element in common with the first, sounds like exactly the same tune; but the sequence E, D, C, C, E, D, C, C, which contains the same elements as the first sequence in a new configuration, sounds like *Three Blind Mice*, an entirely different Gestalt. *See also* autochthonous, bundle hypothesis, Gestalt psychology, *Gestaltqualität*, grouping law, member, membership character, *Prägnanz*, precision law, trait centrality. **Gestalten** *pl.*
[From German *Gestalt* shape or form, from Old High German *stellen* to shape]

Gestalt psychology *n.* A school of psychology concerned largely with emergent *Gestalt phenomena in perception. Its forerunners were the German poet Johann Wolfgang von Goethe (1749–1832), the Austrian physicist, philosopher, and psychologist Ernst Mach (1838–1916), and especially the German philosopher Christian von Ehrenfels (1859–1932), but the emergence of the school is usually traced to 1912 and the publication of a seminal article on *apparent movement by the German psychologist Max Wertheimer (1880–1943). The school was transplanted to the US with the rise of Nazism in Germany, as Wertheimer emigrated there together with the other founding German psychologists Kurt Koffka (1886–1941), Wolfgang Köhler (1887–1967), and Kurt Lewin (1890–1947). The cardinal principles of Gestalt psychology are the primary importance in psychology of subjective experience and of its forms and structures, and a rejection of elementalism. *See also* appurtenance, Bender Gestalt Test, bundle hypothesis, field effect, *Gestaltqualität*, good Gestalt, grouping law, Höffding step, isomorphism (3), Korte's laws, levelling (1), member, membership character, perceptual constancy, *Prägnanz*, precision law, symmetry law, Ternus phenomenon, trait centrality.

Gestaltqualität *n.* A term coined by the German philosopher Christian von Ehrenfels (1859–1932) and later introduced into *Gestalt psychology to denote a perceptual *attribute or quality that emerges from the way in which the elements of an object or image are put together and is not reducible to the sum of those elements, his standard example being *melodic constancy, according to which a tune is recognizably the same when played in a different key without using any of its original elements (tones). Also called *founded content. See* Gestalt. **Gestaltqualitäten** *pl.*
[From German *Gestalt* shape or form, from *stellen* to shape + *Qualität* quality]

Gestalt therapy *n.* A form of *counselling or *psychotherapy, unconnected with Gestalt psychology, developed in the United States during the 1960s by the German-born psychiatrist Fritz (Frederick) Perls (1893–1970), in which clients are encouraged to focus on the immediate present and to express their true feelings openly and honestly. *See also* empty-chair technique, unfinished business.

gesture *n.* **1.** A bodily movement, usually of the hands or the head, that has a communicative function in *kinesics. *See also* amimia, apraxia, asemia, copropraxia, echopraxia, paramimia, Rett's disorder. **2.** Something that is said or done as a formality or without conviction. *vb.* **3.** To make a *gesture (1).
[From Latin *gestura* bearing, from *gestus* carried, from *gerere* to carry or behave]

geusis *n.* The sense of *taste.
[From Greek *geusis* taste, from *geusthai* to taste]

GHB *abbrev.* Gamma-hydroxybutyrate, a colourless, odourless, salty-tasting liquid that acts as an *anaesthetic (1) drug with sedative–hypnotic and antidepressant effects. It became popular as a street drug in the late 1990s, at moderate doses having a general calming effect, lowering inhibitions, and increasing sociability, and at high doses causing nausea, muscle stiffness, confusion, convulsions, and possible coma and respiratory collapse. Also called *gamma-OH* (trademark). Often humorously called *GBH*, especially in the UK. *See also* sedative–hypnotic; sedative-, hypnotic-, or anxiolytic-related disorders, sociabilizer.

ghost in the machine *n.* The term first used by the English philosopher Gilbert Ryle (1900–76) on page 17 of his book *The Concept of Mind* (1949) to describe the dogma of mind–body *dualism, which he interpreted as a *category mistake.

ghost sickness *n.* A *culture-bound syndrome found in many American Indian tribes, characterized by *thanatophobia, *necromania, *nightmares (1), *asthenia, feelings of danger, *anorexia, fainting, dizziness, *anxiety, and *hallucinations, the *symptoms often being attributed by the afflicted person to witchcraft.

Gibsonian *adj*. Pertaining to or resembling the interpretation of visual perception of the US psychologist James Jerome Gibson (1904–79), according to which information is absorbed from the ambient flow of light, without significant retinal or cognitive processing, by the detection of features of objects that are invariant with motion and rotation. *See also* affordance, air theory, direct perception, global psychophysics, motion perspective.

giftedness *n*. Exceptional intelligence or talent. *See* genius.

gift of tongues *n*. A non-technical name for *glossolalia.

Gilles de la Tourette's syndrome *n*. Another name for *Tourette's disorder. **GTS** *abbrev*.

ginkgo *n*. The ornamental Chinese tree *Ginkgo biloba*, also called the *maidenhair tree*, highly resistant to virus infection, fungi, and effects of pollution and radiation. Also, a herbal substance prepared from it and taken for its alleged *nootropic effect of slowing intellectual decline in old age or as an *aphrodisiac. Also spelt *gingko*. *See also* smart drug.
[From Japanese *ginkyo*, from Chinese *yin* silver + *hing* apricot]

ginseng *n*. A plant of the genus *Panax* (*Panax schinseng* in China or *Panax quinquefolius* in North America) whose roots contain ginsenosides, used in Chinese medicine for their tonic, stimulant, or restorative effects. Its pharmacological action is poorly understood, though it is believed to involve enhancement of *nitric oxide (NO) synthesis in the body. Also taken as a *smart drug with a wide range of supposed mental and physical benefits and as an *aphrodisiac.
[From Mandarin Chinese *jen* a man, from the resemblance of the roots to human legs + *shen* spirit]

give-some game *n*. An experimental game used to represent a *public goods dilemma.

gland *n*. A cell or organ specialized to secrete a substance either through a duct or into the bloodstream. *See* endocrine gland, exocrine gland.
[From Latin *glans* an acorn]

glaucoma *n*. A relatively common disorder of the eye in which fluid pressure increases within the eyeball because of obstruction of the outflow of *aqueous humour, impairing vision and eventually causing *tunnel vision if not corrected. *Acute glaucoma*, accompanied by a dilated *pupil, intense pain, blurred vision, and red eye, results from the pupil dilating in a manner that causes the *iris to fold back against the cornea and to block the exit of aqueous humour, and it results in complete and permanent *blindness within 2–5 days if untreated with eye drops that constrict the pupil and unfold the iris; *chronic glaucoma*, which is much more common and often bilateral, develops insidiously, often without symptoms apart from gradual loss of peripheral vision, and is caused by a genetic factor.
[From Greek *glaukoma* cataract, from *glaukos* bluish-green or grey + *-oma* indicating an abnormality, alluding to the appearance of an eye affected by *cataract, with which glaucoma was confused]

glia *n*. A short name for *neuroglia. Often mistakenly assumed to be a plural of *glion* (a spurious *back formation), but in fact singular like the word *glue*. *See also* macroglia, microglia, neuroglia. **glial** *adj*.
[From Greek *glia* glue]

glide *n*. The transitional sound that is made as the vocal organs move from a position for articulating one speech sound to a position for articulating another, as in any *diphthong, *triphthong, or *semivowel.

glioblastoma *n*. A malignant glioma or tumour of *neuroglia in the brain or spinal cord.
[From *glia* + Greek *blastos* a bud + *-oma* indicating a tumour]

glioma *n*. A tumour affecting the *neuroglia (usually *astrocytes) in the brain or spinal cord. Symptoms include headache, drowsiness, and vomiting, together with other site-dependent signs, such as motor weakness on one side of the body caused by a cerebral glioma on the opposite side, or clumsiness on one side caused by a *cerebellar glioma on the same side. *Compare* glioblastoma.

[From *glia* + Greek *-oma* indicating a tumour]

global amnesia *n*. Severe or total *anterograde amnesia resulting from damage to the *diencephalon or medial *temporal lobe, often accompanied by partial *retrograde amnesia, with *short-term memory and *perceptual–motor skills generally remaining unimpaired. *Compare* transient global amnesia.

global feature *n*. A *feature (1) of a stimulus as a whole, such as its overall circular shape or its symmetry. *Compare* local feature.

global psychophysics *n*. A term used by the US psychologist James Jerome Gibson (1904–79) to characterize his approach to the study of perception, in which an attempt is made to establish psychophysical correspondences between perceptions and behaviour by examining relations between stimulus information and response, in contrast to classical *psychophysics in which relations between stimulus intensity and response are examined. *See also* direct perception.

globus hystericus *n*. The medical name for a lump in the throat.

globus pallidus *n*. One of the *basal ganglia in the lenticular nucleus of the corpus striatum, either of a pair of pale yellow globular masses involved in posture, muscle tonus, and the control of eating and drinking. Also called the *pallidum* or the *palaeostriatum* (US *paleostriatum*). *See also* attention-deficit/hyperactivity disorder.
[From Latin *globus* a sphere + *pallidus* pale]

glomerulus *n*. Any cluster or coil of blood vessels or nerve fibres, especially the clusters of nerve fibres of the *olfactory bulb (containing the primary synapses of the olfactory pathway) and the *cerebellum.
[From Latin *glomerulus* a little ball, diminutive of *glomus* a ball]

glossa *n*. The technical name for the tongue.
glossal *adj*.
[From Greek *glossa* a tongue]

glossogenetics *n*. The study of the origins and development of language.
[From Greek *glossa* a tongue + *genesis* generation or development]

glossograph *n*. An instrument for recording the movements of the tongue during speech.
[From Greek *glossa* a tongue + *graphein* to write]

glossographia *n*. A written variant of *glossolalia.

glossolalia *n*. Speech-like utterances with an impoverished range of syllabic and rhythmic patterns and no systematic grammatical structure, often believed by the speaker to be a real but unknown language, but on analysis quite unlike any *natural language, commonly produced during Pentecostal Protestant and charismatic Roman Catholic religious services. Also called the *gift of tongues* or *speaking in tongues*. Glossolalia should be carefully distinguished from *xenoglossia.
glossolalic *adj*.
[From Greek *glossa* a tongue + *lalein* to babble]

glossopalatine nerve *n*. A branch of the *facial nerve supplying the front two-thirds of the tongue and parts of the palate.
[From Greek *glossa* a tongue + Latin *palatum* the roof of the mouth]

glossopharyngeal nerve *n*. Either of the ninth pair of *cranial nerves, carrying sensations from the pharynx, the back of the tongue, and the middle ear, and supplying the muscles of the pharynx, hence involved in controlling swallowing and, together with the vagus nerve, the *gag reflex.
[From Greek *glossa* a tongue + *pharynx, pharyngos* the throat]

glossosynthesis *n*. Arbitrary invention of new words.

glottal *adj*. Of, relating to, or denoting a speech sound articulated by interrupting the airstream at the *glottis by closing the *vocal folds, as in the *glottal stop used in the *cockney dialect in place of the usual /t/ sounds in utterances such as *Pat's got a lot of bottle* (*Pa's go' a lo' of bo'le*). *See also* place of articulation.

glottis *n*. The opening between the *vocal folds.
[From Greek *glotta*, Attic form of Ionic *glossa* a tongue]

glottochronology *n*. The application of techniques of *lexicostatistics to study the evolution and establish the relationship between languages and therefore populations and to estimate how long ago they diverged from their common source, believed by many authorities to have been in Africa approximately 150,000 years ago. *See also* Indo-European. *Compare* evolutionary clock, mitochondrial DNA.

[From Greek *glotta*, Attic form of Ionic *glossa* a tongue + *chronos* time + *logos* word, discourse, or reason]

glove anaesthesia *n.* Absence of sensation or feeling in the hand, the anaesthetic area ending abruptly at the wrist, invariably a *conversion symptom, the distribution of sensory nerve fibres allowing no possible neurological cause of the symptom, because the nerve that supplies the hand also supplies the lower arm. *Shoe anaesthesia* and *stocking anaesthesia* are defined and interpreted analogously. US *glove anesthesia*. *See also* anaesthesia.

glucagon *n.* A hormone secreted by the *islets of Langerhans in the pancreas that stimulates the release of glucose into the bloodstream.

[From Greek *glykys* sweet + *agein* to lead]

glucocorticoid *n.* Any of a group of *corticosteroids, the principal ones being *cortisol (hydrocortisone) and *corticosterone, that are secreted by the adrenal cortex in response to serious injury or stress and that tend to shift the body from carbohydrate to fat metabolism, to regulate blood pressure, and to have anti-inflammatory effects. *See also* dexamethasone, prednisolone, prednisone, zona fasciculata. *Compare* mineralocorticoid.

[From *gluco(se)* + *cortic(al)* + Greek *-oeides* denoting resemblance of form, from *eidos* shape]

glucose *n.* A white crystalline sugar, the most common form being dextrose, that plays an important part in energy supply and metabolism. *See* glycolysis, Krebs cycle.

[From Greek *gleukos* sweet wine, from *glykys* sweet]

glucostatic theory *n.* A *homeostatic theory of hunger, according to which the brain monitors the difference between the levels of glucose in the arteries and veins as an index of the rate of glucose removal from the blood. A low rate, which indicates that the blood glucose level is low and is probably being replenished by glucose derived from body fat, stimulates hunger and eating behaviour. *Compare* lipostatic theory.

[From *glucose* + *statikos* bringing to a standstill, from *histanai* to cause to stand or to weigh in a balance + *-ikos* of, resembling, or characterized by]

glue-sniffing *n.* The deliberate inhalation of the *psychotropic fumes given off by certain types of adhesives. *See also* inhalant-related disorders, solvent abuse.

glutamate *n.* A salt of glutamic acid, the main excitatory *neurotransmitter for all nerve impulses in the *diencephalon and *telencephalon and for sensory impulses in the *peripheral nervous system. *See also* kainic acid, lithium.

[From *glutamic acid* + *-ate* indicating a salt or ester of an acid]

glutamic acid *n.* A non-essential *amino acid that is a precursor of *glutamate and is believed to function as a *neurotransmitter in the dorsal horns of the spinal cord and in the cerebellum. **Glu** *abbrev.*

[From Latin *gluten* glue + *-amine* indicating an amine + *-ikos* of, resembling, or characterized by]

glutamic acid decarboxylase *n.* An *enzyme that makes *GABA. **GAD** *abbrev.*

glutethimide *n.* One of the *carbamates, a central nervous system *depressant that is prescribed as a *sedative–hypnotic drug in the treatment of anxiety disorders and insomnia. Also called *Doriden* (trademark). *See also* sedative-, hypnotic-, or anxiolytic-related disorders.

[From its chemical name *glut(aryl)* + *eth(yl)* + *imide*]

glycine *n.* A non-essential *amino acid that functions as an inhibitory *neurotransmitter in the spinal cord, binding to the receptor sites on *alpha motor neurons. *See also* strychnine. **Gly** *abbrev.*

[From Greek *glykys* sweet + *-ine* indicating an organic compound]

glycogen *n.* Animal starch, stored in the liver and muscles and converted to *glucose by *hydrolysis.

[From Greek *glykys* sweet + *genein* to produce]

glycol n. A chemical used as antifreeze and as a solvent, containing volatile substances that are *psychotropic when inhaled. See also inhalant-related disorders, solvent abuse.
[From Greek glykys sweet]

glycolysis n. The metabolism, by enzymes, of *glucose with the production of pyruvic acid and the liberation of energy in the form of *ATP. Depending on the cell type and conditions, the pyruvate may then be converted to *ethanol (an *anaerobic process), lactic acid (an anaerobic process), or acetyl coenzyme A which enters the *Krebs cycle, initiating a process of *aerobic respiration.
[From glucose + Greek lysis loosening]

GnRH abbrev. Gonadotrophin-releasing hormone. See gonadotrophin.

Gödel's theorem n. A term that usually refers to Gödel's first incompleteness theorem, the proposition that, in any formal system rich enough to incorporate arithmetic, it is possible to formulate statements that are true but that cannot be proved within the system. Slightly more precisely, in such a system S, there must be a sentence p such that if S is consistent, then neither p nor its negation (not-p) can be proved within S. This theorem is a genuine *paradox, has far-reaching implications for the foundations of arithmetic and logic, and has (controversially) been used, informally by the Czech-born US philosopher Ernest Nagel (1901–85) and James R(oy) Newman (1907–66) in their book Gödel's Proof (1958), more formally by the British philosopher John R(andolph) Lucas (born 1929) in an article in the journal Philosophy in 1961, and most formally by the mathematical physicist Roger Penrose (born 1931) in his book The Emperor's New Mind (1989) and especially in his later book Shadows of the Mind (1994), to argue against the *strong AI position that conscious thought can be explained in terms of computational principles, and also against the *weak AI position that conscious thought can be simulated by computational procedures, and in favour of the view that a fundamental difference therefore exists between human and *artificial intelligence. Gödel's second incompleteness theorem is the proposition that the consistency of a formal system rich enough to incorporate arithmetic cannot be proved within the system itself.
[Named after the US logician and mathematician Kurt Gödel (1906–78), born in Brno, Austria–Hungary (now in the Czech Republic), who published it in the journal Monatshefte für Mathematik und Physik in 1931]

God-image n. In *analytical psychology, an image of God that, when it appears spontaneously in a dream or fantasy, symbolizes the self. Carl Gustav Jung (1875–1961) borrowed this term from medieval Christian theology, in which the Latin version imago Dei (image of God) was believed to be imprinted on the human soul.

Goldstein–Scheerer tests n. A set of tests requiring abstract thinking and *concept formation, used to diagnose *neurological damage. The tests require the respondent to copy coloured designs, to sort items into categories according to colour, form, and material, and to reproduce designs from memory by arranging sticks. They were developed in the US by the German-born psychiatrist Kurt Goldstein (1878–1965) and the German-born psychologist Martin Scheerer (1900–61) and first published by them in the journal Psychological Monographs in 1941. Later editions of the test are also called the Weigl–Goldstein–Scheerer tests.

Golgi apparatus n. A complex of easily stained stacks, called Golgi bodies or dictyosomes, of flattened membrane sacs, called Golgi vesicles, in the *cytoplasm of most cells, involved in transport of *lipids and *proteins. Also called a Golgi complex. **GA** abbrev.
[Named after the Italian cytologist Camillo Golgi (1844–1926) who discovered it]

Golgi cell n. A type of *interneuron found in the cerebellum that acts on *granule cells. Compare basket cell, stellate cell.
[Named after the Italian cytologist Camillo Golgi (1844–1926) who discovered it]

Golgi stain n. A method of staining neurons with potassium bichromate and silver nitrate, introduced in 1900 by the Italian cytologist Camillo Golgi (1844–1926), affecting only a tiny fraction of the neurons in the stained region but revealing them fully or almost fully, exposing their cell bodies, dendrites, and axons. Compare Nissl stain.

Golgi tendon organ n. A *sensory receptor that is located in a muscle, near a junction with a tendon, and is sensitive to contractions of the muscle, producing *action potentials when compressed by muscle tension. Also called an *organ of Golgi* or a *tendon organ. See also* Ib fibre. *Compare* muscle spindle.

[Named after the Italian cytologist Camillo Golgi (1844–1926) who gave the first complete description of it in 1880]

gonad *n.* Any organ that produces *gametes, including a human *testis or *ovary. The word is often mistakenly believed to apply to male organs only. **gonadal, gonadial,** or **gonadic** *adj.*

[From Greek *gonos* seed]

gonadotrophin *n.* Any of a number of hormones secreted by the pituitary gland and the placenta that stimulate the activity of the *gonads. Also spelt *gonadotropin. See also* chorionic gonadotrophin, follicle-stimulating hormone, luteinizing hormone, prolactin. **gonadotrophic** or **gonadotropic** *adj.*

[From *gonad* + Greek *trophe* nourishment + *-in(e)* indicating an organic compound]

gonadotrophin-releasing hormone *n.* Another name for *luteinizing-hormone releasing hormone. Also spelt *gonadotropin-releasing hormone.* **GnRH** *abbrev.*

good breast *n.* In *psychoanalysis, a concept introduced by the British-based Austrian psychoanalyst Melanie Klein (1882–1960) to denote one aspect of the mother's breast as a *part object in an infant's fantasies after *splitting of the object into a good breast and a bad breast as a defence against *ambivalence and consequent *anxiety. Gratification of hunger tends to produce an *imago (1) of a good breast, and withdrawal generates the bad breast through a vicious circle involving *projection (1) in which the infant comes to believe that the breast is withdrawn because it is hated. In the theory of *defensive techniques of the Scottish psychoanalyst W. Ronald D. Fairbairn (1889–1964), the location of the good breast and the bad breast define the particular defensive technique adopted by a person with a mental disorder. *See also* good object.

good continuation *n.* One of the four original *grouping laws of *Gestalt psychology, formulated in 1923 by the German psychologist Max Wertheimer (1880–1943) to explain the organization of parts into wholes by the visual system. According to the law, elements that move in the same direction tend to be grouped perceptually, hence the symbol × is perceived as being composed of two straight lines rather than (for example) two wedges > and <, and the symbol ∅ is perceived as a circle crossed by a straight line. A special case of this law for elements moving in time is called *common fate. *See also* common region, connectedness grouping law, *Prägnanz. Compare* closure grouping law, proximity grouping law, similarity grouping law.

Goodenough Draw-a-Man test *See* Draw-a-Man test.

[Named after the US psychologist Florence Laura Goodenough (1886–1959) who introduced it in 1926]

good-enough mother *n.* A concept introduced in 1953 by the English psychoanalyst Donald Woods Winnicott (1896–1971) to denote a mother who initially behaves towards a totally dependent infant just how the infant wishes, allowing the infant to feel all-powerful and to maintain the fantasy that the mother is a part of itself, and who later allows the child to abandon this fantasy and separate from her in an orderly way. A mother who is too intrusive (too good) interferes with the child's separation and development of selfhood, and a mother who is too distant (not good enough) generates anxiety in the child; in either case the failure to supply good-enough mothering can disrupt the development of the child's self-concept, and as an adult the ability to form meaningful relationships.

good figure *n.* Another name for *good Gestalt.

good Gestalt *n.* A law of *Gestalt psychology according to which shapes, contours, and patterns tend to be perceived in the most simple, stable, and balanced form compatible with the sensory information. Also called *good figure* or *good shape. See also* levelling (1), *Prägnanz*, precision law.

Goodman–Kruskal gamma *n.* Another name for the *gamma statistic.

[Named after the US statisticians Leo A. Goodman (born 1928) and William Henry Kruskal (born 1919) who developed it in a series of articles beginning in 1954, and *gamma* (γ), the third letter of the Greek alphabet]

Goodman–Kruskal lambda *n.* In descriptive statistics, a measure of the degree of similarity between binary or dichotomous variables. It provides an index, on a scale ranging from 0 to 1, of the presence or absence of a characteristic on one variable given its presence or absence on the other variable. Also called the *lambda statistic* L_B.
[Named after the US statisticians Leo A. Goodman (born 1928) and William Henry Kruskal (born 1919) who discussed it in a series of articles beginning in 1954 and *lambda* (λ), the eleventh letter of the Greek alphabet]

Goodman's paradox *n.* A *paradox of *induction (1). Suppose that someone notes that all emeralds that have ever been observed are green, and argues inductively to conclude that all emeralds are green. Now suppose we define *grue* as the property of being green up to time *t* (say, the beginning of the year 2050) and blue thereafter. All our inductive evidence supports the conclusion that all emeralds are grue just as well as it supports the conclusion that all emeralds are green, therefore we have no grounds for preferring either conclusion. Many people (though not Goodman) interpret this as a refutation of induction. Also called the *grue paradox*. *Compare* Hempel's paradox.
[Named after the US philosopher Nelson Goodman (1906–98) who published it in 1955 in his book *Fact, Fiction, and Forecast* (pp. 74–5)]

goodness of fit *n.* **1.** In statistics, the closeness of agreement between observed and expected frequencies, usually measured by the *chi-square test or the *Kolmogorov–Smirnov test. **2.** In fitting a line or a curve to a set of data points, the degree of closeness of the points to the curve, often measured by the *least-squares method or *maximum likelihood method.

good object *n.* In *psychoanalysis, a concept introduced by the British-based Austrian psychoanalyst Melanie Klein (1882–1960) to denote a *part object or *whole object as it appears in an infant's fantasies. According to Klein, the *splitting of the object into a good object and a bad object is a defence against ambivalence and the *anxiety that it generates, the first object to undergo splitting being

the mother's breast. A person's handling of the good object and the bad object defines the four *defensive techniques in the theory of mental disorders of the Scottish psychoanalyst W. Ronald D. Fairbairn (1889–1964). *See also* good breast, imago (1).

good shape *n.* Another name for *good Gestalt.

goofers *n.* A street name for *barbiturate drugs in general.

goose pimples *n.* A colloquial name for *piloerection when it occurs in skin that is not thickly covered in hair. Also called *goose flesh* or *goose bumps*. *See also* tickle.
[So called because of resemblance to the skin of a freshly plucked fowl]

Gottschaldt figures test *n.* Another name for the *embedded-figures test.
[Named after the German psychologist Kurt Gottschaldt (1902–91) who published it in the journal *Psychologische Forschung* in 1926]

Gough Adjective Check List *n.* Another name for the *Adjective Check List.
[Named after the US psychologist Harrison G. Gough (born 1921) who introduced it in 1952 and discussed its psychometric properties in an article in the journal *Psychological Reports* in 1960]

government and binding *n.* A class of linguistic theories, derived from *transformational grammar, based on the assumption that any syntactic operation can be interpreted as a transformation involving the movement of some linguistic element(s) such as a noun phrase. *See also* binding problem. **GB** *abbrev.*

Graafian follicle *n.* A fluid-filled sac in the *ovary within which an *ovum develops. Also called a *Graafian vesicle* or *ovarian follicle*. *See also* zona granulosa.
[Named after the 17th-century Dutch anatomist Regnier de Graaf (1641–73) who discovered it in 1672]

graceful degradation *n.* A principle proposed by the English psychologist David Courtenay Marr (1945–80) according to which an efficient information processing system should be able to respond to minor errors without generating completely incorrect output. The human mind appears to have this property, but most computers do not.

gracile nucleus *n.* Either of two areas of the *medulla oblongata where the *fasciculus gracilis terminates. Also called the *nucleus gracilis*.
[From Latin *gracilis* slender]

gradation method *See* method of gradation.

graded potential *n.* A *depolarization or *hyperpolarization of a neuron that varies in amplitude according to the intensity of stimulation and that does not produce a conventional nerve impulse or action potential but is itself conducted passively along the axon as a nerve signal, declining with time and distance. Some cells with very short axons, including *rods, *cones, and *bipolar cells, show only graded potentials and function without conventional nerve impulses, whereas others generate nerve impulses only when their graded potentials reach some threshold as a consequence of *spatial summation or *temporal summation. *Compare* action potential.

grade-equivalent score *n.* A measure of a person's ability, skill, or knowledge, expressed in terms of the grade level in school at which the average person attains that level of performance. Also called a *grade score*. *Compare* age-equivalent score.

gradient descent *n.* A numerical method for minimizing a function by invariably moving downwards along a steepest path from the current position. The method does not guarantee to reach a global minimum because, like a mountaineer who tries to reach the lowest point by always going down a steepest slope from any given point and who gets trapped in a local basin separated by hills from lower valleys, the process may get trapped in a local minimum far above the global minimum. It is used in *connectionism (1) and *parallel distributed processing to minimize the discrepancy between the output of a *network model and the desired state for a given input. Also called *steepest descent*. *See also* annealing (1), back-propagation algorithm. *Compare* hill climbing.

gradient of texture *See* texture gradient.

Gräfenberg spot *See* G spot.

gram calorie *See under* Calorie.

grammar *n.* **1.** The branch of *linguistics concerned with sentence structure, especially *syntax and *morphology (2). **2.** The system of implicit rules governing a speaker's use of a language, especially *semantics and *phonology. *See also* case grammar, context-dependent grammar, context-free grammar, finite-state grammar, generative grammar, phrase-structure grammar, pivot grammar, transformational grammar, universal grammar.
[From Greek *grammatikos* concerning letters]

grandeur, delusion of *See* grandiose delusion.

grandiose delusion *n.* A *delusion of inflated importance, power, wealth, knowledge, or identity, or of having a great but unrecognized talent or intelligence, having made a significant discovery, or of being or having a special relationship with a prominent person. *See also* grandiose delusional disorder, megalomania. *Compare* grandiose ideas or actions.

grandiose delusional disorder *n.* A type of *delusional disorder in which the central delusion is a *grandiose delusion. *Compare* grandiose ideas or actions.

grandiose ideas or actions *n.* A pattern of thought or behaviour, falling short of being classified as a *delusion, seen in *manic episodes, *narcissistic personality disorder, and other mental disorders and states, characterized by feelings of being superbly healthy, exceptionally intelligent, or extraordinarily talented, often associated with overspending, excessive gambling, and similar extravagant behaviour. *See also* grandiose self. *Compare* grandiose delusion, grandiose delusional disorder.

grandiose self *n.* In *self-psychology, a term introduced by the Austrian-born US psychoanalyst Heinz Kohut (1913–81) to denote a protective and inflated self-image that a child develops when its natural *narcissism is inevitably undermined by the mother's occasional failure to respond adequately. This grandiose self normally moderates as the child grows older and its parents' responses change; but it is liable to remain unaltered if the normal developmental sequence is disrupted, especially if the mother never responds adequately or responds unpredictably or unrealistically, and in such cases the child may develop *narcissistic personality disorder. Also called the *grandiose-exhibitionist self*. *See also* grandiose ideas or actions, self-psychology.

grand mal *n*. An obsolescent synonym for *tonic–clonic.
[French: literally big illness]

grandmother cell *n*. Based on the discovery of *feature detectors, a hypothetical cell (improbably exaggerated, but based on reality) in the *visual cortex that might respond maximally to a highly specific stimulus such as the viewer's own grandmother.

granule cell *n*. Any of the small *multipolar neurons that are the principal *interneurons of the neocortex and are abundantly present in the cerebellum. *See also* parallel fibre. *Compare* pyramidal cell.
[From Latin *granulum* a small grain]

granulocyte *n*. Any of a group of *leucocytes with granules in their cytoplasm that play a part in the immune system as *phagocytes by consuming foreign or malfunctioning cells. *See also* lymphocyte, monocyte.
[From Latin *granulum* a small grain + Greek *kytos* a vessel]

grapheme *n*. The smallest unit in the written form of a language, usually a letter or combination of letters representing a single *phoneme, such as the *b* in *book*, the *s* in *sip*, the *sh* in *ship*, or the *ph* in *photograph*.
[From Greek *graphema* a letter, from *graphein* to write]

graphic rating scale *n*. Any *rating scale in which a response is indicated by marking a position on a line, such as one anchored by *strongly disagree* at one end and *strongly agree* at the other, or some other *analogue (2) representation of the dimension being rated. *Compare* numerical rating scale, verbal rating scale.

graphology *n*. The study of handwriting from all angles, including its relationship with character or personality. Speculation about this possibility can be traced to ancient Rome, where in the second century Seutonius Tranquillus remarked on peculiarities in Augustus Caesar's handwriting, and modern interest in graphology was stimulated by the French Abbot Jean Hippolyte Michon (1806–81), who coined the word in the title of his book *Système de Graphologie* (1875). Graphologists study variations of size, layout, slant, connectedness, speed, regularity, letter forms, angularity, and shading of handwriting, but relationships with objective measures of personality have generally produced only weak and unstable correlations. None the less, graphology has been popular as a selection tool in Germany and other continental European countries since the publication of the influential book *Handschrift und Charakter* (1940, Handwriting and Character) by the German philosopher and psychologist Ludwig Klages (1872–1956).
[From Greek *graphein* to write + *logos* word, discourse, or reason]

graphomania *n*. Overpowering urge to write, often leading to *graphorrhoea.
[From Greek *graphein* to write + *mania* madness]

graphorrhoea *n*. Excessive, uncontrolled, incoherent writing; a written counterpart of *logorrhoea. US *graphorrhea*.
[From Greek *graphein* to write + *rhoia* a flow]

grasp reflex *n*. A type of reflex in which the fingers flex in a clutching motion in response to stroking of the palm of the hand. It is normal in young infants from birth to about four months of age, during which time the grip is strong enough to support the infant's own weight, but in older people it is a neurological sign of a lesion in the premotor cortex (*see under* motor cortex). Also called the *Darwinian reflex* or the *grasping reflex*.

grass *n*. A common street name for *cannabis, especially in the form of *marijuana.

Grassmann's law (linguistics) *n*. A modification of *Grimm's law, devised to explain exceptions to it, such as the English *daughter*, which was *duhita* in Sanskrit but according to Grimm's law should have been *dhuhita*. Grassmann's law asserts that a sequence of two *aspirates (2) in a word is sufficient to block the sound shift of Grimm's law.

[Named after the German–Polish mathematician and physicist Hermann G(ünther) Grassmann (1809–77) who formulated it in 1863]

Grassmann's laws (perception) *n.* Three basic laws of colour mixing. If *x*, *y*, and *z* are distinct stimulus colours, and if the symbol = indicates visual matching, then the laws state that: (a) If $x = y$, then $x + z = y + z$ (if equivalent colours are added to equivalent colours, then the sums are also equivalent); (b) If $x = y$, then $x - z = y - z$ (if equivalent colours are subtracted from equivalent colours, then the differences are also equivalent); (c) If $x = z$ and $y = z$, then $x = y$ (colours that are equivalent to the same colour are equivalent to each other). *See also* additive primary, primary colour (1, 2), subtractive primary.

[Named after the German–Polish mathematician and physicist Hermann G(ünther) Grassmann (1809–77) who formulated them in 1853]

grating *n.* A framework of parallel bars serving as a cover or hatch, hence figuratively an image consisting of alternating dark and light bars used for studying spatial vision. *See also* acuity grating, diffraction grating, McCollough effect, phantom grating, sinusoidal grating, spatial frequency, tilt aftereffect.

gray matter *See* grey matter.

Great Vowel Shift *n.* A change in the pronunciation of English that took place at the end of the Middle Ages: most long *vowels, such as the vowel in *see* (which before the shift rhymed with the modern French *thé*), were raised, and the already *close vowels in *shine* (which was pronounced like today's *sheen*) and *mouse* (which was pronounced like today's *moose*) became the *diphthongs that they now are.

Greenspoon effect *n.* Modification of the content of conversational speech, without the speaker's awareness, through *reinforcement given by the listener in the form of nods, smiles, or expressions of approval such as 'mmm-hmm'. Such reinforcers have been used to increase the speaker's use of a certain

word, or a category of words such as plural nouns, or the frequency with which the speaker expresses personal opinions, and so on.

[Named after the US psychologist Joel Greenspoon (born 1921) who reported the effect in articles in the *American Psychologist* in 1954 and the *American Journal of Psychology* in 1955, although previous studies had already demonstrated the effect]

Grelling's paradox *n.* A *paradox of non-self-descriptive adjectives. Some adjectives are self-descriptive: the adjective *short* is short, the adjective *English* is English, and the adjective *polysyllabic* is polysyllabic, and each of these adjectives is therefore *autological, because each is self-descriptive. In contrast, some adjectives are *heterological: the adjective *long* is not long, *Russian* is not Russian, and *monosyllabic* is not monosyllabic. Is the adjective *heterological* autological or heterological? If it is autological, then it is self-descriptive, which means that it must be heterological; and if it is heterological, then it must be non-self-descriptive, in which case it is autological.

[Named after the German mathematician Kurt Grelling (1886–1942) who published it in 1908]

grey matter *n.* The greyish nerve tissue of the brain and spinal cord, containing neuronal cell bodies, unmyelinated axons, and dendrites. US *gray matter*. Also called (technically) the *substantia grisea*. *Compare* white matter.

Gricean maxims *n.* Another name for *conversational maxims.

grid analysis *n.* A collection of techniques for analysing data generated by the *Repertory Grid Test.

grid test *See* Repertory Grid Test.

grief reaction *n.* Distress and intense sorrow in response to the loss of someone or something to which one is strongly attached, usually through *bereavement. In severe cases it can amount to an *adjustment disorder.

Grimm's law *n.* A proposition about various shifts that occurred in the pronunciation of *plosive consonants between the Proto-Indo-European language and the various Indo-European languages, including English,

that are descended from it, based on a set of nine correspondences observed between Sanskrit, Latin and Greek on the one hand and the Germanic languages such as English on the other, including the change from [p] to [f] as in Latin *pater* becoming English *father* and the change from [t] to [θ] as in Latin *tres* becoming English *three*. The other correspondences are [k] to [x] (the final phoneme in the Scots *loch*), [b] to [p], [d] to [t], [g] to [k], [bʰ] (aspirated, that is, accompanied by a brief [h]-sound) to [b], [dʰ] to [d], and [gʰ] to [g]. *See also* Grassmann's law (linguistics).
[Named after the German philologist Jakob Ludwig Karl Grimm (1785–1863) who formulated it in 1822]

grooming *n*. **1.** A pattern of behaviour whereby an animal cleans and maintains the hair or surface of its body or that of another member of the same species (a conspecific). **2.** In humans, cleaning and tidying one's hair, clothes, and general appearance (also called *self-grooming*), or rubbing down and smartening a horse, dog, or other domesticated animal.
[From Middle English *grom* a manservant]

grounded theory *n*. A *theory built up from *naturalistic observations of phenomena, generally reflecting the participants' own interpretations, rather than being introduced or imposed by the investigator, sometimes used in *qualitative research.

group dynamics *n*. The social interactions and influences in small groups and the study of these phenomena.

group factor *n*. In *factor analysis, a *factor (2) that accounts for the intercorrelations between a subset of the variables but not all of them.

grouping law *n*. Any of the four laws formulated in 1923 by the Gestalt psychologist Max Wertheimer (1880–1943) to explain the organization of parts into wholes by the visual system, or one of the two additional laws suggested in 1990 by the US psychologists Irvin Rock (1922–95) and Stephen E. Palmer (born 1948). Also called a Gestalt *principle of organization*. *See* closure grouping law, common region, connectedness grouping law, good continuation, proximity grouping law, similarity grouping law. *See also* associationism,

Bender Gestalt Test, common fate, Gestalt psychology.

group inhibition of helping *See under* bystander effect.

group movement *n*. A form of *apparent movement that occurs in the *Ternus phenomenon when an intermediate interstimulus interval is used, all three elements appearing to move together in step. *Compare* element movement.

group polarization *n*. The tendency for involvement in a group to cause the attitudes and opinions of the group members to become more extreme, in the direction of the predominant attitudes and opinions in the group. The phenomenon is explained by collective involvement and group participation making salient the group *norms (1), amplifying normative individual attitudes and opinions and causing them to shift even further in the direction of the group norms. The concept was introduced in 1969 by the Romanian-born French social psychologist Serge Moscovici (born 1920) and the Italian-born Canadian social psychologist Marisa Zavalloni (born 1929), who provided evidence, for example, that the generally favourable attitudes of French students towards de Gaulle became even more positive, on average, and their generally hostile attitudes towards Americans became even more hostile, following group discussion. *See also* risky shift, social influence.

group selection *n*. A form of *natural selection favouring characteristics that benefit the group or species as a whole, rather than any individual organism, put forward to explain the evolution of *altruistic behaviour such as the alarm calls of birds responding to the presence of predators, but rejected by most contemporary biologists because of the problem of explaining how it could evolve, except in highly unusual circumstances. *Compare* kin selection.

group stereotype *See* stereotype.

group test *n*. A test of *intelligence, *personality, or any other psychological attribute that is presented in *multiple-choice format and can be administered to groups of respondents simultaneously. The first widely used group tests were the *Army Alpha and Beta Tests. *Compare* individual test.

group therapy n. A generic term for various techniques of *psychotherapy in which clients or patients are treated together in groups, including traditional therapies adapted for application in groups, *encounter groups, *est, *milieu therapy, *psychodrama, *sociodrama, *T-groups, and a myriad of more unconventional marathon, growth, and confrontation therapies. Its first use is believed to have been by the Scottish psychiatrist William (Alexander Francis) Browne (1805–85) at the Crichton Royal Hospital in Dumfries, Scotland, in 1855. Also called *group psychotherapy*, the original term introduced in 1932 by the Romanian-born US psychiatrist Jacob L(evy) Moreno (1892–1974). *See also* conjoint therapy, sociodrama, systems theory.

groupthink n. A collective pattern of defensive avoidance, characteristic of group decision making in organizations in which group members develop rationalizations supporting shared illusions of their own infallibility and invulnerability within the organization. The US psychologist Irving Lester Janis (1918–90), who introduced the term in his book *Victims of Groupthink* (1972), listed eight characteristic features: an illusion of invulnerability; collective efforts to rationalize in order to discount warnings; an unquestioned belief in the group's inherent morality; stereotyped views of rivals and enemies; direct pressure on any member who dissents from the consensus view; self-censorship of disagreements with the apparent group consensus; a shared illusion of unanimity; and the emergence of self-appointed protectors of the group from adverse information that might undermine the existing complacency.

growth hormone n. A *hormone secreted by the *anterior pituitary that acts directly on somatic cells, promoting the synthesis of proteins essential to growth of muscles and long limb bones, sometimes used as a *performance enhancer. Also called *somatotrophin*. **GH** abbrev.

growth hormone releasing hormone n. A *releasing hormone secreted by the hypothalamus that induces the anterior pituitary to secrete *growth hormone. Also called *somatotrophin releasing hormone*. *Compare* somatostatin. **GHRH** abbrev.

Grübelsucht n. A type of *obsession in which even simple and obvious things are compulsively questioned.
[From German *grübeln* to ponder + *Sucht* mania]

grue paradox n. Another name for *Goodman's paradox.

G spot abbrev. A region of spongy tissue on the front wall of the vagina, behind the pubic bone, surrounding the urethra approximately two inches from the mouth of the vagina, that when stimulated by firm pressure swells into a ridge, becomes a focus of sexual excitement in some women, and has been claimed to be a source of fluid, similar in composition to a man's prostate fluid, released through the urethra. *See also* erogenous zone.
[An abbreviation of *Gräfenberg spot*, named after the German gynaecologist Ernst Gräfenberg (1881–1957) who first drew attention to it in 1950]

guanine n. One of the constituent *bases (1) of the nucleic acids *DNA and *RNA, having an affinity for cytosine, also found in the liver, pancreas, and other organs of animals, in the germ cells of plants, and in guano. **G** abbrev.
[From Spanish *guano* the dung of fish-eating sea-birds + Greek *-ine* indicating an organic compound]

guided discovery n. A technique used in *cognitive behaviour modification for helping a client to recall the steps that led to a particular instance of feeling anxious or depressed, with a view to locating potentially changeable elements in the client's thinking patterns.

guiding fiction n. In the *individual psychology of the Austrian psychiatrist Alfred Adler (1870–1937) and his followers, a term used to denote the characteristic form of a person's *self-image. Also called a *guiding idea*. *See also* neurotic fiction.

Guilford's cube n. A multifactorial model of the *structure of intellect* (SOI) developed and refined from 1946 onwards by the US psychologist J(oy) P(aul) Guilford (1897–1987) and usually depicted as an object loosely called a cube.

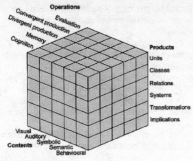

Guilford's cube

According to the theory, intelligence comprises 120 independent abilities, extended in 1982 to 150. In the extended version of the theory, a given mental task may involve any of five possible kinds of mental *operations* (cognition, memory, divergent production, convergent production, or evaluation); five different kinds of mental representations or *contents* (visual, auditory, symbolic, semantic, or behavioural); and six different kinds of *products* (units, classes, relations, systems, transformations, or implications). Multiplying these together yields 150 different cognitive factors, each of which can be assessed by a different task, and the theory can be represented by a $5 \times 5 \times 6$ 'cube' composed of 150 smaller units (see illustration). Also called the *structure-of-intellect model*. *See also* convergence–divergence, Merrill–Palmer scale. *Compare* multiple intelligences.

Gulf War Syndrome *n.* A disorder controversially claimed to have been contracted by soldiers involved in the Gulf War in 1991, characterized by fatigue, muscle and joint pains, headaches, memory loss, insomnia, skin complaints, depression, and irritability, possibly caused by multiple vaccinations, nerve gas, interaction of vaccinations with anti-nerve-gas medication, or *organophosphate insecticides. *Compare* chronic fatigue syndrome. **GWS** *abbrev.*
[Named after the 1991 Gulf War between an international force led by the US on the one side and Iraq on the other, following Iraq's invasion of Kuwait in 1990]

guppy effect *n.* An anomaly in *prototype theory, in which an item is more prototypical of a conjunctive concept than of either (or any) of its constituent concepts. Thus a *guppy* is supposedly more prototypical of the conjunctive concept *pet fish* than of either of the constituent concepts *pet* or *fish*, and if prototype theory is formulated in the theory of *fuzzy sets, this leads to a contradiction, implying that either the apparently natural formulation in the theory of fuzzy sets, or prototype theory itself, must be fundamentally flawed. The concept of *goldfish* has also been claimed to manifest the guppy effect, because it is a more prototypical instance of a pet fish than of a pet or a fish, and empirical research has uncovered many other examples, such as *atlas*, more prototypical of *reference books* than of *references sources* or *books*. The anomaly was first uncovered and the example of the guppy suggested in 1981 by the US psychologists Daniel N. Osherson (born 1949) and Edward E. Smith (born 1940).

gustation *n.* The act or process of tasting or the sense of *taste. **gustatory** *adj.*
[From Latin *gustare* to taste + *-ation* indicating a process or condition]

gustatory acuity *n.* Keenness or sharpness of the sense of *taste. *See also* acuity.

gustatory hallucination *n.* A *hallucination of a taste, usually experienced as unpleasant.
[From Latin *gustare* to taste]

gustatory receptor *n.* A *sensory receptor specialized for binding to molecules of sapid chemical substances and responding with nerve impulses that generate experiences of *taste. The term is used sometimes for a *taste bud and sometimes for a *taste cell. Also called a *gustatory cell* or *taste cell*.

Guttman scale *n.* A type of *attitude scale, the items of which can be arranged in a hierarchical order such that agreement with any particular item implies probable agreement with all those below it in the hierarchy, as would apply to the following (non-attitudinal) items: *I am over 5 feet tall; I am over 5 feet 6 inches tall; I am over 6 feet tall; I am over 6 feet 6 inches tall*. It is constructed by the method of *scalogram analysis* in which a large pool of candidate statements about an attitude object (such as *Euthanasia is morally wrong; Euthanasia should be legalized*, and so on) are administered to a group of respondents who mark just those items with which they agree, and from these responses a set of items is selected that can be arranged into a hierarchy with as few errors (deviations from a perfect linear hierarchy) as possible, a satisfactory Guttman scale having relatively few errors as indexed by a *reproducibility (Rep) of at least 0.90, implying that the scale is unidimensional, measuring only one major attitude variable. The process of constructing a Guttman scale is called *scalogram analysis*. A simple example of a Guttman scale is a *social distance scale.

[Named after the US (later Israeli) psychologist Louis H. Guttman (1916–87) who introduced it in an article in the *American Sociological Review* in 1944]

gyrus *n*. A ridge, especially one of the convolutions on the surface of the brain that are separated by *sulci. *See* angular gyrus, cingulate gyrus, dentate gyrus, Heschl's gyrus, inferior temporal gyrus, parahippocampal gyrus, postcentral gyrus, precentral gyrus, superior temporal gyrus. **gyri** *pl*.

[From Latin *gyrus* a circle or turning, from Greek *gyros* a circle or ring]

H *abbrev*. A common street name for *heroin.

Haab's pupillary reflex *n*. Another name for the *pupillary light reflex.
[Named after the Swiss ophthalmologist Otto Haab (1850–1931) who drew attention to it]

habenula *n*. A small triangular area of the *epithalamus on each side of the base of the pineal gland. **habenulae** *pl*.
[From Latin *habenula* a little strap or thong, from *habena* a strap or thong]

habenular nucleus *n*. A collection of nerve cells in each half of the *habenula, connected by nerve fibres, functioning as a correlation centre for olfactory information.

habit *n*. A disposition to behave in a particular way, or an established practice or custom. In learning theory, a learned behavioural *response associated with a particular situation, especially a response that has been subject to *reinforcement (1, 2) or a *conditioned response.

habitat *n*. The natural locality in which an organism lives, or the environment of a community; the place in which a person or group of people are normally to be found. *Compare* biotope, ecosystem.
[From Latin *habitat* it dwells, from *habitare* to dwell]

habit disorders *n*. Any *impulse-control disorders involving habitual maladaptive behaviour, apart from the *paraphilias and *substance-related disorders. Examples include *Internet addiction syndrome, *kleptomania, *pathological gambling, *pyromania, and *trichotillomania. In careful usage, this term should not be applied to stereotyped movements or to stereotypic movement disorder.

habit reversal *n*. A form of *learning (1) in which an organism choosing repeatedly between two alternatives *A* and *B* is initially rewarded for choosing alternative *A* rather than *B* until a behavioural preference for *A* is established, and is then rewarded for choosing *B* rather than *A* until the preference is reversed, and so on. Birds and mammals show progressive improvement in switching from *A* to *B* and back again, whereas fish show little or no improvement. Also called *reversal learning*. *See also* overtraining reversal effect, serial learning (2). *Compare* non-reversal shift.

habit strength *n*. The term used in *Hullian learning theory to denote the strength of a connection between a *stimulus (1) and a *response, determined by the number of *reinforcements (1). *See also* generalized habit strength. $_sH_R$ *abbrev*.

habituation *n*. **1.** The process of making or becoming used to something. **2.** More specifically the temporary diminution in the strength or frequency of an *unconditioned response by repeated exposure to the *stimulus (1) that evokes it. **3.** A mild form of *tolerance (3) of the effects of a drug. *See also* inhibition (3). *Compare* dishabituation, extinction (2).

haemoglobin *n*. A protein present in *erythrocytes (red blood corpuscles). It consists of haem, a red organic pigment containing iron, and globin, a protein, and it combines reversibly with oxygen and plays a vital role in the transport of oxygen through the bloodstream to the tissues. US *hemoglobin*. **Hb** *abbrev*.
[From Greek *haima* blood + Latin *globus* a sphere]

hair cell *n*. Any of the cylindrical or flask-shaped *sensory receptor cells for hearing in the *organ of Corti of the *cochlea, or any of the similar cells in the *vestibular system that are involved in the sense of balance and orientation and that enable human beings to walk upright, certain animals to detect vibrations in the ground, and fishes to detect displacements of water. The cell is divided into three sections: a front end consisting of a cone-shaped bundle of 30 to 150 *stereocilia (which are not true cilia) together with a single true cilium called a *kinocilium, a middle section containing the cell nucleus, *mitochondria, and *Golgi apparatuses, and a back section consisting of nerve endings that feed in to the nervous system, the cell as a whole functioning as an extremely sensitive mechano-electrical *transducer that converts kinetic energy into electrical nerve impulses. A mammalian hair cell responds along its axis of maximum sensitivity to movements of its tip of 100 picometres (trillionths of a metre, about the same distance as the diameter of some atoms), but is totally insensitive to movement along the perpendicular axis. *See also* Deiters' cell, inner hair cell, outer hair cell.

hair-pulling, pathological *n*. Another name for *trichotillomania.

Halcion *n*. A proprietary name for the benzodiazepine drug *triazolam.
[Trademark, from *halcyon*, peaceful and carefree, from Greek *alkyon* a kingfisher, once believed to make a secure floating nest for its eggs]

Haldol *n*. A proprietary name for the neuroleptic drug *haloperidol.
[Trademark]

halfway house *n*. A residential centre offering temporary accommodation and rehabilitation to people recently released from prison or recovering from a mental disorder not requiring full hospitalization.

hallucination *n*. A perceptual experience similar to a true perception but not resulting from stimulation of a sense organ, generally occurring under a *hallucinogen or *hypnosis, or as a symptom of *schizophrenia or a *neurological disorder, but excluding dreams occurring while asleep, *hypnagogic images experienced while falling asleep, and *hypnopompic images experienced while awakening. To be distinguished in careful usage from an *illusion, in which a real object or event is misperceived or misinterpreted. *See also* alcohol hallucinosis, audible thought, auditory hallucination, delirium tremens, gustatory hallucination, hallucinogen, hallucinosis, mood-congruent, mood-incongruent, odour hallucination, organic hallucinosis, pseudohallucination, schizophrenia, somatic hallucination, tactile hallucination, visual hallucination. *Compare* delusion.
[From Latin *alucinari* to wander in the mind + *-ation* indicating a process or condition]

hallucinogen *n*. Any of a number of drugs that induce *hallucinations or perceptual alterations, the most common examples being *phenylalkylamines such as *mescaline and *STP; *indole alkaloids such as *bufotenin, *harmine, *LSD, *psilocybin, and *DMT; and various other compounds such as *ibotenic acid, *myristin, and *ololiuqui. Also called a *psychodysleptic*, a *psycholytic*, or a *psychotomimetic*. *See also* Amanita muscaria, cannabis, fly agaric, hallucinogen-related disorders, magic mushroom, morning glory, muscimol, phencyclidine, teonanactyl, travel agent, trip. *Compare* phantasticant, psychedelic. **hallucinogenic** *adj*.
[From Latin *alucinari* to wander in the mind + Greek *genes* born or produced]

hallucinogen-related disorders *n*. *Substance-related disorders associated specifically with the consumption of *hallucinogens. *See* substance abuse, substance dependence, substance-induced disorders, substance use disorders.

hallucinosis *n*. A mental condition in which *hallucinations occur frequently. *See also* alcohol hallucinosis, organic hallucinosis.

halo effect *n*. In *person perception, a generalization from the perception of one prominent or salient characteristic, trait, or personality attribute to an impression of the personality as a whole, leading to inflated correlations between rated characteristics. The effect was first reported by the US psychologist Frederick Lyman Wells (1884–1964) in a study of ratings of the literary merit of authors published in the *Archives of Psychology* in 1907. The US psychologist Edward Lee Thorndike (1874–1949) introduced the term *halo error* in 1920. The term is sometimes restricted to instances in which it leads to an overvaluation of the personality as a whole. *See also* atmosphere effect, trait centrality.

haloperidol *n*. A central nervous system *depressant and *neuroleptic (1) agent, belonging to the class of *butyrophenones, that blocks *dopamine neuroreceptors and is used in the treatment of *schizophrenia and other psychotic disorders and in the control of symptoms in *Tourette's disorder. Also called *Haldol* (trademark). *Compare* droperidol.
[From *hal-* indicating a halogen, from Greek *hals* salt + English *(pi)perid(ine)* + *-ol* denoting a compound containing a hydroxyl group, from *(alcoh)ol*]

hammer *n*. A non-technical name for the *malleus of the *middle ear. *See also* anvil.
[So called because of its resemblance to a blacksmith's hammer]

handedness *n*. **1.** A preference for using one hand rather than the other, or a tendency to use one hand more skilfully or comfortably than the other, depending on which *cerebral hemisphere is dominant for motor control, approximately 90 per cent of people showing right handedness or left hemisphere dominance for motor control. Also called *lateral dominance*. *See also* cerebral dominance, laterality. **2.** A property of some molecules of having an inherent asymmetry in their three-dimensional structure depending on the direction of rotation or twist, such molecules often having both left-handed and right-handed *enantiomorphs.

handicapped *adj*. An obsolescent term meaning afflicted by a physical disability or mental retardation.

Hanoi, Tower of *See* Tower of Hanoi.

Hans, Little *See* Little Hans.

haphalgesia *n*. A condition in which stimuli that would ordinarily elicit sensations of touch are experienced as painful.
[From Greek *haphe* touch + *algesis* sense of pain, from *algos* pain + *-ia* indicating a condition or quality]

haplodiploid *adj*. Of or relating to a species, including many ants, bees, and wasps, and some bugs, beetles, mites, ticks, and rotifers, in which males emerge from unfertilized eggs and are *haploid whereas females emerge from fertilized eggs and are *diploid. This explains how, in a haplodiploid species, females inherit only half their genes from their fathers, although fathers pass all their genes on to their daughters. **haplodiploidy** *n*. The state or condition of being *haplodiploid.
[From *haplo(id)* + *diploid*]

haplography *n*. An error in writing a word containing a repeated letter or syllable, only one instead of both of the repeated letters or syllables being written, as in *ocurrence* instead of the correct *occurrence*, or *autopagnosia* instead of the correct *autotopagnosia* (this example occurring even in dictionaries of psychology). Also called *lipography*. *Compare* haplology.
[From Greek *haplous* single + *graphein* to write]

haploid *adj*. Of or relating to a cell that has a single set of unpaired *chromosomes, as in the sex cells or *gametes of humans and other sexually reproducing animals, rather than the full complement of paired chromosomes; also of or relating to an organism such as a fungus or a male bee whose body cells are haploid. *Compare* diploid, haplodiploid. **haploidy** *n*. The state or condition of being *haploid.
[From Greek *haploeides* single, from *haplos* one + *-oeides* denoting resemblance of form, from *eidos* shape]

haplology *n*. An error in fluent speech, especially in *allegro speech, in pronouncing a word containing a repeated sound or syllable, only one of the repeated sounds or syllables being articulated, as when *library* is pronounced as if it were written *libry* or *probably* as if it were written *probly*. Also called *syncope*. *Compare* elision, haplography.
[From Greek *haplous* single + *logos* a word]

haptic *adj*. Of or relating to the sense of *touch. *See also* haptic touch.
[From Greek *haptein* to touch + *-ikos* of, relating to, or resembling]

haptic agnosia *n*. Another name for *tactile agnosia.
[From Greek *haptein* to touch + *agnosia*]

haptic touch *n*. One of the major forms of *touch, involving active exploration, usually by the hands, or the experience that arises when one's hands envelop an object and explore its surface freely, providing information about its general shape or form and allowing object recognition to occur, even if the object is larger than any area of the skin. *See also* astereognosis, eccentric projection, stereognosis. *Compare* cutaneous sense, dynamic touch.

hard AI *n.* Another name for *strong AI.

hard drug *n.* An imprecise term for a drug such as heroin or cocaine that is highly addictive, but excluding highly addictive drugs such as alcohol or nicotine. *Compare* soft drug.

hard of hearing *n.* Partially deaf. *See* deafness.

hard sign *n.* An obvious or unambiguous *sign (1) of a *neurological disorder, such as an absent or pathological *reflex, an abnormal *EEG, a unilateral *paralysis, or a loss of function of one or more of the *cranial nerves. *Compare* soft sign.

hard-wired *adj.* Of, relating to, or consisting of a circuit or instruction that is built into the hardware of a computer and is therefore effectively unmodifiable; figuratively, of or relating to an innate and unmodifiable response or pattern of behaviour, such as a *fixed-action pattern.

Hardy–Weinberg equilibrium *n.* The stable state of a population in which the *Hardy–Weinberg law holds, also called a *balanced polymorphism.*

Hardy–Weinberg law *n.* The law according to which relative *gene frequencies in a population remain stable from generation to generation provided that mating occurs randomly and there is no *selection (1), *migration, or *mutation. If the relative frequency of one *allele at a particular gene locus is p and that of another is q, then it is easy to prove that the population will contain p^2 homozygotes with two p genes, q^2 homozygotes with two q genes, and $2pq$ heterozygotes with one p and one q gene. *See also* balanced polymorphism, population genetics.
[Named after the English mathematician G(odfrey) H(arold) Hardy (1877–1947) and the German physician Wilhelm Weinberg (1862–1937) who discovered the law independently of each other in 1908]

harmine *n.* A *psychedelic drug and *indole alkaloid obtained from the seeds of the plant *Peganum harmala* native to India and the Levant. Formula $C_{13}H_{14}N_2O$. *See also* hallucinogen.
[From *harmala* the specific part of the plant's name + -*ine* indicating an organic compound]

harmonic *n.* A component of a *complex tone, having a frequency that is an integral multiple of the *fundamental frequency. The *first harmonic* is the fundamental tone; the *second harmonic*, also called the *first overtone*, has twice the frequency of the fundamental and is therefore an *octave higher; the *third harmonic* or *second overtone* has three times the frequency of the fundamental; and so on (see illustration). *See also* missing fundamental illusion.
[From Latin *harmonicus* of or relating to harmony]

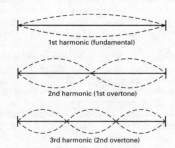

1st harmonic (fundamental)

2nd harmonic (1st overtone)

3rd harmonic (2nd overtone)

Harmonic. Fundamental and two overtones.

harmonic mean *n.* In descriptive statistics, the average value of a set of scores calculated by taking the reciprocal of the arithmetic mean of the reciprocals of the scores. The scores 3, 4, 5 have reciprocal 1/3, 1/4, 1/5, and the arithmetic mean of these reciprocals is 0.261, so the harmonic mean of the set of scores is 1/0.261 = 3.831. *Compare* arithmetic mean, geometric mean.

harp theory *n.* Another name for the *place theory.

Hartley's *F* max *n.* In statistics, a test for *homogeneity of variance in several samples based on the ratio of the largest variance to the smallest variance. Also called *F max*, *Hartley's largest F*.

[Named after the US statistician Herman Otto Hartley (1912–80) who published the test in 1950]

hashish *n*. The dried resinous exudate of the flowering tops of the female *cannabis plant and the undersides of its leaves, smoked with tobacco or added to foods and eaten as a psychotropic drug.
[From Arabic *hashish* dried hemp]

Hawk–Dove game *n*. Another name for the *Chicken game, especially in biological literature, where it was rediscovered and interpreted as follows. The Hawk strategy involves *escalated fighting until the individual adopting it is forced to withdraw or its opponent gives way; the Dove strategy involves *conventional fighting—the individual adopting it retreats before getting injured if its opponent escalates. The highest payoff, in terms of *Darwinian fitness, goes to the Hawk strategy pitted against Dove, the second-highest payoff to Dove against Dove, the third-highest to Dove against Hawk, and the lowest to Hawk against Hawk. The English biologist John Maynard Smith (born 1920) and the US physicist and chemist George R. Price (1922–75) first analysed this game in 1973 and showed that the *evolutionarily stable strategy is a mixture of Hawk and Dove.

Hawk–Dove–Retaliator game *n*. An extension of the *Hawk–Dove game, with the additional strategy available of fighting conventionally and escalating only if the adversary escalates: a Retaliator normally plays Dove but responds to a Hawk opponent by playing Hawk. The game was introduced in 1973 by the English biologist John Maynard Smith (born 1920) and the US physicist and chemist George R. Price (1922–75), who showed that the *evolutionarily stable strategy is Retaliator.

Hawthorne effect *n*. Improvement in the performance or productivity of workers or students resulting from the introduction of new working methods or conditions, irrespective of the nature of the changes, the effect often being attributed to the feeling of being under concerned observation. In the mid 1920s, informal tests at the Hawthorne works of the effects of changes in lighting on the productivity of women factory workers inspecting parts, assembling relays, and winding coils suggested that the women worked faster irrespective of the lighting changes that were introduced. The first formal investigation of the effect was the Relay Assembly Test Room experiment, focusing on the effects of rest pauses and changes in hours of work, which ran from 1927 to 1932 under the directorship of the Australian psychologist Elton Mayo (1880–1949), with the collaboration of the US human relations researcher Fritz J(ules) Roethlisberger (1898–1974) and others. The interpretation of all the Hawthorne studies has been a matter of controversy, especially since the mid 1970s.
[Named after the Hawthorne works in Chicago where the Western Electric Company manufactured equipment for Bell Telephone Systems and where seven separate studies on the effects of changes in working conditions were carried out between 1924 and 1932]

heading vector *n*. A fixed direction of travel towards a goal, used as a crude method of navigation. *Compare* cognitive map.
[From Latin *vector* a carrier or bearer, from *vehere, vectum* to convey]

head rotation illusion *See* rotating head illusion.

health psychology *n*. A field of *applied psychology concerned with psychological aspects of physical health, including health promotion and the prevention and treatment of illness and the identification of psychological causes and correlates of health and illness. *See also* medical psychology.

hearing *n*. One of the five classical *senses (1), responsive to sound waves within the normal *audibility range of *frequencies (1) from 16 hertz to about 20,000 hertz, the human organ of hearing being the *ear, within which periodic variations in air pressure are amplified in the *outer ear and *middle ear and transmitted to the *inner ear where *hair cells in the *organ of Corti located in the *cochlea convert the vibrations into nerve impulses that are transmitted by the *vestibulocochlear nerve to the *inferior colliculi in the tectum of the midbrain and thence to the *auditory cortex located on *Heschl's gyrus. Also called *audition*. *See also* amblyacusia, anacusia, deafness, diplacusis, dysacusia, hypacusia, hyperacusis, Ohm's acoustic law, paracusia, presbyacusis.

hearing impairment *n.* Partial *deafness.
hearing-impaired *adj.*

hearing loss *n.* *Deafness or partial deafness.

heat grill *n.* A device consisting of closely packed alternating warm and cold bars. When applied to the skin it stimulates both *cold spots and *warm spots and creates a sensation of intense heat called *paradoxical heat.*

Hebbian rule *n.* In *connectionism (1) and *parallel distributed processing, a rule governing the alteration of weights of connections between units in order to adjust a *network model in the direction of a target pattern of activation. For example, the *Hopfield rule* strengthens the connection between two units whenever both are simultaneously active or both are simultaneously inactive, and weakens the connection whenever one is active and the other inactive; the *Stent–Singer rule* strengthens the weight of a connection between two units whenever one is active and the other is capable of sending a signal to it and is also active, and it decreases the weight whenever the unit capable of sending the signal is inactive.
[Named after the *Hebb synapse]

Hebb synapse *n.* A special type of excitatory *synapse (1) that tends to be strengthened whenever the *postsynaptic cell fires shortly after the *presynaptic cell, even when the firing of the postsynaptic cell occurs in response to an input from a different cell. Such synapses are believed to underlie *long-term potentiation in the hippocampus. Also called a *Hebbian synapse. See also* cell assembly.
[Named after the Canadian psychologist Donald O(lding) Hebb (1904–85) who identified and discussed it in his book *The Organization of Behavior* (1949)]

hebephrenia *n.* An obsolescent term for a form of insanity with onset in childhood.
hebephrenic *adj.*
[From Greek *hebe* youth, from *Hebe* in Greek mythology, the cup-bearer of Olympus and the personification of youth + *phren* mind, originally midriff, the supposed seat of the soul + *-ia* indicating a condition or quality]

hebephrenic schizophrenia *n.* A form of *schizophrenia in adolescents and young adults in which *affective flattening or inappropriate *affect are prominent, *delusions and *hallucinations relatively insignificant, behaviour irresponsible and erratic, and mannerisms common.

hebetude *n.* Emotional dullness, listlessness, or lethargy.
[From Latin *hebetare* to dull or blunt]

height in the visual field *n.* Another name for *elevation in the visual field.

Heimdallr sensitivity *n.* Any extremely low *absolute threshold, especially for hearing; another name for *hyperacusis, *hyperaesthesia, *hyperalgesia, *thermalgesia, and other forms of sensory hypersensitivity. Also spelt *Heimdal sensitivity* or *Heimdall sensitivity*.
[Named after Heimdallr in Norse mythology, the god of light and the dawn, guardian of the rainbow bridge Bifrost between heaven and Earth, who could hear the wool growing on a sheep's back]

Heisenberg uncertainty principle *n.* Another name for the *uncertainty principle.

helicotrema *n.* The tiny opening within the apex of the *cochlea where the *scala tympani and *scala vestibuli communicate.
[From Greek *helix* a spiral + *trema* a hole]

Heller's syndrome *n.* An alternative name for *childhood disintegrative disorder.
[Named after the Austrian neuropsychiatrist Theodor O. Heller (1869–1938) who first described it in 1908]

Helmholtz illusion *n.* An *irradiation illusion consisting of a light square on a dark background and a dark square on a light background, the two squares being equal in size but the light one appearing larger than the dark one (see illustration). Also called *Helmholtz's flags.*

Helmholtz illusion. The small black square is the same size as the small white square.

[Named after the German physiologist, physicist, and mathematician Hermann Ludwig Ferdinand von Helmholtz (1821–94) who first drew attention to it]

helper T cell *See under* T lymphocyte.

helplessness, learned *See* learned helplessness.

hemeralopia *n.* A form of partial *blindness in which bright light causes blurring of vision, resulting from a malfunction of the *photopic visual system, often as a side-effect of *anticonvulsant medication prescribed for people with *epilepsy. The term is sometimes misapplied to *nyctalopia, but this is avoided in careful usage. Also called *day blindness*. *Compare* nyctalopia.
[From Greek *hemera* day + *alaos* blind + *ops* an eye + *-ia* indicating a condition or quality]

hemianopia *n.* Blindness in the left or right *visual field affecting one or both eyes, *left hemianopia* referring to loss of the left visual field and *right hemianopia* to loss of the right visual field. Also called *hemianopsia, hemiamblyopia,* or *hemiopia. See also* homonymous hemianopia, nasal hemianopia, spatial neglect.
[From Greek *hemi-* half + *an-* without + *ops* an eye + *-ia* indicating a condition or quality]

hemiballism *n.* A form of *ballism resulting from unilateral subthalamic haemorrhage and affecting one side of the body only, caused by a lesion in the *subthalamic nucleus of the brain.
[From Greek *hemi-* half + *ballein* to throw]

hemifield *n.* Half a field, usually referring to the left or right *visual field.
[From Greek *hemi-* half + English *field*]

hemineglect *n.* Another name for *spatial neglect.

hemiopia *n.* Another name for *hemianopia.

hemiparesis *n.* Partial paralysis or muscular weakness confined to one side of the body. *Compare* hemiplegia.
[From Greek *hemi-* half + Latin *paresis* relaxation, from Greek *para* beside or beyond + *hienai* to release]

hemiplegia *n.* Paralysis of one side of the body, usually as a result of a lesion in the contralateral cerebral hemisphere. *Compare* diplegia, monoplegia, ophthalmoplegia, paraplegia, quadriplegia, triplegia. **hemiplegic** *adj.*
[From Greek *hemi-* half + *plege* a blow + *-ia* indicating a condition or quality]

hemisphere *n.* Any half sphere, including either of the two *cerebral hemispheres.
[From Greek *hemi-* half + *sphaira* a sphere or globe]

hemispherectomy *n.* A radical surgical operation involving removal of the cortical structures of one *cerebral hemisphere, usually leaving subcortical structures in place, to restrict the spread of tumours or to relieve very severe epilepsy associated with damage to one hemisphere.

hemizygous *adj.* Having only one *gene or *chromosome, without its *homologous counterpart. Thus, for example, males of the human and other mammalian species are hemizygous for their X and Y chromosomes, and consequently for certain genes carried on those chromosomes.
[From Greek *hemi-* half + Greek *zygon* a yoke + *-ous* having or characterized by]

hemoglobin *See* haemoglobin.

Hempel's paradox *n.* A *paradox of *induction (1). Suppose a researcher wishes to confirm the hypothesis that all ravens are black, using the logic of induction. The more black ravens that are observed, the more probable the hypothesis becomes. But instead of going outside and examining ravens, the researcher may just as well stay indoors and observe a green carpet, a blue skirt, a brown egg, a grey telephone, and so on, because each of these is also a confirming instance of the hypothesis. The reason is that the propositions *All ravens are black* and *All non-black objects are not ravens* are logically equivalent: they are identical in meaning, different merely in wording. Logicians agree that there is no flaw in this reasoning; the difficulty is a purely psychological one arising from misguided intuition. Also called the *confirmation paradox* or the *raven paradox. See also* confirmation bias. *Compare* Goodman's paradox.
[Named after the German-born US philosopher Carl (Gustav) Hempel (1905–97) who first

expounded it in 1937 in the Swedish journal *Theoria*]

henbane *n.* A poisonous Mediterranean plant *Hyoscyamus niger* from which the drugs *hyoscyamine and *scopolamine are obtained.
[So called because of its capacity to poison poultry]

Henning's prism *n.* A classification of *odours according to six primary odours: fragrant (like lavender or rose petals), ethereal (like ether or cleaning fluid), resinous (like resin or turpentine), spicy (like cinnamon or nutmeg), putrid (like faeces or rotten eggs), and burnt (like tar oil), the first four being closely related and depicted as the vertices of one face of a prism (see illustration). Also called the *odour prism* or *smell prism*. Compare Crocker–Henderson system, stereochemical theory, Zwaardemaker smell system.
[Named after the German psychologist Hans Henning (1885–1946) who presented it in his book *Der Geruch* (Smell) in 1915]

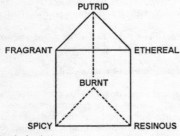

Henning's prism

Henning's tetrahedron *n.* A classification of tastes in terms of a pyramid with a triangular base, its corners representing the fundamental or primary tastes, namely sweet (like sugar or *aspartame), sour (like vinegar or lemon juice), salty (like sea water or table salt), and bitter (like quinine or orange peel), and points elsewhere representing other tastes, assumed to be blends of the four primaries. Also called the *taste tetrahedron*. See also umami.
[Named after the German psychologist Hans Henning (1885–1946) who published it in 1927]

hepatic portal vein *n.* A vein that carries newly absorbed food nutrients from the small intestine to the liver.

[From Greek *hepar*, *hepatos* the liver + Latin *porta* a gate]

herbal ecstasy *n.* A street name for *ephedrine.

herbivore *n.* An animal that feeds on plants, especially grass. Compare carnivore, omnivore. **herbivorous** *adj.*
[From Latin *herba* a herb + *vorare* to devour]

hereditarianism *n.* The belief that *heredity is the predominant factor determining behaviour or individual differences.

heredity *n.* The transmission from parents to their offspring of genetic factors that partly determine individual characteristics. **hereditary** *adj.* Of or relating to characteristics that can be transmitted genetically from parents to offspring. See also gene, heritability, Mendel's laws.
[From Latin *hereditas* inheritance, from *heres* an heir]

Hering grey *n.* Any of a set of 50 neutral-grey papers, carefully graded in steps of equal subjective *lightness from black to white, representing the range of *achromatic (1) colours. US *Hering gray*.
[Devised by the German psychologist and physiologist Ewald Hering (1834–1918)]

Hering illusion *n.* A visual illusion in which a pair of parallel straight lines appear to be bowed outwards when superimposed on a series of straight lines radiating like spokes of a wheel from a central point between the parallel lines (see illustration). It is closely related to the *Wundt illusion.

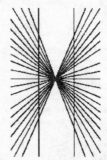

Hering illusion. The vertical lines are straight and parallel.

[First reported in 1861 by the German psychologist and physiologist Ewald Hering (1834–1918)]

Hering image *n.* The first *afterimage in the sequence of afterimages that follow brief exposure to a bright light, a *positive afterimage provided that the original stimulus was lighter than its surroundings, otherwise a *negative afterimage (1), usually appearing in the same colour as the original stimulus but sometimes colourless, persisting for only about 50 milliseconds. Also called a *Hering afterimage. Compare* Hess image, Purkinje image. [Named after the German psychologist and physiologist Ewald Hering (1834–1918) who first reported it]

heritability *n.* The proportion of *variance, symbolized by h^2, in a *phenotypic variable that is explained by, attributable to, or shared with *genetic variance in a specified population at a particular time. Thus if $h^2 = 0.30$ for a particular *trait, this means that 30 per cent of the total phenotypic variance in that trait is explained by genetic factors. The broad heritability h^2 of a trait is the ratio of genetic variance V_G to total phenotypic variance V_P, and its definition is: h^2 (broad) $= V_G/V_P$. Narrow heritability is the ratio of *additive genetic variance V_A, excluding the effects of *dominance (genetic), *epistasis, and *assortative mating, to total phenotypic variance V_P, its definition being: h^2 (narrow) $= V_A/V_P$. *See also* adoption study, DF extremes analysis, kinship study, population genetics, twin study. *Compare* environmentability. The term *hereditability*, although found in some textbooks and dictionaries, is a barbarism that is avoided in careful usage. **heritable** *adj.* Capable of being inherited. [From Old French *heriter* to inherit, from Latin *hereditas* inheritance, from *heres* an heir + *-abilitas* capacity, from *habilis* able]

Hermann grid *n.* A visual illusion induced by a pattern of black squares separated by narrow white channels, at the intersections of which illusory grey spots appear (see illustration). The illusion is believed to be caused by the fact that both ON and OFF regions of *centresurround receptive fields are stimulated by white light at the intersections, whereas when the gaze is fixed on other parts of the white channels, the edges of the black squares fall on the OFF regions and the white chan-

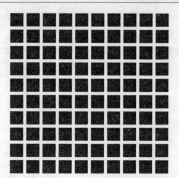

Hermann grid. Illusory grey spots appear at the corners of the black squares.

nels on the ON regions, producing stronger responses from both types of retinal neurons. [Named after the German physiologist Ludimar Hermann (1838–1914) who first observed it in a design on a book cover and reported his observation in 1870]

hermaphrodite *n.* **1.** Any plant or animal with the reproductive organs of both sexes; in the case of humans, usually having a female sex chromosome but being partly masculinized by abnormally high levels of *androgens in the womb. *Compare* pseudohermaphrodite. *adj.* **2.** Of, relating to, or resembling a hermaphrodite. *Compare* epicene (1). **hermaphroditism** *n.* The congenital condition of being a *hermaphrodite. [Named after Hermaphroditos in Greek mythology, so called because he was the son of Hermes and Aphrodite, who merged with a female nymph to form one person]

hermeneutics *n.* **1.** A term first used by the German philosopher Wilhelm Dilthey (1833–1911) to denote the art, skill, or theory of interpreting human behaviour, speech, and writing in terms of intentions and meanings, using methods of understanding that are inapplicable to the natural sciences. *See also* Verstehen. **2.** The branch of knowledge that deals with interpretation, especially of literary texts and Scripture. **3.** In *existentialism, discussion of the meaning of life. [From Greek *hermeneutikos* of or relating to interpretation, from *hermeneuein* to interpret, from *hermeneus* an interpreter + *-ikos* of, relating to, or resembling]

heroin *n*. A bitter-tasting white or brown crystalline powder diacetylmorphine, derived from *morphine, a powerful *narcotic analgesic with *psychotropic effects when consumed as a street drug, either by intravenous injection or, if very pure, by smoking or snorting through the nostrils. It is often used as a street drug, although it is highly addictive, and its street names include *gear*, *H*, *horse*, *junk*, *skag*, and *smack*. *See also* addiction, dependence (2), opioid-related disorders, substance dependence, substance-induced disorders, substance-related disorders, substance use disorders.
[Coined as a trademark from Greek *heros* a hero, probably alluding to its aggrandizing effects + English *(morph)-in(e)*]

herpes *n*. Any of a group of seven viruses, including herpes simplex viruses 1 and 2, and *cytomegalovirus, associated mostly with skin diseases but also with other disorders. *See also* herpes simplex encephalitis.
[From Greek *herpein* to creep]

herpes simplex encephalitis *n*. A condition caused by *herpes simplex virus 1 in people with severely compromised immune systems, usually from *AIDS or intensive chemotherapy for cancer. It is characterized by variable lesions in the temporal lobes, parietal lobes, and orbitofrontal cortex, leading to *anterograde amnesia and *retrograde amnesia but without loss of short-term memory, sometimes producing signs and symptoms resembling those of *Klüver–Bucy syndrome. **HSE** *abbrev*.

herstory *n*. Feminist history, or history viewed from a female or feminine perspective. The word was coined by militant feminists in the US in 1970. *See also* political correctness, pseudomorpheme.
[From *her* + *story*, following the model of *history*]

hertz *n*. The unit of *frequency (1) known non-technically as cycles per second. Alternating current cycles at 50 hertz in the UK and at 60 hertz in the US, Middle C has a frequency of 256 hertz, and EEG alpha waves have frequencies in the region of 8–10 hertz. **Hz** *abbrev*.
[Named after the German physicist Heinrich Rudolph Hertz (1857–94) who discovered radio waves in 1887]

Heschl's gyrus *n*. A small *gyrus running transversely across the *superior temporal gyrus (temporal operculum) on the upper surface of each temporal lobe immediately in front of the planum temporale. It is occupied by the primary *auditory cortex and arranged in isofrequency stripes, each stripe responding to a particular tonal frequency, both ears being represented in each cerebral hemisphere because of incomplete crossing of the auditory nerve fibres.
[Named after the Austrian pathologist Richard Ladislas Heschl (1824–81)]

Hess image *n*. A third *positive afterimage occurring in the sequence of afterimages that result from exposure to a brief light stimulus. Also called a *Hess afterimage*. *See also* afterimage. *Compare* Hering image, Purkinje image.
[Named after the German ophthalmologist Carl von Hess (1863–1923) who drew attention to it]

heteroduplex DNA *n*. Double-stranded *DNA produced by *annealing (2) two single DNA strands from different organisms in genetic engineering. *See also* DNA hybridization, hybridization, recombinant DNA.
[From Greek *heteros* other + Latin *duplex* twofold or double]

heterogeneity of variance *n*. Another name for *heteroscedasticity.

heterographs *n*. Words that have the same pronunciation but different spelling, such as *write* and *right*. *Compare* homophones.
[From Greek *heteros* other + *graphein* to write]

heterological *adj*. Of or relating to an adjective that is non-self-descriptive, such as the adjective *long* (which is not long), *Russian* (which is not Russian), and *monosyllabic* (which is not monosyllabic). *See also* Grelling's paradox. *Compare* autological.
[From Greek *heteros* other + *logos* a word + Latin *-icalis* of, relating to, or resembling]

heteronyms *n*. Words that are spelt the same but pronounced differently, such as *sow* (an adult female pig) and *sow* (to scatter seed). *See also* polysemy. *Compare* homographs, homonyms.
[From Greek *heteros* other + *onoma* a name]

heterophoria *n*. A form of *strabismus in which one eye tends to deviate either outwards or inwards. Also called *heterotropia*. *Compare* cyclophoria, esotropia, exophoria, hyperphoria, hypophoria. **heterophoric** *adj*.
[From Greek *heteros* other + *-phoros* carrying, from *pherein* to bear + *-ia* indicating a condition or quality]

heteroscedasticity *n*. In statistics, the degree to which the *variances of two or more variables differ. Many distribution-dependent statistical tests, such as *analysis of variance and the *t test assume *homoscedasticity. *Compare* homoscedasticity. **heteroscedastic** *adj*.
[From Greek *heteros* other + *skedasis* a scattering or dispersion]

heterosexism *n*. Prejudice or discrimination in favour of *heterosexuals (1) and against *homosexuals (1). It first appeared in a paper given to the National Council of Teachers of English in San Francisco in 1979 by the US linguist and English teacher Julia Penelope (born 1941). *Compare* ableism, ageism, ethnocentrism, fattism, racism, sexism, speciesism. **heterosexist** *n*. **1.** One who practises or advocates *heterosexism. *adj*. **2.** Of or relating to *heterosexism.
[From *heterosexuality* + Greek *-ismos* indicating a state or condition, on the model of words such as *racism*]

heterosexual *n*. **1.** A person who is sexually attracted to members of the opposite sex. *Compare* bisexual (1), homosexual (1). *adj*. **2.** Of or relating to heterosexuals or heterosexuality. *Compare* bisexual (2), homosexual (2). **heterosexuality** *n*. Attraction to or sexual activity between members of opposite sexes.
[From Greek *heteros* other + Latin *sexus* sex]

heterosis *n*. The increased size, robustness, or health often found in a *hybrid (1, 2) compared with a pure genetic form, also called *hybrid vigour*. A well-known example is associated with the gene that causes the disease sickle-cell anaemia, which is endemic in parts of Africa: individuals who are *homozygous for this gene develop the disease and tend to die young, whereas *heterozygous individuals do not normally develop the disease and are significantly more resistant to malaria than other members of the population. Heterosis is a factor that can contribute towards *balanced polymorphism.

[From Greek *heteros* other + *-osis* indicating a process or state]

heterotropia *n*. Another name for *heterophoria.
[From Greek *heteros* other + *tropos* a turn, from *trapein* to turn + *ops* an eye + *-ia* indicating a condition or quality]

heterozygote *n*. An organism that is *heterozygous. *Compare* homozygote.

heterozygous *adj*. Having a different *allele of a specified gene inherited from each parent at the same chromosomal *locus, one normally being a *dominant gene and the other *recessive. *Compare* homozygous. **heterozygosis** or **heterozygosity** *n*. The condition of having inherited a different *allele of a specified gene from each parent; the state or condition of being *heterozygous.
[From Greek *heteros* other + *zygon* a yoke + *-ous* having or characterized by]

heuristic *n*. A rough-and-ready procedure or rule of thumb for making a decision, forming a judgement, or solving a problem without the application of an *algorithm or an exhaustive comparison of all available options, and hence without any guarantee of obtaining a correct or optimal result. The concept can be traced to the work of the US economist and decision theorist Herbert A(lexander) Simon (1916–2001) who first suggested in 1957 that human decision makers with *bounded rationality use such procedures when thorough examination of all available options is infeasible. The concept was introduced into psychology in the early 1970s by the Israeli psychologists Amos Tversky (1937–96) and Daniel Kahneman (born 1934), and the most important heuristics initially identified and studied by them were the *anchoring and adjustment heuristic, the *availability heuristic, and the *representativeness heuristic. Also called a *cognitive heuristic*. *See also* base-rate fallacy, cancellation heuristic, dual-process model, means–end analysis, regression fallacy, sample size fallacy, satisficing, simulation heuristic. *Compare* algorithm. **heuristic** *adj*.
[From Greek *heuriskein* to find]

hibernate *vb*. To pass the winter in a dormant state with greatly reduced metabolism, as do some amphibians, reptiles, and mammals. **hibernation** *n*.

[From Latin *hibernare* to spend the winter, from *hibernus* wintry, from *hiems* winter]

Hick's law *n.* The proposition that *choice reaction time increases as the logarithm of the number of alternatives. The law is usually expressed by the formula $RT = a + b\log_2(n + 1)$, where a and b are constants representing the intercept and slope of the function, respectively, and n is the number of alternatives. It was first documented by the German psychologist Julius Merkel (1834–1900) in the journal *Philosophische Studien* in 1885, therefore the name by which it is usually known is a misnomer and there is a strong case for calling it *Merkel's law*. Compare Fitts' law.

[Named after the English physician W(illiam) Edmund Hick (1912–74) who reformulated it in 1952]

hidden figure *n.* Another name for an embedded figure. *See under* embedded-figures test.

hidden observer *n.* In a person who is hypnotized, a part of the mind that functions separately, experiencing things of which the hypnotized person appears to be unaware. For example, a person under hypnotic *analgesia who is subjected to *cold pressor pain may report no pain sensation and may appear quite undisturbed, but if the hypnotist says, 'When I place my hand on your shoulder, I shall be able to talk to a hidden part of you that knows things that are going on in your body, things that are unknown to the part of you to which I am now talking', then the hidden observer may emerge and the person may report strong pain sensations. The phenomenon was observed in 1899 by the US psychologist William James (1842–1910) and by several subsequent researchers, but it was first studied experimentally in 1973 by the US psychologist Ernest R(opiequit) Hilgard (1904–2001), who had rediscovered it by chance during a laboratory demonstration in which a hypnotically deaf subject was asked, in a quiet voice, to raise his right forefinger if 'some part' of him could hear the hypnotist's voice, whereupon the finger rose and the subject immediately asked to have his hearing restored because he had felt his finger move and wanted to know what had been done to him. *See also* neodissociation theory.

higher-order conditioning *n.* A form of *classical conditioning in which a *conditioned stimulus CS1 is first paired with an *unconditioned stimulus, in the usual way, until CS1 elicits a *conditioned response, then a new conditioned stimulus CS2 is paired with CS1, without the unconditioned stimulus, until CS2 elicits the original conditioned response. For example, the ticking of a metronome may be paired with food powder until it elicits salivation, then a bell may be paired with the metronome until the bell elicits salivation, and so on. This process can be extended further back. The corresponding phenomenon in *operant conditioning is *secondary reinforcement.

higher-order reinforcement schedule *n.* In *operant conditioning, any *reinforcement schedule that incorporates two or more simple schedules. Also called a *higher-order schedule* or a *compound reinforcement schedule. See* chained reinforcement schedule, tandem reinforcement schedule. *Compare* simple reinforcement schedule.

high-pass filter *See under* band-pass filter.

high vowel *n.* Another name for a *close vowel.

hill climbing *n.* A numerical method for maximizing a function by invariably moving upwards along a slope of steepest ascent from the current position. The method does not guarantee to reach a global maximum because, like a mountaineer who tries to reach the highest point by always climbing up a slope of steepest ascent from any given point and who gets trapped on a local mound separated by valleys from higher peaks, the process may get trapped at a local maximum nowhere near the global maximum or summit. It is used in *connectionism (1) and *parallel distributed processing to maximize the correlation between the output of a *network model and the desired state for a given input. Also called *steepest descent. See also* annealing (1), back-propagation algorithm. *Compare* gradient descent.

hindbrain *n.* The *cerebellum, *pons, and *medulla oblongata, responsible for unconscious control functions such as regulation of muscle tonus, posture, heartbeat, blood pressure, and respiration. Also called the *rhomben-

cephalon, especially in a developing embryo. *Compare* forebrain, midbrain.

hindsight bias *n*. The tendency for people who know that a particular event has occurred to overestimate in hindsight the probability with which they would have predicted it in foresight. It was first reported in 1975 by the US psychologist Baruch Fischhoff (born 1946), who initially invited people to predict the likelihood of events (such as the US president's visit to China) before they occurred and later to recall their predictions. Their recall of their predictions was biased towards what had actually occurred, and they were therefore insufficiently surprised by the events, given their earlier predictions. In a later experiment, participants read descriptions of historical events, judged the likelihoods of various possible outcomes, and were then told what had actually happened. When they were invited to estimate the likelihoods of the possible outcomes once again in the light of this additional information—with the benefit of hindsight—they tended to assign higher likelihoods to outcomes they were told had occurred, and they justified this to themselves by perceiving information supporting this outcome as more relevant than other information that they had been given. *See also* overconfidence effect.

hippocampal commissure *n*. A thin triangular band of transverse nerve fibres connecting the two cerebral hemispheres at the level of the hippocampus. *See also* commissure.

hippocampal formation *n*. *Ammon's horn (the hippocampus proper) and its associated structures, namely the *subiculum and the *dentate gyrus.

hippocampus *n*. A phylogenetically primitive structure in the *limbic system of the brain, folded into the inner surface of each temporal lobe between the thalamus and the main part of the cerebral cortex, having a cross-section shaped like a sea horse, involved in emotion, motivation, navigation by *cognitive maps, learning, and the *consolidation of long-term memory (only *declarative memory and not *procedural memory). The entire hippocampal formation consists of *Ammon's horn (the hippocampus proper) together with the *subiculum and the *dentate gyrus. *See also* archaecortex, entorhinal cortex, fimbria, hip-

pocampal commissure, kindling, long-term potentiation, Papez circuit, parahippocampal gyrus, theta wave, uncus. **hippocampi** *pl*. [From Greek *hippokampos* a fabulous sea horse, from *hippos* a horse + *kampos* a sea monster]

hiragana *See under* kana.

Hiskey–Nebraska Test of Learning Aptitude *n*. A non-linguistic *intelligence test for deaf children, constructed by the US psychologist Marshall S. Hiskey (1908–98).

histamine *n*. A *base (1) that is present in all body tissues and is released by *mast cells during allergic reactions and when the skin is injured or burnt, causing blood vessels to dilate and smooth muscles outside blood vessels to contract, resulting in the accumulation of tissue fluid and the weal response; it is also a *biogenic amine belonging to the class of imidazoleamines and functioning as a *neurotransmitter in certain areas of the brain. *See also* antihistamine, axon reflex. [From Greek *histos* tissue + English *amine*, from *am(monium)* + Greek *-ine* indicating an organic compound]

histocompatibility antigen *n*. Any of a number of genetically determined and highly variable proteins, including the major histocompatibility antigens, that are displayed on the surface of almost every body cell, defining tissue type, and are involved in antigen recognition. [From Greek *histos* tissue + Latin *compatibilis* agreeable]

histogram *n*. In descriptive statistics, a graph in which the values of scores of a quantitative variable are plotted, usually on the horizontal axis, and their *frequencies are represented by the heights of the bars on the vertical axis. Also called a *block diagram*. *Compare* bar chart. [Perhaps from *history* + Greek *gramme* a line]

histrionic personality disorder *n*. A *personality disorder characterized by a pervasive pattern of excessive emotionality and attention-seeking behaviour, beginning by early adulthood and indicated by such signs and symptoms as discomfort when not being the centre of attention, inappropriate sexually seductive interactions with others, labile and shallow emotional expression, consistent use of physical appearance to attract attention, impressionistic speech style with insufficient detail, self-dramatization and theatricality, suggestibility, and a tendency to consider relationships to be more intimate than they really are. **HPD** *abbrev.*

[From Latin *histrionicus* like an actor, from *histrio* an actor]

hit *n.* An impact or blow; a musical, theatrical, or literary creation that gains great popularity; or a shot that reaches its target. In *signal detection theory, a correct detection of a signal when it is present. *See also* memory operating characteristic, receiver operating characteristic. *Compare* correct rejection, false alarm (2), miss.

HIV *abbrev.* Human immunodeficiency virus, a *retrovirus that is transmitted through sexual contact, infected blood or blood products, and from mother to child via the placenta, and that breaks down the human body's immune system, sometimes producing symptoms of *dementia, and often leading to *AIDS. **HIV positive** *adj.* Infected by *HIV according to the positive result of a blood test.

HIV dementia *n.* Human immunodeficiency virus dementia resulting from infection with *HIV, a rapidly progressive *dementia experienced by almost one-third of people with *AIDS, characterized by cognitive deficits such as *amnesia and motor abnormalities such as *tremor and *ataxia. Also called *AIDS dementia complex* (*ADC*).

hoarding orientation *n.* In *neo-Freudian theory, a term used by the German-born US psychoanalyst Erich Fromm (1900–80) to denote a character type in which security is obtained by holding on to possessions, spending is felt to be threatening and anxiety-arousing, and miserliness extends to feelings as well as material things. *Compare* exploitative orientation, marketing orientation, productive orientation, receptive orientation.

hodological space *n.* In the *topological psychology of the Polish/German-born US psychologist Kurt Lewin (1890–1947), a special form of topological geometry in which paths and vectors are defined psychologically, the distance between one hodological region and another being not the shortest path but the path of least effort given the attractive and repulsive valences of the regions making up the space. *See also* principle of least effort.

[From Greek *hodos* a way + *logos* word, discourse, or reason + Latin *-al* from *-alis* of or relating to]

Höffding step *n.* According to a theory in *Gestalt psychology, a mental step in which one *memory trace makes contact with another, such a step being required for the association of ideas to occur, as when the perception of bread elicits the associated idea of butter, a memory trace of bread having first to be activated and to make contact with a memory trace of butter before the association can occur.

[Named after the Danish philosopher and psychologist Harald Höffding (1843–1931) who suggested it]

hog *n.* A common street name for the depressant drug *phencyclidine.

holandric *adj.* Transmitted only from fathers to sons by genes carried on the *Y chromosome that do not have counterparts on the *X chromosome. *See also* sex-linked, Y-linked. *Compare* hologynic.

[From Greek *holos* whole + *andros* a man + *-ikos* of, relating to, or resembling]

hold-out sample *n.* In statistics, a *sample of observations withheld from estimation when multiple regression, discriminant function analysis, or any other type of analysis designed to yield a predictive model is being developed, so that the model's ability to predict future scores can be estimated by its ability to predict the data of the hold-out sample.

hole-in-the-hand illusion *n.* A visual illusion produced by holding a tube to the right eye, placing the edge of the left hand against the far end of the tube, and looking at a distant object or surface with both eyes open, whereupon the left hand appears to have a circular hole through it. A cardboard tube from the middle of a roll of kitchen towel or foil is ideal for this demonstration. The illusion, which results from *binocular rivalry, was first described in print in 1871 in the *Philosophical Magazine* by the US physician and geologist Joseph LeConte (1823–1901).

hollow squares illusion *n.* A visual illusion in which columns of staggered hollow squares appear to be misaligned on the horizontal

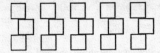

Hollow squares illusion. The figure is composed of identical perfect squares.

axis (see illustration). It is essentially a variant of the *Münsterberg illusion without alternating colours. Also called the *Taylor–Woodhouse illusion*.
[First published in 1980 by the English optometrists Stephen P(hilip) Taylor (born 1951) and J(oy) Margaret Woodhouse (born 1948)]

Holmgren test *n*. One of the first scientific tests of colour vision, still in use, involving the selection of coloured woollen skeins to match three standard skeins. *Compare* Ishihara test, Stilling test.
[Named after the Swedish physiologist Alarik Frithiof Holmgren (1831–97) who introduced it in 1879 following a railway disaster at Lagerlunda, Sweden, that was believed to have resulted from the driver's colour-blindness]

holocrine *adj*. Of or relating to a gland, such as the sebaceous gland, whose secretions contain the whole of the secreting cell. *Compare* apocrine, merocrine.
[From Greek *holos* whole + *krinein* to separate]

hologynic *adj*. Transmitted only from mothers to daughters by recessive genes carried on the *X chromosome that do not have counterparts on the *Y chromosome. *See also* sex-linked, X-linked. *Compare* holandric.
[From Greek *holos* whole + *gyne* a woman + *-ikos* of, relating to, or resembling]

holophrase *n*. A grammatically unstructured speech segment, usually a single word, characteristic of the earliest stage of language acquisition in children, such as *mama* or *allgone*, according to some authorities analysable as one-word sentences (as in *mama = There is mama* or *allgone = It is all gone*) and sometimes found in the language of adults in utterances such as *thanks* and *sorry*. *Compare* pivot grammar, telegraphic speech. **holophrastic** *adj*.
[From Greek *holos* whole + *phrazein* to express]

Holtzman Inkblot Technique *n*. A *projective test, designed to overcome the psychometric

weaknesses of the *Rorschach test, introduced by the US psychologist Wayne H(arold) Holtzman (born 1923) and several colleagues in 1961, comprising two parallel sets of 45 ink blots and an elaborate scoring procedure. **HIT** *abbrev*.

homeopathy *n*. An unconventional or alternative form of drug therapy for physical and mental disorders devised by the German physician Christian Samuel Hahnemann (1755–1843), based on the dictum of the Greek father of medicine Hippocrates (?460–?377 BC) that 'like cures like' (*similia similibus curantur*), in which a drug that produces a particular pattern of symptoms in a healthy person is used in an extremely dilute form to treat disorders characterized by similar symptoms. Successive dilutions of the drug produce a solution containing virtually no molecules of the original active substance but are believed to have therapeutic properties none the less. Also spelt *homoeopathy*. *Compare* allopathy. **homeopath** or **homoeopath** *n*. One who practises *homeopathy. **homeopathic** or **homoeopathic** *adj*.
[From Greek *homoio-* similar to, from *homos* the same + *pathos* suffering]

homeostasis *n*. The maintenance of equilibrium in any physiological, psychological, or social process by an automatic *feedback mechanism compensating for disrupting changes. The word was coined by the US physiologist Walter Bradford Cannon (1871–1945) and became popular after the publication in 1932 of his book *The Wisdom of the Body*, in which the process is described in relation to the automatic maintenance of the temperature and components of blood, including water, salt, sugar, proteins, fat, calcium, oxygen, hydrogen ions—the list could be extended in the light of subsequent discoveries. *See also* appestat, closed-loop control, cybernetics, feedback, principle of constancy, thermoregulation, set point. **homeostatic** *adj*.
[From Greek *homos* same + *stasis* a standing]

homeothermic *See* homoiothermic.

hominid *n*. Any member of the *family (2) Hominidae, including modern humans and their extinct ancestors such as *australopithecines. **hominid** *adj*. Belonging to the family Hominidae.

[From Latin *homo* man + *-ida* indicating offspring]

hominoid *n.* **1.** Any member of the superfamily Hominoidea, including both *hominids and *anthropoid (1) apes. *adj.* **2.** Belonging to the superfamily Hominoidea; apelike.
[From Latin *homo* man + Greek *-oeides* denoting resemblance of form, from *eidos* shape]

Homo *n.* A *genus of *hominids that includes the *species *Homo sapiens* (modern man) and various extinct forerunners such as *H. erectus* (increasingly called *H. ergaster*), *H. habilis*, *H. neanderthalensis* (Neanderthal man), and *H. heidelbergensis*, the last of these being a probable ancestor of both *H. neanderthalensis* and *H. sapiens*, the human species that evolved in Africa about 150,000 years ago. *See also* mitochondrial DNA.
[From Latin *homo* a man]

homoeopathy *See* homeopathy.

homogeneity of variance *n.* Another name for *homoscedasticity.

homogeneous subset *n.* In statistics, after calculating a *multiple comparison, a set of groups that have means which are not significantly different from one another.

homographs *n.* Words that are spelt the same but have different meanings, such as *content* (what is inside) and *content* (satisfied) or *wind* (air) and *wind* (twist). Homographs are one of the two major classes of *homonyms. *Compare* heteronyms, homophones.
[From Greek *homos* same + *graphein* to write]

homoiothermic *adj.* Warm-blooded, or having a body temperature that remains constant with changes in ambient temperature. Also called *homeothermal*, *homeothermic*, *homothermal*, or *homothermous*. *Compare* poikilothermic. *See also* thermoregulation. **homoiothermy** or **homoiothermism** *n.*
[From Greek *homos* the same + *therme* heat + *-ikos* of, relating to, or resembling]

homologous *adj.* Having a related, similar, or corresponding position, structure, or origin.

homologous chromosomes *n.* Any pair of *chromosomes, one from the father and one from the mother, that are similar in appearance and pair with each other during *meiosis (1), one member of each pair being carried by every *gamete.

homologue *n.* Anything that is *homologous to something else. Also spelt *homolog*.
[From Greek *homologos* agreeing, from *homos* the same + *legein* to speak]

homonymous hemianopia *n.* Blindness in the left or right *visual field affecting both eyes, caused by unilateral damage to the visual cortex or the nerve fibres with projections there, often resulting from a massive *stroke in one side of the brain. A person with this condition may be unaware of being totally blind in half the visual field, because the blindness is not like a conspicuous black curtain draped over half a television screen, as many people assume, but is simply a portion of the immediate environment that is not visible, as is the area behind the head of a person with normal vision; but a person with left homonymous hemianopia who gazes fixedly at the dot in the printed sequence *L.R* will see the *R* but not the *L*, and a person with right homonymous hemianopia will see the *L* but not the *R*. To test for these forms of *hemifield blindness, the person is usually asked to close one eye and fixate on a point directly ahead with the other eye while a conspicuous object is waved in the area to the left and right of the fixation point, and then the procedure is repeated with the other eye. Another method is the *line bisection test. Also called *homonymous hemianopsia*, *homonymous hemiopia*, *homonymous hemiamblyopia*, or *spatial neglect*. *See also* divided visual field. *Compare* hemianopia.
[From Greek *homos* same + *onoma* a name + *hemi-* half + *a-* without + *opsis* sight, from *ops* an eye + *-ia* indicating a condition or quality]

homonyms *n.* Words that are spelt the same way but have different meanings, such as *bear* (animal) and *bear* (carry), also called *homographs, or that have the same pronunciation but different spelling or meaning, such as *rest* (relaxation) and *wrest* (take by force), also called *homophones. *See also* polysemy. *Compare* heteronyms.
[From Greek *homos* same + *onoma* a name]

homonym symptom *n.* A pattern of speech, associated with *thought disorder in general and *loosening of associations in particular, in which the speaker hops from one topic to another via *homonyms, as in: *The pain is hard to bear, doctor, a koala bear came to the zoo from China cups and saucers for the goose is sauce for the gander.*

homophones *n.* Words that have the same pronunciation but different spelling or meaning or both, such as *write* and *right*, *threw* and *through*, or *rest* (relaxation) and *rest* (remainder). Homophones are one of the two major classes of *homonyms. *Compare* heterographs, homographs, homonyms.
[From Greek *homos* same + *phone* sound]

homoscedasticity *n.* In statistics, the degree of similarity in the *variances of two or more variables. Many distribution-dependent statistical tests, such as *analysis of variance and the *t test, assume homoscedasticity. *Compare* heteroscedasticity. **homoscedastic** *adj.*
[From Greek *homos* same + *skedasis* a scattering or dispersion]

homosexual *n.* **1.** A person who is sexually attracted to members of the same sex. *Compare* bisexual (1), heterosexual (1). *adj.* **2.** Of or relating to homosexuals or homosexuality. *Compare* bisexual (2), heterosexual (2). **homosexuality** *n.* Attraction to or sexual activity with members of one's own sex. *See also* egodystonic sexual orientation, latent homosexuality, lesbian, narcissism.
[From Greek *homos* the same + Latin *sexus* sex]

homothermic *See* homoiothermic.

homozygote *n.* An organism that is *homozygous for a specified factor, thus having *gametes of only one kind for that factor and consequently breeding true to type. *Compare* heterozygote.

homozygous *adj.* Having identical *alleles of a specified gene at the same chromosomal *locus, as in an individual who inherits the same gene for blue eye colour from both parents and is therefore blue-eyed, although the gene is *recessive. *Compare* heterozygous. **homozygosis** or **homozygosity** *n.* The condition of having inherited identical *alleles of a specified gene from both parents; the state or condition of being *homozygous.
[From Greek *homos* the same + *zygon* a yoke + *-ous* having or characterized by]

homunculus *n.* A tiny man, especially the completed homunculus depicting the surface of the human body, with each part drawn in proportion to its representation in the *somatosensory cortex (see illustration), or the *somatosensory homunculus often used to depict the layout of the *sensory projection areas of the somatosensory cortex. The term was formerly used to denote the minute but fully formed human form that was believed by the *preformationists to be present in every spermatozoon or ovum.
[From Latin *homunculus* a little man, diminutive of *homo* a man]

Homunculus. The distorted body parts indicate the relative sizes of their sensory projection areas in the somatosensory cortex; adapted from Penfield and Rasmussen's *The Cerebral Cortex of Man* (1950).

honestly significant difference test *See* Tukey-HSD test.

honey-bee dance *See* round dance, waggle dance.

Honi phenomenon *n.* An effect of viewing a very familiar person in the *Ames room, the illusory distortion usually created by the abnormal perspectives of the room being partly or wholly suppressed.
[Named after the family nickname of a woman who first experienced and reported the phenomenon when she observed both a stranger and her husband in the Ames room in 1949 and saw a size distortion in the stranger but not in her husband]

hook order *n.* A *dominance hierarchy in a herd of cattle in which each animal is able to gore only those lower in the hierarchy without retaliation and is liable to be gored only by those above. *Compare* pecking order.
[From *hook* to catch or gore with the horns]

Hopfield rule *See under* Hebbian rule.

horizon *n.* The circle at which the Earth and sky appear to meet and on which the *vanishing point is usually located, also called the *apparent horizon* or the *visible horizon*; a plane forming a tangent to the Earth at the position of an observer, also called a *sensible horizon*; a plane through the centre of the Earth parallel to the apparent horizon, also called the *celestial horizon* or *rational horizon*; figuratively, the limit or scope of a person's perception, knowledge, interest, experience, or expectation. **horizontal** *adj.*
[From Greek *horizon* *(kyklos)* limiting (circle), from *horizein* to limit, from *horos* a limit]

horizontal cell *n.* A type of cell in the *retina that lacks an *axon, lying perpendicular to the sensory pathway and linking *photoreceptors and *bipolar cells, one of its important functions being to inhibit neurons outside the immediate zone of excitation. *Compare* amacrine cell.

horizontal décalage *See under* décalage.

horizontal icicle plot *n.* In statistics, a graphical representation of successive steps of a *cluster analysis in which the individuals or cases are represented in the display by the rows, and the steps of the analysis by the columns, with individuals or cases in the same cluster being joined by a vertical line. A horizontal icicle plot is especially useful when there are many individuals or cases so that a *vertical icicle plot cannot fit across a single page. *Compare* vertical icicle plot.

horizontal plane *n.* A plane parallel to the horizon dividing the brain or any other organ or organism into top and bottom parts. *Compare* coronal plane, sagittal plane, transverse plane.

horizontal section *n.* A cutting through a *horizontal plane. *Compare* coronal section, sagittal section, transverse section.

horizontal–vertical illusion *n.* A visual illusion that causes a vertical distance to appear greater than an equal horizontal distance, usually illustrated with an inverted T whose horizontal and vertical lines are of equal length (see illustration), first reported in 1858 by the German psychologist Wilhelm (Max)

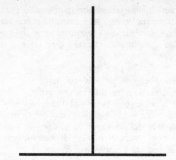

Horizontal–vertical illusion. The horizontal and vertical lines are the same length.

Wundt (1832–1920). *See also* teacup illusion, top hat illusion.

horme *n.* In *analytical psychology, a word introduced by Carl Gustav Jung (1875–1961) to denote vital or purposeful energy. Also spelt *hormé*.
[From Greek *horme* animal impulse]

hormonagogue *n.* A substance that stimulates the secretion of a hormone, a typical example being nicotine, which stimulates the secretion of vasopressin.
[From *hormone* + Greek *agogos* leading, from *agein* to lead]

hormone *n.* Any of a large number of chemical substances secreted into the bloodstream by an *endocrine gland and transported to another part of the body where it binds to a specific type of receptor and exerts a particular effect, enabling the endocrine system to function as a communication system between cells alongside and independently of the nervous system. Most hormones are either *peptide hormones or *steroid hormones, and among the most important are the *androgens, *corticosteroid hormones, *gonadotrophins, *masculinizing hormones, *neurohormones *neuropeptides, *releasing hormones, *sex hormones, and *trophic hormones. *See also* adrenalin, adrenocorticotrophic hormone, aldosterone, androsterone, angiotensin II, calcitonin, cholecystokinin, corticosterone, corticotrophin-releasing hormone, cortisol, cortisone, dexamethasone, dopamine, enkephalin, follicle-stimulating hormone, glucagon, gonadotrophin-releasing hormone, growth hormone, growth hormone releasing hormone, insulin, luteinizing hormone, luteinizing-hormone releasing hormone, melanocyte-stimulating hormone, melatonin, Müllerian inhibiting substance, noradrenalin, oestradiol, oestrogen, oestrone, oxytocin, parathyroid hormone, progesterone, prolactin, relaxin, renin, testosterone, thyroid-stimulating hormone, thyrotrophin-releasing hormone, thyroxine, vasopressin. [Coined in 1904 by the British physiologist Ernest Henry Starling (1866–1927) from Greek *horman* to stir up or urge on]

Horner's law n. The proposition that the most common forms of *colour-blindness are transmitted from males to males through female carriers. *See also* daltonism, X-linked. [Named after the Swiss ophthalmologist Johann Friedrich Horner (1831–86) who formulated it]

Horner's syndrome n. A *neurological condition caused by damage to or malfunction of the *sympathetic nervous system, often associated with a spinal cord injury, characterized by *ptosis of one eyelid, constriction of the corresponding pupil, and inability to sweat on that side of the face. [Named after the Swiss ophthalmologist Johann F. Horner (1831–86) who first described it]

horologagnosia *See under* agnosia.

horopter n. The curved surface of points in space that, for a given degree of *ocular convergence, are projected on to *corresponding retinal points, all points on the horopter being perceived as the same distance away as the point being fixated. Points close to the horopter within *Panum's fusion area give rise to *binocular disparity and produce sensations of three-dimensional depth, and points far from the horopter outside Panum's fusion area fail to result in *binocular fusion and produce double images or *diplopia. *See also* correspondence problem, stereopsis. [From Greek *horos* boundary + *optos* seen, from *ops* an eye]

horse n. A street name for *heroin.

hospice n. A nursing home for the care of people who are terminally ill. [From Latin *hospes* a guest]

hospital hopper syndrome n. A colloquial name for *factitious disorder.

hospitalism n. A term introduced in 1945 by the Austrian psychoanalyst René A. Spitz (1887–1974) to denote the physical and psychological effects on an infant (up to 18 months old) of prolonged and total separation from its mother, due to hospitalization or some other similar cause. According to Spitz, the characteristics include retarded physical development and disruption of perceptual–motor skills and language. *See also* anaclitic depression, attachment theory, maternal deprivation, separation anxiety, separation anxiety disorder.

hot spot n. In genetics, a region of a chromosome or a gene that has a propensity for *recombination or *mutation. Also written *hotspot.*

HOUND abbrev. Humble, old, unattractive, non-verbal, and dumb, the syndrome of personal qualities that counsellors, therapists, and people in general supposedly find most unappealing in their clients or associates. *Compare* YAVIS.

House–Tree–Person technique n. A *projective test developed by the US psychologist John N. Buck (1906–83) and first published in the journal *Clinical Psychology Monographs* in 1948 in which the respondent is asked to make freehand drawings of a house, a tree, and a person, first in pencil, then in crayon, and is then asked 20 questions about each drawing. Interpretations of the drawings are based on the assumptions that the drawing of the house reveals aspects of the respondent's home life and family relationships, the tree reflects unconscious feelings about the self, and the person shows aspects of the self, interpreted similarly to the *Draw-a-Person test. The test gained a certain notoriety during the 1990s when it was recommended as a device for discovering evidence of sexual abuse in children but was criticized for lack of *validity. **H–T–P** abbrev.

HPA axis abbrev. The hypothalamic-pituitary–adrenal axis, a self-regulating system, based on negative *feedback, in which *hormones are released from the *hypothalamus, stimulating the release of a different class of hormones from the *pituitary gland, which in turn stimulate secretions of a third class of hormones from the *adrenal glands and the *testes, or *ovaries, the whole cycle playing an important role in the regulation of hunger, thirst, sleep, mood, sexual activity, learning, and memory.

hue *n.* The dimension of a *colour that is determined by the wavelength of the light in relation to the wavelengths reflected from objects or surfaces in other parts of the visual field and that gives rise to a qualitative sensation such as red or blue, the other major dimensions of colour being *saturation (1) and *lightness. The *Munsell hue scale* contains five principal hues (red, yellow, green, blue, purple) and five intermediate hues (yellow-red, green-yellow, blue-green, purple-blue, red-purple). *See also* chroma, chromatic (1), chromaticity, Munsell colour system, non-spectral colour.
[From Old English *hīw* beauty, cognate with Old Norse *hȳ* fine hair]

hug drug *n.* A street name sometimes used for *ecstasy (2), because of the feelings of empathy and benevolence that it induces.

Hullian learning theory *n.* An elaborate theory of *learning (1) formulated in 1940 by the US psychologist Clark L. Hull (1884–1952), published in his book *Principles of Behavior* (1943), and presented in a modified form in *A Behavior System* (1952). In the final version, the *independent variables are stimulus energy (*S*), work involved in response (*W*), number of reinforcements (*N*), and difference between the current stimulus and the stimulus used in training (*d*); the *dependent variables are *reaction latency ($_st_R$), *response amplitude (*A*), and number of unreinforced responses required to produce extinction (*n*); and the theory also has scores of *intervening variables. The gist of the theory is as follows: learning is represented by *habit strength ($_sH_R$), the *S* and the *R* nestling on either side of the *H* to symbolize the role of a habit in linking stimuli to responses, and $_sH_R$ is a logarithmic function of *N*. *Generalized habit strength ($_s\bar{H}_R$) is determined jointly by $_sH_R$ and *d*. *Generalized reaction potential ($_sE_R$) is a multiplicative function of $_s\bar{H}_R$ and three other intervening variables: $_sE_R = _s\bar{H}_R \times D \times K \times V$, where *D* is *drive strength, *K* is *incentive motivation (determined in turn by *W*) and *V* is *stimulus intensity dynamism (determined in turn by *S*). *Net reac-

tion potential is defined as follows: $_s\bar{E}_R = _sE_R - _s\dot{I}_R$, where $_s\dot{I}_R$ is aggregate inhibitory potential (determined in turn by *d* and *W* acting via various intervening variables). Finally, $_s\bar{E}_R$ interacts with *behavioural oscillation ($_sO_R$) and *reaction threshold ($_sL_R$) to determine the dependent variables $_st_R$, *A*, and *n*.

human factors psychology *n.* Another name for *ergonomics.

human immunodeficiency virus *See* HIV.

human interest score *n.* One of the *Flesch indices of the readability of text, defined by the formula $HI = (3.635 \times$ average number of personal words per 100 words) + (0.314 × average number of personal sentences per 100 sentences), where personal words are pronouns referring to people, words of identifiable masculine or feminine gender (such as *Mary*, *sister*, or *iceman*), and the words *people* and *folks*, and personal sentences are spoken sentences in quotation marks, questions, commands, requests, other sentences addressed directly to the reader, and also exclamations and grammatically incomplete sentences whose meaning has to be inferred from their contexts. A human interest score of zero indicates that the text has no human interest, 30 that it is interesting, 50 that it is very interesting, and 80 that it is dramatic. Although the theoretical upper limit is about 395, in practice human interest scores are almost always below 100. *See also* reading ease score.

humanistic psychology *n.* An approach to psychology that became popular in the 1960s, influenced by *existentialism and *phenomenology, stressing individual free will, responsibility, and *self-actualization. *See also* client-centred therapy, need-hierarchy theory, neurolinguistic programming, peak experience.

human relations group *See* T-group.

Hume's fork *n.* The argument first advanced by the Scottish philosopher David Hume (1711–76) in section IV, part I of his *Inquiry Concerning Human Understanding*, that the only legitimate sources of knowledge or belief are *reason and *empirical evidence, an often-quoted synopsis of the argument occurring at the end of the book: 'If we take in our hand any volume; of divinity or school metaphysics, for instance; let us ask, *Does it contain any abstract reasoning concerning quantity or number?* No. *Does it contain any experimental reasoning concerning matter of fact and existence?* No. Commit it then to the flames: for it can contain nothing but sophistry and illusion' (section XII, part III, italics in original). In *logical positivism, a strong form of Hume's fork was used as a criterion for distinguishing sense from nonsense, the assumption being that any assertion that failed the test was literally nonsensical. *See also* empiricism, rationalism (1).

Hume's problem *n.* The problem of *induction (1).

humour *n.* **1.** Anything that is funny, witty, or amusing, or that has the capacity to make people laugh. Most forms of humour can be classified into the following categories: slapstick, misunderstanding/farce, innuendo, pun/wordplay, mimicry/parody/satire, irony/sarcasm, exaggeration, analogy/comic metaphor, inappropriate response, comic repetition, reversal of reality, black humour. **2.** A state or disposition of mind or mood, as in the phrases *bad humour* or *good humour*. **3.** According to a doctrine propounded by pre-Socratic philosophy and widely accepted until the Renaissance, any of the four cardinal bodily fluids, the balance of which was believed to determine a person's *temperament or *personality: people were thought to be more or less sanguine (optimistic), melancholic (depressive), choleric (short-tempered), or phlegmatic (unemotional) according to the balance in their bodies of blood (*sanguis*), black bile (*melaina chole*), yellow bile (*chole*), and phlegm (*phlegma*). Also called a *cardinal humour*. US *humor, cardinal humor*. *See also* aqueous humour, complexion (2), temperament, vitreous humour. *Compare* yin and yang.
[From Latin *umere* to be moist]

Humphrey's law *n.* The proposition that consciously thinking about one's performance of a task that involves *automatic processing impairs one's performance of it. For example, golfers who think too closely about their golf swings may find that they cannot swing properly, and a man who thinks too closely about how he knots a bow tie may find that he cannot do it. *See also* centipede effect, hyper-reflection.

[Named after the English psychologist George Humphrey (1889–1966) who propounded it in 1951]

hunger *n.* **1.** Appetite, craving, desire, or need for food; figuratively, a strong desire for anything else. *vb.* **2.** To have a hunger for something. *See also* 2-deoxyglucose, glucostatic theory, HPA axis, hypothalamus, limbic system, lipostatic theory, medial forebrain bundle, specific hunger. **hungry** *adj.*
[From Old English *hungor* a hunger, *hyngran* to hunger]

Huntington's disease *n.* A rare hereditary disorder transmitted by a single *dominant gene, with damage to the *basal ganglia, characterized by widespread degeneration of the brain, *dementia, and *chorea, with onset after the age of 40 and slow progression leading to death usually within 10–15 years. Also called *Huntington's chorea*. **HD** *abbrev.*
[Named after the US neurologist George S. Huntington (1850–1916) who described it in 1872, though it had already been described in 1841 by Charles Oscar Waters (1816–92)]

Hunt–Minnesota test *n.* A psychometric test constructed by the US psychologist Howard Francis Hunt (born 1918), designed to detect organic brain damage, including a vocabulary test (taken from the *Stanford–Binet intelligence scale), six memory and recall tests, and nine further tests.

Hurler's syndrome *n.* A hereditary metabolic disorder transmitted by a recessive gene resulting in the absence of an enzyme and leading to severe *mental retardation, swelling of the liver and spleen, low forehead, enlarged head, often clouding of the corneas of the eyes, and usually death during childhood from heart or lung complications. Also called *gargoylism*.
[Named after the German paediatrician Gertrud Hurler (1889–1965) who first described it in 1919]

hwa-byung *n.* A *culture-bound syndrome of Korea and emigrant Korean communities in other countries, attributed locally to suppression of anger, characterized by *panic attacks, *dyspnoea, *thanatophobia, *insomnia, *anorexia, *palpitation, *fatigue (1), joint or muscle pains, indigestion, and a sense of fullness in the pit of the stomach.
[Korean *hwa-byung* anger syndrome]

hyalophagia n. Eating glass. *See also* pica.
[From Greek *hyalos* glass + *phagein* to consume + *-ia* indicating a condition or quality]

hybrid n. **1.** In genetics, the offspring of a cross between genetically dissimilar forms, such an organism being necessarily sterile if the cross is between different *species; also, a molecule of *DNA composed of portions from different organisms. *See also* dihybrid. **2.** Any organism of mixed ancestry. **3.** A word formed by combining parts from different languages, as in *bureaucracy*, from French *bureau* a department or office + Greek *kratos* power; or *amoral*, from Greek *a-* not + Latin *moralis* moral. *adj.* **4.** Of or relating to an organism of genetically mixed parentage or a word of linguistically mixed origin.
[From Latin *hibrida* the offspring of a mixed union, originally a tame sow and a wild boar]

hybridization n. A technique of *genetic engineering for determining the degree of relatedness of two DNA or RNA samples by *annealing (2) them to form hybrid molecules of *heteroduplex DNA, the stability of which indicates the degree of relatedness. *See also* DNA hybridization, recombinant DNA.

hybridize vb. To produce a *hybrid (1, 2) or to interbreed.

hybrid sterility n. Inability of an organism to produce offspring owing to the fact that it is a *hybrid (1, 2), as in a cross between two different *species. *Compare* hybrid vigour.

hybrid vigour n. The increased size, robustness, and health often found in a *hybrid (1, 2) compared with its parents. Also called *heterosis*. *Compare* hybrid sterility.

hydraulic theory n. Any theory based on liquid in motion or under pressure, either literally as in certain theories of hearing, or figuratively as in the *economic aspects of *psychoanalysis that are more correctly called the *principle of constancy and the *quota of affect.
[From Greek *hydraulikos* hydraulic, from *hydor* water + *aulos* a pipe + *-ikos* of, relating to, or resembling]

hydrazine n. A colourless liquid *base (1) made from sodium hydrochlorite and ammonia and used in the manufacture of certain monoamine oxidase inhibitor drugs such as *isocarboxazid and *phenelzine.
[From Greek *hydor* water + *azo* indicating a compound containing the divalent group —N:N—+ *-ine* an organic compound]

hydrocephalus n. A disorder sometimes caused by a mutant gene on the *X chromosome, associated with obstruction of the flow of *cerebrospinal fluid and its accumulation in the *ventricles of the brain, causing increased intracranial pressure, leading in infants to an enlargement of the head and a wide range of impairments and disorders. Also written *hydrocephaly*, and referred to nontechnically as *water on the brain*. *Compare* macrocephaly. **hydrocephalic** *adj.*
[From Greek *hydor* water + *kephale* the head]

hydrocortisone n. Another name for *cortisol.
[From Greek *hydor* water + English *cortisone*]

hydrolysis n. Chemical decomposition caused by reaction with water, as when a salt is decomposed into an acid and a base, or an ester to an acid and an alcohol. **hydrolyse** or, especially in the US, **hydrolyze** *vb.*
[From Greek *hydor* water + *lysis* loosening]

hydromorphone n. Hydromorphone hydrochloride, a *narcotic analgesic drug, used in the management of moderate and severe pain and sometimes taken as a street drug.
[From Greek *hydor* water + English *morphine* + Greek *-one* indicating a chemical compound that is a ketone, from *-one* a feminine name suffix]

hyoscine n. Another name for *scopolamine.

hyoscyamine n. A poisonous *alkaloid occurring in *henbane, *deadly nightshade, and related plants, with similar pharmacological properties to *atropine.
[From Greek *hyoskyamos*, from *hys* a pig + *kyanion* cyanide, from *kyamos* a bean, alluding to the fact that the plant is poisonous to pigs + English *amine*]

hypacusia n. Partial deafness. Also spelt *hypacousia* or *hypoacousia*. Also called *hypacusis*. **hypacusic** *adj.*
[From Greek *hypo* under + *akousis* hearing, from *akouein* to hear + *-ia* indicating a condition or quality]

hypaesthesia *n.* Abnormally diminished touch sensitivity. US *hypesthesia.* Also called *hypoaesthesia* or *hypoesthesia.* **hypaesthesic** or **hypesthesic** *adj.*
[From Greek *hypo* under + *aisthesis* sensation + *-ia* indicating a condition or quality]

hypalgesia *n.* Abnormally diminished sensitivity to pain. **hypalgesic** *adj.*
[From Greek *hypo* under + *algesis* sense of pain, from *algos* pain + *-ia* indicating a condition or quality]

hyperactivity *n.* Abnormal or pathological overactivity; a prominent feature of *attention-deficit/hyperactivity disorder and *hyperkinetic disorders.

hyperacusis *n.* Abnormally sensitive hearing resulting in uncomfortable sensitivity to sounds, a common symptom of *Bell's palsy and *Williams syndrome. Also spelt *hyperacousis.* Also called *hyperacusia* or *hyperacousia.* *See also* Heimdallr sensitivity. **hyperacusic** *adj.*
[From Greek *hyper* over + *akousis* hearing, from *akouein* to hear + *-ia* indicating a condition or quality]

hyperaesthesia *n.* Increased sensitivity of any of the sense organs, especially touch. US *hyperesthesia.* Also called *superaesthesia* or *superesthesia.* *See also* Heimdallr sensitivity. **hyperaesthesic** or **hyperesthesic** *adj.*
[From Greek *hyper* over + *aisthesis* sensation, from *aisthanesthai* to feel + *-ia* indicating a condition or quality]

hyperalgesia *n.* Abnormally heightened sensitivity to pain. *See also* Heimdallr sensitivity. **hyperalgesic** *adj.*
[From Greek *hyper* over + *algesis* sense of pain, from *algos* pain + *-ia* indicating a condition or quality]

hypercathexis *n.* In *psychoanalysis, additional *cathexis invested in any object that is already cathected. Sigmund Freud (1856–1939) used the concept especially for explaining *attention, his most detailed account of this theory appearing in 1895 in his 'Project for a Scientific Psychology' (*Standard Edition*, I, pp. 177–397).

hypercolumn *n.* An aggregation of *ocular-dominance columns containing cells whose *receptive fields overlap on the same region of the retina.

hypercomplex cell *n.* A type of cell in the *primary visual cortex (Area V1) that is similar to a *simple cell or a *complex cell except that it has an *end-stopped receptive field, ceasing to fire if the line, edge, or bar that excites it exceeds a certain length. Hypercomplex cells are sensitive to corners, curvature, or to sudden breaks in straight images. *See also* bar detector, edge detector, end-stopped receptive field, feature detector, orientation-specific cell.

hypercomplex receptive field *n.* The *receptive field of a *hypercomplex cell.

hypercorrection *n.* A mistaken attempt to correct an imagined error in the use of language, such as the erroneous use of *I* instead of *me* in *The party will be hosted by Jessica and I*, or the pronunciation by people from the North of England, where *cut* rhymes with *but*, of words such as *put* as if they also rhymed with *but*. Also called *overcorrection.* **hypercorrect** *adj.vb.*
[From Greek *hyper* over + English *correction*]

hypergasia *n.* Frenzied *psychomotor agitation.
[From Greek *hyper* over + *ergasia* work or business + *-ia* indicating a condition or quality]

hypergeusia *n.* Abnormally heightened taste sensitivity. *Compare* ageusia, cacogeusia, dysgeusia, hypogeusia, parageusia, taste blindness. **hypergeusic** *adj.*
[From Greek *hyper* over + *geusis* taste + *-ia* indicating a condition or quality]

hyperglycaemia *n.* An abnormally high level of sugar in the blood, often caused by a deficiency of insulin secretion by the islets of Langerhans due to *diabetes mellitus, leading to a failure of carbohydrate metabolism. US *hyperglycemia.* *Compare* hypoglycaemia.
[From Greek *hyper* over + *glykys* sweet + *haima* blood + *-ia* indicating a condition or quality]

hypericum *n.* The pharmacologically active ingredient of *St John's wort. *See also* orphan drug.
[From Latin *Hypericum* the generic name of St John's wort, from Greek *hypereikon*, from *hyper* over + *ereike* heath]

hyperkinaesthesis *n*. Abnormally heightened sense of body movement or *kinaesthesis. US *hyperkinesthesis*. Also called *hyperkinaesthesia* or *hyperkinesthesia*.
[From Greek *hyper* over + *kineein* to move + *aisthesis* sensation, from *aisthanesthai* to feel]

hyperkinesis *n*. Excessive movement, as in such conditions as *athetosis or *ballism, or in *hyperkinetic disorders and *attention-deficit/hyperactivity disorder in children.
[From Greek *hyper* over + *kinesis* movement]

hyperkinetic disorders *n*. A class of disorders with early onset (in the first five years of life) characterized by persistent inattention and lack of persistence in activities requiring concentration, together with excessive, disorganized, and unregulated physical activity or *hyperkinesis, and often impulsivity, recklessness, and accident-proneness. *See also* attention-deficit/hyperactivity disorder.

hyperlexia *n*. A *reading disorder characterized by advanced word-recognition skills in a person with pronounced cognitive and language deficits. People with hyperlexia manifest word-recognition skills by their ability to pronounce single words presented to them out of context, but they lack the ability to understand printed words and texts and therefore have poor reading comprehension. The condition was first identified and named by Norman E. Silberberg and Margaret C. Silberberg in 1967. *See also* attentional dyslexia, dyslexia.
[From Greek *hyper* over + *lexis* a word + *-ia* indicating a condition or quality]

hypermania *n*. An exaggerated or extreme form of mania; often confused with *hypomania. *See* manic episode.
[From Greek *hyper* over + *mania* madness]

hypermetamorphosis *n*. A tendency to attend indiscriminately and react to every visual stimulus. It is characteristic of *Klüver–Bucy syndrome.
[From Greek *hyper* over + *meta* among, with, or beside + *morphe* form + *-osis* indicating a process or state]

hypermetropia *n*. Another name for *hyperopia. Also written *hypermetropy*. **hypermetrope** *n*. A long-sighted person. **hypermetropic** *adj*. Long-sighted.

[From Greek *hypermetros* beyond the measure, from *hyper* over + *metron* a measure + *ops* an eye + *-ia* indicating a condition or quality]

hypermnesia *n*. Enhanced power of memory, usually under the influence of *hypnosis or *truth drugs, though the effects may be illusory. The term is also used to denote a form of *reminiscence (2), for material such as pictures or prose passages, in *successive reproduction with short intervals between successive tests. For example, people who view a video recording of a burglary and are then tested repeatedly over a few hours or days for their recall of critical details have shown steady improvement across the repeated tests. If the interval between tests is increased to a week, then recall tends to decline. *Compare* amnesia.
[From Greek *hyper* over + *mnasthai* to remember + *-ia* indicating a condition or quality]

hypermotility *n*. Another name for *hyperkinesis.

hyperopia *n*. Long-sightedness (far-sightedness) or difficulty in accommodating the eyes for *near vision, resulting from light rays that enter the eye being focused behind the retina, most often because of *presbyopia. Also called *hypermetropia* or *hypermetropy*. *See also* aphakia. *Compare* emmetropia, myopia. **hyperope** *n*. A long-sighted person. **hyperopic** *adj*. Long-sighted or far-sighted.
[From Greek *hyper* over + *ops* an eye + *-ia* indicating a condition or quality]

hyperorexia *n*. Excessive appetite; another name for *bulimia (1). The term is usually restricted to cases in which it is not caused by a brain lesion. *Compare* hyperphagia.
[From Greek *hyper* over + *orexis* appetite + *-ia* indicating a condition or quality]

hyperosmia *n*. Abnormal acuteness of the sense of smell. *See also* anosmia, cacosmia, dysosmia, parosmia, specific anosmia. *Compare* hyposmia. **hyperosmic** *adj*.
[From Greek *hyper* over + *osme* a smell + *-ia* indicating a condition or quality]

hyperphagia *n*. Compulsive overeating; another name for *bulimia (1), but usually reserved for cases in which it is caused by a lesion in the medial forebrain bundle, the hypothalamus, or some other part of the brain involved in appetite. *Compare* hyperorexia.

[From Greek *hyper* over + *phagein* to consume + *-ia* indicating a condition or quality]

hyperphoria *n*. A form of *strabismus in which the eye tends to deviate upwards. *Compare* cyclophoria, esotropia, exophoria, heterophoria, hypophoria.
[From Greek *hyper* over + *-phoros* carrying, from *pherein* to bear + *-ia* indicating a condition or quality]

hyperphrasia *n*. Excessive volubility or talkativeness, as often occurs in *manic episodes.
[From Greek *hyper* over + *phrazein* to express + *-ia* indicating a condition or quality]

hyperphrenia *n*. Mental overactivity such as occurs in *flight of ideas or, more generally, in a *manic episode.
[From Greek *hyper* over + *phren* mind, originally midriff, the supposed seat of the soul + *-ia* indicating a condition or quality]

hyperpnoea *n*. Another name for *hyperventilation. US *hyperpnea*.
[From Greek *hyper* over + *pnein* to breathe]

hyperpolarization *n*. An increase in the *membrane potential of a neuron relative to its *resting potential, reducing its propensity to generate a nerve impulse, such as occurs in an *inhibitory postsynaptic potential. *Compare* depolarization.
[From Greek *hyper* over + English *polarization*]

hyperprosexia *n*. Excessive and sometimes debilitating attention to trivial matters, such as the sound of a dripping tap. *Compare* aprosexia, hypoprosexia.
[From Greek *hyper* over + *prosexis* heedfulness, from *prosechein* to heed + *-ia* indicating a condition or quality]

hyper-reflection *n*. Over-consciousness of one's own behaviour, to the point that it interferes with sexual performance, social interaction, or other activities involving skills. The idea can be traced back to the ancient Sanskrit scriptures of the Vedanta, one of the philosophical schools of Hinduism, according to which the knower cannot be known, and the one that sees cannot be seen, but it was first investigated in clinical psychology by the Austrian psychiatrist Viktor E. Frankl (1905–97). It is countered by the therapeutic

technique of *de-reflection. *See also* centipede effect, Humphrey's law.

hyper-reflexia *n*. Overactive or exaggerated reflexes, usually occurring during a period of recovery from spinal injury.
[From Greek *hyper* over + English *reflex* + *-ia* indicating a condition or quality]

hypersomnia *n*. Excessive sleepiness, usually manifested as prolonged nocturnal sleep followed by difficulty in staying awake during the day. *See also* disorder of excessive somnolence, dyssomnias, narcolepsy, primary hypersomnia. *Compare* insomnia.
[From Greek *hyper* over + *somnus* sleep + *-ia* indicating a condition or quality]

hypertension *n*. Abnormally high blood pressure, persistently exceeding 140/90 millimetres of mercury, the first figure being pressure during systole (contraction of the heart muscle) and the second the pressure during diastole (the period of time between contractions), typical values for a healthy young adult being 120/70.

hyperthymia *n*. Excessive emotionalism.
[From Greek *hyper* over + *thymos* spirit + *-ia* indicating a condition or quality]

hyperthyroidism *n*. Overproduction by the thyroid gland of *thyroxine, leading to increased metabolic rate, insomnia, palpitations, tremor, nervousness, weight loss, sweating, hypersensitivity to heat, and possibly swelling of the eyeballs (exophthalmic goitre). *See also* deep tendon reflex.

hypertonia *n*. Abnormally high muscle tone or tension. *See* hypertonic (1). *Compare* hypotonia, isotonia.

hypertonic *adj*. **1.** Of or relating to muscles that are abnormally tensed. *Compare* hypotonic (1), isotonic (1). **2.** Of or relating to a solution having a greater concentration than another and hence exerting more *osmotic pressure than the other. A hypertonic saline solution (more than 0.9 per cent) is more concentrated than the *intracellular fluid, so that cells shrink when immersed in it. *See also* osmosis. *Compare* hypotonic (2), isotonic (2).
[From Greek *hyper* over + *tonos* tension + *-ikos* of, relating to, or resembling]

hypertrophy *n*. Abnormal enlargement of an organ, structure, or part. *Compare* atrophy.
[From Greek *hyper* over + *trophe* nourishment]

hypertropia *n*. Another name for *anoopsia.
[From Greek *hyper* over + *tropos* a turn + *ops* an eye + *-ia* indicating a condition or quality]

hyperventilation *n*. Abnormally increased depth or rate of breathing, often associated with *anxiety, leading to a reduction in blood carbon dioxide, sometimes causing dizziness and muscle cramps. Also called *hyperpnoea*.

hypesthesia *n*. Another name for *hypaesthesia.

hypnagogic image *n*. A dreamlike image, often vivid and resembling a *hallucination, generally accompanied by *sleep paralysis, experienced by a person in the transition state from wakefulness to sleep. *See also* Isakower phenomenon. *Compare* hypnopompic image.
[From French *hypnagogique* hypnagogic, from Greek *hypnos* sleep + *agogos* bringing + *-ikos* of, relating to, or resembling]

hypnoanalysis *n*. A form of *psychoanalysis in which *hypnosis is used to facilitate the uncovering of repressed memories, especially from infancy and early childhood.

hypnogenic *adj*. Tending to cause sleep or *hypnosis.
[From Greek *hypnos* sleep + *genein* to produce + *-ikos* of, relating to, or resembling]

hypnoid hysteria *n*. In *psychoanalysis, one of three types of *hysteria that were distinguished in 1895 by the Austrian physician Josef Breuer (1842–1925) and Sigmund Freud (1856–1939) in *Studies on Hysteria* (*Standard Edition*, II), supposedly originating in a state similar to a hypnotic state. However, Freud wrote: 'Strangely enough, I have never in my own experience met with a genuine hypnoid hysteria. Any that I took in hand has turned into a defence hysteria' (p. 286). After 1895 Freud came to believe that all hysteria is defence hysteria, and he abandoned the tripartite distinction. *See also* hypnoid state. *Compare* defence hysteria, retention hysteria.

hypnoid state *n*. In *psychoanalysis, a concept introduced by the Austrian physician Josef Breuer (1842–1925) to denote a state of consciousness resembling *hypnosis, occurring when an emotion intrudes into a reverie or daydream. Breuer's theory is set out in Freud's *Standard Edition*, II, pp. 183–252. The concept was later (1901/5) repudiated by Sigmund Freud (1856–1939) in his 'Fragment of an Analysis of a Case of Hysteria' (*Standard Edition*, VII, pp. 7–122, at p. 27n). *See also* hypnoid hysteria.

hypnopompic image *n*. A dreamlike image, often vivid and resembling a *hallucination, sometimes accompanied by *sleep paralysis, experienced by a person in transition from sleep to wakefulness. *Compare* hypnagogic image.
[From Greek *hypnos* sleep + *pompos* a guide + *-ikos* of, relating to, or resembling]

hypnosis *n*. Alterations in sensations, perceptions, thoughts, feelings, or behaviour brought about by suggestion, often (though controversially) interpreted as a trance-like altered state of consciousness characterized by heightened suggestibility, associated with such phenomena as suggested *hallucinations, hypnotic *analgesia, hypnotic *amnesia, and *hypnotic age regression. Also called *hypnotism* or *mesmerism*. *See also* animal magnetism, autohypnosis, hidden observer, hypermnesia, hypnotherapy, hypnotic amnesia, hypnotic susceptibility, neodissociation theory. **hypnoid** *adj*. Resembling *hypnosis.
[From Greek *hypnos* sleep + *-osis* indicating a process or state]

hypnotherapy *n*. A form of *psychotherapy in which *hypnosis is used, sometimes (controversially) with the aim of recovering repressed memories. *See also* recovered memory.

hypnotic *adj*. **1.** Of, relating to, or tending to produce *hypnosis or *sleep. *n*. **2.** Any drug that is used primarily to induce sleep, especially a *barbiturate acting via the *GABA receptor complex. In careful usage, the word is reserved for sleeping pills or draughts and is not applied to *sedatives, *narcotics, and *anxiolytics that may induce sleep incidentally to their main function. *See also* narcotic, sedative-, hypnotic-, or anxiolytic-related disorders.
[From Greek *hypnos* sleep + *-itikos* resembling or marked by]

hypnotic age regression *n*. The re-experiencing or re-enacting of experiences or patterns of behaviour from earlier life in response to suggestions given under *hypnosis, usually involving a guided year-by-year retracing of life. *See also* neodissociation theory.

hypnotic amnesia *n.* The inability of a person who has been hypnotized to recall, after the hypnotic session, all or part of what took place during the session. It usually occurs as a consequence of a direct suggestion given by the hypnotist during the hypnotic session but can also occur spontaneously. Also called *posthypnotic amnesia*.

hypnotic analgesia *See under* analgesia.

hypnotic susceptibility *n.* Responsivity or openness to *hypnosis, some people being significantly more easily or successfully hypnotized than others. Also called *hypnotizability*.

hypnotism *n.* An obsolescent name for the state of *hypnosis.

hypnotist *n.* A person who induces *hypnosis in another.

hypnotizability *n.* Another name for *hypnotic susceptibility.

hypnotize *vb.* To induce *hypnosis in a person or an animal.

hypoactive sexual desire disorder *n.* One of the *sexual dysfunctions, characterized by persistent or recurrent absence or deficiency of sexual fantasy and desire, causing significant distress or problems of interpersonal interaction. It is not diagnosed if it is attributable to a drug or a *general medical condition.
[From Greek *hypo* under + Latin *activus* in a state of action, from *actus* a doing + -*ivus* tending]

hypoaesthesia *n.* Another name for *hypaesthesia. US *hypoesthesia*.
[From Greek *hypo* under + *aisthesis* sensation, from *aisthanesthai* to feel + -*ia* indicating a condition or quality]

hypochondria *n.* Preoccupation and worry about apparently normal *somatic sensations or physical manifestations, which are interpreted as symptoms of a serious illness. *See also* actual neurosis, hypochondriasis, medical student syndrome. **hypochondriac** *n.* **1.** A

sufferer from *hypochondria. *adj.* **2.** Of or relating to a sufferer from *hypochondria.
hypochondriacal *adj.*
[From Greek *hypochondrion* the region of the abdomen under the costal cartilages and short ribs, from *hypo* under + *chondros* a cartilage + -*ia* indicating a condition or quality]

hypochondriasis *n.* A *somatoform disorder characterized by pathological *hypochondria, intense preoccupation and worry about apparently normal *somatic sensations or physical signs, which are interpreted as symptoms of a serious illness, in spite of appropriate medical investigation and reassurance that the fear is groundless. In most severe cases the preoccupation can become a hypochondriacal *delusional disorder involving a false belief that a disease is present. *See also* medical student syndrome.

hypochondriasis scale *See* MMPI.

hypoergastia *n.* Depression, especially the depressive phase of a *bipolar disorder.
[From *hypo* under + *ergasia* work or business, from *ergon* work + -*ia* indicating a condition or quality]

hypoesthesia *See* hypaesthesia.

hypogeusia *n.* Abnormally diminished taste sensitivity. *Compare* ageusia, cacogeusia, dysgeusia, hypergeusia, parageusia, taste blindness. **hypogeusic** *adj.*
[From Greek *hypo* under + *geusis* taste + -*ia* indicating a condition or quality]

hypoglossal nerve *n.* Either of the twelfth pair of *cranial nerves arising from the medulla oblongata, controlling the muscles of the tongue, and essential for swallowing.
[From Latin *hypo* under + *lingua* a tongue]

hypoglycaemia *n.* Abnormally low blood glucose, usually caused either by an overdose of insulin taken therapeutically in the treatment of *diabetes mellitus or by an excessive secretion of insulin by the pancreas, generally resulting from a pancreatic tumour, alcoholism, or liver disease. The signs and symptoms include asthenia, palpitations, tachycardia, sweating, tremor, ataxia, slowed thinking, confusion, irritability, and aggressiveness, terminating if untreated in delirium, coma, and occasionally death. US

hypoglycemia. *See also* insulin shock. *Compare* hyperglycaemia.
[From Greek *hypo* under + *glykys* sweet + *haima* blood + -*ia* indicating a condition or quality]

hypohedonia *n*. Abnormally reduced ability to experience pleasure or enjoyment in ordinarily pleasurable activities, falling short of *anhedonia or *depression. **hypohedonic** *adj*.
[From Greek *hypo* under + *hedone* pleasure + -*ia* indicating a condition or quality]

hypokinaesthesia *n*. Reduced sensitivity to positions or movements of body parts. US *hypokinesthesia*.
[From Greek *hypo* under + *kinesis* movement + *aisthesis* sensation, from *aisthanesthai* to feel + -*ia* indicating a condition or quality]

hypokinesis *n*. Diminished bodily movement.
[From Greek *hypo* under + *kinesis* movement]

hypolexia *n*. Another name for *dyslexia.
[From Greek *hypo* under + *lexis* a word + -*ia* indicating a condition or quality]

hypologia *n*. Another name for *poverty of speech.
[From Greek *hypo* under + *logos* a word or discourse + -*ia* indicating a condition or quality]

hypomania *n*. Another name for a *hypomanic episode.

hypomania scale *See* MMPI.

hypomanic episode *n*. A *mood episode with similar symptoms to a *manic episode but not sufficiently severe to cause marked impairment in social or occupational functioning or to require hospitalization, though characterized by unrealistic optimism, overactivity, a decreased need for sleep, and often reckless spending of money. Also called *hypomania* or *hypomanic disorder*.
[From Greek *hypo* under + *mania* madness]

hypomnesia *n*. Partial *amnesia.
[From Greek *hypo* under + *mnasthai* to remember + -*ia* indicating a condition or quality]

hypophoria *n*. A form of *strabismus in which the eye tends to deviate downwards. *Compare* cyclophoria, esotropia, exophoria, heterophoria, hyperphoria.

[From Greek *hypo* under + -*phoros* carrying, from *pherein* to bear + -*ia* indicating a condition or quality]

hypophrasia *n*. Another name for *poverty of speech or *hypologia.
[From Greek *hypo* under + *phrazein* to express + -*ia* indicating a condition or quality]

hypophrenia *n*. Another name for *mental retardation.
[From Greek *hypo* under + *phren* mind, originally midriff, the supposed seat of the soul + -*ia* indicating a condition or quality]

hypophysis *n*. Short for hypophysis cerebri, a technical name for the *pituitary gland.
[From Greek *hypophysis* an attachment underneath, from *hypo* under + *phyein* to grow]

hypoprosexia *n*. Reduced ability to attend or concentrate. *Compare* aprosexia, hyperprosexia.
[From Greek *hypo* under + *prosexis* heedfulness, from *prosechein* to heed + -*ia* indicating a condition or quality]

hyposmia *n*. Abnormally diminished sensitivity to all or a limited number of odorants. *See also* anosmia, cacosmia, dysosmia, parosmia, specific anosmia. *Compare* hyperosmia. **hyposmic** *adj*.
[From Greek *hypo* under + *osme* a smell + -*ia* indicating a condition or quality]

hyposthenia *n*. Debilitation or lack of strength.
[From Greek *hypo* under + *sthenos* strength + -*ia* indicating a condition or quality]

hypothalamic hyperphagia *n*. Another name for *ventromedial hypothalamic syndrome.

hypothalamic–hypophyseal portal system *n*. A system of blood vessels connecting capillaries of the *hypothalamus and the *anterior pituitary (hypophysis) through which hypothalamic hormones travel to the anterior pituitary.

hypothalamic–pituitary–adrenal axis *See* HPA axis.

hypothalamic syndromes *n*. Disorders associated with damage to the *hypothalamus arising from tumours, congenital malformations, or head injury, with signs and symptoms such as gross obesity, disturbances of *autonomic control, *hypersomnia, and *amnesia.

hypothalamus n. A fingernail-sized area of the diencephalon at the base of the brain in the limbic system, occupying the side walls and floor of the third ventricle, situated below both sides of the thalamus and above the pituitary gland, consisting of two halves with paired right and left nuclei, crucially involved in the regulation of the *endocrine glands and the *autonomic nervous system and implicated in the control of temperature, heart rate, blood pressure, hunger, thirst, sexual arousal, predatory aggression, and fight-or-flight responses. See arcuate nucleus, lateral hypothalamic feeding centre, medial forebrain bundle, median eminence, osmoreceptor (2), paraventricular nucleus, preoptic nucleus, satiety centre, suprachiasmatic nucleus, supraoptic nucleus, ventromedial hypothalamus, zona incerta. **hypothalamic** adj. [From Greek hypo under + English thalamus, so called because of its situation]

hypothesis n. A tentative explanation for a *phenomenon, subject to criticism by rational argument and refutation by *empirical evidence. See also alternative hypothesis, hypothetico-deductive method, null hypothesis. Compare model, theory (2). **hypotheses** pl. [From Greek hypo under + tithenai to place]

hypothetical construct n. A conjectured entity, process, or event that is not observed directly but is assumed to explain an observable phenomenon. It is not merely a summary of the relationships between observable variables but contains surplus meaning over and above such relationships. Typical examples are the *echoic store, *logogen, *primal sketch, and *superego. The distinction between hypothetical constructs and *intervening variables was first made explicit by the US psychologists Kenneth MacCorquodale (1919–85) and Paul Everett Meehl (born 1920) in an influential article in the journal Psychological Review in 1948, in which they used the examples from physics of an electron (a hypothetical construct that is assumed to be an entity, although it is not observed directly) and the resistance of a wire (an intervening variable that merely specifies the amperage of

current that will be carried by the wire for any given voltage). See also construct, convergent validity, discriminant validity, nomological network.

hypothetico-deductive method n. The standard research method of empirical science in which *hypotheses are formulated and tested by deducing predictions from them and then testing the predictions through controlled *experiments, hypotheses that are falsified being rejected and replaced by new ones. Also called scientific method. See also confirmation bias, falsifiability, induction (1).

hypothymia n. Diminished emotional response or *depression. [From Greek hypo under + thymos spirit + -ia indicating a condition or quality]

hypothyroidism n. An underproduction of *thyroxine by the *thyroid gland, leading to decreased metabolic rate, asthenia, weight gain, constipation, and sometimes mental retardation, coma, and death. Compare hyperthyroidism.

hypotonia n. Abnormally low muscle *tonus or tension. See hypotonic (1). Compare hypertonia, isotonia.

hypotonic adj. **1.** Of or relating to muscles that are abnormally flaccid. Compare hypertonic (1), isotonic (1). **2.** Of or relating to a solution having a lower concentration than another and hence exerting less *osmotic pressure than the other. A hypotonic saline solution (less than 0.9 per cent) is less concentrated than the *intracellular fluid, so that cells expand when immersed in it. See also osmosis. Compare hypertonic (2), isotonic (2). [From Greek hypo under + tonos tension + -ikos of, relating to, or resembling]

hypovolaemic thirst n. A form of thirst triggered by decreased blood volume sensed by *baroreceptors. US hypovolemic thirst. Also called extracellular thirst or volumetric thirst. Compare intracellular thirst. [From Greek hypo under + volumen a roll + haima blood]

hypoxyphilia n. A *paraphilia characterized by recurrent sexually arousing fantasies, sexual urges, or behaviour involving a dangerous and sometimes fatal form of *sexual masochism in which self-stimulation is sought by oxygen deprivation through the use of a noose, ligature, plastic bag, or chemical substance such as *amyl nitrite.

[From Greek *hypo* under + *oxy-* denoting oxygen + *philos* loving, from *phileein* to love + *-ia* indicating a condition or quality]

hysteria *n*. A once-popular name for a *mental disorder characterized by emotional outbursts, fainting, heightened *suggestibility, and *conversion symptoms such as *paralysis, nowadays generally not viewed as a coherent *syndrome but rather as aspects of *conversion disorder, *dissociative disorders, and *histrionic personality disorder. It has been traced back to the ancient Greek physician Hippocrates (?460–?377 BC). Also called *hysterical neurosis*. *See also* anxiety hysteria, conversion hysteria, defence hysteria, dissociation theory, hypnoid hysteria, hysterical technique, hysterogenic zone, retention hysteria. **hysteric** *n*. A person with *hysteria. **hysterical** *adj*. [From Greek *hysteria* the womb, which was formerly thought to underlie the disorder because it occurred mainly in women]

hysteria scale *See* MMPI.

hysterical paralysis *n*. Any *paralysis of *psychogenic rather than organic aetiology. *See* psychogenesis. *Compare* organic disorders.

hysterical personality *n*. An obsolescent name for *histrionic personality disorder.

hysterical technique *n*. In *psychoanalysis, one of the four *defensive techniques proposed by the Scottish psychoanalyst W. Ronald D. Fairbairn (1889–1964). It involves *externalization of the *good object and *internalization of the bad object, causing the hysterical person to consider internal impulses as bad. *See also* splitting of the object. *Compare* obsessional technique, paranoid technique, phobic technique.

hysterogenic zone *n*. In *psychoanalysis, areas of the body identified in 1890 by the French neurologist Jean Martin Charcot (1825–93) as the focal points for symptoms of conversion hysteria (*conversion disorder). According to Charcot, the patient describes them as painful but experiences sexual pleasure if they are stimulated (they function as *erotogenic zones), although this can precipitate a hysterical attack. Sigmund Freud (1856–1939) endorsed this theory in 1895 in *Studies on Hysteria* (*Standard Edition*, II, at p. 137) and in 'Some General Remarks on Hysterical Attacks' (1908/9), where he describes such a hysterical attack as 'an equivalent of coition' (*Standard Edition*, IX, pp. 227–34, at p. 234).

Ia fibre *n.* A large-diameter, thickly myeli-nated type of *afferent nerve fibre with high conduction velocity, such as that innervating a *muscle spindle. US *Ia fiber. Compare* alpha fibre, C fibre, delta fibre, gamma fibre, Ib fibre, II fibre.

iatrogenic *adj.* Of or pertaining to a disorder, *sign (1), or *symptom caused by a physician's treatment or management of a patient; doctor-induced.
[From Greek *iatros* a physician + *genes* born + *-ikos* of, relating to, or resembling]

Ib fibre *n.* A large-diameter, thickly myeli-nated type of *afferent nerve fibre with high conduction velocity, such as that innervating a *Golgi tendon organ. US *Ib fiber. Compare* alpha fibre, C fibre, delta fibre, gamma fibre, Ia fibre, II fibre.

ibotenic acid *n.* The *psychedelic drug α-amino-3-hydroxy-5-isoxazole-acetic acid, found in the *fly agaric mushroom *Amanita muscaria*, a potent excitatory amino acid *an-tagonist (3) that causes initial drowsiness, depression of motor activity, and ataxia, followed by hyperactivity and excitability ac-companied by changes in perceptions and emotions and delirium. It is also used as a *neurotoxin to destroy neuron cell bodies while leaving nerve fibres intact in the area where it is applied. *See also* hallucinogen.

ICD-10 *abbrev.* The *International Classi-fication of Diseases and Related Health Problems* (10th edition) issued by the World Health Organization in Geneva, Chapter 5 of which is devoted to mental and behavioural disorders. Along with *DSM-IV, it is one of the most authoritative reference works on matters of definition and classification of mental disorders. The tenth edition appeared in 1992–3.

ice *n.* Frozen water. Also, a street name for a very pure form of *methamphetamine. Because of its purity and low vaporization point, like crack cocaine it produces a rapid and powerful effect when smoked.
[So called because of the appearance of its crystals when seen under magnification]

icicle plot *See* horizontal icicle plot, vertical icicle plot.

iconic memory *See* iconic store.

iconic store *n.* One of the *sensory registers, allowing a visual image to persist for about half a second (depending on brightness) after its stimulus has ceased. It enables television, which presents 25 still images per second, each given twice to raise the flicker rate to 50 per second (British standard), to convey the illusion of a single continuous image, which, owing to *apparent movement, can be per-ceived as a moving image. In 1740, the Hungarian physicist Johann Andreas von Segner (1704–77) was the first to measure the duration of iconic memory traces (about half a second) by attaching a glowing ember to the rim of a wheel and determining the mini-mum speed of rotation (about 120 revolutions per minute) at which a complete circle was perceived. Interest in iconic memory was re-vived by a classic experiment devised by the US psychologist George Sperling and reported in the journal *Psychological Monographs* in 1960 in which three rows of four random letters were exposed for approximately 50 millisec-onds; when viewers attempted to recall as many letters as possible from all three rows, they typically reported no more than four or five items, but when they attempted to recall as many letters as possible from a single specified row, cued after the offset of the display, their recall was virtually perfect, provided that the row number was cued immediately, but recall declined steadily with increasing cue delay up to about 500 milliseconds, suggesting (in line with von Segner's earlier finding) that more information is available immediately after the stimulus offset than can be reported before it fades from memory and that much of it has disappeared after about half a second. Also called *iconic memory*, a term introduced by the US psychologist Ulrich (Richard Gustav) Neisser (born 1928) in his book *Cognitive Psychology* (1967). *See also* sensory memory. *Compare* echoic store.

[From Greek *eikon* an image + -*ikos* of, relating to, or resembling]

ictal *adj*. Of or relating to a sudden acute onset or attack, especially of an epileptic seizure or *convulsion. **ictus** *n*. A sudden acute onset or attack.

[From Latin *ictus* struck, from *icere* to strike + -*alis* of or relating to]

id *n*. In *psychoanalysis, one of the three components of the human mental apparatus in the second formulation of Sigmund Freud (1856–1939), after he replaced the *topography of unconscious–preconscious–conscious with the structural model of id–ego–superego in 1920. It is a reservoir of energy derived from *instincts (3), governed by the *pleasure principle, and its contents are *unconscious (1), some being *innate and others derived from experience but submerged by *repression, and it is in constant conflict with the *ego and the *superego, both of which originate from it during the course of development. Freud used the German word *das Es* (the it) in 1923 in his book *Das Ich und das Es*, translated as *The Ego and the Id* (*Standard Edition*, XIX, pp. 12–66, at p. 23), where he revealed that he borrowed the term from the German psychiatrist Georg Groddeck (1866–1934) but attributed it ultimately to the German philosopher Friedrich Wilhelm Nietzsche (1844–1900), and Freud's translator James Strachey (1887–1967) chose the word *id*, imbuing it with an aura of obscurity and technicality that the original German word lacks. The id is insulated from the *preconscious and *consciousness by *censorship, but it is not synonymous with the unconscious, as stated in many elementary expositions of Freud's theory, because the repressive functions of the *ego and many of the functions of the superego are also unconscious. The functions of the id are governed by the *primary process.

[From Latin *id* it]

idea, guiding *See* guiding fiction.

idealization *n*. In *psychoanalysis, a process whereby the attributes of an *instinctual object, especially another person, are represented mentally in a perfected form. Sigmund Freud (1856–1939) defined it as follows in an article 'On Narcissism: An Introduction' (1914): 'Idealisation is a process which concerns the *object*; by it that object, without any alteration in its nature, is aggrandised and exalted in the subject's mind' (*Standard Edition*, XIV, pp. 73–102, at p. 94). Many subsequent psychoanalysts, including the British-based Austrian psychoanalyst Melanie Klein (1882–1960) in a chapter in a co-authored book *Developments in Psycho-Analysis* in 1952, have interpreted it as a *defence mechanism. *See also* imago (1).

ideal observer *n*. In *signal detection theory, a hypothetical observer who has complete knowledge of the detection problem and who responds optimally in the light of this knowledge.

ideal self *n*. A conception of oneself as one would most like to be, in contradistinction to how one actually is or how one sees oneself.

ideas of reference *n*. A pattern of beliefs that external events and activities have a special significance for the person. *Compare* delusion of reference.

ideational apraxia *See under* apraxia.

idée fixe *n*. A fixed idea or *obsession. ***idées fixes*** *pl*.

[From French *idée* idea + *fixe* fixed]

identical twins *n*. A non-technical name for *monozygotic twins. It is a misleading term, avoided in careful scientific usage, because monozygotic twins, though similar, are never identical, phenotype being influenced not only by genetic but also by environmental factors.

identification *n*. **1.** The act or process of recognizing or distinguishing something or someone. **2.** The deliberate adoption of another person's behaviour or ideas as one's own. In *psychoanalysis, a *defence mechanism whereby one unconsciously incorporates attributes or characteristics of another person into one's own personality. Sigmund Freud (1856–1939) expounded his theory of identification most fully in his book *Group Psychology and the Analysis of the Ego* (1921, *Standard Edition*, XVIII, pp. 69–143, at pp. 105–9). *See also* identification with the aggressor, incorporation, introjection, primary identification, projective identification, secondary identification.

identification task *n*. A task in which the subject or participant tries to recognize a stimulus or discriminate it from other stimuli. *Compare* detection task.

identification with the aggressor *n*. In *psychoanalysis, a *defence mechanism first named and described in 1936/7 by the Austrian-born British psychoanalyst Anna Freud (1895–1982) in her book *The Ego and the Mechanisms of Defence* whereby a person facing an external threat, such as disapproval or criticism from an authority figure, identifies with the source of the threat, either by appropriating the aggression or else by adopting other attributes of the threatening figure. Anna Freud and the Austrian psychoanalyst René A. Spitz (1887–1974) argued that this mechanism plays an important part in the early development of the *superego, before criticism is turned inward at a later stage of development. The Austrian-born US psychologist Bruno Bettelheim (1903–90) described in an article in the *Journal of Abnormal and Social Psychology* in 1943 and in Chapter 4 of his book *The Informed Heart* (1960) how even in Nazi concentration camps, some inmates came to identify with their SS guards. *See also* identification (2).

identity crisis *n*. A state of confusion arising from an inability to reconcile conflicting aspects of one's personality. The concept was popularized by the German-born *ego psychologist Erik H. Erikson (1902–94) in his book *Identity: Youth and Conflict* (1968). *See* developmental crises, ego identity. *See also* dissociative identity disorder, gender identity disorder.

identity disorder *See* dissociative identity disorder, gender identity disorder.

identity theory *n*. An approach to the *mind–body problem, a form of *materialism holding that mental states have no separate existence but are identical to physical brain states. *See also* double-aspect theory, monism.

identity versus role confusion *n*. One of the crises in the developmental theory of the German-born *ego psychologist Erik H. Erikson (1902–94). *See* developmental crises.

ideograph *n*. A character or symbol used in a system of writing to represent directly a concept, idea, or object rather than a word or a sound. Characters in the writing systems of China and Japan are often called ideographs, but because the characters actually represent linguistic units rather than concepts they are therefore more properly called *logographs. Also called an *ideogram*. *See also* kanji. *Compare* logograph, pictograph. **ideographic** *adj*. Of or relating to *ideographs, not to be confused with *idiographic.
[From Greek *idea* idea + *graphein* to write]

ideokinetic apraxia *n*. Another name for *ideomotor apraxia. *See under* apraxia.

ideomotor aphasia *n*. Another name for *transcortical motor aphasia. *See* under aphasia.

ideomotor apraxia *See under* apraxia.

idioglossia *n*. Another name for *autonomous speech.

idiographic *adj*. Of or relating to the study of individuals or anything unique, especially approaches to the study of *personality that deny the possibility of general laws or *traits and stress the uniqueness of individuals. Not to be confused with *ideographic. The term was coined in 1904 by the German philosopher Wilhelm Windelband (1848–1915). *Compare* nomothetic.
[From Greek *idios* own or private + *graphein* to write + *-ikos* of, relating to, or resembling]

idiolect *n*. A variety of a language peculiar to an individual speaker. *Compare* acrolect, basilect, dialect, lect, mesolect.
[From Greek *idios* private or separate + *legein* to speak]

idiopathic *adj*. Of unknown or uncertain cause. Hence terms such as *idiopathic epilepsy*,

idiopathic convulsion, *idiopathic seizure* exclude cases resulting from known head injury or other identifiable causes.
[From Greek *idios* separate + *pathos* suffering + *-ikos* of, relating to, or resembling]

idioretinal light *n*. Another name for *dark light or *intrinsic light.
[From Greek *idios* private or separate + English *retina* + *-al* from Latin *-alis* of or relating to]

idiot *n*. An obsolete term for a person with *profound mental retardation; also an abusive term for a fool. **idiocy** *n*. Profound mental retardation. **idiotic** *adj*.
[From French *idiot* an idiot, from Latin *idiota* an ignorant person, from Greek *idiotes* a private person, or one who has no professional knowledge]

idiot savant *n*. A person with *mental retardation who can perform at a high level in some restricted domain of intellectual functioning, such as memorizing vast bodies of information, musical or artistic performance, or calendar calculating—naming the day of the week for a specified date in the past or future. It is not unusual for an idiot savant to suffer from *autistic disorder. **idiots savants** *pl*.
[From French *idiot* an idiot + *savant* wise or knowledgeable]

IE scale *n*. A scale derived from the *MMPI (Minnesota Multiphasic Personality Inventory) to measure *introversion–extraversion.

iff *conj*. In logic and mathematics, if and only if. It indicates that the two sentences that it conjoins are necessary and sufficient conditions for each other. *See* biconditional.

iich'aa *n*. A variant name for *amok among the Navajo indians of North America.
[Navajo]

II fibre *n*. A medium-diameter, partly myelinated type of *afferent nerve fibre with intermediate conduction velocity, such as those of the sensory receptors located in the skin, extrafusal muscles, and joints. US *II fiber*. *Compare* alpha fibre, C fibre, delta fibre, gamma fibre, Ia fibre, Ib fibre.

ikota *See* latah.

ill-defined problem *n*. In the study of *problem solving, any problem in which either the starting position, the allowable operations, or the goal state is not clearly specified, or a unique solution cannot be shown to exist. A typical example is the problem of overpopulation, which satisfies none of these criteria. Also called an *ill-structured problem*. *Compare* well-defined problem.

Illinois Test of Psycholinguistic Abilities *n*. A test for the assessment of psycholinguistic disabilities in children, consisting of 10 ordinary subtests plus a further two optional subtests for children between the ages of 2 and 10. **ITPA** *abbrev*.

illocutionary act *n*. A form of *speech act that does not convey information like a statement but functions as an action in itself. For example, a request, a threat, a welcome, a warning, or an apology cannot be considered as true or false like a statement, but such utterances none the less bring about new psychological or social realities—saying is equivalent to doing. *Compare* locutionary act, perlocutionary act.
[From *in-* into + Latin *locutio* an utterance, from *loqui* to speak]

illuminance *n*. The amount of light falling on a surface, measured in *lux. Also called *illumination*.

illumination *n*. **1.** Another name for *illuminance. **2.** Another name for *insight (2).

illusion *n*. According to a narrow definition, a misperception or misconception of a stimulus object, image, event, experience, or problem, or a stimulus that generates such a misperception or misconception; more generally, any misleading, deceptive, or puzzling stimulus or the experience that it generates. *Perceptual illusions can arise through any *sensory modality, but the most prominent are the *auditory illusions, *tactile illusions, and above all *visual illusions. Illusions of conception rather than of perception are called *cognitive illusions. Delusions of identification and memory such as *Capgras syndrome, *déjà vu, and the other *paramnesias (1) are often referred to as illusions, but this is avoided in careful usage. *See also* postural aftereffect, space–time illusion. *Compare* delusion, hallucination.

[From Latin *illusio, illusionis* deceit, from *illudere* to mock or make sport with, from *ludere* to play]

illusion of circular pitch *n*. Another name for the *auditory staircase illusion.

illusion of control *n*. The belief that one has control over events that are actually determined by chance. For example, choosing a 'lucky' number when buying a lottery ticket does not increase the probability of winning, and throwing dice with great effort does not increase the probability of winning numbers coming up, but people often behave as if such actions influence the events in question. People who are presented with a simulation of coin-tossing on a computer and who try to influence the outcomes—for example, to increase the number of heads—by *psychokinesis often believe that they have had an effect even when the computer has behaved perfectly randomly. The English psychologist Susan J. Blackmore (born 1951) and a colleague provided evidence in 1985 that this occurs especially in people who believe strongly in *extra-sensory perception (ESP). The concept of illusion of control was introduced and named in 1975 in an article in the *Journal of Personality and Social Psychology* by the US psychologist Ellen J. Langer (born 1947), who was also the first to study it experimentally. Research by Langer and others suggests that it occurs most frequently in situations that resemble tasks involving skill, appear familiar, allow free choice, involve competition with apparently incompetent opponents, include foreknowledge of the desired outcome, and emphasize the importance of success. There is also evidence to suggest that depressive mood reduces the illusion of control. *See also* depressive realism, just world hypothesis.

illusion of doubles *See* Capgras syndrome.

illusory conjunction *n*. Mistakenly merging attributes of two distinct stimuli in perception, for example, perceiving a red circle when a blue circle and a red square were displayed.

illusory contour *n*. A visual *contour in the absence of a lightness or colour gradient in the stimulus, computed in Area V2 of the *visual cortex, generating form perception

without a corresponding retinal image, the best-known example being the contour of a *Kanizsa triangle. Also called an *imaginary contour*, a *Kanizsa contour*, or a *subjective contour*. *See also* anorthoscopic, cognitive invention, Ehrenstein's brightness illusion, random-dot kinematogram, random-dot stereogram.

illusory correlation *n*. An apparent correlation that does not actually exist in the data being judged. In the classic demonstration of the illusion in 1967, the US psychologists Loren J(ames) Chapman (born 1927) and Jean Chapman (born 1929) presented experienced clinicians and students with information about a number of mental patients—for each patient, diagnostic statements and a drawing of a person made by that patient. The clinicians and students then estimated, from memory, the frequency with which different diagnostic statements (such as *The man who drew this is suspicious of other people*) had been associated with specific characteristics of the drawings (such as peculiar eyes in the drawing). Both groups of judges vastly overestimated the co-occurrences that fitted in with their *implicit personality theories, and this illusion was extremely resistant to change, persisting even when the actual correlations were negative. For example, 91 per cent of the experienced clinicians and 58 per cent of the students reported that peculiar eyes had been associated with suspiciousness, and 80 per cent of the clinicians and 76 per cent of the students reported that broad shoulders had been associated with being worried about manliness. The illusion helps to underpin superstitions and prejudices, and it is usually explained by the *availability heuristic, the assumption being that co-occurrences that seem likely are easier to remember than unlikely ones.

illustrator *n*. Anything that elucidates or amplifies, especially by visual signs, or anyone who produces pictures to clarify or explain a written text. In social psychology, a *gesture (1) that accompanies speech and that depicts, clarifies, or amplifies what is being said, as when a person locks two hands together to illustrate a phrase referring to a powerful bond between two people, or punches the fist of one hand into the palm of the other to accompany a description of a car crash. *See also* kinesics.

image n. **1.** A depiction or likeness of an object. **2.** An optically formed representation of an object, such as a *retinal image projected by the crystalline lens of the eye on to the retina. **3.** A mental representation of a stimulus in the absence of the physical stimulus, formed by imagination or memory. Also called a *mental image. See also* afterimage, eidetic image, Hering image, Hess image, hypnagogic image, hypnopompic image, imagery, Purkinje image, Purkinje–Sanson image, representation (1, 2), stabilized retinal image. **4.** The appearance or character that a person or an organization presents in public (as in *Speaking out in favour of legalizing cannabis wouldn't be good for my image*). **5.** Another name for a *figure of speech in which a word or phrase is applied to something other than its usual or literal meaning. **imaging** n. Creating or forming *images (1, 2, 3). See also* brain imaging.
[From Latin *imago* an image]

imageless thought n. *Thinking without mental *imagery. The *Würzburg school believed this form of thinking to be possible but never managed to provide evidence persuasive enough to convince sceptics.

imagen n. A representation of a visual image in long-term memory. *Compare* logogen.
[From Latin *imago* a copy or representation + Greek *genes* born]

image–retinal system n. A subsystem of the visual system, based on *direction-sensitive neurons, that computes the movement of objects from the movement of images across the retina, but that is unable on its own to distinguish between retinal movements caused by movements in the environment and those caused by movements of the observer's eyes and head. *See also* eye–head movement system, reafference.

imagery n. The act or process of forming mental *images (3) without stimulation of sense organs, or the mental images formed by *memory and *imagination, including not only visual images but also images from the other senses, such as hearing, taste, smell, and touch. The German psychologist Wilhelm (Max) Wundt (1832–1920) believed that images are one of the three basic elements of consciousness, together with sensations and feelings. *See also* dual-code theory (1), eidetic image, functional equivalence hypothesis, imagen, logogen, mental model, mental rotation.

imaginary companion n. A child's fanciful or invented friend, playmate, or associate, often believed in with *delusional conviction.

imaginary contour n. Another name for an *illusory contour.

imagination n. **1.** The act or process of *imagery, especially of generating mental *images (3) of stimuli that are not being or have never been experienced in perception; more generally creative ability or resourcefulness. **2.** In approaches to literary criticism influenced by the English romantic poet and critic Samuel Taylor Coleridge (1772–1834), a creative joining of active and passive perceptual elements that imposes unity on poetic material. **imaginary** adj.

imago n. **1.** In *psychoanalysis, an idealized image of another person, such as a parent, or of an *instinctual object, acquired in infancy and maintained in the *unconscious (2) in later life. The concept was introduced in 1911 by Carl Gustav Jung (1875–1961), who believed that some imagos are derived from *archetypes (2) rather than from personal experiences, and it became a key concept of his *analytical psychology. In the writings of the British-based Austrian psychoanalyst Melanie Klein (1882–1960), it is a fantastically distorted picture of the real object on which it is based. *See also* anima, animus (3), idealization. **2.** A mature adult insect produced by metamorphosis.
[From Latin *imago* a likeness, from *imitari* to copy]

imbecile n. An obsolete term for a person with *mild mental retardation; also, an abusive term for a person of low intelligence. **imbecility** n. Mild mental retardation. **imbecilic** adj.
[From Latin *imbecillus* feeble]

imidazoleamine n. A *biogenic amine such as *histamine derived from the five-member imidazole ring $C_3H_4N_2$.
[From *imidazole* a white crystalline base + *amine*]

imipramine n. A commonly prescribed *tricyclic antidepressant drug that acts by block-

ing the reuptake mechanism of amine neuro-transmitters, allowing them to accumulate at *synapses (1) in the central nervous system. Also called *Amitril*, *Elavil*, *Endep*, *Laroxyl*, *Saroten*, *Tofranil*, and *Triptafen* (trademarks). Formula $C_{19}H_{24}N_2$. *See also* clomipramine.
[From *imi(de)* indicating a compound containing the divalent group —CONHCO— + *pr(opyl)* indicating a compound containing the monovalent group C_3H_7 + *amine*]

imitation game *n.* The name used by the English mathematician Alan Mathison Turing (1912–54) to refer to what others have always called the *Turing test.

immediate memory *n.* Another name for *short-term memory.

immune response *n.* The production of *antibodies within the body as a defensive reaction to the presence of an *antigen, as when *B lymphocytes produce *immunoglobulin molecules with combining sites that fit shapes on the surface of the antigen and that bind to the antigen, setting in train a process that can neutralize and destroy it. A *primary immune response* follows first exposure to an antigen, usually takes several days to develop, and is mediated initially by immunoglobulin M (IgM), whereas a *secondary immune response* occurs after a second or subsequent exposure, develops much more rapidly, and is mediated primarily by immunoglobulin G (IgG). Also called an *antigen–antibody response*. *See also* granulocyte, interleukin, monocyte, prion disease, T lymphocyte.
[From Latin *immunis* exempt or immune, from *in-* not + *munis* serving]

immune system *n.* The structures, substances, and processes within the body that are responsible for *immune responses.

immunoglobulin *n.* Any of a group of Y-shaped protein molecules synthesized in blood plasma by B lymphocytes and functioning as an *antibody in an *immune response. Immunoglobulins are made up of two pairs of molecular chains, one light pair and one heavy pair, linked by disulphide bonds and containing variable regions providing differently shaped combining sites for different *antigens, the number and positions determining the particular class. Among the most important classes are immunoglobulin G

(IgG), an antibody produced towards the end of a primary immune response and the main antibody in a secondary response; immunoglobulin A (IgA), secreted locally in the gut and occurring in bodily fluids such as saliva, tears, and milk; and immunoglobulin M (IgM), the first class of immunoglobulin appearing in a primary immune response. *See also* B lymphocyte, T lymphocyte. **Ig** *abbrev.*
[From Latin *immunis* exempt or immune, from *in-* not + *munis* serving + *globulus* a little globe, diminutive of *globus* a globe + *-in(a)* indicating an organic compound, referring to globulins, proteins soluble in dilute salt solutions but not in pure water]

immunology *n.* The study of the nature, functions, and phenomena of the *immune system and *immune responses.
[From *immune* + Greek *logos* word, discourse, or reason]

impairment *n.* Any diminution in quality or strength; more specifically, any diminution in the quality or strength of physical or psychological functioning in some specified domain. *Compare* deficit. **impair** *vb.*
[From Latin *im-* indicating intensive + *peiorare* to make worse, from *peior* worse]

implicational universals *n.* One of the classes of *linguistic universals, taking the form *if A, then B*, where *A* and *B* are two properties of languages. A typical example, suggested by the US linguist Joseph H. Greenberg (1915–2001), is the following: If a language has *gender (2) categories in nouns, then it has gender categories in pronouns.

implicit memory *n.* A type of memory that is revealed when learning facilitates performance on a task that does not require conscious or intentional recollection of what was learnt. In a typical test, learners are shown a list of words or pictures, and then they are given an ostensibly unrelated task of recognizing fragmented forms of words or pictures in brief displays, and evidence for implicit memory is found in their ability to recognize the fragmented forms better if they have previously studied them. Evidence suggests that densely amnesic patients, who perform badly on standard memory tests, often perform normally on tests of implicit memory. The term was introduced by the Canadian psychologist Peter Graf (born 1951) and the US psychologist Daniel L. Schacter (born 1952) in an article in the *Journal of Experimental Psychology: Learning, Memory, and Cognition* in 1985. *Compare* explicit memory.

implicit personality theory *n.* A set of assumptions that a person makes, often unconsciously, about the *correlations between personality *traits, including such widespread assumptions as that *warmth* is positively correlated with *generosity*, so that a person who is warm is perceived as being likely also to be generous, and that *coldness* is positively correlated with *seriousness*, so that a person who is cold is perceived as being likely also to be serious. Some implicit personality theories also include correlations between psychological and physiognomic traits, such as the belief that intelligence is positively correlated with forehead height or that meanness is negatively correlated with distance between the eyes. The concept was introduced in 1954 by the US psychologist Jerome S(eymour) Bruner (born 1915) and the Italian-born US psychologist Renato Tagiuri (born 1919), who called it a *lay personality theory*, and in 1955 by the US psychologist Lee J(oseph) Cronbach (1916–2001), who introduced the term *implicit personality theory*. *See also* illusory correlation, trait centrality.

implosion therapy *n.* Another name for *flooding.
[From Latin *in* in + *plodere* to clap]

impossible figure *n.* A drawing or other representation of an object that could not exist in actual three-dimensional space, the best known examples being the *Freemish crate, *impossible trident, the *Penrose triangle, and the *staircase illusion. It is a misnomer, because what is impossible is not the figure but what it represents. Impossible figures feature strongly in the work of the Swedish artist Oscar Reutersvärd (1915–2001) and the Dutch artist Maurits C(ornelis) Escher (1898–1970). Also called an *Escher figure* or an *undecidable figure*. *See also* visual illusion. *Compare* ambiguous figure.

impossible triangle *n.* Another name for the *Penrose triangle.

impossible trident *n.* An *impossible figure representing a three-pronged (or two-pronged) object that emerged from an ob-

scure source in the US in 1964 and appeared on the cover of *Mad* magazine in 1965. It has been incorporated into several of the paintings, drawings, and etchings of the Swedish artist Oscar Reutersvärd (1915–2001) and some of the works of the Dutch graphic artist Maurits C(ornelis) Escher (1898–1970). Also called a *blivet*. *See also* visual illusion.

impotence *n.* **1.** Weakness or powerlessness. **2.** More specifically in relation to males, incapacity to perform sexual intercourse owing to an inability to achieve or to maintain an erection, believed to affect approximately 10 per cent of adult males, also called *erectile dysfunction* (*ED*), *male erectile disorder*, or *erectile impotence*; also, less commonly, an inability to have an *orgasm or to ejaculate, also called *orgasmic impotence*, *ejaculatory impotence*, or *male orgasmic disorder*. Both forms of impotence may be classified either as *primary impotence* if successful intercourse has never been possible and *secondary impotence* if at least one successful intercourse has been possible. *See also* cyclic GMP, de-reflection, male erectile disorder, premature ejaculation, Viagra. **impotent** *adj.*
[From Latin *in-* not + *potentia* power]

impoverished stimulus *n.* Another name for a *degraded stimulus.

impression formation *n.* The rapid creation of a unified perception or understanding of the character or personality of another person on the basis of a large number of diverse characteristics. One of the main problems in this area has been to determine whether people use *additive or non-additive models to combine the information. *See also* attribution theory, implicit personality theory, impression management, person perception, primacy effect (2), self-presentation, trait centrality.

impression management *n.* Control and regulation of information in order to influence *impression formation or the attitudes or opinions of the people on whom such behaviour is targeted. Through impression management one seeks to shape other people's impressions of a person (such as oneself, a friend, or an enemy) or of an event (such as an achievement or a failure). Impression management that is focused on controlling impressions of oneself is called *self-presentation.

imprinting n. In ethology, a form of rapid *learning (1) that takes place during a *critical period of development immediately or shortly after birth and is extremely resistant to *extinction (2), the most familiar example being the behaviour of newly hatched ducklings that become imprinted on, and subsequently follow around, virtually any moving object to which they are exposed during the critical period following hatching. It was first studied in detail in 1935 by the Austrian zoologist Konrad (Zacharias) Lorenz (1903–89). Also called *filial imprinting*. Compare attachment theory.

impulse-control disorders n. A class of *mental disorders characterized by a failure to resist impulses, drives, or temptations to behave in ways that are damaging to self or others. See antisocial personality disorder, conduct disorder, intermittent explosive disorder, kleptomania, paraphilias, pathological gambling, pyromania, substance-related disorders, trichotillomania. See also Internet addiction syndrome, road rage.

imu See latah.

inadequate personality n. A term occasionally used for a condition, without evidence of any *mental disorder, characterized by lack of judgement, ambition, and initiative, leading to failure at almost everything attempted.

inadequate stimulus n. A term sometimes used for a *stimulus (1) that is incapable of evoking a *response from an organism, such as visible light or sound that is too faint for the visual or auditory receptors to detect. It is an *oxymoron and is avoided in careful usage. Compare adequate stimulus.

inadmissible alternative/strategy n. In decision theory and game theory, an alternative or *strategy (2) that is dominated by a *dominant alternative/strategy.

inappropriate affect See under affect.

inbred strain n. A group of organisms produced by or resulting from *inbreeding.

inbreeding n. Producing offspring from closely related parents over a number of generations. See inbreeding depression.

inbreeding depression n. Loss of vigour resulting from *inbreeding, due to the loss of *heterozygosity and the expression of deleterious *recessive genes in *homozygous state. See also incest taboo.

incapacitant n. A substance that temporarily disables people and is used for personal protection, crowd control, or biological warfare. Also called an *incapacitating agent* or a *disabling agent*. See BZ gas, CN gas, CS gas, Mace, pepper spray, tear gas.

incentive motivation n. In *Hullian learning theory, an *intervening variable between the work involved in a response and the *generalized reaction potential. *K* abbrev.

incest taboo n. The custom or law in all societies prohibiting sex and marriage between members of the *nuclear family, the universality of the taboo being notoriously difficult to explain. According to the *functional theory*, the taboo creates and maintains networks of social relationships without which societies disintegrate into separate nuclear families and are eliminated, but this theory rests on the controversial assumption that without the incest taboo people would naturally want to mate with close relatives, and it fails to explain why the taboo governs sexual intercourse rather than marriage. According to the *inbreeding depression theory*, inbreeding leads to the genetic deterioration and ultimate extinction of any society that practises it, because harmful *recessive genes are more likely to come together, and the taboo may thus have evolved by natural selection, but this leaves open the question as to why few non-human animals have incest taboos and why some successful human societies, such as the Sotho people of southern Africa, have a positive obligation to marry cousins. The most persuasive explanation is the *prepubertal interaction theory*, put forward in 1894 by the Finnish social philosopher Edvard Alexander Westermarck (1862–1939), based on the psychological observation that intimate contact between children at a critical period before puberty, now believed to be between 2 and 6 years of age, results in a lack of sexual attraction between them in adult life. See also adelphogamy (2), inbreeding depression.

incidence n. In *epidemiology, the frequency of occurrence or onset of new cases of a disorder as a proportion of a population in a specific time period, usually expressed as the number of new cases per 100,000 per annum. *Compare* prevalence.

incidental learning *n.* Human *learning (1) that is unintentional and unmotivated or that occurs without any apparent *reinforcement (1, 2). In animal learning, the phenomenon is called *latent learning. Also called *passive learning*.

incident light *n.* Light falling on or striking a surface.
[From Latin *incidere* to fall into, from *in* into + *cadere* to fall]

inclusive disjunction *See* disjunction (2).

inclusive fitness *n.* The degree of *adaptation (1) of an organism to its environment, measured in terms of the average number of genes belonging to its *genotype that are passed on to the next generation, relative to those of other genotypes, taking into account not only the genes that it passes on directly but also those that it shares with close relatives and are passed on by them. *See also* kin selection. *Compare* Darwinian fitness, fitness.

incoherence *n.* Loose, rambling speech that lacks meaningful connections between words or phrases within sentences or clauses and is incomprehensible to others. Extreme instances are sometimes called *word salad*. *See also* disorganized speech. *Compare* cognitive derailment, loosening of associations.
[From Latin *in-* not + *cohaerere* to stick together or be consistent, from *co-* together + *haerere* to stick]

incomplete-pictures test *n.* A non-verbal test or subtest, often included in an *IQ test, in which the respondent tries to identify or fill in a part that is missing from a picture of a familiar object, such as a pig without a tail or a revolver without a trigger.

incomplete-sentences test *n.* Another name for a *sentence completion test.

incongruity of affect *See under* affect.

incorporation *n.* In *psychoanalysis, a *defence mechanism whereby a person mentally ingests or swallows another person, an *in-

stinctual object, or a *part object. Its *instinctual aim is characteristic of the *oral stage, and it provides a model for *identification (2) and *introjection.

incremental validity *n.* In psychometrics, the degree to which a test improves on decisions that can be made from existing information, such as the *base rate of the attribute being measured and other measures that are available. The term is also used to denote the *validity of a test arising from successive refinements or improvements of it in the light of experience or evidence, usually including the removal or replacement of test items that turn out to be problematic or that yield different results from the others.

incubation *n.* One of the *problem-solving stages, coming after preparation and before *insight (2), characterized by creative thinking while the problem is turned over in the mind, often unconsciously.
[From Latin *incubare* to lie on, from *in* to or on + *cubare* to lie down, alluding to the incubation of eggs before they hatch]

incus *n.* The middle of the three small bones in the *middle ear, transmitting sound vibrations from the malleus to the stapes. Referred to non-technically as the *anvil. *Compare* malleus, stapes.
[From Latin *incus* an anvil, from *incudere* to forge, alluding to its resemblance to a blacksmith's anvil]

independent assortment *n.* The law of independent assortment, the second of *Mendel's laws, stating that the separation at *meiosis (1) of any pair of hereditary units for a *trait or characteristic is not affected by the separation of any other pair, so that each unit is inherited independently of every other unit. This law had to be modified when *linkage was discovered. Also called the *law of independent assortment of genes*. *See also* DNA recombination, segregation of alleles.

independent samples *t* test *n.* In inferential statistics, a version of the *t test used for comparing means from two independent samples. *Compare* related scores *t* test.

independent variable *n.* In *experimental design, a variable that is varied by the experimenter independently of the *extraneous variables in order to examine its effects on the *dependent variable. In *multiple regression, it is a variable that has a potential effect on the *dependent variable. Also called an *experimental variable*. *See also* intervening variable. **IV** *abbrev.*

indeterminacy principle *n.* Another name for the *uncertainty principle.

index case *n.* Another name for a *proband.

indicator variable *n.* In statistics, a variable with just two possible values, sometimes represented by the symbols 0 and 1, used (for example) to represent categorical variables in *regression analysis.

indifference interval *n.* A time interval that, according to *Vierordt's law, is neither systematically overestimated nor systematically underestimated, usually found by experiment to be in the region of 0.7 second, though varying from one person to another and from one occasion to another.

indifference, principle of *n.* Another name for the principle of *insufficient reason.

indirect scaling *n.* In *psychophysics, any scaling method, such as the *method of bisection, in which an observer's judgement of stimulus magnitude is inferred rather than being simply estimated as in direct scaling or *magnitude estimation.

indirect speech act *n.* An utterance whose communicative purpose is masked by its grammatical form. For example, the utterance *Would you like to set the table?* is grammatically a question, but it masks the speaker's real communicative purpose, which is not to enquire about the listener's likes or dislikes but to tell the listener to do something. *See also* speech act.

indissociation *n.* The term used by the Swiss psychologist Jean Piaget (1896–1980) to refer to the failure of young children to differentiate themselves from their environments or objects from one another.

individual differences *n.* All of the ways in which people differ from one another, especially psychological differences. Included

are all differences in *personality and *intelligence.

individual differences scaling *See* INDSCAL.

individual psychology *n.* The school of *psychoanalysis, also called *Adlerian psychoanalysis, founded in 1911 by the Austrian psychiatrist Alfred Adler (1870–1937). *See* compensation, Diana complex, fictional finalism, guiding fiction, inferiority complex, life lie, masculine protest, neurotic character, neurotic fiction, will to power.

individual test *n.* A test of *intelligence, *personality, or any other psychological attribute, designed to be administered to one respondent at a time. *Compare* group test.

individuation *n.* The act or process of giving individuality to someone or something. In *analytical psychology it is the process occurring by degrees over the lifespan whereby an individual achieves wholeness through the integration of *consciousness and the *collective unconscious, and it is symbolized by the *mandala. In a key passage, Carl Gustav Jung (1875–1961) described it as follows: 'Individuation means becoming a single, homogeneous being, and, in so far as "individuality" embraces our innermost, last, and incomparable uniqueness, it also implies becoming one's own self. We could therefore translate individuation as "coming to selfhood" or "self-actualization"' (*Collected Works*, 7, paragraph 266). Jung borrowed the word from the German philosopher Arthur Schopenhauer (1788–1860), but it has been traced back to 16th-century alchemy. In *neo-Freudian theory, the German-born US psychoanalyst Erich Fromm (1900–80) used the term slightly differently to denote the gradual attainment by a growing child of awareness of being a particular, individual person. *Compare* deindividuation.
[From Latin *individuare* to single out, from *in-* into + *dividuus* divisible, from *dividere* to divide]

Indo-European *adj. n.* (Of, relating to, or belonging to) a family of languages spoken by almost half the world's population, descended from a common tongue called *Proto-Indo-European* that is believed to have existed in the fifth millennium BC and subsequently to have fragmented into Germanic, Italic, Celtic,

Baltic, Slavic, Albanian, Greek, Armenian, Iranian, and Indic, and later still into many different languages, including English and all descendants from Greek, Latin, and Sanskrit. By working backwards, linguists have reconstructed much of the structure and vocabulary of Indo-European; thus the word for god is believed to have been *deiw-os* (cognate with Latin *deus* and Greek *theos*), the word for father *p'tēr-* (cognate with Latin and Greek *pater*), and hence the word for the patriarchal god of Indo-European religion *Dyeu p'ter-*, from which *Zeus pater* found its way into Greek, *Dyaus pitar* into Sanskrit, and *Jupiter* into Latin and then English. *See also* glottochronology, Grimm's law, lexicostatistics.

indole *n.* A crystalline substance C_8H_7N forming the basis of the indigo molecule, occurring naturally in coal tar, some plants such as jasmine, and the urine of civets and other mammals, also an important constituent of *indoleamine. Also spelt *indol*.
[From *indigo* + Latin *oleum* oil]

indole alkaloids *n.* A group of *alkaloids forming one of the major groups of *hallucinogens and *psychedelic drugs, including *bufotenin, *DMT, *harmine, *LSD, and *psilocybin. *See also* phantasticant.

indoleamine *n.* Any of a group of *biogenic amines, including *serotonin and *tryptamine, containing an *indole ring with five members and an amine group (NH_2).
[From *indole* + *amine*]

indoleamine hypothesis *n.* The conjecture that abnormalities in the metabolism of *indoleamines are implicated in the aetiology of *depression, *mania, and other mental disorders.

INDSCAL *abbrev.* Individual differences scaling, one of the most powerful and popular methods of *multidimensional scaling, created in 1970 by the US statistician J(ohn) Douglas Carroll (born 1939) in collaboration with Jih-Jie Chang, used for analysing several proximity matrices simultaneously.

induced colour *n.* A colour arising from *colour induction. US *induced color*.

induced delusional disorder *n.* Another name for a *shared psychotic disorder (folie à deux). Also called *induced psychotic disorder*.

induced motion *n.* Another name for *vection; more generally, any illusion of movement of a stationary object caused by movement of its background or surrounding context.

induction *n.* **1.** A form of reasoning, also called *empirical induction*, in which a general law or principle is inferred from particular instances that have been observed. Many people believe that this form of reasoning works in practice, and it is widely believed to form the basis of all empirical sciences, but the Scottish philosopher David Hume (1711–76) showed in *A Treatise of Human Nature* in 1739 that induction is logically invalid: from the premise *All swans that have been observed are white* it is not valid to conclude that *Therefore, all swans are white*. There is a missing premise, that *All swans have been observed*, which is not true and could never be true of any universal proposition in science that is supposed to apply throughout time and space. Hume pointed out that the uniformity of nature might justify induction, in the form of the premise *Future observations will resemble past observations*, but this could be justified only by a question-begging appeal to induction itself, and in any event it is not true in general—for example, there are black swans in Australia. This apparent inconsistency is called the *problem of induction* or *Hume's problem*, and it is solved by the insight that empirical evidence is used to falsify rather than to confirm hypotheses. *See also* falsifiability, Goodman's paradox, Hempel's paradox, hypothetico-deductive method. *Compare* deduction. **2.** A mathematical technique, also called *mathematical induction*, for proving that a statement or *proposition (1) is true in general, or (equivalently) that each of an infinite sequence of statements is true, by proving that the first statement in the sequence is true, and then that if any one of the statements is true it follows that the next one is also true. **3.** Indirect generation of a sensory experience without direct stimulation of the corresponding sensory receptors, by stimulation of adjacent or related sensory processes. *See* colour induction, induced motion, visual induction, warmth contrast. **4.** The name given by the Russian physiologist Ivan Petrovich Pavlov (1849–1936) to *positive induction*, in which the response to an excitatory *conditioned stimulus is increased if it is immediately preceded by an inhibitory one, and to *negative induction*, in which the response to

an inhibitory conditioned stimulus is increased if it is immediately preceded by an excitatory one. **5.** The process whereby morphogenic differentiation is stimulated in a developing *embryo by *Müllerian inhibiting substance, *testosterone, or other hormones or substances. **6.** A formal process of introduction to membership of a group or organization. **7.** A shortened name for *enzyme induction. **induce** *vb.* **inductive** *adj.*
[From Latin *inducere* to lead in, from *in* in + *ducere, inductum* to lead + *-ion* indicating an action, process, or state]

inductive reasoning *n.* Another name for *induction (1, 2).

inductive statistics *n.* Another name for *inferential statistics.

industrial/organizational psychology *n.* A field of applied psychology in which the results of basic and applied research into the well-being and efficiency of people in work is applied to problems arising in industry and in non-industrial organizations. Work in this field focuses on vocational guidance and selection, problems of work motivation and *job satisfaction, absenteeism in organizations, improvement of communication within organizations, design and implementation of training courses, teaching of social and human relations skills, improvement of promotion structures, evaluation of job performance, and problems of safety and welfare. Its major branches are *personnel psychology, *ergonomics or human factors psychology, and *organizational psychology. It corresponds roughly to *occupational psychology, the term often preferred in the UK and the rest of Europe, and it falls under the umbrella of *work psychology. **I/O psychology** *abbrev.*

industry versus inferiority *n.* One of the crises in the developmental theory of the German-born *ego psychologist Erik H. Erikson (1902–94). *See* developmental crises.

infantile amnesia *n.* The inability of human adults to retrieve genuine memories for events that occurred before about three years of age. Also called *childhood amnesia*. Faced with overwhelming evidence for this phenomenon, even the Austrian neurologist Sigmund Freud (1856–1939) was forced to ac-

cept it in his book *Three Essays on the Theory of Sexuality* (1905) (*Standard Edition*, VI, pp. 130–243, at pp. 174–6). *See also* false memory, false memory syndrome, paramnesia (1), Piaget kidnapping memory, screen memory.

infantile autism *n.* An alternative name for *autistic disorder manifested during infancy. *Compare* childhood autism.

infantile sexuality *n.* In *psychoanalysis, the sexual drive or *libido in infants. *See* anal stage, oral stage.

infarct *n.* A localized area of dead tissue resulting from the interruption of its blood supply. When it occurs at multiple sites in the brain it can lead to *dementia. Also called an *infarction*. *See also* vascular dementia.
[From Latin *infarctus* stuffed into, from *in* in or into + *farcire* to stuff]

infatuation *n.* Foolish or unreasoning passion; a type of love characterized by erotic passion but lacking other components. *See under* love.
[From Latin *in* in + *fatuus* foolish]

inference *n.* Reasoning from premises to conclusions; or a conclusion arrived at by this process. When the premises are particular observations and the conclusion a general law or principle, then the mode of inference is called *induction (1); when the premises are axioms, postulates, or assumptions and the conclusion a logical inference or theorem, then the mode of inference is called *deduction. **infer** *vb.* To make *inferences. This word is sometimes used as a synonym for *imply* (as in *Her replies inferred that she disagreed*), but this is avoided in careful usage.
[From Latin *inferre* to bring in, bring about, or deduce, from *in-* into + *ferre* to bear or carry]

inferential statistics *n.* Techniques for inferring conclusions about *populations on the basis of data from *samples. The major objective is usually to decide whether the results of research are statistically significant. Also called *inductive statistics*. *See also* significance test, statistical inference. *Compare* descriptive statistics.

inferior *adj.* Lower in any respect; towards the bottom of a body, organ, or part, or situated below another homologous structure. *Compare* superior.

[From Latin *inferior* lower, from *inferus* low]

inferior colliculus *n*. Either of two hillock-shaped small bumps on the tectum (the roof of the midbrain), below and behind the superior colliculi, functioning as an intermediate nucleus for processing auditory signals before they are transmitted to the primary *auditory cortex. The four colliculi are collectively called the corpora quadrigemina. **inferior colliculi** *pl*.

[From Latin *inferior* lower + *colliculus* a small hill, from *collis* a hill]

inferiority complex *n*. In the *individual psychology of the Austrian psychiatrist Alfred Adler (1870–1937) and his followers, a *complex (2) of emotionally toned ideas arising from repressed fear and resentment associated with real or imagined inferiority, resulting either in *compensation, in the form of pugnacity, or withdrawal into oneself. Adler introduced the concept in 1907 in a book translated as *Study of Organ Inferiority and its Psychical Compensation* (1917). In a later book *The Neurotic Constitution* (1926, original work 1912), he described it as follows: 'The constitutional inferiority and similarly effective childhood situations give rise to a feeling of inferiority which demands a compensation in the sense of an enhancement of the self-esteem' (p. 111). In an article in 1935 Adler distinguished between natural feelings of inferiority and the inferiority complex proper.

inferior longitudinal fasciculus *n*. A bundle of nerve fibres in each cerebral hemisphere linking the *temporal lobe to the *occipital lobe. *Compare* superior longitudinal fasciculus.

[From Latin *inferior* lower + *longitudo* length, from *longus* long + *fasciculus* a little bundle, diminutive of *fasculus* a bundle]

inferior oblique muscle *n*. The lower of the two *oblique muscles attached externally to the eyeball.

inferior olivary nucleus *n*. Either of two wrinkled olive-shaped clumps of neurons in the upper part of the medulla oblongata, just below the pons, connected to the thalamus, cerebellum, and spinal cord, implicated in motor coordination. Also called an *inferior olivary complex* or an *inferior olive*. *Compare* superior olivary nucleus. **ION** *abbrev.*

inferior rectus *n*. The lower of the four *rectus muscles attached externally to the eyeball.

inferior temporal cortex *n*. Another name for the *inferior temporal gyrus. **ITC** *abbrev.*

inferior temporal gyrus *n*. The lowest *gyrus running horizontally on the lateral (outer) surface of the *temporal lobe, implicated in visual pattern recognition. Also called the *inferior temporal cortex (ITC)* or *inferotemporal cortex*. **ITG** *abbrev.*

infinite regress *n*. An argument consisting of or implying an endless sequence of steps. An argument of this kind shows, for example, that *introspection cannot be a valid and complete source of self-knowledge, because it requires that it be possible to perform a mental act (such as remembering one's last birthday) while at the same time observing oneself doing it; but then the act of introspection is part of the mental process, and for a complete understanding it would be necessary to observe the act of observation, and so on, which in this case is clearly impossible. This is an example of a *vicious* infinite regress: an infinite regress is vicious only if it leads to an absurd conclusion, and in other cases it is often unproblematic.

inflation of consciousness *n*. In *analytical psychology, the expansion of a person's consciousness beyond its normal limits, arising through *identification (2) with an *archetype (2), the *persona (1) or, in certain mental disorders, a famous person, resulting in an exaggerated sense of importance that is generally compensated for by feelings of inferiority. Carl Gustav Jung (1875–1961) described how it arises when the archetypal content 'seizes hold of the psyche with a kind of primeval force and compels it to transgress the bounds of humanity. The consequence is a puffed-up attitude, loss of free will, delusion and enthusiasm for good and evil alike' (*Collected Works*, 12, paragraph 563).

inflecting language *n*. A language such as Latin, German, or Arabic in which grammatical relationships are indicated by altering the internal structure of words, often by changing their endings. English has some features of an inflecting language, as is shown in the two sentences *I ask you* and *I asked you*. Also called a *synthetic language* or a *fusional language*. *Compare* agglutinative language, isolating language.

influence, delusion of *See* delusion of control.

information *n*. **1.** *Knowledge acquired by *learning (2). **2.** In *information theory, a numerical quantity indicating the degree of uncertainty in a *signal, such that if the signal occurs with probability p, then the information that it conveys, symbolized by H, is equal to $\log_2(1/p)$, the units of measurement being binary digits or *bits. *See also* byte, information technology, information theory, nybble. [From Latin *informare* to give form or shape to, from *in* into + *formare* to form, from *forma* a form or shape + *-ation* indicating a process or condition]

information processing *n*. Cognitive functioning or *cognition interpreted with the help of concepts borrowed from computer science. It includes all of the processes studied within *cognitive psychology, such as *attention, *perception, *learning (1, 2), *memory, *thinking, *problem solving, *decision making, and *language (1). *See* ACT*, automatic processing, bottom-up processing, cascade processing, cognitive miser, cognitive psychology, controlled processing, discrete processing, distributed cognition, neural network, parallel distributed processing, stereotype, top-down processing.

information technology *n*. The study or use of computers, telecommunication systems, and other devices for storing, retrieving, and transmitting *information (2). *See also* information theory. **IT** *abbrev*.

information theory *n*. A theory of *information (2) in which the amount of information, symbolized by H, in a signal is defined as the smallest number of binary digits or *bits that are required to encode it. If a signal specifies a choice of one of N equiprobable alternatives, then the amount of information that it contains is $H = \log_2 N$; hence, for example, if 16 people are equally likely to have committed a crime, a signal specifying the guilty person

conveys $H = \log_2 16 = 4$ bits of information, which may be interpreted as four successive binary divisions of the set of suspects. As a second example, in a signal in which each letter of the English alphabet is equally probable, the information content of a single letter is $H = \log_2 26 = 4.70$ bits. A more general definition, applicable where the alternatives are not equiprobable, is given by the Wiener–Shannon formula $H = -\Sigma p_i \log_2 p_i$, where p_i is the probability of the ith alternative, and in the light of this formula information is sometimes defined as negative *entropy. The theory was developed independently in the late 1940s and early 1950s by the English statistician and geneticist Ronald Aylmer Fisher (1890–1962) and the US mathematicians Norbert Wiener (1894–1964) and Claude E(lwood) Shannon (1916–2001), and it was Shannon's work that had the greatest influence in psychology. *See also* byte, information technology, nybble.

informed consent *n*. Voluntary agreement by a patient to undergo a medical treatment or procedure, or by a research participant or subject to take part in an experiment or other research study, given in full knowledge of the nature of the procedure and its potential risks and benefits. It is acknowledged in the ethical principles for research published by the American Psychological Association and the British Psychological Society that informed consent, while desirable, is sometimes either infeasible (as when the research participants lack the capacity to give it, through youth or mental disorder), or impractical (as when the nature of the investigation relies on deception). *See also* Ulysses contract.

infradian rhythm *n*. Any *biological rhythm with a period of less than a day. *See* alpha wave, basic rest–activity cycle, beta wave, delta wave, gamma wave, sensorimotor rhythm, theta wave. *See also* biological clock, chronobiology, *Zeitgeber*. *Compare* circadian rhythm, circannual rhythm, ultradian rhythm. [From Latin *infra* under + *dies* a day]

infra-red *adj. n*. (Of or relating to) electromagnetic radiation with wavelengths longer than the longest radiation in the *visible spectrum but not as long as radio waves, hence within the range 750 nanometres to 1 millimetre, such radiation being perceived as heat. *See*

also infra-red vision. *Compare* ultraviolet. **IR** *abbrev.*
[From Latin *infra* below or under + English *red*]

infra-red vision *n.* A form of perception found in all snakes of the subfamily Crotalinae, the pit vipers, including rattlesnakes and pythons, in which *infra-red radiation emitted by warm objects such as prey animals is detected by a snake's pit organs, a pair of deep cavities in the sides of its head below its eyes.

infrasound *n.* A pressure wave of the same physical character as sound but with a frequency below the lower limit of the *audibility range—below about 16 hertz. Such waves are capable of travelling relatively great distances, and if intense enough, they can induce *dysphoria and can even damage internal organs of the body although they cannot be heard. African and Indian elephant families in the wild communicate with sounds that are partly infrasonic, ranging from 35 hertz down to 12 hertz. *Compare* ultrasound. **infrasonic** *adj.*
[From Latin *infra* below or under + English *sound*]

infundibulum *n.* The funnel-shaped stalk connecting the *pituitary gland to the *hypothalamus at the base of the brain.
[From Latin *infundibulum* a funnel, from *in* into + *fundere* to pour]

ingratiation *n.* A form of *self-presentation calculated to increase one's attractiveness in the eyes of another person. It was first investigated experimentally in the early 1960s by the US psychologist Edward Ellsworth Jones (1926–93), who observed three major classes of tactics commonly used by ingratiators who are motivated to win the favour of a target person: other-enhancement, in which the ingratiator flatters and compliments the target person; opinion conformity, in which the ingratiator pretends to share the target person's attitudes on important issues; and biased self-presentation, in which ingratiators of both sexes emphasize their most attractive qualities and play down their weak points. In addition, if circumstances allow, an ingratiator often renders favours to the target person. Research has revealed that such ingratiation tactics are often successful in eliciting liking,

and that when they succeed, ingratiators often come to believe, presumably out of vanity, that they did not use any tactics. **ingratiate** *vb.*
[From Latin *in* into + *gratia* favour]

inhalant *n.* Any volatile chemical substance that is inhaled, whether for medicinal or therapeutic purposes or as a street drug. *See also* aliphatic, inhalant-related disorders, ketone, nitrite inhalant, solvent abuse.
[From *in-* into + Latin *halare* to breathe]

inhalant-related disorders *n.* *Substance-related disorders induced by inhaling the *aliphatic and *aromatic hydrocarbons in petrol or gasoline, glue, paint, and some aerosols or, less commonly, the halogenated hydrocarbons in cleaning fluids and other volatile substances in *esters, *ketones, and *glycols. *See* glue-sniffing, solvent abuse, substance abuse, substance dependence, substance-induced disorders, substance use disorders.

inhibited orgasm *n.* Another name for *female orgasmic disorder and *male orgasmic disorder.

inhibited sexual desire *n.* Another name for *female sexual desire disorder and *hypoactive sexual desire disorder.

inhibition *n.* **1.** The act or process of restraining or preventing something, or the state of being restrained or prevented. **2.** A stopping or checking of a physiological process, as when the action of a neuron, organ, or gland is interrupted by the action of a nerve impulse or a hormone. *See also* inhibitory postsynaptic potential. *Compare* excitation. **3.** The weakening of a *conditioned response by *extinction (2) or an *unconditioned response by *habituation (2) or by the occurrence of a distracting stimulus. *See also* reciprocal inhibition. *Compare* excitation. **4.** A psychological state or condition characterized by lack of confidence and restriction of the range of *expressive behaviour. *See also* avoidant personality disorder, reactive attachment disorder. **5.** In *psychoanalysis, the unconscious restraint of a drive or impulse. *See also* aim-inhibition. **inhibit** *vb.*
[From Latin *inhibere, inhibitum* to restrain, from *habere* to have + *-ion* indicating an action, process, or state]

inhibition of inhibition *n.* Another name for *disinhibition.

inhibition, proactive *See* proactive interference.

inhibition, retroactive *See* retroactive interference.

inhibitor *n.* A substance or gene that inhibits a specific process.

inhibitory *adj.* Tending to cause *inhibition (1, 2, 3, 4, 5). In neurophysiology, characteristic of *neurons that restrain other neurons from firing, or *neurotransmitters such as GABA, the action of which tends to prevent neurons from firing, or *synapses (1) at which the transmission of nerve impulses tends to prevent postsynaptic neurons from firing. *See also* inhibitory postsynaptic potential. *Compare* excitatory.

inhibitory postsynaptic potential *n.* A graded hyperpolarization or increase in the electrical potential across the membrane of a *postsynaptic neuron, occurring in response to a signal transmitted across a *synapse (1) by a *presynaptic neuron and reducing the propensity of the postsynaptic neuron to initiate a nerve impulse. Also called *postsynaptic inhibition*. *See also* action potential, resting potential. *Compare* excitatory postsynaptic potential. **IPSP** *abbrev.*

inhibitory priming *See under* priming (1).

initial insomnia *See under* insomnia.

initial letter priming *See under* priming (1).

Initial Teaching Alphabet *n.* An alphabet containing 44 characters, each of which corresponds to a single sound or *phoneme of English, designed to simplify and facilitate the teaching of reading. **ITA** *abbrev.*

initial values law *n.* In the study of drug effects, the notion that the effect of a drug on a measurable variable may depend on the level of that variable at the time of administration or, more generally, that the *dose–response curve of a drug may depend on the starting level of the effect variable. As an example, a central nervous system stimulant may have a strong positive effect on the arousal of a drowsy person but may have very little effect, or even a depressant effect, on a highly aroused person. In relation to behaviour, the law is also called the *rate-dependency effect*. *See also* methylphenidate (Ritalin).

initiation codon *n.* Another name for a *start codon. Also called an *initiator codon*.

initiative versus guilt *n.* One of the crises in the developmental theory of the German-born *ego psychologist Erik H. Erikson (1902–94). *See* developmental crises.

injury feigning *See under* factitious disorder, malingering.

inkblot test *See* Holtzman Inkblot Technique, Rorschach test.

innate *adj.* Present in an organism from birth, hence inborn or congenital. Also, loosely, genetically determined rather than acquired by learning or attributable to environmental factors, though this meaning is avoided in careful usage, because a congenital characteristic is not necessarily genetic in origin.
[From Latin *innatus* inborn, from *in* in or into + *nasci, natus* born]

innate releasing mechanism *n.* In ethology, a hypothetical *hard-wired device in the *central nervous system of an animal that causes a *sign stimulus or *releaser to evoke *fixed-action pattern. *See also* vacuum activity. **IRM** *abbrev.*

inner ear *n.* The internal fluid-filled part of the *ear containing the *cochlea and the *vestibular system, including the *semicircular canals, separated from the middle ear by the round window (fenestra rotunda) and the oval window (fenestra ovalis). Also called the *internal ear* or *labyrinth*. *See* ear (illustration). *See also* scala. *Compare* middle ear, outer ear.

inner hair cell *n.* Any of approximately 3,500 *hair cells, situated in the *organ of Corti, specialized as *transducers of sound waves into nerve impulses and believed to encode information about the frequency of sound. *Compare* outer hair cell. **IHC** *abbrev.*
[So called because they are further from the outside of the cochlea than are the outer hair cells]

inner nuclear layer *n*. A stratum of the *retina containing the cell bodies of *amacrine cells, *bipolar cells, *horizontal cells, and *interplexiform cells.

inner plexiform layer *n*. A thin stratum separating the inner and middle layers of the *retina and containing synaptic connections between *amacrine cells, *bipolar cells, and *ganglion cells. *See also* interplexiform cell.
[From Latin *plexus* a network, from *plectere* to weave]

inner speech *n*. The mental use of words or language without physical articulation of speech sounds. *See also* phonological loop.

innervate *vb*. **1.** To supply an organ, structure, or body part with nerves or with nerve impulses. **2.** To excite or stimulate a nerve. When used by the Austrian neurologist Sigmund Freud (1856–1939), the word always had this meaning. **innervation** *n*.
[From Latin *in* in or into + *nervus* a nerve]

innervation ratio *n*. A number indicating the density of *innervation (1) of a specified muscle by motor neurons, especially the average number of muscle fibres contacted by each motor neuron (the total number of muscle fibres contacted divided by the number of motor neurons), a low ratio being indicative of a lack of precise control and a high ratio, greater precision of control.

inoculation theory *n*. A theory of resistance to *persuasion according to which most ordinary attitudes and beliefs are more or less resistant to change through having been exposed to repeated mild attacks. The theory predicts that *cultural truisms* that most people have never heard being questioned, such as *It is a good idea to brush your teeth three times a day if possible*, should be more vulnerable to persuasion, and this counter-intuitive prediction has been confirmed by experiments. The theory is based on the biological analogy of an organism that has been raised in a sterile, germ-free environment and that appears robust and healthy but is in reality vulnerable to infection, because it has not had the opportunity to develop defensive antibodies. Cultural truisms have also never been attacked, and defensive arguments have therefore never been developed, but their resistance to persuasion can be markedly increased by a process of in-

oculation, which involves exposing the recipients to relatively weak arguments against the truisms together with rebuttals that the recipients are either presented with or are required to think up for themselves. When the cultural truisms are later exposed to strong persuasive attacks, they turn out to be much more resistant to persuasion, even when the arguments used in the attacking messages are different from those presented in the inoculation procedure. The theory was formulated in 1964 by the US psychologist William J(ames) McGuire (born 1925). *See also* attitude change.
[From Latin *inoculare, inoculatum* to implant, from *in* into + *oculus* an eye or a bud]

inositol *n*. A substance closely related to glucose that occurs in most body tissues, at high levels in people with *mania and at low levels in people with *depression. The richest dietary sources are fruits, nuts, beans, and grains. *Compare* antidepressant.
[From Greek *is, inos* a sinew + *-ite* indicating a part of the body *-ol* denoting a compound containing a hydroxyl group, from *(alcoh)ol*]

insanity *n*. Another name for *mental disorder, especially in legal contexts, where it refers specifically to conditions that impair one's ability to discharge one's legal responsibilities. *See also* McNaghten rules, mens rea. **insane** *adj*.

insanity of negation *n*. Another name for *Cotard's syndrome.

insight *n*. **1.** Clear and deep understanding or perception. **2.** The process by which the meaning or significance of a pattern or the solution of a problem suddenly becomes clear, often accompanied by an *aha experience. A famous and dramatic example is that of the ancient Greek mathematician and physicist Archimedes of Syracuse (?287–212 BC), who was asked by King Hiero II (308–216 BC) to determine whether his gold crown was alloyed with silver. Archimedes could not at first think how to perform such a test, but when getting into a bath that was full to its brim, he had an aha experience, realizing suddenly that a body heavier than water must displace its own volume of water when immersed, and that because silver is lighter than gold, a pound weight of gold/silver alloy must displace more water than a pound weight of gold, enabling the crown to be tested against a piece of pure gold of equal weight, whereupon (according to Vitruvius Pollio) he jumped out of the bath crying 'Eureka! Eureka!' (I've found it! I've found it!) and ran home naked to perform the experiment. **3.** The capacity to understand oneself, especially the abnormal or pathological nature of aspects of one's behaviour or mental experience that result from a *mental disorder; often used to distinguish *neurosis, in which insight is typically present, from *psychosis (1), in which it is typically absent. In *psychoanalysis, conscious understanding of unconscious reasons for maladaptive behaviour is believed to be curative in itself. *See also* Anton's syndrome, interpretation (2), problem-solving stages.

insomnia *n*. Inability to fall asleep or to maintain restful sleep, the condition usually being chronic. *Initial insomnia* (also called *sleep-onset insomnia*) is difficulty in falling asleep; *middle insomnia* is waking up in the middle of the night and having difficulty going back to sleep; and *terminal insomnia* is waking up at least two hours before one's normal waking time and being unable to fall asleep again. *See also* delayed sleep-phase syndrome, dyssomnias, fatal familial insomnia, primary insomnia. *Compare* hypersomnia, pseudoinsomnia. [From Greek *insomnus* sleepless, from *in-* not + *somnus* sleep + *-ia* indicating a condition or quality]

inspection time *n*. An aspect of *processing speed, usually measured with the help of *visual masking. A test stimulus consisting of two vertical lines is exposed very briefly on each trial and is immediately followed by a masking stimulus. The task is to judge which line was shorter, and a person's inspection time is usually taken as the minimum exposure duration (up to the onset of the masking stimulus) required for a predetermined level of accuracy, such as 90 per cent correct responses. Inspection time is consistently though weakly correlated (approximately $r = -0.30$) with psychometric measures of *intelligence, especially with performance subtests. **IT** *abbrev*.

instinct *n*. **1.** An *innate propensity to emit a relatively fixed *response to a stimulus. **2.** Any natural and apparently innate drive or motivation, such as those associated with sex,

hunger, and self-preservation. **3.** In *psychoanalysis, a dynamic force of biological origin, represented mentally by ideas and images having an emotional charge called *cathexis, generating psychological pressure and directing a person towards its aim. Sigmund Freud (1856–1939) originally identified it with *libido but later (beginning with the publication of his book *Beyond the Pleasure Principle* in 1920) with both *Eros and *Thanatos. The German word that Freud used was *Trieb*, which his translator James Strachey (1887–1967) rendered in English as *instinct*, but some scholars believe that *drive* would have been a better choice. Also called *instinctual drive* or simply *drive*. *See also* instinctual aim, instinctual source, instinctual object. **instinctive** or **instinctual** *adj*. [From Latin *instinctus* roused, from *instinguere* to instigate]

instinct, component *See* component instinct.

instinct, death *See* death instinct, Thanatos.

instinct, life *See* Eros, life instinct.

instinctual aim *n*. In *psychoanalysis, behaviour or activity that an *instinct (3) exerts pressure on a person to perform, performance of the behaviour resulting in resolution of internal tension. Sigmund Freud (1856–1939) introduced the distinction between the instinctual aim, the *instinctual object, and the *instinctual source in his book *Three Essays on the Theory of Sexuality* (1905). *See also* aim-inhibition.

instinctual component *n*. Another name for a *component instinct.

instinctual drive *n*. Another name for *instinct (3).

instinctual energy *n*. Energy associated with an *instinct (3).

instinctual object *n*. In *psychoanalysis, anything through which an *instinct (3) seeks to attain its *instinctual aim, including a person, a *part object, or either of these in a person's fantasy. It is not necessarily a physical object but rather an object in the sense of a phrase such as *object of her desire*. Sigmund Freud (1856–1939) introduced the distinction between the *instinctual aim, the instinctual object, and the *instinctual source in his book *Three Essays on the Theory of Sexuality* (1905). *See also* good object, object-cathexis, object-choice, object-relationship, primary object, splitting of the object, transitional object, whole object.

instinctual source *n*. In *psychoanalysis, the particular internal origin of an *instinct (3), being either the site of its origin, such as an *erotogenic zone, including a sexual organ, or the physiological process assumed to occur at such a site and to be experienced as excitation. Sigmund Freud (1856–1939) introduced the concept in 1905 in his book *Three Essays on the Theory of Sexuality* and developed it fully in 1915 in an article on 'Instincts and their Vicissitudes' (*Standard Edition*, XIV, pp. 117–40, at pp. 123, 132). *Compare* instinctual aim, instinctual object.

instrumental conditioning *n*. Another name for *operant conditioning.

insufficient reason *n*. The principle introduced by the English mathematician and Presbyterian clergyman Thomas Bayes (1702–61), and championed by the French mathematician Pierre Simon Laplace (1749–1827), according to which we are entitled to consider two events as equally probable if we have no reason to consider one more probable than the other. It enables *uncertainty (2) to be transformed into *risk (2) and provides a justification for *prior probabilities (2) in *Bayesian inference in the absence of other grounds for estimating them. Its critics have shown that it leads to contradictions, and they deny that anything can be inferred from ignorance. Also called the principle of *indifference*.

insula *n*. The large pyramid-shaped structure in the limbic system of the brain that lies deep between the opercula or lips of the lateral sulcus of each cerebral hemisphere and that is exposed by retracting the temporal lobe. The anterior part functions as the cortical *pain centre, and the posterior part is implicated in language functions. Also called the *island of Reil*.
[From Latin *insula* an island]

insulin *n*. A polypeptide *hormone that is secreted by the *islets of Langerhans in the pancreas and that lowers the concentration of *glucose in the blood. A deficiency of insulin leads to *diabetes mellitus. *See also* hypoglycaemia.
[From Latin *insula* an island (referring to the islets of Langerhans) + *-in(a)* indicating an organic compound]

insulin shock *n*. A formerly popular method of treating *schizophrenia and other disorders by injecting *insulin into the bloodstream to induce *hypoglycaemia, resulting in *coma. Also called *insulin coma*.

integral attribute *n*. An *attribute that is inherent in a *phenomenon, without which the phenomenon cannot occur or exist. For example, *amplitude is an integral attribute of any sound, because without amplitude there can be no sound wave and therefore no sound, but *frequency (1) is not an integral attribute of sound, because *noise (1) is sound without any definite frequency. In the visual modality, *lightness is an integral attribute of colour, but *saturation (1) is not. *Compare* separable attribute.

integral stimulus dimension *n*. An *integral attribute of any measurable aspect of a *stimulus (1). *Compare* separable stimulus dimension.

integrative agnosia *n*. Intact ability to recognize elements of perceptual forms with impaired ability to integrate the elements into perceptual wholes. *See also* agnosia.

intellect *n*. The faculty of reasoning and understanding, as distinct from feeling and wishing; a term used in general discourse for what in psychology is usually called *intelligence. In personality theory and psychometrics, another name for *openness to experience.
[From Latin *intellectus* understanding, from *intellegere* to understand, from *inter* between + *legere* to choose]

intellectualization *n*. In *psychoanalysis, a *defence mechanism involving excessive abstract thinking designed to block out disturbing emotions or conflicts, in therapy usually a device for evading the *fundamental rule of psychoanalysis. The concept was introduced by the Austrian-born British psychoanalyst Anna Freud (1895–1982) in her book *The Ego and the Mechanisms of Defence* (1937), her father never having used the term in writing.

intelligence *n*. Cognitive ability. In a symposium published in the *Journal of Educational Psychology* in 1921, fourteen of the world's leading authorities suggested definitions of intelligence, which included 'the ability to carry on abstract thinking' (Lewis Madison Terman, 1877–1956); 'the power of good responses from the point of view of truth or fact' (Edward Lee Thorndike, 1874–1949); and 'the capacity to inhibit an instinctive adjustment, the capacity to redefine the inhibited instinctive adjustment in the light of imaginally experienced trial and error, and the volitional capacity to realize the modified instinctive adjustment into overt behaviour to the advantage of the individual as a social animal' (Louis Leon Thurstone, 1887–1955). Since then, one of the most influential definitions was the one put forward in 1944 by the Romanian-born US psychologist David Wechsler (1896–1981): 'the aggregate or global capacity of the individual to act purposefully, to think rationally, and to deal effectively with his environment.' However, just as a triangle is defined simply as a plane figure with three angles and three sides, ignoring its many other interesting and important but non-defining properties, good lexicographic practice suggests that it may be best to define intelligence simply as cognitive ability. *Factor-analytic studies by the US psychologist Robert J(effrey) Sternberg (born 1949) and others have suggested that the major components of intelligence as it is conceived by experts and lay people are verbal intelligence, problem solving, and practical intelligence; but during the 1990s some authorities began to consider *emotional intelligence as another form of intelligence. The standard index of intelligence is the *IQ score. *See also* A/S ratio, crystallized intelligence, emotional intelligence, encephalization quotient, fluid intelligence, g, Guilford's cube, inspection time, intelligence test, multiple intelligences, nerve conduction velocity, N140, primary mental abilities, processing speed, progression index, P200, social intelligence, string length, triarchic theory of intelligence.
[From Latin *intelligere* to understand, from *inter* between + *legere* to choose]

intelligence quotient *See* IQ.

intelligence test *n*. A test designed to measure *intelligence, often but not invariably an *IQ test.

intension *n*. The sum of properties by which the referent or referents of a given word or expression are determined, including both defining and non-defining properties; thus, *having interior angles equal to 180 degrees* is part of the intension of the word *triangle*, although it is not part of the definition of that concept, and *suckling its young* and *having a pouch* are both parts of the intension of the word *marsupial*. It is distinguished from the *extension* of a word, expression, or concept, which consists of all those entities to which the word or expression applies or that fall under the concept: the extension of *wife of King Henry VIII* is precisely the set {Catherine of Aragon, Anne Boleyn, Jane Seymour, Anne of Cleves, Catherine Howard, Catherine Parr}. The distinction between intension and extension, which is close to the distinction between *connotation (2) and *denotation (2), was introduced by the French theologians/logicians Antoine Arnauld (1612–94) and Pierre Nicole (1625–95) in the *Port Royal Logic* in 1662, where intension was called *comprehension*. **intensional** *adj*.
[From Latin *intensus* stretched or given one's attention, from *intendere* to stretch forth or give one's attention to, from *in-* towards + *tendere* to stretch]

intentional forgetting *n*. Deliberately erasing something from memory. In *psychoanalysis, forgetting something as a consequence of *repression.

intentionality *n*. **1.** According to the German psychologist and philosopher Franz Brentano (1838–1917), the property of mental experiences whereby they refer to objects or entities outside themselves: it is impossible to hear without hearing a sound, to believe without believing a statement or a proposition, to hope without hoping for something, to strive without striving for a goal, to feel joy without feeling joyful about something, and so on (these examples are all Brentano's). The concept was introduced by Brentano in 1874 in his book *Psychologie vom empirischen Standpunkt* (Book II, Chapter I, section 5, pp. 125ff.) to distinguish psychological from

physical phenomena, which lack this property of outward-directedness. It is a key concept of *phenomenology. *See also* act psychology. **2.** The property of an action that is performed deliberately rather than accidentally or without purpose.
[From Latin *intentus* aim or intent, from *intendere* to stretch forth or give one's attention to, from *in-* towards + *tendere* to stretch]

intention tremor *n*. A form of *tremor characterized by fine rhythmic movements that tend to increase during voluntary movements, as in some cases of *alcohol dependence, *cerebellar syndrome, and *senile dementia. Also called *movement tremor*. *See also* delirium tremens. *Compare* parkinsonism, resting tremor.

interaction effect *n*. In statistics, a pattern of data obtained from multifactorial *analysis of variance (ANOVA) or *log-linear analysis in which the effect of an *independent variable or *factor (1) varies across levels of another independent variable, or across combinations of levels of other independent variables or factors. When this occurs, variation in the *dependent variable is not the result of a simple additive combination of the independent variables or factors. For example, suppose a well-practised skill is performed better in front of an audience than alone, whereas an unpractised skill is performed better alone than in front of an audience. In this case the independent variables or factors may be the audience condition and the level of practice, and the effect of the audience factor on the dependent variable varies across levels of the practice factor, leading to improved performance at one level of the practice factor (well practised) and worse performance at the other level (unpractised). In this case, performance is not a simple additive effect of audience condition and level practice. Interactions are notoriously difficult to interpret, and an *interaction graph is usually helpful. A *main effect*, in contrast to an interaction effect, is a significant difference between two or more means; a *two-way interaction* is a significant difference between two or more *differences* between means (as in the above example, in which one difference is positive and the other negative); a *three-way interaction* is a significant difference between two or more differences between two or more differences between means, and so on, but after

that it begins to become too complex to grasp or to depict graphically. *Compare* main effect.

interaction graph *n*. A diagram representing an *interaction effect in multifactorial *analysis of variance (ANOVA). For the simplest two-way interaction, the vertical axis represents scores on the *dependent variable, the horizontal axis different levels of one *independent variable, and each line on the graph a different level of another independent variable. If the lines are parallel, there is no interaction effect; if the lines cross or are non-parallel, then there is an interaction effect that can be tested for *statistical significance.

interactionism *n*. **1.** An approach to the *mind–body problem, a form of *dualism according to which events or processes in the mental and physical realms influence or interact with each other. *See also* epiphenomenalism. **2.** An interpretation of the contributions of *personality according to which human behaviour is dependent partly on internal personality factors, partly on external situational factors, and partly on interactions between the two. *Compare* situationist critique.

interaction process analysis *n*. A technique for studying interaction in small groups. Observers record the source and target of every expressive act and classify the acts into the following twelve categories: shows solidarity, shows tension release, agrees, gives suggestion, gives opinion, gives orientation, asks for orientation, asks for opinion, asks for suggestion, disagrees, shows tension, and shows antagonism. Analysis of protocols has revealed, among other things, two principal types of group leader, namely the task specialist and the social specialist, and leadership in groups is often shared between two people filling these roles. The technique was introduced in 1947 by the US social psychologist Robert Freed Bales (born 1916) and described in his book *Interaction Process Analysis: A Method for the Study of Small Groups* (1950). Bales initially studied meetings of Alcoholics Anonymous, the effectiveness of which he was anxious to understand. **IPA** *abbrev*.

interaural intensity difference *n*. Another name for a *sonic shadow. Also called a *binaural intensity difference*. **IID** *abbrev*.

interaural time difference n. A generic name for both *phase delay or *transient disparity. Also called a *binaural time difference*. **ITD** abbrev.

interblob See under blob.

intercorrelations n. The *correlations of several variables with one another.

interest inventory n. Any questionnaire designed to assess interests, including especially any *occupational interest inventory. See also Allport–Vernon–Lindzey Study of Values.

interference theory n. The proposition that forgetting is caused by *proactive interference and *retroactive interference. *Compare* decay theory.

interhemispheric fissure n. Another name for the *longitudinal fissure.
[From Latin *inter* between + English *hemisphere*]

interictal syndrome n. A condition sometimes observed in people with *temporal lobe epilepsy, characterized by intense productiveness, often in writing or artistic work, between *convulsions. Also called *Dostoevsky syndrome*.
[From Latin *inter* between + *ictus* struck, from *icere* to strike + *-alis* of or relating to]

interleukin n. A group of peptides present in white blood cells or leucocytes, produced mainly by neuroglial cells, that play a part in the *immune system by mobilizing *lymphocytes. **interleukin-1** n. An *interleukin produced by *macrophages and *monocytes that regulates immune responses by activating lymphocytes, and by playing a part in other reactions to infection and inflammation, and that increases sleep. **interleukin-2** n. An *interleukin that is produced by helper *T lymphocytes, after their activation by an *antigen, and that in the presence of interleukin-1 stimulates the production of T lymphocytes carrying antigen-specific receptors and plays a part in the production of *B lymphocytes and *macrophages. It is used in the treatment of cancer and AIDS. **interleukin-3** n. A substance involved in the maturation of *stem cell populations of *T lymphocytes.
[From Latin *inter* among + Greek *leukos* white, alluding to its presence among the white blood cells]

intermediary neuron n. Another name for an *interneuron

intermetamorphosis n. A *delusional misidentification in which a familiar person appears to change into someone else. *Compare* Capgras syndrome, Frégoli syndrome.
[From Latin *inter* between or among + Greek *meta* with or beside + *morphe* form + *-osis* indicating a process or state]

intermittent explosive disorder n. An *impulse-control disorder characterized by repeated outbursts of aggression, grossly out of proportion to the precipitating events or provocations, resulting in serious assaults or destruction of property. *See also* road rage.

intermittent reinforcement n. Another name for *partial reinforcement.

internal auditory canal n. A passageway located in the *temporal bone and containing the *vestibulocochlear nerve that transmits impulses from the *inner ear to the brain. Also called the *internal meatus*. *Compare* external auditory canal.

internal capsule n. Either of two neural pathways in the brain between the thalamus and the lenticular nucleus containing nerve fibres running from the thalamus to the left or right cerebral cortex and from the cerebral cortex to the thalamus, brainstem, and spinal cord. It is a common site for a *stroke.

internal consistency n. In psychometrics, an aspect of *reliability associated with the degree to which the items of a test measure the same *construct or *attribute. It is indexed by *Cronbach's alpha, the *Kuder–Richardson coefficient, or the *split-half reliability.

internal ear n. Another name for the *inner ear.

internal–external control of reinforcement n. Another name for *locus of control. **I–E** abbrev.

internal-external scale n. A 29-item questionnaire designed to measure *locus of control. The respondent chooses one statement that 'I believe more strongly' from each of the 29 pairs, 23 of the items measuring locus of control and the remaining six being fillers unrelated to locus of control. A typical item from the scale is: *I believe more strongly that: (a) Whether I make a success of my life is entirely up to me; (b) Success is a matter of being lucky enough to be in the right place at the right time*. Another typical item is: *I believe more strongly that: (a) Pressure groups can influence government decisions; (b) The government is beyond the influence of the ordinary person*. In both examples, (a) indicates internal and (b) external locus of control. The scale was introduced in an article in the journal *Psychological Monographs* in 1966 by the US psychologist Julian B(ernard) Rotter (born 1916). **I–E scale** *abbrev*.

internalization *n*. In *psychoanalysis, absorbing a relationship or an *instinctual object into one's mental apparatus, as when a child's relationship with an authoritarian father is internalized as the relationship between an *ego and a strict *superego. In *Kleinian analysis the term is used more broadly as simply another name for *introjection: fantasizing the absorption of a *whole object or a *part object. *See also* defensive technique. **internalize** *vb*.

internal meatus *n*. Another name for the *internal auditory canal.
[From Latin *meatus* a course]

internal rectus *n*. Another name for the medial *rectus muscle attached externally to the eyeball. *See under* rectus muscle.

internal reliability *n*. Another name for *internal consistency.

internal sense *n*. A generic name for *kinaesthesis, *proprioception, and *interoception.

internal validity *n*. The extent to which the conclusions of an empirical investigation are true within the limits of the research methods and subjects or participants used. *See also* validity. *Compare* ecological validity (1), external validity.

International Classification of Diseases *See* ICD-10.

International Phonetic Alphabet *n*. A set of symbols, based on the Roman alphabet but supplemented with modified Roman letters

and characters from other writing systems, designed for the representation of human speech sounds in all languages. The IPA, first published by the International Phonetic Association in 1888 and revised many times since then, is accepted as the standard phonetic alphabet almost universally except in the United States, where it is only slowly gaining acceptance. **IPA** *abbrev*.

Internet addiction syndrome *n*. A condition resembling an *impulse-control disorder, first identified in the US in 1994 and not included in *DSM-IV or *ICD-10, characterized by excessive or pathological Internet surfing, indicated by such signs and symptoms as being preoccupied with the Internet; recurrent dreams and fantasies about the Internet; lying to family members or therapists to conceal the extent of time spent online; attempting repeatedly and unsuccessfully to cut down or to stop spending time online, and becoming restless or irritable while doing so; using the Internet as an escape from worry or unhappiness; and jeopardizing a significant job, relationship, or educational opportunity by spending excessive time online. *See also* dataholic. *Compare* impulse-control disorders. **IAS** *abbrev*.

interneuron *n*. A neuron that is itself neither sensory nor motor but forms a synapse with an afferent and/or an efferent neuron and lies in the path of a *reflex arc, its axon not projecting outside the structure in which its cell body is located. Also called an *internuncial neuron*, an *intrinsic neuron*, an *intermediary neuron*, or a *relay cell*. *See also* reflex.
[From Latin *inter* between + Greek *neuron* a nerve]

internuncial *adj*. Interconnecting, of or relating to an *interneuron interposed between two other neurons.
[From Latin *inter* between + *nuntius* a messenger]

interoception *n*. Any form of sensation arising from stimulation of *interoceptors and conveying information about the state of the internal organs and tissues, blood pressure, and the fluid, salt, and sugar levels in the blood. *See also* internal sense. *Compare* exteroception, kinaesthesis, proprioception.
[From *inter(i)o(r) (re)ception*]

interoceptor *n*. A *sensory receptor, specialized for *interoception, that transmits impulses from organs or tissues within the body, excluding receptors in the vestibular system and in the tendons, muscles, and joints (which are *proprioceptors), but including other receptors in the internal organs, tissues, and blood vessels. *See* area postrema, baroreceptor, blood-flow receptor, Golgi tendon organ, muscle spindle, organum vasculosum lamina terminalis, osmoreceptor, stretch receptor, subfornical organ. *Compare* exteroceptor, proprioceptor. **interoceptive** *adj*.

interpersonal trust scale *n*. A scale developed by the US psychologist Julian B(ernard) Rotter (born 1916) for measuring the degree to which a person judges others to be believable or trustworthy.

interplexiform cell *n*. A type of cell in the *retina that conveys signals across the middle layer from the *inner plexiform layer to the *outer plexiform layer, in the opposite direction to the rest of the neural information flow in the retina, and whose functions are poorly understood.
[From Latin *inter* between *plexus* a network, from *plectere* to weave + *forma* a shape]

interposition *n*. The placement of something between other things; specifically (in psychology) one of the monocular cues of visual *depth perception, an object that appears in front of and overlapping another object being perceived as closer than the object that it occludes.
[From French *interposer* to interpose, from Latin *inter* between + French *poser* to place]

interpretation *n*. **1.** The act or process of explaining, elucidating, or clarifying, or the product of such activity. **2.** In *psychoanalysis, a process of decoding the latent meaning of a patient's speech and actions, thereby revealing *unconscious (1) conflicts, exposing the underlying wishes that maintain them, and allowing the patient to gain *insight (3). Sigmund Freud (1856–1939) first described it in 1900 in relation to dreams in his book *The Interpretation of Dreams* (*Standard Edition*, IV–V), where the *latent content of dreams is derived from its *manifest content through interpretation. *See also* active analysis, overinterpretation, passive analysis, reductive interpretation, resistance, third ear, working

through. *Compare* psychoanalytic construction. **3.** In *logic, the allocation of specific meanings to the terms of a purely abstract or formal system. **interpret** *vb*. **interpretational** *adj*.

interquartile range *n*. In descriptive statistics, a measure of the degree of dispersion, variability, or scatter in a group of scores, defined as the difference between the third and the first *quartiles. *Compare* probable error, range, semi-interquartile range, standard deviation, variance. **IQR** *abbrev*.

inter-rater reliability *n*. A measure of the consistency of ratings, equal to the correlation between the ratings given by different raters of the same people or stimuli.

interrupted time-series design *n*. A *quasi-experimental research design similar to a *one-group pretest–posttest design except that instead of a single pretest and a single posttest, the data consist of a *time series in the form of a sequence of baseline measurements, followed by a change in the independent variable, usually called an intervention, and then a sequence of post-intervention measurements. *Compare* non-equivalent groups design.

intersex condition *n*. A condition in which a person displays a mixture of both male and female physical forms, reproductive organs, and sexual behaviour.

intersexuality *n*. Another name for *intersex condition.

interspecific competition *n*. Competition between or among species. *Compare* intraspecific competition.
[From Latin *inter* between + *specificus* specific, from *species* appearance or kind, from *specere* to look]

interstimulus interval *n*. The time interval between the termination of one stimulus and the beginning of another. *Compare* stimulus onset asynchrony. **ISI** *abbrev*.

interstitial-cell-stimulating hormone *n*. Another name for *luteinizing hormone, especially in males. **ICSH** *abbrev*.
[From Latin *inter* within + *sistere* to stand]

intertectal commissure *n*. Another name for the *posterior cerebral commissure.
[So called because it lies between the two halves of the *tectum]

interval of uncertainty *n*. In *psychophysics, the range of stimulus differences that are detected between 25 per cent and 75 per cent of the time. **IU** *abbrev*.

interval scale *n*. A scale of measurement in which differences between values can be quantified in absolute terms but the zero point is fixed arbitrarily, familiar examples being Fahrenheit or Celsius temperature scales and calendar dates. In an interval scale, equal differences between scale scores correspond to equal differences in the *attribute being measured, but there is no score corresponding to the total absence of the attribute. *See also* measurement level, method of equal-appearing intervals, scale, unfolding technique. *Compare* absolute scale, log-interval scale, nominal scale, ordinal scale, ratio scale. [From Latin *intervallum* space between, from *inter* between and *vallum* a rampart]

intervening region *n*. In genetics, another name for an *intron.

intervening variable *n*. In a formal model, a *variable whose value is determined by a specified manipulation or combination of *independent variables and/or other intervening variables, without any hypotheses about the existence of unobserved entities or processes, and that plays a part in explaining the value of a *dependent variable, although it has no factual content apart from the empirical relationships that it summarizes. A typical example is the concept of broad *heritability (h^2), which is defined as the ratio of genetic variance V_G to total phenotypic variance V_P, so that, formally, h^2 (broad) $= V_G/V_P$. Another example is that of the *therapeutic ratio of a drug, defined as the ratio of the *median lethal dosage (LD-50) to the *median effective dosage (ED-50). *Hullian learning theory has scores of intervening variables. The term was introduced in 1938 by the US psychologist Edward C(hace) Tolman (1886–1959), and the distinction between hypothetical constructs and intervening variables was first made explicit in 1948 by the US psychologists Kenneth MacCorquodale (1919–85) and Paul Everett Meehl (born 1920)—*see* hypothetical construct.

interview *n*. A structured meeting in which a person is questioned as part of a process of choosing among candidates for a position, or a journalistic or other form of enquiry; more specifically a method of data collection involving face-to-face or telephone questioning of subjects or respondents by the researcher. An interview may be relatively structured or unstructured. *See also* depth interview, focus group.

intestine *n*. The section of the *alimentary canal between the stomach and the anus. *See also* large intestine, small intestine.
[From Latin *intestinum* gut, from *intestinus* internal]

intimacy versus isolation *n*. One of the crises in the developmental theory of the German-born *ego psychologist Erik H. Erikson (1902–94). *See* developmental crises.

intolerance of ambiguity *n*. A *cognitive style characterized by an inability to accept without discomfort situations or stimuli that allow alternative interpretations, and a preference for situations or stimuli that appear black and white to those that consist of shades of grey. It is often considered as characteristic of *authoritarianism.

intonation *n*. The distinctive modulation of vocal pitch in speech, functioning like punctuation to signal grammatical structure, as for example in the utterance *It's big, isn't it*, in which a rising pitch would be used to indicate a question and a falling pitch an assertion, and used also to express attitudes or emotions such as sarcasm, puzzlement, or anger.
intonology *n*. The study of *intonation.
[From Latin *intonare* to intone, from *in* in + *tonus* a tone + -*ation* indicating a process or condition]

intoxication *n*. The state of being inebriated or poisoned by a drug or other substance taken into the body. **intoxicant** *n*. Anything that causes *intoxication.
[From Latin *intoxicare* to poison, from *toxicum* a poison + -*ation* indicating a process or condition]

intracellular *adj*. Inside cells.
[From Latin *intra* within + *cella* a room, from *celare* to hide]

intracellular fluid *n*. Fluid inside the cells of the body, separated from the extracellular fluid by semipermeable cell membranes. *See also* osmosis, sodium pump. *Compare* extracellular fluid. **ICF** *abbrev.*

intracellular thirst *n*. A form of thirst arising from depletion of fluid within cells and triggered by *osmoreceptors (2), as after ingestion of salt, which accumulates in the extracellular fluid and creates *osmotic pressure, forcing fluid out of the cell. Also called *osmometric thirst* or *osmotic thirst*. *Compare* hypovolaemic thirst.

intraception *n*. Subjectivity and imagination. *See* anti-intraception, F scale.
[From Latin *intra* within + *capere, ceptum* to take + *-ion* indicating an action, process, or state]

intracortical *n*. Within the *cerebral cortex.
[From Latin *intra* within + *cortex* bark or outer layer + *-icalis* of, relating to, or resembling]

intracranial *n*. Inside the skull.
[From Latin *intra* within + *cranium* a skull, from Greek *kranion* a skull]

intrafusal *adj*. Of, relating to, or consisting of small muscle fibres, up to a dozen of which are enclosed in each *muscle spindle embedded within extrafusal muscle fibres of *skeletal muscles. They signal information about the degree of stretch of the muscle. *Compare* extrafusal.
[From Latin *intra* within + *fusus* a spindle]

intragenic region *n*. Another name for an *intron.

intralaminar nucleus *n*. Either of two tiny clusters of nerve cell bodies on each side of the dorsal thalamus that receive inputs from the cerebral hemispheres, brainstem, cerebellum, and spinal cord and that project to the striatum, being involved in higher motor control.
[From Latin *intra* within + *lamina* a plate or layer, so called because they are contained within the internal layers of white matter in the thalamus]

intransitive preferences *n*. Preferences violating the condition that if one alternative is preferred to a second, and the second is preferred to a third, then the first should be preferred to the third. The following is the simplest example of intransitive preferences: x is preferred to y, y to z, and z to x. It is often interpreted as necessarily irrational, but it can arise from the aggregation of rational individual preferences into a group preference ranking, as in *Condorcet's paradox, and it can even arise plausibly in an individual's preferences from a *lexicographic semiorder, or when multiple *attributes are involved, as in a person who rates three similarly priced cars, x, y, and z on three equally important attributes as follows:

	Speed	Comfort	Fuel Economy
x	excellent	satisfactory	good
y	good	excellent	satisfactory
z	satisfactory	good	excellent

This person evidently prefers x to y because it is better on two of the three equally valued attributes, y to z for the same reason, and z to x for the same reason. *See also* Arrow's impossibility theorem, cyclic preferences, decision theory, money pump. *Compare* transitive preferences.
[From Latin *in-* not + *transitivus* going over, from *transiens* going over, *transire* to pass over, from *trans* across + *ire* to go]

intraspecific competition *n*. Competition between or among organisms within a species. *Compare* interspecific competition.
[From Latin *intra* within + *specificus* specific, from *species* appearance or kind, from *specere* to look]

intrinsic light *n*. The impression of a dim cloud of light that is generated in complete darkness by the spontaneous activity of neurons in the visual system. Also called *dark light* or *idioretinal light*.

intrinsic neuron *n*. Another name for an *interneuron.

intrinsic nucleus *n*. Any of a number of clusters of nerve cell bodies within the *thalamus that do not relay information to the cortex but make connections with other thalamic nuclei.

intrinsic validity *n*. In psychometrics, a form of *validity that is said to exist when the test items necessarily or inherently measure the construct in question. For example, a test to measure children's ability to recognize and name letters of the alphabet has intrinsic validity if it involves presenting each of the letters in turn and asking the child to try to name it. The line between intrinsic validity on the one hand and *face validity or *consensual validity on the other is often blurred.

introjection *n.* In *psychoanalysis, a *defence mechanism whereby an *instinctual object is symbolically, or in fantasy, absorbed by a person, or instinctual energy is turned inward, as when a depressed person turns aggression back on the self. The term was introduced in 1909 by the Hungarian psychoanalyst Sandor Ferenczi (1873–1933) in an article entitled 'Introjection and Transference', where he contrasts it with *projection (1): 'Whereas the paranoiac expels from his ego the impulses that have become unpleasant, the neurotic helps himself by taking into the ego as large as possible a part of the outside world, making it the object of unconscious phantasies' (*First Contributions to Psycho-Analysis*, 1952, p. 43). *See also* identification (2), incorporation, internalization.

intron *n.* Any segment of *DNA that does not carry coded information about the synthesis of proteins and that is removed by *snurps before translation by *messenger RNA, such segments interrupting the coding sequences in most DNA molecules. Also called an *intragenic region*, an *intervening region*, or (especially in reference to long introns) *junk DNA*. *See also* repetitive DNA. *Compare* exon.
[From *intr(agenic) (regi)on* on the model of *codon*]

introspection *n.* A method of data collection in which observers examine, record, and describe their own internal mental processes and experiences. It can be traced back to the writings of the Greek philosopher Aristotle (384–322 BC), who described in his essay *On Memory* in his *Parva Naturalia* how the process of recalling *autumn* was preceded by related thoughts such as *milk*, *white*, *air*, *fluid*, and only then *autumn*. When psychology emerged as an independent empirical science in Germany in the 1880s, Wilhelm (Max) Wundt (1832–1920) and other experimental researchers regarded uncontrolled introspection as unreliable and introduced methods based on introspection by trained observers under experimental conditions. In 1913 the US psychologist John

B(roadus) Watson (1878–1958) launched an attack on introspection, declaring that psychology ought to be confined to the prediction and control of overt behaviour, but he advocated the study of reasoning processes via think-aloud methods, on which modern techniques of *protocol analysis are based. *See also* infinite regress, metacognition, phenomenology, structuralism (2). *Compare* free association. **introspect** *vb.*
[From Latin *intro-* towards the inside + *specere*, *spectum* to look + *-ion* indicating an action, process, or state]

introspectionism *n.* The doctrine that the fundamental research technique of psychology must be *introspection.

introversion *n.* A predominant concern with one's own thoughts and feelings rather than the outside world and social interaction, characterized by *traits such as reserve, passivity, and silence, the negative pole of one of the *Big Five personality factors, namely *extraversion. The term first appeared in the mid 17th century, in a purely descriptive sense of turning one's thoughts inwards in spiritual contemplation, and it was introduced in its modern psychological sense in 1910 by Carl Gustav Jung (1875–1961). Also called *introversion–extraversion* or *extraversion–introversion*. **introvert** *n.* A person prone to *introversion. **introverted** *adj.* Characterized by *introversion.
[From Latin *intro* towards the inside or within + *vertere* to turn]

intrusion *n.* The insertion of a speech sound, especially in *allegro speech, between two syllables, neither of which contains the sound when the syllable is spoken in isolation, or the letter representing it in that position, such as the /r/ often heard in such phrases as *the idea(r) of it*, *law(r) and order*, *India(r) and Pakistan*, *visa(r) application*, and *the Shah(r) of Iran*. *Compare* linking r.

intuition *n.* Immediate understanding, knowledge, or awareness, derived neither from perception nor from reasoning. Immediate knowledge of a *concept exists when a person can apply the concept correctly but cannot state the rules of its application; this form of intuition has been shown experimentally in studies of *concept formation. The Chomskyan notion of *competence

(2), for example, implies intuitive knowledge of grammatical concepts. Immediate awareness of the truth of a *proposition (1) (*I have an intuition that I will win the lottery today*) is essentially an unjustified *opinion, in contradistinction to a *belief or an item of *knowledge. *Compare* attuition. **intuitive** *adj.*

[From Latin *intuitio* a contemplation, from *intueri* to gaze at, from *tueri* to look at]

intuitive physics *n.* Assumptions about the motion of objects that are commonly held but that sometimes violate the known laws of Newtonian mechanics, as in the following three examples. If a person drops a ball from an outstretched hand while walking briskly, then the ball will continue moving forward until it hits the ground approximately alongside the walker, but a majority of people who have been questioned believe that the ball will drop straight down and will hit the ground directly below the point at which it was released. If a stone is tied to a string and whirled around one's head, and the string suddenly breaks, then the horizontal motion of the stone will be a straight line at a tangent to its original circular path, but many people believe that it will continue along a curved path. If a bullet dropped from shoulder height takes about half a second to reach the ground, then the same bullet fired horizontally at shoulder height from a high-powered rifle will also take about half a second to reach the ground, but many people falsely believe that it will take much longer. Such misconceptions embedded in intuitive physics are believed to be influenced by the discredited medieval impetus theory of motion. Also called *naive physics. See also* knowledge representation.

intuitive type *n.* One of the subsidiary personality types in *analytical psychology. *See* function type.

invariable hue *n.* Any colour that is not markedly affected by changes in the brightness of illumination, notably the *psychological primary colours. *See also* Bezold–Brücke phenomenon.

inventory *n.* Any list or schedule of items. In psychometrics, a *questionnaire or checklist usually functioning as a self-report test of abilities, aptitudes, or intelligence. Tests designed to measure interests, attitudes, personality traits, preferences, and psychological attributes are also sometimes called inventories, but tests designed to measure abilities, aptitudes, and intelligence are usually called questionnaires.

[From Latin *inventorium* a list of things found, from *invenire, inventum* to find or come upon, from *in* on + *venire* to come]

inverse square law *n.* The principle according to which the intensity of a wave, including a light wave or a sound wave, decreases in proportion to the square of the distance from its source.

invertebrate *n.* **1.** Any animal without a backbone, comprising all those not classified as *vertebrates (1). *adj.* **2.** Without a backbone; hence, figuratively, weak, indecisive, or lacking in courage or conviction.

[From Latin *in-* not + *vertebra* a spinal joint, from *vertere* to turn]

inverted Oedipus complex *n.* In *psychoanalysis, sexual desire for the same-sex parent and hatred of the opposite-sex parent. *See under* Oedipus complex.

inverted qualia *n.* A hypothetical state of affairs in which one person experiences *qualia in the opposite way to another, as would be the case if one person always experienced as red those stimuli that another always experienced as green. The possibility of inverted qualia, and the apparent impossibility of knowing if they exist, have been used by philosophers to argue that mental experiences are not reducible to physical states or events.

inverting spectacles *n.* Eyeglasses incorporating *prisms that have the effect of inverting the images projected on the retinas and the visual images seen by the wearer, first worn by the US psychologist George Malcolm Stratton (1865–1957) in an experiment performed in 1895 and published in the journal *Psychological Review* in 1897. Stratton wore the spectacles, which in that case inverted the visual field and also reversed left and right, continuously during waking hours for seven days, and towards the end of this time the world looked almost normal to him, a finding that refuted the view held by some people at the time that an inverted retinal image was necessary for perceiving the world the right way up. *See also* prism adaptation.

investigative psychology *n.* A branch of *criminological psychology in which psychological principles are applied to the investigation of crimes and the apprehension of criminals, especially serial murderers and rapists. The pattern of behaviour of serial criminals sometimes enables an investigative psychologist to engage in *criminal profiling.

in vitro *adj.* Of or relating to biological processes or experiments that occur outside the organism in artificial environments. *Compare* in vivo.
[Latin: in glass, alluding to test-tubes]

in vitro fertilization *n.* Fertilization of an *ovum by a *spermatozoon *in vitro before implanting it in a woman's uterus. **IVF** *abbrev.*

in vivo *adj.* Of or relating to biological processes or experiments that occur in living organisms. *Compare* in vitro.
[Latin: in living]

in vivo desensitization *See under* systematic desensitization.

involuntary muscle *n.* Any muscle controlling automatic functions and not under voluntary control, usually (with the notable exception of *cardiac muscle) consisting of *smooth muscle. *See also* muscle. *Compare* voluntary muscle.

involutional depression *n.* A form of *depression occurring in both sexes during the *menopause or in middle life, with feelings of anxiety, futility, and guilt. Also called *involutional melancholia*. *Compare* involutional psychosis.
[From Latin *involutum* rolled up, from *involvere* to roll up + *-ion* indicating an action, process, or state + *-alis* of or relating to]

involutional psychosis *n.* A variant form of *involutional depression accompanied by *persecutory delusions.

iodopsin *n.* The violet *cone pigment in the retina of the eye that was the first cone pigment studied chemically; also, a generic name for any cone pigment, though this sense

is avoided in careful usage. Also called *visual violet*.
[From *iodine* + Greek *ops* an eye + *-ine* indicating an organic compound, so called because the element iodine is violet in colour]

ion *n.* An electrically charged particle that is either a *cation, having lost one or more electrons and therefore carrying a positive electrical charge, or an *anion, having gained one or more electrons and therefore carrying a negative electrical charge. The movement of ions across cell membranes is the main mechanism of electrical signalling in the nervous system. *See also* action potential, ion channel.

ionization *n.* The production of *ions. **ionize** *vb.* To produce *ions or turn into ions.
[From Greek *ion* going, from *ienai* to go]

ion channel *n.* A pore in the *cell membrane of a neuron allowing passive flow across it of particular *ions or groups of ions when it opens in response to a specific stimulus, resulting in either *depolarization or *hyperpolarization of the neuron, ion channels being divided broadly into *anion channels and *cation channels. *See also* action potential, calcium channel, chemically gated ion channel, sodium channel, voltage-gated ion channel.

ionizing radiation *n.* Radiation such as X-ray or gamma-ray radiation of sufficiently high energy to cause *ionization.

ionophore *n.* A chemical compound capable of combining with an *ion and transporting it across a biological membrane. *See also* active transport, carrier protein.
[From *ion* + Greek *-phoros* carrying, from *pherein* to bear]

Iowa Manifest Anxiety Scale *n.* Another name for the *Manifest Anxiety Scale.

iproniazid *n.* An *antidepressant drug, the first of the *monoamine oxidase inhibitors (MAOIs), originally developed in 1951 for the treatment of tuberculosis. Also called *Marsilid* (trademark).
[From *i(so)niazid* an earlier compound used for treating tuberculosis + *pro(pyl)* indicating a compound containing the monovalent group C_3H_7]

ipsative *adj.* In psychometrics, a property of a multi-score measuring instrument in which responses that increase one of the scores necessarily reduce one or more of the others, so that the various scores must be interpreted relative to one another rather than in absolute terms. For example, the *Edwards Personal Preference Schedule (EPPS) measures 15 needs, but by endorsing items pertaining to certain needs, a respondent necessarily rejects items pertaining to others, and it is impossible to score high (or low) on all the needs. *Compare* normative (2).

[From Latin *ipso facto* by that very fact, so called because a high score on one scale by that very fact implies a lower score on another]

ipsilateral *adj*. On, pertaining to, or affecting the same side of the body. *Compare* contralateral.

[From Latin *ipse* self + *lateralis* of or relating to a side, from *lateris* a side]

IQ *abbrev*. Intelligence quotient, an index of *intelligence having a *normal distribution with a mean of 100 and a *standard deviation of 15 (usually). As a consequence, about 68 per cent of IQ scores in a population fall between 85 (one standard deviation below the mean) and 115 (one standard deviation above the mean), about 95 per cent fall between 70 and 130, about 99.74 per cent between 55 and 145, and so on. The concept was first proposed in 1912 by the German psychologist (Louis) William Stern (1871–1938), who defined it as *mental age (MA) divided by actual or *chronological age (CA): IQ = MA/CA, and that is how it came to be called a quotient. In 1916 the US psychometrician Lewis M(adison) Terman (1877–1956) introduced the convention of multiplying the ratio by 100, to eliminate unwanted decimals and to express IQ as a percentage of chronological age, so that IQ = (MA/CA) × 100, and this means that a score of 100 is average for the age group by definition. That definition was used until the Romanian-born US psychologist David Wechsler (1896–1981) introduced the modern statistical definition, sometimes called the *deviation IQ because it is based on standard deviations, in 1939. *See also* developmental quotient, genius, norm-referenced test, ratio IQ. *Compare* emotional quotient, social quotient.

IQ test *n*. An *intelligence test that yields *IQ scores. *See also* norm-referenced test.

iris *n*. The opaque contractile diaphragm suspended in *aqueous humour between the cornea and the crystalline lens of the eye, surrounding and controlling the variable diameter of the *pupil, attached around its rim to the *ciliary body, its deeply pigmented appearance determining the colour of the eye, containing the *dilator pupillae* muscle that contracts the iris and thus dilates the pupil and the *sphincter pupillae* muscle that expands the iris and thus constricts the pupil. *See also* glaucoma. **irises** or **irides** *pl*.

[From Greek *iris* a rainbow]

irkunii *See* latah.

irradiation *n*. **1.** The act or process of treating something with electromagnetic waves or beams of particles. **2.** The name used in the literature of art criticism for what psychologists call *Mach bands. **3.** A shortened name for the *irradiation illusion.

[From *ir-* intensifier + Latin *radiatus* rayed, from *radiare* to shine + *-ation* indicating a process or condition]

irradiation illusion *n*. Any visual illusion arising from the fact that light areas of an image tend to appear larger than dark areas (see illustration), a classic example being the *Helmholtz illusion. *See also* star illusion.

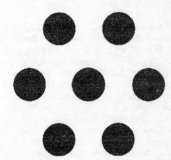

Irradiation illusion. The diameter of the discs is the same as the distance between them.

irrational type *n*. One of the basic personality types in *analytical psychology. *See* function type.

irritable bowel syndrome *n*. A chronic condition of recurrent abdominal pain, with constipation or diarrhoea, without any known organic cause and poorly understood.

irritable mood *n.* An irascible *mood (1) of angry impatience and hasty temper in which a person is easily annoyed or roused to anger or aggression.

Isakower phenomenon *n.* A type of *hypnagogic image in which a soft, doughy mass appears to be moving towards one's face. It was first reported in 1938 by the Austrian psychoanalyst Otto Isakower (1899–1972), who attributed it to a revival of the infantile experience of feeding at the mother's breast.

ischaemia *n.* Obstruction of the flow of blood to an organ or tissue of the body. Also spelt *ischemia*. **ischaemic** or **ischemic** *adj.*
[From Greek *ischein* to restrain + *haima* blood + *-ia* indicating a condition or quality]

ischaemic pain *n.* Pain induced by applying a tourniquet to the arm just above the elbow to obstruct the flow of blood, then squeezing a hand-exercising device for a minute or two. When the exercising stops, pain begins to mount and typically becomes unbearable after about eight minutes. It is used in experimental studies of pain because it causes no permanent tissue damage. US *ischemic pain*. *See also* algesimeter, cold pressor pain, dolorimeter.

Ishihara test *n.* A popular test for the detection and characterization of *colour-blindness or *colour deficiency, consisting of a series of coloured plates each composed of small blobs of different colours closely packed together, each plate having a large numeral clearly visible to viewers with normal colour vision but invisible to those with a form of colour deficiency associated with that plate, the pattern of responses across the complete set of plates enabling the form of colour deficiency to be specified reasonably precisely. *See also* pseudo-isochromatic. *Compare* Holmgren test, Stilling test.
[Named after the Japanese ophthalmologist Shinobu Ishihara (1897–1963) who devised it]

island of Reil *n.* Another name for the *insula.
[Named after the Dutch-born German physician Johann Christian Reil (1759–1813) who drew attention to it]

islets of Langerhans *n.* Groups of endocrine glands in the *pancreas that secrete *insulin and *glucagon into the bloodstream, and whose failure leads to *diabetes mellitus. Also called *islands of Langerhans*.
[Named after the German pathologist Paul Langerhans (1847–88) who discovered them]

isocarboxazid *n.* A *monoamine oxidase inhibitor (MAOI), derived from *hydrazine, used as an *antidepressant drug. Also called *Marplan* (trademark).

isocortex *n.* Another name for the *neocortex.
[From Greek *isos* equal or the same + Latin *cortex* bark or outer layer]

isogenic *adj.* Derived from the same source, as are organs derived from the same embryonic tissue. Also written *isogenous*.
[From Greek *isos* equal or the same + *genein* to produce + *-ikos* of, relating to, or resembling]

isogloss *n.* A line on a map enclosing an area within which a particular linguistic *feature (1) is found. Various types of isogloss are distinguished: an *isophone* is a feature of pronunciation, an *isolex* an item of vocabulary, an *isomorph* a feature of word-formation, and an *isoseme* a particular word meaning.
[From Greek *isos* equal + *glossa* a tongue]

isolating language *n.* A language such as Chinese, Vietnamese, and Samoan in which words are invariable, there are no inflections or changeable endings, and grammatical relations are indicated by word order. English has some features of an isolating language, as shown by the two sentences *The burglar killed the woman* and *The woman killed the burglar*. Also called an *analytic language* or a *root language*. *Compare* agglutinative language, inflecting language.

isolating mechanism *n.* A topographic, ecological, physical, or psychological barrier that prevents breeding between two populations and thereby allows differentiation into distinct *taxonomic groups and that sometimes causes *speciation to occur.

isolation *n.* The act or process of separating or placing apart; in reproductive biology, the prevention of interbreeding between populations resulting from one or more *isolating mechanism.

isolation effect n. Another name for the *von Restorff effect.

isolation of affect n. In *psychoanalysis, a *defence mechanism in which *emotion is detached from an idea and rendered unconscious, leaving the idea bland and emotionally flat. It is especially important in *obsessive–compulsive disorder, and in non-disordered people it most often occurs following a traumatic experience. The mechanisms by which the detachment is effected include repetitive intrusive thoughts and ritualistic behaviour. Sigmund Freud (1856–1939) expressed his ideas about isolation most clearly in his book *Inhibitions, Symptoms and Anxiety* (1926, *Standard Edition*, XX, pp. 77–175, at pp. 120–2). Also called *isolation. See also* decathexis.

isoluminant adj. Having uniform light intensity, pertaining to visual stimuli in which shapes or forms are defined by variations in colour without any contrasts in *lightness. If red and green stripes in motion on a television screen are adjusted so that they are isoluminant, then although the viewer can see that they have changed position from one moment to the next, the sensation of movement is either greatly reduced or entirely eliminated, because information about movement is processed by the colour-blind *magnocellular system; and for the same reason, binocular *stereopsis and the other binocular and monocular cues used for *depth perception do not function with isoluminant stimuli, which invariably appear flat and two-dimensional. Also called *equiluminant. See also* dark focus. **isoluminance** n.
[From Greek *isos* equal or the same + Latin *lumen* light]

isomorphism n. **1.** A one-to-one correspondence between the elements of two or more sets or classes and between the sums or products of the elements of one set and the sums or products of the equivalent elements of the other set. A typical isormorphism exists between the Arabic numerals 1, 2, 3, 4, . . . and the Roman numerals I, II, III, IV, ... **2.** A similarity in form or structure between two or more substances or entities, including abstract structures or problems that look superficially different but turn out, on analy-

sis, to be different versions of the same problem. *See also* Boolean. **3.** The doctrine of *Gestalt psychology according to which a mental experience such as a perception is invariably accompanied by a neurophysiological *representation (1) that is similar to it in structure. *See also Prägnanz.* **isomorph** n. Anything that exhibits *isomorphism with something else. *See also* isogloss. **isomorphic** adj. Manifesting *isomorphism. Also called *isophorphous*.
[From Greek *isos* equal or the same + *morphe* a shape or form + -*ismos* indicating a state or condition]

isophonic contour n. Another name for an *equal-loudness contour.
[From Greek *isos* equal or the same + *phonikos* of or relating to sound, from *phone* a voice or sound + -*ikos* of, relating to, or resembling]

isoquinoline n. Any of a number of nitrogenous bases that can be formed from catecholamines and indoleamines and that, when treated with formaldehyde gas, fluoresce under ultraviolet light, the wavelength of the emitted light depending on the specific catecholamine or indoleamine involved, providing a method of tracking these neurotransmitters in the nervous system.
[From Greek *isos* equal or the same + *quinoline*, from Spanish *quina* kinchoma bark, from Quechua *kina* bark]

isotonia n. The state or condition of equal tone or tension in two or more muscles. *See* isotonic (1). *Compare* hypertonia, hypotonia.

isotonic adj. **1.** Of, relating to, or comprising two or more muscles that are equally tense. *Compare* hypertonic (1), hypotonic (1). **2.** Of or relating to two or more solutions having equal concentration and hence exerting the same *osmotic pressure as each other, such as a 0.9 per cent sodium chloride (salt) solution and the *intracellular fluid of the body. *See also* osmosis. *Compare* hypertonic (2), hypotonic (2).
[From Greek *isos* equal or the same + *tonos* tension + -*ikos* of, relating to, or resembling]

isotropic adj. Having the same properties in all directions or with respect to all axes. *Compare* anisotropic. **isotropism** or **isotropy** n.

[From Greek *isos* equal or the same + *tropos* a turn, from *trapein* to turn]

Issawi's law of social motion *n*. The following proposition: 'In any dispute, the intensity of feeling is inversely proportional to the value of the stakes at issue. That is why academic politics are so bitter.' It was first published by the Egyptian-born US economist Charles Philip Issawi (1916–2000) in his book *Issawi's Laws of Social Motion* (1973), although it had been formulated earlier by the US political scientist Wallace Stanley Sayre (1905–72), without written publication, and is also called *Sayre's law*.

item analysis *n*. In psychometrics, a set of techniques for determining the psychometric properties of test items, including the *discriminating power of attitude scale items or the correlation of item scores with an external criterion.

item bias *n*. In psychometrics, a form of *test bias restricted to specific test items.

item characteristic curve *n*. Another name for an item response function. *See* item response theory.

item discrimination index *n*. In psychometrics, a measure of the extent to which test respondents who are known to be high on the attribute being measured exhibit different responses to a test item than people who are known to be low on the attribute. It is a measure of the *discriminating power of the item.

Item Group Checklist *n*. A list of *signs (1) and *symptoms used in evaluating patients with mental disorders as part of the *SCAN system. **IGC** *abbrev*.

item response curve *n*. Another name for an item response function. *See* item response theory.

item response theory *n*. An approach to the theory of psychological testing based on the assumption that the probability of a particular response to a test item is a joint function of one or more characteristics of the individual respondent and one or more characteristics of the test item. The relationship of these parameters to the probability of a particular response is defined by an *item response function*, and their values are estimated from the observable responses of respondents to the test item. It is the principal alternative to *classical test theory. Also called *latent trait theory*. *See also* Rasch scale. **IRT** *abbrev*.

I–thou relation *n*. A term coined in 1923 by the Austrian theologian and philosopher Martin Buber (1878–1965) in his book *Ich und du* (I and Thou) to denote a relationship based on mutuality and reciprocity rather than utilitarian objectives.

Jacksonian epilepsy *n.* A form of *epilepsy that is associated with abnormal neuronal activity in a localized area of the brain and that typically begins with spasmodic contractions in a finger, toe, or corner of the mouth and then spreads throughout the body, usually with loss of *consciousness. Also called *focal epilepsy* or *focal seizure*.
[Named after the English neurologist J(ohn) Hughlings Jackson (1835–1911) who studied it]

Jackson's principle *n.* The notion that deterioration of psychological functions through mental disorders or neurological impairments retraces in reverse the order of evolutionary development, so that the most recently evolved are the first to be lost. Also called *Jackson's law*. *Compare* Ribot's law.
[Formulated by the English neurologist J(ohn) Hughlings Jackson (1835–1911)]

Jacobson's organ *n.* Another name for the *vomeronasal organ.
[Named after the Danish anatomist Ludvig Levin Jacobson (1783–1843) who discovered it]

Jacobson's progressive relaxation *n.* Another name for *progressive relaxation.
[Named after the US physician Edmund Jacobson (1888–1983) who introduced it in 1938]

jactation *n.* Jerky, convulsive bodily movements characteristic of severe fevers, some mental disorders, and neurological damage to the *subthalamic nucleus. *See also* ballism.
[From Latin *iactare* to throw + *-ation* indicating a process or condition]

jamais vu *n.* A form of *paramnesia (1) characterized by an erroneous belief of having never before seen or experienced something that one has in reality encountered before. *Compare* déjà vu.
[From French *jamais* never + *vu* seen]

James–Lange theory *n.* The proposition that *emotions are caused by bodily sensations. It was first propounded by the US psychologist William James (1842–1910) in the journal *Mind* in 1884 and most famously expounded in his *Principles of Psychology* (1890): 'Our natural way of thinking . . . is that the mental perception of some fact excites the mental affection called the emotion, and that this latter state of mind gives rise to the bodily expression. My thesis, on the contrary, is that *the bodily changes follow directly the perception of the exciting fact, and that our feeling of the same changes as they occur IS the emotion*. . . . We feel sorry because we cry, angry because we strike, afraid because we tremble' (volume 2, p. 449, italics in original). The Danish psychologist Carl (Georg) Lange (1834–1900) independently put forward a somewhat similar theory in his book *Om Sindsbevägelser* in 1885, although Lange's theory places no emphasis on emotion as a mental state, equating emotion with the bodily (especially visceral) events themselves. The main problem with the theory, first pointed out in 1927 by the US physiologist Walter Bradford Cannon (1871–1945), is that the physiological changes accompanying qualitatively different emotions are often very similar. *Compare* Cannon–Bard theory. *See also* cognitive–appraisal theory.

Japanese writing *See* kana, kanji.

jargon *n.* **1.** The specialized language associated with a particular profession or field of activity. *See also* psychobabble, register (2). **2.** In developmental psychology, an unintelligible but well-articulated utterance of a child

learning to speak. **3.** Meaningless gibberish.
See also jargon aphasia.
[French *jargon*, origin obscure]

jargon aphasia *n.* A form of *fluent aphasia*
characterized by a copious flow of unintelligible speech. Jargon-aphasic speech may be
subdivided into semantic jargon, in which ordinary words are strung together to form unintelligible utterances, such as *automatic
winding voice and the very very recording,* and
phonemic jargon involving neologisms, such
as *I've not norter with the verker. See also* aphasia.

Jastrow illusion *n.* A visual illusion in which
two identical tapering annular or ring
segments placed one above the other appear
unequal in size (see illustration).
[Named after the Polish-born US psychologist
Joseph Jastrow (1863–1944) who first published it in 1891]

Jastrow illusion. The two figures are identical.

jealous delusional disorder *n.* A type of
*delusional disorder in which the central
theme of the *delusion is that the sexual
partner is being unfaithful.

jealousy, morbid *n.* Another name for
*jealous delusional disorder.

Jerusalem syndrome *n.* A non-technical
name for a condition not infrequently affecting Christian pilgrims to Jerusalem who develop (usually) transient *delusions of being
biblical personalities such as Jesus Christ,
John the Baptist or, worryingly for respectable
Israeli guest-houses, Mary Magdalene.

jet lag *n.* A condition of fatigue and disorientation brought about by travelling across several time zones in a short period, especially
in an eastward direction, resulting in a mis-

match between exogenous temporal cues
and endogenous *circadian rhythms. *See also*
melatonin. **jet-lagged** *adj.*

Jimmy *n.* A nickname used by psychologists to
refer to the best-selling textbook *Psychology:
Briefer Course* (1892) by the US psychologist
William James (1842–1910). His monumental
two-volume *Principles of Psychology* appeared
in 1890, after a gestation period of 12 years,
and comments such as *You'll find it in James*
were so common that the book gradually
came to be known as *James.* When the
abridged version appeared in 1892, it was immediately nicknamed *Jimmy.*

jinjinia bemar *See* koro.

jiryan *See* dhat.

job analysis *n.* In *personnel psychology, the
process of determining the characteristics of
a job and the *attributes required to perform
it for purposes of selection and placement of
employees, evaluation of employee productivity for purposes of promotion, and design of
training programmes for employees. It usually begins with a *job description*—a detailed description, often agreed between management
and workforce, of the work normally done
by a person carrying out the job, including all
relevant duties and responsibilities. The next
step is the construction of a *job specification*—
a record of the work that a person in the
job ought ideally to do. The final step is
the specification of a set of *job requirements*—
skills, competencies, and qualifications
needed by a person to perform the job
satisfactorily. The list of job requirements may
be viewed as a distillation of the personal
factors that are important in carrying out
the work.

Job Descriptive Index *n.* A scale used widely
in *personnel psychology to measure five
major factors associated with *job satisfaction: the nature of the work itself, wages and
salaries, attitudes towards supervisors, relations with co-workers, and opportunities
for promotion. **JDI** *abbrev.*

job satisfaction *n.* In *personnel psychology
and *industrial/organizational psychology
or *occupational psychology, the degree to
which employees are contented with their

jobs. It tends to be low when experience in a job fails to live up to expectations, although the same work might produce higher levels of job satisfaction among employees with more realistic expectations. Low job satisfaction leads to high absenteeism and labour turnover, but the relationship between job satisfaction and productivity is not straightforward. *See also* Job Descriptive Index.

Jocasta complex *n.* In *psychoanalysis, sexual desire of a mother for her son. *Compare* Oedipus complex.
[Named after Jocasta, Queen of Thebes in Greek mythology, who married Oedipus without realizing that he was her son]

John Henry effect *n.* A tendency for members of the *control group in certain experiments to adopt a competitive attitude towards the *experimental group, thereby negating their status as controls. In an industrial setting, for example, if members of the experimental group are provided with a powerful new tool, members of the control group may treat this as a challenge and, using the old tool, may try to beat the experimental group members in productivity.
[Named after John Henry, an enormously strong and hard-working African–American railroad worker and folk tale hero of the late 19th century, possibly based on a real person]

joint *n.* A place where two things, especially bones, meet, allowing a hingelike movement. Also, a common street name for a hand-rolled cigarette containing *cannabis.
[Perhaps from *joint* American slang for penis, alluding to its appearance]

joint sense *n.* A form of *proprioception and *kinaesthesis mediated by receptors in the joints and stimulated by flexion. *See also* Golgi tendon organ, Pacinian corpuscle.

Jost's law *n.* **1.** The proposition that if two learnt associations are of equal strength but of different durations, then repetition will increase the strength of the older one more than that of the more recent one. **2.** The proposition that if two learnt associations are of equal strength but of different durations, then the older one will decay more slowly than the more recent one.
[Named after the German psychologist Adolph Jost (1874–1920) who propounded

both laws in an article in the journal *Zeitschrift für Psychologie* in 1897]

Julesz stereogram *n.* Another name for a *random-dot stereogram.
[Named after the Hungarian-born US radar engineer and psychologist Bela Julesz (born 1928) who invented it in 1960]

jumping gene *n.* A plasmid, transposon, or other fragment of DNA that can migrate to a gene locus from somewhere else, sometimes causing a mutation and disrupting normal gene function.

Jungian *adj.* Of or relating to the school of *psychoanalysis founded in 1913 by the Swiss psychologist Carl Gustav Jung (1875–1961). *See* analytical psychology.

Jungian analysis *n.* A form of *psychoanalysis based on *Jungian theories or *analytical psychology.

junk *n.* Rubbish. Also, a common street name for *heroin.
[From the obsolete word *jonke* useless old rope]

junk DNA *n.* Long sections of *DNA that consist of highly repetitive non-coding *introns having no apparent effect on the *phenotype but having important uses in *genetic fingerprinting. *See also* repetitive DNA.

junkie *n.* An informal name for a drug user, especially an injecting heroin user.

just noticeable difference *n.* Another name for a *difference threshold. **jnd** *abbrev.*

just world hypothesis *n.* The widespread but false belief that the world is essentially fair, so that the good are rewarded and the bad are punished. One consequence of this belief is that people who suffer misfortunes are assumed to deserve their fates: a person involved in a traffic accident must have been driving carelessly, a victim of burglary could not have taken adequate precautions, a woman who was raped must have acted provocatively and led her attacker on, and so on, and even the victims often blame themselves. This phenomenon, which is usually interpreted as a consequence of the *illusion of control, was first identified and named by the Canadian psychologist Melvin J. Lerner in an article in the *Journal of Personality and Social Psychology* in 1965. *See also* blaming the victim, Just World Scale.

Just World Scale *n.* A questionnaire designed to measure the extent to which the respondent believes in a just world. It contains statements such as *Basically, the world is a just place*; *When parents punish their children, it is almost always for good reasons*; and *By and large, people get what they deserve*. It was designed by the US psychologist Zick Rubin (born 1944) and the English-born US psychologist (Letitia) Anne Peplau (born 1945) and was published by them in two articles in the *Journal of Social Issues* in 1973 and 1975. *See also* just world hypothesis.

kainic acid *n*. A neurotoxic amino acid that is found in the Japanese red alga or seaweed *Digenia simplex* and that acts as a powerful central nervous system *stimulant by potentiating the neurotransmitter *glutamate, causing destruction to postsynaptic cells with glutamate receptors.
[From Japanese *kainin-so* red alga]

kairomone *n*. A *pheromone or *allomone that has a detrimental affect on the animal that emits it, for example, a chemical that attracts not only mates but also predators.
[From Greek *kairos* opportunity + *horman* to stir up or urge on]

kakosmia *See* cacosmia.

Kamin effect *n*. The finding that, after *avoidance conditioning, an animal tested repeatedly shows a U-shaped performance curve, performing well at first, then performing much worse after about an hour, then finally performing well again after about two hours.
[Named after the US psychologist Leon J. Kamin (born 1927) who discovered it]

kana *n*. A syllabic writing system, used in conjunction with *kanji in Japanese writing. It consists of two written forms: *hiragana*, used to express particles and grammatical distinctions, is based on Chinese cursive script and is widely used in newspapers and general literature, and *katakana*, an angular script based mainly on Chinese *logographs, is used mainly for loan words and foreign words. *See also* kanji.
[Japanese: literally borrowed or provisional characters, distinguishing them from kanji, regarded as real characters]

Kanizsa triangle *n*. A visual illusion of a triangle without a corresponding retinal image, induced by three dark *Pac-Man icons at the corners of an imaginary triangle, oriented to give the impression that they are discs with segments occluded by the vertices of the triangle (see illustration). The *illusory contour arises from processing that occurs in Area V2 of the *visual cortex of information sent there from the primary visual cortex. The other major example of form perception without a retinal image is *anorthoscopic vision. *Compare* Ehrenstein's brightness illusion, random-dot stereogram.
[Named after the Italian psychologist Gaetano Kanizsa (1913–93), born in Trieste when it was part of the Austro-Hungarian Empire, who discovered it in 1971]

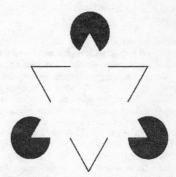

Kanizsa triangle. A figure with illusory contours and no corresponding retinal image.

kanji *n*. The Japanese *logographic writing system based mainly on Chinese logographs. A character in this system is also called a *kanji*. *See also* kana.
[From Chinese *han* Chinese + *zi* a character]

Kanner's syndrome *n*. An alternative name for *autistic disorder.
[Named after the Austrian-born US child

psychiatrist Leo Kanner (1894–1981) who first described it in 1943]

kappa effect *n.* A relation between perceived space and time, demonstrated most simply by placing three light sources A, B, and C at different positions, with A and B closer together than B and C, and then flashing the lights successively in the dark, with equal time intervals between the three flashes, creating the *space–time illusion that the time interval between A and B is shorter than that between B and C. *Compare* tau effect.

kappa statistic *n.* In statistics, an index of the degree of agreement between two raters classifying the same set of items, ranging from zero when agreement is no better than chance to 1 (except in certain special cases) when agreement is perfect. It is calculated by dividing the difference between the observed proportion of cases in which the raters agree and the proportion expected by chance by the maximum difference possible between the observed and expected proportions, assuming fixed row and column totals (marginals). Symbol: *K. See also* Kendall coefficient of concordance.
[From *kappa* (K), the tenth letter of the Greek alphabet]

Kardos effect *n.* The appearance of a white surface as black when it is precisely covered by a small region of shadow and is viewed among a collection of brightly illuminated objects. If the screen that casts the shadow is adjusted so that its edge is visible on the white surface, then the whole of the white surface is immediately perceived as white and partly in shadow, but as soon as the shadow is returned to its original position to cover the whole of the white surface, the surface instantly reverts to its previous black appearance. This phenomenon, like its counterpart the *Gelb effect, demonstrates that the lightness dimension of colour is not determined straightforwardly by physical light intensity but is subject to *context effects, as are other dimensions of colour. *See also* lightness, luminance. *Compare* Land effect.
[Named after the Hungarian psychologist Lajos (Ludwig) Kardos (1899–1985) who published his experiment in 1934]

karyotype *n.* **1.** The number, size, shape, and general appearance of the *chromosomes in a

*somatic cell of an organism; or a diagram or photograph of the complete set of chromosomes. *vb.* **2.** To determine the karyotype of a cell.
[From Greek *karyon* a kernel or nut + Greek *typos* a mark]

Kaspar Hauser experiment *n.* An experiment in which an animal is reared in isolation from members of its own species (conspecifics), for example, the experiments carried out in the 1950s by the British ethologist William H. Thorpe (1902–86) in which birds were reared in isolation to determine which aspects of their songs are *innate. *See also* feral child, Psammetichus experiment.
[Named after Kaspar Hauser (?1812–33), a teenage boy who appeared mysteriously in Nuremberg in 1828 and was believed to be a feral child, having grown up virtually without human contact]

kat *See* khat.

katakana *See under* kana.

katasexualism *n.* A generic name for the *paraphilias *necrophilia and *zoophilia.
[From Greek *kata* down + English *sexualism*]

kava *n.* The aromatic pepper plant *Piper methysticum*, indigenous to the south Pacific islands of Fiji, Tonga, Vanuatu, and Samoa, or a drink prepared by grinding its roots and stems, mixing them with water, and sieving the resulting liquid. It induces euphoria, sedation, incoordination, and other effects, some of them possibly harmful. It is a traditional ceremonial drug in Fiji and elsewhere, and in the late 1990s a demand for it began to emerge in Western cultures. *See also* substance abuse, substance-related disorders.
[From Polynesian (Tongan) *kava* bitter]

K complex *n.* A brief high-amplitude *EEG wave occurring at approximately one-minute intervals during Stage II *NREM sleep.

Keeler polygraph *n.* An instrument for recording changes in respiration rate, pulse rate, and blood pressure, used as a *lie detector during interrogations. *See also* polygraph.
[Named after the US criminologist Leonarde Keeler (1903–49) who invented it]

Kelley's cube *n*. An influential contribution to *attribution theory, formulated by the US psychologist Harold H. Kelley (born 1921) and first published in the *Nebraska Symposium on Motivation* in 1967, according to which people integrate three types of information in explaining an observed item of behaviour: *consensus*, the proportion of other people who have performed the same behaviour, providing an estimate of how unusual the behaviour in question is; *consistency*, the extent to which the behaviour is typical of the past behaviour of the person in similar situations; and *distinctiveness*, the extent to which the behaviour is peculiar to the particular situation in which it occurred. For example, a person may observe a friend losing her temper in response to her mother criticizing her in public, and the observer may judge this behaviour to be low on consensus (unusual for people in general), high in consistency (typical of that woman in that type of situation), and low in distinctiveness (something that she does in many other situations as well). Each of the three variables can be judged to be high or low, leading to eight possible combinations, often depicted as a $2 \times 2 \times 2$ cube. According to Kelley, observers tend to attribute behaviour to internal, dispositional causes within the actor when consensus is low, consistency is high, and distinctiveness is low, as in the example; conversely, observers tend to attribute behaviour to external, situational causes when consensus is high, consistency low, and distinctiveness high. Also called *Kelley's ANOVA model*. *See also* attribution, causal schema, covariation principle, fundamental attribution error, self-serving bias.

Kendall coefficient of concordance *n*. In statistics, an index of the degree of agreement between several variables measured on an *ordinal scale or transformed to *ranks, ranging from 0 (no agreement) to 1 (complete agreement). It may be thought of as similar to *Kendall's tau but suitable for measuring the association between more than two variables at a time. Symbol: *W*. *See also* kappa statistic.
[Named after the English statistician Maurice George Kendall (1907–83) who introduced it in 1948]

Kendall correlation coefficient *n*. Another name for *Kendall's tau.

Kendall's tau *n*. In statistics, an index of the degree of association between two variables measured on an *ordinal scale or transformed to *ranks. Its computation involves examining every pair of items and counting the number of pairs that are similarly ranked (concordant) and the number differently ranked (discordant) relative to each other on the two variables, and the difference between the number of concordant and discordant pairs is then divided by the total number of pairs. *See also* Kendall coefficient of concordance.
[Named after the English statistician Maurice George Kendall (1907–83) who introduced it in 1938]

Kent–Rosanoff Free Association Test *n*. A popular *word-association test consisting of 100 nouns, adjectives, and verbs selected by the US psychologist Grace H. Kent (1875–1973) and the Russian-born US psychologist Aaron J. Rosanoff (1878–1943) and published in the *American Journal of Insanity* in 1910. The words are all emotionally neutral, unlike some other word-association tests, and norms obtained by counting and classifying the associations given by 1,000 normal respondents are supplied.

kernel *n*. A basic form of sentence structure (simple, active, declarative) used as a starting point in some forms of *generative grammar.
[Old English *cyrnel* a little seed, from *corn* seed]

ketamine *n*. A drug closely related to *phencyclidine, developed originally as an *anaesthetic (1) and adopted as a street drug in the 1960s, often called *Special K*. *See also* phencyclidine-related disorders.
[From *ket*(one) + *amine*]

ketone *n*. A chemical compound consisting of a carbonyl group joined to two like or unlike alkyl radicals and containing volatile substances that are *psychotropic when inhaled. *See also* inhalant-related disorders, solvent abuse.
[German *Keton*, from *Aketon* acetone]

keyword mnemonic *n*. Another name for the *peg-word mnemonic.

khat *n*. An evergreen shrub *Catha edulis* native to Africa and Arabia that has *stimulant effects when its leaves are chewed or used to make tea.
[From Arabic *qat*]

Kiddie Mach *n*. A version of the *Mach scale designed for children.

killer T cell *See under* T lymphocyte.

kilocalorie *n*. Another name for a *Calorie.

kinaesthesis *n*. The sensation that is stimulated by movements of the body or parts of the body and is mediated by *proprioceptors in the *vestibular system and in the muscles, tendons, and joints. The term is sometimes used as a synonym for *proprioception, thus including sensations of position and orientation rather than just movement, but this ignores the etymology of the word and sacrifices a useful distinction, and the over-extended sense is therefore avoided in careful usage. US *kinesthesis*. Also called *kinaesthesia* or *kinesthesia*. *See* joint sense, muscle sense, static sense, tendon sense. **kinaesthetic** or **kines-thetic** *adj*.
[From Greek *kineein* to move + *aisthesis* sensation, from *aisthanesthai* to feel]

kinaesthetic method *n*. **1.** A method of correcting faulty speech by teaching the learner to sense the differences between the sensations of movement of the vocal apparatus in correct and faulty speech. **2.** A technique for treating *reading disorder by encouraging the reader to trace the outlines of letters and words. US *kinesthetic method*.

kindling *n*. A progressively increasing response of a group of neurons when exposed to a repetitive electrical stimulation of unchanging strength, sometimes leading to a *psychomotor seizure or *convulsion, a phenomenon mediated by neurons in the *hippocampus and *amygdala.
[From Old Norse *kyndill* to set fire to or inflame, from Latin *candela* a candle]

kineme *n*. The most basic component of *kinesic behaviour, distinguishing one kinesic signal or gesture from another. *Compare* phoneme.
[A blend of *kin(esic)* and *(phon)eme*]

kinemorph *n*. The smallest unit of *kinesic behaviour having a distinctive function. *Compare* morpheme.
[A blend of *kine(sic)* and *morph(eme)*]

kinephantom *n*. A misperception of visual movement such as occurs when viewing the *trapezoidal window or *Pulfrich effect.
[From Greek *kinesis* movement, from *kineein* to move + *phantasma* an illusion, from *phantazein* to make visible, from *phainein* to show, from *phaein* to shine]

kinesics *n*. The study of the role of *gestures (1) and other body movements in *non-verbal communication. Gestures are often classified into *emblems (gestures that substitute for words, such as waving the hand for 'goodbye' or putting a forefinger to the lips for 'silence'); *illustrators (gestures that accompany speech and depict what is being said, such as moving the hands apart to illustrate a description of a big fish); *adaptors (gestures, usually involving self-touching, that help one to cope with emotional reactions, such as covering the eyes with shock or putting a hand over the mouth with surprise); and *regulators (gestures that accompany speech and help to coordinate turn-taking, including raising a hand in the air to indicate that one has not finished speaking). In addition to these, *affect displays are *facial expressions that convey emotional states. Also called *body language*. *See also* amimia, apraxia, asemia, copropraxia, echopraxia, kineme, kinemorph, paramimia, Rett's disorder, semiotics. **kinesic** *adj*. Of or relating to *kinesics.
[From Greek *kinesis* movement, from *kineein* to move]

kinetic depth effect *n*. A phenomenon, discovered by the German-born US psychologist Hans Wallach (1904–98) and co-workers in 1953, in which a moving two-dimensional shadow cast by a three-dimensional object such as a rod appears three-dimensional when the object is held obliquely and rotated about its centre, causing complex transformations that make the shadow appear to move in front and behind the surface on which it is cast. The three-dimensional effect disappears if the rod stops moving, or if it rotates in a plane perpendicular to the surface on which the shadow is cast, causing the shadow merely to lengthen and shorten as the rod rotates. It is closely related to the *windmill illusion. *See also* structure from motion. **KDE** *abbrev*.

kingdom *n*. **1.** A state or nation ruled by a king or queen. **2.** Any of the highest *taxonomic groups into which nature is divided, traditionally the animal, vegetable, and mineral kingdoms, but now comprising animals, plants, fungi (which resemble plants but lack chlorophyll and do not grow by photosynthesis), protists (single-celled eukaryotic organisms such as protozoans), monera (single-celled prokaryotes such as bacteria), and viruses (subcellular organisms). Animal and plant kingdoms are further subdivided into *phyla.

kinin n. Any of a group of *polypeptides functioning as local hormones, manufactured in the blood or tissues as and when needed, causing *smooth muscles to contract and blood vessels to dilate. Two important kinins found in human and animal tissue are *cholecystokinin and *bradykinin.
[From Greek kineein to move + -in(e) indicating an organic compound]

kinocilium n. A long hair with a bulbous tip that projects from every *hair cell. In the *vestibular system, in the *macula within the *saccule in the *membranous labyrinth of the *inner ear, it is embedded in a gelatinous matrix containing crystals of calcium carbonate that exert gravitation drag on it and on the shorter *stereocilia. **kinocilia** pl.
[From Greek kineein to move + Latin cilium an eyelash]

kin selection n. A form of *natural selection involving *altruism shown by animals towards their siblings or other close relatives, thereby increasing their own *inclusive fitness indirectly by helping their relatives to propagate genes that they share. The concept was introduced by the British biologist William D(onald) Hamilton (1936–2000) in two articles in the Journal of Theoretical Biology in 1964. Compare group selection.
[From Old English cynn people belonging to the same family]

kinship, coefficient of See coefficient of consanguinity.

kinship study n. In behaviour genetics, a comparison of the correlations between relatives of different known degrees of genetic relatedness on a measurable *trait in order to estimate the *heritability of that trait, the assumption being that the higher the heritability of the trait the more closely will the

correlations correspond to degrees of relatedness. For example, because children share on average half their genes with each parent and with each sibling, the highest correlation between such relatives that could be expected for a trait with very high heritability is 0.5, and a substantially lower correlation would suggest low heritability. Also called a consanguinity study or a family study. Compare adoption study, twin study.

Kleine–Levin syndrome n. A disorder often associated with *psychotic (1) symptoms, with recurrent *hypersomnia, *bulimia (1), and *hyperkinesis.
[Named after the German psychiatrist Willi Kleine who first described it in 1925 and the Russian-born US neurologist Max Levin (born 1901) who studied it further in 1929]

Kleinian adj. Of or relating to the school of *psychoanalysis founded by the British-based Austrian psychoanalyst Melanie Klein (1882–1960). See combined parent-figure, depressive position, good breast, good object, idealization, imago (1), internalization, object relations, oral sadistic phase, paranoid–schizoid position, part object, projective identification, reparation, splitting of the object, whole object. See also early oral phase, Oedipus complex, oral sadistic phase, penis envy, primary narcissism, superego, Thanatos, urethral erotism.

kleptolagnia n. A *paraphilia characterized by recurrent sexually arousing fantasies, sexual urges, or behaviour involving stealing. See also kleptomania.
[From Greek kleptein to steal + lagneia lust]

kleptomania n. An *impulse-control disorder characterized by repeated stealing of objects not needed for personal use or for their intrinsic value, with emotional tension before the commission of a theft, followed by pleasure, gratification, or relief after its completion, the behaviour being generally experienced as *ego-dystonic. See also kleptolagnia.
[From Greek kleptein to steal + mania madness]

K-line n. In an associative *network model, a connection that reactivates a memory. The term was introduced by the US cognitive scientist Marvin (Lee) Minsky (born 1927).
[Abbreviation of knowledge-line]

Klinefelter's syndrome *n*. A disorder of males resulting from the presence of two or more *X chromosomes, causing small testicles, female physical characteristics, long legs, and mental retardation. Also called *XXY syndrome*. *Compare* Turner's syndrome, XXX syndrome, XYY syndrome.
[Named after the US physician Harry Fitch Klinefelter (born 1912) who first described it in 1942]

klinokinesis *n*. Movement in which an organism travels in a straight line except when it encounters an unfavourable environment or an aversive stimulus, when it turns at random to remain in the favourable environment, the frequency of turning depending on the environmental variability and the direction or angular velocity of turning, which depends in turn on the intensity of the environmental stimulus.
[From Greek *kleinein* to incline + *kinesis* movement]

Klüver–Bucy syndrome *n*. A syndrome resulting from bilateral damage to the *temporal lobes of the brain, characterized by increased and indiscriminate sexual activity, excessive oral behaviour, visual agnosia (*see under* agnosia), and *hypermetamorphosis. *See also* herpes simplex encephalitis.
[Named after the US-based German psychologist Heinrich Klüver (1898–1979) and the US neurosurgeon Paul Clancy Bucy (1904–92) who first described the condition in monkeys following surgical removal of the temporal lobes]

klysmaphilia *n*. A *paraphilia characterized by recurrent sexually arousing fantasies, sexual urges, or behaviour involving enemas.
[From Greek *klysma* an enema + *philos* loving, from *phileein* to love + *-ia* indicating a condition or quality]

knee-jerk reflex *n*. A non-technical name for the *patellar reflex.

knobs-and-dials psychology *n*. An aspect of *ergonomics or human factors psychology concerned with the optimal design of human–machine interfaces, including the design and placement of instrument panels and controls, taking into account *population stereotypes and findings from research

into perception and other relevant areas of psychology. *See also* population stereotype.

knowing how *n*. Another name for *procedural knowledge.

knowing that *n*. Another name for *declarative knowledge.

knowledge *n*. Anything that is known. The three major classes of knowledge are *declarative knowledge (knowing that), *procedural knowledge (knowing how), and *acquaintanceship knowledge (knowing people, places, and things). *See also* information (1). *Compare* belief, opinion.
[From Latin *noscere* to come to know]

knowledge representation *n*. The encoding and storage of *knowledge in computational models of cognition. It is a major branch of *artificial intelligence and is also studied in cognitive psychology, logic, computer science, and linguistics. The representation of informal and intuitive human knowledge is one of its major unsolved problems. *See also* ACT*, analogue (2), binding problem, conceptual dependency theory, connectionism (1), frame (2), frame problem, fuzzy logic, intuitive physics, K-line, neural network, nonmonotonic reasoning, symbolic representation. **KR** *abbrev*.

Kohlberg stage *n*. Any of the three stages of moral development, each divided into two levels, proposed by the US psychologist Lawrence Kohlberg (1927–87) on the basis of research in which he confronted children with stories that posed moral dilemmas. Kohlberg developed his theory in a series of investigations, beginning with his doctoral dissertation in 1958 and culminating in his book *Stages in the Development of Moral Thought and Action* (1969). *See* conventional morality, postconventional morality, preconventional morality.

Kohnstamm effect *n*. A dramatic phenomenon of involuntary movement. Stand with one shoulder about a foot from a wall and, with your arm rigidly extended downwards, press the back of your hand hard against the wall for about two minutes. If you then stand away from the wall with your arm hanging loosely by your side, it will rise up into the air, spontaneously and involuntarily. A double-arm version of the effect can be produced by standing in an open doorway and pressing the backs of both hands against the door frame. The phenomenon has been exploited in preparing people for *hypnosis, by deluding them into believing that they are responding involuntarily to a suggestion from the hypnotist for their arms to rise. The phenomenon has been interpreted as a *postural aftereffect. Also called the *Kohnstamm phenomenon* or *Kohnstamm manoeuvre*.

[Named after the German physician Oskar Kohnstamm (1871–1917) who drew attention to it]

Kohs Block Design Test *n.* A *psychometric test in which the respondent has to arrange groups of 4, 9, or 16 multi-coloured blocks to copy patterns presented on test cards, designed originally to differentiate brain-damaged from psychiatric patients, later adapted as an *intelligence subtest and incorporated into the *Wechsler scales, the *Goldstein–Scheerer tests, and other *IQ tests.

[Named after the US psychologist Samuel Calmin Kohs (1890–1984) who introduced it]

Kohutian *adj.* Of or relating to *self-psychology and the theories of the Austrian-born US psychoanalyst Heinz Kohut (1913–81) and his followers. *See* grandiose self, narcissism, narcissistic personality disorder, self-object.

Kolmogorov's axioms *n.* Four propositions about *probabilities from which all major theorems can be derived: (1) the probability of any event is equal to or greater than zero; (2) the probability of a certain event is 1; (3) if E and F are two mutually exclusive events (events that cannot both occur), then the probability of the disjunction (the probability of either E or F occurring) is equal to the sum of their individual probabilities: $P(E$ or $F) = P(E) + P(F)$; and (4) the probability of a conjunction of two events E and F (the probability that both E and F occur) is equal to the probability of E assuming that F occurs multiplied by the probability of F: $P(E$ and $F) = P(E|F)P(F)$.

[Named after the Soviet mathematician Andrei Nikolaevich Kolmogorov (1903–87) who formulated them in 1933]

Kolmogorov–Smirnov test *n.* In statistics, a *goodness of fit (1) test to determine whether a single sample fits some theoretical distribution or whether two independent samples have been drawn from the same population (or populations with the same distribution). *See also* chi-square test, independent samples *t* test.

[Named after the Soviet mathematicians Andrei Nikolaevich Kolmogorov (1903–87), who proposed the test in 1933, and Nikolai Vasilevich Smirnov (1900–66) who developed it further in 1939]

König bars *n.* A diagram depicting a set of bars subtending *visual angles of 3 minutes (sixtieths of a degree), separated by distances of 1 minute, used for measuring *visual acuity. *See also* acuity grating.

[Named after the German physiologist and psychologist Arthur König (1856–1901) who devised them]

koro *n.* A *culture-bound syndrome included in CCMD-2 (the *Chinese Classification of Mental Disorders*, 2nd ed.), restricted mainly to male members of ethnic Chinese communities in southern and eastern Asia and elsewhere, sometimes occurring in localized *epidemics (1), characterized by sudden and intense anxiety that the penis is shrinking and is liable to retract into the abdomen, resulting in death. In an effort to prevent this from happening, afflicted men often hold on to their penises during the day and wear commercially available bamboo clamps while sleeping. A less common female variant of the syndrome, focused on fear of the nipples or vulva retracting, is also recognized. Also called *shook yong*, *shuk yang*, *suk yeong*, or *suo yang* in Chinese-speaking areas, *rok-joo* in Thailand, and *jinjinia bemar* or *jinjin* in north-eastern India.

[From Malay *koro* to shrink]

Korsakoff's psychosis *n.* A *mental disorder characterized by *amnesia, especially an impairment in ability to retain newly acquired information, typically accompanied by confabulation—a tendency to invent explanations to cover areas of memory loss—but with other *cognitive functions usually well preserved, in contrast to *dementia. It is caused by a deficiency of thiamine (vitamin B_1) usually resulting from *alcohol dependence. Also called *alcohol amnestic disorder* or *Korsakoff's syndrome*. *See also* dorsomedial thalamus.

[Named after the Russian neuropsychiatrist Sergei Sergeievich Korsakoff (1854–1900) who first described it in 1887]

Korte's laws n. Laws governing the illusion of *apparent movement when two stimuli are exposed in alternation. If s is the spatial distance between the stimuli, t is their exposure time (assumed to be the same for both stimuli), i is their intensity (assumed equal), and p the interstimulus interval or pause between exposures, then for critical values of s, i, and t yielding *optimal movement, the four basic laws are as follows. (a) s increases as i increases, p and t remaining constant; (b) i decreases as p increases, s and t remaining constant; (c) s increases as p increases, i and t remaining constant; (d) t increases as p increases, i and s remaining constant. The laws apply approximately to *partial movement and *phi movement also. *See also* alpha movement, beta movement, gamma movement, delta movement, phi movement.
[Named after the German Gestalt psychologist Adolf Korte who formulated the earliest version of them in the journal *Zeitschrift für Psychologie* in 1915]

Krebs cycle n. A complex sequence of biochemical reactions in the *mitochondria of living cells whereby acetyl coenzyme A, derived by *glycolysis from *glucose, which in turn is derived from the *metabolism of amino acids, fatty acids, and carbohydrates in foodstuffs, is oxidized into carbon dioxide and water, with the release of minute quantities of stored energy in the form of *ATP. Any interference with the Krebs cycle, as by swallowing a poison such as potassium cyanide, is fatal within minutes. *See also* oxidative phosphorylation. Also called the *citric acid cycle* or the *tricarboxylic acid cycle*.
[Named after the German-born British biochemist Hans Adolf Krebs (1900–81) who discovered it in 1934 and shared a Nobel prize for so doing in 1953]

Kretschmer constitutional type n. Any of the four basic body types, each associated with its own distinctive pattern of personality characteristics, in the theory propounded by the German psychiatrist Ernst Kretschmer (1888–1964) in his book *Körperbau und Character* (1948, Body Build and Character). *See* asthenic body type, athletic body type, dysplastic body type, pyknic body type. *Compare* Sheldon's constitutional psychology.

Kruskal–Wallis 1-way analysis of variance n. In statistics, a test used with scores mea-sured on an *ordinal scale, or with data converted to *ranks, to determine whether several independent samples are from populations with the same *median. It is a nonparametric equivalent of one-way *analysis of variance (ANOVA). Also called *Kruskal–Wallis 1-way ANOVA*.
[Named after the US statisticians William Henry Kruskal (born 1919) and Wilson Allen Wallis (born 1912) who developed it in 1952]

K-selection n. A form of *natural selection that is typical of organisms in relatively stable, constant, and predictable ecological conditions in which rapid population growth is unimportant, and that is characterized by slow development, long life, large size, late reproduction, intensive parental care, and high learning capacity. *See also* r–K continuum. *Compare* r-selection. **K-selected** *adj*. Selected for superiority in such environments.

Kuder Preference Record n. An *occupational interest inventory designed to measure the respondent's relative levels of interest in ten occupational areas: clerical, computational, art, music, social service, outdoor, science, persuasive, literary, mechanical. Each item of the scale consists of three activities from which the respondent selects the least liked and the most liked. **KPR** or **KPR-V** *abbrev*.
[Named after the US psychologist George Frederic (Fritz) Kuder (1903–2000) who published it as a commercial test in 1960]

Kuder–Richardson coefficient n. In psychometrics, *Cronbach's alpha coefficient of reliability in the special case of a scale with pass/fail, yes/no, or other dichotomous test items. There are two slightly different versions based on different statistical assumptions: the Kuder–Richardson 20 formula and the Kuder–Richardson 21 formula. **K-R 20** or **K-R 21** *abbrev*.
[Named after the US psychologists George Frederic (Fritz) Kuder (1903–2000) and Marion Webster Richardson (1891–1965) who introduced it in an article in the journal *Psychometrika* in 1937]

Kuhnian *adj*. Of or relating to the ideas and writings of the US historian and philosopher of science Thomas S(amuel) Kuhn (1922–96), especially his distinction between *normal science and *scientific revolution and his doctrine of the *paradigm shift presented in his influential book *The Structure of Scientific Revolutions* (1962).

kula ring *n.* A ceremonial gift exchange among tribes in the western Pacific, practised alongside normal trading, functioning to establish and maintain friendly relations between islands.
[From Melanesian *kula*]

Kuleshov experiment *See under* dialectical montage.

Kundt's rules *n.* The propositions that (a) a distance or space divided into parts looks greater than the same distance or space undivided; and (b) an attempt to bisect a line with one eye closed usually results in a division too close to the nasal side of the open eye. *See also* filled-space illusion.
[Named after the German physicist August Adolph Eduard Eberhardt Kundt (1838–94) who formulated them in the early 1860s]

kurtosis *n.* In statistics, a measure of the peakedness of a distribution indicating the degree to which a set of scores is concentrated around its mean. A distribution that is more concentrated about its mean than the *normal distribution is *leptokurtic*, one that is concentrated like the normal distribution is *mesokurtic*, and a distribution that is flatter than the normal distribution is *platykurtic*. *Compare* skewness.
[From Greek *kurtos* arched + *-osis* indicating a process or state]

kuru *n.* A human *prion disease affecting the nervous system, restricted to the Fore highlanders of Papua New Guinea who used to practise a form of ritual cannibalism involving the eating of the brains of deceased relatives as an act of homage. It is characterized by *tremor, *ataxia, *dementia, and death usually within months of the onset of symptoms.
[Native Fore word: literally, the trembles]

kymograph *n.* An early device consisting of a rotating drum covered with paper on which a tracking stylus records continuous measurements of blood pressure, heart rate, respiration, variations in the muscular action of the organs of speech, or other physiological data.
[From Greek *kyma* a wave + *graphein* to write]

la belle indifférence *n.* An abnormal lack of concern about one's afflictions or disabilities, characteristic of some *conversion disorders.
[French: literally beautiful indifference]

labia majora *n.* The two outer folds surrounding the vaginal orifice of the female *vulva. *Compare* labia minora.
[From Latin *labia* lips + *majora* larger]

labia minora *n.* The two inner folds surrounding the vaginal orifice of the female *vulva. *Compare* labia majora.
[From Latin *labia* lips + *minora* smaller or lesser]

labile affect (mood) *See under* affect.

labiodental *adj.* Of, relating to, or denoting a speech sound articulated with the lower lip touching the upper teeth, as in the initial *phonemes in *fine* and *vine*. *See also* place of articulation.
[From Latin *labium* a lip + *dens, dentis* a tooth + *-alis* of or relating to]

labiovelar *adj.* Of, relating to, or denoting a speech sound articulated with the back of the tongue against the soft palate and the lips rounded, as in the initial *phoneme in the words *win*. *See also* place of articulation.
[From Latin *labium* a lip + *velum* a veil]

labyrinth *n.* Any mazelike structure or network of interconnecting chambers, especially the system of cavities of the *inner ear. *See* bony labyrinth, dynamic labyrinth, membranous labyrinth, static labyrinth. *See also* vestibular system.
[From Greek *labyrinthos* a maze, especially in Greek mythology the huge maze in Crete that Daedalus built for King Minos to contain the Minotaur]

labyrinthine nystagmus *n.* A form of *nystagmus resulting from damage to the *labyrinth.

Lacanian *adj.* Of or relating to the approach to *psychoanalysis adopted by the French psychoanalyst Jacques Lacan (1901–81). *See* foreclosure, mirror phase. *See also* condensation, deferred action, displacement, phallus.

lacrimator *n.* Another name for a *tear gas.
[From Latin *lacrima* a tear]

lactation *n.* Secretion of milk from *mammary glands after giving birth.
[From Latin *lac, lactis* milk + *-ation* indicating a process or condition]

lacunar amnesia *n.* Another name for *episodic amnesia.
[From Latin *lacuna* a hole or cavity]

Ladd-Franklin theory *n.* A speculative theory of colour vision according to which the first photoreceptors to evolve yielded only *achromatic (1) vision, receptors for blue and yellow evolved next, and receptors for red and green evolved most recently, the central area of the retina, where all colours are perceived, being the most evolutionarily advanced.
[Named after the US psychologist and logician Christine Ladd-Franklin (1847–1930) who first published it in her book *Colour and Colour Theories* in 1929]

lallation *n.* **1.** A speech defect in which the *phoneme /l/ is substituted for /r/, as in *velly solly*. **2.** Another name for *pseudolalia.
[From Latin *lallare* to sing a lullaby + *-ation* indicating a process or condition]

laloplegia *n.* A form of *aphasia resulting from *paralysis of the muscles of the vocal tract and not those of the tongue.
[From Greek *lalia* speech + *plege* stroke, from

language

plessein to strike + *-ia* indicating a condition or quality]

Ialorrhoea *n.* Another name for *logorrhoea.
US *lalorrhea.*
[From Greek *lalia* speech + *rhoia* a flow]

Lamarckism *n.* The theory of evolution, largely obsolete in biology but still relevant to social or cultural evolution (*see* meme), according to which acquired characteristics resulting from adaptations to new environments may be inherited. *See also* Lysenkoism, neo-Lamarckism. *Compare* Darwinian evolution, neo-Darwinism. **Lamarckian** *adj.*
[Named after the French naturalist Jean Baptiste Pierre Antoine de Monet Lamarck (1744–1829) who propounded it in his book *Philosophie Zoologique* (1809)]

lambda statistic *n.* Another name for the *Goodman–Kruskal lambda.

lambert *n.* A unit of light intensity or illumination, equal to one *lumen per square centimetre. **millilambert** *n.* 1/1,000 of a lambert.
[Named after the German mathematician and physicist Johann H. Lambert (1728–77)]

Land effect *n.* A vivid impression of a full range of colours created from monochromatic light. The effect is produced by taking two black-and-white photographs of a coloured display such as a bowl of fruit, the first with a green filter over the camera lens and the second from the identical position with a red filter, and then superimposing images of the two resulting black-and-white transparencies on a screen with slide projectors, the first without any filter over its lens and the second with a red filter. Although in terms of absolute wavelength all the light falling on the screen and being reflected from it is red, pink, or white, apples look green, plums blue, bananas yellow, and so on, disproving the common misconception that the colour of an object in the visual field is fully explained by the wavelength of the light reflected from it. In reality, the visual system assigns colours according to the relative balance of short, medium, and long wavelengths across the whole visual field, so that light of a particular wavelength has no inherent colour in itself but may be perceived as any colour depending on the range of wavelengths in the surrounding visual field, and this is why the effect disappears if the screen is viewed in *void mode. *See also* colour constancy, cone, retinex theory. *Compare* Gelb effect, Kardos effect.
[Named after the US physicist Edwin H(erbert) Land (1909–91), inventor of the Polaroid Land camera and president of the Polaroid Corporation, who discovered the effect and published it in the *Proceedings of the National Academy of Sciences* in 1959 and in *Scientific American* magazine later in the same year]

Landmark Forum *n.* The official name, since 1984, for *est.

Landolt circle *n.* A circle with a tiny part of its circumference missing, easily perceived as a circle in spite of the fact that it is not a closed curve, illustrating the *closure grouping law and the phenomenon of *Prägnanz. It is used mainly to test *visual acuity, the respondent being shown a series of small differently oriented Landolt circles and asked to say where the gaps appear, choosing from alternatives such as twelve o'clock, three o'clock, six o'clock, and nine o'clock. Also called a *Landolt C.*
[Named after the Swiss-born German physical chemist Hans Heinrich Landolt (1831–1910) who devised it]

langage *n.* A term introduced in 1915 by the Swiss linguist Ferdinand de Saussure (1857–1913) to denote the faculty of speech present in all human beings and acquired through heredity, which is divided into two major aspects, namely *langue and *parole, often said to correspond roughly to the *competence (2) and *performance (2) of the US linguist and philosopher (Avram) Noam Chomsky (born 1928), but there are important differences between *langue* and competence.
[Old French *langage* language, from Latin *lingua* the tongue]

language *n.* **1.** A conventional system of communicative sounds and sometimes (though not necessarily) written symbols capable of fulfilling the following hierarchy of functions suggested by the German-born Austrian psychologist Karl Bühler (1879–1963) and the Austrian-born British philosopher Karl R(aimund) Popper (1902–94): expressing a communicator's physical, emotional, or cognitive state; issuing signals that can elicit responses from other individuals; describing

a concept, idea, or external state of affairs; and commenting on a previous communication. The concept of language is often interpreted loosely to embrace codes devised for specific purposes, as in expressions such as *programming languages*, and forms of communication that fulfil some but not all of the four listed functions, including *body language* and the *language of the bees* (*see* waggle dance), neither of which can fulfil the fourth and highest function. **2.** The particular system of verbal communication, such as the English language, that is used by a specific nation or people.
[From Old French *langage*, from Latin *lingua* the tongue]

language acquisition device *n.* A hypothetical mechanism, based on *generative grammar, introduced in 1964 by the US linguist and philosopher (Avram) Noam Chomsky (born 1928) to explain how children acquire internalized knowledge of grammar with remarkable speed on the basis of fragmentary and degenerate input data. The language acquisition device is assumed to be a biologically based innate capacity for language, independent of any specific *natural language, that enables a child exposed to adult speech to implement certain general principles for discovering the grammatical rules of the specific language in question. Also called a *language acquisition system (LAS)*. **LAD** *abbrev.*

language disorders *n.* Disorder of the expression or understanding of language, including *dyslexia, *expressive language disorder, *hyperlexia, *mixed receptive–expressive language disorder, *phonological disorder, *reading disorder, *receptive language disorder, *specific spelling disorder, and *stuttering. *See also* aphasia. *Compare* communication disorders.

Language Personality Sphere *n.* The set of 4,505 trait names with distinct meanings, located by an exhaustive dictionary search in 1936. The dictionary search located 17,953 *trait names, but the number was reduced to 4,505 by eliminating synonyms. This study was carried out by the US psychologists Gordon W(illard) Allport (1897–1967) and Henry S(ebastian) Odbert (1909–95) and published in the journal *Psychological Monographs* in 1936. *See also* 16PF.

langue *n.* A term introduced in 1915 by the Swiss linguist Ferdinand de Saussure (1857–1913) to denote language as an abstract communicative system or social institution that is the common possession of a particular speech community and is one of the two major aspects of *langage, the other being *parole.
[French *langue* language]

lanugo *n.* Fine hair or down, especially the woolly covering of a human foetus at birth and the fluffy hair that often appears on the faces of people with *anorexia nervosa.
[From Latin *lanugo* down, from *lana* wool]

lapsus calami *n.* Another name for a *slip of the pen.
[From Latin *lapsus* an error + *calamus* a reedpen]

lapsus linguae *n.* Another name for a *slip of the tongue.
[From Latin *lapsus* an error + *lingua* a tongue]

lapsus memoriae *n.* Another name for a *slip of memory.
[From Latin *lapsus* an error + *memoria* a memory]

Largactil *n.* A proprietary name for the neuroleptic drug *chlorpromazine, used in the treatment of schizophrenia.
[Trademark, from *larg(e)* + *act(ion)* + Latin *-il(is)* indicating capability or relationship]

large intestine *n.* The section of the *alimentary canal between the small intestine and the anus.

Laroxyl *n.* A proprietary name for the tricyclic antidepressant drug *amitriptyline.
[Trademark]

larynx *n.* The upper part of the windpipe, behind the Adam's apple, containing and protecting the *vocal folds. Its non-technical name is the *voice box*.
[From Greek *larynx* the throat]

Lashley jumping stand *n.* A device used to study visual discrimination in rats. It comprises a platform on which the rat is placed and two vertical cards, each containing a visual stimulus, towards which the rat jumps. If the rat chooses the right card, then a door

swings open and the rat lands in a chamber and receives a food reward; if it chooses wrongly, it bumps against a fixed door and falls into a net below.
[Named after the US physiological psychologist Karl Spencer Lashley (1890–1958) who invented it]

latah *n.* A *culture-bound syndrome found mainly in Malaysian and Indonesian cultures, most often among middle-aged women, but reported occasionally in Thailand (where it is called *bah tschi* or *baah-ji*), the Philippines (*mali-mali* or *silok*), among the native Ainu people of Japan (*imu*), in Siberia (*amurakh, irkunii, ikota, olan, myriachit*, or *menkeiti*), and in southern Africa (*latah*), in which a person after experiencing a sudden fright or shock displays abnormal *suggestibility, accompanied by *echolalia, *echopraxia, and a state resembling a *trance. Also spelt *lattah*.
[From Malay]

late luteal phase dysphoric disorder *n.* Another name for *premenstrual syndrome with prominent symptoms of *mood episodes. **LLPDD** *abbrev.*
[Referring to the *luteal phase of the menstrual cycle]

latency *n.* The interval between a *stimulus (1) and a *response. Also called *latent time, reaction time*, or *response latency*.
[From Latin *latere* to lie hidden or to escape attention]

latency period *n.* In *psychoanalysis, a period of development from the dissolution of the *Oedipus complex at the end of the *phallic stage around 5 or 6 years of age until the *genital stage at puberty. It is characterized by a decrease in sexual activity, a decline in sexual investment in *object relations, and the emergence of emotions such as shame and disgust. Sigmund Freud (1856–1939) presented the concept in its fully developed form in 1924 in an article entitled 'The Dissolution of the Oedipus Complex' (*Standard Edition*, XIX, pp. 173–9). He attributed the term *latency period* to his friend, the German physician Wilhelm Fliess (1858–1928), and he used the term *period* rather than *stage* because no new organization of sexuality takes place at this time—it is not a turning point. *See also* castration complex.

latent content *n.* In *psychoanalysis, the underlying hidden meaning of a *dream (1) or other psychological phenomenon exposed by *interpretation (2) of the *dreamwork.

latent homosexuality *n.* A form of *homosexuality that is not recognized as such by the person concerned but is *repressed and manifested indirectly through various *defence mechanisms, generally including *projection (1). *See also* Schreber case.

latent inhibition *n.* In *classical conditioning, the retardation of learning caused by repeated presentation of the *conditioned stimulus before the beginning of the conditioning process. **LI** *abbrev.*

latent learning *n.* Animal *learning (1) that occurs without any apparent *reinforcement (1, 2) or reward, as when a rat explores a maze and is later shown to have learned to find its way around it. In human learning, the phenomenon is called *incidental learning. Also called *passive learning*.

latent time *n.* Another name for *reaction time.

latent trait theory *n.* Another name for *item response theory.

latent variable *n.* Another name for a *construct.

lateral *adj. n.* Situated at the side or oriented towards the side; the opposite of *medial. In phonetics, (pertaining to) a consonant articulated with the tip of the tongue touching the *alveolar ridge, allowing the airstream to pass on one or both sides of this central obstruction. The initial phoneme in the English word *low* is a voiced lateral consonant, whereas the phoneme represented twice by *ll* in the name of the Welsh town *Llanelli* is a voiceless lateral consonant.
[From Latin *lateralis* situated on the side, from *latus* the side]

lateral dominance *n.* Another name for *handedness (1) or *cerebral dominance.

lateral eye movement *n.* A deflection of gaze to the left or right, sometimes claimed to indicate an increase of activity in the contralateral *cerebral hemisphere, so that a person will tend to show a rightward deflection of gaze when preparing to answer a question requiring verbal processing and a leftward deflection when thinking about a spatial problem. **LEM** *abbrev.*

lateral fissure *n.* Another name for the *lateral sulcus.

lateral funiculus *See under* funiculus.

lateral geniculate nucleus *n.* A peanut-sized structure at the side of each lobe of the *thalamus, receiving most of its input via the *optic tract from the opposite half of the visual field as represented on the *retinas of both eyes, these inputs preserving the *centre-surround receptive fields of the retinal *ganglion cells and being arranged in a *topographic map so that points close together on the retina are close together in the lateral geniculate nucleus, and relaying most of them to the *primary visual cortex (Area V1), where the topographic order is preserved. It contains six layers of cells, three receiving inputs from the left (L) eye alternating with three from the right (R) eye, in the order from top to bottom LRLRRL in the left geniculate or RLRLLR in the right geniculate, with the six maps of the visual field superimposed exactly. It also receives inputs from the primary visual cortex to which it projects and from the brainstem *reticular formation, affecting visual attention. Also called the *lateral geniculate body*. *See also* magnocellular system, parvocellular system, pretectal pathway, retinotopic map. **lateral geniculate nuclei** *pl.* **LGN** *abbrev.* [From Latin *lateralis* situated on the side, from *latus* the side + *geniculatus* knee-shaped, from *geniculum* a little knee, diminutive of *genus* a knee]

lateral hypothalamic feeding centre *n.* One of the two parts of the *appestat on each side of the hypothalamus, stimulation of which increases eating and destruction of which inhibits eating. US *lateral hypothalamic feeding center*. *Compare* ventromedial hypothalamus.

lateral hypothalamic syndrome *n.* A constellation of signs and symptoms including *anorexia, *aphagia, and *adipsia associated with lesions in the *lateral hypothalamic feeding centres on both sides of the thalamus. *Compare* ventromedial hypothalamic syndrome.

lateral inhibition *n.* Suppression by a neuron of the response of a neighbouring neuron at the same level in a sensory system, such as the suppression by neurons receiving information from the OFF region of a *centre-surround receptive field of neurons in the ON region if both regions are stimulated simultaneously. This phenomenon occurs in certain neural structures in which receptor cells are arranged to represent points along a *continuum, as in the *retina and the *organ of Corti, and in which excitation at one point produces inhibition at adjacent points, leading to enhancement or sharpening of differences between neighbouring regions.

laterality *n.* The asymmetry in functions between the two *cerebral hemispheres, including *handedness (1) and language functions, the left hemisphere being dominant for language in approximately 90 per cent of people—over 95 per cent of right-handers and about 70 per cent of left-handers. Laterality of functions has been studied via cognitive deficits in people with unilateral brain damage and electrical brain stimulation, and through other specialized research techniques: *dichotic listening studies, *dichhaptic techniques, *divided visual field studies, *split-brain preparations, *EEG studies, examinations of *evoked potentials, and *brain imaging techniques. *See also* Broca's area, Wada test, Wernicke's area.

lateral lemniscus *n.* Either of the two bands of nerve fibres in the *lemniscus connecting the *cochlear nuclei to the *inferior colliculi and the *thalamus on each side of the brain, involved in the processing of auditory signals. *Compare* medial lemniscus, trigeminal lemniscus.

lateral sulcus *n.* The deep horizontal cleft in the outside wall of each *cerebral hemisphere, separating the frontal lobe and part of the parietal lobe from the temporal lobe. Also called the *fissure of Sylvius*, the *lateral fissure*, or the *Sylvian fissure*. *See also* insula, operculum.

lateral surface *n.* The surface of an organ or structure situated or oriented towards the side of the body, such as the outer surface of each cerebral hemisphere.

lateral thinking *n.* Creative *problem solving, usually by reformulating the problem or viewing it from a fresh angle. It is contrasted with *vertical thinking*, which involves finding methods for overcoming obstacles in the chosen line of approach. The distinction was first made explicit by the Maltese-born British psychologist and author Edward (Francis Charles Publius) de Bono (born 1933) in his book *Lateral Thinking* (1970).

lateral ventricle *See under* ventricle.

late selection *n.* In the study of *attention, the filtering out of unwanted information at a late stage in the process of information processing.

Latin square *n.* In statistics and experimental design, a square array of letters (or occasionally numbers or other symbols) such that no symbol occurs more than once in any row or column. The following is a 4×4 Latin square:

A B C D
B C D A
C D A B
D A B C

A *Latin square design* is a type of *within-subjects design in which research participants or subjects are allocated to treatment conditions according to a Latin square with as many rows or columns as there are treatment conditions in order to control for *order effects. Usually equal numbers are assigned to each of the rows of a Latin square and are exposed to the treatments in the order of the letters in the row. *See also* randomized blocks design.
[So called because letters from the Roman alphabet are conventionally used to represent it]

lattah *See* latah.

laudanum *n.* Tincture (solution in alcohol) of *opium, containing *morphine and *codeine as active ingredients, first prepared by the Swiss physician and alchemist Philippus Aureolus Paracelsus (1493–1541) and used as a *narcotic analgesic. Formerly and more loosely, any medication containing opium as its main component.
[Coined by Paracelsus, probably from *labdanum* or *ladanum* a juice obtained from rockroses, from Greek *ledon* a rockrose]

laughing gas *n.* A non-technical name for *nitrous oxide.

[So called because it sometimes induces giggling or laughter]

lavatory wall illusion *n.* A variant of the *hollow squares illusion and the *Münster-berg illusion, created by an alternating arrangement of square two-tone tiles, each changing smoothly from light to dark along one axis, the effect being that the tiles appear misaligned and non-parallel. It was first reported in 1987 by the English optometrists J(oy) Margaret Woodhouse (born 1948) and Stephen P(hilip) Taylor (born 1951), who reproduced a photograph of a bathroom decorated with such tiles. *See also* cafe wall illusion.

law of comparative judgement *n.* The proposition that in any *comparative judgement, the magnitude of the psychological or subjective difference corresponds to the relative frequency with which the stimuli are discriminated.

law of effect *n.* A proposition formulated by the US psychologist Edward Lee Thorndike (1874–1949) in his book *Animal Intelligence: Experimental Studies* (1911) as follows: 'Of several responses made to the same situation, those which are accompanied or closely followed by satisfaction [are] more firmly connected with the situation . . . ; those which are accompanied or closely followed by discomfort . . . have their connections with the situation weakened' (p. 244). According to this law, responses that lead to reward tend to increase in strength, whereas those that lead to punishment tend to decrease in strength. The first part of the law has been amply corroborated by empirical studies and is one of the foundation stones of modern behaviourism. *See also* associationism, connectionism (2), reinforcement (1). *Compare* law of exercise.

law of exercise *n.* A proposition formulated in 1911 by the US psychologist Edward Lee Thorndike (1874–1949) according to which repetition tends to strengthen the association between a *stimulus (1) and a *response, making the response more likely to occur on the next presentation of the stimulus. *Compare* law of effect.

law of forgetting *See* forgetting law.

law of independent assortment *See* independent assortment.

law of segregation *See* segregation of alleles.

law of social impact *n.* A proposition introduced by the US psychologist Bibb Latané (born 1937) in an article in the journal *American Psychologist* in 1981, designed to explain *social influence effects, including *persuasion, *conformity, *compliance, and *obedience. It is usually expressed by the equation $T = f(SIN)$, where T is the magnitude of the impact, f indicates a function, S is the strength of the influence sources (for example, their *credibility in the case of attitude change), I is the immediacy of the influence sources (face-to-face communication being the most immediate and the print media the least immediate), and N is the number of influence sources. The analogy of electric lamps shining on a sheet of paper helps to explain the law: the amount of light reaching the paper is a function of the strength (wattage) of the lamps, the immediacy of the lamps (how close they are to the paper), and the number of lamps. The law embodies a *multiplicative model, because if S, I, or N is zero, the magnitude of the impact is zero.

law of the excluded middle *See* excluded middle law.

lay personality theory *n.* Another name for an *implicit personality theory.

L-dopa *abbrev.* Laevo-dihydroxyphenylalanine, a substance that is synthesized in the body from tyrosine and is an immediate precursor of *dopamine. Dopamine cannot cross the *blood–brain barrier, but L-dopa can, therefore a synthetic form of L-dopa is used in the treatment of *Parkinson's disease, which arises from a failure of dopamine production in the brain. Also called *levodopa. See also* antiparkinsonian, aphrodisiac, dopa.
[From *laevo-* indicating a left-handed form, from Latin *laevus* left + *d(ihydr)o(xy)p(henyl)-a(lanine)*]

learned food/flavour/taste aversion *See* food aversion learning.

learned helplessness *n.* An apathetic condition in an animal or a human being resulting from exposure to insoluble problems or inescapable physical or emotional stress, believed by some psychologists to underlie *depression. The term was introduced in 1968 by the US psychologist Martin E. P. Seligman (born 1942) and his colleagues, whose early experiments involved strapping experimental dogs into harnesses to prevent them escaping, and then exposing them to inescapable electric shocks. When the dogs were later placed in a situation in which they had to respond to a warning signal by jumping over a low barrier in order to avoid further shocks, most became apathetic and listless and failed to learn this simple avoidance response, whereas a control group of dogs that had not been exposed to the inescapable shocks learned the avoidance response quickly and easily. Learned helplessness has been demonstrated in humans as well as animals, and Seligman and his followers believe that it reduces the motivation to solve problems, interferes with the ability to learn from experience, and produces depression. It is very occasionally spelt *learnt helplessness*, which is arguably preferable inasmuch as it avoids the implication that the helplessness is knowledgeable and well read.
[So called because it is acquired by *learning (1)]

learning *n.* **1.** Any lasting change in behaviour resulting from experience, especially *conditioning (1). **2.** The act or process of acquiring knowledge or skill, or knowledge gained by study (*He had several university degrees and was a man of learning*).

learning curve *n.* A mathematical expression of the change in behaviour occurring as a function of practice, usually represented by a graph showing a measure of performance on the vertical axis and amount of learning, represented by trials or time, on the horizontal axis. The best example is a *cumulative record. The concept was introduced by the US psychologist Louis Leon Thurstone (1887–1955) in an article entitled 'The Learning Curve Equation' in the journal *Psychological Monographs* in 1919. Also called a *practice curve*.

learning difficulties *n.* A term used by *educational psychologists in the UK since the 1980s to refer to *mental retardation; thus *moderate learning difficulties* corresponds approximately to *moderate mental retardation, *severe learning difficulties* to *severe mental retardation, and *profound learning difficulties* to *profound mental retardation. *Compare* learning disability.

learning disability *n.* A generic name for disorders characterized by substantial deficits in scholastic or academic skills, including *reading disorder, *mathematics disorder, and *disorder of written expression. Also called *academic skills disorders* or *learning disorders. See also* specific learning disability. *Compare* learning difficulties. **LD** *abbrev.*

Learning Potential Assessment Device *n.* A device intended for *dynamic testing of children, adolescents, and adults for potential cognitive growth. It comprises a battery of 15 instruments designed to challenge the respondent's ability to use different cognitive operations (serialization, classification) in different *content domains (numerical, verbal, logico-deductive, and figural), while the examiner detects errors and helps the respondent to find ways to remedy them. **LPAD** *abbrev.*

least-effort principle *See* principle of least effort.

least-significant difference test *n.* In statistics, a method of *multiple comparisons in which all possible *t tests between group means are performed without adjustment of the significance levels for the fact that multiple, non-independent comparisons are being made, and therefore without adequate protection against a *Type I error. *Compare* Bonferroni correction, Duncan's multiple range test, Newman–Keuls test, Scheffé test, Tukey-HSD test.

least-squares method *n.* In statistics, a technique for estimating the value of an unknown quantity from a number of observations or scores, especially for finding the line or curve that best fits a set of data points, by finding the values that minimize the sum of the squared deviations of the observed scores from their expected values.

lecithin *n.* A phosphorous-based chemical substance found in egg yolk, soybeans, corn, and liver, the main dietary source of *choline, used as an emulsifier and stabilizer (E322) in manufactured foodstuffs.
[From Greek *lekithos* egg yolk]

lect *n.* A general term for any variety of a language that can be identified in a speech community. *Compare* acrolect, basilect, dialect, idiolect, mesolect.
[From Greek *legein* to speak]

Lee–Boot effect *n.* The suspension of *oestrous cycles in a group of females housed together in the absence of males of the same species or their *pheromones. *Compare* Whitten effect.
[Named after the Dutch biologists S. van der Lee and I. M. Boot who first reported it in 1955]

left-sided apraxia *n.* An impairment of ability to carry out verbal requests with the left hand, resulting from damage to the *corpus callosum, preventing impulses from the left hemisphere, where language is processed, from reaching the right *motor cortex, where control of the left side of the body is located. Also called *callosal apraxia, sympathetic apraxia, unilateral limb apraxia. See also* apraxia, disconnection syndrome.

legasthenia *n.* A term introduced in 1916 (in the German form *Legasthenie*) by the Hungarian psychiatrist Paul Ranschburg (1870–1945) to denote specific *reading disorder.
[From Latin *legere* to read + Greek *astheneia* weakness, from *a-* without + *sthenos* strength + *-ia* indicating a condition or quality]

legend, urban *See* urban legend.

lek *n.* A small area of ground where certain species of birds such as grouse gather for *courtship (1) and *display (1), or the behaviour that occurs at such a location, or the season during which such behaviour takes place.
[From Old English *lacan* to frolic, perhaps from Swedish *leka* to play]

lemma *n.* **1.** In logic and mathematics, a preliminary *proposition (1) on which the proof of a subsequent proposition depends. **2.** In linguistics, a word in its *citation form, together with all its inflected forms, such as *do* together with *doing, does, did,* and *done.* **lemmatize** *vb.*
[From Greek *lambanein* to take for granted]

lemniscus *n.* A band of ascending sensory nerve fibres connected to the thalamus, including the *lateral lemniscus, *medial lemniscus and *trigeminal lemniscus, the

whole lemniscus being referred to non-technically as the *fillet*. Also called the *lemniscal system*.
[From Greek *lemniskos* a ribbon]

lenis *adj*. Of or relating to a *consonant speech sound articulated with relatively weak muscular tension of the organs of speech and breath pressure, such as the initial phonemes in *bee, die, go, vow, though*, and *zoo. See also* clipping. *Compare* fortis.
[From Latin *lenis* gentle]

lens *n*. A transparent structure, with one or more convex or concave surfaces, that *refracts light passing through it, causing either convergence or divergence of rays. The *crystalline lens of the *eye converges light rays on to the retina. *See also* dioptre, refraction.
[From Latin *lens, lentis* a lentil, alluding to the shape of a biconvex lens]

lens model *n*. A metaphor proposed by the Hungarian-born US psychologist Egon Brunswik (1903–55) to highlight the probabilistic relationships between, on the one hand, an *ecological criterion, and on the other, the sensory *cues (2) of imperfect *ecological validity (2) that an organism uses to judge the ecological criterion, the cues being focused on cognitive processes like rays of light on to the ecological criterion. *See also* Brunswikian.

lenticular nucleus *n*. One of the *basal ganglia comprising the *putamen and the *globus pallidus in each cerebral hemisphere, implicated in the control of movement. Also called the *lentiform nucleus. See also* corpus striatum.
[From Latin *lens, lentis* a lentil, alluding to its double-convex shape]

lento speech *n*. Slow, deliberate, careful speech lacking the features typical of rapid, casual, connected *allegro speech.
[Italian *lento* slow, from Latin *lentus* slow]

leptokurtic *See* kurtosis.

Lerntest *n*. A collection of *dynamic testing procedures developed in Germany in the early 1990s, administered with repetitions, prompts, and systematic feedback.
[From German *Lerntest* learning test, from *lern* learn + *Test* a test]

lesbian *n*. A *homosexual woman. **lesbianism** *n*. The practice of being a *lesbian, also called *sapphism*.
[From the name of the Greek island of Lesbos, home of the lyric poet Sappho, believed to have been a lesbian]

Lesch–Nyhan syndrome *n*. A hereditary disorder of purine metabolism, affecting young boys, transmitted by a *sex-linked *recessive gene, characterized by mental retardation, self-mutilation of lips and fingers by biting, abnormal physical development, often leading to death.
[Named after the US paediatricians Michael Lesch (born 1939) and William L. Nyhan, Jr (born 1926), who first studied it]

lesion *n*. Any structural alteration of an organ or tissue of the body brought about by injury or disease.
[From Latin *laesio* an injury, from *laedere* to hurt + *-ion* indicating an action, process, or state]

lesion experiment *n*. Another name for an *ablation experiment.

lethal dosage *n*. The minimum dosage of a drug required to kill an organism. **LD** *abbrev.* **lethal dosage 50** *n*. Another name for the *median lethal dosage. *See also* therapeutic index, therapeutic ratio. *Compare* effective dosage, toxic dosage. **LD-50** or **LD$_{50}$**. *abbrev.*

letter-by-letter reading *n*. An alternative name for *spelling dyslexia.

leucocyte *n*. Any of the various types of large white corpuscles of the blood and lymph in humans and other vertebrates, including *phagocytes with granular cytoplasm and other immunologically active cells with clear cytoplasm. US *leukocyte*. Also called a *white blood cell* or *white blood corpuscle. See also* granulocyte, lymphocyte, monocyte, stem cell. *Compare* erythrocyte.
[From Greek *leucos* white + *kytos* a vessel]

leucotomy *n*. A shortened name for *frontal leucotomy. Also spelt *leukotomy*.

leu-enkephalin *See under* enkephalin.

leukocyte *See* leucocyte.

levelling *n*. **1.** The tendency to perceive or to remember material in a form closer to a *good Gestalt than is objectively the case, unimportant and incongruous details gradually disappearing over time, such alteration also occurring in *serial reproduction and *rumour transmission. *Compare* assimilation (5), sharpening. **2.** In the terminology of some forms of therapy and counselling, speaking frankly and openly (being level in the sense of straightforward). **3.** In linguistics, the gradual loss of linguistic distinctions, such as the loss of the distinction between the nominative and accusative forms of nouns in Old English, which have generally been levelled to a single form, although the distinction has been preserved in some pronouns (*I/me*, *he/him*, *she/her*, *they/them*) though not in *you*. US *leveling*.

level of measurement *See* measurement level.

levels of processing *n*. The depth with which incoming information is analysed and *encoded, ranging from superficial processing of sensory *features (1) to semantic and conceptual processing, with deeper levels of processing leading to longer-lasting memories. According to this interpretation, incoming verbal information may be analysed in terms of its sensory and surface features but may also be processed at progressively deeper levels in terms of its *phonemic, *semantic, and *conceptual properties, the early sensory analyses being relatively automatic and effortless and the later deeper analyses requiring attention and effort. The concept was introduced in 1972 by the Canadian-based Scottish psychologist Fergus I. M. Craik (born 1935) and the Canadian-based Australian psychologist Robert S. Lockhart (born 1939). In 1975 Craik and the Estonian-born Canadian psychologist Endel Tulving (born 1927) published a classic experiment in which people first answered yes–no questions about a list of words and then tried to recall as many of them as possible. Some of the words were accompanied by questions asked about their visual appearance (*Is the word in lower case?* or *Is the word in upper case?*), others their sound (*Does the word rhyme with dog?* and so on), and still others their meaning (*Is it the name of an animal?* and so on). Recall was very poor for words that had been processed according to visual appearance, slightly better for words

processed according to sound, and best by far for words processed according to meaning. This approach is sometimes seen as an alternative to the conventional model of three separate memory stores, namely *sensory memory, *short-term memory, and *long-term memory. *See also* attenuation theory, bottleneck theory, depth of processing, domains of processing theory, elaboration, proofreader's illusion (1, 2). **LOP** *abbrev*.

levodopa *n*. Another name for *L-dopa.

Lewinian *adj*. Of, relating to, or resembling the psychological approach of Kurt Lewin (1890–1947), a US psychologist born in a part of Germany that is now in Poland. *See* action research, approach-approach conflict, field theory, hodological space, life space, T-group, topological psychology.

Lewy body *n*. A microscopic particle with a characteristic dark core and pale halo found abundantly in cortical neurons of people with *Lewy body dementia.
[Named after the German-born US neurologist Frederick H. Lewy (1885–1950) who discovered the particle]

Lewy body dementia *n*. A form of *dementia, distinct from Alzheimer's disease, associated with *Lewy bodies in cortical neurons, especially in the *frontal lobes, characterized by rapid and unpredictable fluctuations in levels of cognitive functioning and extremely poor reactions to *neuroleptic (1) drugs.

lexeme *n*. The basic unit of semantic analysis, roughly equivalent to a *word* in the everyday sense but referring more precisely to the abstract unit postulated to underlie a set of grammatical variants such as *write*, *writes*, *writing*, *wrote* or *loud*, *louder*, *loudest*; the smallest unit of language with a distinctive meaning that cannot be inferred from the meanings of its component *morphemes. Many lexemes consist of single words (such as *game*, *castle*, or *sing*), but multi-word lexemes also exist (as in *kick the bucket*, meaning die). Also called a *lexical item*.
[From Greek *lexis* a word, from *legein* to speak + a suffix on the model of *phoneme*]

lexical access *n*. The process by which a person retrieves items from a *lexicon (2).
[From Greek *lexis* a word, from *legein* to speak]

lexical access time *n.* The time taken to retrieve information from a *lexicon (2).

lexical ambiguity *n.* The property of a word that has more than one meaning. In written language it arises from *homographs, and in spoken language from *homonyms. *See also* polysemy.

lexical decision task *n.* An experimental task in which participants or subjects are required to decide as quickly as possible whether strings of letters are or are not words. **LDT** *abbrev.*

lexical word *n.* Another name for a *content word.

lexicographic *adj.* Of, relating to or consisting of a method of arranging a set of items in the manner of a dictionary, by ordering them first according to one *attribute, then according to a second, and so on. Thus the words *cab*, *dab*, *den*, and *fag* are lexicographically ordered, and so are the vectors (3, 1, 2), (4, 1, 2), (4, 5, 14), and (6, 1, 7), and the relation between the two systems of ordering can be seen by setting $a = 1, b = 2, \ldots, z = 26$. Also called *lexical*, though this is liable to cause confusion and is avoided in careful usage, because this adjective usually refers to *lexemes or words. *See also* lexicographic choice, lexicographic semiorder.
[From Greek *lexikon* a dictionary, from *lexis* a word, from *legein* to speak + *graphein* to write + *-ikos* of, relating to, or resembling]

lexicographic choice *n.* Any method of *multi-attribute decision making that is *lexicographic inasmuch as the decision maker proceeds by first comparing the alternatives on the most important *attribute, and if more than one alternative is best on the first attribute, the decision maker then compares them on the next most important attribute, and so on until just one alternative emerges as best or the list of attributes is exhausted without a definite first preference emerging. Suppose a decision maker has to choose between two travel agencies, namely A_1 offering a tour only to destination D_1 (Africa), and A_2 offering tours to both D_1 (Africa) and D_2 (the Far East). The decision maker is equally attracted by Africa and the Far East and is indifferent between the travel agencies. According to the conventional linear value-maximization model of decision making, the three alternatives A_1D_1, A_2D_1, A_2D_2 are equally valued and are therefore equally likely to be chosen; but it is intuitively obvious that most human decision makers would choose first between destinations D_1 and D_2, because this attribute is most important, and only then between travel agencies A_1 and A_2, and consequently the probability of choosing A_2D_2 would be greater than that of the other two alternatives. Also called *lexicographic decision making* or *lexical choice*, although the latter is avoided in careful usage, because it causes confusion with *lexical decision task*. *See also* elimination by aspects, lexicographic semiorder.

lexicographic semiorder *n.* A *lexicographic preference ordering applied to a set of elements differing on two or more *attributes, at least one of which yields a *semiorder. It is noteworthy because it can generate an *intransitive preference ordering from intuitively reasonable transitive preferences within each separate attribute. For example, suppose three job applicants x, y, and z are ranked according to aptitude test scores and interview performance, and interview performance is taken into account only if the difference in aptitude test score between two candidates is less than five points and is therefore considered to be negligible. Suppose that the data are as follows:

Candidate	Aptitude	Interview
x	70	good
y	73	moderate
z	76	weak

Then x is preferred to y, y is preferred to z, and z is preferred to x. Also called a *lexical semiorder*, though this is apt to cause confusion.

lexicology *n.* The study of the development and present state of the *lexicon (1) of a language.
[From Greek *lexis* a word, from *legein* to speak + *logos* word, discourse, or reason]

lexicon *n.* **1.** The entire vocabulary of a language, especially one that is listed alphabetically like a dictionary. English is believed to have the largest lexicon of any language: *The Oxford English Dictionary* (2nd ed.) defines more than 500,000 words. **2.** The entire vocabulary of an individual. The US psychologist George A(rmitage) Miller (born 1920)

estimated in 1991 that the average high-school graduate has a passive lexicon of about 60,000 words that are understood but not necessarily used. Also called a *mental lexicon*. **3.** A list of words relating to a particular subject. **lexical** *adj.*
[From Greek *lexikon* a dictionary, from *lexis* a word, from *legein* to speak]

lexicostatistics *n.* A technique devised by the US linguists Morris Swadesh (1909–67) and Robert Benjamin Lees (1922–96) in the late 1940s for studying the vocabularies of languages, especially to trace historical links with other languages through *glottochronology. Using a list of 100 basic words (such as *I, you, not, tree, father, two*), the number of words in the two languages that are recognizably similar or cognate can be counted, and the fewer the cognate words, the longer they are assumed to have been separated: on average, two languages have 86 per cent in common after 1,000 years of separation. *See also* Indo-European.
[From Greek *lexis* a word, from *legein* to speak + *statistics*]

liar paradox *n.* A profound and intractable though simple *paradox discovered by ancient Greek thinkers. Epimenides, the Cretan, says that all Cretans are liars; if he is telling the truth, then he must be a liar, and if he is lying, then he must be telling the truth. The simplest version of the paradox is the statement *This statement is false*; if it is true, then it must be false, and if it is false, then it must be true. The paradox was mentioned by St Paul in his epistle to Titus (1 : 12), although Paul evidently failed to grasp its point. *See also* metalanguage.

liberty cap *n.* The slightly poisonous mushroom *Psilocybe semilanceata*, sometimes eaten as a *hallucinogenic drug. Also called *magic mushroom*. Its common street name is *mush*. *See also* fly agaric.
[So called because of its resemblance to the soft felt cap worn during the French Revolution as a symbol of liberty]

libidinal regression *See under* regression (2).

libidinal stage *n.* In *psychoanalysis, any stage or phase of *psychosexual development when *libido is focused specifically on one *erotogenic zone and in which one mode of *object-relationship predominates. Also called a *libidinal phase* or a *psychosexual stage*. *See* anal stage, genital stage, latency period, oral stage, phallic stage, polymorphous perversity. *See also* fixation (2), regression (2).

libido *n.* Sexual desire. In *psychoanalysis, the energy of the *sexual instinct as a component of the *Eros. Sigmund Freud (1856–1939) introduced the concept in his book *Three Essays on the Theory of Sexuality* (1905), in a passage added to the 1915 edition (*Standard Edition*, VII, pp. 130–243, at p. 217), and he expanded his explanation in his book *Group Psychology and the Analysis of the Ego* (1921), where he gave the following definition: 'Libido is an expression taken from the theory of the emotions. We call by that name the energy, regarded as a quantitative magnitude, (though not at present actually measurable), of those instincts which have to do with all that may be comprised under the word "love"' (*Standard Edition*, XVIII, pp. 69–143, at p. 90). Freud attributed the term to the book *Untersuchungen über die Libido sexualis* (1898, Researches into the Sexual Libido) by the German psychiatrist Albert Moll (1862–1939), but Freud had already used the word several times in letters (*Standard Edition*, I, pp. 173ff.) to his friend, the German physician Wilhelm Fliess (1858–1928), the earliest occurrence being in June 1894, several years before the publication of Moll's book. *See also* ego libido, object libido. *Compare* destrudo, mortido, self-preservation instinct. **libidinal** *adj.* Of or relating to the *libido. **libidinous** *adj.* Lustful, lascivious, or lewd.
[From Latin *libido* desire or lust]

Librium *n.* A proprietary name for the benzodiazepine drug *chlordiazepoxide.
[Trademark]

lie detector *n.* A type of *polygraph sometimes used in police interrogations to detect untrue or deceptive answers by recording involuntary stress-induced physiological responses, typically including changes in galvanic skin response (GSR), respiration rate, blood pressure, and heart rate. Responses to test questions relevant to the crime or matter at issue are compared with responses to unrelated control questions, and the most advanced polygraph lie detectors incorporate computer software, based on data from confirmed polygraph test results, designed to analyse the waveforms and eliminate subjectivity from their interpretation. The original polygraph lie detector was called the *Keeler polygraph*. Also called simply a *polygraph*. *See also* bogus pipeline, word-association test.

lie scale *n.* In psychometrics, a set of items included in a test to provide an indication of the extent to which the respondent has answered truthfully in other parts of the test. Some lie scales consist of repetitions of the same or closely similar items, to check for consistency of responses; others are made up of items to which certain responses may be assumed to be evidence of *social desirability response set, or some other *response bias, for example *I always smile at strangers in the street* (True) or *I never regret things that I have said* (True); and there are other more devious and subtle types of lie scales.

life instincts *n.* Another name for *Eros.

life lie *n.* In *individual psychology, a term introduced by the Austrian psychiatrist Alfred Adler (1870–1937) to denote the false belief, functioning as a means of evading responsibility, that one cannot achieve any of one's goals.

life space *n.* A term introduced in 1936 by the Polish/German-born US psychologist Kurt Lewin (1890–1947) to refer to the psychological *field, comprising the person *P* and the person's environment *E*, jointly determining the person's behaviour *B* at a given moment, this relation being expressed by the equation $B = f(P, E)$, certain regions of the life space having *valence* and thus being either attractive or repulsive to the person and determining *locomotion* from one region to another. *See also* approach–approach conflict, approach–avoidance conflict, avoidance–avoidance conflict, field theory, hodological space, Lewinian, topological psychology.

life table *n.* Another name for a *mortality table.

ligand *n.* An atom, molecule, ion, or radical that binds with a central atom; more specifically, any such element that binds with a specific *neuroreceptor.
[From Latin *ligandum* binding, from *ligare* to bind]

light adaptation *n.* A form of *adaptation (2) in which the visual system is adjusted for efficient response to light under conditions of strong illumination, including the constriction of the *pupil, a rapid increase in the *absolute threshold for vision, and the switch from the *scotopic system to the *photopic system. *See also* Purkinje shift. *Compare* dark adaptation. **light-adapted** *adj.* Of or relating to the eye or the visual system after it has undergone *light adaptation.

lightness *n.* The *achromatic (1) dimension of *colour, ranging from black (0) to white (10) in the *Munsell value scale of lightness, being one of the three major dimensions of colour together with *hue and *saturation (1). It is the psychological counterpart of physical *luminance, but the fact that it does not correspond in a simple way to physical light intensity can be demonstrated by first noting the lightness of a television screen when the power is turned off—it is usually not very dark—and then switching on the power and observing that parts of the picture appear much darker and even pitch black, despite the fact that the transmitted images can only increase and never reduce the intensity of the light coming from any part of the screen. Also called *Munsell value* or *brightness*, although brightness is specifically related to luminance, which as explained above is a different though closely related physical property. *See also* Gelb effect, Hering grey, Kardos effect.

lightness constancy *n.* The apparent stability of an object's *lightness despite changes in illumination. Also called *brightness constancy* or *whiteness constancy*. *See also* perceptual constancy.

lightness contrast *n.* The apparent darkening of an object or image when viewed against, alongside, or immediately after a lighter one, or an apparent lightening of an object or image juxtaposed with a darker one. Also called *brightness contrast*. *See also* contrast (2), simultaneous contrast, successive contrast, visual induction.

light reflex *n.* Another name for the *pupillary light reflex.

likelihood function *n.* In statistics, the probability of obtaining a given set of observed scores in a random sample as a function of the *parameter(s) of the population from which the scores are drawn. *See also* likelihood ratio (1).

likelihood principle *n.* A hypothesis first proposed in 1866 by the German physiologist, physicist, and mathematician Hermann Ludwig Ferdinand von Helmholtz (1821–94) that a perception is inferred unconsciously to correspond to the most likely physical events or circumstances that could have produced the pattern of sensations that generated it. *Compare Prägnanz.*

likelihood ratio *n.* **1.** In statistics, the ratio of two *likelihood functions at a given value, especially the ratio of a likelihood function to the *maximum likelihood, or in *Bayesian inference, the ratio between (a) the probability of an observation or datum conditional on a hypothesis and (b) the probability of the same observation or datum conditional on an alternative hypothesis: $P(D \mid H_1)/P(D \mid H_2)$. **2.** In *signal detection theory, the ratio (at a particular cutoff or criterion level of sensory activation) given by the probability of a response being due to signal plus noise divided by the probability of its being due to noise alone. Symbol: β.

likelihood ratio chi-square test *n.* A statistical test of association or *goodness of fit (1) that is based on the *likelihood ratio (1) and is thought by many statisticians to be preferable to the conventional Pearson *chi-square test for the simultaneous analysis of several overlapping associations in a multiple-classification table, because under certain conditions it has the property of *additivity of effects. The statistic, which is distributed like chi-square, is computed from the natural logarithms of observed and (in goodness of fit tests) expected frequencies. *Compare* Pearson chi-square test.

Likert scale *n.* One of the most popular types of attitude scale, constructed by the method of *summated ratings in which a sample of respondents are given a large number of candidate statements about an attitude object (such as *Homosexuality is acceptable in today's society, Homosexuality should be outlawed*) to which they respond with their own attitudes by choosing one of the response categories attached to each item, for example, *strongly disagree, disagree, neutral, agree, strongly agree.* Items that are worded positively towards the

attitude object, such as the first of the examples above, are assigned positively increasing scores to their response categories such as 0, 1, 2, 3, and 4, respectively, and for negatively worded items such as the second example the scoring is reversed (4, 3, 2, 1, 0). Each respondent's scores on all the candidate items are summed to yield a total score, the candidate items are then subjected to *item analysis, and those with the highest discriminating power are retained for the final scale.
[Named after the US sociologist and economist Rensis Likert (1903–81) who introduced it in an article in the *Archives of Psychology* in 1932]

liking scale *n.* A questionnaire designed to measure interpersonal liking, defined in terms of fondness and respect for the liked person and a feeling that the liked person is similar to oneself, the scale being specifically intended to distinguish liking from loving, which is measured by a *romantic love scale. Both scales were constructed by the US psychologist Zick Rubin (born 1944) and published in the *Journal of Personality and Social Psychology* in 1970.

l'illusion de sosies *n.* Another name for *Capgras syndrome.
[From French *l'illusion* the illusion + *de* of + *sosies* doubles, from *Socias* in Greek mythology, the identity that Zeus persuaded Mercury to adopt to help him seduce Alcmene by impersonating her husband]

limbic system *n.* A ring of cortical and subcortical structures folded into the inner surface of the *temporal lobe surrounding the brainstem and bordering on the corpus callosum, including the *amygdala, *cingulate gyrus, *fornix, *hippocampus, *parahippocampal gyrus, and *septum pellucidum, implicated in basic emotions, hunger, sex, and memory. *See also* Papez circuit, pleasure centre.
[From Latin *limbicus* bordering, from *limbus* a border]

limen *n.* Another name for a *threshold.
[From Latin *limen* a threshold]

limits, method of *See* method of limits.

Linda problem *n.* A classic problem of judgement. *See under* conjunction fallacy.

[Named after a fictitious bank teller called Linda]

linear model *n.* A mathematical model represented by a linear equation of the form $Y = b_1X_1 + b_2X_2 + \ldots + b_nX_n$, or by a system of such linear equations. The relationship between the variables in a linear equation is a straight line when plotted on a graph. In *multiple regression, Y represents the estimated value of the *dependent variable, each of the X_i represents a *predictor variable, and the b_i are regression coefficients or weights. If they are expressed as *standardized regression coefficients, then they are represented by the Greek letter beta (β) instead of b and are called *beta weights. *See also* bootstrapping.

linear perspective *n.* One of the monocular cues of visual *depth perception, a form of *perspective closely related to *aerial perspective and *texture gradient, arising from the fact that an object of a fixed size subtends a smaller *visual angle when it is far away than when it is relatively close, so that parallel lines such as rail tracks appear to converge towards a *vanishing point at the horizon. *See also* carpentered world.

linear regression *See* regression analysis.

line bisection test *n.* A simple test in which a person is asked to mark the approximate midpoint of a straight line. People with *spatial neglect perform badly on this test, tending to ignore part of the line and consequently to divide it too far towards the other side.

lingam *n.* The Hindu phallic symbol representing the god Shiva, associated with the powers of reproduction and dissolution. *See* phallus.
[From Sanskrit *linga* a mark or sexual characteristic]

linguistic competence *n.* Another name for *competence (2).

linguistic determinism *n.* The theory propounded originally by the US fire prevention officer and linguist Benjamin Lee Whorf (1897–1943) that language determines the way people perceive the world and think, rather than vice versa. Whorf argued that because the North American Hopi Indians have only one word (*masa'ytaka*) for everything that flies, apart from birds, they do not perceive and conceptualize the distinctions between insects, aircraft, bats, and aviators that English-speakers do; and analogously, English-speakers do not perceive and conceptualize the distinctions between different kinds of snow that are distinguished in the language of the Inuit Eskimos, who have twelve separate words for specific kinds of snow (although only one word meaning snow in general), the popular myth that the Eskimos have hundreds of words for snow having originated in 1911 in the introduction by the German-born American anthropologist Franz Boas (1858–1942) to his *Handbook of North American Indian Languages*. The theory of linguistic determinism has been undermined by evidence such as that of the Dani tribesmen in Papua New Guinea, who have only two words for colours (usually translated as *light* and *dark*), but can distinguish between colours as well as people from Western cultures. *See also* linguistic relativity, polyonymy, Sapir–Whorf hypothesis.

linguistic performance *n.* Another name for *performance (2).

linguistic relativity *n.* The hypothesis first suggested by the German ethnologist Wilhelm von Humboldt (1767–1835) and reformulated in the 20th century by the US fire prevention officer and linguist Benjamin Lee Whorf (1897–1943) that people who speak different languages perceive reality and think differently, because categories and distinctions encoded in one language are not necessarily available in another. For example, the language of the North American Hopi Indians has no forms corresponding to English tenses and no words for conceptualizing time as a dimension; therefore, Whorf argued, it would be difficult for a Hopi and an English-speaking physicist to understand each other's thinking about time. *See also* linguistic determinism, Sapir–Whorf hypothesis.

linguistics *n.* The scientific study of language, the major branches of which include *phonetics, *phonology, *semantics, *syntax, and *pragmatics. *Compare* psycholinguistics.

linguistic universals *n.* Linguistic features that are believed to be common to all *natural languages. They are usually divided into three classes: *substantive universals; *formal universals; and *implicational universals. *See also* creole.

linkage *n*. In genetics, the occurrence of two *genes close together on the same *chromosome, so that they are unlikely to become separated during *crossing over and tend to be inherited together. *See also* gene mapping, independent assortment.

linking *r* *n*. A type of *intrusion in fluent speech, especially *allegro speech, in which the phoneme /r/ is pronounced in such phrases as *the car in the photo* or *the floor of the House*, even by a non-*rhotic speaker (such as one who uses *Received Pronunciation) who does not normally pronounce the /r/ in *car* or *floor*. *Compare* intrusion.

lipid *n*. Any of a group of organic compounds, including especially fats and waxes that are esters of fatty acids, that together with carbohydrates and proteins are the principal constituents of living cells and are soluble in alcohol and other solvents but not in water. [From French *lipide*, from Greek *lipos* fat]

lipid bilayer *n*. A double layer of *amphipathic lipid molecules that forms a *cell membrane (see illustration).

lipogram *n*. A written text from which a specific letter is absent throughout. The most ambitious example is the 50,000-word novel *Gadsby* (1939) by Ernest Vincent Wright (1872–1939) in which the letter *e*, normally the most frequent in English, does not appear; this is a serious novel intended to present a different picture of the US from *The Great Gatsby* (1925) by (Francis) Scott (Key) Fitzgerald (1896–1940). A more recent novel entitled *A Void* (1995), a translation by the British writer

Gilbert Adair (born 1944) of *La Disparation* (1969) by the French novelist Georges Perec (1936–82), also omits the letter *e* throughout. The accidental omission of letters or words from writing is called *lipography* or *haplography.
[From Greek *leipein* to omit + *gramma* a letter]

lipostatic theory *n*. A *homeostatic theory of hunger according to which the brain monitors the level in the blood of free fatty acids that result from the metabolism of fat. A low level indicates that fat has not recently been metabolized, and this leads to a lessening of hunger, whereas a high level indicates recent fat metabolism and increases hunger. *Compare* glucostatic theory.
[From Greek *lipos* fat + *statikos* bringing to a standstill, from *histanai* to cause to stand or to weigh in a balance + -*itikos* resembling or marked by]

liquid *n*. A speech sound articulated by narrowing the mouth passage but allowing the airstream to escape without turbulence. In English, there are two liquids /l/ and /r/ as in the initial *phonemes in the words *lung* and *rung*, and both are *approximants. *See also* manner of articulation.

Lissajous figure *n*. A curve traced out by a point moving in simple harmonic motion in two directions perpendicular to each other, the shape of the curve being determined by the relative frequencies and phases of the motion. If the motion is observed for some time on an oscilloscope screen, the direction of apparent rotation appears to reverse spontaneously.
[Named after the French physicist Jules Antoine Lissajous (1822–80) who first constructed it]

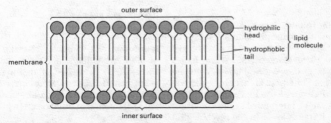

Lipid bilayer

lithium *n*. A soft, silvery, *alkaline metal, lighter than any other yet discovered. *See also* lithium carbonate.
[From Greek *lithos* stone + Latin *-ium* indicating a metallic element]

lithium carbonate *n*. A salt of *lithium, used as a mood stabilizer in the treatment of acute *manic episodes and *bipolar disorders in general, by replacing sodium in body tissues, thereby affecting the permeability of their membranes. It curbs both manic and depressive episodes by stabilizing levels of the neurotransmitter *glutamate in the brain. It, or its close relative lithium citrate, is also used in the treatment of *hypomanic episodes and (more controversially and at best indirectly) *depressive disorders. Also called simply *lithium*. *See also* antimanic, mood stabilizer, orphan drug.

Little Hans *n*. In *psychoanalysis, the pseudonym of a 5-year-old boy with an irrational fear of horses (hippophobia) who was analysed by his father in 1906–8 with the advice of Sigmund Freud (1856–1939) and discussed in an article by Freud in a famous case study in 1909 entitled 'Analysis of a Phobia in a Five-Year-Old Boy' (*Standard Edition*, X, pp. 5–149), in which the phobia was traced to a *castration complex.

little thirty *n*. Specific personality *traits associated with the *Big Five personality factors. Each of the Big Five is described by six traits on which it loads most heavily, for example, *extraversion is associated with warmth, sociability, positive emotions, excitement-seeking, activity, and assertiveness. The little thirty is a finer-grained way of describing personality than the Big Five, which tend to obscure anomalies such as that of the *passive–aggressive personality disorder, which is characterized by high assertiveness but low warmth.

Lloyd Morgan's canon *n*. A frequently paraphrased doctrine propounded in 1894 by the British comparative psychologist C(onway) Lloyd Morgan (1852–1936) in his *Introduction to Comparative Psychology*: 'In no case may we interpret an action as the outcome of the exercise of a higher psychical faculty, if it can be interpreted as the exercise of one which stands lower in the psychological scale' (p. 53). It is an application of *Ockham's

razor, implying as it does that psychology must seek the simplest explanations. Morgan was anticipated by the German psychologist Wilhelm (Max) Wundt (1832–1920) who wrote in 1863 in his *Vorlesungen über die Menschen- und Tierseele* (translated into English as *Lectures on Human and Animal Psychology*) that in psychological matters recourse should be had to 'complex principles of explanation [only] when the simplest ones have proved inadequate' (p. 350 of the English translation).

loan translation *n*. A word or phrase borrowed from another language by translating its component parts separately and literally, as in the English word *superman* taken from the German *Übermensch*. Also called a *calque*.

lobe *n*. A structurally distinct and usually rounded part of any larger organ or body part. The four lobes of each *cerebral hemisphere are the *frontal lobe, the *parietal lobe, the *temporal lobe, and the *occipital lobe (see illustration).
[From Latin *lobus* a lobe, from Greek *lobos* an earlobe]

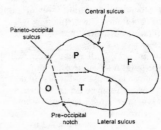

Lobes of the brain. F, frontal lobe; P, parietal lobe; O, occipital lobe; T, temporal lobe.

lobectomy *n*. Surgical excision of a lobe of an organ, especially excision of the prefrontal areas of the *frontal lobe of the brain. *Compare* prefrontal leucotomy.
[From Greek *lobos* a lobe + *ectome* an excision, from *tome* a cut]

lobotomy *n*. **1.** Surgical severing of one or more nerve fibres in the *frontal lobe of the brain as a method of treating intractable *mental disorders. More correctly called *frontal lobotomy or *frontal leucotomy. **2.** Surgical removal or disconnection of a lobe of any organ.
[From Greek *lobos* a lobe + *tome* a cut]

local feature n. A stimulus *feature (1), such as an indentation in the outline of a visual image or a click in an auditory tone, that is characteristic of part of the stimulus rather than of the stimulus as a whole. *Compare* global feature.

localization n. 1. Determining the position of something. *See also* eccentric projection, egocentric localization, sound localization. 2. Becoming characteristic of a particular region in attitudes or behaviour. 3. Restricting something to a particular region.

localization of function n. The specialization of different areas of the brain for different operations, activities, or processes. *Compare* equipotentiality, mass action.

local sign n. Information from a *photoreceptor in the eye indicating direction in space, or from a *touch receptor indicating a specific point on the body.

loci, method of *See* method of loci.

lock-and-key theory n. Another name for the *stereochemical theory of odour, so called because molecules with particular shapes are assumed to fit specific olfactory receptors as keys fit locks.

locked-in syndrome n. A condition resulting from bilateral destruction of the *medulla oblongata or base of the *pons, resulting in *paralysis of all voluntary muscles except those of the eyes, with intact consciousness but loss of speech, and communication only through blinking or eye movements. Also called *pseudocoma*. *Compare* persistent vegetative state.

locomotor ataxia n. A form of *ataxia resulting from syphilis, with slow degeneration of nerve fibres, muscular *atrophy, and gradual loss of deep tendon reflexes. Also called *tabes dorsalis*. *Compare* gait ataxia.

locura n. A *culture-bound syndrome resembling a chronic *psychosis (1) found in several parts of Latin America and among Latino communities in the United States and elsewhere, with signs and symptoms such as *incoherence, *psychomotor agitation, auditory and visual *hallucinations, and sometimes outbursts of violent or aggressive behaviour. It is

often interpreted as a form of *schizophrenia. [Spanish *locura* madness]

locus n. 1. A specific place or region, especially the position occupied by a particular *gene or *allele on a *chromosome, as in a locus for eye colour. Also called a *gene locus*. 2. In mathematics, a set of points satisfying a specified condition, such as all points whose distance from a fixed point P is a constant, or all points satisfying the equation $r^2 = x^2 + y^2$, where r is a constant, both of which conditions define a circle. **loci** pl. [From Latin *locus* a place]

locus coeruleus n. A small region on either side of the *pons containing neurons that secrete *noradrenalin (norepinephrine) and *serotonin, prominently implicated in anxiety and fear, and responsible for initiating *REM sleep after a period of slow-wave sleep. Also spelt *locus ceruleus*. *See also* subcoerulear nucleus. [From Latin *locus* a place + *caelum* sky, referring to its deeply pigmented appearance]

locus of control n. A *cognitive style or personality *trait characterized by a generalized expectancy about the relationship between behaviour and the subsequent occurrence of *reinforcement (1) in the form of reward and punishment. People with *internal* locus of control tend to expect *reinforcements (1) to be the consequences of their own efforts or behaviour, whereas people with *external* locus of control expect them to be the consequences of chance, luck, fate, or the actions of powerful others. Between these two extremes lies a *continuum of intermediate cognitive styles. The concept was introduced in an article in the journal *Psychological Monographs* in 1966 by the US psychologist Julian B(ernard) Rotter (born 1916), who also provided the *internal–external scale to measure it. Also called *internal–external control of reinforcement*. *See also* social learning.

locutionary act n. The *speech act of uttering a meaningful sentence. *Compare* illocutionary act, perlocutionary act. [From Latin *locutio* an utterance, from *loqui* to speak]

logagnosia n. Another name for *Wernicke's aphasia. Also called *logamnesia*. *See under* aphasia.

logic *n.* The branch of philosophy devoted to the study of valid arguments, or (equivalently) of consistent sets of beliefs, involving the application of rules of *inference to draw valid conclusions from sets of *premises. An argument is a set of statements purporting to provide a reason for believing a certain statement, and it is valid if its *counterexample set is inconsistent. More specifically, a logic is any particular formal system of axioms and rules of inference, or the arrangement of elements in a computer designed to perform a specified computation; and more generally logic is any sound or valid method of argument or reasoning, or *rational thinking as distinct from irrationality. *See also* analytic statement, biconditional, Boolean, fuzzy logic, interpretation (3), lemma (1), logical analysis, logical positivism, monotonicity, mood (3), negation (3), propositional calculus, quantifier (1), sentence functor, syllogism, synthetic statement, truth functor, truth table. **logical** *adj.*
[From Greek *logike (techne)* (art) of reason, from *logikos* of or relating to speech or reasoning, from *logos* word, discourse, or reason]

logical analysis *n.* In *logic, the process of combining short sentences into longer sentences and then finding other sentences that mean the same as the sentences built up in this way. It is an activity somewhere between translating and paraphrasing, and it can be performed quite mechanically, according to strict rules. Some logicians believe that it uncovers the true underlying forms of the sentences that they analyse, whereas others believe that it is part of an enterprise to replace natural languages such as English with a new and more rational language. *See also* propositional calculus, truth table.

logical empiricism *n.* An influential approach to the philosophy of science, less radical than *logical positivism, associated especially with the writings of three US philosophers of science, namely the German-born Rudolph Carnap (1891–1970), the Czechoslovakian-born Ernest Nagel (1901–85), and the German-born Hans Reichenbach (1891–1953), according to which the aim of research in both the natural and social sciences is the discovery and justification (testing) of general laws, a sharp distinction being drawn between the context of discovery and the context of justification. *See also* empiricism, falsifiability.

logical positivism *n.* A largely obsolete philosophical doctrine that rejected metaphysics, theology, and ethics as meaningless and held that the only meaningful *propositions (1) are those consisting of elementary propositions that are either tautological or empirically verifiable. *See also* confirmation bias, empiricism, falsifiability, Hume's fork, operationalism. *Compare* logical empiricism, positivism (1).

log-interval scale *n.* A scale of measurement in which numbers are assigned so that ratios between values reflect ratios in the *attribute being measured, familiar examples being density (mass divided by volume) and fuel efficiency in miles per gallon or kilometres per litre. *See also* measurement level, scale (1). *Compare* absolute scale, interval scale, nominal scale, ordinal scale, ratio scale.
[So called because the logarithms of the scale scores form an interval scale, the reason being that the ratio $a/b = \log a - \log b$]

log-linear analysis *n.* In statistics, a technique for analysing *frequency (2) data to investigate the relationships among the variables in a cross-tabulation by modelling the logarithm of the frequency in a cell as a function of *main effect and *interaction effects. Unlike the *chi-square test, log-linear analysis is capable of analysing the effects of more than one independent variable on a dependent variable and of estimating not only *main effects but also *interaction effects. *See also* multiway frequency analysis, saturation (2).

logogen *n.* A representation of a word or other verbal unit in long-term memory, activated by speech sounds, writing, or an object or event to which it refers. In *tachistoscopic word recognition, for which the concept was originally devised, each logogen has a resting activation level, and if it receives evidence that it corresponds to the stimulus presented, its activation level increases: for example, if the observer recognizes the first letter of the display as a *p*, then in the observer's long-term memory all the logogens beginning with *p* are slightly activated, and as further evidence accumulates, if the activation level of a logogen

exceeds a certain threshold level (threshold levels being lower for more common verbal expressions), then the logogen 'fires' and the corresponding verbal unit is recognized. The term was introduced by the English cognitive psychologist John Morton (born 1933) in an article in the journal *Psychological Review* in 1969, and the theory has been modified several times since then by Morton and others. *Compare* imagen.
[From Greek *logos* a word + *genes* born]

logograph *n*. A representation of a complete *morpheme, word, or phrase in a single character or symbol, as in the writing systems of China and Japan or internationally recognized symbols such as % for *per cent*, ÷ for *divided by*, @ for *at*, © for *copyright*, and so on. The great Chinese dictionary of K'ang Hsi (1662–1722) contains almost 50,000 logographs, but basic literacy in modern Chinese is usually assumed to require knowledge of some 2,000 basic logographs, and the Japanese Ministry of Education prescribes 1,850 characters as essential for everyday use, of which 881 are taught to elementary schoolchildren. Also called a *logogram*. *See also* kanji. *Compare* ideograph, pictograph. **logographic** *adj*.
[From Greek *logos* a word + *graphein* to write]

logography *n*. A system of writing based on *logographs. *Compare* phonography. **logographic** *adj*.

logorrhoea *n*. Excessive, uncontrollable talking or verbal diarrhoea. US *logorrhea*. Also called *lalorrhoea*.
[From Greek *logos* a word + *rhoia* a flow]

logotherapy *n*. A form of *psychotherapy developed by the Austrian psychiatrist Viktor E. Frankl (1905–97) that capitalizes on people's will to meaning (rather than their will to power or the will to pleasure), attempts to restore a sense of meaning by encouraging meaningful and creative activities and experiences of art, nature, and culture, and encourages self-acceptance and an appreciation of one's place in the world by a close study of one's attitudes to work, love, and life in general, using techniques such as *paradoxical intention and *de-reflection.
[From Greek *logos* word, discourse, or reason + English *therapy*, intended to denote meaning-centred therapy]

Lomotil *n*. A proprietary name for a *narcotic drug containing an antiperistaltic agent (diphenoxylate hydrochloride) and an anticholinergic agent (atropine sulphate), used in the treatment of diarrhoea and sometimes taken as a street drug for its psychotropic effects.
[Trademark]

longitudinal fissure *n*. The long deep groove separating the two *cerebral hemispheres of the brain. Also called the *interhemispheric fissure*, *principal sulcus*, *longitudinal sulcus*, or *sulcus principalis*.
[From Latin *longitudo, longitudinis* length, from *longus* long]

longitudinal study *n*. A research design in which the same sample of research participants or subjects is examined repeatedly over an extended span of time, typically to investigate problems of developmental psychology. *See also* panel study. *Compare* cross-sectional study.

long-sightedness *n*. A non-technical name for *hyperopia.

long-term memory *n*. A type of *memory containing information that is stored for periods ranging from about 30 seconds to many decades, often differentiated into *episodic memory for events and experiences and *semantic memory for information about the world, although *perceptual memory may not fall into either category. Also called *secondary memory*. *See also* ACT*, declarative memory, episodic memory, levels of processing, procedural memory, semantic memory, working memory. *Compare* sensory memory, short-term memory. **LTM** *abbrev*.

long-term potentiation *n*. A process necessary for *consolidation of certain types of memory traces, occurring prominently in the *hippocampus but also in other brain regions, involving cells showing increased sensitivity to new stimulation as a result of prior excitation, believed to be based on *Hebb synapses. It is promoted by *opiates, *noradrenalin (norepinephrine), and *dopamine. **LTP** *abbrev*.
[From Latin *potentia* power or force + -*ation* indicating a process or condition]

long-term store *n*. Another name for *long-term memory. **LTS** *abbrev*.

look-and-say method n. Another name for the *whole-word method.

looming n. Accelerating increase in the *angular size of a visual image, usually indicating that an object is approaching the face and that a collision is imminent, eliciting reflex avoidance reactions in most animals, including humans even in early infancy, but triggering landing behaviour in flies and other insects. Also called *retinal expansion*.

loosening of associations n. A form of *thought disorder, closely related to *cognitive derailment, characterized by speech that shifts between topics only minimally related to one another, usually without the speaker being aware of the disconnectedness of the stream of ideas. *Compare* disorganized speech, incoherence.

lorazepam n. A *benzodiazepine drug used as an *anxiolytic and *sedative. Also called *Ativan* (trademark).

lordosis n. Arching of the spine with a concave back and raised pelvis, a posture adopted by females of many animal species when sexually aroused. It is contrasted with kyphosis (hunchback curvature), or scoliosis (lateral curvature).
[From Greek *lordos* bent back + -*osis* indicating a process or state]

lordosis quotient n. A standard index of the relative sexual receptivity of a female animal in the presence of males, given by the number of times the female adopts a posture of *lordosis in a specified time period divided by the number of times a male mounts her.

loss aversion n. The observation that a loss generally has a greater subjective effect than an equivalent gain. *See* prospect theory. *See also* endowment effect. *Compare* risk aversion. **loss-averse** adj.

lost-letter technique n. An *unobtrusive measure of attitudes in which stamped addressed envelopes are scattered in public places, as if left by accident, the proportion being posted by members of the public and turning up at the addresses on the envelopes providing a crude index of attitudes in the community. For example, if half the envelopes are addressed to a pro-abortion organization and half to an anti-abortion organization, and if equal numbers of pro-abortion and anti-abortion envelopes are distributed but significantly more of the anti-abortion envelopes are returned, then it may be concluded that members of the community are more favourably disposed towards the anti-abortion than the pro-abortion cause. The technique was introduced by the US psychologist Stanley Milgram (1933–84) and colleagues in an article in the journal *Public Opinion Quarterly* in 1965.

loudness n. The experienced or subjective intensity of sound, corresponding to its *decibel sound pressure level, its standard unit of measurement being the *phon. Also called *volume*, though that word carries further connotations. *See also* amplitude, decibel, equal-loudness contour, loudness level, recruitment (2), volume (2). **loud** adj.

loudness level n. In relation to any specified sound, the intensity level in *decibel sound pressure level of a *pure tone with a frequency of 1,000 hertz (about two octaves above Middle C) that is judged by the listener to be equivalent to it in loudness. *See also* equal-loudness contour, phon.

loudness matching n. In *psychophysics, a procedure in which a listener adjusts the intensity of a tone until it seems equal in loudness to a comparison tone, used to map *equal-loudness contours.

loudness recruitment n. Another name for *recruitment (2).

Lou Gehrig's disease n. Another name for *amyotrophic lateral sclerosis.
[Named after an American baseball player Henry Louis Gehrig (1903–41), known as the Iron Horse, who died of it]

love n. An intense feeling of fondness or attraction, deeper and stronger than liking, especially when associated with a romantic or sexual attachment to someone. According to a popular taxonomy proposed by the Canadian sociologist John Alan Lee in *The Colors of Love: An Exploration of the Ways of Loving* (1973), there are three primary and three secondary types of love that blend into different shades like colours, the three primary types being *eros* (erotic or passionate love), *ludus* (ludic or playful love), and *storge* (storgic or friendly/affectionate love), and the three secondary types *pragma* (pragmatic or utilitarian love, a combination of ludus and storge), *mania* (manic or obsessive/possessive love, a combination of eros and ludus), and *agape* (agapic or brotherly love, an altruistic or selfless combination of eros and storge). According to the *triangular theory* of love proposed in 1986 by the US psychologist Robert J(effrey) Sternberg (born 1949), there are three basic components of love, namely *passion* (sexual desire), *intimacy* (confiding and sharing feelings), and *commitment* (intention to maintain the relationship), different combinations of the three components yielding eight basic types: *non-love* (none of the three components present), *infatuated love* (passion only), *liking/friendship* (intimacy only), *empty love* (commitment only), *romantic love* (passion and intimacy), *companionate love* (intimacy and commitment), *fatuous love* (passion and commitment), and *consummate love* (passion, intimacy, and commitment). *See also* attachment theory, Eros, genital love, libido. *Compare* romantic love scale.

love, genital *See* genital love.

love scale *See* romantic love scale.

lowball technique *n.* A technique for eliciting *compliance that is most often used in commercial transactions. A customer is first induced to agree to purchase an item by being quoted an unrealistically low price. Before the deal is completed, the salesperson claims to have discovered a mistake and tells the customer that the sale can go ahead only at a much higher price. Having made a commitment, the customer is more likely to agree than if the true price were revealed at the outset. The technique was named and first studied experimentally in 1978 by the US social psychologist Robert B(eno) Cialdini (born 1945), who discovered it while being trained as a car salesman. Cialdini and several colleagues performed a field experiment in which they first tried to persuade students to agree to volunteer to serve as experimental participants, and 56 per cent agreed. They then told the volunteers that the study was scheduled for 7 a.m., and the volunteers were given the opportunity to withdraw, but none did so, and 95 per cent of them actually turned up at the appointed time. However, when a control group were asked to partici-

pate and were told the unsocial timing of the experiment up front, only 24 per cent agreed to participate. *See also* door-in-the-face technique, foot-in-the-door technique. **lowballing** *n.* Using the *lowball technique.
[From *lowball* in baseball, a ball pitched to pass over the plate below the level of the batter's knees, alluding to a quoted price or estimate that is deceptively or misleadingly low]

lower threshold *n.* The lesser of the two thresholds determined by the *method of limits.

low-pass filter *See under* band-pass filter.

low vowel *n.* Another name for an *open vowel.

LSD *abbrev.* Lysergic acid diethylamide, a crystalline compound first synthesized from lysergic acid in 1943 and since the 1960s widely used as a street drug. It acts as a *serotonin *agonist (3) and has powerful *hallucinogenic and *psychedelic effects that can mimic *psychotic (1) states. Its most common street name is *acid*. *See also* hallucinogen-related disorders, phantasticant.

lucid dream *n.* A *dream (1) in which the dreamer is aware of being asleep and dreaming and is sometimes able to control the course of events in the dream.
[From Latin *lucidus* clear, from *lucere* to shine, from *lux* light]

luciferase *n.* An enzyme that is present in all *bioluminescent organisms and that reacts with *luciferin, producing light as the luciferin returns to its ground state after enzymatic oxidation.
[From Latin *lucifer* light-bearer + Greek *-ase* denoting an enzyme, from *diastasis* separation]

luciferin *n.* A chemical compound involved in *bioluminescence, present in certain organisms such as deep-sea fishes, fireflies, and glow-worms. It is oxidized by the enzyme *luciferase and emits light on decaying to its ground state.
[From Latin *lucifer* light-bearer + *-in(a)* indicating an organic compound]

Luckiesh illusion *n.* A more appropriate name for what is usually called the *Sander parallelogram.

[First published by the US lighting engineer and psychologist Matthew Luckiesh (1883–1967) in his book *Visual Illusions: Their Causes, Characteristics and Applications* (1922, p. 58)]

ludic love *n*. A primary type of *love that is playful and flirtatious. *Compare* agapic love, erotic love, manic love, pragmatic love, storgic love.
[From Latin *ludere* to play + *-ikos* of, relating to, or resembling]

lumen *n*. **1.** A unit of *luminous intensity, equal to the *luminous flux emitted or reflected in a solid angle of one steradian (a stereo radian or solid angle with its vertex at the centre of a sphere cutting off an area of the sphere's surface equal to the square of its radius) by a point source having a uniform intensity of one *candela. *See also* bril, foot-candle. **lm** *abbrev*. **2.** A cavity within an organ, such as any of the hollows within the *central nervous system filled with cerebrospinal fluid, including the cerebral *ventricles and the *central canal of the spinal cord.
[From Latin *lumen* light or aperture]

Luminal *n*. A proprietary name for the barbiturate drug *phenobarbital (phenobarbitone).
[Trademark]

luminance *n*. The amount of light per unit area emitted or reflected by an object or surface, hence the intensity of the emitted or reflected light, giving rise to the visual sensation of *brightness or *lightness, its standard measure being in *candelas per square metre. *See also* contrast ratio, Gelb effect, Kardos effect, reflectance, Troland. *Compare* luminosity, luminous flux, luminous intensity. **L** *abbrev*.

luminosity *n*. The perceived *brightness or *lightness of an object or surface emitting or reflecting light, corresponding to its physical *luminance.

luminosity coefficient *n*. Any of the weights attached to a wavelength in the *luminous efficiency function.

luminosity curve *n*. A graph depicting the intensity of light that is required at each point in the visible spectrum for the colours to appear equally bright, a *photopic luminosity curve being required for vision in bright light

and a *scotopic luminosity curve for vision in dim light.

luminous efficiency function *n*. A function that predicts the perceived *brightness of light as a weighted combination of its component wavelengths, the weights or luminosity coefficients being derived from averaged *luminosity curves of representative viewers. A *photopic luminous efficiency function* is required for cone-mediated vision in bright light and a *scotopic luminous efficiency function* for rod-mediated vision in dim light.

luminous flux *n*. A measure of the rate of emission or reflection of light from an object or surface, its standard unit of measurement being in *lumens. Symbol: Φ. *Compare* luminance, luminous intensity.

luminous intensity *n*. The amount of light per unit area emitted or reflected by an object or surface, expressed in terms of *luminous flux per steradian (a stereo radian or solid angle with its vertex at the centre of a sphere cutting off an area of the sphere's surface equal to the square of its radius), its standard unit of measurement being the *candela. *See also* photometer. *Compare* luminance, luminous flux. **I** *abbrev*.

lunacy *n*. An obsolete term for any severe *mental disorder, thought to be associated with phases of the moon. Empirical studies have consistently failed to find any significant correlation between phases of the moon and admissions to mental hospitals, suicides, or any other objective index of mental disorder. **lunatic** *n*. One afflicted with *lunacy.
[From Latin *luna* the moon]

lunatic asylum *n*. An obsolete term for a mental hospital.

lunatic fringe *n*. An abusive term for people who adopt or support views that others consider extreme or fanatical.

luteal phase *n*. The second phase of the *oestrous cycle or *menstrual cycle, characterized by the formation of the *corpus luteum and secretion of *progesterone from it. In the absence of pregnancy, it culminates in a rapid fall in progesterone and the onset of *menstruation, which in turn is followed by the *follicular phase. Also called the *secretory*

phase. *See also* late luteal phase dysphoric disorder, luteinizing-hormone releasing hormone. *Compare* follicular phase, menstrual phase.
[Named after the corpus luteum]

luteinizing hormone *n.* A gonadotrophic hormone secreted by the anterior pituitary. In females, it stimulates *ovulation and the formation of the *corpus luteum; in males it stimulates *androgen secretion. Also called *interstitial-cell-stimulating hormone (ICSH)*, especially in males. *See also* luteinizing-hormone releasing hormone, oestrous cycle. *Compare* follicle-stimulating hormone. **LH** *abbrev.*
[From Latin *luteum* egg yolk, from *luteus* yellow]

luteinizing-hormone releasing hormone *n.* A *releasing hormone that is secreted by the hypothalamus in response to a *biological clock at the beginning of a woman's *menstrual cycle and that in turn stimulates the pituitary gland to secrete *luteinizing hormone. Also called *gonadotrophin-releasing hormone* **LH-RH** *abbrev.*

luteotrophic hormone *n.* Another name for *prolactin. Also spelt *luteotropic hormone*. Also called *luteotrophin* (or *luteotropin*). **LTH** *abbrev.*
[From Latin *luteum* egg yolk, from *luteus* yellow + *trophe* nourishment]

Luvox *n.* A proprietary name for the antidepressant drug *fluvoxamine.
[Trademark]

lux *n.* The standard SI unit of *illuminance or illumination, equal to 1 *lumen per square metre, equivalent to 0.0929 foot-candle.
[From Latin *lux* light]

lycanthropy *n.* **1.** The magical transformation of a person into a wolf. **2.** A *delusion

that one is a wolf. Cases have been traced back to Nebuchadnezzar II (605–562 BC), King of Babylon, who was apparently so deluded.
[From Greek *lykos* a wolf + *anthropos* a person]

lymph *n.* The pale yellow fluid, consisting chiefly of a liquid similar to blood plasma and white blood cells or leucocytes, that is collected from body tissues and transported through a network of capillary vessels called the lymphatic system before flowing passively into the bloodstream through the thoracic duct.
[From Latin *lympha* water, cognate with Greek *nymphe* a nymph]

lymphocyte *n.* Any of a group of *leucocytes, including *B lymphocytes and *T lymphocytes, that are present in the blood and lymph and that play an important part in the *immune system. *See also* granulocyte, monocyte.
[From Latin *lympha* water + Greek *kytos* a vessel]

Lysenkoism *n.* A form of *neo-Lamarckism, based on the assumption that acquired characteristics can be passed on by heredity. It seriously handicapped Soviet biology and agricultural production from 1948 until the death of Stalin in 1953.
[Named after the Russian geneticist and agronomist Trofim Denisovich Lysenko (1898–1976) who propounded it in his book *Agrobiology* in 1948, which earned him the Stalin Prize in 1949]

lysergic acid diethylamide *See* LSD.

lysosome *n.* Any of the tiny particles containing digestive enzymes that are present in the cytoplasm of most cells, contained within membranes to prevent self-digestion of the cells. *See also* retrograde transport.
[From Greek *lysis* loosening + *soma* a body]

mace *n.* A spice prepared by grinding the dried, reddish, fleshy outer covering of the nutmeg. *See* myristin.
[From Latin *macir* mace]

Mace *n.* A liquid that, when sprayed in a person's face, acts as a type of *tear gas, causing temporary blindness, dizziness, immobilization, and sometimes nausea, and that is used as an *incapacitant for personal defence and crowd control. *Compare* BZ gas, CN gas, CS gas, pepper spray.
[Trademark]

Mach band *n.* An illusory light or dark strip along the edge of a blurred contour between light and dark areas of an image, the strip on the light side being lighter than the light area of the image and the strip on the dark side darker than the dark area, familiar examples being the light and dark strips that can be seen at the outer and inner edges, respectively, of a blurred shadow cast by the sun or by a table lamp. Such bands have been incorporated deliberately into paintings by artists such as the French neo-impressionist and pointillist Georges Seurat (1859–91), and the phenomenon is called *irradiation* in the literature of art criticism. *See also* Craik–O'Brien effect.
[Named after the Austrian physicist, philosopher, and psychologist Ernst Mach (1838–1916) who first drew attention to the phenomenon in 1865]

Machiavellianism *n.* A strategy of social conduct that involves manipulating others for personal advantage, often to the detriment of the people being thus exploited. The concept was introduced by the US psychologists Richard Christie (1918–92) and Florence L. Geis (1933–93) in a book chapter in 1968 and discussed in their edited book *Studies in Machiavellianism* (1970), and it is sometimes in-

terpreted as a personality trait. In an experiment in which groups of three players had to reach agreements as to how to divide $10 among themselves, people who had scored high on the *Mach scale tended to end up with significantly more money ($5.57 on average) than low scorers ($1.29 average), the chance expectation, had Machiavellianism been unrelated to outcomes, being $3.33, and other evidence has accumulated to show that high scorers have a propensity to manipulate others to their own advantage, often by lying and cheating.
[Named after the Florentine statesman and political philosopher Niccolò Machiavelli (1469–1527) who advocated manipulative political behaviour in his posthumous book *Il Principe* (The Prince, 1532)]

Mach illusion *n.* A visual illusion consisting of an ambiguous line drawing of a folded sheet of paper. *See also* ambiguous figure.
[Named after the Austrian physicist, philosopher, and psychologist Ernst Mach (1838–1916) who published it in 1866]

machine intelligence *n.* Another name for *artificial intelligence.

Machover Draw-a-Person Test *See* Draw-a-Person test.

Mach scale *n.* A questionnaire designed to measure *Machiavellianism as a personality trait. It contains items such as the following (agreement indicating high Machiavellianism): *The best way to handle people is to tell them what they want to hear*; *Anyone who completely trusts anyone else is asking for trouble*; and *It is safest to assume that all people have a vicious streak that will come out when it is given a chance*. The scale also contains items such as the following, agreement with which indicates low Machiavellianism: *When you ask some-*

one to do something for you, it is best to give the real reasons, rather than giving reasons that might carry more weight; One should take action only when sure it is morally right; and There is no excuse for lying to someone. People who score high on the scale are called *high Machs* and people who score low are called *low Machs.* The scale was introduced in a book chapter in 1968 by the US psychologists Richard Christie (1918–92) and Florence L. Geis (1933–93) and discussed in their edited book *Studies in Machiavellianism* (1970). A version of the scale for use with children is called the *Kiddie Mach.* Also called the *Machiavellianism scale.*

macrocephaly *n.* Congenital enlargement of the head without increased intracranial pressure (*compare* hydrocephalus), resulting in some degree of *mental retardation. **macrocephalic** *adj.*
[From Greek *makros* large + *kephale* head]

macroevolution *n.* A relatively slow change brought about by *natural selection, leading to the emergence of a *genus, *family (2), *order (3), or *class (2) of organisms. *Compare* microevolution.
[From Greek *makros* large + English *evolution*]

macroglia *n.* A generic name for three types of *neuroglia found in the central nervous system, namely *astrocytes, *ependymal cells, and *oligodendrocytes. *See also* glia. *Compare* microglia.
[From Greek *makros* large + *glia* glue]

macromania *n.* An unusual name for *megalomania.
[From Greek *makros* large + *mania* madness]

macrophage *n.* A large *phagocytic *leucocyte that is abundantly present in the blood, lymph, and connective tissues of most body organs and that ingests invading microorganisms and scavenges damaged cells and cellular debris. *See also* stem cell.
[From Greek *makros* large + *phagein* to eat]

macropsia *n.* Visual perception of objects as larger than they really are, usually resulting from damage to the *retinas, *epilepsy, or one of the *somatoform disorders. Also called *macropsy. Compare* micropsia.
[From Greek *makros* large + *opsis* sight, from *ops* an eye + *-ia* indicating a condition or quality]

macula *n.* A patch or spot, especially the patch of *hair cells aligned approximately horizontally in the *utricle and approximately vertically in the *saccule when the head is upright, projecting into the gelatinous otolith membrane in the *vestibular system. Also an abbreviated name for the *macula lutea of the retina. **maculae** *pl.*
[From Latin *macula* a spot or stain]

macula lutea *n.* A small yellowish oval-shaped area in the centre of the *retina, where *cones are especially plentiful and vision most distinct, located 2 millimetres from the *optic nerve, containing the *fovea. Also called the *yellow spot. See also* Arago phenomenon, colour zone. **maculae luteae** *pl.* **macular** *adj.*
[From Latin *macula* spot + *lutea* yellow]

Madame Butterfly fantasy *n.* A recurrent *daydream that a departed loved one will return, found most often in 5–8-year-old children of divorced parents who fantasize about the absent parent returning.
[Named after the eponymous heroine of Puccini's opera, *Madame Butterfly*]

mad cow disease *n.* A non-technical name for *BSE.

magazine training *n.* In experimental research with an animal in a *Skinner box, a preparatory process during which food is delivered without the animal having to press a lever, peck a key, or make any other response. Its purpose is to accustom the animal to the sound and sight of the food being delivered from the magazine to the food hopper so that this does not cause disturbance during the subsequent learning process.

Magendie's foramen *n.* The central opening in the roof of the fourth cerebral *ventricle, interconnecting with the *subarachnoid space.
[Named after the French physiologist François Magendie (1783–1855) + Latin *foramen* a hole, from *forare* to bore or pierce]

Maggie illusion *n.* Another name for the *Margaret Thatcher illusion.

magical number seven *n.* A general limitation on human information processing capacity, according to a classic article in the journal *Psychological Review* in 1956 entitled 'The

Magical Number Seven Plus or Minus Two: Some Limits on Our Capacity for Processing Information' by the US psychologist George A(rmitage) Miller (born 1920), who assembled evidence suggesting that the human mind has a span of absolute judgement that can distinguish about seven distinct categories, a span of *short-term memory for about seven items, and a *span of apprehension or attention that can encompass about six items at a time. *See also* chunking, dynamic memory span, iconic store, subitize.

magical thinking *n.* *Thinking that one's thoughts on their own can bring about effects in the world or that thinking something amounts to doing it.

magic mushroom *n.* Any of a number of mushrooms containing substances that are taken as *psychedelic or *hallucinogenic drugs, notably the *fly agaric mushroom *Amanita muscaria* and the *liberty cap mushroom *Psilocybe semilanceata*. *See also* teonanactyl.

Magnan sign *n.* A name given to *formication when it occurs as a *withdrawal symptom in cocaine users. Also called the *cocaine bug*.
[Named after the French physician Valentin Magnan (1835–1916) who first described it in a co-authored article in 1889]

magnetic resonance imaging *See* MRI.

magnetic sense *n.* A capacity possessed by some species of bacteria, bees, snails, birds, and fishes to detect the Earth's magnetic field, which acts as an aid to navigation. The navigation of European robins (*Erithacus rubecula*) can be altered by superimposing an artificial magnetic field, and homing pigeons with magnets attached to their heads become disoriented when the sky is overcast and they cannot use the sun as a compass. This sense modality has been most extensively studied in the rainbow trout, which can be conditioned to press a bar for food whenever it detects one magnetic field rather than another, and nerve impulses in response to magnetic fields have been detected in its *trigeminal nerve, which branches over the front of its head. The magnetic sense organ is believed to contain crystals of magnetite or loadstone, the mineral first used by humans to construct compasses. Chains of these crystals have been located in a discrete layer of the rainbow trout's snout, and they move when the fish changes its orientation to the Earth's magnetic field. Also called the *electromagnetic sense*. *Compare* electroreceptor.

magnetoencephalography *n.* A method of *brain imaging through the recording of magnetic fields induced by the electrical activity of brain cells. **MEG** *abbrev.*
[From Greek *magnetis (lithos)* magnesian (stone) + *enkephalos* the brain, from *en* in + *kephale* the head + *graphein* to write]

magnitude estimation *n.* A scaling method used in *psychophysics in which an observer assigns numbers to a *variable stimulus according to its apparent intensity, often after being presented with a *standard stimulus and told what number to assign to it, as when an observer is told that a standard light stimulus should be assigned a brightness rating of 10 and the variable stimulus should be assigned numbers in relation to it. *See also* cross-modal matching, direct scaling. *Compare* magnitude production.

magnitude production *n.* A *psychophysical technique in which an observer adjusts a *variable stimulus until it stands in some prescribed relation of magnitude to a *standard stimulus, as when an observer adjusts a sound stimulus until it appears equal in loudness, twice as loud, or half as loud as a comparison sound. Also called the *production method*. *See also* cross-modal matching. *Compare* magnitude estimation.

magnocellular nucleus *n.* A nucleus in the *medulla oblongata, connected to the *subcoerulear nucleus, responsible for *REM atonia.
[From Latin *magnus* large + *cella* a room, from *celare* to hide, alluding to the fact that it contains large cells]

magnocellular system *n.* The earlier evolved of the two major visual pathways, originating in large *ganglion cells in the *retina, projecting to the bottom two layers of the *lateral geniculate nucleus that contain neurons with large cell bodies, and thence to layer 4Cα of the *primary visual cortex (Area V1). It is characterized by colour-blindness, rapidly conducting axons responsible for perception of movement, high contrast-sensitivity re-

sponsive to small differences in brightness, and low resolution. Magnocellular neurons carry information about movement and depth but not colour, whereas some *parvocellular neurons carry high-resolution information about shape and others low-resolution information about colour and shades of grey. Also called the *magno system*. *See also* M cell (Y cell), MT, parasol cell. *Compare* parvocellular system. **M system** *abbrev.*
[From Latin *magnus* large + *cella* a room, from *celare* to hide]

main effect *n*. In statistics, in data obtained from an *analysis of variance (ANOVA) or the transformed scores of a *log-linear analysis, the mean change in scores resulting from a change in the level of a single independent variable or factor, averaged over all combinations of levels of the other factor(s). *Compare* interaction effect.

mainline *vb*. In drug-culture slang, to inject a drug intravenously (into a vein). *Compare* skin-pop.

maintenance behaviour *n*. Behaviour carried out by an animal for basic subsistence, including searching for food, finding or constructing suitable shelter, and mating. US *maintenance behavior*.

maintenance rehearsal *n*. The simple repetition (without elaboration) of items that need to be remembered in order to prevent them fading from *short-term memory, as when a person repeats a telephone number over and over while searching for a pen and paper to write it down. It develops spontaneously in children at 6–7 years of age. *See also* phonological loop, rehearse (2). *Compare* elaborative rehearsal.

major affective disorders *n*. A generic name sometimes used to cover *major depressive disorder and *bipolar disorders.

major depressive disorder *n*. A *depressive disorder characterized by one or more *major depressive episodes without any history of *manic, *mixed, or *hypomanic episodes. Up to fifteen per cent of people with severe major depressive disorder commit suicide each year. Also called *major depression*. *See also* antidepressant, cognitive therapy, inositol, MHPG. *Compare* dysthymic disorder. **MDD** *abbrev.*

major depressive episode *n*. A *mood episode, lasting at least two weeks, characterized by five or more of the following symptoms, including at least one of the first two, for at least two weeks: depressed mood or *depression most of the day, almost every day (possibly manifested as irritability in children and adolescents); markedly diminished interest or pleasure in almost all activities for most of the day; loss of appetite or a marked increase in appetite almost every day, leading to significant weight loss or gain; *insomnia (especially middle or terminal insomnia) or *hypersomnia; *psychomotor agitation (manifested by such behaviour as hand-wringing) or *psychomotor retardation (manifested by slowness of movement or speech); fatigue or loss of energy (*asthenia); feelings of worthlessness or excessive or inappropriate guilt; indecisiveness or diminished ability to think or concentrate; recurrent thoughts of death or suicide. At some time in their lives, 5–10 per cent of men and 10–20 per cent of women in the US, the UK, and comparable industrialized countries experience a major depressive episode.

major epilepsy *n*. A form of *epilepsy in which *tonic–clonic convulsions occur. Formerly called *grand mal epilepsy*.

majority preference cycle *See under* Condorcet's paradox.

major solution *n*. In the *neo-Freudian theory of the German-born US psychoanalyst Karen Horney (1885–1952), the repression of aspects of one's self that are in conflict with one's *idealization of oneself.

major tranquillizer *n*. An obsolescent name for a *neuroleptic (1) drug. US *major tranquilizer*. *Compare* minor tranquillizer.

Make-a-Picture-Story Test *n*. A *projective test devised by Edwin S. Schneidman and first published in 1947, often described as a cousin of the *TAT, consisting of a series of background pictures—a living room, a street, a bridge, and so on—together with 67 human and animal cutout figures, the respondent's task being to place one or more of the figures on a background and then to tell a story about the resulting picture. **MAPS** *abbrev.*

maladjustment *n*. Failure to deal adequately with problems of adaptation to physical, emotional, social, economic, or occupational circumstances, events, or experiences, generally leading to coping difficulties or symptoms of *stress (1).

malapropism n. The unintentional replacement of a word with another word of similar sound, especially when the effect of the error is humorous, as in the phrase *expletive delighted* instead of *expletive deleted*. Compare catachresis (a more general term).
[Named after Mrs Malaprop in Sheridan's play, *The Rivals* (1775), from French *mal à propos* out of place or inappropriate]

mal de ojo n. A *culture-bound syndrome, sometimes referred to in English as the *evil eye*, widespread throughout Mediterranean cultures and Latino communities in other parts of the world, to which children are supposed to be especially vulnerable, believed to be caused by a malignant look or glance from a malevolent person, leading to insomnia, crying without provocation, diarrhoea, vomiting, and fever.
[From Spanish *mal* illness + *de* of + *ojo* an eye]

mal de pelea n. A variant name for *amok in Puerto Rico.
[From Spanish *mal* illness + *de* of + *pelea* tussle or quarrel]

male erectile disorder n. A *sexual dysfunction characterized by persistent or recurrent inability to attain or maintain an adequate erection of the penis until completion of sexual activity, believed to affect approximately ten per cent of adult males, causing significant distress or problems of interpersonal interaction. It is not diagnosed if it is attributable to a drug or a *general medical condition. Also called *erectile dysfunction* (*ED*), *erectile impotence*, or *impotence*. See also cyclic GMP, de-reflection, impotence (2), Viagra. Compare male orgasmic disorder.

male menopause See under climacteric.

male mouse effect n. Another name for the *Whitten effect.

male orgasmic disorder n. A *sexual dysfunction characterized by a persistent or recurrent delay or absence of *orgasm following the excitement phase of the male *sexual response cycle, causing significant distress or in-

terpersonal problems. It is not diagnosed if it is attributable to a drug or a *general medical condition. Also called *orgasmic impotence*, *ejaculatory impotence*, or *impotence*. See also dereflection, impotence (2). Compare male erectile disorder.

mali-mali See latah.

malingering n. Intentional feigning or exaggeration of physical or psychological symptoms, motivated by external incentives such as avoidance of work or military service, receipt of financial compensation, evasion of criminal prosecution, or procurement of prescription drugs. Compare compensation neurosis, factitious disorder, somatoform disorders. **malinger** vb.
[From French *malingre* sickly, perhaps from *mal* badly + Old French *haingre* feeble]

malleus n. The outermost and largest of the three small bones in the *middle ear, connected to the *tympanic membrane and capable of transmitting sound vibrations to the incus. Referred to non-technically as the *hammer*. Compare incus, stapes.
[From Latin *malleus* a hammer, alluding to its resemblance to a blacksmith's hammer]

mal puesto n. A name for *rootwork in Spanish-speaking communities of the Caribbean and the southern United States, where it is also called *brujeria*.
[Spanish *mal puesto* badly placed, from, *mal* badly + *poner* to place]

mamillary body n. An alternative spelling of *mammillary body*.

mammary gland n. The distinctive milk-producing *exocrine gland of mammals, consisting in humans of a network of tubes and cavities feeding the external nipple of the breast.
[From Latin *mamma* a breast]

mammillary body n. Either of two small rounded protrusions from the back of the *hypothalamus, forming the terminal pillars of the *fornix, implicated in emotion, sexual arousal, and memory. Also spelt *mamillary body*.
[From Latin *mammilla* a nipple, diminutive of *mamma* a breast]

mammillothalamic tract n. A bundle of nerve fibres connecting the *mammillary bodies to the *thalamus.

mana n. A Melanesian and Polynesian word (also found in Maori), imported into *analytical psychology by Carl Gustav Jung (1875–1961), denoting a supernatural life force, normally originating from the head or the spirit world, that can be concentrated in other people or objects and inherited and transmitted between people, and that confers high social status and ritual power.

mand n. In the writings of the US psychologist B(urrhus) F(rederic) Skinner (1904–90), a verbal utterance that makes a demand and is reinforced by fulfilment of the demand, a typical example being *Please shut the door.* Compare tact (2).
[From (de)mand]

mandala n. In Hindu and Sanskrit art, a design, usually circular in form, symbolizing the universe. A version of it, comprising a circle divided into four equal sectors (or a circle inscribed in a square, or a square inscribed in a circle), was imported into *analytical psychology by Carl Gustav Jung (1875–1961) as a symbol of the self as a psychic unity, which can appear in dreams or paintings during *Jungian analysis. *See also* individuation.
[From Sanskrit mandala a circle]

mania n. A *mood disorder characterized by *manic episodes. **maniac** n. A person with *mania. *See also* antimanic, inositol. **manic** adj. Of or pertaining to *mania. **maniacal** adj. Of, pertaining to, or resembling a *maniac.
[From Greek mania madness]

manic–depressive psychosis n. Another name for *bipolar disorders. Also called manic–depressive disorder or manic–depressive reaction. **MDP** abbrev.

manic episode n. A *mood episode lasting at least one week, characterized by continuously elevated, expansive, or irritable mood, sufficiently severe to cause marked impairment in social or occupational functioning or to require hospitalization, during which there may be inflated *self-esteem or *grandiose ideas or actions, decreased need for sleep (almost invariably), increased talkativeness, *flight of ideas, distractibility, increased goal-oriented activity, *psychomotor agitation, and risky pleasure-seeking activities such as spree shopping, sexual indiscretions, or imprudent financial investments. *See also* antimanic, inositol. Compare major depressive episode, mixed episode.
[From Greek mania madness]

manic love n. A secondary form of *love that is obsessive and/or possessive, often being associated with jealousy, and is a combination of *erotic love and *ludic love. Compare agapic love, pragmatic love, storgic love.

Manifest Anxiety Scale n. A questionnaire designed to measure the personality trait of overt or conscious anxiety, developed by the US psychologist Janet A. Taylor (born 1923, later called Janet Taylor Spence) from the pool of items used in the *MMPI, and published by her in the Journal of Abnormal and Social Psychology in 1953. Also called the Taylor Manifest Anxiety Scale or the Iowa Manifest Anxiety Scale. **MAS** abbrev.

manifest content n. In *psychoanalysis, the narrative substance of a *dream (1) as it is recalled by the dreamer, in contradistinction to the *latent content that may be exposed by *interpretation (2) of the *dreamwork.

manner of articulation n. The way in which the airstream, usually from the lungs, is interfered with in order to produce a speech sound. In English, there are five or six manners of articulation: *plosive, *fricative, *affricate, *nasal (2), *liquid, and *semivowel, the last two usually being combined as *approximant. *See also* articulation.

Mann–Whitney U test n. In statistics, a widely used *distribution-free test, more powerful than the *median test, of the null hypothesis that two independent samples come from the same population. The distribution-dependent alternative is the *independent samples t test.
[Named after the Austrian-born US mathematician Henry Berthold Mann (1905–2000) and the US statistician Donald Ransom Whitney (1915–2001) who jointly published the test in 1947]

Mantel–Haenszel chi-square n. In statistics, an index of linear association between the row and column variables in a cross-tabulation, calculated by multiplying the

*product–moment correlation coefficient by one less than the number of scores.
[Named after the US biostatistician Nathan Mantel (1919–2002) and epidemiologist William Haenszel (1910–98) who published it in 1959]

map distance *n.* A measure of the relative distance or separation of two *gene loci in terms of the percentage of progeny inheriting one but not the other. It ranges from zero to 100, thus 10 map units represents ten per cent *discordant progeny, 15 map units represents fifteen per cent discordant progeny, and so on.

Marbe's law *n.* The proposition that the higher the population frequency of a particular response to an item in a *word-association test, the shorter the *response latency when that response is given by an individual respondent. Also called the *Marbe–Thumb law*.
[Named after the French-born German psychologist Karl Marbe (1869–1953) who formulated it in 1901]

Margaret Thatcher illusion *n.* The natural appearance of an inverted image of a human face in which the eyes (with their eyebrows) and mouth are inverted relative to the face, although the image appears grotesquely hideous when the face as a whole is viewed the right way up, so that only the eyes and mouth are inverted (see illustration). The illu-

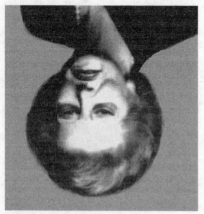

Margaret Thatcher illusion. The inverted face looks almost normal, but it becomes grotesquely hideous when turned the right way up.

sion of normality in the inverted image is believed to be due to the *differential inversion effect and the associated difficulty of recognizing configurational incongruities in an inverted face. Also called the *Maggie illusion* or the *Thatcher illusion*.
[So called because the British psychologist Peter G. Thompson (born 1950) who discovered it in 1980 originally used a photograph of the newly installed UK Prime Minister Margaret Thatcher]

marginal consciousness *n.* The portion of consciousness that is not the focus of *attention and of which one is only dimly aware.

marginals *n.* In statistics, the row and column totals of a cross-tabulation.

margin of attention *n.* Another name for *marginal consciousness.

margin of consciousness *n.* Another name for *marginal consciousness.

marijuana *n.* The cut and dried upper leaves, flowering tops, and young stems of the female *cannabis plant, rolled into cigarettes and smoked as a psychotropic drug.
[From Mexican Spanish *marihuana*, from Portuguese *mariguango* intoxicant]

marital therapy *n.* Any form of *psychotherapy aimed at treating problems of married couples. *Compare* couples therapy.

marketing orientation *n.* In *neo-Freudian theory, a term used by the German-born US psychoanalyst Erich Fromm (1900–80) to denote a category of people who consider their personalities as commodities to be bought and sold and who mould themselves to fit whatever qualities are demanded by others, with consequent superficiality and lack of individuality. *Compare* exploitative orientation, hoarding orientation, productive orientation, receptive orientation.

marketing research *n.* Research designed to estimate the size and location of markets or the cost of products or services, distinguished in careful usage from *market research.

market research *n.* A form of *survey research into the attitudes, opinions, and behaviour of consumers towards products and services, distinguished in careful usage from *marketing research.

Marplan n. A proprietary name for the antidepressant drug *isocarboxazid. [Trademark]

marriage counselling n. A form of *counselling offered to people with marital or relationship problems. US *marriage counseling*. Also called *marital counselling* (US *marital counseling*), *marriage guidance*, or *marriage guidance counselling* (US *marriage guidance counseling*).

Marr's computational theory of vision See $2\frac{1}{2}$-D sketch, 3-D model description, primal sketch. See also computational theory, generalized cone.

Marsilid n. A proprietary name for the antidepressant drug *iproniazid. [Trademark]

masculine protest n. In *individual psychology, a term introduced by the Austrian psychiatrist Alfred Adler (1870–1937) to denote a cluster of personality traits in either sex arising as overcompensations for feelings of inferiority and rejection of the feminine role. In later writings, Adler and his followers used the term more specifically to denote the rejection by women of the feminine role. Adler used the term for the first time in a paper read to the Viennese Psychoanalytic Society in 1911, and he developed and modified the concept further in his book *Individual Psychology* (1924), where he identified it as the main source of *neuroses. See also Diana complex, gender identity disorder.

masculinity–femininity scale n. Any scale designed to measure this dimension of personality, including the masculinity–femininity scale of the *MMPI.

masculinizing hormone n. A *hormone that causes masculine *traits to develop in an embryo. See Müllerian inhibiting substance, testosterone.

masked depression n. A form of *depression that is disguised or concealed behind *affective flattening, a different *mood (1) such as irritability, or some other symptom.

masking n. The blocking or suppression of the perception of a stimulus, often called the *test stimulus*, by the presentation of another stimulus, called the *masking stimulus*. Complete masking occurs when the test stimulus is not perceived, and partial masking occurs when its *absolute threshold is raised or its perceived intensity is reduced by the masking stimulus. The masking effect arises from swamping of the neural activity evoked by the test stimulus and/or suppression of the neural activity that test stimulus would have evoked if presented alone. See also auditory masking, backward masking, binaural unmasking, brightness masking, central masking, critical band, dichoptic masking, inspection time, metacontrast, paracontrast, pattern masking, Perky phenomenon, subliminal perception, visual masking.

masochism n. Another name for *sexual masochism. The term is also used loosely to denote extreme self-damaging behaviour not accompanied by sexual gratification. **masochistic** adj. [Named after the Austrian historian and novelist Leopold von Sacher-Masoch (1836–95) who wrote about it, notably in his novel *Venus in Pelz* (1870), translated into English as *Venus in Furs* (1902), in which the heroine Wanda subjects the narrator to sexually stimulating suffering]

masochistic personality n. Another name for *self-defeating personality disorder. It is misleading in view of the fact that no *paraphilia resembling *sexual masochism is involved.

mass action n. The doctrine propounded by the US physiological psychologist Karl Spencer Lashley (1890–1958) that the *cerebral cortex functions as a coordinated unit, with large areas being involved in all complex functions, and that consequently, within limits, the degree of deficit resulting from a localized lesion depends on the amount of cortex rather than the specific region affected. This doctrine is now known to have many exceptions, *localization of function being common in the cerebral cortex. See also equipotentiality.

massa intermedia n. A *commissure, not present in all human (especially male) brains, connecting the *thalamus in one cerebral hemisphere with its counterpart in the other.

[From Latin *massa* a mass + *inter* between + *media* the middle]

massed practice *n*. Learning that takes place in a single block rather than being divided into sessions separated by rest intervals or gaps, generally leading to inferior recall, after a delay, relative to *distributed practice. *See also* reminiscence (2).

mast cell *n*. A type of cell that is present in connective tissue and that responds to inflammation and allergens by releasing *histamine and *serotonin. *See also* axon reflex.
[Coined in 1879 by the German bacteriologist and immunologist Paul Ehrlich (1854–1915) from German *Mast* a fattening]

masturbation *n*. Sexual stimulation of the genitals, either one's own or another person's. *See also* auto-erotic. **masturbate** *vb*.
[From Latin *masturbari* to masturbate, of unknown origin, formerly believed to derive from *manus* a hand + *stuprare* to have sexual intercourse]

matched guise *n*. A research technique in which a bilingual or bidialectal person speaks the same words in two or more different languages or speech styles in order to compare listeners' responses while controlling for the effects of other factors.

matching bias *n*. In the *Wason selection task, a tendency to focus attention on evidence containing the letters and numbers mentioned in the rule. *Compare* confirmation bias.

Matching Familiar Figures Test *n*. An instrument designed to measure *reflection–impulsivity by requiring the respondent to select repeatedly from several alternative figures the one that matches a standard. The number of errors and the time required to complete the test are recorded, and people with below-median errors and above-median response times are classified as *reflective*; people with above-median errors and below-median response times *impulsive*; people with below-median errors and below-median response times *quick*; and people with above-median errors and above-median response times *slow*. The test was developed in 1966 by the US psychologist Jerome Kagan (born 1929). **MFFT** *abbrev*.

matching to sample *n*. A task in which a person or animal is presented with a series of trials, on each of which the task is to choose a test stimulus that is the same as a sample stimulus, the sample stimulus being presented simultaneously with the test stimulus in *simultaneous matching to sample*, or some time before the test stimulus in *delayed matching to sample*. In *generalized matching to sample*, the several different matching tasks are presented in sequence, and the increase in speed of learning across the series of tasks is measured.

materialism *n*. An approach to the *mind–body problem according to which only the physical realm is real and mental phenomena are merely functions or aspects of it. *See also* double-aspect theory, identity theory, monism.

maternal deprivation *n*. Inadequate mothering, whether delivered by the mother or another primary caretaker, during the first six months of life, leading to a failure of attachment, or more generally inadequate mothering during the first five years of life. The concept was introduced by the English psychiatrist (Edward) John (Mostyn) Bowlby (1907–90) who argued in his book *Child Care and the Growth of Love* (1953) that it could seriously affect the child's development and lead to psychological problems and juvenile delinquency. Early research tended to support the theory, but subsequent research suggested that the adverse effects were often caused by other factors that tend to accompany maternal deprivation, such as physical neglect. *See also* anaclitic depression, attachment theory, hospitalism, separation anxiety, separation anxiety disorder.

maternal inheritance *n*. Inheritance of characteristics through genes that are carried by *mitochondrial DNA, or by DNA in *plasmids in the cytoplasm outside the cell nucleus, and that are transmitted exclusively through the female line, because only the mother's ovum contributes cytoplasm to the *zygote.

mathematical induction *n*. Another name for *induction (2).

mathematics disorder *n*. A *learning disability characterized by substantially below-average mathematical ability for the given age, intelligence, and education; the *deficit interfering substantially with scholastic or academic achievement or everyday life and not being due merely to a sensory deficit.

matriarchy n. Literally, a community of related families under the authority of a female head called a *matriarch*; applied more generally to any form of social organization in which women have predominant power, there being controversy as to whether a matriarchy has ever existed, although there is no doubt that *matrilineal societies have existed. *Compare* patriarchy. **matriarchal** adj.
[From Latin *mater, matris* a mother + Greek *arche* a rule]

matrilineal adj. Of or relating to descent, kinship, or inheritance through the female line, as occurs in some non-western societies. *Compare* patrilineal.
[From Latin *mater, matris* a mother + *linea* a line]

matrix n. In mathematics, any rectangular array or elements, usually numbers.
[From Latin *matrix* womb or female animal used for breeding, from *mater* mother]

maturation n. The process of growing or ripening towards a fully developed state.
[From Latin *maturus* ripe + *-ation* indicating a process or condition]

Maudsley Personality Inventory n. A questionnaire designed to measure two major dimensions of personality, namely *extraversion and *neuroticism, according to the theory of personality of the German-born British psychologist Hans J(ürgen) Eysenck (1916–97), first propounded in his books *Dimensions of Personality* (1947) and *The Scientific Study of Personality* (1952). Eysenck published the test initially in the journal *Rivista di Psicologia* in 1956. Later versions of it were called the *Eysenck Personality Inventory and the *Eysenck Personality Questionnaire. **MPI** abbrev.
[Named after the Maudsley Hospital in Denmark Hill, south London, where Eysenck worked, and which in turn is named after the English psychiatrist Henry Maudsley (1835–1918) who founded it]

maximin n. In decision theory and game theory, an alternative or *strategy (2) that ensures the best of the worst possible payoffs, thereby maximizing the minimum possible payoff. Thus if there are three available alternatives, and if the worst that can happen is a small loss if the first alternative is chosen, a medium loss if the second alternative is chosen, and a large loss if the third alternative is chosen, then the first alternative is the maximin alternative irrespective of what other payoffs are possible. *See also* Ellsberg paradox, minimax, modified Ellsberg paradox.

maximum likelihood n. In statistics, the probability of obtaining a given set of observed scores in a random sample of a population maximized over the possible values of the *parameter(s) of the population from which the scores are drawn; also, a method of estimation used in *multiple regression and elsewhere based on this concept.

Maxwell disc n. A rotating disc on to which radially slit and overlapping discs of paper, cardboard, or plastic can be mounted to divide the surface into sectors of different colours for investigating *colour mixing. US *Maxwell disk*. Also called a *colour wheel*. *See also* associationism, Talbot's law.
[Named after the Scottish physicist James Clerk Maxwell (1831–79) who invented it and published it in 1855]

maze n. A network of passages and blind alleys, either a simple *T-maze or a more intricate labyrinth, introduced into psychology in an article in the *American Journal of Psychology* in 1901 by the US psychologist Willard Stanton Small (1870–1943) for studying animal learning and behaviour, a reward usually being provided for an organism that solves the maze and finds the goal box. Small constructed his original maze, which he used for studying 'the mental processes of the rat', as an exact replica in miniature of the famous garden maze at Hampton Court in Richmond-upon-Thames, England.
[From Old English *amasian* to amaze]

McCarthy Scales of Children's Abilities n. A set of scales for measuring the development of intellectual abilities of children between $2\frac{1}{2}$ and $8\frac{1}{2}$ years of age, divided into verbal ability, perceptual ability, quantitative ability, memory, and motor ability, also providing a score for general cognitive ability based on pooling the other scores.

[Named after the US developmental psychologist Dorothea McCarthy (1906–74) who introduced them]

McCollough effect *n.* A visual illusion that is seen by a viewer who stares for half a minute or more at two differently oriented and differently coloured grating patterns, such as vertical red and black stripes and horizontal green and black stripes, shifting attention back and forth between the two, and then looks at a figure containing a grating of vertical black and white stripes and a grating of horizontal black and white stripes. The white areas of the black and white gratings appear tinged with the *complementary colours of the corresponding (vertical or horizontal) coloured gratings, so that the vertical white stripes appear pale green and the horizontal white stripes pink. The fact that the illusory colours depend on the particular black and white grating patterns shows that they cannot be explained by depletion of pigment or any other gross retinal process. *See also* contingent aftereffect.

[Named after the US psychologist Celeste F(aye) McCollough (born 1926) who first reported the illusion in the journal *Science* in 1965]

M cell *abbrev.* A type of ganglion cell belonging to the *magnocellular system. Also called a *Y cell. Compare* P cell.

McGurk effect *n.* A phenomenon that occurs when a speech sound does not match the shape of the lips producing it, as when a sound corresponding to the usual pronunciation of the word *gay* is dubbed on to a video image of a person uttering the word *bay*, causing the listener to hear a word intermediate between the two (*day*). This effect shows that the visual channel conveys important information not just to deaf people but also to listeners with normal hearing.

[Named after the Scottish psychologist Harry McGurk (1936–98) who co-authored the first article on it, entitled 'Hearing Lips and Seeing Voices' in the journal *Nature* in 1976]

McNaghten rules *n.* A set of rules, established in English law in *Regina* v. *McNaghten* (1843) and followed in many jurisdictions throughout the world, according to which legal proof of *insanity, and thus lack of criminal responsibility, requires evidence that the accused either did not know what he or she was doing or was incapable of understanding that what he or she was doing was wrong. Also spelt *McNaughten rules* or *M'Naghten rules. See also* mens rea.

[Established by the House of Lords following the case of *R* v. *McNaghten* (1843) in which the defendant, Daniel McNaghten, shot and killed the private secretary of the British Prime Minister Sir Robert Peel but was found to have been of unsound mind at the time]

McNemar test *n.* In statistics, a *distribution-free test of the significance of changes, especially applicable to before–after designs of the effects of particular treatments in which scores are dichotomous and measurement is made on a *nominal scale or an *ordinal scale. It tests the *null hypothesis that unlike pairs of responses (0, 1) and (1, 0) are equally likely.

[Named after the US psychologist and statistician Quinn McNemar (1900–86) who developed it in 1947]

MDA *abbrev.* Methyl-dioxy amphetamine, a synthetic *designer drug derived from *amphetamine. *See also* amphetamine-related disorders, empathogen, substance-related disorders.

MDMA *abbrev.* 3,4-methylene-dioxy-methamphetamine, a central nervous system *stimulant and *designer drug commonly called *ecstasy (2).

mean *n.* Short for *arithmetic mean: in descriptive statistics, the average value, calculated for a finite set of scores by adding the scores together and then dividing the total by the number of scores. *See also* geometric mean, harmonic mean, trimmed mean. *Compare* median, mode. **M** *abbrev.* **mean** *adj.*

[From Old French *moien*, from Latin *medius* middle]

mean error method *n.* Another name for the *method of average error.

mean length of utterance *n.* The mean or average number of *morphemes or words in a sample of speech, often used as a crude index of the level of linguistic development of a child. **MLU** *abbrev.*

mean lethal dosage *n.* Another name for the *median lethal dosage (LD-50).

means–end analysis n. A cognitive *heuristic implemented by the *General Problem Solver to deal with practical problems when the *problem space is too large for exhaustive search to be used. The problem space is represented by an initial state (such as the starting position in a game of chess), a goal state (such as checkmating the opponent), and all possible intervening states that are achieved by actions involving the application of operators (such as chess moves) to existing states. If there is an action that immediately solves the problem, then it is implemented immediately; if not, the problem solver establishes the subgoal of maximally reducing the difference between the current state and the goal state; if an action can be found to achieve this subgoal, then it is implemented immediately; if not, the problem solver establishes the sub-subgoal of removing the constraints on achieving the subgoal; and so on. See also General Problem Solver.

mean square n. In statistics, the *arithmetic mean of the squared *deviation scores in a data set, used as an estimate of variance in *analysis of variance (ANOVA). See also sum of squares.

measurement n. The systematic assignment of numbers to represent quantitative *attributes of objects or events. The US psychologist S(tanley) S(mith) Stevens (1906–73) defined measurement in an article in the journal Science in 1946 and in an influential chapter in his Handbook of Experimental Psychology as 'the assignment of numerals to objects or events according to rules', and this definition is repeated in many textbooks, but it is avoided by many experts because it ignores a crucial (defining) aspect of measurement, namely its connection with quantity or magnitude, and because it includes rule-governed assignments of numbers that do not represent quantities or magnitudes, such as the assignment of telephone numbers to subscribers or of ISBN numbers to books. See also axiomatic measurement theory, conjoint measurement theory, measurement level, measurement model, scale (1).
[From Latin mensura a measure, from metiri to measure]

measurement level n. The type of measurement scale used for generating scores, which determines the permissible transformations that can be performed on the scores without changing their relationship to the *attributes being measured. For example, it is meaningless to calculate the mean of a collection of telephone numbers, because the level of measurement involved in the numbers (a nominal scale) renders the operations of addition and division meaningless. Level of measurement is not a property of the data themselves, but of the data and their interpretation considered together: the same scores can represent different levels depending on their interpretation. Among the most important measurement levels, with separate entries, are the following, arranged from lowest to highest level of measurement: *nominal scale, *ordinal scale, *interval scale, *ratio scale, *absolute scale. Another, at the same level as the interval scale, is the *log-interval scale. See also measurement, scale (1).

measurement model n. The relationship that is believed or assumed to exist between numerical scores recorded as data in an empirical investigation and the *attribute that is being measured. See also measurement, measurement level, model.

mechanism of defence See defence mechanism.

mechanoreceptor n. A type of *sensory receptor that converts kinetic energy from mechanical stimulation including touch, pressure, vibration, acceleration, or gravity into nerve impulses, such receptors being either *touch receptors in the *skin, *auditory receptors in the *organ of Corti, or receptors that respond to mechanical stimulation in the *vestibular system.
[From Greek mechane a machine + Latin recipere, receptum to receive, from re- back + capere, ceptum to take]

Mecholyl n. A proprietary name for the parasympathomimetic drug *methacholine. [Trademark]

MED-50 abbrev. The dosage of a drug that produces a specified effect in 50 per cent of the population. Also called the median effective dosage or ED-50. See also effective dosage, therapeutic index, therapeutic ratio.

medial adj. Situated in the middle or oriented towards the midline; the opposite of *lateral.

[From Latin *medialis* of or relating to the middle, from *medius* the middle]

medial forebrain bundle *n*. A tract of nerve fibres on each side of the *hypothalamus involved in the control of hunger and predatory aggression, and functioning more generally as a major reward centre through the action of the catecholamines *dopamine and *noradrenalin (norepinephrine). *See also* pleasure centre, quiet-biting attack. **MFB** *abbrev*.
[From Latin *medialis* situated in the middle, from *medius* the middle + English *forebrain*]

medial geniculate nucleus *n*. A structure at the back of each lobe of the *thalamus, close to the lateral geniculate nucleus, that receives inputs from the *inferior colliculus and relays them to the primary *auditory cortex. Also called the *medial geniculate body*. **medial geniculate nuclei** *pl*. **MGN** *abbrev*.
[From Latin *medialis* situated in the middle, from *medius* the middle + *geniculatus* knee-shaped, from *geniculum* a little knee, diminutive of *genus* a knee]

medial lemniscus *n*. Either of the two bundles of nerve fibres of the *lemniscus ascending through the medulla oblongata and pons and continuing to the somatosensory cortex in each cerebral hemisphere. *Compare* lateral lemniscus, trigeminal lemniscus.

medial rectus *n*. One of the four *rectus muscles attached externally to the eyeball.

medial surface *n*. The surface of an organ or structure situated or oriented towards the midline of the body, such as the inner surface of each *cerebral hemisphere, exposed only by a *midsagittal section dividing the brain through its longitudinal fissure. *See also* sagittal section.

median *n*. In descriptive statistics, a measure of *central tendency that is the middle value of the set of scores arranged in order of magnitude, or the mean of the two middle scores if there is an even number of scores and therefore no single middle score. *Compare* mean, mode. **median** *adj*.
[From Latin *medius* middle]

median effective dosage *n*. The dosage that produces a specified effect in 50 per cent of the population. *See also* effective dosage, therapeutic index, therapeutic ratio. *Compare* median lethal dosage, median toxic dosage, minimum effective dosage, minimum lethal dosage, minimum toxic dosage. **ED-50** or **ED$_{50}$** *abbrev*.

median eminence *n*. A swelling at the base of the *hypothalamus, immediately above the infundibulum, secreting hormones into the *hypothalamic–hypophyseal portal system.
[From Latin *medius* the middle + *eminentia* a prominence]

median lethal dosage *n*. The dosage of a drug or other substance that kills 50 per cent of experimental animals in a specified time. Also called the *mean lethal dosage*. *See also* lethal dosage, therapeutic index, therapeutic ratio. *Compare* median effective dosage, median toxic dosage, minimum effective dosage, minimum lethal dosage, minimum toxic dosage. **LD-50** or **LD$_{50}$** *abbrev*.

median plane *n*. Another name for the *midsagittal plane.

median section *n*. Another name for the *midsagittal section.

median temporal gyrus *n*. Another name for the *middle temporal gyrus.

median test *n*. In statistics, a *distribution-free test of the null hypothesis that two or more independent samples come from populations with the same *median. *See also* Mann–Whitney *U* test.

median toxic dosage *n*. The quantity of a drug or other substance that produces signs or symptoms of toxicity in 50 per cent of human or animal experimental subjects in a specified time. Also called the *mean toxic dosage*. *See also* therapeutic index, therapeutic ratio, toxic dosage. *Compare* median effective dosage, median lethal dosage, minimum effective dosage, minimum lethal dosage, minimum toxic dosage. **TD-50** or **TD$_{50}$** *abbrev*.

mediating variable *n*. A *variable, the value of which is determined by one or more *independent variables and/or other mediat-

ing variables and that in turn affects the value of a *dependent variable not directly affected by the independent variables. For example, the independent variable wealth has a measurable effect on the dependent variable life expectancy inasmuch as wealthy people tend to live longer than poor people, and the effect is indirect, one mediating variable that plays a part being medical care: wealthy people tend to receive more and better medical care than poor people, and this in turn increases life expectancy. The chain of causation is thus wealth → medical care → life expectancy, and medical care is a mediating variable. Often confused with *intervening variable.
[From Latin *mediare, mediatum*, to be in the middle, from *medius* the middle]

medical psychology *n.* A branch of *applied psychology devoted to psychological problems arising in the practice of medicine, including psychological aspects of pain, terminal illness, bereavement, disability, and reactions to medical advice. It overlaps to some extent with *health psychology.

medical student syndrome *n.* A form of *hypochondria in medical students, occasionally developing into full-blown *hypochondriasis, characterized by anxiety about having one or more (often several) of the disorders that are being studied. It often occurs as students begin studying mental disorders, when they begin to believe that they are suffering from the disorders that they are reading about in textbooks, and in this form it is also found among psychology students. Also called *medical student hypochondria*.

meditation *See* transcendental meditation.

medulla *n.* The internal part of any structure or organ, such as the adrenal medulla. Usually short for the *medulla oblongata, though this abbreviation is avoided in careful usage whenever its meaning is ambiguous. **medullae** or **medullas** *pl.*
[From Latin *medulla* marrow or innermost part]

medulla oblongata *n.* The lower, tapering part of the *brainstem, attached to the spinal cord, involved in the control of vegetative processes such as heartbeat, blood pressure,

breathing, and consciousness. Often shortened to *medulla*, though this is avoided in careful usage whenever ambiguity would result (*see* medulla). *See also* locked-in syndrome. **medullae oblongatae** or **medulla oblongatas** *pl.* **medullary**, **medullar**, or **bulbar** *adj.*
[From Latin *oblongus* elongated, from *longus* long]

medulloblastoma *n.* A quick-growing malignant brain tumour, usually originating in the *cerebellum, most common in children (especially boys) between 5 and 9 years old, responsive to radiotherapy but with poor long-term prognosis. Its name does not refer to the medulla oblongata.
[From *medulla* + *blastos* a bud + *-oma* indicating a tumour]

megalomania *n.* A pathological condition of *grandiose delusions. Also called *macromania*.
[From Greek *megas* great + *mania* madness]

megavitamin therapy *n.* Another name for *orthomolecular therapy.

meiosis *n.* **1.** A form of cell division such as that of *gametes in sexually reproducing species in which the nucleus divides into four daughter nuclei each containing half the *chromosomes of the parent nucleus (see illustration overleaf). It consists of two successive divisions: during the first, *homologous chromosomes pair up, exchange genetic material by *crossing over, then during the *anaphase* part of the cycle move apart by *disjunction (1) to form separate *haploid nuclei; during the second phase these daughter nuclei divide by *mitosis (with a further anaphase), producing four haploid cells. Also called *reduction division*. *Compare* mitosis. **2.** A figure of speech characterized by understatement or litotes. **meiotic** *adj.*
[From Greek *meiosis* diminution, from *meion* less + *-osis* indicating a process or state]

Meissner's corpuscle *n.* An egg-shaped *sensory receptor in hairless *skin, found most abundantly in the finger pads but also present in the skin of the inner forearm, foot, breast nipple, and lips, containing a single nerve fibre that spirals around the interior of the capsule and ends in a globular mass, sensitive to vibration when moving over

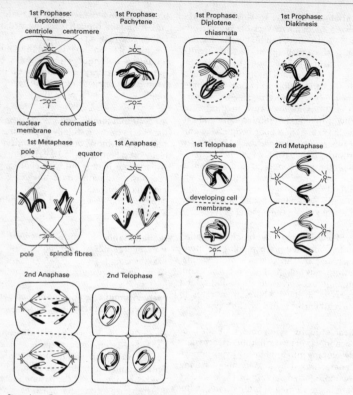

Meiosis. Stages in a cell containing two pairs of homologous chromosomes.

textured or embossed surfaces. Also called a *tactile corpuscle* or a *Wagner–Meissner corpuscle. Compare* free nerve ending, Golgi tendon organ, Merkel cell, Pacinian corpuscle, Ruffini corpuscle.
[Named after the German anatomist Georg Meissner (1829–1905) who discovered it]

mel *n.* A unit of subjective *pitch, arbitrarily anchored so that a 1,000-hertz tone at 40 decibels has a value of 1,000 mels by definition, other values being determined by *fractionation, the resulting graph of pitch in mels as a function of frequency in hertz usually being approximately S-shaped.
[From Greek *melos* a song]

melancholia *n.* A severe form of *depression; more specifically, a *major depressive

episode. **involutional melancholia** *n.* Another name for *involutional depression.
[From Greek *melas* black + *chole* bile + -*ia* indicating a condition or quality, referring to the ancient doctrine of the four *temperaments, according to which depression was attributed to an excess of black bile]

melanocyte-stimulating hormone *n.* A polypeptide *hormone that is secreted by the *anterior pituitary and that controls the degree of colouring in pigmented cells. **MSH** *abbrev.*
[From Greek *melas, melanos* black + *kytos* a vessel or hollow]

melatonin *n.* The *hormone *N*-acetyl-5-methoxytryptamine secreted by the *pineal gland only at night (hence sometimes called the Dracula hormone), lightening skin pigment in some organisms such as tadpoles, though apparently not in humans, affecting sexual development by inhibiting development of gonads in males and the oestrous cycle in females, perhaps promoting sleep (thus used for treating *jet lag), and probably fulfilling other unknown functions.

[From Greek *mela(s)* black + English *(sero)tonin*, alluding to its ability to lighten melanocytes]

Mellaril *n.* A proprietary name for the neuroleptic drug *thioridazine.

[Trademark]

melodic constancy *n.* A form of *perceptual constancy according to which a melody or tune tends to remain recognizably the same when it is played in another key with entirely different notes (*see* Gestaltqualität), at a different tempo (speed), or on another instrument with entirely different *timbre. *See also* Gestalt.

melodic paradox *n.* A phenomenon in the perception of musical tones that are clearly defined in terms of pitch class (the twelve notes of the octave that are normally labelled C, C#, D, . . . , B) but are ambiguous as regards the octaves to which they belong, each tone being composed of equal *sinusoidal waves from octaves spanning the auditory range. Using such ambiguous tones, if a sequence of chords (tones sounded together simultaneously) such as B with D, then A with E, then G with F, are presented to listeners, then the listeners clearly perceive the sequence as either converging or diverging in contrary motion, although the sequence could be either converging or diverging depending on the octaves to which the notes belong, and the stimulus tones lack the cues required to determine octave pitch. It is a surprising phenomenon rather than a true *paradox. *See also* auditory illusion. *Compare* semitone paradox, tritone paradox.

member *n.* A constituent part of a whole, especially a limb, an individual who belongs to a group or organization, or a political representative in a parliament. The term is used in *Gestalt psychology in preference to *part*, which has connotations of separateness denied by Gestalt theory. *See also* membership character.

[From Latin *membrum* a limb, member, or part]

membership character *n.* Any *attribute by which a *member (in the *Gestalt sense) is recognized as belonging to a whole; specifically, any attribute of an element that results directly from its belonging to a Gestalt.

membrana tympani *n.* Another name for the *tympanic membrane.

[From Latin *membrana* a membrane + *tympanum* a drum]

membrane *n.* A thin film, skin, or layer of (usually) fibrous tissue that covers, lines, or connects biological organs or cells. *See also* cell membrane, membrane potential, osmosis, semipermeable membrane, skin. **membranous** *adj.* Of or relating to a *membrane.

[From Latin *membrana* skin covering a body part, from *membrum* a member]

membrane potential *n.* The difference in electrical voltage across the membrane of a living cell, controlled by a *sodium pump and momentarily reversed in a *neuron when it transmits a nerve impulse. *See also* action potential, cell membrane, depolarization, resting potential.

membranous labyrinth *n.* The system of ducts, filled with *endolymph, suspended within the three *semicircular canals of the *bony labyrinth in the inner ear, containing the *vestibular system. *See also* labyrinth.

meme *n.* A self-replicating cultural element or pattern of behaviour, analogous to a gene but passed from one individual to another by imitation rather than genetic transmission. Memes are subject to inheritance and evolution through a form of *natural selection according to their likelihood, relative to the alternatives available in the meme pool, of being reproduced or of multiplying. Typical examples are tunes, ideas, beliefs, catchphrases, stories, hairstyles, clothing fashions, recipes, inventions, skills, traditions, and theories. Whereas genes propagate themselves in a gene pool by migrating from one body to the next, memes propagate themselves in a meme pool by migrating from one brain to the next; but unlike genes, memes are subject to *Lamarckian inheritance, because acquired characteristics can be incorporated into a meme and passed on. **memeplex** *n.* (Contraction of *meme complex*), a collection of mutually adapted *memes that tend to be transmitted together, such as those constituting a religion or political ideology. **meme pool** n. The sum total of all *memes in a population at a given time. *Compare* gene pool. **memetic** adj. Of, relating to, or consisting of a *meme or memes. **memetic engineering** n. Deliberate and systematic manipulation of *memes or *memeplexes, as in education, psychotherapy, advertising, or brainwashing. *Compare* genetic engineering. **memetics** n. The science of *memes.

[From Greek *mimema* something that is imitated, from *mimeisthai* to imitate, coined in 1976 by the British ethologist Richard Dawkins (born 1941) to sound like *gene* and to be reminiscent of *memory* and French *même* same, because memes are sustained and replicated by memory and imitation]

memory n. The psychological function of preserving information, involving the processes of *encoding, *storage, and *retrieval. Human memory consists of a series of interconnected systems serving different functions, one of the most basic divisions being into *declarative memory for factual information about the world and *procedural memory for information about how to carry out sequences of operations; another basic division being between *long-term memory for information stored for more than a few seconds, *short-term memory for temporary storage of information for briefer periods, and *sensory memory (including the *iconic store) for very brief storage of visual and possibly other sensory information; and a third basic division being into *episodic memory for events and experiences and *semantic memory for information about the world, although *perceptual memory may not fall into either category. The power of the chemical senses to reawaken distant memories is discussed under *redintegration. *See also* amnesia, blocking memory, confabulation, cued recall, deferred action, dual-code theory (2), dual-process model, encoding specificity, free recall, Höffding step, levels of processing, memory drum, memory operating characteristic, memory organization packet, memory trace, method of savings, mnemonic, recall, recognition, screen memory, state-dependent memory, tip-of-the-tongue phenomenon, ugly sister effect, working memory.

[From Latin *memoria* memory, from *memor* mindful]

memory drum n. A rotating cylinder on to which may be attached a list of words, nonsense syllables, or other items that are visible one at a time for a fixed time period through a hole in a screen. Before the advent of desktop computers, it was widely used to study *memory.

memory operating characteristic n. A *receiver operating characteristic applied to experimental data from *recognition experiments. *Target items correctly recognized are counted as *hits, and non-target items incorrectly identified as target items are counted as *false alarms (2). Also written *memory-operating characteristic*. *See also* signal detection theory. **MOC** abbrev.

memory organization packet n. A collection of *scripts (3) relating to a particular class of situations, such as shopping or going to the cinema, enabling a person to exhibit appropriate behaviour without having to think about it. Each memory organization packet is assembled from existing scripts, and different packets often have scripts in common: shopping and going to the cinema, for example, both include a script for paying for goods and services. The inclusion of an inappropriate script in a packet can cause interaction problems, as when a husband treats his wife like a waiter in a restaurant. **MOP** abbrev.

memory span n. The number of items, such as words, numbers, or letters, that a person can recall immediately after presentation. It is a measure of the capacity of *short-term memory. *Compare* dynamic memory span.

memory trace n. A physiological alteration or process occurring in the nervous system and underlying the storage of a *memory. Also called a *trace*, an *engram*, or a *neurogram*. *See also* Höffding step.

menarche n. A female's first *menstruation when she reaches puberty.
[From Greek *men* month + *arche* beginning]

Mendelian adj. Of or relating to a form of genetics or a mechanism of inheritance through pairs of non-blending discrete hereditary factors, now called genes, one member of each pair being inherited from each parent. *See also* Mendel's laws, non-Mendelian gene. *Compare* blending inheritance.

Mendel's laws *n*. Two major principles of heredity proposed by Mendel on the basis of his breeding experiments with peas and other plants, the first of which is the law of *segregation of alleles, the second the law of *independent assortment, and the third the proposition that some alleles show *dominance (genetic) over others. *Compare* non-Mendelian gene.
[Named after the Austro-Hungarian Augustinian monk Gregor Johann Mendel (1822–84) who published them in 1865 in an article in the *Proceedings of the Natural Science Society of Brünn* that was neglected by biologists for 35 years]

meninges *n. pl.* The three *membranes covering the brain and spinal cord. *See* arachnoid membrane, dura mater, pia mater. **meninx** *sing.*
[From Greek *meninx, meningos* a membrane]

meningioma *n*. A tumour of the meninges of the brain or, rarely, of the spinal cord.
[From Greek *meninx, meningos* a membrane + *-oma* indicating a tumour]

meningitis *n*. Inflammation of the meninges.
[From Greek *meninx, meningos* a membrane + *-itis* inflammation]

meninx *n*. The singular of *meninges.
[From Greek *meninx* a membrane]

menkeiti *See* latah.

menopause *n*. The natural cessation of a woman's *menstrual cycle occurring usually between 45 and 50 years of age. Also called the *change of life* or *climacteric*.
[From Greek *men* a month + *pausis* a halt]

menses *n*. Another name for *menstruation or menstrual periods.
[From Latin *menses* months, from *mensis* a month]

mens rea *n*. A legal term denoting criminal intent and knowledge of the wrongness of a criminal act, the criminal act itself being called the *actus reus. For a defendant to be convicted of a crime, both an actus reus and a mens rea must normally be proved. *See also* insanity, McNaghten rules.
[From Latin *mens* mind + *rea* guilty]

menstrual cycle *n*. The monthly *oestrous cycle in a woman or other female primate, consisting of the *follicular phase, the *luteal phase, and the *menstrual phase. *See also* pheromone.
[From Latin *menstruus* monthly, from *mensis* a month + Greek *kyklos* a circle or cycle]

menstrual phase *n*. The third and last of the three phases of the *menstrual cycle, characterized by *menstruation. *Compare* follicular phase, luteal phase.

menstrual synchrony *See* Whitten effect.

menstruation *n*. The *vaginal discharge from the uterus of a non-pregnant woman occurring monthly from puberty to the *menopause as the final phase of the *menstrual cycle, containing blood and cellular debris from the shedding of the endometrium (the *mucous membrane lining the uterus). **menstruate** *vb*.

mental age *n*. A child's performance on a test of mental ability expressed as the average age of children who achieved the same level of performance in a standardization sample. Thus a 10-year-old child who achieves the same score as the average 12-year-old child in a standardization sample has a mental age of 12. The concept was introduced in 1905 by the French psychologists Alfred Binet (1857–1911) and Théodore Simon (1873–1961). *See also* Binet–Simon scale, IQ. *Compare* chronological age, social age. **MA** *abbrev*.

mental chemistry *n*. In the doctrine of *associationism, an idea introduced by the English philosopher John Stuart Mill (1806–73) to replace the *mental mechanics* of his father, the Scottish philosopher James Mill (1773–1836). The idea was borrowed from chemistry, in which compounds often have properties that are qualitatively different from the elements of which they are composed, a familiar example being water, the properties of which are not found in its constituent elements hydrogen or oxygen, which are both gases. According to John Stuart Mill, simple ideas combine to form complex ideas that are qualitatively different from their constituent elements, as when, according to the *contiguity law, the idea of whiteness arises from the association of several different colours seen in rapid succession on a *Maxwell disc, as the

English physicist and mathematician Sir Isaac Newton (1642–1727) had demonstrated in his *Opticks* in 1704.

mental defective *n*. A person manifesting *mental retardation.

mental deficiency *n*. Another name for *mental retardation.

mental disorder *n*. According to *DSM-IV, a psychological *syndrome associated with distress, impairment in an important area or areas of functioning, or significantly increased risk of death, disability, or loss of freedom, occurring not merely as a predictable response to a disturbing life event such as a bereavement but assumed to be a manifestation of a psychological or biological *dysfunction. According to *ICD-10, a mental disorder is a clinically recognizable collection of symptoms or behaviour associated in most cases with distress or interference with personal functions. A deviant pattern of behaviour, whether political, religious, or sexual, or a conflict between an individual and society, is not a mental disorder unless it is symptomatic of a dysfunction in the individual.

mental handicap *n*. Another name for *mental retardation.

mental illness *n*. Another name for *mental disorder, with medical connotations that some consider misleading or tendentious.

mental image *n*. Another name for an *image (3).

mental imagery *See* imagery.

mental lexicon *n*. Another name for a *lexicon (2).

mental map *n*. Another name for a *cognitive map.

mental model *n*. An internal representation having—in some abstract sense—the same structure as the aspect or portion of external reality that it represents, such as the *3-D model description that the English psychologist David Courtenay Marr (1945–80) posited as the basis of visual perception. According to a theory put forward in 1983 by the British psychologist Philip N(icholas) Johnson-Laird

(born 1936), people need to construct mental models in order to carry out deductive and inductive reasoning on the basis of *propositions (1), which are not themselves mental models but generally give rise to mental models. For example, the proposition *Alex is to the left of Bernie, and Bernie is to the left of Charlie* may give rise to a mental model in which three men are standing in a row, with Alex to the left of Charlie; but a different mental model would have them arranged anticlockwise around a table, in which case Alex is to the right of Charlie—and in some mental models they could even be three women. According to some researchers, mental models are required to comprehend *discourse, to have a *body image, and even to experience *consciousness. The concept was suggested in 1943 by the Scottish experimental psychologist Kenneth J(ohn) W(illiam) Craik (1914–45) in his book *The Nature of Explanation. See also* mental rotation. *Compare* frame (2), schema.

mental operation *n*. In the writings of the Swiss psychologist Jean Piaget (1896–1980) and his followers, a mental procedure that can be carried out in reverse. Also called an *operation. See* concrete operations, formal operations, pre-operational stage.

mental retardation *n*. A *mental disorder characterized by arrested or incomplete mental development, with onset before age 18, leading to significantly below-average intellectual functioning (specifically, *IQ below 70), accompanied by deficits in adaptive functioning in such areas as interpersonal communication, self-care, home living, social skills, use of public amenities, self-direction, scholastic or academic performance, work, leisure, health, or safety. According to the World Health Organization, an IQ between 50 and 70 is approximately indicative of mild mental retardation, 35–50 moderate mental retardation, 20–35 severe mental retardation, and below 20 profound mental retardation. *See* cerebral gigantism, cerebral palsy, cretinism, *cri du chat*, Down's syndrome, foetal alcohol syndrome, fragile X syndrome, Hurler's syndrome, idiot savant, Klinefelter's syndrome, Lesch–Nyhan syndrome, macrocephaly, microcephaly, mild mental retardation, moderate mental retardation, phenylketonuria, profound mental retardation, severe mental retardation, Tay–Sachs disease, Williams syndrome, zombie (2). *See* *also* idiot savant. *Compare* borderline intelligence.

mental rotation *n*. The imagined turning of a form or shape from one orientation in space to another, believed to involve the mental image passing through all intermediate positions. The original study of this process by the US psychologist Roger N. Shepard (born 1929) and his student Jacqueline Ann Metzler, published in the journal *Science* in 1971, used stimuli consisting of pairs of computer-generated perspective drawings of three-dimensional objects, each constructed by joining ten cubical blocks face to face to form an arm-like structure with three right-angle bends. People were asked to decide as quickly as possible whether each pair depicted identical structures in different orientations or mirror-image *enantiomorphs, and mean response times in recognizing identical structures to be identical were found to increase linearly in almost exact proportion to their angular difference in orientation, from approximately one second for pairs in the same orientation to approximately 4.4 seconds for the maximum angular rotation of 180 degrees, suggesting that the viewers had to mentally rotate one shape through intermediate positions until its orientation matched that of the other shape in order to check for similarity. Men tend to perform significantly better at this task than women. The novel *Dirk Gently's Holistic Detective Agency* (1987) by the English novelist Douglas (Noel) Adams (1952–2002) is devoted largely to the mental rotation of a sofa that has become stuck on a stairway landing. *See also* cognitive penetrability, mental model, mirror reversal problem.

mental set *n*. Another name for a *set (2).

mental subnormality *n*. Another name for *mental retardation.

mental test *n*. Any instrument designed to measure intelligence or any other mental ability or aptitude.

meperidine *n*. Meperidine hydrochloride, a synthetic white crystalline *narcotic analgesic drug with a *morphine-like action, used as an *analgesic and *sedative. Also called *pethidine* or *Demerol* (trademark). *See also* opioid-related disorders.
[From *me(thyl)* the alkyl radical CH_3 derived

from methane by removal of one hydrogen atom, from Greek *methy* wine + *hyle* wood + *(pi)peridine*]

meprobamate *n*. A bitter-tasting *carbamate that acts as a central nervous system *depressant and is used as a sedative and muscle relaxant, the best known of the class of *propanediols. *See also* sedative-, hypnotic-, or anxiolytic-related disorders. Also called *Miltown* (trademark). **MPB** *abbrev*.
[From *me(thyl)* the alkyl radical CH_3 derived from methane by removal of one hydrogen atom, from Greek *methy* wine + *hyle* wood + *pro(pyl)* + *(dicar)bamate*]

mere exposure effect *n*. The tendency for repeated exposure to a stimulus to be sufficient to enhance an observer's liking for it or attitude towards it. The effect was first referred to by the German philosopher, physician, psychologist, and mystic Gustav Theodor Fechner (1801–87) in *Vorschule der Aesthetik* (1876, pp. 240–3), and the US psychologist William James (1842–1910) independently rediscovered it and discussed it in *Principles of Psychology* (1890, volume 2, p. 672), but the first quantitative investigation of it was carried out by the US-based Polish psychologist Robert B(oleslaw) Zajonc (born 1923) and published in the journal *Psychological Monographs* in 1968. Zajonc examined *antonym pairs and found that the positively toned words were more frequent in the language according to word counts than negatively toned words: *happiness* occurs more than 15 times as frequently in written English as *unhappiness*, *beauty* 41 times as frequently as *ugliness*, *love* almost 10 times as frequently as *hate*, and so on, and similar relationships between frequency and favourability have been found in French, German, Spanish, Russian, Urdu, and other languages. Zajonc also reported experimental evidence using pseudo-Turkish nonsense words such as *iktitaf* and diagrams resembling Chinese *logographs. Participants were exposed to different stimuli different numbers of times, and they then guessed the degree of favourability of the meanings of these items. The results showed almost linear relationships between (log transformed) exposure frequency and rated favourability. *See also* Pollyanna effect, preference-feedback hypothesis.

Merkel cell *n*. A touch receptor deep in the skin, and in the mucous membrane of the

mouth, with a flattened or slightly cupped body and a large modified epithelial ending, especially sensitive to the edges of objects held in the hand or mouth. Also called a *Merkel corpuscle*, *Merkel disc*, or *Merkel–Ranvier corpuscle*. Compare free nerve ending, Golgi tendon organ, Meissner's corpuscle, Pacinian corpuscle, Ruffini corpuscle.
[Named after the German anatomist Friedrich Sigmund Merkel (1845–1919) who discovered it in 1880]

Merkel's law n. In *psychophysics, the proposition that equal differences in the magnitude of a sensation correspond to equal differences in the intensity of the stimulus causing it. It was not well corroborated by subsequent experimental tests. The term *Merkel's law* is also an arguably preferable name for *Hick's law, because it was first formulated by Merkel. *See also* psychophysical function. *Compare* Fechner's law, power law.
[Named after the German psychologist Julius Merkel (1834–1900) who formulated it in 1888]

merocrine adj. Of or relating to glands such as sweat glands that produce secretions without undergoing degeneration. *Compare* apocrine, holocrine.
[From Greek *meros* part or share + *krinein* to separate]

Merrill–Palmer scale n. A scale for measuring mental abilities in preschool children from 18 months to 6 years of age (in the Merrill–Palmer Scale of Mental Tests), or 3 to 5 years of age (in the revised version, called the Extended Merrill–Palmer Scale), designed to provide a broader assessment than can be gained from a conventional IQ test. The Merrill–Palmer Scale of Mental Tests, introduced originally in 1926, comprises 93 tasks, grouped into clusters labelled Language, All-or-None, Form Board and Picture, and Motor Coordination, and grouped into six-month age ranges. The Extended Merrill–Palmer Scale comprises 16 tasks grouped into Semantic Production, Figural Production, Semantic Evaluation, and Figural Evaluation, based on Guilford's structure-of-intellect model. *See also* Guilford's cube.
[Named after the Merrill-Palmer school in Detroit, Michigan, where the scale was developed in 1931]

mescaline n. A *psychotropic *alkaloid, chemically related to *adrenalin (epinephrine), derived from the flowering heads of the mescal or peyote cactus *Lophophora williamsii* native to Mexico and the south-western US, used for religious ceremonies in some Native American cultures, usually eaten or dissolved in a drink, acting as a central nervous system *stimulant causing pupil dilation and palpitations, together with *psychedelic and *hallucinogenic effects and feelings of *euphoria. Also called *peyote*. *See also* phantasticant.
[From Spanish *mezcal*, from Nahuatl *mexcalli* mescal liquor, from *metl* the tropical American agave plant + *ixcalli* a stew or concoction]

mesencephalic locomotor region n. An area of the *reticular formation in the mesencephalon or midbrain that, when stimulated, generates alternating limb movements normally seen in walking or running.

mesencephalon n. A technical name for the *midbrain, especially in a developing embryo. *Compare* prosencephalon, rhombencephalon.
[From Greek *mesos* middle + *enkephalos* the brain, from *en* in + *kephale* the head]

mesmerism n. An obsolete term for *animal magnetism or *hypnosis.
[Named after the Viennese physician Franz Anton Mesmer (1734–1815) who practised animal magnetism, though not hypnosis, in the 1770s]

mesocortex n. The five-layered cortex found mainly in the *cingulate gyrus, which evolved in humans earlier than most of the *cerebral cortex but not as early as the *archaecortex. *See also* neocortex, palaeocortex.
[From Greek *mesos* middle + Latin *cortex* bark or outer layer]

mesocortical system n. A system of *dopamine-secreting neurons with cell bodies in the *ventral tegmental area of the midbrain (mesencephalon) and terminal boutons in the *cerebral cortex, involved in experiences of pleasure and reward. *See also* mesolimbic system, mesotelencephalic pathway.

mesoderm n. The middle germ layer of a human or animal *embryo, from which the

muscles, blood, bone, and connective tissue are formed. *Compare* ectoderm, endoderm.
[From Greek *mesos* middle + *derma* skin]

mesokurtic *See* kurtosis.

mesolect *n.* A speech style intermediate between the *acrolect and the *basilect within a speech community. *See also* dialect, idiolect, lect.
[From Greek *mesos* middle + *legein* to speak]

mesolimbic system *n.* A system of *dopamine-secreting neurons with cell bodies in the *ventral tegmental area of the midbrain (mesencephalon) and terminal boutons in the *limbic system, widely believed to be the ultimate common pathway for experiences of pleasure and reward in the brain. *See also* mesocortical system, mesotelencephalic pathway.

mesomorph *n.* A muscular physique or body build, believed by the US psychologist William H. Sheldon (1899–1977) and followers of his *constitutional psychology to be associated with such personality characteristics as extraversion and aggressiveness. *Compare* ectomorph, endomorph. **mesomorphic** *adj.* **mesomorphy** *n.* The state or condition of being a mesomorph.
[From Greek *mesos* middle + *morphe* a form or shape]

mesopic *adj.* Of or relating to vision that is intermediate between *photopic and *scotopic vision and is mediated by both *rods and *cones.
[From Greek *mesos* middle + *ops* an eye + *-ikos* of, relating to, or resembling]

mesotelencephalic pathway *n.* A major *dopamine pathway in the brain that includes the *nigrostriatal bundle and parts of the *telencephalon, portions of which are involved in experiences of pleasure and reward. *See also* mesocortical system, mesolimbic system.
[From Greek *mesos* middle + *telos* end + *enkephalos* the brain, from *en* in + *kephale* the head]

messenger RNA *n.* A short-lived form of *RNA found in all cells, functioning as a template for *protein synthesis by transcribing genetic information from *DNA and carrying the information to a *ribosome, where the specified *proteins are then synthesized. *See also* snurp. *Compare* transfer RNA. **mRNA** *abbrev.*

meta-analysis *n.* A set of techniques for combining the results of a number of research studies and analysing them statistically as a single data set. Often confused with *metanalysis. *See also* file drawer problem.
[From Greek *meta* among, beside, after + English *analysis*]

metabolism *n.* The sum total of biological processes occurring in a living organism that result in growth and energy production, more specifically the processes of *anabolism whereby foods are converted into body cells and *catabolism whereby substances are broken down to release energy. *See also* aerobic, anaerobic, basal metabolic rate, Krebs cycle. **metabolic** *adj.* **metabolite** *n.* A substance produced by *metabolism. **metabolize** *vb.* To cause to be changed by *metabolism.
[From Greek *metabole* change, from *meta* among, with, or beside + *ballein* to throw]

metachrosis *n.* The ability of chameleons and certain other reptiles and fishes to change colour by expanding and contracting specialized pigment cells on the outsides of their bodies.
[From Greek *meta* beside + *chrosis* colouring, from *chros* colour + *-osis* indicating a process or state]

metacognition *n.* Knowledge and beliefs about one's own cognitive processes, an important class of metacognition being *metamemory. The term is also sometimes applied to regulation of cognitive functions, including planning, checking, or monitoring, as when one plans one's cognitive strategy for memorizing something, checks one's accuracy while performing mental arithmetic, or monitors one's comprehension while reading, and these forms of metacognition are called *metacognitive regulation* in contradistinction to *metacognitive knowledge*. Writings on metacognition can be traced back at least as far as *De Anima* and the *Parva Naturalia* of the Greek philosopher Aristotle (384–322 BC), and the phenomenon was brought to prominence during the 1970s largely by the US psychologist John H. Flavell (born 1928), who focused attention especially on developmental aspects of metacognition. In an influential article in the journal *Psychological Review* in 1977, the US psychologists Richard E. Nisbett (born 1941) and Timothy D. Wilson (born 1951) summarized a range of evidence suggesting that people are often unaware of the factors influencing their own choices, evaluations, and behaviour, and that the verbal reports that they give when questioned are often quite erroneous and misleading. *See also* reality monitoring.

[From Greek *meta* beside or beyond + English *cognition*]

metacontrast *n*. A type of *backward masking in which the test stimulus and masking stimulus do not overlap spatially in the visual field. The term is often applied to visual masking by a non-overlapping figure irrespective of the temporal order of test stimulus and masking stimulus, but in careful usage the term *paracontrast is used when the test stimulus precedes the masking stimulus. *See also* masking, visual masking. *Compare* paracontrast.

[From Greek *meta* beyond + Latin *contra* against + *stare* to stand]

metalanguage *n*. A language used to refer to statements made in another language, called in this context the *object language. If the statements being referred to are in French and the statements referring to them are in English, for example, then the distinction between object language (French) and the metalanguage (English) is clear, but if object language and metalanguage are both expressed in English, or both in a formal language such as the *predicate calculus, then confusion can arise. Quotation marks can sometimes help, as in the sentence 'Snow is white' is true if and only if snow is white, in which the statement belonging to the object language is enclosed in quotation marks. Many paradoxes, including debatably the *liar paradox, arise from a failure to distinguish object language from metalanguage: expressions involving *true* and *false*, when applied to a sentence, must always be expressed in a metalanguage and not in the object language of the sentence. The ideas behind the concept of a metalanguage are traceable to an article 'On Denoting' by the Welsh philosopher Bertrand (Arthur William) Russell (1872–1970) in the journal *Mind* in 1905, and the concept was fully developed by the Polish logician and mathematician Alfred

Tarski (1902–83) in his monograph *Der Wahrheitsbegriff in den formalisierten Sprachen* (The Concept of Truth in Formalized Languages) in 1933.

metamemory *n*. Knowledge or beliefs about one's own memory, its strengths and weaknesses, whether one has remembered particular items, and so on. The word is also used to denote regulation or control of memory, as described under *metacognition. *See also* mnemonic, reality monitoring.

[From Greek *meta* beside or beyond + English *memory*]

metamer *n*. Either of a pair of colours that appear identical but have different spectral compositions and are therefore composed of different wavelengths. A mixture of two non-complementary colours produces a colour that appears identical to a pure colour intermediate on the *colour circle between the component colours of the mixture but that has a different spectral composition from the pure colour.

[From Greek *meta* beside + English *(iso)mer*, from Greek *isos* equal or the same + *meros* a part]

metameric match *n*. A comparison colour that a viewer considers identical to both members of a pair of *metamers.

metametric pair *n*. Two colours that are *metamers of each other.

metanalysis *n*. The formation of a new word through a mistaken analysis of a boundary between existing words. A typical example is the word *adder*, derived from Middle English *naddre* through people mishearing the phrase *a naddre* as *an adder*. A second example is the word *apron*, derived from a mistaken division into *an apron* of the Middle English *a napron*, from Old French *naperon* a little cloth, from Latin *nappa* a napkin. Often confused with *meta-analysis. *Compare* back formation, folk etymology (2).

[From Greek *meta* beside or beyond + English *analysis*]

metaphase *n*. The second phase of *mitosis, during which the *nuclear spindles are formed and the *chromosomes attach themselves to the equator of the spindles by their *centromeres.

[From Greek *meta* beside + *phasis* an aspect, from *phainein* to show]

metaphor *n.* A *figure of speech in which a word or phrase is stated to mean something that it resembles but does not literally denote, as in *Life is just a bowl of cherries* (song title) or *Life is just a bowl of cheerios* (graffito). *See also* condensation. *Compare* simile.
[From Greek *meta* beside or beyond + *pherein* to carry]

metapsychology *n.* The study of the underlying conceptual questions or principles of psychology. The term was first used in *psychoanalysis by Sigmund Freud (1856–1939) to denote his own theory of psychology, especially its more abstract conceptual assumptions, in a letter to his friend, the German physician Wilhelm Fliess (1858–1928) in 1898 (*Standard Edition*, I, p. 274), and later given the following definition in his article on 'The Unconscious' (1915): 'I propose that when we have succeeded in describing a psychical process in its dynamic, topographical and economic aspects, we should speak of it as a *metapsychological* presentation' (*Standard Edition*, XIV, pp. 166–215, at p. 181). *See also* dynamic, economic, topography.
[From Greek *meta* among, beside, after + English *psychology*]

metathetic stimulus dimension *n.* Any stimulus dimension that can vary continuously and in so doing produce discrete or qualitative changes in perception, the standard example being the wavelength or frequency of visible light, which produces qualitatively different hues or colours as it varies continuously, whereas sound produces continuous or quantitative perceptual changes. *Compare* prothetic stimulus dimension. *See also* categorical perception.
[From Greek *metathetikos* able to change, from *meta* beside + *tithenai* to place + *-ikos* of, relating to, or resembling]

metencephalon *n.* A part of the *rhombencephalon hindbrain or of an embryo that develops later into the *cerebellum and *pons.
[From Greek *meta* among, with, or beside + *enkephalos* the brain, from *en* in + *kephale* the head]

met-enkephalin *See under* enkephalin.

methacholine *n.* A *parasympathomimetic drug that mimics *acetylcholine at *muscarinic receptor sites. Also called *Mecholyl* (trademark). *See also* cholinomimetic.
[From *meth(yl)* the alkyl radical CH_3 derived from methane by removal of one hydrogen atom, from Greek *methy* wine + *hyle* wood + *a(cetyl)choline*]

methadone *n.* A synthetic *narcotic analgesic with similar effects to *morphine but believed by some to be less harmful, often used as a replacement for *heroin in the treatment of heroin dependency. Also called *Dolophine* (trademark). *See also* cross-dependence, opioid-related disorders.
[From *(di)meth(yl)* + *a(mino)* + *d(iphenyl)* + Greek *-one* indicating a chemical compound that is a ketone, from *-one* a feminine name suffix]

methamphetamine *n.* A drug that is closely related to *amphetamine and that has a long-lasting action, used as a central nervous system *stimulant and appetite suppressant. A common street name for it is *speed*. *See also* amphetamine-related disorders, ice.
[From *meth(yl)* the alkyl radical CH_3 derived from methane by removal of one hydrogen atom, from Greek *methy* wine + *hyle* wood + English *amphetamine*]

methaqualone *n.* A central nervous system *depressant that is used as a sedative and a hypnotic drug. Also called *Quaalude* (trademark).
[From its chemical name *meth(yl)* the alkyl radical CH_3 derived from methane by removal of one hydrogen atom, from Greek *methy* wine + *hyle* wood + *qu(in)a(zo)l(ine)* + *-one* indicating a ketone, from *-one* a feminine name suffix]

method of absolute judgement *n.* In *psychophysics, a procedure in which judgements are made without any explicit standards of comparison, as when an observer is asked to rate a sound for loudness on a scale from 0 to 100. Also called the *method of single stimuli*. *Compare* method of comparative judgement.

method of adjustment *n.* Another name for the *method of average error.

method of average error *n.* One of the three classical methods of *psychophysics introduced in 1860 by the German philosopher, physician, psychologist, and mystic Gustav

Theodor Fechner (1801–87) for determining *difference thresholds. It involves repeatedly adjusting a *variable stimulus until it appears equal (or stands in some other prescribed relation of magnitude) to a *standard stimulus, a difference threshold being calculated as the *probable error of the adjustment—the absolute error exceeded in 50 per cent of such matches. Also called the *method of adjustment*, *method of mean error*, or *method of reproduction*. *Compare* method of constant stimuli, method of limits.

method of bisection *n.* In *psychophysics, a technique for measuring sensations on an *interval scale by having the observer repeatedly select or adjust a stimulus until it appears to be exactly half-way between two others. It is a form of the *method of equal-appearing intervals. *See also* indirect scaling.

method of comparative judgement *n.* In *psychophysics, a procedure in which a *variable stimulus is judged in relation to a *standard stimulus. *See also* comparative judgement, difference threshold, law of comparative judgement. *Compare* method of absolute judgement.

method of constant stimuli *n.* One of the three classical methods of *psychophysics introduced in 1860 by the German philosopher, physician, psychologist, and mystic Gustav Theodor Fechner (1801–87) for determining *absolute thresholds and *difference thresholds. It involves presenting *variable stimuli in random order and determining the smallest intensity that can be detected in the case of an absolute threshold or the smallest difference from a *standard stimulus that can be detected in the case of a difference threshold, the criterion used nowadays usually being correct detection or discrimination on 75 per cent of presentations, although other percentages are sometimes used. *See also* method of equal and unequal cases. *Compare* method of average error, method of limits.

method of equal and unequal cases *n.* In *psychophysics, a version of the *method of constant stimuli in which a *difference threshold is determined by presenting stimuli in pairs and requiring the observer to decide in each case whether they are the same or different.

method of equal-appearing intervals *n.* Any method of *psychophysical scaling in which an observer adjusts the differences between stimuli, or chooses stimuli from a set, so that the differences between the magnitudes of the stimuli appear equal, thereby producing an *interval scale. A *Thurstone scale is a special form of equal-appearing interval scale. *See also* method of bisection.

method of gradation *n.* Any method of *psychophysics in which an observer's judgement is determined by a succession of increasingly narrow approximations, a typical example being the *method of limits.

method of limits *n.* One of the three classical methods of *psychophysics introduced in 1860 by the German philosopher, physician, psychologist, and mystic Gustav Theodor Fechner (1801–87) for determining *absolute thresholds and *difference thresholds. It involves the presentation of an ascending series in which the intensity of a *variable stimulus is increased by predetermined steps until it can be perceived on 50 per cent of presentations (for an absolute threshold determination) or until a difference between it and a *standard stimulus can be perceived on 50 per cent of presentations (for a difference threshold), and a descending series in which the intensity is reduced by corresponding steps until the stimulus or the difference can be perceived on only 50 per cent of presentations. The threshold from the ascending series is called the *upper threshold* and is usually higher than the threshold from the descending series, called the *lower threshold*, and when a single threshold is required it is usually taken as the midpoint between the upper and lower thresholds. *Compare* method of average error, method of constant stimuli.

method of loci *n.* A technique for memorizing lists of items, first introduced in about 500 BC by the poet Simonides of Ceos (556–468 BC). *See under* mnemonic.

method of mean error *n.* Another name for the *method of average error.

method of paired comparisons *n.* In *psychophysics, a method of scaling in which pairs of stimuli are presented, every stimulus in the set being paired with every other stimulus, a judgement being made in each case as to which of the two is greater with regard to the *attribute being scaled (for example, which is heavier, brighter, or preferable). Provided the judgements satisfy certain assumptions, an *ordinal scale is established. The technique is practical only if the number of stimuli is relatively small, because the number of pairs in a set of n stimuli is $n!/2(n-2)!$ and hence for $n = 8$ there are 28 pairs, for $n = 10$ there are 45 pairs, for $n = 20$ there are 190 pairs, for $n = 50$ there are 1,225 pairs, and so on. See also unfolding technique.

method of reproduction n. Another name for the *method of average error.

method of savings n. A technique for studying *memory by measuring the amount of time or the number of trials required to learn a certain amount of information or a certain skill and then determining how much less time or how many fewer trials are required to relearn the material or skill to the same standard after a period of forgetting, the reduction providing an index of the extent of the original learning.

method of single stimuli n. In *psychophysics, a procedure in which judgements are made without explicit standard of comparison, as when an observer is asked to rate a sound for loudness on a scale from 0 to 100. Also called the method of absolute judgement.

methyl atropine n. A form of *atropine, biochemically modified by the addition of a methyl radical, leaving the molecule with a positive charge and rendering it incapable of crossing the *blood–brain barrier, so that it blocks peripheral acetylcholine neuroreceptors but allows brain acetylcholine systems to function normally. Compare methyl scopolamine.
[From methyl the alkyl radical CH_3 derived from methane by removal of one hydrogen atom, from Greek methy wine + hyle wood + English atropine]

methylphenidate n. Methylphenidate hydrochloride, an analogue of *amphetamine, being a mild central nervous system *stimulant drug that blocks the reuptake of *noradrenalin and *dopamine and is often prescribed in the treatment of attention-deficit/hyperactivity disorder (ADHD) in children and narcolepsy in adults. Commonly called Ritalin (trademark). See also amphetamine-related disorders, initial values law.
[From methyl + phen(yl) + (piper)id(ine) + (acet)ate]

methylphenylpyridine n. The chemical name of *MPP$^+$.

methylphenyltetrahydropyridine n. The chemical name of *MPTP.

methyl scopolamine n. A form of *scopolamine, biochemically modified by the addition of a methyl radical, leaving the molecule with a positive charge and rendering it incapable of crossing the *blood–brain barrier, so that it blocks peripheral acetylcholine neuroreceptors but allows brain acetylcholine systems to function normally. Compare methyl atropine.
[From methyl the alkyl radical CH_3 derived from methane by removal of one hydrogen atom, from Greek methy wine + hyle wood + English scopolamine]

methylxanthine n. Another name for a *xanthine.

metonymy n. A *figure of speech in which a word denoting an *attribute comes to be substituted for the thing referred to, as in the phrase the crown, denoting the king or queen, or the bench, denoting a collection of judges or magistrates. See also displacement. Compare synecdoche.
[From Greek meta beside + onoma a name]

Metrazol n. A proprietary name for the stimulant drug *pentylene tetrazol.
[Trademark, from (penta)met(hylene) + (tet)razol(e)]

MHPG abbrev. 3-Methoxy-4-hydroxyphenylethylene glycol, a metabolite of *dopamine and *noradrenalin (norepinephrine) that is believed to be a biochemical marker for the diagnosis of depression.

mianserin n. A *tetracyclic antidepressant drug, used to treat *depression, especially when it is accompanied by a *sleep disorder, and other disorders of which depression is a feature.

Michelangelo phenomenon n. A pattern of relationship interdependence in which close partners influence each other's dispositions, values, and behavioural patterns in such a manner as to bring both people closer to their *ideal selves. The concept was introduced by the US psychologist Stephen Michael Drigotas (born 1966) and several collaborators in an article in the *Journal of Personality and Social Psychology* in 1999 reporting the results of four experiments designed to elucidate the phenomenon.

[Named after the Italian sculptor Michelangelo Buonarroti (1475–1564) who is said to have conceived of sculpture as a process of bringing out figures already hidden in stone by chipping away the excess]

microcephaly n. A congenital condition characterized by an abnormally small head and underdeveloped brain, resulting in some degree of *mental retardation. **microcephalic** adj.

[From Greek *mikros* small + *kephale* head]

microelectrode n. A fine insulated wire with an extremely narrow tip, usually between one-half and five microns (micrometres or millionths of a metre) in diameter, that when inserted close enough to a *neuron can detect its individual electrical signals or can be used to stimulate the neuron.

[From Greek *mikros* small + *elektron* amber (in which electricity was first observed) + *hodos* a way]

microevolution n. A relatively rapid change in a species or subspecies brought about by *natural selection operating intensively on a characteristic or characteristics. *Compare* macroevolution.

[From Greek *mikros* small + English *evolution*]

microfilament n. A slender threadlike structure containing *actin that is abundantly present in *muscle tissue.

[From Greek *mikros* small + Latin *filum* a thread, from *filare* to spin]

microglia n. A type of *neuroglial cell found in the central nervous system, more abundant in *grey matter than in *white matter, functioning as a *phagocyte, scavenging dead or damaged cells or encircling them, and proliferating when the brain is injured or infected. *See also* glia. *Compare* macroglia.

[From Greek *mikros* small + *glia* glue]

micropsia n. A condition, caused either by a lesion in the retina or by a neurological disorder, in which everything in the *visual field appears smaller than normal. Also called *micropsy*. *Compare* macropsia.

[From Greek *mikros* small + *opsis* sight, from *ops* an eye + *-ia* indicating a condition or quality]

microsaccade n. One of the forms of *physiological nystagmus, consisting of a tiny *saccade, usually through a visual angle between 1 and 2 minutes of arc (sixtieths of a degree), occurring in random directions three or four times a second while an observer fixates an object visually, necessary to prevent the visual image from disappearing, as an artificially *stabilized retinal image does after about a second. *See also* ocular drift, ocular tremor.

[From Greek *mikros* small + French *saccade* a jerk, from Old French *saquer* to pull]

microsleep n. A very brief period of sleep, occurring without awareness in a person who is apparently awake, often associated with fatigue or alcohol intoxication.

microsome n. Any of the small fragments that can be isolated from biological cells by centrifugal action. They consist of *ribosomes with scraps of *endoplasmic reticulum attached to them.

[From Greek *mikros* small + *soma* a body]

microspecies n. A taxonomic category below the level of a *species, hence a race, subspecies, or variety.

[From Greek *mikros* small + Latin *species* appearance or kind, from *specere* to look]

microtome n. An instrument for cutting thin slices of brain tissue or other material for microscopical examination. **microtomy** n. The slicing of sections with a *microtome.

[From Greek *mikros* small + *tome* a cut]

microtubule n. Any of the comparatively rigid, hollow protein tunnels, with an outside diameter of approximately 25 nanometres and an inside diameter of approximately 14 nm, up to several millimetres in length, forming part of the *cytoskeleton within the cytoplasm of almost all cells, including *neurons, where such tunnels are involved in *anterograde transport and *retrograde

transport within *axons and *dendrites. The molecules of *tubulin*, the protein of which it is composed, can exist in at least two different geometrical configurations, in one of which it bends about 30 degrees from the direction of the microtubule, enabling movement to occur, for example during *mitosis, and possibly encoding and transmitting signals within the cell like a *cellular automaton. The *cilia of *paramecia consist of bundles of microtubules. *See also* neurofibril, paramecium.
[From Greek *mikros* small + Latin *tubulus* a little pipe, diminutive of *tubus* a pipe]

midbrain *n.* The middle part of the brain, connecting the diencephalon to the hindbrain, including the *tectum, *tegmentum, *cerebral peduncles and the *aqueduct of Sylvius, also called the *mesencephalon*, especially in a developing embryo. *Compare* forebrain, hindbrain.

middle commissure *n.* A band of grey matter connecting the two *thalami across the third *ventricle of the brain. *See also* commissure.

middle ear *n.* The sound-transmitting intermediate part of the ear, filled with air and containing the *malleus, *incus, and *stapes, separated from the outer ear by the *tympanic membrane and from the inner ear by the *round window (fenestra rotunda) and *oval window (fenestra rotunda). *See also* Eustachian tube.

middle insomnia *See under* insomnia.

middle temporal gyrus *n.* The middle of the three gyri on the lateral surface of each *temporal lobe, running horizontally between the superior temporal gyrus (temporal operculum) and the inferior temporal gyrus, occupied at its posterior extremity by Area V5 of the *visual cortex, which is responsible for visual perception of motion. Also called the *median temporal gyrus* or the *middle temple*. **MT** *abbrev.*

midget cell *n.* A small retinal *ganglion cell in the *parvocellular system, with a *centre-surround receptive field, its centre receiving input from only one of the three types of *cone (blue, green, or red) and the surround from the other two types of retinal cones. *Compare* parasol cell.

midsagittal plane *n.* A *sagittal plane passing through the middle of an organ or organism, dividing it into equal right and left halves.

midsagittal section *n.* A *sagittal section dividing an organ or organism down the middle into left and right halves. In the case of the brain it exposes the *medial surfaces of the cerebral hemispheres. Also called the *median section*. *See* sagittal section.

mid vowel *n.* A *vowel (see the diagram accompanying that entry) produced at a position in the vocal tract that is mid-way between the position of a *close vowel and that of an *open vowel, such as the initial vowel in the word *about* (a *schwa) or the vowel in *get*.

Mignon delusion *n.* The delusion that the parents who brought one up are not one's natural parents and that one really belongs to a more distinguished family.
[Named after a character of mysterious origins in Goethe's novel *Wilhelm Meister*, and the eponymous heroine of the opera *Mignon* based on it, who pines away and dies without her longings being fulfilled]

migraine *n.* A recurrent headache originating on one side of the head, characterized by severe throbbing pain and an aversion to bright light, sometimes preceded or accompanied by visual disturbances such as prodromal *auras (2) such as *scotomas or *phosphenes, nausea, vomiting, sweating, chills, and exhaustion. *See also* Möbius syndrome.
[From Greek *(he)mi* half + *kran(ion)* skull]

migration *n.* The movement from one region, place, or country to another, including the seasonal movement of a population of animals to a different environment, most common in certain species of birds (such as Arctic terns, which migrate annually 17,600 km between their breeding ground in the Arctic circle and the Antarctic), but observed also in mammals (such as porpoises), fish (such as eels, salmon), and some insects. *See also* population genetics.

mild mental retardation *n.* A level of *mental retardation associated with an *IQ approximately between 50 and 69 (in adults, *mental age from 9 to 12 years), equivalent to the educational category of educable mentally retarded. Sometimes called *feeble-mindedness* or *mild mental subnormality*.

Milgram experiment *n.* A famous experimental procedure introduced in 1963 by the US psychologist Stanley Milgram (1933–84) to study obedience to authority. *See* obedience.

milieu therapy *n.* A form of *psychotherapy, usually conducted in a hospital or other facility that can function as a *therapeutic community and provide a stable environment, in which personal growth and behaviour change may be promoted through interaction of individuals within the total therapeutic environment. *See also* group therapy.

Mill Hill Vocabulary scale *n.* An *intelligence test designed to measure verbal intelligence, consisting of a list of 88 words divided into two sets of 44, published by the English psychologist John C(arlyle) Raven (1902–70) in its original form in 1944 as a companion to *Raven's Progressive Matrices. The respondent's task is to explain the meanings of the words or (in an alternative form of presentation) to select the correct synonym for each word from a list of six alternatives provided. Most children with a *mental age of 5 years can explain the meanings of the first few words (*cap*, *loaf*, *unhappy*), and between the ages of 5 and 16 children of average intelligence can usually define about three additional words per year. The most difficult words in the list, which only a small minority of adults can define, include *recondite*, *exiguous*, and *minatory*. The *correlation between scores on the Mill Hill Vocabulary scale and Raven's Progressive Matrices is approximately 0.75, notwithstanding the utterly different ways in which the two tests measure intelligence. **MHV** *abbrev.*
[Named after the Mill Hill Emergency Hospital in London, the wartime location of the Maudsley Hospital, where it was developed]

millimicron *n.* Another (obsolescent) name for a *nanometre.

Miltown *n.* A proprietary name for the depressant drug *meprobamate.
[Trademark]

mimesis *n.* Imitation or *mimicry. **mimetic** *adj.* Imitative; of or relating to *mimesis.

[From Greek *mimesis* imitation, from *mimeisthai* to imitate]

mimicry *n.* Imitation or *mimesis; more specifically the deceptive resemblance of one animal species to another to protect it from *predators, common especially among butterflies and other insects. *See also* Batesian mimicry, Müllerian mimicry.
[From Greek *mimos* a mime]

mind-blindness *n.* A specific inability to appreciate other people's mental states. The term was introduced in 1990 by the British psychologist Simon Baron-Cohen (born 1958). *See* theory of mind. **mind-blind** *adj.*

mind–body problem *n.* The philosophical problem, usually attributed to the French philosopher René Descartes (1596–1650) of explaining the apparent interaction of mental and physical events, which appear to belong to two quite separate realms of existence, as when a (mental) wish gives rise to a (physical) bodily movement or a (physical) pinprick to a (mental) sensation of pain. The problem was appreciated by Descartes only after he received a letter in 1643 from Princess Elizabeth of Bohemia (1596–1662), the daughter of King James I of England and VI of Scotland, pointing it out. *See also* Cartesian dualism, double-aspect theory, dualism, epiphenomenalism, identity theory, interactionism (1), materialism, monism, neutral monism, psychophysical parallelism.

mineralocorticoid *n.* Any *corticosteroid that maintains the body's electrolyte and fluid balance, especially by promoting the retention of sodium in the kidney tubules, the most significant one in humans being *aldosterone. *See also* zona glomerulosa. *Compare* glucocorticoid.
[From *mineral* + *cortico(stero)id*]

miniature end-plate potential *n.* A small variation in the electrical potential across the membrane of a resting muscle cell, below the threshold required to trigger a contraction of the muscle fibre, caused by the release of a small quantity of *acetylcholine by a *motor neuron at the *motor end plate. *Compare* end-plate potential. **MEPP** *abbrev.*

minimal audible angle *See* minimum audible angle.

minimal audible field *See* minimum audible field.

minimal audible pressure *See* minimum audible pressure.

minimal brain dysfunction *n.* Another name for *attention-deficit/hyperactivity disorder. Also called *minimal cerebral dysfunction* (or *damage*). **MBD** *abbrev.*

minimal group situation *n.* An experimental procedure in which mere *social categorization elicits intergroup discrimination. It was introduced in 1970 and 1971 in articles in *Scientific American* magazine and the *European Journal of Social Psychology* respectively by the British-based Polish psychologist Hanri Tajfel (1919–82) and several colleagues, who performed the following experiment with a group of 64 schoolboys who knew one another very well. The boys were divided into two groups on arbitrary and insignificant criteria and were then presented with a series of two-row matrices, on each of which they were asked to choose a column specifying amounts of money to be assigned to two members of their own group (ingroup choices), two members of the other group (outgroup choices), or one member of their own group and one member of the other group (intergroup choices). The boys did not know the identity of the individuals who were affected by their choices but only which groups they belonged to, and their own interests were not affected by their choices, because no one could know their choices. Nevertheless, when they made intergroup choices, a large majority of the boys gave slightly more money to members of their own group than to members of the other group, even when they could have chosen columns in which members of their own group would have got more in absolute terms but the other group would have done even better. In contrast, when they made ingroup choices or outgroup choices, they tended to select columns that distributed the money with maximum fairness. This effect has been replicated with children and adults of both sexes in many different countries. Also called the *minimal group paradigm*, and often confused with the *minimal social situation. See also* social identity theory.

minimal pair *n.* A pair of words that differ in only one speech sound but have distinct meanings, thus establishing that the speech sounds in question are different *phonemes. For example, the fact that *cap* and *cab* have different meanings establishes that /p/ and /b/ are different phonemes in English. In English, /r/ and /l/ give distinct meanings to minimal pairs (such as *row* and *low*) and are therefore distinct phonemes, whereas in Japanese they do not and are therefore *allophones, which explains why they are often confused by native Japanese speakers of English. *See also* acoustic cue (1), acquired similarity, distinctive feature, neutralization.

minimal social situation *n.* An interactive decision in which each decision maker is ignorant of the interactive nature of the decision and even of the existence of another decision maker whose actions affect the outcomes, first investigated by the US psychologist Joseph B. Sidowski (born 1925) and his colleagues and published in the *Journal of Abnormal and Social Psychology* in 1956 and the *Journal of Experimental Psychology* in 1957. In the original experiment, pairs of participants or subjects were seated in separate rooms, unaware of each other's existence, with electrodes attached to their bodies, each individual operating an apparatus with a pair of buttons labelled *L* and *R* and a digital display showing the cumulative number of points scored. They pressed one button at a time as often as required with the twin goals of obtaining rewards (points) and avoiding punishments (electric shocks). The rewards and punishments were arranged according to a *mutual fate control* payoff structure such that whenever either individual pressed *L*, the other was rewarded with points, and whenever either pressed *R*, the other was punished with electric shock; but a choice had no direct effect on the individual who made it. As Sidowski and his colleagues were the first to demonstrate, in such situations people generally learn to coordinate their choices to their mutual benefit, although they are unaware of their interdependence, and in the long run pairs often settle down to choosing *L* on every occasion. The minimal social situation is often confused with the *minimal group situation. *See also* win-stay, lose-change strategy.

minimax *n.* In two-person game theory, a *strategy (2) that *minimizes* the *maximum* payoff to the co-player. In a two-person *zero-sum game, it is equivalent to a *maximin strategy, because each player's gains are the co-player's losses.

minimax theorem *n.* A fundamental result in *game theory, establishing that every finite, strictly competitive (two-person *zero-sum) game has what later came to be called a *Nash equilibrium, provided that *mixed strategies may be used, and that the corresponding strategies are *minimax strategies. The theorem was first proved by the Hungarian-born US mathematician John von Neumann (1903–57) and published in the journal *Mathematische Annalen* in 1928.

minimum audible angle *n.* A measure of the *acuity of binaural *sound localization in the horizontal plane, equal to the smallest difference in the direction of two sound sources that can be reliably detected. In humans it is usually in the region of two degrees under ideal conditions, whereas in the barn owl, which relies entirely on its hearing to locate fieldmice and other prey in total darkness, it is close to one degree in both the horizontal and vertical dimensions, more acute than that of any other species whose hearing has been tested. Also called the *minimal audible angle*. **MAA** *abbrev.*

minimum audible field *n.* The smallest sound intensity that can be detected reliably by a listener facing the sound source under ideal listening conditions. Also called *minimal audible field*. *See also* acuity. **MAF** *abbrev.*

minimum audible pressure *n.* The sound pressure on the tympanic membrane corresponding to the *minimum audible field. Also called the *minimal audible pressure*. *See also* acuity. **MAP** *abbrev.*

minimum effective dosage *n.* The smallest dosage of a particular drug that produces a specified effect in an organism. Also called *minimal effective dosage*. *See also* effective dosage, therapeutic index, therapeutic ratio. *Compare* median effective dosage, median lethal dosage, median toxic dosage, minimum lethal dosage, minimum toxic dosage. **MED** *abbrev.*

minimum lethal dosage *n.* The smallest dosage of a drug that kills an experimental animal. Also called *minimal fatal dosage*. *See also* lethal dosage, therapeutic index, therapeutic ratio. *Compare* median effective dosage, median lethal dosage, median toxic dosage, minimum effective dosage, minimum toxic dosage. **MLD** *abbrev.*

minimum separable *n.* A measure of *visual acuity, usually determined with an *acuity grating, equal to the *visual angle corresponding to the finest grating in which separate bars can be distinguished. A person with normal 20/20 vision according to the *Snellen fraction has a minimum separable of approximately 1/60 of a degree or one minute of arc. *Compare* minimum visible.

minimum toxic dosage *n.* The smallest dosage of a drug that produces signs or symptoms of toxicity in an organism. Also called *minimal toxic dosage*. *See also* therapeutic index, therapeutic ratio, toxic dosage. *Compare* median effective dosage, median lethal dosage, median toxic dosage, minimum effective dosage, minimum lethal dosage. **MTD** *abbrev.*

minimum visible *n.* A measure of *visual acuity in terms of the *visual angle subtended by the finest hair-line that can be reliably detected. Under ideal viewing conditions it is in the region of one-half of one second of arc or about 1/7000 of a degree. *Compare* minimum separable.

Minnesota Multiphasic Personality Inventory *See* MMPI.

minor depressive disorder *n.* A term used to denote subthreshold cases of *major depressive disorder. Also called *dysthymic disorder*.

minor epilepsy *n.* A form of *epilepsy characterized by *absences, without *convulsions. Formerly called *petit mal epilepsy*.

minority social influence *n.* A form of *social influence in which the deviant subgroup rejects the established group *norm (1, 2) and persuades the majority to the minority attitude, opinion, belief, or behaviour pattern, thereby changing the norm. The concept was introduced by the Romanian-born French social psychologist Serge Moscovici (born 1920) in his book *Social Influence and Social Change* (1976), in which he argued that the conflict caused by minorities is a force for innovation.

Minorities are most influential when they are consistent, consensual, and in line with the underlying values of the group.

minor tranquillizer n. An obsolescent name for an *anxiolytic. US *minor tranquilizer*. *Compare* major tranquillizer.

miracle berry n. The fruit of the tropical African tree *Synsepalum dulcificum* that contains the protein *miraculin. Also called the *miraculous fruit* or *miraculous berry*.

miraculin n. A protein found in the *miracle berry that alters the taste buds, causing bland or acid foods eaten after it to taste sweet. *Compare* monosodium glutamate.
[From *miracul(ous)* + *-in(e)* indicating an organic compound]

mirror drawing n. Tracing shapes such as stars and circles with a pencil while the writing hand and the shapes are screened from sight but can be viewed via a reflection in a mirror. The discovery in 1960 that the ability to learn such automatic skilled movements is not impaired by bilateral *temporal lobe lesions, whereas memories requiring conscious cognitive processes are abolished by such lesions, gave the first hint of the existence of two distinct types of learning systems involving *declarative knowledge and *nondeclarative knowledge.

mirror focus n. A region of abnormal electrical activity in the cerebral cortex, corresponding to a region in the opposite cerebral hemisphere that has been stimulated to produce a focal epileptic *seizure, or an abnormal region of the cerebral cortex developing in response to a *lesion in the corresponding region of the opposite cerebral hemisphere.

mirror phase n. In *psychoanalysis, a concept introduced in 1936 by the French psychoanalyst Jacques Lacan (1901–81) to denote the stage of human development between 6 months and 18 months, when the infant, though still helpless, is capable of recognizing its body as a unity and imagining a state of being able to master it. According to Lacan, this phase forms the basis on which the *ego develops, and it is called the mirror phase because it is evidenced by the infant's jubilant response to its own mirror reflection, with which it is believed to identify.

mirror reversal problem n. The problem of explaining why a mirror appears to reverse left and right but not up and down. This question, often loosely labelled a *paradox, has been discussed ever since the Greek philosopher Plato (?427–?347 BC) answered it incorrectly in his dialogue *Timaeus*. According to a widely accepted explanation in *The Ambidextrous Universe* (1964) by the best-selling US science writer Martin Gardner (born 1914), the fact that the image appears behind the mirror causes the viewer to perform a *mental rotation of it, using the vertical axis of rotation because the human body is nearly left–right symmetrical and this is therefore the easiest mental rotation to perform; but this explanation fails because mental rotation is too slow to account for the phenomenon and because it relies on an awareness that what is seen is a mirror image, whereas the apparent left–right reversal is experienced as usual by a viewer who lacks this awareness. Others have offered explanations based on the fact that we have a pair of horizontally separated eyes; but the apparent reversal is unaffected by closing one eye. Further fallacious explanations have relied on physics or linguistics (the ambiguity of the words *left* and *right*). The correct solution to the problem, first published by the English psychologist Richard L(angton) Gregory (born 1923) in his book *Mirrors of the Mind* in 1997, with an added discussion of faces in 1999, is surprisingly simple. A mirror does not reverse left and right or top and bottom, but in order to see the reflection of an object we have to rotate it physically to face the mirror, and we usually perform this rotation about the horizontal axis, therefore the image appears left–right reversed because the object is indeed left–right reversed relative to the orientation of the reflected image. If, instead, we turned an object over about its horizontal axis to face a mirror, then its reflection would appear upside-down but not left–right reversed. Mirror images of our own faces appear left–right reversed for the same reason: to look in a mirror, we turn horizontally through 180 degrees relative to the reflected image we are about to produce; we cannot face the same way as the reflected image, because then we would be facing away from the mirror. *See also* enantiomorph.

mirror writing n. Handwriting that runs back-to-front. Also called *palingraphia*.

misidentification disorders *See* delusional misidentification.

misinformation effect *n*. Another name for the *eyewitness misinformation effect.

mismatch *n*. An incorrect pairing of a word and a *concept, usually by a child during the course of language development, as when a child calls a toy drum a car. It is seldom possible to trace the source of such misnomers. *See also* concept formation. *Compare* overextension, overgeneralization, underextension.

miss *n*. A failure to hit a target; hence, especially in *signal detection theory, a failure to detect a signal when it is present. Also called a *false negative*. *See also* receiver operating characteristic. *Compare* correct rejection, false alarm (2), hit.

missing fundamental illusion *n*. An *auditory illusion of pitch perception that arises if the set of *overtones or harmonics associated with a certain *fundamental frequency are presented to a listener without the fundamental frequency: the listener perceives the sound as having the pitch of the fundamental although the fundamental frequency is not present in the sound. *See also* combination tone, otogenic tone.

mitochondrial DNA *n*. A form of *DNA found in *mitochondria, having its own genetic code, slightly different from the universal code of nuclear DNA and subject to variation between species, encoding subunits of vital respiratory enzymes. It is inherited only from mothers, because only the mother's ovum contributes cytoplasm to the *zygote, it consists of several loops, each containing 37 genes, and it is present in every mitochondrion. Mutations in mitochondrial DNA caused by *free radicals have been linked to ageing and to several chronic degenerative diseases of the muscles and brain, including *dystonia, *Alzheimer's disease, and *diabetes mellitus. Comparisons of harmless mutations or changes in *introns that have accumulated, apparently at a fairly constant rate, in the mitochondrial DNA of people from around the world have been used to trace the prehistoric migrations of populations from the emergence of *Homo sapiens in Africa about 150,000 years ago. Mitochondrial DNA is also used in *genetic fingerprinting when nuclear DNA cannot be extracted in sufficient quantity, as often occurs when DNA is taken from solid bone, tooth fragments, hair, or faeces, rather than from blood, saliva, or semen. *See also* Eve, evolutionary clock, maternal inheritance, non-Mendelian gene, parsimony principle, plasmagene. *Compare* plasmid. **mtDNA** *abbrev*.

mitochondrion *n*. Any of the tiny (from two to five micrometres long) bean-shaped bodies that are evolutionarily descended from a free-living bacterium and are present in the cytoplasm of every cell, in large numbers in cells with heavy energy demands, releasing through the *Krebs cycle most of the energy that cells, tissues, and organs of the body require to function. *See also* crista, mitochondrial DNA, plasmagene. **mitochondria** *pl*. **mitochondrial** *adj*.
[From Greek *mitos* a thread + *chondros* cartilage, as the German biologist C. Benda (1857–1933) mistakenly thought it was when he discovered mitochondria in 1898]

mitosis *n*. A form of *cell division of *somatic cells in which each of the daughter nuclei contains the same number of *chromosomes as the parent nucleus, this being the normal form of cell division except for the formation of *gametes (see illustration). During *prophase* the nuclear membrane disappears and the chromosomes divide lengthwise into *chro-

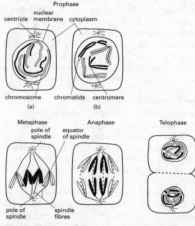

Mitosis. The stages of mitosis in a cell containing two pairs of homologous chromosomes.

matids, which become the chromosomes of the daughter cells; during *metaphase* *nuclear spindles are formed, and the chromosomes attach themselves to the equator of the spindles by their *centromeres; during *anaphase* the newly duplicated chromosomes separate and migrate to opposite ends of the spindles; and during the final *telophase* the cell pinches in the middle and a nuclear membrane forms around the chromosomes at each end. The movements taking place during mitosis are controlled by the cell's *cytoskeleton, and especially by movements of *microtubules. *Compare* meiosis (1). **mitotic** *adj.* **mitotic clock** *See under* telomere.

[From Greek *mitos* a thread + -*osis* indicating a process or state]

mitral cell *n.* A type of *pyramidal cell that is found abundantly in the *olfactory bulbs and that receives inputs from the olfactory receptors and sends information to other parts of the brain.

[*Mitral* mitre-shaped, from Latin *mitra* a turban]

Mitwelt *n.* In *phenomenology and *existentialism, the social environment as it is experienced. *See also* existential analysis, existential therapy. *Compare Eigenwelt, Umwelt.*

[From German *mit* with + *Welt* world]

mixed episode *n.* A *mood episode lasting at least one week during which the criteria of both *manic episode and *major depressive episode are met.

mixed-motive game *n.* In *game theory, any game in which the players' preferences among the outcomes are partly coincident and partly opposed, motivating the players both to cooperate and to compete, as in the *Prisoner's Dilemma game. A player in a mixed-motive game has to contend with *intra*personal, psychological conflict arising from this clash of motives in addition to the *inter*personal conflict of the game. At an abstract level, a mixed-motive game can be distinguished from a zero-sum game by the fact that the sum of the payoffs differs from one outcome to another, so that it is not the case that what one player gains the other(s) must necessarily lose. Mixed-motive games are therefore sometimes called *variable-sum* or *non-zero-sum* games. *Compare* zero-sum game.

mixed receptive-expressive language disorder *n.* A *communication disorder characterized by levels of language comprehension and expressive language development substantially below the level of non-verbal intelligence; the deficit interfering substantially with scholastic, academic, or occupational achievement or social interaction and not being due solely to mental retardation, speech-motor or sensory deficit, environmental deprivation, or a *pervasive developmental disorder. *See also* aphasia.

mixed strategy *n.* In *game theory, a strategy that is chosen with a randomizing device, by assigning a certain probability to each pure strategy. For example, in the children's game of *handy-dandy*, mentioned by Shakespeare in *King Lear* (I.iv.94), one player conceals a small object in one fist and the second player guesses left or right. The first player wins if the guess is wrong, and the second if it is right. Any player who chooses according to any deliberate procedure risks being outguessed by the opponent, and for both players, the game-theoretic solution is a randomized 50–50 mixed strategy that assigns equal probabilities to left and right. *See also* minimax theorem.

mixed transcortical aphasia *See under* aphasia.

mixture suppression *n.* A phenomenon of *olfaction in which the strength of an odour is reduced by the simultaneous presence of a different odour.

MMPI *abbrev.* The Minnesota Multiphasic Personality Inventory, one of the most widely used paper-and-pencil tests of personality, especially in the US, consisting of 566 (originally 504, later 550) statements, including 16 that are repeated, to which the respondent answers *True or mostly true (T), False or not usually true (F),* or *Cannot say (?),* typical items being similar to the following: *I feel contented most of the time; I have never had a fainting spell,* and *I believe I am cursed.* The instrument provides scores on 10 clinical scales: Hypochondriasis (Hs), Depression (D), Hysteria (Hy), Psychopathic deviate (Pd), Masculinity–femininity (Mf), Paranoia (Pa), Psychasthenia (Pt), Schizophrenia (Sc), Hypomania (Ma), and Social introversion (Si). In addition there are four validity (test-taking attitude) scales: a score for the number of questions left unanswered (?); a Lie scale (L) containing items describing socially desirable but unlikely behaviour, such as *I always tell the truth* (True); an Infrequency scale (F) of items answered in the keyed direction by ten per cent or less of normal people, such as *I see things, animals, or people around me that others do not see* (True); and a Correction factor (K) reflecting defensiveness in admitting to problems, containing items such as *At times I feel like swearing* (False). Numerous other scales have been derived from the MMPI test items. The MMPI was developed and first published in 1942 by the US clinical psychologist Starke Rosecrans Hathaway (1903–84) and the US neuropsychiatrist John Charnley McKinley (1891–1950); a revised version, called *MMPI-2*, was issued in 1989.

mneme *n.* The capacity to retain the aftereffects of an experience or stimulus. **mnemic** *adj.* Of or relating to *mneme. See also* mnemic symbol.
[From Greek *mnemon* mindful, from *mnasthai* to remember]

mnemic symbol *n.* In *psychoanalysis, a *hysterical symptom arising from a memory of a trauma or a conflict that has been repressed. In a key passage in an article on 'The Neuro-Psychoses of Defence' (1894), Sigmund Freud (1856–1939) described it as follows: 'By this means the ego succeeds in freeing itself from the contradiction; but instead, it has burdened itself with a mnemic symbol which finds a lodgement in consciousness, like a sort of parasite, either in the form of an unresolvable motor innervation or as a constantly recurring hallucinatory sensation' (*Standard Edition*, III, pp. 45–61, at p. 49).

mnemon *n.* A basic unit of memory, or the minimum physical change in the nervous system that encodes a memory.
[From Greek *mneme* memory, from *mnasthai* to remember]

mnemonic *adj. n.* (Of or relating to) a technique used to aid memory, such as the *rhyming method* familiar to most English-speaking people in the mnemonic *Thirty days hath September* . . . for remembering how many days there are in each month, or the *acronym method* known by most musicians in the mnemonic *Every Good Boy Deserves Favour* for remembering the

five lines of the treble clef in musical notation (E, G, B, D, F). The English physicist Sir James (Hopwood) Jeans (1877–1946) suggested the following *word-length mnemonic* for remembering the first 15 digits of the transcendental number pi, represented by the number of letters in each successive word: *How I want a drink, alcoholic of course, after the heavy chapters involving quantum mechanics*, yielding π = 3.14159265358979. In the same spirit, a US correspondent to *Scientific American* magazine suggested the following word-length mnemonic for the first 10 digits of the transcendental number *e*: *To express e, remember to memorize a sentence to simplify this*, yielding *e* = 2.7182818284. The use of mnemonics can be traced to ancient Greece, where, in about 500 BC, the poet Simonides of Ceos (556–468 BC) invented the *method of loci*, a useful and effective technique for memorizing collections of items such as shopping lists: the items are visualised at specific locations in a familiar building, and they are recalled by revisiting the locations in a systematic tour round the building carried out in one's imagination. A similar but more flexible and even more effective technique—the method of choice of serious *mnemonists and professional memory performers—is the *peg-word mnemonic. **mnemonics** *n.* The practice of using *mnemonic techniques.
[From Greek *mnemonikos* mnemonic, from *mneme* memory, from *mnasthai* to remember + -*ikos* of, relating to, or resembling]

mnemonist *n.* A person who uses *mnemonics. Research has shown that most if not all professional memory performers use mnemonics. One of the most phenomenal and most thoroughly investigated of mnemonists, the Russian man usually referred to as S (actually called Shereshevskii), studied in depth by the Russian neuropsychologist Alexandr Romanovich Luria (1902–77) and described in his book *The Mind of a Mnemonist* (1968), relied heavily on mnemonics, including the method of loci.

mobbing *n.* The coordinated activity of a large number of birds or other small animals in harassing or driving away a *predator.

Möbius syndrome *n.* A rare neurological disorder caused by a defect in the prenatal development of the motor nuclei of the cranial nerves and characterized by loss of

control of facial muscles, resulting in an inability to express emotion through *facial expression and in most cases a diminished ability to interpret emotion in other people's faces, often associated with oculomotor dysfunction and periodic *migraine headache. Also called *congenital facial diplegia, congenital oculofacial paralysis, nuclear agenesis*. Compare Bell's palsy.
[Named after the German neurologist Paul Julius Möbius (1853–1907) who first described it in 1884]

modality *See* sensory modality.

modality effect *n.* Any effect of the presentation of information via different *sensory modalities, one example being the superior immediate recall of simple verbal information presented in the auditory rather than the visual modality, although the effect is restricted to the terminal part of the message, and another example being the superior long-term recall of complex verbal information presented via the visual rather than the auditory modality. *See also* cross-modal transfer.

modal logic *n.* The logic of necessity and possibility, first developed in 1912 by the US logician and philosopher C(larence) I(rving) Lewis (1883–1964), in which a *modal proposition* is a *proposition (1) that asserts something to be necessarily or possibly true, and a *modal syllogism* is a *syllogism in which at least one of the premises is a modal proposition or statement. If p is a proposition, then p *is possible* means the same as *it is not necessary that not-p*, and p *is contingent* means the same as *it is not necessary either that p or that not-p*. *See also* categorical syllogism, deductive reasoning, epistemic reasoning. *See also* possible world.
[From Latin *modus* a measure or manner + *-alis* of or relating to]

modal verb *n.* An auxiliary verb that modifies a main verb, expressing necessity or possibility. In English, the modal verbs are *can, could, may, might, will, would, shall, should, must, ought*, and sometimes *dare, need*, and *used to*.

mode *n.* In descriptive statistics, a measure of *central tendency that is the most frequently occurring score or scores among a collection of scores. *Compare* mean, median. **modal** *adj.* Of or relating to a (or the) mode.
[From Latin *modus* measure]

model *n.* A deliberately simplified and usually idealized and imaginary *representation (1) of a *phenomenon, with fundamental properties that are explicitly defined (or physically built) and from which other properties can be deduced by logical reasoning (or by empirical observation if the model is a physical object). Inferences from the model apply only to the model and not necessarily to the reality that it purports to represent, but if the model captures the important features of the phenomenon, then such inferences may apply also to the phenomenon itself. Among the most successful abstract models in the history of science are Euclid's geometry, which models spatial relationships, and Newton's theory of mechanics, which models the interaction of physical objects and forces operating on them. *See also* additive model, construct, linear model, measurement model, multiplicative model, quadratic model. *Compare* hypothesis, theory.

modelling *n.* A technique of *behaviour therapy in which the client or patient learns appropriate patterns of behaviour by imitating another person demonstrating the target behaviour either live or on video; often used in *assertiveness training. US *modeling*.

moderate mental retardation *n.* A level of *mental retardation associated with *IQ approximately between 35 and 50 (in adults, *mental age from 6 to under 9 years), equivalent to the educational category of trainable mentally retarded. Also called *moderate mental subnormality*.

modified Ellsberg paradox *n.* A version of the *Ellsberg paradox in which the failure of *expected utility theory and of *subjective expected utility theory is especially clear. Two urns are each filled with white, red, and green balls. Urn *A* contains 50 white balls, 25 red balls, and 25 green balls; Urn *B* contains 50 white balls and 50 red and green balls, the ratio of red to green balls being unknown. You are offered a choice between the following three bets, each of which carries the same prize if you win.

X: You draw a ball at random from Urn *A*, and you win the prize if it is white or red.
Y: You draw a ball at random from Urn *B*, and you win the prize if it is white or red.
Z: You draw a ball at random from Urn *B*,

and you win the prize if it is white or green.

Most people prefer X. In X, the probability of winning the prize is obviously 0.75, whereas in Y or Z the probability could be as low as 0.50 or as high as 1.00, depending on the unknown proportions of red and green balls. If the decision maker's subjective probability of drawing a red ball from Urn B is p, then the preference for X over Y implies that $0.75 > 0.50 + p$, which means that $p < 0.25$. But if $p < 0.25$, then the probability q of drawing a green ball from Urn B must be greater than 0.25, and the decision maker should therefore prefer Z to X, because $0.75 < 0.50 + q$. The usual preference of X over both Y and Z violates the axioms of expected utility theory, though it is consistent with Ellsberg's suggestion that human decision makers use *maximin strategies in choices involving *uncertainty (2). See also risk aversion. Compare Allais paradox, common ratio effect, St Petersburg paradox.
[Named after the US political analyst Daniel Ellsberg (born 1931) who published the original version of the paradox in the *Quarterly Journal of Economics* in 1961]

modified LSD test n. In statistics, the modified least significant difference test, another name for a Bonferroni t test. See Bonferroni correction.

modifier gene n. Any gene that affects the *phenotypic expression of another gene. See also regulator gene.

modularity of mind n. The notion that cognitive processes are controlled by subsystems that operate as distinct units and with a significant degree of independence from one another. This notion can be traced to the Greek philosopher Aristotle (384–322 BC), who discussed a division of mental functions in *De Anima*; it formed the basis of the pseudoscience of *phrenology, and in more recent times it has been chiefly associated with the writings of the US philosopher Jerry Fodor (born 1935), especially his book *The Modularity of Mind* (1983).

modulation transfer function n. Another name for the *contrast sensitivity function. **MTF** abbrev.

modulator n. Anything that modulates; in visual perception a hypothetical retinal *ganglion cell that transmits discrete sensations of colour and regulates the responses of *dominator cells.

modus ponens n. Any argument taking the form: *If p, then q; p; Therefore, q*. For example, *If it is Sunday, then the restaurant is closed; It is Sunday; Therefore, the restaurant is closed*. Such an argument is logically valid. See also affirming the antecedent. Compare modus tollens.
[Latin: mood that affirms]

modus tollens n. Any argument taking the form: *If p, then q; Not-q; Therefore not-p*. For example, *If it is Sunday, then the restaurant is closed; The restaurant is not closed; Therefore, it is not Sunday*. Such an argument is logically valid. See also denying the consequent. Compare modus ponens.
[Latin: mood that denies]

molecular biology n. The study of biological molecules, especially *proteins and *nucleic acids.

molecular genetics n. The study of structure and function of the molecules of *genes and *chromosomes.

Molyneux's question n. The question regarding how the world would look to a person who acquired the gift of sight late in life, and in particular whether such a person would at first be able to distinguish a globe (ball) from a cube by sight alone. The English philosopher John Locke (1632–1704), a proponent of *empiricism, hypothesized in 1690 that the answer was no: 'For, though he has obtained the experience of how a globe, how a cube affects his touch, yet he has not yet obtained the experience that what affects his touch so or so must affect his sight so or so' (*Essay Concerning Human Understanding*, Book 2, Chapter 9, section 8), but research into *crossmodal transfer in the 1960s proved him wrong.
[Named after the Irish philosopher, astronomer, and politician William Molyneux (1656–98), referred to by Locke as 'the learned and worthy Mr Molineux' [sic], who first posed the question to Locke in 1688]

monad n. Literally, a group of one, but more usually denoting a fundamental or indivisible metaphysical unit. According to the German rationalist philosopher and mathematician

Gottfried Wilhelm von Leibniz (1646–1716), it is an elementary indestructible element, not belonging to ordinary space, of which reality is composed. *See also* entelechy. **monadic** *adj.* Of or relating to *monads, or (in logic and mathematics) having only one term.
[From Greek *monas*, *monados* a unit, from *monos* alone]

monaural *adj.* Of, relating to, or involving the use of one ear. *Compare* binaural.
[From Greek *monos* alone or single + Latin *auris* an ear + -*alis* of or relating to]

money pump *n.* A pattern of intransitive or *cyclic preferences causing a decision maker to be willing to pay repeated amounts of money to have these preferences satisfied without gaining any benefit. The simplest example is a person who evaluates three commodities x, y, and z and prefers x to y, y to z, and z to x. A person may, for example, prefer one lawnmower x to another y because it is larger, and may prefer y to z for the same reason, but may prefer z to x because x would be extremely difficult to take to a repair shop if it were to break down. If the person owns x, then a salesman could offer to replace it with z in return for a fee (there must be *some* price that a person who prefers z to x is willing to pay for this improvement), then the salesman could offer to replace z with y for a fee, then to replace y with x for a fee, and so on indefinitely or until the money runs out. The concept was introduced by the English philosopher, mathematician, and economist Frank (Plumpton) Ramsey (1903–30) and published posthumously in 1931. Also called a *Dutch book*, especially when the price of each replacement is reduced until the person is willing to pay for it. *See also* decision theory, intransitive preferences.

mongolism *n.* An obsolete name for *Down's syndrome.
[Referring to the supposed resemblance of people with the disorder to Mongolians, a comparison now considered offensive]

monism *n.* Any approach to the *mind–body problem according to which there is no essential difference between the mental and physical realms. *See also* double-aspect theory, identity theory, materialism, neutral monism.
[From Greek *monos* single or alone]

monoamine *n.* An *amine such as *adrenalin (epinephrine), *noradrenalin (norepinephrine), *serotonin, or *dopamine containing only one amino group (NH_2).

monoamine oxidase *n.* An *enzyme that is located between the outer and inner membranes of *mitochondria in almost all tissues and that metabolizes *monoamines, notably *catecholamines, within neurons. *See also* monoamine oxidase inhibitor. *Compare* catechol-o-methyl-transferase (COMT). **MAO** *abbrev.*
[From Greek *monos* single or alone + English *amine* + *oxid(ation)* + Greek -*ase* denoting an enzyme, from *diastasis* separation]

monoamine oxidase inhibitor *n.* Any of a group of *antidepressant drugs that inhibit the action of the intracellular enzyme *monoamine oxidase in neurons of the central nervous system, thereby slowing the metabolism of neurotransmitters such as *adrenalin (epinephrine), *noradrenalin (norepinephrine), and *dopamine and allowing their concentrations to increase at the *synapses (1). When taken with foods containing *tyramine or *dopa, it produces acute *hypertension. Also called a *psychoenergizer*. *See* iproniazid, isocarboxazid, phenelzine, St John's wort, tranylcypromine. *See also* cheese effect. *Compare* selective serotonin reuptake inhibitor (SSRI), tetracyclic antidepressant, tricyclic antidepressant. **MAOI** or **MAO inhibitor** *abbrev.*

monoblepsis *n.* A condition in which vision is clearer when one rather than both eyes are used. Also called *monoblepsia*.
[From Greek *monos* alone or single + *blepsis* sight]

monochromatic *adj.* All of one colour, or pertaining to light consisting of a single wavelength.
[From Greek *monos* alone or single + *chroma*, *chromatos* a colour + -*ikos* of, relating to, or resembling]

monochromatism *n.* A form of *colour-blindness characterized by *monochromatic vision in which all colours are perceived as different shades of the same colour. Also called *monochromasy*. *Compare* achromatopsia. **monochromat** or **monochromate** *n.* A person with *monochromatism.

monoclonal antibody *n*. An *antibody, produced by a single *clone (1) of *B lymphocytes fused with malignant tumour cells and grown in a culture, consisting of a population of identical molecules all specific for a single *antigen and capable of proliferating indefinitely to produce unlimited copies of itself; widely used in biotechnology, genetic engineering, and the diagnosis of disorders.
[From Greek *monos* single or alone + English *clone*]

monocular *adj*. Of, relating to, or involving the use of only one eye. Also called *uniocular*. *Compare* binocular, dichoptic.
[From Greek *monos* alone or single + Latin *oculus* an eye]

monocular cue *n*. Any of the visual *cues (2) functioning as indications or hints of distance that contribute towards visual *depth perception and that do not depend on integration of information from both eyes. *See* accommodation (1), aerial perspective, chiaroscuro, elevation in the visual field, interposition, linear perspective, monocular parallax, relative size, and texture gradient. *Compare* binocular cue.

monocular parallax *n*. One of the monocular cues of visual *depth perception, depending on the fact that movement of the head produces relatively large apparent displacement of nearby objects in the opposite direction and relatively small displacement of distant objects in the same direction. Also called *motion parallax* or *movement parallax*. *See also* motion perspective, parallax, reduction screen. *Compare* binocular parallax.

monocyte *n*. A giant *leucocyte with a round nucleus, playing a part in the immune system as a *phagocyte by consuming foreign or malfunctioning cells. *See also* granulocyte, lymphocyte, stem cell.
[From Greek *monos* single + *kytos* a vessel]

monogamy *n*. The custom or practice of having only one spouse at a time or, in animals, of having only one mate during a breeding season. *Compare* polygamy.
[From Greek *monos* single + *gamos* marriage]

monogenic inheritance *n*. Inheritance of a characteristic through a single *gene, such as occurs in the inheritance of haemophilia or

phenylketonuria. *See also* qualitative inheritance. *Compare* polygenic inheritance, quantitative inheritance.
[From Greek *monos* single + German *Gen* a gene, from Greek *genein* to produce]

monomania *n*. Pathological preoccupation with a single idea or fanatical devotion to a single activity.
[From Greek *monos* single + *mania* madness]

monopede mania *n*. Another name for *acrotomorphilia.

monopedophilia *n*. Another name for *acrotomorphilia.

monophthong *n*. A single vowel sound with no detectable change within it, such as the vowel sounds in *seat, set, sat, coot, caught, cot*, and *cut*. *Compare* diphthong, triphthong.
[From Greek *monos* one + *phthongos* a sound]

monoplegia *n*. Paralysis of one limb or a single muscle group, usually as a result of a lesion in a *motor nerve. *Compare* diplegia, hemiplegia, ophthalmoplegia, paraplegia, quadriplegia, triplegia. **monoplegic** *adj*.
[From Greek *monos* single + *plege* a blow + -*ia* indicating a condition or quality]

monopolar neuron *n*. Another name for a *unipolar neuron. Also called a *monopolar cell*.

monoptic *adj*. **1.** Having one eye. **2.** Of or relating to the (usually successive) presentation of different stimuli to the same eye. *Compare* dichoptic, monocular.
[From Greek *monos* alone or single + *optikos* of or relating to vision, from *optos* visible, from *ops* an eye]

monosemy *n*. The property of a word of having only one meaning. *Compare* polysemy.
[From Greek *monos* one + *sema* a sign]

monosodium glutamate *n*. A white crystalline flavour enhancer that is often added to foods in restaurants and supermarkets and that, on its own, elicits all four primary taste sensations, namely sweet, sour, salty, and bitter. It intensifies the taste of food to which it is added and may have a distinctive taste of its own called *umami. Formula: $NaC_5H_8O_4$. Also called *sodium glutamate*. *Compare* miraculin. **MSG** *abbrev*.

[So called because it is the sodium salt of glutamic acid]

monosomy X n. Another name for *Turner's syndrome.

monosynaptic reflex n. A reflex involving just one *synapse (1) between a sensory neuron and a motor neuron, without the involvement of any *interneurons. *Stretch reflexes are the only monosynaptic reflexes in humans. Strictly speaking the term is a misnomer and is avoided in careful usage, because there must also be a synapse between the motor neuron and the muscle, hence any reflex necessarily involves at least two synapses. Also called a *single-synapse reflex. Compare polysynaptic reflex.
[From Greek monos single + neuron a nerve]

monotonic adj. The property of a sequence or a function of consistently increasing in value or staying the same, or of consistently decreasing in value or staying the same. Also called a monotone sequence or function. See also monotonicity.
[From Greek monos single, solitary, or alone + tonos a tone + -ikos of, relating to, or resembling]

monotonicity n. The property of being *monotonic. In *logic, it refers to the fact that a valid argument cannot be made invalid, nor an invalid argument made valid, by adding new *premises. More precisely, monotonicity in logic is the property of obeying the *extension theorem of semantic entailment. See also non-monotonic reasoning.

monozygotic adj. Developed from one *zygote. Compare dizygotic. **MZ** abbrev.
[From Greek monos single + zygotos yoked, from zygon a yoke + -itikos resembling or marked by]

monozygotic twins n. Twins that are *monozygotic, being formed when a single *ovum or egg is fertilized by a single *spermatozoon and then splits and develops into two separate individuals sharing identical genes. The relative frequency of monozygotic twins is quite stable at about 1 pair per 250 births. Also called identical twins, but this is avoided in careful scientific usage, because they are never identical, having been influenced by environmental as well as genetic factors. See also twin studies. Compare dizygotic twins.

Monte Carlo method n. Any of a range of heuristic techniques of statistical analysis, used especially when an *algorithm or formula is unavailable, in which the phenomenon or process of interest is simulated, usually on a computer, by the generation of random numbers. For example, to estimate the probability of five heads in five successive coin tosses, an analyst unfamiliar with the *binomial test could simulate five coin tosses thousands of times on a computer and count the proportion that consist of five heads. This would amount to performing a *randomization test.
[Named by its pioneer, the Hungarian-born US mathematician John von Neumann (1903–57), after the casino at Monte Carlo where randomization determines outcomes]

Monty Hall problem n. A problem of decision making and probability judgement, first discussed by the US columnist Marilyn vos Savant (born 1946) in Parade magazine in September 1990, the solution to which is notoriously difficult to believe—when it was first published, thousands of people (including many university professors) wrote in refusing to accept it. In the simplest version, a game show host invites you to choose among three doors, behind just one of which is a car. After your initial choice, the host, who knows where the car is, opens one of the other doors to show that the car is not there and invites you to switch your choice to the remaining unopened door if you wish. The problem is: should you switch? Surprisingly, switching doubles your probability of winning the car from 1/3 to 2/3. The reason is that there is one chance in three that the car is behind your originally chosen door, and accepting the invitation to switch loses only if your original choice is right; if the car is not there and you switch, then the host's action will direct you to the right door, because in that case there is only one door that the host can open, and you will choose the other, where the car is. In many descriptions of the problem, there is a car behind one of the doors and a goat behind each of the others. The probabilistic phenomenon underlying the problem can be traced to Bertrand's box paradox, first discussed by the French mathematician Joseph (Louis François) Bertrand (1822–1900) on pages 3–4 of his book Calcul des Probabilités in 1889. Also called the Monty Hall dilemma. See also principle of restricted choice.

[Named after the US entertainer Monty Hall (born 1923) who hosted the television game show *Let's Make a Deal* in which the problem was first noticed]

mood *n.* **1.** A temporary but relatively sustained and pervasive affective state, often contrasted in psychology and psychiatry with a more specific and short-term *emotion. See also* affect, depression, dysphoric mood, elevated mood, euthymic mood, expansive mood, irritable mood. **2.** In linguistics, a category of verb expressing a mode or manner of action or being, typical grammatical moods being indicative, subjunctive, and imperative. **3.** In logic, the form of a *syllogism, depending on the nature of its three constituent *propositions (1).
[Sense 1 from Old English *mod* mind or feeling; senses 2 and 3 from Latin *modus* manner]

mood-congruent *adj.* Of or relating to a *delusion or *hallucination whose content is consistent with the depressed or manic mood of the person experiencing it. *Compare* mood-incongruent.

mood-dependent memory *n.* A form of *state-dependent memory associated with effects of moods or emotional states during learning and recall.

mood disorders *n.* A class of *mental disorders with disturbance of *mood (1) as the predominant feature. *See* bipolar disorders, cyclothymic disorder, depressive disorder, mania, mood episodes, seasonal affective disorder (SAD), substance-induced disorders, unipolar depression. *See also* schizoaffective disorder.

mood episodes *n.* A class of *mental disorders comprising *depressive episode, *major depressive episode, *manic episode, *mixed episode, and *hypomanic episode.

mood-incongruent *adj.* Of or relating to a *delusion or *hallucination whose content is inconsistent with the depressed or manic mood of the person experiencing it. *Compare* mood-congruent.

mood stabilizer *n.* Any drug, such as *lithium carbonate, that is used in the treatment of *bipolar disorders. *Compare* antimanic.

moon illusion *n.* A visual illusion that causes the moon to appear relatively larger when it is near the horizon than when it is at its zenith, although in both cases it subtends the same *visual angle of about one-half of a degree or 30 minutes of arc, and although it does not necessarily appear any further away at its zenith. The sun is much larger than the moon but by remarkable coincidence almost identical to it in *angular size, fitting behind the moon almost perfectly in a total eclipse, and it is also subject to the moon illusion, appearing much larger shortly after sunrise or shortly before sunset than at its zenith. The illusion first appeared in print in the *Meteorology* of the Greek philosopher Aristotle (384–322 BC), who described its effect on the sun and stars but oddly omitted to mention the moon: 'The sun and stars seem bigger when rising and setting than on the meridian' (Book 3, Chapter 4, Bekker edition, p. 373b). Also called the *celestial illusion*, especially when referring to the illusion in a stimulus other than the moon. *See also* Emmert's law, horizontal–vertical illusion, perspective illusion, size–distance invariance, visual angle.

moral development *n.* The formation and maturation of a sense of right and wrong in children in the normal course of cognitive development. *See also* Kohlberg stage.

morbid jealousy *n.* Another name for *jealous delusional disorder.

Morgan–Murray Thematic Apperception Test *n.* The original name by which the *TAT was generally known prior to 1943.

Morgan's canon *See* Lloyd Morgan's canon.

Morinaga misalignment illusion *n.* A visual illusion in which three or more arrowheads, some pointing to the left and some to the right, aligned with their apexes or tips in vertical straight lines, appear to be out of alignment, with the left-pointing apexes further to the left than the right-pointing ones. Pairs of arrowheads can be constructed such that the apparent misalignment is opposite to what would be expected from the *Müller-Lyer illusion (see illustration).
[Named after the Japanese Gestalt psychologist Shiro Morinaga (1908–64) who first drew attention to it in 1941]

Morinaga misalignment illusion. The distance between each of the three pairs of arrowheads is identical, and their apexes are vertically aligned.

Morita therapy *n.* A form of *psychotherapy, used especially to treat *hypochondriasis. It begins with 4–7 days of absolute bed rest without reading, talking, or other active pursuits, to be followed by a programme of progressively difficult or demanding work, usually in a communal setting. It is based on Buddhist beliefs.
[Named after the Japanese psychiatrist Shoma Morita (1874–1938) who originated it]

morning glory *n.* Any of a number of tropical plants of the family Convolvulaceae, including the Mexican vine *Rivea corymbosa* containing the *psychedelic and *hallucinogenic drug *ololiuqui.
[So called because its trumpet-shaped flowers close in the late afternoon]

moron *n.* An obsolete term for a person with *moderate mental retardation; also, an abusive term for a person of low intelligence. **moronic** *adj.*
[From Greek *moros* foolish]

Moro reflex *n.* A form of the *startle reflex displayed by infants up to about 12 months of age, elicited by making a sudden loud noise or raising the infant's head slightly and allowing it to drop back on to a pillow, consisting of flexion (bending) of the legs, drawing the arms across the chest, and usually a brief cry. It is often absent in premature babies, and it is sometimes used to test infants for deafness. Also called the *embrace reflex*.
[Named after the German paediatrician Ernst Moro (1874–1951) who first drew attention to it]

morpheme *n.* The smallest distinctive unit of a language having a definite grammatical function. For example, *unhappiness* contains three morphemes: *un-* (a morpheme denoting negation) + *happi* (happy) + *-ness* (a morpheme denoting a state); and *Helen's brother is crying* contains six: *Helen* + *'s* (a morpheme denoting possession) + *brother* + *is* + *cry* + *ing* (a morpheme indicating the present participle). *See also* allomorph, bound form, pseudomorpheme. *Compare* kinemorph.
[From Greek *morphe* form + a suffix on the model of *phoneme*]

morphine *n.* A bitter crystalline *alkaloid, being a *narcotic analgesic extracted from *opium, in which it occurs in amounts up to fifteen per cent, used as a *narcotic analgesic and *sedative. *See also* addiction, dependence (2), opioid-related disorders, substance dependence, substance-induced disorders, substance-related disorders, substance use disorders.
[From Greek *Morph(eus)* the god of sleep and dreams + *-ine* indicating an organic compound]

morphology *n.* **1.** A branch of biology devoted to the form and structure of organisms. **2.** The study of the form and structure of words, especially in terms of *morphemes. **morphological** *adj.*
[From Greek *morphe* form + *logos* word, discourse, or reason]

mortality table *n.* An actuarial table showing people's life expectancies and death rates depending on demographic factors such as sex, age, and occupation, used for calculating life insurance premiums.

mortido *n.* In *psychoanalysis, a term coined by the Austrian physician Paul Federn (1871–1950) to denote the form of energy associated with *Thanatos, intended as a counterpart to *libido. *See also* destrudo.
[From Latin *mors*, *mortis* death + *-ido* on the model of *libido*]

morula *n.* A solid ball of cells that results from the cleavage of a *zygote or fertilized ovum and that later develops into a *blastocyst. *See also* embryo, foetus.
[From Latin *morula* a little mulberry, diminutive of *morum* a mulberry]

mosaic *n.* An organism composed of two or more genetically distinct tissue types or created by combining genes from two or more different species. Also called a *chimera*.
[From Latin *mosaicus* a mosaic, from Greek

mouseios of the Muses, from *mousa* a Muse + -*ikos* of, relating to, or resembling]

Moses test of extreme reaction *n*. In statistics, a *distribution-free *non-parametric test of the difference between two independent groups in the extremity of scores (in both directions) that the groups contain. Scores from both groups are pooled and converted to *ranks, and the test statistic is the span of scores (the range plus 1) in one of the groups chosen arbitrarily. An exact probability is computed for the span and then recomputed after dropping a specified number of extreme scores from each end of its range.
[Named after the US statistician Lincoln Ellsworth Moses (born 1921) who introduced it in 1952]

mossy fibre *n*. One of the two types of *afferent neurons conveying signals to the *cerebellum, projecting from sites other than the inferior olivary nuclei on to tiny *granule cells in the cerebellar cortex, situated immediately under the layer of *Purkinje cells with which the granule cells form many synapses, each mossy fibre indirectly exciting many Purkinje cells. US *mossy fiber*. *Compare* climbing fibre.
[So called because of its appearance]

mother complex *n*. In *psychoanalysis, *ambivalence in a girl's feelings towards her mother, being one of the elements of the *Oedipus complex. *See also* complex (2).

motherese *n*. A popular alternative name for *caretaker speech, misleading because it is used also by fathers when talking to young children, although fatherese tends to be more intense and demanding. Even *parentese* is too restrictive a term, because the major features of motherese have been observed in the speech of unrelated adults and of older children talking to younger siblings. Also called *child-directed speech* or (ambiguously) *baby talk*.
[From *mother* + -*ese* indicating style]

mother, phallic *See* phallic woman.

motile *adj*. **1.** Exhibiting or capable of motion. *n*. **2.** A person whose characteristic style of mental imagery is motor rather than visual, auditory, or tactile, taking the form of feelings of motion such as limb movements or muscular movements associated with the pronunciation of words. *Compare* audile (2), tactile (2), visualizer.

motion aftereffect *n*. An illusion of movement resulting from prolonged perception of motion in the opposite direction, as occurs with the *Plateau spiral or the *waterfall illusion. Also called a *movement aftereffect*. **MAE** *abbrev*.

motion capture *n*. A phenomenon of *apparent movement in which a target image moving in one direction against a background of randomly moving elements causes those elements to appear to be moving in the same direction as the target.

motion detector *n*. Another name for a *direction-sensitive neuron.

motion parallax *n*. Another name for *monocular parallax.

motion perspective *n*. A term used by the US psychologist James Jerome Gibson (1904–79) to denote the *optical flow pattern in the visual field resulting from *monocular parallax. *See also* direct perception.

motion sickness *n*. A debilitating condition brought about by *passive movement or the illusory perception of passive movement, characterized by pallor, vertigo, hyperventilation, nausea, and sometimes vomiting. It is often associated with vehicular transport, people suffering from it being described as being *airsick*, *carsick*, or *seasick*, and *antihistamine drugs or *scopolamine are often prescribed for its prevention. *See also* sensory conflict theory.

motivated error *n*. Another name for a *parapraxis.

motivation *n*. A driving force or forces responsible for the initiation, persistence, direction, and vigour of goal-directed behaviour. It includes the biological *drives such as hunger, thirst, sex, and self-preservation, and also social forms of motivation such as *need for achievement and *need for affiliation. **motivational** *adj*.
[From Latin *motivus* moving, from *motus* moved, from *movere* to move + -*ation* indicating a process or condition]

motivational research n. An approach to the study of consumer behaviour, especially advertising and marketing, based loosely on assumptions and concepts of *dynamic psychology in general and *psychoanalysis in particular. It seeks to uncover the unconscious motives through the use of *naturalistic observation, *focus groups, *depth interviews, and *projective tests, and it tends often to focus on sexual factors. It was pioneered in the 1930s by the Austrian-born US psychologist Ernest Dichter (1907–91), one of whose early claims was that, for a woman, baking a cake unconsciously symbolizes having a baby, and that ready-mix cakes, which did not sell as well as expected when they were first introduced, could be made more appealing to housewives by allowing them to add the basic ingredient that they expect to contribute when having a baby, namely a fresh egg. Motivational research has attracted criticism from psychologists and others and was scathingly attacked by the Canadian-born US economist John Kenneth Galbraith (born 1908) in the first edition of *The Affluent Society* (1958). *See also* subliminal perception. **MR** *abbrev.*

motoneuron n. The unit formed by a *motor neuron or *efferent neuron and the muscle fibre to which it is connected. Also called a *motor unit*.
[A term coined by the British neurophysiologist Sir Charles Scott Sherrington (1857–1952) from *moto(r)* + *neuron*]

motor aphasia *See under* aphasia.

motor apraxia n. Another name for *ideomotor apraxia. *See under* apraxia.

motor area n. Any area of the *cerebral cortex responsible for the initiation, coordination, or regulation of nerve impulses transmitted to muscles or glands, especially the areas of the *motor cortex.

motor cortex n. Areas in the *cerebral cortex, namely the primary motor cortex, premotor cortex, supplementary motor area, and frontal eye field, devoted to the control of bodily movements. The primary motor cortex occupies the *precentral gyrus immediately in front of the *central sulcus, directly opposite the primary somatosensory cortex, containing in each cerebral hemisphere an inverted

representation of the opposite side of the body with the hand and tongue disproportionately overrepresented. The premotor cortex, in front of the primary motor cortex, is about six times as large as the primary motor cortex and is concerned with postural coordination and execution of movements controlled by visual or tactile feedback. The supplementary motor area (SMA), still further forward in the frontal lobe, is concerned with the coordination of preplanned or preprogrammed movements. The frontal eye field, immediately in front of the area where the head is represented in the premotor cortex, is responsible for voluntary *saccadic eye movements, as when tracking moving images or reading. *See also* sensorimotor cortex.
[From Latin *motor* a mover, from *motus* moved, from *movere* to move]

motor dissociative disorders *See* dissociative movement disorders.

motor end plate n. The flattened *neuromuscular junction at which the *bouton of a *motor neuron synapses with the squad of muscle fibres that it innervates.

motor nerve n. Any of a number of nerves comprising the axons of *motor neurons that transmit signals from the *motor cortex or *spinal cord to the muscles and glands.

motor neuron n. Any of the nerve cells of the *peripheral nervous system that transmit signals from the *motor cortex or the *spinal cord to the muscles or glands (see illustration overleaf). Also called an *efferent neuron*. *See* alpha motor neuron, gamma motor neuron, Renshaw cell. *Compare* motoneuron.
[From Latin *motor* a mover, from *motus* moved, from *movere* to move]

motor neuron disease n. A progressive, degenerative, and ultimately fatal disease of the *motor neurons affecting approximately 10 people per 100,000, resulting in gradual weakening and wasting of muscles and death usually from respiratory failure after 2–5 years, the cause of the disease being unknown but assumed to be a virus or environmental toxin. *See also* amyotrophic lateral sclerosis. **MND** *abbrev.*

motor set n. A temporary readiness for a particular muscular movement. *See also* Aufgabe, set (2).

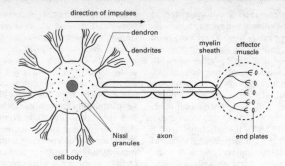

direction of impulses

dendron

dendrites

myelin sheath

effector muscle

Nissl granules

axon

end plates

cell body

Motor neuron

motor skills disorder *n.* A group of *mental disorders associated with motor skills, by far the most prominent being *developmental co-ordination disorder, characterized by *deficits in activities involving motor coordination.

motor unit *n.* Another name for a *moto-neuron.

movement aftereffect *n.* Another name for *motion aftereffect.

movement detector *n.* Another name for a *direction-sensitive neuron.

movement disorders *n.* Disorders of voluntary movements, including all the *apraxias, *dissociative movement disorders, and *stereotypic movement disorder.

movement illusion *n.* Any misperception of movement, notably any of the phenomena of *apparent movement, including *alpha movement, *beta movement, *gamma movement, *delta movement, *optimal movement, *partial movement, and *phi movement. *See also* audiogyral illusion, auto-kinetic effect, kinetic depth effect, Lissajous figure, motion capture, oculogyral illusion, Ouchi illusion, phantom grating, Plateau spiral, random-dot kinematogram, rotating head illusion, sensory saltation, Ternus phenomenon, vection, wagon wheel illusion, waterfall illusion, windmill illusion.

movement parallax *n.* Another name for *monocular parallax.

movement perception *n.* The perception of motion, processed by the *magnocellular system, which can be shown through *isolumi-nant displays to be totally colour-blind. *See also* direction-sensitive neuron.

movement tremor *n.* Another name for *intention tremor.

moving average *n.* In statistics, a sequence of numbers consisting of the averages of successive subsequences of a sequence of numbers, often computed from *time series to smooth out short-term fluctuations and make underlying trends clearer. For example, the three-term moving average of the sequence 1, 7, 4, 10, 4 is obtained by taking the mean of the first three numbers, then the mean of the second, third, and fourth, then the mean of the third, fourth, and fifth, yielding 4, 7, 6, which is much smoother. More generally, especially in *time-series analysis, a moving average is a sequence of numbers consisting of *weighted* sums of successive subsequences of a sequence of numbers, whether or not the weights sum to unity as they do for simple averages. *See also* ARIMA, white noise.

Mozart effect *n.* A finding, first reported in the journal *Nature* in 1993, that listening to compositions by Mozart increases scores on tests of spatial ability for a short while. In the original experiment, college students were given various tests after experiencing each of the following for ten minutes: listening to Mozart's sonata for two pianos in D major K488, listening to a relaxation tape, or silence. Performance on the paper-folding subtest of the *Stanford–Binet intelligence scale was significantly better after listening to Mozart than after the other two treatments, but the effect dissipated after about 15 minutes, and

other (non-spatial) tasks were unaffected. The finding has been contested by other researchers and has been widely misinterpreted to imply that listening to Mozart (or listening to classical music) increases one's intelligence. Several independent research studies have shown that children who receive extensive training in musical *performance* achieve significantly higher average scores on tests of spatial ability, but that long-term consequence is not the Mozart effect.
[Named after the Austrian composer Wolfgang Amadeus Mozart (1756–91)]

MPP⁺ *abbrev*. Methylphenylpyridine, a substance that is produced in the body from *MPTP and that selectively destroys neurons in the *substantia nigra, causing *Parkinson's disease.

MPPP *abbrev*. 1-Methyl-4-phenyl-4-propionoxy-piperidine, a *designer drug similar to *pethidine (meperidine) and often described as synthetic heroin. It is often contaminated with *MPTP.

MPTP *abbrev*. 1-Methyl-4-phenyl-1,2,3,6-tetrahydropyridine, a substance that is found as a contaminant in some *designer drugs, notably *MPPP, and is converted in the body to *MPP⁺, causing *Parkinson's disease.

MRI *abbrev*. Magnetic resonance imaging, a non-invasive method of *brain imaging or examination of other body organs by recording the responses to radio waves, or other forms of energy, of different kinds of molecules in a magnetic field. An MRI machine is a cylindrical magnet, large enough to contain a human body, producing a constant magnetic field in which protons (subatomic charged particles) spin like tops. A pulse of energy causes the spinning particles to tilt momentarily and then to regain their original orientations, giving up a detectable amount of energy as they do so. Different tissues emit different amounts of energy in response to the pulses, and the tissues that emit the greatest energy appear as the brightest regions in the resulting MRI scan. A series of two-dimensional slices are combined by a computer into a three-dimensional image. MRI can be used for imaging brain structure or (indirectly) brain function. When it is used to provide a dynamic picture of oxygen metabolism during specific mental activities it is called func-

tional MRI or fMRI; this involves imaging blood oxygenation, which is of interest because it correlates with levels of neuronal activity in specific brain regions. *See also* nuclear magnetic resonance.

MT *abbrev*. Median or middle temporal, another name for Area V5 of the *visual cortex, receiving inputs chiefly from the *magnocellular system, concerned mainly with movement perception. Also called *MT/V5*.

mucous membrane *n*. A thin sheet of tissue consisting of a surface layer of *epithelial tissue and a deeper layer of connective tissue covering or lining the cavities and canals of the body that open to the outside, including the mouth, nose, digestive tract, genitourinary tract, and uterus, secreting mucus and absorbing water, salts, and other solutes. *See also* common chemical sense.
[From Latin *mucus* slime + *membrana* a skin or parchment]

MUD *abbrev*. Multi-user dungeon or multi-user dimension, a class of *virtual reality constructions accessible simultaneously by several users via the Internet, allowing the playing of fantasy adventure games involving simulated interaction, combat, traps, puzzles, and magic, originally developed at the University of Essex in England in the early 1980s. Also written *mud*, and also used as a verb, meaning to play MUD. *See also* teledildonics.
[Named after the prototype fantasy game Dungeons and Dragons]

muddy children problem *n*. A logical problem illustrating that all members of a group may know a *proposition (1) to be true without that proposition being *common knowledge in the group. Suppose that all children in a classroom can see one another's foreheads but not their own, and that exactly two of them have muddy foreheads. The teacher asks all those who know they have muddy foreheads to put up their hands. The two muddy children, who are assumed to be perceptive, intelligent, and honest, have no reason to own up. The teacher then repeats the request a second time, and the two muddy children still have no reason to own up. Now suppose that the teacher had first announced to the class as a whole that at least one child in the class is muddy, turning a proposition that every child already knows to be true—because every child can see at least one muddy child—into an item of common knowledge. When the teacher asked all those with muddy foreheads to put up their hands, the two muddy children would not own up the first time the question was asked, but they would both own up when it was repeated a second time, because at that point each would realize that the failure of the other muddy child to own up the first time implied that there must be two muddy children in the class. It can be proved that if n of the children are muddy, then they will all own up when the question is asked for the nth time. The problem is sometimes cast in terms of a group in which some members have cheating spouses that the others all know about, and it is also called the *unfaithful wives problem* or the *cheating husbands problem*. It is a classic problem in *epistemic reasoning.

muina *See* bilis.

Müllerian duct *n.* Either of the pair of ducts that are present in a human embryo, alongside the pair of *Wolffian ducts, and that in a female develop by default into Fallopian tubes, uterus, and the upper part of the vagina, and in a male atrophy and disappear under the influence of *Müllerian inhibiting substance secreted by the embryonic testes while the Wolffian ducts develop into the male internal sex organs. Also called the *Müllerian system*.
[Named after the German physiologist Johannes Peter Müller (1801–58) who discovered them]

Müllerian inhibiting substance *n.* A *hormone that is produced by the *testes of a male embryo and that inhibits the development of the *Müllerian ducts into Fallopian tubes, uterus, and the upper part of the vagina. Also called *anti-Müllerian hormone (AMH)* or *Müllerian regression hormone (MRH)*. *See also* masculinizing hormone. **MIS** *abbrev.*

Müllerian mimicry *n.* A form of *mimicry in which two or more organisms that are harmful or unpalatable to a *predator resemble one another in shape or coloration and thereby jointly deter predation. *Compare* Batesian mimicry.
[Named after the German zoologist Johann F. T. Müller (1821–97) who first described it]

Müller-Lyer illusion *n.* The best known of all visual illusions, in which a line with inward-pointing arrowheads appears shorter than a line of the same length with reversed or outward-pointing arrowheads (see illustration). *See also* carpentered world, Morinaga misalignment illusion, star illusion, Zanforlin illusion.
[Named after the German sociologist and psychiatrist Franz Carl Müller-Lyer (1857–1916) who discovered the illusion and published 15 versions of it in the journal *Zeitschrift für Psychologie* in 1889]

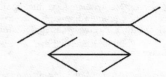

Müller-Lyer illusion. The horizontal lines are equal in length.

multi-attribute decision making *n.* Decisions made from sets of alternatives that vary on a number of attributes, aspects, or criteria. Familiar examples include choosing a house by comparing alternatives according to price, location, and number of rooms; selecting a marriage partner by comparing suitors on attributes such as physical attractiveness, intelligence, and sense of humour; and hiring an employee by comparing candidates on various qualifications. According to the standard linear additive value-maximization model, the decision maker simply weights the attributes according to their perceived importance, then sums the weights, then finally chooses the alternative with the highest aggregate weight; but there is evidence to suggest that human decision makers do not always behave according to this model. Also called *multi-attribute choice* or *multiple-attribute decision making* or *choice*. *See* elimination by aspects, lexicographic choice, lexicographic semiorder. **MADM** *abbrev.*

multidimensional scaling *n.* In statistics, a form of statistical data analysis for analysing similarities and dissimilarities among a collection of elements (organisms, objects, or events) in order to identify and model the dimensional structure underlying the elements, including the number of underlying dimensions, the location of each element on the dimensions, and the nature of the dimensions. The input data are usually represented by a *proximity matrix* showing the degree of similarity between every pair of elements. Multidimensional scaling has been likened to reconstructing a map of an unknown country from information about the distances between pairs of its towns and cities. *See also* INDSCAL. *Compare* cluster analysis, factor analysis. **MDS** *abbrev*.

multifactorial analysis *n*. Any form of *analysis of variance involving more than one *independent variable. *See also* repeated-measures analysis of variance.

multifactorial inheritance *n*. Inheritance of characteristics that are determined by multiple genes.

multiframe task *n*. A *visual search task in which different groups of stimuli are presented in successive displays. *Compare* single-frame task.

multi-infarct dementia *n*. Another name for *vascular dementia. **MID** *abbrev*.

multimodal therapy *n*. An approach to *psychotherapy, developed in 1972 by the South African-born US psychologist Arnold A. Lazarus (born 1932), based partly on *behaviour therapy, but more eclectic in its range of techniques and more concerned with the unique requirements of particular cases, the functional character of symptoms, and the importance of cognitive factors. *See also* BASIC-ID. **MMT** *abbrev*.

multiple-choice *adj*. In psychometrics, pertaining to a question that is accompanied by two or more *response categories of which the respondent chooses one. A multiple-choice questionnaire, made up of such questions, can be scored automatically. *Compare* free response.

multiple comparisons *n*. In statistics, tests of the significance of pairwise differences between more than two means, often conducted after *analysis of variance. Significance tests designed for comparisons between just one pair of means cannot be used for this purpose without violating the assumptions of the tests, because if three comparisons are made between three means, for example, then even if the data were completely random, the probability that one of the comparisons would be significant at $p < 0.05$ by chance alone would be greater than 0.05, because there would be three ways in which this could happen: Mean 1 could be significantly different from Mean 2, Mean 1 from Mean 3, or Mean 2 from Mean 3. This means that there would be inadequate protection against a *Type I error. Various specialized procedures have therefore been devised for handling multiple comparisons. *See also* Bonferroni correction, Duncan's multiple range test, least-significant difference test, Newman–Keuls test, Scheffé test, Tukey-HSD test. *Compare* a priori test.

multiple correlation coefficient *R* *n*. In statistics, an index of how well a *dependent variable can be predicted from a linear combination of *independent variables. It ranges from 0 (zero multiple correlation) to 1 (perfect multiple correlation), and the value of R^2 is the *coefficient of determination. *See also* regression analysis.

multiple determination *n*. In *psychoanalysis, another name for *overdetermination.

multiple intelligences *n*. An interpretation of *intelligence put forward by the US psychologist Howard (Earl) Gardner (born 1943) in his book *Frames of Mind: The Theory of Multiple Intelligences* (1983, 1993), taking account of abilities of gifted people and virtuosos or experts in various domains, abilities valued in different cultures, and abilities of individuals who have suffered brain damage. In addition to the linguistic, logical–mathematical, and spatial abilities incorporated in conventional interpretations of intelligence, Gardner's taxonomy includes *musical intelligence* (used in musical appreciation, composition, and performance), *bodily-kinaesthetic intelligence* (used in sport, dancing, and everyday activities requiring dexterity), *interpersonal intelligence* (used in relating to others, interpreting social signals, and predicting social outcomes), and *intrapersonal intelligence* (used in understanding and predicting one's own behaviour). In 1997 Gardner added *naturalist intelligence* (used in discriminating among plants, animals, and other features of the natural world, and in classifying objects in general) as an eighth intelligence and *spiritual intelligence* and *existential intelligence* as 'candidate' intelligences. Critics have argued that some of these abilities are better interpreted as special talents than as aspects of intelligence. *See also* creativity. *Compare* Guilford's cube.

multiple linear regression analysis *See* multiple regression.

multiple personality disorder *n.* Another name for *dissociative identity disorder. **MPD** abbrev.

multiple range test *n.* In statistics, a procedure for making *multiple comparisons, that is, for comparing all possible pairs of a set of group means. *See also* Duncan's multiple range test.

multiple regression *n.* Multiple linear regression analysis, a statistical method for analysing the joint and separate influences of two or more *predictor variables (also called *independent variables) on a *dependent variable, usually through a *linear model. It is a generalization of bivariate *regression analysis. The form of a multiple regression equation for k independent variables is a weighted sum:

$$Y = \beta_0 + \beta_1 X_1 + \beta_2 X_2 + \ldots + \beta_k X_k,$$

where Y is the *predicted* score on the dependent variable, each X_i is one of the predictor variables, β_0 is the intercept indicating the value of Y when all of the predictor variables are equal to zero, and each β_i is a *standardized regression coefficient indicating the relative importance of the corresponding independent variable in determining the predicted value of the dependent variable. *See also* beta coefficient, cross-validation (2), discriminant function analysis.

multiple sclerosis *n.* A chronic progressive autoimmune disease, triggered by bacteria that mimic the molecular structure of *myelin, causing the immune system to attack both the bacteria and normal myelin. It is associated with patchy deterioration of the myelin sheath surrounding neurons in the *white matter of the *central nervous system and is characterized by muscle weakness or *paresis, especially in the legs, clumsiness, numbness or *paraesthesia, *diplopia, *scotoma, and *tremor. *See also* BSE. **MS** abbrev.
[From Greek *sklerosis* a hardening, from *skleros* hard + -*osis* indicating a process or state]

multiplicative model *n.* Any statistical or mathematical model in which an effect can be expressed as a weighted product of *independent variables, so that if any of the independent variables is zero, then the value of the dependent variable is also zero, because any number multiplied by zero is zero. In *axiomatic measurement theory, multiplicative models are divided into those that can be converted into additive models by means of monotonic transformations of their independent and dependent variables and those that cannot, only the latter being considered fundamentally non-additive. *Compare* additive model.

multipolar neuron *n.* A *neuron with more than one *neurite, invariably a single *axon and one or more *dendrites, projecting from its *soma (1). Also called a *multipolar cell.* *Compare* bipolar cell, unipolar neuron.

multistage cluster sampling *n.* A form of *cluster sampling involving drawing a cluster sample in two or more successive stages. For example, to survey hospital patients throughout a country, a survey researcher might select a sample of hospitals randomly, then within each hospital select a single ward randomly, then select individual patients from each ward randomly.

multitrait–multimethod matrix *n.* A method of interpreting *construct validity in terms of the *convergent validity and *discriminant validity of several different methods of measuring several different psychological *attributes or *traits. It consists of a matrix (a rectangular table) of correlations between two or more theoretically distinct traits, each measured by two or more different methods. For example, the traits might be extraversion and conscientiousness, assumed on theoretical grounds to be distinct (*see* Big Five), and each of these traits might be measured by three methods, namely a multiple-choice test, a projective test, and peer ratings; this would produce a matrix with two rows and three columns. The figures along the main diagonal of the matrix, called *monotrait–monomethod* scores, are estimates of the *validity coefficients of the six measures, and for the measurements to be considered satisfactory they should be the highest in the matrix. Correlations between measures of the same trait by different methods, called *monotrait–heteromethod* scores, provide data about the *convergent validity of the measures, on the assumption that if they validly measure the same trait they should correlate with each other, and for the measurements to be considered satisfactory these scores should be reasonably high. Correlations between different traits measured by the same method, called *heterotrait–monomethod* scores, provide evidence of the degree to which the results are due to a methods factor, irrespective of what is being measured, and if measures of theoretically different traits, using the same method, do not correlate highly with one another, this constitutes evidence of *discriminant validity. Finally, correlations between different traits measured by different methods, called *heterotrait–heteromethod* scores, are generally the lowest in the matrix, and they should not be higher than the validity coefficients in their own rows or columns. The technique was introduced by the US psychologists Donald T(homas) Campbell (1916–96) and Donald W(inslow) Fiske (born 1916) in an article in the journal *Psychological Bulletin* in 1959. **MTMM** *abbrev.*

multi-user dungeon *See* MUD.

multivariate analysis of variance *n.* A statistical procedure that is closely related to *analysis of variance (ANOVA) and that determines the significance of differences among several group means, but unlike the standard (univariate) analysis of variance analyses more than one *dependent variable simultaneously. **MANOVA** *abbrev.*

multivariate statistics *n.* The branch of statistics devoted to investigating the influence of one or more *independent variable acting on more than one *dependent variable. The *multi-* in the name refers to the multiplicity of dependent variables. *See also* multivariate analysis of variance (MANOVA). *Compare* bivariate statistics, univariate statistics.

multiway frequency analysis *n.* Statistical analysis of frequency data involving more than one *independent variable and a *dependent variable, the most common technique being *log-linear analysis.

Munchausen by proxy syndrome *n.* Another name for *factitious disorder by proxy;

named after the disorder of *Munchausen syndrome, but not itself a mental disorder or syndrome according to the British paediatrician (Samuel) Roy (later Sir Roy) Meadow (born 1933) who named it in 1977. Also called *Münchhausen syndrome by proxy*. **MBPS** *abbrev.*

Munchausen syndrome *n.* Another name for *factitious disorder. Also spelt *Münchhausen syndrome*, especially in continental Europe, and more correctly in terms of its etymology. Also called *pathomimicry*. *See also* Munchausen by proxy syndrome. *Compare* compensation neurosis, malingering, pseudologia fantastica.
[First described and named, with the misspelling that has been widely adopted, by the British physician Richard (Alan John) Asher (1912–69) in a three-page article in the *Lancet* in 1951, alluding to Baron Münchhausen, a teller of tall stories in the fiction of the German novelist Rudolf Erich Raspe (1737–94), published in 1785, based on a real Baron Münchhausen (1720–97) who served in the Russian army fighting against the Turks and is said to have recounted extravagant tales of his prowess]

Munsell colour system *n.* A method of specifying colours in terms of the three dimensions of *hue, *lightness, and *saturation (1), standardized to the *CIE colour system and defined to theoretical limits in 1943, the *Munsell hue* scale containing five principal hues (red, yellow, green, blue, purple) and five intermediate hues (yellow-red, green-yellow, blue-green, purple-blue, red-purple); the *Munsell value* scale containing ten steps of lightness from black (zero) to white (10); and the *Munsell chroma* scale showing fourteen steps of saturation from the equivalent neutral grey (zero) to the most saturated level (14). US *Munsell color system*.
[Named after the US inventor Albert Henry Munsell (1858–1918) who developed it in 1915]

Münsterberg illusion *n.* A visual illusion created by a pattern of alternating columns of staggered light and dark rectangles whose rows are horizontally aligned but appear non-horizontal and non-parallel. Also called the *cafe wall illusion*, the *eccentric chessboard figure* (its original name), the *shifted checkerboard figure*,

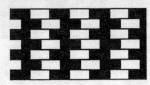

Münsterberg illusion. The figure is composed of rectangles in perfect horizontal alignment.

or the *Münsterberg figure*. *See also* hollow squares illusion, lavatory wall illusion.
[Named after the German-born US psychologist Hugo Münsterberg (1863–1916) who published it in 1894 and 1897]

muscarine *n*. A toxic *alkaloid drug, chemically related to *choline, that was originally derived from the *fly agaric mushroom *Amanita muscaria*, and that mimics *acetylcholine at certain receptor sites in the parasympathetic and central nervous systems, stimulating smooth muscle activity. When ingested it causes abdominal contractions, evacuation of bowels and bladder, constricted pupils, blurred vision, sweating, salivation, bradycardia, and decreased respiration. Formula: $C_8H_{19}NO_3$. *See also* cholinomimetic, muscarinic receptor, parasympathomimetic.
[From Latin *muscar(ius)* of flies, from *musca* a fly + *-ine* indicating an organic compound]

muscarinic receptor *n*. One of two types of *neuroreceptors for *acetylcholine found in the central nervous system and the parasympathetic branch of the peripheral nervous system, stimulated by *muscarine and inhibited by *atropine. The smooth muscles that are target organs of the autonomic nervous system (such as the pupils, blood vessels, and glands) use muscarinic receptors. Also called a *muscarinic cholinoceptor*. *Compare* nicotinic receptor.
[From Latin *muscarius* the alkaloid poison muscarine found in some mushrooms, so named because muscarine mimics acetylcholine at such a site]

muscimol *n*. A *hallucinogenic plant alkaloid found in the *fly agaric mushroom that binds to *GABA receptor complex in the brain.
[From Latin *musca* a fly + English *molecule*]

muscle *n*. Contractile tissue composed of bundles of elongated cells, some with multiple nuclei, by which movement of organs and parts of the body is effected; or a structure such as the biceps consisting of muscle tissue. The three main types of muscle tissue are *cardiac muscle, *smooth muscle, and *striped muscle. *See also* actin, actomyosin, creatine, extrafusal, fast-twitch fibre, Golgi tendon organ, intrafusal, involuntary muscle, miniature end-plate potential, motor end plate, muscle spindle, myofibril, myosin, phosphocreatine, sarcomere, skeletal muscle, slow-twitch fibre, tonus, voluntary muscle. **muscular** *adj*.
[From Latin *musculus* a little mouse, diminutive of *mus* a mouse, alluding to the supposed resemblance of some muscles to mice]

muscle relaxant *n*. Any drug that causes relaxation of *striped muscles, apart from the heart muscle.

muscle sense *n*. A form of *proprioception and *kinaesthesis mediated by *sensory receptors in the muscles and stimulated by contraction. The term is also used non-technically to denote proprioception or kinaesthesis in general, but this is avoided in careful usage. *See also* Golgi tendon organ, muscle spindle.

muscle spindle *n*. Any of the stretch receptors composed of *intrafusal fibres, up to one centimetre long, that are embedded in *skeletal muscles and oriented in parallel with the *extrafusal muscles to generate *action potentials whenever the muscles stretch. *See also* Ia fibre. *Compare* Golgi tendon organ.
[So called because of its shape, tapering at each end]

muscular dystrophy *n*. A hereditary disease caused by a mutant gene on the *X chromosome, characterized by progressive wasting of muscle tissue, the most common form being *Duchenne muscular dystrophy.
[From Greek *dys-* bad or abnormal + *trophe* nourishment]

mush *n*. A street name for the *liberty cap mushroom.
[Abbreviation of *mushroom* and also descriptive of the psychological state that it induces]

music therapy *n*. A form of *psychotherapy in which clients or patients are encouraged to express their feelings and inner conflicts through music.

mutagen n. Any substance or other agent, including X-rays and other forms of *ionizing radiation, that can cause genetic *mutations. *See also* teratogen.
[From *muta(tion)* + Greek *genein* to produce]

mutant n. **1.** An organism or gene that has undergone genetic *mutation. *adj.* **2.** Of, relating to, undergoing, or resulting from genetic mutation.
[From Latin *mutare* to change]

mutation n. A change in the *genes or *chromosomes of a cell, capable of being transmitted to offspring as a *heritable alteration of the organism, including a change in an *intron. *See also* back mutation, *cis–trans* complementation test, deletion mutation, frameshift mutation, hot spot, jumping gene, mutagen, neutral mutation, nonsense mutation, point mutation, reversion, saltation (2), silent mutation.
[From Latin *mutare, mutatus* to change + -*ation* indicating a process or condition]

mutism n. A refusal or inability to speak although the organs of speech are undamaged. Also called *aphrasia*. *See* selective mutism.
[From Latin *mutus* silent]

mutual gaze n. The event of two people simultaneously looking at each other in the vicinity of each other's eyes. Also called *eye contact*. *See also* gaze.

myalgic encephalomyelitis n. Another name for *chronic fatigue syndrome. *Compare* encephalomyelitis. **ME** *abbrev.*
[From Greek *mys* a muscle + *algos* pain + *encephalos* a brain + *myelos* the spinal cord]

myasthenia gravis n. A chronic and progressive disease in which the muscles, especially those of the head and face, gradually become weak and easily fatigued.
[From Greek *mys* a muscle + *astheneia* weakness, from *a-* without + *sthenos* strength + Latin *gravis* grave]

myelencephalon n. A part of the *rhombencephalon or hindbrain of an embryo that develops later into the *medulla oblongata.
[From Greek *myelos* marrow or spinal cord + *enkephalos* the brain, from *en* in + *kephale* the head]

myelin n. White lipid-based tissue produced by *oligodendrocytes in the central nervous system and by *Schwann cells in the peripheral nervous system, forming a protective covering called a myelin sheath around the neural *axons. Damage to the myelin sheath is found in neurological disorders such as *multiple sclerosis. *See also* neurolemma.
myelinated *adj.* Having a *myelin sheath.
[From Greek *myelos* marrow or spinal cord + -*in(e)* indicating an organic compound]

Myers–Briggs Type Indicator n. One of the most popular personality questionnaires, especially in commercial and industrial contexts, designed to implement the theory of *function types first suggested in 1923 by the Swiss psychologist Carl Gustav Jung (1875–1961). It contains 126 items in its standard form (G) and 132 in its advanced form (K), all the items being concerned with preferences and inclinations, and it measures four bipolar dimensions: extraversion (E) versus introversion (I), sensing (S) versus intuition (N), thinking (T) versus feeling (F), and judging (J) versus perceiving (P). These four dimensions are combined to yield 16 types, each characterized by a different score pattern represented by a four-letter type description: ESTJ, ESTP, . . . , INFP. *See also* cognitive style, temperament theory. **MBTI** *abbrev.*
[Named after the US novelist and playwright Isabel McKelvey Myers (1897–1980) and her mother, the self-taught US psychologist Katharine Elizabeth Briggs (1875–1968), who jointly introduced the earliest version of it in 1943]

myoclonic *adj.* Of, relating to, or resembling an involuntary contraction of the skeletal muscles, such as occurs in a *convulsion.
[From Greek *mys* a muscle + *klonos* contraction]

myofibril n. Any of the long contractile cells with multiple nuclei of which *striped muscle is composed. *See* actin, myosin.
[From Greek *mys, myos* a muscle + Latin *fibrilla* a little fibre, diminutive of *fibra* a fibre]

myopia n. Short-sightedness or difficulty in seeing distant objects clearly, caused by an excessively elongated eyeball in which light rays entering the eye are focused in front of the retina. Also called *brachymetropia* or *near-sightedness*. *See also* anomalous myopia. *Compare* emmetropia, hyperopia, presbyopia.

myope or **myops** n. A short-sighted person.
myopic adj. Short-sighted.
[From Greek *myops* short-sighted, from *myein* to close + *ops* an eye + *-ia* indicating a condition or quality]

myosin n. A protein that reacts with *actin to form the contractile protein *actomyosin in muscles and that is also present in other body cells.
[From Greek *mys* a muscle + *-in(e)* indicating an organic compound]

myostatic reflex n. Another name for a *stretch reflex. *See also* deep tendon reflex.
[From Greek *mys* a muscle + *statikos* bringing to a standstill, from *histanai* to cause to stand or to weigh in a balance + *-itikos* resembling or marked by]

myotonia n. Prolonged spasm or rigidity of a muscle. *See* catalepsy, cerea flexibilitas, clasp-knife rigidity, cogwheel rigidity. **myotonic** adj.
[From Greek *mys* a muscle + *tonos* tension, from *teinein* to stretch + *-ia* indicating a condition or quality]

myriachit n. The name usually given to the version of *latah found in Siberia.
[From Russian *myriachit* to fool or play the fool]

myristin n. A *psychedelic and *hallucinogenic drug obtained from *nutmeg and *mace.
[From Greek *myristikos* fragrant, from *myron* an ointment or perfume]

myth, urban *See* urban legend.

N140 *abbrev.* The first major negative deflection in an *event-related potential or an *average evoked potential, occurring about 140 milliseconds after the onset of the stimulus. Some researchers have claimed that either its magnitude, or the acuteness of the angle between the N140 and the *P200, correlates with *IQ, but empirical findings are inconsistent. Also called the *N140 potential* or *N140 wave*. *Compare* string length.
[From *n(egative) 140 (milliseconds)*]

naive participant *n.* In research methodology, a participant or subject who has no previous experience of the procedure, or one who is unaware of the purpose of the research or the hypothesis being tested. In research involving *confederates, the term is used to denote a participant who is not one of the confederates.

naive physics *n.* Another name for *intuitive physics.

naive realism *n.* The philosophical doctrine that perception of a physical object is direct awareness of the object itself rather than of a *representation (1) of it, a view that is seriously challenged and in the opinion of many philosophers refuted by *perceptual illusions in general and *visual illusions in particular.

naive subject *See* naive participant.

nalorphine *n.* A white crystalline compound, derived from morphine by substituting an allyl group (C_3H_5) for a methyl group (CH_3), used as a respiratory stimulant and *narcotic *antagonist (3) in the treatment of narcotic poisoning and *opioid-related disorders, also used to detect morphine addiction quickly through the short-lived *withdrawal reaction that it elicits from a morphine addict. *Compare* naloxone, naltrexone.
[From its chemical name *N-al(lyln)or(mor)phine*]

naloxone *n.* A potent, short-acting *narcotic *antagonist (3) that acts by binding to the *opiate *neuroreceptors on cells, often used for treating acute narcotic overdose and *opioid-related disorders. *Compare* nalorphine, naltrexone.
[From its conventional chemical name *N-al(lylnor)ox(ymorph)one*]

naltrexone *n.* A long-acting *narcotic antagonist that blocks the action of *opiates, including the *euphoria that they induce, and that is thus used in the treatment of narcotic overdose and *opioid-related disorders. *Compare* nalorphine, naloxone.
[A blend of *naloxone* and *Trexan* a trademark]

NANC *abbrev.* Non-*adrenergic, non-*cholinergic, of or relating to peripheral nerve fibres whose neurotransmitter is neither adrenalin nor acetylcholine.

nanometre *n.* One billionth of a metre (10^{-9} metre, or one millionth of a millimetre), used mainly for expressing wavelengths of light and other electromagnetic radiation. The *visible spectrum extends from approximately 390 nanometres at the violet end of the spectrum to 740 nanometres at the red end. US *nanometer*. Also (formerly) called a *millimicron*. *Compare* angstrom. **nm** *abbrev.*
[From Greek *nanos* a dwarf + *metron* a measure]

narcissism *n.* Self-love, or sexual gratification obtained by contemplating oneself. In *psychoanalysis, *cathexis of the *ego by *sexual instincts, as occurs in *homosexuality, according to Sigmund Freud (1856–1939) in his book *Three Essays on the Theory of Sexuality* (1905, *Standard Edition*, VII, pp. 130–243, at p. 145n). Freud later formed the view that it is a normal *psychosexual stage of development, between stages of *auto-erotism and *object libido, and in 1914 he published an entire article entitled 'On Narcissism: An Introduction' (*Standard Edition*, XIV, pp. 73–102) in which he expounded at length his theory at that time. The Austrian-born US psychoanalyst Heinz Kohut (1913–81) viewed narcissism as a natural part of development, but the British-based Austrian psychoanalyst Melanie Klein (1882–1960) and her followers questioned Freud's theory, arguing that *object-relationships are evident from the earliest stages of sucking. The concept of narcissism was originally introduced in 1898 by the English sexologist Havelock Ellis (1859–1939) in an article entitled 'Auto-erotism: A Psychological Study'. *See also* ego libido, grandiose self, narcissistic neurosis, narcissistic object-choice, narcissistic personality disorder, primary narcissism, secondary narcissism. *Compare* object relations. **narcissistic** *adj.*

[Named after *Narkissos*, a beautiful youth in Greek mythology who pined away for love of his own reflection in a pool and was punished by being transformed into the flower that bears his name]

narcissistic libido *n.* Another name for *ego libido.

narcissistic neurosis *n.* In *psychoanalysis, a category of *psychoneuroses that Sigmund Freud (1856–1939) distinguished from the *transference neuroses. In an article 'On Narcissism: An Introduction' (1914, *Standard Edition*, XIV, pp. 73–102), he described its salient characteristic to be the turning of *libido from external *instinctual objects on to the *ego, and he identified it with *paraphrenia. The concept lost popularity among psychoanalysts after the Second World War. *See also* decathexis, narcissism, narcissistic personality disorder.

narcissistic object-choice *n.* In *psychoanalysis, a type of *object-choice in which one chooses a love-object according to characteristics that the person shares with oneself. Sigmund Freud (1856–1939) introduced this concept in 1911 in an article 'Psycho-analytic Notes on an Autobiographical Account of a Case of Paranoia (Dementia Paranoides)' (*Standard Edition*, XII, pp. 9–82, at pp. 60–1) and developed it fully in 1914 in an article 'On Narcissism: An Introduction' (*Standard Edition*, XIV, pp. 73–102, at pp. 88–91), citing the fact that homosexuals take themselves as models in object-choices as 'the strongest of the rea-

sons that have led us to adopt the hypothesis of narcissism' (p. 88). *See also* narcissism. *Compare* anaclitic object-choice.

narcissistic personality disorder *n.* A *personality disorder characterized by *grandiose ideas or actions, beginning by early adulthood, indicated by such signs and symptoms as self-importance and boastfulness; preoccupation with fantasies of unlimited success, power, beauty, or other desirable attributes; self-image as someone who should associate only with high-status people or institutions; excessive need for admiration; unreasonable expectations of favourable treatment; interpersonal exploitativeness; lack of empathy; envy; and patronizing arrogance. The term was introduced by the Austrian-born US psychoanalyst Heinz Kohut (1913–81). *See also* grandiose self, narcissism. **NPD** *abbrev.*

narcoanalysis *n.* A technique of *psychotherapy in which an attempt is made to bring out repressed emotions in an altered state of consciousness induced by narcotic drugs (usually short-acting *barbiturates), originally used in the treatment of mental disorders in military personnel. Also called *narcosynthesis*. *Compare* narcosynthesis, narcotherapy.

[A blend of *narco(tic)* and *(psycho)analysis*]

narcolepsy *n.* One of the *dyssomnias, in which sudden and unpredictable lapses occur from wakefulness directly into *REM sleep or from wakefulness into paralysis and *atonia without loss of consciousness. It is characterized by frequent, involuntary episodes of refreshing sleep, together with either *cataplexy (1) or recurrent intrusions of *REM sleep during the transition between sleep and wakefulness, accompanied by *hypnopompic images, *hypnagogic images, or *sleep paralysis. It is believed to be caused by a malfunction of the mechanisms in the *subcoerulear nuclei or *magnocellular nuclei responsible for *REM atonia. *Compare* cataplexy (1), Kleine–Levin syndrome, hypersomnia, primary hypersomnia.

[From Greek *narke* numbness or torpor + *lepsis* a seizure, from *lambanein* to seize]

narcosis *n.* Drug-induced loss of *consciousness.

[From Greek *narke* numbness or torpor + *-osis* indicating a process or state]

narcosynthesis n. Another name for *narco-analysis, especially when the explicit goal is the reintegration of the patient's *personality. Compare narcotherapy.
[A blend of narco(tic) and syntheses]

narcotherapy n. Psychotherapy conducted with the help of narcotic drugs (usually short-acting *barbiturates); also, treatment of mental disorders by prolonged *narcosis. Compare narcoanalysis, narcosynthesis.

narcotic adj. n. (Of or relating to) a class of drugs that produce *narcosis, or at least drowsiness, torpor, and numbness, and are sometimes prescribed medicinally as *analgesics (1), *anaesthetics (1), or *hypnotics (2) and sometimes taken as street drugs, high dosages leading to depressed respiration, convulsions, coma, and death, and prolonged use often resulting in addiction or *dependence (2). The word is often misapplied, even by government agencies, to addictive drugs in general, excluding alcohol but including stimulant drugs such as cocaine or amphetamine, or to illegal drugs in general, including cannabis and LSD, whether or not they have narcotic or depressant effects, but such abuses of language are avoided in careful usage. See codeine, fentanyl, heroin, hydromorphone, Lomotil, methadone, morphine, nalorphine, opium, oxycodone, oxymorphone, paregoric, pentazocine, pethidine (meperidine), phenazocine, propoxyphene. See also narcotic analgesic, narcotic antagonist, opiate, opioid-related disorders, substance abuse, substance-related disorders. Compare naloxone, naltrexone, tranquillizer.
narcotize vb. To place a person or an animal under the influence of a *narcotic drug.
[From Greek narkotikos of or relating to numbness, from narke numbness or torpor + -ikos of, relating to, or resembling]

narcotic analgesic n. Any *narcotic such as *morphine that is used as an *analgesic (1) in cases of severe pain and is sometimes taken as a street drug. See Dover's powder, fentanyl, heroin, hydromorphone, laudanum, meperidine, methadone, morphine, oxycodone, oxymorphone, paregoric, pentazocine, pethidine (meperidine), phenazocine, propoxyphene. See also codeine (a mildly narcotic analgesic).

narcotic antagonist n. Any drug such as *nalorphine, *naloxone, or *naltrexone that binds to the *neuroreceptor sites of the *opiates in the *central nervous system and thereby blocks their action. Also called an opioid antagonist. See also antagonist (3).

narrow heritability See under heritability.

nasal adj. 1. Of or relating to the *nose. n. 2. In phonetics, a *consonant speech sound articulated by obstructing the mouth passage completely while allowing the airstream to pass through the nose, as in the final *phonemes in the words sum, sun, and sung. See also manner of articulation.

nasal epithelium n. Another name for the *olfactory epithelium.

nasal hemianopia n. Loss of vision of one nasal field (the right field of the left eye or the left field of the right eye) resulting from damage to the lateral region of the *optic chiasm. Also called nasal hemianopsia. See also hemianopia.
[So called because the affected area lies on the side nearest the nose]

nasal retina n. The half of the retina of each eye that is nearest to the nose and from which nerve fibres are projected to the opposite cerebral hemisphere after crossing over in the *optic chiasm. Compare temporal retina.

Nash equilibrium n. In game theory, a profile of *strategy (2) choices such that every player's strategy is a best reply to the strategies chosen by the other players. Given the strategies chosen by the other players (or, if there is only one, the strategy chosen by the other player), a best reply is a strategy that gives the player choosing it at least as good a payoff as any other strategy. A key property of a Nash equilibrium is that no player has any incentive to deviate unilaterally from it, so that it gives the players no cause to regret their strategy choices when the other players' choices are revealed. It is a basic tenet of game theory that a *rational solution to any game must be a Nash equilibrium, but many games have multiple Nash equilibria. Also called an equilibrium point or an equilibrium. See also minimax theorem.
[Named after the US mathematician John F(orbes) Nash (born 1928) who introduced it in articles in the Proceedings of the National

Academy of Sciences in 1950 and the *Annals of Mathematics* in 1951]

National Intelligence Test *n.* A civilian version of the *Army Alpha and Beta tests, published in 1919 by the US psychologist Robert Mearns Yerkes (1876–1956), and widely used in schools, universities, and commercial firms.

nativism *n.* The doctrine that the mind contains knowledge that is not derived from the senses; more generally, the theory that the mind and its capacities are innately determined, or any theory emphasizing heredity or biological constitution as determinants of perceptions, attitudes, personality, or behaviour. *See also* rationalism (1, 2). *Compare* empiricism.

NATO phonetic alphabet *n.* The standard list of words used to identify letters of the alphabet unambiguously in police and maritime communications, air traffic control, and military contexts: Alpha, Bravo, Charlie, Delta, Echo, Foxtrot, Golf, Hotel, India, Juliet, Kilo, Lima, Mike, November, Oscar, Papa, Quebec, Romeo, Sierra, Tango, Uniform, Victor, Whiskey, X-ray, Yankee, Zulu.
[Named after NATO, the North Atlantic Treaty Organization, which standardized it]

natural category *n.* **1.** A category imposed by the sense organs, such as the class of visual sensations giving rise to the sensation of blue or the class of taste sensations giving rise to the sensation of saltiness, in contradistinction to an artificially chosen category. **2.** Another name for a *basic-level category, but this is avoided in careful usage.

naturalistic fallacy *n.* The mistake of deriving what ought to be from what is, or occasionally vice versa. It was named and discussed at length by the English philosopher G(eorge) E(dward) Moore (1873–1958) in his book in *Principia Ethica* (1903), without reference to what came to be regarded as the basic authority, namely *A Treatise of Human Nature* (1739) by the Scottish philosopher David Hume (1711–76): 'In every system of morality that I have hitherto met with . . . I am surprised to find, that instead of the usual copulations of propositions, *is*, and *is not*, I meet with no proposition that is not connected with an *ought*, or and *ought not*. This change is imperceptible; but is, however, of the last consequence' (Book III, part 1, section 1).
[So called because examples usually centre on what is natural, as in the argument that it is right to eat meat because human beings have always naturally done so]

naturalistic observation *n.* A research method involving the passive observation of behaviour in naturally occurring situations, rather than any active intervention from the researcher such as occurs in an *experiment. *See also* observational study.

natural language *n.* A language that has evolved spontaneously within a community and that has native speakers. *See also* language (1). *Compare* artificial language.

natural-level category *n.* Another name for a *basic-level category. Also called a *natural-level concept.

natural selection *n.* The basic mechanism of *evolution whereby those individuals in a population that are best adapted to the environment survive and produce more offspring than others, thereby altering the composition of the population and eventually the characteristics of the *species. The term was introduced by the English naturalist Charles (Robert) Darwin (1809–82) in his book *The Origin of Species by Means of Natural Selection or the Preservation of Favoured Races in the Struggle for Life* (1859). *See also* apostatic selection, blind watchmaker, canalizing selection, counteracting selection, Darwinian evolution, directional selection, disruptive selection, frequency-dependent selection, group selection, kin selection, *K*-selection, meme, reinforcing selection, *r*-selection, selection pressure, selfish gene, sexual selection, stabilizing selection.

nature–nurture controversy *n.* The debate about the relative contributions of heredity and environment to a psychological characteristic, such as *intelligence. The juxtaposition of the words *nature* and *nurture* in this sense was introduced by the English schoolmaster Richard Mulcaster (1530–1611), though the phrase had already been used in Greek by the philosopher Socrates (469–399 BC). It became popular in psychology after being adopted by the English explorer, amateur scientist, and psychologist Sir Francis Galton (1822–1911). *See also* heritability, nurture.

Navane *n.* A proprietary name for the neuroleptic drug *thiothixene.
[Trademark]

nearest neighbour method *n.* In statistics, any technique of *cluster analysis in which the distance between two clusters is defined as the distance between their two closest members. Also called *single-linkage clustering*.

near point *n.* The closest point to the eye at which an object or image can be focused on the retina with maximum *accommodation (1) of the crystalline lens. It is about 10 centimetres (4 inches) in infancy, 25 centimetres (10 inches) in adulthood if vision is normal, and 33 centimetres (13) inches in old age. *See also* range of accommodation. *Compare* far point.

near sense *n.* Any of the senses such as touch or taste that are mediated by *proximoreceptors and that require close proximity between the perceiver and the object or event being perceived. *Compare* far sense.

near-sightedness *n.* A non-technical name for *myopia.

near vision *n.* Close-up viewing, usually defined for objects less than 2 feet or about 60 centimetres from the eyes. *See also* accommodation (1), accommodation reflex, ciliary reflex, hyperopia, parasympathetic nervous system, presbyopia. *Compare* far vision.

nebbies *n.* A street name for the barbiturate drug *pentobarbital (pentobarbitone).

Necker cube *n.* A simple line drawing of a transparent cube that, when viewed continuously, appears to alternate between two different spatial orientations, a classic example of an *ambiguous figure and more specifically of *perspective reversal (see illustration).
[Named after the Swiss mineralogist Louis Albert Necker (1786–1861) who in 1832 reported his observation that line drawings of crystals appeared to reverse spontaneously]

Necker cube. The figure alternates spontaneously between two perspectives of the cube.

necromania *n.* A pathological preoccupation with dead bodies, or another name for *necrophilia.
[From Greek *nekros* a dead body + *mania* madness]

necrophilia *n.* A *paraphilia characterized by recurrent sexually arousing fantasies, sexual urges, or behaviour involving intercourse with dead bodies. **necrophiliac** *n.* A person with *necrophilia.
[From Greek *nekros* a dead body + *philos* loving, from *phileein* to love + *-ia* indicating a condition or quality]

need *n.* **1.** A lack of something that is required for survival. **2.** A motivational state resulting from the lack of something that an organism requires or desires, also called a *drive*. **3.** In the *personology of the US psychologist Henry Alexander Murray (1893–1988), a general course of action or behavioural tendency. *See also* Edwards Personal Preference Schedule, need-press, press.

need complementarity hypothesis *n.* The proposition that people tend to be attracted to others who have complementary needs to their own, a person with a high need for dominance, for example, being attracted to a person with a high need for submission, and vice versa. Despite its superficial plausibility, the theory has received only weak and inconsistent empirical support. Also called the *complementarity hypothesis*. *Compare* attitude similarity hypothesis.

need for achievement *n.* A social form of *motivation involving a competitive drive to meet standards of excellence, traditionally measured with a projective test such as the *TAT. The concept was introduced by the US psychologist Henry Alexander Murray (1893–1988) in his book *Explorations in Personality* (1938). Also called *achievement motivation*. **N Ach** or **nAch** *abbrev.*

need for affiliation *n.* A social form of *moti-vation involving a need to seek out and enjoy close and cooperative relationships with other people, and to adhere and remain loyal to a friend. The concept was introduced by the US psychologist Henry Alexander Murray (1893–1988) in his book *Explorations in Personality* (1938). Also called *affiliation need.* **N Aff** or **nAff** *abbrev.*

need-hierarchy theory *n.* The proposition put forward by the US psychologist Abraham Maslow (1908–70) in his book *Motivation and Personality* (1954, 1970) that human needs fall into five categories that form the following hierarchy. The strongest and most imperative are the *physiological needs* for food, water, oxygen, and sex; if the physiological needs are gratified, the *needs for safety* emerge, and the person begins to seek out safe environments; next to emerge are *needs for love and belonging,* and the person yearns for a friend, a lover, a place in a group; then *needs for esteem* come to the fore, and the person seeks self-respect, respect from others, status, and achievement; then last, and usually only if all the others have been reasonably well satisfied, there emerges a need for *self-actualization.*

need-press *n.* In the *personology of the US psychologist Henry Alexander Murray (1893–1988), a *need (3) evoked by environmental circumstances, such as a poor person's need for money or a lonely person's need for affiliation. Also called a *press-need. See also* press.

neencephalon *n.* Another name for the *neocortex.

negation *n.* **1.** The contradiction, or denial, or reversal of something, or the act or process of contradicting. **2.** In *psychoanalysis, a process whereby one continues to defend oneself against a formerly *repressed wish, thought, or feeling that has come to consciousness by disavowing or disowning it, as when a patient says during therapy 'You might expect me to have felt angry with him, but I never felt any anger'. Sigmund Freud (1856–1939) expounded his theory in an article entitled 'Negation' in 1925, where he asserted somewhat cryptically: 'Only one consequence of the process of negation is undone—the fact, namely, of the ideational content of what is repressed not reaching

consciousness. The outcome of this is a kind of intellectual acceptance of the repressed, while at the same time what is essential to the repression persists' (*Standard Edition*, XIX, pp. 235–9, at pp. 235–6). Some psychoanalysts consider it as a *defence mechanism. Also called *disavowal.* **3.** In *logic, the operator that reverses the meaning of a proposition *p*, or the resulting proposition *not-p* that is true precisely when *p* is false and vice versa.

negative adaptation *n.* A gradual diminution in sensitivity of a *sensory receptor or neuron resulting from prolonged or repeated stimulation.

negative afterimage *n.* **1.** An *afterimage in which the lightness contrasts are reversed, light areas of the original stimulus appearing dark and dark areas appearing light. *See also* complementary afterimage. *Compare* positive afterimage. **2.** Another name for a *complementary afterimage, though this usage undermines an important distinction and is avoided in careful usage.

negative capability *n.* Suspension of critical rationality coupled with calm and unquestioning acceptance of uncertainty and doubt. The term, frequently used in British *psychoanalysis to describe an attitude adopted by some analysts, is taken from a letter of the English poet John Keats (1795–1821) to his younger brother Tom, who was dying of consumption: 'Negative Capability, that is, when a man is capable of being in uncertainties, mysteries, doubts, without any irritable reaching after fact or reason' (letter dated 21 December 1817).

negative feedback *See under* feedback.

negative induction *See under* induction (4).

negative Oedipus complex *See under* Oedipus complex.

negative practice *n.* A form of *paradoxical therapy in which the patient or client is enjoined to practise the very behaviour that needs to be eliminated. *See also* paradoxical intention.

negative priming *n.* Increased reaction time (slower responding) to a stimulus resulting from attention recently having been focused on stimuli belonging to a different class. It is a form of inhibitory *priming (1) arising from the suppression of irrelevant internal representations. For example, if someone is presented with a picture of a green owl and a red cat and is asked to name the red object, internal representations activated by the green owl will tend to be inhibited, causing increased reaction time in an immediately following task requiring rapid identification of a bird or something green.

negative reference group n. A *reference group that an individual disapproves of and uses as a standard representing opinions, attitudes, or behaviour patterns to avoid. Compare positive reference group.

negative reinforcement n. In *operant conditioning, the strengthening of a response as a consequence of its being followed by the cessation or avoidance of an aversive stimulus. See avoidance conditioning, escape conditioning. Compare punishment.

negative symptoms n. In the diagnosis of *schizophrenia, symptoms such as *affective flattening, *alogia, and *avolition. Compare positive symptoms.

negative therapeutic reaction n. A temporary worsening of symptoms as a result of treatment. Sigmund Freud (1856–1939) described this phenomenon in his book The Ego and the Id (1923): 'Every partial solution that ought to result, and in other people does result, in an improvement or a temporary suspension of symptoms produces in them for the time being an exacerbation of their illness; they get worse during the treatment instead of getting better' (Standard Edition, XIX, pp. 12–66, at p. 49). Freud attributed it to *resistance and to the patient's preference for suffering over being cured.

negative transfer n. A form of *transfer of training in which learning or performance of a task is impaired by training on a different but related task, as when a spell of driving on the right-hand side of the road temporarily impairs one's ability to drive on the left, or vice versa. Transfer tends to be negative when the two tasks involve similar stimuli and different responses. See also proactive interfer-ence, retroactive interference. Compare positive transfer.

negative transference n. In *psychoanalysis, hostility on the part of the patient towards the analyst, interpreted as *displacement of hostility towards other significant figures, especially parents. See also transference. Compare positive transference.

negativism n. **1.** Refusal to do what is suggested or advised or a tendency to do the opposite, a symptom of some forms of *schizophrenia and *catatonia. **2.** An attitude of unconstructive criticism. **negativistic** adj.
[From Latin negare to deny + Greek -ismos indicating a state or condition]

negativistic personality disorder n. Another name for *passive–aggressive personality disorder.

neglect dyslexia n. A type of *dyslexia in which either the initial parts of words are misread (left neglect dyslexia) or the terminal parts of words are misread (right neglect dyslexia), the errors not being simple deletions but typically guesses of real though incorrect words with approximately the right number of letters.

Nembutal n. A proprietary name for the barbiturate drug *pentobarbital (pentobarbitone).
[Trademark]

nemesism n. Frustration expressed as aggression turned inward against the self. **nemesistic** adj.
[From Nemesis the Greek goddess of vengeance]

NEO abbrev. *Neuroticism, *extraversion, *openness to experience: a questionnaire designed to measure the *Big Five personality factors, namely those three plus *agreeableness, and *conscientiousness. The original NEO Five-Factor Inventory (NEO-FFI), constructed by the US psychologists Paul T. Costa (born 1942) and Robert R. McCrae and first published in the journal Psychological Assessment in 1992, comprised 60 items, and the subsequent longer version, called the NEO Personality Inventory-Revised (NEO-PI-R) comprises 243 items.

neobehaviourism *n.* Any form of *behaviourism coming after that of the founding father, the US psychologist John B(roadus) Watson (1878–1958), the most influential being that of the US psychologist B(urrhus) F(rederic) Skinner (1904–90). Most neobehaviourists, while agreeing with Watson that psychology should be restricted to the study of overt behaviour, have accepted the existence of hidden psychological processes that can be inferred from behaviour. US *neobehaviorism*. **neobehaviourist** or **neobehaviorist** *adj.* *n.* (Of or relating to) one who advocates or practises *neobehaviourism.

neo-catastrophism *See* catastrophism (1).

neocerebellum *n.* The most recently evolved functional part of the *cerebellum, comprising the lateral areas of the cerebellar hemispheres, receiving inputs from the *pons and projecting to the *motor cortex also via the pons. Lesions in this area lead to ipsilateral (same side of the body) incoordination of movements, especially in the upper limbs, *adiadochokinesia, *intention tremor, and *dysarthria. *See also* cerebellar syndrome. *Compare* spinocerebellum, vestibulocerebellum.
[From Greek *neos* new + Latin *cerebellum* a little brain, diminutive of *cerebrum* a brain]

neocortex *n.* The most recently evolved part of the *cerebral cortex, composed of six layers of cells, including the *lateral surfaces of the frontal, parietal, temporal and occipital lobes. The older parts of the cerebral cortex, all with fewer than six layers and collectively called the allocortex, are the palaeocortex or olfactory cortex at the front of each temporal lobe, the mesocortex mainly in the cingulate gyrus, and the archaecortex mainly in the hippocampus, which is the oldest of all. In humans, over 90 per cent of the cerebral cortex is neocortex (*see also* progression index). Also called *isocortex*, *neencephalon*, or *neopallium*.
[From Greek *neos* new + Latin *cortex* bark or outer layer]

neo-Darwinism *n.* A modern version of *Darwinian evolution that emerged in the 1920s and 1930s, incorporating the processes of *gene transmission and *mutation that were unknown to Darwin, and denying the possibility (which Darwin accepted) of the inheritance of acquired characteristics. *See also* Darwinian evolution. *Compare* Lamarckism, Lysenkoism, neo-Lamarckism.

neodissociation theory *n.* A leading interpretation of *hypnosis, first proposed in 1973 in an article in the journal *Psychological Review* by the US psychologist Ernest R(opiequit) Hilgard (1904–2001), according to which hypnosis involves a form of divided consciousness, as in *hypnotic analgesia, when a hypnotized person is unaware of the pain being caused by a stimulus that would normally be painful but the *hidden observer is aware of the pain; or in *hypnotic amnesia, in which a person who has recently been hypnotized is unable to recall what happened during the hypnotic session. It is called *neo*dissociation theory to distinguish it from *dissociation theory. *See also* dissociation.

neo-Freudian *adj.* *n.* (Of or relating to) any of the theorists in the US who reformulated *psychoanalysis on a more sociological and humanistic basis, notably the German-born US psychoanalysts Karen Horney (1885–1952), Erich Fromm (1900–80), and Erik H. Erikson (1902–94), and the US psychiatrist Harry Stack Sullivan (1892–1949).

neo-Lamarckism *n.* A modern version of *Lamarckism based on the assumption that genetic changes can be brought about by environmental factors and that *natural selection operates on acquired characteristics. *See also* Lysenkoism. **neo-Lamarckian** *adj.*

neologism *n.* A newly coined word or phrase or a new meaning given to an established word or phrase.
[From Greek *neos* new + *logos* a word]

Neonatal Behavioral Assessment Scale *n.* A simple and straightforward system for assessing newborn infants by examining their reactions to 27 types of stimuli, including a pinprick, a rattle, a light, a moving ball, the sound of a bell, and so on. It was introduced in 1969 by the US paediatrician T(homas) Berry Brazelton (born 1918) in his book *Infants and Mothers: Differences in Development*, and it is capable of detecting a wide range of abnormalities. Also called the *Brazelton assessment*.

neonate *n.* A newborn baby up to four weeks old. **neonatal** *adj.*
[From Greek *neos* new + Latin *natus* born]

neopallium *n*. Another name for the *neocortex.
[From Latin *neo* new + *pallium* a cloak]

neostriatum *n*. The more recently evolved part of the *corpus striatum, consisting of the *caudate nucleus and *putamen (and excluding the globus pallidus). *Compare* palaeostriatum. **neostriata** or **neostriatums** *pl*.

neoteny *n*. Persistence in the adult form of attributes of the foetal form, or attributes that were confined to the foetal form in ancestors, such as the tadpole form of the mature adults of some amphibian species, or the lack of body hair in humans. **neotenous** *adj*.
[From Greek *neos* new + *teinein* to stretch]

neothalamus *n*. The most recently evolved parts of the *thalamus comprising the lateral group of nuclei that function as relay stations for sensory and optic projections to the cerebral cortex.
[From Greek *neos* new + *thalamos* an inner room or chamber, from *thalos* a vault]

nephron *n*. Any of the tiny tubules of the kidney that filter blood to produce urine.
[From Greek *nephros* a kidney]

nerfiza *See* nervios.

Nernst heat theorem *n*. The third law of *thermodynamics, according to which as a homogeneous system approaches a temperature of absolute zero its *entropy tends to zero.
[Named after the German physical chemist Walther Hermann Nernst (1864–1941) who formulated it in 1906]

nerve *n*. A cordlike band of *axon fibres that transmits impulses of sensation (if it is an *afferent nerve) or movement (if it is an *efferent nerve) between a sensory receptor and the central nervous system, or between the central nervous system and a muscle or gland. It is often confused with a *neuron, which has a soma and only one axon. *See* cranial nerve, spinal nerve.
[From Latin *nervus* a nerve, from Greek *neuron* a nerve]

nerve cell *n*. A *neuron.

nerve conduction velocity *n*. A neural measure of *processing speed proposed in 1992 by

the US psychologist Arthur R(obert) Jensen (born 1923), obtained by dividing a person's head length (distance from the eye to the *primary visual cortex) by the latency of an early component of the visual *evoked potential, usually N70 or P100. It yields consistent though small correlations with psychometric measures of *intelligence. **NCV** *abbrev*.

nerve deafness *n*. Another name for *sensorineural deafness.

nerve ending *n*. The terminal part of a *nerve, usually consisting of an *end organ, but *see also* free nerve ending.

nerve fibre *n*. An *axon. US *nerve fiber*. *See* alpha fibre, association fibre, C fibre, climbing fibre, delta fibre, gamma fibre, Ia fibre, Ib fibre, II fibre, mossy fibre.

nerve gas *n*. Any gas, especially an *organophosphate *anticholinesterase agent such as *sarin (isopropyl methylphosphonofluoridate) or the more potent agent *VX, that may be used as a chemical weapon and that, if absorbed through the skin or inhaled, occupies the active sites of *acetylcholinesterase molecules and thereby interferes with the enzyme's ability to break down the neurotransmitter *acetylcholine after nerve impulses, causing the neurotransmitter to accumulate at the *synapses (1) between motor nerve fibres and muscles, and leading to muscle cramps and asphyxia. Also called a *nerve agent*. *See also* neurotoxin.

nerve growth factor *n*. A substance that is produced by *smooth muscles and other tissues stimulated by neurons and is necessary for the maintenance of sympathetic and sensory neurons. *See also* apoptosis. **NGF** *abbrev*.

nerve impulse *n*. An electrical impulse travelling along an *axon when a *neuron is stimulated, also called an *action potential*. *Compare* graded potential.

nervios *n*. A *culture-bound syndrome widespread throughout Latin America and among Latino communities in the United States and elsewhere, also found in Egypt (where it is called *nerfiza*) and Greece (*nevra*), characterized by chronic *anxiety and sorrowfulness, interpreted as a general state of vulnerability to *psychosocial stressors brought about by

personal or family difficulties, with a broad range of signs and symptoms, commonly including *anorexia, *dyssomnias, headaches, irritability, stomach upsets, tearfulness, loss of concentration, *tremor, *paraesthesia, and dizziness or *vertigo.
[Spanish *nervios* nerves, from Latin *nervus* a nerve]

nervous *adj.* **1.** Of, relating to, or consisting of nerves or nerve fibres. **2.** Apprehensive, agitated, or timid.

nervous breakdown *n.* A non-technical term for any severe *mental disorder involving a marked impairment in functioning and impaired *reality testing.

nervous system *n.* The sensory and control system enabling *neurons to communicate with one another in most animals, consisting in humans of the *brain, *spinal cord, and *nerves. It is divided anatomically into the *central nervous system and the *peripheral nervous system, and functionally into the *autonomic nervous system and the *somatic nervous system. The autonomic nervous system is further subdivided into the *sympathetic nervous system and the *parasympathetic nervous system. The other major intercellular communication system is the *endocrine system. These are not the only sensory and control systems: *see* paramecium. *See also* endocrine glands.

net benefit index *n.* In *cost–benefit analysis, the difference between total present benefits (*B*) and total present costs (*C*) given by the formula $B - C$, a project being more worthwhile the higher the index. *Compare* benefit-cost ratio.

net reaction potential *n.* In *Hullian learning theory, the strength of the propensity of the organism to respond after subtracting inhibitory factors from the *generalized reaction potential. $_S\bar{E}_R$ *abbrev.*

network model *n.* Any *model consisting of a collection of units, each joined to one or more other units that it may excite or inhibit. *See* ACT*, connectionism (1), neural network, parallel distributed processing.

neural *adj.* Of, relating to, or resembling *neurons in the nervous system.

neural adaptation *n.* Another name for *field adaptation.

neural computer *n.* Another name for a *neurocomputer.

neural Darwinism *n.* The proposition that synaptic connections in the nervous system are shaped by competition, only those that turn out to be relatively useful surviving, the others disappearing through *apoptosis or neural *pruning.
[So called by analogy with the competitive struggle for existence between organisms in Darwinian evolution]

neuralgia *n.* Intermittent paroxysmal pain following the course of a nerve, often caused by neural damage or malfunction.
[From Greek *neuron* a nerve + *algos* pain + *-ia* indicating a condition or quality]

neural network *n.* A system of interconnected *neurons, as in the brain or nervous system, or (especially in cognitive science and artificial intelligence) an analogous system of interconnected *neurochips constituting a *neurocomputer designed to simulate the human brain, or a design for such a system. According to neural network theorists, mental experiences arise from the interaction of many interconnected computing units (or neurons), each in a specified state of activation (or firing rate), and each having the capacity to affect others by either excitatory or inhibitory connections (or synapses), the entire system being activated by a stimulus that affects a subset of the units, activation then propagating through the network until an equilibrium state of minimum energy is attained. The concept of a neural network was foreshadowed by the US psychologist William James (1842–1910) in his *Principles of Psychology* (1890, volume 2, pp. 563–6), and the first neural logic circuit based on a binary code was proposed in 1938 by the Russian-born US mathematical biologist Nicolas Rashevsky (1899–1972). The first detailed neural network was developed in 1943 by the US neurophysiologist Warren S(turgis) McCulloch (1898–1968) and the self-taught US logician Walter Pitts (1923–69), but that early version lacked the ability to learn, which was introduced in 1948 in an article on 'Intelligent Machinery' by the English mathematician Alan Mathison Turing (1912–54) and independently in 1949 by the Canadian psychologist Donald O(lding) Hebb (1904–85). The concept of the neural network became popular only after the publication in 1981 of a connectionist model of human memory developed by the US cognitive scientist James L(loyd) McClelland (born 1948). Still more advanced neural networks often make use of *fuzzy logic. Also called an *artificial neural network* (drawing attention to the fact that it consists of artificial rather than natural structures) or a *neural net*. *See also* connectionism (1), network model, parallel distributed processing, perceptron, spreading activation. **ANN** *abbrev*.

neurasthenia *n*. A *mental disorder characterized by persistent and distressing complaints of exhaustion following expenditure of insignificant amounts of mental or physical effort, including the performance of everyday tasks, with such additional signs and symptoms as muscular aches and pains, *tension headaches, *dyssomnia, restlessness, and irritability. The word was coined by the US physician George Beard (1839–83) in his book *American Nervousness: Its Causes and Consequences* (1881). *See also* actual neurosis, asthenia.
[From Greek *neuron* a nerve + *astheneia* weakness, from *a-* without + *sthenos* strength + *-ia* indicating a condition or quality]

neurilemma *n*. A variant spelling of *neurolemma.

neurite *n*. A *process (2) of a *neuron, whether an *axon or a *dendrite.
[From Greek *neur(on)* a nerve + *-ite(s)* indicating a part of an organ or biological structure]

neurobiology *n*. The study of the anatomy, physiology, biochemistry, and development of the *nervous system, including the biochemical and cell biological basis of brain functioning.
[From Greek *neuron* a nerve + *bios* life + *logos* word, discourse, or reason]

neuroblast *n*. An embryonic nerve cell.
[From Greek *neuron* a nerve + *blastos* a bud]

neurochip *n*. A computer microchip used in an electronic *neural network.

neurocomputer *n*. An electronic computer that uses a *neural network to mimic or sim-

ulate the operation of the human brain. Also called a *neural computer*. *See also* connectionism (1).
[From Greek *neuro(n)* a nerve + English *computer*]

neuroendocrine *adj*. Of or relating to certain functions that are under dual control of the *nervous system and the *endocrine glands. The term has become popular as it has become increasingly apparent that the endocrine system cannot be considered separately from the nervous system, because the same chemical compound (for example, noradrenalin) can function both as a neurotransmitter and as a hormone.
[From Greek *neuron* a nerve + *endon* within + *krinein* to separate]

neuroendocrine cell *n*. A cell that is a true *neuron, with axon and dendrite(s), and also a true *endocrine gland, secreting a hormone into the bloodstream. Such cells are found especially in the hypothalamus, secreting hormones that in turn affect secretions of the pituitary gland.

neuroendocrine system *n*. The *nervous system and the *endocrine glands considered as a functional unit.

neuroendocrinology *n*. The study of the interaction of the *nervous system, especially the brain, and the *endocrine system, especially the *HPA axis.

neurofibril *n*. Any of the fibres composed chiefly of *neurofilaments and *microtubules, forming a cross-hatched pattern of the *cytoskeleton within the cell body of a neuron and extending longitudinally along its axon and dendrites.
[From Greek *neuron* a nerve + *fibrilla* a small fibre]

neurofibrillary tangle *n*. A knotty mass of *neurofibrils and insoluble fibres composed chiefly of breakdown products of the tau protein, occurring in the brains of most people over 70 years old and found abundantly in the hippocampi and amygdalae of patients with *Alzheimer's disease and other disorders. *See also* amyloid plaque, progressive supranuclear palsy. **NFT** *abbrev*.

neurofilament *n*. Any of the minute thread-like fibres found in all parts of a neuron, with side-arms that keep them apart and evenly spaced. *See also* microtubule, neurofibril.

[From Greek *neuron* a nerve + *filum* a thread]

neuroglia *n*. The web of non-neural cells forming the connecting tissue that surrounds and supports *neurons in the *nervous system, outnumbering neurons by about 10 to 1, and divided into *macroglia and *microglia. Also called *glia* for short. Often mistakenly assumed to be a plural of *neuroglion* (a spurious *back formation), but in fact singular like the phrase *nerve glue*. *See also* astrocyte, ependymal cell, oligodendrocyte, satellite cell, Schwann cell. **neuroglial** *adj*.

[Coined in 1846 by the German pathologist Rudolf Ludwig Karl Virchow (1821–1902) from Greek *neuron* a nerve + *glia* glue]

neurogram *n*. Another name for an *engram or a *memory trace.

[A blend of *neural* and *engram*]

neurohormone *n*. A *hormone such as *noradrenalin (norepinephrine) or *serotonin that is produced by specialized cells in the nervous system rather than endocrine glands and that functions as a chemical messenger, interacting with a variety of cell types, in contrast to other *neurotransmitters that interact only with neurons, muscles, and glands. Also called a *neurohumour* (US *neurohumor*). *Compare* hormone.

[From Greek *neuron* a nerve + English *hormone*]

neurohumour *n*. Another name for a *neurohormone. US *neurohumor*.

[From Greek *neuron* a nerve + Latin *umere* to be moist]

neurohypophysis *n*. The posterior lobe of the hypophysis (pituitary gland), usually called the *posterior pituitary. *Compare* adenohypophysis.

[From Greek *neuron* a nerve + *hypophysis* an attachment underneath, from *hypo* under + *phyein* to grow]

neurolemma *n*. The external *myelin sheath of a neuron in the peripheral nervous system, made up of chains of *Schwann cells. Also spelt *neurilemma*. Also called an *axolemma*.

[From Greek *neuron* a nerve + *eilema* a covering]

neuroleptic *n*. **1**. Any of the *dopamine antagonist drugs, including any of the *phe-nothiazines, *butyrophenones, *dibenzodiazepines, or *thioxanthenes, that are used in the treatment of *psychoses. Also called an *antipsychotic drug* or a *major tranquillizer*. *See also* atypical antipsychotic, fentanyl, neurolepticinduced. *adj*. **2**. Capable of affecting the brain or nervous system, especially by reducing the activity of neurons.

[Adopted at the Second International Congress of Psychiatry in 1957, from Greek *neuron* a nerve + *lepsis* a taking hold or seizure + *-ikos* of, relating to, or resembling]

neuroleptic-induced *adj*. Of or relating to mental disorders or signs and symptoms induced as side-effects of *neuroleptic (1) medication, including neuroleptic-induced *parkinsonism, neuroleptic malignant syndrome (severe *myotonia and elevated temperature), *tardive dyskinesia, *extrapyramidal syndrome, *akinesia, *dystonia, acute *akathisia, *amnesia, dry mouth, blurred vision, difficulty urinating, or constipation.

neurolinguistic programming *n*. A form of *psychotherapy and a model of interpersonal communication in the tradition of *humanistic psychology based on elements of *transformational grammar and preferred sensory representations for learning and self-expression. **NLP** *abbrev*.

neurolinguistics *n*. The study of *language (1) through an analysis of *deficits and *impairments of language function resulting from *neurological damage. *See* cognitive neuropsychology.

neurology *n*. The study of the *nervous system; the branch of medicine concerned with disorders of the nervous system. **neurological** *adj*.

[From Greek *neuron* a nerve + *logos* word, discourse, or reason]

neurolymph *n*. Another name for *cerebrospinal fluid.

[From Greek *neuron* a nerve + Latin *lympha* water]

neurometrics *n*. A group of techniques involving measurements of the activity of neurons in the nervous system, including *EEG, *evoked potentials (EPs), and *event-related potentials (ERPs).

[From Greek *neuron* a nerve + *metron* measure + *-ikos* of, relating to, or resembling]

neuromodulation *n*. Alteration in the number or sensitivity of *neuroreceptor sites on *postsynaptic neurons caused by exposure to a chemical substance. It is one of the mechanisms of drug *tolerance (3). *See also* neuromodulator.

neuromodulator *n*. A chemical substance that amplifies or dampens the activities of neurons but is not a *neurotransmitter. *See also* neuromodulation.
[From Greek *neuron* a nerve + English *modulator*, from Latin *modulari, modulatus* to regulate]

neuromuscular junction *n*. A synapse between a terminal bouton of a neural axon and a squad of muscle fibres, normally situated at a *motor end plate.

neuron *n*. A nerve cell specialized to transmit nerve impulses in the form of *action potentials, the basic functional unit of the *nervous system, normally consisting of a cell body or soma together with *dendrites receiving signals from other neurons via *synapses (1), typical neurons being involved in 1,000–10,000 synapses, and an *axon ranging in length from 3 micrometres to more than a metre, often splitting into many branches near its end, transmitting signals away from the soma to one or more other neurons, a muscle, or a gland. Often confused with a *nerve, which has no cell bodies or somata and is made up of bundles of axons. Also spelt *neurone*. *See* basket cell, Betz cell, bipolar cell, Golgi cell, granule cell, horizontal cell, interneuron, Merkel cell, mitral cell, motor neuron, multipolar neuron, non-opponent cell, opponent cell, pacemaker neuron, Purkinje cell, pyramidal cell, Renshaw cell, sensory neuron, spindle cell, spiral ganglion cell, stellate cell, unipolar neuron. *See also* cytoskeleton, microtubule, postsynaptic, presynaptic. **neuronal** *adj*.
[Greek *neuron* a nerve]

neuronal oscillator *n*. The neural circuitry underlying the execution of any rhythmic activity, such as walking or running, chewing, or (in airborne species) flying.

neuronal transplantation *See* foetal brain transplantation.

neuron receptor site *n*. Another name for a *neuroreceptor.

neuropathic *adj*. Of or related to disorders of the *nervous system. **neuropath** *n*. A person suffering from or predisposed to *neuropathy. **neuropathy** *n*. Disease or disorder of the nervous system.
[From Greek *neuron* a nerve + *pathos* suffering + *-ikos* of, relating to, or resembling]

neuropathology *n*. The study of disorders of the *nervous system. **neuropathological** *adj*.
[From Greek *neuron* a nerve + *pathos* suffering + *logos* word, discourse, or reason]

neuropathy *n*. Any disorder of the *nervous system.
[From Greek *neuron* a nerve + *pathos* suffering]

neuropeptide *n*. A *peptide produced in the *nervous system and functioning either as a *neurotransmitter or as a *hormone.
[From Greek *neuron* a nerve + *peptein* to digest]

neurophysiology *n*. The study of the working of the nervous system.

neuropil *n*. A dense network of unmyelinated neurons and glia found in areas of concentrated nervous tissue at various sites in the central nervous system, especially in the *reticular formation, where it is interwoven with myelinated nerve fibres, and other parts of the brain.
[From Greek *neuron* a nerve + *pilos* hair or felt]

neuropsychiatry *n*. The branch of medicine dealing with *mental disorders and disorders of the *nervous system; a generic name for *psychiatry and *neurology.

neuropsychology *n*. The interface between *neurology and *psychology; the study of the effects of disorders of the brain and nervous system on behaviour and mental experience.

neuropsychosis *n*. Another name for a *psychoneurosis.

neuroreceptor *n*. A site on the surface or inside a neuron to which a *neurotransmitter, a *hormone, or a *psychotropic drug may bind, either exciting or inhibiting *action potentials. Also called a *neuron receptor site* a *receptor site*, or simply a *receptor*.

neuroregulator *n*. A general term for any of the substances that affect neuronal activity, including a *neurotransmitter, *neuromodulator, or *neurohormone.

neuroscience *n*. An interdisciplinary field of study concerned with the anatomy, physiology, and biochemistry of the *nervous system and its effects on behaviour and mental experience.
[From Greek *neuron* a nerve + English *science*, from Latin *scientia* knowledge, from *scire* to know]

neurosis *n*. An imprecise term for a relatively mild *mental disorder with predominantly distressing symptoms and without loss of *insight (3) or *reality testing, and without apparent *organic *aetiology, including anxiety neurosis (*see* generalized anxiety disorder); depersonalization neurosis (*see* depersonalization disorder); depressive neurosis (*see* dysthymic disorder); hysterical neurosis, conversion and dissociative types (*see* conversion disorder, dissociative disorders, histrionic personality disorder); obsessive–compulsive neurosis (*see* obsessive–compulsive disorder); and phobic neurosis (*see* phobia). The word was coined in 1777 by the Scottish physician William Cullen (1710–90) in a medical treatise entitled *First Lines of the Practice of Physic*. *See also* actual neurosis, choice of neurosis, failure neurosis, family neurosis, psychoneurosis. *Compare* psychosis (1). **neuroses** *pl*.
[From Greek *neuron* a nerve + *-osis* indicating a process or state]

neurosis, actual *See* actual neurosis.

neurosurgery *n*. A branch of surgery devoted to treating disorders of the brain, spinal cord, and other parts of the *nervous system. *Compare* psychosurgery.

neurotic *adj*. **1.** Of or pertaining to a *neurosis. *n*. **2.** A person afflicted with a *neurosis.

neurotic anxiety *n*. In *psychoanalysis, a form of *anxiety arising from fear of losing control of the instincts of the *id. *Compare* realistic anxiety.

neurotic character *n*. In *individual psychology, a term introduced by the Austrian psychiatrist Alfred Adler (1870–1937) to denote the personality characteristics that protect a person from feelings of inferiority. *See also* neurotic fiction.

neurotic depression *n*. Another name for *dysthymic disorder.

neurotic fiction *n*. In the *individual psychology of the Austrian psychiatrist Alfred Adler (1870–1937) and his followers, a person's *self-image that is unrealistic and false, serving to reduce anxiety about the self. *See also* guiding fiction.

neuroticism *n*. A psychological condition or state characterized by *neurosis. Also, one of the *Big Five personality factors, ranging from one extreme of neuroticism, including such *traits as nervousness, tenseness, moodiness, and temperamentality, to the opposite extreme of emotional stability.

neurotic paradox *n*. The persistence of *neurotic (1) symptoms or behaviour despite their distressing qualities and the desire of the afflicted person to be rid of them. For example, a man with *obsessive–compulsive disorder may wash his hands many times a day until they bleed, and may consider this behaviour unnecessary and maladaptive, or even ridiculous, yet feel compelled to continue doing it, and this appears paradoxical.

neurotic solution *n*. In the *neo-Freudian theory of the German-born US psychoanalyst Karen Horney (1885–1952), a method of dealing with a conflict by *repression.

neurotoxin *n*. Any substance such as *6-hydroxydopamine, *ibotenic acid, *kainic acid, *saxitoxin, or *tetrodotoxin that is poisonous to neurons or that interferes with their electrochemical functioning. The venom of many poisonous snakes, spiders, and scorpions contains neurotoxins. *See also* nerve gas. **neurotoxic** *adj*.
[From Greek *neuron* a nerve + *toxikon* arrow-poison, from *toxon* a bow]

neurotransmitter *n*. Any of about 50 chemical substances, usually a small *amine or a *peptide but also a substance such as the gas *nitric oxide, by which a neuron communicates with another neuron or with a muscle or gland via a *synapse (1). In the central nervous system *glutamate is the main excitatory neurotransmitter and *GABA the main inhibitory one; in the peripheral nervous system *acetylcholine is predominant for *motor neurons and glutamate for *sensory neurons. *Dopamine functions as a neurotransmitter in the midbrain, *noradrenalin (norepinephrine) mainly in the peripheral nervous system and in the pons and medulla oblongata, and *serotonin mainly near the midline of the brainstem. Other important neurotransmitters include *adenosine, *adrenalin (epinephrine), *aspartic acid, *glutamic acid, *histamine, *oxytocin, *substance P, and *vasopressin. See also excitatory postsynaptic potential, inhibitory postsynaptic potential, isoquinoline. Compare false neurotransmitter, neurohormone, neuromodulator. **neurotransmission** n. The communication of nerve impulses across a *synapse (1).

neurotropic virus n. Any of a number of viruses that have a strong affinity for neurons in the central nervous system, as contrasted with pantropic viruses, which attack body tissues indiscriminately.
[From Greek neuron a nerve + tropos a turn, from trapein to turn]

neutral colour n. Another name for an *achromatic (1) colour. US neutral color.

neutral grey n. Another name for an *achromatic (1) colour. US neutral gray.

neutralization n. The process by which two *phonemes, which by definition have the power to distinguish *minimal pairs, can become indistinguishable. For example, in English /p/ and /b/ are different phonemes, as can be seen in the different meanings of pan and ban or cap and cab, but following /s/ this opposition is neutralized, and from a phonetic point of view span could just as well be written sban. See also acoustic cue (1).

neutralization of libido n. In *psychoanalysis, the expression of *libido in non-sexual activities, such as artistic creation.

neutral monism n. An approach to the *mind–body problem that is a version of *monism, asserting that the mental and the physical are both constructs of the same elements that are in themselves neither mental nor physical.

neutral mutation n. A *mutation that is neither advantageous nor disadvantageous in terms of *Darwinian fitness but can lead to *genetic drift and contribute to *genetic polymorphism. A *silent mutation is one kind of neutral mutation.

nevra See nervios.

Newcomb's problem n. One of the most difficult problems of logic and decision making. On the table is a transparent box containing $1000 and an opaque box containing either $1 million or nothing. A decision maker has the choice of taking either the opaque box only or both boxes. The decision maker is told, and believes, that a predictor of human behaviour, such as a sophisticated computer programmed with psychological information, has already put $1 million in the opaque box if and only if it has predicted that the decision maker will take only that box, and not the transparent box as well, and the decision maker knows that the predictor is correct in most cases (95 per cent of cases, say, although the exact figure is not critical). Both strategies can apparently be justified by simple and apparently irrefutable arguments: *expected utility theory supports the strategy of taking the opaque box only, but the strategy of taking both boxes is a strongly *dominant alternative/strategy. Also called Newcomb's paradox. See also sure-thing principle.
[Named after the US theoretical physicist William A(drian) Newcomb (1927–99) who discovered it in 1960 while pondering the paradox of the Prisoner's Dilemma game, although it was first published in 1969 in a book chapter by the US philosopher Robert Nozick (1938–2002), who commented in a footnote: 'It is a beautiful problem. I wish it were mine.']

Newman–Keuls test n. In statistics, a method of *multiple comparisons in which the group means are ranked from smallest to largest, and then the statistic that is used to test for a significant difference between a pair of means is computed on the basis of the number of steps between the two means in the rank order. Also called Student–Newman–Keuls procedure. Compare Bonferroni correction, Duncan's multiple range test, least-significant difference test, Scheffé test, Tukey-HSD test.

[Named after the English statistician D. Newman and the Dutch horticulturalist M. Keuls who developed the test in 1952]

newton n. The derived SI unit of force required to accelerate a mass of 1 kilogram by 1 metre per second per second, equivalent to 100,000 *dynes.
[Named after the English physicist and mathematician Sir Isaac Newton (1642–1727)]

new-variant Creutzfeldt–Jakob disease See Creutzfeldt–Jakob disease.

next-in-line effect n. Impaired recall for an event immediately preceding an anticipated public performance. The effect was first reported in 1973 by the US postgraduate student Malcolm Brenner, who performed an experiment in which a group of participants sat around a circular table taking turns reading words aloud, trying to remember as many words as possible. After going round the table several times, so that each participant had read out several words and there were many more read out by others to remember, the participants' recall was tested. Recall tended to be best for the words that the participants had read out themselves (the *von Restorff effect) and worst for the words immediately preceding the words that they had read out (the next-in-line effect). The effect is believed to be due to both attention distraction and *retrograde amnesia. See also audience effect.

nibble See nybble.

nicotine n. A colourless, oily, toxic liquid that turns yellow on exposure to air and light and is the principal *alkaloid in tobacco, being ingested when tobacco is smoked, chewed, or snuffed. It is a powerful central nervous system *stimulant, mimicking *acetylcholine at certain neuroreceptor sites in both sympathetic and parasympathetic divisions of the autonomic nervous system, triggering the release of *dopamine and *noradrenalin (norepinephrine) and stimulating the release of *vasopressin. Prolonged tobacco use often leads to nicotine *dependence (2) or *addiction. See also cholinomimetic, nicotine-related disorders, nicotinic receptor.
[French, from Latin herba nicotiana Nicot's plant, named after the 16th-century French diplomat Jaques Nicot (1530–1600) who supplied tobacco to Catherine de Medici and introduced it into France in 1560 + -ine indicating an organic compound]

nicotine-related disorders n. *Substance-related disorders induced by consuming *nicotine. See substance abuse, substance dependence, substance-induced disorders, substance use disorders.

nicotinic receptor n. One of two types of receptors for *acetylcholine found in the central nervous system and in motor neurons controlling skeletal muscles, stimulated by *nicotine and inhibited by *curare. Nicotinic receptors are used by the striped voluntary muscles, and slightly different types of nicotinic receptors are found at the autonomic ganglia, relaying both sympathetic and parasympathetic signals. Also called a nicotinic cholinoceptor. Compare muscarinic receptor.
[So named because nicotine mimics acetylcholine at such a site]

nictitating membrane n. A thin membrane beneath the eyelids of birds, reptiles, and some mammals such as cats and rabbits that can be drawn across the eye. Also (non-technically) called a third eyelid.
[From Latin nictitare to wink repeatedly, from nictare to wink]

night blindness n. A non-technical name for *nyctalopia.

nightmare n. **1.** A terrifying or extremely upsetting *dream (1), or figuratively an event or experience resembling such a dream. **2.** An evil spirit believed to torment and suffocate sleepers. See also nightmare disorder.
[From night + Old English maere an evil spirit or incubus]

nightmare disorder n. A *parasomnia characterized by recurrent awakening from sleep, alert and oriented but with vivid recall of long and extremely frightening *nightmares (1). Compare sleep terror disorder.

nightshade n. Any of a number of plants including the *deadly nightshade Atropa belladonna.

night terrors n. Another name for *sleep terror disorder. Also called pavor nocturnus.

night vision n. A non-technical name for *scotopia.

nigrostriatal bundle n. A bundle of *dopaminergic nerve fibres in each cerebral hemisphere, originating in the *substantia nigra and terminating in the *striatum in the same hemisphere. See also mesotelencephalic pathway. **NSB** abbrev.

nihilistic delusion n. A *delusion that nothing exists, or that a significant aspect of the self (such as one's brain or the outside world) does not exist.

nirvana principle n. In *psychoanalysis, the tendency for the quantity of energy in the mental apparatus to reduce to zero. Sigmund Freud (1856–1939) introduced the concept in 1920 in his book Beyond the Pleasure Principle (Standard Edition, XVIII, pp. 7–64, at pp. 55–6). In 1924, in an article on 'The Economic Problem in Masochism', he defined it ambiguously as the principle of the mental apparatus 'of extinguishing, or at least of maintaining at as low a level as possible, the quantities of excitation flowing into it' (Standard Edition, XIX, pp. 159–70, at pp. 159–60). The term itself, which Freud attributed to the British psychoanalyst Barbara Low (1877–1955), relates to Buddhism and Hinduism, in which nirvana is the longed-for release from the cycle of reincarnation, attained by the extinction of all desires and individual existence. See also bound energy, free energy, Thanatos. Compare principle of constancy.
[From Sanskrit nirvana extinction or a blowing out, from nir- out + vati it blows]

Nissl body n. Any of the large granular structures consisting of clumps of *endoplasmic reticulum in the *cytoplasm of neurons.
[Named after the German neurologist Franz Nissl (1860–1919)]

Nissl granule n. Any of the small grains now identified as *ribosomes in the *endoplasmic reticulum of a *Nissl body. Also called a Nissl substance or chromatin granule.

Nissl stain n. A histological stain, usually using methylene blue or cresyl violet, that affects mainly *Nissl bodies, exposing neuron cell bodies but not their axons and dendrites. Compare Golgi stain.

nitric oxide n. A gas with *free-radical chemical properties that functions as a *neurotransmitter in the brain, believed to be involved in *long-term potentiation, and also released in response to sexual stimulation, activating *cyclic GMP in the penis and causing vasodilation (expansion of blood vessels) in the *corpora cavernosa and *corpus spongiosum. It should not be confused with *nitrous oxide (N_2O), the chemically stable laughing gas that is used as an anaesthetic. Formula: NO. See also ginseng.

nitrite inhalant n. Any amyl, butyl, or isobutyl nitrite that is inhaled as a drug, causing peripheral vasodilation and a temporary reduction in oxygen supply to the brain, leading to mild *euphoria, a change of time perception, relaxation of smooth muscles, and in some people an intensification of sexual sensations. Known colloquially as poppers. See also amyl nitrite, inhalant-related disorders, substance abuse, substance-related disorders.

nitrogenous base n. Any *base (1) containing nitrogen, specifically three found in both DNA and RNA (*adenine, *guanine, and *cytosine), one found only in DNA (*thymine), and one found only in RNA (*uracil). See also purine, pyrimidine.

nitrous oxide n. A gas that is used as an *anaesthetic (1), especially in dentistry, and that when inhaled causes rapid intoxication, characterized by loss of sensation, lightheadedness, and a floating sensation, sometimes accompanied by laughter, such effects disappearing a few minutes after the inhalation is stopped. Also called laughing gas. Often confused with *nitric oxide (NO), a chemically unstable gas that functions as a neurotransmitter. Formula: N_2O. See also substance abuse, substance-related disorders.

nociceptive adj. Sensitive to or causing *pain. **nociception** n. Pain perception. **nociceptor** n. Another name for a *pain receptor.
[From Latin nocere to injure + English (re)ceptive]

nocireceptor n. Another name for a *pain receptor.

noctambulation n. Another name for *sleepwalking. Also called noctambulism or somnambulism. **noctambulate** vb.

[From Latin *nox, noctis* night + *ambulare* to walk + *-ation* indicating a process or condition]

Noctec *n.* A proprietary name for the depressant drug *chloral hydrate.
[Trademark]

nocturnal *adj.* Occurring or active during the night or nightly. *Compare* diurnal.
[From Latin *nocturnalis* nocturnal, from *nox, noctis* night]

nocturnal myoclonus *n.* The technical name for night cramps.
[From Greek *mys* a muscle + *klonos* contraction]

node *n.* **1.** Any natural anatomical swelling or bulge. **2.** Any point in a *network model or graph where lines or pathways intersect or branch, especially (in cognitive psychology) an element representing a concept in a semantic network of relations between nodes (relations such as *x is a member of y* or *x is an attribute of y*), each node being linked to certain other nodes in the network. *See also* ACT*, closed node, fan effect, open node.
[From Latin *nodus* a knot]

node expansion *n.* Examining the successor nodes to a *node (2) in a network.

node of Ranvier *n.* Any of the gaps that occur at regular intervals along the *myelin sheath of a myelinated nerve fibre, exposing the *axon. Also called *Ranvier's node*. *See also* saltation (1).
[Named after the French histologist Louis-Antoine Ranvier (1835–1922) who drew attention to them]

nodulus *n.* A small *node (1).

noesis *n.* The act or process of *thinking or *perceiving, the functioning of intellect, or the exercise of *reason.
[From Greek *noesis* thought, from *noein* to think].

noise *n.* **1.** Any unwanted or disturbing sound, or any sound without any definite frequency or pitch. *See also* noise (2). *Compare* tone (1). **2.** Random disturbances in any communication channel in addition to the *signal that is being transmitted, or more generally any random component in a *time series that degrades its periodicity. *See* coloured noise,

frozen noise, pink noise, white noise. *See also* decibel, signal detection theory, signal-to-noise ratio.
[From Latin *nausea* the sensation of being about to vomit]

nominal aphasia *See* aphasia.

nominalism *n.* In scholastic philosophy, the doctrine propounded by the English philosopher William of Ockham (?1285–?1349) and others that only individual things exist and that universal concepts such as redness have no independent existence beyond being mere names. In modern philosophy, an interpretation of general concepts such as redness in terms of the mutual resemblance of the specific things to which they apply.

nominal scale *n.* A discrete form of data classification in which items are not quantified or even arranged in order but are merely allocated to different (often numbered) categories as, for example, in assigning numbers to categories of books in a library classification system. In nominal scaling, the numbers serve only as names for the categories to which the items belong. *See also* measurement level, scale (1). *Compare* absolute scale, interval scale, log-interval scale, ordinal scale, ratio scale.
[From Latin *nomen* a name]

nomological network *n.* A lawful pattern of interrelationships that exists between *hypothetical constructs and observable *attributes and that guides a researcher in establishing the *construct validity of a psychological test or measure. According to the US psychologists Lee J(oseph) Cronbach (1916–2001) and Paul Everett Meehl (born 1920), who introduced the concept in an article in the journal *Psychological Bulletin* in 1955, a nomological network includes a theoretical framework for what is being measured, specifying linkages between different hypothetical constructs, between different observable attributes, and between hypothetical constructs and observable attributes. Qualitatively different measurement operations may be said to measure the same attributes if their locations in the nomological network link them to the same hypothetical construct variable. Also called a *nomological net*. *Compare* trait validity.
[From Greek *nomos* a law + *logos* word, discourse, or reason + Latin *-icalis* of, relating to, or resembling]

nomological validity n. In psychometrics, a form of *validity established via a *nomological network.

nomothetic adj. Of or relating to the general case, especially in relation to the search for general laws or *traits in the study of *personality. The term was coined in 1904 by the German philosopher Wilhelm Windelband (1848–1915). See also ecological fallacy. Compare idiographic.
[From Greek nomothetes a lawgiver, from nomos a law + titheneai to set + -ikos of, relating to, or resembling]

non-adaptive adj. In genetics and evolutionary theory, pertaining to any gene that, relative to its alleles, reduces an organism's fitness.

non-additivity See additivity.

non-classical receptive field See under receptive field.

non-competitive antagonist n. An *antagonist (3) drug that depresses the effect of the *agonist (3) by acting at different *neuroreceptor sites. Compare competitive antagonist.

non compos mentis n. Not of sound mind; incapable of managing one's own affairs.
[Latin: not in control of one's mind]

non-Darwinian evolution n. Changes in the relative frequencies of genes in a population resulting not from natural selection but from *neutral mutation. Also called genetic drift or random drift. Compare Darwinian evolution, natural selection.
[So called because the Darwinian mechanism of natural selection does not drive it]

non-declarative knowledge n. Knowledge that does not involve awareness and understanding of factual information about the world, including especially *procedural knowledge. See also non-declarative memory. Compare declarative knowledge.

non-declarative memory n. Memory for *non-declarative knowledge, involving memory systems that do not draw on the individual's general knowledge. See also mirror drawing, procedural memory.

non-directional test See under directional test.

non-directive therapy n. Another name for *client-centred therapy.

non-discrimination point See point of subjective equality.

non-disjunction n. The failure of paired *chromosomes to separate and move to opposite poles during *mitosis or *meiosis (1).

non-equivalent groups design n. A *quasi-experimental research design in which the investigator does not manipulate the *independent variable but compares existing groups that differ on it. In this research design, the groups may differ in many other ways apart from the independent variable being investigated, and this limits the confidence with which the results can be attributed to the independent variable. See also one-group pretest–posttest design, interrupted time-series design.

non-essential amino acids See under amino acid.

non-fluent aphasia See under aphasia.

non-identical twins n. A non-technical name for *dizygotic twins.

non-Mendelian gene n. Any gene that does not conform to a *Mendelian mechanism of inheritance or is not inherited in accordance with *Mendel's laws, notably the genes encoded in *mitochondrial DNA and in *plasmids.

non-metric analysis n. In statistics, an approach to *multidimensional scaling in which analysis is performed on qualitative rather than quantitative dissimilarities.

non-monotonic reasoning n. Any of a number of systems of reasoning that violate the principle of *monotonicity. Formalizations of non-monotonic reasoning are designed to capture some of the features of commonsense reasoning. The canonical example consists of the two *premises Birds fly and Tweety is a bird together with the conclusion Tweety can fly. In this example, Birds fly is interpreted to mean Normally, birds fly, or Typically, birds fly, or

If x is a bird, then assume by default that x flies: it is a default assumption that we adopt provisionally, in the absence of information that might override it. An additional premise that Tweety is a penguin, or an ostrich, or an emu, or is coated in heavy crude oil, or is dead, would render the conclusion invalid. This form of reasoning is non-monotonic because it violates the *extension theorem of semantic entailment in propositional calculus, so that additional premises can negate conclusions derived from a smaller set of premises. Also called *non-monotonic logic*, but this is avoided in careful usage, because it violates monotonicity, which is a fundamental principle of logic. *See also* default reasoning, knowledge representation.
[From Greek *monos* single + *tonos* a tone + *-ikos* of, relating to, or resembling]

Nonne's syndrome *n*. Another name for *cerebellar syndrome.
[Named after the German neurologist Max Nonne (1861–1939) who studied and wrote about it]

non-opponent cell *n*. A type of neuron in the *lateral geniculate nucleus that is excited or inhibited by light of widely differing different wavelengths. Also called a *non-opponent neuron*. *Compare* opponent cell.

non-paralytic strabismus *n*. A hereditary form of *strabismus characterized by an inability to use both eyes together, so that objects or images have to be fixated with one eye or the other. A person with *alternating strabismus* tends to alternate fixation between the eyes, the eyes taking turns of approximately a second each as long as the object is fixated, whereas a person with *monocular* or *non-alternating strabismus* fixates continuously with one eye, the other eye often becoming blind as a result of disuse. *See also* amblyopia ex anopsia. *Compare* paralytic strabismus.

non-parametric statistics *n*. A branch of statistics that does not rely on assumptions about the parameters of the distributions from which scores are drawn and usually deals with data measured on *ordinal scales or *nominal scales to which arithmetic operations like addition and multiplication cannot meaningfully be applied. The term was introduced in 1942 by the Polish-born US statistician Jacob Wolfowitz (1910–81). *Compare* distribution-free test.

[From Latin *non* not + Greek *para* beside or beyond + Greek *metron* measure + English *statistics*]

non-probability sample *n*. Any sample drawn by a technique that does not involve randomization, so that the probabilities of inclusion of members of the population or sub-groups within it are not equal. *See* accidental sample, convenience sample, opportunity sample, quota sample, self-selected sample, snowball sample. *Compare* cluster sample, probability sample, random digit dialling, simple random sample, stratified random sample.

non-reactive measure *n*. Any measure of behaviour that is not influenced by awareness on the part of the participants or subjects that their behaviour is being observed or measured. In general, *unobtrusive measures are considered non-reactive, and some other techniques, such as *randomized response, are also intended to be non-reactive. *See also* reactivity.

non-regressiveness bias *n*. A tendency to make insufficient allowance for *regression towards the mean when predicting from an imperfectly reliable predictor. Suppose that a student is described by a tutor as being much more intelligent, hard-working, and self-confident than the average student on the course. (a) What percentage of students on the course would you expect to be described even more favourably by the tutor? (b) What percentage of students on the course would you predict to obtain a higher aggregate mark or grade point average? There is more uncertainty about (b) than (a), because a tutor's ratings are an imperfectly reliable predictor of academic performance, and your prediction (b) should therefore be more regressive, and hence closer to 50 per cent, than your expectation (a). In practice, most people show little or no difference between the two percentages, and this is usually interpreted as being due to their use of the *representativeness heuristic, in which evaluation and prediction coincide. *Compare* regression fallacy.

non-REM sleep *See* NREM sleep.

non-reversal shift *n*. A form of *serial learning (2) in which the set of stimuli is changed, but the rewarded and non-rewarded items are not simply interchanged, a typical example being an experiment in which organisms are trained to choose the round rather than the square containers, irrespective of their colours, and are then presented with stimulus sets in which the reward is associated with the yellow rather than the blue containers irrespective of their shapes. *Compare* habit reversal.

nonsense codon n. Another name for a *stop codon.
[So called because it does not specify any amino acid but is none the less a *codon]

nonsense mutation n. Any *mutation that produces one of the *stop codons, causing premature termination of protein synthesis by the gene in which it occurs.
[So called because a stop codon is also called a nonsense codon]

nonsense syllable n. A *CVC trigram that forms a meaningless non-word (such as *KEB*) rather than a meaningful word (such as *DOG*). It was introduced into psychology in about 1878 by the German psychologist Hermann von Ebbinghaus (1850–1909) for studying memory. Ebbinghaus had begun by experimenting with fragments of poetry but had found that they aroused mental associations, influencing their ease of learning, so he constructed lists of nonsense syllables, which provided material that was relatively homogeneous, evoked few mental associations, and could easily be broken into objectively equal units for quantitative research, and he reported his results in his book *Über das Gedächtnis* (On Memory) in 1885. *See also* association value, consonant trigram.

nonsense syndrome n. Another name for *Ganser syndrome.

non-spectral colour n. Any colour that does not occur in the *visible spectrum and that cannot be produced by light of a single wavelength, for example purple, which can be generated only by a mixture of red and blue (*see* complementary colours). US *non-spectral color*. Also called an *extra-spectral colour/hue* or *extraspectral color/hue*. *Compare* spectral colour.

non-taster *See under* propylthiouracil, PTC.

non-verbal communication n. Any form of communication apart from *language (1), including *paralanguage (non-verbal aspects of speech), *facial expression, communicative *gaze and *eye contact, *kinesics (gestures and other communicative bodily movements), and *proxemics (communicative use of personal space). *See also* Clever Hans, equilibrium hypothesis, expressive behaviour, semiotics, social skills training. **NVC** *abbrev*.

non-verbal test n. In psychometrics, any test that does not require language skills on the part of the respondent, including *intelligence tests that do not depend on any knowledge of language or linguistic skills, such as *Raven's Progressive Matrices, the *Cattell Culture-Fair Test, and other pychometric tests such as the *Porteus Maze Test. *See also* culture-fair.

non-zero-sum game n. Another name for a *mixed-motive game.
[So called because the sum of the payoffs to the players is not zero in every outcome of the game]

nootropic *adj*. Affecting the intellect or enhancing cognitive performance. *See* smart drug.
[From Greek *nous* intellect + *tropos* a turn, from *trapein* to turn + *-ikos* of, relating to, or resembling]

noradrenalin n. A *biogenic amine and one of the *catecholamine hormones, chemically related to adrenalin and crucial to the maintenance of alertness, drive, and motivation, synthesized from tyrosine in the presence of the cofactor vitamin C, and secreted by the *chromaffin cells of the adrenal medulla, widely distributed between the brainstem and most areas of the cerebral cortex, stimulating the heart muscle to contract, the blood vessels to constrict, the bronchial tracts of the lungs to dilate, and the contractile strength of the skeletal muscles to increase, also functioning as an important *neurotransmitter in the sympathetic nervous system and in the central nervous system mainly through circuits originating in the *locus coeruleus of the pons and projecting to many areas of the brain, levels of noradrenalin often being significantly reduced in people with depression or attempting suicide. Formula: $(HO)_2C_6H_3CH(OH)CH_2NH_2$. Also spelt *noradren-*

aline. Also, especially in US, called *norepineph-rine* (*NE*). **NA** *abbrev*.

[From *nor(mal)* + *adrenalin*]

noradrenergic *adj*. Releasing *noradrenalin (norepinephrine); also activated by or responding to noradrenalin, this extended usage being widespread but consistently rejected by the English physiologist Sir Henry Hallet Dale (1875–1968), who coined the suffix *-ergic*, and by many other authorities. The term applies especially to nerve fibres such as those of the *sympathetic nervous system or the *locus coeruleus and many other areas in the central nervous system that use noradrenalin as their *neurotransmitter. *Compare* adrenergic, cholinergic, dopaminergic, GABAergic, serotonergic.

[From *noradrenalin* + Greek *ergon* work + *-ikos* of, relating to, or resembling]

norepinephrine *n*. Another name for *noradrenalin, especially in US usage. **NE** *abbrev*.

[From *nor(mal)* + Greek *epi* on + *nephros* a kidney + *-ine* indicating an organic compound]

norm *n*. **1.** A generally accepted standard of behaviour within a society, community, or group. *See also* social influence. **2.** A typical or most common value, pattern, state, condition, or event. In *psychometrics, an average score on a test determined by applying the test to a standardization sample. *See also* standardized test.

[From Latin *norma* a carpenter's square or a rule]

normal distribution *n*. In statistics, a symmetrical, bell-shaped *probability distribution, also called the *Gaussian distribution*, the *normal curve*, or colloquially the *bell curve*, with the most probable scores concentrated around the *mean (average) and progressively less probable scores occurring further from the mean (see illustration). In this distribution, 68.26 per cent of scores fall within one *standard deviation on either side of the mean, 95.44 per cent within two standard deviations, and 99.74 within three standard deviations. For a reason explained by the *central limit theorem, the normal distribution approximates the observed *frequency distribution of many psychological and biological variables and is by far the most widely used probability distribution in inferential statistics. *See also* deviation IQ. **normally dis-**

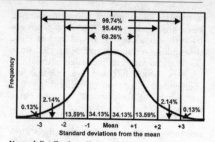

Normal distribution. Showing the percentages of observations occurring within various distances from the mean, measured in standard deviations.

tributed *adj*. Distributed according to the *normal distribution.

[From Latin *norma* a carpenter's square or a rule + *-alis* of or relating to]

normal probability plot *n*. In statistics, a graph used to detect departures from normality in a set of scores whose cumulative proportion at various points is plotted against the expected cumulative proportion based on the *normal distribution of *standardized (1) scores. The points should fall close to a straight line if the scores are a sample from a normal distribution. *See also* detrended normal plot.

normal science *n*. According to an influential idea first presented by the US historian and philosopher of science Thomas S(amuel) Kuhn (1922–96) in his book *The Structure of Scientific Revolutions* (1962), a period in the development of any scientific discipline in which there is general acceptance and agreement as to the basic concepts and steady cumulative progress is made. *See also* Kuhnian, paradigm shift, scientific revolution.

normative *adj*. **1.** Prescribing or establishing *norms (1) or standards; prescriptive. For example, *decision theory and classical *game theory are normative inasmuch as they seek to prescribe how rational decision makers ought to choose in order to optimize their own interests. Such theories are sometimes contrasted with *descriptive* or *positive* theories that seek to explain and predict the behaviour of actual agents. In an edited book entitled *Decision Making: Descriptive, Normative, and*

Prescriptive Interactions (1988), the US decision theorists David E. Bell (born 1949) and Howard Raiffa (born 1924) and the US-based Israeli psychologist Amos Tversky (1937–96) distinguished a third category of *prescriptive* theories that offer advice as to how to act, given our acknowledged cognitive limitations, but some other authorities (and Tversky himself) consider them to be essentially normative theories. **2.** Of or relating to data providing *norms (2) or average scores, as in the standardization of a psychological test. *Compare* ipsative.
[From Latin *norma* a carpenter's square or a rule + *-ivus* indicating a tendency, inclination, or quality]

normative reference group See *under* reference group.

norm-referenced test *n.* A test that measures an *attribute of a respondent relative to *norms (2) derived from a standardization sample rather than by reference to any predefined absolute standard. Modern *IQ tests are among the best known examples of norm-referenced tests. *Compare* criterion-referenced test, domain-referenced test.

nose *n.* The organ of *olfaction and entrance to the respiratory tract, its smaller external portion protruding from the front of the face and its larger internal portion lying over the roof of the mouth, divided into two hair-lined mucous membranes separated by a nasal septum and containing the *olfactory receptors. *See also* common chemical sense, dirhinic, vomeronasal organ.

nosology *n.* The classification of disorders, or more generally the study of disorders.
[From Greek *nosos* a disorder + *logos* word, discourse, or reason]

***N*-person Prisoner's Dilemma** *n.* The first and most fundamental type of multi-person *social dilemma, a generalization of the *Prisoner's Dilemma game to include more than two players, discovered simultaneously and independently in 1973 by the US psychologist Robyn Mason Dawes (born 1936), the US mathematician Henry Hamburger (born 1940), and the US economist Thomas C. Schelling (born 1921). It is an interactive decision involving three or more players who each face a choice between a cooperative *strategy

(2) labelled *C* and a non-cooperative or defecting strategy labelled *D*. The *payoff structure is such that *D* is a *dominant strategy for each player in the sense that each player obtains a better payoff by choosing *D* than *C* no matter how many of the other players choose *C*; but the outcome if all players choose their dominated *C* strategies is preferable from every player's point of view to the outcome if everyone chooses *D*. Apart from the Prisoner's Dilemma game, which is a special (two-person) case, the simplest example is the three-person game in which, if three players choose *C*, then each gets a payoff of 3; if two players choose *C*, then each *C*-chooser gets 2 and the *D*-chooser gets 4; if one player chooses *C*, then the *C*-chooser gets 1 and each *D*-chooser gets 3; and if no player chooses *C*, then each *D*-chooser gets 2. *See also* sure-thing principle. **NPD** *abbrev.*

NREM sleep *abbrev.* Non-rapid-eye-movement sleep, in which four progressively deepening stages can be distinguished by *EEG measurements: Stage I NREM sleep, without *delta waves, is the stage of transition between wakefulness and sleep, and it occupies about 5 per cent of sleeping time in healthy adults; Stage II NREM sleep, with delta waves 20 per cent of the time, is characterized by *sleep spindles and *K complexes, and it occupies about 50 per cent of normal adult sleeping time; and Stages III and IV NREM sleep, or *slow-wave sleep, with delta waves more than 50 per cent of the time, are the deepest levels, and they occupy about 10–20 per cent of normal adult sleeping time. Also called *quiet sleep* or *synchronized (S) sleep*. *See also* sleep. *Compare* REM sleep.

nuclear agenesis *n.* Another name for *Möbius syndrome.

nuclear family *n.* The basic family unit consisting of a mother and father with their immediate children. *Compare* extended family.
[From Latin *nux, nucis* a nut]

nuclear magnetic resonance *n.* A phenomenon that occurs when the nuclei of molecules resonate during exposure to high-frequency (usually radio-wave) radiation in a strong magnetic field. In strong magnetic fields, certain protons (subatomic particles) spin like tops, and pulses of radiation cause them to tilt momentarily and then to regain their original orientations, giving off detectable amounts of energy as they do so. Different molecules absorb different frequencies of the radiation as the protons tilt, depending on the magnetic properties of their nuclei, and from the precise frequencies of radiation that they absorb, information concerning the bonds between their atoms can be deduced, thus enabling the structure of the material to be determined. Magnetic resonance imaging or *MRI, one of the techniques of *brain imaging, is based on this phenomenon. **NMR** *abbrev*.

nuclear self *n*. In *self-psychology, the initial organization of the self that emerges in the second year of life.

nuclear spindle *n*. A spindle-shaped structure, formed from *microtubules, that draws the newly duplicated *chromosomes apart during *mitosis and *meiosis (1). Also called a *spindle*.

nucleic acid *n*. A generic name for several complex compounds, especially *DNA, *RNA, *messenger RNA, and *transfer RNA, that play important roles in living cells. *See also* nucleotide.
[From Latin *nucleus* a kernel, from *nux*, *nucis* a nut, so called because they are found in the nuclei of cells]

nucleoplasm *n*. The *protoplasm in the *nucleus (1) of a cell.
[From Latin *nucleus* a kernel + *plasma* a form]

nucleotide *n*. A basic building block of *DNA or *RNA, consisting of a *base (1) linked to a sugar (*deoxyribose or *ribose respectively) and a *phosphate, long chains of such units constituting *nucleic acids.
[From Latin *nucleus* a kernel, from *nux*, *nucis* a nut + -*ide* indicating membership of a particular group of chemical compounds]

nucleotide sequence *n*. Another name for a *DNA sequence or an equivalent sequence of RNA.

nucleus *n*. **1.** The spherical or egg-shaped compartment in the *protoplasm of a cell, enclosed in a membrane, containing the chromosomes and other important structures that determine the behaviour of the cell. *See also* eukaryote, prokaryote. **2.** More generally, the central or core part or element of any structure, especially an anatomically or func-

tionally distinct area of *grey matter containing a collection of *neuron cell bodies. *See* caudate nucleus, dentate nucleus, inferior olivary nucleus, lateral geniculate nucleus, lenticular nucleus, medial geniculate nucleus, nucleus accumbens, nucleus basalis of Meynert, nucleus cuneatus, nucleus gigantocellularis, nucleus gracilis, raphe nuclei, subthalamic nucleus, superior olivary nucleus, suprachiasmatic nucleus. **nuclei** *pl*.
[From Latin *nucleus* a kernel, from *nux*, *nucis* a nut]

nucleus accumbens *n*. Either of two clusters of neuron cell bodies and *opiate receptors in the basal forebrain near the septum pellucidum, where *dopamine-secreting neurons originating in the *ventral tegmental area terminate. This dopamine pathway is thought to be involved in reward and *reinforcement (1) and appears to be implicated in most if not all *addictions. It is also involved in attention. Also called the *accumbens nucleus*.

nucleus basalis of Meynert *n*. Either of two small regions in the forebrain with a high concentration of *cholinergic neurons that undergoes profound cell loss in *Alzheimer's disease. **nbM** *abbrev*.
[Named after the German neurologist and psychiatrist Theodor Hermann Meynert (1833–92) who drew attention to it]

nucleus cuneatus *n*. Either of two areas of the *medulla oblongata where the left or right *fasciculus cuneatus terminates, functioning as a relay station for somatosensory information. Also called the *cuneate nucleus*.
[From Latin *cuneatus* wedge-shaped, from *cuneus* a wedge]

nucleus gigantocellularis *n*. Either of two clusters of neurons in the *pons that are thought to generate *PGO spikes during *REM sleep.
[From Latin *gigantis* a giant + *cellularis* of cells, from *cellula* a cell, from *cella* a room]

nucleus gracilis *n*. Either of two areas of the *medulla oblongata where the *fasciculus gracilis terminates. Also called the *gracile nucleus*.
[From Latin *gracilis* slender]

NUD*IST *abbrev*. Non-numerical unstructured data indexing, searching, and theory-building, a popular software package for the analysis of textual data in *qualitative research.

nuisance variable *n*. Another name for an *extraneous variable.

null hypothesis *n*. In *inferential statistics, the provisional hypothesis that there is no difference or no relationship and that the observed experimental results can therefore be attributed to chance alone. If the statistical test rejects the null hypothesis, then the *alternative hypothesis may be accepted and the effect that has been observed may be considered statistically significant. *See also* significance test.
[From Latin *nullus* none, from *ne* not + *ullus* any + *hypothesis*]

null hypothesis significance testing *n*. The process of applying a *significance test. **NHST** *abbrev*.

number-completion test *n*. A type of *intelligence test item or subtest in which the respondent has to find a number to complete a sequence of numbers. A typical example is: *What is the missing number in the following sequence? 0, 2, 8, 18, . . .* Although there is always an infinity of mathematically justifiable answers, the 'correct' answer in this case is 32, because the steps between adjacent numbers are 2, 6, 10, which are alternate even numbers, so the step between 18 and the missing number should be 14, making the missing number 32. *See also* completion test. Also called a *number sequence*, a *number series*, a *sequence completion*, or a *series completion*.

number sequence *n*. Another name for a *number-completion test. Also called a *number series*.

numerical rating scale *n*. Any *rating scale in which the *response categories are identified by numbers, such as a scale from −3 to +3 or from 0 to 10. The main alternatives are rating scales with unlabelled response categories, indicated by a row of boxes, dashes, or other symbols; *verbal rating scales; and *graphic rating scales.

numeric variable *n*. In statistics and measurement theory, any *variable whose values are numbers. *Compare* string variable.

numinosum *n*. In *analytical psychology, a type of involuntary mystical or religious experience described by Carl Gustav Jung (1875–1961) in 1937 as 'a dynamic agency or effect not caused by an arbitrary act of will. On the contrary, it seizes and controls the human subject, who is always rather its victim than its creator. The *numinosum*—whatever its cause may be—is an experience of the subject independent of his will' (*Collected Works*, 11, paragraph 6).
[From Latin *numen* divine will or a nod (indicating a command), from *nuere* to nod + *-osus* having or characterized by]

Numorphan *n*. A proprietary name for the narcotic analgesic drug *oxymorphone.
[Trademark]

nurture *n*. The sum total of all *environmental factors that contribute to the physical and psychological characteristics of an individual, including upbringing or rearing. It is often contrasted with *nature*: the genetic factors that contribute to an individual's characteristics. *See* nature–nurture controversy.
[From Latin *nutrire* to nourish]

nutmeg *n*. The hard, round, seed of a tropical tree, or a spice prepared from it. *See* myristin.
[From Latin *nux* nut + *muscus* musk]

nybble *n*. A measure of *information (2) equivalent to four *bits. It suffices to represent a decimal digit. Also spelt *nibble*, though this is avoided in careful usage and is to be deprecated, because it obscures the pleasing analogy with *byte*. *Compare* byte.
[An arbitrary formation based on *nibble*, alluding to the fact that it is half a *byte*]

nyctalopia *n*. A form of partial blindness characterized by poor vision in dim light or at night, resulting from inadequate synthesis of *rhodopsin, or from *vitamin A deficiency, retinal degeneration, or a congenital defect. Also called *night blindness*. *Compare* hemeralopia.
[From Greek *nyx*, *nyktos* night + *alaos* blind + *ops* an eye + *-ia* indicating a condition or quality]

nymphomania *n*. A psychological condition of women characterized by uncontrollable sexual desire and an inability to have lasting sexual relationships. *Compare* satyriasis.

nymphomaniac *n.* A woman who displays
*nymphomania.
[From Greek *nymphe* a bride or nymph + *mania*
madness]

nystagmus *n.* Spasmodic involuntary eye
movements. Also called *ocular nystagmus*. *See*
caloric nystagmus, central nystagmus,
labyrinthine nystagmus, optokinetic nystagmus, physiological nystagmus, post-
rotational nystagmus, vestibular nystagmus.
See also Bárány test, reafference.
[From Greek *nystagmos* drowsiness, from
nystazein to nap]

obedience *n*. A form of *social influence in which a person yields to explicit instructions or orders from an authority figure. Experimental research into this phenomenon was pioneered by the US psychologist Stanley Milgram (1933–84) who conducted a series of experiments, the first of which was published in the *Journal of Abnormal and Social Psychology* in 1963, in which approximately two-thirds of participants administered what they believed to be extremely painful and possibly lethal electric shocks to an innocent victim when instructed to do so by an authoritative experimenter. *See also* law of social impact. *Compare* compliance, conformity.

object assembly test *n*. A type of *intelligence test item or subtest in which the respondent tries to fit a number of shapes together to form a recognizable object.

object blindness *n*. A form of *agnosia characterized by an inability to identify objects that are clearly perceived.

object-cathexis *n*. In *psychoanalysis, the investment of *libido in an *instinctual object.

object-choice *n*. In *psychoanalysis, the action of selecting a person or a type of person as a love-object. The element *object* refers not to an inanimate thing but to an *instinctual object. *See* anaclitic object-choice, narcissistic object-choice, Oedipus complex. *See also* good object, instinctual object, part object, splitting of the object, transitional object, whole object.

object constancy *n*. The tendency for an object to retain its perceived identity and form despite being briefly occluded or altered in appearance because of a change in orientation, distance, illumination, or movement.

See also perceptual constancy, phenomenal regression.

object instinct *n*. In *psychoanalysis, a type of instinct that is concerned with relations to an external object, distinguished by Sigmund Freud (1856–1939) in his early (1910–15) classification from an *ego instinct, which is a *self-preservation instinct. Freud introduced the concept (though not yet the term) in 1910 in an article on 'The Psycho-Analytic View of Psychogenic Disturbance of Vision' (*Standard Edition*, XI, pp. 211–18, at pp. 214–15). After 1920, he recognized two varieties of object instincts, namely libidinal instincts, driven by *Eros (the life instincts), and destructive instincts, driven by *Thanatos (the death instinct).

objective psyche *n*. In *analytical psychology, another name for the *collective unconscious, so called because it is not personal and therefore not subjective. Carl Gustav Jung (1875–1961) introduced this term (*Collected Works*, 7, paragraph 103*n*).

object language *n*. A language being referred to in a *metalanguage. The sentence '*Snow is white' if and only if snow is white* is expressed in a metalanguage, and the sentence that it contains, enclosed in quotation marks, belongs to the object language. Such an object language may be a metalanguage relative to a third language.

object libido *n*. In *psychoanalysis, *libido involved in the *cathexis of an external *instinctual object, in contradistinction to *ego libido, which is libido involved in the cathexis of oneself. According to Sigmund Freud (1856–1939), object libido decreases as ego libido increases, and vice versa. Freud expounded these ideas in 1914 in his article 'On Narcissism: An Introduction' (*Standard

Edition, XIV, pp. 73–102, at pp. 77–81). *See also* narcissism.

object loss *n*. In *psychoanalysis, loss of an *instinctual object, such as the loss of a loved one or of a relationship with a loved one.

object of instinct *See* instinctual object.

object, part *See* part object.

object permanence *n*. A cognitive ability associated with *working memory, first identified by the Swiss psychologist Jean Piaget (1896–1980). To test for this ability in a child, the child is shown two boxes, one of which contains a toy, then the boxes are closed and the child is deliberately distracted for a short while, and the child is asked to choose the box containing the toy. After several correct choices, the toy is transferred to the other box while the child watches, and further trials are carried out to determine whether the child is able to switch responses in accordance with the updated information. This ability, and the ability to perform *delayed-response tasks, depends on maturity of the *prefrontal cortex: in children under about 8 months this area is not fully developed, and they perform poorly on such tasks, behaving as though 'out of sight is out of mind', as do monkeys with surgical lesions in the prefrontal cortex.

object recognition *n*. The identification of something as a particular object (such as one's own jacket) or as a member of a particular class of objects (such as a tabby-cat) in spite of wide variations in the precise pattern of sensory stimulation, which depends on the angle from which it is viewed, lighting conditions, distance, and so on. *Compare* pattern recognition.

object relations *n*. In *psychoanalysis, the emotional bonds that people form with *instinctual objects, in contradistinction to interest in and love of oneself. It is given expression through capacity to form loving relationships with other people, any such bond being called an *object-relationship. The concept is associated with the work of the British-based Austrian psychoanalyst Melanie Klein (1882–1960) as set forth in her books *The Psycho-Analysis of Children* (1932) and

Contributions to Psycho-Analysis, 1921–1945 (1948), and her followers. *See* defensive technique, Kleinian, schizoid personality, Winnicottian. *See also* object instinct, object-relations theory. *Compare* narcissism.

object-relationship *n*. In *psychoanalysis, a relationship experienced, or an emotion directed, by the *ego towards an *instinctual object. Barely mentioned in the writings of Sigmund Freud (1856–1939), it has played a central role in the theories of later psychoanalysts such as the British-based Hungarian psychiatrist Michael Balint (1896–1970), who pointed out in his book *Primary Love and Psychoanalytic Technique* (1952) that it is virtually the only concept in classical psychoanalysis that does not refer to the individual in social isolation, and the Austrian psychoanalyst René A. Spitz (1887–1974), who made a similar observation. *See also* fixation (2), libidinal stage, object instinct, primary identification, object-relations theory, primary object.

object-relations theory *n*. A theory of *object relations developed in the UK by the British-based Austrian psychoanalyst Melanie Klein (1882–1960), the English psychoanalyst Donald Woods Winnicott (1896–1971), the Scottish psychoanalyst W. Ronald D. Fairbairn (1889–1964), the British-based Hungarian psychiatrist Michael Balint (1896–1970), and others. Also called *object theory*.

object superiority effect *n*. Another name for the *configural superiority effect.

object theory *n*. Another name for *object-relations theory.

object, transitional *See* transitional object.

oblique *décalage* *See under décalage*.

oblique effect *n*. A visual defect in which slanted lines or edges are harder to see than horizontal or vertical lines or edges. [From Latin *obliquus* slanting]

oblique muscle *n*. A muscle attached at an oblique angle to the structure that it controls, especially two of the *extra-ocular muscles that are attached externally to each eyeball and that roll the eyeball about the visual axis, namely the *superior oblique muscle* that passes through an eyelet above the eyeball and works like a pulley and the *inferior oblique muscle* that is wrapped at an angle round the bottom of the eyeball. *See also* cyclophoria, diplopia, rectus muscle, trochlear nerve.

obliviscence *n*. Forgetfulness or forgetting. Also spelt *oblivescence*. *Compare* reminiscence (2).
[From Latin *oblivisci* to forget]

observational study *n*. A research methodology most often used in certain areas of *social psychology, *developmental psychology, and *ethology in which the investigator records behaviour as far as possible without influencing it. An observational field study is conducted in a naturally occurring situation (*compare* naturalistic observation), and an observational laboratory study is carried out in an artificial laboratory environment.

obsession *n*. A recurrent and persistent thought, impulse, or idea that causes significant distress, is experienced as intrusive or inappropriate (*ego-dystonic), is not merely an exaggerated worry about a genuine problem, and is recognized by the afflicted person as internally generated. *See also* Grübelsucht, obsessional technique, obsessive–compulsive disorder. *Compare* compulsion. **obsess** *vb*. **obsessional** or **obsessive** *adj*.
[From Latin *obsessus* besieged, from *ob* in front + *sidere* to sit + *-ion* indicating an action, process, or state]

obsessional neurosis *n*. Another name for an *obsessive–compulsive disorder. The term was introduced in German (*Zwangsneurose*) by Sigmund Freud (1856–1939) in an article on 'Heredity and the Aetiology of the Neuroses' (1896): 'I was obliged to begin my work with a nosolographic innovation. I found reason to set alongside of hysteria the obsessional neurosis as a self-sufficient and independent disorder' (*Standard Edition*, III, pp. 143–56, at p. 146). *See also* transference neurosis.

obsessional technique *n*. In *psychoanalysis, one of the four *defensive techniques proposed by the Scottish psychoanalyst W. Ronald D. Fairbairn (1889–1964). It involves *internalization of both the *good object and the bad object, causing the obsessional person to consider bad objects as alien internal forces that need to be controlled. *See also* splitting of the object. *Compare* hysterical technique, paranoid technique, phobic technique.

obsessive–compulsive disorder *n*. An *anxiety disorder characterized by either *obsessions or *compulsions, recognized by the afflicted person (if an adolescent or adult) as excessive or unreasonable, causing significant distress, wasting significant amounts of time, or markedly interfering with everyday life, occupational or academic performance, or social interaction. Also called *anankastic neurosis, obsessive–compulsive neurosis*. *See also* defusion of instincts, isolation of affect, obsessional neurosis, obsessional technique, paradoxical intention, Rat Man. *Compare* obsessive–compulsive personality disorder. **OCD** *abbrev*.
[From Latin *obsessus* besieged, from *ob* in front + *sidere* to sit + *compulsare* to compel frequently or habitually, from *compellere* to compel]

obsessive–compulsive personality disorder *n*. A *personality disorder characterized by a pervasive pattern of preoccupation with orderliness, perfectionism, and control, at the cost of flexibility, openness, and efficiency, beginning by early adulthood and indicated by such signs and symptoms as excessive preoccupation with details, rules, and order; perfectionism that interferes with task completion; excessive devotion to work at the expense of leisure; excessive conscientiousness and scrupulousness; tendency to hoard worthless objects; reluctance to delegate tasks to others; thrifty or stingy attitude towards money; rigidity and stubbornness. The absence of true *obsessions or *compulsions makes this condition easily distinguishable from *obsessive–compulsive disorder, despite the similarity of their names, and also suggests that *obsessive–compulsive personality disorder* is a misnomer. Also called *anankastic personality disorder*. *See also* anal character, anal triad.

obstacle sense *n*. Another name for *facial vision.

obstructive sleep apnoea *n*. A form of *sleep apnoea, occurring usually in overweight people, in which the recurrent episodes of breathing cessation during sleep are associated with obstruction to the upper airway and are followed by loud snores or gasps as breathing resumes. US *obstructive sleep apnea*. *Compare* central sleep apnoea.

obstruent *n.* A *consonant involving substantial obstruction of the airstream through the *vocal tract. All *plosives, *fricatives, and *affricates are obstruents; *nasals (2) and *approximants are not.
[From Latin *obstruere* to obstruct, from *ob* in the way of + *struere* to pile up]

Occam's razor *n.* A variant spelling of *Ockham's razor.

occipital *adj.* Of or relating to the back of the head, which is called the occiput.
[From Latin *ob* against + *caput* the head]

occipital bone *n.* The saucer-shaped bone that forms the back of the skull.

occipital lobe *n.* The *lobe at the back of each cerebral hemisphere, separated on its lateral or outer surface from the parietal lobe and temporal lobe by an imaginary line from the top of the *parieto-occipital sulcus to the *pre-occipital notch and on its medial surface by the *parieto-occipital sulcus. It is devoted almost entirely to vision and contains the *primary visual cortex (Area V1) in the gyri on both sides of the *calcarine sulcus. *See also* lobe.

occupational interest inventory *n.* Any questionnaire designed to measure respondents' likes and dislikes for the types of activities involved in different jobs. *See* Kuder Preference Record, Strong Interest Inventory, Strong Vocational Interest Blank. *See also* Allport–Vernon–Lindzey Study of Values, interest inventory.

occupational psychology *n.* A field of applied psychology in which the results of psychological research are applied to all problems related to people in work and unemployment, including vocational guidance and selection, problems of work motivation and job satisfaction, absenteeism, design and implementation of training courses, teaching of social and human relations skills, improvement of promotion structures, evaluation of job performance, and problems of safety and welfare. Its major branches are *personnel

psychology, *ergonomics or human factors psychology, and *organizational psychology. It corresponds roughly to *industrial/organizational psychology, the term usually preferred in the US, and it falls under the umbrella of *work psychology.

occupational therapy *n.* A method of treating a *mental disorder or a *general medical condition by a programme of useful or productive work. **OT** *abbrev.*

oceanic feeling *n.* In *psychoanalysis, a term suggested by the French novelist, dramatist, and essayist Romain Rolland (1866–1944) to Sigmund Freud (1856–1939), who discussed it as a basis of religion in his book *Civilization and its Discontents* (1930, *Standard Edition*, XXI, pp. 64–145 at pp. 64–5, 72). It is a transcendental sense of a limitless and indissoluble bond between oneself and the external world that Freud believed to underlie religious sentiments (which he could not discover in himself). *See also* peak experience.

Ockham's razor *n.* The principle of economy of explanation according to which entities (usually interpreted as assumptions) should not be multiplied beyond necessity (*Entia non sunt multiplicanda praeter necessitatem*), and hence simple explanations should be preferred to more complex ones. Another version of the principle attributed to Ockham is that 'What can be explained by the assumption of fewer things is vainly explained by the assumption of more things'. Because it is useful in so many fields, the English psychologist Richard L(angton) Gregory (born 1923) referred to it in 1999 as an 'eclectic razor'. Also spelt *Occam's razor. See also* Lloyd Morgan's canon.
[Named after the English philosopher William of Ockham (?1285–?1349), so called because he was born in the English village of Ockham, near Guildford, Surrey, perhaps the most influential of the later medieval philosophers, although the words attributed to him are not found in any of his surviving works]

octave *n.* The interval between two tones, one of which is twice the frequency or pitch of the other; also, a name for all the tones contained within that interval. An octave contains twelve *semitones.
[From Latin *octavus* eighth, from *octo* eight]

ocular apraxia See under apraxia.

ocular convergence n. The turning inwards of the eyes in order to fixate an object or image that is closer than the previous fixation point, also called simply *convergence*. It is one of two binocular cues of visual *depth perception, in which kinaesthetic information about the degree of ocular convergence indicates the distance of objects being fixated. See also accommodation reflex, horopter, oculomotor cue, reduction screen, vergence. Compare ocular divergence.
[From Latin *convergere* to bend together, from *con-* together + *vergere* to incline]

ocular divergence n. The turning outwards of the eyes in order to fixate an object or image that is further away than the previous fixation point, also called simply *divergence*. See also horopter, vergence. Compare ocular convergence.
[From Latin *divergere* to move apart, from *di-* apart + *vergere* to incline]

ocular dominance n. The degree to which a *binocular cell located in the *visual cortex and receiving inputs from both eyes responds primarily to one eye or the other, usually measured on a seven-point scale in which 1 indicates responsivity to inputs from the left eye only, 4 indicates equal responsivity to inputs from both eyes, and 7 indicates receptivity to inputs from the right eye only. See also ocular-dominance column.

ocular-dominance column n. Any of the alternating slabs of cells perpendicular to the surface of the *primary visual cortex (Area V1), approximately half a millimetre wide and extending through all six cortical layers, appearing after special staining procedures as orderly stripes, with all the cells in a slab responding mainly to inputs from the same eye, and in layer 4C, which receives inputs directly from the *lateral geniculate nuclei, responding only to inputs from the dominant eye for that particular slab. The anatomical basis of this alternation is that each axon from the lateral geniculate nucleus, after ascending through the deep layers of the cortex, terminates in layer 4C in two or three half-millimetre wide clusters of synaptic endings, such clusters being separated by half-millimetre gaps that are occupied by clusters of synaptic endings of axons from the other eye,

resulting in an orderly alternation of left and right dominance columns. Also called an *eye-dominance column*. See also ocular dominance. Compare orientation column.

ocular drift n. One of the forms of *physiological nystagmus, consisting of a random movement of the eyes through a *visual angle of up to 5 minutes of arc (sixtieths of a degree). Such movements occur while an observer fixates an object and are necessary to prevent the visual image from disappearing, as an artificially *stabilized retinal image does after about a second. See also microsaccade, ocular tremor.

ocular nystagmus n. Another name for *nystagmus.

ocular pursuit movement n. Another name for a *pursuit movement.

ocular tremor n. One of the forms of *physiological nystagmus, consisting of a continuous high-frequency *tremor with a frequency between about 60 and 120 hertz and an amplitude of about 30 seconds of arc (1/120 of a degree) that is present when the gaze is fixated on a stationary object or image. See also microsaccade, ocular drift.

oculogyral illusion n. A visual illusion of motion that arises when a person's body rotates in darkness together with a small light rotating at the same velocity as the body. The impression is created of the light moving horizontally with respect to the body, as adaptation of the *vestibular system causes the person to underestimate the velocity of the body's rotation.
[From Latin *oculus* the eye + *gyrus* a circle + *-alis* of or relating to]

oculomotor apraxia See under apraxia.

oculomotor cue n. *Kinaesthetic information about *ocular convergence received from the *extra-ocular muscles of the eyes, providing a *cue (2) for visual *depth perception.
[From Latin *oculus* the eye + *motor* a mover, from *movere, motus* to move]

oculomotor nerve n. Either of the third pair of *cranial nerves, arising from the *superior colliculus and supplying some of the *extra-ocular muscles, the ciliary muscles that increase the convexity of the lens for *near vision, and the sphincter muscle of the *pupil. Paralysis of this nerve causes pupil dilation and divergent squint. *See also* Argyll Robertson pupil, ptosis.

[From Latin *oculus* the eye + *motor* a mover, from *movere* to move]

oddity problem *n.* A discrimination task in which an organism learns to select from a set of stimuli the one that differs from all of the others. It was first used in psychology in an experiment carried out by the US psychologist Andrew Janeway Kinnaman and reported in the *American Journal of Psychology* in 1902 in which food was hidden in a coloured beaker and presented to macaque monkeys among four grey beakers carefully matched for brightness with the coloured beaker, and the monkeys learned to choose the coloured beakers quickly and easily, which established their ability to perceive colours. *See also* dimension-abstracted oddity, generalized oddity problem.

odd-one-out test *n.* A type of *intelligence test item or subtest in which the respondent has to choose which of several alternatives is the odd one out. A typical (difficult) example is: *Which of the following is the odd one out? DET, DIS, EOJ, GEM, NEK.* Although various choices could be justified, the 'correct' answer to this item is *GEM*, because this is an abbreviated female name written backwards, and all the others are abbreviated male names written backwards.

odor *See* odour.

odorimetry *n.* The measurement of the characteristics of *odours. Also called *olfactometry*. *See also* Crocker–Henderson system, Henning's prism, olfactie, stereochemical theory, Zwaardemaker olfactometer, Zwaardemaker smell system.

odour *n.* The property of an aromatic substance associated with its characteristic smell, scent, fragrance, or aroma, perceived through the *olfactory receptors in the *nose. US *odor*. *See* olfaction. *See also* Crocker–Henderson system, cross-adaptation, flavour, Henning's prism, mixture suppression, odorimetry, odour adaptation, odour constancy, odour hallucination, stereochemical theory, Zwaardemaker smell system.

[From Latin *odor* a smell or odour]

odour adaptation *n.* A temporary reduction in sensitivity to an odour following prolonged exposure to it, the phenomenon that causes workers in noisome factories to be oblivious of the stench, except for a short while after they first arrive for work, and that makes people in general insensitive to their own body odours. US *odor adaptation*.

odour constancy *n.* The tendency for the perceived intensity of an odour to remain the same despite differences in the volume of air being drawn into the nose and therefore the amount of stimulation of the olfactory receptors. US *odor constancy*. *See also* perceptual constancy.

odour hallucination *n.* An odour experienced in the absence of any *olfactory stimulus, often a symptom of a neurological disorder. US *odor hallucination*. *See also* hallucination.

odour prism *n.* Another name for *Henning's prism. US *odor prism*.

odour square *n.* Another name for the *Crocker–Henderson system. US *odor square*.

Oedipal phase *n.* Another name for the *phallic stage, during which the *Oedipus complex is assumed to develop. According to Sigmund Freud (1856–1939), girls develop *penis envy during this phase.

Oedipus complex *n.* In *psychoanalysis, an organized collection of loving and hostile feelings of a child towards its parents, reaching its peak during the *phallic stage between 3 and 5 or 6 years of age, dissolving with the onset of the *latency period, and then re-emerging during the *genital stage, after which it is mastered with greater or lesser success through mature *object-choices. It manifests itself in its *positive* form as a sexual desire for the opposite-sex parent and a jealous hatred of the same-sex parent, in its *negative* (or *inverted*) form as a desire for the same-sex parent and hatred of the opposite-sex parent, and in its *complete* form as a blend of the positive and negative forms. Sigmund Freud (1856–1939) introduced the term in 1910 in an article entitled 'A Special Type of Choice of Object Made by Men' (*Standard Edition*, XI, pp. 165–75, at p. 171), and in a note added in 1920 to his book *Three Essays on the Theory of Sexuality* (1905) he as-

serted the universality of the complex: 'Every new arrival on this planet is faced with the task of mastering the Oedipus complex' (*Standard Edition*, VII, pp. 130–243, at p. 226*n*); but he never fully clarified his views regarding the nature of the complex in girls, and in an article on 'Female Sexuality' in 1931, he wrote: 'It is only in the male child that we find the fateful combination of love for one parent and simultaneous hatred for the other as a rival' (*Standard Edition*, XXI, pp. 225–43, at p. 229). The British-based Austrian psychoanalyst Melanie Klein (1882–1960) deviated from Freud in dating the onset of the complex to the first year of life. *See also* castration complex, complex (2), Electra complex, father complex, mother complex, phallus, superego. *Compare* Jocasta complex, Orestes complex.
[Named after the Greek legendary figure Oedipus, who killed his father Laius, married his mother Jocasta, and then blinded himself when the truth about his parenthood emerged, as recounted most famously in the play *Oedipus Rex* by Sophocles]

Oedipus effect *n.* In psychology and the social sciences, the effect of a prediction on the predicted event, the prediction either causing or preventing the event that it predicts, or more generally the influence of an item of information on the situation to which the information refers. The term was coined in 1936 by the Austrian-born British philosopher Karl R(aimund) Popper (1902–94) and published in a journal article in 1944, reprinted in book form in *The Poverty of Historicism* (Chapter 1, section 5) in 1957, and from it he deduced that '*exact and detailed* scientific social predictions are therefore impossible' (p. 14, italics in original). *See* self-defeating prophecy, self-fulfilling prophecy. *See also* experimenter expectancy effect, Pygmalion effect, unexpected hanging paradox.
[So called because the Greek legendary figure Oedipus killed his father, whom he had never seen before, as a direct result of the prophecy that had caused his father to abandon him]

oesophagus *n.* The section of the *alimentary canal between the *pharynx and the *stomach. US *esophagus*. Also called the *gullet*.
[From Greek *oisein* to be carried, from *pherein* to carry + *phagein* to eat]

oestradiol *n.* A potent *oestrogenic *steroid *sex hormone secreted by the *ovaries, a syn-

thetic form of which is used to treat oestrogen deficiency, especially in menopausal women, and breast cancer. US *estradiol*. *Compare* oestrone.
[From Latin *oestrus* a gadfly or frenzy + English *diol* a compound containing two hydroxyl groups, from Greek *dis* twice + English *-ol* denoting a compound containing a hydroxyl group, from *(alcoh)ol*]

oestrogen *n.* Any of a group of steroid hormones that are secreted by the ovaries during the female *oestrous cycle and that stimulate the development of female *secondary sexual characteristics. US *estrogen*, *estrogenic*. *See also* DHEA, stilboestrol. *Compare* testosterone. **oestrogenic** *adj.*
[From Latin *oestrus* a gadfly or frenzy, from Greek *oistros* a gadfly + Greek *genes* born or produced]

oestrone *n.* An *oestrogenic hormone secreted by the ovaries and found in the urine of pregnant females, having similar action and uses to *oestradiol. US *estrone*.
[From Latin *oestrus* a gadfly or frenzy + *-one* indicating a ketone, from Greek *-one* a feminine name suffix]

oestrous cycle *n.* The *feedback-controlled cycle of changes in the reproductive organs of many female mammals, consisting of a *follicular phase and a *luteal phase. It includes the menstrual cycle in women (and many female *anthropoid apes), in whom there is also a *menstrual phase. The anterior pituitary initially releases *follicle-stimulating hormone; this causes the ovary to produce *oestrogen; the oestrogen acts on the hypothalamus to inhibit further release of follicle-stimulating hormone and to stimulate the release of *luteinizing hormone instead by the anterior pituitary; this hormone triggers *ovulation and causes the ovary to produce *progesterone; when this hormone reaches the hypothalamus it inhibits further release of luteinizing hormone, thereby completing the cycle. US *estrous cycle*. *See also* menstrual cycle, pheromone.
[From Latin *oestrus* a gadfly or frenzy, from Greek *oistros* a gadfly + *kyklos* a circle or cycle]

oestrus *n.* The cyclically recurring period of fertility and sexual receptivity associated with the *oestrous cycle in most female mammals. In humans, fertility fluctuates but the effect on receptivity is a matter of controversy. US *estrus*.

[From Latin *oestrus* a gadfly or frenzy, from Greek *oistros* a gadfly]

off-centre cell *n.* A type of retinal *ganglion cell having a *centre-surround receptive field consisting of a central OFF area, in which stimulation tends to suppress neural responses by *lateral inhibition, and a surrounding ON area, in which stimulation tends to excite neural responses, so that the strongest response occurs when only the surrounding ring is stimulated. US *off-center cell*. Compare on-centre cell.

offender counselling *n.* A form of *counselling offered to people with criminal convictions. US *offender counseling*.

Ohm's acoustic law *n.* The proposition that the human auditory system responds to a complex sound by generating sensations of the separate components of the sound rather than a sensation of a single integrated sound; thus when we listen to an orchestra we hear the separate instruments although the ears receive only a single complex sound wave. *See also* Fourier analysis.

[Named after the German physicist Georg Simon Ohm (1784–1854) who formulated it in 1843]

olan *See* latah.

olanzapine *n.* An *atypical antipsychotic drug that blocks both *dopamine receptors and (more strongly) *serotonin receptors in the brain and is used in the treatment of *schizophrenia and other *psychotic (1) disorders. *See also* dopamine antagonist. Also called *Zyprexa* (trademark).

old woman/young girl figure *n.* Another name for the *young girl/old woman figure.

olfactie *n.* In *psychophysics, the smallest unit of odour intensity that can be detected reliably, expressed in terms of the tube length in the *Zwaardemaker olfactometer. *See also* difference threshold, odorimetry.

olfaction *n.* The sense of smell or the act or process of smelling, occurring when molecules of an aromatic substance are drawn into the upper nasal cavity and are captured by *olfactory receptor neurons that are specialized for specific kinds of *odours and that respond by generating nerve impulses and transmitting them to the *olfactory bulbs, the type or types of activated neurons indicating the quality of the odour and the number of activated neurons indicating its intensity, the input pattern being analysed in the olfactory bulbs and transmitted directly to the *olfactory cortex and the *amygdala, and from there to the *entorhinal cortex, where information from disparate sensory receptors is integrated. It is more effective than any other sense in reawakening memories from the distant past, especially the emotions associated with past experiences, though the literary passage most often cited in support of this phenomenon, quoted under *redintegration, actually refers to taste rather than smell. *See* chemoreceptor, olfactory bulb, olfactory cortex, olfactory epithelium, olfactory lobe, olfactory nerve, olfactory tract, rhinencephalon. *See also* Crocker–Henderson system, cross-adaptation, flavour, Henning's prism, mixture suppression, nose, odorimetry, odour, odour adaptation, odour constancy, odour hallucination, olfactory acuity, osmoreceptor (1), parosmia, pheromone, stereochemical theory, vomeronasal organ, Zwaardemaker smell system. **olfactory** *adj.* Of or relating to the sense of smell.

[From Latin *olfacere* to smell, from *olere* to smell + *facere*, *factum* to make + *-ion* indicating an action, process, or state]

olfactology *n.* The study of smells and of *olfaction.

olfactometry *n.* The measurement of *olfactory acuity and of the characteristics of odours. Also called *odorimetry*.

olfactory acuity *n.* Keenness or sharpness of the sense of smell. *See* olfaction, acuity.

olfactory bulb *n.* The slightly enlarged front end of the *olfactory tract, resembling a match head projecting from the front lower margin of each cerebral hemisphere, receiving nerve impulses from the olfactory receptors and sending impulses via the *olfactory nerve directly to the *olfactory cortex and the *amygdala, unique among sensory pathways in bypassing the thalamus entirely. *See also* olfaction.

olfactory cortex n. The *piriform cortex in the anterior temporal lobes and the hippocampal convolution, concerned mainly with the sense of smell, connected directly to the *amygdala, which controls the experience and expression of emotion, and the *hippocampus, which is responsible for the *consolidation of long-term memory. See also olfaction.

olfactory epithelium n. The *mucous membrane in the upper nasal cavity where the *olfactory receptors are situated. Also called the nasal epithelium. See also olfaction.

olfactory lobe n. Another name for the rhinencephalon, part of the forebrain in each cerebral hemisphere containing the *olfactory bulb, *olfactory tract, and *olfactory cortex, concerned largely with the sense of smell, but in humans also with *emotions. See also olfaction.

olfactory nerve n. Either of the first pair of *cranial nerves, supplying the organ of smell and unusual among sensory pathways in being connected via the *olfactory tract directly to the brain from the *olfactory bulb. See also olfaction.

olfactory receptor n. A type of *sensory receptor that is associated with *olfaction and that responds to aromatic substances drawn into the upper nasal cavity, where molecules bind to *bipolar neurons in the *olfactory epithelium, specialized for specific kinds of *odours, whose *axons are part of the *olfactory nerve, and the bipolar neurons respond by generating nerve impulses and transmitting them to the *olfactory bulbs. Also called an osmoreceptor, though that usage is ambiguous.

olfactory tract n. A band of nerve fibres clearly visible on the bottom of each cerebral hemisphere, resembling a long matchstick extending back from the *olfactory bulb to the *olfactory cortex and the *amygdala. See also olfaction.

oligodendrocyte n. A type of *neuroglial cell with few *dendrites and few branches, responsible for wrapping *myelin sheaths around *axons in the *central nervous system. Also called oligodendroglia. Compare Schwann cell.

[From Greek oligos few or little + dendron a tree + kytos a vessel]

oligophrenia n. An old-fashioned term for *mental retardation. **phenylpyruvic oligophrenia** n. Another name for phenylketonuria.
[From Greek oligos little or few + phren mind, originally midriff, the supposed seat of the soul + -ia indicating a condition or quality]

olivary nucleus See inferior olivary nucleus, superior olivary nucleus.

ololiuqui n. A *psychedelic and *hallucinogenic drug obtained from the seeds of the *morning glory plant Rivea corymbosa.
[From Nahuatl ololiuhqui one that covers, from ololoa to cover, alluding to the fact that the plant is a clinging vine]

omega process n. In *psychoanalysis, a term used by Sigmund Freud (1856–1939) to denote any function of the *perception–consciousness system. Also called a W process or a Pcpt-Cs process.

ommatidium n. Any of the simple eyes that make up the *compound eye of insects and some crustaceans, consisting typically of an external corneal lens beneath which is a crystalline *cone and a fourfold *rod called a rhabdom attached to a *photoreceptor and enclosed in a dark pigment. Compare eye. **ommatidia** pl.
[Latin ommatidium, from Greek ommatidion, from omma an eye]

omnivore n. An animal that eats both flesh and plants; more generally, a person or animal with indiscriminate eating habits. Compare carnivore, herbivore. **omnivorous** adj.
[From Latin omnis all + vorare to devour]

onanism n. Another name for *coitus interruptus or (less correctly) *masturbation.
[Named after Onan in Genesis 38:9 who deliberately spilled his seed on the ground when having intercourse with his brother's wife]

on-centre cell n. A type of retinal *ganglion cell having a *centre-surround receptive field consisting of a central ON area, in which stimulation tends to excite neural responses, and a surrounding OFF area, in which stimulation tends to suppress neural responses by *lateral inhibition, so that the strongest response occurs when only the central region is stimulated. US *on-center cell*. Compare off-centre cell.

one-group pretest–posttest design *n*. One of the most frequently used *quasi-experimental research designs in which a single group of research participants or subjects is pretested, given some treatment or *independent variable manipulation, then posttested. If the pretest and posttest scores differ significantly, then the difference may be attributed to the independent variable, but because the research design is not strictly experimental and there is no control group, this inference is uncertain, and the difference may be due to *extraneous variables such as *order effects or *regression towards the mean. *See also* interrupted time-series design, non-equivalent groups design.

oneiric *adj*. Of or relating to dreams. **oneirocritic** *n*. A dream-interpreter. **oneirocriticism** *n*. Dream interpretation. **oneirodynia** *n*. Troubled sleep. **oneiromancy** *n*. Divination through dream-interpretation. **oneiroscopy** *n*. Examination of dreams.
[From Greek *oneiros* a dream]

oneirophrenia *n*. A dreamlike state of consciousness. Also called *oneirism*.
[From Greek *oneiros* a dream + *phren* mind, originally midriff, the supposed seat of the soul + *-ia* indicating a condition or quality]

one-sample *t* test *n*. In statistics, a version of the *related scores *t* test to evaluate the significance of the departure of the mean of a single sample of scores from some specified value. *See also t* test.

1-tailed probability *n*. In *inferential statistics, the probability of obtaining a result as extreme as the one observed, and in the same direction, if the *null hypothesis is true. If the probability is small (by convention, often less than $p < 0.05$), then the null hypothesis may be rejected. Compare 2-tailed probability.
[The name refers to one tail of the relevant *probability distribution]

1-tailed test *n*. In *inferential statistics, a test of the significance of a departure from the *null hypothesis in one direction only, so that

a departure in the opposite direction, no matter how large, is attributed to chance. In a *2-tailed test*, a departure from the null hypothesis in either direction results in its rejection. Also called a *directional test*. *See also* 1-tailed probability.

one-way analysis of variance *See under* analysis of variance (ANOVA).

one-way screen *n*. A sheet of glass or other transparent material that both reflects and transmits light. If the area on one side of the screen is brightly lit and the area on the other dimmed, then it is possible to see through the screen from the dimmed side but not from the bright side. This device is used for research in which it is useful to be able to observe people without being observed. If the screen is made of half-silvered glass, then it is often called a *one-way mirror*.

ongoing time disparity *n*. Another name for *phase delay. Also called *ongoing disparity*.

onomastics *n*. The study or science of names and naming. It is usually divided into *anthroponomastics*, the study of personal names, and *toponomastics* or *toponymy*, the study of place names, but onomastics is often interpreted loosely as the study of personal names.
[From Greek *onoma* name]

onomatopoeic theory *n*. A theory of the origins of language, according to which words originated as imitations of natural sounds in the environment. US *onomatopeic theory*. Also (dismissively) called the *bow-wow theory* or *ding-dong theory*.
[From *onomatopoeia* the formation of words that are imitative of the sound of the concept designated]

ontogeny *n*. The sequence of development of an individual organism as distinguished from the evolution of a *species or other *taxonomic group. Also called *ontogenesis*. Compare phylogeny. **ontogenetic** or **ontogenic** *adj*.
[From Greek *on*, *ontos* being, present participle of *einai* to be + *genes* born]

ontology *n*. The branch of metaphysics devoted to the study of the nature of being or existence or the essence of things, including the

distinction between reality and appearance and whether mathematical entities exist outside of people's minds.
[From Greek *on, ontos*, the present participle of *einai* to be + *logos* word, discourse, or reason]

onychophagia *n.* Nail biting.
[From Greek *onyx, onychos* a nail or claw + *phagein* to consume + *-ia* indicating a condition or quality]

open-ended question *n.* A question framed in such a way as to encourage a full expression of an opinion rather than merely a yes/no answer or otherwise constrained response. An open-ended question allows the respondent to answer freely, without having to select an answer from a predetermined set or *response categories. Such questions are commonplace in *qualitative research, although responses to them present formidable problems of data analysis. In interviews or informal conversations, open-ended questions such as *What do you feel about X?* are more effective than *closed questions in initiating interactions or encouraging discussion. Also called an *open question*.

open-field test *n.* A procedure for measuring the activity of a rat or other small animal by placing it in an enclosed area of floor space, divided into squares, and counting the number of squares that it crosses in a specified time period.

open-loop control *n.* In *cybernetics, a control process in which there is no *feedback of the system's output to its input, such control being characteristic of *ballistic movements, *action slips, and some forms of *automatic processing. *Compare* closed-loop control.

openness to experience *n.* One of the *Big Five personality factors, characterized at the one extreme by such *traits as imagination, curiosity, and creativity, and at the other by shallowness and imperceptiveness. Also called *intellect*.

open node *n.* A *node (2) that is awaiting processing. *Compare* closed node.

open study *n.* A research design in which both the experimenter and the research participants or subjects know the purpose of the study and which experimental treatment has been applied to which individuals. *Compare* double-blind study, single-blind study.

open vowel *n.* A *vowel (see the diagram accompanying that entry) produced at a low position in the mouth with the tongue low in the mouth and the jaw lowered, such as the vowels in *father* and *lot*, or the first element of the *diphthongs in *price* and *mouth*, which is the same as the vowel in the German *Mann*. Also called a *low vowel*. *Compare* close vowel, mid vowel.

operant *n.* Any *response by an organism that is not directly caused by a *stimulus (7) but is freely *emitted behaviour.

operant conditioning *n.* One of the two major forms of *conditioning (1), the *learning (1) process whereby the relative frequency of a *response increases as a result of reward or *reinforcement (1) that is contingent on the response being emitted. Also called *instrumental learning, respondent conditioning,* or *Skinnerian conditioning. See also* avoidance conditioning, behaviourism, cumulative record, escape conditioning, reinforcement schedule, secondary reinforcement, shaping (1), Skinner box.

operating characteristic *See* memory operating characteristic, receiver operating characteristic.

operation *See* mental operation.

operational definition *n.* A definition of a concept couched in terms of the operations or procedures by which it may be observed, measured, or distinguished from other things, a standard example being 'intelligence is what intelligence tests measure'. *See also* operationalism.

operationalism *n.* A largely abandoned doctrine of *logical positivism, propounded by the US philosopher of science Percy W. Bridgman (1882–1961) in his book *The Logic of Modern Physics* (1927), according to which concepts derive their meaning solely from the operations through which they are observed so that, for example, intelligence is defined as whatever intelligence tests measure. Also called *operationism. See also* operational definition. **operationalistic** *adj*. Of or relating to *operationalism. **operationalize** *vb*. To make operational or to formulate an *operational definition of something.

operational research *n*. A mathematically based approach to corporate decision making using techniques of optimization, dynamic programming, control theory, computer simulation, and statistical analysis. The term was coined and the technique introduced during the Second World War when scientific planning and management of military operations was first implemented. Also (especially in the US) called *operations research. See also* Monte Carlo method. **OR** *abbrev*.

operational stage *n*. A general term for *concrete operations and *formal operations.

operator (gene) *See* gene operator.

operatory stage *n*. Another name for an *operational stage. *See* concrete operations, formal operations.

operculum *n*. Any outer covering or lid of a structure in a living organism, such as one of the flaps covering the gill slits in a fish, and especially the parietal operculum and the temporal operculum that are the upper and lower lips of the *lateral sulcus in each cerebral hemisphere of the brain. **opercula** or **operculums** *pl*.
[From Latin *operculum* a lid, from *operire* to cover]

operon *n*. A group of adjacent *structural genes that are transcribed into a single molecule of *RNA and that function as a unit under the control of a single *gene operator.
[From *operate*, on the model of *codon*]

ophthalmic *adj*. Of or relating to the *eye. **ophthalmologist** *n*. A medical practitioner specializing in disorders of the *eye. **ophthalmology** *n*. The branch of medicine concerned with disorders of the *eye. **ophthalmoscope** *n*. An instrument for examining the interior of the *eye, comprising a light, a mirror perforated by a hole through which the examiner looks, and a rotating disc for positioning lenses of varying strengths in front of the hole.
[From Greek *ophthalmos* an eyeball, from *op(sethai)* to see + *thal(a)m(os)* an inner room or chamber, from *thalos* a vault + *-ik(os)* of, relating to, or resembling]

ophthalmoplegia *n*. Paralysis of the *extraocular muscles. *Compare* diplegia, hemiplegia, monoplegia, paraplegia, quadriplegia, triplegia. **ophthalmoplegic** *adj*.
[From Greek *ophthalmos* an eye + *plege* a blow + *-ia* indicating a condition or quality]

opiate *n*. Any of a group of chemical substances that contain *opium or an *alkaloid of opium and that tend to have *narcotic effects and are sometimes used as *analgesics (1), *anaesthetics (1), or cough suppressants. Also called *opioids*, especially when referring to the *endogenous opioids produced naturally in the brain. *See* heroin, morphine. *See also* nucleus accumbens, opioid antagonist, opioid-related disorders.
[From Latin *opium* poppy juice, from Greek *opion* diminutive of *opos* sap]

opinion *n*. A *proposition (1) that is accepted as true without compelling grounds, therefore falling short of being a *belief and far short of constituting *knowledge. **opine** *vb*.

opinion leader *n*. An individual belonging to a small minority in any community who tend to respond to messages in the mass media and to have a disproportionate effect on public opinion and behaviour through face-to-face communication with many friends, relatives, and acquaintances and by setting behavioural examples. *See* two-step flow.

opioid *See* opiate.

opioid antagonist *n*. Any drug such as *nalorphine, *naloxone, or *naltrexone that binds to the neuroreceptor sites of the *opiates in the central nervous system and thereby blocks their action. Also called a *narcotic antagonist*. *See also* antagonist (3).

opioid-related disorders *n*. *Substance-related disorders induced by consuming *opiates or opioids, including natural opiates such as *morphine, semi-synthetic compounds such as *heroin, and fully synthetic compounds with morphine-like effects such as *codeine, *methadone, and *meperidine. *See* substance abuse, substance dependence, substance-induced disorders, substance use disorders.

opium *n.* A *narcotic drug extracted as a bitter-tasting, yellow-brown milky juice from the unripe seed pods of the opium poppy *Papaver somniferum*, containing *alkaloids such as *morphine and *codeine, used medicinally to induce *analgesia, also smoked as an intoxicant with euphoric effects, often leading to *dependence (2). *See also* Dover's powder, laudanum, opiates, opioid-related disorders, paregoric, substance dependence.
[From Latin *opium* poppy juice, from Greek *opion* diminutive of *opos* vegetable juice or sap]

Oppel illusion *n.* Another name for the *filled-space illusion.
[Named after the German physicist Johann Joseph Oppel (1815–94) who first reported it in 1860–61]

Oppel–Kundt illusion *n.* Another name for the *filled-space illusion. Also called the *Oppel illusion*.
[So called because it was first described in 1860–61 by the German physicist Johann Joseph Oppel (1815–94) and further investigated in 1863 by the German physicist August Adolph Eduard Eberhardt Kundt (1838–94)]

opponent cell *n.* A type of neuron in the *lateral geniculate nucleus that responds maximally to light of one particular range of wavelengths and is maximally inhibited by light of a different range of wavelengths. Also called an *opponent neuron*. *Compare* non-opponent cell.
[From Latin *opponere* to oppose, from *ob* against + *ponere* to place]

opponent-process theory *n.* The theory of colour vision put forward by the German psychologist and physiologist Ewald Hering (1834–1918), or any of its more recent variants, according to which there are three classes of bipolar *photoreceptors or visual *afferent neurons responding to white versus black, red versus green, and blue versus yellow differences in visible light. Physiological research has shown this theory to be essentially correct for stages of the visual system after the initial receptor stage, whereas the *trichromatic theory, according to which colour vision depends on three types of receptors responsive to the *primary colours (1), is essentially correct at the receptor level. Also called the *tetrachromatic theory*. *See also* achro-

matic system, blue–yellow cell, red–green cell.

opportunity sample *n.* A *non-probability sample comprising a pre-existing serviceable group, such as the children on a school outing or the patients on a hospital ward. *See also* accidental sample, convenience sample, quota sample, self-selected sample, snowball sample. *Compare* cluster sample, probability sample, random digit dialling, simple random sample, stratified random sample.

opposites test *n.* Another name for an *antonym test.

oppositional defiant disorder *n.* A *conduct disorder of childhood characterized by recurrent negativistic, defiant, disobedient, or hostile behaviour towards authority figures, including such signs and symptoms as temper tantrums, arguing with adults, actively defying rules, deliberately annoying people, unfairly blaming others for mistakes or misbehaviour, being touchy or easily annoyed, angry, resentful, spiteful, or vindictive, with the pattern of behaviour leading to significant impairment in social, academic, or occupational functioning.

opsin *n.* A protein that is one of the two constituents of *rhodopsin. *See also* retinene.
[A *back formation from *rhodopsin*, as if it were the opsin of the r(h)ods]

optacon *n.* An electronic aid for blind people that transforms a pattern of light-intensity differences into a pattern of vibrations that can be felt by the fingertips, making possible such activities as reading printed text. *Compare* Braille, optohapt.
[Coined from Greek *optikon* neuter of *optikos* of or relating to vision, modified to avoid *opticon*, a word already in use for an enlargement of the optic lobe in an insect brain associated with its compound eye]

optic agnosia *See under* agnosia.

optical character recognition *n.* The process whereby a device called an *optical character reader* scans printed characters, or occasionally and less successfully handwriting, performs some form of *template matching to identify letters, numbers, or other characters, and inputs the information to a computer or other storage system. *See also* Pandemonium (1). **OCR** *abbrev.*

optical flow *n.* The instantaneous velocity of points in a retinal image or visual field, resulting either from movements of objects or images in the visual field or from movements of the head or eyes. Also called *optic flow*.

optical illusion *n.* Another name for a *visual illusion.

optic apraxia *See under* apraxia.

optic ataxia *n.* A form of *ataxia involving a selective inability to integrate information about the position of an object from *proprioceptive information about the position of one's hand or arm.
[From Greek *a-* without + *taxis* order + *-ia* indicating a condition or quality]

optic chiasm *n.* An area at the bottom of the brain immediately below the hypothalamus where *decussation (partial decussation in humans and other animals with forward-pointing eyes and therefore overlapping visual fields) of the *optic nerve fibres occurs, with approximately half the fibres from each eye (the fibres from the *nasal retina of each eye) crossing over to the opposite *cerebral hemisphere. The effect of this is that images from the left visual field of both eyes are transmitted to the right cerebral hemisphere and images from the right visual field to the left cerebral hemisphere, enabling information from corresponding points in the visual fields of the eyes to come together in the visual cortex for binocular depth perception. In animals such as rabbits with much smaller overlap of visual fields, almost all the fibres are crossed. Also called the *optic chiasma*. *See also* binocular cell.
[From Greek *optikos* optic, from *optos* seen + *chiasma* a cross, named after the shape of the upper-case letter chi (X)]

optic disc *n.* Another name for the *blind spot (1). US *optic disk*.

optic nerve *n.* Either of the second pair of *cranial nerves, carrying the entire output of the visual receptors in the retina, consisting of the axons of retinal *ganglion cells, passing through the *optic chiasm and terminating chiefly in one of the *lateral geniculate nuclei.

Some fibres of the optic nerve terminate in the *suprachiasmatic nucleus of the hypothalamus, which is implicated in the control of biological rhythms, and some travel by the *pretectal pathway and terminate in the pretectal nuclei. *See also* optic tract.

optic radiation *n.* A fibre of the visual system projecting from the *lateral geniculate nucleus to the *visual cortex.

optic tectum *n.* Part of the *tectum at the base of the pons in the roof of the midbrain containing the two *superior colliculi involved in visual orienting and localizing behaviour.
[From Greek *optikos* optic, from *optos* seen + Latin *tectum* a roof or canopy]

optic tract *n.* The part of each *optic nerve between the *optic chiasm and the *lateral geniculate nucleus. *See also* optic radiation, tectal pathway.

optimal foraging *n.* Searching for food using strategies that are most efficient or cost-effective in terms of minimizing metabolic energy or maximizing *Darwinian fitness, a phenomenon that has been demonstrated empirically in various species of animals although it is not a necessary prediction of the theory of evolution by *natural selection, which does not require that optimality ever be attained.

optimal movement *n.* A form of *apparent movement, indistinguishable from real movement, that occurs when two visual stimuli a few centimetres apart are presented in an alternating pattern with an interstimulus interval too long for the stimuli to appear simultaneous or for *partial movement to occur but not long enough for *phi movement or the disappearance of apparent movement and the veridical perception of the stimuli simply alternating. In optimal movement, a single stimulus appears to move smoothly and continuously back and forth across the space between the two actual stimuli. Also called *beta movement, stroboscopic movement*, or *optimal motion*. Often misleadingly called the *phi phenomenon*, a term that in careful usage is reserved for the phenomenon of *phi movement. *See also* Korte's laws.

optimism, unrealistic *See* unrealistic optimism.

optional stopping n. In sequential data-collection, halting the process in the light of the data collected up to that point, as when a researcher continues collecting scores just until the data support the hypothesis under investigation. This procedure is unacceptable, and it undermines the validity of any statistical tests that are later performed on the data.

optogram n. An image fixed or imprinted on the retina by the photochemical action of light on *rhodopsin.
[From Greek *optikos* of or relating to vision, from *optos* seen, from *ops* an eye + *gramme* a line]

optohapt n. An electronic device for blind people that converts printed text into vibrations that are transmitted to various locations on the body. Also called an *optophone*. Compare Braille, optacon, teletactor (for deaf people).
[Named by the US psychologist Frank A. Geldard (1904–84) who, with several colleagues, developed it in 1966, from Greek *optos* seen, from *ops* an eye + *haptein* to touch]

optokinetic nystagmus n. A form of *nystagmus characterized by smooth tracking movements of the eyes interspersed with *saccades, enabling an object or image moving across the visual field to be perceived more or less continuously. **OKN** abbrev.
[From Greek *optos* seen + *kinetikos* of or relating to motion, from *kineein* to move + *nystagmos* nystagmus, from *nystazein* to nap]

oral adj. Of or relating to the mouth, or expressed in spoken rather than written form (as in an *oral agreement* or an *oral examination*). Compare parenteral.
[From Latin *os, oris* the mouth]

oral–aggressive character n. In *psychoanalysis, a personality type resulting from *fixation (2) at the *oral sadistic phase and *sublimation of the impulses of that phase in later life. It is characterized by aggressiveness, exploitativeness, ambition, and envy. Also called an *oral–aggressive personality*.

oral apraxia n. A syndrome characterized by a reduced ability or inability to produce, on command, voluntary movements of the mouth, such as sticking the tongue out or opening the mouth, although these movements may be produced without difficulty in natural circumstances such as eating and drinking. See also apraxia.
[From Latin *os, oris* the mouth]

oral character n. In *psychoanalysis, a personality pattern determined by *fixation (2) in early childhood at the *oral stage, such a person being extremely dependent on others for maintenance of self-esteem and tending to relieve stress and depression by eating, drinking, talking, or smoking. Also called the *oral personality* or *oral–passive character*. See also oral–aggressive character, oral dependence.

oral dependence n. In *psychoanalysis, marked reliance on other people resulting from *fixation (2) at the *oral stage.

oral erotism n. In *psychoanalysis, sensuous pleasure derived from stimulation of the mouth and lips by kissing, smoking, eating, drinking, talking, engaging in *fellatio or *cunnilingus, or playing a wind instrument, and focusing of *libido on the mouth during the *oral stage. Also called *oral eroticism*. **oral–erotic** adj.

oral-incorporative phase n. Another name for the *early oral phase.

oral–passive character n. Another name for the *oral character. Also called the *oral–passive personality*.

oral primacy n. In *psychoanalysis, the phenomenon of *libido being focused first on the mouth and lips.

oral sadistic phase n. The second of the two phases of the *oral stage, corresponding to the teething period, according to a subdivision suggested in 1924 by the German psychoanalyst Karl Abraham (1877–1925) in his book *Versuch einer Entwicklungsgeschichte der Libido* (A Study of the Developmental History of the Libido). It is characterized by biting, in contrast to the *early oral phase, which is characterized by sucking. In a chapter in a co-authored book *Developments in Psycho-Analysis* in 1952, the British-based Austrian psychoanalyst Melanie Klein (1882–1960) rejected Abraham's distinction between the early sucking and later biting phases of the oral stage, and she declared the oral stage to be sadistic from the start: 'aggression forms part of the infant's earliest relation to the breast, though it is not usually expressed in biting at [the early] stage'. Also called the *oral sadistic stage* or the *cannibalistic stage*. *See also* oral–aggressive character.

oral stage *n*. In *psychoanalysis, the first *libidinal stage of *psychosexual development, occupying the first year of life, during which *libido is focused on the mouth and lips, as they are stimulated during feeding, through which the *object-relationship is expressed, the loving relationship towards the mother being experienced through ideas of eating and being eaten. During this stage, the *instinctual source is the oral zone, the *instinctual object is food, and the *instinctual aim is *incorporation. Sigmund Freud (1856–1939) had not developed this concept when the first edition of his book *Three Essays on the Theory of Sexuality* appeared in 1905, but the revised edition of 1915 included a full and detailed exposition of the theory. *See* early oral phase, oral sadistic phase. *See also* anal stage, genital stage, latency period, oral–aggressive character, oral character, phallic stage, polymorphous perversity. Also called the *oral phase*.

Orbison illusion *n*. A visual illusion caused by overlaying a simple geometric figure such as a circle or a square on a pattern of concentric circles or radiating lines, the effect being to distort the apparent shape of the figure (see illustration). It is closely related to *Ehrenstein's square illusion and the *Ponzo illusion.
[Named after US psychologist William Dillard Orbison (1911–52) who first drew attention to it in 1939]

orbitofrontal cortex *n*. The area of the *prefrontal cortex at the base of the anterior frontal lobes.
[From Latin *orbis* a circle, alluding to the bony cavities of the eye sockets]

order *n*. **1.** An arrangement or sequence of objects or elements; or an established or customary social system or structure, especially a social hierarchy. **2.** A command or instruction issued by a person in a position of authority over another. **3.** In biology, a *taxonomic group into which a *class (2) is divided, containing one or more *families (2). Thus the class of Mammalia (mammals) includes the orders Carnivora and Primates, each of which is divided into families.
[From Latin *ordo* an order]

ordered recall *n*. A test of *short-term memory in which the respondent is presented with a sequence of items, usually numbers, and then tries to repeat them back in the same order. The *Wechsler scales include both ordered recall and *backward span subtests.

order effect *n*. In research methods, any *extraneous variable arising from the serial order in which the procedures are administered or the measurements taken, for example fatigue (which may lead to a decline in performance on later measurements) or learning and practice (which may lead to improved performance on later measurement). *See also* counterbalancing (1), Latin square, one-group pretest–posttest design.

ordinal scale *n*. A scale of measurement in which data are arranged in order of magnitude but there is no standard measure of degrees of difference between them, for example a ranking of tennis players. *See also* measurement level, rank, scale (1), unfolding technique. *Compare* absolute scale, interval scale, log-interval scale, nominal scale, ratio scale.
[From Latin *ordinalis* of the order in a sequence, from *ordo* a row or order]

orectic *adj*. Of or relating to appetite or desire.
orexis *n*. Appetite or desire.
[From Greek *orexis* appetite, from *oregein* to reach for]

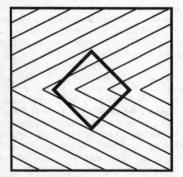

Orbison illusion. The inner square and the bounding square both appear distorted.

Orestes complex n. In *psychoanalysis, a son's desire to kill his mother. *Compare* Oedipus complex.
[Named after Orestes in Greek mythology, the son of Agamemnon and Clytemnestra, who killed his mother and her lover in revenge for the murder of his father]

organelle n. A specialized structure such as a *mitochondrion, having a particular function or group of functions within a cell.
[From Latin *organella* a little organ, diminutive of *organum* an organ]

organ erotism n. In *psychoanalysis, the focusing of *libido in specific organs at different stages or phases of development. Also called *organ eroticism* or *organ libido*. *See* anal erotism, oral erotism, phallic erotism, urethral erotism.

organic affective disorders n. Another name for organic *mood disorders. *See* organic disorders.

organic brain syndrome n. Another name for an *organic disorder. **OBS** abbrev.

organic disorders n. Disorders involving a physical *lesion in an organ or body part. An organic mental disorder is one involving disease, dysfunction, or damage affecting the brain, arising from a primary brain disorder or injury, a disorder in another part of the body with secondary effects in the brain, or the effects of a toxic substance. Included in this category are various forms of *dementia, *cerebral arteriosclerosis, organic *affective disorders, organic *anxiety disorder, organic *catatonic disorder, organic *delusional disorder, organic *dissociative disorder, *organic hallucinosis, organic *mood disorder, organic *personality disorder, *postencephalitic syndrome, and *postconcussional disorder. Also called *organic brain syndromes* (OBS).
[From Greek *organikos* of or pertaining to an organ, from *organon* an implement, from *ergein* to work]

organic hallucinosis n. A *mental disorder of persistent or recurrent *hallucinations occurring in clear consciousness, sometimes not recognized by the hallucinator as such, arising as a consequence of an *organic disorder. *See also* alcohol hallucinosis, hallucinosis.

organic mental disorders *See under* organic disorders. *Compare* psychogenesis.

organism n. Any living thing, including a human or other animal, a plant, a fungus, a protist, a bacterium, or a virus. *See also* kingdom (2).
[From *organize*]

organizational psychology n. The field of applied psychology devoted to the structures and functions of organizations and the activities of the people within them. It is applied not only in industrial organizations, but also in schools, hospitals, prisons, military units, and other non-industrial organizations. It focuses on such psychological problems as job satisfaction, employee attitudes and motivation, and their effects on absenteeism, labour turnover, and organizational productivity and efficiency. *See also* industrial/organizational psychology.

organization, Gestalt principle of n. Another name for a Gestalt *grouping law.

organ libido n. Another name for *organ erotism.

organ neurosis n. A term used in *psychoanalysis to denote a *psychosomatic disorder.

organ of Corti n. A spiral structure within the *cochlea of the inner ear, containing the *basilar membrane in which are situated *hair cells that convert sound waves into nerve impulses. Also called *Corti's organ*.
[Named after the Italian anatomist Alfonso Corti (1822–76) who was the first to describe the structure of the inner ear in detail in 1851]

organ of Golgi n. Another name for a *Golgi tendon organ.
[Named after the Italian cytologist Camillo Golgi (1844–1926) who gave the first complete description of it in 1880]

organophosphate n. Any of a group of *anticholinesterase compounds used as insecticides and pesticides that cause irreversible suppression of *cholinesterase. Also called an *organophosphorus compound*. *See also* nerve gas, organophosphate poisoning. **OP** abbrev.
[From *organo-* indicating a compound containing an organic group + *phosphate*]

organophosphate poisoning *n*. A condition resulting from exposure to *organophosphates, with signs and symptoms such as amnesia, anxiety, depression, aphasia, and asthenia. *See also* Gulf War Syndrome, nerve gas. *Compare* chronic fatigue syndrome.

organum vasculosum lamina terminalis *n*. A structure bordering the third *ventricle of the brain, believed to contain receptors for *angiotensin II and thus to play a part in *hypovolaemic thirst. **OVLT** *abbrev*.
[Latin: vascular organ end plate]

orgasm *n*. The culminating phase of the *sexual response cycle in which sexual pleasure reaches a peak with release of tension and rhythmic contraction of the *perineal muscles and sex organs, accompanied in the male by a sensation of ejaculatory inevitability followed by *ejaculation (1) of semen and contraction of the anal sphincter, and in the female by contractions of the wall of the *vagina and the anal sphincter. **orgasmic** *adj*. Of or relating to an *orgasm. **orgasmic phase** *n*. The third phase of the *sexual response cycle, when *orgasm occurs.
[From Greek *orgasmos* a swelling]

orgasmic dysfunctions *n*. Another name for *female orgasmic disorder and *male orgasmic disorder. Also called *orgasm disorders* or *orgasmic disorders*. *See also* impotence (2).

orgasmic impotence *See under* impotence (2).

orgone therapy *n*. A form of *psychotherapy and cure for physical ailments proposed by the Austrian (later US-based) psychiatrist Wilhelm Reich (1897–1957) in his book *The Function of the Orgasm* (1927/42), involving a specially constructed orgone box or orgone accumulator designed to capture a supposed vital substance called orgone energy. Reich believed that mental and physical health depended on having as many orgasms as possible. Also called *Reichian therapy*. *See also* body therapies.
[Coined as a blend of *org(asm)* and *(horm)one*]

orientation column *n*. A slender slab, extending through the full thickness of the *primary visual cortex (Area V1), consisting of cells that are selectively responsive to stimuli oriented at a particular angle in their *recep-

tive fields, the specific angle changing from one orientation column to the next by a regular amount of 10 degrees clockwise or anticlockwise for every horizontal movement of 0.05 millimetre, or a full circuit of 180 degrees per millimetre (approximately). With appropriate biochemical staining, orientation columns in the primary visual cortex of an organism being stimulated by parallel stripes oriented at a particular angle show up as a complex but regular configuration of 1-millimetre stripes unrelated to the pattern of *ocular-dominance columns.

orientation-specific cell *n*. A general term for a *simple cell, *complex cell, or *hypercomplex cell that responds selectively to stimuli oriented at a specific angle in its *receptive field. Also called an *orientation-selective cell*. *See also* twisted-cord illusion.

orienting response *n*. The characteristic behavioural and physiological *response to a novel or potentially threatening stimulus, including focusing attention on the source of the stimulus, turning the head and body towards it, and arousal of the *reticular activating system and the *sympathetic nervous system. Also called the *orienting reaction* or *orienting reflex*.
[From Latin *oriens, orientis* rising, present participle of *oriri* to rise]

orphan drug *n*. A potentially useful drug that the major pharmaceutical companies are unwilling to market or promote, typical examples being *inositol, *lithium carbonate, and *St John's wort, none of which can be patented because they occur naturally.

orthodromic *adj*. Of or relating to a nerve impulse conducted in the normal direction, from the axon hillock towards the axon terminal. *Compare* antidromic.
[From Greek *orthos* right + *dromos* a course or run + *-ikos* of, relating to, or resembling]

orthogonal *adj*. **1**. Of, relating to, or consisting of right angles. **2**. In mathematics, (of a pair of vectors) having a scalar product equal to zero. **3**. In statistics, in relation to a *contrast (3), having coefficients that sum to zero.
[From Greek *orthos* straight, right, upright + *gonia* an angle]

orthographic agraphia *See under* agraphia.

orthography n. **1.** Correct spelling or the principles underlying spelling. *Compare* cacography. **2.** A system of writing.
[From Greek *orthos* straight, right + *graphein* to write]

orthomolecular therapy n. An approach to the treatment of *mental disorders based on the doctrine that every disorder can be alleviated with a specific chemical substance. The approach was developed by the Nobel prizewinning US chemist Linus (Carl) Pauling (1901–94). Also called *megavitamin therapy*, *orthomolecular psychiatry*, *vitamin therapy*.
[From Greek *orthos* right + English *molecular*]

orthopsychiatry n. An approach to *psychiatry that emphasizes preventive techniques and collaboration between psychiatry, psychology, social work, and other behavioural, social, and clinical sciences.
[From Greek *orthos* right + English *psychiatry*]

oscillating figure n. Another name for an *ambiguous figure.

osmometric thirst n. Another name for *intracellular thirst.
[From *osmosis* + Greek *metron* a measure]

osmoreceptor n. **1.** Another name for an *olfactory receptor. **2.** A type of neuron located primarily in the *preoptic nuclei at the front of the hypothalamus, sensitive to cellular dehydration, able to signal changes in *osmotic pressure, triggering *intracellular thirst, and also monitoring concentrations of substances in the blood and regulating the secretion of *vasopressin.
[A blend of Greek *osme* a smell (sense 1) or English *osmosis* (sense 2) + English *receptor*]

osmosis n. The diffusion of a solvent such as water across a *semipermeable membrane from the side where the solution is less concentrated to the side where it is more concentrated until the concentration and the *osmotic pressure on both sides is equalized. *See also* cell membrane. *Compare* dialysis. **osmotic** adj.
[From Greek *osmos* thrust or impulse + *-osis* indicating a process or state]

osmotic pressure n. The pressure exerted by a solution through the motion of its molecules, measured according to the pressure required

to prevent *osmosis of the pure solvent into it. *See also* hypertonic (2), hypotonic (2), isotonic (2), osmoreceptor (2), sodium pump.

osmotic thirst n. Another name for *intracellular thirst.

osphresiolagnia n. A *paraphilia characterized by recurrent sexually arousing fantasies, sexual urges, or behaviour involving smells. *See also* renifleur.
[From Greek *osphresis* a smell + *lagneia* lust]

osphresis n. Another name for *olfaction.
osphretic adj. Capable of being smelled.
[From Greek *osphresis* sense of smell]

osseous labyrinth n. Another name for the *bony labyrinth.
[From Latin *osseus* bony, from *os* a bone]

ossicle n. Any of the three tiny bones in the *middle ear, the *malleus (hammer), *incus (anvil), or *stapes (stirrup).
[From Latin *ossiculum* a little bone, from *os* a bone]

Othello syndrome n. Morbid and irrational jealousy or, if sufficiently severe, *jealous delusional disorder.
[Named after Shakespeare's play *Othello* and the eponymous character whose sexual jealousy leads him to murder his innocent wife]

other, significant *See* significant other.

otic adj. Of or relating to the ear.
[From Greek *otikos* of or relating to the ear, from *ous, otos* an ear + *-ikos* of, relating to, or resembling]

otitis n. Inflammation of the ear, sometimes causing deafness. **otitis externa** n. Inflammation of the external canal or the pinna of the outer ear, causing itching, weeping or discharge, and sometimes hearing loss and pain, often related to anxiety or stress. **otitis media** n. Inflammation of the middle ear, generally causing hearing loss and pain, a common affliction of childhood.
[From Greek *ous* an ear + *-itis* indicating an inflammation]

otoconium n. Another name for an *otolith.
otoconia pl.

[From Greek *ous, otos* an ear + *konis, konia* ashes, alluding to their appearance when viewed without magnification]

otogenic tone *n.* A *tone (1) that is not present in the sound wave entering the ear but is generated by the ear or the auditory system itself. *See also* combination tone, missing fundamental illusion.
[From Greek *ous, otos* an ear + *genes* born or produced + *-ikos* of, relating to, or resembling]

otolith *n.* Any of the tiny crystals of calcium carbonate, with a density of 2.95 grams per cubic centimetre, almost three times the density of water, in the *utricle and *saccule within the *vestibular system of a vertebrate animal, playing an important part in the vestibular system of the inner ear, responsive to linear acceleration, and partly responsible for the sense of balance and orientation. Linear acceleration of the head causes the *hair cells embedded in the *otolith receptor* to move with it, but the dense otoliths resist acceleration and tend to hold the gelatinous membrane stationary, causing the hair cells that protrude into the membrane to bend backwards and trigger adjacent neurons to transmit nerve impulses to the brainstem and cerebellum. The otolith organs are also responsive to gravity, which according to the general theory of relativity formulated by the German-born US physicist Albert Einstein (1879–1955) is equivalent to accelerating an object upwards at 9.8 metres per second squared. Also called a *statolith*. *See also* saccule, statocyst. *Compare* endolymph.
[From Greek *ous, otos* an ear + *lithos* a stone]

otology *n.* The study of the ear, including prevention, diagnosis, and treatment of its disorders.
[From Greek *ous, otos* an ear + *logos* word, discourse, or reason]

otosclerosis *n.* A hereditary disorder of the middle ear, usually appearing before age 30 years, affecting twice as many women as men and often worsening during pregnancy. When it occurs, parts of the *bony labyrinth become irregularly ossified and the *stapes (stirrup) becomes immobilized, causing tinnitus and then deafness.
[From Greek *ous, otos* an ear + *sklerosis* a hardening, from *skleros* hard + *-osis* indicating a process or state]

ototoxic *adj.* Damaging to the *vestibulocochlear nerve or the organs of hearing or balance, characteristic of drugs including *aspirin, *quinine, and many antibiotics if taken in excess. **ototoxic deafness** *n.* Deafness caused by *ototoxic drugs. *See also* sensorineural deafness.
[From Greek *ous, otos* an ear + *toxikon* arrow-poison, from *toxon* a bow + *-ikos* of, relating to, or resembling]

Ouchi illusion *n.* A visual illusion in which a chequered pattern of small black and white rectangles, containing a circular region in which the rectangles are oriented at right-angles to those in the rest of the figure, creates an impression of relative motion when the whole pattern is moved (see illustration), the illusion being caused by the excitation of spatially overlapping ON and OFF regions of *centre-surround receptive fields of retinal neurons. Also spelt *Ōuchi illusion*.
[Named after the Japanese graphic artist Hajime Ōuchi who first published it in a book of graphic designs in 1973]

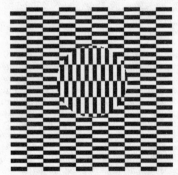

Ouchi illusion. An illusion of relative motion, most vividly seen if the image is moved slowly from side to side or in a circle.

Ouija board *n.* A board marked with letters of the alphabet, used in *parapsychology to spell out answers to questions with a pointer or inverted glass held by the fingertips of a group of participants, the answers supposedly coming from the spirits of dead people.
[From French *oui* yes + German *ja* yes]

outbreeding *n.* Producing offspring through mating between parents that are not closely related. Also called *exogamy*.

outer ear n. The sound-collecting part of the *ear, comprising the *pinna and the *external auditory canal, separated from the middle ear by the *tympanic membrane. Also called the *external ear*. *Compare* inner ear, middle ear.

outer hair cell n. Any of approximately 25,000 *hair cells in the *organ of Corti, specialized as *transducers of sound waves into nerve impulses and sensitive to low sound levels, easily damaged by loud noise (over 85 decibels), and probably involved in encoding information about the loudness of sounds. *Compare* inner hair cell. **OHC** *abbrev.*
[So called because they are nearer to the outside of the cochlea than are the inner hair cells]

outer nuclear layer n. A stratum of the *retina containing the cell bodies of the *photoreceptors.
[So called because the nuclei of the rods and cones are situated there]

outer plexiform layer n. A thin stratum of the *retina, separating the middle and outer retinal layers, within which the *photoreceptors terminate and make synaptic connections with *bipolar cells and *horizontal cells. *See also* interplexiform cell.
[From Latin *plexus* a network, from *plectere* to weave]

outlier n. In statistics, an extreme score that is widely separated from the rest of the scores and raises the possibility of an error in measurement, recording, or data entry.

out-of-body experience n. A form of *depersonalization characterized by a sense of detachment from one's body and perception of oneself from a distance, usually from above. It is often associated with sleep deprivation, some forms of drug intoxication, or mental disorders such as *schizophrenia and certain *dissociative disorders. It is sometimes (and perhaps generally) triggered by *sleep paralysis. **OBE** or **OOBE** *abbrev.*

out-of-level testing n. In psychometrics, administering a test that is designed for a different age of grade level from that of the respondent.

outplacement counselling n. A form of *counselling offered to people facing redundancy from work. US *outplacement counseling*.

oval window n. An opening in the wall of the *middle ear, leading to the *inner ear, containing the footplate of the *stapes, which transmits vibrations to the *cochlea. Also called the *fenestra ovalis*. *See also* round window.
[So called because of its elliptical shape]

ovarian follicle n. Another name for a *Graafian follicle.

ovary n. Either of the two female sex glands or gonads that secrete sex hormones such as *oestrogen, *progesterone, and *oestrone into the bloodstream and release *ova. *Compare* testis. **ovarian** *adj.*
[From Latin *ovarium* an egg-container, from *ovum* an egg]

overanxious disorder n. A childhood *anxiety disorder, not included in the *DSM-IV classification, corresponding to *generalized anxiety disorder in adults, in which anxiety is focused on such matters as personal appearance, health, and academic or sporting achievement at school.

overattribution bias n. Another name for the *fundamental attribution error.

overconfidence effect n. Unwarranted belief in the correctness of one's judgements or beliefs. Many studies have used general knowledge quiz questions to which respondents give answers and also confidence ratings indicating their estimates of their probability of being correct, from 0 per cent certain to 100 per cent certain. Average estimates of probability of being correct—confidence ratings—tend to be much higher than average percentages of responses that turn out actually to be correct. For moderately difficult items, average confidence ratings tend to be around 90 per cent when approximately 65 to 70 per cent of the answers are correct, and to approach 100 per cent when approximately 80 per cent of the answers are correct. *Anchoring and adjustment may account for the effect, and *hindsight bias is closely related to it. Research in this area can be traced to 1957 and was revived in the late 1970s following extensive research by the US psychologists Sarah C. Lichtenstein (born 1933) and Baruch Fischhoff (born 1946). *See also* depressive realism. *Compare* unrealistic optimism.

overcorrection *n.* Another name for *hypercorrection.

overdetermination *n.* In *psychoanalysis, a characteristic of dreams, symptoms, and other psychological phenomena of manifesting their causative factor more than once or providing more than one outlet for a wish or need. In his book *The Interpretation of Dreams* (1900), Sigmund Freud (1856–1939) described it as follows: 'Each of the elements of the dream's content turns out to have been "overdetermined"—to have been represented in the dream-thoughts many times over' (*Standard Edition*, IV–V, at p. 283). Overdetermination is a consequence of *condensation. Also called *multiple determination*. *See also* overinterpretation, psychical determinism. **overdetermined** *adj.*

overdominance *n.* A phenomenon associated with certain *heritable *traits in which a *heterozygote has a phenotype that is more extreme on some measurable dimension than either of the corresponding *homozygotes. Also called *superdominance*. *See also* dominance (genetic). *Compare* filial regression, regression towards the mean.

overextension *n.* The interpretation of a word, usually by a child during the course of language development in the second or third year, to denote more than it normally denotes, as when a child understands the word *daddy* to denote all men, or *cat* to denote all animals. *See also* concept formation. *Compare* mismatch, overgeneralization, underextension.

overflow response *n.* Another name for *vacuum activity.

overgeneralization *n.* In language acquisition, the extension of a grammatical rule beyond its range of applicability in standard usage, as in the use by a child of such formations as *foots* instead of *feet* and *goed* instead of *went*, or in response to a request to behave, *I am being have* instead of *I am behaving*. *Compare* mismatch, overextension, underextension.

overinclusiveness *n.* The use of a concept to encompass too broad a range of items, indicating an inability to preserve conceptual boundaries, so that distantly associated items become incorporated into concepts, making them abstract and obscure. It is characteristic of *thought disorder in *schizophrenia.

overinterpretation *n.* Deriving more meaning than the information warrants. In *psychoanalysis, it denotes an additional *interpretation, especially of a dream, following one that has already proved to be illuminating, the additional interpretations sometimes being worthwhile and sometimes not. In a key passage in his book *Introductory Lectures on Psycho-Analysis* (1916–17) Sigmund Freud (1856–1939) described it thus: 'The achievements of condensation can be quite extraordinary. It is sometimes possible by its help to combine two quite different latent trains of thought into one manifest dream, so that one can arrive at what appears to be a sufficient interpretation of a dream and yet in doing so can fail to notice a possible "overinterpretation"' (*Standard Edition*, XV–XVI, at p. 173). But in a famous passage in his book *The Interpretation of Dreams* (1900), he wrote: 'There is often a passage in even the most thoroughly interpreted dream which has to be left obscure; this is because we become aware during the work of interpretation that at that point there is a tangle of dream-thoughts which cannot be unravelled and which moreover adds nothing to our knowledge of the content of the dream. This is the dream's navel, the spot where it reaches down into the unknown' (*Standard Edition*, IV–V, at p. 525). *See also* overdetermination. **overinterpreted** *adj.*

overjustification *n.* Rewarding a person for performing a task that the person considers adequately rewarded or worth doing for its own sake, often resulting in a reduction in the person's liking for the task. Also called *oversufficient justification*.

overlearning *n.* Additional learning carried out after a skill has been learned to a high criterion. Although the skill does not improve as a result of overlearning, its long-term retention is generally improved and its vulnerability to distractors such as the *audience effect is generally reduced, as professional musicians and other performing artists are aware. *See also* overtraining extinction effect, overtraining reversal effect. **overlearn** *vb.*

overregularization *n.* A form of language, sometimes generated by children, in which grammatical rules are extended to irregular cases where they do not apply, leading to expressions such as *I eated my ice cream*. Also called *overregulation*.

oversufficient justification *n*. Another name for overjustification.

overtone *n*. A component of a *complex tone, having a frequency that is an integral multiple of the *fundamental frequency. The *first overtone*, also called the *second harmonic*, has twice the frequency of the fundamental and is therefore an *octave higher; the *second overtone* or *third harmonic* has three times the frequency of the fundamental; and so on. Also called a *harmonic*. *See also* missing fundamental illusion.

overtraining *n*. The continuation of *conditioning (1) beyond the point at which the organism shows no further increase in response rate. *See also* overlearning. **overtrain** *vb*.

overtraining extinction effect *n*. The tendency for an animal that has been subjected to *overtraining to show more rapid *extinction (2) than one that has not been overtrained. **OEE** *abbrev*.

overtraining reversal effect *n*. The tendency for an animal that has been subjected to *overtraining and is then presented with a *habit reversal learning task to learn to reverse its responses more quickly than an animal that has not been overtrained. **ORE** *abbrev*.

overvalued idea *n*. An irrational and sustained belief, not generally accepted by members of the culture or subculture of the person who holds it, falling short of being a *delusion inasmuch as the person is willing to entertain the possibility of its falsity.

ovulate *vb*. To release an *ovum from the *ovary. **ovulation** *n*. *See* oestrous cycle.
[From Latin *ovulum* a little egg, diminutive of *ovum* an egg]

ovum *n*. An unfertilized female gamete or egg. *Compare* zygote.
[From Latin *ovum* an egg]

oxidative metabolism *See* oxidative phosphorylation.

oxidative phosphorylation *n*. The process whereby energy released by oxidation is used to synthesize the energy-storing molecule *ATP. Also called *oxidative metabolism*. *See also* Krebs cycle.
[From *oxidation* + *phosphorus*, alluding to the fact that ATP is a phosphate, + *-ation* indicating an action, process, state, condition, or result]

oxycodone *n*. Oxycodone terephthalate, a *narcotic analgesic that is sometimes used as a street drug. Also called *Percodan* (trademark).

oxymoron *n*. A *figure of speech involving the combination of semantically contradictory elements, thus forcing a figurative interpretation, as in Milton's *living death* or, according to some, *British intelligence*. **oxymoronic** *adj*.
[From Greek *oxys* sharp + *moros* stupid]

oxymorphone *n*. Oxymorphone hydrochloride, a *narcotic analgesic drug, prescribed for moderate or severe pain and as a preoperative medication. Also called *Numorphan* (trademark).

oxytocin *n*. The *hormone and *neurotransmitter alphahypophame secreted by the posterior pituitary and also manufactured synthetically. In females it is secreted in response to sucking of the breast, stimulating lactation and contractions of the muscles of the uterus, and in males it is implicated in the ejaculatory response during sexual activity.
[From Greek *oxys* sharp + *tokos* birth]

P200 *n*. The first major positive deflection in an *event-related potential or an *average evoked potential, occurring about 200 milliseconds after the onset of the stimulus. Some researchers have claimed that its magnitude, or the acuteness of the angle between the *N140 and the P200, correlates with *IQ, but empirical findings are inconsistent. *Compare* string length. Also called the *P200 potential* or *P200 wave*.
[From p(ositive) 200 (milliseconds)]

P300 *n*. A large positive *evoked potential that occurs approximately 300 milliseconds after the presentation of a stimulus, especially one that is unexpected, interesting, or potentially important, and that is believed to indicate that the stimulus has been appraised. The P300 latency increases between 1 and 2 milliseconds per year of the adult lifespan. Also called the *P300 potential* or *P300 wave*.

pacemaker neuron *n*. Any of a number of different nerve cells in the autonomic nervous system that trigger regular cyclic activities, such as heartbeat, breathing, and EEG waves. The *suprachiasmatic nucleus is thought to have a role in regulating them. *See also* biological clock, biological rhythm.

pachymeninx *n*. Another name for the *dura mater.
[From Greek *pachys* thick + Greek *meninx* a membrane]

Pacinian corpuscle *n*. A type of sensory nerve ending, the size and colour of a grain of rice, attached to the end of a single nerve fibre in the *skin and joints, abundantly present along the sides of the fingers, in the palms, and in the joints, sensitive to pressure and vibration. Also called a *Pacinian body*, *Pacini's corpuscle*, or a *Vater–Pacini corpuscle*. *See also* pallaesthesia. *Compare* free nerve ending, Golgi tendon organ, Meissner's corpuscle, Merkel cell, Ruffini corpuscle.
[Named after the Italian anatomist Filippo Pacini (1812–83) who rediscovered it in the fingers in 1835 and gave a full description of it in 1840, although the German anatomist Abraham Vater (1684–1751) had discovered it some time prior to 1741]

Pac-Man *n*. A shape consisting of a circular disc with a missing segment, used as an icon in an electronic computer game in which the player's task is to guide the icon through a maze while devouring other icons and eluding attacks; also, because of its resemblance in shape, the name given to the symbol used at each vertex of a *Kanizsa triangle to create illusory contours. Also spelt *PacMan*, *Pacman*, or *pacman*.
[Trademark]

paedophilia *n*. A *paraphilia characterized by recurrent, intense sexual fantasies, urges, or behaviour involving sexual activity with prepubescent girls or boys. US *pedophilia*.
[From Greek *pais, paidos* a boy or child + *philos* loving, from *phileein* to love + *-ia* indicating a condition or quality]

pagophagia *n*. A form of *pica characterized by the eating of ice.
[From Greek *pagos* ice + *phagein* to consume + *-ia* indicating a condition or quality]

pain *n*. An unpleasant sensation usually caused by noxious stimulation of sensory nerve endings, defined in the *Classification of Nursing Diagnoses* of the North American Nursing Diagnosis Association as a state in which severe discomfort or an unpleasant sensation is experienced and signalled by the following: verbal and non-verbal communication, including self-protective behaviour; nar-

rowed attentional focus evidenced by altered time perspective, social withdrawal, or impaired thought processes; distraction behaviour such as moaning, crying, pacing, restlessness; a facial expression of pain characterized by dull and lustreless eyes, a beaten appearance, and fixed or scattered facial movements or grimaces; alteration of muscle tone ranging from listlessness to rigidity; and autonomic responses such as increased blood pressure and pulse rate, pupil dilation, and increased or decreased respiration rate. *See* acute pain, analgesia, chronic pain, cold pressor pain, ischaemic pain, pain receptor, referred pain, substance P. *See also* adaptation (2), algesimeter, audioanalgesia, C fibre, cingulate gyrus, delta fibre, dolorimeter, endorphin, enkephalin, flexion reflex, free nerve ending, gate-control theory, insula, neuralgia, peptide, periaqueductal grey matter, phantom limb, prostaglandin, somatosensory cortex, spinoreticulothalamic system, spinothalamic tract, substantia gelatinosa, vasopressin. **painful** *adj.*
[From Latin *poena* punishment or grief, from Greek *poine* penalty]

pain disorder *n.* A *somatoform disorder characterized by pain, causing clinically significant distress or impairment in social, occupational, or other important areas of functioning, with psychological factors judged to play an important role in the onset or maintenance of the pain. *Compare* factitious disorder, malingering.

pain principle *n.* In *psychoanalysis, the initial form of *Thanatos, when the destructive instinct is turned on oneself.

pain receptor *n.* Any of the *free nerve endings located throughout the body that function as *sensory receptors, transmitting sensations of *pain in response to noxious stimulation, one type (the *monomodal nocireceptor*) being a thinly myelinated *delta fibre that responds to severe mechanical deformation, the other (the *polymodal nocireceptor*) being a *C fibre that responds to mechanical deformation, excessive heat or cold, and irritant chemical stimulation, and is responsible for the *axon reflex. In the epidermis and dermis of the skin and in the mucous membranes, any form of stimulation, if intense enough, can stimulate pain receptors, whereas in the viscera only severe mechanical

deformation and certain chemicals are adequate stimuli for pain receptors. *Referred pain arises only from stimulation of deeplying pain receptors in viscera, joints, and muscles, and never from pain receptors in the skin. *See also* substance P.

paired-associate learning *n.* Learning connections between pairs of items, usually words, until one member of the pair elicits recall or recognition of the other. For example, the learner may be presented with a list of pairs such as *green—box, long—rope, heavy—stone*, and so on, and recall may be tested by listing the first member of each pair with a list of alternatives, for example *green—apple/box/dress/paper*, the learner trying to recognize the correct alternative. Such memory is called *associative memory. See also* serial anticipation method. **PA** or **PAL** *abbrev.*

paired comparisons *See* method of paired comparisons.

paired samples *t* test *n.* Another name for the *related scores *t* test.

palaeocortex *n.* The three-layered *olfactory cortex that evolved in humans earlier than most of the human cerebral cortex but not as early as the archaecortex. The word is sometimes used loosely for any part of the cerebral cortex that is not *neocortex. US *paleocortex*. Also called the *paleencephalon. See also* piriform cortex. *Compare* neocortex, mesocortex.
[From Greek *palaios* old + Latin *cortex* bark or outer layer]

palaeostriatum *n.* The *globus pallidus, which is the phylogenetically older part of the *corpus striatum. US *paleostriatum*. *Compare* neostriatum.
[From Greek *palaios* old + *striatus* streaked, from *stria* a furrow or a flute of a column]

palatal *adj.* Of or relating to speech sounds articulated with the front body of the tongue raised towards the hard palate, as in the initial *phoneme in the word *yes*. *See also* place of articulation.

palato-alveolar *adj.* Of or relating to speech sounds articulated with the tip of the tongue against the *alveolar ridge and hard palate (usually with some lip rounding), as in the initial *phonemes in the words *chin, judge*,

and *shin*, and the second phoneme in *azure*. *See also* place of articulation.
[From *palate* + Latin *alveolus* a small depression, referring to the tooth sockets]

paleencephalon *n*. Another name for the *palaeocortex.
[From Greek *palaios* old + *enkephalos* the brain, from *en* in + *kephale* the head]

pa-leng *n*. A *culture-bound syndrome found in China and southeast Asia, characterized by pathological fear of cold (frigophobia) and of wind (anemophobia), believed to produce fatigue, impotence, and death. Also called *frigophobia*.
[From Chinese *pa* fear + *leng* cold or the cold season]

paleocortex *See* palaeocortex.

paleostriatum *See* palaeostriatum.

palilalia *n*. A speech abnormality symptomatic of some forms of *tic disorder and other mental disorders, characterized by repetition of words or speech fragments with a characteristic acceleration during each cluster of repeated speech.
[From Greek *palin* back or again + *lalia* speech]

palinacousis *n*. Hearing voices repeating words that were spoken a short while earlier, or a similar repetition of other types of sounds, a rare neurological symptom of damage into the temporal lobe.

palingenesis *n*. **1.** Another name for *recapitulationism. **2.** In theology, spiritual rebirth through reincarnation or transmigration of souls into other bodies.
[From Greek *palin* again + *genesis* birth]

palingraphia *n*. Mirror writing.
[From Greek *palin* back or again + *graphein* to write + *-ia* indicating a condition or quality]

pallaesthesia *n*. Sensation of vibration transmitted through the *skin and bones. US *pallesthesia*. Also called *palmaesthesia* or *palmesthesia*. *See also* Meissner's corpuscle, Pacinian corpuscle, vibration receptor, vibratory sense. *Compare* pallanaesthesia.
[From Greek *pallein* to shake + *aisthesis* feeling + *-ia* indicating a condition or quality]

pallanaesthesia *n*. Diminished or nonfunctional *pallaesthesia. US *pallanesthesia*. Also called *palmanaesthesia* or *palmanesthesia*.
[From Greek *pallein* to shake + *an-* without + *aisthesis* feeling + *-ia* indicating a condition or quality]

pallidum *n*. An abbreviated name for the *globus pallidus.
[From Latin *pallidus* pale]

palmaesthesia *n*. Another name for *pallaesthesia. US *palmesthesia*. **palmanaesthesia** *n*. Another name for *pallanaesthesia. US *palmanesthesia*.
[From Greek *palmos* vibration + *aisthesis* feeling + *-ia* indicating a condition or quality]

palpitation *n*. Abnormally rapid or pounding heartbeat.
[From Latin *palpitare* to throb, from *palpare* to stroke + *-ation* indicating a process or condition]

palsy *n*. A *paralysis of the skeletal muscles of the body, as in *cerebral palsy. *See* Bell's palsy, cerebral palsy, Möbius syndrome, Parkinson's disease, progressive supranuclear palsy, pseudobulbar palsy.
[A corruption of *paralysis*]

pancreas *n*. An elongated organ, situated behind the stomach, containing the *islets of Langerhans that secrete *insulin and *glucagon into the bloodstream and digestive enzymes into the duodenum. **pancreatic** *adj*.
[From Greek *pan-* all + *kreas* flesh]

pandemic *n*. **1.** Any disorder occurring in a wide area, in many populations, or universally. *Compare* epidemic (1). *adj*. **2.** In *epidemiology, of or relating to a pandemic (1). *Compare* endemic, epidemic (2).
[From Greek *pandemos* universal, from *pan* all + *demos* the people + *-ikos* of, relating to, or resembling]

Pandemonium *n*. **1.** In *artificial intelligence, an *optical character recognition system that operates in successive stages, by first checking for *features (1) of the letter such as diagonal lines (as in *X* or *K*); then the output is fed to letter detectors that have been activated in the first stage and that match the letter shape to their templates; and finally recognition is achieved by identifying the letter de-

tector that is most strongly activated. **2.** Any very noisy or disorderly state of affairs.
[Named after *Pandemonium*, the capital of Hell in Milton's *Paradise Lost*, from Greek *pas, pan* all + *daimon* a spirit]

panel study *n.* A research method in which a sample of research participants or subjects is followed over an extended period of time in order to monitor changes in judgements, attitudes, opinions, developmental changes, or other variables of interest. *See also* longitudinal study.

pangram *n.* A sentence containing every letter of the alphabet, sometimes used for teaching writing or keyboard skills. The most familiar example in English is the 37-letter typists' sentence: *The quick brown fox jumped over the lazy dogs*. A 26-letter pangram in which each letter occurs just once is: *Jump dogs! Why vex Fritz Blank QC?*, but the use of personal names and abbreviations renders it imperfect, though easily memorable. The only known perfect pangram in English is: *Veldt jynx grimps waqf zho buck* (which means grassland wryneck causes charitable-land hybrid cattle buck to mount), and the words can all be found in large dictionaries, such as the *Oxford English Dictionary* (unabridged): *veldt* is open grassland in South Africa, a *jynx* is a wryneck bird, to *grimp* is to cause something or someone to mount, *waqf* is land given to a religious institution for charitable purposes in Islamic countries, a *zho* is a hybrid bovine animal bred from a yak bull and a common cow, and a *buck* is a male member of a species.
[From Greek *pan* all + *gramma* a letter]

panic attack *n.* A period during which there is a sudden onset of intense terror, fear, or apprehension, accompanied by signs and symptoms such as a feeling of impending doom, *thanatophobia, fear of going insane, shortness of breath, smothering or choking sensations, increased heart rate and *palpitation, chest pain or discomfort, dizziness, trembling, sweating, and nausea. Panic attacks occur in several *anxiety disorders, including *panic disorder, *agoraphobia, *social phobia, and *specific phobia, and they may also occur in *post-traumatic stress disorder.

panic disorder *n.* An *anxiety disorder characterized by recurrent, unexpected *panic attacks, followed by persistent apprehension about further attacks, concern about the possible effects of the attacks (such as having a heart attack or going insane), or a significant alteration in behaviour brought about by the attacks (such as resigning from a job). Panic disorder may occur with or without *agoraphobia. **PD** *abbrev.*

pansexualism *n.* The doctrine that all mental activity arises from the sexual instinct, a term often used to describe *psychoanalysis, although even in its early (pre-1920) form, before the introduction of *Thanatos, the conception of the life instincts in *Eros was not restricted to the sexual drive.
[From Greek *pantos* all + English *sexualism*]

panting centre *n.* A region of the hypothalamus that when stimulated quickens the rate of breathing. US *panting center*.
[From Old French *pantaisier* to pant, from Greek *phantasioun* to have visions, from *phantasia* a fantasy, from *phantazein* to make visible, from *phainein* to show, from *phaein* to shine]

Panum phenomenon *See* Panum's limiting case.

Panum's fusion area *n.* An area of space, surrounding the *horopter for a given degree of *ocular convergence, within which different points projected on to the left and right retinas result in *binocular fusion, producing a sensation of visual depth, and points lying outside the area result in *diplopia. It is really a volume rather than an area, because it is curved and has a three-dimensional shape. Near the fovea, the maximum binocular disparity resulting in binocular fusion corresponds to a *visual angle of about 10 minutes of arc or 1/6 of one degree. **PFA** *abbrev.*
[Named after the Danish physician and physiologist Peter Ludvig Panum (1820–85) who first described it in 1858]

Panum's limiting case *n.* A visual sensation of three-dimensional depth that occurs when two lines or other elements are presented, one to each eye, at positions allowing *binocular fusion to occur, and at the same time a third is presented to one of the eyes at a different position, generating a perception in which the fused line appears nearer than the single line. The explanation, and the reason for its being called a limiting case, is that it mimics the stimulus pattern that occurs when two objects at different distances are viewed from such an angle that one of the objects is hidden behind the other from the vantage point of one eye whereas the other eye sees both of them. Also called the *Panum phenomenon* or the *Wheatstone–Panum limiting case*. *See also* Panum's fusion area, stereopsis.

[Named after the Danish physician and physiologist Peter Ludvig Panum (1820–85) who rediscovered it in 1858, although the English physicist and inventor Sir Charles Wheatstone (1802–75) had already discovered and reported it in 1838]

Papez circuit *n*. A neural pathway closely associated with emotional experiences, including many of the structures of and around the limbic system, running from the *thalamus through the *cingulate gyrus, *entorhinal cortex, *hippocampus, *septum pellucidum, *hypothalamus, and *mammillary bodies, before returning to the thalamus.

[Named after the US neuroanatomist James W. Papez (1883–1958) who first described it in 1937]

papilla *n*. A small nipple-shaped protuberance, including any of the lingual papillae situated chiefly within pits in the surface of the *tongue but also on the soft palate, throat, pharynx, and insides of the cheeks, most papillae being studded with *taste buds around their bases. Approximately 12 *circumvallate papillae are concentrated at the back of the tongue, numerous *fungiform papillae and *filiform papillae in the middle and front of the tongue, and pairs of *foliate papillae on the sides of the back part of the tongue, the only ones without taste buds being filiform papillae. **papillae** *pl*.

[From Latin *papilla* a nipple, diminutive of *papula* a pimple]

paracentral vision *n*. Vision arising from images falling in the parafoveal area of the retina immediately surrounding the *fovea.

[From Greek *para* beside or beyond + *kentron* a sharp point]

parachlorophenylalanine *n*. A substance that inhibits the activity of *tryptophan hydroxylase and is used as a drug to reduce levels of *serotonin in the brain. **p-CPA** or **PCPA** *abbrev*.

parachromatopsia *n*. Partial or incomplete *colour-blindness. *Compare* achromatopsia.

[From Greek *para* beside + *chroma* colour + *ops* an eye + *-ia* indicating a condition or quality]

paracontrast *n*. A type of *forward masking in which the test stimulus and masking stimulus do not overlap spatially. *See also* masking, visual masking. *Compare* metacontrast.

[From Greek *para* beside + Latin *contra* against + *stare* to stand]

paracusia *n*. Disordered hearing. Also spelt *paracousia*. Also called *paracusis* or *paracousis*. **paracusic** *adj*.

[From Greek *para* beside + *akousis* hearing, from *akouein* to hear + *-ia* indicating a condition or quality]

paradigm *n*. **1.** A pattern, stereotypical example, model, or general conceptual framework within which theories in a particular area of research are constructed. *See also* paradigm shift. **2.** (Originally) the set of inflected forms of a word, or a table displaying these forms, such as the conjugation of the regular French verb meaning to speak: *je parle, tu parles, il parle, nous parlons, vous parlez, ils parlent*. **paradigmatic** or **paradigmatical** *adj*.

[From Greek *para* beside or beyond + *deiknynai* to show]

paradigm shift *n*. According to a doctrine propounded by the US historian and philosopher of science Thomas S(amuel) Kuhn (1922–96) in his book *The Structure of Scientific Revolutions* (1962), a rapid change, marking the culmination of a *scientific revolution, from one *paradigm (1) to another, such as occurred in physics when Einstein's theory replaced Newton's in 1916. *See also* Kuhnian, normal science.

paradox *n*. A logically valid argument based on premises that are generally accepted as true, yielding either a contradiction or a conclusion that conflicts with other generally accepted beliefs. The US philosopher and logician Willard Van Orman Quine (1908–2000) introduced a threefold classification into *veridical paradoxes*, whose conclusions are true, such as *Hempel's paradox; *falsidical paradoxes*, whose conclusions are false, such as the *unexpected hanging paradox or the *sorites paradox; and *antinomies*,

whose conclusions are mutually contradictory, such as *Russell's paradox, the *liar paradox, or *Grelling's paradox. The term is also used more loosely for any argument that yields a surprising conclusion, or even for a fact or phenomenon that seems surprising, but the latter is avoided in careful usage. *See also* Allais paradox, Aubert–Fleischl paradox, barber's paradox, Condorcet's paradox, duration estimation paradox, Ellsberg paradox, Fechner's paradox, Gödel's theorem, Goodman's paradox, melodic paradox, metalanguage, mirror reversal problem, modified Ellsberg paradox, Monty Hall problem, neurotic paradox, Newcomb's problem, paradoxical injunction, paradoxical intention, paradoxical therapy, Prisoner's Dilemma game, semitone paradox, Simpson's paradox, Skaggs–Robinson paradox, sociology of knowledge, sorites paradox, St Petersburg paradox, tritone paradox. **paradoxical** *adj.*
[From Greek *paradoxos*, beyond belief, from *para* beyond + *doxa* a belief]

paradoxical cold *n.* A sensation of coldness that is experienced when a warm stimulus touches a *cold spot on the skin. *Compare* paradoxical heat, paradoxical warmth.

paradoxical heat *n.* A sensation of intense heat that is experienced in the absence of a hot stimulus if an area of the skin containing both *cold spots and *warm spots is stimulated with a *heat grill* of closely packed alternating warm and cold bars. *Compare* paradoxical cold, paradoxical warmth.

paradoxical injunction *n.* An instruction to do something that is rendered impossible by the instruction itself, as in *Do not think of a giraffe!*

paradoxical intention *n.* A technique of *logotherapy and *behaviour therapy, used in the treatment of *obsessive–compulsive disorder, in which the client or patient deliberately and repeatedly rehearses a habit or unwanted pattern of thought or behaviour, with the aim of developing a less fearful attitude towards it, gaining control over it, or bringing about its elimination or *extinction (2). Also called *negative practice*. *See also* paradoxical therapy.

paradoxical sleep *n.* Another name for *REM sleep.

[So called because its characteristic EEG pattern is similar to that of the waking state, but the sleeper is none the less especially difficult to awaken]

paradoxical therapy *n.* Any form of *psychotherapy involving techniques that appear on the surface to contradict the goals of the treatment, such as *negative practice and *paradoxical intention.

paradoxical warmth *n.* A sensation of warmth that is experienced when a cold stimulus touches a *warm spot on the skin. *Compare* paradoxical cold, paradoxical heat.

paradox of voting *n.* Another name for *Condorcet's paradox.

paraesthesia *n.* An abnormal sensation such as tingling, burning, prickling, pins and needles, or numbness in an area of the skin or a part of the body. US *paresthesia*. *See also* acroparaesthesia, dysaesthesia.
[From Greek *para* beside or beyond + *aisthesis* sensation + -*ia* indicating a condition or quality]

parafovea *n.* The area of the retina immediately surrounding the *fovea. *See also* paracentral vision. **parafoveal** *adj.*
[From Greek *para* beside or beyond + Latin *fovea* a pit]

parageusia *n.* Abnormal taste sensation. *See* ageusia, cacogeusia, dysgeusia, hypergeusia, hypogeusia, taste blindness.
[From Greek *para* beside or beyond + *geusis* taste + -*ia* indicating a condition or quality]

parahippocampal gyrus *n.* The gyrus of the cerebral cortex immediately adjacent to the *hippocampus, considered as part of the *limbic system. It receives a constant stream of information from the association areas that it transmits to the hippocampus, mainly via the entorhinal cortex, for consolidation in long-term memory, and it is also involved in the control of aggression. *See also* entorhinal cortex.

paralanguage *n.* The non-verbal aspects of speech that convey information to listeners, including *accent (1), *loudness, *pitch, *rhythm, *tempo, *timbre. *See also* non-verbal communication, prosody.

[From Greek *para* beside or beyond + English *language*]

paraldehyde n. A colourless strong-smelling liquid obtained from *acetaldehyde and sulphuric acid that acts as a central nervous system *depressant and is used as a *sedative–hypnotic drug. Formula $C_6H_{12}O_3$.
[From Greek *para* beside or beyond + English *aldehyde*, from Latin *al(cohol) dehyd(rogenatum)* dehydrogenated alcohol]

paralexia n. A disordered or defective form of reading in which words or syllables are meaninglessly transposed.
[From Greek *para* beside or beyond + *lexis* a word]

paralinguistics n. The study of *paralanguage.

parallax n. Apparent movement of an object resulting from a change in the vantage point from which it is viewed. *See also* binocular parallax, monocular parallax.
[From Latin *parallaxis* parallax, from Greek *parallassein* to change, from *para* beside or beyond + *allassein* to alter, from *allos* another]

parallel distributed processing n. A model of *knowledge representation and *information processing according to which items of knowledge are represented by patterns of connections of varying strengths between locations within a *network model, information processing taking the form of parallel processing of collections of activated connections. The term is almost synonymous with *connectionism (1). *See also* back-propagation algorithm, cascade processing, content-addressable memory, delta rule, distributed network model, gradient descent, Hebbian rule, hill climbing, neural network, teacher unit. *Compare* distributed cognition. **PDP** *abbrev.*

parallel fibre n. Any of the axon branches arising from *granule cells that run horizontally near the cortical surface of the *cerebellum and synapse on *Purkinje cells. US *parallel fiber*.

parallel-form reliability n. Another name for *equivalent-form reliability.

parallel forms n. In psychometrics, *alternative forms of a test that have similar *means, *standard deviations, and *correlations with other tests. Also called *equated forms*.

parallelism n. Another name for *psychophysical parallelism.

parallelogram illusion n. Another name for the *Sander parallelogram.

parallel processing n. Computational processing in which a process is split into subunits that are executed simultaneously by independent processing units. *See also* cascade processing, connectionism, discrete processing, parallel distributed processing. *Compare* serial processing.

paralysis n. An impairment or loss of function of one or more voluntary muscles, usually resulting from a disorder of the muscle, a neurological disorder, or a mental disorder.
[From Greek *para* beside or beyond + *lysis* a loosening]

paralysis agitans n. Another name for *Parkinson's disease.

paralytic strabismus n. A form of *strabismus associated with a malfunction of the ocular muscles resulting from a neurological or muscular disorder or dysfunction. *Compare* non-paralytic strabismus.

paramecium n. A freshwater, single-celled creature having a bean-shaped body covered with *cilia that are used for swimming, the cilia being composed of bundles of *microtubules. It moves about, avoiding obstacles by swimming round them, darts for bacterial food, retreats from danger, turns itself round to escape if enclosed in a glass tube, and is probably capable of learning from experience, according to the results of experiments dating back to 1908, though some authorities have disputed that it is capable of true learning. Yet it has no *nervous system, its single cell not even being a *neuron, which proves that rather complex behaviour can occur without a nervous system. *See also* cytoskeleton. **paramecia** *pl.*
[From Greek *paramekes* elongated, from *para* beside or beyond + *mekos* length]

parameter n. In statistics, a property of a *population distribution, such as the population mean or population standard deviation, as distinct from a property of a *sample.

[From Greek *para* beside or beyond + *metron* a measure]

parametric statistics *n.* A branch of statistics that makes assumptions about the *parameters of the distributions from which the data are drawn, often including the assumption that variables conform to the *normal distribution. It deals mainly with data measured on interval or ratio scales that are suitable for the application of ordinary arithmetic operations such as addition and multiplication, so that parameters such as the *mean and *standard deviation can be meaningfully defined.

paramimia *n.* A form of *apraxia in which there is an impairment in the ability to imitate *gestures (1).
[From Greek *para* beside or beyond + *mimos* a mime, from *mimesis* imitation + *-ia* indicating a condition or quality]

paramnesia *n.* **1.** A belief that one is recalling events or experiences that never really occurred. *See also* experimentally induced false memory, false memory, false memory syndrome, reality monitoring. **2.** Any disorder of memory involving misremembering rather than failing to remember, including *déjà vu and *jamais vu.
[From Greek *para* beside + *mnasthai* to remember + *-ia* indicating a condition or quality]

paramnesia, reduplicative *See* reduplicative paramnesia.

paranoia *n.* Another name for *delusional disorder or, more generally, any mental disorder characterized by *delusions, including *paranoid personality disorder, *paranoid schizophrenia, or *shared psychotic disorder. *See also* paranoid technique, Schreber case.
[From Greek *paranoia* frenzy, from *para* beside + *nous* intellect or sense + *-ia* indicating a condition or quality]

paranoia scale *See* MMPI.

paranoid *adj.* Of, relating to, characterized by, or resembling *paranoia or *delusional disorder.

paranoid disorder *See* delusional disorder, paranoia, paranoid personality disorder, paranoid schizophrenia, shared psychotic disorder.

paranoid disorder, shared *See* shared psychotic disorder.

paranoid ideation *n.* Suspicious ideas and beliefs falling short of *delusions that one is being harassed, persecuted, or treated unfairly.

paranoid personality disorder *n.* A *personality disorder characterized by *paranoid ideation, indicated by such signs and symptoms as unwarranted suspicion of being exploited, harmed or plotted against; unjustified doubts about the trustworthiness of friends and associates; reluctance to confide in others because of unwarranted fear of the information being maliciously exploited; tendency to interpret innocent remarks or events as demeaning or threatening; persistent bearing of grudges for past insults, injuries, or slights; tendency to perceive personal attacks that are not apparent to others; tendency to become angry, and to counterattack; and harbouring of unjustified suspicions about the faithfulness of sexual partners. *Compare* delusional disorder, paranoid schizophrenia.

paranoid–schizoid position *n.* In *Kleinian analysis, a mode of *object relations occurring during the first 4 months of life, before the *depressive position, recurring occasionally in later childhood and adulthood, and becoming dominant in states of *paranoid personality disorder and *schizophrenia. It is characterized by *ambivalence arising from the coexistence of aggressive and libidinal drives directed at an *instinctual object, namely the mother's breast, that is a *part object and is split into a *good object* and a *bad object*, because it both gratifies and frustrates, and because it evokes emotions of love and hate. The concept was introduced in 1932 by the British-based Austrian psychoanalyst Melanie Klein (1882–1960) and fully developed in a contribution to a co-authored book in 1952 on 'Some Theoretical Conclusions Regarding the Emotional Life of the Infant', where she explained her preference for the word *position* to *stage* or *phase*: 'these groupings of anxieties and defences, although arising first during the earliest stages, are not restricted to them but occur and recur during the first years of childhood and under certain circumstances in later life' (*Developments in Psycho-Analysis*, p. 236). Also called the *paranoid position*, the element *schizoid* being added to allude to the splitting of the object that it involves.

paranoid schizophrenia *n*. One of the major types of *schizophrenia, the essential feature being the presence of prominent *delusions or *auditory hallucinations involving *paranoid ideation in the context of otherwise normal *cognition and *affect. *Compare* delusional disorder, paranoid personality disorder.

paranoid technique *n*. In *psychoanalysis, one of the four *defensive techniques proposed by the Scottish psychoanalyst W. Ronald D. Fairbairn (1889–1964). It involves *internalization of the *good object and *externalization of the bad object, causing the paranoid person to feel persecuted by external forces. *See also* splitting of the object. *Compare* hysterical technique, obsessional technique, phobic technique.

paranormal *adj*. Beyond the normal; supernatural or inexplicable by the laws of science or reason. *See also* parapsychology. Also called *psychic* or *psychical*.
[From Greek *para* beside or beyond + English *normal*, from Latin *normalis* conforming to a carpenter's square or rule, from *norma* a carpenter's square or a rule + *-alis* of or relating to]

paranosic gain *n*. Another name for *primary gain.
[From Greek *para* beside or beyond + *nosos* a disorder]

paraphasia *n*. A form of *aphasia characterized by the habitual substitution of one word for another.
[From Greek *para* beside or beyond + English *aphasia*]

paraphemia *n*. Disordered speech, characterized by misuse of *phonemes and words.
[From Greek *para* beside or beyond + *pheme* speech, from *phanai* to speak]

paraphilias *n*. A group of *mental disorders characterized by recurrent sexually arousing fantasies, sexual urges, or behaviour involving non-human objects, children or other non-consenting sexual partners, or suffering or humiliation of oneself or a sexual partner, causing clinically significant distress or impairment in social, occupational, or other important areas of functioning. *See* acrotomorphilia, apotemnophilia, bestiality (1), coprophilia, exhibitionism (1), fetishism, fetishistic transvestism, frotteurism, hypoxyphilia, katasexualism, kleptolagnia, klysmaphilia, necrophilia, osphresiolagnia, paedophilia, renifleur, scopophilia, sexual masochism, sexual sadism, telephone scatalogia, urophilia, voyeurism, zoophilia. Also called *sexual deviations* or *sexual preference disorders*. Formerly called *sexual perversions* or *perversions*. **paraphiliac** *n*. A person with a *paraphilia.
[From Greek *para* beside or beyond + *philos* loving, from *phileein* to love + *-ia* indicating a condition or quality]

paraphobia *n*. An irrational fear of some object, activity, or situation, falling below the threshold of being labelled a true *phobia.
[From Greek *para* beside or beyond + *phobos* fear + *-ia* indicating a condition or quality]

paraphrenia *n*. A term introduced in 1904 by the German psychiatrist Emil Kraepelin (1856–1926) to denote chronic *delusional disorder without intellectual deterioration or *dementia. *See also* narcissistic neurosis.
[From Greek *para* beside or beyond + *phren* mind, originally midriff, the supposed seat of the soul + *-ia* indicating a condition or quality]

paraplegia *n*. Paralysis of the lower limbs, usually as a result of lesions in the middle or lower part of the spinal cord. *Compare* diplegia, hemiplegia, monoplegia, ophthalmoplegia, quadriplegia, triplegia. **paraplegic** *adj*.
[From Greek *para* beside or beyond + *plege* a blow + *-ia* indicating a condition or quality]

parapraxis *n*. In *psychoanalysis, a minor error in speech or action, such as a *slip of the tongue, a *slip of the pen, an *action slip, or a *slip of memory. In his book *The Psychopathology of Everyday Life* (1901, *Standard Edition*, VI), Sigmund Freud (1856–1939) advanced the theory that such errors are not random but often represent fulfilments of unconscious wishes, and the book is crammed with anecdotal examples. Parapraxes can be analysed for possible clues to repressed thoughts and desires by a method similar to *dream analysis. Freud's original German word for this phenomenon was *Fehlleistung*, combining two ordinary words and meaning simply a faulty performance. Also called a *mo-

tivated error, and (colloquially) a *Freudian slip*. *See also* acting out (2), déjà vu. **parapraxes** *pl*. [From Greek *para* beside or beyond + *praxis* a deed, from *prassein* to do]

parapsychology *n*. The study of apparently *paranormal psychological phenomena or *psi phenomena, especially *extra-sensory perception (telepathy, clairvoyance, and pre-cognition) and *psychokinesis. Also called *psychical research*. *See also* file drawer problem, Ouija board, psi, psi-missing. **parapsychological** *adj*. [From Greek *para* beside or beyond + English *psychology*]

parasitosis *n*. Infestation with parasites; also, figuratively, another name for *formication.

parasol cell *n*. A large retinal *ganglion cell in the *magnocellular system, with a *centre-surround receptive field, receiving input from all three types of retinal *cones. *Compare* midget cell.

parasomnias *n*. Abnormal physiological or psychological reactions associated with sleep or the transition between wakefulness and sleep, causing significant distress or impairment in social, occupational, or other important areas of functioning. In *DSM-IV they form a subcategory of *sleep disorders, including *nightmare disorder, *sleep terror disorder, and *sleepwalking disorder. *See also* bruxism, central alveolar hypoventilation syndrome, central sleep apnoea, obstructive sleep apnoea, pavor diurnus, pavor nocturnus, sleep apnoea. *Compare* dyssomnias. [From Greek *para* beside or beyond + *somnus* sleep]

parasuicide *n*. A deliberate self-inflicted injury or poisoning resembling a suicide attempt but probably not intended to be successful. [From Greek *para* beside + English *suicide*]

parasympathetic nervous system *n*. One of the two major subdivisions of the *autonomic nervous system whose general function is to conserve metabolic energy, acting in opposition to and with more specificity than the *sympathetic nervous system by slowing pulse rate, stimulating the smooth muscles of the alimentary canal (*see* peristalsis), promoting secretion of salivary and intestinal juices

and voiding of urine, constricting the pupils, and preparing the eyes for *near vision. *See also* cholinergic. *Compare* sympathetic nervous system. **PNS** *abbrev*. [From Greek *para* beside + *syn* with + *pathos* suffering]

parasympatholytic *adj*. *n*. (Of, relating to, or having an effect similar to) a drug or other agent that acts against or inhibits the activity of the *parasympathetic nervous system, usually by blocking *muscarinic receptors. *Compare* parasympathomimetic, sympatholytic. [From *parasympathetic* + Greek *lysis* loosening + *-ikos* of, relating to, or resembling]

parasympathomimetic *adj*. *n*. (Of, relating to, or having an effect similar to) a drug such as *carbachol, *methacholine, or *muscarine that mimics or increases the activity of *acetylcholine, the major neurotransmitter of the *parasympathetic nervous system, with effects such as constriction of the pupils of the eyes and preparation for close-up vision, salivation, slowing of the heart, secretion of gastric juices, and voiding of urine. *Compare* parasympatholytic, sympathomimetic. *See also* cholinergic. [From Greek *para* beside + *syn* with + *pathos* suffering + *mimetes* an imitator + *-ikos* of, relating to, or resembling]

parathyroid gland *n*. Any of the small ovoid endocrine glands, usually four in number, attached to the sides of the thyroid gland at the base of the neck. They secrete *parathyroid hormone into the bloodstream. [From Greek *para* beside + *thyreoeides* a door-shaped shield, from *thyra* a door + *eidos* form]

parathyroid hormone *n*. A hormone secreted by the *parathyroid glands that increases the level of *calcium and *phosphate in the blood and whose action is regulated by *calcitonin secreted by the thyroid glands. **PTH** *abbrev*.

paraventricular nucleus *n*. A cluster of neurons at the back of each side of the hypothalamus, synthesizing *vasopressin and *oxytocin and transporting them through their axons to the *posterior pituitary. [From Greek *para* beside + Latin *ventriculus* a little belly, diminutive of *venter, ventris* a belly, alluding to its location near the walls of the third ventricle]

paregoric *n.* A *narcotic analgesic containing *opium, formerly prescribed in the treatment of coughing and diarrhoea in children.
[From Greek *paregoreein* to exhort or comfort, from *para* beside + *agoreuein* to speak publicly, from *agora* an assembly or marketplace + *-ikos* of, relating to, or resembling]

parental investment *n.* Any contribution that a parent makes towards an individual offspring and that increases the offspring's chances of survival and reproduction at the cost of the parent's ability to contribute to other offspring, including producing sex cells and later feeding and guarding the young. According to the US biologist Robert L. Trivers (born 1943), who introduced the term into ethology in 1972, in species in which females provide more parental investment than males, males compete among themselves for female mates and females are vulnerable to mate desertion. *See also* sexual selection. **PI** *abbrev.*

parenteral *adj.* By a route other than the mouth or alimentary canal, referring to the mode of administration of a drug, usually implying administration by injection. *Compare* oral.
[From Greek *para* beside + *enteron* the alimentary canal or gut]

parent-figure, combined *See* combined parent-figure.

paresis *n.* Partial *paralysis, as in *general paralysis (paresis) of the insane.
[From Latin *paresis* relaxation, from *para* beside or beyond + *hienai* to release]

paresthesia *See* paraesthesia.

Pareto-optimal *adj.* Of or relating to a distribution of *payoffs such that any redistribution that benefited one individual would be detrimental to one or more others. **Pareto optimality** *n.*
[Named after the French-born Italian economist and sociologist Vilfredo Pareto (1848–1923) who introduced the concept in his mathematical treatment of income distribution]

parietal lobe *n.* The upper *lobe on the side of each cerebral hemisphere, separated on its lateral or outer surface from the frontal lobe by the *central sulcus, from the temporal lobe by the *lateral sulcus and an imaginary line extending it horizontally towards the occipital lobe, and from the occipital lobe by an imaginary line from the top of the *parieto-occipital sulcus to the *pre-occipital notch. The right parietal lobe is especially involved in appreciation of spatial relationships. Lesions in either hemisphere in the somatosensory association area *(see* somatosensory cortex) can result in *astereognosis, and lesions in the parietal operculum immediately above the lateral sulcus can lead to *spatial neglect. *See also* aphasia, autotopagnosia, Gerstmann syndrome, lobe, operculum.
[From Latin *parietalis* of a wall, from *paries* a wall]

parietal operculum *See under* operculum.

parieto-occipital sulcus *n.* A *sulcus towards the back of each cerebral hemisphere on its *medial surface (hence not visible on the outside), marking the boundary between the parietal lobe and the occipital lobe.

parkinsonism *n.* Mild regular *resting tremor of the limbs, head, jaw, mouth, or lip (the so-called *rabbit syndrome*), characteristic of *Parkinson's disease but associated also with other neurological disorders, with oscillations of 3–6 hertz, exacerbated by cold, fatigue, or strong emotion, usually suppressed during voluntary movements and sleep. *See also* antiparkinsonian, neuroleptic-induced, postural tremor. *Compare* intention tremor.
[Named after Parkinson's disease]

Parkinson's disease *n.* A progressive, degenerative neurological disorder affecting two per cent of people over 65 in the developed world, associated with malfunction (usually resulting from damage caused by *free radicals but occasionally due to a genetic mutation) to neurons that produce *dopamine in the *substantia nigra and the extended projections into the *striatum, which in turn relays signals to the higher motor centres of the brain. The disease is characterized by *parkinsonism, often occurring first in one hand, where it resembles pill-rolling movements of the thumb and forefinger, masklike facial expression, shuffling gait or *festination, *cogwheel rigidity of muscles and difficulty rising from a sitting position, shrinkage of handwriting, *bradykinesia or *akinesia, drooling,

profuse sweating, lability of *affect, and defective judgement. Also called *paralysis agitans*. *See also* amantadine, antiparkinsonian, foetal brain transplantation, ʟ-dopa, MPP⁺, progressive supranuclear palsy. **PD** *abbrev*.
[Named after the English surgeon James Parkinson (1755–1824) who first described it in 1817 and called it the shaking palsy]

Parlodel *n*. A proprietary name for the dopamine agonist *bromocriptine.
[Trademark]

parole *n*. A term introduced in 1915 by the Swiss linguist Ferdinand de Saussure (1857–1913) to denote language as manifested in concrete utterances of particular speakers. *Parole* is seen as one of the two major aspects of *langage*, the other being *langue*, and it is analogous to the concept of *performance (2).
[Old French *parole* speech]

paronomasia *n*. Any form of word-play, especially a pun.
[From Greek *para* beside or beyond + *onoma* a name + *-ia* indicating a condition or quality]

parosmia *n*. Any abnormality in *olfaction or the sense of smell. *See* anosmia, cacosmia, dysosmia, hyperosmia, hyposmia, specific anosmia.
[From Greek *para* beside or beyond + *osme* a smell + *-ia* indicating a condition or quality]

parotid gland *n*. A large salivary gland situated in the oral cavity just below and in front of each ear.
[From Greek *para* beside + *ous, otos* an ear]

paroxetine *n*. An antidepressant drug with anxiolytic effects belonging to the group of *selective serotonin reuptake inhibitors (SSRIs), used especially to treat *social phobia and shyness in general. Also called *Paxil* or *Seroxat* (trademarks).

parsimony principle *n*. The proposition that closely related organisms, having diverged comparatively recently in evolutionary history, have fewer differences in their *DNA than more distantly related organisms. *See also* mitochondrial DNA.

parthenogenesis *n*. A form of reproduction in some insects from a female *gamete without fertilization by a male gamete.

Distinguished in careful usage from *asexual reproduction, in which gametes are not formed. *Compare* sexual reproduction. **parthenogenetic** or **parthenogenic** *adj*.
[From Greek *parthenos* a virgin + *genesis* birth]

partial correlation *n*. In statistics, a *correlation between two variables with the effect of a third variable controlled or *partialled out*. For example, if *x*, *y*, and *z* represent the heights, weights, and ages of children, respectively, then a significant positive correlation between *x* and *y* may be due in part to the correlation of each of these variables with *z*. A partial correlation coefficient between *x* and *y* with *z* partialled out, written r_{xyz}, shows the degree of linear relationship between height and weight irrespective of age.

partial instinct *n*. Another name for a *component instinct.

partial movement *n*. A form of *apparent movement that occurs when two visual stimuli a few centimetres apart are presented in an alternating pattern with an interstimulus interval too long for the stimuli to appear simultaneously but not long enough for *optimal movement, *phi movement, or the disappearance of apparent movement and the veridical perception of the stimuli simply alternating. In partial movement, the first stimulus appears to move part of the distance towards the second and then to disappear, then the second stimulus appears in the space between the two stimuli and moves towards its own location, then this cycle is repeated in the opposite direction, and so on. Also called *partial motion*. *See also* Korte's laws.

partial reinforcement *n*. In *operant conditioning, any *reinforcement schedule in which the organism is not rewarded after every response. Also called *intermittent reinforcement*. *See also* partial reinforcement effect. *Compare* continuous reinforcement. **PR** *abbrev*.

partial reinforcement effect *n*. The finding that responses established by *partial reinforcement are more resistant to *extinction (2) than responses established by continuous reinforcement. **PRE** *abbrev*.

partial tone *n*. Any *pure tone that is a component of a *complex tone. Also called a *partial*. *See also* Fourier analysis.

participant observation n. A research methodology in which the investigator participates in the activities of a group while recording the behaviour of the other group members. See also ethnomethodology, naturalistic observation, observational study.

participant (research or experimental) n. Another name for a *subject (research or experimental) or volunteer.

participation mystique n. In *analytical psychology, a term introduced in 1912 by Carl Gustav Jung (1875–1961) to denote a form of *projective identification in which a person gains influence over another. Jung borrowed the term from the French anthropologist Lucien Lévy-Bruhl (1857–1939) who used it to denote a phenomenon whereby people identify themselves with a physical object such as a holy artefact or a *totem.
[French: literally mystical involvement]

participatory action research n. A form of *action research in which the researchers and the people being studied collaborate in defining the research problem, choosing the research methodology and method of data analysis, and disseminating the findings. **PAR** abbrev.

particular complex n. In *psychoanalysis, a *complex (2) that is peculiar to an individual and, unlike the *Oedipus complex, for example, is not universal.

particulate inheritance n. Inheritance of discrete characteristics through factors now identified as *genes, in contrast to the discredited doctrine of *blending inheritance.

partile n. In statistics, one of a number of scores that divide a distribution into equal parts, the most common being the *decile, *percentile, and *quartile.

part instinct n. Another name for a *component instinct.

part object n. In *Kleinian analysis, any part of a person that serves as an *instinctual object satisfying another person's sexual *instinct (3), the first instance in human development being the mother's breast. See also good object, instinctual object, object re-

lations, paranoid–schizoid position, splitting of the object. Compare whole object.

parvocellular system n. The more recently evolved of the two major visual pathways, originating in small *ganglion cells in the *retina, projecting to the uppermost four layers of the *lateral geniculate nucleus that contain neurons with small cell bodies, and terminating in layer $4C\beta$ of the *primary visual cortex (Area V1). It is characterized by colour-sensitivity, slowly conducting axons, low contrast sensitivity, and high resolution of fine detail. Parvocellular neurons that project on to interblobs between the *blobs in layers 1 and 2 of the primary visual cortex carry high-resolution information about shape, and parvocellular neurons that project on to blobs carry lower-resolution information about colour and shades of grey but not about shape, movement, or depth, whereas *magnocellular neurons carry information about movement and depth but not colour. Also called the **parvo system**. See also midget cell, P cell (X cell), W cell. Compare magnocellular system. **P system** abbrev.
[From Latin parvus small + cella a room, from celare to hide]

Pascal's wager n. The argument that it is in one's rational self-interest to assume that God exists, because however small the probability is that God does indeed exist, provided that it is not zero, the infinite gain from belief and the infinite punishment from disbelief outweigh any advantage of disbelief if God does not exist. In modern terms, the argument purports to show that the *expected utility of assuming that God exists must be greater than the expected utility of believing that God does not exist. The argument was formulated by the French philosopher, mathematician, and physicist Blaise Pascal (1623–62) and published posthumously in Pensées (1670): 'God is or he is not. . . . What is your wager? . . . Let us weigh the gain and the loss in choosing "heads" that God is. . . . If you gain, you gain all. If you lose, you lose nothing. Wager, then, unhesitatingly that he is' (Thought 233). Critics have claimed that there are not merely two possibilities—that the Christian God exists or does not exist—but an infinite number, and that this undermines the argument. See also rational choice theory.

passing stranger effect n. Another name for the *ancient mariner effect.

passive–aggressive personality disorder n. A *personality disorder (not included in the *DSM-IV classification) characterized by a pervasive pattern of *negativism (1), with passive resistance, complaints of being misunderstood, sullenness and argumentativeness, unreasonable scorn for authority, envy and resentment, alternation between hostile defiance and contrition, and general discontentment. People with the disorder tend to obtain high scores on measures of assertiveness and low scores on measures of warmth. Also called *negativistic personality disorder. See also* little thirty.

passive analysis n. A style of *psychoanalysis in which the analyst offers a minimum of *interpretations (2).

passive avoidance conditioning n. Learning to abstain from a particular response in order to avoid a punishing or aversive stimulus. Also called *passive avoidance learning. Compare* active avoidance conditioning, escape conditioning. *See also* avoidance conditioning.

passive-dependent personality disorder n. Another name for *dependent personality disorder.

passive learning n. Another name for *incidental learning and *latent learning.

passive movement n. Movement of an organism resulting from external force and not from the organism's own locomotion or muscular activity, as when a person is transported in a vehicle. Also called *passive motion. See also* motion sickness, vection.

passive tremor n. Another name for *resting tremor.

passive vocabulary n. The set of words that a person can understand. *Compare* active vocabulary.

pastoral counselling n. A form of *counselling given by ministers of religion to help members of their congregations with emotional problems. US *pastoral counseling.

patellar reflex n. A *deep tendon reflex elicited by tapping the tendon immediately below the knee-cap, normally resulting in contraction of the quadriceps muscle and extension of the leg in a kicking movement. Lesions in the *pyramidal tract are associated with a hyperactive patellar reflex. Also called the *knee-jerk reflex* or the *quadriceps reflex. See also* stretch reflex.
[From Latin *patella* a small dish, diminutive of *patina* a dish or pan, alluding to the shape of the knee-cap]

path analysis *See* path diagram.

path diagram n. A graphic representation of a causal *model derived from a *correlational study, showing the strengths of hypothesized *causal effects of certain variables on certain other variables. The results of *multiple regression, *structural equation models, and simple *analysis of covariance structures are often depicted by path diagrams, and such analyses are therefore called *path analysis.

pathergasia n. A physical defect or abnormality that limits a person's capacity for psychological adjustment.
[From Greek *pathos* suffering + *ergasia* work or business]

pathetic fallacy n. Attributing to inanimate objects feelings, dispositions, and reactions that can be manifested only by animate creatures or human beings, as when a person accuses a computer of being vindictive for deleting an important file. It is a mistake rather than a fallacy, because it does not arise from any invalid form of reasoning. The term was first used in 1843 by the English author and art critic John Ruskin (1819–1900) in his book *Modern Painters*.

pathetic nerve n. Another name for the *abducens nerve (the sixth cranial nerve).

pathogenesis n. The *aetiology of a disorder.
pathogenic adj. Capable of causing a disorder or disease.
[From Greek *pathos* suffering + *genes* born]

pathognomonic adj. Of or relating to a group of *signs (1) and *symptoms that are indicative of a specific disorder.

[From Greek *pathos* suffering + *gnomon* a judge or index + -*ikos* of, relating to, or resembling]

pathological fire-setting *n.* Another name for *pyromania.

pathological gambling *n.* An *impulse-control disorder characterized by persistent and maladaptive gambling, indicated by such signs and symptoms as being preoccupied with gambling; needing increasing amounts of money to achieve the desired level of excitement; attempting repeatedly and unsuccessfully to cut down or to stop gambling; becoming restless or irritable while desisting from gambling; using gambling as an escape from worry or unhappiness; attempting to recoup gambling losses by further gambling; lying to family members or therapists to conceal the extent of gambling; committing illegal acts such as fraud or theft to finance gambling; jeopardizing a significant job, personal relationship, or educational opportunity by gambling; or relying on others to relieve financial crises caused by gambling.

pathological hair-pulling *n.* Another name for *trichotillomania.

pathological stealing *n.* Another name for *kleptomania.

pathomimicry *n.* A less common name for *factitious disorder or *Munchausen syndrome.
[From Greek *pathos* suffering + *mimos* a mime]

patient *n.* A person receiving medical, surgical, or other form of treatment for a disorder or illness. Also called a *client*, especially when the treatment is not medical or surgical.

patriarchy *n.* Literally, a community of related families under the authority of a male head called a *patriarch*; applied more generally to any form of social organization in which men have predominant power. *Compare* matriarchy. **patriarchal** *adj.*
[From Greek *patria* a family + Greek *arche* a rule]

patrilineal *adj.* Of or relating to descent, kinship, or inheritance through the male line, as in most Western societies. *Compare* matrilineal.

[From Latin *pater, patris* a father + *linea* a line]

pattern discrimination *n.* Distinguishing consistently between two or more patterns, or consistently making different responses to them.

pattern-induced flicker colour *n.* A colour produced by *Benham's top. US *pattern-induced flicker color*. Also called a *Fechner–Benham colour* or a *subjective colour*. **PIFC** *abbrev.*

patterning *n.* A method of retraining brain-injured children who have suffered disruption of sensory-motor functions by guiding them through developmental sequences of behaviour, starting with early behavioural patterns such as crawling, the object being to enable undamaged brain tissue to take over the functions previously controlled by tissue that has become non-functional.

pattern masking *n.* *Visual masking using a differentiated image as a masking stimulus. *See also* inspection time. **pattern masking by noise** *n.* *Pattern masking using a masking stimulus that consists of visual *noise (2) in the form of a random array of light and dark areas. **pattern masking by structure** *n.* *Pattern masking using a masking stimulus that consists of an array of light and dark areas each of which is similar to an element of the test stimulus.

pattern recognition *n.* Identification of a pattern as the same as one previously encountered despite modifications, as when a printed character or symbol is presented in a different font, colour, or size, or is viewed from a different angle. *See also* perceptron. *Compare* object recognition.

Pavlovian conditioning *n.* Another name for *classical conditioning.
[Named after the Russian physiologist Ivan Petrovich Pavlov (1849–1936) who introduced it in 1923]

pavor diurnus *n.* A daytime counterpart of pavor nocturnus or *sleep terror disorder; a form of sleep terror disorder associated with daytime sleep, usually in children.
[From Latin *pavor* fear or dread + *diurnalis* of the day]

pavor nocturnus *n.* Another name for *sleep terror disorder. Also called *night terrors*.
[From Latin *pavor* fear or dread + *nocturnus* of the night]

Paxil *n.* A proprietary name for the antidepressant drug *paroxetine.
[Trademark]

payoff *n.* A gain or loss resulting from a particular action or event, especially (in *game theory) a gain or loss of *utility (1) associated with the outcome of a strategic *game (1).

P cell *abbrev.* A type of ganglion cell belonging to the *parvocellular system. Also called an *X cell*. *See also* midget cell. *Compare* M cell.

Pcpt-Cs process *n.* In *psychoanalysis, a term used by Sigmund Freud (1856–1939) to denote any function of the *perception–consciousness system. Also called a *ω process* or a *W process*.

Peabody Picture Vocabulary Test *n.* A multiple-choice test, suitable for children from $2\frac{1}{2}$ to 18 years of age, designed to measure the respondent's receptive vocabulary, generally interpreted as verbal intelligence. It is untimed but takes 15 minutes or less to administer, it is issued in two parallel forms, and like a standard IQ test it yields scores on a scale with a *mean of 100 and a *standard deviation of 15. Administration of the test requires no reading by the respondent: the examiner reads aloud a series of stimulus words, and in each case the respondent selects a picture corresponding to the word from a set of four alternatives, the words being arranged within the test in ascending order of difficulty. The test was developed by the Canadian-born psychologist Lloyd M. Dunn (born 1917) and published in 1959, and a revised version (with the suffix *-Revised*) was issued in 1981. **PPVT** or **PPVT-R** *abbrev.*
[So called because it was constructed at George Peabody College in Nashville, Tennessee, where Lloyd M. Dunn was Professor of Special Education]

peace pill *n.* A common street name for the depressant drug *phencyclidine. Also spelt *PC pill*.

peak clipping *n.* A common form of distortion in telephones and other auditory transmission systems in which the peaks of the waveform are flattened off—to only one or two per cent of their original height in severe peak clipping—transforming the waveform into a sequence of rectangular pulses. When applied to speech it has surprisingly little effect on its intelligibility, 80 or 90 per cent of words still being correctly interpreted by listeners when the clipping is severe.

peak experience *n.* An *altered state of consciousness resembling a form of *oceanic feeling, in which a person experiences an ecstatic dissolution of the usual bonds of space and time and an attitude of wonderment and awe. The concept was introduced by the US psychologist Abraham Maslow (1908–70) in his book *Religions, Values, and Peak-Experiences* (1964, pp. 59–68).

peak shift *n.* A phenomenon of *discrimination learning, when an animal has learnt to distinguish between a positive and a negative stimulus lying on the same stimulus dimension, such as light stimulus associated with reward and a dark stimulus not associated with reward. If the animal is then tested with a variety of stimuli spanning the stimulus dimension (in this example, stimuli of various shades of lightness), it responds maximally not to the original positive stimulus but to a stimulus further from the negative stimulus (a stimulus even lighter than the original positive stimulus).

Pearson chi-square test *n.* Another name for the *chi-square test when the Pearson formula is used. *Compare* likelihood ratio chi-square test.
[Named after the English statistician Karl Pearson (1857–1936) who developed it in 1900]

Pearson's correlation coefficient *See* product–moment correlation coefficient.

pecking order *n.* A *dominance hierarchy within a flock of poultry in which each bird is able to peck without retaliation only those lower in the hierarchy and is liable to be pecked only by those above. There are usually separate pecking orders for males and females, with all the males dominating all the females, and the highest-ranked (alpha or α) male, often with the largest comb (itself determined by high *testosterone level), dominating all the others but in practice pecking only his nearest rivals. Also called a *peck order*. Compare hook order.

[A literal translation of the German *Hackordnung*, the name given to it in 1922 by the Norwegian psychologist Thorleif Schjelderup-Ebbe (1894–1976) following his pioneering study of domestic hens]

PEC scale *abbrev.* A scale to measure political and economic conservatism of attitudes first published by the German philosopher, sociologist, and psychologist Theodor W(iesengrund) Adorno (1903–69) and several colleagues in the book *The Authoritarian Personality* (1950). *See also* authoritarianism.

pederasty *n.* Sex between a man and a boy, especially involving anal intercourse.
[From Greek *pais, paidos* a boy + *erastes* a lover]

pedophilia *n.* An alternative spelling, especially in the US, of *paedophilia.

peduncle *n.* Any stalklike structure, especially a bundle of white nerve fibres in the brain. *See* cerebellar peduncle, cerebral peduncle. **peduncular** *adj.*
[From Latin *pedunculus* a corruption of *pediculus* a little foot, from *pes, pedis* a foot]

peeping Tom *n.* Another name for a *voyeur.
[Named after a 13th-century English legend according to which Lady Godiva rode naked through the marketplace of Coventry in response to a promise from her husband, Leofric, Earl of Mercia, that he would reduce taxes if she did so. In a later version of the legend, all the townspeople averted their eyes except a tailor called Tom, who was struck blind for his sin]

pegboard test *n.* A test of perceptual-motor skill in which pegs have to be inserted into holes as quickly as possible.

peg-word mnemonic *n.* A flexible and effective *mnemonic for memorizing long lists of items in a specific numerical sequence by forming mental associations with a list of words that are already known or can be generated to order. A popular set of peg-words, easy to remember because they rhyme with the names of the first ten natural numbers, is: one

is a *bun*, two is a *shoe*, three is a *tree*, four is a *door*, five is a *hive*, six is *sticks*, seven is *heaven*, eight is a *gate*, nine is *wine*, ten is a *hen*. To memorize the ten commandments, one might form vivid mental images such as these: (1) a *bun* inscribed with *One God* in icing; (2) a *shoe* decorated with *graven images* of gods, animals, and fishes; (3) a *tree* into which children have climbed and are loudly *taking God's name in vain*; (4) a *door* hung with a calendar showing the *Sabbath days* blacked out; (5) a *hive* being presented to *honour one's father and mother*; (6) *sticks* being used to *kill* someone; (7) *heaven* up above, with a sign *No Adultery* written in the clouds; (8) a *gate* with a thief climbing over it to *steal* something; (9) a *wine* bottle sticking out of the pocket of a witness giving *false testimony* in court; (10) a *hen* being *coveted* by a neighbour over a garden fence. When the time comes to recall them, *bun* should bring back the image of the inscription *One God*, *shoe* should remind one of the graven images decorating it, and so on. For lists of unlimited length, the standard system used by experts is to generate peg-words from numbers by using a technique introduced in 1634 by the French mathematician Pierre Hérigone (1580–1643) in which each of the ten digits has one or more consonants assigned to it, and then words lending themselves to vivid images are formed from numbers by inserting vowels freely. In the modern version of the Hérigone code, 1 is associated with *t* or *d*; 2 with *n*; 3 with *m*; 4 with *r*; 5 with *l*; 6 with *ch, j,* or *sh*; 7 with *k*, hard *c*, or hard *g*; 8 with *f* or *v*; 9 with *p* or *b*; and 0 with *s* or *z*. The peg-word for the number 1 might be *toe*, 31 might be *mat*, and 131 might be *tomato*, and so on. The system is also useful for memorizing numbers, such as 1879, the year in which the world's first psychological laboratory was opened in Leipzig, which might be translated into a mental image of a *dove cup*—a trophy cup engraved with an image of the dove of peace to commemorate the event; but one's own images always work best, especially if they are more bizarre than that. Also called *keyword mnemonic*. *See also* mnemonist.

pellagra *n.* A disease that is caused by dietary deficiency of niacin or nicotinic acid, a member of the *vitamin B complex contained in milk, liver, yeast, and other foods, and that results in wasting of the body, itching and scaling of the skin, inflammation of the mouth, diarrhoea, and mental retardation.

[From Italian *pelle* skin + *agra* rough, or Greek *pella* skin + *agra* seizure]

penetrability, cognitive *See* cognitive penetrability.

penetrance *n.* The degree to which a *gene is expressed in the *phenotype, often indexed by the proportion of organisms with the specified genotype who show the characteristic. *See also* dominance (genetic).

penile plethysmograph *n.* An instrument for recording changes in the volume of the *penis, generally used to study sexual responses of men to various stimuli. *See also* plethysmograph.
[From *penis* + Greek *plethysmos* enlargement + *graphein* to write]

penis *n.* The external male sexual organ, in humans and other mammals also used for excretion of urine. *See also* phallus, Wolffian duct. *Compare* clitoris. **penile** *adj.*
[Latin *penis* originally a tail]

penis dentata *n.* A fantasy of a toothed penis encountered in some women with neurotic sexual fears. *See also vagina dentata.*
[From Latin *penis* originally a tail + *dentata* toothed, from *dens, dentis* a tooth]

penis envy *n.* In *psychoanalysis, a key aspect of female psychology, originating in a girl's discovery of the anatomic differences between the sexes, causing her to feel deprived, and later, during the *Oedipal phase, to develop a desire for a penis, manifested symbolically as a desire to have a child or to possess a penis in sexual intercourse. Sigmund Freud (1856–1939) introduced the concept in 1914 in connection with the *castration complex in girls in his article 'On Narcissism: An Introduction' (*Standard Edition*, XIV, pp. 73–102, at p. 92) and developed it further in an article in 1917 'On the Transformations of Instinct, as Exemplified in Anal Erotism' (*Standard Edition*, XVII, pp. 127–33). The concept was rejected by the German-born US psychoanalyst Karen Horney (1885–1952) and the Welsh psychoanalyst Ernest Jones (1879–1958), among others, and was given less prominence by the British-based Austrian psychoanalyst Melanie Klein (1882–1960). *See also* phallic stage.

Penrose staircase *n.* Another name for the *staircase illusion.

Penrose triangle *n.* An *impossible figure of a solid triangular frame that could not exist in actual space although each of its corners, considered on its own, is feasibly constructed (see illustration). Also called an *impossible triangle* or a *tribar*. The first recognizable version of it was depicted in 1934 as an impossible arrangement of nine cubes by the Swedish artist Oscar Reutersvärd (1915–2001) and was used as a design for a postage stamp issued in Sweden in 1982.
[Named after the English psychologist/geneticist Lionel S. Penrose (1898–1972) and his mathematical physicist son Roger Penrose (born 1931) who, unaware of Reutersvärd's earlier work, published a version of it in 1958]

Penrose triangle

pentazocine *n.* A synthetic *opiate drug, being a *narcotic analgesic that is less addictive than morphine and is sometimes taken as a street drug. Also called *Talwin* or *Fortral* (trademark). Formula: $C_{19}H_{27}NO$. *Compare* phenazocine.
[From Greek *pente* five + *azocine* a chemical compound]

pentobarbital *n.* Pentobarbitone sodium, a short-acting *barbiturate drug and central nervous system *depressant, used as a sedative and hypnotic, and sometimes taken as a street drug. Also called *Nembutal* (trademark) or *pentobarbitone*. Street names include *nebbies, yellow bullets.* Formula: $C_{11}H_{17}N_2O_3Na$.
[From Greek *pente* five + *barbit(uric) acid* + *-al* indicating a pharmaceutical product]

pentobarbitone *n. See* pentobarbital.

Pentothal n. Sodium Pentothal, a proprietary name for the barbiturate drug *thiopental sodium (thiopentone sodium). See also truth drug.
[Trademark]

pentylene tetrazol n. A synthetic, white, crystalline, bitter-tasting drug that functions as a central nervous system *stimulant by reducing the recovery time of neurons following *action potentials, this effect being brought about by increasing the permeability of the neurons' cell membranes to potassium. Also called Metrazol (trademark).
[From its chemical name pent(ameth)ylene tetrazol(e)]

Pepper's ghost n. A spectral image produced by a large sheet of clear glass positioned at an angle, allowing people and objects to be seen through it while an image of a person situated elsewhere, if brightly lit, is simultaneously reflected from it. It was used in Victorian theatre productions to project an image of an actor from a well beneath the front of the stage, the lighting on the actor being brightened or dimmed to make the image appear or disappear, the image itself having the quality of an apparition through which other actors on the stage could walk. The device is often wrongly described as being made from half-silvered glass. It should, perhaps, be called Dircks's ghost (see etymology immediately below).
[Named after the English analytical chemist John Henry Pepper (1821–1900) who improved it and was the first to demonstrate it in public at the Royal Polytechnic in London in 1862, although it had been invented earlier that year by the retired English civil engineer and patent agent Henry Dircks (1806–73) and was patented jointly by Pepper and Dircks in 1863]

pepper spray n. Oleoresin capsicum (OC), a mixture of the resin and essential oil of the cayenne pepper plant, developed in the 1980s as a dog repellent and later adapted for personal defence and crowd control, sprayed as an aerosol causing immediate but temporary inflammation (rather than irritation as with other *incapacitants) of the mucous membranes of the eyes, nose, throat, and lungs, with accompanying pain, blindness, and breathing difficulty. Compare BZ gas, CN gas, CS gas, Mace, tear gas.

pepsin n. Any of a group of digestive enzymes produced in the stomach in the inactive form pepsinogen and activated by the presence of acids to contribute to digestion by breaking down proteins into their component amino acids. Also spelt pepsine. See also gastric gland. **peptic** adj. Of or relating to *pepsin or digestion.
[From Greek peptein to digest]

peptide n. Any chemical compound of two or more *amino acids linked by chemical bonds between their respective amino and carboxyl groups, including a substance such as an *endorphin that regulates various bodily functions and plays an important part in the experience of *pain. See also polypeptide.
[From Greek peptein to digest]

peptide hormone n. Any *hormone that is a *peptide or *polypeptide, in contrast to a *steroid hormone; the hormones of the hypothalamus and most of the endocrine glands being *peptide hormones, apart from those of the adrenal cortex, testes, and ovaries, which are steroid hormones. Many peptide hormones function also as *neurotransmitters.

perceive vb. To become aware or gain knowledge of something through the senses, or to comprehend or grasp a stimulus. See also perception.
[From Latin percipere to seize thoroughly, from per thoroughly + capere to grasp]

percentile n. Any of the 100 equal groups into which a distribution of scores can be divided, or the value of a variable such that a specified percentage of scores, arranged in order or magnitude, fall below that value, the 95th percentile, for example, being the value of the variable such that 95 per cent of the other scores fall below that value. The 25th, 50th, and 75th percentiles are also *quartiles, and the 50th percentile is the *median of any distribution. A percentile is also called a centile. See also partile. Compare decile, quartile.
[From Latin per centum out of every hundred]

percept n. The mental representation of something that is *perceived, an object or image as perceived by the senses rather than the physical stimulus that generates it, distinct from both the *proximal stimulus and the *distal stimulus. See also perception.

perception *n*. The act, process, or product of *perceiving, the ability or capacity to perceive, or a particular way of perceiving (*Newspapers influenced the public's perception of Princess Diana*). In psychology, a distinction is conventionally drawn between *sensation, the subjective experience or feeling that results from excitation of *sensory receptors, and perception, sensory experience that has been interpreted with reference to its presumed external stimulus object or event, this distinction having first been made in 1785 by Thomas Reid (1710–96), founder of the Scottish school of psychological philosophy, who pointed out that the agreeable fragrance of a rose is merely a sensation inasmuch as it can be experienced without thinking of a rose or of any other object, whereas the perception of a rose or of anything else always refers to the external object that is its cause. *Compare* apperception. **perceive** *vb*. To engage in *perception. **perceptual** *adj*. Of or relating to *perception.
[From Latin *percipere, perceptum* to perceive, from *per* through or thoroughly + *capere, ceptum* to take + *-ion* indicating an action, process, or state]

perception–consciousness system *n*. In the *psychoanalysis of Sigmund Freud (1856–1939), a subsystem of the mental apparatus characterized by *consciousness, receiving input from the outside world via the *sensory receptors and from the *preconscious via the activation of memories, and playing a dynamic role in avoidance of unacceptable thoughts or ideas and control of the *pleasure principle. In *An Outline of Psycho-Analysis* (1938), Freud considered the existence of this system to be 'a fact without parallel, which defies all explanation or description. . . . Nevertheless, if anyone speaks of consciousness we know immediately and from our most personal experience what is meant by it' (*Standard Edition*, XXIII, pp. 144–207, at p. 157). *ω* or *W* or **Pcpt-Cs** *abbrev*.

perceptron *n*. In *artificial intelligence, a pattern-recognition machine into which distinctive *features (1) of a target pattern are input with weights reflecting their relative importance. The machine is programmed to signal a decision that the target pattern is present whenever the sum of the weights of features in a test pattern presented to it exceeds a critical level, and a process of learning takes place as the weights of features present in a test pattern are increased after every *hit and decreased after every *false negative. The first version was introduced in an article in the journal *Psychological Review* in 1958 by the US psychologist Frank Rosenblatt (1928–71) and is an early example of a *neural network. *See also* computer vision, pattern recognition.
[From Latin *percipere, perceptum* to perceive, from *per* through + *capere, ceptum* to take + Greek *-tron* denoting an instrument, from *arotron* a plough]

perceptual constancy *n*. The tendency for a perceived object or a perceptual quality to appear the same when the pattern of sensory stimulation or *proximal stimulus alters through a change in orientation, distance, illumination, or some other extraneous influence or factor. *See* colour constancy, lightness constancy, melodic constancy, object constancy, odour constancy, person constancy, position constancy, shape constancy, size constancy, velocity constancy, word constancy. *See also* Brunswik ratio, Land effect, phenomenal regression, retinex theory, shape–slant invariance, template matching, Thouless ratio.

perceptual cycle *n*. A term introduced by the US psychologist Ulrich (Richard Gustav) Neisser (born 1928) for (a) the set of cognitive *schemata that direct perceptual processes, (b) the perceptual responses through which perceptual information is sampled, and (c) the physical stimuli that give rise to perception, the assumption being that a cyclic *feedback mechanism causes a change in (c) to lead to a change of (a), which in turn leads to a change in (b), which affects (c), and so on indefinitely. Also called the *cyclic model of perception*. *See also* constructivism.

perceptual defence *n*. The process by which stimuli that are potentially threatening, offensive, or unpleasant are either not perceived or are distorted in perception, especially when presented as brief flashes in a *tachistoscope. US *perceptual defense*.

perceptual differentiation *n*. The process by which exposure to a range of stimuli belonging to a particular class increases one's ability to discriminate between them.

perceptual field *n*. A general term for the *visual field or the analogous range of stimuli available to any other sense organ. *Compare* receptive field.

perceptual illusion *n*. A misperception of a stimulus object, event, or experience, or a stimulus that gives rise to such a misperception or misconception; more generally any misleading, deceptive, or puzzling stimulus or the perceptual experience that it generates. *See* auditory illusion, tactile illusion, visual illusion. *See also* constant error, naive realism. [From Latin *illusio, illusionis* deceit, from *illudere* to mock or make sport with, from *ludere* to play]

perceptual memory *n*. Long-term memory for visual, auditory, and other perceptual information, including memory for people's faces and voices, the appearance of buildings, familiar tunes, the flavours of particular foods and drinks, and so on. Stored information of this type does not fall into the category of *episodic memory, and it is therefore often included in *semantic memory, but this is avoided in careful usage because it is not (and in some cases cannot be) encoded in words. It should not be confused with *sensory memory.

perceptual–motor skill *n*. Any ability or capacity involving the interaction of *perception and voluntary movement, typical examples being the ability to type and the ability to play a ball game.

perceptual schema *n*. A structured internal *representation (1) of an object or image acquired through perception. *See also* schema.

perceptual sensitization *n*. An abnormally lowered threshold for the perception of certain stimuli, tending to result in *false alarms (2). Also called *perceptual vigilance*.

perceptual set *n*. A temporary readiness or predisposition to perceive in a particular way. *See also* Aufgabe, Einstellung, set (2).

perceptual speed *n*. A skill involving the rapid identification of matching items, incorporated into many IQ tests, women tending to outperform men on measures of this skill.

perceptual vigilance *n*. Another name for *perceptual sensitization.

percipient *adj*. **1.** Perceptive, observant, or able to perceive. *n*. **2.** A person, organism, or machine that perceives.
[From Latin *percipiens* observing, from *percipere* to perceive, from *per* through or thoroughly + *capere* to take]

Percodan *n*. A proprietary name for a drug containing the narcotic analgesic *oxycodone that is sometimes taken as a street drug. [Trademark]

perdeviation effect *n*. A form of *adaptation (2) to an eccentric body posture held for some time, the sensation gradually developing that the posture is normal. *See also* Kohnstamm effect, postural aftereffect.
[From Latin *per* through or thoroughly + *de* from + *via* a way + *-ation* indicating a process or condition]

perdida del alma *n*. Another name for *susto. [From Spanish *perdida* loss + *del* of + *alma* soul]

peregrinating patient *n*. Another name for a person with *Munchausen syndrome.

perfect pitch *n*. Another name for *absolute pitch, but a term that is avoided in careful usage. Absolute pitch could never be exact, because the *frequency (1) of a sound wave is a continuous variable, and differences in frequency can be arbitrarily small.

perforant pathway *n*. A major tract of afferent nerve fibres from the *entorhinal cortex to the *hippocampus.
[From Latin *per* through + *forare* to bore]

performance *n*. **1.** The act or process of carrying out a sequence of behaviour, especially the presentation of a dramatic role or piece of music. **2.** In linguistics, especially in *generative grammar and *transformational grammar, a term introduced by the US linguist and philosopher (Avram) Noam Chomsky (born 1928) to denote the specific utterances of a native speaker of a language, including hesitations, false starts, and speech errors, in contrast to their underlying *competence (2). It is analogous to the concept of *parole. Also called *linguistic performance*.

performance anxiety *n*. A form of *anxiety preceding or accompanying participation in a musical, theatrical, sporting, or other activity involving public self-presentation before an audience. Also called *stage fright*. *See also* audience effect, beta-blocker, drive theory of social facilitation.

performance enhancer *n*. Any drug or treatment that improves an athlete's level of achievement. Among the drugs that have been used for this purpose are *anabolic steroids, *creatine, *erythropoietin, *testosterone, *growth hormone, *stimulant drugs, *beta-blockers, and *smart drugs. Also called a *performance-enhancing drug*.

performance operating characteristic *n*. A graph showing the performance of one task plotted against the performance of a different task, when both tasks are performed at the same time. In general, it shows a trade-off, with relatively good performance on one task being associated with relatively poor performance on the other. *See also* attention operating characteristic. **POC** *abbrev*.

performance test *n*. In psychometrics, any *non-verbal test of aptitude, ability, or intelligence.

periaqueductal grey matter *n*. An area surrounding the *cerebral aqueduct in the pons and thalamus. It contains opiate *neuroreceptors and neurons that release *endorphins and is thus implicated in the sensation and suppression of *pain, and it is also implicated in the control of aggression and in female sexual behaviour. US *periaqueductal gray matter*. **PAG** *abbrev*.
[From Greek *peri* around + Latin *aqua* water + *ductus* a leading, from *ducere, ductus* to lead]

periglomerular cell *n*. A type of horizontally oriented cell in an *olfactory bulb responsible for lateral interactions within the bulb.
[From Greek *peri* around + Latin *glomerulus* a little ball, diminutive of *glomus* a ball]

perikaryon *n*. The part of a cell surrounding the *nucleus (1). Also called the *cytoplasm*.
[From Greek *peri* around + *karyon* a kernel]

perilymph *n*. The fluid contained within the *scala tympani and the *scala vestibuli in the space between the membranous labyrinth and bony labyrinth of the *inner ear. *Compare* endolymph.

[From Greek *peri* around + Latin *lympha* water, alluding to the fact that it lies outside the membranous labyrinth, unlike endolymph]

perimetry *n*. Mapping the limits of the *visual field for stimuli of various kinds (especially colours) with a *perimeter*, a device consisting of a light stimulus on the end of an adjustable arm that moves to various positions while the person being tested maintains a steady fixation on a point immediately ahead and reports visual sensations, the resulting map of the visual field being projected on to the inside of a spherical surface.
[From Greek *perimetros* a boundary, from *peri* around + *metron* a measure]

perineal *adj*. Of or relating to the perineum (or perinaeum), the diamond-shaped part of the body between the genital organs and the anus.
[From Greek *perinaion* the perineum, from *peri* around + *inein* to empty out]

perineural *adj*. Of or relating to the connective tissue that forms a sheath around a bundle of nerve fibres. Also written *perineurial* or *perineuronal*. **perineurium** *n*.
[From Greek *peri* around + *neuron* a nerve]

peripheral dyslexia *n*. Another name for *visual word-form dyslexia.

peripheral nerve *n*. Any nerve belonging to the *peripheral nervous system.

peripheral nervous system *n*. All of the *nervous system outside the brain and spinal cord, including the *cranial nerves apart from the *optic nerves (the second pair of cranial nerves), the *spinal nerves, and the *autonomic nervous system. *Compare* central nervous system. **PNS** *abbrev*.

peripheral vision *n*. Perception of stimuli that are not being fixated directly and are projected on to the retina outside the *macula lutea. *See also* Arago phenomenon. *Compare* central vision.

peristalsis *n*. Travelling waves of involuntary contractions along the *alimentary canal, controlled by the parasympathetic nervous system, causing food and waste products to move down it; also similar contractions in other tubular organs. **peristaltic** *adj*.

[From Greek *peristellein* to wrap around, from *peri* around + *stellein* to press together]

Perky phenomenon *n*. The act or process of mistaking a physical stimulus for an image of imagination, an effect first demonstrated in a group of viewers who were instructed to stare fixedly at a mark on a ground glass screen and to imagine a red tomato as vividly as possible while a very faint (sub-threshold) and slightly blurred image of a red tomato was back-projected on to the screen and its illumination gradually increased until the observer reported experiencing an image of a tomato, the procedure then being repeated with images of a blue book, a banana, an orange, a leaf, and a lemon, whereupon the observers all mistook the visual stimuli for images of imagination, and not one of them realized that light stimuli were being projected on to the screen. In almost all cases the observers reported the images only after the illumination had been increased well above the threshold at which the stimuli were perceived by a control group of viewers who were not vividly imagining the objects, therefore the phenomenon is interpreted by some authorities as a type of *visual masking by imaginary mental images, the perception of stimuli apparently being partially suppressed by vividly imagined visual images.
[Named after US psychologist Cheves West Perky (1874–1940) who first reported it in 1910, while she was a postgraduate student under the English psychologist Edward Bradford Titchener (1867–1927) at Cornell University]

perlocutionary act *n*. The effect of a *speech act on a listener. An *illocutionary act may not produce the intended perlocutionary act on the part of the listener, as when a threat fails to induce fear. *Compare* locutionary act.
[From Latin *per* through + *locutio* an utterance, from *loqui* to speak]

perphenazine *n*. A *neuroleptic (1) drug belonging to the class of *phenothiazines, used in the treatment of anxiety, tension, and agitation in *schizophrenia and other *psychotic (1) disorders and in the control of nausea, vomiting, and hiccups. Also called *Trilafon* (trademark).
[A blend of *piperazine* and *phene* an old name for benzene, from Greek *phainein* to show, al-

luding to its use in manufacturing illuminating gas]

persecution, delusion of *See* persecutory delusion.

persecutory delusion *n*. A *delusion of being conspired or plotted against, cheated, spied on, stalked, poisoned, drugged, slandered, harassed, or obstructed.

persecutory delusional disorder *n*. A type of *delusional disorder in which the central delusion is a *persecutory delusion.

perseveration *n*. **1.** The continuance or recurrence of a sensation, impression, or idea during subsequent activity; the automatic repetition of an action, utterance, thought, or other form of behaviour; or the difficulty experienced in switching from one pattern of behaviour or method of working to another. **2.** Meaningless or pointless repetition of words, phrases, ideas, or actions, characteristic of some forms of *thought disorder and some neurological disorders such as *frontal lobe syndrome.
[From Latin *perseverare* to remain steadfast or to persist, from *per* through or thoroughly + *severus* strict + *-ation* indicating a process or condition]

persistent vegetative state *n*. A generally irreversible condition resulting from severe brain damage in which a person is alive, has spontaneous breathing, heartbeat, and sleep–wake cycle, but is incapable of voluntary movement and is judged to lack conscious awareness. Also called *persistent vegetative syndrome* or (especially if it has not persisted for long) a *vegetative state*. *Compare* locked-in syndrome. **PVS** *abbrev*.

persona *n*. **1.** In *analytical psychology, the mask or face that a person presents to the world, often derived from a sense of gender identity (as when a woman plays the role of a loyal wife), or a stage of development (a rebellious adolescent), or an occupation (as in a trustworthy doctor), and over the lifespan a person may adopt various different personas derived from *archetypes (2). Carl Gustav Jung (1875–1961) believed that a persona can become pathological if a person identifies too closely with it, causing it to stifle awareness of anything beyond the social role and reducing the person's ability to adapt to changing circumstances. **2.** A character in a play or other work of fiction, as in *dramatis personae*, a list of characters. **3.** An assumed identity. **personas** or **personae** *pl.*

[From Latin *persona* an actor's mask]

personal constructs therapy *n.* A technique of *psychotherapy based on the *personal construct theory of the US psychologist George A(lexander) Kelly (1905–66) in which the client or patient is encouraged to formulate hypotheses and try out new constructs for interpreting experience. *Compare* cognitive therapy, fixed-role therapy.

personal construct theory *n.* A theory or personality, formulated by the US psychologist George A(lexander) Kelly (1905–66) and published in his book *The Psychology of Personal Constructs* (1955), according to which people think like incipient scientists in construing their worlds, constantly formulating hypotheses and testing their predictions against experience. The fundamental postulate of the theory is that 'a person's processes are psychologically channelized by the ways in which he anticipates events' (Vol. 1, p. 46), and this postulate is extended by eleven corollaries, including the individuality corollary: 'Persons differ from each other in their construction of events' (p. 55), and the dichotomy corollary: 'A person's construction system is composed of a finite number of dichotomous constructs' (p. 59), a dichotomous construct being a way of construing reality such that any pair of elements of experience may be classified as being either similar or different. Personal constructs are elicited and studied with the help of the *Repertory Grid Test. The theory interprets emotion as follows: *threat* is an awareness of an imminent comprehensive change in one's core constructs when they appear inadequate; *anxiety* is an awareness of the existence of important elements that lie outside the range of convenience of one's construct system; *guilt* is an awareness of being dislodged from one's core role structure; and *hostility* is an effort to extort validational evidence in favour of a social prediction that has already failed. Two treatment techniques based on personal construct theory are *fixed-role therapy and *personal constructs therapy. **PCT** *abbrev.*

Personal Data Sheet *n.* The first *personality questionnaire of significance ever devised, and the first to be administered to large numbers of respondents, designed to measure maladjustment or neurosis, described as 'emotional fitness for warfare' but completed too late to be used in the First World War, constructed by the US psychologist Robert S(essions) Woodworth (1869–1962) and published in the journal *Psychological Bulletin* in 1919. It consists of 116 yes/no questions, many of them based on common neurotic symptoms (such as *Do you feel low-spirited most of the time? Do you ever feel an awful pressure in or about your head? Did you have a happy childhood?*) and only items that were answered in the keyed direction by fewer than 25 per cent of a control group of normal respondents were included in the final test. *Compare* Bernreuter Personality Inventory.

personal equation *n.* A person's characteristic *reaction time, or a correction for it, first investigated after an incident in which Neville Maskelyne (1732–1811), the eighth Astronomer Royal at Greenwich, reported in 1799 that he had found discrepancies averaging 0.8 second between his own observations of the transit times of stars across a hair-line, measured by counting the ticks of a pendulum clock, and those of his assistant, whom he had therefore fired, but in 1820 the German astronomer and mathematician Friedrich Wilhelm Bessel (1784–1846) followed up this report and discovered that even skilled astronomers vary consistently in the transit times that they report, and on the basis of this finding he introduced the personal equation for calibrating individuals to reflect these differences in what later came to be called reaction time. *See also* prior entry law.

personality *n.* The sum total of the behavioural and mental characteristics that are distinctive of an individual. Also, informally, the personal qualities that make a person socially popular, as in *Princess Diana had a lot of personality*, but this sense is avoided in careful psychological usage. *See also* interactionism (2), situationist critique.

[From Latin *personalitas* personality, from *personalis* of or relating to a person, from *persona* an actor's mask]

personality disorders *n.* A category of *mental disorders, with onset no later than early childhood, characterized by pervasive, inflexible, and enduring patterns of cognition, affect, interpersonal behaviour, or impulse control that deviate markedly from culturally shared expectations and lead to significant distress or impairment in social, occupational, or other important areas of functioning. *See* antisocial personality disorder, avoidant personality disorder, borderline personality disorder, dependent personality disorder, dissocial personality disorder, histrionic personality disorder, narcissistic personality disorder, obsessive–compulsive personality disorder, paranoid personality disorder, passive–aggressive personality disorder, psychopathy, schizoid personality disorder, schizotypal personality disorder, self-defeating personality disorder. Also called *character disorders. See also* inadequate personality.

personality inventory *n.* A *questionnaire designed to measure one or more personality characteristics, usually *traits.

personality, multiple (split) *See* dissociative identity disorder.

personal space *n.* The area round a person's or an animal's body into which other people or *conspecifics (1) may not normally intrude without provoking a negative reaction. In special circumstances, such as crowded situations, contact sports, or sexually intimate interactions, invasions of personal space need not cause negative reactions. *See also* proxemics.

personal unconscious *n.* In *analytical psychology, another name for the *unconscious (2), introduced by Carl Gustav Jung (1875–1961) to distinguish it from the *collective unconscious.

person-centred therapy *n.* Another name for *client-centred therapy. US *person-centered therapy.*

person constancy *n.* A form of *perceptual constancy through which a familiar person tends to remain recognizably the same individual in spite of large variations in such factors as clothes, hairstyle, and facial expression.

personification *n.* The attribution of human characteristics to non-human entities, as when the dying English television dramatist Dennis (Christopher George) Potter (1935–94) named his cancer Rupert, after a media mogul whom he hated; or a *figure of speech in which a non-human entity is referred to as though it were human, as in the phrases *merciful death* and *angry thunder*.

personnel psychology *n.* A branch of *occupational psychology or *industrial/organizational psychology devoted to *job analysis, *job satisfaction, personnel selection and placement, and training of employees in industry. *See also* ergonomics.

personology *n.* In *psychoanalysis, a term introduced by the US psychologist Henry Alexander Murray (1893–1988) to denote a theory of personality and social behaviour in which a person's needs and personality are considered as an integrated whole. *See also* Edwards Personal Preference Schedule, need (3), need-press, press, TAT.

person perception *n.* The area of social psychology concerned with how people perceive one another, factors such as *impression formation and *attribution operating in addition to the normal processes of perception. *See also* atmosphere effect, balance theory, dual-process model, halo effect, implicit personality theory, social perception, trait centrality.

perspective *n.* A point of view or way of regarding something; specifically, the appearance of objects relative to their distance from the viewer, or the effects of distance on their appearance, including especially *aerial perspective, *linear perspective, and *texture gradient.
[From Latin *ars perspectiva* the art of perspective, from *perspicere, perspectum* to inspect thoroughly, from *per* through + *specere* to see + *-ivus* indicating a tendency, inclination, or quality]

perspective illusion *n.* Any illusion in the perception of *perspective. *See* Ames room, corridor illusion, horizontal–vertical illusion, moon illusion, Necker cube, Ponzo illusion, Schröder staircase, Scripture's blocks, teacup illusion, trapezoidal window.

perspective reversal *n.* A phenomenon that occurs while viewing certain *ambiguous figures such as the *Necker cube, *Schröder staircase, or *Scripture's blocks, in which a change occurs in the apparent spatial orientation of the depicted object. Also called *alternating perspective* or *reversible perspective*. See Necker cube, Schröder staircase, Scripture's blocks.

persuasion *n.* The process by which *attitude change is brought about, usually by the presentation of a message containing arguments in favour or against the person, object, or issue to which the attitude applies. *See also* elaboration likelihood model, forced compliance, inoculation theory, law of social impact, rhetoric (1), sleeper effect, social influence.

pervasive developmental disorders *n.* In the classification of *DSM-IV, *mental disorders characterized by severe and extensive impairment in the development of social interaction and communication skills or by the presence of stereotyped behaviour, interests, and activities. See Asperger's disorder, autistic disorder, childhood disintegrative disorder, Rett's disorder. *Compare* specific developmental disorder.

perversion, sexual *n.* An obsolescent term, often considered offensive nowadays, for a *paraphilia. **pervert** *n.* One who practises a *perversion.
[From Latin *per-* wrongly + *vertere* to turn]

pethidine *n.* Meperidine hydrochloride, a synthetic, white, crystalline, *narcotic analgesic drug with a morphine-like action, used as a narcotic analgesic and sedative. US *meperidine*. Also called *Demerol* (trademark). *See also* MPPP, opioid-related disorders.
[A blend of *piperidine* and *methyl*]

petit mal seizure *n.* An obsolescent name for an *absence.
[From French *petit mal* little illness]

PET scan *abbrev.* Positron emission tomography scan, a non-invasive technique of *brain imaging that monitors *regional cerebral blood flow in the brain by recording the emission of gamma rays when radioactively labelled *glucose or some other substance introduced into the bloodstream is metabolized by neurons as they are activated. The radioactive atoms used in a PET scan emit subatomic particles called positrons (positive

electrons), which collide with their negatively charged counterparts, namely electrons. The two particles annihilate each other and emit two gamma rays that radiate in opposite directions and can be recorded by a ring of detectors round the person's head and traced back to their point of origin. A PET scan is expensive, requiring an on-site *cyclotron because of the short half-life of the radioactive materials produced, but it provides a dynamic record, usually colour-coded, of brain activity and can also be used to study other organs such as the heart and lungs. *Compare* radioisotope scan, SPECT scan.

peyote *n.* Another name for *mescaline or the cactus from which it is extracted.
[Mexican Spanish, from Nahuatl *peyotl*]

PGO spike *abbrev.* Pontogeniculo-occipital spike, a brief high-amplitude *EEG wave, representing an alerting response, occurring spontaneously during *REM sleep in the pons (where it is believed to originate), in the lateral geniculate nuclei, and in the occipital cortex, elicited in all phases of sleep by sounds or tactile stimuli. It is identical in appearance and probably similar in significance to an *eye-movement potential. Also called a *PGO wave* or *pontogeniculo-occipital wave*. *See also* nucleus gigantocellularis.
[From *p(ons)* + *(lateral) g(eniculate nucleus)* + *o(ccipital cortex)*]

pH *abbrev.* A measure of the acidity/alkalinity of a solution, originally the logarithm to the base 10 of the reciprocal of the concentration of hydrogen *ions in moles per cubic decimetre, now indexed to a standard solution of potassium hydrogen phthalate at 15°C, which has a pH of 4 by definition. *Acid (1) solutions have pH less than 7, pure water pH equal to 7, and *alkaline solutions have pH more than 7.
[Abbreviation of *potential of hydrogen*]

Phaedra complex *n.* The sexual love of a mother for her son.
[Named after Phaedra, the wife of Theseus in Greek mythology, who accused her stepson Hippolytus of raping her after he declined her sexual advances]

phagocyte *n.* Any cell such as a *macrophage, *astrocyte, *granulocyte, *monocyte, or *microglial cell that is specialized to absorb large

solid particles such as invading microorganisms or debris from dead cells. **phagocytic** *adj*. **phagocytosis** *n*. The process whereby a *phagocyte engulfs particles.
[From Greek *phagein* to consume + *kytos* a vessel or hollow]

phallic character *n*. In *psychoanalysis, a personality pattern determined by *fixation (2) at the *phallic stage, characterized by reckless, resolute, and self-assured adult personality traits, and sometimes also vanity, exhibitionism, and touchiness. Also called the *phallic personality*.

phallic erotism *n*. In *psychoanalysis, sensuous pleasure derived from stimulation of the penis or clitoris, and focusing of *libido in that region during the *phallic stage. **phallic-erotic** *adj*.

phallic stage *n*. In *psychoanalysis, the *libidinal stage of *psychosexual development from about 3–5 or 6 years of age, following the *oral stage and the *anal stage but before the *latency period and the *genital stage. Sigmund Freud (1856–1939) introduced the concept late in his writings, in articles entitled 'The Infantile Genital Organization' (1923), 'The Dissolution of the Oedipus Complex' (1924), and 'Some Psychical Consequences of the Anatomical Distinction Between the Sexes' (1925), all of which are in volume XIX of the *Standard Edition* (pp. 141–5, 173–9, 248–58). During the phallic stage, libido is centred on the genital organs but the child, whether male or female, recognizes only the male organ and the difference between the sexes is interpreted as phallic versus castrated. It is during this stage that the *castration complex predominates and the *Oedipus complex flourishes and then dissolves. Also called the *phallic phase. See also* penis envy, phallic character, phallic woman.

phallic symbol *n*. Any object that is taken as a symbol of a *phallus.

phallic woman *n*. An image or fantasy of a woman endowed with a *phallus, often discussed in *psychoanalysis, where it is given an *interpretation (2) in the light of the *phallic stage. Also called a *phallic mother. See also* combined parent-figure.

phallocentric *adj*. Focused on or obsessed with the *phallus, or biased towards cultural assumptions of male dominance symbolized by the phallus.

phallocrat *n*. A believer in or supporter of male superiority or dominance in social, economic, or political spheres.
[From Greek *phallos* a phallus + *kratos* power]

phallus *n*. Another name for the *penis, especially the erect penis considered as a symbol of masculinity, potency, or generation. The Hindu equivalent is *lingam, the phallic image of the god Shiva. The French psychoanalyst Jacques Lacan (1901–81) developed a theory, published in the *Bulletin de Psychologie* in 1958, of the phallus as a signifier of desire, the *Oedipus complex being reformulated as a conflict between being versus not being a phallus (or having versus not having a phallus), which plays a different role in the desires of each of the three parties involved in the complex. *See also* foreclosure, phallic character, phallic erotism, phallic stage, phallic symbol, phallic woman, phallocentric. **phallic** *adj*. Of or pertaining to the *phallus. **phalluses** or **phalli** *pl*.
[From Greek *phallos* a phallus]

phantasmagoria *n*. A fantastic or dreamlike sequence of real or imagined images. *See also* phantasticant. **phantasmagoric** or **phantasmagorical** *adj*.
[From French *phantasmagorie* production of phantasms, from Greek *phantasma* an appearance, from *phantazein* to make visible + *agora* an assembly or marketplace + *-ia* indicating a condition or quality]

phantasticant *n*. Any drug that induces vivid perceptual experiences or *phantasmagoria, the most common examples being *phenylalkylamines such as *mescaline, *STP, and *ecstasy (2); *indole alkaloids such as *psilocybin and *DMT; and various other compounds such as *LSD, *bufotenin, *harmine, *ibotenic acid, *myristin, *ololiuqui, and *phencyclidine. Also spelt *fantasticant. See also* Amanita muscaria, fly agaric, magic mushroom, morning glory, teonanactyl. *Compare* hallucinogen, psychedelic.
[From Greek *phantastikos* capable of imagining, from *phantazein* to make visible + *-ikos* re-

lating to or resembling + -*ant* indicating an agent]

phantasy *n.* An alternative spelling of *fantasy (1, 2, 3). This spelling tends to be favoured by British-based psychoanalysts when referring to unconscious thought processes.

phantom grating *n.* An illusory grating of vertical bars that is seen in a blank area of an image when the rest of the image, on both sides of the blank area, consists of a real grating moving slowly in one direction. The phantom grating moves along with the real grating, as if the real grating were moving under the paper and could be seen faintly through it, but the phantom disappears if the real grating stops moving, suggesting that the phantom is activated by *direction-sensitive neurons in the retina. *See also* apparent movement.
[From Greek *phantasma* an illusion, from *phantazein* to make visible, from *phainein* to show, from *phaein* to shine]

phantom limb *n.* An illusory sensation, experienced by an amputee, of the limb still being attached to the body, even when all sensory nerve fibres associated with the limb have been removed. It is experienced by almost all amputees, and the sensations include *pain in approximately 70 per cent of cases. *See also* pseudaesthesia.

phantom phoneme effect *n.* Another name for *phonemic restoration.

pharmacodynamics *n.* The interaction of drugs with the *neuroreceptors that mediate *drug action. *Compare* pharmacokinetics.
[From Greek *pharmakon* a drug + *dynamikos* of or relating to strength or power, from *dynamis* strength or power + -*ikos* of, relating to, or resembling]

pharmacokinetics *n.* The mathematical analysis of the absorption, movement through the body, metabolism, and excretion of drugs. *Compare* pharmacodynamics.
[From Greek *pharmakon* a drug + *kinetikos* of or relating to motion, from *kinesis* movement + -*ikos* of, relating to, or resembling]

pharmacology *n.* The study of drugs. *See also* behavioural pharmacology, psychopharmacology. **pharmacological** *adj.* Of or relating to drugs or the study of drugs. **pharmacologist** *n.* A specialist in *pharmacology.
[From Greek *pharmakon* a drug + *logos* word, discourse, or reason]

pharyngeal reflex *n.* Another name for the *gag reflex.

pharynx *n.* The section of the *alimentary canal between the mouth and the *oesophagus. **pharyngeal** *adj.*
[From Greek *pharynx* the throat]

phase *n.* Any distinct or characteristic period or stage in a process or a sequence of development or evolution, including especially a particular stage (such as the peak or the trough) in the cycle of a periodic oscillation or wave.
[From Greek *phasis* a phase, from *phaein* to shine, alluding to the phases of the moon]

phase delay *n.* A continuous or ongoing binaural difference in the *phase of a sound wave arising from the fact that the peaks arrive momentarily sooner at the nearer ear than the further ear. It is used in conjunction with *transient disparity as a *cue (2) for localization of sounds below about 1,000 hertz (about two octaves above Middle C) that have wavelengths longer than the diameter of the head, bending round the head rather than being absorbed or reflected by it, and that therefore do not cast *sonic shadows on the side further from the sound source. It is one of the *binaural time differences* or *interaural time differences* used in sound localization. Also called *phase difference*, *ongoing disparity*, or *ongoing time disparity*. *See also* binaural shift, biosonar, cone of confusion, sound localization.

phase-locking *n.* The synchronization of the phases of two or more waveforms, so that their peaks and troughs occur simultaneously, as when auditory receptors in the *organ of Corti synchronize their receptor potentials with the vibration of the *basilar membrane for sounds below about 4,000 hertz.

phase sequence *n.* A group of *cell assemblies that tend to excite one another and that constitute a neural basis for the *consolidation of learning and memory, according to an influential hypothesis of the Canadian psychologist Donald O(lding) Hebb (1904–85). *See also* reverberating circuit.

phenazocine *n.* An *opiate drug and *narcotic analgesic with a greater analgesic effect and a slightly lesser narcotic effect than morphine. Formula: $C_{22}H_{27}NO$. *Compare* pentazocine.

[From *phen(e)* an old name for benzene, from Greek *phainein* to show, alluding to its use in manufacturing illuminating gas + *azocine* a chemical compound]

phencyclidine *n.* 1-1-Phenycyclohexyl-piperidine, or phencyclidine hydrochloride for short, a central nervous system *depressant developed in the 1950s as an *anaesthetic (1) and used in veterinary medicine to produce trancelike anaesthetic states in animals, adopted in the 1960s as a *psychedelic street drug capable of inducing vivid imagery. Street names include *hog*, *peace pill*, *tranq*, and most commonly *angel dust*. Formula $C_{17}H_{25}N$. *See also* hallucinogen, phantasticant, phencyclidine-related disorders. *Compare* ketamine. **PCP** *abbrev.*

phencyclidine-related disorders *n.* *Substance-related disorders induced by consuming *phencyclidine or phencyclidine-like compounds such as *ketamine, which may be taken orally, injected intravenously, or smoked. *See* substance abuse, substance dependence, substance-induced disorders, substance use disorders.

phenelzine *n.* Phenelzine sulphate (US *sulfate*), a *monoamine oxidase inhibitor (MAOI) derived from *hydrazine, used in the treatment of severe depression and panic disorder. [From its chemical name *phen(yl)* + *e(thy)l* + *(hydra)zine*]

phenmetrazine *n.* Phenmetrazine hydrochloride, a *sympathomimetic central nervous system *stimulant used as an appetite suppressant for weight control and sometimes taken as a street drug. Also called *Preludin* (trademark). Formula: $C_{11}H_{15}NO$. [From its chemical name *phen(yl)* + *me(thyl)* + *(te)tra* + *(oxa)zine*]

phennies *n.* A common street name of the barbiturate drug *phenobarbital (phenobarbitone).

phenobarbital *n.* Phenobarbital sodium, a long-acting *barbiturate drug and central nervous system *depressant, used as a sedative and hypnotic, especially in major epilepsy with tonic–clonic convulsions, and sometimes taken as a street drug. Also called *Luminal* (trademark) or *phenobarbitone*. Street names include *phennies*, *purple hearts*. Formula: $C_{12}H_{12}N_2O_3Na$.

[From *phen(e)* an old name for benzene, from Greek *phainein* to show, alluding to its use in manufacturing illuminating gas + *barbital*, from *barbit(uric) (acid)* + *-al* indicating a pharmaceutical product]

phenobarbitone *n. See* phenobarbital.

phenome *n.* The full set of characteristics constituting the *phenotype of an organism. *Compare* genome.
[From *phenotype*, on the model of *genome*]

phenomenal field *n.* The sum total of consciousness at a given moment. Also called the *phenomenological field*.

phenomenal motion *n.* Another name for *apparent movement.

phenomenal regression *n.* The tendency for one's perceptions of an object viewed obliquely or at a distance to be intermediate in shape or size between the *proximal stimulus and the actual object, or between the proximal stimulus and the perception that would occur if there were perfect *object constancy, as when a plate viewed at an angle and from a distance yields a proximal stimulus that is elliptical and small, but the perception is somewhat rounder and larger. Also called *phenomenal regression to the real object*, the term used by the English psychologist Robert Henry Thouless (1894–1984) when he introduced the concept in 1931.

phenomenal self *n.* The self as experienced or apprehended directly.

phenomenistic causality *n.* An important aspect of *phenomenistic thought, according to the Swiss psychologist Jean Piaget (1896–1980), in which events or processes that co-occur are interpreted as being causally linked, as when a child believes that trains go fast because they are big.

[From Greek *phainomenon* a thing shown, from *phainein* to show + *istikos* like]

phenomenistic thought *n.* A term introduced by the Swiss psychologist Jean Piaget (1896–1980) to characterize the reasoning of young children, whose cognitive processes focus on the physical appearances of objects in the environment. One important aspect of phenomenistic thought is *phenomenistic causality.

phenomenological field *n.* Another name for the *phenomenal field.

phenomenology *n.* A philosophical method of enquiry, introduced in 1901 by the German philosopher Edmund (Gustav Albert) Husserl (1859–1938), that concentrates on the detailed description of conscious experience while suspending or bracketing all preconceptions, interpretations, and explanations; more generally a *qualitative research method in psychology that concentrates on the analysis of mental experience rather than behaviour. *See also* act psychology, *Eigenwelt*, *epoche*, existentialism, intentionality (1), introspectionism, *Mitwelt*, sociology of knowledge, *Umwelt*.
[From Greek *phainomenon* a thing shown, from *phainein* to show + *logos* word, discourse, or reason]

phenomenon *n. sing.* Anything that can be perceived or observed. **phenomena** *pl.* **phenomenal** *adj.*
[From Greek *phainomenon* a thing shown, from *phainein* to show]

phenothiazine *n.* Any of a number of drugs such as *chlorpromazine, *fluphenazine, *perphenazine, *thioridazine, or *trifluoperazine that are derived from the phenothiazine compound $C_{12}H_9NS$ and that belong to the *neuroleptic (1) subgroup of psychotropic drugs, having a strong affinity for *dopamine neuroreceptors, which they block. *See also* dopamine antagonist, thioxanthene.

phenotype *n.* The characteristics of an organism, determined jointly by its genetic constitution and its environment, including such physical characteristics as stature and eye colour and such psychological characteristics as intelligence and extraversion; more specifically the outward manifestations of a

*gene, in comparison to its *alleles, in an organism that possesses it. *See also* extended phenotype, phenome. *Compare* genotype. **phenotypic** *adj.*
[From Greek *phainein* to show + *typos* a mark]

phenylalanine *n.* An essential *amino acid and precursor of *tyrosine, contained in milk, eggs, cheese, and many food proteins. People with *phenylketonuria cannot metabolize it and have to exclude it from their diets. Also spelt *phenylalanin*. *See also* aspartame. **Phe** *abbrev.*
[From *phene* an old name for benzene, from Greek *phainein* to show, alluding to its use in manufacturing illuminating gas + *hyle* material + German *Alanin(e)*, from *al(dehyde)* + Greek *-in(e)* indicating an organic compound]

phenylalkylamines *n.* One of the major groups of *hallucinogens and *psychedelic drugs, including especially *mescaline, *STP, and *ecstasy (2) or MDMA. *See also* phantasticant.

phenylethanolamine - N - methyltransferase *See* PNMT.

phenylethylamine *n.* An *amine that resembles *amphetamine chemically and pharmacologically and that functions as a *neurotransmitter in the nervous system. **PEA** *abbrev.*
[From *phenyl* (as in phenylalanine) + *ethyl*, from Greek *aither* ether, from *aithein* to burn + *hyle* wood or substance + English *amine*, from *am(monium)* + Greek *-ine* indicating an organic compound]

phenylketonuria *n.* A hereditary disorder caused by a single recessive gene, leading to the absence or deficiency of an enzyme required for the metabolism of *phenylalanine, an amino acid found in many proteins, to *tyrosine. Unless treated by dietary restriction of phenylalanine, it leads to a deficiency of *serotonin and the accumulation in all body fluids of phenylalanine, which is toxic to brain tissue and causes mental retardation. When two carriers of the gene have a child, there is a 1 in 4 chance that it will have the disorder, a 1 in 2 chance that it will be a carrier, and a 1 in 4 chance that it will be normal; and because approximately 1 in 50 people carry the recessive gene, the incidence of the

disorder is about 1 in 10,000 births. Also called *phenylpyruvic oligophrenia*. **PKU** *abbrev*.
[From *phenyl(alanine)* + *keton(e)* + *-uria* indicating a diseased state of the urine, from Greek *ouron* urine + *-ia* indicating a condition or quality]

phenylpyruvic oligophrenia *n*. Another name for *phenylketonuria.

phenylquinine writing test *n*. Observation of writhing in an experimental animal injected with phenylquinine, which normally causes pain and suffering, to test the efficacy of an *analgesic (1) drug or procedure.

phenylthiocarbamide *See* PTC.

phenytoin *n*. An anticonvulsant drug that is used in the treatment of *epilepsy and that acts by stabilizing neuron cell membranes, decreasing the intracellular concentration of sodium and thereby causing *hyperpolarization and preventing *action potentials. It is also taken as a supposedly *smart drug to improve IQ, concentration, verbal performance, and long-term memory.
[A contraction of its chemical name, *(di)pheny(lhydan)toin*]

pheromone *n*. Any of a number of chemical substances with communicative functions, secreted externally by an organism and affecting the behaviour or physiology of other members of the same species. Human pheromones are poorly understood, the best documented though controversial examples being the *Whitten effect, manifested as the synchronization of *menstrual cycles among women living together, occurring only when a man is also present, and the increased regularity of menstrual cycles of women living with men, both effects apparently being mediated by *steroid pheromones. *See also* alarm pheromone, Bruce effect, kairomone, Lee–Boot effect, sex pheromone, vomeronasal organ. *Compare* allomone. **pheromonal** *adj*.
[From Greek *pherein* to bear + *horman* to stimulate]

phi coefficient *n*. In statistics, an index of the degree of association between two truly dichotomous variables, such as male/female or pass/fail. Mathematically it is equivalent to the *product–moment correlation coefficient applied to two dichotomous variables, and in practice it is most often used to analyse data in *contingency tables. Symbol: ϕ. *Compare* Cramér's *C*, contingency coefficient.

philosophy *n*. The study of the nature of knowledge and beliefs, the intelligibility of concepts, and the validity of arguments. Its main branches include *metaphysics*, the study of the nature and phenomena of reality; *epistemology*, the theory of knowledge, especially the investigation of what distinguishes mere belief from knowledge; *ethics*, the study of moral principles and judgements; and *semantics*, the study of the relationship between linguistic expressions and their meanings. A useful informal definition of philosophy is thought about thought.
[From Greek *philosophia* love of wisdom, from *philos* loving, from *phileein* to love + *sophia* wisdom]

phi movement *n*. A form of pure objectless *apparent movement, without the appearance of any entity actually moving, that occurs when two visual stimuli a few centimetres apart are presented in an alternating pattern with an interstimulus interval too long for the stimuli to appear simultaneous or for *partial movement or *optimal movement to occur but not long enough for the disappearance of apparent movement and the veridical perception of the stimuli simply alternating. The term is often applied to any form of apparent movement, but it was defined precisely by the German psychologist Max Wertheimer (1880–1943) when he introduced it in 1912, and its indiscriminate application is avoided in careful usage. Wertheimer believed movement to be an immediate sense experience (a *quale*) like colour or lightness that under appropriate conditions may be perceived in a pure form as sheer objectless movement. The following demonstration provides an easy way to experience something similar to phi movement: hold a finger close enough to the eyes for a double image to be seen, then alternately open and close the left and right eyes—for some people, the finger appears to leap from one place to another without any image moving across the space. Also called *phi motion*, the *phi phenomenon*, or *pure phi*. *See also* Korte's laws.

phi phenomenon *n*. Another name for *phi movement. It is also applied to *apparent movement in general, but this is avoided in careful usage because it blurs the distinction between phi movement and other forms of apparent movement.

phlegm *n*. The slimy, viscous substance secreted in the throat and discharged by coughing, formerly believed to be one of the four cardinal humours of the body. *See also* humour (3). **phlegmatic** *adj*. Calm, unemotional, or cool-headed.
[From Latin *phlegma* phlegm, from Greek *phlegma* flame, inflammation, or phlegm (thought to be produced by heat), from *phlegein* to burn]

phobia *n*. A persistent, irrational fear of an object, event, activity, or situation called a *phobic stimulus*, resulting in a compelling desire to avoid it. The presence or anticipation of the phobic stimulus triggers *anxiety or a *panic attack, although the person acknowledges the fear to be irrational, and the phobic stimulus is either avoided or endured with dread. A phobia that leads to clinically significant distress or impairment in social, occupational, or other important areas of functioning may be diagnosed as a *mental disorder—either a *specific phobia or a *social phobia. A comprehensive list of phobias and phobic stimuli is provided in Appendix I at the back of this dictionary. According to the National Phobics Society, the eight most common phobias in the UK (in descending order) are: arachnophobia, social phobia, aeronausiphobia, agoraphobia, carcinophobia, brontophobia, thanatophobia, and cardiophobia. Also called a *phobic neurosis*. *See also* (in the main body of the dictionary) agoraphobia, dysmorphophobia, Little Hans, paleng, paraphobia, phobic technique, social phobia, specific phobia, thanatophobia. **phobic** *adj*.
[From Greek *phobos* fear + -*ia* indicating a condition or quality]

phobic stimulus *n*. Any object, event, or situation that functions as the focus of a *phobia, eliciting persistent, irrational fear.

phobic technique *n*. In *psychoanalysis, one of the *defensive techniques proposed by the Scottish psychoanalyst W. Ronald D. Fairbairn (1889–1964). It involves *externalization of both the *good object and the bad object, causing the phobic person to feel threatened by external forces. *See also* splitting of the object. *Compare* hysterical technique, obsessional technique, paranoid technique.

phon *n*. The standard unit of *loudness level, ranging upwards from zero for the faintest audible sound. The loudness in phons of a sound is defined as the intensity level in units of *decibel sound pressure level (dB SPL) of a comparison pure tone of 1,000 hertz that is judged by the listener to be equally loud. Thus if the comparison tone is 20 dB SPL, then the loudness of any tone of another frequency that is judged to be equally loud is defined to be 20 phons; if the comparison tone is 40 dB SPL, then any tone judged equally loud is 40 phons, and so on. *See also* equal-loudness contour.
[From Greek *phone* sound or voice]

phonagnosia *n*. A form of agnosia involving an impaired ability to identify people by their voices. *See also* agnosia. *Compare* prosopagnosia.
[From Greek *phone* a voice + *a*- without + *gnosis* knowing + -*ia* indicating a condition or quality]

phone *n*. The smallest perceptible discrete segment of sound in a stream of speech. A phone is a physical realization of a *phoneme, and different phones representing the same phoneme are *allophones.
[From Greek *phone* a voice or sound, from *phonein* to speak]

phoneme *n*. A basic speech sound, with an average duration of 70 to 80 milliseconds at normal speaking rate, distinguishing one word from another in a given language, although it may have various phonetically distinct articulations, called *allophones, that are regarded as functionally identical by native speakers of the language. Phonemes are defined by the *distinctive features that allow *minimal pairs in a language to be distinguished. *See also* neutralization, phone. *Compare* kineme. **phonemic** *adj*.
[From Greek *phonema* a sound or utterance, from *phone* a voice or sound]

phonemic restoration *n*. An *auditory illusion that occurs when a single *phoneme is deleted from a recording of a sentence (in the original experiment, the first /s/ of the word *legislatures* in the sentence *The state governors* *met with their respective legislatures convening in the capital city*) and is replaced by a recording of a cough or other intrusive sound; when this doctored recording is played to listeners, the missing phoneme is perceived as clearly as if it were physically present, even when the listeners hear the recording again after being told that the sound is missing. The cough cannot be clearly located in the sentence by listeners, but if the deleted sound is replaced by a silent gap it can be located easily and phonemic restoration does not occur. In spite of its name, the phenomenon is not restricted to single phonemes, a whole syllable such as the *-gis-* in the word *legislatures* being heard clearly when replaced by an extraneous sound of the same length. The phenomenon was discovered by the US psychologist Richard M. Warren (born 1925) and two colleagues and first reported in articles in the journals *Science* and *Scientific American* in 1970. Also called the *phantom phoneme effect. Compare* amodal completion.

phonemics *n*. The study of the *phonemes of a language.

phonetics *n*. The study of speech sounds, including their production, their use in language, their perception by listeners, and their transcription.
[From Greek *phonetikos* of or relating to speech, from *phone* a voice or sound + *-itikos* resembling or marked by]

phonics *n*. **1.** The science of spoken sounds, or of sounds in general. **2.** A method of teaching reading by concentrating on the sounds associated with specific letters or groups of letters. *Compare* whole-word method.
[From Greek *phonikos* of or relating to speech, from *phone* a voice or sound + *-ikos* of, relating to, or resembling]

phonogram *n*. A character or symbol, or a sequence of characters or symbols, representing a speech sound, such as (in English) *a, b, c, ch, ei,* or *th*. Some languages (including German or Spanish) are regular in the sense of having an unvarying correspondence between phonograms and *phonemes, while others (including English) are more or less irregular. *Compare* ideograph, logograph.
[From Greek *phonein* to make sounds or to speak + *gramma* a character]

phonography *n*. A system of writing based on *phonograms. Compare* logography.

phonological buffer store *n*. One of the two components of the *phonological loop of *working memory, holding phonologically coded information but capable of maintaining the information only for brief periods. Also called a *rehearsal buffer*.

phonological disorder *n*. A *communication disorder characterized by failure to use appropriate speech sounds (such as pronouncing the word *sea* like *she*), the deficit interfering with scholastic, academic, or occupational achievement or social communication and not being due solely to mental retardation, a speech-motor or sensory deficit, or environmental deprivation. Also called *articulation disorder. See also* aphasia.

phonological dyslexia *n*. A form of *dyslexia involving an impaired ability to read by using spelling-to-sound correspondences, and an over-reliance on established spelling vocabulary. Closely related to *deep dyslexia.

phonological loop *n*. A subsystem of *working memory that functions as a *buffer store, holding information with the help of *inner speech, as when a person mentally rehearses a telephone number over and over while searching for a pen and paper to write it down. It contains two components, a short-term *phonological buffer store, holding phonologically coded information for very short periods only, and a *subvocal rehearsal loop that maintains information by repeating it mentally from time to time.

phonological reading *n*. Another name for *surface dyslexia.

phonology *n*. The study of the sound systems of languages, especially the study of *phonemes. *See also* addressed phonology, assembled phonology. **phonological** *adj*.
[From Greek *phonein* to make sounds or to speak + *logos* word, discourse, or reason]

phonoreceptor *n*. Another name for an *auditory receptor. **phonoreception** *n*. The perception of high-frequency variations in air pressure through *auditory receptors.
[From Greek *phone* a sound or voice + English

receptor, from Latin *recipere, receptum* to receive, from *re-* back + *capere, ceptum* to take]

phosphate *n.* Any salt or *ester of phosphoric acid.
[From Greek *phosphoros* light-bringing, from *phos* light + *pherein* to bring]

phosphene *n.* The perception of a flash of light resulting from anything other than excitation of the photoreceptors of the retina by light, the most common causes being pressure on an eyeball behind closed lids, a blow to the head resulting in pressure of the visual cortex against the inside of the skull (the effect often described as seeing stars), electrical stimulation of the visual cortex, or an *aura (2) heralding an *epileptic seizure or a *migraine headache. Also called a *photoma*.
[From Greek *phos* light + *phainein* to show, from *phaein* to shine]

phosphocreatine *n.* Another name for *creatine phosphate, the *phosphate of creatine stored in muscles to enable adequate quantities of *ATP to be produced.
[From *phosphate* + Greek *kreas, kreatos* flesh]

phosphodiesterase type 5 *n.* An *enzyme that metabolizes *cyclic GMP. *See also* Viagra. **PDE5** *abbrev.*

phot *n.* An obsolescent unit of illumination equal to one *lumen per square centimetre, 1 phot being equal to 10,000 lux.
[From Greek *phos, photos* light]

photism *n.* **1.** A form of *synaesthesia (1) in which a visual sensation accompanies stimulation of another *sensory modality. **2.** The experience of a *phosphene.

photochemical *adj.* Of or relating to the production of light by a chemical process. *See also* bioluminescence.
[From Greek *phos, photos* light + English *chemical*]

photochromatic interval *n.* The range of light intensity that is sufficiently high to stimulate *rods but not *cones in the retina of the eye and that therefore produces vision without colour. *See also* scotopic.
[From Greek *phos, photos* light + *chroma, chro-*

matos a colour + *-ikos* of, relating to, or resembling]

photographic memory *n.* A colloquial term for the ability to remember visual images very accurately. The technical term for such an image remembered in vivid detail is an *eidetic image.

photoma *n.* Another name for a *phosphene.
[From Greek *phos, photos* light + *-oma* indicating an abnormality]

photometer *n.* An instrument for measuring *luminous intensity, older types usually involving visual comparisons of the illumination from a specified light source with that from a standard comparison source, and more modern types using photoelectric cells that generate electrical signals in response to light. **photometry** *n.* The measurement of *luminous intensity, *luminous flux, and related phenomena, or the branch of physics concerned with these phenomena.
[From Greek *phos, photos* light + *metron* a measure]

photon *n.* The basic unit or quantum of light or other electromagnetic radiation, considered as a particle with zero rest mass and energy equal to hf, where h is Planck's constant (6.6262×10^{-34} Joule seconds) and f is the *frequency (1) of the radiation in hertz.
[From Greek *phos, photos* light + *-on* by analogy with *electron*]

photopic *adj.* Of, relating to, or governed by the *cone-mediated visual system that functions when the eyes are light-adapted for bright illumination or day vision. It is maximally sensitive to light falling on the *fovea, and it has peak sensitivity at a wavelength of 555 nanometres (green light), but it responds to light across the entire *visible spectrum, operating with three different types of photoreceptors that normally provide colour vision, and it is less sensitive than the scotopic system except for wavelengths above 650 nanometres (in the red region of the spectrum), where the sensitivities of the two systems are similar. *See also* duplexity function, field adaptation, hemeralopia, light adaptation, photopic luminosity curve, Purkinje shift, Stiles–Crawford effect. *Compare* mesopic, scotopic. **photopia** *n.* *Photopic vision, also called *daylight vision. Compare* scotopia.

[From Greek *phos, photos* light + *ops* an eye + -*ikos* of, relating to, or resembling]

photopic luminosity curve *n.* A *luminosity curve depicting the intensity of light that is required at each point in the visible spectrum for the colours to appear equally bright in bright light, under *photopic vision mediated by *cones. *Compare* scotopic luminosity curve.

photopigment *n.* Any light-sensitive *pigment, including the *visual pigments found in the *photoreceptors of the eye.

photoreceptor *n.* A *sensory receptor situated at the back of the *retina, either a large cylindrical *rod or a smaller tapering *cone, specialized to convert light stimulation into electrical nerve impulses or *action potentials. The human retina contains approximately 120 million rods and 6 million cones. Also called a *visual receptor.

[From Greek *phos, photos* light + English *receptor*, from Latin *recipere, receptum* to receive, from *re-* back + *capere, ceptum* to take]

photosensitive epilepsy *n.* A form of *epilepsy in which seizures are precipitated by bright flashing or flickering lights, often from strobe lighting or television images. The physiological effects can be observed in *EEG recordings from the *occipital lobes of the brain.

phototherapy *n.* Controlled exposure to extremely bright light (generally 10,000 lux), simulating daylight, used especially to treat *seasonal affective disorder (SAD) and certain *sleep disorders. Also called *bright light therapy*.

[From Greek *phos, photos* light]

phrase marker *n.* A representation, usually in the form of a tree diagram, of the grammatical structure of a sentence (see illustration). The sentence is conventionally labelled S; a noun, N; a verb, V; a noun phrase, NP; a verb phrase, VP; a determiner, DET; and so on. *See also* constituent.

phrase-structure grammar *n.* A form of *generative grammar that describes the relations between words and *morphemes of a sen-

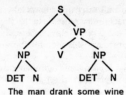

Phrase marker: S = sentence, NP = noun phrase, VP = verb phrase, DET = determiner, N = noun, V = verb.

tence, but does not analyse syntactic relations in greater depth.

phrase-structure rule *n.* Another name for a *rewrite rule.

phrenology *n.* A discredited doctrine of mental faculties supposedly located in specific areas of the brain and detectable through bumps at the corresponding points on the external skull. Founded in Germany by the physiologist Franz Joseph Gall (1758–1828) and the physician Johann Kaspar Spurzheim (1809–72), it flourished in the early decades of the 19th century, especially in the United States and Britain, where at one time there were 29 phrenological societies simultaneously active. *See also* faculty psychology.

[From Greek *phren* mind, originally midriff (the supposed seat of the soul) + *logos* word, discourse, or reason]

phylogeny *n.* The evolution of a *phylum or other *taxonomic group, as distinguished from the development of an individual organism. *Compare* ontogeny. **phylogenetic** or **phylogenic** *adj.*

[From Greek *phylon* a race + *genes* born]

phylum *n.* Any of the primary taxonomic groups into which the animal and plant *kingdoms (2) are divided, each containing one or more *classes (2). Thus the phylum Platyhelminthes contains flatworms, flukes, and tapeworms. **phyla** *pl.*

[From Greek *phylon* a race]

physical anthropology *n.* The branch of anthropology devoted to the study of physical and biological characteristics of humans, especially genetic traits, as opposed to cultural or social attributes. *Compare* cultural anthropology, social anthropology.

physiognomy *n.* **1.** A person's physical features or habitual expression. **2.** The art or pseudoscience of judging *personality from physical appearance, especially from the face. **3.** The outward appearance or gross physical structure of anything. **physiognomic** or **physiognomical** *adj.* **physiognomist** *n.* One who practises *physiognomy (2).
[From Greek *physis* nature + *gnomon* an interpreter]

physiological arousal *See* arousal.

physiological nystagmus *n.* A form of *nystagmus occurring continuously during visual *fixation (1), consisting of *ocular drifts with *visual angles up to about 5 minutes of arc (5/60 of a degree), *microsaccades between 1 and 2 minutes of arc, and *ocular tremors of about 30 seconds of arc (1/120 of a degree). That these eye movements are essential to vision is shown dramatically by experiments on *stabilized retinal images. *See also* autokinetic effect, filling-in illusion, reafference, saccade, visual suppression.

physiological psychology *n.* The branch of psychology devoted to the relations between physiological and psychological processes and events.

physiological time *n.* The fraction of *reaction time taken up by the passage of a nerve impulse from the *sensory receptor to the brain and of another nerve impulse from the brain to the muscle. According to an analysis introduced in 1868 by the Dutch ophthalmologist Franciscus Cornelius Donders (1818–89), total reaction time is physiological time plus *central reaction time.

physiological zero *n.* The temperature at which an object touching the *skin feels neither warm nor cold, its precise value not being fixed but approximating the surface temperature of the skin and depending on its state of adaptation to warmth. *See also* successive contrast, thermal adaptation.

physiology *n.* The study of the functioning of *organisms; also the working of a particular organism or one of its organs or parts (as in *the physiology of the human ear*).
[From Greek *physio-* of or relating to nature or natural processes, from *physis* nature, from

phyein to cause to grow + *logos* word, discourse, or reason]

physostigmine *n.* An *alkaloid extracted from the *Calabar bean that functions as a reversible *anticholinesterase drug, inhibiting the breakdown of *acetylcholinesterase. Also called *eserine*. Formula $C_{15}H_{21}N_3O_2$.
[From Latin *Physostigma venenosum* the Calabar bean plant, from Greek *physa* a bladder + *stigma* a mark]

Piagetian *adj.* Of, relating to, or resembling the theory of cognitive development of the Swiss psychologist Jean Piaget (1896–1980). *See* accommodation (2), adaptation (3), animism (1), assimilation (2), centration, concrete operations, conservation, constructivism, *décalage*, egocentrism, equilibration, formal operations, genetic epistemology, indissociation, mental operation, object permanence, phenomenistic causality, phenomenistic thought, preconcept, predicate thinking, pre-operational stage, scheme, sensorimotor stage, structuralism (1), transductive reasoning. *See also* Piaget kidnapping memory.

Piaget kidnapping memory *n.* A classic example of a *false memory from the second year of life described by the Swiss psychologist Jean Piaget (1896–1980) and reproduced in English translation by the US psychologist Elizabeth F. Loftus in her book *Eyewitness Testimony* (1979): 'I was sitting in my pram, which my nurse was pushing in the Champs Élysées, when a man tried to kidnap me. I was held in by the strap fastened round me while my nurse bravely tried to stand between me and the thief. She received various scratches, and I can still see vaguely those on her face. Then a crowd gathered, a policeman with a short cloak and a white baton came up and the man took to his heels. I can still see the whole scene, and can even place it near the tube station. When I was about fifteen my parents received a letter from my former nurse saying that she had been converted to the Salvation Army. She wanted to confess past faults, and in particular to return the watch she had been given on this occasion. She had made up the whole story, faking the scratches. I, therefore, must have heard, as a child, the account of the story, which my parents believed, and projected it into the past in the form of a visual memory' (pp.

62–3). *See also* constructive memory, deferred action, eyewitness misinformation effect, infantile amnesia, reality monitoring, recovered memory.

pia mater *n.* A delicate vascular membrane enclosing the brain and spinal cord, forming the innermost of the three *meninges, below the *arachnoid space. *Compare* arachnoid membrane, dura mater.
[Latin *pia mater* tender mother, a literal translation of the Arabic name *umm raqiqah*]

piano theory *n.* Another name for the *place theory.

pibloktoq *n.* A *culture-bound syndrome, sometimes called *arctic hysteria* in English, restricted mainly to Eskimo communities of North America and Greenland, characterized by a period of fatigue, social withdrawal, confusion, and irritability lasting for a few hours or days, leading up to an abrupt episode of *dissociation that usually lasts only minutes, during which the afflicted person may strip or tear off clothes, roll in the snow, run about in a frenzied state, shout obscenities, destroy property, engage in other violent, dangerous, or antisocial forms of behaviour, and manifest *pseudolalia, *echolalia, and *echopraxia, before lapsing into *convulsions and losing consciousness, followed typically by complete *amnesia for the dissociative episode.
[From Inuit *piblokto* frenzy]

pica *n.* An *eating disorder of infancy or early childhood characterized by persistent eating of inappropriate substances such as paint, plaster, string, hair, cloth, animal droppings, sand, insects, leaves, pebbles, clay, soil, or other non-nutritive matter, but without any aversion to conventional foods, the behaviour not occurring as part of a culturally sanctioned practice. *See also* coprophagia, geophagia, hyalophagia, pagophagia.
[From Latin *pica* a magpie, referring to its fondness for inedible objects]

Pick's disease *n.* A progressive disorder commencing in middle age, caused by predominantly *frontal lobe or *temporal lobe impairment, characterized by *dementia with gradual personality change and deterioration of *intelligence, *memory, and *language (1). *Compare* Alzheimer's disease.
[Named after the Czech neurologist Arnold Pick (1851–1924) who first described it in 1892]

picrotoxin *n.* A bitter-tasting crystalline compound extracted from the seeds of the climbing plant *Cocculus indicus* (the *fishberry shrub) that functions as a central nervous system *stimulant and *convulsant by blocking the neuroreceptors that normally mediate the inhibitory effects of *GABA. It is used as an antidote to *barbiturate poisoning. *Compare* strychnine, tetanus toxin.
[From Greek *pikros* bitter + *toxikon pharmakon* arrow-poison, from *toxon* a bow]

pictogram *n.* Another name for a *pictograph.

pictograph *n.* A symbol used in picture writing, typical examples being the images of human figures, body parts, animals, and other objects used in the writing of the Minoan period of ancient Crete, or the stylized images used in many countries to label men's and women's toilets. *Compare* ideograph, logograph. **pictographic** *adj.* Of or relating to *pictographs.

pictorial depth *n.* *Depth perception arising from cues presented in two-dimensional pictures or images, only some of the monocular cues being functional under such conditions, namely *aerial perspective, *chiaroscuro, *elevation in the visual field, *interposition, *linear perspective, *relative size, and *texture gradient. *See also* carpentered world.

picture-arrangement test *n.* A type of *intelligence test item or subtest in which the respondent tries to arrange a number of pictures into a sequence that tells a meaningful story.

picture-completion test *n.* A type of *intelligence test item or subtest in which the respondent tries to point out missing elements in pictures, such as a numeral missing from a clock face or a leg missing from an insect.

picture-frustration test *See* Rosenzweig Picture-Frustration Study.

pidgin *n.* A language constructed from elements taken from two or more other languages and used for communication, especially trade, between members of two language communities. In contrast to a *creole, a pidgin is not the mother tongue of any speech community.

[From Chinese pronunciation of the English word *business*]

pie chart *n*. A circular graph divided into segments, resembling slices of a pie, proportional to the sizes of the various categories represented. This method of displaying data was popularized, if not invented, by the Italian-born British philanthropist Florence Nightingale (1820–1910) and the English medical statistician William Farr (1807–83) in a report on categories of morbidity and mortality in the British army issued in 1860.

pigment *n*. Any substance, including the *visual pigments contained in the rods and cones in the retina of the eye, whose constituent molecules absorb some wavelengths of light and reflect others. *See also* chromophore.

[From Latin *pigmentum* painted, from *pingere* to paint]

pigment epithelium *n*. The light-absorbing dark lining at the back of the retina of diurnal animals. *Compare* tapetum (1).

piloerection *n*. Raising of hair into an upright position as a result of contraction of *smooth muscles attached to the base of hair follicles, usually in response to cold or as part of a *startle reflex, in humans often accompanied by *goose pimples. Also called a *pilomotor response*.

[From Greek *pilos* hair + English *erection*]

pilot study *n*. A preliminary and usually small-scale research study designed to try out procedures, calibrate measures, and generally serve as a dress rehearsal before a major study. Also called simply a *pilot*.

[From Medieval Latin *pilotus* a steersman, from Greek *pedon* an oar]

pineal gland *n*. The pea-sized *endocrine gland, shaped like a miniature pine cone, attached to the base of the brain in the roof of the third ventricle below the anterior part of the *corpus callosum, receiving information from the *suprachiasmatic nucleus and secreting *melatonin into the bloodstream at night, involved in *circadian rhythms and probably in the promotion of sleep. It tends to

calcify during middle age. It is one of the *circumventricular organs and is also called the *pineal body*. Its rarely used technical name is the *epiphysis* or *epiphysis cerebri*. *See also* Cartesian dualism, epithalamus.

[From Latin *pinea* a pine cone, from *pinus* pine]

pink lady *n*. A street name for *secobarbital (quinalbarbitone) or *Seconal.

pink noise *n*. A sound wave or any other *time series that resembles *white noise, being essentially random, but with intensity or energy in inverse proportion to frequency, and hence more energy in the bass than the treble because high-frequency sound is more energetic than low-frequency sound. The sound of a waterfall, or waves crashing on a beach, is pink noise. *See also* noise (2). *Compare* coloured noise, frozen noise.

[So called by analogy with white light in which higher frequencies (shorter waves) are damped, leading to a pink tinge]

pinna *n*. Any feather, leaflet, or feather-shaped structure, especially the external part of the ear, also called the *auricle*. *See also* ear. **pinnae** *pl*.

[From Latin *pinna* a feather]

Piper's law *n*. In *psychophysics, a law relating either the *absolute threshold or the *difference threshold for visual brightness sensation to the intensity of the stimulus and the area of the retina that is stimulated, usually expressed as $\sqrt{A} \times I = k$, where A is the area of the retina stimulated, I is the intensity of the stimulus, and k is a constant. It is valid for stimuli subtending *visual angles from about 6 minutes of arc (1/10 of a degree) to about 20 degrees. *Compare* Ricco's law.

[Named after the German physiologist Hans Edmund Piper (1877–1915) who formulated it]

piriform cortex *n*. An area in the anterior temporal lobe of each cerebral hemisphere forming part of the *olfactory cortex, receiving nerve impulses from the olfactory receptors via the olfactory bulb without the prior involvement of the thalamus as in other sensory systems. It is not part of the *neocortex but is a three-layered *palaeocortex. Also spelt *pyriform cortex*, an etymologically incorrect but common form.

[From Latin *pirum* a pear + *forma* a form or shape]

pitch *n*. The perceived height or depth of a *tone (1), determined largely though not exclusively by the *frequency (1) of the vibration that gives rise to it. According to an international standard adopted in 1939, a vibration of 440 hertz is identified as the A above Middle C, and all other notes of the musical scale are defined in relation to it. *See also* absolute pitch, mel, pitch perception, relative pitch.

pitch perception *n*. The process whereby the frequency of a sound wave entering the ear is converted into a sensation of pitch. *See also* frequency theory, place theory, volley theory.

pituitary gland *n*. The master *endocrine gland, shaped like a miniature bulb of garlic about the size of a pea, suspended by a stalk (the infundibulum) within a specialized bony cavity of the skull (the sella turcica) below the *hypothalamus, to which it is connected beneath the centre of the brain, and from where it secretes into the bloodstream hormones that affect other endocrine glands throughout the body and that also influence bodily growth. Also called the *pituitary body, hypophysis*, or *hypophysis cerebri*. *See also* anterior pituitary, posterior pituitary.
[From Latin *pituita* phlegm, which it was once mistakenly thought to produce owing to its location just above the back of the nasal passage]

pivot grammar *n*. A grammar, first suggested by the Singaporean-born US psychologist Martin D. S. Braine (1926–96) in an article in the journal *Language* in 1963, based on two grammatical classes of words, namely pivot (*P*) and open (*O*), to describe two-word utterances of children at an early stage of language development, from about 18 months to 2 years of age. The *P* words are taken from a small vocabulary of high-frequency words that seldom occur as single-word utterances, and the *O* words from large, open classes of nouns, verbs, and adjectives. Typical *P* + *O* constructions recorded by Braine and later researchers are *Pretty fan, Night-night boat*, and *Allgone ball*. *Compare* holophrase, telegraphic speech.

placebo *n*. **1.** An assumedly inactive substance or dummy treatment administered to a *control group to serve as a baseline for comparison of the effects of an active drug or treatment. *See also* placebo effect, randomized controlled trial. **2.** A psychological treatment, in contrast to a pharmacological treatment.
[From Latin *placebo* I shall please, the opening word of the Roman Catholic office or service for the dead: *Placebo Domino*, I shall please the Lord]

placebo effect *n*. A positive or therapeutic effect resulting solely from the administration of a *placebo (1). Across a wide range of mental and physical symptoms and disorders, between 30 and 40 per cent of patients show improvement following the administration of a placebo.

place of articulation *n*. The location within the mouth where a speech sound is made. In English, there are ten places of articulation for *consonants: *bilabial, *labiodental, *dental, *alveolar, *post-alveolar, *palato-alveolar, *palatal, *velar, *glottal, and *retroflex. There are a few additional places of articulation in other languages.

place theory *n*. A theory of pitch perception first proposed in 1865 by the German physiologist, physicist, and mathematician Hermann Ludwig Ferdinand von Helmholtz (1821–94) according to which the perceived pitch of a tone depends on the position or place on the *basilar membrane of the auditory receptors that transmit nerve impulses. Physiological evidence for the place theory was provided by the Nobel prizewinning Hungarian physicist and physiologist Georg von Békésy (1899–1972) and summarized in his book *Experiments in Hearing* (1962). Because the *cochlea tapers from one end to the other, the part of the basilar membrane that vibrates the most depends on the frequency of the sound. Resting on the basilar membrane are *hair cells with auditory nerve cells connected to their bases, and vibrations of the basilar membrane cause the hair cells to bend back and forth, triggering nerve impulses to the brain. For tones above about 5,000 hertz, the pitch that is heard depends on which part of the basilar membrane vibrates the most and which nerve cells are therefore excited. Also called the *harp theory*, the *piano theory*, or the *resonance theory. Compare* frequency theory, volley theory.

planned behaviour, theory of *See* theory of planned behaviour.

planned comparison n. A statistical test of a difference between two means, usually carried out after *analysis of variance but planned before the data were collected, and therefore validly using a t test. Also called an *a priori test*. *See also* multiple comparisons. *Compare* a posteriori test.

plantar response n. A curling inwards of the toes when the sole of the foot is stroked with a hard object such as a key, replacing the infantile *Babinski reflex from about 2 years of age in neurologically normal infants. Also called the *plantar reflex*.
[From Latin *plantaris* of the sole of the foot, from *planta* the sole of the foot]

planum temporale n. The flat upper surface at the back of the temporal *operculum in the region of *Wernicke's area, extending to the end of the lateral sulcus, crucially involved in language comprehension. It is the most asymmetrical structure in the brain, much larger (approximately nine millimetres longer, on average) in the linguistically dominant (usually left) than the non-dominant cerebral hemisphere, resulting in a significantly longer left lateral sulcus in the left hemisphere. Also called the *temporal plane*.
[From Latin *planum* a flat surface + *temporalis* of the temple, from *tempus, temporis* the temple (on the side of the head)]

plasma n. **1.** The clear, pale yellow liquid component of blood (blood plasma) or lymph (lymph plasma), within which corpuscles and cells are suspended. **2.** An obsolescent name for the *cytoplasm of a cell, surviving in a combining form in the word *plasmagene. **3.** In physics, a hot ionized gas (*see* ion).
[From Greek *plasma* a form, from *plassein* to form or mould]

plasmagene n. Any *gene located in the cytoplasm outside the *nucleus (1) of a cell, in a *plasmid or a *mitochondrion, consisting of *DNA that self-replicates independently of chromosomal DNA. *See also* mitochondrial DNA.
[From *plasma* cytoplasm + *gene*]

plasma membrane n. Another name for a *cell membrane.

plasmid n. A circular fragment of *DNA that is not part of a *chromosome but exists and reproduces autonomously in the *cytoplasm of a cell. Bacterial plasmids can be transmitted between bacteria of the same or different species and are useful in *genetic engineering. *See also* jumping gene, plasmagene. *Compare* mitochondrial DNA.
[From *(cyto)plasm* + *-is, -idos* daughter of, indicating a particle, body, or structure]

Plateau spiral n. An *Archimedes spiral or some other spiral that is attached to a circular disc and, when rotating, appears to be continuously expanding from its centre or contracting towards its centre depending on the direction of rotation. After being observed for several seconds it induces a powerful opposite *motion aftereffect in which an object or surface that is fixated appears to be contracting or expanding, so that a person's face (for example) appears to shrink or enlarge while remaining paradoxically the same size, and this aftereffect is called the *spiral aftereffect*. It is also called a *Talbot–Plateau spiral* or *Archimedes spiral*, though the latter term is misleading, partly because the Archimedes spiral is a mathematical concept predating the illusion by many centuries, and partly because other spirals are often used to produce the effect. *See also* visual illusion. *Compare* waterfall illusion.
[Named after the Belgian physicist Joseph Antoine Ferdinand Plateau (1801–83) who produced the first version of it with the help of an assistant in 1849, although he never saw it himself because he had blinded himself six years earlier by staring at the sun]

platelet n. Particles in the blood of vertebrates that are responsible for blood clotting.
[So called because of their shape]

platoon-volley theory *See* volley theory.

platykurtic *See* kurtosis.

player n. **1.** A person who takes part in a game; more specifically a decision maker in an interactive decision problem of the type analysed within *game theory. A player in this sense may be a person, a committee or other decision making group, an animal, or any other entity that functions as a decision maker in a strategic *game (1). **2.** An actor or one who plays a musical instrument.

play therapy *n*. A form of *psychotherapy used with children in which play is used to facilitate communication between client or patient and therapist.

pleasantness *n*. The quality of being pleasing or satisfying. Also, another name for *agreeableness.

pleasure centre *n*. Any region of the brain in which electrical stimulation is rewarding or in which implanted electrodes tend to elicit self-stimulation from experimental animals provided with levers with which they can stimulate the area. The most important pleasure centres are in areas of the *hypothalamus and the *limbic system, especially the *septum pellucidum and the *medial forebrain bundle (MFB). US *pleasure center*. *See also* priming (3).

pleasure-ego *n*. In *psychoanalysis, one of the two major aspects of the *ego, based on the *pleasure principle, differentiated by Sigmund Freud (1856–1939) from the *reality-ego, based on the *reality principle. In his article on 'Formulations on the Two Principles of Mental Functioning' (1911), he summed up the distinction as follows: 'Just as the pleasure-ego can do nothing but *wish*, work for a yield of pleasure, and avoid unpleasure, so the reality-ego need do nothing but strive for what is *useful* and guard itself against damage' (*Standard Edition*, XII, pp. 218–26, at p. 223).

pleasure-pain principle *n*. Another name for the *pleasure principle.

pleasure principle *n*. In *psychoanalysis, the precept according to which psychological processes and actions are governed by the gratification of needs and the avoidance or discharge of unpleasurable tension. It is the governing principle of the *id, in contrast to the *reality principle, which is a governing principle of the *ego. Sigmund Freud (1856–1939) borrowed the concept from the German philosopher, physician, psychologist, and mystic Gustav Theodor Fechner (1801–87) who, in an article in the journal *Zeitschrift für Philosophie und philosophische Kritik* in 1848, introduced the term (in its German form *Lustprinzip*) and noted that motives underlying actions can be unconscious. Freud introduced the concept in his book *The Interpretation of Dreams* (1900), where he initially called it the unpleasure principle (*Standard Edition*, IV–V, at p. 574), but later he fell in with Fechner's more natural terminology. Also called the *pleasure–pain principle* or (awkwardly but closer to Freud's original German) the *pleasure–unpleasure principle*. *See also* free energy, perception–consciousness system, pleasure-ego, primary process, principle of constancy.

pleasure–unpleasure principle *n*. Another name for the *pleasure principle.

pleiotropic *adj*. Of or relating to a *gene or a *mutation that has a simultaneous effect on more than one *phenotypic trait. **pleiotropism** or **pleiotropy** *n*.
[From Greek *pleion* more + *tropos* a turn, from *trapein* to turn + *-ikos* of, relating to, or resembling]

plethysmograph *n*. An instrument for recording changes in the size or volume of the penis (*penile plethysmograph) or another body organ or part, especially changes resulting from variations in blood content.
[From Greek *plethysmos* enlargement + *graphein* to write]

plexiform layer *n*. Either of two thin strata in the *retina, the *inner plexiform layer and the *outer plexiform layer, that separate the three major retinal layers and are connected by *interplexiform cells conveying information backwards towards the *photoreceptors.
[From Latin *plexus* a network, from *plectere* to weave]

plexus *n*. Any complex network of nerves, ganglia, blood vessels, or lymphatic vessels, such as the *choroid plexus.
[From Latin *plexus* a weaving, from *plectere* to weave]

plosive *n*. A *consonant speech sound articulated by completely blocking the airstream through the mouth and nose for a moment, as in the initial *phonemes in the words *bee*, *dear*, *gear*, *key*, *pea*, *tea*. *See also* manner of articulation.
[French, from *(ex)plosif*]

pneumoencephalogram *n*. An X-ray image of the brain with its *cerebrospinal fluid replaced with air to show the *ventricles clearly.

Also called a *pneumoencephalograph* or an *air encephalogram*. *See also* encephalogram. **pneumoencephalography** *n*. The production and interpretation of *pneumoencephalograms.
[From Greek *pneuma, pneumatos* breath, from *pneein* to breathe + *en* in + *kephale* the head + *gramme* a line]

pneumograph *n*. An instrument for recording respiratory movements, usually from straps fitted around the chest or abdomen. **pneumogram** *n*. A recording from a *pneumograph. *See also* polygraph.
[From Greek *pneuma, pneumatos* breath, from *pneein* to breathe + *graphein* to write]

pneumotachograph *n*. An instrument for measuring and recording the airflow from the nose and mouth during speech.
[From Greek *pneuma* breath + *tachos* speed + *graphein* to write]

PNMT *abbrev*. An enzyme contained in adrenergic neurons of the adrenal medulla that synthesize *adrenalin (epinephrine). It functions as a catalyst in the conversion of noradrenalin (norepinephrine) to adrenalin.
[From its chemical name *p(henylethanolamine)-N-m(ethyl)t(ransferase)*]

Poetzl phenomenon *n*. The reappearance in dreams of images or information previously perceived *subliminally. Also spelt *Pötzl phenomenon*.
[Named after the Austrian neurologist Otto Poetzl (born 1877) who first reported the phenomenon in 1917]

Poggendorff illusion *n*. A visual illusion in which a diagonal line appears displaced when interrupted by a rectangle appearing to occlude the middle part of it (see illustration).
[Named after the German physicist Johann Christian Poggendorff (1796–1877) who discovered it, although the German astronomer Johann Karl Friedrich Zöllner (1834–82) first published it in 1860 after Poggendorff had drawn his attention to it]

poikilitic function *n*. Another name for a *psychometric function.
[From Greek *poikilos* various + *-itikos* resembling or marked by]

poikilothermic *adj*. Cold-blooded, or having a body temperature that varies with the ambi-

Poggendorff illusion. The lower of the two lines on the right is a continuation of the line on the left.

ent temperature. Also called *poikilothermal. Compare* homoiothermic. **poikilothermy** or **poikilothermism** *n*.
[From Greek *poikilos* various + *therme* heat + *-ikos* of, relating to, or resembling]

point-light display *n*. A moving image of small light sources attached to the principal joints of a person's body (usually shoulders, elbows, wrists, hips, knees, and ankles), filmed as the person moves around in the dark, introduced by the Swedish psychologist Gunnar Johansson (born 1911) and first published in the journal *Perception and Psychophysics* in 1973. Static point-light displays, even when several are viewed as a sequence, look like meaningless constellations, but the moving image is almost instantly (after two or three frames) and irresistibly interpreted as a human body in motion, and from such displays familiar people can be recognized easily from their characteristic gaits, the sexes of unknown people can be reliably judged even when cues relating to physical size are eliminated, and the weights of objects being lifted can be accurately judged to within 3–4 kg. The perception created by a point-light display is also called *biological motion* or *biomechanical motion*.

point mutation *n*. A *mutation involving the alteration of a single base pair in a segment of *DNA.
[So called because it occurs at a single point in the sequence of bases]

point of non-discrimination *n*. Another name for a *point of subjective equality.

point of subjective equality n. Any of the points along a stimulus dimension at which a *variable stimulus is judged by an observer to be equal to a *standard stimulus; also, any point along a stimulus dimension at which no relevant differences between responses to a variable stimulus and a standard stimulus can be detected in the behaviour of an animal. Also called a *non-discrimination point* or a *point of non-discrimination*. **PSE** *abbrev.*

point source n. A light source that is sufficiently small to be considered as having negligible size.

Poisson distribution n. In statistics, a very skewed *probability distribution representing the number of discrete events occurring randomly but at a constant average rate in a specified continuous interval of time or space, for example. It is often used to model the random occurrence of rare events with fixed probability of occurrence.
[Named after the French mathematician Siméon-Denis Poisson (1781–1840) who published the results of his researches in a book in 1837]

political correctness n. The avoidance of verbal expressions or actions that may be interpreted as prejudicial or offensive to minorities or groups considered to be disadvantaged by race, sex, disability, sexual orientation, social class, or appearance. As a consequence of political correctness, some *epicene (2) words have become commonplace (for example, *flight attendant* in preference to *air stewardess* and *firefighter* in preference to *fireman*), but certain other manifestations of political correctness have been ridiculed, as when a US television reporter, referring to the South African president Nelson Mandela (born 1918) and wishing to refer to the fact that he was black without uttering the word *black*, referred to him as African American. *See also* ableism, fattism, herstory, heterosexism. **politically correct** *adj.* **PC** *abbrev.*
[Coined by the US journalist Elinor Langer (born 1939) in the *New York Times* in 1984, alluding to social conventions in the liberal establishment]

Pollyanna effect n. A tendency for people to pay more attention in their thought and speech to positive than negative aspects of their conceptual worlds and to process positive information more easily than negative information. The term was coined in 1964 by the US psychologist Charles E(gerton) Osgood (1916–91) to explain the greater frequency of positive than negative words in written language: *good* occurs almost 10 times as frequently as *bad*, *love* almost 10 times as frequently as *hate*, and so on. *See also* mere exposure effect, trait negativity bias.
[Named after Pollyanna Whittier, known as the 'glad girl', whose blindly optimistic and Panglossian disposition always led her to look on the bright side of things, in the novels *Pollyanna* (1913) and *Pollyanna Grows Up* (1915) by the US writer Eleanor H(odgman) Porter (1868–1920)]

polyandry n. The custom or practice of having more than one husband at the same time or, in female animals, of mating with more than one male during the same breeding season. *See also* adelphogamy (1), polygamy. *Compare* polygyny.
[From Greek *polys* many + *andros* a man]

polydipsia n. Excessive thirst, symptomatic of several disorders including *diabetes mellitus and certain mental disorders. *Compare* adipsia.
[From Greek *polys* much or many + *dipsa* thirst + *-ia* indicating a condition or quality]

polyethism n. Division of labour, especially in reference to the *social insects.
[From Greek *polys* many + *ethos* a custom]

polygamy n. The custom or practice of having more than one spouse (whether husband or wife) at the same time or, in animals, of having more than one mate during the same breeding season. *See* polyandry, polygyny. *Compare* monogamy.
[From Greek *polys* many + *gamos* marriage]

polygenic inheritance n. Inheritance of a characteristic that depends on the cumulative effects of several or many *genes each having a small individual effect, such as physical stature or intelligence. *See also* quantitative inheritance. *Compare* monogenic inheritance, qualitative inheritance.
[From Greek *polys* many + German *Gen* a gene, from Greek *genein* to produce]

polygraph n. An instrument for the simultaneous recording of several largely involuntary physiological responses controlled by the autonomic nervous system, usually skin conductance or *galvanic skin response (GSR), respiration rate (monitored by a *pneumograph and producing separate traces for chest movement and abdominal movement), blood pressure, and heart rate. It is sometimes used as a *lie detector. The original instrument of this type was the *Keeler polygraph.

[From Greek *polygraphos* writing copiously, from *polys* many + *graphein* to write]

polygyny *n.* The custom or practice of having more than one wife at the same time or, in male animals, of mating with more than one female during the same breeding season. *See also* polygamy. *Compare* polyandry.

[From Greek *polys* + *gyne* a woman]

polymerase chain reaction *n.* A technique for synthesizing numerous copies of a sequence of *DNA without *genetic engineering by repeatedly separating it into its two complementary strands and using *DNA polymerase to catalyse the synthesis of double-stranded DNA from each single strand. *See also* genetic fingerprinting, transcription (2). **PCR** *abbrev.*

[From *polymer* a large molecule consisting of repeating subunits, from Greek *polys* many + *meros* a part + *-ase* denoting an enzyme, from *diastasis* separation]

polymorphic gene *n.* A gene such as any of the human genes for eye colour or the ABO blood groups that occurs as two or more different *alleles at the same gene locus within a species or population. *See* genetic polymorphism. *See also* race (2).

[From Greek *polys* many + *morphe* a form or shape]

polymorphism *See* genetic polymorphism.

polymorphous perversity *n.* In *psychoanalysis, the earliest *libidinal stage of *psychosexual development, during the *oral stage, characterized by undifferentiated sexual desire that finds gratification through any *erotogenic zone. The term is also used to denote the varied bodily sources and styles of libidinal gratification in the course of early psychosexual development. *Compare* anal stage, genital stage, latency period, oral stage, phallic stage.

[From Greek *polys* many + *morphe* a shape or form]

polyonymy *n.* The property of having several names. English has no equivalents for the many words for *camel* in Arabic, *snow* in the language of the Inuit Eskimos of Greenland, Canada, and Northern Alaska, or *hole* in the Australian aboriginal Pintupi; but on the other hand few languages have the polyonymy that English has for different types of vehicles (*car*, *lorry*, *bus*, *motorbike*, *go-cart*, and so on). *See also* linguistic determinism. *Compare* polysemy. **polyonymous** *adj.*

[From Greek *polys* many + *onoma* a name]

polypeptide *n.* A molecule that is smaller than a *protein, consisting of a *peptide chain composed of *amino acids linked together. If the molecular weight (in units of the weight of a single hydrogen atom) is less than 10,000, corresponding to about 100 amino acids, it is arbitrarily called a polypeptide; if the molecular weight exceeds 10,000, corresponding to over 100 amino acids, it is called a protein. The basis for the dividing line is the fact that molecules lighter than 10,000, when in solution, will pass through cellophane, providing a simple discriminative test.

[From Greek *polys* many + English *peptide*]

polyphagia *n.* The habit of some creatures (omnivores) of eating many different kinds of foods. Also, loosely, another name for *bulimia (1).

[From Greek *polys* much + *phagein* to consume + *-ia* indicating a condition or quality]

polysemy *n.* The property of a word or *lexeme of having several different meanings, a typical English example being the word *kind*, which can mean type (*a different kind of food*); quality (*a difference of kind rather than degree*); goods or services (*payment in kind*); something similar (*respond to the attack in kind*); compassionate (*a kind gesture*); or cordial (*kind regards*). Also called *polysemia*. *See also* heteronyms, lexical ambiguity. *Compare* monosemy, polyonymy. **polysemous** *adj.*

[From Greek *polys* many + *sema* a sign]

polysomnography *n.* The simultaneous recording of several physiological processes, usually including *EEG and *electro-oculogram (EOG) activity, in a sleeping person.

[From Greek *polys* many + Latin *somnus* sleep + *graphein* to write]

polysubstance dependence *n*. A *substance-related disorder, specifically a form of *substance dependence involving at least three groups of *drugs for at least 12 months without any one of them predominating.
[From Greek *polys* much + Latin *substantia* substance, from *sub* under + *stare* to stand]

polysynaptic reflex *n*. Any reflex with more than one *synapse (1), not counting the synapse between neuron and muscle, and hence involving one or more *interneurons. In humans, all reflexes except *stretch reflexes are polysynaptic. *Compare* monosynaptic reflex.
[From Greek *polys* many + *neuron* a nerve]

POMC *abbrev*. Pro-opiomelanocortin, a large polypeptide present in the *pituitary gland that functions as a precursor of *beta-endorphin and *adrenocorticotrophic hormone (ACTH).

pons *n*. A broad band of mostly white fibres connecting the two halves of the brain at the level of the brainstem above the medulla oblongata, containing the *corticospinal tract and part of the *reticular formation and connected to the cerebral cortex via the *corticopontine tract. Not to be confused with the *PONS. *See also* cerebral peduncle, locked-in syndrome, locus coeruleus, nucleus gigantocellularis, periaqueductal grey matter, subcoerulear nucleus, superior olivary nucleus, tectum, trapezoid body. **pontine** *adj*.
[From Latin *pons* a bridge, short for *pons Varolii* bridge of Varolius, named after the Italian anatomist Costanzo Varolius (?1543–75) who first identified it]

PONS *abbrev*. Profile of non-verbal sensitivity, a test designed to measure ability to decode non-verbal information from the face, body, and voice. It consists of brief film clips of a woman displaying various emotional states, the respondent's task being to identify those states. It was published commercially in 1979 by the German-born US psychologist Robert Rosenthal (born 1933) and several colleagues, who reported that children's PONS scores tend to increase with age, that females tend to score higher than males, and that non-verbal

behaviour of strangers tends to be less accurately decoded than that of familiar people. Not to be confused with the *pons.

pontogeniculo-occipital *adj*. Pertaining to a *PGO spike or wave.
[From *pons* + *(lateral) geniculate nucleus* + *occipital cortex*]

Ponzo illusion *n*. A visual illusion in which two lines of equal length appear unequal when drawn horizontally at different heights between a pair of converging lines (see illustration). It is also called the *railway illusion*, because it is often illustrated with a picture of converging railway lines, and it is closely related to *Ehrenstein's square illusion. *See also* corridor illusion, Orbison illusion, perceptual constancy, size constancy.
[Named after the Italian psychologist Mario Ponzo (1882–1960) who first published it in 1913]

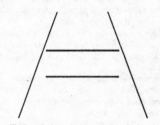

Ponzo illusion. The horizontal lines are equal in length.

pooled variance estimate *n*. In statistics, an estimate of a population's *variance obtained by combining or pooling data from two or more samples. In the *independent samples *t* test, for example, the squared deviations of the scores from their means in both groups are normally pooled to obtain an estimate of what is assumed under the *null hypothesis to be the common population variance. *Compare* separate variance estimates.

poppers *n*. A street name for *nitrite inhalants generally or *amyl nitrite in particular.
[Alluding to the fact that the capsules containing it make a popping sound when they are opened]

pop-type *n*. An informal name for a *population stereotype.

population *n*. All the people inhabiting a country or other area or belonging to a specified group. In statistics, an aggregate of individuals from which a *sample may be drawn and to which the results of a research investigation may be generalized. A population need not encompass every individual in a country: it is quite legitimate to refer to the population of patients diagnosed as schizophrenic or the population of university undergraduates, for example.
[From Latin *populus* people + *-ation* indicating a process or condition]

population genetics *n*. A branch of genetics concerned with the relative frequencies of genes and genotypes in populations, as affected by natural selection under conditions of *mutation, *assortative mating or *disassortative mating, and *migration, focusing especially on phenomena such as *heritability. *See also* Hardy–Weinberg law.

population stereotype *n*. In a situation of seemingly arbitrary choice, a particular option that is chosen by a large proportion of a given population, or an expectation, interpretation, or a manner of perceiving, thinking, or behaving that is statistically prominent within the population. For example, most people in the US and Europe unconsciously expect a knob on an electrical appliance to increase the appliance's output when it is turned clockwise and to decrease the output when it is turned anticlockwise, but they expect a water or gas tap or faucet to function in exactly the opposite way, decreasing the flow when it is turned clockwise and increasing the flow when it is turned anticlockwise, and controls that do not function in the expected ways cause irritation, inefficiency, and operator errors. Another example, often used by conjurors and people pretending to have telepathic powers, is the marked preference that emerges when people are asked to draw two geometric figures, one inside the other: research reveals that more than one-third of people draw a triangle and circle. Also (informally) called a *pop-type*. *See also* three-seven effect.

pornographomania *n*. A pathological impulse to write obscene messages or graffiti.
[From Greek *porne* a prostitute + *graphein* to write + *mania* madness]

pornolagnia *n*. A desire for sexual intercourse with prostitutes.
[From Greek *porne* a prostitute + *lagneia* lust]

porphyria *n*. A group of hereditary disorders in which the body over-produces substances called porphryrins, causing abdominal pain, aversion to bright light, and a variety of neurological symptoms.
[From Greek *porphyra* purple, referring to the colour of the substance excreted by people with the disorders + *-ia* indicating a condition or quality]

Porter's law *n*. Another name for the *Ferry–Porter law.

Porteus Maze Test *n*. The first widely used *non-verbal test of ability, designed to supplement the *Stanford–Binet intelligence scale by measuring aspects of intellectual ability such as foresight, planning, and prudence. It involves finding paths through a series of mazes or labyrinths, and some researchers have considered it *culture-fair. **PMT** *abbrev.*
[Named after the Australian psychologist Stanley D. Porteus (1883–1972) who constructed it in 1914]

portfolio theory *n*. A theory of decision making under risk, based on *unfolding technique, developed in the early 1960s by the US psychologist Clyde Hamilton Coombs (1912–88).

portmanteau word *n*. Another name for a *blend.
[From *portmanteau* a large travelling case, from French *porter* to carry + *manteau* a cloak]

portrait illusion *n*. Another name for the *rotating head illusion.

position constancy *n*. A form of *perceptual constancy through which stationary objects appear stationary in spite of movements of their retinal images caused by movements of the eyes, head, and body. *See also* eye–head movement system, reafference.

position preference *n*. Any consistent tendency to choose an option because of its location, as when a person in a discrimination task tends to favour the right-hand option, or when a person responding to a multiple-choice questionnaire tends to favour the middle option of the response categories presented. See also response style.

positive afterimage n. An *afterimage in which the lightness contrasts of the original stimulus are preserved, light areas of the original stimulus appearing light and dark areas appearing dark. See also complementary afterimage. Compare negative afterimage (1).

positive feedback See under feedback.

positive induction See under induction (4).

positive Oedipus complex See under Oedipus complex.

positive reference group n. A *reference group that an individual admires or aspires to and uses as a standard representing opinions, attitudes, or behaviour patterns to emulate. Compare negative reference group.

positive symptoms n. In the diagnosis of *schizophrenia, the symptoms of *delusions, *hallucinations, *disorganized speech, and *catatonia. Compare negative symptoms.

positive theory See under normative (1).

positive transfer n. A form of *transfer of training in which the learning or performance of a task is facilitated or improves as a result of training on a different but related task, as when learning to speak Italian improves one's ability to speak Spanish, or vice versa. Transfer tends to be positive when the two tasks involve different stimuli and similar responses. Compare negative transfer.

positive transference n. In *psychoanalysis, sexual desire on the part of the patient towards the analyst. See also transference. Compare negative transference.

positivism n. **1.** A philosophical doctrine developed explicitly by the French philosopher and mathematician Auguste Comte (1798–1857), though it can be traced back through the French socialist thinker Claude-Henri de Rouvroy Comte de Saint-Simon (1760–1825) to the English philosopher and statesman Francis Bacon (1561–1626), according to which observation and experiment are the only sources of substantial knowledge. Comte believed that human thought passes

through three stages: theological, metaphysical, then finally positive. See also empiricism. **2.** Another name for *logical positivism. See also Frankfurt school, operationalism.

positivity bias n. **1.** A pervasive tendency for people, especially those with high *self-esteem, to rate positive *traits as being more true of themselves than negative traits. **2.** In *balance theory, a general preference shown by most people for positive relations, especially p–o relations.

positron emission tomography See PET scan.

possession trance n. A *trance associated with the replacement of one's customary personal identity with a new identity, and a belief that this is caused by the influence of a spirit, deity, power, or other person. See also dissociative trance disorder.
[From Old French possesser to possess, from Latin possidere to occupy or inhabit + French transe trance, from Latin transire to go across or to die]

possible world n. In *modal logic, a formalization of an imaginable state of affairs consistent with certain specified assumptions, such that a *proposition (1) is true if and only if it is true in every possible world.

post-alveolar adj. Of or relating to the area immediately behind the *alveolar ridge, the hard, bony part of the palate behind the upper front teeth, and descriptive of speech sounds articulated with the tongue tip in that area, examples being the initial sounds in the words rye, try, and dry. See also place of articulation.
[From Latin post after or behind + alveolus a small depression, referring to the tooth sockets]

postcategorical acoustic store n. A memory store for verbal information that has undergone a degree of *information processing, especially syntactic analysis. Also called postcategorical acoustic memory. Compare precategorical acoustic store.

postcentral gyrus n. The gyrus of the parietal lobe immediately behind the central sulcus, occupied by the primary *somatosensory cortex. Also called the postrolandic gyrus.

[From Latin *post* after or behind + *centrum* the centre]

postconcussional disorder *n.* A condition (included in the *ICD-10 classification and in the *DSM-IV appendix of conditions meriting further study) following head *trauma causing significant *concussion, indicated by *fatigue (1), *dyssomnia, headache, *vertigo or dizziness, irritability, *anxiety, *depression, or labile *affect, changes in personality, and apathy. Also called *postconcussion syndrome*.
[From Latin *post* after + *concussus* violently shaken, from *concutere* to shake violently, from *quatere* to shake]

postconventional morality *n.* The third and final *Kohlberg stage of moral development, characterized by the internalization of moral principles. It is divided into two levels: at Level 5 the child defines moral behaviour in terms of the social contract and what is generally agreed to be for the public good (*I should not tell lies, because it is in all our best interests for everyone to be truthful*), and at Level 6 it is based on genuine ethical principles that determine a person's personal moral code. *Compare* conventional morality, preconventional morality.

postencephalitic syndrome *n.* An *organic mental disorder following recovery from viral or bacterial *encephalitis, characterized by non-specific and variable behavioural change, including paralysis, deafness, *amnesia, *aphasia, *apraxia, or *acalculia.

posterior *adj.* Behind, at the back, or after. *Compare* anterior.
[From Latin *posterus* coming after, later, or following, from *post* after]

posterior cerebral commissure *n.* A band of nerve fibres beneath the pineal gland in the epithalamus, connecting the midbrain regions of the two cerebral hemispheres, including the two superior colliculi. Also called the *intertectal commissure* or simply the *posterior commissure*. *See also* commissure.
[From Latin *commissura* a joining together, from *com-* together + *mittere* to send]

posterior funiculus *See under* funiculus.

posterior horn *n.* Either of the two dorsal ends of the H-shaped column of grey matter

running throughout the length of the spinal cord and receiving inputs from most of the afferent nerves. It includes the *substantia gelatinosa. *See also* funiculus. *Compare* anterior horn.

posterior pituitary *n.* The back part or lobe of the *pituitary gland that is responsive to a variety of pituitary, adrenal, gonadal, and hypothalamic hormones and that secretes *oxytocin and *vasopressin in response to neural stimulation. It is one of the *circumventricular organs and is called the *neurohypophysis*. *Compare* anterior pituitary.

posterior probability *n.* In *Bayesian inference, the probability assigned to an event, in accordance with *Bayes' theorem, in the light of empirical evidence as to its observed relative frequency. Also called *conditional probability*. *Compare* prior probability (2).

post-Freudian *adj. n.* (Of or relating to) any of the *psychoanalysts who followed Sigmund Freud (1856–1939).

postganglionic *adj.* Pertaining to *efferent neurons of the *autonomic nervous system that are peripheral to *ganglia and that synapse directly on to muscles or glands. *Compare* preganglionic.
[From Latin *post* after or behind + Greek *ganglion* a cystic tumour + *-ikos* of, relating to, or resembling]

posthallucinogen perception disorder *n.* Another name for *flashback (3).

post hoc test *n.* Another name for an *a posteriori test.
[From Latin *post* after + *hoc* this]

posthypnotic amnesia *n.* Another name for *hypnotic amnesia.

postnatal blues *See* postpartum blues.

postnatal depression *See* postpartum depression.

postpartum blues *n.* A common emotional reaction of mothers to childbirth, characterized by transient *depression lasting up to 72 hours. Also called *postnatal blues*. *Compare* postpartum depression.
[From Latin *post* after + *parturire* to give birth]

postpartum depression *n.* A form of *depression occurring occasionally in mothers between three days and six weeks after giving birth, with symptoms ranging from relatively mild to a *major depressive episode. Also called *postnatal depression.* *Compare* postpartum blues.

postrolandic gyrus *n.* Another name for the postcentral gyrus.
[From Latin *post* + English *Rolandic (fissure),* named after the Italian anatomist Luigi Rolando (1773–1831)]

post-rotational nystagmus *n.* A form of *vestibular nystagmus resulting from rotation of the body, occurring when the rotation stops abruptly. Also called *postrotatory optic nystagmus.*

postsynaptic *adj.* Of or relating to a *neuron or part of a neuron, muscle, or gland that receives a signal across a *synapse (1). *Compare* presynaptic. **postsynaptic excitation** *See* excitatory postsynaptic potential. **postsynaptic inhibition** *See* inhibitory postsynaptic potential.
[From Latin *post* after or behind + Greek *synapsis* contact or junction, from *syn* together + *haptein* to fasten + *-ikos* of, relating to, or resembling]

postsynaptic potential *n.* A change in the *membrane potential of a *postsynaptic neuron resulting from a *neurotransmitter or other signal sent across a synapse by a *presynaptic neuron. *See* excitatory postsynaptic potential, inhibitory postsynaptic potential.

postsynaptic receptor *n.* A *neuroreceptor molecule in a *postsynaptic cell membrane specialized to detect and respond to the *neurotransmitter released by a presynaptic neuron.

post-traumatic stress disorder *n.* An *anxiety disorder arising as a delayed and protracted response after experiencing or witnessing a traumatic event involving actual or threatened death or serious injury to self or others. It is characterized by intense fear, helplessness, or horror lasting more than four weeks, the traumatic event being persistently re-experienced in the form of distressing recollections, recurrent dreams, sensations

of reliving the experience, *hallucinations, or *flashbacks (2), intense distress and physiological reactions in response to anything reminiscent of the traumatic event, evidence of persistent avoidance of stimuli associated with the trauma, a numbing of responsiveness, and heightened arousal manifested as insomnia, irritability, difficulty concentrating, hypervigilance, or exaggerated startle response. Formerly called *traumatic neurosis,* and before that *shell shock. See also* battered wife syndrome, combat fatigue, dissociative identity disorder, eye-movement desensitization and reprocessing, flooding, stress. *Compare* acute stress disorder. **PTSD** *abbrev.*
[From Latin *post* after + Greek *trauma* a wound]

postulate *n.* Another name for an *axiom.

postural aftereffect *n.* A subjective feeling that arises after adopting an eccentric or abnormal body posture for some time, and then adopting a normal posture. The sensation is of an abnormal posture that deviates from normality in the opposite direction to the prior abnormal posture, and this aftereffect is a consequence of the *perdeviation effect. *See* Kohnstamm effect.

postural tremor *n.* A form of *tremor not easily classifiable as either a *passive tremor or an *intention tremor, appearing when an attempt is made to maintain a posture, resulting sometimes from lesions in the *basal ganglia as in *parkinsonism, with a typical frequency of 3–6 hertz, or as a sign of *cerebellar syndrome, with a typical frequency of 2.5–4 hertz. *See also* posturography.

posturography *n.* Instrumental recording of the stability of erect posture by means of strain gauges attached to a supporting platform to detect swaying, used to detect *neurological disorders, especially those associated with *postural tremor in *cerebellar syndrome and various forms of *ataxia. In some cases *electromyogram electrodes are also attached to muscles of the ankles and calves.
[From *posture* + *graphein* to write]

postviral syndrome *n.* Another name for *chronic fatigue syndrome.

pot *n.* An obsolescent street name for *cannabis. **pot-head** *n.* A habitual cannabis user.

[Perhaps from the Mexican Indian *potiguaya* cannabis]

potassium *n.* A light, silvery, alkaline, metallic element that is highly reactive chemically and is an important *electrolyte in the body. It is the predominant *cation within cells and is required for contraction of *skeletal muscles and relaxation of *cardiac muscle. **K** *abbrev.*
[From Latin *potassa* potash]

potlatch *n.* A competitive winter festival involving extravagant feasting, ostentatious distribution of gifts, and ceremonial destruction of valuable possessions, performed by the Kwakiutl and other American Indians of the north-west coastal area as a display of wealth and a method of maintaining or enhancing the prestige of chiefs and clans.
[Chinook, from Nootka *patlatsch* to a gift]

Pötzl phenomenon *See* Poetzl phenomenon.

poverty of content *n.* Speech that conveys little information. *Compare* poverty of speech.

poverty of speech *n.* Marked deficit in spontaneous speech, and replies to questions that are perfunctory, monosyllabic, or unforthcoming. Also called *hypologia*, *hypophrasia*. *Compare* poverty of content.

power law *n.* Any law expressed by a mathematical power function, especially the *psychophysical law that was advocated from 1953 onwards by the US psychologist S(tanley) S(mith) Stevens (1906–73) and discussed by him in an influential article in the journal *Psychological Review* in 1957, a century after it was first proposed by the Belgian physicist Joseph Antoine Ferdinand Plateau (1801–83), and that largely replaced *Fechner's law. According to the power law, the magnitude of a sensation is a power function of the intensity of the stimulus causing it, so that equal proportional increases in sensation correspond to equal proportional increases in stimulus intensity, the two proportions not necessarily being the same. It is usually expressed by the equation $\psi = k\phi^n$, where ψ is the magnitude of the sensation, ϕ is the physical intensity of the stimulus, k is a constant scaling factor that depends on the units of measurement, and n is an exponent or power that is constant for a given type of sensory experience but that varies from one type of sensa-

tion to the next, with $n = 0.33$ for visual brightness perception, $n = 0.67$ for loudness perception, $n = 1.45$ for heaviness perception of lifted weights, $n = 1.00$ for visual length perception, of which people have much experience, and so on. Also called *Stevens's law* or *Stevens's power law. See also* prospect theory, psychophysical function.
[So called because ϕ is raised to the *power* of n]

power, statistical *See* statistical power.

power test *n.* In psychometrics, any test in which ability is measured by the degree of difficulty of the items that can be mastered, rather than the speed of performance. *Compare* speed test.

POX triad *See* balance theory.

practice curve *n.* Another name for a *learning curve.

pragmatic love *n.* A secondary type of *love that is practical and utilitarian and is a combination of *ludic love and *storgic love. *Compare* agapic love, erotic love, manic love.
[From Greek *pragma* a deed + *-ikos* of, relating to, or resembling]

pragmatics *n.* The study of social and behavioural aspects of practical language usage, the factors governing speakers' choices of words and expressions in particular circumstances, and the effects of such choices on listeners. This was clarified by the English philosopher Peter (Frederick) Strawson (born 1919) in a famous article 'On Referring' in the journal *Mind* in 1950 in which he pointed out that a phrase such as *the woman in the blue dress* does not, by itself, refer to a particular woman but that it acquires a clear meaning from the circumstances in which it is spoken. *See also* cooperative principle.
[From Greek *pragma* an act or deed + *-itikos* resembling or marked by]

Prägnanz *n.* A principle or law of perception of *Gestalt psychology according to which perception of ambiguous stimuli tends to be as 'good' (meaning simple, regular, and symmetric) as the sensory input allows. The Gestalt psychologist Wolfgang Köhler (1887–1967) grounded this principle on the doctrine of *isomorphism (3), coupled with a belief that electrical brain fields, like other systems, evolve to physical Gestalten representing minimal energy states, a standard example being a soap bubble, which invariably evolves to a perfect sphere—the minimal energy state of a soap film. Köhler's theory was discredited as neuroscience advanced, but the principle of *Prägnanz* was widely embraced, and the underlying notion of a 'good' perception has been clarified in terms of *information theory as one encoded with the minimum *bits of information. Also spelt *Praegnanz* or *pregnance*, though the latter in particular is avoided in careful usage. *See also* good Gestalt, Landolt circle, precision law. *Compare* likelihood principle.

[From German *Prägnanz* pithiness or terseness]

prandial drinking *n*. Drinking stimulated by the eating of dry food.
[From Latin *prandium* lunch]

pre-attentive processing *n*. Another name for *automatic processing.

precategorical acoustic store *n*. An *echoic store that is believed to hold auditory information for brief periods before it has been subjected to significant *information processing. Evidence for it comes from experiments on serial digit recall, showing that the final two items in a list of digits are recalled better when the list is heard than when it is read but that this effect is suppressed if the auditory list is followed by a verbal suffix (such as *that's the end of the list*) that need not be recalled. This *auditory suffix effect suggests the existence of an auditory memory trace that decays quickly and can be overwritten by other verbal information, but doubt was cast on its existence during the 1990s. Also called a *precategorical acoustic memory* (PAM). *Compare* postcategorical acoustic store. **PAS** *abbrev*.

precedence effect *n*. Hearing only the first of two sounds or sound patterns when the second is similar to the first and follows it within about 50 milliseconds. *Compare* auditory fusion.

precentral gyrus *n*. The gyrus of the frontal lobe immediately in front of the *central sulcus, occupied by the primary *motor cortex.
[From Latin *prae* in front + *centrum* the centre]

precision law *n*. The most general law of perceptual organization in *Gestalt psychology, according to which a Gestalt tends to become as sharply defined, stable, strong, regular, symmetrical, simple, meaningful, and economical as the sensory information allows, these properties being characteristics or features of *Prägnanz. Also called the *simplicity principle*. *See also* good Gestalt.
[From Latin *praecision* a cutting off, from *prae* before + *caedere* to cut]

precocial *adj*. Of or relating to species of birds whose young are hatched with a covering of down and open eyes and are capable of leaving the nest alone within a few days. *Compare* altricial.
[From Latin *praecox* early maturing, from *prae* early + *coquere* to ripen]

precognition *n*. *Extra-sensory perception of objects or events in the future, or of another person's future mental processes, a conjectural *paranormal phenomenon. *Compare* clairvoyance, telepathy. **precognitive** *adj*. Of or relating to *precognition. **precognitive clairvoyance** *n*. *Extra-sensory perception of objects or events in the future. **precognitive telepathy** *n*. *Extra-sensory perception of another person's future mental processes.
[From Latin *prae* before + *cognoscere, cognitum* to get to know, from *com*- together + *noscere* to know + *-ion* indicating an action, process, or state]

preconcept *n*. A term introduced by the Swiss psychologist Jean Piaget (1896–1980) to denote any of the primitive action-based concepts developed during the *pre-operational stage of development.

preconscious *adj*. *n*. In *psychoanalysis, (of or relating to) mental contents that are not currently in *consciousness but are accessible to consciousness by directing attention to them, such as memories that are not at present being recalled but that can be recalled at will. Sigmund Freud (1856–1939) developed the theory of the preconscious early in his career and set it out fully in his book *The Interpretation of Dreams* (1900, *Standard Edition*, IV–V). A barrier of *censorship exists between the preconscious and the *unconscious (2), and a second barrier exists between the preconscious and consciousness, though this second barrier differs from the first inasmuch as it selects more than it distorts. In 1920 Freud abandoned this *topography in favour of the structural model of id–ego–superego. *See also* perception–consciousness system, subconscious (2), thing-presentation, word-presentation. **pcs** *abbrev. (adj.)*, **Pcs** *abbrev. (n.)*.

preconscious processing *n.* **1.** *Information processing occurring without conscious awareness, as in *subliminal perception and various phenomena that have been observed in the study of memory and emotion. **2.** Another name for *automatic processing.

preconventional morality *n.* The most primitive *Kohlberg stage of moral development, in which the child interprets moral behaviour entirely in terms of personal gain and loss. It is divided into two levels: at Level 1 the child's moral behaviour is guided by the avoidance of punishment (*I should not tell lies because I might get into trouble*), and at Level 2 it is influenced also by the desire for gain (*I should not tell lies because then my parents will reward me*). *Compare* conventional morality, postconventional morality.

precursor *n.* A forerunner, or something that precedes or heralds something else; in particular, a chemical substance from which another more important substance is derived or synthesized.
[From Latin *praecursor* one who runs in front, from *prae* before + *currere, cursum* to run]

predator *n.* Any *species of animal that hunts and kills members of another species for food. Also called a *carnivore*. **predation** *n.* The hunting and killing for food by one animal species (the *predator) of another (the *prey). **predatory** or **predacious** *adj.* Habitually hunting and killing animals of other species for food.
[From Latin *praedator* a plunderer or hunter, from *praeda* booty]

predicate calculus *n.* An advanced form of symbolic *logic incorporating not only *propositions (1), relations between propositions (*and, or, not*, and *if . . . then*), axioms, and rules of inference, but also *quantifiers (1). First-order predicate calculus is obtained by extending *propositional calculus to include quantifiers, and it is widely regarded as the most powerful form of symbolic logic. The first systematic description of this form of

logic was introduced in 1928 by the German mathematical logicians David Hilbert (1862–1943) and Wilhelm Ackermann (1896–1962).
[From Latin *praedicatum* something declared, from *prae* before + *dicare* to declare]

predicate thinking *n.* The fallacy of considering two things to be the same merely because they have attributes in common. According to the Swiss psychologist Jean Piaget (1896–1980), it is characteristic of *preoperational stage of development. Also called *predicative thinking*.

predicative *adj.* Of or relating to a part of a sentence that asserts or denies something about the subject of the sentence and is located outside the noun phrase that it refers to. For example, the adjective *good* is *attributive in the phrase *the good terrorist*, but it is predicative in *the terrorist is good*.
[From Latin *praedicare* to assert publicly, from *prae* before + *dicare* to proclaim + *-ivus* indicating a tendency, inclination, or quality]

prediction paradox *n.* Another name for the *unexpected hanging paradox.

predictive validity *n.* In psychometrics, a form of *criterion validity in which the predictor scores are obtained in advance of the criterion scores, as when a test of scholastic aptitude is validated against scores on tests of school performance obtained months or years later. *Compare* concurrent validity.

predictor variable *n.* The name often given in *regression analysis and *multiple regression to an *independent variable whose effect on the *dependent variable is examined. The term *predictor variable* is preferred by many statisticians because it is not varied independently by the investigator.

prednisolone *n.* A synthetic *corticosteroid hormone derived from *prednisone and having similar effects to *cortisone.

prednisone *n.* A synthetic *corticosteroid hormone derived from and having similar effects to *cortisone.
[Perhaps from *pre(gnant)* + *d(ie)n(e)* a hydrocarbon with two double bonds between carbon atoms + *(cort)isone*]

preference-feedback hypothesis *n.* A conjecture put forward by the South African-born British psychologist Andrew M(ichael) Colman (born 1944), the English psychologist David J(ohn) Hargreaves (born 1948), and the Polish-born British psychologist Wladyslaw Sluckin (1919–85) in articles in the *British Journal of Psychology* and the *British Journal of Social Psychology* in 1981 to explain the fact that for certain classes of stimuli (such as surnames) the relationship between rated familiarity and attractiveness is an inverted U, with both very unfamiliar and very familiar surnames receiving lower ratings of attractiveness than stimuli of intermediate familiarity, whereas for other classes of stimuli (such as first names) the relationship is *monotonic, with attractiveness increasing indefinitely with familiarity. According to the hypothesis, the underlying relationship is an inverted U, but the decrease in attractiveness for high levels of familiarity does not occur in stimuli such as first names whose frequency of exposure and therefore familiarity is significantly controlled by human choice, because as soon as such stimuli begin to decrease in attractiveness through over-exposure, they tend to be chosen less often and their frequency of exposure in the culture is thus damped by a *feedback mechanism, the net effect being a monotonic empirical relationship. The *mere exposure effect is explained partly by this mechanism and partly by the fact that, for complex stimuli, extremely high levels of exposure are required before the peak of the inverted U is passed.

preference reversal *n.* **1.** A tendency, when facing a choice between gambles of nearly equal expected values in certain circumstances, to prefer one gamble but to place a higher monetary value on the other. Reversals occur when one gamble offers a high probability of winning a small prize and the other offers a low probability of winning a large prize. In a typical example, the high-probability H gamble offered an 8/9 probability of winning $4 and the L gamble a 1/9 probability of winning $40, and most participants preferred H; but when they were asked to place a monetary value on each gamble—to state the lowest price at which they would exchange it for cash—most put a higher value on L. The phenomenon was first reported in the *Journal of Experimental Psychology* in 1971 by the US psychologist Sarah C. Lichtenstein (born

1933) and the US-based Israeli psychologist Paul Slovic (born 1938), who attributed it to a finding that they had earlier (in 1968) reported, namely that preferences for gambles (and ratings of their attractiveness) are more highly correlated with probabilities of winning than with payoff sizes, whereas buying and selling prices of gambles are more highly correlated with payoff sizes than with probabilities of winning. Subsequent research, beginning with an experiment reported in 1990 by the Israeli psychologists Amos Tversky (1937–96), Paul Slovic, and Daniel Kahneman (born 1934) showed that most preference reversals are not caused by violations of *expected utility theory but by overpricing of low-probability gambles relative to the choice preference: a person who chooses between (H) $10 for sure and ($L$) a 1/3 probability of winning $40 is quite likely to prefer H but nevertheless to assign a value above $10 to L, which implies an overpricing of L relative to the choice preference. This may be a result of *anchoring and adjustment on the money scale. **2.** A tendency to prefer one alternative when a set of alternatives is presented simultaneously and evaluated jointly but to prefer a different one when the same alternatives are presented in isolation and evaluated separately. The phenomenon was first published in an article in the *Administrative Science Quarterly* in 1992 by the US decision theorists Max H. Bazerman (born 1955), George F. Loewenstein (born 1955), and Sally Blount White (born 1961), who presented decision makers with a hypothetical dispute between neighbours and two potential resolutions involving splitting proceeds from the sale of vacant land between the two properties:

> A: $600 for yourself and $800 for your neighbour;
> B: $500 for yourself and $500 for your neighbour.

The results were that 75 per cent of decision makers who were presented with the two alternatives simultaneously and were asked which they considered more acceptable preferred A, but 71 per cent who were presented with the alternatives one at a time and were asked to indicate the acceptability of each on a rating scale preferred B.

preformationism *n.* A discredited theory that organisms are fully formed in miniature within the *ovum (according to the ovists) or within the *spermatozoon (according to the animalculists), and that development following fertilization involves mere enlargement and not differentiation or formation of new structures. *See also* homunculus. *Compare* epigenesis (1). **preformationist** *n.* One who propounds or believes in *preformationism.

pre-fortis clipping *See* clipping.

prefrontal cortex *n.* The frontmost portion of the *frontal lobe, in front of the primary and secondary motor cortex, uniquely large in the human brain, involved in anxiety and also in brain functions such as *working memory, abstract thinking, social behaviour, and executive functions such as decision making and strategic planning, any or all of which are affected by lesions in this area. The right prefrontal cortex is involved in monitoring behaviour, resisting distractions, and providing an awareness of self and of time. *See also* attention-deficit/hyperactivity disorder, delayed-response task, object permanence, orbitofrontal cortex.

prefrontal leucotomy *See* frontal leucotomy.

prefrontal lobotomy *See* frontal lobotomy.

preganglionic *adj.* Pertaining to *efferent neurons of the *autonomic nervous system that synapse on to other neurons in peripheral *ganglions. *Compare* postganglionic.
[From Latin *prae* in front or before + Greek *ganglion* a cystic tumour + *-ikos* of, relating to, or resembling]

pregenital *adj.* In *psychoanalysis, pertaining to any stage or phase of *psychosexual development before the *genital stage. *See* anal stage, latency period, oral stage, phallic stage, polymorphous perversity.

pregnance *See* Prägnanz.

pregnancy blockage *n.* Another name for the *Bruce effect.

prehensile *adj.* Capable of grasping or holding, as in the prehensile tail of a monkey.
[From Latin *prehendere* to seize or grasp]

prejudice *n.* A preconceived opinion or judgement, formed without adequate consideration of relevant evidence, especially an unfavourable judgement based on group membership, including *racialism, *ethnocentrism, *sexism, or *ageism. The US psychologist Gordon W(illard) Allport (1897–1967) defined it in his seminal book *The Nature of Prejudice* (1954) as 'a feeling, favourable or unfavourable, toward a person or thing, prior to, or not based on, actual experience' (p. 7), but he also suggested a rougher definition that is more often quoted: 'being down on what you're not up on' (p. 8). *See also* ableism, authoritarianism, confirmation bias, fattism, heterosexism, speciesism, social categorization, social identity theory, stereotype. **prejudiced** *adj.* Characterized by *prejudice. **prejudicial** *adj.* Tending to cause *prejudice.
[From Latin *praeiudicium* a previous judgement or precedent, from *prae* before + *iudicium* a trial or sentence, from *iudex* a judge]

Preludin *n.* A proprietary name for the stimulant drug *phenmetrazine.
[Trademark]

premature ejaculation *n.* A *male orgasmic disorder characterized by persistent or recurrent *orgasm and *ejaculation following minimal sexual stimulation and before they are wanted, usually prior to or around the time of penetration, making sexual intercourse difficult or impossible and causing significant distress or problems of interpersonal interaction. It is not diagnosed if it is attributable to a drug, many medicinal drugs producing these symptoms as a side-effect. Also called *ejaculatio praecox. *See also* squeeze technique.
[From Latin *praematurus* unduly early, from *prae* before + *maturus* ripe + *e* from + *iaculatus* thrown, from *iacere* to throw + *-ation* indicating a process or condition]

premenstrual syndrome *n.* A condition of women (included in the *ICD-10 classification and in the *DSM-IV appendix of conditions meriting further study) in which signs and symptoms such as the following tend to appear regularly during the week before and disappear within a few days of the onset of *menstruation: *depressed mood, *anxiety, labile *affect, persistent anger and irritability, decreased interest in usual activities, difficulty in concentrating, *fatigue (1), *hypersomnia or *insomnia, and somatic symp-

toms such as breast tenderness, headaches, joint or muscle pain, and a sensation of bloating. Also called *late luteal phase dysphoric disorder, premenstrual dysphoric disorder* (PMDD), *premenstrual tension (PMT)*. **PMS** *abbrev*.
[From Latin *prae* before + *menstrualis* monthly, from *mensis* a month]

premise *n*. In *logic, a stated reason for believing the conclusion of an argument. In some contexts it refers to a statement or *proposition (1) that is assumed to be true for the purpose of drawing a conclusion in an argument. Also spelt *premiss*, especially in formal logic. *See also* monotonicity, non-monotonic reasoning, syllogism.
[From Latin *praemissa* sent on before, from *prae* before + *mittere, missum* to send, meaning a statement to set before a conclusion]

premotor cortex *See under* motor cortex. **PMC** *abbrev*.

pre-occipital notch *n*. An indentation in the base of each cerebral hemisphere towards the back, marking the boundary between the temporal lobe and the occipital lobe.

pre-Oedipal *adj*. In *psychoanalysis, pertaining to the period of *psychosexual development before the development of the *Oedipus complex, when attachment to the mother predominates in both sexes.

pre-operational stage *n*. In the theory of cognitive development of the Swiss psychologist Jean Piaget (1896–1980), the period between the *sensorimotor stage and the stage of *concrete operations, from about 2 to 7 years of age. *See also* centration, conservation, egocentrism, preconcept, predicate thinking, transductive reasoning.

preoptic nucleus *n*. A region in the front of the *hypothalamus, sometimes regarded as being apart from the hypothalamus proper, implicated in sexual behaviour, aggression, slow-wave sleep, and thirst, containing *osmoreceptors (2). Also called the *preoptic area*.
[So called because it lies above the optic chiasm]

presbyacusis *n*. Loss of hearing sensitivity as a result of ageing, usually characterized by gradual loss of sensitivity to high-frequency sounds through deterioration of the *organ of Corti. Also spelt *presbyacousis*. Also called *presbyacusia* or *presbyacousia. See also* deafness, sensorineural deafness. **presbyacusic** *adj*.
[From Greek *presbys* old + *akousis* hearing, from *akouein* to hear + *-ia* indicating a condition or quality]

presbyopia *n*. Loss of ability to accommodate the eyes to *near vision, caused by loss of elasticity of the crystalline lens as a result of ageing and usually associated with hyperopia (long-sightedness). *Compare* hyperopia. **presbyopic** *adj*.
[From Greek *presbys* old + *ops* an eye + *-ia* indicating a condition or quality]

prescriptive theory *See under* normative (1).

presenile dementia *n*. A chronic, progressive form of *dementia starting before 65 years of age with no clear physical cause; another name for *Alzheimer's disease.
[From Latin *prae* before + *senilis* old, from *senex* an old man]

Present State Examination *n*. A semi-structured interview, intended to provide an objective evaluation of *symptoms associated with mental disorders. It contains 140 items, each scored on a 3-point or 4-point scale, and it is designed for use by experienced clinicians. It was constructed by the English psychiatrist John Kenneth Wing (born 1923) and several colleagues, an early version being published in the *British Journal of Psychiatry* in 1967 and a widely used revision as a separate publication in 1974. *See also* SCAN. **PSE** *abbrev*.

press *n*. Anything that exerts pressure. In the *personology of the US psychologist Henry Alexander Murray (1893–1988), another name for a *stimulus (1) or a configuration or pattern of stimuli that, in conjunction with *needs (3), determine behaviour. *See also* need-press.

press-need *n*. Another name for a *need-press.

pressured speech *n*. Continuous, excessive, rapid, loud, and sometimes incoherent speech that is difficult to interrupt and may continue even when no one is listening, often seen in *manic episodes and other mental disorders. Also called *pressure of speech. See also* logorrhoea.

pressure receptor *n.* Any of a number of different kinds of *touch receptors that are sensitive to pressure stimulation. *See* Golgi tendon organ, Meissner's corpuscle, Merkel cell, Pacinian corpuscle, Ruffini corpuscle. *See also* pressure-sensitive spot.

pressure-sensitive spot *n.* A small area of the *skin that is abundantly supplied by *pressure receptors and is especially sensitive to pressure stimulation, such spots occurring most numerously in the hands and mouth.

prestige suggestion *n.* A persuasive message delivered by or attributed to a highly respected or admired source to maximize its *credibility, as when a celebrity endorses a commercial product on television.

prestriate cortex *n.* A generic name for Areas V2, V3, V4, and V5, of the *visual cortex, sometimes excluding V2. *See under* visual cortex.
[So called because it is adjacent to the striate cortex or primary visual cortex (Area V1)]

presynaptic *adj.* Of or relating to a *neuron that transmits a signal across a *synapse (1). *Compare* postsynaptic.
[From Latin *prae* before or in front + Greek *synapsis* contact or junction, from *syn* together + *haptein* to fasten + *-ikos* of, relating to, or resembling]

presynaptic facilitation *n.* An increase in the effect of a *presynaptic neuron on a *postsynaptic neuron caused by a third neuron that makes an *axoaxonic synapse with the presynaptic neuron near its terminal bouton.

presynaptic inhibition *n.* A diminution in the effect of a *presynaptic neuron on its *postsynaptic neuron caused by a third neuron that makes an *axoaxonic synapse with the presynaptic neuron near its terminal bouton.

pretectal pathway *n.* Either of the pathways of nerve fibres of the *optic tracts that do not reach the lateral geniculate nuclei but proceed instead to the pretectal nuclei, which are collections of nerve cell bodies in front of the tectum in the midbrain. *Compare* tectal pathway.
[From Latin *prae* before or in front + *tectum* a roof or canopy]

prevalence *n.* In *epidemiology, the total number of existing cases of a disorder as a proportion of a population (usually per 100,000 people) at a specific time. *Compare* incidence.

prey *n.* An animal species that is hunted and killed for food by a *predator. **prey on** or **prey upon** *vb.* To hunt and kill for food, as in *Barn owls prey on fieldmice*.
[From Latin *praeda* booty]

priapism *n.* A condition resulting from a disorder within the penis or the central nervous system, characterized by prolonged erection of the penis, seldom accompanied by sexual arousal, but usually causing pain.
[From Greek *priapizein* to be lewd, from *Priapos* Priapus, the ancient deity personifying male fertility and generative power]

primacy effect *n.* **1.** In *serial learning (1), a tendency for the items near the beginning of the series to be better recalled than those near the middle. *See also* serial position effect. *Compare* recency effect. **2.** In *impression formation, the tendency for information about a person that is presented first to have a larger effect on the overall impression of the person that the recipient forms than information presented later.

primacy, law of *See* primacy effect (1, 2).

primacy, oral *See* oral primacy.

primal anxiety *n.* In *psychoanalysis, *anxiety resulting from the *birth trauma.
[From Latin *primalis* of or relating to the first, from *primus* first + *-alis* of or relating to]

primal fantasy *n.* In *psychoanalysis, a primitive *fantasy (2) of the *primal scene, infantile seduction, castration, or similar experiences, believed by Sigmund Freud (1856–1939) to be universal and to be transmitted by genetic inheritance from practices that were common occurrences in prehistory. Freud introduced the concept in an article on 'A Case of Paranoia Running Counter to the Psycho-Analytic Theory of the Disease' (1915): 'I call such phantasies—of the observation of sexual intercourse between the parents, of seduction, of castration, and others—"primal phantasies"' (*Standard Edition*, XIV, pp. 263–72, at p. 269), and he expounded this genetic theory in his book *Introductory Lectures on*

Psycho-Analysis (1916–17, *Standard Edition*, XV–XVI, at p. 371). *See also* seduction theory.

primal father *n*. In *psychoanalysis, the head of the *primal horde. *See also* totem.

primal horde *n*. In *psychoanalysis, an obsolete concept of a state of nature assumed to have existed in the distant past.

primal repression *n*. In *psychoanalysis, a form of *repression, when wishes emanating in the *id are blocked from reaching *consciousness. Sigmund Freud (1856–1939) introduced the concept in the *Schreber case in 1911. *Compare* primary repression, secondary repression.

primal scene *n*. In *psychoanalysis, the spectacle of intercourse between one's parents. *See* primal fantasy, Wolf Man.

primal sketch *n*. In the *computational theory of vision pioneered in the late 1970s by the English psychologist David Courtenay Marr (1945–80), the first stage in the perceptual process, similar to a rough line drawing, its function being to represent the variations in *luminance present in the image after eliminating extraneous visual *noise (2) such as glare that does not convey useful information about the image. The sketch is constructed by first blurring or smoothing the image with *filters (2) of different *spatial frequencies, capable of detecting information at different levels of resolution, and then locating regions of maximum change in luminance by finding *zero-crossings, the result of this process being a two-dimensional black-and-white *representation (2) of *contours and shapes present in the image. The *raw primal sketch* incorporates edges and lines (formed wherever a zero-crossing emerges under a blur filter or pairs of zero-crossings emerge in the same place under two adjacent blur filters), bars (formed wherever a line detected under a filter that transmits only low-frequency information is flanked by two edges detected under a filter that transmits only high-frequency information), terminations (ends of bars), and blobs (areas enclosed in single edges). The *full primal sketch* joins together lines and edges that belong with one another, groups other items that appear to be associated, and locates the apparent boundaries of objects. *Compare* 3-D model description, $2\frac{1}{2}$-D sketch.

primal therapy *n*. A form of *psychotherapy, developed by the US psychologist Arthur Janov in 1970, in which clients or patients are encouraged to scream about their parents and their painful re-experiencing of birth and infancy. Also called *primal scream therapy* or *scream therapy*. *See also* birth trauma, body therapies, rebirthing.

primary abilities *See* primary mental abilities.

primary anxiety *n*. In *psychoanalysis, *anxiety arising from failure to control the impulses of the *id, its name alluding to the *primary process. *Compare* signal anxiety.

primary auditory cortex *See under* auditory cortex.

primary colour *n*. **1.** Any of the shades of red, green, or blue that can be mixed equally to form white or in different proportions to match all other *spectral colours and also certain *non-spectral colours such as purple. The wavelengths often used to define the primary colours are 670, 535, and 470 nanometres respectively. Also called an *additive primary*. *See also* chromaticity, CIE colour system, colour equation, complementary colour, Grassmann's laws (perception), Rayleigh equation, spectrum, trichromacy, tristimulus values. *Compare* psychological primary, secondary colour, subtractive primary. **2.** Any of the *complementary colours of red, green, and blue, namely green–blue (cyan), deep bluish purple (magenta), and yellow respectively, that can be subtracted from white light, equally to form black, or in different proportions (usually by mixing pigments) to match any other spectral colour. Also called a *subtractive primary*. **3.** Any of the four colours red, yellow, green, or blue that are basic to the processing of colour in the visual system and that are perceived as being basic or fundamental, the wavelengths often used to define them being 670, 589, 535, and 470 nanometres respectively. Also called a *principal colour* or a *psychological primary*. US *primary color*. *See also* Bezold–Brücke phenomenon.

primary drive *See under* drive.

primary emotions *n*. According to a classification suggested in 1971 by the US psychologists Paul Ekman (born 1934) and

Wallace V(erne) Friesen, the six *emotions of happiness, sadness, disgust, fear, anger, and surprise, so called partly because their associated *facial expressions appear to be innate, the evidence for this being that they appear soon after birth, even in infants born blind and deaf who could not have learnt them from others, and that they are expressed and decoded similarly in relatively isolated cultures that have been studied by anthropologists. Some researchers believe that other emotions or *affects are blends of these six.

primary gain n. In *psychoanalysis, an immediate benefit, such as relief from *anxiety, resulting from a *neurosis or a *defence mechanism. Sigmund Freud (1856–1939) drew the distinction between primary gain and *secondary gain in 1916–17 in his book *Introductory Lectures on Psycho-Analysis* (*Standard Edition*, XV–XVI, at pp. 381–5). Also called *paranosic gain*. *See also* flight into illness. *Compare* secondary gain.

primary hypersomnia n. One of the *dyssomnias, with excessive sleepiness or *hypersomnia as the major symptom. Also called *disorder of excessive somnolence (DOES)*. *Compare* narcolepsy.

primary identification n. In *psychoanalysis, a primitive form of *identification (2), occurring during the *oral stage, before any other type of *object-relationship is formed. Sigmund Freud (1856–1939) described this phenomenon in his book *The Ego and the Id* (1923): 'At the very beginning, in the individual's primitive oral stage, object-cathexis and identification are no doubt indistinguishable from each other' (*Standard Edition*, XIX, pp. 12–66, at p. 29). *Compare* secondary identification.

primary immune response *See under* immune response.

primary impotence *See under* impotence (2).

primary insomnia n. An *insomnia that is not related to another mental disorder or a *general medical condition and is not induced by a drug.

primary integration n. In *psychoanalysis, an infant's first recognition of itself as a unitary being, separate from its environment.

primary memory n. The content of consciousness supplied by *memory rather than direct perception. *See also* working memory. *Compare* secondary memory.

primary mental abilities n. A set of seven basic or fundamental cognitive capacities proposed in 1938 by the US psychologist Louis Leon Thurstone (1887–1955), on the basis of *factor analysis, as an interpretation of the group factors or clusters of correlations between certain types of test items and subtests. They are labelled verbal comprehension (V), word fluency (W), number (N), spatial ability (S), associative memory (M), perceptual speed (P), and reasoning (R) or induction (I). *Compare* g. **PMA** *abbrev.*

primary motor cortex *See under* motor cortex.

primary narcissism n. In *psychoanalysis, a form of *narcissism involving *cathexis of the self with the whole of the *libido in an early phase of development. The British-based Austrian psychoanalyst Melanie Klein (1882–1960) and her followers rejected the concept, arguing that object-relationships are evident from the earliest stages of sucking. *Compare* secondary narcissism.

primary object n. In *psychoanalysis, the first *instinctual object, usually the mother or the mother's breast, in an infant's libidinal development. *See also* object-relationship.

primary odour n. Any of the fundamental odours of which other odours are believed to be formed by combination, especially the six primary odours of *Henning's prism: fragrant (like lavender or rose petals), ethereal (like ether or cleaning fluid), resinous (like resin or turpentine), spicy (like cinnamon or nutmeg), putrid (like faeces or rotten eggs), and burnt (like tar oil). *See also* Crocker–Henderson system, stereochemical theory, Zwaardemaker smell system.

primary prevention n. Measures taken to prevent the occurrence of a disorder. *Compare* secondary prevention, tertiary prevention.

primary process n. In *psychoanalysis, an unconscious, irrational mode of mental functioning, based on the *pleasure principle, involving *free energy governed by mechanisms such as *condensation and *displacement. Sigmund Freud (1856–1939) developed the concept at the beginning of his psychological work and expounded it at length in Chapter VII of his book *The Interpretation of Dreams* (1900, *Standard Edition*, IV–V). *See also* binding. *Compare* secondary process.

primary projection area *n*. An area of the brain, such as the primary *somatosensory cortex, *primary visual cortex (Area V1), or primary *auditory cortex, that is the first to receive information from another system before relaying it elsewhere. *Compare* secondary projection area, tertiary projection area.

primary quality *n*. In philosophy, a property such as solidity, physical extension, shape, motion or rest, or number that is inherent in an object or a group of objects and is capable of being experienced directly by an observer. It is distinguished from a *secondary quality*, such as sound, colour, taste, smell, warmth, or cold that is merely a property capable of producing in an observer a sensation that does not correspond to the property itself. This distinction was first made by the Greek philosopher Democritus of Abdera (?460–?370 BC) and was accepted by the French philosopher René Descartes (1596–1650) and the English physicist and mathematician Sir Isaac Newton (1642–1727) before being fully developed and given its most influential formulation in 1690 by the English philosopher John Locke (1632–1704) in his *Essay Concerning Human Understanding* (Book 2, Chapter 8). *See also* successive contrast.

primary repression *n*. In *psychoanalysis, a form of *repression in which anxiety-arousing information already in *consciousness is removed and blocked from returning. *Compare* primal repression, secondary repression.

primary sexual characteristic *n*. Any difference between the sexes in their sexual organs or gametes. *Compare* secondary sexual characteristic.

primary sleep disorders *n*. A generic term for the *dyssomnias and the *parasomnias.

primary somatosensory cortex *See under* *somatosensory cortex.

primary taste *n*. Any of the fundamental tastes that are believed to underlie all tastes, usually the four vertices of *Henning's tetrahedron: sweet (like sugar or *aspartame), sour (like vinegar or lemon juice), salty (like sea water or table salt), and bitter (like quinine or orange peel). *See also* umami.

primary visual cortex *n*. The part of the *visual cortex to which the *photoreceptors in the retinas of the eyes are eventually projected, occupying the gyri on both sides of the deep *calcarine sulcus in the *occipital cortex, containing 200 million cells within a total area of 25 square centimetres and arranged in an inverted *topographic map of the object or scene being viewed, with neighbouring cells having *receptive fields close together and being stacked vertically in *ocular-dominance columns and *orientation columns. It contains six layers of cells numbered 1 to 6 from the top, layer 4 being subdivided into three sublayers 4A, 4B and 4C, layer 4C receiving inputs from the photoreceptors in the retina via the *lateral geniculate nuclei, the upper part 4Cα receiving inputs from the *magnocellular layer and the lower part 4Cβ from the *parvocellular layer of the geniculate nuclei. All layers except layers 1 and 4A have neuronal connections outside the primary visual cortex: layers 1 and 2, which contain *blobs for colour vision and are concerned with both form and colour, receive inputs from layers 4Cα and 4Cβ, and layer 2 projects to Area V2 of the visual cortex; layer 4B, concerned with movement and stereopsis, receives inputs from layer 4Cα and projects to Areas V2 and V5 (or MT) of the visual cortex, layer 4Cα (in the magnocellular pathway) projects to layer 4A, and layer 4Cβ (in the parvocellular pathway) projects to layers 2 and 3 and thence to Area V2. Layers 5 and 6 are less well understood but are known to project to deep structures within the brain, layer 5 to the *superior colliculus and layer 6 back to the lateral geniculate nuclei. Also called the *striate cortex* and known technically as *Area V1* or *Brodmann area 17*. *See also* retinotopic map, visual cortex.

primary zone *n*. Another name for an *erotogenic zone.

primate *n*. Any member of the order Primates, including humans, anthropoid apes, monkeys, lorises, and lemurs.

[From Latin *primates* plural of *primas* principal, from *primus* first]

prime *n.* **1.** A *cue (3) given to facilitate a particular response. *See* priming (1). **2.** A *prime number*, that is, any number that is evenly divisible only by itself and 1. **3.** A typographical symbol (′) affixed to a mathematical symbol as a modifier, as in *d′*—*see* d prime.

priming *n.* **1.** In a task involving recall, recognition, or some other form of cognitive performance, the provision of a contextual *cue (3), *prime (1), or *prompt that provides information about either the identity or the time of appearance of a target stimulus and that may facilitate a response (in *facilitative priming*) or inhibit it (in *inhibitory priming*). When primes provide information that influences expectancies of targets, as in *associative priming* in which primes are meaningfully related to targets, *expectation-dependent* or *strategic priming* may occur, whereas when primes are unrelated to targets only *automatic priming* can occur, though it occurs more quickly. Associative priming that is dependent on verbal meaning, as when the prime *bread* is provided for the target *butter*, is called *semantic priming*; and a common type of associative priming that is not dependent on verbal meaning is *initial letter priming*, when the first letter of the word to be remembered is provided as a cue. **2.** Reduced reaction time (quicker responding) resulting from a signal warning of the imminent presentation of the stimulus. *Compare* negative priming. **3.** In research involving animals self-stimulating their *pleasure centres, the provision of an initial stimulatory impulse at the start of the session to encourage the animal to provide further impulses on its own.
[From Latin *primus* first]

primordial image *n.* In *analytical psychology, a term originally introduced by the Swiss historian Jacob Christopher Burckhardt (1818–97) and adopted in 1912 by Carl Gustav Jung (1875–1961) for what he later came to call an *archetype (2).

principal colour *n.* Another name for a *psychological primary. US *principal color*.

principal-components analysis *n.* A statistical technique applied to a correlation matrix to combine observed variables into weighted linear combinations of the original variables called *principal components*, which are all uncorrelated with one another. The first principal component explains the maximum proportion of the variance, and successive principal components explain progressively smaller portions of the variance. This technique is closely related to *factor analysis. *See also* cluster analysis, correspondence analysis. **PCA** *abbrev.*

principal sulcus *n.* Another name for the *longitudinal fissure.

principle of constancy *n.* In *psychoanalysis, the proposition that the quantity of psychic energy within the mental apparatus remains constant, regulation being achieved through discharge of excess energy in *abreaction and avoidance of increase through *defence mechanisms. This *economic concept is derived loosely from the first law of *thermodynamics, the *conservation of energy law, and may be thought of as a form of *homeostasis, but the formulations of it by the Austrian physician Josef Breuer (1842–1925) in *Studies on Hysteria* (1895, *Standard Edition*, II, at pp. 183–252) and by Sigmund Freud (1856–1939) in his book *Beyond the Pleasure Principle* (1920, *Standard Edition*, XVIII, pp. 7–64, especially at pp. 9, 55–6) are ambiguous and contradictory; in particular, Freud appears to confuse the regulation of energy with its reduction. *See also* bound energy, ego libido, free energy, hydraulic theory, metapsychology, object libido, quota of affect. *Compare* nirvana principle.

principle of equipotentiality *See* equipotentiality.

principle of least effort *n.* The proposition that, in striving for a goal, an organism generally seeks a method involving the minimum expenditure of energy. The concept was named in 1954 by the US psychologist Gordon W(illard) Allport (1897–1967). *See* cognitive economy, cognitive miser, elaboration likelihood model, hodological space.

principle of mass action *See* mass action.

principle of psychical determinism *See* psychical determinism.

principle of reinstatement of stimulating conditions *n.* Another (obsolete) name for *encoding specificity.

principle of restricted choice *n.* A rule influencing the play of certain card combinations in the game of bridge, first discussed by the British-born US bridge expert Alan F(raser) Truscott (born 1925) and later developed and named by the English player and author (John) Terence Reese (1913–96) in his book *The Expert Game* (1958), based on the same probabilistic phenomenon as the *Monty Hall problem, according to which if a certain action could have been taken *either* because there was no alternative *or* as a result of a choice between two alternatives, then the first possibility is twice as likely as the second, other things being equal.

principle of the excluded middle *See* excluded middle law.

prion *n.* An infectious particle of protein that is not a virus or a bacterium and does not contain *nucleic acid but is none the less capable of self-replication. The normal (alpha) form is harmless, but the rogue (beta) form, when it occurs in the brain and spinal cord, is believed to be a cause of *prion diseases. *See also* PrP.
[Coined in the 1980s from *proteinaceous infectious particle* to denote a mutant or rogue protein]

prion disease *n.* Any of a number of disorders of the nervous system, all fatal, believed to be caused by rogue *prions, including scrapie in sheep, BSE in cattle, and the human prion diseases new-variant *Creutzfeldt–Jakob disease (nvCJD), *fatal familial insomnia (FFI), *Gerstmann–Sträussler–Scheinker syndrome (GSS), and *kuru. Unlike all other infectious diseases they do not provoke *immune responses, and they are therefore difficult to detect because tests based on antibody production cannot be developed.

prion protein *See* PrP.

prior entry law *n.* The principle according to which, if two events occur simultaneously, then a person who is attending primarily to one of them will usually perceive that event as occurring before the other. This is believed to be one factor accounting for the *personal

equation in astronomy, because some observers of star transits apparently attended primarily to the stars and others primarily to the ticking clock.

prior probability *n.* **1.** The *base rate or relative frequency of an event or characteristic in a *population. **2.** In *Bayesian inference, the probability assigned to an event before taking empirical evidence into account. Also called an *a priori probability* or simply a *prior. See also* insufficient reason. *Compare* posterior probability.

prism *n.* A transparent solid, usually with triangular or wedge-shaped cross-section and rectangular sides, through which white light is diffracted into a *spectrum. It is also used to reflect rays of light, as in *inverting spectacles. *Compare* diffraction grating.
[From Greek *prisma* something sawn off, from *prizein* to saw]

prism adaptation *n.* A form of *adaptation (2) in which a person wearing wedge-shaped *prism spectacles, resulting in displacement of the visual field usually about 10 degrees to one side, becomes accustomed to the distortion, making normal body movements and no longer reaching out for objects at incorrect positions in space. *See also* inverting spectacles.

Prisoner's Dilemma game *n.* A two-person game in which each player chooses between a cooperative *C* *strategy (2) and a defecting *D* strategy, each receiving a higher payoff from *D* than *C* irrespective of whether the other player chooses *C* or *D*, but each receiving a higher payoff if both choose *C* than if both choose *D*. Its name derives from an interpretation first applied to it by the US mathematician Albert W(illiam) Tucker (1905–95) in a seminar at the Psychology Department of Stanford University in 1950: Two people, charged with involvement in a serious crime, are arrested and prevented from communicating with each other. There is insufficient evidence to obtain a conviction unless at least one of them discloses incriminating information, and each prisoner has to choose between concealing the information (*C*) and disclosing it (*D*). If both conceal, both will be acquitted, the second-best payoff for each; if both disclose, both will be convicted, the third-best payoff for each; and if only one discloses and one conceals, then according to a deal offered to them, the one who discloses will be acquitted and will receive a reward for helping the police, the best possible payoff, and the other will receive an especially heavy sentence from the court, the worst possible payoff. The game is *paradoxical, because D is a *dominant strategy for both players, so that it is *rational for each player to choose it whatever the other player does, but each player receives a higher payoff if they both choose their dominated C strategies than if they both choose D. The game was discovered in 1950 by the US mathematician Merrill M(eeks) Flood (1908–91) and the Polish-born US mathematician Melvin Dresher (1911–92). *See also* mixed-motive game, Newcomb's problem, N-person Prisoner's Dilemma, social dilemma, sure-thing principle, tit for tat strategy. **PD** or **PDG** *abbrev*.

prison psychosis *n*. A misleading name for *Ganser syndrome, which is not classified as a *psychosis (1) and is not peculiar to prisoners. [So called because Ganser's original description of it was based on three prisoners awaiting sentence]

proactive interference *n*. Impairment of learning or performance of a task caused by having previously learnt similar information or a similar task. Also called *proactive inhibition*. *See also* Ranschburg inhibition, Skaggs–Robinson paradox. *Compare* retroactive interference. **PI** *abbrev*.

probabilistic functionalism *n*. A theory of perception formulated by the Hungarian-born US psychologist Egon Brunswik (1903–55) according to which perception involves the selection of environmental *cues (2) that are most useful or functional in responding, the validity of all perceptions and beliefs being necessarily probabilistic rather than certain. *See also* Brunswikian.

probability *n*. A measure or index of degree of certainty regarding the occurrence of an event, on a scale from zero (indicating impossibility) to 1 (indicating certainty), interpreted as the relative frequency of the event (in classical statistics) or as one's subjective belief regarding the likelihood of the event (in *Bayesian inference). Probabilities are nowadays usually assumed to obey *Kolmogorov's axioms. The theory of probability is the foun-

dation on which the whole of *statistics is constructed.
[From Latin *probabilis* that may be proved, from *probare* to prove + *-abilitas* capacity, from *habilis* able]

probability distribution *n*. In statistics, the probability or relative frequency of a variable for all possible values that the variable can assume.

probability learning *n*. A form of *discrimination learning in which the positive stimulus is rewarded on a randomized proportion of trials. In humans, this is usually achieved with variations of the light-guessing experiment first described by the US psychologist Lloyd G(irton) Humphreys (born 1913) in the *Journal of Experimental Psychology* in 1939. An observer tries to predict which of two light bulbs will light up on each trial, and the bulbs are lit up randomly, 80 per cent left and 20 per cent right, for example. People typically began by distributing their guesses roughly equally between the two options, then they increase the frequency of choosing the bulb that is being lit up more often, and finally after very many trials, by which time they have enough information to judge the probabilities reasonably accurately, they usually settle into a non-optimal *matching strategy* of choosing 80 per cent left and 20 per cent right in the example above. This matching strategy yields a probability of $(0.8)(0.8) + (0.2)(0.2)$ of being correct, which is 68 per cent correct guesses. This is non-optimal, because the strategy of choosing the more frequently illuminated bulb on every single trial yields 80 per cent correct guesses. Animals also tend to respond non-optimally, and when the responses of many animals are pooled, they sometimes correspond to probability matching.

probability matching *See under* probability learning.

probability sample *n*. Any sample drawn by a technique involving *randomization, so that members of the population or subgroups within it have known probabilities of inclusion. *See* cluster sample, random digit dialling, simple random sample, stratified random sample. *Compare* accidental sample, convenience sample, non-probability sample, opportunity sample, quota sample, self-selected sample, snowball sample.

probable error n. A measure of the degree of dispersion, variability, or scatter in a group of scores, equal to half the *interquartile range. It can be calculated by multiplying the *standard deviation by 0.6745. *Compare* interquartile range, range, semi-interquartile range, variance. **PE** *abbrev.*

proband n. A person with a particular trait or disorder, serving as the starting point for a study in which the person's blood relatives are investigated in order to obtain information about the genetic transmission of the characteristic in question. Also called an *index case.*
[From Latin *probandus* to be proved, from *probare* to prove]

probe n. Anything that is used to examine or explore, especially (in cognitive psychology) a *cue (3) in the form of an item in a list immediately preceding the item to be recalled.

problem solving n. Cognitive processing directed at finding solutions to *well-defined problems, such as the *Tower of Hanoi, *Wason selection task, or a *water-jar problem, by performing a sequence of operations. Problem solving by means of *logic or *logical analysis is usually called *reasoning. *See also* 2-4-6 problem, algorithm, brute force algorithm, convergence–divergence, functional fixedness, General Problem Solver, ill-defined problem, insight (2), intelligence, lateral thinking, Monty Hall problem, muddy children problem, Newcomb's problem, oddity problem, problem-solving stages, taxicab problem, travelling salesman problem, well-defined problem.

problem-solving cycle *See* problem-solving stages.

problem-solving stages n. The successive phases that can be observed in the process of *problem solving. According to the most influential scheme, proposed by the English psychologist Graham Wallas (1858–1932) in his book *The Art of Thought* (1921), the stages are preparation, *incubation, illumination or *insight (2), and verification. According to the US philosopher John Dewey (1859–1952) in his book *How We Think* (1933), the stages are suggestion, translation of a difficulty into a *well-defined problem, framing of a hypothesis, *reasoning, and testing.

problem space n. In *problem solving, the set of all possible operations that can be performed in an attempt to reach a solution.

procedural knowledge n. Information about how to carry out sequences of operations—*knowing how* in contrast to *knowing that*—sometimes lacking awareness and understanding of how to perform certain tasks and therefore being a form of *non-declarative knowledge. The English philosopher Gilbert Ryle (1900–76) argued in *The Concept of Mind* (1949) that it cannot be reduced to declarative knowledge of facts. *See also* knowledge, mirror drawing, procedural memory. *Compare* acquaintanceship knowledge, declarative knowledge.

procedural memory n. A storage system for *procedural knowledge, information within it being acquired through a form of learning that is relatively slow, requiring repetition over many trials, often involving associations of sequential stimuli and permitting storage of information about predicative relations between events, expressed primarily by improved performance at skilled tasks, often occurring without conscious awareness or understanding of what is being learned and therefore being a form of *non-declarative memory. It is distinguished from *episodic memory and *semantic memory. *See also* ACT*, mirror drawing. *Compare* declarative memory.

proceptive behaviour n. Behaviour of a female that facilitates mating. US *proceptive behavior. See also* lordosis.
[From Latin *pro* for + *(con)ceptus* becoming pregnant]

process n. **1.** A sequence of events leading to some change or alteration in the state of a dynamic system. **2.** In anatomy, a projecting part, especially a fine threadlike protrusion from a *neuron, being an *axon, a *dendrite, or one of their branches, also called a *neurite.*
[From Latin *processus* an advance, from *procedere* to proceed]

processing speed n. The rate at which a person performs simple perceptual or cognitive tasks such as apprehension, scanning, retrieval, and response to stimuli. Measures of processing speed correlate weakly with psychometric measures of intelligence. *See also* choice reaction time, inspection time, nerve conduction velocity.

process, primary *See* primary process.

process, secondary *See* secondary process.

proclitic *n.* A monosyllabic *clitic that precedes the word on which it depends, such as the English 't, standing for *it* in the word 'twas. *Compare* enclitic.
[From Greek *pro* before + *enklinein* to cause to lean + -*itikos* resembling or marked by]

procyclidine *n.* Procyclidine hydrochloride, an *anticholinergic drug that is used in the treatment of *parkinsonism. *See also* antiparkinsonian.

prodrome *n.* A precursor or premonitory *sign (1) or *symptom of a developing disorder or attack, such as an *aura (2) before an attack of *epilepsy. **prodromal** *adj.* Of or denoting a *prodrome.
[From Greek *prodromos* a forerunner, from *pro* before + *dromos* a run + -*alis* of or relating to]

production method *n.* Another name for *magnitude production.

production rule *n.* In cognitive psychology, a condition–action or *if–then* sequence (*if X occurs or obtains, then do Y*) designed to implement a procedure, often incorporated in a *production system.

production system *n.* In cognitive psychology, an ordered set of *production rules that are implemented by locating the first production rule in the list whose condition is satisfied, implementing its procedure, then beginning again at the top of the list, and so on. *See also* ACT*.

productive orientation *n.* In *neo-Freudian theory, a term used by the German-born US psychoanalyst Erich Fromm (1900–80) to denote a character type manifesting full use of potential and realization of latent potentialities, independent thinking, respect for self and others, enjoyment of sensual pleasures without anxiety, and delight in nature and works of art. *Compare* exploitative orientation, hoarding orientation, marketing orientation, receptive orientation.

product–moment correlation coefficient *n.* A statistic representing the degree of linear relationship between two variables. It is defined as the *covariance of the two variables divided by the product of their standard deviations, hence it may be thought of as a measure of *standardized (1) covariance. It is symbolized by r, and it ranges from 1.00 for perfect positive correlation, through zero for uncorrelated variables, to -1.00 for perfect negative correlation. When one variable is being used to predict another, the square of r indicates the proportion of variance in one variable that is explained by the other (given certain linear assumptions), or the proportion of variance shared by the two variables: if $r = 0.50$, then $r^2 = 0.25$, indicating that 25 per cent of the variance in one of the variables is explained by the other, or that 25 per cent of the variance is shared by the two variables. Also called *Pearson's correlation coefficient*. *See also* correlation. *Compare* correlation ratio, partial correlation, Spearman rank correlation coefficient.

profile *n.* An outline, especially of a person's face in side view. In psychometrics, a graphic representation of a person's scores on several tests or subtests using a common scale. *See also* criminal profiling. **profiler** *n.* One who creates *profiles.
[From Italian *profilo* a profile, from Latin *pro* forth + *filare* to spin or draw a line, from *filum* a thread]

profile of non-verbal sensitivity *See* PONS.

profiling *See* criminal profiling.

profound mental retardation *n.* A level of *mental retardation associated with *IQ below approximately 20 (in adults, *mental age below 3 years). Also called *profound mental subnormality*.

progeria *n.* A congenital condition of premature ageing, characterized by small stature and the appearance during childhood of grey hair, wrinkled skin, and the posture and general demeanour of an old person.
[From Greek *pro* before + *geras* old age + -*ia* indicating a condition or quality]

progesterone *n.* A female *steroid *sex hormone secreted especially by the *corpus luteum in the ovary to prepare the uterus for a fertilized ovum and to maintain pregnancy. When it reaches the hypothalamus, it inhibits the release of *luteinizing hormone from the pituitary gland. *See also* DHEA, oestrous cycle. [From *proge(stin)*, from *pro* before + *gestation* + *ster(ol)* + *-one* indicating a ketone, from Greek *-one* a feminine name suffix]

prognosis *n.* A prediction or forecast of the course or outcome of a disorder. **prognostic** *adj.*
[From Greek *pro* before + *gnosis* knowing]

prognostic test *n.* In psychometrics, any test that is designed to predict the likely outcome for the respondent of a programme of therapy, education, or training.
[From Greek *pro* before + *gnosis* knowing + *-ikos* of, relating to, or resembling]

programmed strategy *n.* A predetermined pattern of *strategy (2) choices used in experimental studies of players' choices in repeated *strategic games. In a two-person experimental game, a player may be pitted against a simulated co-player in the form of a computer or an accomplice of the experimenter's, programmed in advance to make a predetermined sequence of choices that may or may not depend on the player's choices. In many such experiments the players are led to believe that they are playing against ordinary co-players. The most thoroughly researched programmed strategy for repeated *Prisoner's Dilemma games is *tit for tat.

progression index *n.* An index of the comparative *intelligence of mammalian species, based on a modification of the *encephalization quotient, defined as volume of *neocortex in the animal in question divided by volume of neocortex in a standard comparison animal belonging to the same order, correcting for body size. If a chimpanzee is arbitrarily assigned a standard progression index for primates of 1.0, then humans score 3.2. *Compare* A/S ratio, encephalization quotient.

Progressive Matrices test *See* Raven's Progressive Matrices.

progressive relaxation *n.* A form of *psychotherapy used for treating *anxiety disorders, in which skeletal muscles throughout the body, often beginning with the feet and legs and working upwards, are first tensed and then deeply relaxed. It is also used as an adjunct to other forms of psychotherapy, especially *systematic desensitization. It was introduced by the US physician Edmund Jacobson (1888–1983) and was described in his book *Progressive Relaxation* (1938). Also called *Jacobson's progressive relaxation* or *relaxation therapy*.

progressive supranuclear palsy *n.* A neurological disorder of unknown cause, first described in 1964 by the Canadian neurologists John C. Steele and John Clifford Richardson (1909–86) and the Polish-born Canadian neurologist Jerzy Olszewski (1913–66), characterized by loss of balance while walking, a gradual paralysis of the *extra-ocular muscles, making upward and downward eye movements difficult or impossible, *dysarthria, and stiffness of the neck and trunk muscles, followed eventually by loss of memory and mild *dementia. It strikes in middle or old age, and its associated pathology includes degeneration of neurons in the *basal ganglia, *brainstem, and *cerebellum, with subcortical *amyloid plaques and *neurofibrillary tangles. It is estimated to affect approximately 1.4 per 100,000 people, slightly more women than men, and it is related to (though much less common than) *Parkinson's disease. Also called *supranuclear palsy* or (especially in the UK) *Steele–Richardson–Olszewski syndrome (SRO)*. **PSP** *abbrev.*
[So called because the paralysis, especially of the eye muscles, occurs above nuclei of the central nervous system]

projection *n.* **1.** In *psychoanalysis, a *defence mechanism in which intolerable feelings, impulses, or thoughts are falsely attributed to other people. Sigmund Freud (1856–1939) developed the concept initially in relation to paranoia (*delusional disorder), and later extended it to a wide range of psychological phenomena, but never provided a detailed analysis of it: in his celebrated case study entitled 'Psycho-Analytic Notes on an Autobiographical Account of a Case of Paranoia (Dementia Paranoides)' published in 1911, he wrote: 'let us make up our minds to postpone the investigation of it (and with it that of the mechanism of paranoiac symptom formation in general) until some other occasion' (*Standard Edition*, XII, pp. 9–82, at

p. 66), but he never published any such investigation. *See also* externalization, projective identification, projective test, Schreber case. **2.** An area where *axons from a sense organ or another part of the nervous system terminate.

projection area *n.* Another name for a *sensory projection area.

projective identification *n.* In *Kleinian analysis, a *fantasy (2) in which one inserts oneself, or part of oneself, into an *instinctual object in order to possess it, control it, or harm it. The British-based Austrian psychoanalyst Melanie Klein (1882–1960) introduced the concept in 1932 in her book *The Psycho-Analysis of Children*, in which she described a child's fantasy of invading its mother's body and attacking it sadistically, but she did not introduce the term *projective identification* until 1952, when she described it in a chapter in a co-authored book *Developments in Psycho-Analysis* as 'a particular form of identification which establishes the prototype of an aggressive object-relation'. *See also* identification (2), *participation mystique*.

projective test *n.* Any of a variety of personality tests in which the respondent gives *free responses to a series of stimuli such as inkblots, pictures, or incomplete sentences. Such tests are based loosely on the psychoanalytic concept of *projection (1), the assumption being that respondents project unconscious aspects of their personalities on to the test items and reveal them in their responses. Among the best known projective tests are the *Blacky pictures, *Draw-a-Person test, *Holtzman Inkblot Technique, *House–Tree–Person Technique, *Make-a-Picture-Story Test, *Rorschach test, *Rosenzweig Picture-Frustration Study, *sentence completion test, *Szondi test, *TAT, and *word-association test. Also called a *projective technique* or a *projective method*. The term *projective method* first appeared in print in the title of an article in the *Journal of Experimental Education* in 1938, where the authors attributed it to the US psychologist Lawrence K. Frank (1890–1968), who published an article entitled 'Projective Methods for the Study of Personality' in the *Journal of Psychology* in 1939 and later published a book entitled *Projective Methods* (1948) in which he suggested that projective tests provide X-ray images of

the unconscious mind. *See also* motivational research.

prokaryote *n.* A bacterium or a cyanobacterium (blue-green alga) composed of cells each containing genetic material in a single filament, not enclosed in a well defined *nucleus (1). *Compare* eukaryote.
[From Greek *pro* before + *karyon* a kernel]

prokaryotic cell *n.* A biological cell without a *membrane separating the genetic material from the rest of the cell.

prolactin *n.* A *gonadotrophic hormone secreted by the anterior pituitary, stimulating the secretion of *progesterone by the *corpus luteum, initiating and maintaining lactation and functioning as a contraceptive. Also called *luteotrophic hormone (LTH)* or *luteotrophin*. **PrL** *abbrev.*
[From Latin *pro* before + *lac, lactis* milk]

proliferative phase *n.* Another name for the *follicular phase of the *oestrous cycle or *menstrual cycle.

Prolixin *n.* A proprietary name for the neuroleptic drug *fluphenazine.
[Trademark]

promnesia *n.* The sensation of remembering something that is being experienced for the first time; the sense of *déjà vu.
[From Greek *pro* before + *mneme* memory + *-ia* indicating a condition or quality]

prompt *n.* Anything that urges someone to act or that functions as a reminder, especially (in cognitive psychology) a *cue (3, 4) intended to aid recall or as a hint to guide performance of a task. *See also* priming (1).
[From Latin *promptus* evident, from *promere* to bring forward, from *pro* before + *emere* to buy]

pronation *n.* Lying in a prone (belly-down) position or, if standing with one's arms at one's sides, turning the palms backwards. *Compare* supination.
[From Latin *pronus* bent forward or bowed + *-ation* indicating a process or condition]

proof-reader's illusion *n.* **1.** The failure of a proof-reader to notice gross errors in the meaning of the text being checked, because different and incompatible *levels of processing are required for checking meaning and orthography. **2.** The tendency of a proofreader to overlook small errors of orthography because of the difficulty of suppressing higher *levels of processing while checking orthography, especially when one is the author of the text. Some professional proofreaders read text backwards to avoid this problem.

pro-opiomelanocortin *See* POMC.

propanediol *n.* An early class of minor tranquillizers or *sedative drugs, the best known example being *meprobamate (Miltown).
[So called because it is derived from propane-diol]

prophase *n.* The first phase of *mitosis, when the nuclear membrane disappears and the chromosomes divide lengthwise into *chromatids, which become the chromosomes of the daughter cells.
[From Greek *pro* before + *phasis* an aspect, from *phainein* to show]

proposition *n.* **1.** The meaning conveyed by a declarative sentence, a declarative sentence being one that asserts or denies something, or in other words one that is capable of being true or false. The proposition is not the sentence itself but its meaning. The sentences *Snow is white* and *Schnee ist weiß* are obviously different, but they express the same proposition in two different languages, and the proposition is true if and only if snow is indeed white. *See also* categorical syllogism, mental model, modal logic, possible world, propositional calculus, sentence functor, syllogism, truth functor, truth table, Venn diagram. **2.** More generally, any deal proposed for consideration. **3.** An invitation to engage in sexual intercourse.
[From Latin *propositio* a setting forth, from *proponere* to display, from *pro* before + *ponere* to place]

propositional calculus *n.* Any formal system of symbolic *logic providing a language for expressing *propositions (1) and the relations between them (*and, or, not,* and *if ... then*), without regard to the internal structure or content of the propositions, together with a set of axioms and rules of inference, enabling the process of constructing a valid argument to be reduced to a mechanical process. *See*

also logical analysis, sentence functor, truth functor, truth table. *Compare* predicate calculus.

propositional representation *n.* Another name for *symbolic representation.

propositus *n.* A person from whom a genealogical lineage is traced when delineating the pattern of inheritance of a psychological or physical trait.
[From Latin *propositus* placed before, from *pro* before + *ponere* to place]

propoxyphene *n.* Propoxyphene hydrochloride, a *narcotic analgesic that is sometimes taken as a street drug. Also called *Darvon* (trademark).
[From *propoxy-* composed of propyl united with oxygen + *phene* an old name for benzene, from Greek *phainein* to show, alluding to its use in manufacturing illuminating gas]

propranolol *n.* Propranolol hydrochloride, the most commonly prescribed *beta-blocker.
[From *pro(pyl)* containing the monovalent group C_3H_7 + *pr(op)anol*, from *propane* + *-ol* denoting a compound containing a hydroxyl group, from *(alcoh)ol*]

proprioception *n.* The form of sensation through which one is aware of the position and orientation of one's body relative to the direction of gravity, of one's body parts relative to one another, and of acceleration and changes in position, the information being supplied by *proprioceptors. *See* joint sense, muscle sense, static sense, tendon sense. *See also* internal sense, kinaesthesis. *Compare* exteroception, interoception. **proprioceptive** *adj.*
[From Latin *proprius* one's own + English *receptor* + Latin *-ion* indicating an action, process, or state]

proprioceptor *n.* Any *sensory receptor that supplies information for *proprioception, especially receptors in the *vestibular system and in the muscles, tendons, and joints. *Compare* exteroceptor, interoceptor.

propylthiouracil *n.* A crystalline compound that is used to treat abnormal swelling of the thyroid gland and that, depending on a simple hereditary factor, tastes very bitter to some people and tasteless to others, roughly 25 per cent of people being non-tasters, 50 per cent

tasters, and 25 per cent supertasters. Formula: $C_7H_{10}N_2OS$. *Compare* PTC. **PROP** *abbrev*.
[From *pro(pyl)* containing the monovalent group C_3H_7 + Greek *theion* sulphur + English *uracil*, from *ur(ea)* + *ac(etic)* + Latin *-il(is)* indicating capability or relationship]

prosencephalon *n.* A technical name for the *forebrain, especially in a developing embryo. *Compare* mesencephalon, rhombencephalon.
[From Greek *proso* forward + *enkephalos* the brain, from *en* in + *kephale* the head]

prosimian *n.* A primate of the primitive suborder Prosimii, including lemurs, tree shrews, lorises, and tarsiers. *Compare* anthropoid (2).
[From Latin *pro* before + *simia* an ape]

prosocial behaviour *n.* Helping behaviour, *altruism, or more generally any behaviour that is positive and calculated to promote the interests of society. US *prosocial behavior*.

prosody *n.* A generic name for the qualities of speech involving *loudness, *pitch, *rhythm, and *tempo. *See also* paralanguage.
[From Greek *prosoidia* a song set to music, from *pros* towards + *oide* a song]

prosopagnosia *n.* A form of agnosia involving an impaired ability to recognize or identify previously familiar faces, sometimes even those of close relatives, such faces being identified as faces but not faces of particular known people, usually associated with damage to the posterior right hemisphere of the brain. *See also* agnosia. *Compare* phonagnosia.
[From Greek *prosopon* a face + *a-* without + *gnosis* knowledge + *-ia* indicating a condition or quality]

prospective study *n.* A type of research investigation in which a *cohort of participants is examined over a period of time in an effort to discover the factor(s) that cause a particular disorder or characteristic to emerge. The initial sample is often selected from groups of participants relatively likely to develop the disorder or characteristic being studied; for example, in a prospective study of *anorexia nervosa, young women learning to be models might be used. Results from prospective studies carry more persuasive weight than those from *retrospective studies.

[From Latin *pro* before or in front + *specere, spectum* to look]

prospect theory *n.* A theory of preferences among outcomes involving *risk (2) formulated in 1979 by the Israeli psychologists Daniel Kahneman (born 1934) and Amos Tversky (1937–96) as an alternative to *expected utility theory. According to prospect theory, human preferences tend to violate expected utility (SEU) theory in the following ways: people tend to evaluate outcomes as gains or losses relative to their current situation or the status quo rather than in terms of absolute value; they tend to attach greater weight to losses than to corresponding gains; they tend to show *risk aversion for gains but *risk seeking for losses; and they tend to overweight very small probabilities and underweight moderate and high probabilities. The theory is usually depicted by an S-shaped *utility function that associates a subjective utility to any amount that may be gained or lost (see illustration); the part of the function representing gains is a concave power function (*see* power law) with an exponent of 2/3, and the part representing losses is a convex power function with an exponent of 3/4, though some researchers have reported slightly smaller exponents. The slope is

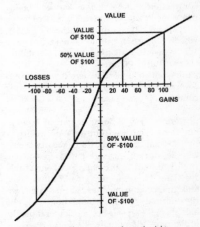

Prospect theory. The concave section to the right represents risk aversion for gains, with a sure gain of $35 having the same value as a 50 per cent probability of gaining $100; the steeper convex section to the left represents risk seeking for losses, with a sure loss of $40 having the same value as a 50 per cent probability of losing $100.

greater for losses than for gains, depicting the observation that a loss has a greater subjective effect than an equivalent gain (loss aversion). In 1981 Tversky and Kahneman provided experimental data showing that 84 per cent of the undergraduate students preferred a sure gain of $240 to a gamble involving a 25 per cent chance of gaining $1,000 and a 75 per cent chance of gaining nothing (risk aversion for gains), but 87 per cent preferred a gamble involving a 75 per cent chance of losing $1,000 and a 25 per cent chance of losing nothing to a sure loss of $750 (risk seeking for losses). Combining these prospects, most of these students were expressing a preference for a portfolio containing a 25 per cent chance of winning $240 and a 75 per cent chance of losing $760 over a portfolio containing a 25 per cent chance of winning $250 and a 75 per cent chance of losing $750, thus violating the principle of rationality according to which a *dominant alternative/strategy should invariably be preferred. See also endowment effect, framing effect.

prostaglandin n. Any of a group of substances, composed mostly of fatty acids, present in semen and secreted into the bloodstream at various sites in the body, causing fever and inflammation and also playing a part in *pain perception, muscle contraction, and various other bodily processes. Prostaglandins are produced by the enzyme prostaglandin H_2 synthase or PGHS, which converts arachidonic acid from the *endoplasmic reticulum to prostaglandins. See also aspirin. **PG** abbrev.
[From prosta(te) + gland (where it was first discovered) + Greek -in(e) indicating an organic compound]

protanomaly n. A form of partial *colour-blindness resulting from an abnormality in the *visual pigment that absorbs long-wave light, resulting in a partial loss of sensitivity to light in the red part of the visible spectrum, a tendency to confuse reds and greens, and matches that deviate from the normal *Rayleigh equation. See also daltonism. Compare deuteranomaly, protanopia, tritanomaly.
[From Greek protos first, from pro before, alluding to the first of the three *primary colours (1) red, green, and blue + anomalos uneven or inconsistent, from an- without + homalos even, from homos the same]

protanopia n. A form of *anomalous dichromacy in which the *visual pigment that absorbs long-wave light is non-functional, leading to a loss of sensitivity to red light and a tendency to confuse reds and greens. See also daltonism. Compare deuteranopia, protanomaly, tritanopia.
[From Greek protos first, from pro before, alluding to the first of the three *primary colours (1) red, green, and blue + anopia blindness, from an- without + ops an eye + -ia indicating a condition or quality]

protein n. Any of a group of complex nitrogenous compounds that are encoded by genes and are the main constituents of living organisms. Every protein is composed of a chain of a hundred or more *amino acids (if it contains fewer it is a *polypeptide), linked by *peptide bonds and folded into a distinctive three-dimensional shape, and some proteins are *enzymes. The human body is composed of more than 50,000 proteins.
[From Greek proteios primary, from protos first]

protein binding n. The attachment of molecules of a drug in the bloodstream to molecules of protein, especially albumin, effectively inactivating the drug by fixing it to a molecule that is too large to reach the target receptor sites. A dynamic equilibrium usually arises in which a portion of the drug is bound and a portion remains in the free form, the strength of the binding determining the quantity of the drug available in its active free form.

protein kinase C n. A protein that can move from the cytoplasm of a neuron to the membrane, changing the neuron's electrical and molecular properties and increasing its propensity to respond to stimulation by triggering nerve impulses, such changes providing physical substrates of certain types of memories in dendritic trees. **PKC** abbrev.

protensity n. The subjective or psychological experience of duration as opposed to objective duration or time.
[From Latin protendere to extend or prolong, from pro forward + tendere to stretch]

protest, masculine See masculine protest.

prothetic stimulus dimension n. Any stimulus dimension that varies continuously and produces continuous changes in perception, the standard example being the wavelength or frequency of sound, which produces continuous changes in perceived pitch as it varies continuously, whereas light produces qualitative perceptual changes. *Compare* categorical perception, metathetic stimulus dimension. [From Greek *prothetikos* placed in front, from *pro* before + *tithenai* to place + *-ikos* of, relating to, or resembling]

protocol analysis *n.* Any of a number of techniques of *qualitative research in which thought processes elicited from research participants or subjects while they were performing a mental task are studied and classified, often by means of *content analysis. *See also* introspection.

Proto-Indo-European *See under* Indo-European.

protoplasm *n.* The living substance of a *cell, consisting of the *cytoplasm and the *nucleoplasm. **protoplasmic** *adj.*
[From Greek *protos* first + *plasma* a form]

prototype *n.* **1.** A preliminary version of a product, suitable for testing and modification before the product is manufactured and marketed commercially. **2.** An object or item that serves as an example or typical representative of its type or class. *See also* focal colour, prototype theory, schema. *Compare* exemplar. **3.** In biology, the ancestral or original form of a species or other taxonomic category. **prototypical**, **prototypic**, or **prototypal** *adj.*
[From Greek *protos* first, from *pro* before, + *typos* a mark]

prototype matching *n.* Another name for *template matching.

prototype theory *n.* A theory of *concepts and *concept formation introduced in 1973 by the US psychologist Eleanor Rosch (born 1938) to overcome problems inherent in the classical *componential theory originally put forward by the Greek philosophers Plato (?427–?347 BC) and Aristotle (384–322 BC). According to the componential theory, concepts can be expressed in terms of their *defining properties, which are the necessary and sufficient *attributes that items must have to be instances of the concept. But the Austrian-born British philosopher Ludwig

(Josef Johann) Wittgenstein (1889–1951) argued in his *Philosophical Investigations* (1953, paragraph 66) that a concept such as that of a *game* has no necessary or sufficient attributes, and hence no defining properties, and that instances of games are linked to one another by family resemblance, just as some members of the family may share the same build, others the same eye colour, and others the same gait, without any characteristic being shared in common by all members of the family. According to prototype theory, instances of a natural concept are defined by their resemblance to a *prototype (2) that is a best or most typical example of the concept, sharing the maximum number of *features (1) or attributes with other instances and a minimum number with instances of other concepts. Thus a prototype consists of *characteristic features rather than defining properties, and according to this interpretation concepts have indistinct boundaries and may be represented by *fuzzy sets (but *see* guppy effect). If an item is clearly similar to a prototype, as *table* is to the prototypical *furniture*, then it is likely to be perceived as belonging to the concept, whereas if it is somewhat (but not entirely) dissimilar to the prototype, as *carpet* is to *furniture*, then it may be unclear whether or not it belongs to the concept. *See also* basic-level category, schema. *Compare* componential theory.

proverbs test *n.* Any test in which the respondent is asked to explain the figurative meaning of a series of proverbs. For example, the figurative meaning of the proverb *A rolling stone gathers no moss* is that a restless or wandering person does not become prosperous. In clinical practice it is sometimes used as a rough-and-ready test of *thought disorder, the assumption being that people with thought disorder often have difficulty distinguishing between the literal and figurative meanings of proverbs.

proxemics *n.* A branch of *non-verbal communication concerned with the study of *personal space and other spatial aspects of human and animal interaction.
[From Latin *proximus* nearest, superlative of *prope* near + Greek *-ikos* of, relating to, or resembling]

proximal *adj.* Nearer or nearest to the centre, point of attachment, or origin. *Compare* distal.

[From Latin *proximus* next, superlative of *prope* near]

proximal stimulus *n.* The pattern of physical energy that stimulates or excites a *sensory receptor. *See also* reafference. *Compare* distal stimulus.
[From Latin *proximus* next + -*al* from Latin -*alis* of or relating to]

proximity grouping law *n.* One of the four original *grouping laws of *Gestalt psychology formulated in 1923 by the German psychologist Max Wertheimer (1880–1943) to explain the organization of parts into wholes by the visual system. According to the law, elements close together tend to be grouped perceptually, so that the array OO OO OO OO tends to be perceived as four pairs rather than eight separate elements. *See also* Prägnanz, common fate, common region, connectedness grouping law. *Compare* closure grouping law, good continuation, similarity grouping law.

proximodistal *adj.* From the centre of the body towards the extremities, referring to the development of an embryo, and also later stages of development, in which growth is fastest near the head and torso and progressively slower towards the feet and hands. *Compare* cephalocaudal.
[From Latin *proximus* next + *distare* to be distant, from *dis-* apart + *stare* to stand]

proximoreceptor *n.* A *sensory receptor such as a *somatic receptor that can be stimulated only by nearby stimuli and that mediates a *near sense. Also called a *proximoceptor. *Compare* telereceptor.
[From Latin *proximus* next + *recipere*, *receptum* to receive, from *re-* back + *capere*, *ceptum* to take]

Prozac *n.* Fluoxetine hydrochloride, an *antidepressant drug belonging to the group of *selective serotonin reuptake inhibitor (SSRI) agents, used in the treatment of depression, obsessive–compulsive disorder, bulimia nervosa, and panic disorder.
[Trademark]

PrP *abbrev.* Prion protein, a glycoprotein (a protein in which the amino acid units are bound to sugars) that forms the major or only component of a *prion. In brain tissue molecules of PrP tend to aggregate into rod-shaped structures, and the rods collect in clumps that appear in photomicrographs as fluffy tufts resembling *amyloid plaques.

pruning *n.* Trimming by removing superfluous parts, including naturally occurring neuronal death or *apoptosis resulting in the elimination of redundant synapses, also occurring excessively in certain pathological states. *See also* neural Darwinism.
[From Old French *proignier* to clip, from Latin *propago* a cutting]

Psammetichus experiment *n.* The earliest recorded psychological experiment, reported about 429 BC in *The Histories* (part 1, book 2, paragraph 2) of the Greek historian Herodotus (?485–425 BC), the world's first history book. According to Herodotus, the Egyptian Pharaoh Psammetichus I (664–610 BC) performed the experiment to determine whether human beings have an innate capacity for speech, and if so, which particular language is innate. He ordered two infants to be brought up in a remote place by a shepherd who was forbidden to speak in their presence. After two years the children began to speak, and the word that they repeated most often was *becos*, which turned out to be the Phrygian word for bread. Psammetichus concluded that the capacity for speech is innate, and that the natural language of human beings is Phrygian. The experiment is conceptually similar to the *Kaspar Hauser experiments by the British ethologist William H. Thorpe (1902–86), published in 1958, in which birds were reared in isolation to determine which aspects of their songs are innate.

pseudaesthesia *n.* An illusory tactile sensation without any physical basis, such as a *phantom limb. US *pseudesthesia*. Also called *pseudoaesthesia* or *pseudoesthesia*.
[From Greek *pseudes* false + *aisthesis* feeling + -*ia* indicating a condition or quality]

pseudoangina *n.* Chest pain suggestive of a heart attack in a person without any coronary heart disease; a common symptom of *hypochondria and *hypochondriasis.
[From Greek *pseudes* false + Latin *angustia* tightness]

pseudoanorexia *n.* A condition in which a person eats secretly while claiming to have no appetite and to be unable to eat. Also called

false anorexia. See also factitious disorder, malingering. *Compare* anorexia.
[From Greek *pseudes* false + *an-* not or without + *orexis* appetite + *-ia* indicating a condition or quality]

pseudoataxia *n.* Loss of ability to coordinate voluntary movements without any lesion in the *central nervous system. *Compare* ataxia.
[From Greek *pseudes* false + *a-* without + *taxis* order + *-ia* indicating a condition or quality]

pseudobulbar palsy *n.* A neurological condition, resulting from a lesion in the *corticobulbar pathway, in which the voluntary muscles of the face are paralysed, resulting in *dysarthria and *dysphagia, but involuntary facial movements such as facial expressions, coughing, and sneezing are unaffected. Also called *pseudobulbar paralysis.*
[From Greek *pseudes* false + English *(cortico)bulbar (pathway)*]

pseudocoma *n.* Another name for *locked-in syndrome.

pseudocyesis *n.* A *somatoform disorder involving a phantom pregnancy, with a false belief of being pregnant together with many of the physical signs of pregnancy. Also called *false pregnancy, pseudopregnancy.*
[From Greek *pseudes* false + *kyesis* pregnancy]

pseudodementia *n.* A syndrome, usually associated with *depression, in which the symptoms of *dementia are mimicked but evidence for an *organic disorder is lacking.
[From Greek *pseudes* false + Latin *dementare* to drive mad, from *de* from + *mens, mentis* mind + *-ia* indicating a condition or quality]

pseudodepression *n.* A condition following a massive lesion in the *frontal lobe of the brain, characterized by apathy, indifference, and loss of initiative but no experience of *depression.

pseudohallucination *n.* A type of *hallucination that seems to come from within one's mind rather than from outside as in a true hallucination, although some authorities consider this distinction obscure and unhelpful.

pseudohermaphrodite *n.* A person who has the reproductive organs of one sex and the external genitalia of the other. *Compare* hermaphrodite (1). **pseudohermaphroditism** *n.* The congenital condition of being a *pseudohermaphrodite.
[From Greek *pseudes* false + English *hermaphrodite*]

pseudoinsomnia *n.* A condition characterized by recurrent dreams of lying awake, creating the delusion of insomnia. *Compare* insomnia.

pseudo-isochromatic *adj.* Of or relating to a plate or image of two or more colours that appears isochromatic (uniform in colour) to a person with a particular form of *colour-blindness and is included in a set of plates such as the *Ishihara test or the *Stilling test used to test colour vision.

pseudolalia *n.* Speechlike sounds that are not interpretable as language.
[From Greek *pseudes* false, from *pseudein* to lie + *lalein* to babble + *-ia* indicating a condition or quality]

pseudolinguistic *adj.* Resembling language superficially, but lacking one or more of the defining properties of true *language (1).

pseudologia fantastica *n.* A syndrome characterized by habitual telling of implausible lies and fantastic exaggerations, usually half believed by the teller but often transparently improbable to the recipients. *Compare* factitious disorder. **pseudologue** *n.* A person with *pseudologia fantastica; a liar.
[From Greek *pseudes* false + *logos* discourse + *phantastikos* imaginary, from *phantazein* to make visible + *-ikos* of, relating to, or resembling]

pseudology *n.* The study of lying; the art or science of lying.
[From Greek *pseudes* false + *logos* discourse]

pseudomemory *n.* Another name for a *false memory. Also called *pseudomnesia.*
[From Greek *pseudes* false + English *memory*]

pseudomnesia *n.* Another name for a *false memory.
[From Greek *pseudes* false + *a-* without + *mnasthai* to remember + *-ia* indicating a condition or quality]

pseudomorpheme *n.* A portion of a word that resembles a *morpheme but is not, in fact, one. For example, in the word *history*, the portion *his* is a pseudomorpheme, appearing to some people to be a morpheme and encouraging the coinage *herstory* to denote history viewed from a feminine or a feminist perspective.

pseudomutuality *n.* A relationship between marriage partners, family members, or other people closely involved with each other in which surface harmony and agreement cloaks deep and damaging interpersonal conflicts that are not confronted openly.

pseudophone *n.* A device that transposes the sounds entering the left and right ears, used for studying *sound localization. *Compare* pseudoscope.
[From Greek *pseudes* false + *phone* a sound or voice]

pseudopregnancy *n.* Another name for *pseudocyesis.

pseudoscope *n.* A device that transposes the images projected on to the retinas of the left and right eyes, causing distance relations to be inverted so that convex objects appear concave and vice versa. *Compare* pseudophone.
[From Greek *pseudes* false + *skopeein* to view]

psi *n.* A generic term for *paranormal phenomena, including especially *extra-sensory perception (telepathy, clairvoyance, and precognition) and *psychokinesis. It is often preferred to more specific terms on the ground that it is difficult or impossible to distinguish between alternative manifestations of psi, as when an apparent demonstration of telepathy in a card-guessing experiment could be explicable by clairvoyance (paranormal perception of the cards themselves rather than of the sender's thoughts) or psychokinesis (paranormal control of the order of the cards during the shuffling process).
[Named after *psi* (Ψ), the 23rd letter of the Greek alphabet, alluding to the adjective *psychic* or *psychical*]

psilocybin *n.* A *hallucinogen belonging to the group of *indole alkaloids, occurring in the form of a crystalline phosphate ester in the magic mushroom *Psilocybe mexicana*. *See also* phantasticant, psychedelic, teonanactyl.

[From Greek *psilos* bare + *kybe* head, alluding to the appearance of the magic mushroom]

psi-missing *n.* A *psi or parapsychological effect that is statistically significant in the opposite direction to the experimental hypothesis, such as a significantly below-chance number of hits in an experiment on telepathy or clairvoyance. *See also* miss.

psittacism *n.* Meaningless, repetitive speech. [From Latin *psittacus* a parrot]

psychasthenia scale *See* MMPI.

psyche *n.* The human mind or soul. In Greek mythology, the soul was personified by Psyche, a young woman who was loved by Eros, the god of love who married Psyche but visited her only at night and insisted that she should never see his face. One night Psyche lit an oil lamp while Eros was asleep, fell in love with him at first sight, and was so startled by his beauty that she spilt a drop of hot oil on his shoulder and awakened him, whereupon he immediately abandoned her. To win him back, Psyche had to endure many trials and dangers, but eventually she was transformed into a goddess and joined him in heavenly bliss. Psyche is often depicted in works of art with butterfly wings or as a butterfly, because she symbolizes the human soul, suffering hardship and struggle in life but re-emerging after death in a new and better existence, like a caterpillar reborn as a butterfly. **psychic** or **psychical** *adj.*
[From Greek *psyche* breath, from *psychein* to breathe, alluding to the ancient belief that breathing was evidence that the soul had not yet left the body]

psychedelic *adj.* Of, relating to, or resembling a state of subjectively heightened perception and awareness associated with certain drugs, including *phenylalkylamines such as *mescaline, *STP, and *ecstasy (2); *indole alkaloids such as *bufotenin, *DMT, *harmine, *LSD, and *psilocybin; and various other compounds such as *ibotenic acid, *myristin, *ololiuqui, and *phencyclidine. Also spelt *psychodelic*. *See also* Amanita muscaria, fly agaric, magic mushroom, morning glory, teonanactyl. *Compare* hallucinogen, phantasticant.
psychedelia *n.* The culture and phenomena associated with *psychedelic experiences and

drugs. Also spelt *psychodelia*, but this is avoided in careful usage.

[From Greek *psyche* mind + *delos* visible or clear + *-ikos* of, relating to, or resembling]

psychiatry *n*. The branch of medicine devoted to the diagnosis, classification, treatment, and prevention of *mental disorders. *Compare* clinical psychology, neurology, neuropsychiatry. **psychiatric** *adj*. **psychiatrist** *n*. A physician who practises *psychiatry.

[From Greek *psyche* mind + *iatros* a physician]

psychic *adj*. **1.** Another word for *paranormal, or sensitive to paranormal or spiritual phenomena, influences, or forces. Also written *psychical*. **2.** Mental as opposed to physical. *n*. **3.** A person who professes paranormal or spiritual powers or abilities.

[From Greek *psychikos* of or relating to the soul, from *psyche* the soul + *-ikos* of, relating to, or resembling]

psychical apparatus *n*. In *psychoanalysis, a term used prolifically by Sigmund Freud (1856–1939) and his followers for the mind, including its various conscious and unconscious components. Also called *psychic apparatus*.

psychical conflict *n*. In *psychoanalysis, the situation that exists when two contradictory tendencies oppose each other in a person's mind. Some such conflicts are conscious, as when a desire is opposed by a moral constraint, but it is unconscious conflicts that are assumed to generate *neurotic (1) symptoms. In an article on 'The Psycho-Analytic View of Psychogenic Disturbances of Vision' (1910), Sigmund Freud (1856–1939) argued that conflicts between ideas are invariably traceable to conflicts between instincts: 'We have discovered that every instinct tries to make itself effective by activating ideas that are in keeping with its aims. These instincts are not always compatible with one another; their interests often come into conflict. Opposition between ideas is only an expression of struggle between the various instincts' (*Standard Edition*, XI, pp. 211–18, at p. 213.) Also called *psychic conflict*.

psychical determinism *n*. In *psychoanalysis, the assumption, first introduced by Sigmund Freud (1856–1939), that no psychological phenomena, not even *dreams,

*symptoms, or *parapraxes, occur by chance, but that they can always be assigned definite causes. Freud discussed this concept at length in his book *The Psychopathology of Everyday Life* (1901, *Standard Edition*, VI), citing numerous anecdotal instances. Also called *psychic determinism*. *See also* overdetermination, reductive interpretation.

psychical reality *n*. In *psychoanalysis, anything that strikes a person as real, including fantasies that are experienced as memories of actual occurrences, including those of sexual seduction in childhood, whether or not they are based on real events. Sigmund Freud (1856–1939) claimed in his book *Introductory Lectures on Psycho-Analysis* (1916–17) that 'phantasies possess *psychical* as contrasted with material reality' and that '*in the world of the neuroses it is the psychical reality which is the decisive kind*' (*Standard Edition*, XV–XVI, at p. 368, italics in original). This concept has been attacked as an absurd and dangerous blurring of the distinction between truth and fantasy arising from Freud's discovery that his patients' claims of childhood seduction were untrue. Also called *psychic reality*. *See also* seduction theory.

psychical research *n*. An obsolescent name for *parapsychology. The world's first Society for Psychical Research was formed in Cambridge, England, in 1882; the American Society for Psychical Research was founded in 1885.

psychic apparatus *See* psychical apparatus.

psychic conflict *See* psychical conflict.

psychic determinism *See* psychical determinism.

psychic reality *See* psychical reality.

psychoacoustics *n*. The study of the relationship between sounds and their psychological effects.

[A blend of *psycho(logy)* + *acoustics*]

psychoactive *adj*. Another word for *psychotropic.

psychoanaleptic *adj. n*. (Of or relating to) a *stimulant drug.

[From Greek *psyche* the mind + *analeptikos*

restorative, from *analambanein* to take up, from *ana* up + *lambanein* to take + *-ikos* of, relating to, or resembling]

psychoanalysis *n.* A theory of mental structure and function, consisting of a loosely connected set of concepts and propositions, a theory of mental disorders, and an associated method of *psychotherapy (the 'talking cure') based on the writings of Sigmund Freud (1856–1939), its distinctive character residing in the emphasis that Freud placed on unconscious mental processes and the various mechanisms people use to repress them. As a therapeutic method, its major techniques are *free association, *dream analysis, the *interpretation (2) of *parapraxes, and the analysis of the *transference. The Austrian neurologist Sigmund Freud (1856–1939) introduced the term in 1896 in an article on 'Heredity and the Aetiology of the Neuroses' (*Standard Edition*, III, pp. 143–56). Also spelt *psycho-analysis. See also* Adlerian, ego psychology, Eriksonian, Freudian, insight (3), Jungian, Kleinian, Kohutian, Lacanian, neo-Freudian, object-relations theory, psychoanalytic construction, resistance, self-analysis, self-psychology, wild psychoanalysis, Winnicottian. *Compare* psychoanalytic psychotherapy. **psychoanalytic** *adj.*

psychoanalyst *n.* One who practises *psychoanalysis. Also called an *analyst.*

psychoanalytic construction *n.* In *psychoanalysis, an explanation of a person's verbal utterances and actions that is more extensive and further removed from the empirical material than an *interpretation (2). Sigmund Freud (1856–1939) introduced this concept in 1937 in an article entitled 'Constructions in Analysis' (*Standard Edition*, XXIII, pp. 257–69), where he suggested that when a correct construction is put to a patient it sometimes results in the emergence of a repressed memory, and that it can be useful even when that does not happen: 'Quite often we do not succeed in bringing the patient to recollect what has been repressed. Instead of that, if the analysis is carried out correctly, we produce in him an assured conviction of the truth of the construction which achieves the same therapeutic result as the recaptured memory' (pp. 265–6). Freud's articles 'Psycho-analytic Notes on an Autobiographical Account of a Case of Paranoia (Dementia Paranoides)' (1911,

Standard Edition, XII, pp. 9–82) and 'A Child is Being Beaten' (1919, *Standard Edition*, XVII, pp. 179–204) contain virtuosic examples of psychoanalytic construction.

psychoanalytic psychotherapy *n.* A form of *psychotherapy that evolved out of *psychoanalysis and that uses many of its assumptions and techniques but that falls short of formal psychoanalysis. It tends to focus on specific problems—often a single conflict such as an inability to respond appropriately to criticism—and on aspects of the client's social interactions. Also called *analytic therapy.*

psychobabble *n.* A term coined by the US writer Richard Dean Rosen (born 1949) in the title of his book *Psychobabble* (1977) for excessive or superfluous psychological *jargon (1), especially in connection with various forms of *psychotherapy.

psychobiology *n.* A term coined by the Swiss-born US psychiatrist and neurologist Adolf Meyer (1866–1950) for the study of the relationships between psychological and biological phenomena.

psychodrama *n.* A form of *group therapy in which people act out their own emotional problems and conflicts in front of audiences in order to gain objectivity and understanding of them. *See also* drama therapy, sociodrama.

psychodynamic *adj.* Of or relating to the *dynamic interplay of psychological processes. *See* dynamic psychology.

psychodysleptic *adj. n.* (Of or relating to) a *hallucinogen.
[From Greek *psyche* the mind + *dys-* bad or abnormal + *lepsis* a seizure, from *lambanein* to take + *-ikos* of, relating to, or resembling]

psychoendocrinology *n.* The interface between *psychology and *endocrinology; the study of the interaction between hormones, behaviour, and mental experience.

psychoenergizer *n.* An *antidepressant drug belonging to the class of *monoamine oxidase inhibitors (MAOIs).

psychogalvanic response *n.* Another name for a *galvanic skin response. **PGR** *abbrev.*

[From Greek *psyche* the mind + *galvanic* of or relating to current electricity, named after the Italian physiologist Luigi Galvani (1737–98) who first showed that muscles contract when electricity is passed through them]

psychogenesis *n.* The production of a disorder, including a *mental disorder, or a *sign (1) or *symptom, by a psychological rather than a physical process. **psychogenic** *adj.* Compare organic mental disorder.
[From Greek *psyche* mind + *genes* born]

psychogenic amnesia *n.* Any form of *amnesia arising by *psychogenesis rather than as part of an *organic disorder, similarly *psychogenic fugue, psychogenic pain disorder*, and so on.

psychogeriatrics *n.* The branch of medicine devoted to the prevention, diagnosis, and treatment of mental disorders affecting old people. Compare geriatrics.
[From Greek *psyche* mind + *geras* old age + *iatros* a doctor + *-ikos* of, relating to, or resembling]

psychoid *adj.* In *analytical psychology, soul-like, a term that Carl Gustav Jung (1875–1961) applied to the *collective unconscious, which 'cannot be directly perceived or "represented", in contrast to the perceptible psychic phenomena, and on account of its "unrepresentable" nature I have called it "psychoid"' (*Collected Works*, 8, paragraph 840).
[From Greek *psyche* the soul + *-oid* indicating likeness or resemblance, from *eidos* shape or form]

psychoimmunology *n.* The interface between *psychology and *immunology; the study of the interaction between behaviour, mental experience, and the immune system. Compare psychoneuroimmunology.
[From *psycho(logy)* + *immunology*]

psychokinesis *n.* The movement or change of physical objects by mental processes without the application of physical force, a conjectural *paranormal phenomenon. See also illusion of control, telekinesis. Compare extra-sensory perception. **PK** *abbrev.* **psychokinetic** *adj.*
[From Greek *psyche* mind + *kinesis* movement]

psycholinguistics *n.* A word introduced by collective agreement at an academic conference in 1953 to denote the psychology of language, including language acquisition by children and all aspects of the production and comprehension of speech and writing.

psychological autopsy *n.* A postmortem study of the possible reasons for a person's death, especially after a suspected suicide, by interviewing relatives and acquaintances, examining diaries and letters, and making other personal inquiries.

psychological decision theory *n.* A *normative (2) and descriptive approach to judgement and decision introduced in the early 1970s by the Israeli psychologists Amos Tversky (1937–96) and Daniel Kahneman (born 1934) and the US psychologists Paul Slovic (born 1938), Sarah C. Lichtenstein (born 1933), and Baruch Fischhoff (born 1946). See base-rate fallacy, causal schema, conjunction fallacy, elimination by aspects, framing effect, heuristic, hindsight bias, non-regressiveness bias, prospect theory, regression fallacy, sample size fallacy, taxicab problem. See also bounded rationality, satisficing. Compare behavioural decision theory, decision theory.

psychological differentiation *n.* Another name for field independence. See under field dependence–independence.

psychological primary *n.* Any of the colours red, yellow, green, or blue that are basic to the processing of colour in the visual system and are perceived as cardinal or fundamental rather than as mixtures of other colours. Also called a *unique colour, unique hue*, or *primary colour*, though the latter term is ambiguous. See also Bezold–Brücke phenomenon, spectrum. Compare additive primary, primary colour (1, 2), subtractive primary.

psychological refractory period See under refractory period (3). **PRP** *abbrev.*

psychologism *n.* An exaggeration of the importance or significance of psychology; a belief that psychology is the basis of philosophy or of all natural and social sciences; any unjustified or fanciful psychological explanation for a non-psychological phenomenon, such as *drapetomania or *dysaesthesia aethiopis.

psychology *n.* The study of the nature, functions, and phenomena of behaviour and mental experience. The etymology of the word (see below) implies that it is simply the study of the mind, but much of modern psychology focuses on behaviour rather than the mind, and some aspects of psychology have little to do with the mind. Many textbooks define psychology simply as the study of behaviour, or the science of behaviour, but that too is to exclude much of psychology: the study of *cognition, for example, is concerned with behaviour only indirectly, as evidence of mental processes. The establishment of psychology as an independent discipline, separate from the disciplines of philosophy and biology from which it emerged, is attributable to the German psychologist Wilhelm (Max) Wundt (1832–1920), who stated in the opening sentence of his book *Principles of Physiological Psychology* (1873), the first major textbook of experimental psychology: 'The book that I herewith offer to the public attempts to mark out a new domain of science', and who founded the first psychological laboratory in Leipzig in 1879. *See also* psyche.
[From Greek *psyche* soul or mind + *logos* word, discourse, or reason. The Latin *psychologia* emerged from obscure origins in Germany in the 16th century; the English word *psychology* first appeared in 1693 in Steven Blankaart's *The Physical Dictionary: Wherein the terms of Anatomy, the names and causes of Diseases, chyrugical Instruments and their Use; are accurately Describ'd*: Blankaart refers to '*Anthropologia*, the Description of Man, or the Doctrin concerning him [which is divided] into Two Parts; viz. *Anatomy*, which treats of the Body, and *Psychology*, which treats of the Soul' (p. 13, italics in original)]

psycholytic *adj.* *n.* (Of or relating to) a *hallucinogen.
[From Greek *psyche* the mind + *lysis* loosening]

psychometric function *n.* In *signal detection theory, a plot of the intensity of stimuli on the horizontal axis against the percentage of correct detections of the stimuli on the vertical axis, the resulting curve being generally S-shaped. Also called a *poikilitic function*.
[From Greek *psyche* mind + *metron* a measure + -*ikos* of, relating to, or resembling]

psychometrics *n.* The construction and application of psychological tests; mental measurement.
[From Greek *psyche* mind + *metron* a measure + -*ikos* of, relating to, or resembling]

psychomotor *adj.* Of or relating to the relationship between mental activity and bodily movements.
[From Greek *psyche* mind + Latin *motus* a movement, from *movere* to move]

psychomotor agitation *n.* Excessive motor activity, usually consisting of purposeless behaviour such as pacing, fidgeting, or hand-wringing, accompanied by a feeling of *anxiety or tension. *Compare* psychomotor retardation.
[From Latin *agitatus* stirred, from *agitare* to set into motion + -*ion* indicating an action, process, or state]

psychomotor depressant *n.* Another name for a central nervous system *depressant drug.

psychomotor epilepsy *n.* Another name for *temporal lobe epilepsy.

psychomotor retardation *n.* A general slowing of bodily movements, including eye blinking and speech, often associated with *depression. *Compare* psychomotor agitation.
[From Latin *retardare, retardatum* to slow down, from *re-* again + *tardare* to slow + -*ation* indicating a process or condition]

psychomotor seizure *n.* A *seizure of the type found in *temporal lobe epilepsy, without any evidence of a *convulsion. Also called a *temporal lobe seizure*.

psychomotor stimulant *n.* Another name for a central nervous system *stimulant drug.

psychoneuroimmunology *n.* The study of the interactions between psychological phenomena, the *nervous system, and the *immune system, including especially psychological effects such as *stress (1) on immune responses. This field of research emerged in the US in the early 1970s. *Compare* psychoimmunology. **PNI** *abbrev.*
[From *psycho(logy)* + Greek *neuro(n)* a nerve + English *immunology*]

psychoneurosis n. Another name for a *neurosis. In *psychoanalysis, it is any neurosis that is not an *actual neurosis, and it is also called a *neuropsychosis*. It includes *narcissistic neuroses and *transference neuroses.
[From Greek *psyche* mind + *neuron* a nerve + *-osis* indicating a process or state]

psychopathic deviate scale See MMPI.

psychopathic personality n. A personality disorder characterized by *psychopathy.

psychopathology n. The study of *mental disorders; another name for *abnormal psychology.
[From Greek *psyche* mind + *pathos* suffering + *logos* word, discourse, or reason]

psychopathy n. A *mental disorder roughly equivalent to *antisocial personality disorder, but with emphasis on affective and interpersonal *traits such as superficial charm, pathological lying, egocentricity, lack of remorse, and callousness that have traditionally been regarded by clinicians as characteristic of psychopaths, rather than social deviance traits such as need for stimulation, parasitic lifestyle, poor behavioural controls, impulsivity, and irresponsibility that are prototypical of antisocial personality disorder. Whether psychopathy and antisocial personality disorder share a common referent is an open question. *Compare* sociopathy.
psychopath n. A person with *psychopathy.
psychopathic adj.
[From Greek *psyche* mind + *pathos* suffering]

psychopharmacology n. The study of the effects of drugs on behaviour and mental experience, with particular emphasis on changes in mood, emotions, and psychomotor functions and abilities.
[From *psycho(logy)* + *pharmacology*]

psychophysical function n. In *psychophysics, a mathematical expression of the relation between the magnitude of sensations and the intensity of the stimuli that excite them, for example a relation between loudness and sound intensity or between perceived heaviness and mass. See Fechner's law, Fullerton–Cattell law, Merkel's law, Piper's law, power law, Ricco's law, Weber's law. See also psychophysical scale.

psychophysical parallelism n. An approach to the *mind–body problem first suggested by the German philosopher Gottfried Wilhelm Leibniz (1646–1716) in the early 18th century, a form of *dualism according to which mental and physical processes are perfectly correlated but not *causally connected, like the movements of two clocks standing side by side. Also called *parallelism*. *Compare* epiphenomenalism, interactionism (1).

psychophysical scale n. In *psychophysics, a specification of the values of a psychological dimension of perceived magnitude (such as brightness, loudness, or heaviness) corresponding to values of a physical dimension of stimulus intensity (such as luminous intensity, sound intensity, or mass). See direct scaling, fractionation, indirect scaling, loudness matching, magnitude estimation, magnitude production, method of absolute judgement, method of bisection, method of equal and unequal cases, method of equal-appearing intervals, method of gradation, method of paired comparisons, production method, sense ratio method, staircase method, unfolding technique. See also psychophysical function.

psychophysics n. The oldest branch of experimental psychology, concerned with the relationship between the psychological magnitude of sensations and the physical intensity (broadly interpreted to include any perceptible stimulus dimension) of the stimuli that produce them. It is concerned partly with the determination of *absolute thresholds and *difference thresholds, using variations of three classical methods called the *method of constant stimuli, the *method of limits, and the *method of average error, and partly with the establishment of *psychophysical functions and *psychophysical scales. Among its greatest achievements are *Weber's law, *Fechner's law, and the *power law, and one of its most important modern forms is *signal detection theory. See also absolute error, ABX paradigm, catch trial, constant error, cross-modal matching, direct scaling, fractionation, Fullerton–Cattell law, global psychophysics, indirect scaling, interval of uncertainty, loudness matching, magnitude estimation, magnitude production, Merkel's law, method of absolute judgement, method of bisection, method of equal and unequal cases, method of equal-appearing intervals, method of gradation, method of paired comparisons, olfactie, Piper's law, production method, relative error, Ricco's law, sense ratio method, staircase method, standard stimulus, unfolding technique, variable error, variable stimulus, Weber fraction. **psychophysical** *adj.*

psychophysiology *n.* The branch of psychology devoted to studying the physiological correlates of psychological functions and phenomena.

psychoplegic *adj. n.* (Of or relating to) a *neuroleptic (1) drug.
[From Greek *psyche* the mind + *plege* a blow + *-ikos* of, relating to, or resembling]

psychopomp *n.* One who conducts souls to the other world after death, a function ascribed in Greek mythology to Hermes. In *analytical psychology, the word used by Carl Gustav Jung (1875–1961) to describe the role of the *anima and *animus (3) as go-betweens, linking the *ego and the *unconscious (2). **psychopomps** or **psychopompoi** *pl.*
[From Greek *psyche* a soul + *pompos* a guide, from *pompein* to send or conduct]

psychoprophylaxis *n.* A training system based on breathing and relaxation exercises designed to prepare women for childbirth.
[From Greek *psyche* the mind + *prophylaxis* protecting against affliction, from *pro* before + *phylax* a guard]

psychose passionelle *n.* Another name for *erotomanic delusional disorder.
[French, literally insanity of passion]

psychosexual development *n.* In *psychoanalysis, the progress during infancy and childhood through a sequence of *libidinal stages. *See* anal stage, genital stage, latency period, oral stage, phallic stage, polymorphous perversity. *See also* mirror phase, narcissism.

psychosexual dysfunctions *n.* Another name for *sexual dysfunctions.

psychosexual stage *n.* Another name for a *libidinal stage.

psychosis *n.* **1.** Any mental disorder characterized by *delusions and/or prominent *hallucinations with or, in the narrowest

definition of the term, without *insight (3) into their pathological nature. Broader definitions include mental disorders characterized by other *positive symptoms of *schizophrenia such as *disorganized speech or *catatonia. **2.** In older psychological and psychiatric literature, mental impairment grossly interfering with the capacity to meet ordinary demands of life, or gross impairment in *reality testing. *Compare* neurosis. **psychoses** *pl.*
[A word introduced in 1845 by the Austrian psychiatrist Ernst von Feuchtersleben (1806–49) in his *Lehrbuch der ärztlichen Seelkunde* (translated into English in 1847 as *The Principles of Medical Psychology*), from Greek *psyche* mind + *-osis* indicating a process or state]

psychosocial moratorium *n.* In *ego psychology, a term introduced by the German-born psychoanalyst Erik H. Erikson (1902–94) to denote a 'time out of life' during which a person can retain a fluid identity, such a period often being a feature of early post-adolescent life in modern industrial societies, when young adults can take time out by travelling, for example, before settling into more fixed identities constrained by work and relationships.

psychosocial stressor *n.* Any life event or change, such as divorce, marriage, bereavement, loss or change of a job, or moving house, that causes *stress (1) and may be associated with the onset or deterioration of a *mental disorder. *See also* adjustment disorder.

psychosomatic *adj.* Of or relating to certain *organic disorders, such as *hypertension, that are believed to be caused or aggravated by psychological factors, such as *stress (1).
[From Greek *psyche* mind + *soma* body + *-itikos* resembling or marked by]

psychosomatic disorder *n.* Any disorder that is *psychosomatic. Also, in *psychoanalysis, called an *organ neurosis*.

psychosomatic medicine *n.* The branch of medicine devoted to *psychosomatic disorders.

psychostimulant *n.* Another name for a central nervous system *stimulant drug.

psychosurgery *n.* Surgical operations such as *frontal leucotomy performed on physically normal brain tissue to treat mental disorders rather than brain pathologies. *Compare* neurosurgery.

psychotherapy n. The treatment of *mental disorders and allied problems by psychological methods. *See* analytic psychology, art therapy, assertiveness training, autogenic training, behaviour therapy, bibliotherapy, bioenergetics (2), body therapies, brief psychotherapy, client-centred therapy, co-counselling, cognitive-analytic therapy, cognitive behaviour modification (CBM), cognitive therapy, conjoint therapy, contingency management, couples therapy, crisis intervention, dance therapy, drama therapy, est, existential therapy, experiential therapy, eye-movement desensitization and reprocessing (EMDR), facilitated communication (FC), family therapy, fixed-role therapy, focal therapy, Gestalt therapy, group therapy, hypnotherapy, logotherapy, marital therapy, milieu therapy, modelling, Morita therapy, multimodal therapy (MMT), music therapy, narcoanalysis, narcosynthesis, narcotherapy, orgone therapy, paradoxical therapy, personal constructs therapy, phototherapy, play therapy, primal therapy, progressive relaxation, psychoanalysis, psychoanalytic psychotherapy, rational emotive behaviour therapy (REBT), rebirthing, rolfing, sex therapy, sociodrama, T-group, transactional analysis (TA), transcendental meditation (TM), will therapy. *See also* distress relief quotient, negative therapeutic reaction. **psychotherapeutic** adj. **psychotherapist** n. One who practises *psychotherapy.
[From Greek *psyche* mind + *therapeia* service or treatment, from *therapeuein* to take care of or to heal]

psychotic adj. **1.** Of, pertaining to, or resembling *psychosis (1). n. **2.** A person with a *psychosis (1).
[From Greek *psyche* mind + *-osis* indicating a process or state + *-itikos* resembling or marked by]

psychotic depression n. A form of *depression accompanied either by symptoms of *psychosis (1) such as *delusions or *hallucinations or by depressive *stupor.

psychoticism n. A psychological condition or state characterized by *psychosis (1). Also, one of the three major dimensions of personality in the later writings (from 1975 onwards) of the German-born British psychologist Hans J(ürgen) Eysenck (1916–97), characterized by *traits such as aggressiveness, coldness, impulsiveness, antisocial behaviour, tough-mindedness, and creativity. Also called *tough-mindedness*.

psychotogen n. A chemical substance or drug that induces a *psychotic (1) state. **psychotogenic** adj.
[From *psychotic* + Greek *genein* to produce]

psychotomimetic n. Another name for a *hallucinogen.
[From *psychotic* + Greek *mimesis* imitation, from *mimeisthai* to imitate + *-ikos* of, relating to, or resembling]

psychotropic adj. Affecting mental experience or behaviour, generally referring to a *drug that has such effects. Also called *psychoactive*. *See* anaesthetic (2), analgesic (2), anticholinergic, anticonvulsant, antidepressant, antimanic, antiparkinsonian, anxiolytic, aphrodisiac, beta-blocker, calcium antagonist, cholinomimetic, convulsant, depressant drug, empathogen, endogenous opioid, euphoriant, false neurotransmitter, hallucinogen, hypnotic (2), indole alkaloids, monoamine oxidase inhibitor, mood stabilizer, narcotic, narcotic analgesic, narcotic antagonist, nerve gas, neuroleptic (1), opiate, opioid antagonist, phantasticant, phenylalkylamines, psychedelic, sedative, selective serotonin reuptake inhibitor, smart drug, sociabilizer, stimulant drug, sympathomimetic, tricyclic antidepressant, truth drug.
[From Greek *psyche* mind + *tropos* a turn, from *trapein* to turn + *-ikos* of, relating to, or resembling]

PTC abbrev. Phenylthiocarbamide, a crystalline compound that is tasteless to some people and intensely bitter-tasting to others, the difference being due to a recessive gene. Approximately one-third of Caucasian and Asian populations are *non-tasters* and two-thirds are *tasters*, but almost all members of African and native South American populations are *tasters*. Also called *phenylthiourea*. Formula: $C_6H_5NHCSNH_2$. *Compare* propylthiouracil (PROP).

ptosis n. Drooping of one eyelid, partially or completely closing the eye. When the *pupil of the eye is normal and there is only partial drooping, it is usually a sign of fatigue; if the pupil is constricted and there is only partial drooping, it may be a sign of *Horner's syndrome; when the pupil is dilated and especially if the eye is completely closed and the eyeball is turned outwards, it may be a sign of malfunction of the *oculomotor nerve, which travels from the brainstem directly to the eye. [From Greek *ptosis* a falling, from *piptein* to fall + -*osis* indicating a process or state]

puberty n. The stage of development at the beginning of *adolescence when the glands that secrete *sex hormones mature and *secondary sexual characteristics appear. Also called *pubescence*. **pubertal** adj.
[From Latin *pubertas* maturity, from *puber* grown-up]

public goods dilemma n. A type of *social dilemma in which members of a group choose whether or how much to contribute to something from which all group members benefit equally. In a classical (and typical) experiment, nine participants or subjects were given $5 each, and the rules specified that if five or more of them contributed their money to a central fund, then all nine participants would receive a $10 bonus whether or not they had contributed. If enough people contributed, the net payoff, taking into account contributions paid in, was $10 to a contributor and $15 to a non-contributor, but if too few contributed, the payoff was zero to a contributor and $5 to a non-contributor. Public goods games are designed to simulate subscription payments to unions and other social dilemmas in which all members of a group benefit from actions that are costly to the individuals who make them. They are also called *free-rider problems*, and the corresponding experimental games are sometimes called *give-some* games.

puer aeternus n. In *analytical psychology, an *archetype (2) of eternal youth, viewed by Carl Gustav Jung (1875–1961) as a *neurotic (1) component of personality, arising from an inability to come to terms with ageing.
[From Latin *puer* a boy + *aeternus* eternal or everlasting]

Pulfrich effect n. A visual illusion that is seen when a pendulum such as a length of string with a weight attached to one end is swung from side to side in a plane perpendicular to the line of vision. If it is viewed from a distance with a lens from a pair of sunglasses or a similar dark filter over one eye but with both eyes open, and with attention focused on the centre of the swing, the pendulum appears to move in an ellipse parallel to the floor, clockwise as seen from above if the dark lens is over the left eye and anticlockwise if it is covers the right eye. Any object moving across the line of vision is similarly affected, so that if the dark filter covers the left eye, objects moving from left to right on a television screen appear to recede and objects moving from right to left appear to be displaced forward. Since 1966 this effect has been exploited periodically by companies marketing expensive spectacles that are claimed to make ordinary television images three-dimensional but that consist merely of one dark and one plain lens. *See also* kinephantom.
[Named after the German psychologist Carl Pulfrich (1858–1927) who first described it in 1922, although he was born blind in one eye and never saw the effect himself]

pulvinar n. The cushion-shaped bulge at the back of the *thalamus above the midbrain that receives projections from the auditory, somatosensory, and visual cortex, and also from the superior colliculus, and is believed to be implicated in visual attention, especially the suppression of attention to irrelevant stimuli.
[From Latin *pulvinus* a cushion]

punch-drunk adj. Manifesting the characteristic signs of some professional boxers and others who have suffered repeated blows to the head and contusions of the brain, including *clouding of consciousness, *ataxia, and *tremor.

punctuated equilibrium n. A form of *evolution characterized by short bursts of radical change interrupted or punctuated by long periods of stability; or a theory according to which evolution occurs in this way.
[From Latin *punctuare, punctuatum* to prick, from *pungere, punctum* to puncture]

punctuationist n. One who believes in *punctuated equilibrium.

punishment n. Any *stimulus (1) that an organism seeks to avoid or escape. *Negative reinforcement is not punishment but almost the reverse, namely the withdrawal of punishment. *See also* avoidance conditioning, escape conditioning, law of effect, locus of control.

pupil *n.* The dark central opening in the *iris through which light enters the eye, its variable diameter being controlled by the *dilator pupillae* and *sphincter pupillae* muscles of the iris. *See also* accommodation reflex, Argyll Robertson pupil, dark adaptation, depth of field, glaucoma, light adaptation, oculomotor nerve, pupillary light reflex, sympathetic nervous system. **pupillary** *adj.*
[From Latin *pupilla* a pupil, diminutive of *pupa* a girl or a doll, alluding to the tiny reflection in the eye]

pupillary light reflex *n.* A reflex in which light shone into one eye causes the pupils of both eyes to constrict involuntarily, protecting against damage to the retina and causing a temporary threshold shift (TTS), similar to the acoustic reflex in response to loud noise. The reflex is found even in people whose primary visual cortex is destroyed, rendering them totally blind. *Optic nerve damage results in equal pupils, neither responding to light shone into the eye on the damaged side but both responding normally to light shone into the other eye, whereas *oculomotor nerve damage results in a dilated pupil on the damaged side that does not respond to light shone into either eye. Also called the *consensual pupillary reflex*, the *consensual light reflex*, *Haab's pupillary reflex*, the *light reflex*, or the *pupillary reflex*. *See also* reflex.

pure erotomania *n.* Another name for *erotomanic delusional disorder.

pure hue *n.* A hue consisting of *monochromatic light.

pure light *n.* In the terminology introduced by the English physicist and mathematician Sir Isaac Newton (1642–1727) in his *Opticks* (1704), any light that cannot be broken down into constituent colours, thus the same as a pure hue consisting of *monochromatic light. *Compare* composite light.

pure phi *n.* Another name for *phi movement.

pure tone *n.* A sound wave such as that generated by a tuning fork or oscillator whose pressure variation as a function of time is a sine wave. Also called a *simple tone*. *See also* Fourier analysis, tone (1). *Compare* complex tone.

purine *n.* A white crystalline substance or any of several *bases (1) derived from it, including *adenine and *guanine, which are constituents of *DNA and *RNA, in which they are paired with pyrimidine bases. *Compare* pyrimidine.
[From *pure (uric acid)* + Greek *-ine* indicating an organic compound]

Purkinje cell *n.* A type of large efferent neuron that has dense *dendrites forming as many as 100,000 synapses with afferent neurons, although it is not bushlike but lies flat in one plane and has an axon that breaks up into numerous branches near its end, its cell body being found in the middle layer of the *cerebellar cortex, its action being inhibitory, and its neurotransmitter being *GABA. Axons of Purkinje cells provide the only output from the cerebellar cortex after it has processed sensory and motor information from other parts of the nervous system. It was discovered in 1837 by the Czech-born German physiologist Johannes E(vangelista) Purkinje (Purkyně) (1787–1869). Also spelt *Purkyně cell*. Also called a *Purkinje neuron* or a *Purkyně neuron*.

Purkinje figure *n.* An image of the network of retinal blood vessels that is made visible in one's own eye if light is shone on to the eyeball at an oblique angle from a pinhole close to its surface. The best way of seeing the image is by darkening the room and holding a torch or flashlight against the outer corner of one closed eye, and then moving the torch from side to side. Also spelt *Purkyně figure*.
[Named after the Czech-born German physiologist Johannes E(vangelista) Purkinje (Purkyně) (1787–1869) who discovered it]

Purkinje image *n.* A secondary *positive afterimage occurring after the primary afterimage following exposure to a brief light stimulus, appearing in the *complementary colour to that of the original stimulus, the primary (Hering) afterimage generally being either in the same colour as the stimulus or colourless. Depending on the intensity of the original stimulus, the Purkinje image may persist for several seconds if the gaze is held steady, but it tends to disappear as soon as the eyes are moved, though blinking may briefly restore it. Also spelt *Purkyně image*. Also called the *Purkinje afterimage. See also* afterimage, Bidwell's ghost. *Compare* Hering image, Hess image.

[Named after the Czech-born German physiologist Johannes E(vangelista) Purkinje (Purkyně) (1787–1869) who first drew attention to it in 1823]

Purkinje–Sanson image *n.* Any of three images that can be seen reflected from the eye of a person who is looking at an illuminated object such as a flame in a dark room. The first is a bright image reflected from the convex surface of the cornea; the second is a large, dim image reflected from the convex front surface of the *crystalline lens; and the third is a small, bright, inverted image that is reflected from the rear (posterior) surface of the lens and that enlarges with *accommodation (1) of the eye for close viewing, because the curvature of the lens increases, such accommodation also causing the distance between the second and third images to change. Also spelt *Purkyně–Sanson image*. Also called a *Purkinje image* or a *Sanson image*.

[So called because it was first observed in 1823 by the Czech-born German physiologist Johannes E(vangelista) Purkinje (Purkyně) (1787–1869) and investigated further in 1838 by the French surgeon Louis Joseph Sanson (1790–1841)]

Purkinje shift *n.* A change in peak sensitivity to light under changing illumination, from wavelengths close to 555 nanometres (green) in *photopic (light-adapted) vision to 505 nanometres (blue–green) in *scotopic (dark-adapted) vision, resulting from the predominance of *cone vision in bright illumination and *rod vision in dim illumination. Thus reds, oranges, and yellows appear relatively light in bright illumination whereas blues and greens appear relatively light in dim illumination, as can be demonstrated by finding red and blue objects that appear equally light under bright daylight illumination and then viewing them in twilight or dim illumination, where the red will appear very much darker than the blue. Also called the *Purkinje effect* or *Purkinje phenomenon*. Also spelt *Purkyně shift. See also* Bezold–Brücke phenomenon.

[Named after the Czech-born German physiologist Johannes E(vangelista) Purkinje (Purkyně) (1787–1869) who first drew attention to it in 1825 after noticing that in the dim light of early dawn, when one's eyes are usually dark adapted, red flowers look inky black]

purple hearts *n.* A street name for the barbiturate drug *phenobarbital (phenobarbitone).

pursuit movement *n.* A *smooth following movement of the eyes, used when tracking a moving object and sometimes accompanied by *saccades. Also called an *ocular pursuit movement*.

pursuit rotor *n.* A device for measuring a person's skill at tracking a moving target, usually consisting of an object or image moving either smoothly or irregularly and a stylus that the person being tested tries to keep on the target, the device keeping an automatic record of time on target.

push-down stack *n.* Any storage system from which items are withdrawn in reverse order to the order in which they were entered, so that the last item in is the first one out, and so on. In computing, temporary memory stores are often push-down stacks, and human *short-term memory operates mainly in this way.

[Named after a type of spring-operated device for stacking trays in canteens]

pusher *n.* Someone or something that pushes. In informal usage, a person who sells illegal drugs, especially *narcotics. *See also* travel agent.

putamen *n.* One of the *basal ganglia in the *corpus striatum, a large reddish structure surrounding the globus pallidus on three sides in each cerebral hemisphere, consisting of the lateral part of the *lenticular nucleus, implicated in posture and movement control.

[From Latin *putamen* clippings, from *putare* to prune]

putrid odour *n.* One of the six primary odours in *Henning's prism and one of the seven in the *stereochemical theory, resembling the odour of faeces or rotten eggs. US *putrid odor*.

p value *abbrev.* Probability value: in *inferential statistics, the probability of obtaining, by chance alone, results at least as extreme as those obtained; equivalently, the probability of a *Type I error. *See also* significance test.

Pygmalion effect *n.* A *self-fulfilling prophecy whereby people tend to behave the way others expect them to. In a famous field experiment on the Pygmalion effect in children, carried out by the German-born US psychologist Robert Rosenthal (born 1933) and the US schoolteacher Lenore F. Jacobson (born 1926) and published in a book entitled *Pygmalion in the Classroom* (1968), the researchers applied a standard IQ test to children in an elementary school in San Francisco at the beginning of an academic year, selected 20 per cent (about five children per class) at random, and told their teachers that the tests suggested that these children were potential academic 'spurters' who could be expected to show unusual intellectual gains in the year ahead. When the children were retested at the end of academic year, the 'spurters' showed massive IQ gains relative to the other children, especially in the first and second grades (6–7-year-old children): 20 per cent of the 'spurters' gained at least 30 IQ points, and 80 per cent gained at least 10 IQ points. These gains were presumably due to subtle effects of the teachers' expectations on the way they handled the children, but the experiment has been criticized on methodological grounds. *See also* experimenter expectancy effect, Oedipus effect.
[Named after George Bernard Shaw's play *Pygmalion* (1912), in which the linguist Professor Henry Higgins gives elocution lessons to a cockney flower-girl Eliza Dolittle and passes her off in high society as an upper-class lady—see also etymology of *Pygmalionism*]

Pygmalionism *n.* **1.** Sexual attraction to a statue, dressmaker's dummy, or other representation of the human form. **2.** Falling in love with one's own handiwork.
[Named after Pygmalion, the king of Cyprus in a Greek myth, who fell in love with his own ivory sculpture of a woman, later brought to life as Galatea]

pyknic body type *n.* A short, squat, rounded *somatotype believed by the German psychiatrist Ernst Kretschmer (1888–1964) and his followers to be prone to manic–depressive psychosis (*bipolar disorders). *See also* Kretschmer constitutional type. *Compare* asthenic body type, athletic body type, dysplastic body type.
[From Greek *pyknos* thick]

pyramidal cell *n.* Any of the large neurons that are the principal output neurons of the *neocortex, each having long *dendrites ascending towards and branching near the surface of the cortex, smaller basal dendrites near the pyramid-shaped cell body, and a long, slender *axon emerging from the base of the cell body, continuing for centimetres or in some cases more than a metre before terminating in a dense brush of branches. Most of the nerve fibres leaving the cerebral cortex are composed of the axons of pyramidal cells. Pyramidal cells are also found in the hippocampus, olfactory bulb, and elsewhere. *See also* Betz cell. *Compare* bipolar cell, granule cell, stellate cell.
[So called because of the pyramidal shape of its soma]

pyramidal decussation *n.* The partial *decussation of the *corticospinal tract in the medulla oblongata, just above its junction with the top of the spinal cord, where the fibres of *pyramidal cells divide into three, with 80 per cent crossing the left–right midline of the body.
[So called because it forms a pyramid-shaped cross-section of pyramidal cell axons]

pyramidal tract *n.* Another name for the *corticospinal tract.
[So called because it contains mostly the axons of *pyramidal cells, and also because it forms a pyramidal structure where it splits into three strands at the *pyramidal decussation just above the top of the spinal cord]

pyramid of numbers *n.* The characteristic decrease in the relative numbers of animals at each successively higher level in the *food chain of a natural ecosystem (see illustration overleaf).

pyridoxine *See* vitamin B₆.

pyriform cortex *See* piriform cortex.

pyrimidine *n.* A type of crystalline nitrogenous *base (1) or a derivative of it such as

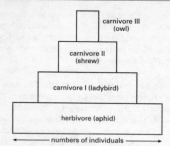

Pyramid of numbers. A woodland food chain.

*cytosine, *thymine, and *uracil, which are found in *DNA and *RNA, where they are paired with purine bases. *Compare* purine.

[A variant of *pyridine*, from Greek *pyr* fire + *-ide* indicating membership of a particular group of chemical compounds + *-ine* indicating an organic compound]

pyromania *n.* An *impulse-control disorder characterized by multiple episodes of deliberate and purposeful fire setting, with emotional tension before the act, followed by pleasure, gratification, or relief while committing the act or watching its aftermath, and general interest in or preoccupation with fire and matters associated with fire. *See also* urethral erotism.

[From Greek *pyr* fire + *mania* madness]

qi-gong psychotic reaction *n.* A *culture-bound syndrome included in CCMD-2 (the *Chinese Classification of Mental Disorders*, 2nd ed.), restricted mainly to Chinese communities in southern and eastern Asia and elsewhere, the onset invariably following participation in qi-gong, a system of meditational exercises involving deep breathing believed to promote physical and spiritual well-being, characterized by a time-limited period of *paranoid ideation, *dissociation, and *psychotic (1) signs and symptoms.
[From Chinese *qi-gong* exercise of vital energy, from *qi* energy + *gong* skill or exercise]

Q-methodology *n.* A form of *factor analysis in which the correlations between individuals rather than tests are analysed. It was introduced by the US-based English psychologist William Stephenson (1902–89) in an article entitled 'Correlating Persons Instead of Tests' in the journal *Character and Personality* in 1935 and expounded at length in his book *The Study of Behavior: Q-Technique and its Methodology* (1953). Also called *Q-technique*. *See also* Q-sort. *Compare* R-methodology.

Q-sort *n.* In psychometrics, a test in which the respondent classifies items into categories along a dimension such as *Agree/Disagree*, often by arranging a deck of cards showing trait-descriptive statements into a fixed number of piles, such classifications being suitable for analysis by *Q-methodology. It amounts to a kind of *rating scale.
[From q(uestionnaire) sort]

Quaalude *n.* A proprietary name for the depressant drug *methaqualone.
[Trademark]

quadrantic hemianopsia *n.* Loss of vision for one quadrant of the visual field, usually associated with a lesion in *optic radiations from a lateral geniculate nucleus to the visual cortex.

quadratic model *n.* A mathematical model represented by a quadratic equation such as $Y = aX^2 + bX + c$, or by a system of quadratic equations. The relationship between the variables in a quadratic equation is a parabola when plotted on a graph. *Compare* linear model.

quadriceps reflex *n.* An informal name for the *patellar reflex.
[Named after the quadriceps muscle that extends the leg at the knee joint]

quadriplegia *n.* Paralysis of all four limbs, usually as a result of an injury to the upper part of the spine. Also called *tetraplegia*, which is a less common but more correct form because it is not a neoclassical *hybrid (3). *Compare* diplegia, hemiplegia, monoplegia, ophthalmoplegia, paraplegia, triplegia. **quadriplegic** *adj.*
[From Latin *quadrans* a quarter + Greek *plege* a blow + -*ia* indicating a condition or quality]

qualia *n. pl.* A philosophical term for sensory experiences that have distinctive subjective qualities but lack any meaning or external reference to the objects or events that cause them, such as the painfulness of pinpricks or the redness of red roses. The term is virtually synonymous with *sense data. *See also* inverted qualia, phi movement, sensation, sensibilia. **quale** *sing.*
[From Latin *qualis* of what kind]

qualitative inheritance *n.* Inheritance of an all-or-nothing *phenotypic characteristic through an *allele at a single locus, as contrasted with *quantitative inheritance of a characteristic that varies on a *continuum from one extreme to another. *See also* monogenic inheritance. *Compare* polygenic inheritance.

qualitative research *n*. Research that focuses on non-numerical data, such as verbal protocols or reports, and that uses such techniques and approaches as *content analysis, *conversation analysis, *critical theory, *deconstruction, *discourse analysis, *ethnomethodology, *focus groups, *grounded theory, *hermeneutics (1), *interviews, *motivational research, *phenomenology, *protocol analysis, *psychoanalytic construction, *sociology of knowledge, and *Verstehen. *See also* NUD*IST, open-ended question.

quantifier *n*. **1.** In *logic, a symbol denoting the degree of generality of an expression, the most important being the *existential quantifier* ∃ and the *universal quantifier* ∀. ∃x means approximately *there exists an x such that* … ; and ∀x means approximately *for every x,* …. The universal quantifier is also written (x), for example, the sentence *All students are friendly* may be written either ∀x: $Sx \rightarrow Fx$ or (x)($Sx \rightarrow Fx$), where S stands for *is a student*, F stands for *is friendly*, and the arrow stands for *if* … *then* or material implication; literally, *For every x, if x is a student, then x is friendly*. *See also* predicate calculus. **2.** In linguistics, a word or phrase referring to the number or amount of anything (*all, some, a few, every, many, any*), an example in context being the first word in the sentence *All generalizations are false.*

quantitative inheritance *n*. Inheritance of a phenotypic characteristic that varies on a *continuum from one extreme to another and is determined by multiple genes, as contrasted with *qualitative inheritance of an all-or-nothing characteristic. *See also* polygenic inheritance. *Compare* monogenic inheritance.

quantized image *n*. Another name for a *block portrait.
[From Latin *quantum*, neuter of *quantus* how much + *-izare* from Greek *-izein* to cause to become]

quartile *n*. In descriptive statistics, a score such that one-quarter, one-half, or three-quarters of a set of scores, arranged in order, fall below it, these being the first, second, and third quartiles respectively, symbolized by Q_1, Q_2, and Q_3. The second quartile is identical to the *median. *See also* partile. *Compare* decile, percentile.

quasi-experiment *n*. Any research method that has some of the features of an *experiment but is not strictly experimental inasmuch as the investigator either does not manipulate the *independent variable directly or does not have full control over the *extraneous or nuisance variables that might influence the results. *See also* non-equivalent groups design, one-group pretest–posttest design, interrupted time-series design. *Compare* correlational study. **quasi-experimental** *adj*. [From Latin *quasi* as if]

questionnaire *n*. In psychometrics, a set of questions specially designed to provide objective information about some characteristic of a respondent, such as attitudes, preferences, interests, values, or personality. Also called an *inventory*, particularly when used to measure abilities, aptitudes, or intelligence, such instruments seldom being called questionnaires.
[From French *questionner* to ask questions]

quiet-biting attack *n*. The organized pattern of behaviour of a *predator stalking and killing its *prey. This type of behaviour has been elicited in animals by stimulating the *medial forebrain bundle of the hypothalamus.
[So called because other forms of aggression are characteristically accompanied by vocalization]

quiet sleep *n*. Another name for *NREM sleep.

quinalbarbitone *n*. Another name for *secobarbital.

quinine *n*. A very bitter-tasting crystalline *alkaloid extracted from the bark of trees belonging to the genus *Cinchona* and used as an *analgesic (1), antipyretic, and muscle relaxant. *See also* ototoxic.
[From Spanish *quina* cinchona bark, from Quechua *kina* bark]

quinone *See* vitamin K.

quota of affect *n*. In *psychoanalysis, a quantity of instinctual energy that remains constant despite *displacement and various qualitative transformations that it undergoes. It is an *economic concept related to the *principle of constancy. Sigmund Freud (1856–1939) defined it in an important though confused passage (because it seems to allow the quota to increase or diminish) in an article on 'The Neuro-Psychoses of Defence' (1894): 'In mental functions something is to be distinguished—a quota of affect or sum of excitation—which possesses all the characteristics of a quantity (though we have no means of measuring it), which is capable of increase, diminution, displacement and discharge, and which is spread over the memory-traces of ideas somewhat as an electric charge is spread over the surface of a body' (*Standard Edition*, III, pp. 45–61, at p. 60).

quota sample *n.* A *non-probability sample drawn from a population so that its composition in terms of sex, age, social class, or other demographic characteristics matches the known proportions in the population. *See also* accidental sample, convenience sample, opportunity sample, self-selected sample, snowball sample. *Compare* cluster sample, probability sample, random digit dialling, simple random sample, stratified random sample.
[From Latin *quota pars?* how large a share?]

rabbit syndrome *n.* A form of *parkinsonism affecting the lip, arising as a side-effect of prolonged *neuroleptic (1) medication.
[So called because of its resemblance to the quivering of a rabbit's lip]

race *n.* **1.** A competitive trial of speed in running, swimming, driving, etc; more generally, any manifestation of rivalry or contest. *See also* arms race. **2.** In biology, a *taxonomic group into which a *species is divided, arising from relative reproductive isolation of populations from one another owing to geographic and other barriers, containing organisms that are genetically differentiable from other members of the same species by the relative frequencies of their *polymorphic genes. Thus in humans the relative percentages of the A, B, and O *blood group genes are 28, 6, 66 in Caucasian populations; 18, 11, and 71 in African populations; and 19, 17, and 64 in Oriental populations; and many other polymorphic genes show similar racial differences, but across all polymorphic genes, only about 6 per cent of genetic *variance among humans is due to racial differences. Also called a *microspecies*, *subspecies* or *variety*. *See also* ethnic, racialism, racism. **racial** *adj.*
[From Italian *razza*, origin uncertain]

racialism *n.* *Prejudice, discrimination, stereotyping, or condescension on the basis of *race (2), usually accompanied by a belief in the intrinsic superiority of one race over another or others or by race hatred. Also called *racism*, but distinguished from it in careful usage. *See also* authoritarianism, stereotype. *Compare* ethnocentrism, racism. **racialist** *n.* **1.** One who manifests or practises *racialism. *adj.* **2.** Manifesting or practising *racialism.
[From *racial* + Greek *-ismos* indicating a state or condition]

racial memory *n.* Another name for the *collective unconscious. Also called the *racial unconscious*.

racism *n.* A belief that *races (2) are inherently different from one another and that people's characteristics and capacities are determined largely by race, usually accompanied by a belief in the intrinsic superiority of one particular race over another or others. Also called *racialism*, but distinguished from it in careful usage. *See also* authoritarianism, stereotype. *Compare* ableism, ageism, ethnocentrism, fattism, heterosexism, sexism, speciesism. **racist** *n.* **1.** A person with opinions or attitudes that are characterized by *racism. *adj.* **2.** Of, relating to, or manifesting *racism.
[From race + Greek *-ismos* indicating a state or condition]

radical *adj.* **1.** Relating to, consisting of, or going to the root or fundament; necessitating, entailing, or favouring fundamental social, economic, or political change. *n.* **2.** A group of atoms that is unstable in the free state but when bound together in a molecule behaves as a single unit, such as the *acetyl group —COCH$_3$. *See also* free radical.
[From Latin *radix* a root + *-icalis* of, relating to, or resembling]

radical constructivism *See under* constructivism.

radioisotope scan *n.* A method of examining the brain by passing a Geiger counter over the cranium after the intravenous injection of a radioisotope, used to detect tumours, vascular disturbances, cerebral atrophy, and other abnormalities.

railway illusion *n.* Another name for the *Ponzo illusion.

ramp movement *n.* A slow, deliberate, sustained bodily movement thought to be controlled by the *basal ganglia. Also called a *smooth movement*. Compare ballistic movement. [From French *ramper* to creep or clamber]

random digit dialling *n.* A technique used by some public opinion polling organizations to draw a *probability sample of telephone subscribers within a telephone exchange by dialling the last few digits randomly. A variation of this technique is *directory plus one sampling. See also cluster sample, simple random sample, stratified random sample. Compare accidental sample, cluster sample, convenience sample, non-probability sample, opportunity sample, quota sample, self-selected sample, snowball sample. **RDD** *abbrev.*

random-dot kinematogram *n.* Two or more patterns of random dots presented in sequence, each having an area or shape within it that has no visible border but is identical in both or all the patterns and is displaced a short distance from one pattern to the next. If viewed singly or in slow succession, the patterns appear random and the displaced area remains totally invisible, but if viewed in rapid succession, with interstimulus intervals between approximately 10 and 100 milliseconds for displacements of 5 to 40 minutes of arc (sixtieths of a degree) of *visual angle, the displaced area stands out from the background pattern of dots with an *illusory contour and appears to move as a block. In some displays the area of identical dots changes slightly in outline, though not in the relative positions of its dots, from one frame to the next, and in one popular example it depicts a Dalmatian dog walking in a spotty environment. See also apparent movement, visual illusion. Compare random-dot stereogram, Ternus phenomenon. [From Greek *kinema, kinematos* motion + *gramme* a line]

random-dot stereogram *n.* A type of *anaglyph for studying binocular depth perception invented by the Hungarian-born US radar engineer and psychologist Bela Julesz (born 1928) at Bell Telephone Laboratories in 1960, consisting of two random arrays of dots that when viewed stereoscopically, one array being viewed by each eye, appears to contain a form such as a triangle or square lying in a plane either in front or behind the rest of the dots, bounded by an *illusory contour. It is constructed by generating two arrays of randomly placed dots, identical except for a clearly defined region that is slightly shifted sideways in one of the arrays, and it is usually presented for viewing by printing one of the arrays in red and the other in green or cyan (blue–green), with a slight horizontal displacement so that the unshifted dots do not fall exactly on top of one another, and it is viewed with spectacles having one red and one green or cyan lens. Also called a *Julesz stereogram. See also Cyclopean perception, stereopsis, visual illusion. Compare random-dot kinematogram. [From Greek *stereos* solid + *gramme* a line]

random drift *n.* Another name for *genetic drift.

randomization *n.* A technique of particular importance in *experimental design, introduced by the English statistician and geneticist Ronald Aylmer Fisher (1890–1962) in an article in the *Journal of the Ministry of Agriculture* in 1926, in which experimental subjects are assigned to *treatment conditions strictly at random in order to control for the influence of *extraneous variables and to enable *inferential statistics to be used to determine the significance of any effects that are then observed. The control of extraneous variables through random assignment to treatment groups can be demonstrated by choosing a page from a telephone directory, assigning all the entries on it to two groups by tossing a coin, and then comparing the two groups for the number of surnames containing the letter *p*, or the number of telephone numbers ending in 6, or the number of addresses in a particular sector of the area covered by the directory, or any other characteristic of the entries whatsoever: in each case the two groups will turn out to be roughly similar, especially if the groups are large. See also randomized controlled trial. [From Old French *randon* random, from *randir* to gallop + *-izare* from Greek *-izein* to cause to become + Latin *-ation* indicating a process or condition]

randomization test *n.* In statistics, a *distribution-free approach to *significance testing that is carried out either by forming all possible permutations of all possible scores, or by selecting a random sample of all possible permutations of all possible scores, and then counting the proportion that are at least as extreme as the observed score, either in terms of raw scores or a test statistic, such as the *t test value, derived from the raw scores. It is similar to *resampling statistics but differs from it in using all possible permutations of scores, or a random sample of these, rather than restricting the permutations to the actual scores obtained in the study. The prototypical randomization test is *Fisher's exact test. *See also* Monte Carlo method.

randomized blocks design n. A research design in which research participants or subjects are assigned to blocks according to a pretest, the members of each block being roughly matched on a variable assumed to be related to the *dependent variable, and each block containing as many members as there are treatment conditions, and then the members of each block are randomly assigned to treatment conditions. *See also* Latin square.

randomized controlled trial n. A research design used for testing the effectiveness of a drug, or any other type of treatment, in which research participants are assigned randomly to treatment and control or *placebo (1) groups and the differences in outcomes are compared. The idea of *randomization as a method of control was introduced by the English statistician and geneticist Ronald Aylmer Fisher (1890–1962) in an article in the *Journal of the Ministry of Agriculture* in 1926, and the first randomized controlled trial was designed by the English medical statistician Sir Austin Bradford Hill (1897–1991) and carried out in 1948 by the Medical Research Council of the UK to study the therapeutic efficacy of the antibiotic drug streptomycin. Hill gave a full account of this historic drug trial in an article in the journal *Controlled Clinical Trials* in 1990. Also called a *randomized clinical trial*. *See also* double-blind study, randomized double-blind experiment, single-blind study. **RCT** *abbrev*.

randomized double-blind experiment n. A type of *double-blind study, often used in conducting drug trials and trials of other forms of treatment, in which participants or subjects are randomly assigned to *treatment conditions, usually an *experimental group and a *control group, and neither they nor the experimenter knows, until the data have been collected, which groups they have been assigned to. *See also* randomized controlled trial.

randomized response n. A technique designed to reduce or eliminate evasive *response bias in *survey research on sensitive issues by preserving respondent confidentiality through randomization. For example, an investigator might instruct the respondents as follows: Toss a coin privately and then answer *Yes* if *either* your coin fell heads *or* you have smoked cannabis, otherwise answer *No*. With a sample size of 1,000, we would expect 500 *Yes* replies if none of the respondents had smoked cannabis; additional *Yes* responses would suggest that some respondents whose coins fell tails also replied *Yes*, and the proportion who had smoked cannabis could be estimated from the results without identifying the individuals concerned. If 580 answered *Yes*, then we might assume that approximately 80 of the 500 whose coins fell tails answered *Yes*, and we could therefore estimate the proportion of the population who have smoked cannabis to be $80/500 = 16$ per cent, and this conclusion could be reached without having identified any individual cannabis smokers. The technique was first proposed by the US economist Stanley Leon Warner (1928–92) in an article in the *Journal of the American Statistical Association* in 1965. *See also* non-reactive measure, reactivity.

random lottery incentive system n. A method of rewarding experimental participants or subjects for taking part in a research study by using a chance device. For example, participants may be rewarded with points or tokens on the understanding that one in ten of them, selected at random, will be paid at a specified rate for the points that they accumulate. This technique is supposed to save money while retaining a real financial incentive for the participants.

random sample n. A *probability sample drawn from a *population in such a way that every member of the population is equally likely to be selected. Also called, especially in the context of *survey research, a *simple random sample*.

range n. In descriptive statistics, a crude measure of the degree of dispersion, variability, or scatter in a group of scores, defined as the difference between the highest and lowest score in the group. *Compare* interquartile range, probable error, semi-interquartile range, standard deviation, variance.

range of accommodation *n.* The distance between the *near point and the *far point of the eye, the limits within which *accommodation (1) is able to adjust the crystalline lens so that an image is sharply focused on the retina.

rank *n.* Position or status within a social organization. In statistics and measurement theory, an ordinal number (1, 2, 3, . . .) often used in place of measurements made on an *ordinal scale to represent the order of magnitude of the scores. If two or more raw scores are equal, then they are both assigned a rank that is the mean of the ranks they would have had if the raw scores had been slightly different. Many *non-parametric statistical procedures work with ranks.
[Old French *ranc* a row or tier]

rank correlation *n.* A shortened name for *Spearman rank correlation coefficient.

Rankian *adj.* Of or relating to the Austrian *psychoanalyst Otto Rank (1884–1939) or his writings and doctrines. *See* will therapy.

Ranschburg inhibition *n.* The difficulty of recalling lists of similar items relative to clearly differentiated items; thus a list of *nonsense syllables such as *BEX, DOV, DEX, BOV, DEV* takes longer to learn and tends to result in more errors on recall than *DEG, VOK, NUX, ZAJ, KIF*, or a list of words such as *big, immense, large, great, vast* is similarly harder than *cold, red, quiet, clever, hungry*. A special case of this phenomenon is the *repetition effect. Also called the *Ranschburg effect, Ranschburg phenomenon, Ranschburgsches Phänomen*, or *Ranschburgsches phenomenon*, though the latter mixture of two languages is a barbarism that is avoided in careful usage. *See also* proactive interference, retroactive interference.
[Named after the Hungarian psychiatrist Paul Ranschburg (1870–1945) who reported it in 1901]

Ranvier's node *n.* Any of the spaces that occur at regular intervals along the *myelin sheath of a nerve fibre, where the *axon is exposed. Also called a *node of Ranvier. See also* saltation (1).

[Named after the French histologist Louis-Antoine Ranvier (1835–1922) who studied them]

raphe nuclei *n. pl.* A series of neuron clusters resembling stitches connecting the two halves of the *medulla oblongata. They release *serotonin and may be implicated in *slow-wave sleep. Also called the *raphe system*, and sometimes spelt *raphé nuclei* or *raphé system*, probably in the mistaken belief that the word is of French origin. **raphe nucleus** *sing.*
[From Greek *rhaphe* a seam, from *rhaptein* to sew together]

rapid eye movement *n.* Any of the quick, jerky, synchronized rotations of the eyeballs behind closed lids that occur throughout *REM sleep and are associated with dreaming. **REM** *abbrev.*

rapidly adapting *adj.* Of or relating to a *afferent neurons from *sensory receptors in the *skin that respond only to the onset and offset of stimulation and not to sustained stimulation. *See also* transient responder. *Compare* slowly adapting. **RA** *abbrev.*

rapport *n.* A sympathetic or harmonious relationship or state of mutual understanding. The word was introduced into psychology by the Viennese physician Franz Anton Mesmer (1734–1815), and the French psychologist and neurologist Pierre Janet (1859–1947) confined its meaning specifically to the relationship between a hypnotist and a hypnotized subject; then Sigmund Freud (1856–1939) eventually widened its meaning and described it as the *prototype (2) of the *transference.
[From French *rapporter* to bring back, from *re-* again + *aporter* to carry to, from Latin *apportare* to bring to, from *ad* to + *portare* to bring or carry]

Rasch scale *n.* In psychometrics, a simple application of *item response theory based on the assumption that the probability of a particular response to a test item depends on two parameters that can be estimated independently: the extent to which the item elicits a latent trait, and the status of the respondent on that latent trait, the latter being constant across test items. The *British Ability Scales were among the first to be constructed according to Rasch scales.

[Named after the Danish psychometrician Georg Rasch (1901–80), who expounded this approach in his book *Probabilistic Models for Some Intelligence and Attainment Tests* (1960)]

rate-dependency effect *n*. Another name for the *initial values law, as it applies to the effects of drugs on behaviour.

rating scale *n*. In psychometrics, any device for quantifying a respondent's subjective judgement or response to a stimulus. Some rating scales consist of a row of unlabelled boxes or lines on which the respondent marks a chosen point, whereas others provide the respondent with sets of alternatives labelled with numbers or words. In all of these cases, the end-points of the scale are generally anchored with labels such as *Strongly Disagree* and *Strongly Agree*. *See also* bipolar rating scale, graphic rating scale, numerical rating scale, Q-sort, Repertory Grid Test, response category, semantic differential, verbal rating scale.

ratio IQ *n*. The original but now obsolete conception of *IQ, introduced in 1912 by the German psychologist (Louis) William Stern (1871–1938), as a ratio of *mental age (MA) to *chronological age (CA). Although Stern's original quotient was this MA/CA, in 1916 the US psychologist Lewis Madison Terman (1877–1956) modified it to (MA/CA) ×100, to express mental age as a percentage of chronological age and to eliminate awkward decimals. Since the publication of *The Measurement of Intelligence* in 1944 by the Romanian-born US psychologist David Wechsler (1896–1981), the standard definition of IQ has been the purely statistical *deviation IQ.

ratiomorphic *adj*. Of or relating to psychological processes that appear *rational but are inaccessible to consciousness, especially the computational processes involved in perception. The word was coined by the Hungarian-born US psychologist Egon Brunswik (1903–55). *See also* Brunswikian. **ratiomorphism** *n*.
[From Latin *ratio* reason + Greek *morphe* form]

rational *adj*. *Thinking or behaving reasonably or logically. Rational decisions or choices are those that are in the best interests of the agent who makes them, relative to the information available to the agent at the time of acting; or more specifically, rational decisions

or choices are those that maximize *expected utility. In addition, rational *beliefs are those that are internally consistent; rational preferences are those that are *transitive; rational probability judgements are those that obey *Kolmogorov's axioms; and rational *inferences or arguments are those that obey the rules of *logic. *See also* bounded rationality, dominant alternative/strategy, Nash equilibrium, rational choice theory, rationalism (1, 2, 3), reason, sure-thing principle, transitive preferences. **rationality** *n*. The state or quality of being *rational. *Compare* negative capability.
[From Latin *rationalis* rational, from *ratio, -onis* reason or reckoning, from *reri, ratus* to think]

rational choice theory *n*. A theory of *decision making according to which, when faced with several options or possible courses of action, a decision maker chooses an option that is believed to offer the best outcome from that agent's own point of view. The fundamental assumption is that agents are *rational in the sense of maximizing *expected utility, but this is often interpreted as a *normative (1) assumption rather than one that accurately describes human behaviour. Many writers use the term synonymously with *decision theory. The theory has been particularly influential in economics and in branches of psychology closely associated with economics. *See also* expected utility theory, intransitive preferences, money pump, Pascal's wager. *Compare* behavioural decision theory, psychological decision theory.

rational emotive behaviour therapy *n*. A form of *psychotherapy or *cognitive therapy developed by the US psychologist Albert Ellis (born 1913) and introduced in 1961, based on the assumption that psychological problems often arise from people's interpretations of events in their lives rather than the events themselves, and that irrational interpretations (as when people who are rejected in love irrationally infer that they are intrinsically worthless and unlovable) cause psychological problems; the therapy involves challenging irrational belief systems in an extremely directive manner by explicit confrontation, suggestion, argument, and various specialized procedures. US *rational emotive behavior therapy*. *See also* ABC (1), cognitive restructuring, rational emotive therapy. **REBT** *abbrev*.

rational emotive therapy n. The term used by the US psychologist Albert Ellis (born 1913) for a new form of *psychotherapy that he introduced in 1961 and that from 1993 he began calling *rational emotive behaviour therapy. **RET** abbrev.

rationalism n. **1.** The doctrine associated especially with the French philosopher René Descartes (1596–1650), the Dutch philosopher Baruch Spinoza (1632–77), and the German philosopher and mathematician Gottfried Wilhelm von Leibniz (1646–1716) that it is possible to obtain knowledge by *reason alone, that there is only one valid system of reasoning and it is deductive in character, and that everything is explicable in principle by this form of reasoning. See also a priori, Hume's fork, nativism. Compare empiricism. **2.** The more general view that everything is explicable in principle by one system of reasoning. **3.** A general commitment to *reason as opposed to faith, religious belief, prejudice, tradition, or any other source of belief that is without foundation in reason. **rationalist** n. One who believes in or practises *rationalism (1, 2, 3). **rationalistic** adj.
[From Latin rationalis of or relating to reason, from ratio reason]

rationality, bounded See bounded rationality.

rationalization n. The act of justifying discreditable actions after the event, or a justification or excuse put forward in this way. In *psychoanalysis, a *defence mechanism in which a false but reassuring or self-serving explanation is contrived to explain behaviour that in reality arises from a repressed wish. The term was first used in the narrower psychoanalytic sense in 1908 by the Welsh psychoanalyst Ernest Jones (1879–1958) in an article in the Journal of Abnormal Psychology entitled 'Rationalisation in Everyday Life'. **rationalize** vb.

rational type n. One of the basic personality types in *analytical psychology. See function type.

ratio scale n. A scale of measurement in which differences between values can be quantified in absolute terms and a fixed zero point is defined, as for example in measurements of length in centimetres or age in years. In a ratio scale, equal differences between scores represent equal differences in the *attribute being measured, and a zero score represents complete absence of the attribute. It is only when measurement reaches the level of a ratio scale that it is meaningful to describe a score as twice the value of another score, for example. See also measurement level, scale (1). Compare absolute scale, interval scale, log-interval scale, nominal scale, ordinal scale.
[From Latin ratio a reckoning]

Rat Man n. The nickname used in the literature of *psychoanalysis to refer to an early patient of Sigmund Freud (1856–1939). The Rat Man was tormented by fantasies of rats gnawing at his father's anus and that of a woman to whom he was attracted. Freud's case study, published in 1909, entitled 'Notes upon a Case of Obsessional Neurosis' (Standard Edition, X, pp. 155–320), is a classic text on the psychoanalytic theory of *obsessive–compulsive disorder. See also undoing.

rausch n. A state of diminished consciousness characteristic of light general *anaesthesia, often defined in anaesthesiology as the point at which a patient fails to respond to questions.
[From German Rausch intoxication or ecstasy]

Rauwolfia n. A genus of tropical trees and shrubs including the south-east Asian species Rauwolfia serpentina from the powdered roots of which *reserpine is derived.
[Named by the French botanist and monk Charles Plumier (1646–1704), after the German Botanist Leonhard Rauwolf (1535–96) who had travelled to Africa and Asia to study such plants]

raven paradox n. Another name for *Hempel's paradox.

Raven's Progressive Matrices n. A nonverbal *intelligence test requiring inductive reasoning about abstract geometric patterns, first published in 1938 and revised several times since then, designed to cover a very wide range of mental ability and to be usable with subjects irrespective of age, sex, nationality, or education. The respondent is presented with 60 abstract geometric patterns, and in each case tries to select from several alternatives the one that fits in a missing part of the pattern. Some psychologists believe that it provides the purest available measure of general intelligence, uncontaminated by cultural and educational influences, but there is evidence to suggest that it is not entirely *culture-fair. Also called the *Progressive Matrices test. See also* Cattell Culture-Fair Test, Mill Hill Vocabulary scale. **RPM** *abbrev.*

[Named after the English psychologist John C(arlyle) Raven (1902–70), who developed it in 1938]

raw primal sketch *See under* primal sketch.

raw score *n.* In statistics and measurement theory, a numerical result of an empirical investigation in the form in which it was recorded. *See also* data, scoring formula, transformation. *Compare* derived score.

Rayleigh equation *n.* An index of a person's colour vision given by the proportion of light from the red and green parts of the visible spectrum that need to be mixed to match a standard yellow. Usually 670 nanometres (spectral red) is mixed with 535 nm (spectral green) until it matches 589 nm (spectral yellow). Also called the *Rayleigh match. See also* additive primary, anomaloscope, colour-blindness, colour equation, primary colour (1), tristimulus values.

[Named after the English physicist Lord (John William Strutt) Rayleigh (1842–1919) who introduced it in 1881]

reaction formation *n.* In *psychoanalysis, a *defence mechanism whereby a person replaces a repressed thought, feeling, or behavioural act with one that is diametrically opposed to it, as when a shy person behaves in an exhibitionist manner or a repressed homosexual denounces homosexuality. According to the Austrian psychoanalyst Otto Fenichel (1898–1946), it is a form of permanent *countercathexis: 'The person who has built up reaction-formations does not develop certain defence mechanisms for use when an instinctual danger threatens; he has changed his personality structure as if the danger were continually present, so that he may be ready whenever the danger occurs' (*The Psychoanalytic Theory of Neuroses*, 1945, p. 151).

reaction latency *n.* In *Hullian learning theory, the time elapsing between a *stimulus (1) and a *response. $_s t_R$ *abbrev.*

reaction threshold *n.* In *Hullian learning theory, the strength of an organism's momentary reaction potential that must be reached for it to respond to a *stimulus (1). $_s L_R$ *abbrev.*

reaction time *n.* The time elapsing between the onset of a *stimulus (1) and a *response to it, sometimes broken down into *physiological time plus *central reaction time. *Simple reaction time applies when there is only one possible stimulus requiring only one type of response; *choice reaction time (also called *complex reaction time*) when there are two or more possible stimuli requiring different responses; and *discrimination reaction time when the response depends on the detection of a difference in an objectively measurable perceptual dimension such as brightness, length, or weight. Also, especially in relation to animal behaviour, called *latency, latent time*, or *response latency. See also* Fitts' law, Hick's law, personal equation, physiological time, subtraction method. **RT** *abbrev.*

reactive attachment disorder *n.* A *mental disorder of infancy or early childhood (beginning before age 5 years) characterized by disturbed and developmentally inappropriate patterns of social relating, not resulting from *mental retardation or *pervasive developmental disorder, evidenced either by a persistent failure to initiate or respond appropriately in social interactions (inhibited type), or by indiscriminate sociability without appropriate selective attachments (uninhibited type). By definition, there must also be evidence of pathogenic care, assumed to be responsible for the disturbed social relating, in the form of persistent disregard for the child's basic emotional or physical needs or repeated changes of major attachment figures. *See also* attachment theory.

reactive depression *n.* A form of *depression that arises as a consequence of some upsetting event or experience. Also called *exogenous depression. Compare* endogenous depression.

reactive synaptogenesis *n.* The spontaneous formation of new *synapses (1) in reaction to axon terminal degeneration at nearby receptor sites.

[From Greek *synapsis* contact or junction, from *syn* together + *haptein* to fasten + *genesis* birth]

reactivity *n.* The property of being responsive to stimuli, or (in relation to a mental disorder) of being precipitated by an external cause, notably with reference to *reactive depression. In psychometrics, the property of some psychological measures of yielding scores that are influenced by the participants' or subjects' knowledge that their behaviour is being observed or measured. *See* non-reactive measure. *See also* demand characteristics.

readability formulas *See* Flesch indices.

readiness potential *n*. A large negative difference in voltage across the cerebral cortex, believed to indicate attention, developing approximately 0.8 seconds before a person makes a preplanned bodily movement. *Compare* contingent negative variation.

reading by sound *n*. Another name for *surface dyslexia.

reading disorder *n*. A *learning disability characterized by a level of reading ability (accuracy, speed, and comprehension) substantially below what is expected for the child's age, intelligence, and education, the reading difficulty interfering substantially with scholastic or academic achievement or everyday life and not being attributable to neurological or sensory impairment, mental retardation, or environmental deprivation. Also called *legasthenia*, *reading disability*, *specific developmental dyslexia*, *specific reading disorder*. *See also* dyslexia, hyperlexia, specific spelling disorder.

reading ease score *n*. One of the *Flesch indices of the readability of text, defined by the formula $RE = 206.835 - (1.015 \times$ average number of words per sentence$) - (84.6 \times$ average number of syllables per word$)$. In practice, reading ease scores almost always lie between zero and 100. A reading ease score of zero indicates that the text is practically unreadable, 40 that it is difficult, 65 that it is standard, 85 that it is easy, and 95 that it is very easy. Reading ease scores have been found to correlate highly with ratings of readability and with measures of comprehension and retention. *See also* human interest score.

reading span *n*. The number of words that can be apprehended in a single *fixation (1) while reading. Most adults have an average reading span of about three.

reafference *n*. Changes in *proximal stimuli resulting from self-produced movements rather than any movements or changes in the *distal stimuli, including especially the changes in visual stimulation resulting from head and eye movements. **reafferent** *adj.* [From Latin *re-* back again + *aferre* to carry to, from *ad* to + *ferre* to carry]

realistic anxiety *n*. In *psychoanalysis, any *anxiety resulting from an external danger that poses a real threat, in contrast to an internally generated anxiety. *Compare* neurotic anxiety.

reality-ego *n*. In *psychoanalysis, one of the two major aspects of the *ego, based on the *reality principle, differentiated by Sigmund Freud (1856–1939) from the *pleasure-ego, based on the *pleasure principle. In his article on 'Formulations on the Two Principles of Mental Functioning' (1911), he summed up the distinction as follows: 'Just as the pleasure-ego can do nothing but *wish*, work for a yield of pleasure, and avoid unpleasure, so the reality-ego need do nothing but strive for what is *useful* and guard itself against damage' (*Standard Edition*, XII, pp. 218–26, at p. 223).

reality monitoring *n*. The act or process of discriminating between genuine memories that are acquired through perception from external reality and apparent memories that are generated internally by imagination. It tends to break down in *schizophrenia, *delusional disorder, *Alzheimer's disease, and other mental disorders characterized by *hallucinations, *delusions, and *dementia, and it is temporarily disrupted by intoxication with some types of drugs, especially *hallucinogens. Research into *constructive memory has shown that the sources of many memories are neither purely external nor purely internal, and the distinction between external and internal memory sources is therefore considered relative rather than absolute. Reality monitoring is a form of *metacognition that was named in 1981 by the US psychologists Marcia K. Johnson (born 1943) and C. L. Raye, who were also the first to study it systematically. The term is widely used in cognitive psychology and is closely related to *reality testing in clinical psychology. *See also* déjà vu, eyewitness misinformation effect, false memory, paramnesia (1), Piaget kidnapping memory, recovered memory, source memory.

reality principle *n*. In *psychoanalysis, the chief governing principle of the *ego, exercising control over behaviour to meet the conditions imposed by external reality, thereby acting as a moderating influence on the *pleasure principle. The Irish dramatist George Bernard Shaw (1856–1950) expressed its essence with remarkable clarity and brevity in his play *Man and Superman: A Comedy and a Philosophy* (1901–3), in the discussion about the Life Force near the end of Act III, when the Devil asks Don Juan what the use is of knowing oneself, and Don Juan replies: 'Why, to be able to choose the line of greatest advantage instead of yielding in the direction of the least resistance'. The reality principle involves the conversion of *free energy into *bound energy. Sigmund Freud (1856–1939) gave a full account of this aspect of his theory in 1915 in an article on 'Instincts and their Vicissitudes' (*Standard Edition*, XIV, pp. 117–40). *See also* reality-ego, reality testing.

reality, psychical *See* psychical reality.

reality testing *n*. Objective differentiation between the external world and one's inner imaginative world, loss of which in a *mental disorder tends to indicate lack of *insight (3) and is often taken to be indicative of *psychosis (1). The term is used widely in clinical psychology and is closely related to *reality monitoring in cognitive psychology. The concept was introduced by the Austrian neurologist Sigmund Freud (1856–1939) in his article on 'Formulations on the Two Principles of Mental Functioning' (1911, *Standard Edition*, XII, pp. 218–26).

reason *n*. The faculty of *rational thought; rational grounds for a belief, or a *premise of an argument supporting a belief; a rational motive or cause for an action or a choice; sanity or soundness of mind.
[From Old French *reisun* reason, from Latin *ratio* reckoning, from *reri* to think]

reasoned action, theory of *See* theory of reasoned action.

reasoning *n*. Cognitive processing directed at finding solutions to problems by applying formal rules of *logic or some other *rational procedure. *See* conditional reasoning, counterfactual reasoning, deduction, deductive reasoning, default reasoning, epistemic reasoning, induction (1, 2), inference, logic, logical analysis, modal logic, non-monotonic reasoning, syllogism. *See also* mental model, premise, rational, rationalism (1, 2). *Compare* problem solving.

rebirthing *n*. A technique of *psychotherapy based on and similar to *primal therapy, but concentrating specifically on reliving and coming to terms with one's birth pains and involving total body immersion in warm water.

rebound effect *n*. A pattern of effects, opposite to those produced by a drug or some other special treatment, that occur when the drug or treatment is abruptly withdrawn, typical examples being rebound insomnia following sudden withdrawal from a *hypnotic (2) drug and *REM rebound following the cessation of a period of REM deprivation. *See also* delirium tremens.

rebound REM *n*. Another name for *REM rebound.

rebus *n*. A representation of a word or sentence by a combination of *pictographs, *logographs, or other symbols in the form of a puzzle. A typical example is h@b& to represents the word *hatband*. **rebuses** *pl*.
[French *rébus*, from Latin *rebus* by things]

recall *n*. The act or process of retrieving information from memory spontaneously, either without *cues (3) in the case of *free recall* or with cues in the case of *cued recall*. It involves reproduction of the remembered information, in contrast to *recognition, which involves identification of a match between the remembered information and newly presented information, recognition generally being easier than recall and producing higher memory scores in formal tests. *See also* encoding specificity, memory, mnemonic, serial recall, state-dependent memory.

recapitulationism *n*. The doctrine that the development of an organism from conception to maturity repeats the same sequence of stages as have occurred during the evolution of its *species or *race (2). Also called *palingenesis* or *recapitulation theory*.

[From Latin *recapitulare* to reinstate headings in a document]

Received Pronunciation *n*. The standard, regionally neutral, prestige *accent (1) of British English, sometimes (misleadingly) called BBC English. **RP** *abbrev*.

receiver operating characteristic *n*. In *signal detection theory, a plot of the proportion of *false alarms (2) on the horizontal axis against the proportion of *hits on the vertical axis (see illustration), the diagonal from bottom left (0, 0) to top right (1, 1) corresponding to a *d prime of zero, and the curve obtained from a particular experiment always describing an arc above this diagonal, its precise form depending on the value of *d* prime, which in turn depends on the *signal-to-noise ratio and the observer's sensitivity to the signal, different points on the curve representing variations in the observer's attitude towards the relative importance of *misses and false alarms. *See also* memory operating characteristic. **ROC** *abbrev*.

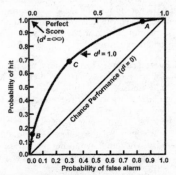

Receiver operating characteristic. The observer at *A* is concerned to avoid misses and is willing to risk many false alarms, and at *B* is concerned to avoid false alarms and is willing to risk many misses; the observer at *C* is equally concerned about misses and false alarms.

recency effect *n*. In *serial learning (1), enhanced memory for the last items in a series of items that have been learned. *See also* serial position effect. *Compare* primacy effect (1).

recency law *n*. The principle according to which the more recently information was learned the better it tends to be remembered.

receptive aphasia *n*. Another name for Wernicke's aphasia. *See under* aphasia.

receptive–expressive language disorder *n*. *See* mixed receptive–expressive language disorder.

receptive field *n*. An area of the retina or any other receptor surface that when stimulated increases or decreases the propensity of a neuron at a higher level in the sensory system to discharge a nerve impulse, the receptor area thus being the receptive field of that neuron. The term is sometimes applied in the same way to the neurons in the *sensory projection areas of receptors. A *classical receptive field* is one within which stimulation invariably excites the neuron or invariably inhibits the neuron; a *non-classical receptive field* is an area that surrounds or is adjacent to a classical receptive field and within which stimulation cannot influence the neuron directly but can modulate the firing of neurons in the associated classical receptive field. A receptive field is sometimes defined in terms of an external area of the perceptual field that stimulates a specified neuron rather than in terms of an internal area of the receptor surface. *See also* auditory receptive field, centre-surround receptive field, complex cell, double-opponent receptive field, end-stopped receptive field, hypercomplex cell, simple cell. *Compare* perceptual field, visual field.

receptive language disorder *n*. A *specific developmental disorder characterized by language comprehension substantially below that of expressive language ability and nonverbal intelligence, the deficit not being due solely to a speech or sensory deficit or a physical impairment. *See also* aphasia. *Compare* expressive language disorder.

receptive orientation *n*. In *neo-Freudian theory, a term used by the German-born US psychoanalyst Erich Fromm (1900–80) to denote a passive-dependent character type who leans on authority for knowledge and help, and on people in general for support, usually accompanied by a chronic inability to say no to requests and an inordinate fondness for food and drink. *Compare* exploitative orientation, hoarding orientation, marketing orientation, productive orientation.

receptor n. **1.** An abbreviated name for a *sensory receptor. **2.** An abbreviated name for a *neuroreceptor.
[From Latin *recipere, receptum* to receive, from re- back + *capere, ceptum* to take]

receptor blocker n. Another name for a *competitive antagonist.

receptor potential n. Another name for *generator potential.

receptor site n. Another name for a *neuroreceptor.

recessive gene n. A *gene that is inherited from one parent and that produces its characteristic *phenotype only in a homozygous organism, that is, only when the corresponding *allele inherited from the other parent is the same. Also (more accurately but less commonly) called a *recessive allele. See also complementation. Compare dominant gene.

reciprocal altruism n. A form of *altruism or helping behaviour whose performance or continuation is conditional on the recipient behaving altruistically or helpfully in return. See also tit for tat strategy.

reciprocal inhibition n. A technique of *behaviour therapy used especially to treat *phobias by repeatedly evoking a response that is physiologically incompatible with anxiety, such as deep muscular relaxation, simultaneously with the anxiety-provoking *phobic stimulus, usually imagined rather than actually present. A specialized application of this technique, with a hierarchy of increasingly anxiety-provoking imaginary situations involving the phobic stimulus, is called *systematic desensitization.

recoding test n. Another name for a *coding test.

recognition n. The act or process of perceiving or identifying information as matching or being the same as information that has been remembered. It is often contrasted with *recall, which involves reproduction of remembered information without *cues (3), and it is generally easier than recall, producing higher memory scores in formal tests. See also memory, memory operating characteristic. **recognize** vb.

[From Latin *recognoscere* to know again, from *re-* again + *cognoscere* to know, from *com-* together + *noscere* to know]

recombinant DNA n. A form of *genetic engineering in which genetic material is produced by combining *DNA extracted from different sources, often combining *genes from a human or animal with those from a bacterium, using *restriction enzymes to cut DNA chains and *DNA ligase to unite strands that have been cut. Not to be confused with *DNA recombination. See also annealing (2), heteroduplex DNA, hybridization.

recombination n. Another name for *DNA recombination, not to be confused with *recombinant DNA.

reconstructive memory n. An active process whereby various strategies are used during the process of memory *retrieval to rebuild information from memory, filling in missing elements while remembering. It was first differentiated from *reproductive memory in 1932 by the English psychologist Sir Frederic Charles Bartlett (1886–1969), who studied it with the technique of *successive reproduction. See also constructivism, deferred action, false memory, War of the Ghosts. Compare constructive memory.

recovered memory n. A memory, usually for a traumatic event or experience, such as being sexually abused as a child, retrieved after having been forgotten or repressed, often for many years. Unless it is verified, what appears to be a recovered memory may in fact be a *false memory. See also deferred action, false memory syndrome, hypnotherapy, paramnesia (1), Piaget kidnapping memory. Compare eyewitness misinformation effect.

recruitment n. **1.** The process or practice of enlisting people, especially for military service or employment. **2.** A symptom of certain forms of hearing disorder in which there is a greater than normal increase in loudness with increasing stimulus intensity, resulting in a distressing exaggeration of loud sounds, while soft sounds may be comfortably audible. Also called *loudness recruitment*. **3.** An increase in the number of neurons firing as a stimulus is prolonged.
[From French *recroître* to reinforce, from Latin *recrescere* to grow again, from *re-* again + *crescere* to grow]

rectus muscle *n*. A straight muscle, especially one of the *extra-ocular muscles attached externally to each eyeball along its front-to-back axis: the *superior rectus*, *medial rectus* (also called *internal rectus*), *lateral rectus* (also called *external rectus*), or *inferior rectus*. Together with the two *oblique muscles, the rectus muscles control eye movements, the lateral and medial recti moving the visual axis from side to side, and the superior and inferior recti moving the axis up and down. *See also* abducens nerve, diplopia.
[From Latin *rectus* straight]

red blood cell *n*. Another name for an *erythrocyte. Also called a *red blood corpuscle*.

red devils *n*. A street name for *secobarbital (quinalbarbitone) or *Seconal.

red–green cell *n*. A neuron that is located in the visual system and is excited by red light and inhibited by green light or vice versa. Such *opponent cells are not found in the retina, where the *trichromatic theory applies, but at higher levels in the visual system. *See also* blue–yellow cell. *Compare* cone.

red–green colour-blindness *n*. Another name for *daltonism. US *red–green color-blindness*.

redintegration *n*. The restoration of a complete mental state when only a single element of it is experienced. A classic literary example, often quoted as an illustration of the power of the chemical senses to reawaken memories from the distant past, occurs at the end of the 'Overture' to the vast novel *A la Recherche du Temps Perdu* (Remembrance of Things Past) by the French novelist Marcel Proust (1871–1922), where the taste of a madeleine cake soaked in lime tea evokes vivid memories of childhood: 'I had recognized the taste of the crumb of madeleine soaked in her concoction of lime-flowers which my aunt used to give to me. . . . Immediately the old grey house upon the street, where her room was, rose up like the scenery of a theatre to attach itself to the little pavilion, opening on to the garden, which had been built out behind it for my parents', and so on for thirteen volumes. *See also* state-dependent memory.
[From Latin *re-* again + *integrare* to make whole, from *integer* whole]

red nucleus *n*. A large *nucleus (2) in the front of the *tegmentum of the midbrain in each hemisphere, receiving inputs from the motor cortex and the cerebellum and sending outputs to the inferior olivary nucleus on the same side and also to the cerebellum, the reticular formation, and the thalamus. It is involved in movement control in distal muscles, including those of the hands and feet. *See also* rubrospinal tract.
[So called because of its reddish appearance, which results from its high iron content]

Red Queen hypothesis *n*. The proposition that any evolutionary advance by one species is ipso facto detrimental to other species in the same *ecosystem, so that species are involved in a competitive evolutionary race in which they must continually evolve merely to survive and maintain their positions.
[Alluding to the passage in Chapter 2 of Lewis Carroll's *Through the Looking Glass* in which Alice first finds herself on a chessboard and the Red Queen says: 'Now, *here*, you see, it takes all the running *you* can do, to stay in the same place. If you want to get somewhere else, you must run at least twice as fast as that!']

reduced reaction time *n*. Another name for *central reaction time.

reductional division *n*. Another name for *meiosis (1).

reductionism *n*. An attempt to provide a complete explanation of a phenomenon in terms of events or processes occurring at a lower or more basic level. Thus a psychological phenomenon may be reduced to neurophysiological processes, which in turn are correlated in detail with biochemical processes, and these may be similarly reduced to chemical processes, and the chemical processes to physical processes. Reductionism usually entails a belief that the lower or more basic processes in some sense explain the higher; but critics argue that such correlations cannot amount to a complete explanation any more than a specification of the electronic or electrical processes taking place in a computer could explain the computations that it performs. **reductionist** or **reductionistic** *adj*.

reduction screen *n*. A visual barrier perforated by a pinhole through which an observer can view a scene while eliminating several important depth cues, namely monocular (movement) *parallax, *ocular convergence, and *stereopsis. Also called an *artificial pupil*. *Compare* void mode.

reductive interpretation *n*. In *analytical psychology, a term used dismissively by Carl Gustav Jung (1875–1961) to characterize *interpretation in classical *psychoanalysis, in which the doctrine of *psychic determinism encourages analysts to explain everything causally in terms of unconscious instinctual processes. According to Jung, on the contrary, 'No psychological fact can ever be explained in terms of causality alone; as a living phenomenon, it is always indissolubly bound up with the continuity of the vital process, so that it is not only something evolved but also continually evolving and creative' (*Collected Works*, 6, paragraph 717).

reduplicative paramnesia *n*. A disorder of *memory in which a person may believe that familiar objects such as buildings are not the ones they know but merely resemble them. *Compare* Capgras syndrome, Doppelgänger.

reefer *n*. An obsolescent street name for a hand-rolled cigarette containing *cannabis. [From *reef* the part of a sail gathered in when there is high wind, alluding to the resemblance of a cannabis cigarette to a rolled-up sail]

reference, delusion (ideas) of *See* delusion of reference, ideas of reference.

reference group *n*. Any group that an individual takes as a standard in adopting opinions, attitudes, or patterns of behaviour or in self-judgement of social standing. The term was introduced in 1942 by the US sociologist Herbert H(iram) Hyman (born 1918). The US psychologist Harold H. Kelley (born 1921) later distinguished between *normative reference groups*, which set standards that individuals use as positive or negative models, and *comparative reference groups*, which are used by individuals to judge their own income, status, education, and so on. *See also* anticipatory socialization, negative reference group, positive reference group, relative deprivation.

referred pain *n*. Pain felt at a site in the body some distance from a *lesion that gives rise to it, well-known examples being *angina, which originates from coronary artery disease but may be felt in the left arm, shoulder, or jaw, and pain in the right shoulder often felt by a person with disease of the *gall bladder. It arises only from stimulation of deeplying *pain receptors in viscera, joints, and muscles, and never from pain receptors in the skin. Also called *telalgia*. *See also* pain, synaesthesia (2).

reflectance *n*. The degree to which a surface reflects light, sound, or any other form of radiant energy. Radiation striking a surface that is not reflected is either absorbed, depending on the *absorbance* of the surface, or transmitted, depending on its *transmittance*, which is the reciprocal of its *opacity*, the degree to which it reflects or absorbs incident light. *See also* luminance.
[From Latin *reflectere* to turn back, from *re-* again + *flectere* to bend]

reflecting back *n*. In client-centred therapy or counselling, a process whereby the therapist or counsellor puts into words and feeds back, without *interpretation (2) or judgement, the emotional content of the client's words and behaviour. The therapist might say, for example, 'You are angry because I am not taking your side against your husband'. Also called *reflection of feeling*.

reflection–impulsivity *n*. A *cognitive style, first identified in 1958 by the US psychologist Jerome Kagan (born 1929), characterized by either *reflection* or *reflectivity*, a tendency to consider and deliberate over alternative solutions to problems, or *impulsivity*, a tendency to respond spontaneously without deliberation, especially in situations of uncertainty. It is usually measured by analysing patterns of response latencies and errors in simple tasks, a reflective person generally producing relatively few errors but long response times, and an impulsive person more errors but shorter response times. *See also* Matching Familiar Figures Test. Also called *conceptual tempo*.

reflex *n*. **1.** An immediate involuntary stereotyped *response to a *stimulus (1), such as blinking both eyes when something touches the cornea of either eye. In spite of being involuntary, many reflexes are effected by voluntary (striped) muscles, but some (such as the axon reflex) do not involve voluntary muscles. Also called a *reflex action* or a *reflex response*.

See accommodation reflex, Achilles tendon reflex, acoustic reflex, audio-oculogyric reflex, axon reflex, Babinski reflex, biceps reflex, blink reflex, ciliary reflex, corneal reflex, deep tendon reflex, flexion reflex, gag reflex, grasp reflex, Moro reflex, patellar reflex, pupillary light reflex, rooting reflex, spinal reflex, startle reflex, stretch reflex, triceps reflex, vestibulo-ocular reflex. *See also* conditioned reflex, looming, reflex arc, unconditioned reflex. *adj.* **2.** Of, relating to, or resembling a *reflex (1).

[From Latin *reflexus* bent back, from *reflectere* to bend back, from *flectare* to bend]

reflex arc *n.* A simple model of a neural pathway underlying a *reflex, regarded by some psychologists as the basic element of behaviour: *stimulus (1) → *sensory receptor → *afferent nerve → *interneuron(s) → *efferent nerve → *effector → *response. According to this model, a reflex carries an impulse from a sensory receptor to the spinal cord, where it connects either directly or via one or more interneurons with an efferent neuron that transmits the impulse to an appropriate muscle, gland, or other effector organ. The mechanism of the *axon reflex does not conform to this pattern. *See also* conditioned response, monosynaptic reflex, polysynaptic reflex, unconditioned response. *Compare* TOTE.

refraction *n.* A deflection in the direction of propagation of a light wave, sound wave, or other wave, caused by passing from one medium of transmission to another in which it is propagated at a different velocity, the degree of refraction depending on the relative *refractive indices of the two media, the angle of incidence to the second medium, and the wavelength of the radiation. This phenomenon explains the working of a *lens, including the *crystalline lens of the eye, and the optical defect of chromatic aberration. *See also* aberration (3), refractive index. **refract** *vb.*

[From Latin *refractus* broken up, from *refringere* to break up, from re- again + *frangere* to break + *-ion* indicating an action, process, or state]

refractive index *n.* A measure of the degree of *refraction of light or other radiation at the interface of two media, equal to the ratio of the sine of the angle of incidence to the sine of the angle of refraction, which in turn is equal to the ratio of the wave propagation speed in the first medium to the wave propagation speed in the second. *See also* dioptre.

refractory period *n.* **1.** A variable period of time following *orgasm during which males lack sexual desire and are incapable of achieving erection of the penis. *See also* Coolidge effect. **2.** A period up to approximately 2 milliseconds after an *action potential (the firing of a neuron) before the neuron recovers its capacity to fire again (the *absolute refractory period) or the subsequent period of up to 10 milliseconds during which its propensity to fire again is diminished (the *relative refractory period). **3.** A period following a response to a stimulus during which reaction time to a further stimulus is increased. Also called a *refractory phase* or, in sense 3, a *psychological refractory period* or *PRP*.

[From Latin *refractum* broken, from *frangere* to break]

regeneration *n.* The process whereby a damaged *axon of a sensory or motor neuron in the peripheral nervous system grows a new connection to the organ, tissue, or cell that it previously innervated. In the central nervous system, damaged neurons do not usually regenerate.

regenerative sprouting *n.* The growth of offshoots or sprouts from a severed axon initiating a process of *regeneration.

regional cerebral blood flow *n.* Blood flow in localized areas of the brain during specific mental states or activities, recorded by a noninvasive *brain imaging technique such as a *PET scan or a *SPECT scan, usually after introducing a radioactive substance, or by *MRI. **rCBF** *abbrev.*

register *n.* **1.** In computer technology, a specialized memory location. **2.** A speech style associated with a particular topic or class of social interactions, such as legal *jargon (1), the *argot of a particular group, or *slang. **3.** The anatomically determined range of a human voice. **4.** Another name for a *sensory register.

regression *n.* **1.** A reversion to an earlier, more immature mode of thinking, feeling, or behaving. **2.** In *psychoanalysis, a *defence mechanism whereby a person reverts to a form of behaviour, thinking, or *object-

relationship characteristic of an earlier stage of development in order to avoid or reduce *anxiety. *Libidinal regression* is a retreat to an earlier *libidinal stage, and tends to occur in response to conflict if there has been an earlier *fixation (2); *ego regression* is a return to earlier modes of mental functioning, as when an adult behaves in a childlike manner under stress. The concept was introduced by Sigmund Freud (1856–1939) in 1900 in his book *The Interpretation of Dreams* (*Standard Edition*, IV–V, at pp. 533–48). *See also* regression in the service of the ego. **3.** In statistics, a technique for analysing the association between one or more *independent variables and a *dependent variable. *See* multiple regression, regression analysis, regression towards the mean. **4.** A backward glance while reading a line of text.
[From Latin *regressus* a retreat + *-ion* indicating an action, process, or state]

regression analysis *n*. In statistics, the analysis of the relationship between a *predictor variable (or *independent variable) and a *dependent variable, usually expressed as a *linear model in which the value of the dependent variable is equal to a weighted value of the independent variable plus a constant. It was originally put forward in a primitive form by the English explorer, amateur scientist, and psychologist Sir Francis Galton (1822–1911) at a meeting of the Royal Institution in London in 1877. When more than one predictor variable is involved, it is called *multiple regression. Also called *linear regression*. *See also* cross-validation (2).
[From Latin *regressus* a retreat]

regression fallacy *n*. An erroneous interpretation of *regression towards the mean as being caused by something other than chance. A frequently quoted example reported in 1973 by the Israeli psychologists Daniel Kahneman (born 1934) and Amos Tversky (1937–96) comes from the experience of flying instructors. Experienced instructors noticed that praise given to a trainee pilot for an exceptionally smooth landing was usually followed by a rougher landing on the following attempt, and harsh criticism for an unusually rough landing was usually followed by a smoother landing on the following attempt, and the instructors therefore came to believe that praise was not merely ineffective but counter-productive and that punishment

was highly effective, whereas in reality an unusually smooth or rough landing is likely to be followed by a more average one because of regression towards the mean. The fallacy is usually explained by the use in judgements of this kind of the *representativeness heuristic. *Compare* non-regressiveness bias.

regression in the service of the ego *n*. A term introduced into *ego psychology by the US-based German psychologist Ernst Kris (1901–57) to denote the use of *regression (2) as a means of facilitating creativity.

regression towards the mean *n*. In statistics, the tendency for the value of a variable predicted probabilistically and with random error to be closer to its mean than predicted. When a *predictor variable is used to predict the value of a *dependent variable with which it is imperfectly correlated, and then the actual value of the dependent variable is observed and compared with its predicted value, the observed value turns out most often to be somewhere between the predicted value and the mean. To clarify this phenomenon, consider the limiting case of a totally unreliable predictor variable that has a zero correlation with the dependent variable. Suppose a fair coin is tossed ten times, and the number of heads (the predictor variable) is used to predict the number of heads in the following ten tosses (the dependent variable). In this case there is *complete* regression to the mean, the expected value of the dependent variable being *equal* to its mean, namely five heads. The higher the correlation between the predictor variable and the dependent variable, the less the regression towards the mean, but unless the correlation is perfectly reliable, the expected value of the dependent variable is always somewhere between its predicted value and its mean. One manifestation of this phenomenon is the fact that when values fluctuate randomly around a mean value, an extreme score is relatively improbable, so that if such a score is observed, then the following observation is likely to be a less extreme score. A familiar instance of regression towards the mean is *filial regression. US *regression toward the mean*. *See also* non-regressiveness bias, one-group pretest–posttest design, regression fallacy. *Compare* overdominance.
[From Latin *regressus* a retreat + Old French *moien*, from Latin *medius* middle]

regulator *n*. A person who regulates or controls, or anything that regulates or controls, especially (in social psychology) a *gesture (1) that accompanies speech and helps to coordinate turn-taking, including raising a hand in the air to indicate that one has not finished speaking, and establishing *eye contact at the beginning and end of a speaking turn. *See also* kinesics.

regulator gene *n*. A gene that controls the expression of a *structural gene by directing the synthesis of a *gene regulator that binds to a *gene operator and affects the synthesis of the structural gene's protein product. *See* activator gene, repressor gene. *See also* operon. *Compare* structural gene.

rehabilitation *n*. The process of helping a person who has been ill, disabled, hospitalized, or imprisoned to re-adapt to society or find employment; more generally, the process of restoring the status or reputation of a person or thing. *See also* halfway house. **rehabilitate** *vb*.
[From Latin *rehabilitare* to restore, from *re-* again + *habilitas* skill + *-ation* indicating a process or condition]

rehearsal buffer *n*. Another name for a *phonological buffer store.

rehearse *vb*. **1.** To repeat or go over something, usually in order to commit it to memory or to retain it in memory. **2.** To recall or enumerate items of information repeatedly in order to retain them in *short-term memory. Such repetition is called *maintenance rehearsal* when it is simple repetition and *elaborative rehearsal* when deeper processing is involved. *See also* phonological loop. **3.** To practise a speech or a musical or dramatic act in preparation for a performance of it. **rehearsal** *n*.
[From Old French *rehercier* to harrow again, from *re-* again + *hercer* to harrow, from Latin *hirpex, hirpicis* a rake or harrow]

Reichian therapy *n*. Another name for *orgone therapy.
[Named after the Austrian (later US-based) psychiatrist Wilhelm Reich (1897–1957), who introduced it in 1927 in a book translated into English in 1942 as *The Function of the Orgasm*]

reify *vb*. To treat an abstract concept as something concrete, as when a child asks what

colour sadness is. *See also* category mistake.
reification *n*. The act or process of *reifying.
[From Latin *res* a thing, on the model of the English word *deify*]

reinforcement *n*. **1.** In *operant conditioning, any *stimulus (1) that, if it is presented soon after a *response, increases the relative frequency with which that response is emitted in the future; also the process whereby a response is strengthened in this way. *See also* cumulative record, differential reinforcement, law of effect, negative reinforcement, reinforcement schedule, Skinner box, social learning. **2.** In *classical conditioning, an *unconditioned stimulus that, if paired repeatedly with a *conditioned stimulus, causes the conditioned stimulus to elicit a *conditioned response. **reinforce** *vb*. To provide *reinforcement (1, 2). **reinforcer** *n*. A *stimulus (1) that provides *reinforcement (1, 2).

reinforcement schedule *n*. In *operant conditioning, a particular arrangement of the contingency of *reinforcement (1), relating an organism's responses to the frequency and timing of the reinforcement. In *continuous reinforcement*, the organism is rewarded after every response, whereas in *partial reinforcement* or *intermittent reinforcement* the organism is rewarded after a certain amount of time has elapsed or a certain number of responses have been made. The most important *simple reinforcement schedules* are the *fixed-interval schedule, *fixed-ratio schedule, *variable-interval schedule, and *variable-ratio schedule. *See also* compound reinforcement schedule, differential reinforcement of high response rates, differential reinforcement of low response rates, differential reinforcement of other responses, differential reinforcement of paced responses.

reinforcing selection *n*. Pressures of *natural selection operating at two or more levels (individual, family, population) in such a way that certain genes are favoured at all levels and their spread through the population is accelerated. *Compare* counteracting selection.

Reissner's membrane *n*. A membrane separating the vestibular and cochlear canals of the inner ear.
[Named after the German anatomist Ernst Reissner (1824–78) who discovered it and published his finding in 1851]

Reiz *n*. Stimulus. This causes confusion in English-speaking countries where *R* is an abbreviation for *response*. **R** *abbrev*.
[From German *Reiz* stimulus]

Reiz limen *n*. Absolute threshold. **RL** *abbrev*.
[From German *Reiz* stimulus + Latin *limen* a threshold]

rejection-then-retreat technique *n*. Another name for the *door-in-the-face technique.

related scores *t* test *n*. In *inferential statistics, a version of the *t* test used for comparing means from two statistically related samples, such as two sets of scores taken from a single group of research participants or subjects. Also called a *paired samples t test*. *Compare* independent samples *t* test.

relationship, coefficient of *See* coefficient of relationship.

relative deprivation *n*. The discrepancy that one perceives between what one has and what one could or should have, in contradistinction to absolute deprivation of the bare necessities for living. *Egoistic relative deprivation* arises from unfavourable comparisons between one's individual circumstances and those of a comparative *reference group, and it tends to generate personal dissatisfaction and unhappiness; *fraternal relative deprivation* arises from unfavourable comparisons between the circumstances of one's group (social class, racial group, occupational group, and so on) and a reference group, and it tends to generate protest behaviour, rebellion, and in extreme cases revolution. The concept was introduced by the US sociologist Samuel Stouffer (1900–60) and several co-authors in their study of *The American Soldier* (1949), where it was reported that army units with the highest rates of promotion also had the highest levels of dissatisfaction among those not promoted. The US sociologist Robert K(ing) Merton (born 1910) developed the idea further in his book *Social Theory and Social Structure* (1957), arguing that high rates of social mobility raised hopes and expectations and encouraged over-optimistic social comparisons. The British sociologist Walter G. Runciman (born 1934), in his book *Relative Deprivation and Social Justice* (1966), provided further evidence that workers' feelings of deprivation and class consciousness tend to be relative rather than absolute. Subsequent researchers have generally corroborated and extended these basic ideas and findings. *See also* equity theory.

relative error *n*. In *psychophysics, the *absolute error divided by the true value of a stimulus.

relative pitch *n*. The ability to recognize the *pitch of a *tone (1), or to produce a tone at its correct pitch, by referring it to a tone of known pitch. Thus a person with relative pitch who is presented with a C and told that it is a C can recognize another tone as an F or can hum an F. *Compare* absolute pitch.

relative refractory period *n*. A *refractory period (2), lasting up to 10 milliseconds, immediately after the *absolute refractory period, during which a neuron will fire only in response to a very strong stimulus, well above the normal threshold strength. This allows frequency of neuron firing to be used by the nervous system to signal stimulus strength in spite of the *all-or-none law.

relative size *n*. The *angular size of an object as compared with that of another; specifically, one of the monocular cues of visual *depth perception, useful only with objects that are familiar or of known size, objects with relatively large angular sizes being perceived as closer than objects with relatively small angular sizes.

relaxation technique *n*. In *connectionism (1) and *parallel distributed processing, the use of iterated propagation of signals through a network of connected units until they are all responding as consistently as possible to signals received from one another and no further adjustments in connections and firing rates can lead to further improvements. If some connections between units are excitatory and others are inhibitory, then a single signal propagated through the network will cause some of the units to increase their strength of firing in response to excitatory input from other units, and will cause other units to decrease their strength of firing because of inhibitory input, but the resulting pattern will not necessarily be stable or settled, because a second signal propagated through the network will in most cases result in further changes, but after a number of iterations the system will usually settle down to an equilibrium state. *Compare* annealing (1).

relaxation therapy *n*. Another name for *progressive relaxation.

relaxin *n*. A polypeptide hormone that is secreted by the corpus luteum of a pregnant woman and that relaxes the pelvic ligaments, allowing the pelvis to dilate during childbirth.

relay cell *n*. Another name for an *interneuron. Also called a *relay neuron*.

releaser *n*. In ethology, a *sign stimulus that is contained in a structure, crest, colouring pattern, call, or scent and that evokes an immediate innate response or *fixed-action pattern, having evolved specifically as a signal to communicate with *conspecifics (1). Not all sign stimuli are releasers: the speckling pattern on some birds' eggs is a sign stimulus for incubation behaviour, but it is believed to have evolved as camouflage. *See also* innate releasing mechanism, vacuum activity.

releasing hormone *n*. Any of several *peptide hormones secreted by the hypothalamus and transmitted to the anterior pituitary via the hypothalamic-hypophyseal portal system, where it stimulates the release of a *trophic hormone. *See* corticotrophin-releasing hormone, growth hormone releasing hormone, luteinizing-hormone releasing hormone, thyrotrophin-releasing hormone. Also called a *releasing factor*.

reliability *n*. The quality of being trustworthy or dependable. In psychometrics, the *internal consistency and *stability with which a measuring instrument performs its function, corresponding roughly to the everyday concept of accuracy. *See* Cronbach's alpha, equivalent-form reliability, Kuder-Richardson coefficient, split-half reliability, test–retest reliability. *See also* classical test theory, generalizability theory. *Compare* validity. [From Old French *relier* to rely, from Latin *religare* to tie back + -*abilitas* capacity, from *habilis* able]

reliability coefficient *n*. In psychometrics, a *correlation coefficient or other numerical index of the *reliability of a test or measure.

REM atonia *abbrev.* An inhibition of skeletal muscles (but not *extra-ocular muscles) during *REM sleep, manifested as complete *atonia, that is governed by a small inhibitory centre in the pons called the *subcoerulear nucleus and by the *magnocellular nucleus in the medulla oblongata to which it is connected, and that prevents spinal nerves from activating skeletal muscles and thereby stops dreams from being acted out by the sleeper. The only observable bodily movements in a person in REM sleep, apart from breathing and rapid eye movements, are occasional twitches of the extremities, except in people with *REM behaviour disorder. The French physiologist Michel Jouvet (born 1925) discovered the mechanism in 1965 by performing experiments on cats in which he used a heated wire to destroy a small volume of the subcoerulear nucleus or of the magnocellular nucleus to which it is linked. This caused the cats to move about during REM sleep, stand up, twitch their whiskers, hiss, paw the air, and make movements typical of stalking and attacking prey—a phenomenon called *REM sleep without atonia. See also* narcolepsy, sleep paralysis. [From *rapid eye movement* + *atonia*, from Greek *a-* without + *tonos* tension or tone + -*ia* indicating a condition or quality]

REM behaviour disorder *abbrev.* A condition is which *REM atonia does not function during episodes of dreaming. People with this disorder thrash violently about, leap out of bed, and sometimes attack bed-partners during REM sleep. It is assumed to be due to a lesion in the *subcoerulear nucleus or the *magnocellular nucleus. US *REM behavior disorder*. **RBD** *abbrev.*

remember *n*. To maintain in or recall to consciousness something previously experienced or learned, or to retain information. *See* memory. [From Latin *re-* again + *memor* mindful]

reminiscence *n*. **1.** The act or process of recalling or recounting a past experience; the event recalled or recounted, or something that reminds one of a past experience. *See also* anamnesis (1). **2.** In *cognitive psychology, an improvement in memory for material or performance of a task some time after learning it, compared to the level of performance immediately after learning, especially when the learning was carried out by *massed practice. The concept was introduced in 1913 by the Welsh schoolteacher Philip Boswood Ballard (1865–1950), who reported that schoolchildren who memorized passages of poetry and were tested repeatedly for periods up to a week could often recall lines on later tests that they could not recall on earlier tests. Ballard contrasted this phenomenon with *obliviscence. Reminiscence of some items of information can be offset by forgetting of others, so that the overall performance may not improve over time; however, under some conditions there may be an overall gain in performance over successive tests, in which case the phenomenon is called *hypermnesia. *See also* successive reproduction. **reminiscent** *adj*.

[From Latin *reminisci* to call to mind, from *re*- again + *mens* mind]

remote viewing *n*. A conjectural *paranormal phenomenon involving *extra-sensory perception of distant objects or events, especially of large environmental features such as lakes or prominent buildings. Also called *clairvoyance*.

REM rebound *abbrev*. The tendency for a person or animal deprived of *REM sleep to spend an increased proportion of sleeping time in REM sleep during immediately succeeding sleeping periods. In research into this phenomenon, the person or animal is awakened whenever a period of REM begins and then allowed to go back to sleep, carefully curtailing the amount of REM sleep but not the total amount of sleep. Also called *rebound REM*. *See also* rebound effect.

REM sleep *abbrev*. Rapid-eye-movement sleep, a stage of sleep occurring in progressively lengthening episodes roughly every 90 minutes throughout the night in human adults and occupying about twenty per cent of sleeping time, strongly associated with vivid *dreams (1), and characterized by *rapid eye movements, *theta waves, absence of *delta waves, penile erections in males, and *REM atonia of the skeletal muscles preventing dreams being acted out. REM sleep does not occur in reptiles but has been found in birds and almost all mammals, including dogs and cats (whose eyelids can be lifted gently to reveal darting eyes during REM episodes) and also in bats, moles, and whales, but not in the

Australian spiny anteater or echidna of the genus *Tachyglossus*, which is exceptional in this regard. Also called *active sleep*, *desynchronized (D) sleep* or *paradoxical sleep*. *See also* REM rebound, sleep. *Compare* NREM sleep.

renifleur *n*. A person with *osphresiolagnia; one given to recurrent sexually arousing fantasies, sexual urges, or behaviour involving smells.

[French *renifleur* a sniffer]

renin *n*. A hormone secreted by the kidneys in response to signals from *baroreceptors and *blood-flow receptors, indicating falling blood pressure or blood flow or a rise in the concentration of *vasopressin in the blood. Its secretion causes the synthesis of *angiotensin II, which leads to the constriction of blood vessels, compensating for the lowered blood pressure, and angiotensin II also precipitates the release of *aldosterone, leading to decreased sodium excretion in urine, therefore increased whole-body sodium and the stimulation of the *subfornical organ, which tends to initiate drinking.

[From Latin *renes* kidneys, from *ren* a kidney]

Renshaw cell *n*. A type of spinal *motor neuron that releases glycine as a neurotransmitter, inhibiting the activity of *alpha motor neurons and preventing their repeated firing. *See also* gamma motor neuron.

[Named after the US neurologist Birdsey Renshaw (1911–48)]

reparation *n*. The act or process or repairing, compensating, or making amends. In *Kleinian analysis, a mechanism associated with depressive anxiety and feelings of guilt whereby one repairs the damage done by destructive fantasies to an *instinctual object, enabling the *depressive position to be overcome.

[From Latin *reparare* to mend, from *parare* to prepare]

repeated-measures analysis of variance *n*. A form of *analysis of variance that is used to analyse the difference between three or more means when the sets of scores are not independent, data that require this type of analysis most often arising in *within-subjects designs when several measurements of a variable are taken from a single group of individuals at different times. *Multifactorial analysis of variance may involve repeated measures on one or more of its independent variables.

repeated reproduction See successive reproduction.

Repertory Grid Test n. A test designed to reveal the respondent's ways of construing the world according to *personal construct theory. The respondent is presented with three elements from the domain of interest (people, events, or objects) and is asked to indicate in what way any two of the elements are similar to each other and different from the third. For example, if the three elements are *my father*, *my boss*, and *my husband*, then the respondent may reply that *my father* and *my boss* are both unfriendly and in that way different from *my husband*, thereby eliciting the personal construct *friendly–unfriendly* among the respondent's ways of construing people. Then the respondent answers the same question with regard to a second group of three elements, and so on, until all the respondent's important constructs in the relevant domain have been elicited, whereupon a grid is constructed, with elements running across the top, elicited constructs down the side, and each cell marked with a tick if the construct applies to the element, a cross if it does not apply, or unmarked if the respondent has not used the construct to judge the element. After the repertory grid has been drawn up, the constructs may be presented as *rating scales on which the respondent rates each of the elements on each of the constructs. What is unusual about this test is that it is tailored to the individual respondent's way of construing or interpreting the world. The earliest form of the test was first described by its inventor, the US psychologist George A(lexander) Kelly (1905–66), in his book *The Psychology of Personal Constructs* (1955, Vol. 1, pp. 219–66). See also grid analysis, Role Construct Repertory Test. **Rep test** abbrev.
[From *repertory* an entire stock of things available, from Latin *repertorium* a storehouse, from *reperire* to obtain, from *re-* again + *parere* to bring forth]

repetition compulsion n. In *psychoanalysis, a type of *compulsion characterized by a tendency to place oneself in dangerous or distressing situations that repeat similar experiences from the past. Sigmund Freud

(1856–1939) introduced it in 1914 in an article on 'Remembering, Repeating and Working-Through' (*Standard Edition*, XII, pp. 147–56) and discussed it at length in his book *Beyond the Pleasure Principle* (1920). In analysis, the *transference often contains elements that involve recreations of past conflicts with parents and other family members. Also called a *compulsion to repeat*. See also fate neurosis.

repetition effect n. In *serial recall of a string of letters, numbers, or other items, the phenomenon of generally superior performance when none of the items occurs more than once than when some items are repeated. It is a special case of *Ranschburg inhibition.

repetitive DNA n. Any segment of *DNA containing stuttering duplications of a sequence of base pairs that may be from tens to hundreds of base pairs long. Most repetitive DNA does not code for proteins but consists of *introns or *junk DNA with no apparent function, and because it tends to be highly variable and individually distinctive, it is useful in *DNA fingerprinting. Also called a *VNTR locus*. See also centromere.

replication n. **1.** The reproduction of exact copies of complex *DNA or other molecules such as occurs during the growth of living tissue. **2.** The repetition of an experiment or other research procedure to check the *external validity of the results.

representability n. In *psychoanalysis, an aspect of *dreamwork denoting the quality of ideas that have been transformed so as to be capable of representation by visual images. Sigmund Freud (1856–1939) discussed considerations of representability in 1900 in his book *The Interpretation of Dreams* (*Standard Edition*, IV–V, at pp. 539–49).

representation n. **1.** Anything that corresponds to something else in certain specified ways, or that serves as an *image (1, 2, 3) of it. **2.** More specifically a formal system for making explicit a certain class of information together with a specification of how the system achieves this, typical examples being representations of the natural numbers by systems of Arabic numerals (1, 2, 3, 4, . . .), Roman numerals (I, II, III, IV, . . .), or binary digits (1, 10, 11, 100, . . .), each system having its own explicit rules for constructing an integer of any desired size. *Computational theories of vision seek to construct representations of visual information.

representativeness heuristic *n*. A cognitive *heuristic through which people estimate the probability that *A* belongs to (or originates from) a particular class *B* by judging the degree to which *A* is representative or typical of *B*. It can lead to errors of judgement because it ignores *prior probabilities (1) and can thus cause people to commit the *base-rate fallacy, and if it is used to estimate the probability of obtaining a particular value in a sample drawn from a known population, then it is insensitive to information about the sample size and may therefore cause people to commit the *sample size fallacy. *See also* conjunction fallacy, non-regressiveness bias, regression fallacy.

repressed gene *n*. A *gene that has been inactivated by a *gene repressor.

repression *n*. In *psychoanalysis, a *defence mechanism whereby unacceptable thoughts, feelings, or wishes are banished from *consciousness. In an article entitled 'Repression' in 1915, Sigmund Freud (1856–1939) gave the following brief and frequently quoted definition: *'The essence of repression lies simply in turning something away, and keeping it at a distance, from the conscious'* (*Standard Edition*, XIV, pp. 146–58, at p. 147, italics in original). In *primal repression, wishes emanating from the *id are blocked from reaching consciousness; in *primary repression, anxiety-arousing information already in consciousness is removed and blocked from returning; and in *secondary repression conscious material that is reminiscent of repressed material is also removed from consciousness. The term (German *Verdrängung*) was introduced in its psychological sense in 1806 by the German philosopher and psychologist Johann Friedrich Herbart (1776–1841) (*Samtliche Werke*, V, p. 19) and repeated in 1824 in his book *Psychologie als Wissenschaft* (Psychology as Science), and it has not been established whether Freud knew of this work when he began using the term in 1894. *See also* countercathexis. *Compare* foreclosure, suppression (with which this concept is often confused). **repress** *vb*. **repressed** *adj*.

repression–sensitization scale *n*. A personality questionnaire designed to measure a re-

spondent's characteristic mode of reacting to threatening stimuli or ideas, typical *repressors* tending to react by blocking, denial, and repression, that is, by putting threatening ideas out of their minds, and *sensitizers* tending to react by approaching, facilitating, and increasing vigilance, that is, by confronting the threatening stimuli directly. It was developed by the US psychologist Donn Byrne (born 1931), on the basis of items taken from the *MMPI, and published in the *Journal of Personality* in 1961. **R–S scale** *abbrev*.

repressor gene *n*. A *regulator gene that synthesizes a *gene repressor capable of binding to a *gene operator and preventing the expression of a *structural gene by suppressing the synthesis of its protein product. *Compare* activator gene.

reproducibility *n*. In a *Guttman scale, the degree to which the items can be arranged in a hierarchy such that a respondent's agreement to an item implies agreement to all items below it in the hierarchy, deviations from this pattern being counted as errors. It is often abbreviated to *Rep* and defined as *Rep* = 1 − (number of errors)/(total number of responses), a Guttman scale being considered satisfactory if it has been administered to a large group of respondents and its reproducibility is at least 0.90, implying that the scale is reasonably unidimensional, measuring mainly one major variable. *See also* unidimensionality. **Rep** *abbrev*.

reproduction method *n*. Another name for the *method of average error.

reproductive interference *n*. Impairment of the reproduction of learned material caused by the learning of other material. *See* proactive interference, retroactive interference.

reproductive memory *n*. Accurate retrieval of information from memory, without significant alteration. The English psychologist Sir Frederic Charles Bartlett (1886–1969) first differentiated it from *reconstructive memory in 1932.

Rep test *See* Repertory Grid Test.

resampling statistics *n*. A general approach to statistical analysis in which, given a set of scores, new data are generated by repeated random sampling with replacement from the existing scores (the bootstrapping technique) or by using a data-generating mechanism such as a computer's random number generator (the *Monte Carlo method or simulation technique), and the results of the new samples are then examined. Thus if 7/10 patients given a drug and 2/10 given a *placebo (1) improved, a researcher could randomly select 10 balls with replacement from an urn containing 9 white balls (representing the improved patients) and 11 black balls (representing the unimproved patients) and count the proportion of these samples containing 7 or more white balls; if the proportion is less than 5 per cent, then the observed result is statistically significant. The procedure would normally be performed using a computer rather than a physical urn and balls. It is similar to *randomization statistics but differs from it in using the observed scores rather than all possible scores that could be generated. See also Monte Carlo method.

research hypothesis n. Another name for an *alternative hypothesis.

reserpine n. An *alkaloid extracted from the roots of the south-east Asian plant *Rauwolfia serpentina*, used for the treatment of hypertension and as a sedative and tranquillizer. It has a broad spectrum of pharmacological actions, including especially the progressive depletion of the neurotransmitters *noradrenalin (norepinephrine), *dopamine, and *serotonin from synaptic vesicles in the central nervous system, and it tends to cause severe depression.
[From German *Reserpin* an irregular blend of Latin *Rauwolfia* and *serpentina*]

residual n. **1.** In statistics, especially in *regression analysis and *analysis of variance (ANOVA), short for residual variance, that part of the variance in the dependent variable unaccounted for by the independent variables and thus attributed to chance variation. **2.** The difference between a score and its expected value according to a theoretical model. [From Latin *residuus* remaining over, from *residere* to stay behind + -*alis* of or relating to]

residual schizophrenia n. A form of *schizophrenia without *positive symptoms, that is, without *delusions, *hallucinations, *disorganized speech, or *catatonia, but with evidence of *negative symptoms such as *affective flattening, *alogia, or *avolition.

resinous odour n. One of the six primary odours in *Henning's prism, resembling the odour of resin or turpentine. US *resinous odor*.

resistance n. The process of striving against, opposing, or withstanding something. In *psychoanalysis, the tendency to strive against the transition of *repressed thoughts, feelings, or wishes from the *unconscious (2) to *consciousness, especially an attempt to prevent this happening while undergoing psychoanalysis. The *interpretation (2) of resistance is an important aspect of psychoanalytic technique. Sigmund Freud (1856–1939) discussed a number of forms of resistance in *Studies on Hysteria* (1895, *Standard Edition*, II, at pp. 278–87) and in *Inhibitions, Symptoms and Anxiety* (1926, *Standard Edition*, XX, pp. 77–175, at pp. 158–60). In an article on 'A Difficulty in the Path of Psycho-Analysis' in 1917, he interpreted hostility to his work as further evidence of resistance (*Standard Edition*, XVII, pp. 137–44). When it occurs during psychoanalysis, it is also called *transference resistance*. See also negative therapeutic reaction, working through.

resistance stage n. The second stage of the *general adaptation syndrome to *stress (1), during which the body copes actively with a stressor by mechanisms such as sending *leucocytes to the site of an injury or infection. See also alarm reaction, exhaustion stage.

resolution phase n. The fourth phase of the *sexual response cycle, occurring after the *orgasmic phase.

resonance theory n. Another name for the *place theory of pitch perception. Also called *resonance place theory*.

resource dilemma n. A type of *social dilemma in which players harvest resources (usually tokens representing money) from a common resource pool of known size, and after each trial the pool is replenished at a predetermined rate. Players are free to choose, within limits, how much to take from the pool, and it is in each player's individual self-interest to take as much as possible, but if everyone behaves greedily, then the pool is exhausted and every player suffers. One popular type of resource dilemma is the *commons dilemma. The resource dilemma research paradigm provides a useful model of everyday social dilemmas involving conservation of natural resources. It is also called a *resource management dilemma* or a *resource conservation dilemma*, and the corresponding experimental games are sometimes called *take-some* games.

resource-holding potential *n*. A measure of an animal's capacity to win a fight against an opponent, assuming that both adopt the same behavioural strategy. It is often equivalent simply to the animal's *escalated fighting ability, which in turn derives from its strength, size, and experience, but it is sometimes affected by other factors, as when a male insect in possession of a female has greater chances of winning, even against a stronger opponent, because it is easier to hold on to something than to wrest it from the grip of an opponent. Also called *resource-holding power* or *relative holding power*. **RHP** *abbrev*.
[Coined in 1974 by the British biologist Geoffrey A. Parker (born 1944)]

respiration *n*. Breathing, or more generally any process by which an organism generates usable energy, usually in the form of molecules of *ATP, from the oxidative metabolism of food. *See also* Krebs cycle.
[From Latin *respirare* to breathe + *-ation* indicating a process or condition]

respondent conditioning *n*. Another name for *operant conditioning.

response *n*. Any physical or psychological reaction of an organism to a *stimulus (1). It may include a behavioural, muscular, glandular, or neurophysiological reaction caused by stimulation of a *sensory receptor, and in the *behaviourism of the US psychologist B(urrhus) F(rederic) Skinner (1904–90) and his followers, it also includes a purely mental reaction. *See also* conditioned response, discriminative response, fight-or-flight response, fixed-action pattern, reaction time, reflex (1), unconditioned response. **R** *abbrev*.
[From Latin *respondere* to reply, from *re-* back + *spondere* to promise]

response amplitude *n*. In *Hullian learning theory, the magnitude or intensity of an organism's response to a *stimulus (1). **A** *abbrev*.

response bias *n*. In psychometrics, any systematic tendency of a respondent to choose a particular response category in a multiple-choice questionnaire for an extraneous reason, unrelated to the variable that the response is supposed to indicate but related to the content or meaning of the question. A typical example is *social desirability response set. *See also* lie scale, response set (2). *Compare* response style.

response category *n*. One of the alternatives from which a respondent must select in responding to a *closed question. For example, in the questionnaire item *I enjoy working with numbers (YES, NO)*, the response categories are *YES* and *NO*. *See also* multiple-choice, numerical rating scale, verbal rating scale. *Compare* free response, graphic rating scale, open-ended question.

response competition *n*. A condition in which a *stimulus (1) activates more than one *response in an organism, so that the responses vie with one another for dominance. For example, a person performing a difficult task in front of an audience may need to concentrate on the task but may also wish to concentrate on aspects of self-presentation and may therefore experience response competition, leading to an *audience effect.

response latency *n*. The interval of time elapsing between a *stimulus (1) and a *response, a term used in preference to *reaction time when referring to animal behaviour. Also called *latency* or *latent time*.

response set *n*. **1.** A bias disposing an organism to respond in a particular way to a stimulus, especially if the organism is concentrating on the *response rather than the *stimulus (1). *Compare* stimulus set (1, 2). **2.** In psychometrics, a type of *response bias such as *acquiescence response set or *social desirability response set in which a respondent replies to items in a multiple-choice questionnaire by choosing or avoiding certain response categories for reasons related or unrelated to their content or meaning. *Compare* response style.

response style *n*. In psychometrics, any consistent tendency on the part of a respondent to choose a particular response category in a multiple-choice questionnaire irrespective of the content of the question or item, as in *acquiescence response set or *position preference, rather than a tendency to choose a particular type of response determined by the content of the item or question, as in *social desirability response set. *See also* response set (2). *Compare* response bias.

rest–activity cycle *See* basic rest–activity cycle.

resting potential *n.* The voltage difference of about −70 millivolts (mV) across the cell membrane of a neuron (negative on the inside) maintained by the *sodium pump when it is not transmitting a nerve impulse. Given that it occurs across the very thin membrane of a tiny cell, it equates to about 10,000 volts per millimetre. It represents stored energy, and its momentary reversal when the nerve is stimulated constitutes the firing of the neuron. Also called *equilibrium potential* or *resting membrane potential*. *See also* depolarization, refractory period (2), sodium channel. *Compare* action potential.

resting tremor *n.* A form of *tremor characterized by fine, quick quavering movements that tend to disappear during purposeful movements, this type of tremor being characteristic of *parkinsonism. Also called *passive tremor*. *See also* postural tremor. *Compare* intention tremor.

Restorff effect *See* von Restorff effect.

Restoril *n.* A proprietary name for the benzodiazepine drug *temazepam.
[Trademark]

restricted affect *See under* affect.

restricted choice principle *See* principle of restricted choice.

restricted code *n.* A concept introduced by the English sociologist Basil Bernstein (1924–2000) in an article to denote an informal use of language, linked to immediate situations (context bound), with a reduced semantic and syntactic range, supposedly characteristic of lower-working-class speakers, in contrast to middle-class speakers who have access to both a restricted and an *elaborated codes. The theory is often reduced to the proposition that, owing to differences in the linguistic resources available to them, middle-class people are capable of abstract reasoning, whereas lower-working-class

people are not; but Bernstein has argued vigorously against this interpretation. Bernstein first drew attention to social class differences in language in an article in the *British Journal of Sociology* in 1958, and he developed the concept further in two articles in the journal *Language and Speech* in 1962 and in numerous subsequent publications.

restriction analysis *n.* Another name for *restriction mapping.

restriction enzyme *n.* Any of a number of *enzymes that are produced by bacteria and are used to cut DNA in *genetic engineering, *genetic fingerprinting, and *gene mapping. Each restriction enzyme cuts DNA at a different point defined by a different palindromic sequence of bases. Also called a *restriction endonuclease*. *See also* restriction mapping. *Compare* DNA ligase. **restriction fragment** *n.* A section of DNA cut by a *restriction enzyme.

restriction mapping *n.* Determination of the distinctive features of a segment of *DNA by treating it with different *restriction enzymes to produce restriction fragments of different lengths, which are then separated and sized by *electrophoresis to produce a map of the segment with distances between restriction sites measured in base pairs (bp) or thousands of base pairs (kbp). Used in *genetic fingerprinting and research. Also called *restriction analysis*.

retardation, mental *See* mental retardation.

retardation, psychomotor *See* psychomotor retardation.

retarded depression *n.* A form of *depression occurring during the depressive phase of a *bipolar disorder.

rete mirabile *n.* A network of fine blood vessels in the base of the brain within which the temperature of arterial blood is lowered before entering the brain.
[From Latin *rete* a net + *mirabile* wonderful]

retention hysteria *n.* In *psychoanalysis, one of three types of *hysteria distinguished in 1895 by the Austrian physician Josef Breuer (1842–1925) and Sigmund Freud (1856–1939) in *Studies on Hysteria (Standard Edition*, II, at pp. 169–73), supposedly characterized by emotions that have not undergone *abreaction and are therefore retained, Freud's case of Rosalia H (pp. 169–73) being the classic example. After 1895 Freud came to believe that all hysteria is defence hysteria, and he abandoned the tripartite distinction. *Compare* defence hysteria, hypnoid hysteria.

reticular activating system *n.* An abbreviated name for the *ascending reticular activating system. **RAS** *abbrev.*

reticular formation *n.* A small, thick bundle of ascending and descending axons running through the length of the brainstem, interwoven with nerve cells having predominantly horizontal and evenly spaced dendrites producing a netlike pattern, responsible for controlling breathing, heartbeat, blood pressure, swallowing, urination, movements of the face, eyes, and tongue, sleep and wakefulness, and other vital functions. Also called the *brainstem reticular formation (BSRF)*. *See also* ascending reticular activating system, de-

scending reticular formation, neuropil. **RF** *abbrev.*

[From Latin *reticulum* a little net, diminutive of *rete* a net, alluding to its appearance]

reticular nucleus *n.* Any of the clusters of nerve cell bodies belonging to the *reticular formation and situated in the pons or the medulla oblongata.

reticular nucleus of the thalamus *n.* A network of nerve cell bodies surrounding the front and sides of the *thalamus, receiving impulses ascending to and descending from the cerebral cortex and inhibiting neurons in the thalamus.

retina *n.* A platelike structure, a quarter of a millimetre thick, at the back of each eye, technically part of the brain, responsible for converting light into nerve impulses, arranged in three principal layers separated by two thin strata of synaptic connections called *plexiform layers (see illustration). The outer layer

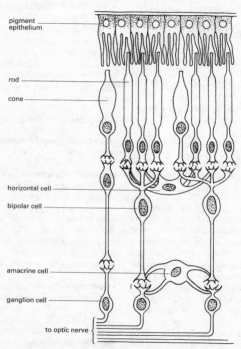

pigment
epithelium

rod

cone

horizontal cell

bipolar cell

amacrine cell

ganglion cell

to optic nerve

Retina. Basic structure (light enters from the bottom of the diagram).

nearest the *pigment epithelium has an array of 126 million photoreceptors (*rods and *cones), the middle layer contains *bipolar cells that receive inputs from photoreceptors immediately in front of them, and the inner layer facing the *crystalline lens contains *ganglion cells, interlaced with *horizontal cells and *amacrine cells, and receives inputs from retinal *bipolar cells. This arrangement of layers is found in all vertebrates and is unexpected, because light has to pass through a forest of neurons before reaching the photoreceptors, and because fibres from ganglion cells have to burrow back through the layers of the retina to feed into the optic nerve, thereby creating the *blind spot (1). This seems so illogical that diagrams appearing in textbooks sometimes incorrectly show light entering from the outer layer where the photoreceptors are located, and various arguments have been put forward to explain why the layers have to be arranged back to front, but such arguments are beside the point because, quite independently of vertebrates, squids and octopuses have evolved eyes that are very similar to those of vertebrates but have retinal layers arranged the other way round, avoiding the drawbacks mentioned above. *See also* colour zone, duplexity theory, fovea, inner nuclear layer, inner plexiform layer, interplexiform cell, macula lutea, outer nuclear layer, outer plexiform layer. **retinas** or **retinae** *pl.* **retinopathy** *n.* Disorder of the *retina. *See also* solar retinopathy.
[Probably from Latin *rete* a net]

retinal *adj.* **1.** Of or relating to the retina. *n.* **2.** Another name for *retinene.

retinal cone *See* cone.

retinal disparity *n.* Another name for *binocular disparity.

retinal expansion *n.* Another name for *looming.

retinal ganglion cell *See* ganglion cell.

retinal image *n.* The inverted image of the *visual field that is focused on to the *retina by the crystalline lens of the eye.

retinal painting *n.* An explanation of *anorthoscopic perception in terms of a hypothetical process by which the extended image of a figure viewed through a moving slit is gradually spread over the retina and imprinted on to it part by part, resulting in a retinal imprint of the whole figure whose form is then perceived. This hypothesis was championed by the German physiologist, physicist, and mathematician Hermann Ludwig Ferdinand von Helmholtz (1821–94) and other 19th-century researchers, but it was subsequently discredited by studies of eye movements that occur during anorthoscopic perception and that would disrupt the process.

retinal rivalry *n.* Another name for *binocular rivalry.

retinene *n.* A form of *retinol that combines with the protein *opsin to form *rhodopsin, the visual purple pigment. Also called *retinal*. [From *retin(a)* + *-ene* indicating an unsaturated compound with double bonds, from Greek *-ene* a feminine name suffix]

retinex theory *n.* A theory of colour vision according to which the visual system includes three separate eye–brain systems called *retinexes*, each with a peak sensitivity to longwave light (560 nanometres), medium-wave light (530 nm), or short-wave light (430 nm) and inhibitory effects on the other systems, operating to assign a colour to each spot in the visual field according to the ratio, for each of the three retinexes, of light reflected from that spot to the average of the light reflected from its surround, the resulting triplet of ratios uniquely defining the colour at each spot. The theory, which was put forward by the US physicist Edwin H(erbert) Land (1909–91), inventor of the Polaroid Land camera and president of the Polaroid Corporation, in the *Journal of the Optical Society of America* in 1971, accounts for the *Land effect and for *colour constancy, because relative rather than absolute wavelengths determine perceived colour, the perceived colour of an object remaining constant as long as the reflectance ratios are unchanged, even if the total amount of light of any given wavelength varies markedly, and this explains why colour constancy is disrupted and some colours cannot be perceived at all when surfaces are viewed in *void mode.
[Coined by its inventor from *retin(a)* + *(cort)ex*]

retinitis pigmentosa *n.* Any of a group of disorders, often hereditary, characterized by bilateral degeneration of the retinas, with onset in childhood, often manifested initially as night blindness or reduction in visual field, leading to *blindness in middle age.

[From *retin(a)* + *-itis* indicating an inflammation + Latin *pigmentum* paint, alluding to the reddish pigmentation of the retina associated with the disease]

retinol *n.* A fat-soluble vitamin necessary for *scotopic vision, formed by *hydrolysis of beta-carotene (*see under* carotene), found in carrots and other yellow and green vegetables, butter, eggs, and fish oil. Also called *vitamin A. See also* retinene, vitamin.

[From Greek *rhetine* resin + English *-ol* denoting a compound containing a hydroxyl group, from *(alcoh)ol*]

retinotopic map *n.* An inverted *topographic map of the object or scene being viewed with the eyes, with neighbouring cells having *receptive fields close together, in the *lateral geniculate nucleus or in the *primary visual cortex where the neurons are stacked vertically in *ocular-dominance columns and *orientation columns.

[Probably from Latin *rete* a net + Greek *topos* a place + *-ikos* of, relating to, or resembling]

retrieval *n.* The act or process of retrieving anything, especially (in psychology) the act or process of recovering *encoded information from *storage in *memory and bringing it into *consciousness. **retrieve** *vb.*

retroactive association *n.* Another name for a *backward association.

retroactive facilitation *n.* Facilitation or improvement in the learning or performance of a task caused by *positive transfer from training on a different task occurring later in time.

retroactive inhibition *n.* Another name for *retroactive interference.

retroactive interference *n.* Impairment of memory for previously learnt information, or performance of a previously learnt task, caused by subsequent learning of similar information or a similar task. Also called *retroactive inhibition. See also* Ranschburg inhibition, Skaggs–Robinson paradox. *Compare* proactive interference. **RI** *abbrev.*

retroflex *adj.* Of or relating to speech sounds articulated with the tip of the tongue curled back towards the front part of the hard palate behind the *alveolar ridge, as in the *r* sounds in North American English and some *rhotic varieties of British English, especially the south-west of England. *See also* place of articulation.

[From Latin *retroflexus* bent back, from *retro-* back + *flectere* to bend]

retrograde amnesia *n.* Loss of memory for events or experiences before a traumatic event or incident that causes the amnesia. The memories are generally recovered gradually over time, starting with early memories, and the traumatic event itself is often, though not always, recalled eventually. *See also* global amnesia, next-in-line effect, transient global amnesia. *Compare* anterograde amnesia.

[From Latin *retro* behind + *gradus* a step]

retrograde transport *n.* The movement of worn-out components of neurons along *microtubules from *axons and *dendrites back to the cell body or soma for degradation by *lysosomes. *Compare* anterograde transport.

[From Latin *retro* backwards + *gradi* to go]

retrospective falsification *n.* Unconscious alteration or distortion of memories to make them satisfy present wishes or needs.

[From Latin *retro* backwards + *specere, spectum* to look]

retrospective study *n.* A type of research investigation in which participants with a particular disorder or characteristic are recruited and their past histories are examined in an effort to discover the relevant causal factor(s). The findings of such an investigation carry less persuasive force than those of a *prospective study, partly because they rely on the fallible memories of the participants, which may be influenced by their own theories about the causative factors.

retrovirus *n.* Any of a group of viruses, notably *HIV, whose genetic code is carried in *RNA rather than *DNA and is transcribed by *reverse transcriptase into DNA, thereby reversing the normal direction in which it was once thought that genetic information invariably flows. *See also* central dogma. **retroviral** *adj.*

[From *re(verse) tr(anscriptase)* + *virus*]

Rett's disorder n. A *pervasive developmental disorder found only in girls, characterized by the appearance, between 5 months and 4 years of age, of accelerated head growth and *psychomotor retardation, replacement of purposeful hand movements with stereotyped *gestures (1) such as hand-wringing, poorly coordinated gait, withdrawal from social interaction, and impairment in speech and language comprehension.
[Named after the German-born Austrian paediatrician Andreas Rett (1924–97) who first described the disorder in 1965]

return of the repressed n. In *psychoanalysis, the reappearance in *dreams (1), *symptoms, or *parapraxes of material that has been subject to *repression. See also choice of neurosis, compromise formation.

reuptake n. The reabsorption by a *presynaptic neuron of a *neurotransmitter substance recently released from its terminal *bouton, thereby halting the *action potential in the *postsynaptic cell.

revealed preference n. A preference inferred from observations of a decision maker's actual choices. The notion was introduced in 1931 by the English philosopher, mathematician, and economist Frank (Plumpton) Ramsey (1903–30) and later popularized by the US economist Paul Anthony Samuelson (born 1915). It underlies the modern form *utility theory introduced in 1947 by the Hungarian-born US mathematician John von Neumann (1903–57) and the German-born US economist Oskar Morgenstern (1902–77). Consider a woman facing a decision involving several alternatives. We may assign a value of 0 to her least preferred alternative L and 1 to her most preferred alternative M. Then, to determine her degree of preference for another alternative X we may find a gamble involving L and M that she considers equally as attractive as X. For example, she may turn out to be indifferent between X for certain and roll of a die resulting in L if one spot comes up and M if any other number of spots come up, in which case the utility of X according to revealed preference is 5/6 or 0.83 on the scale from 0 to 1. A strong interpretation of revealed preference holds that it is meaningless to assert that a decision maker's choice of X rather than Y can be explained by a preference for X over Y, because the choice literally determines the prefer-

ence, and hence decision makers choose according to their preferences by definition. However, the strong interpretation leads to difficulties in interpreting inconsistent preferences such as those induced by the *Allais paradox or *modified Ellsberg paradox. See also anchoring and adjustment, expected utility theory, subjective utility.

reverberating circuit n. A *cell assembly that continues to respond after the original stimulus that excited it has ceased, providing a neural basis for *short-term memory, according to a hypothesis of the Canadian psychologist Donald O(lding) Hebb (1904–85). Also called a reverberatory circuit. See also phase sequence.

reversal n. **1.** The act or process of turning round. In *psychoanalysis, a *defence mechanism whereby an *instinctual aim changes into its opposite, usually from an active to a passive form, as when *sexual sadism turns to *sexual masochism or *voyeurism to *exhibitionism (1). Also called reversal into the opposite. **2.** Another name for a *reversal error in reading or writing.

reversal error n. An error of reading or writing in which a letter, group of letters, or word is read or written backwards, as when a d is read or written as a b or the word bed is read or written as deb. Also called simply a reversal.

reversal into the opposite See reversal (1).

reversal learning n. Another name for *habit reversal.

reverse tolerance n. Another name for *sensitization.

reverse transcriptase n. An enzyme present in *retroviruses that transcribes information from *RNA into *DNA, thereby reversing the usual direction of transcription of genetic information from DNA to RNA. Compare RNA polymerase.

reversible figure n. Another name for an *ambiguous figure.

reversible goblet n. An *ambiguous figure introduced in 1915 by the Danish psychologist Edgar Rubin (1886–1951), a classic demonstration of *figure–ground reversal, its appearance alternating between a goblet and a pair of facial profiles in silhouette. Also called the *face–goblet illusion* or *Rubin's figure*.

reversible perspective See perspective reversal.

reversion *n.* A turning back, reverse, or recurrence. In genetics, the restoration of a *mutant (2) phenotype to the normal form by a further mutation of the same gene. Also called a *back mutation*.
[From Latin *re-* back + *vertere* to turn + *-ion* indicating an action, process, or state]

rewrite rule *n.* A rule in *generative grammar of the form $A \rightarrow X$, where *A* represents a syntactic category such as a sentence or a noun phrase and *X* a sequence of syntactic categories. The rule expresses an instruction to replace *A* by *X*. For example, a sentence (S) can be rewritten as a noun phrase (NP) plus a verb phrase (VP): $S \rightarrow NP + VP$; and the verb phrase can be rewritten as a verb (V) plus a noun phrase (NP): $VP \rightarrow V + NP$. Also called a *phrase-structure rule*. See also phrase marker.

rhetoric *n.* **1.** The art of persuasive, influential, or entertaining speech or oratory, or the study of effective language use. See also attitude change, persuasion. **2.** Bombastic or mannered speech or writing, or language that seems impressive but lacks true meaning (*the Chinese claims are mere rhetoric*). **rhetorical** *adj.*
[From Greek *rhetor* a teacher of rhetoric + *-ikos* of, relating to, or resembling]

rhetorical question *n.* A question asked for dramatic effect and not requiring an answer.

rheumatic chorea *n.* Another name for *Sydenham's chorea.

rhinencephalon *n.* The olfactory lobe in the *forebrain of each cerebral hemisphere containing the *olfactory bulb, *olfactory tract, and *olfactory cortex, concerned largely with the sense of smell, but in humans also with *emotions. The meaning is sometimes restricted to the olfactory cortex alone and is sometimes taken to be nearly synonymous with the limbic system, which was once believed to be devoted to olfaction.
[From Greek *rhis, rhinos* the nose + *enkephalos* the brain, from *en* in + *kephale* the head]

rhodopsin *n.* The *visual pigment found in *rods in the retina, with peak sensitivity to light of approximately 505 nanometres in the blue–green part of the visible spectrum. Also called *visual purple*, not because it is sensitive to light in the purple part of the spectrum, but on the contrary because it reflects blue and red light and therefore looks purple. See also nyctalopia, opsin, optogram, retinene. Compare cone pigment.
[From Greek *rhodon* a rose + *opsis* sight, from *ops* and eye]

rhombencephalon *n.* A technical name for the *hindbrain, especially in a developing embryo. Compare mesencephalon, prosencephalon.
[From Greek *rhombos* a rhombus (alluding to the shape of the fourth ventricle that it contains) + *enkephalos* the brain, from *en* in + *kephale* the head]

rho (Spearman's) See Spearman rank correlation coefficient.

rhotic *adj.* Denoting an *accent (1) or *dialect in which an *r* following a vowel (as in the words *car* and *cart*) is pronounced. In *Received Pronunciation *r* is pronounced only before a vowel and never before a consonant or a pause; but rhotic pronunciation is found in most varieties of English in the United States and Canada, Ireland, Scotland, and parts of England including the area to the south and west of London. **rhotacism** *n.* Defective or non-standard pronunciation or *r*.
[From the name of the Greek letter *rho*, corresponding to the roman *r* + *-itikos* resembling or marked by]

rhyming method *n.* A memory aid based on rhymes. See under mnemonic.

rhyming slang *n.* A form of *slang characteristic of the *cockney dialect of the East End of London, in which a word is replaced by another word or phrase that rhymes with it, for example, *apples and pears* meaning stairs, *Jimmy Riddle* meaning piddle, *dicky-bird* meaning word, and *boat race* meaning face. In practice, the rhyming part is often dropped, originally to hide the meaning from the uninitiated, so that (for example) *apples* means stairs and *Jimmy* means piddle. Some of the shortened forms have become common words, including as the familiar *loaf* (from *loaf* *of bread*) and the surprisingly offensive *berk* (from *Berkshire hunt*).

rhythm *n.* An ordered arrangement of stressed and unstressed or long and short sounds in speech or music, or any analogous regularly occurring sequence of events, including a *biological rhythm. **rhythmic** or **rhythmical** *adj.*
[From Greek *rhythmos* a measure or measured motion, from *rhein* to flow]

riboflavin *See* vitamin B$_2$.

ribonucleic acid *See* RNA.
[From *ribo(se)* + *nucleic acid*]

ribose *n.* A sugar that occurs in *RNA. *See also* deoxyribose.
[Changed from *arabinose* a sugar found in cedar and pine gum]

ribosome *n.* Any of the tiny particles that are found in abundance in the *cytoplasm of a cell, some being attached to the *endoplasmic reticulum, and that contain *RNA and *protein and are the construction sites where proteins are synthesized according to information carried to them by *messenger RNA.
[From *ribo(nucleic acid)* + Greek *soma* a body]

Ribot's law *n.* The principle that, during *retrograde amnesia, the oldest memories are most resistant to disruption or impairment. *Compare* Jackson's principle.
[Named after the French psychologist Théodule Armand Ribot (1839–1916), who formulated it]

Ricco's law *n.* In *psychophysics, a law relating the *absolute threshold or *difference threshold for visual brightness to the intensity of the stimulus and the area of the retina that is stimulated, usually expressed as $A \times I = k$, where A is the area of the retina stimulated, I is the intensity of the stimulus, and k is a constant. It is valid for small retinal areas centred on the fovea, corresponding to stimuli subtending *visual angles up to about 6 minutes of arc (1/10 of a degree). *Compare* Piper's law.
[Named after the Italian astronomer Annibale Ricco (1844–1911) who formulated it]

Ringelmann effect *n.* Another name for *social loafing.

[Named after the French agricultural engineer Maximilien (Max) Ringelmann (1861–1931) who first investigated the phenomenon in 1882–7]

risk *n.* **1.** Danger or hazard; or a situation or factor involving danger or hazard, or one likely to cause loss or injury. **2.** A situation in which an action will result in an outcome that is not known with certainty, but the set of possible outcomes and their associated probabilities are known or can be estimated. For example, betting on the outcome of the roll of a die involves risk inasmuch as the particular outcome is not known in advance, but the possible outcomes {1, 2, 3, 4, 5, 6} and their associated probabilities (1/6 each) are known. The US economist Frank H. Knight (1885–1972) was the first to distinguish between risk and *uncertainty (2) in his book *Risk, Uncertainty, and Profit* (1921), and the distinction is maintained in careful usage, but many writers use the terms interchangeably. *See also* common ratio effect, Ellsberg paradox, insufficient reason, modified Ellsberg paradox. **risky** *adj.*
[From French *risque* risk, from Italian *risco* danger, from Greek *rhiza* a cliff]

risk aversion *n.* A widespread characteristic of human preferences, first discussed in 1738 by the Swiss mathematician and physicist Daniel Bernoulli (1700–82), according to which most people tend to value gains involving *risk (2) less than certain gains of equivalent monetary expectation. A typical example is a choice between a sure gain of 50 units (Swiss francs, dollars, pounds sterling, or any other units) and a gamble involving a 50 per cent probability of winning 100 units and a 50 per cent probability of winning nothing. The two prospects are of equivalent monetary expected value, but most people prefer the sure gain to the gamble, which they typically value equally to a sure gain of about 35 units. *See also* Allais paradox, certainty effect, framing effect, modified Ellsberg paradox, prospect theory, St Petersburg paradox. *Compare* risk seeking. **risk-averse** *adj.*

risk seeking *n.* A tendency among human decision makers to prefer losses involving risk (2) to sure-thing losses of equivalent monetary expectation. Experiments have shown that human decision makers typically prefer a gamble involving a 50 per cent probability of losing 100 units (such as dollars or pounds) to a sure loss of 50 units, although these two prospects are of equivalent monetary expectation; in fact, people typically value a 50 per cent probability of losing 100 units equally to a sure loss of about 40 units. *See also* framing effect, prospect theory. *Compare* risk aversion. **risk-seeking** *adj*.

risky shift *n*. In decisions involving risk, a tendency for involvement or participation in a group to cause the individual opinions of the group members to change in the direction of greater risk, causing group decisions to be generally riskier than the average of the individual decisions of the participating group members. It was discovered independently in 1957 by the US psychologist Robert Charles Ziller (born 1924) and in 1961 by a US graduate student James (Arthur Finch) Stoner (born 1935), who used quite different methods and who both expected the opposite effect. The finding has been replicated many times and holds true for most decisions involving risk, although dilemmas have been found that reliably produce cautious shifts. It is explained partly by a *social comparison* effect, based on a cultural tendency for people to admire riskiness rather than caution in most circumstances, as a result of which most people like to consider themselves at least as willing to take risks as their peers, but during group discussion some group members discover that others are riskier than themselves, and they therefore alter their opinions in a risky direction to restore their self-images, causing a risky shift in the group decision. A second explanatory mechanism is the *persuasive argumentation* effect, which arises from the same cultural tendency to admire riskiness rather than caution, causing group members to be more willing to voice pro-risk than pro-caution persuasive arguments during the group discussion, resulting in more persuasive arguments in a risky than a cautious direction. Social comparison and persuasive argumentation effects can also explain cautious shifts, and some authorities believe that they can also explain the more general *group polarization phenomenon. Also called a *choice shift*.

risperidone *n*. A *dibenzodiazepine drug belonging to the group of *atypical antipsychotics that acts as a *serotonin and a *dopamine antagonist and is used in the treatment of *schizophrenia with fewer *neu-

roleptic-induced side-effects than are associated with conventional neuroleptic drugs. Also called *Risperdal* (trademark).

Ritalin *n*. A proprietary name for the stimulant drug *methylphenidate.
[Trademark]

ritualized fighting *n*. Another name for *conventional fighting.

r–K continuum *n*. A dimension along which *natural selection is claimed by some *sociobiologists to vary according to ecological conditions, from *r-selection at one extreme to *K-selection at the other. *See also* continuum.

R-methodology *n*. Regular *factor analysis, in which correlations between tests are analysed. Also called *R-technique. Compare* Q-methodology.
[Arbitrary symbol, presumably chosen because it follows Q in the alphabet]

RNA *abbrev*. Ribonucleic acid, a type of *nucleic acid present in all living cells, playing an important part in the synthesis of *proteins within the cells' *ribosomes. Hydrolysis of RNA yields the bases *adenine, *guanine, *cytosine, and *uracil, together with ribose and phosphoric acid (see illustration). *See also* AMP, codon, complementary base pairing, double helix, gene expression, nitrogenous base, nucleotide, polymerase chain reaction, RNA polymerase. *Compare* messenger RNA, transfer RNA.

RNA polymerase *n*. An enzyme that catalyses the synthesis of *RNA from a *DNA template by a process of *transcription (2). Also called *transcriptase* or *RNA transcriptase. See also* polymerase chain reaction. *Compare* DNA polymerase, reverse transcriptase.
[From *RNA* + *polymer* + Greek -*ase* denoting an enzyme, from *diastasis* separation]

RNA transcriptase *n*. Another name for *RNA polymerase.

road rage *n*. A grossly disproportional outburst of aggression by the driver of a motor vehicle in response to a perceived discourtesy or transgression by another road user, sometimes indicative of an *intermittent explosive disorder or other form of *impulse–control disorder.

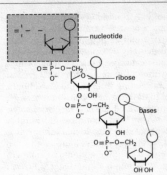

Detail of molecular structure of sugar–phosphate backbone. Each ribose unit is attached to a phosphate group and a base, forming a nucleotide.

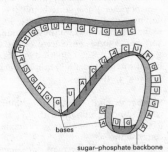

Single-stranded structure of RNA

The four bases of RNA

RNA. Molecular structure.

rocks *n*. A street name for *crack cocaine. [Referring to its appearance]

rod *n*. One of the two major classes of *photoreceptors at the back of the *retina, absent from the *fovea, long and cylindrical in shape, with an outer segment at its back end containing photosensitive membranes arranged like an orderly stack of discs studded with light-absorbing pigment molecules of *rhodopsin and a synaptic ending at the other end transmitting nerve impulses to *bipolar cells and *horizontal cells in the retina. A rod is totally unresponsive to colour; it mediates *scotopic vision, functioning only in dim light, and is extremely sensitive, being capable of excitation by a single *photon. The human retina contains some 120 million rods, far outnumbering the 6 million retinal

cones. *See also* dark adaptation, photochromatic interval. *Compare* cone.

rod-and-frame test *n*. A test of *field dependence–independence in which the respondent, seated in a completely darkened room, attempts to adjust a luminous rod to a vertical position within a tilted luminous frame. Field-dependent people are more strongly influenced by the frame and less able to discount it in judging the upright. *Compare* tilting-room test. **RFT** *abbrev*.

rod pigment *n*. Rhodopsin.

Rogerian *adj*. Of, relating to, or resembling the *client-centred therapy of the US psychologist Carl Rogers (1902–87).

Rohypnol *n*. A proprietary name for *fluni-trazepam, a benzodiazepine drug approximately ten times as potent as Valium, that when taken orally induces within 15 minutes slight nausea, dizziness, and a form of drowsiness and immobility resembling mild general anaesthesia lasting from two to eight hours. It is used in the treatment of insomnia, and it is sometimes called the *date rape drug* on account of having been implicated in a number of incidents of rape and sexual assault: it is tasteless, odourless, and colourless and can easily be used to spike a potential rape victim's drink without her knowledge; all traces of it disappear from the bloodstream within 36 hours; and people who take it with alcohol generally experience amnesia lasting at least 12 hours. It is sometimes taken as a street drug, and its most common street name is *roofies*.
[Trademark]

rok-joo *See* koro.

Rolandic fissure *n*. Another name for the *central sulcus. Also written *Rolando's fissure*.
[Named after the Italian anatomist Luigi Rolando (1773–1831)]

Role Construct Repertory Test *n*. Another name for the *Repertory Grid Test when the elements presented to the respondent are role titles such as *A teacher you liked*, *Your mother*, *A neighbour with whom you get along well*, and so on. Its inventor, the US psychologist George A(lexander) Kelly (1905–66), listed 24 role titles, including the three quoted here, in the original publication of the test in his book *The Psychology of Personal Constructs* (1955, Vol. 1, pp. 221–2).

rolfing *n*. A technique of *psychotherapy based on body manipulation and massage, using fingers, knuckles, and elbows, designed to correct postural faults and to realign the body vertically and symmetrically. Also written *Rolfing*. *See also* body therapies.
[Named after the US physiotherapist Ida P. Rolf (1897–1979) who invented and promoted it from the 1970s]

romantic love *n*. A type of love characterized by erotic passion and intimacy but lacking commitment. *See under* love.

romantic love scale *n*. A questionnaire designed to measure romantic *love, defined in terms of three components labelled affiliative/dependent needs (needing to be with the loved person), predispositions to help (willingness to make sacrifices for the loved person), and exclusivity (desire to be intimately involved with the loved person to the exclusion of others), the scale being specifically designed to distinguish romantic love from liking, which is measured by the *liking scale. Both scales were constructed by the US psychologist Zick Rubin (born 1944) and published in the *Journal of Personality and Social Psychology* in 1970.

Romberg's sign *n*. Swaying or falling over when standing upright with eyes shut and feet together; a sign of *sensory ataxia or *locomotor ataxia.
[Named after the German pathologist and neurologist Moritz Heinrich Romberg (1795–1873) who gave the first clinical description of *locomotor ataxia (tabes dorsalis)]

roofies *n*. A street name for the benzodiazepine drug *Rohypnol, the date rape drug.

rooting reflex *n*. A reflex in which a newborn infant responds to being touched or stroked on the cheek by turning its head towards the stimulated side and making sucking movements. The reflex usually disappears at around 3 or 4 months of age but can persist until 12 months.
[From Old English *wrotan* to burrow with the snout, from *wrot* a snout]

root language *n*. Another name for an *isolating language.

rootwork *n*. A *culture-bound syndrome found in the Caribbean and among African American and Latino communities in the southern United States, where it is generally attributed to witchcraft, sorcery, or hexing, characterized by *anxiety, gastrointestinal complaints such as nausea, vomiting, and diarrhoea, weakness, dizziness, and fear of being poisoned or killed, the symptoms generally persisting unless the spell is removed by a healer called a *root doctor*. Also called *mal puesto* or *brujeria* in Spanish-speaking communities. *Compare* voodoo death.
[From Old English *rot* a root, from Old Norse *rot* a root]

Rorschach test *n*. A *projective test consisting of ten symmetric ink blots varying in shape and colour. The respondent examines each one in turn and interprets it by saying what it looks like. The test is designed to yield information about unconscious mental processes. It was developed in 1911 and published in 1921 in a book entitled *Psychodiagnostik* (Psychodiagnostics) by the Swiss psychiatrist Hermann Rorschach (1884–1922). Rorschach was not the first to experiment with the interpretation of ink blots, his most famous forerunner having been the Italian polymath Leonardo da Vinci (1452–1519). *See also* Holtzman Inkblot Technique.

Rosencrantz and Guildenstern effect *n*. A type of *approach–avoidance conflict and entrapment experienced by a person who is kept waiting while attempting to achieve a particular goal, as when a person waiting at a bus stop faces the choice of waiting or walking but as time passes feels increasingly unwilling to leave the bus stop because of the increasing likelihood that a bus will arrive. In such situations, time is simultaneously an investment that increases the likelihood of goal attainment and an expense that increases the likelihood of failing to attain the goal, and as time passes, the conflict increases.
[Named after the following passage in the play *Rosencrantz and Guildenstern are Dead* (1967) by the Czechoslovakian-born British playwright Tom Stoppard (born 1937): 'We've travelled too far, and our momentum has taken over; we move idly towards eternity, without possibility of reprieve or hope of explanation.']

Rosenthal effect *n*. Another name for the *experimenter expectancy effect.
[Named after the German-born US psychologist Robert Rosenthal (born 1933) who pioneered research on it]

Rosenzweig Picture-Frustration Study *n*. A *projective test, designed to measure characteristic modes of responding to frustration, in which the respondent is presented with 24 cartoon drawings, each depicting one person saying something frustrating to the other, the second person being shown with a blank speech bubble. The respondent's task is to fill in each of the 24 blank speech bubbles with the first response that comes to mind, and from the responses the direction of aggression (directed inwards, directed outwards, or

repressed) and type of aggression, including obstacle-dominance (frustrating objects stand out), ego-defence (the respondent's ego predominates to protect itself), and need-persistence (the respondent pursues goals despite frustration) are scored. In addition, a group conformity rating is provided, indicating how closely the responses resemble the most common responses or population norms. **RPFS** *abbrev*.
[Named after the US psychologist Saul Rosenzweig (born 1907) who published early accounts of research using the test in the *Journal of Experimental Psychology* in 1943 and the *Journal of Personality* in 1945 and adult and child versions of the test itself in 1948]

Ross–Jones test *n*. A test for excess of globulin in the *cerebrospinal fluid. Cerebrospinal fluid is floated on a solution of ammonium sulphate, and globulin forms a greyish-white ring at the junction of the two liquids, the width of the ring providing an index of excess of globulin.
[Named after the Scottish pathologist Hugh Campbell Ross (1875–1926) and the Welsh psychoanalyst Ernest Jones (1879–1958) who introduced it]

rostral *adj*. Of, relating to, or situated towards the *anterior end or side of a body, organ, or part; or, in the human brain, towards the top, as if humans walked on all fours like other animals. *Compare* caudal.
[From Latin *rostrum* a beak]

rostrum *n*. **1.** Any beak or beak-shaped structure, such as the rostrum of the *corpus callosum, the front tip below the genu. **2.** A platform for public speaking, named after the *rostrum* of the Roman forum, which was festooned with beaks plundered from the bows of captured ships.
[From Latin *rostrum* a beak]

rotating head illusion *n*. A visual illusion in which a two-dimensional painting or photograph of a head (or of any three-dimensional object) appears to rotate in the same direction as a viewer who moves in front of it from one side to the other. The illusion results from the fact that if the head were three-dimensional, then the viewer, moving from side to side, would see it first from one side, then from the front, then finally from the other side, as if the head were rotating in the opposite direction, and the head would appear stationary, therefore with a two-dimensional painting or photograph, the absence of any apparent contrary rotation causes the head to appear to rotate in the same direction as the viewer, and the sitter's *gaze seems to follow the viewer around. Also called the *portrait illusion*.

rotation *n*. Application of any of several statistical techniques in *factor analysis for making a factor solution easier to interpret by rotating the axes of the factor loadings to achieve a simple or meaningful structure. *See* simple structure.

rotation, mental *See* mental rotation.

rote learning *n*. Memorization through repetition and reproduction without attention to meaning. In psychology, the term is applied especially to the learning of inherently meaningless information such as *nonsense syllables.
[Perhaps from Latin *rota* a wheel]

rote memory *n*. Mechanical memory based on *rote learning.

Rotter Incomplete Sentences Blank *n*. A *sentence completion test designed to measure psychological adjustment, available in three forms (high school, college, and adult), each consisting of 40 truncated sentences, such as *I hate . . .* ; *The best . . .* ; and *Most girls. . . .* It is scored for conflict, positive responses, and neutral responses, from which an overall adjustment score is calculated. **RISB** *abbrev*.
[Named after the US psychologist Julian B(ernard) Rotter (born 1916) who published the earliest version of it in the journal *American Psychologist* in 1946 and, with two colleagues, issued a revised version commercially in 1992]

rough endoplasmic reticulum *See under* endoplasmic reticulum. **RER** *abbrev*.

round dance *n*. One of two patterns of movement, first described by the Austrian zoologist Karl von Frisch (1886–1982) in a series of publications from 1924 to 1955, through which a female honey-bee communicates to other members of her hive the direction and distance of a source of nectar or sometimes a new nesting site less than a certain distance away—

Round dance

less than about 5–80 metres away, depending on the bee species or subspecies—the more elaborate and specific *waggle dance being reserved for targets further away. In the round dance, the bee moves in circles on a (usually) vertical surface of the honeycomb, alternating clockwise and anticlockwise, the liveliness and length of her dance indicating how rich the food source is (see illustration). Also called a *circling dance*.
[Translated from von Frisch's German *Rundtanz* literally round dance, from *rund* round + *Tanz* a dance]

round window *n*. An opening in the wall of the middle ear leading to the cochlea, covered by a membrane, functioning to reduce pressure caused by vibration of the *oval window. Also called the *cochlear window*, *fenestra cochleae* or *fenestra rotunda*.
[So called because of its circular shape]

r-selection *n*. A form of *natural selection that is typical of organisms in relatively unstable, variable, and unpredictable ecological conditions in which rapid population growth is crucial, and that is characterized by fast development, small size, early reproduction, perfunctory parental care, limited learning capacity, and generally opportunistic behaviour. *See also* r–K continuum. *Compare* K-selection. **r-selected** *adj*. Selected for superiority in environments favouring r-selection.

R squared *n*. In statistics, the square of the *multiple correlation coefficient. *See* coefficient of determination. Symbol: R^2.

Rubin's figure *n*. Another name for the *reversible goblet.

[Named after the Danish psychologist Edgar Rubin (1886–1951) who introduced it in 1915]

rubrospinal tract *n*. A bundle of efferent nerve fibres connecting the *red nucleus to the *spinal cord.

[From Latin *ruber* red + English *spinal*]

Ruffini corpuscle *n*. An oval-shaped sensory nerve ending in subcutaneous tissue of hairy *skin and near fingernails, similar in structure to a *Golgi tendon organ, sensitive to drag or shearing stress. Also called a *Ruffini ending*. *Compare* free nerve ending, Meissner's corpuscle, Merkel cell, Pacinian corpuscle.

[Named after the Italian histologist Angelo Ruffini (1864–1929) who discovered it and published his findings in 1892]

rule of abstinence *See* abstinence rule.

rumination disorder *n*. An *eating disorder of infancy or (less often) early childhood characterized by a persistent pattern of repeated regurgitation, chewing, and swallowing or spitting out of partly digested food, without apparent nausea, retching, or disgust, the behaviour not occurring as a result of *anorexia nervosa, *bulimia nervosa or a gastrointestinal or other medical condition.

[From Latin *ruminare* to chew the cud, from *rumen* the gullet]

rumour *n*. An unverified story or report circulating in a community, usually by word of mouth. It tends to focus on people or events about which there is interest or concern but not much concrete evidence, and as it is propagated, it undergoes the same processes of *assimilation (5), *levelling (1), and *sharpening as are found in other forms of *serial reproduction. US *rumor*. *See also* rumour intensity formula, urban legend.

[From Latin *rumor* noise]

rumour intensity formula *n*. A proposition formulated by the US psychologists Gordon W(illard) Allport (1897–1967) and Leo (Joseph) Postman (born 1918) in their book *The Psychology of Rumor* (1947) that the strength of a *rumour depends on its importance multiplied by the difficulty of falsifying it. US *rumor intensity formula*.

Rumpelstiltskin phenomenon *n*. The tendency for the naming of something to create the impression of imparting an understanding of it. It applies, for example, to the naming of mental disorders: a person who tells implausible lies may be said to be suffering from *pseudologia fantastica, but that term is nothing more than a name for implausible lying, and any impression that it imparts an understanding of the phenomenon is a *cognitive illusion.

[Named after Rumpelstiltskin in a famous fairly tale, called Rumpelstilzchen in the German version collected by the brothers Grimm, a strange dwarf who exerts a baleful influence over a miller's daughter until she eventually gains power over him by learning his name]

run *n*. The act or process of running, or a journey, trip, or spell. In statistics, any succession of observations of one specified type in an ordered sequence of observations, preceded and followed by observations of a different type or by no observations at all. For example, a succession of heads in a sequence of coin tosses is a run, and so is a succession of failures in a sequence of trials of a treatment. *See also* runs test.

runs test *n*. In statistics, a test of the randomness of an ordered sequence of binary or dichotomous observations, in which the number of *runs expected on the basis of chance is calculated and compared with the observed number of runs. Also called the *Wald–Wolfowitz runs test*.

Russell's paradox *n*. The most famous *paradox of *set theory. Some sets are members of themselves and others are not: for example, the set of all sets is a member of itself, because it is a set, whereas the set of all penguins is not, because it is not a penguin. Now consider the set of all sets that are not members of themselves; is it a member of itself or is it not? If it is a member of itself, then it is not a member of itself, because it is one of those that are not members of themselves; and if it is not a member of itself, then it is a member of itself. It was discovered in 1901 by the Welsh philosopher Bertrand (Arthur William) Russell (1872–1970), and it undermined the attempt by the German logician and mathematician Friedrich Ludwig Gottlob Frege

(1848–1925) to derive the whole of arithmetic from logic via set theory. When the second volume of Frege's monumental *Grundgesetze der Arithmetik* was in press, he received a letter from Russell describing the paradox; he replied that 'arithmetic totters' and was forced to add an appendix to the book explaining why the ambitious project had to be abandoned. Russell's paradox is closely related to the *barber's paradox.

saccade *n.* A rapid *ballistic movement of the eyes, lasting 20 to 100 milliseconds, as they jump from one fixation point to the next when reading or tracking a moving object or image. A *microsaccade is a small saccade occurring as part of *physiological nystagmus during visual fixation of a stationary object. *See also* autokinetic effect, feedforward, visual suppression. *Compare* smooth eye movement. **saccadic** *adj.*
[French *saccade* a jerk, from Old French *saquer* to pull]

saccadic suppression *n.* Another name for *visual suppression.

saccule *n.* A small sac, especially the smaller of the two sections of the *membranous labyrinth of the inner ear that functions as an *otolith receptor in the *vestibular system. **saccular** *adj. Compare* utricle.
[From Latin *sacculus* a little sac, diminutive of *saccus* a sack]

sadism *n.* Another name for *sexual sadism. The term is also used loosely to denote extreme cruelty not motivated by sexual desire. *See also* oral sadistic phase. **sadistic** *adj.*
[Named after the French writer Comte Donatien François de Sade (1740–1814), also known as Marquis de Sade, who described it in his novels, notably *Les 120 Journées de Sodome* (1785, The 120 Days of Sodom) and *Juliette* (1796)]

sadistic–anal stage *n.* Another name for the *anal sadistic stage. *See* anal stage.

sadistic–oral phase *See* oral sadistic phase.

sadomasochism *n.* A generic name for *sexual sadism and *sexual masochism, alluding to the fact that they are often combined in the same person. **sadomasochistic** *adj.* **SM** *abbrev.*

sagittal plane *n.* The vertical plane dividing the body, the brain, or any other organ into left and right parts, the *midsagittal plane* (also called the *median plane*) dividing the structure along its midline. *Compare* coronal plane, horizontal plane, transverse plane.
[From Latin *sagitta* an arrow]

sagittal section *n.* A cutting through a *sagittal plane. The midsagittal section (also called the *median section*) of the brain passes through the *longitudinal fissure and exposes the *medial surfaces of the cerebral hemispheres. *Compare* coronal section, horizontal section, transverse section.

sagittal suture *n.* The serrated line along the middle of the top of the skull where the left and right *parietal bones join together.

Saint John's wort *See* St John's wort.

Saint Vitus' dance *n.* A disorder of the motor nerves leading to jerky, *choreiform movements of the limbs and face; also an obsolete name for *Sydenham's chorea.
[So called because of an early confusion with *tarantism in pilgrims to the shrine of St Vitus at Ulm]

saka *See* ufufunyane.

salience *n.* **1.** The protruding or jutting-out property of a physical structure; hence figuratively the prominence, conspicuousness, or striking quality of a *stimulus (1). **2.** In relation to animal behaviour, leaping. **salient** *adj.*
[From Latin *saliens* leaping, from *salire* to leap]

salivary gland *n.* Any of the *exocrine glands that secrete saliva into the oral or mouth cavity. Human salivary glands include the parotid glands in front and below each ear, the sublingual gland below the tongue, and the submaxillary glands below each side of the jaw.

saltation *n.* **1.** The manner in which a nerve impulse is propagated along a *myelinated nerve fibre in a sequence of jumps from one *node of Ranvier to the next, greatly increasing its speed of propagation. Also called *saltatory conduction.* **2.** A sudden variation in the structure or behaviour of an organism, species, or subspecies resulting from genetic *mutation. **3.** Another name for *sensory saltation.
[From Latin *saltus* a leap, from *saltare* to dance + *-ation* indicating a process or condition]

salty *n.* One of the primary tastes in *Henning's tetrahedron, the characteristic taste of sodium chloride or table salt.

sample *n.* In research methods and statistics, a number of individuals selected from a *population to test hypotheses about the population or to derive estimates of its *parameters. *See* accidental sample, cluster sample, convenience sample, hold-out sample, nonprobability sample, opportunity sample, probability sample, quota sample, random digit dialling, self-selected sample, simple random sample, snowball sample, stratified random sample.
[From Latin *exemplum* an example]

sample size fallacy *n.* A failure to take account of sample size when estimating the probability of obtaining a particular value in a sample drawn from a known population. Research into the fallacy was first reported by the Israeli psychologists Daniel Kahneman (born 1934) and Amos Tversky (1937–96) in an article in the journal *Cognitive Psychology* in 1972 describing an experiment in which participants were asked to estimate the probability of a group of people having an average height over 6 feet. The participants produced almost identical estimates for group sizes of 10, 100, and 1,000, whereas in reality the probability of an unusually high sample average, relative to the population average, is much greater in a small sample than in a large one. The fallacy is explained by the use of the *representativeness heuristic, which is insensitive to sample size. The most common form of the fallacy is the tendency to assume that small samples should be representative of their parent populations, the *gambler's fallacy being

a special case of this phenomenon. *Compare* base-rate fallacy.

sampling frame *n.* A list of members of a *population from which members of a *sample are selected, especially when a *simple random sample (SRS) is drawn.

Sander parallelogram *n.* A visual illusion in which the long diagonal of a parallelogram appears much longer than that of a smaller parallelogram contiguous to it, one of the large parallelogram's short sides forming one of the long sides of the smaller parallelogram and the two long diagonals being of equal length (see illustration). Also called the *parallelogram illusion.*
[Named after the German Gestalt psychologist Friedrich Sander (1889–1971) by one of his students, who published it in 1926, although it had already been published by the US lighting engineer and psychologist Matthew Luckiesh (1883–1967) in his book *Visual Illusions: Their Causes, Characteristics and Applications* (1922, p. 58) and should arguably be called the Luckiesh illusion]

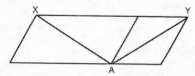

Sander parallelogram. The distances AX and AY are equal.

sangue dormido *n.* A *culture-bound syndrome largely confined to Portuguese-speaking Cape Verde islanders and emigrant Cape Verde communities in other parts of the world, the symptoms of which may include muscle and joint pain, numbness, trembling, paralysis, convulsions, stroke, blindness, heart attack, and (among pregnant women) miscarriage.
[From Spanish *sangue* blood, from Latin *sanguis* blood + Spanish *dormido* sleeping, from Latin *dormire* to sleep]

Sanson image *n.* Another name for a *Purkinje–Sanson image.
[So called because it was investigated in 1838 by the French surgeon Louis Joseph Sanson (1790–1841), having been first observed in

1825 by the Czech-born German physiologist Johannes E(vangelista) Purkinje (1787–1869)]

sapid *adj*. Tastable; in non-technical discourse also tasty or pleasant-tasting.
[From Latin *sapidus* tastable, from *sapere* to taste]

Sapir–Whorf hypothesis *n*. The two-pronged theory that language determines the way people perceive the world and think, rather than the other way round (*see* linguistic determinism), and that people who speak different languages perceive reality and think differently, because categories and distinctions encoded in one language are not necessarily available in another (*see* linguistic relativity). Also called the *Whorfian hypothesis*. *See also* polyonymy.
[Named after the US anthropologist Edward Sapir (1884–1939) and the US fire prevention officer and linguist Benjamin Lee Whorf (1897–1943) who formulated it in the 1920s]

sapphism *n*. A less common name for *lesbianism. **sapphic** *adj*.
[Named after the lyric poet Sappho (born about 650 BC) who lived on the Greek island of Lesbos and expressed love for women in many of her poems]

sarcomere *n*. Any of the transverse segments of *striped muscle tissue, situated between two *Z-discs, that comprise an integrated contractile unit.
[From Greek *sarx, sarcos* flesh + *meros* a part]

sarin *n*. The *organophosphate, *anticholinesterase, *nerve gas isopropyl methylphosphonofluoridate. Formula: $C_4H_{10}FPO_2$.
[German, origin unknown]

Saroten *n*. A proprietary name for the tricyclic antidepressant drug *amitriptyline.
[Trademark]

SAS *abbrev*. Statistical Analysis System, a suite of statistical computer programs often used by psychologists, distributed by SAS Inc. of Cary, North Carolina, USA. *Compare* BMDP, SPSS, SYSTAT.

satellite cell *n*. A type of *neuroglial cell that forms round a damaged cell.
[From Latin *satelles* an attendant]

satiety centre *n*. One of the two structures of the *appestat, situated in each side of the *ventromedial hypothalamus, stimulation of which inhibits eating and destruction increases eating. US *satiety center*. *Compare* feeding centre.

satisficing *n*. A decision making procedure or cognitive *heuristic that entails searching through the available options just long enough to find one that reaches a preset threshold of acceptability, first suggested by the US economist and decision theorist Herbert A(lexander) Simon (1916–2001), in his book *Models of Man: Social and Rational* (1957), to explain the behaviour of human decision makers with *bounded rationality in circumstances in which an optimal solution cannot be determined, often because a thorough examination of all available options would be required but would be infeasible or would consume too much time and energy. Thus a newly married couple looking for a house to buy may accept the first one they find that satisfies certain minimal requirements of price, location, number of rooms, and local amenities; human chess players also usually adopt satisficing moves because it is impossible to analyse all available moves in a typical chess position; and firms often seek satisfactory rather than optimum level of profits and growth. *See also* psychological decision theory. **satisfice** *vb*. **satisficer** *n*. One who *satisfices.
[A blend of *satis(factory)* and *(suf)ficing*, because it involves the choice of options that are satisfactory or that suffice]

saturation *n*. **1**. The amount of *chroma in a colour as a proportion of all the colour, both *chromatic (1) and *achromatic (1), the admixture of grey causing the colour to appear *desaturated*. It is one of the three major dimensions of colour, the other two being *hue and *lightness. The *Munsell chroma scale of saturation ranges from grey (zero) to the most saturated level (14). *See also* chromaticity, Munsell colour system. **2**. In *log-linear analysis, the state of a model that contains all main effects and interactions and in which observed and expected frequencies are therefore equal. **3**. More generally, the state or quality of being soaked or imbued with something to the fullest extent possible.
[From Latin *saturare, -atum* to soak, from *satur* full or sated, from *satis* enough + *-ation* indicating a process or condition]

satyriasis n. A psychological condition of men characterized by uncontrollable sexual desire and an inability to have lasting sexual relationships. Referred to non-technically as *Don Juanism. Compare* nymphomania.
[From Greek *satyros* one of the Greek gods of the woodlands who chase the nymphs]

savings, method of *See* method of savings.

saxitoxin n. A *neurotoxin that is produced by plankton in reddish discoloured sea water and that selectively blocks *sodium channels in neurons, disabling their ability to generate nerve impulses, used as a neurotoxin in experimental neurophysiology. *See also* neurotoxin. **STX** *abbrev.*
[Named after *Saxi(domus) (gigantus)* an Alaskan clam that feeds on it and from which it is isolated + *toxin* poison, from Greek *toxikon* arrow-poison, from *toxon* a bow]

Sayre's law n. Another name for *Issawi's law of social motion.
[Named after the US political scientist Wallace Stanley Sayre (1905–72) who formulated it but did not publish it]

scala n. Any of the three fluid-filled chambers separated by membranes that run through the length of the *cochlea of the inner ear. *See* scala media, scala tympani, scala vestibuli. **scalae** *pl.*
[From Latin *scala* a ladder or staircase, alluding to the cochlea's resemblance to a spiral staircase]

scala media n. A *cochlear chamber bounded by the *organ of Corti and *Reissner's membrane and containing *endolymph.

scala tympani n. A *cochlear chamber lying below the *basilar membrane and containing *perilymph.

scala vestibuli n. A *cochlear chamber situated on the opposite side of Reissner's membrane to the *organ of Corti and containing perilymph.

scale n. 1. In statistics and measurement theory, a rule governing the relationship between numerical scores and the magnitudes of the *attributes or quantities being measured. *See also* absolute scale, interval scale, log-interval scale, measurement level, nomi-

nal scale, ordinal scale, ratio scale. **2.** A test or measuring instrument for implementing a *scale (1). **scaling** n. The development or construction of *scales (1, 2), often by aggregating or ordering responses of individuals.
[From Latin *scala* a ladder, from *scandare* to climb]

scalogram analysis n. The method used to construct a *Guttman scale.

SCAN *abbrev.* Schedules for Clinical Assessment in Neuropsychiatry, a set of instruments and manuals for assessing, measuring, and accurately classifying the *signs (1) and *symptoms of adult mental disorders, with the objective of facilitating valid comparisons across research investigations, published by the World Health Organization in 1994. Its major components are the *Present State Examination (PSE), an *Item Group Checklist (IGC), a *Clinical History Schedule (CHS), and *Catego, a computer software package for processing SCAN data.

scanning speech n. Abnormal speech characterized by staccato articulation, with words clipped and broken into detached syllables with pauses between them, caused by neuromuscular disorder.

scatter n. In descriptive statistics, the degree of dispersion or variability in a set of scores, usually indexed by the *variance or *standard deviation. *See also* interquartile range, probable error, range, semi-interquartile range.

scatterplot n. In statistics, a graph of the relationship between two variables consisting of unconnected points representing individuals or cases, with the horizontal axis usually representing the individuals' scores on one variable and the vertical axis the scores on the other variable. A scatterplot is often useful when the *correlation between two variables is being investigated. Also called a *scatter diagram* or a *scattergram*.

schedule of reinforcement *See* reinforcement schedule.

Scheffé test n. In statistics, a method of *multiple comparisons that can be used for making not only pairwise comparisons but all possible linear combinations of group means. For pairwise comparisons of means it tends to be conservative, inasmuch as it requires larger differences between means for significance than some other methods. *Compare* Bonferroni correction, Duncan's multiple range test, least-significant difference test, Newman–Keuls test, Tukey-HSD test. [Named after the US mathematician Henry Scheffé (1907–77) who developed it in 1959]

schema *n.* A plan, diagram, or outline, especially a mental representation of some aspect of experience, based on prior experience and memory, structured in such a way as to facilitate (and sometimes to distort) perception, cognition, the drawing of inferences, or the interpretation of new information in terms of existing knowledge. The term was first used in a psychological sense by the English neurologist Sir Henry Head (1861–1940), who restricted its meaning to a person's internal *body image, and it was given its modern meaning by the English psychologist Sir Frederic Charles Bartlett (1886–1969) in his book *Remembering: A Study in Experimental and Social psychology* (1932, p. 199) to account for the observation that errors in the recall of stories tend to make them more conventional, which Bartlett attributed to the *assimilation (5) of the stories to pre-existing schemata. The concept of a *frame (2), introduced in 1975 by the US cognitive scientist Marvin (Lee) Minsky (born 1927), is essentially a schema formalized in *artificial intelligence. A *script (3) is a schema of an event sequence. *See also* causal schema, constructivism, perceptual schema, scheme, self-schema, War of the Ghosts. *Compare* mental model, prototype (2). **schemata** or **schemas** *pl.*
[From Greek *schema* a form, from *echein* to have]

scheme *n.* In the writings of the Swiss psychologist Jean Piaget (1896–1980), a concept almost synonymous with *schema but restricted to conscious cognitive representations and plans.

schizoaffective disorder *n.* A *mental disorder characterized by a *major depressive episode, a *manic episode, or a *mixed episode, together with the symptoms of *schizophrenia.

schizoid personality *n.* A concept introduced in 1963 by the Scottish psychoanalyst W. Ronald D. Fairbairn (1889–1964) to denote a type of person who may be outwardly success-ful but is solitary, withdrawn, and unable to relate to people, and even when interacting gives nothing to the other person. Fairbairn linked this to a failure of the person's mother to treat the child as real or to love it for its own sake. *See also* schizoid personality disorder.

schizoid personality disorder *n.* A *personality disorder characterized by a pervasive detachment from social relationships and a restricted range of emotional expression, indicated by such signs and symptoms as a lack of desire for or enjoyment of close relationships; almost exclusive choice of solitary pursuits; little or no interest in having sexual relationships; enjoyment of few activities; lack of close friends or confidants other than immediate family members; apparent indifference to praise and criticism; and emotional coldness, detachment, and *affective flattening. *See also* schizoid personality. *Compare* Asperger's disorder, avoidant personality disorder, schizophrenia, schizotypal personality disorder.

schizophrenia *n.* A major *mental disorder, formerly called *dementia praecox*, characterized by *positive symptoms such as *delusions, *hallucinations, *disorganized speech, grossly disorganized behaviour, or *catatonia; *negative symptoms such as *affective flattening, *alogia, or *avolition; and marked deterioration in work, social relations, or self-care. Associated features include inappropriate *affect, *anhedonia, *dysphoric mood, lack of *insight (3), *depersonalization, and *derealization. Because of its etymology (see below), schizophrenia is often confused with multiple personality disorder or split personality (*dissociative identity disorder), but the Swiss psychiatrist Eugen Bleuler (1857–1939), who coined the term, meant it to refer to the splitting up or disintegrating of the mental functions rather than the cleaving in two of the mind. On page 5 of his book *Dementia praecox oder Gruppe der Schizophrenien* (1911, p. 8 of the English translation *Dementia Praecox or the Group of Schizophrenias*, 1950), he explained: 'I call dementia praecox "schizophrenia" because . . . the "splitting" of the different psychic functions is one of its most important characteristics'. *See also* catatonic schizophrenia, delusional disorder, disorganized schizophrenia, double bind, paranoid schizophrenia, reality monitoring, reality testing, residual schizophrenia, schizoaffective disorder, schizophrenia scale, undifferentiated schizophrenia. *Compare* schizoid personality, schizophreniform disorder, schizotypal personality disorder.

[From Greek *schizein* to split + *phren* mind, originally midriff, the supposed seat of the soul + -*ia* indicating a condition or quality]

schizophrenia scale *n.* Any scale designed to measure schizophrenia, including the schizophrenia scale of the *MMPI.

schizophreniform disorder *n.* A *mental disorder with the same features as *schizophrenia, but lasting for only a short time, usually more than one month but less than six months.

[From *schizophreni(a)* + *form*, from Latin *forma* a form]

schizophrenogenic *adj.* Tending to cause schizophrenia. The word has been used especially to describe mothers or parents who create *double binds for their children.

schizotypal personality disorder *n.* A *personality disorder characterized by behavioural eccentricities and anomalies of cognition and affect that resemble those of *schizophrenia, notably marked discomfort with, and reduced capacity for, close personal relationships together with cognitive or perceptual distortions and eccentric behaviour, beginning by early childhood, indicated by such signs and symptoms as *ideas of reference (but not *delusions of reference); odd beliefs or magical thinking (such as superstitions and beliefs in telepathy or clairvoyance); unusual perceptual experiences; strange speech and thinking; *paranoid ideation; inappropriate *affect or *affective flattening; eccentric or peculiar appearance or behaviour; absence of close friends; and excessive social anxiety that does not decline with intimacy. *Compare* schizoid personality disorder, schizophrenia.

Scholastic Aptitude Test *n.* The most widely used test for selecting candidates for admission to colleges and universities in the US. Its subtests include a verbal and a mathematical aptitude test and an achievement test in each academic subject. *Compare* American College Testing Program. **SAT** *abbrev.*

school psychology *n.* The name given in the US to the field of *applied psychology that in

the UK is called *educational psychology. The work of school psychologists involves the diagnosis and treatment of educational, emotional, and behavioural problems in children of all ages up to the late teens.

Schreber case *n.* A virtuosic *case study in *psychoanalysis by Sigmund Freud (1856–1939), entitled 'Psycho-Analytic Notes on an Autobiographical Account of a Case of Paranoia (Dementia Paranoides)' (1911, *Standard Edition*, XII, pp. 9–82), based on the memoirs of the German magistrate Daniel Paul Schreber (1842–1911). Freud sought to explain why the particular *delusions found in paranoia (now called *delusional disorder) are delusions of jealousy, *erotomania (1), persecution, and grandeur, rather than any others, and he concluded that the following unconscious homosexual wish-fantasy underlies paranoia in a man: *I (a man) love him (a man)*. Homosexuality being socially taboo, the man with paranoia distorts the wish-fantasy into a more acceptable form. First, he may alter the grammatical subject of the wish-fantasy by *projection (1), yielding *It is not I, but she (my sexual partner), who loves him*, and delusions of jealousy arise. Second, he may alter the object of the sentence by *displacement: *I don't love a man, because I love women*. This is still unacceptable to a Victorian married man, so it is distorted further by projection into *Women love me*, and delusions of erotomania arise. Third, the verb may be altered by *reversal (1): *I do not love a man, I hate men*, and this may be changed by projection into the more acceptable form *Men hate me*, yielding delusions of persecution. Finally, he may deny the whole sentence: *I don't love a man, because I love no one*; but for *economic reasons *object libido cannot simply disappear but is diverted into *ego libido, so this is equivalent to *I love no one but myself*, yielding delusions of grandeur. If the person with paranoia is female, then the whole chain of argument applies with the gender terms reversed. The reason for the particular group of delusions found in paranoia was thus explained by Freud. *See also* latent homosexuality.

Schröder staircase *n.* An *ambiguous figure appearing as a staircase viewed either from above or below, a classic illustration of *perspective reversal (see illustration). Also spelt *Schroeder staircase*. Often confused with the *staircase illusion.

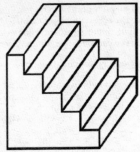

Schröder staircase. The perspective alternates spontaneously between views of a staircase as seen from above and from below.

[Named after the German bacteriologist and psychologist Heinrich G. F. Schröder (1810–85) who first published it in 1858]

schwa *n.* The neutral and central mid *vowel (see also the diagram accompanying that entry) that occurs in the words *the* and *fern*, at the beginning of *about*, and at the end of *sofa*, and the symbol in the *International Phonetic Alphabet (IPA) that represents it, namely an inverted *e*. Statistically, it is the most frequently occurring English vowel (over ten per cent of all vowel sounds), yet it has no corresponding single letter in the standard alphabet. *See also* central vowel, formant, mid vowel.
[From Hebrew *shewa* a mark indicating the absence of a vowel sound]

Schwann cell *n.* A type of large *neuroglial cell responsible for forming the *myelin sheath around nerves in the *peripheral nervous system. *See also* neurolemma. *Compare* oligodendrocyte.
[Named after the German physiologist Theodor Schwann (1810–82) who studied it]

scientific method *n.* Another (less precise) name for the hypothetico-deductive method.

scientific revolution *n.* According to the US historian and philosopher of science Thomas S(amuel) Kuhn (1922–96) in *The Structure of Scientific Revolutions* (1962), a period in which competing *paradigms (1) vie with one another in a scientific discipline, in a manner analogous to *Darwinian evolution, until a new paradigm replaces the old by a process of *survival of the fittest, and a *paradigm shift thus occurs. *See also* Kuhnian, normal science.

sclera *n.* The tough inelastic opaque white membrane that forms the outer covering of the eyeball, apart from one-sixth of the area that is covered by the transparent *cornea. It maintains the eyeball's shape and forms attachments to the *extra-ocular muscles.
[From Greek *skleros* hard]

sclerosis *n.* Hardening of tissue resulting from inflammation, deposits of fat or of *amyloid plaques, infiltration of connective tissue fibres, or other causes. *See also* amyotrophic lateral sclerosis, arteriosclerosis, arteriosclerotic dementia, atherosclerosis, cerebral arteriosclerosis, multiple sclerosis. **sclerotic** *adj.*
[From Greek *skleros* hard + -*osis* indicating a process or state]

scopolamine *n.* A colourless, viscous, liquid *alkaloid that is found in *henbane and other plants and that acts pharmacologically to inhibit muscarinic acetylcholine activity by competing with acetylcholine for receptor sites, having the effect of a central nervous system *depressant that crosses the blood–brain barrier and produces sedation and amnesia, used as an adjunct to analgesics in surgery and obstetrics and as a preventative of motion sickness. Also called *hyoscine*. Formula: $C_{17}H_{21}NO_4$. *See also* methyl scopolamine, truth drug. *Compare* atropine.
[From Latin *Scopolia* the belladonna genus of plants, named after the Italian naturalist Giovanni Scopoli (1723–88) + *amine*]

scopophilia *n.* A *paraphilia characterized by recurrent, intense sexual fantasies, urges, or behaviour involving looking at naked bodies or other arousing stimuli. Also written *scoptophilia*. *See also* voyeurism.
[From Greek *skopeein* to watch + *philos* loving, from *phileein* to love + -*ia* indicating a condition or quality]

scoring formula *n.* In psychometrics, a mathematical rule by which *raw scores are converted to test scores. According to the simplest scoring formula, the test score is simply the sum of the item scores; other scoring formulas involve combining raw scores in various ways other than simple addition, weighting different items of subtests differently, correcting for guessing or for failing to respond to certain items, and so on. *See also* configural scoring rule.

scotoma *n.* A blind spot or area of absent or diminished vision, usually resulting from a lesion in the *retina or *optic nerve, from viewing the sun directly (called *solar retinopathy* or an *eclipse scotoma*, because it often arises from a person trying to watch an eclipse of the sun), or from squinting. Temporary scotomas often arise as *auras heralding *epileptic seizures or *migraine headaches. **scotomas** or **scotomata** *pl.*
[From Greek *skotoma* dizziness, from *skotos* darkness + *-oma* indicating an abnormality]

scotopic *adj.* Of, relating to, or governed by the *rod-mediated visual system that functions when the eyes are dark-adapted for dim illumination or night vision, functioning only outside the *fovea and having peak sensitivity at a wavelength of 505 nanometres (blue–green light) but responding to light across the entire visible spectrum, having only one type of photoreceptor and therefore being completely colour-blind though significantly more sensitive than the *photopic system except for wavelengths above 650 nanometres (in the red region of the spectrum), where the sensitivities of the two systems are similar. *See also* Arago phenomenon, dark adaptation, duplexity function, field adaptation, light adaptation, nyctalopia, photochromatic interval, Purkinje shift, retinol, scotopic luminosity curve, Stiles–Crawford effect. *Compare* mesopic, photopic. **scotopia** *n.* *Scotopic vision. Also called *night vision* or *twilight vision. Compare* photopic.
[From Greek *skotos* darkness + *ops* an eye + *-ikos* of, relating to, or resembling]

scotopic luminosity curve *n.* A *luminosity curve depicting the intensity of light that is required at each point in the *visible spectrum for the colours to appear equally bright in dim light, under *scotopic vision mediated by *rods. *Compare* photopic luminosity curve.

scream therapy *See* primal therapy.

screening test *n.* In psychometrics, a test designed to eliminate a significant proportion of respondents as a preliminary step to a process of *diagnosis or a *selection test.

screen memory *n.* In *psychoanalysis, an innocuous and non-threatening memory of a childhood experience, noteworthy for its sharpness in relation to the insignificance of its content, that signifies an unconscious memory of a significant and threatening kind. Sigmund Freud (1856–1939) introduced the concept in 1899 in an article entitled 'Screen Memories' (*Standard Edition*, III, pp. 303–22). Also called a cover memory. *Compare* blocking memory.

script *n.* **1.** Handwriting in contradistinction to type or printed text. **2.** Any written text. **3.** A *schema of an event sequence, such as paying at the checkout of a supermarket, incorporating assumptions about the characteristic actors, objects, and actions in a prototypical instance of the schema. This usage was introduced in 1977 by the US linguist and cognitive scientist Roger C. Schank (born 1946) and the US psychologist Robert P(aul) Abelson (born 1928) in their book *Scripts, Plans, Goals and Understanding. See also* conceptual dependency theory, frame (3), memory organization packet.
[From Latin *scribere, scriptum* to write]

Scripture's blocks *n.* An *ambiguous figure that can be perceived either as three cubes or as five cubes depending on how the perspective cues are interpreted (see illustration). *See also* perspective reversal.

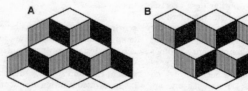

Scripture's blocks. A is identical to B but inverted, as can be confirmed by inverting the page. If one of the groups is seen as three blocks, then the other will be seen as five, and whenever one of the images appears to flip over, so does the other.

[Named after the US-born German/British psychologist Edward Wheeler Scripture (1864–1945) who published it in 1895]

SDAT *abbrev.* Senile dementia of the Alzheimer type; a disorder similar to *Alzheimer's disease but with onset after 65 years of age. *See also* senile dementia.

Seashore Measures of Musical Talent *n.* A set of measures devised by the US psychologist Carl E(mil) Seashore (1866–1949) and discussed in his book *The Psychology of Musical Talent* (1919). They involve controlled procedures for measuring the respondent's ability to discriminate pitch, loudness, tempo, timbre, and rhythm. Also called the *Seashore Tests of Musical Ability*, but Seashore himself deliberately avoided the word *tests* and preferred *measures*, which he thought better captured their character as standardized laboratory procedures.

seasonal affective disorder *n.* A *mood disorder characterized by recurrent *major depressive episodes that tend to occur during the winter months, thought to be related to the reduction in hours of daylight. Also called *seasonal mood disorder*. *See also* phototherapy. **SAD** *abbrev.*

secobarbital *n.* A short-acting *barbiturate drug and central nervous system *depressant, used as a sedative and hypnotic and sometimes taken as a street drug. Also called *quinalbarbitone* or *Seconal* (trademark). Street names include *pink lady*, *red devils*. Formula $C_{12}H_{18}N_2O_3$.
[From *seco-* indicating a chemical compound with an open ring + *barbit(uric) acid* + *-al* indicating a pharmaceutical product]

Seconal *n.* A proprietary name for the barbiturate drug *secobarbital (quinalbarbitone). [Trademark]

secondary advantage *n.* Another name for *secondary gain.

secondary colour *n.* A colour resulting from the mixture of two *primary colours (1). US *secondary color*. Also called a *binary colour*. *See also* metamer.

secondary drive *See under* drive.

secondary elaboration *n.* Another name for *secondary revision.

secondary gain *n.* Any benefit that a person receives as an indirect result of having a disorder, such benefits taking the form of monetary compensation, disability benefits, personal services and attention, or escape from work or onerous responsibilities. Sigmund Freud (1856–1939) drew the distinction between *primary gain and secondary gain in 1916–17 in his book *Introductory Lectures on Psycho-Analysis* (Standard Edition, XV–XVI, at pp. 381–5). Also called *advantage by illness, epinosic gain, gain from illness, secondary advantage*.

secondary identification *n.* In *psychoanalysis, *identification (2) occurring after the establishment of an *object-relationship. *See under* primary identification.

secondary immune response *See under* immune response.

secondary impotence *See under* impotence (2).

secondary memory *n.* Another name for *long-term memory. *Compare* primary memory.

secondary narcissism *n.* In *psychoanalysis, a form of *narcissism in which *libido is withdrawn from external *instinctual objects and turned back on the *ego. *See also* ego libido, object libido. *Compare* primary narcissism.

secondary prevention *n.* Measures taken to limit the spread of an existing disorder. *Compare* primary prevention, tertiary prevention.

secondary process *n.* In *psychoanalysis, a conscious, rational mode of mental functioning, based on the *reality principle, involving *bound energy. Sigmund Freud (1856–1939) developed the concept at the beginning of his psychological work and expounded it at length in Chapter VII of his book *The Interpretation of Dreams* (1900, Standard Edition, IV–V). *See also* binding. *Compare* primary process.

secondary projection area *n.* Any area of the cerebral cortex that receives projections from a *primary projection area. *Compare* tertiary projection area.

secondary quality *See under* primary quality.

secondary reinforcement *n.* In *operant conditioning, *reinforcement by means of a *stimulus (7) that has acquired reinforcing properties by having been paired with a *reinforcer. For example, if a bell is sounded repeatedly before an animal is fed, then the bell becomes a secondary reinforcer that can be used to reinforce a particular response, such as pressing a lever. Secondary reinforcement is especially useful in *shaping (1), because it is often difficult to time primary reinforcers such as food sufficiently precisely. The counterpart of secondary reinforcement in *classical conditioning is *higher-order conditioning. **secondary reinforcer** *n.* A *stimulus (7) that has become a *reinforcer through *secondary reinforcement.

secondary repression *n.* In *psychoanalysis, a form of *repression in which conscious material that is reminiscent of repressed material is removed from consciousness. *Compare* primal repression, primary repression.

secondary revision *n.* In *psychoanalysis, one of the forms of *dreamwork in which the contents of a dream are rearranged to present a more consistent and comprehensible narrative. Also called *secondary elaboration*.

secondary sexual characteristic *n.* Any of the *attributes that distinguish the sexes, apart from differences in their reproductive organs and *gametes, and that develop during *puberty under the influence of *sex hormones. Among the most prominent are facial hair and deep voices in men, and wide hips and breasts in women. *Compare* primary sexual characteristic.

secondary somatosensory area *See under* somatosensory cortex.

second censorship *See under* censorship.

second messenger *n.* Any chemical substance, notably *cyclic AMP, that is synthesized within the *cytoplasm of a cell in response to stimulation by a nerve impulse from a neuron and that has the effect of changing the electrical potential across the *cell membrane of the cell in which it is operating.
[So called because it acts as a neurotransmitter after being activated by a different neurotransmitter or hormone]

second-order approximation to language *See* approximation to language.

secretory phase *n.* Another name for the *luteal phase of the *oestrous cycle or *menstrual cycle.
[So called because of the secretion of progesterone from the corpus luteum during this phase, although hormones are also secreted during the other phases]

sedative *adj. n.* (Of or relating to) a drug or agent that has a calming or soothing effect without a strong hypnotic (sleep-inducing) effect, especially certain of the *benzodiazepine drugs acting via the *GABA receptor complex, a *propanediol drug, or *buspirone. *See also* sedative–hypnotic; sedative-, hypnotic-, or anxiolytic-related disorders.
[From Latin *sedatus* stilled, from *sedare* to still, related to *sedere* to sit + *-ivus* indicating a tendency, inclination, or quality]

sedative–hypnotic *n.* Any of a number of central nervous system *depressant drugs that are used mainly for their calming and sleep-inducing effects, among the most commonly prescribed being the *barbiturates, certain of the *benzodiazepines, the *propanediols, *chloral hydrate, *GHB, *glutethimide, *paraldehyde, and *temazepam. *See also* sedative-, hypnotic-, or anxiolytic-related disorders.

sedative-, hypnotic-, or anxiolytic-related disorders *n.* *Substance-related disorders induced by consuming *sedatives, *hypnotics, and *anxiolytic or anti-anxiety drugs. These drugs, all of which are central nervous system depressants, include the *benzodiazepines, *carbamates, and *barbiturates, comprising all sleeping medications and all anti-anxiety drugs apart from the non-benzodiazepine anxiolytics. *See* substance abuse, substance dependence, substance-induced disorders, substance use disorders.

seduction theory *n.* In *psychoanalysis, a theory propounded by Sigmund Freud (1856–1939) from 1895 to 1897, and then abandoned, according to which *neuroses were attributed to *repressed memories of sexual seduction in childhood. But in 1897 he ceased to believe that the fantasies were based in reality and propounded a theory of *psychical reality to deal with the problem. In his article 'On the History of the Psycho-Analytic Movement' (1914), he wrote: 'If hysterical subjects trace back their symptoms to traumas that are fictitious, then the new fact which emerges is precisely that they create such scenes in *phantasy*, and this psychical reality requires to be taken into account alongside practical reality' (*Standard Edition*, XIV, pp. 7–66, at pp. 17–18).

segregation of alleles *n*. The law of segregation of alleles, the first of *Mendel's laws, stating that every *somatic cell of an organism carries a pair of hereditary units (now identified as *alleles) for each *character (2), and that at *meiosis (1) the pairs separate so that each *gamete carries only one unit from each pair. Also called the *law of segregation*. *See also* independent assortment.

seizure *n*. A sudden attack of a disorder, especially a *convulsion. *See also* audiogenic seizure, psychomotor seizure.

selection *n*. **1.** The act or process of choosing, or the item(s) chosen. **2.** The natural and artificial processes whereby certain organisms or their characteristics or *genotypes are reproduced and perpetuated in a population in preference to others. *See* natural selection. *See also* apostatic selection, canalizing selection, counteracting selection, directional selection, disruptive selection, frequency-dependent selection, group selection, kin selection, *K*-selection, reinforcing selection, *r*-selection, selection pressure, selective breeding, sexual selection, stabilizing selection.
[From Latin *seligere*, *selectum* to sort, from *se-* apart + *legere* to choose + *-ion* indicating an action, process, or state]

selection pressure *n*. Any environmental feature, such as shortage of food, presence of predators, or competition from *conspecifics (1), that drives *natural selection.

selection test *n*. In psychometrics, any test used to choose among candidates for jobs or positions, for promotion, for places on training courses, and so on.

selective advantage *n*. Any characteristic or *trait that gives an organism or a *genotype greater chances of surviving and reproducing than the available alternatives.

selective attention *n*. Focusing concentration on a single stimulus or class of stimuli to the exclusion of others. The US psychologist William James (1842–1910) famously pointed out in his *Principles of Psychology* (1890) that this ability must be acquired: 'The baby, assailed by the eyes, ears, nose, skin and entrails all at once, feels it all as one great blooming, buzzing confusion' (p. 488). *See* attenuation theory, bottleneck theory, cocktail party phenomenon, filter theory.

selective breeding *n*. The artificial mating of organisms with particular *genotypes in order to enhance or suppress certain hereditary characteristics.

selective exposure *n*. The tendency for people to expose themselves to mass media messages that reinforce their pre-existing attitudes. For example, people tend to read newspapers whose editorial opinions are close to their own.

selective mutism *n*. A *mental disorder of childhood or adolescence whose essential feature is a persistent failure to speak in certain social situations in which speaking is expected, such as at school or among peers, despite a proven ability to speak in other situations. To satisfy the diagnostic criteria, the behaviour must interfere with educational or occupational achievement or with social interaction and must not be attributable to a lack of knowledge or facility with the language required in the specified situations, or to embarrassment about a communication disorder such as stuttering. Also called *elective mutism*.
[From Latin *mutus* dumb]

selective serotonin reuptake inhibitor *n*. A class of *antidepressant drugs that have a specific blocking action on the reuptake of *serotonin at *synapses (1) in the central nervous system, allowing ambient concentrations of this neurotransmitter to increase. Side-effects include sexual dysfunction in approximately half of the people who take them. *See* citalopram (Cipramil), clomipramine (Anafranil), fluoxetine (Prozac), fluvoxamine

(Luvox), paroxetine (Paxil), sertraline (Zoloft), St John's wort. *Compare* monoamine oxidase inhibitor (MAOI), tetracyclic antidepressant, tricyclic antidepressant. **SSRI** *abbrev.*

self-actualization *n.* A term introduced by the German psychiatrist Kurt Goldstein (1878–1965) to denote the motive to realize one's latent potential, understand oneself, and establish oneself as a whole person. In the theory of *personality of the US psychologist Abraham Maslow (1908–70), set out in his book *Toward a Psychology of Being* (1962), it represents the highest level of psychological development. The Swiss psychologist Carl Gustav Jung (1875–1961) used the word to define his concept of *individuation (*Collected Works*, 7, paragraph 266). *See also* need-hierarchy theory, peak experience. *Compare* actualization. **self-actualize** *vb.*

self-analysis *n.* The systematic application to oneself of the techniques of *psychoanalysis, apart from the analysis of the *transference.

self-defeating personality disorder *n.* A controversial *personality disorder, not listed in *ICD-10 or *DSM-IV (though listed in an appendix of DSM-III-R), characterized by habitual or recurrent behaviour that leads to failure and invites rejection. Also (misleadingly, since no sexual arousal is implied) called *masochistic personality*.

self-defeating prophecy *n.* A prediction that becomes false as a consequence of having been made. A frequently cited example is the *unexpected hanging paradox, but the prediction in that paradox is not actually self-defeating, although it appears to be. A more natural and less paradoxical example is the following: a doctor may discover that a particular patient has a strong genetic predisposition to breast cancer and may predict that she will develop the disease; but the patient may respond to the prediction by having a double mastectomy, eliminating the possibility of developing breast cancer. Also called a *self-defeating prediction. See also* Oedipus effect. *Compare* self-fulfilling prophecy.

self-esteem *n.* One's attitude towards oneself or one's opinion or evaluation of oneself, which may be positive (favourable or high), neutral, or negative (unfavourable or low).

Also called *self-evaluation. See also* ego involvement, positivity bias (1), self-image.

self-estrangement *n.* A feeling of *depersonalization and detachment from one's natural self, especially as a result of immersion in complex industrial culture.

self-evaluation *n.* Another name for *self-esteem.

self-fulfilling prophecy *n.* A prediction that becomes true as a consequence of having been made. For example, if the president of a large company predicts a fall in the company's share price, then the prediction is likely to bring about a fall in the share price irrespective of any other factors, because investors will be more inclined to sell their shares. The best-known self-fulfilling prophecy effects in psychology are the *experimenter expectancy effect and the *Pygmalion effect. Also called a *self-fulfilling prediction. See also* Oedipus effect. *Compare* self-defeating prophecy.

self-handicapping *n.* Imposing an obstacle to one's successful performance in a particular situation in order to provide an excuse for failure (usually in a person of low self-esteem) or to increase the credit that one can take for success (usually in a person of high self-esteem). Typical examples are going out with friends rather than staying at home and studying the night before an important examination, or becoming intoxicated with alcohol before a date or a potential sexual encounter. It occurs most often when a person is uncertain of success in an *ego-involving endeavour.

self-hypnosis *n.* Self-induced *hypnosis. Also called *autohypnosis*.

self-image *n.* The idea or conception that one has of oneself in general. *See also* guiding fiction, self-esteem, self-perception theory, self-schema.

selfish *adj.* Characterized by self-interest or promotion of one's own interests without regard to the welfare of others. More specifically in social psychology and sociobiology, of or relating to forms of behaviour that benefit an individual in terms of direct advantage or chances of survival and reproduction at some cost to another individual or individuals. *See also* selfish gene. *Compare* altruism.

selfish gene *n*. A way of describing any *gene, drawing attention to the fact that it is the fundamental unit of competition in the process of evolution by *natural selection, increasing in relative frequency in the gene pool by having *phenotypic effects that give it greater chances of survival and replication than its *alleles. *See also* extended phenotype. [Coined in 1976 by the British ethologist Richard Dawkins (born 1941) in the title of his book *The Selfish Gene*]

self-monitoring *n*. Observation and control of *expressive behaviour and *self-presentation. High self-monitors regulate their expressive self-presentation and are highly responsive to social and interpersonal cues to situationally appropriate behaviour, whereas low self-monitors lack these abilities or motivations. The concept was introduced in an article in the *Journal of Personality and Social Psychology* in 1974 by the US-based Canadian social psychologist Mark Snyder (born 1947).

Self-Monitoring Scale *n*. A questionnaire comprising 25 true/false items designed to measure *self-monitoring. It was introduced in 1974 by the US-based Canadian social psychologist Mark Snyder (born 1947).

self-object *n*. In *self-psychology, one's subjective experience of another person who sustains one's self within a social relationship, evoking and reinforcing one's sense of selfhood. The element *object* refers to an *instinctual object, not to an inanimate thing. Also written *selfobject*.

self-perception theory *n*. A theory according to which people infer their own *attitudes (1), *opinions, and other internal states partly by observing their overt behaviour and the circumstances in which that behaviour occurs. A canonical example is of a man who is asked whether he likes brown bread and who replies, 'I must like it; I'm always eating it.' According to the theory, *introspection is a poor guide to one's internal states, because internal cues are weak and ambiguous, and a person is therefore in essentially the same position as an outside observer, who necessarily relies on outward behaviour in interpreting another's internal states. The theory has been

used to provide an alternative interpretation of *cognitive dissonance effects. It was introduced in two influential articles by the US psychologist Daryl J. Bem (born 1938) in the *Journal of Experimental Social Psychology* in 1965 and in *Psychological Review* in 1967. It is sometimes regarded as a *behaviourist type of *attribution theory.

self-presentation *n*. The conscious or unconscious control of the impression that one creates in social interactions or situations. It is one of the important forms of *impression management, namely management of one's own impression on others through role playing. The phenomenon is encapsulated in Shakespeare's famous observation in *As You Like It*: 'All the world's a stage, / And all the men and women merely players: / They have their exits and their entrances; / And one man in his time plays many parts' (II.vii.139–42). It was popularized by the Canadian-born US sociologist Erving Goffman (1922–82) in his influential book *The Presentation of Self in Everyday Life* (1959). *See also* ingratiation, self-monitoring.

self-preservation instinct *n*. In *psychoanalysis, another name for an *ego instinct, as distinct from a *sexual instinct or *libido, the prototypical example of a self-preservation instinct being *hunger (1). The following key passage occurs in an article entitled 'The Psycho-Analytic View of Psychogenic Disturbance of Vision' (1910) by Sigmund Freud (1856–1939): 'From the point of view of our attempted explanation, a quite specially important part is played by the undeniable opposition between the instincts which subserve sexuality, the attainment of sexual pleasure, and those other instincts, which have as their aim the self-preservation of the individual—the ego instincts. As the poet has said, all the organic instincts that operate in our mind may be classified as "hunger" or "love"' (*Standard Edition*, XI, pp. 211–18, at pp. 214–15). Ten years later he began to change his mind on the point made in the last sentence of the quotation—*see* Thanatos.

self-psychology *n*. A version of *psychoanalysis, put forward by the Austrian-born US psychoanalyst Heinz Kohut (1913–81) in his books *The Analysis of the Self* (1971) and *The Restoration of the Self* (1977), and in his edited volumes *The Search for the Self* (1978) and *How*

Does Psychoanalysis Cure? (1984), placing emphasis on the self and the experience of selfhood, the constituent sectors of the self being the *pole of goals and ambitions*, the *pole of ideals and standards*, and the *arc of tension* between the two poles functioning to activate basic talents and skills. Kohut distinguished between the *virtual self* (an image of the neonate's self in the mind of a parent), the *nuclear self* (the initial organization of the self that emerges in the second year of life), the *cohesive self* (a coherent structure representing the normally functioning self), and the *grandiose self* (a normal exhibitionistic and self-centred self in early infancy). *See also* grandiose self, narcissism, narcissistic personality disorder, self-object.

self-report *adj.* In psychometrics, of, relating to, or comprising a questionnaire, inventory, check list, or other measuring instrument in which the respondent rather than the test administrator selects and records the responses.

self-schema *n.* Any mental structure representing knowledge about oneself on a particular dimension or in a particular domain. A person who has a well-developed *self-image in a particular area—for example, a person with a strong self-image of being truthful—is said to be *self-schematic* on that dimension, and such a person is likely to form self-judgements more rapidly and more confidently about information relevant to the self-schema than is a person who is not self-schematic in that area. *See also* cognitive therapy, depressive realism, schema.

self-selected sample *n.* A type of *convenience sample comprising research participants or subjects who have volunteered to participate, often in response to an advertisement calling for people with certain characteristics to come forward. *Compare* accidental sample, cluster sample, non-probability sample, opportunity sample, probability sample, quota sample, random digit dialling, simple random sample, snowball sample, stratified random sample.

self-serving bias *n.* As *attribution bias that leads people to ascribe their own successes to internal personal factors, such as ability, and their failures to external situational causes, such as bad luck. *See also* attribution theory, Kelley's cube.

sella turcica *n.* A saddle-shaped depression enclosing the *pituitary gland in the middle of the sphenoid bone at the base of the skull. Also called the *Turkish saddle.*
[From Latin *sella* a saddle + *turcica* Turkish]

semantic *adj.* Of or relating to meaning in linguistics and philosophy.
[From Greek *semantikos* significant, from *sema* a sign + *-ikos* of, relating to, or resembling]

semantic coding *n.* Remembering a word or verbal expression by storing its meaning rather than its sound or the physical movements required to articulate it. *Compare* acoustic coding, articulatory coding.

semantic component *n.* Another name for a *semantic feature.

semantic confusion *n.* Misperceiving or misremembering a word as one that has a similar meaning, as when *lamp* is perceived or recalled as *light*. *Compare* acoustic confusion.

semantic differential *n.* A device for measuring the *affective or *connotative meaning of words, also widely used for measuring attitudes towards other concepts and objects. It consists of a variable number of seven-point bipolar *rating scales, such as

good -- -- -- -- -- -- -- *bad*
active -- -- -- -- -- -- -- *passive*
strong -- -- -- -- -- -- -- *weak*

on which respondents rate the items under investigation. According to *factor analysis, there are three underlying dimensions of affective or connotative meaning, exemplified by the three core scales shown above, labelled evaluation, activity, and potency, respectively. Scores ranging from −3 at the negative end of each scale to +3 at the positive end are usually assigned. To illustrate how it works, research in the US has shown that average ratings of the word *nurse* tend to be towards the *good, active*, and *weak* poles, whereas the word *policeman* tends to be rated towards the *good, active*, and *strong* poles. The particular adjective pairs used depend on the items being evaluated: *active* versus *passive* could be included among the scales used to measure the activity dimension if the items being rated were political parties, for example, but this might be less appropriate if the items were types of food. The technique was developed by the US psychologist Charles E(gerton) Osgood (1916–91) and published in 1952 in the journal *Psychological Bulletin*, and it became popular with researchers after it was expounded in detail in the book *The Measurement of Meaning* (1957) by Osgood, his US colleague G(eorge) J(ohn) Suci (born 1925), and the Canadian-born US psychologist Percy (Hyman) Tannenbaum (born 1927). *See also* congruity theory. **SD** *abbrev.*

semantic encoding *See* semantic memory.

semantic feature *n.* An element of a word's *denotation or denotative meaning. For example, *young*, *male*, and *human* are semantic features of the word *boy*. Also called a *semantic component*.

semantic-feature hypothesis *n.* The proposition that the order of appearance of words in the course of a child's language acquisition are governed by the type and complexity of the *semantic features that they contain. **SFH** *abbrev.*

semantic generalization *n.* A form of *stimulus generalization in which a learned *response to a particular *stimulus (1) comes to be elicited by another stimulus that resembles it not in its stimulus properties but in its meaning, as when a learned response to the word *shoe*, or to an image of a shoe, comes to be elicited by the word *lace*, or by the image of a shoelace.

semantic memory *n.* A type of *long-term memory for factual information about the world, excluding personal episodes in one's life, typical examples being knowledge of the dates of the Second World War, the chemical formula for water, and the Spanish word for a book. The concept was introduced in 1972 by the Estonian-born Canadian psychologist Endel Tulving (born 1927), who distinguished it from *episodic memory and *procedural memory. *See also* generic knowledge. [From Greek *semantikos* significant, from *sema* a sign + *-ikos* of, relating to, or resembling, so called because it is necessary for the use of language]

semantic priming *See under* priming (1).

semantics *n.* The branch of *linguistics devoted to the study of meaning, including *concept formation, changes in meaning, and the relationship between linguistic expressions and their meanings. *See also* case grammar, componential theory, prototype theory.

semantic satiation *n.* A peculiar sense of loss of meaning that occurs when a word is recited slowly 15 or 20 times in succession. *Compare* verbal transformation effect.

semicircular canal *n.* Any of the three looped, fluid-filled ducts, set at right-angles to one another as if lying in the x, y, and z planes of a three-dimensional graph, forming part of the *vestibular system within the *membranous labyrinth of the inner ear and being partly responsible for the sense of balance and spatial orientation through its responses to angular acceleration, the angle of rotation of the head determining which one, two, or three of the canals in each ear are affected. Each canal has a bulge (*ampulla) on its crest-shaped inner surface in which are embedded *hair cells that project into a gelatinous membrane (the *cupula) where a fluid (*endolymph) within the canal acts as an inertial mass resisting angular acceleration, displacing the cupula and hair cells backwards relative to the direction of movement and causing adjoining neurons to send nerve impulses to the brainstem and cerebellum. *See also* Aubert effect, Bárány test, otolith.

semi-interquartile range *n.* In descriptive statistics, half the *interquartile range, sometimes used as an index of variability.

semiology *n.* The study of signs and signals, especially of spoken and written language, and their relationships to the objects, concepts, and ideas to which they refer. *Compare* semiotics. [From Greek *semeion* a sign + *logos* word, discourse, or reason]

semiorder *n.* A term introduced in 1956 by the US mathematical psychologist Robert Duncan Luce (born 1925) to denote an ordering, such as a preference ordering, in which an element x is ranked above another element y only if it exceeds y by a certain specified threshold value $\in$, and x ties with y if the absolute difference between them falls below $\in$. *See also* lexicographic semiorder.

semiotics n. The study of patterned human communication in all its modes, including touch, facial expression, gestures, and the spoken and written signs and symbols of human languages. See also kinesics, non-verbal communication. Compare semiology.
[From Greek semeiotikos of or relating to signs, from semeion a sign + -ikos of, relating to, or resembling]

semipermeable membrane n. A *membrane that is partly but not fully permeable, especially one through which a solvent but not its solute or dissolved substance can diffuse. See also cell membrane.

semitone n. A musical interval corresponding to a frequency ratio of approximately 17 : 18, the difference in pitch between adjacent keys on a piano, equal to one-twelfth of an *octave, the smallest difference in pitch normally used in Western music. See also tone (2).

semitone paradox n. A phenomenon in the perception of musical tones that are ambiguous as regards the *octaves to which they belong, each tone being composed of equal *sinusoidal waves from octaves spanning the auditory range. Using ambiguous tones of this kind, if two tones such as D and G are presented simultaneously, followed by C# and G#, which differ from the first pair by a *semitone down and up, then the sequence is clearly perceived as either converging or diverging in contrary motion, although the stimulus tones lack the information required to determine pitch: if the D is below the G, then it is divergent motion, but if the D is above the G, then it is convergent motion, and there is no way of knowing whether the D is below or above the G. It is a surprising phenomenon rather than a true *paradox. See also auditory illusion. Compare melodic paradox, tritone paradox.

semivowel n. A speech sound articulated like a *vowel but functioning like a *consonant because it is non-syllabic. In English, there are two semivowels, both of which are *approximants, namely the initial *phonemes in the words wet and yet. See also manner of articulation.

senescence n. The process of growing old and the physical and psychological changes that characterize this process.

[From Latin senescere to grow old, from senex old]

senile dementia n. Any chronic, progressive form of *dementia starting in old age (usually taken to mean from 65 years of age) with no clear physical cause, most commonly due to a late-onset form of *Alzheimer's disease, *vascular or *multi-infarct dementia, dementia resulting from *HIV infection, head trauma, *Parkinson's disease, *Huntington's disease, *Pick's disease, *Creutzfeldt–Jakob disease, or substance-induced persisting dementia resulting from *alcohol, *inhalants, *sedatives, *hypnotics, or *anxiolytics. See also SDAT.
[From Latin senilis old, from senex an old man]

senile plaque n. Another name for an *amyloid plaque.

sensate focus n. A technique used in *sex therapy, consisting of a structured programme of non-genital tactile stimulation, stroking, and pleasuring, with a strict prohibition of intercourse or genital contact. It was introduced by the US gynaecologist and sexologist William Howell Masters (1915–2001) and Virginia (E. Shelman) Johnson (born 1925) in a series of publications including their influential books Human Sexual Response (1966) and On Sex and Loving (1986).

sensation n. A subjective experience or feeling that results from stimulation of a *sense organ, or the capacity to experience through the senses, conventionally distinguished in psychology from *perception, in which sensory experience is not merely experienced as such but is interpreted with reference to its presumed external stimulus, this distinction having first been made in 1785 by Thomas Reid (1710–96), founder of the Scottish school of psychological philosophy. See also aftersensation, qualia, sense (1), sense data, sensibilia.
[From Latin sensation sensation, from sensus felt, from sentire to feel + -ation indicating a process or condition]

sensation level n. The absolute intensity of a sound measured in *decibels relative to the *absolute threshold of the listener. Thus a sensation level of 40 dB indicates a sound 40 dB more intense than the faintest sound of the same frequency that the listener can hear. Compare sound pressure level. **SL** abbrev.

sensation type *n*. Another name for a *sensing type.

sense *n*. **1.** Any of the faculties by which one experiences the external world or the internal state of one's body. In about 350 BC the Greek philosopher Aristotle (384–322 BC) distinguished between five senses, namely vision, hearing, smell, taste, and touch, but he recognized that touch includes more than one sense, and there are now known to be separate touch receptors for heat, cold, pain, and various forms of pressure, and also sensory receptors that respond to mechanical stimulation in the *vestibular system and that supply information about balance, orientation, and movement, and in some species *electroreceptors for detecting electrical discharges, a *magnetic sense that responds to the Earth's magnetic field, or *infra-red vision. *See also* sensation, sense organ, sensory modality. **2.** Moral discernment (*a sense of right and wrong*). **3.** Practical intelligence (*common sense*). **4.** Reason or purpose (*this doesn't make sense*). **5.** The specific meaning of a word (*in what sense do you mean you are sorry?*). **6.** The mathematical property of being positive or negative. *vb*. **7.** To experience something through intuition or extra-sensory perception (*I sensed that something was going to happen*).
[From Latin *sensus* felt, from *sentire* to feel]

sense data *n. pl.* A philosophical term for *sensations detached from their meaning and from any reference to the stimuli that give rise to them, the raw experiences given through the senses of sight, hearing touch, smell, and taste. *See also* qualia, sensibilia. **sense datum** *sing*.
[From *sense* + Latin *data* things given, from *dare* to give]

sense modality *See* sensory modality.

sense organ *n*. An anatomic structure specialized for detecting *stimuli (3) and converting them into nerve impulses that are transmitted to the central nervous system, its sensory components being *sensory receptors. *See also* ear, eye, nose, skin, tongue, vestibular system.

sense ratio method *n*. A *psychophysical method in which an observer is presented with two *standard stimuli *A* and *B* that differ on some perceptible dimension and is then presented with a different pair of stimuli *C* and *D* and is asked to adjust *D* so that it stands in the same relation of magnitude to *C* as *B* does to *A*.

sensibilia *n. pl.* A philosophical term for potential *sense data or *qualia that are not necessarily sensed by any organism and that can therefore exist independently of sensation. **sensibile** *sing*.
[From Latin *sensibilia* things that can be sensed, from *sensibilis* capable of being sensed, from *sentire* to sense or feel]

sensing type *n*. One of the subsidiary personality types in *analytical psychology. *See* function type.

sensitivity training group *n*. Another name for a *T-group.

sensitization *n*. In *addiction or drug *dependence (2), an increase in responsiveness to a drug resulting from repeated use of it, or a tendency to require smaller and smaller dosages of a drug to achieve a desired effect. Also called *reverse tolerance*. *Compare* tolerance (3), which is more common. *See also* substance dependence.

sensitization–repression scale *See* repression–sensitization scale.

sensorimotor *adj*. Of, relating to, or involving both sensory and motor functions or the nerves governing them. Also spelt *sensory-motor*.

sensorimotor cortex *n*. A generic name for both the *somatosensory cortex and the *motor cortex, separated by the *central sulcus.

sensorimotor rhythm *n*. An *EEG rhythm of 12–14 hertz that is generated in the *sensorimotor cortex.

sensorimotor stage *n*. According to the theory of cognitive development of the Swiss psychologist Jean Piaget (1896–1980), the first stage of cognitive development, from birth to approximately 2 years of age, when the infant gradually adapts motor behaviour to sensory input to serve its motivational goals, increasing the number and complexity of its sensory and motor abilities. *Compare* concrete operations, formal operations, pre-operational stage.

sensorineural deafness n. Any form of *deaf-ness in which sound is conducted normally through the external and middle ears but hearing loss occurs as a result of disease or damage in the *cochlea or the neural path-way from it to the brain. Its most common forms are *presbyacusis (high-frequency hear-ing loss in old people resulting from deterio-ration of the *organ of Corti), occupational deafness caused by exposure to noise at work, *ototoxic deafness following excessive intake of drugs such as *quinine or *aspirin, infec-tious deafness from mumps or congenital rubella (German measles) leading to destruc-tion of the cochlea, and a tumour on a nerve supplying the *vestibular system. Also called *nerve deafness*. *See also* decibel. *Compare* central auditory processing disorder, conductive deafness.
[From Latin *sensorius* of the senses, from *sensus* felt, from *sentire* to feel + Greek *neuron* a nerve + *-al* from *-alis* of or relating to]

sensorium n. Any area of the brain responsi-ble for receiving and analysing information from the *sense organs; also the apparatus of perception considered as a whole.
[From Latin *sensorius* of the senses, from *sensus* felt, from *sentire* to sense]

sensory adj. Of or relating to *sensation or the *senses (1).
[From Latin *sensorius* of the senses, from *sensus* felt, from *sentire* to feel]

sensory acuity n. The sharpness or keenness of a sense organ or sensory system. *See also* acuity.

sensory adaptation *See* adaptation (2).

sensory aphasia n. Another name for Wernicke's aphasia. *See under* aphasia.

sensory apraxia n. Another name for *ideational apraxia. *See under* apraxia.

sensory ataxia n. Any form of *ataxia caused by an impairment of sensation, usually *proprioception.

sensory conflict theory n. A proposed explanation for *motion sickness according to which *passive movement creates a mis-match between information relating to orien-tation and movement supplied by the visual and the vestibular systems, and it is this mis-match that induces feelings of nausea.

sensory cortex n. Any area of the *cerebral cortex receiving information from a *sense organ. *See* auditory cortex, olfactory cortex, somatosensory cortex, visual cortex.

sensory decision theory n. Another name for *signal detection theory. **SDT** *abbrev.*

sensory deprivation n. The state of being cut off from almost all sensory stimulation from the external environment, sometimes used as a technique of *brainwashing. The earliest experiments, reported in the mid 1950s, in-volved volunteers lying in small, soundproof cubicles, sometimes immersed in water held at body temperature, wearing translucent goggles that transmitted diffuse light, to pre-vent form perception, and cotton gloves with cardboard cuffs to restrict tactile sensations. The volunteers remained in sensory depriva-tion typically for 2–4 days almost continu-ously (apart from brief periods for eating and visiting the toilet) during which time their thinking usually became undirected and was often replaced by fantasies and hallucina-tions, many of the volunteers becoming unable to distinguish sleep from waking, and some found the experience intensely unpleasant.

sensory homunculus n. Another name for the *somatosensory homunculus.

sensory information store n. Another name for a *sensory register. **SIS** *abbrev.*

sensory memory n. A very short-term mem-ory store for information being processed by the sense organs. The most frequently investi-gated sensory registers are the *iconic store and the *echoic store, though the existence of an echoic store has not been convincingly established. It should not be confused with *perceptual memory. *See also* levels of process-ing, sensory register. *Compare* long-term memory, short-term memory.

sensory modality n. Any of the relatively independent sensory systems such as vision, hearing, smell, taste, and touch, the traditional five senses originally identified in about 350 BC by the Greek philosopher Aristotle (384–322 BC), who recognized that touch includes different senses within itself. In 1904 the Austrian physiologist Max von Frey (1852–1932) identified the four component sensations of touch as heat, cold, pain, and pressure, pressure now being known to include sensations of texture and vibration. The sensory systems associated with the *vestibular system, *kinaesthesis, *proprioception, and the *magnetic sense are also sometimes regarded as sensory modalities. Also called a *modality* or a *sense* or a *communication channel*. *See also* cross-modal matching, cross-modal transfer, egocentre, modality effect, Molyneux's question, synaesthesia (1).

sensory-motor *See* sensorimotor.

sensory neglect *n*. Any condition in which a well-defined class of sensory information is processed normally by *sensory receptors but is persistently ignored or not responded to. It usually arises from a *neurological disorder, and its most common form is *spatial neglect.

sensory nerve *n*. Any *nerve that carries information from a *sensory receptor to the central nervous system. *See* cochlear nerve, facial nerve, glossopalatine nerve, glossopharyngeal nerve, olfactory nerve, optic nerve, trigeminal nerve, vagus nerve, vestibulocochlear nerve.

sensory neuron *n*. A *neuron belonging to a *sensory receptor or a *sensory nerve (see illustration).

sensory preconditioning *n*. Learning of an association between two stimuli that are presented together or in close succession without *reinforcement (2), the learned association

becoming apparent when a response is conditioned to one of the stimuli and is found to be elicited by the other.

sensory projection area *n*. Any area of the cerebral cortex to which information is transmitted by afferent fibres from *sensory receptors. Also called a *projection area*. *See also* homunculus.

sensory receptor *n*. An anatomical structure composed of *sensory nerve endings adapted to respond to specific *stimuli (1) and to convert them into nerve impulses that are transmitted to other parts of the *nervous system, the forms of energy to which they respond being light, kinetic energy, temperature, chemical reactions, in some species of fish electrical discharges, in some snakes infra-red radiation, and in some birds and other species the Earth's magnetic field. *See* auditory receptor, cold spot, cone, electroreceptor, free nerve ending, Golgi tendon organ, gustatory receptor, hair cell, infra-red vision, magnetic sense, mechanoreceptor, Meissner's corpuscle, Merkel cell, muscle spindle, nociceptor, olfactory receptor, osmoreceptor (1, 2), otolith, Pacinian corpuscle, pain receptor, photoreceptor, pressure receptor, rod, Ruffini corpuscle, saccule, tactile receptor, taste bud, temperature receptor, touch receptor, utricle, warm spot. *See also* chemoreceptor, contact receptor, cutaneous sense, distance receptor, exteroceptor, interoceptor, proximoreceptor, receptive field, sense organ, somatic receptor, telereceptor, transducer. Also called a *receptor*. [From *sensory* + *receptor*, from Latin *recipere, receptum* to receive, from *re-* back + *capere, ceptum* to take]

sensory register *n*. Any of the subsystems of *sensory memory such as the *iconic store for vision and the *echoic store for hearing, generally assumed to exist separately for each

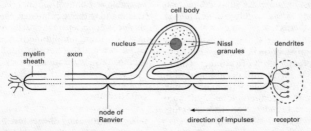

Sensory neuron

sensory modality. Also called a *sensory information store (SIS)*, *sensory store*, or *register*.

sensory relay nucleus *n*. Any of the *nuclei (2) in the *thalamus to which some or all of the information from sensory receptors apart from olfactory receptors is sent before being transmitted to specialized sensory areas of the cerebral cortex.

sensory saltation *n*. A tactile illusion, discovered in 1972 by the US psychologist Frank A. Geldard (1904–84), that occurs if the forearm or other area of the body is given a light tap, then a second and third tap are delivered in quick succession (about one-tenth of a second apart), the second tap in the same spot as the first and the third a few centimetres away. The effect is that the second tap is felt very distinctly to have occurred at a point somewhere between the first and the third taps. Saltatory areas within which the phenomenon occurs differ in size and shape in different parts of the body, but they never cross the *midsagittal plane of the body, and within these areas saltation is experienced even if the area of skin between the taps is anaesthetized, showing that the illusion arises not in the skin but at a higher level of the sensory system. Also called *saltation*.
[From Latin *saltus* a leap, from *saltare* to dance + *-ation* indicating a process or condition]

sensory store *n*. Another name for a *sensory register.

sensory summation *n*. A generic name for *spatial summation and *temporal summation.

sensory suppression *n*. The partial or complete blocking by a stimulus of sensory experience of a different stimulus. *See* binocular rivalry, masking, mixture suppression, taste suppression. *See also* amblyopia ex anopsia, Cheshire Cat effect, hole-in-the-hand illusion.

sensory transduction *n*. The conversion by a *sensory receptor of any of a number of different forms of energy into nerve impulses or *action potentials. Touch receptors supply kinetic energy; photoreceptors, light; auditory receptors, sound; temperature receptors, heat; olfactory and taste receptors, energy from chemical reactions; and electrorecep-

tors in some species of fish, electrical energy. *See also* transducer.
[From *sensory* + Latin *transducere* to lead across, from *trans* across + *ducere*, *ductum* to lead + *-ion* indicating an action, process, or state]

sentence completion test *n*. A type of *projective test in which the respondent is presented with the first few words of a series of sentences and is asked to fill in the missing words. Typical items are *My greatest fear is . . .* ; *I only wish I had. . . .* One of the most carefully constructed versions is the *Rotter Incomplete Sentences Blank. The technique was first used in 1897 by the German psychologist Hermann von Ebbinghaus (1850–1909) as an intelligence test. Also called an *incomplete sentences test*.

sentence functor *n*. In *logic, a string of words and sentence variables (usually represented by Greek letters) such that if the sentence variables are replaced by declarative sentences, then the whole becomes a declarative sentence with the inserted sentences as constituents. A typical example is: *Many people have said that* φ, *but it is a lie that* ψ. Replacing the sentence variables, this might become *Many people have said that fruit is nourishing, but it is a lie that Hitler loved animals. See also* truth functor, truth table.
[From Latin *functio* a function, from *fungi* to perform]

sentient *adj*. Capable of *sensation; conscious or aware. **sentient being** *n*. Any *organism that is *sentient or capable of feeling.
[From Latin *sentiens* feeling, from *sentire* to feel]

separable attribute *n*. An *attribute that is not inherent in a *phenomenon, inasmuch as the phenomenon can occur or exist without the attribute. For example, *frequency (1) is a separable attribute of sound, because *noise (1) is sound without frequency, whereas *amplitude is not a separable attribute of sound, because without amplitude there can be no sound wave and therefore no sound. In the visual modality, *saturation (1) is a separable attribute of colour, but *lightness is not. *See also* separable stimulus dimension. *Compare* integral attribute.

separable stimulus dimension *n*. A *separable attribute of any measurable aspect of a *stimulus (1). *Compare* integral stimulus dimension.

separate variance estimates *n*. In statistics, separate estimates of *variances of two or more populations, used when the population variances cannot be assumed to be equal for testing the null hypothesis that their means are equal. *Compare* pooled variance estimate.

separation anxiety *n*. The normal fear or apprehension of infants when separated from their mothers or other major attachment figures, or when approached by strangers, usually most clearly evident between 6 and 10 months of age or, in later life, similar apprehension about separation from familiar physical or social environments. *See also* separation anxiety disorder.

separation anxiety disorder *n*. A *mental disorder with onset before age 18 years, characterized by developmentally inappropriate and excessive *separation anxiety relating to separation from home or from major attachment figures. Symptoms, which to satisfy the diagnostic criteria must persist for at least 4 weeks and must cause clinically significant distress or social, academic, or occupational problems, may include unrealistic fear of losing major attachment figures or of harm befalling them, refusal to attend school, refusal to sleep alone, repeated nightmares about separation, and complaints of somatic symptoms such as headaches, nausea, or vomiting when separation is threatened. *See also* anaclitic depression, hospitalism.

septal *adj*. Of, relating to, or situated in the *septum pellucidum.

septal rage *n*. Intense *dysphoria, hyperexcitability, and anger resulting from a lesion in the *septum pellucidum. Also called *sham rage*.

septum pellucidum *n*. A thin, double partition extending down from the lower surface of the corpus callosum to the fornix and adjacent structures, separating the lateral ventricles of the brain and enclosing an area above the third ventricle. It is part of the *limbic system and one of the most important of the *pleasure centres of the brain, electrical stimulation of this area producing intensely agreeable sensations of well-being in humans. Experimental rats with access to levers to control the output of electrodes implanted semi-permanently in their septal areas self-stimulate themselves for long periods to the virtual exclusion of food, sex, and sleep, whereas ablation of the area leads to *septal rage. Also spelt *septum pelucidum*. Also called the *septum*, *septal area*, *septal nucleus*, *septal region*, or *septum lucidum*. **septa pellucida** *pl*. [From Latin *saeptum* a fence or enclosure, from *saepire* to fence or enclose + *pellucidus* transparent, from *per* through + *lucere* to shine]

sequence completion *n*. Another name for *number-completion tests.

serial anticipation method *n*. A technique for studying verbal learning in which on each trial the learner is provided with a stimulus word and attempts to provide the next word in the list, or, in the case of *paired-associate learning, the second member of a pair, and after each response the learner is shown the correct word. Also called the *anticipation method*.

serial learning *n*. **1.** Any task that involves learning lists of items and recalling them in the same serial order in which they were presented. *See also* serial anticipation method. **2.** A generic term for any form of *discrimination learning in which the set of stimuli is replaced with a new and unfamiliar set. *See* generalized oddity problem, habit reversal, non-reversal shift.

serial position effect *n*. In *serial learning (1), a tendency for the items near the beginning and end of the series to be recalled best, and those in the middle worst, producing a U-shaped *serial position curve* of recall as a function of serial position. It includes the *primacy effect (1) and the *recency effect. Also called the *edge effect* or *end effect*. *See also* tip-of-the-tongue phenomenon.

serial processing *n*. Computational processing in which steps are executed one at a time in a fixed sequence. This is the way in which ordinary computers function, but the brain is believed to use *parallel processing. *See also* cascade processing, connectionism, discrete processing, neural network, parallel distributed processing. [From Latin *serialis* of or relating to a series, from *series* a row, from *serere* to link + -*alis* of or relating to]

serial recall *n*. Retrieval from memory of a number of items of information in the order in which they were originally presented, in contradistinction to *free recall. *See also* Ranschburg inhibition, recall, repetition effect, serial anticipation method.

serial reproduction *n*. A technique for studying memory in a social context, popularized by the English psychologist Sir Frederic Charles Bartlett (1886–1969) in his book *Remembering: A Study in Experimental and Social Psychology* (1932, Chapters 7–8) and usually attributed to him, but in fact introduced by the US psychologist Ernest Norton Henderson (1869–1967) in an article in the journal *Psychological Review* in 1903, surprisingly not cited by Bartlett. It involves a person reading a short story (typically about 100 words long) and recounting it from memory to a second person, who then recounts it from memory to a third, and so on in the manner of the children's game of Chinese whispers, the phenomena of *assimilation (5), *levelling (1), and *sharpening becoming obvious after about eight transmissions. The technique has been used as a laboratory model of *rumour transmission. In some studies, the original stimulus is a drawing that is serially reproduced from memory by each of the participants or subjects in turn. *See also* War of the Ghosts. *Compare* successive reproduction.

series completion *n*. Another name for *number-completion tests.

Serlect *n*. A proprietary name for the atypical antipsychotic drug *sertindole.
[Trademark]

Seropram *n*. A proprietary name for the anti-depressant drug *citalopram.
[Trademark]

serotonergic *adj*. Releasing *serotonin; also activated by or responding to serotonin, this extended usage being widespread but consistently rejected by the English physiologist Sir Henry Hallet Dale (1875–1968), who coined the suffix *-ergic*, and by many other authorities. The term applies especially to nerve fibres such as those of the *raphe nuclei of the medulla oblongata, the *area postrema, and the *locus coeruleus that use serotonin as a *neurotransmitter and that project to the cerebral cortex, limbic system, thalamus, and cerebellum. *Compare* adrenergic, cholinergic, dopaminergic, GABAergic, noradrenergic.
[From *serotonin* + Greek *ergon* work + *-ikos* of, relating to, or resembling]

serotonin *n*. A *biogenic amine that is a powerful *vasoconstrictor and one of the major neurotransmitter substances in the central nervous system, originating mainly in *raphe nuclei of the brainstem, the *area postrema, and *locus coeruleus, and that is involved in arousal, attention, NREM sleep, and, above all, mood—depression and suicide often being associated with low serotonin levels. It is synthesized in the brain from its precursor *5-hydroxytryptophan (obtained from dietary *tryptophan), an amino acid that, unlike serotonin itself, is able to cross the *blood–brain barrier, and it generates the metabolite 5-hydroxyindoleacetic acid. Formula: $HOC_8H_5NCH_2CH_2NH_2$. Also called *5-hydroxytryptamine* or *5-HT*. *See also* parachlorophenylalanine, Prozac, selective serotonin reuptake inhibitor, serotonergic, tricyclic antidepressant, tryptophan hydroxylase.
[From *serum* the liquid portion of blood, from Latin *serum* whey + Greek *tonos* tone, so called because of its constricting effect on blood vessels]

Seroxat *n*. A proprietary name for the antidepressant drug *paroxetine.
[Trademark]

sertindole *n*. An *atypical antipsychotic drug, used in the treatment of *schizophrenia and other *psychotic (1) disorders. Also called *Serlect* (trademark).

sertraline *n*. An antidepressant drug belonging to the group of *selective serotonin reuptake inhibitors (SSRIs). Also called *Zoloft* (trademark).

set *n*. **1.** A collection of objects or elements that have something in common or that are treated as a unit. *See also* set theory, Venn diagram. **2.** A temporary readiness to perceive, think, or act in a particular way, usually as a result of experimental instructions or an experimental manipulation, hence *perceptual set*, *cognitive set*, *behavioural set*, *motor set*. Also called a *mental set*, formerly called an *Einstellung*. *See also* Aufgabe, functional fixedness, water-jar problem.

set point *n.* A natural state to which a dynamically stable system tends to return if perturbed, such as normal body temperature of 37°C, or the weight to which a person's body tends to revert after loss or gain from unusual or special circumstances or activities such as temporary illness, dieting, or overeating. *See also* appestat, homeostasis.

set theory *n.* A mathematical theory originated by the Russian-born German mathematician Georg Cantor (1845–1918) between 1874 and 1897 to deal with collections of objects, called *sets (1). A set is usually represented by an upper-case letter or by a pair of curly brackets enclosing all of its members; thus the set of all additive primary colours is the set $C = \{$red, green, blue$\}$; the set of natural numbers is $N = \{1, 2, 3, \ldots\}$; and the set of female US presidents is $F = \emptyset$, which is called the *empty set* or *null set*. *See also* barber paradox, Boolean, fuzzy set, Russell's paradox.

severe mental retardation *n.* A level of *mental retardation associated with *IQ approximately between 20 and 35 (in adults, *mental age from 3 to under 6 years). Also called *severe mental subnormality*.

sex *n.* **1.** Either of the categories of male and female or the sum total of biological *attributes on which this distinction is based within a species. *Compare* gender (1). *adj.* **2.** Of or relating to sex, especially *sex (1), as in the phrase *sex differences* or *sex discrimination*, but also *sex (3) as in *sex industry*. **3.** Short for sexual intercourse or any of the activities distinctively associated with it. **sexual** *adj.* Of or relating to sex, especially *sex (3), as in the phrase *sexual abuse*, but also *sex (1) as in *secondary sexual characteristics*.
[From Latin *sexus* sex, perhaps from *secare* to divide]

sex cell *n.* Another name for a *gamete.

sex chromosome *n.* A *chromosome that determines the sex of a human or other organism. *See* X chromosome, Y chromosome. *Compare* autosome.

sex difference *n.* Any of the myriad psychological characteristics that differentiate reliably between women and men or girls and boys, such as the significant superiority of women, on average, at tasks involving decoding non-verbal communication, as in the *PONS, or the significant superiority of men, on average, at *mental rotation. *See also* androgyny, fear of success.

sex hormone *n.* Any *hormone such as *progesterone, *oestrogen (or *oestradiol), *oestrone, *Müllerian inhibiting substance, *testosterone, or *androsterone that is produced by the gonads (ovaries or testes) and controls the development of primary and/or secondary sexual characteristics.

sex-influenced trait *n.* A phenotypic characteristic or *trait such as male pattern baldness that is expressed differently in males and females, usually because its expression depends on androgens or oestrogens, and that is controlled by a single gene that is dominant in males but recessive in females, so that, for example, men who inherit the gene from either parent lose hair as they age, whereas women do so only if they inherit it from both parents and are thus homozygotes. Also called a *sex-limited trait*. *Compare* sex-linked.

sexism *n.* A belief in the intrinsic superiority of one sex over the other, often accompanied by *prejudice, discrimination, or *stereotyping on the basis of sex. *Compare* ableism, ageism, ethnocentrism, fattism, heterosexism, racism, speciesism. **sexist** *n.* **1.** One who manifests or practises *sexism. *adj.* **2.** Of or relating to *sexism.
[Coined from *sex* following the model of *racism*]

sex-limited trait *n.* Another name for a *sex-influenced trait.

sex-linked *adj.* Of or relating to a gene located on a *sex chromosome or a characteristic or *trait inherited along with one's sex through being determined by such a gene. The best known examples in humans are haemophilia and various forms of colour-blindness, which are determined by genes located on the X chromosome, carried by females but expressed mostly by males, because the smaller Y chromosome has no homologous alleles to bring about *complementation. *See also* holandric, hologynic, Horner's law, X-linked, Y-linked. *Compare* sex-influenced trait.

sex pheromone *n.* A *pheromone that is released by an animal and that induces a sexual

response in members of the same species, such as the volatile sexual attractants released by female insects that can attract males from great distances.
[From *sex* + Greek *pherein* to bear + *horman* to stimulate]

sex therapy *n.* Any form of therapy, including *psychotherapy and *sensate focus, offered to people with *sexual dysfunctions. Also called *sexual therapy.*

sexual abuse *n.* The subjection of a child or other vulnerable person to sexual activity liable to cause physical or psychological damage. *See also* child abuse, elder abuse.

sexual anomaly *n.* Another name for a *paraphilia.

sexual arousal disorder *n.* Another name for *hypoactive sexual desire disorder.

sexual aversion disorder *n.* A *sexual dysfunction characterized by persistent or recurrent extreme antipathy to and active avoidance of genital contact with a sexual partner, generally accompanied by anxiety, fear, or disgust at the thought of sexual activity, causing significant distress or problems of interpersonal interaction.
[From Latin *aversus* turned away or hostile, from *avertere* to turn from, from *vertere* to turn]

sexual desire disorder *n.* Another name for *hypoactive sexual desire disorder.

sexual deviation *n.* Another name for a *paraphilia.

sexual dimorphism *n.* The property of some species, including humans, of having differences between males and females in shape, size, or morphology. *See also* dimorphic. **sexually dimorphic** *adj.*
[From *sexual* + Greek *dis* twice + *morphe* a form or shape + *-ismos* indicating a state or condition]

sexual disorder *See* sexual dysfunctions.

sexual dysfunctions *n.* A category of *mental disorders involving disturbances in *sexual response cycle or pain associated with sexual intercourse. *See* dyspareunia, female orgasmic disorder, female sexual arousal disorder, hy-

poactive sexual desire disorder, male erectile disorder, male orgasmic disorder, premature ejaculation, sexual aversion disorder, vaginismus.

sexual harassment *n.* Persistent unwelcome sexual remarks, looks, or advances, especially from a senior colleague in the workplace.

sexual instinct *n.* In *psychoanalysis, one of the two classes of *instincts (3) or *drives in the early classification of Sigmund Freud (1856–1939), the other being the *ego instincts of self-preservation. In Freud's theory, the form of energy driving the sexual instinct is *libido, and it drives a far wider range of activity than is ordinarily understood by sexual behaviour. In his later classification, first introduced in 1920, he distinguished between *Eros (the life instincts, including the sexual instinct) and *Thanatos (the death instinct). Also called the *sex instinct, sexual drive,* or *sex drive.*

sexual involution *n.* The decline in sexual desire and activity manifested by some people of both sexes after the *menopause or in middle life.
[From Latin *involutum* rolled up, from *involvere* to roll up + *-ion* indicating an action, process, or state]

sexual latency *See* latency period.

sexual masochism *n.* A *paraphilia characterized by recurrent, intense sexual fantasies, urges, or behaviour involving submission to pain, humiliation, bondage, or some other form of physical or psychological suffering. Also called simply *masochism,* a term introduced by the German neurologist and sexologist Richard von Krafft-Ebing (1840–1902) in his book *Psychopathia Sexualis* (1886). *See also* fusion of instincts, hypoxyphilia. *Compare* sexual sadism.
[Named after the Austrian historian and novelist Leopold von Sacher-Masoch (1836–95) who wrote about it, notably in his novel *Venus in Pelz* (1870), translated into English as *Venus in Furs* (1902), in which the heroine Wanda subjects the narrator to sexually stimulating suffering]

sexual orientation *n.* Another name for *sexual preference. *See also* ego-dystonic sexual orientation.

[From Latin *sexualis* of or relating to sex + *oriens, orientis* rising, alluding to the rising sun, used to find one's bearings + *-ation* indicating a process or condition]

sexual pain disorder *n*. A non-technical name for *dyspareunia.

sexual perversion *n*. An obsolescent term, often considered offensive nowadays, for a *paraphilia.

sexual preference *n*. The predominant predilection or inclination that defines a person as a *heterosexual (1), *homosexual (1), or *bisexual (1). Also called *sexual orientation*. *See also* heterosexism.

sexual preference disorder *n*. Another name for a *paraphilia.

sexual reproduction *n*. Biological reproduction involving the fusion of male and female *gametes. *Compare* asexual reproduction, parthenogenesis.

sexual response cycle *n*. The cycle of phases associated with sexual activity, classified and labelled differently by different researchers, but roughly as follows: appetitive phase (sexual desire, fantasy, and appetite for sexual activity); arousal phase (sexual excitement accompanied in the male by tumescence and erection of the penis and in the female by vasocongestion in the pelvis, lubrication and expansion of the vagina, and swelling of the external genitalia); orgasmic phase (male climax and ejaculation, female climax); resolution phase (muscular relaxation, feelings of well-being, and detumescence of the male penis); refractory period (lack of sexual desire and incapacity of males to achieve erection of the penis for a time).

sexual sadism *n*. A *paraphilia characterized by recurrent, intense sexual fantasies, urges, or behaviour involving the subjection of another person to pain, humiliation, bondage, or some other form of physical or psychological suffering. Also called *sadism*, a term introduced by the German neurologist and sexologist Richard von Krafft-Ebing (1840–1902) in his book *Psychopathia Sexualis* (1886). *See also* fusion of instincts. *Compare* sexual masochism.

[Named after the French writer Comte Donatien François de Sade (1740–1814), also known as Marquis de Sade, who described it in his novels, notably *Les 120 Journées de Sodome* (1785, The 120 Days of Sodom) and *Juliette* (1796)]

sexual selection *n*. A form of *natural selection operating through the differential success of individuals of different genotypes in acquiring mates. It works largely through mate choices that are made by members of the opposite sex and that are based on perceptible characteristics such as size, plumage, or behaviour. *See also* parental investment.

sexual therapy *See* sex therapy.

shading *n*. The depiction of highlights and shadows in visual art, the effect of light and shade; more specifically, another name for *chiaroscuro, one of the monocular cues of visual *depth perception.

shadow *n*. **1.** A dark shape cast on a surface by an object blocking rays of light; more generally, an area of relative darkness. **2.** In *analytical psychology, the negative side of a person's personality, comprising all personal and collective elements that do not fit in with the person's self-perception and that are therefore denied overt expression but exist in the unconscious as an *archetype (2). It is so called because it is the dark side of one's personality and is interpreted as a shadow cast by the *ego. Carl Gustav Jung (1875–1961) described the shadow in a key passage as 'that hidden, repressed, for the most part inferior and guilt-laden personality whose ultimate ramifications reach back into the realm of our animal ancestors and so comprise the whole historical aspect of the unconscious' (*Collected Works*, 9, part 2, paragraph 422).

shadowing *n*. Repeating out loud words as they are being heard, used in experiments on *dichotic listening to prevent *rehearsal (1) of words presented simultaneously to the other ear.

shaking palsy *n*. The name that the English surgeon James Parkinson (1755–1824) originally gave to the disorder that is now invariably called *Parkinson's disease.

shallow living n. In the *neo-Freudian theory of the German-born US psychoanalyst Karen Horney (1885–1952), a *neurotic (1) method of dealing with a conflict by immersion in trivial though distracting activities.

sham rage n. Unfocused anger or fury in response to any strong stimulus, originally observed in decorticate animals (animals whose cerebral cortex has been removed) and animals in which the pathway between the hypothalamus and pituitary gland has been damaged. It is known to result from more specific lesions, notably ablation of the *septum pellucidum (in which case it is called septal rage) or the *ventromedial hypothalamus, which is responsible for controlling anger and aggression. It has been observed in humans who have suffered extensive cortical damage from prolonged hypoglycaemia or carbon monoxide poisoning.
[So called because it is not triggered by a normal external instigator of anger, such as frustration]

shape constancy n. A form of *perceptual constancy in which a familiar object tends to retain its perceived shape despite radical changes in the pattern of retinal stimulation resulting from differences in its orientation. Thus a dinner plate looks the same shape whether the *proximal stimulus image that it casts on the retina is a circle, an ellipse, or (if it is viewed from the edge) roughly a straight line. Also called *form constancy*. See also shape–slant invariance, template matching.

shape–slant invariance n. A hypothesis, seemingly obvious yet contradicted by experimental evidence, that impressions of the shape and of the slant or orientation of an object are mutually dependent, so that misperceptions of shape should produce misperceptions of slant and vice versa. Also called *shape–tilt invariance*. See also shape constancy. Compare size–distance invariance.

shaping n. **1.** A technique of *operant conditioning that involves gradually building up a desired pattern of behaviour by selectively *reinforcing (1) closer and closer approximations to it, beginning with existing elements of the subject's behavioural repertoire, until the required responses are learned. It can be used to train animals more effectively than any other known method, and is sometimes used as a technique of *behaviour therapy to treat mental disorders and psychological problems in human beings. See also secondary reinforcement. Compare autoshaping. **2.** More generally, moulding something into a particular form.

shared psychotic disorder n. A *mental disorder in which a person develops a *delusion that is similar in content to that of a closely associated person with a pre-established delusion. Also called *folie à deux*, induced delusional disorder, shared paranoid disorder. Compare schizophrenia.

sharpening n. The magnification or exaggeration of certain salient details in perception or memory, and also in *serial reproduction and *rumour transmission. See also weapon focus. Compare assimilation (5), levelling (1).

Sheldon's constitutional psychology n. A theory, especially that of the US psychologist William H. Sheldon (1899–1977), postulating that *personality is dependent on physique or *somatotype. See ectomorph, endomorph, mesomorph. Compare Kretschmer constitutional type.

shell shock n. A name given during the First World War to what came to be called *post-traumatic stress disorder. It resulted from traumatic experiences during military actions and was attributed at that time to noise and concussion associated with exploding shells. Also called *combat fatigue*.

shenjing shuairuo n. A *culture-bound syndrome included in CCMD-2 (the *Chinese Classification of Mental Disorders*, 2nd ed.), found mainly among Chinese communities in southern and eastern Asia, characterized by *fatigue (1), dizziness, headaches, joint and muscle pain, loss of concentration, gastrointestinal complaints, *sexual dysfunctions, assorted *dyssomnias, and *amnesia. It is sometimes interpreted in Western cultures as an *anxiety disorder or a *mood disorder.
[Chinese term for *neurasthenia, from *shenjing* a nerve + *shuairuo* weak]

shen-k'uei n. A *culture-bound syndrome found mainly among men in Thailand and in ethnic Chinese communities in southern and eastern Asia, characterized by *anxiety and *panic attacks accompanied by somatic symp-

toms such as *insomnia, *sexual dysfunctions, dizziness, backache, and *fatigue (1), the symptoms often being attributed to loss of semen brought about by excessive sexual intercourse, masturbation, nocturnal emissions (wet dreams), and the passing of whitish urine believed to contain semen. Spelt *shenkui* in Chinese-speaking communities. *Compare* dhat.
[From Thai or Chinese *shen* spirit + *k'uei* or *kui* deficit or wastage]

shifted checkerboard figure n. Another name for the *Münsterberg illusion.

shin-byung n. A *culture-bound syndrome restricted mainly to Korea and Korean communities living elsewhere, characterized by *anxiety, *dissociation, *insomnia, *anorexia, dizziness, and *fatigue (1), together with somatic symptoms such as gastrointestinal complaints and general *asthenia, the symptoms generally being attributed to possession by the spirits of dead ancestors.
[From Korean *shin* spirit + *byung* possession]

shinkei-shitsu n. Another name for *taijin kyofusho.
[From Japanese *shinkei-shitsu* nervous temperament, from *shinkei* a nerve + *shitsu* constitution or nature]

shock n. **1.** Any sudden and unexpected experience of extreme surprise, horror, or outrage; any violent impact or jarring. **2.** In medical discourse, another name for *traumatic shock.

shock therapy n. Another name for *electroconvulsive therapy. Also called *shock treatment.*

shoe anaesthesia n. A condition analogous to *glove anaesthesia occurring in the foot. US *shoe anesthesia.*

shook yong See koro.

shorthand n. Any method of writing quickly, using special symbols or abbreviations. *See also* brachygraphy (short writing), stenography (narrow writing), and tachygraphy (quick writing).

short-sightedness n. A non-technical name for *myopia.

short-term memory n. A memory system capable of holding a limited amount of information for brief periods, up to a maximum of about 20 or 30 seconds, although it can be renewed indefinitely if the information within it is *rehearsed (2). Its capacity is about seven items or *chunks of information according to evidence first reviewed in an influential article by the US psychologist George A(rmitage) Miller (born 1920) in the journal *Psychological Review* in 1956. Without short-term memory, language would be incomprehensible, because to understand a sentence a listener or reader has to remember its beginning at least until its end. Also called *immediate memory*. *See also* chunking, dynamic memory span, levels of processing, magical number seven, maintenance rehearsal, phonological loop, push-down stack, reverberating circuit, span of apprehension, working memory. *Compare* long-term memory, sensory memory. **STM** *abbrev.*

short-term store n. Another name for *short-term memory. **STS** *abbrev.*

SHRDLU n. A famous *artificial intelligence program devised in 1968–70 by the computer scientist Terry (Allen) Winograd (born 1946) to carry out instructions in a *block world*—a table with blocks of various shapes and colours scattered over it. On the basis of images from a video camera scanning the scene, the program works out the arrangement of blocks, some of which may be lying on top of others, responds to questions in English about the situation, replies to these questions in English, understands requests in English to manipulate the blocks, carries out such requests with a robotic arm, and describes in English its actions and the reasons behind them.
[Named after the printer's code ETAOIN SHRDLU used to indicate typographical errors, representing the twelve most frequent letters in English in descending order]

sibling n. **1.** A brother or sister. *See also* sibling rivalry. **2.** Any member of one's sib, a sib being a group of kinspeople descended from a single ancestor.
[From Old English *sibb* relationship, from *gesibb* related + *-ling* denoting a person associated with the group specified]

sibling rivalry n. Rivalry or competition between brothers, sisters, or brothers and sisters.

sibling rivalry disorder *n.* Abnormally intense negative feeling towards an immediately later-born sibling, manifested in *regression (1), *tantrums, *dysphoria, *dyssomnia, and oppositional, defiant, or attention-seeking behaviour towards one or both parents.

side-effect *n.* Any secondary or incidental effect of a drug or other treatment, especially an unwanted effect in addition to the intended reaction. Also called an *adverse drug effect* or an *adverse drug reaction.*

Sidman avoidance conditioning *n.* A type of *avoidance conditioning in which the organism receives an aversive stimulus (such as an electric shock) at regular fixed intervals, without any warning signal, unless it performs an avoidance response (such as jumping over a barrier), and each avoidance response resets the timer to zero. Also called *free operant avoidance conditioning.*
[Named after the US psychologist Murray Sidman (born 1923) who popularized it in the early 1960s]

sight method *n.* Another name for the *whole-word method.

sight vocabulary *n.* The set of words that a person can recognize as wholes without decomposing them into their elements.

sigma score *n.* Another name for a *standard score.
[Named after *sigma* (σ), the eighteenth letter of the Greek alphabet, the lower-case form of which is often used to symbolize it]

sigmatism *n.* **1.** Abnormal or defective pronunciation of /s/, as in lisping. **2.** The repetitive use of the letter *s* for poetical effect.
[From the name of the Greek letter *sigma*, corresponding to the roman *s*]

sign *n.* **1.** An objective indication of a disorder observed by an examiner rather than reported by the afflicted person. *See also* hard sign, SCAN, soft sign, syndrome. *Compare* symptom. **2.** More generally, any signal, gesture, mark, emblem, or token with an identifiable meaning.
[From Latin *signum* a mark]

signal *n.* Any verbal or non-verbal pattern of sounds, signs, gestures, or other events trans-

mitted through a communication channel and capable of conveying information; more generally any non-random component of a *time series. *See also* receiver operating characteristic, signal detection theory, signal-to-noise ratio. *Compare* noise (2).
[From Latin *signum* a sign]

signal anxiety *n.* In *psychoanalysis, *anxiety activated by the *ego in response to external danger. The concept was introduced by Sigmund Freud (1856–1939) in his book *Inhibitions, Symptoms and Anxiety* (1926, *Standard Edition*, XX, pp. 77–175, at pp. 80–3, 92–4). *Compare* primary anxiety.
[So called because this form of anxiety is a signal of danger]

signal detection theory *n.* A *psychophysical theory of the detectability of stimuli developed in 1952–4 by a number of US researchers led by John A. Swets (born 1928), based on the assumptions that there is a normal probability distribution N of activation of the sensory system by *noise (2) generated externally or by internal random neural activity in the absence of any *signal, that there is a different normal probability distribution (SN) of activation by signal plus noise, and that the difference between the means (or equivalently the separation between the peaks) of the SN and N distributions, divided by the *standard deviation of the N distribution, is an index of detectability called *d prime* or d' that can be estimated experimentally from the relative frequencies of correct detections of the signal when it is present (*hits*) and incorrect detections of the signal when it is absent (*false alarms*), the performance of an observer usually being depicted by means of a *receiver operating characteristic (ROC). According to the theory, an observer sets a criterion level of sensory activation below which the signal is reported as absent and above which it is reported as present, but if the two probability distributions overlap, then stimuli below the criterion must include not only instances of noise (*correct rejections*) but also instances of signal (*misses*), and stimuli above the threshold must include not only instances of signal (*hits*) but also instances of noise (*false alarms*). Also called *sensory decision theory. See also* ideal observer, likelihood ratio (2), memory operating characteristic, psychometric function, signal-to-noise ratio, two-alternative forced-choice task. **SDT** *abbrev.*

signal-to-noise ratio *n.* The ratio of *signal strength to *noise (2) strength in a communication channel or *time series. *See also* receiver operating characteristic.

significance *See* statistical significance.

significance test *n.* In *inferential statistics, any test designed to determine whether an *alternative hypothesis achieved the required level of *statistical significance to justify being accepted in preference to the *null hypothesis. In a classical null hypothesis significance test, the null hypothesis is provisionally assumed to be true, and a calculation is then made of the probability of obtaining a result as extreme as the one actually obtained. If the probability is sufficiently small (by convention this significance level is often set at $p < 0.05$), the investigator is justified in rejecting the null hypothesis and therefore also in accepting its logical negation, namely the alternative hypothesis. Also called a *statistical test*.

significant other *n.* A term used by the US psychiatrist Harry Stack Sullivan (1892–1949) in his book *Conceptions of Modern Psychiatry* (1947) to denote the most influential person—usually the mother—in a child's world. It is used colloquially to denote a person with whom someone is sexually or romantically involved.

sign language *n.* Any system of communication based on hand signals, especially one used by deaf people. There are many such systems, including *American Sign Language and *British Sign Language, and like *natural languages they tend to be mutually unintelligible. *See also* cherology, dactylology.

sign stimulus *n.* In ethology, a *feature (1) of a complex *stimulus (1) that triggers a specific response or *fixed-action pattern. A classic example is the redness of the belly of a male stickleback fish in breeding condition, which elicits aggressive attacks from other male sticklebacks, whereas other features of the stimulus, such as its shape, size, and manner of movement, have little effect on the responses. Similarly, the tactile sensation of prodding by a male stickleback at the base of the tail of a female in the right condition elicits its egg-laying, whereas other features of the stimulus, including its colouring, are irrele-

vant to this response. The Dutch-born British ethologist Niko Tinbergen (1907–88), who first identified sign stimuli in 1951, reported that even a red mail van passing outside the window of his laboratory elicited aggressive *display (1) from his male sticklebacks, and even prodding with a glass rod at the base of a female's tail elicited egg-laying. Many sign stimuli, though not all, are *releasers. *See also* supernormal stimulus, vacuum activity. **sign stimuli** *pl.*

sign test *n.* In statistics, a *distribution-free test applied to two related samples to test the *null hypothesis that the two variables are distributed similarly. Differences between corresponding scores on the two variables are classified as either positive, negative, or tied, and if the two variables are similarly distributed, the numbers of positive and negative differences will not be significantly different.

sildenafil citrate *n.* The chemical name of the drug *Viagra, used for treating *male erectile disorder.

silent mutation *n.* Any *mutation that has no effect on the phenotype, either because the altered *codon happens to specify the same amino acid as the original one (*see* codon family), or because it occurs in an *intron that has no genetic function.
[So called because it is not expressed]

silent receptors *n.* *Neuroreceptors to which substances bind without producing any apparent physiological response.

silok *See* latah.

similarities test *n.* A type of *intelligence test item or subtest in which the respondent tries to explain in what way things are similar or alike. A typical example is: *In what way are fear and happiness similar or the same?* The answer is that they are both emotions.

similarity-attraction hypothesis *See* attitude similarity hypothesis.

similarity grouping law *n.* One of the four original *grouping laws of *Gestalt psychology, formulated in 1923 by the German psychologist Max Wertheimer (1880–1943) to explain the organization of parts into wholes by the visual system. According to the law, elements that are similar tend to be grouped perceptually, so that (for example) the array OOxx tends to be perceived as two pairs. Also called *equality grouping law*. *See also* common fate, common region, connectedness grouping law, *Prägnanz*. *Compare* closure grouping law, good continuation, proximity grouping law.

similarity law *n*. In the doctrine of *association, a law introduced by the English philosopher John Stuart Mill (1806–73) according to which mental elements that are similar tend to become associated. *See also* grouping law. *Compare* contiguity law, frequency law.

similarity paradox *n*. Another name for the *Skaggs–Robinson paradox.

simile *n*. A *figure of speech in which something is explicitly compared to something that it resembles, usually with one of the prepositions *like* or *as*, a typical example being 'Love is like the measles; we all have to go through it'—Jerome K(lapka) Jerome (1859–1927), *Idle Thoughts of an Idle Fellow* (1889). *Compare* metaphor.
[From Latin *simile* something similar, from *similis* like]

simple cell *n*. A type of neuron in the *primary visual cortex (Area V1) that responds maximally to a stationary bar (slit) or straight edge with a particular orientation or slant and position on the *retina and that divides the *receptive field into excitatory and inhibitory regions: excitation within a bar and inhibition outside it, excitation outside a bar and inhibition inside it, or excitation on one side of an edge and inhibition on the other side. *See also* bar detector, edge detector, end-stopped receptive field, feature detector, orientation-specific cell. *Compare* complex cell, hypercomplex cell.

simple deteriorative disorder *n*. A condition (included in the *ICD-10 classification and in the *DSM-IV appendix of conditions meriting further study) characterized by progressive decline in occupational or academic functioning; gradual appearance and exacerbation of *negative symptoms such as *affective flattening, *alogia, and *avolition; poor interpersonal skills; and social isolation and withdrawal. *Compare* schizoaffective disorder,

schizoid personality disorder, schizophreniform disorder, schizotypal personality disorder.
[So called because of the absence of prominent *catatonic, *hebephrenic, or *paranoid symptoms]

simple phobia *n*. Another name for *specific phobia.

simple random sample *n*. A *probability sample drawn from a *population in such a way that every member of the population is equally likely to be selected. Also called a *random sample*. *See also* cluster sample, random digit dialling, stratified random sample. *Compare* accidental sample, convenience sample, non-probability sample, opportunity sample, quota sample, self-selected sample, snowball sample. **SRS** *abbrev*.

simple reaction time *n*. *Reaction time in a situation in which there is only one possible stimulus requiring only one type of response. *Compare* choice reaction time, discrimination reaction time.

simple receptive field *n*. The *receptive field of a *simple cell.

simple reinforcement schedule *n*. A *reinforcement schedule that does not incorporate two or more different schedules. Also called a *simple schedule*. *Compare* compound reinforcement schedule.

simple schizophrenia *n*. Another name for *simple deteriorative disorder.

simple structure *n*. In *factor analysis, a method of *rotation advocated by the US psychologist Louis Leon Thurstone (1887–1955) in which as many factor loadings as possible are zero and none is negative.

simple tone *n*. Another name for a *pure tone.

simplicity principle *n*. Another name for the *precision law of Gestalt psychology.

Simpson's paradox *n*. A statistical *paradox in which two sets of data, considered separately, each support a certain conclusion, but together support the opposite conclusion.

Suppose that a drug trial is run, and drug A is effective in 10 out of 100 patients (10 per cent), whereas drug B is effective in 200 out of 1,000 (20 per cent). Then a second trial is run, and in this case drug A is effective in 400 out of 1,000 patients (40 per cent), whereas drug B is effective in 60 out of 100 patients (60 per cent). Clearly, drug B is superior in each of the two trials, yet if the data are combined, then drug A is superior: drug A is effective in 410 out of 1,100 (37 per cent), whereas drug B is effective in 260 out of 1,100 (24 per cent).
[Named after the British mathematician Edward Hugh Simpson (born 1927) who published it in 1951]

simulation heuristic *n.* A *heuristic whereby people make predictions, assess the probabilities of events, carry out *counterfactual reasoning, or make judgements of causality through an operation resembling the running of a simulation model. The ease with which the mental model reaches a particular state may help a decision maker to judge the propensity of the actual situation to reach that outcome. The Israeli psychologists Daniel Kahneman (born 1934) and Amos Tversky (1937–96), who introduced the heuristic in a lecture in 1979 and published it as a book chapter in 1982, provided empirical evidence that people use it to predict the behaviour of others in certain circumstances and to answer questions involving counterfactual propositions by mentally undoing events that have occurred and then running mental simulations of the events with the corresponding input values of the model altered. For example, when provided with a *vignette describing two men who were delayed by half an hour in a traffic jam on the way to the airport so that both missed flights on which they were booked, one of them by half an hour and the second by only five minutes (because his flight had been delayed for 25 minutes), 96 per cent of a sample of students thought that the second man would be more upset. Kahneman and Tversky argued that this difference could not be attributed to disappointment, because both had expected to miss their flights, and that the true explanation was that the vignette invited the use of the simulation heuristic, in which it would be easier to imagine minor alterations that would have enabled the second man to arrive in time for his flight. The heuristic is often interpreted as a form of *availability heuristic.

simultanagnosia *n.* Impaired ability to perceive more than one object or image at the same time, hence an inability to comprehend a whole picture even when its constituent elements can be recognized, often occurring as a symptom of *Bálint's syndrome or a lesion in the *left temporal lobe. *See also* agnosia.
[From *simultan(eous)* + *agnosia*]

simultaneous contrast *n.* The tendency for a sensation such as lightness, colour, or warmth to induce the opposite sensation in a stimulus with which it is juxtaposed. *See* colour contrast, contrast (2), lightness contrast, warmth contrast. *Compare* successive contrast.

simultaneous masking *n.* A form of *masking that occurs when the perception of a stimulus, called the *test stimulus*, is reduced or eliminated by the simultaneous presentation of a second stimulus, called the *masking stimulus*. *See also* auditory masking, visual masking. *Compare* backward masking, forward masking.

simultaneous matching to sample *See* matching to sample.

single-blind study *n.* A research design in which the research participants or subjects do not know until after the data have been collected, but the experimenter does know, which experimental treatment has been applied to which subjects. This type of design is often used in drug trials involving the comparison of a drug and a *placebo (1), to avoid contamination of the results from biases and preconceptions on the part of the subjects. *See also* randomized controlled trial. *Compare* double-blind study, open study.

single-case design *n.* Another name for a *case study.

single-frame task *n.* A *visual search task in which all stimuli are presented together. *Compare* multiframe task.

single-linkage clustering *n.* In statistics, any technique of *cluster analysis in which the distance between two clusters is defined as the distance between their two closest members. Also called the *nearest neighbour method*.

single photon emission computed tomography *See* SPECT scan.

single stimuli method *See* method of single stimuli.

single-synapse reflex *n*. Another name for a *monosynaptic reflex.

sinusoidal *adj*. Varying according to the regular undulating sine curve $y = \sin x$.
[From Latin *sinus* a curve or bay + *-oid* indicating likeness or resemblance, from Greek *eidos* shape or form + *-al* from Latin *-alis* of or relating to]

sinusoidal grating *n*. A grating in which the *luminance of the image undulates at a regular *spatial frequency along an axis, increasing and decreasing according to the sine curve $y = \sin x$.

sitology *n*. The study of food, nutrition, and diet.
[From Greek *sitos* grain or food + *logos* word, discourse, or reason]

situationist critique *n*. A critique of the concept of *personality, initiated by the US psychologist Walter Mischel (born 1930) in his book *Personality and Assessment* (1968), based on evidence apparently contradicting the fundamental assumption of all personality theories, namely that people display more or less consistent patterns of behaviour across situations. Mischel drew attention to the low correlations between personality test scores and behaviour in everyday situations and concluded that behaviour can be more reliably predicted from past behaviour than from personality test scores. According to the strong form of the situationist critique, behaviour is merely predictive of itself, and theories of personality are futile. *See also* interactionism (2).

6-hydroxydopamine *n*. A *neurotoxin that is closely related to *dopamine and is readily taken into dopaminergic and noradrenergic neurons via their normal reuptake mechanism, whereupon it destroys the neuron terminals, causing the organism to lose the ability to perform simple actions to obtain rewards. **6-OHDA** *abbrev*.

16PF *abbrev*. The Sixteen Personality Factor Questionnaire, a popular personality scale that consists of 185 questions, such as 'I get frustrated when people take too long to explain something', each having three response categories—usually *true*, *?*, *false*—and that yields scores on sixteen primary factors: Warmth, Reasoning, Emotional Stability, Dominance, Liveliness, Rule-consciousness, Social Boldness, Sensitivity, Vigilance, Abstractedness, Privateness, Apprehension, Openness to Change, Self-reliance, Perfectionism, and Tension. Scores on the primary factors can be combined to yield scores on five global factors: Extraversion, Anxiety, Tough-mindedness, Independence, and Self-control, and in addition an Impression Management (lie) score can be calculated. The questionnaire was constructed by the English-born US psychologist Raymond B(ernard) Cattell (1905–98) and first described in an article in the *Journal of Clinical Psychology* in 1956. The sixteen primary factors were derived by successive reduction, using *factor analysis, of the 17,953 trait names, 4,505 with distinct meanings, located by the US psychologists Gordon W(illard) Allport (1897–1967) and Henry S(ebastian) Odbert (1909–95) in an exhaustive dictionary search in 1936. Also called the *Cattell 16PF*. *See also* Language Personality Sphere, trait.

size constancy *n*. A form of *perceptual constancy in which an object tends to retain its perceived size despite changes in its *angular size or the size of the image that it casts on the retina. Thus a football looks the same size whether its *proximal stimulus image covers a large area of the retina when it is viewed close up or a tiny area when it is viewed from a distance.

size–distance invariance *n*. A hypothesis that the perceived size *s* and the perceived distance *d* of an object are associated in such a way that their ratio is a constant, so that $s/d = k$, implying that any misperception of size implies a misperception of distance and vice versa. This relation breaks down in the *moon illusion. *Compare* shape–slant invariance.

size–weight illusion *n*. A powerful *cognitive illusion that causes approximately 98 per cent of people to judge an object to be heavier than another object of the same weight but much larger size when the two are lifted by hand. In a simple home demonstration of the illusion, pieces of lead or other heavy material may be placed in two different-sized containers and surrounded by sand to prevent them from moving about and from being visible if the containers are transparent, and the weights of the containers may be adjusted until they are identical, whereupon the smaller container will feel much heavier than the larger one. In a classic experiment on this illusion, 100 US military officers judged a smaller object to be on average two and a half times as heavy as one that was the same weight but twice the size in each dimension. The illusion was first reported in 1889 by the German psychologists Georg Elias Müller (1850–1934) and Friedrich Schumann (1863–1940). It is sometimes classified as a *tactile illusion. Also called *Charpentier's illusion*.

skag *n*. A street name for *heroin.

Skaggs–Robinson paradox *n*. A surprising fact about the rate at which learning and subsequent recall are affected by the degree of similarity of the material to be learnt in two tasks carried out in close succession. On the one hand, the more similar the material to be learnt in the two tasks, the slower the rate of learning and the worse the subsequent recall, because similarity increases *proactive interference and *retroactive interference; but on the other hand, the rate of learning and the amount of recall are highest when the material in the two tasks is identical, because proactive and retroactive interference cease to operate and each task functions as practice for the other. Also called the *similarity paradox*. [Named after the US psychologists Ernest Burton Skaggs (1892–?1970) and Edward Stevens Robinson (1893–1937) who discussed it in articles in the journal *Psychological Monographs* in 1925 and 1920 respectively]

skeletal muscle *n*. The *striped muscle tissue that is used for voluntary movements of the limbs and other body parts, including the external muscles of the eyes. [So called because most of them move parts of the skeleton]

sketchpad, visuospatial *See* visuospatial sketchpad.

skewness *n*. In statistics, an index of the degree to which a distribution is asymmetric around its mean. The *normal distribution is symmetric and thus has zero skewness, whereas a distribution whose right tail is more prominent than its left tail is positively skewed or skewed to the right, and one whose left tail is comparatively prominent is negatively skewed or skewed to the left. In a positively skewed distribution the mean is larger than the median and the median is larger than the mode, and in a negatively skewed distribution these inequalities are reversed, the order of the parameters often being used as a test for skewness. Skewness is used along with the *kurtosis to assess whether a variable is normally distributed.

skill *n*. Expertise or accomplishment in any field; specifically, any complex, organized pattern of behaviour acquired through training and practice, including cognitive skills such as mathematics or chess, perceptual skills such as radar monitoring, motor skills such as juggling, and social skills such as non-verbal communication. Research into skills can be traced at least as far back as 1820, when the German astronomer Friedrich Wilhelm Bessel (1784–1846) studied the accuracy of difficult astronomical observations requiring judgements of duration (*see* personal equation). In the latter half of the 19th and the early decades of the 20th century investigations continued into how people learn Morse code, typing, and other skills, and research gained considerable momentum during the Second World War with the development of radar, advanced military aircraft, and sophisticated weapon systems, which presented human operators with difficult problems of learning and performance. Since the 1970s, research on skills has been further stimulated by the rise of sport psychology and increased concern about skilled aspects of social interaction. [From Old Norse *skil* distinction, from *skilja* to separate.]

skin *n*. The tough, flexible, cutaneous *membrane that covers the outer surface of the body and that functions as the body's largest *sense organ, occupying a total surface area in a human adult of approximately 1.67 square metres (18 square feet) and being composed of two layers, the outer *epidermis and the inner *dermis (see illustration). *See also* cold spot, cutaneous sense, ectoderm, epicritic, exocrine gland, formication, free nerve ending, galvanic skin response, goose pimples, histamine, mechanoreceptor, Meissner's corpuscle, melatonin, Merkel cell, Pacinian corpuscle, pain receptor, pallaesthesia, paradoxical cold, paradoxical heat, paradoxical warmth, paraesthesia, pellagra, physiological zero, pressure-sensitive spot, rapidly adapting, Ruffini corpuscle, sensory saltation, skin conductance response, slowly adapting, substance P, sweat gland, temperature receptor, touch, touch receptor, two-point threshold, Urbach–Wiethe disorder, warm spot.

skin conductance response *n.* A measure of change in the conductivity of the *skin to a weak electric current. It is usually measured in mhos (*mho* being *ohm* spelt backwards), because it is the reverse of the *galvanic skin response in which change in the electrical resistance of the skin is measured in conventional units of ohms. **SCR** *abbrev.*

Skinner box *n.* A compartment containing a lever, key, or other manipulable device that a rat, pigeon, or other animal can operate in order to receive food delivered from a storage magazine to a hopper, or occasionally to avoid electric shocks delivered through the floor of the compartment. It was invented by the US psychologist B(urrhus) F(rederic) Skinner (1904–90) while he was a postgraduate stu-dent at Harvard University in 1929, and it is often attached to a *cumulative recorder to study *operant conditioning. *See also* maga-zine training, reinforcement (1).

Skinner crib *n.* Another name for an *air crib.

Skinnerian conditioning *n.* Another name for *operant conditioning.
[Named after the US psychologist B(urrhus) F(rederic) Skinner (1904–90) who introduced the procedure in his Ph.D. dissertation in 1931]

skin-pop *vb.* In drug-culture slang, to inject a drug subcutaneously (below the skin) or intra-muscularly (into muscle tissue) rather than intravenously (into a vein). Also called *skin-ning. Compare* mainline.

skin sense *n.* Another name for a *cutaneous sense.

slang *n.* An informal, non-standard variety of a language, or the *jargon (1) of an occupa-tional or social group. *See also* back slang, register (2), rhyming slang. *Compare* argot.

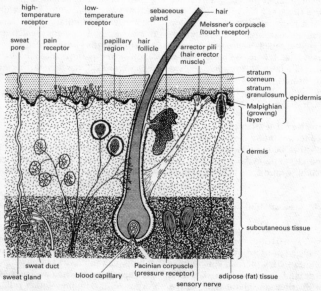

Skin. The structure of mammalian skin.

sleep *n.* A periodic state of muscular relaxation, reduced metabolic rate, and suspended consciousness in which a person is largely unresponsive to events in the environment. Five stages of sleep can be distinguished by psychophysiological measurements, namely *REM sleep and four separate stages of *NREM sleep, called stages I, II, III, and IV NREM sleep respectively. *See also* basal forebrain, basic rest–activity cycle, circadian rhythm, delta sleep-inducing peptide, delta wave, dream (1), dyssomnias, hypnagogic image, hypnopompic image, K complex, locus coeruleus, magnocellular nucleus, melatonin, nucleus gigantocellularis, paradoxical sleep, parasomnias, PGO spike, pineal gland, polysomnography, pseudoinsomnia, REM atonia, REM rebound, sleep spindle, sleep–wake cycle, sleepwalking, slow-wave sleep, subcoerulear nucleus.

sleep apnoea *n.* A *breathing-related sleep disorder characterized by recurrent episodes of breathing cessation during sleep, leading to *hypersomnia during the daytime. US *sleep apnea. See also* central sleep apnoea, obstructive sleep apnoea. *Compare* central alveolar hypoventilation syndrome.
[From Greek *apnoia* cessation of breathing, from *a-* without + *pnein* to breathe]

sleep disorders *n.* A category of *mental disorders prominently associated with disturbances of *sleep patterns. They are subdivided into the *dyssomnias, involving disturbances in the amount, quality, and timing of sleep, and the *parasomnias, characterized by behavioural and physiological abnormalities associated with sleep, although there is overlap between these categories.

sleeper effect *n.* The tendency for the recipients of a persuasive message from a source of low *credibility to show increased *attitude change a few days or weeks after exposure to the message, either relative to recipients of the same message attributed to a source of high credibility (the *relative sleeper effect*) or relative to the amount of attitude change occurring immediately after exposure to the message (the *absolute sleeper effect*). The effect was first reported by the US psychologists Carl I(vor) Hovland (1912–61) and Walter Weiss (born 1925) in the journal *Public Opinion Quarterly* in 1951.

sleep-onset insomnia *n.* Difficulty falling asleep, also called *initial insomnia. See under* insomnia.

sleep paralysis *n.* A condition in which *REM atonia is experienced in the waking state. Such episodes typically occur immediately after waking or shortly before falling asleep. They are often frightening and may be accompanied by *out-of-body experiences. *See also* narcolepsy. *Compare* REM behaviour disorder.

sleep spindle *n.* An *EEG wave form that occurs periodically in brief (approximately 1-second) bursts with a frequency of 12–15 hertz during light Stage II *NREM sleep.
[So called because of the resemblance of its trace to a spindle, tapering at both ends]

sleep terror disorder *n.* A *parasomnia characterized by repeated awakening from sleep, usually during the first part of the night and with a scream or cry, in a state of intense fear, confused, disoriented, and without any vivid recall of a dream, unresponsive to being comforted, and with amnesia for the episode the following morning. Also called *night terrors* or *pavor nocturnus* or, if occurring during the day, *pavor diurnus. Compare* nightmare disorder.

sleep–wake cycle *n.* The *circadian rhythm of sleep and wakefulness that persists even when environmental cues as to the passage of time are removed, although in those circumstances it usually has a period slightly longer than 24 hours.

sleep–wake schedule disorder *n.* Another name for *circadian rhythm sleep disorder.

sleepwalking *n.* A phenomenon occurring occasionally during Stages III and IV *NREM sleep, usually during the first third of the night, in which the sleeper manifests complex motor activity, including rising from bed and walking about with a blank facial expression, and is unresponsive and difficult to awaken, with amnesia for the episode the following morning. Also called *noctambulation* or *somnambulism. See also* sleepwalking disorder.

sleepwalking disorder *n.* A *parasomnia characterized by recurrent episodes of *sleepwalking.

sleepy sickness *n.* A colloquial name for *encephalitis lethargica.

slimmers' disease *n.* A popular name for *anorexia nervosa, misleading because slimmers do not necessarily have it and it is not caused by slimming.

slip of action *See* action slip. *See also* parapraxis.

slip of memory *n.* A minor error of recall, including an instance of *paramnesia (2). Also called a *lapsus memoriae. See also* parapraxis.

slip of the pen *n.* A mistaken piece of writing when something else was intended. Also called a *lapsus calami. See also* parapraxis.

slip of the tongue *n.* A mistaken utterance when something else was intended. Also called a *lapsus linguae. See also* parapraxis.

slowly adapting *adj.* Of or relating to *afferent neurons from *sensory receptors in the *skin that respond constantly to sustained stimulation. *See also* sustained responder. *Compare* rapidly adapting. **SA** *abbrev.*

slow oxidative fibre *n.* Another name for a *slow-twitch fibre. US *slow oxidative fiber*. **SO fibre** *abbrev.*
[So called because it reacts relatively slowly and is adapted for oxidative or aerobic metabolism]

slow-twitch fibre *n.* A dark-coloured *striped muscle fibre, especially in muscles involved in standing and walking, that responds more slowly and is less prone to fatigue but capable of less powerful contractions than *fast-twitch fibre. US *slow-twitch fiber*. Also called a *slow oxidative fibre* or *SO fibre*.

slow-wave sleep *n.* Another name for Stages III and IV of *NREM sleep, characterized by high-amplitude (150 microvolts), low-frequency (1–3 hertz) EEG waves called *delta waves. *See also* delta sleep-inducing peptide. **SWS** *abbrev.*

smack *n.* A common street name for *heroin. [From Yiddish *schmeck* heroin]

small calorie *See under* Calorie.

small intestine *n.* The section of the *alimentary canal between the *stomach and the *large intestine.

small-sample fallacy *n.* Another name for the *sample size fallacy.

smart drug *n.* A non-technical name for any drug believed to have *nootropic effects or to enhance *cognitive ability or performance. Also called a *cognitive enhancer. See* caffeine, deprenyl, ginkgo, ginseng, phenytoin, vasopressin. *See also* performance enhancer.

smell *n.* One of the five classical *senses (1), mediated by *olfactory receptors in the nose. The *olfactory bulb receives impulses from the *olfactory receptors and transmits them via the *olfactory nerves directly to the *olfactory cortex and the *amygdala, this sensory pathway being unique in bypassing the *thalamus entirely. Perhaps for that reason, smell is more effective than any other sense in reawakening memories from the distant past, especially the emotions associated with past experiences, although the literary passage most often cited in support of this phenomenon, quoted under *redintegration, clearly refers to taste rather than smell. *See* olfaction.

smell prism *n.* Another name for *Henning's prism.

smell square *n.* Another name for the *Crocker–Henderson system.

smooth endoplasmic reticulum *See under* endoplasmic reticulum. **SER** *abbrev.*

smooth eye movement *n.* An eye movement that is slow, steady, and controlled by feedback, in contrast to a *saccade. *See also* compensatory eye movement, ocular convergence, ocular divergence, smooth following movement.

smooth following movement *n.* A *smooth eye movement occurring only when tracking a moving object and keeping the gaze fixated on the target. *See also* pursuit movement.

smooth movement *n.* Another name for a *ramp movement.

smooth muscle *n.* Involuntary muscle tissue, capable of slow, rhythmic contractions, such as is found in the muscles that control the walls of blood vessels, the erection of hair cells, the iris, and all internal organs except the heart. *Compare* cardiac muscle, striped muscle.

[So called because it does not have the transversely striped appearance of voluntary muscle and cardiac muscle]

Snellen fraction *n*. An index of visual *acuity based on the familiar *Snellen chart* used by optometrists and opticians, on which are printed upper-case letters arranged in size from the largest at the top to the smallest at the bottom. The person being tested normally stands 20 feet or 6 metres from the chart and reads as many letters as possible starting at the top, and a score is assigned in the form of the ratio or fraction d/d_n, where d is the viewer's distance from the chart and d_n is the distance at which a viewer with normal visual acuity could read the smallest letters that the person being tested can read. On this scale 20/20 vision is normal by definition, and 20/200 vision is a criterion of blindness originally introduced by the American Foundation for the Blind, indicating that the smallest letters read by the person being tested from 20 feet could be read from 200 feet by a viewer with normal (20/20) visual acuity, which means that the letters are approximately ten times as tall as the letters that a viewer with normal visual acuity could read. Normal visual acuity is usually defined as a *minimum separable of one minute of arc or 1/60 of a degree of *visual angle.

[Named after the Dutch ophthalmologist Hermann Snellen (1834–1908) who devised it]

snow *n*. A street name for *cocaine.

snowball sample *n*. A *non-probability sample obtained by recruiting one or more individuals who each recruit one or more individuals, and so on, in the manner of pyramid selling. *Compare* accidental sample, cluster sample, convenience sample, opportunity sample, probability sample, quota sample, random digit dialling, self-selected sample, simple random sample, stratified random sample.

snurp *n*. A small complex of *RNA and protein that helps to clear meaningless *introns from genetic material in cells by splicing *messenger RNA.

[From *snRNP* an abbreviation of small nuclear ribonucleoprotein]

sociabilizer *n*. A drug such as *ecstasy (2) or *GHB that stimulates or enhances natural sociability. *See also* empathogen.

social age *n*. A child's performance on a test of social maturity, such as the *Vineland Social Maturity Scale, expressed as the average age of children who achieved the same level of performance in a standardization sample. The concept is based on that of *mental age. *Compare* chronological age. **SA** *abbrev*.

social anthropology *n*. The branch of anthropology devoted to the study of social and cultural phenomena such as religious beliefs, kinship systems, and political and economic structures, especially (though not exclusively) in non-literate societies. *Compare* cultural anthropology, physical anthropology.

social anxiety disorder *n*. Another name for a *social phobia.

social categorization *n*. The assignment of people to social categories on the basis of skin colour, clothing, speech style, or other signs or indications of group membership, and the consequent *stereotyping of group members according to the supposedly typical characteristics of members of those categories. *See* social identity theory. *See also* minimal group situation.

social class *n*. Another name for *class (1).

social cognition *n*. The cognitive activity that accompanies and mediates social behaviour, including the acquisition of information about the social environment, the organization and transformation of this information in memory, and its effects on social behaviour. It includes *impression formation, *person perception, *attribution, and *social categorization.

social cognitive theory *n*. An approach to *social learning, incorporating findings from research into *learning (1), *memory, and *social cognition, and focusing on people's thoughts and how they affect social behaviour. It was introduced by the Canadian-born US psychologist Albert Bandura (born 1925) in his book *Social Foundations of Thought and Action:*

A Social Cognitive Theory (1986), as a successor to *social learning theory. **SCT** *abbrev.*

social compliance *See* compliance.

social constructivism *See under* constructivism.

social contagion *n.* The spread of ideas, attitudes, or behaviour patterns in a group through imitation and *conformity. Also called *behavioural contagion.*

social desirability response set *n.* A predisposition or readiness to respond to items of a multiple-choice questionnaire with responses calculated to present oneself in a favourable light according to perceived social norms and values. *See also* response set (2).

social dilemma *n.* An interactive decision in which individual interests are at odds with collective interests, the pursuit of individual self-interest by every decision maker leaving everyone worse off than if each had acted cooperatively. In empirical studies, social dilemmas are presented in one of three general forms, called *N-person Prisoner's Dilemmas, *public goods dilemmas, and *resource dilemmas, and they have been used to model problems of inflation and voluntary wage restraint, conservation of scarce natural resources, environmental pollution, arms races and multilateral disarmament, mob behaviour, and many other social problems involving cooperation and trust. The *Prisoner's Dilemma game is a social dilemma restricted to two interacting decision makers. *See also* commons dilemma.
[So called because it is an extension of the Prisoner's Dilemma game and models social problems]

social distance scale *n.* An instrument introduced by the US sociologist Emory S(tephen) Bogardus (1882–1973) in an article in the *Journal of Applied Sociology* in 1925 for measuring attitudes towards social or ethnic groups. Respondents are presented with a number of groups and are asked to indicate which they would willingly admit to various categories of social relationship, varying in level of intimacy. In one of Bogardus's earliest studies, published in his book *Immigration and Race Attitudes* (1928), the groups were Englishmen, Germans, Jews, and Negroes, and the respon-

dents, 1,725 native-born Americans, were asked which they would 'willingly admit' to the following: *to close kinship by marriage, to my club as personal chums, to my street as neighbours, to employment in my occupation,* and *to citizenship in my country.* The percentages for Englishmen were respectively 94, 97, 97, 95, 96; for Germans 54, 67, 79, 83, 87; for Jews 8, 22, 26, 40, 54; and for Negroes 1, 9, 12, 39, 57. A social distance scale is a simple example of a *Guttman scale, although it predates Guttman's formalization of his scale. Also called a *Bogardus social distance scale.*

social exchange theory *n.* A theory of social interaction based on the proposition that people expect rewards and costs from social exchange to be equitable. It was developed by the US sociologist George Caspar Homans (1910–89) and expounded in his books *The Human Group* (1950) and *Social Behavior: Its Elementary Forms* (1961). *See* equity theory.

social facilitation *n.* The term coined in 1920 by the US psychologist Floyd H(enry) Allport (1890–1978) to refer to the phenomena that were later called *audience effects and *coaction effects. Allport's term is a misnomer, because the effects are not invariably facilitative. *See also* drive theory of social facilitation.

social identity theory *n.* A theory of *social categorization based on the concept of social identity, the part of the self-concept that derives from group membership. According to the theory, social categories, including large groups such as nations and small groups such as clubs, provide their members with a sense of who they are, and social identities not only describe but also prescribe appropriate behaviour, and membership of the social category of 'student', for example, determines not only how members define and evaluate themselves but also how others define and evaluate them. According to the theory, the basis of social *prejudice is the enhancement of self-esteem by discrimination against out-groups. The theory was originally formulated in 1978 by the British-based Polish psychologist Hanri Tajfel (1919–82). *See also* minimal group situation. **SIT** *abbrev.*

social impact *See* law of social impact.

social influence *n.* Any process whereby a person's *attitudes (1), *opinions, *beliefs, or behaviour are altered or controlled by some form of social communication. It includes *conformity, *compliance, *group polarization, *minority social influence, *obedience, *persuasion, and the influence of social *norms (1). See also law of social impact.

social insect n. Any of the species of bees, wasps, ants, and termites that live in organized colonies with division of labour. Some species of ants even practise slavery (see dulosis). See also eusocial, polyethism.

social intelligence n. Another name for *emotional intelligence, especially those aspects concerned with the ability to perceive, appraise, and express emotions accurately and the ability to comprehend emotional messages and to make use of emotional information. Its existence as a distinct characteristic would require evidence for high correlations among different measures of social intelligence and low correlations between such measures and conventional measures of *intelligence, and neither of these requirements has been adequately fulfilled.

social introversion scale n. Any scale designed to measure *introversion, including the social introversion scale of the *MMPI.

socialization n. **1.** The process, beginning in infancy, whereby one acquires the attitudes, values, beliefs, habits, behaviour patterns, and accumulated knowledge of one's society, through child-rearing, education, and modification of one's behaviour to conform with the demands of the society or group to which one belongs. See also anticipatory socialization. **2.** The act or process of altering something in accordance with socialist principles, as by transferring an industry to public ownership.

socialize vb. **1.** To train, educate, or prepare someone for life in a particular society or group. See also socialization (1). **2.** To create or alter something according to socialist principles, as by nationalization. See also socialization (2). **3.** To act in a sociable or friendly manner.

social learning n. The processes by which social influences alter people's thoughts, feelings, and behaviour. The earliest social learning theories, put forward in 1950 by the US psychologists John Dollard (1900–80) and Neal E(lgar) Miller (1909–2002) and in 1954 by the US psychologist Julian B(ernard) Rotter (born 1916) were simple *operant conditioning theories based on *reinforcement (1); more recent versions assign a major role to *cognitive processes. In 1969 the Canadian-born US psychologist Albert Bandura (born 1925) argued that imitation and *modelling sometimes occur without reinforcement, through simple observational learning, as in an experiment by Bandura and two colleagues in 1961 in which children who observed the actions of an aggressive adult towards an inflatable five-foot BoBo doll tended later, after they were subjected to mild *frustration, to imitate the hostile behaviour they had observed. See also locus of control.

social learning theory n. The conceptual framework within which the processes of *social learning are studied. See also social cognitive theory. **SLT** abbrev.

social loafing n. The tendency to exert less effort on a task when working as part of a cooperative group than when working on one's own—one reason why many hands make light work. The French agricultural engineer Maximilien (Max) Ringelmann (1861–1931) first investigated this phenomenon in a series of experiments carried out in 1882–7 but not published until 1913, in one of which students pulled as hard as they could on a rope, alone and in groups of two, three, and eight; the results showed that, on average, groups of three exerted only two and a half times as much force as an individual working alone, and groups of eight exerted less than four times the force of a single person. The term social loafing was coined by the US psychologist Bibb Latané (born 1937) and colleagues who performed an experiment, published in the Journal of Personality and Social Psychology in 1979, in which participants attempted to make as much noise as possible, by yelling and clapping, while wearing blindfolds and listening to masking noise through headphones. Compared to the amount of noise that they generated alone, participants made only about 82 per cent as much noise when they believed they were working in pairs and 74 per cent as much noise when they believed they were part of a group of six people working together. The phenomenon has been replicated across a variety of tasks, and evidence has shown that it is greatly reduced by making individual contributions identifiable within the group. Subsequent evidence suggests that social loafing tends to occur when individuals contribute to a group product, whereas *coaction effects tend to occur when individuals work in groups to produce individual products. Also called the *Ringelmann effect*. *See also* diffusion of responsibility.

social perception n. The processes by which people *perceive one another. *See* attribution, attribution theory, false-consensus effect, implicit personality theory, impression formation, person perception, stereotype.

social phobia n. An *anxiety disorder characterized by a *phobia of scrutiny by others or of being the focus of attention in social situations involving strangers. Exposure to such social situations either generates anxiety about behaving in an embarrassing or humiliating way, or triggers a *panic attack, but the reaction is recognized by the afflicted person (if an adolescent or adult) as excessive or irrational, and the avoidance behaviour or anxious anticipation interferes significantly with everyday life, occupational or academic performance, or social relationships. *See also* paroxetine. *Compare* specific phobia.

social psychology n. The branch of psychology devoted to social behaviour in all its forms, including attitudes, social compliance, conformity, obedience to authority, interpersonal attraction, attribution processes, group processes, helping behaviour, and nonverbal communication.

social quotient n. An index of social maturity, based on the ratio definition of the intelligence quotient or *IQ, the social quotient being defined as *social age divided by *chronological age, the ratio then being multiplied by 100. Hence SQ = (SA/CA) × 100. *See also* Vineland Social Maturity Scale. **SQ** *abbrev.*

social skill n. Any *skill necessary for competent social interaction, including both *language (1) and *non-verbal communication. *See also* social skills training.

social skills training n. Any of a number of techniques, often involving practice, feedback, modelling, and *assertiveness training, for teaching the complex patterns of behaviour involved in forms of social interaction such as holding conversations, dating, and being interviewed. **SST** *abbrev.*

sociobiology n. The study of the biological bases of social behaviour. **sociobiological** *adj.* Pertaining to *sociobiology. **sociobiologist** n. One who practises *sociobiology.

sociodrama n. A technique of *group therapy introduced by the Romanian-born US psychiatrist Jacob L(evy) Moreno (1892–1974) as an adjunct to *psychodrama. It differs from psychodrama in the greater importance it places on audience participation and its focus on problems likely to be common to all group members rather than just one. Group members act out the relevant conflicts in an effort to find their own solutions to the problems, while the director keeps the audience constantly involved. *See also* drama therapy.

socio-economic class n. Another name for *class (1).

sociogram n. A chart showing the network of interrelationships in a social group. It is usually constructed by inviting the group members to indicate their choices (or rejections) of one another, in response to a question such as the following, used in a classic study of an air force squadron: *Which member of the squadron would you most like to have flying alongside you during combat?* On the resulting chart, each group member is represented by a circle, with an arrow pointing from each circle to another, indicating which individuals chose which others, and it typically contains one or more *stars* (chosen by many others), one or more *isolates* (chosen by few), and often one or more *cliques* of mutually chosen individuals. The process of mapping social networks in this way, called *sociometry, was introduced by the Romanian-born US psychiatrist Jacob L(evy) Moreno (1892–1974), whose books *Who Shall Survive?* (1934) and *Sociometry, Experimental Method and the Science of Society* (1951) made his ideas available to a wide audience.
[From Latin *socius* a companion + Greek *gramme* a line]

sociolinguistics n. The study of interrelationship between language and its social context, especially the social and cultural factors affecting language.

sociology n. The study of human societies and the structures and processes within them. Classical sociology has been influenced by the writings of three social theorists in particular: the German political philosopher Karl Marx (1818–1883), who argued that economic modes and relations of production are the fundamental bases of the structures and ideologies within all societies, and who drew particular attention to the importance of class conflict in the functioning and change of societies; the French sociologist Émile Durkheim (1858–1917), who challenged the assumption that social processes can be understood in terms of the actions of individuals and argued that even *suicide, apparently the ultimately individualistic act, cannot be fully explained at the purely individual level; and the German economist and sociologist Max Weber (1864–1920), who focused attention on the social implications of rationality, interpreting economics and law as forms of rational human action and religion as a model of non-rational action, and who classified types of authority and bureaucracy according to this distinction. *Social psychology is studied in both sociology and psychology.
[From French sociologie coined in 1837 by the French philosopher and mathematician Auguste Comte (1798–1857) in lectures that were incorporated in his six-volume Cours de Philosophie Positive (Positive Philosophy), from Latin socius a companion + logos word, discourse, or reason]

sociology of knowledge n. The study of the social origins of belief systems and (according to its proponents) *knowledge. The German political philosophers Karl Marx (1818–83) and Friedrich Engels (1820–95) argued in Die Deutsche Ideologie (1846, The German Ideology) and elsewhere that people's ideologies, including their social and political beliefs and opinions, are rooted in their class interests, and more generally in the social and economic circumstances in which they live: 'It is men, who, in developing their material intercourse, change, along with this their real existence, their thinking and the products of their thinking. Life is not determined by consciousness, but consciousness by life' (Marx–Engels Gesamtausgabe 1/5). Under the influence of this doctrine, and of *phenomenology, the Hungarian-born German sociologist Karl Mannheim (1893–1947) gave impetus to the growth of the sociology of knowledge

with his Ideologie und Utopie (1929, translated in 1936 as Ideology and Utopia), although the term had been introduced five years earlier by the co-founder of the movement, the German philosopher and social theorist Max Scheler (1874–1928), in Versuche zu einer Soziologie des Wissens (1924, Attempts at a Sociology of Knowledge). A strong interpretation claims that all knowledge and beliefs are the products of socio-political forces, but this version is self-defeating, because if it is true, then it too is merely a product of socio-political forces and has no claim to truth and no persuasive force. Mannheim sought to escape this paradox by exempting free-floating intellectuals, whom he claimed were only loosely anchored in social traditions, relatively detached from the class system, and capable of avoiding the pitfalls of total ideologies and of forging a 'dynamic synthesis' of the ideologies of other groups. See also epistemology, sociology.

sociometry n. The quantitative study of the interrelations between the members of a social group, especially through the use of a *sociogram. It was introduced by the Romanian-born US psychiatrist Jacob L(evy) Moreno (1892–1974) and became popular after the publication of his books Who Shall Survive? (1934) and Sociometry, Experimental Method and the Science of Society (1951). **sociometric** adj.
[From Latin socius a companion + metron a measure]

sociopathy n. Another name for *antisocial personality disorder. **sociopath** n. A person with *sociopathy. Compare psychopathy. **sociopathic** adj.
[From Latin socius a companion + pathos suffering]

sodium n. A silvery-white, alkaline, metallic element that occurs abundantly in the form of sodium chloride (as in sea water and common table salt) and is required to maintain the electrolyte balance in living cells, also playing an important part in the transmission of nerve impulses and in muscle contractions. See also sodium channel, sodium pump. **Na** abbrev.
[From Latin soda sodium carbonate + -ium indicating a metallic element]

sodium channel n. A *cation channel, such as one of the pores in the *rods and *cones of the retina that is kept open by the substance *cyclic GMP and consequently has an unusually low *resting potential of approximately −50 millivolts in the dark, but when molecules of visual pigment are stimulated by light they activate the enzyme *transducin, which in turn inactivates cGMP so that the pores close and the cell becomes *hyperpolarized. *See also* ion channel, saxitoxin.

sodium current *n*. The flow of sodium through the sodium channels of a cell membrane.

sodium glutamate *n*. Another name for *monosodium glutamate.

sodium inactivation *n*. The momentary interruption of the activity of the *sodium pump during an *action potential.

Sodium Pentothal *n*. A proprietary name for the barbiturate drug *thiopental (thiopentone). *See also* truth drug.
[Trademark]

sodium–potassium pump *n*. Another name for the *sodium pump.

sodium pump *n*. A mechanism for expelling positively charged sodium *ions from inside a neuron, where large negatively charged particles (anions) are trapped by the membrane, across the semipermeable cell membrane to the extracellular fluid, to maintain the interior concentration of positively charged ions far below that of the exterior. When an *action potential occurs, sodium ions are transferred to the inside of the cell, and after an action potential the process of pumping them out is necessary to maintain the *resting potential of the neuron. The mechanism simultaneously drives positively charged potassium ions from the extracellular fluid, where their concentration is low, to the intracellular fluid, where their concentration is high, but this occurs at a lower rate than the outward transfer of sodium ions. Because the pumping process is a form of *active transport against the electrochemical gradient resulting from *osmotic pressure, it requires energy, which is supplied by the hydrolysis of *ATP by certain enzymes that are themselves sometimes called pumps. Also called the *sodium–potassium pump* or *Na⁺-K⁺ pump*.

soft drug *n*. An imprecise term for a drug such as cannabis or LSD that is not addictive. *See also* gateway drug. *Compare* hard drug.

softening of the brain *n*. A non-technical name for *encephalomalacia.

soft sign *n*. A slight abnormality of speech, gait, posture, or behaviour observed during a *neurological examination and judged to be indicative of a mild neurological impairment. Also called an *equivocal sign*. *Compare* hard sign.

solar retinopathy *n*. Damage to the *retina caused by looking at the sun. *See also* scotoma.

solecism *n*. **1.** A grammatical error or non-standard sentence construction. **2.** Any error, mistake, impropriety, breach of etiquette, or departure from good manners.
[From Greek *soloikos* speaking incorrectly, from *Soloi* an Athenian colony where a corrupt form of the Attic dialect of Greek was spoken + *oikizein* to colonize]

soluble RNA *n*. Another name for *transfer RNA.

solvent *n*. Any substance that is capable of dissolving another.

solvent abuse *n*. Self-intoxication by the deliberate inhalation of volatile *solvents such as *toluene that are found in many common household products. Preferred usage *solvent misuse*. *See also* glue-sniffing, inhalant, inhalant-related disorders.

soma *n*. **1.** The central part of a neuron or other cell containing the *nucleus (1) and other structures that keep the cell alive, as distinct from a cell *process (2). Also called a *cell body*. **2.** The body of an organism as distinct from its mind, or (in physiology and genetics) as distinct from its *germ cells. **somata** *pl*. **somatic** *adj*.
[From Greek *soma* a body]

somaesthesis *n*. A generic term for bodily sensations, including the *cutaneous senses, *proprioception, and *kinaesthesis. US *somesthesis*. Also called *somaesthesia* or *somesthesia*.
[From Greek *soma* a body + *aisthesis* sensation, from *aisthanesthai* to feel]

somaesthetic association area n. Another name for the somatosensory association area (see under somatosensory cortex). US somesthetic association area.
[From Greek soma a body + aisthesis sensation, from aisthanesthai to feel]

somaesthetic cortex n. Another name for the primary *somatosensory cortex. US somesthetic cortex.
[From Greek soma a body + aisthesis sensation, from aisthanesthai to feel + Latin cortex bark or outer layer]

somatic adj. **1.** Of or relating to the body as distinct from the mind. **2.** Of or relating to the cell body or *soma (1).
[From Greek somatikos of or relating to the body, from soma a body + -itikos resembling or marked by]

somatic cell n. A body cell as opposed to a *germ cell.

somatic compliance n. In *psychoanalysis, the involvement of the body in the expression of symptoms of *hysteria and other *neurotic (1) disorders. Sigmund Freud (1856–1939) introduced the concept in his celebrated case study of 'Dora' entitled 'Fragment of an Analysis of a Case of Hysteria' (1901/5): 'Every hysterical symptom involves the participation of both sides. It cannot occur without the presence of a certain degree of somatic compliance offered by some normal or pathological process in or connected with one of the bodily organs' (Standard Edition, VII, pp. 7–122, at p. 40, italics in original).
[From Greek soma a body + -ikos of, relating to, or resembling]

somatic delusion n. A *delusion regarding the functioning or appearance of one's body, such as the unfounded belief that one's skin, mouth, vagina, or anus emits a foul smell, that one is infested with insects or parasites, that certain body parts are deformed or unsightly, that one is pregnant when one is not, or that an internal organ is not functioning properly.
[From Greek somatikos of or relating to the body, from soma a body + -itikos resembling or marked by]

somatic delusional disorder n. A type of *delusional disorder in which the central delusion is a *somatic delusion.

somatic hallucination n. A *hallucination of a physical state or event within the body, such as an electrical impulse running down one's arms or an object inside one's chest.

somatic nervous system n. The division of the *nervous system devoted to *sensation from external sense organs and control of *skeletal muscles. Compare autonomic nervous system. **SNS** abbrev.

somatic receptor n. A *sensory receptor mediating a *cutaneous sense, *kinaesthesis, or *proprioception. Also called a somatoreceptor.
[From Greek soma, somat- a body + English receptor]

somatic sensory cortex n. Another name for the *somatosensory cortex.

somatization disorder n. A *somatoform disorder characterized by a history of several years of *somatic symptoms beginning before age 30 and resulting in medical treatment or significant impairment in social, occupational, or other areas of functioning. According to *DSM-IV diagnostic criteria, there must be pain associated with at least four separate bodily sites or functions, and at least two gastrointestinal symptoms apart from pain, at least one reproductive sexual symptom apart from pain, and at least one pseudo-neurological symptom not limited to pain (impairment in coordination or balance, *paralysis, *dysphagia, *diplopia, or some such symptom). Also called Briquet's syndrome. Compare undifferentiated somatoform disorder.
[From Greek soma body + -izein cause to become or to resemble]

somatoform disorders n. A category of *mental disorders characterized by *somatic symptoms suggestive of a *general medical condition, but without independent evidence of any diagnosable general medical condition, and not produced intentionally, but causing clinically significant distress or impairment in social, occupational, or other areas of functioning. See body dysmorphic disorder, conversion disorder, hypochondriasis, pain disorder, pseudocyesis, somatization disorder, undifferentiated somatoform disorder. Compare compensation neurosis, factitious disorders, malingering.
[From Greek soma body + Latin -forma form]

somatosensory association area *See under* somatosensory cortex.

somatosensory cortex *n.* Areas of the *cerebral cortex, namely the primary somatosensory cortex, the secondary somatosensory area, and the somatosensory association area, devoted to processing information from the *somatic receptors. The primary somatosensory cortex, also called the *somaesthetic cortex*, occupying the *postcentral gyrus immediately behind the central sulcus of the temporal lobe in both cerebral hemispheres, is an area in which parts of the body are mapped contralaterally, with disproportionately large representations of hands, lips, and tongue. The small secondary somatosensory area in the parietal lobes responds specifically to *painful stimuli relayed by the peripheral nervous system. The somatosensory association area, also called the *somaesthetic association area* or the *supplementary sensory area*, lies just behind the primary somatosensory cortex and provides a basis for *stereognosis. Also called the *somatic sensory cortex*. *See also* cutaneous sense, sensorimotor cortex, somatosensory homunculus.

[From Greek *soma*, *somat-* a body + Latin *sensorius* of the senses, from *sensus* felt, from *sentire* to sense]

somatosensory homunculus *n.* A standard depiction of the primary *somatosensory cortex of each cerebral hemisphere as a human figure lying supine along the *postcentral gyrus immediately behind the central sulcus with its toes deep in the longitudinal fissure towards the midline of the brain (see illustration). Each part of the figure represents the area of the somatosensory cortex receiving

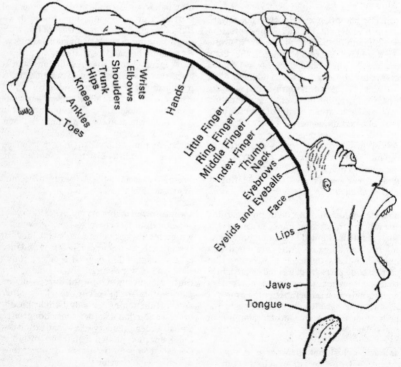

Somatosensory homunculus. A version adapted from Penfield and Rasmussen's *The Cerebral Cortex of Man* (1950).

sensations from the corresponding (contralateral) part of the body, and it has disproportionately large hands, lips, and tongue, which gives it a grotesque appearance. The best known version was developed by the US-born Canadian neurosurgeons Wilder Graves Penfield (1891–1976) and the US neurologist Theodore B(rown) Rasmussen (1910–2002) and published in their book *The Cerebral Cortex of Man* in 1950. Also called a *sensory homunculus*. *See also* homunculus.
[From Latin *homunculus* a little man, diminutive of *homo* a man]

somatostatin *n.* A peptide hormone that inhibits the release of *growth hormone by the anterior pituitary and *insulin by the pancreas. *Compare* growth hormone releasing hormone.

somatotrophin *n.* Another name for *growth hormone. Also spelt *somatotropin*.
[From Greek *soma, somat-* a body + *trophe* nourishment + *-in(e)* indicating an organic compound]

somatotrophin-releasing hormone *n.* Another name for growth hormone releasing hormone. Also spelt *somatotropin-releasing hormone*. **STRH** *abbrev.*

somatotrophin release inhibiting factor *n.* Another name for somatostatin. Also spelt *somatotropin release inhibiting factor*. **SRIF** *abbrev.*

somatotype *n.* Any of the types of human physique or body build distinguished within a classificatory scheme, sometimes associating specific physical types with corresponding psychological types. *See* constitutional psychology. *See also* asthenic body type, athletic body type, dysplastic body type, pyknic body type. **somatotypology** *n.* The study of *somatotypes.
[From Greek *soma* a body + *typos* a mark]

Somers' *D* *n.* In descriptive statistics, an asymmetric index of association, closely related to the gamma statistic, between an *independent variable and a *dependent variable measured on *ordinal scales with ties allowed. If two pairs of scores are examined, they must either be concordant, in the sense that the one ranked higher than the other on the independent variable is also ranked higher than the other on the dependent vari-

able, or discordant. Somers' *D* is defined as the difference between the number of concordant pairs and the number of discordant pairs divided by the total number of pairs not tied on the independent variable, and it ranges from −1 to +1. *See also* Kendall's tau.
[Named after the US sociologist and statistician Robert Hough Somers (born 1929) who developed it in 1962]

somesthesis *See* somaesthesis.

somesthetic *See* somaesthetic.

somnambulism *n.* Another name for *sleepwalking. **somnambulist** *n.* One who engages in *somnambulism or sleepwalking.
[From Latin *somnus* sleep + *ambulare* to walk]

sonar *n.* Any device or system for detecting or locating objects by *echolocation, especially such devices on submarines and the systems of *biosonar used by some organisms.
[From so(und) na(vigation and) r(anging)]

sone *n.* A unit of loudness equivalent to 40 *phons.
[From Latin *sonus* a sound]

sonic shadow *n.* An area of reduced sound intensity around the ear that is further from a sound source, as a result of reflection and absorption of sound waves by the head, leading to a binaural difference in loudness that is used as a *cue (2) for localizing sounds above about 1,000 hertz (about two octaves above Middle C), which have wavelengths shorter than the diameter of the head, but not for longer waves that bend round the head and do not produce sonic shadows. It is less accurate than localization based on *transient disparity and *phase delay, except for very high-pitched sounds with frequencies above 8,000 hertz, when the *pinna becomes effective as a focusing device. Animals with very small heads, such as rodents, cannot use transient disparity or phase delay, because the time differences are too tiny to be detected accurately, but their ears are sensitive to very high-pitched sounds whose wavelengths are shorter than the diameter of their heads, which enables them to use sonic shadows to locate sounds. Also called a *binaural intensity difference*, an *interaural intensity difference*, or a *sound shadow*. *See also* binaural ratio, biosonar, cone of confusion, sound localization.

sorites *n.* A string of *syllogisms in which the conclusion of each forms a premise of the next, arranged with the intermediate conclusions omitted and only the final conclusion stated explicitly. For example: *All true believers shall be saved; Anyone who is saved must be free from sin; Anyone who is free from sin is innocent in the eyes of God; All those who are innocent in the eyes of God go to heaven when they die; Therefore, all true believers go to heaven when they die. See also* sorites paradox. **soritical** or **soritic** *adj.*
[From Greek *soreites* heaped, from *soros* a heap]

sorites paradox *n.* A sophistical argument in the form of a *sorites, the most familiar example being the following. One grain of sand is clearly not a heap of sand, and the addition of one grain to something that is not a heap can never transform it into a heap; therefore there can never be a heap of sand, and it would be futile to try to make one. A similar argument can be used to prove that no man is bald or that no one is old. It is considered by some to be a *paradox but is more correctly classified as a fallacy.

Sotos syndrome *n.* Another name for *cerebral gigantism, often spelt incorrectly as *Soto's syndrome*.
[Named after the US paediatrician Juan Fernandez Sotos (born 1927) who, with four colleagues, first described it in 1964]

soul talk *n.* A non-technical name for *Black English Vernacular.

sound localization *n.* The perception of the position of a sound source in space. Sounds below about 1,000 hertz (about two octaves above Middle C) are located in the horizontal plane by momentary *binaural time differences* called *transient disparity and *phase delay, and high-pitched sounds are located through *binaural intensity differences* called *sonic shadows. Humans have a *minimum audible angle in the horizontal plane of about 2 degrees, but like other terrestrial animals are not good at locating sound in the vertical dimension, whereas the barn owl, which hunts fieldmice and other prey in total darkness, can locate sound sources to within about one degree in both the horizontal and vertical dimensions (azimuth and elevation), more accurately than any other species that has been tested, its left ear pointing downwards and its right ear upwards to aid localization in the vertical dimension. Also called *auditory localization* or *auditory space perception. See also* audiogravic illusion, auditory receptive field, biosonar, cone of confusion, pseudophone, superior olivary nucleus, trapezoid body.

sound pressure level *n.* The absolute intensity of a sound in decibels relative to a reference level of $10^{-16} W/cm^2$ (watts per square centimetre), slightly below the average human *absolute threshold for a sound of 1,000 hertz (about two octaves above Middle C). Thus a sound of 60 dB SPL is 60 dB higher than the reference level and has an intensity of $10^{-10} W/cm^2$, and a doubling or halving of absolute sound intensity always corresponds to a change of 3 dB. *See also* decibel. **SPL** *abbrev.*

sound shadow *n.* Another name for a *sonic shadow.

sound spectrogram *n.* A diagram produced by a *sound spectrograph showing the intensities of the frequency components of a sound as a function of time, with time represented on the horizontal axis, frequency on the vertical axis, and intensity by the darkness of the line. Often called a *speech spectrogram* when representing speech sounds.
[From Latin *spectrum* a spectacle, from *spectare* to watch, from *specere* to look at + Greek *gramme* a line]

sound spectrograph *n.* An electronic device incorporating a large number of sound *filters (2), each responsive to a narrow band of frequencies, used for producing *sound spectrograms. Also called a *speech spectrograph* when used to analyse speech sounds. *See also* voiceprint.

sound spectrum *n.* The distribution of *pure tones in a sound wave, usually represented as a plot of power or *amplitude as a function of frequency. *See also* sound spectrogram.

sour *n.* One of the primary tastes in *Henning's tetrahedron, the characteristic taste of vinegar or lemon juice.

source amnesia *n.* A form of *amnesia in which information is remembered, but the person who remembers it is unable to recall where, from whom, or how the information was obtained.

source memory n. Memory for where, from whom, or how certain knowledge or information was acquired. For example, a person who knows that all insects have six legs, and also remembers learning this fact from *Gardeners' Question Time* on the radio while driving to a family gathering on Christmas day in 1995, has excellent source memory for this particular item of knowledge. *Reality monitoring is a special form of source memory that involves distinguishing between genuine external sources and one's own imagination as sources of information.

source of instinct See instinctual source.

space–time illusion n. An *illusion in which perception of space interferes with perception of time or vice versa. See kappa effect, tau effect.

Spanish fly n. Another name for *cantharides.

span of apprehension n. The number of items that a person can apprehend or grasp at one time, which in turn determines the number of items that can be stored in *short-term memory. Also called an *attention span* or a *span of attention*. See also chunking, iconic store, magical number seven, subitize. **SOA** abbrev.

spasm n. An involuntary muscular contraction, such as a *tic, a *convulsion, or a hiccup.
spasmodic adj. Of, relating to, or occurring in *spasms.
[From Greek *spasmos* a cramp]

spasmodic torticollis n. A *psychogenic condition characterized by sustained or episodic *spasms of the neck muscles, causing the head to be twisted out of alignment. Also called *torticollis*, *wryneck*.
[From Greek *spasmos* a cramp + Latin *tortus* twisted + *collum* neck]

spasmophemia n. A form of *aphasia in which speech is impaired by *spasms of the muscles in the *vocal tract, causing stammering or laboured speech.
[From Greek *spasmos* a cramp + *phanai* to speak + *-ia* indicating a condition or quality]

spastic n. **1.** A derogatory term for a person afflicted by *spasms, especially one with *cerebral palsy. adj. **2.** Afflicted by or resembling *spasms.
[From Greek *spastikos* of or relating to spasms, from *spasmos* a cramp + *-ikos* of, relating to, or resembling]

spastic paralysis n. Permanent contraction of a muscle or group of muscles caused by damage to the *motor cortex.

spastic speech n. Another name for *spasmophemia.

spatial ability n. The capacity to perform tasks requiring the mental manipulation of spatial relationships, such as *mental rotation, *mirror drawing, map-reading, or finding one's way around an unfamiliar environment. See also agnosia, cognitive map, Mozart effect, primary mental abilities.

spatial frequency n. The inverse of the wavelength in a visual image that has been transformed into a *sinusoidal grating of varying *luminance, a high spatial frequency capturing fine detail and a low spatial frequency coarse detail in the image, the luminance variation across any image being decomposable into sinusoidal components by *Fourier analysis. See also contrast sensitivity function, primal sketch, sinusoidal grating. Compare frequency (1).

spatial neglect n. A *neurological disorder characterized by a partial or complete lack of awareness of sensory information in (usually) one half of the *visual field. It is possible for a person to be totally blind in half the visual field without being aware of this fact, though it is easily demonstrated by the *line bisection test. Lesions in either of the *cerebral hemispheres in the *visual cortex or secondary somatosensory area (see somatosensory cortex) are usually responsible for spatial neglect on the opposite side. Also called *unilateral neglect*, or *unilateral spatial neglect*. See homonymous hemianopia.

spatial summation n. The simultaneous action of two or more *afferent neurons that combine additively to produce a *graded potential in a *postsynaptic neuron and that may cause it to transmit a nerve impulse or *action potential that could not be generated by impulses from a single neuron. See *also* graded potential. *Compare* temporal summation.

speaking in tongues *n.* A non-technical name for *glossolalia.

Spearman rank correlation coefficient *n.* In statistics, a correlation coefficient computed on scores that consist of or have been converted to *ranks. It is mathematically equivalent to the *product–moment correlation coefficient after converting the raw scores to ranks. Also called *rho*. Symbol: ρ. *See also* correlation.
[Named after the English statistician and psychologist Charles Spearman (1863–1945) who devised it]

Spearman's rho *n.* Another name for the *Spearman rank correlation coefficient.
[Named after the English statistician and psychologist Charles Spearman (1863–1945) who devised it and *rho* (ρ), the seventeenth letter of the Greek alphabet, which is used to symbolize it]

Special K *n.* A common street name for the drug *ketamine.

speciation *n.* The process of evolutionary divergence whereby new *species are formed. *See also* isolating mechanism.

species *n.* A *taxonomic group containing individuals capable of interbreeding and producing fertile offspring. A species is a subdivision of a *genus, and it may contain one or more *subspecies, *varieties, or *races (2). By convention, following the system put forward by the Swedish botanist Carolus Linnaeus (1707–78) in his book *Systema Naturae* (1737), a species is always given a double name, comprising the generic name with an upper-case initial letter followed by the specific name with a lower-case initial letter, like an entry in a telephone directory comprising a surname followed by a first name, hence *Cannabis sativa*, the common hemp plant, or *Homo sapiens*, the human species. *See also* genus. **species** *pl.* **specific** *adj.*
[From Latin *species* appearance or kind, from *specere* to look]

speciesism *n.* The belief in the intrinsic superiority of the human *species over all others, often accompanied by an assumption that

human beings are therefore justified in exploiting non-human animals for their own advantage. *Compare* ableism, ageism, ethnocentrism, fattism, heterosexism, racism, sexism. **speciesist** *n.* **1.** One who advocates or practises *speciesism. *adj.* **2.** Of or relating to *speciesism.
[Coined from *species* on the model of *racism*]

species-specific *adj.* Of or relating to a characteristic, trait, or pattern of behaviour that is peculiar to a species. **species specificity** *n.* The quality of being *species-specific.

specific anosmia *n.* A selective inability to smell a particular odorant. *See also* anosmia, cacosmia, dysosmia, hyperosmia, hyposmia, parosmia.

specific developmental disorder *n.* Any disorder in which some distinctive and circumscribed ability or function fails to develop properly from an early age, the deficit not being attributable to any other disorder. *Compare* pervasive developmental disorders.

specific developmental disorder of language *n.* A term sometimes used (in *ICD-10 and elsewhere) to refer to disorders in which language acquisition is disturbed from the early stages of development, the deficit not being attributable to neurological or sensory impairment, mental retardation, or environmental deprivation. *See* expressive language disorder, reading disorder, receptive language disorder, specific disorder of arithmetic skills, specific spelling disorder.

specific developmental dyslexia *n.* Another name for *reading disorder.

specific disorder of arithmetic skills *n.* A specific developmental disorder characterized by a significant impairment in arithmetic skills (addition, subtraction, multiplication, and division) that is not explicable by *mental retardation or inadequate schooling. *See also* acalculia, dyscalculia.

specific hunger *n.* A craving for a particular food or nutrient, especially one in which the body is deficient, the most obvious and well-established example being specific hunger for salt.

specific language disability *n.* Any or all of *expressive language disorder, *receptive language disorder, *reading disorder, *specific spelling disorder.

specific learning disability n. A *learning disability in a circumscribed area of functioning, such as a *specific developmental disorder of language, *specific disorder of arithmetic skills, or a *specific language disability, not caused by any general deficit. **SLD** abbrev.

specific nerve energies n. The doctrine formulated in 1826 by the German physiologist Johannes Peter Müller (1801–58), elaborated by him in 1838, and later firmly established by research, that the qualitative differences between visual, auditory, tactile, olfactory, and gustatory sensations are determined by the particular *sensory receptors that are stimulated.

specific phobia n. An *anxiety disorder characterized by a *phobia in which the *phobic stimulus is a specific type of object (such as spiders), event (such as thunder), activity (such as flying), or situation (such as enclosed spaces), exposure to the phobic stimulus almost invariably triggering an anxiety response or *panic attack and being recognized by the afflicted person (if an adolescent or adult) as excessive or irrational but being either avoided or tolerated only with intense anxiety or dread, the avoidance behaviour or anxious anticipation of it interfering significantly with everyday life, occupational or academic performance, or social relationships. Some classifications (including *ICD-10) exclude *agoraphobia. A comprehensive table of phobias and phobic stimuli is provided in Appendix I at the back of this dictionary. Also called a simple phobia. Compare social phobia.

specific spelling disorder n. A *specific developmental disorder characterized by a significant impairment in the development of spelling skills without any history of *reading disorder, the *deficit not being attributable to *neurological or *sensory impairment, *mental retardation, or environmental deprivation.

spectral colour n. Any colour found in the *visible spectrum, thus excluding colours such as purple (a mixture of red and blue). US

spectral color. Also called a spectral hue. Compare non-spectral colour.

spectrogram n. A graphic representation of a *spectrum. A graphic representation of the frequency components in a sound as a function of time is called a *sound spectrogram. [From Latin spectrum a spectacle, from spectare to watch, from specere to look at + Greek gramme a line]

spectrum n. The range of colours produced by passing white light through a *prism or a *diffraction grating, the *visible spectrum extending from a wavelength of about 390 nanometres at the short end to about 740 nm at the long end. Perceived colour depends on the balance of wavelengths across the whole visual field, and most people who are asked what colours they can see in a spectrum name the *psychological primaries red, yellow, green, and blue, but the following breakdown and labelling has become conventional: red, 740–620 nm; orange, 620–585 nm; yellow, 585–575 nm; green, 575–500 nm; blue, 500–445 nm; indigo, 445–425 nm; violet, 425–390 nm. This sevenfold breakdown can be traced to the English physicist and mathematician Sir Isaac Newton (1642–1727), who first studied the spectrum scientifically in 1666 and who attributed magical properties to the number seven, which he pointed out was also the number of notes in a (*diatonic) musical scale. See also categorical perception, infra-red, metathetic stimulus dimension, sound spectrum, spectral colour, ultraviolet. **spectral** adj. [From Latin spectrum a spectacle, from spectare to watch, from specere to look at]

SPECT scan abbrev. Single photon emission computed tomography, a technique of *brain imaging similar to a *PET scan, also indicating *regional cerebral blood flow, but using longer-lived radioactive isotopes and producing less clearly defined images than a PET scan, though at much lower cost because it does not require the use of an on-site cyclotron. Also written SPET scan, probably to resemble PET scan. Compare radioisotope scan.

speech act n. A verbal utterance defined in terms of its content, the intention of the speaker, and the effect on the listener. A speech act necessarily involves a *locutionary act and may or may not involve an *illocutionary act and a *perlocutionary act. The term was introduced in 1961 by the English philosopher John Langsham Austin (1911–60).

speech apraxia n. A form of speech *impairment resulting not from any language deficit but from difficulty in making the required voluntary movements of the tongue, lips, and lower jaw. See also apraxia.

speech spectrogram n. A graph of speech sounds produced by a *sound spectrograph (called a speech spectrograph when used for this purpose).

speech stretcher n. A device that produces slowed but otherwise undistorted recordings of sounds, especially human speech.

speech synthesizer n. A device that generates sound waves of varying frequency and intensity. It can be used to simulate the production of human speech, making possible experiments on the perception of speech sounds, and enabling people who are paralysed to communicate verbally.

speed n. A common street name for *amphetamine, *methamphetamine, and other closely related drugs.
[So called because of their stimulant effects]

speed-accuracy trade-off n. The tendency for increased speed of performance to lead to more errors.

speedball n. A street name for a drug consisting of *cocaine hydrochloride mixed with *heroin.

speed test n. Any test in which the rapidity of responses, rather than their accuracy, is measured. Compare accuracy test, power test.

spell n. A *culture-bound syndrome widespread in sub-Saharan Africa and among African American and Latino communities in the southern United States and elsewhere, characterized by brief episodes of personality change during which the person experiencing the spell believes that some form of communication is taking place with dead relatives or their spirits. A person with this pattern of experiences is endowed locally with dignity and respect, and usually considers it a privilege resulting from being appointed by dead ancestors as a diviner; hence this disorder is distinguished sharply from *ufufunyane, which is feared and despised and is associated with evil spirits. Also (in southern Africa) called thwasa.
[From Old English spell speech, from spellian to speak or announce]

spelling disorder See specific spelling disorder.

spelling dyslexia n. A form of *dyslexia, also called letter-by-letter reading, usually not accompanied by *dysgraphia, in which reading proceeds literally letter by letter and is therefore slow and manifests grave impairment. See also simultanagnosia.

spermatozoon n. A male *gamete or reproductive cell, with a small, flattened head, a long neck, and a very long tail in the form of a whiplike *filament that provides motility, large numbers of which are contained in the semen that is *ejaculated during *coitus although only one at most can penetrate and fertilize the much larger female ovum. **spermatozoa** pl. See also zygote.
[From Greek sperma, spermatos seed, from speirein to sow]

SPET scan abbrev. Another name for a *SPECT scan.
[Presumably to emphasize its relation to a PET scan]

spherical aberration See under aberration (3).

sphincter pupillae n. The muscle that expands the *iris and thereby constricts the *pupil of the eye. Compare dilator pupillae.
[From Greek sphinkter a tightener, from sphingein to bind tight + Latin pupillae of the pupil, from pupilla a pupil, diminutive of pupa a girl or a doll, alluding to the tiny reflection in the eye]

spicy odour n. One of the six primary odours in *Henning's prism, resembling the odour of cinnamon or nutmeg. US spicy odor.

spinal accessory nerve n. Another name for either of the pair of *accessory nerves that supply muscles in the side and front of the neck, the shoulder, and the upper back.

spinal canal *n*. The channel down the middle of the spinal column or backbone containing the *spinal cord.

spinal cord *n*. The thick band of nerve tissue that runs through the spinal canal and to which 31 pairs of *spinal nerves are attached. The spinal cord and the brain together constitute the *central nervous system. *See also* anterior horn, Bell–Magendie law, central canal, corticospinal tract, funiculus, posterior horn, pyramidal decussation, spinal canal, spinal nerve, spinal reflex, substantia gelatinosa.

spinal nerve *n*. Any of the 31 pairs of nerves connected to the *spinal cord, serving the striped muscles, the skin, and the autonomic nervous system, numbered according to the level at which they emerge: 8 cervical pairs, 12 thoracic, 5 lumbar, 5 sacral, and 1 coccygeal pair. *Compare* cranial nerve.

spinal reflex *n*. Any *reflex arc that passes through the spinal cord but avoids the brain.

spinal root *n*. The point of attachment of a *spinal nerve to the *spinal cord. *See* dorsal root, ventral root.

spindle *See* nuclear spindle, sleep spindle, spindle cell.

spindle cell *n*. A type of neuron found in the sixth and deepest (fusiform) layer of the cerebral cortex, with two short *processes (2) that divide into multiple long fibres. Also called a *fusiform cell*.
[So called because it tapers at each end like a spindle]

spinocerebellar tract *n*. A bundle of nerve fibres connecting afferent nerve fibres in the spinal cord to the cerebellum.

spinocerebellum *n*. The functional area of the *cerebellum adjacent to both sides of the midline *vermis, including most of the anterior lobe, receiving inputs from the spinal cord and controlling posture and gait. Lesions in this area lead to *gait ataxia and impairment of posture. *See also* cerebellar syndrome. *Compare* neocerebellum, vestibulocerebellum.

spinoreticulothalamic system *n*. A system of nerve fibres connecting the spinal cord, reticular formation, and thalamus, thought to be involved in the processing of bodily sensations such as *pain.

spinothalamic tract *n*. A bundle of nerve fibres connecting each *posterior horn of the spinal cord to the opposite side of the *thalamus, carrying information about *pain and temperature and some information about touch. It is one of two major routes by which afferent spinal nerve fibres carrying sensations of *somaesthesis are transmitted to the *thalamus. *Compare* dorsal column.

spiny I *n*. A type of neuron with spiny projections on its *dendrites, found abundantly in the *striatum, projecting to the *globus pallidus and *substantia nigra.

spiral aftereffect *n*. The visual aftereffect that is induced by exposure to the *Plateau spiral.

spiral ganglion cell *n*. Any of a large number of *bipolar neurons that have their cell bodies just outside the *cochlea of each ear and that transmit auditory information from the cochlea to the central nervous system via the *vestibulocochlear nerve.
[So called because they occupy the spiral-shaped cochlear canal]

spiral test *n*. In psychometrics, any test of aptitude, ability, or intelligence in which a number of items are presented in sequence, and then the sequence is repeated with more difficult instances of each item type, and so on, with each cycle containing more difficult items than the last.

spiroperidol *n*. A *neuroleptic (1) drug belonging to the class of *butyrophenones that blocks *dopamine neuroreceptors and is used in the treatment of schizophrenia. *See also* dopamine antagonist.

spite *n*. **1.** An *emotion of malicious ill will characterized by an urge to cause harm to another person, especially when this necessitates some harm to oneself as well. **2.** In sociobiology, behaviour of an organism towards another that reduces the *Darwinian fitness of both. **spiteful** *adj*. Filled with or motivated by *spite (1, 2).
[A variant of *despite*]

splenium *n*. The rounded tip at the back of the *corpus callosum, primarily concerned with integrating visual information from the left and right visual fields.
[From Greek *splenion* pad or plaster]

splicing, gene *See* gene splicing.

spliff *n*. A common street name for a *cannabis cigarette.
[Rastafarian slang]

split brain *n*. Another name for *commissurotomy or *split-brain preparation.

split-brain preparation *n*. A surgical operation in which the two *cerebral hemispheres of a person's brain are separated by cutting the *corpus callosum, usually to relieve the symptoms of epilepsy, or in which an animal is treated in this way for research purposes. Also called a *commissurotomy* or *commissurectomy*. *See also* disconnection syndrome.

split-half reliability *n*. A measure of the *reliability of a test based on the correlation between scores on two arbitrarily formed halves of the test, often the odd-numbered and even-numbered test items. More sophisticated versions of this technique are the *Kuder–Richardson coefficient and *Cronbach's alpha.

split personality *n*. Another name for *dissociative identity disorder.

split-span *See under* filter theory.

splitting of the ego *n*. In *psychoanalysis, the coexistence within the *ego of two attitudes towards external reality, functioning side by side without influencing each other, one taking reality into account and the other disavowing reality. According to Sigmund Freud (1856–1939), it is peculiar to the disorder of *fetishism and certain of the *psychoses. He presented his theory in various publications, including an article on 'Splitting of the Ego in the Process of Defence' (*Standard Edition*, XXIII, pp. 275–8). In *object-relations theory it is seen as a more normal mode of psychological functioning.

splitting of the object *n*. In *Kleinian analysis, the most primitive of all *defence mechanisms, in which *instinctual objects that evoke *ambivalence and therefore *anxiety are dealt with by compartmentalizing positive and negative emotions, leading to images of self and others that are not integrated. Splitting plays a central role in the theory of *defensive techniques proposed by the Scottish psychoanalyst W. Ronald D. Fairbairn (1889–1964). *See also* good breast, good object.

spontaneous remission *n*. Recovery from a disorder occurring without treatment. The rate of spontaneous remission ranges from about 30 per cent to about 60 per cent for the various classes of mental disorders.

sports psychology *n*. Application to the performance of competitors in all types of sports of research into *skills and into psychological factors associated with athletic performance. Also called *sport psychology*.

spouse abuse *n*. Any form of physical or mental exploitation or cruelty towards a husband or wife, causing significant harm to its victim. *See also* battered wife syndrome, sexual abuse.

spreading activation *n*. An increase in activity in part of a network caused by increased activity in adjacent units or areas. The term is applied to *neural network models and also to biological networks such as the *central nervous system. *Compare* spreading depression.

spreading depression *n*. An inhibition of the activity of part of the *nervous system induced by the application of a solution of potassium chloride (or another salt), which causes the inhibition to spread slowly from the point of application into neighbouring *neurons. Also called *cortical spreading depression*. *See also* action potential, sodium pump. *Compare* spreading activation.

SPSS *abbrev*. Statistical Product and Service Solutions (formerly, Statistical Package for the Social Sciences), the most popular set of statistical computer programs among psychologists, distributed by SPSS Inc. of Chicago, Illinois, USA. *Compare* BMDP, SAS, SYSTAT.

squeeze technique *n*. A procedure for preventing *premature ejaculation, in which the partner squeezes the neck of the penis tightly until the urge to ejaculate subsides.

SQUID *abbrev.* Superconducting quantum interference device, an instrument for detecting changes in minute magnetic fields generated by the brain.

squiggle game *n.* In *psychoanalysis, a procedure introduced by the English psychoanalyst Donald Woods Winnicott (1896–1971) for therapeutic consultations with children: the therapist begins by drawing a random scribble on a sheet of paper, and the child responds by making it into a meaningful drawing on the basis of what it seems to suggest; and then it is the child's turn to make a random scribble for the therapist to complete, and so on, the drawings serving as points of departure for therapeutic interchanges. Winnicott's researches with the game were published posthumously in his book *Therapeutic Consultations in Child Psychiatry* (1971).

squint *n.* Another name for *strabismus. Also, the act of half-closing the eyes in bright light, but this usage is avoided in technical discourse.

stability *n.* The state or quality of being stable, steady, or dependable. In psychometrics, an aspect of *reliability, according to which a test or measuring instrument yields approximately the same scores when administered to the same respondents on separate occasions. *See also* test–retest reliability.

stabilized retinal image *n.* A visual image that is prevented from moving on the retina by means of specially constructed contact lenses, so that the eye movements that occur continually during visual *fixation (1), owing to various forms of *physiological nystagmus, do not cause the image to move across the retina, the result being that vision fades away after about one second and is replaced by undifferentiated *Eigengrau, although brief glimpses of the image or parts of it may reappear periodically, especially if the stabilization is not complete. This phenomenon, which was discovered simultaneously and independently by researchers in the US and England in 1952, is also called a *fixed image*, a *stabilized image*, or a *stopped image*. *See also* filling-in illusion.

stabilizing selection *n.* A form of *natural selection that operates against the extremes of the range of variation of a characteristic,

thereby tending to stabilize the population close to the mean. *See also* frequency-dependent selection. *Compare* apostatic selection, disruptive selection.

stage fright *n.* A form of *anxiety preceding or accompanying participation in any activity involving public self-presentation before an audience. Also called *performance anxiety*. *See also* audience effect, drive theory of social facilitation.

stage, libidinal *See* libidinal stage.

stages of problem solving *See* problem-solving stages.

staircase illusion *n.* An *impossible figure based on a staircase in the form of a continuous loop that apparently rises endlessly (see illustration), first devised in 1958 by the English psychologist/geneticist Lionel S. Penrose (1898–1972) and his mathematical physicist son Roger Penrose (born 1931), later incorporated into *Ascending and Descending*, one of the best known etchings of the Dutch graphic artist Maurits C(ornelis) Escher (1898–1970). Also called the *Penrose staircase*. Often confused with the *Schröder staircase. *See also* auditory staircase illusion.

Staircase illusion. An impossible figure in which a flight of stairs appears to rise endlessly.

staircase method *n.* A *psychophysical method introduced in 1962 by the US cognitive scientist Tom Norman Cornsweet (born 1929) in which, for *absolute thresholds, a *variable stimulus is presented repeatedly and is adjusted upwards whenever it is not perceived and downwards whenever it is perceived, and for *difference thresholds a variable stimulus is adjusted to increase its absolute difference from a *standard stimulus whenever the difference is not discriminated or is adjusted to decrease its absolute difference from the standard stimulus whenever the difference is discriminated. Also called the *up-and-down method*. *Compare* method of average error, method of constant stimuli, method of limits.

stammering *n*. Another name for *stuttering.

standard deviation *n*. In descriptive statistics, a measure of the degree of dispersion, variability, or scatter in a set of scores, expressed in the same units as the scores themselves, defined as the square root of the *variance. The term was coined in 1893 by the English statistician Karl Pearson (1857–1936). Symbol: *SD* or *σ*. *Compare* interquartile range, probable error, range, semi-interquartile range.

standard error *n*. In statistics, a measure of degree of uncertainty about the value of a *parameter of a population estimated from a sample *statistic, defined as the *standard deviation of values of the statistic observed in a large number of random samples from the population. If the parameter being referred to is the *arithmetic mean, then its standard error is called the *standard error of the mean*, and similarly for any other parameter. *SE* abbrev.

standardize *vb*. **1.** In statistics, to convert a score or value to a *standard score. **2.** In *psychometrics, to establish population *norms (2) for a test by applying it to standardization samples. **standardized** *adj*.

standardized regression coefficient *n*. Another name for a *beta coefficient. Also called a *standardized regression weight*.

standardized test *n*. In psychometrics, a test for which population *norms (2) have been established.

standard score *n*. In statistics, any score expressed in units of *standard deviations of the distribution of scores in the population, with the mean set at zero. Also called a *sigma score* or a *z score*. *See also* stanine score, sten score, T score.

standard stimulus *n*. In *psychophysics, a *stimulus (1) to which an observer attempts to match a *variable stimulus, or an anchoring stimulus that is assigned a number by the experimenter and that an observer uses as the basis in *magnitude estimation by assigning numbers to a variable stimulus in relation to it. **S** or **St** abbrev.

Stanford–Binet intelligence scale *n*. The first *standardized (2) English-language *intelligence test and the prototype of most subsequent intelligence tests, based on a translation of the *Binet–Simon scale, introduced in the United States in 1916 by the psychologist Lewis Madison Terman (1877–1956) and revised several times since then, one of the first to attempt to eliminate cultural and gender bias from its test items. *See also* Porteus Maze Test. **S-B scale** abbrev.
[Named after Stanford University, California, where Terman was working when the test was introduced, and the French psychologist Alfred Binet (1857–1911)]

stanine score *n*. In psychometrics, a test score converted to an equivalent *standard score in a *normal distribution with values 1, 2, . . . , 9, a *mean of 5, and a *standard deviation of 1.96. *See also* derived score. *Compare* IQ, sten score, T score, z score.
[A blend of *Sta(ndard) nine score*]

stapedius *n*. A small muscle in the middle ear that pulls the *stapes backwards and acts in conjunction with the *tensor tympani in the *acoustic reflex to protect the ear from damage when exposed to loud sounds.

stapes *n*. The innermost of the three small bones in the *middle ear, transmitting sound vibrations from the *incus to the inner ear. Referred to non-technically as the *stirrup*. *Compare* incus, malleus. **stapedes** *pl*.
[From Latin *stapes* a stirrup, from *stare* to stand + *pes* a foot, alluding to its resemblance to a stirrup]

star illusion *n*. A form of *irradiation illusion in which a central dark star is surrounded by dark diamonds, the spaces between the star and each of the diamonds being equal to the diameter of the star and the longest diameter of a diamond but appearing much larger (see illustration). The illusion is enhanced by an effect related to the *Müller-Lyer illusion

Star illusion. The white space between the points of the star and of each of the diamonds is equal to the diameter of the star and the longest diameter of a diamond.

arising from the arrowhead shapes formed by the star and the diamonds.

start codon *n.* The *codon or triplet of bases AUG (adenine, uracil, guanine) in a segment of *RNA, or its equivalent in *DNA, signalling the beginning of a protein-coding sequence and specifying the amino acid methionine. Also called an *initiation codon* or an *initiator codon*. *See also* TATA box. *Compare* stop codon.

startle reflex *n.* A reflex pattern of responses to a sudden unexpected stimulus such as a loud noise, including physiological signs of *arousal, flexion of the trunk and limbs, *piloerection, and closing of the eyes. Also called the *startle response* or *startle reaction*. *Compare* Moro reflex.

state anxiety *n.* A temporary form of *anxiety related to a particular situation or condition that a person is currently in, a typical example being *test anxiety. *See also* State-Trait Anxiety Inventory. *Compare* trait anxiety.

state-dependent memory *n.* The tendency for information learnt in a particular mental or physical state to be most easily remembered in a similar state. The phenomenon was first investigated systematically in 1964 by the US psychologist Donald Overton (born 1935), who focused on *drug-dependent memory* in rats, and this was later demonstrated in humans: material learnt in a drunken state is best remembered in a later drunken state, and so on. Clinical evidence has been cited of heavy drinkers who hide alcohol or money when drunk and are unable to find it when sober but remember where it is as soon as they become drunk again. It has since been established that many classes of drugs produce the effect, that the effect is dose-dependent, that it affects recall but not recognition, and that non-pharmacological states can also elicit the effect demonstrated: in a frequently cited British experiment on *context-dependent memory*, lists of words that were learned by divers while they were underwater were best recalled when they were again underwater, and conversely words learned on land were best recalled on land. Emotional states can also produce the effect—*mood-dependent memory*—and this helps to explain why pleasant experiences are more likely to be remembered by a person who is happy, and unpleasant experiences by someone who is unhappy and is likely to become even more unhappy as a result. Also called *state-dependent learning*. *See also* cognitive interview, encoding specificity, redintegration.

State-Trait Anxiety Inventory *n.* A questionnaire comprising two separate self-rating scales, one measuring *state anxiety and the other *trait anxiety, each scale containing 20 items. The inventory was first published by the US psychologist Charles D(onald) Spielberger (born 1927) and several colleagues in 1970. **STAI** *abbrev.*

static assessment environment *n.* A typical context for test administration in which the tester does not respond interactively to a respondent's incorrect answers but merely proceeds to the following question. *Compare* dynamic testing.

static labyrinth *n.* The *maculae in the *utricle and *saccule, functioning to control balance by increasing muscle *tonus to counteract the effect of gravity on the side to which the head is tilted. *See also* vestibular system.

static sense *n.* A form of *proprioception and *kinaesthesis providing information about orientation, balance, and acceleration, mediated by the *vestibular system.

statistic *n.* Any numerical value representing a property of a *sample of scores. Examples of statistics in this sense are the *arithmetic mean, the *variance, and the minimum (lowest score).

[From Latin *statisticus* concerning affairs of state, from *status* a state + -*icus* of, relating to, or resembling]

Statistical Analysis System *See* SAS.

statistical inference *n*. Estimating the *parameters of a population, or forming a judgement about whether an observed relationship or difference can be attributed to chance, usually from the observed properties of a *random sample. *See also* inferential statistics.

Statistical Package for the Social Sciences *See* SPSS.

statistical power *n*. In inferential statistics, the probability that a *significance test will reject the *null hypothesis when it is in fact false. Significance tests vary in power, but all tests increase in power with increasing sample sizes. The power of a test depends on the particular *alternative hypothesis against which it is tested. *See also* Type II error.

statistical prediction *n*. Another name for *actuarial prediction.

Statistical Product and Service Solutions *See* SPSS.

statistical significance *n*. In statistics, a property of the results of an empirical investigation suggesting that they are not due to chance alone. The 5 per cent level of significance has become conventional in psychology; this means that results are normally considered to be statistically significant if statistical tests show that the probability of obtaining, by chance alone, results at least as extreme as those obtained is less than 5 per cent, usually written $p < 0.05$. If the probability is not sufficiently small, then the correct interpretation is that there is no evidence of an effect, not that there is evidence of no effect. *See also* alternative hypothesis, inferential statistics, null hypothesis, *p* value, significance test. **statistically significant** *adj*. [From Latin *significare* to signify]

statistical test *n*. A procedure for deciding whether or not to reject the *null hypothesis and conclude that an observed difference or relationship is not due to chance. *See also* significance test.

statistics *n*. The science of describing and interpreting numerical data in accordance with the theory of *probability, and the application of analytical techniques such as *significance tests, determination of *confidence intervals, and *parameter estimation to such data. The two major branches of statistics are *descriptive statistics and *inferential statistics.
[From Latin *statisticus* concerning affairs of state, from *status* a state + -*icus* of, relating to, or resembling]

statocyst *n*. An organ of equilibrium containing *otoliths, found in crustaceans and other invertebrates; also a gravity-sensitive plant cell containing starch grains enabling the plant to maintain its orientation or direction of growth.
[From Greek *statos* set or placed + *kystis* a bladder]

statolith *n*. Another name for an *otolith.
[From Greek *statos* set or placed + *lithos* a stone]

status epilepticus *n*. A dangerous condition characterized by *convulsions continuing without interruption, caused by sudden withdrawal from anticonvulsant medication, a lack of glucose in the body, a brain tumour, head injury, fever, or poisoning.
[From Latin *status* condition + *epilepticus* epileptic]

status quo bias *n*. Another name for the *endowment effect.

stealing, pathological *See* kleptomania.

Steele–Richardson–Olszewski syndrome *n*. Another name (especially in the UK) for *progressive supranuclear palsy. **SRO syndrome** *abbrev*.
[Named after the Canadian neurologists John C. Steele and John Clifford Richardson (1909–86) and the Polish-born Canadian neurologist Jerzy Olszewski (1913–64) who first described it in 1964]

steepest descent *n*. Another name for *gradient descent.

Stelazine *n*. A proprietary name for the *neuroleptic (1) drug *trifluoperazine.
[Trademark]

stellate cell n. Any of a class of small *interneurons in the *cerebellum, with multiple processes that synapse on the dendrites of *Purkinje cells, the action of which they inhibit, also found in the cerebral cortex, where spiny stellates are excitatory and non-spiny stellates are inhibitory. They are especially abundant in the somatosensory cortex, the primary visual cortex (Area V1), and the primary auditory cortex. *Compare* basket cell, Golgi cell, pyramidal cell.
[From Latin *stellatus* starry, from *stella* a star]

stem-and-leaf display n. In descriptive statistics, a method of tabulating scores that consist of two or more digits. The initial digits (the stems) determine the rows in which the scores are placed and the remaining digits (the leaves) are listed in order within their respective rows, so that the display resembles a *histogram lying on its side with the scores in each class interval listed in order, in place of the bars of the histogram (see illustration). A stem-and-leaf display provides an informative picture of the distribution of a variable. Also called a *stem-and-leaf diagram*.

Raw data		Stem-and-leaf display	
177	171	10	7
118	174	11	1228
122	121	12	12355
178	194	13	3
112	125	14	
107	123	15	
183	182	16	8
111	112	17	1478
125	133	18	233
183	168	19	4

Stem-and-leaf display. The hidden bimodal distribution of the data, with no scores falling between 134 and 167, emerges when the raw data on the left, displayed for convenience in two columns, are rearranged without loss of information on the right.

stem cell n. A master cell that resides in bone marrow and that replicates repeatedly and differentiates to create many different kinds of blood cells and cells of the immune system, and that, unlike other body cells, divides to produce not only new cells of its own type (new stem cells) but also other types of cells, including monocytes, erythrocytes, B lymphocytes, T lymphocyte, and macrophages.

stem completion task n. Another name for a *word-stem completion task.

stenography n. Shorthand writing, especially with the use of a *Stenotype, specially designed for this purpose. *Compare* brachygraphy, tachygraphy. **stenographer** n. A person skilled in the use of *stenography.
[From Greek *stenos* narrow + *graphein* to write]

Stenotype n. A small silent keyboard machine with 22 keys for recording shorthand, invented in 1906 by a US court reporter Ward Stone Ireland (born 1883) and still used for making court records. The fingers of the left hand type consonants appearing before vowels, and these are printed on the left of the paper, the fingers of the right hand consonants after vowels, and these appear on the right, and the thumbs of both hands type all the vowels, which are printed in the middle. An experienced stenographer can operate comfortably at a normal conversational speed of about 150 words per minute. *See also* stenography.
[Trademark, from Greek *stenos* narrow + *typos* type]

sten score n. In psychometrics, a test score converted to an equivalent *standard score in a *normal distribution with values 1, 2, . . . , 10, a *mean of 5.5, and a *standard deviation of approximately 2. *See also* derived score. *Compare* IQ, stanine score, T score, z score.
[A blend of *sta(ndard) ten score*]

Stent–Singer rule *See under* Hebbian rule.

stereoacuity n. Another name for *stereoscopic acuity.

stereoblindness n. An inability to perceive depth on the basis of *binocular disparity, owing to a reduction in the number of functioning *disparity-selective cells in the *visual cortex, usually as a result of *strabismus during infancy. The condition is believed to be quite common (perhaps 4 or 5 per cent of the population) but is generally unrecognized because other depth cues compensate, though it is immediately apparent under examination with *stereograms or *anaglyphs. *See also* depth perception.

stereochemical theory n. An explanation for odour in terms of a small number of odorant molecules with distinctive three-dimensional structures that are assumed to bind to *olfactory receptors, owing to ultramicroscopic slots in their cell membranes specialized to respond to those specific molecular structures. The seven primary odours according to this theory are camphoraceous (like moth balls), musky (like musk), floral or fragrant (like rose or lavender petals), minty (like menthol or peppermint), ethereal (like ether or cleaning fluid), pungent (like vinegar or roasted coffee), and putrid (like faeces or rotten eggs). Also called the *lock-and-key theory*.

stereocilium n. Any of the approximately 100 threadlike structures, not true cilia in spite of their name, projecting from each *hair cell in the *saccular macula within the *membranous labyrinth of the *inner ear and in other epithelia in which hair cells are located. In the inner ear they are embedded in a gelatinous matrix containing crystals of calcium carbonate that exert gravitation drag on them. *Compare* kinocilium. **stereocilia** *pl.*
[From Greek *stereos* solid + Latin *cilium* an eyelash]

stereognosis n. The identification and recognition of solid or three-dimensional objects by touch alone. *Compare* astereognosis.
[From Greek *stereos* solid + *gnosis* knowledge]

stereogram n. A double picture made up of slightly different images that when viewed through a *stereoscope or special spectacles produces a three-dimensional visual image. *See also* anaglyph, random-dot stereogram, stereopsis.

stereopsis n. Depth perception based on *binocular disparity, resulting from the slightly different viewpoints of the side-by-side eyes of humans, monkeys, and some other species, discovered in 1838 by the English physicist and inventor Sir Charles Wheatstone (1802–75). It is served by the *magnocellular system, which is colour-blind (*see* isoluminant). The *visual cortex contains *disparity-selective cells that respond only to particular binocular disparities and are thus tuned to respond to stimuli at particular distances. Also called *stereoscopic vision*. *See also* anaglyph, binocular parallax, horopter, Panum's fusion area, Panum's limiting case, random-dot stereogram, reduction

screen, stereoblindness, stereoscope, stereoscopic acuity.
[From Greek *stereos* solid + *opsis* sight, from *ops* and eye]

stereoscope n. An optical device for displaying a *stereogram so that its two slightly different images of the same object or scene are presented one to each eye, enabling three-dimensional perception to be experienced through *stereopsis.
[From Greek *stereos* solid + *skopeein* to view]

stereoscopic acuity n. Keenness or sharpness of *stereopsis, measured by the subtended angle corresponding to the minimum *binocular disparity sufficient to produce a sensation of depth. Under good viewing conditions, stereoscopic acuities corresponding to *visual angles in the region of 2 seconds of arc, equivalent to 1/1,800 of a degree, have been found. Also called *stereoacuity*. *See also* acuity.

stereoscopic illusion n. Any *visual illusion in which three-dimensional depth is misperceived, or any visual illusion that arises from a phenomenon peculiar to binocular vision. *See* anaglyph, Cheshire cat effect, floating-finger illusion, hole-in-the-hand illusion, Lissajous figure, Pulfrich effect, random-dot kinematogram, random-dot stereogram.

stereoscopic vision n. Another name for *stereopsis.

stereotactic adj. Of or relating to precise three-dimensional localization, especially of brain structures. Also written *stereotaxic*.
[From Greek *stereos* solid + *taktos* arranged (for battle), from *tassein* to arrange + *-ikos* of, relating to, or resembling]

stereotactic instruments n. Devices designed to facilitate precise three-dimensional localization of tissues for brain surgery and research.

stereotype n. A relatively fixed and oversimplified generalization about a group or class of people, usually focusing on negative, unfavourable characteristics, although some authorities recognize the possibility of positive stereotypes as well. The word originally denoted a solid metallic printing plate containing a masthead or other stock image that was difficult to change once cast, and the psycho-

logical meaning was introduced by the US journalist Walter Lippmann (1899–1974) in his book *Public Opinion* (1922), where he also articulated the *cognitive miser theory of stereotyping. Early empirical studies stressed the remarkable consensus in the stereotypes of various ethnic groups in the US; research into the *frustration–aggression hypothesis from the 1940s onwards found evidence for the motivated nature of some stereotypes; and research using the *F scale after its publication in 1950 found stereotypic thinking to be characteristic of people with *authoritarian personalities and fascist belief systems. In 1954, a book entitled *The Nature of Prejudice* by the US psychologist Gordon W(illard) Allport (1897–1967) popularized the interpretation of stereotypes as nothing more than cognitive categories that simplify *information processing and are quite resistant to disconfirming information. There is evidence that some people are capable of maintaining strong stereotypes of typical group members without these stereotypes necessarily influencing how they perceive and evaluate particular members of those groups. *See also* confirmation bias, dual-process model, social categorization. **stereotypic** *adj.* **stereotyping** *n.* The act or process of forming a *stereotype.
[From *stereotype* a fixed, stock plate used for printing a masthead or other standardized text, from Greek *stereos* solid + *typos* type, from *typtein* to strike]

stereotyped movements *n.* Repetitive, non-functional, self-injurious bodily movements such as hand waving, body rocking, head banging, self-biting, or hitting parts of the body, sometimes using an object. *See also* stereotypic movement disorder.

stereotypic movement disorder *n.* A *mental disorder of infancy, childhood, or adolescence, persisting for at least four weeks, involving *stereotyped movements that interfere with normal activities and result (or could result) in injury requiring medical treatment.

Sternberg task *n.* A recognition task in which a number of items are presented and then removed; a single item is then presented, and the respondent has to decide whether or not it was part of the group seen earlier.

[Named after the US psychologist Robert J(effrey) Sternberg (born 1949) who popularized it]

steroid *n.* Any of a group of fat-soluble organic substances with a characteristic chemical structure of 17 carbon atoms bound in four closely linked rings, including the *sterols, *vitamin D, and many *hormones.
[From *sterol* + Greek *-oeides* denoting resemblance of form, from *eidos* shape]

steroid hormone *n.* Any *hormone such as a glucocorticoid, aldosterone, or a sex hormone (androgen or oestrogen) that is synthesized from cholesterol and is a *steroid. The hormones of the adrenal cortex, testes, and ovaries are steroid hormones, whereas those of all other endocrine glands and of the hypothalamus are *peptide hormones. Synthetic analogues include *dexamethasone, *prednisone, *prednisolone, and a synthetic form of *cortisone. *See* aldosterone, corticosterone, cortisol, oestradiol, progesterone, testosterone. *See also* corticosteroid DHEA. *Compare* anabolic steroid.

steroid receptor *n.* A specific region in a cell specialized for *steroid hormone binding.

steroid-regulated gene *n.* A gene whose expression is modified by one or more *steroid hormones.

sterol *n.* Any *steroid alcohol such as *cholesterol.
[Contraction of *cholesterol*, *ergosterol*, and cognate words]

Stevens's law *n.* Another name for the *power law in psychophysics. Also called *Stevens's power law.
[Named after the US psychologist S(tanley) S(mith) Stevens (1906–73) who formulated it in 1953 and discussed it in an influential article in the journal *Psychological Review* in 1957]

stilboestrol *n.* Diethylstilboestrol, a synthetic form of oestrogen, used as a 'morning after' or post-coital contraceptive, especially in cases of rape or incest. US *stilbestrol.
[From Greek *stilb(os)* glittering + English *(o)estr(ogen)* + *-ol* denoting a compound containing a hydroxyl group, from *(alcoh)ol*]

Stiles–Crawford effect *n.* The differential effectiveness of light entering through the centre rather than through the edge of the pupil, bright light that is effective for *cones and that is mediated by the *photopic system being less effective when entering through the edge than the centre, but dim light effective for *rods and mediated by the *scotopic system not showing this differential effect. It is explained by the fact that cones have inner segments serving to channel light travelling directly down their axes, whereas rods are adapted to exploit every scrap of light that falls on them and do not have any channelling mechanism.

[Named after the English physiologists Walter Stanley Stiles (1901–85) and Brian Hewison Crawford (1948–63) who discovered the effect in 1933]

Stilling test n. A test for *colour-blindness and *colour deficiency in the form of a *pseudo-isochromatic chart composed of dots of equal brightness but different hues arranged to form large numerals visible to viewers with normal vision. This test, the first to use a pseudo-isochromatic chart, was modified and adapted by the Japanese ophthalmologist Shinobu Ishihara (1897–1963) to form his famous *Ishihara test. Also called the *Stilling Colour Chart* or *Stilling's Colour Table*. *Compare* Holmgren test.

[Named after the German ophthalmologist Jacob Stilling (1842–1915) who developed it]

stimulant drug n. Any drug that increases or tends to increase the activity of a system or organ of the body, especially one that increases or speeds up the activity of the *central nervous system by boosting *catecholamine transmission, producing an exaggeration of the characteristic features of alert wakefulness, and that in high dosages can cause hallucinations, convulsions, and death. Also called a *psychoanaleptic drug*, a *psychomotor stimulant*, or a *psychostimulant*. A common street name for stimulant drugs in general is *uppers*. *See* amphetamine, caffeine, cocaine, dextroamphetamine, digitalis, ecstasy (2), ephedrine, kainic acid, khat, mescaline, methamphetamine, methylphenidate (Ritalin), nicotine, pentylene tetrazol, phenmetrazine, picrotoxin, strychnine, theobromine, theophylline, xanthine, yohimbine. *See also* performance enhancer, substance abuse, substance-related disorders, sympathomimetic, tachyphrenia. *Compare* depressant drug.

stimulus n. **1.** Any event, agent, or influence, internal or external, that excites or is capable of exciting a *sensory receptor and of causing a *response in an organism. **2.** An object or event in the external environment that causes a response* in an organism, also called a *distal stimulus*. **3.** A pattern of physical energy that stimulates or excites a *sensory receptor, also called a *proximal stimulus*. **4.** Any class of events, agents, or influences that elicit the same type of response* in an organism. **5.** Any occurrence that excites or inhibits the firing of a neuron. **6.** Anything that rouses an organism or goads it into action. **7.** In the *behaviourism of the US psychologist B(urrhus) F(rederic) Skinner (1904–90) and his followers, any event, whether physical or mental, that evokes a *response. *See also* adequate stimulus, conditioned stimulus, reaction time, sign stimulus, supernormal stimulus, unconditioned stimulus. **stimuli** pl. **S** abbrev.

[From Latin *stimulus* a cattle goad or spur]

stimulus generalization n. The tendency for a learned *response to a particular *stimulus (1) to be elicited by other stimuli that resemble it. In *operant conditioning, it is the tendency to respond, after conditioning, to stimuli that were present during *reinforcement (1). *See also* acoustic generalization, generalization gradient, semantic generalization.

stimulus intensity dynamism n. In *Hullian learning theory, the strength of a *stimulus (1), playing a part with other *intervening variables in determining the *generalized reaction potential. *V* abbrev.

stimulus onset asynchrony n. The time interval between the beginning of one stimulus and the beginning of another. *Compare* interstimulus interval. **SOA** abbrev.

stimulus set n. **1.** In experiments on *reaction time, a predisposition to concentrate on the *stimulus (1) rather than the *response. In *reaction time experiments it generally leads to slower reactions but fewer errors than a *response set (1). **2.** A bias disposing an organism to respond in a particular way to a stimulus or class of *stimuli (1). **3.** A group of *stimuli (1) used in a particular empirical investigation.

stirrup n. A non-technical name for the *stapes of the middle ear.

[So called because of its resemblance to a stirrup]

St John's wort *n.* A shrub of the genus *Hypericum*, especially *H. perforatum*, popular in Europe as an *antidepressant with relatively few side-effects compared with the more common types, its action combining mild serotonin reuptake inhibition and monoamine oxidase inhibition. *See also* orphan drug. *Compare* monoamine oxidase inhibitor (MAOI), selective serotonin reuptake inhibitor (SSRI), tetracyclic antidepressant, tricyclic antidepressant.
[So called because it used to be collected on St John's Eve (23 June) to ward off evil spirits and as a medicinal herb]

stochastic *adj.* Randomly determined, of or relating to a process or variable that has a probability distribution subject to statistical regularities but that cannot be predicted precisely. *Compare* deterministic.
[From Greek *stochastikos* capable of guessing, from *stochazesthai* to conjecture or aim at, from *stochos* a target]

Stockholm syndrome *n.* A psychological condition in which hostages or victims of kidnappings sometimes develop positive feelings towards their captors, on whom they depend for their survival, especially after being released.
[Named after a siege in the Swedish capital Stockholm in 1973 in which people were taken hostage by bank robbers and later refused to cooperate with police]

stocking anaesthesia *n.* A condition analogous to *glove anaesthesia occurring in the foot and lower leg. US *stocking anesthesia*.

stomach *n.* The section of the *alimentary canal between the *oesophagus and the *small intestine, consisting of a strong, muscular sac where food is partially digested.
[From Greek *stomachos* the throat, later the stomach, from *stoma* the mouth]

stoned *adj.* In drug-culture slang, under the influence of drugs.
[From a sense of *stone* to numb or desensitize]

stooge *n.* In experimental methodology, another name for a *confederate.

stop codon *n.* Any member of the RNA *codon family UAA, UAG, and UGA (involving the bases uracil, adenine, and guanine), or any of their three equivalents in DNA, signalling the end of a protein-coding sequence. Also called a *nonsense codon*, a *termination codon*, or a *terminator codon*. *See also* nonsense mutation. *Compare* start codon.

stopped image *n.* Another name for a *stabilized retinal image.

storage *n.* The act or process of storing anything, especially (in psychology) storing *encoded information in *memory for subsequent *retrieval, or (in computer technology) storing information in a computer or on a magnetic disk or tape. **store** *vb.*

storge *n.* Natural fondness, especially parental affection.
[From Greek *storge* affection]

storgic love *n.* A primary type of *love that is friendly/affectionate and is based on caring and nurturing. *Compare* agapic love, erotic love, ludic love, manic love, pragmatic love.

STP *n.* A common name for 2,5-dimethoxy-4-methylamphetamine, one of the *phenylalkylamines among the *hallucinogens. Also called *DOM*.
[A trademark for a motor oil additive]

St Petersburg paradox *n.* A *paradox of decision making first presented to the St Petersburg Academy in 1738 by the Swiss mathematician and physicist Daniel Bernoulli (1700–82). A coin is tossed, if it falls heads then the player is paid one rouble and the game ends. If it falls tails then it is tossed again, and this time if it falls heads the player is paid two roubles and the game ends. This process continues, with the payoff doubling each time, until heads comes up and the player wins something, and then it ends. How much should a player be willing to pay for the opportunity to play this game? According to the principles of probability theory, the player wins one rouble with probability 1/2, two roubles with probability 1/4, four roubles with probability 1/8, and so on, therefore the game's *expected value is $(1/2)(1) + (1/4)(2) + (1/8)(4) + \ldots$, and this sum is infinite because each of its terms is equal to 1/2. But it would obviously be absurd to pay a large amount for the privilege of playing the game, because there is a high probability of losing everything, including a 50 per cent chance of losing it on the very first toss, and the game is fatally damaging to the principle of maximizing expected value. The discovery of the paradox led directly to Bernoulli's introduction of 'moral worth', which later came to be called *utility (1). Also called the *St Petersburg game*. *See also* risk aversion. *Compare* Allais paradox, common ratio effect, Ellsberg paradox, modified Ellsberg paradox.

strabismus *n*. A condition in which the orientation of the eyes is abnormal, so that they are not parallel. *Paralytic strabismus* is associated with a malfunction of the ocular muscles resulting from a neurological or muscular disorder or dysfunction. *Non-paralytic strabismus* is an inherited defect in the positioning of the eyes relative to each other, resulting in an inability to use both eyes together, causing the person to fixate with one eye or the other, sometimes leading to *stereoblindness. A person with *alternating strabismus* fixates objects in the visual field first with one eye and then with the other, the eyes taking turns for approximately a second each as long as the object is fixated. A person with *monocular* or *non-alternating strabismus* fixates continuously with one eye, the other eye often becoming blind as a result of disuse. Also called *squint*. *See also* amblyopia ex anopsia, anoopsia, cyclophoria, esotropia, exophoria, heterophoria, hyperphoria, hypophoria. **strabismic** *adj*. [From Greek *strabismos* squinting, from *strabizein* to squint, from *strabos* cross-eyed, related to *straphein* to twist]

stranger anxiety *n*. A form of *anxiety occurring in response to the appearance of an unfamiliar person, normally developing in infants between 6 and 8 months of age, manifested by avoidance of *eye contact, hiding, or crying. It was first discussed in 1957 by the Austrian psychoanalyst René A. Spitz (1887–1974). Also called *eight-month anxiety*.

strategic dominance *n*. The property of being a *dominant alternative/strategy.

strategic game *n*. An interactive decision problem of the type analysed within *game theory. Also called a *game*.

strategic priming *See under* priming (1).

strategy *n*. **1.** The art or science of generalship or military planning, or a specific long-term plan in a military conflict, business, politics, or social affairs, often distinguished from *tactics*, the detailed manoeuvres carried out to achieve immediate or short-term objectives. **2.** In *game theory, a complete plan of action, specifying in advance what moves a player will make in every possible situation that might arise in the course of a game. If each player has only one move to make, and if the moves are made simultaneously or in ignorance of the moves chosen by the other player(s), then the available strategies are simply the available moves, but in other cases a strategy specifies a complete contingency plan covering all possible replies by the co-player(s). *See also* dominant alternative/strategy, mixed strategy, programmed strategy. **strategic** or **strategical** *adj*. **strategies** *pl*. **strategist** *n*. One who devises or implements *strategies (1, 2). [From Greek *strategia* generalship, from *strategos* a general, from *stratos* an army + *agein* to lead]

stratified random sample *n*. A *probability sample in which random sampling is applied piecewise to each stratum of the population to ensure that all subgroups are adequately represented. It resembles a *quota sample, except that the respondents within each category are selected by simple random sampling rather than haphazardly. *See also* cluster sample, random digit dialling, simple random sample. *Compare* accidental sample, convenience sample, non-probability sample, opportunity sample, self-selected sample, snowball sample.

Stratton experiment *n*. A classic experiment involving inverted visual images carried out in 1895 by the US psychologist George Malcolm Stratton (1865–1957) and published in 1897. *See* inverting spectacles.

stream of consciousness *n*. The continuous flow of sensations, images, thoughts, ideas, and feelings that occupy one's *consciousness. The concept was introduced by the US psychologist William James (1842–1910) in his book *Principles of Psychology* (1890, p. 237). It was first used as a device in fictional literature by the English novelist Dorothy Miller Richardson (1873–1957) in her sequence of novels under the collective title *Pilgrimage*

(1915–38), and it was made famous by two writers who are also linked by the remarkable coincidence of identical dates, the English novelist (Adeline) Virginia Woolf (1882–1941) and the Irish novelist James (Augustine Aloysius) Joyce (1882–1941), especially in the last 50 pages of *Ulysses* (1922).

street drug *n*. Any drug that is taken for its *psychotropic effects or for recreational purposes, often though not always illegally.

street name *n*. An unofficial name by which a street drug is referred to by its users and dealers. *See* Adam, acid (2), angel dust, barbs, bennies, benzos, candy (2), Charlie, China white, coke, crack, dolls, dope, downers, Einsteins, ganja, gear, goofers, grass, H, hog, horse, hug drug, ice, joint, junk, mush, nebbies, peace pill, phennies, pink lady, poppers, pot, purple hearts, red devils, reefer, rocks, roofies, skag, smack, snow, Special K, speed, speedball, spliff, tranq, uppers, weed, yellow bullets.

strephosymbolia *n*. A typical symptom of *dyslexia in which letters are transposed, reversed, or confused; more generally a disorder in which objects are perceived in mirror image.
[From Greek *strephein* to twist + *symbolon* a symbol]

stress *n*. **1.** Psychological and physical strain or tension generated by physical, emotional, social, economic, or occupational circumstances, events, or experiences that are difficult to manage or endure. *See also* acute stress disorder, burnout, general adaptation syndrome, post-traumatic stress disorder, psychoneuroimmunology, psychosocial stressor. *Compare* eustress. **2.** In phonetics, the degree of force used in uttering a syllable, stressed syllables being more prominent than unstressed syllables, the prominence being due not only to increased loudness but also sometimes increased length and raised pitch. Also called *accent*.
[From C14 English *stresse*, shortened from *distress*, from Latin *strictus* tightened, from *stringere* to draw tight]

stress interview *n*. An interview specifically designed to create *stress (1) in order to assess the interviewee's capacity to withstand stress in other situations. *See also* stress test.

stressor *See* psychosocial stressor.

stress test *n*. Any of a number of tests designed to create either physical or psychological stress in order to assess a person's capacity to withstand stress in other situations. *See also* stress interview.

stretch receptor *n*. A receptor such as (in mammals) a *muscle spindle that responds to the stretching of a muscle.

stretch reflex *n*. A reflex contraction of a muscle in response to sudden stretching, controlled by a reflex arc involving just one sensory nerve fibre from a *muscle spindle and one motor neuron. Numerous stretch reflexes help to maintain posture against gravitational and other forces, and *deep tendon reflexes are special examples of stretch reflexes. Also called a *myostatic reflex*. *See also* monosynaptic reflex, reflex.

striate cortex *n*. Another name for the *primary visual cortex (Area V1), showing in cross-section alternating bands of *white matter and *grey matter unrelated to the striped *ocular-dominance columns and *orientation columns that are made visible only by special staining procedures. Often confused with the corpus striatum and the striatum.
[From Latin *striatus* streaked, from *stria* a furrow or a flute of a column]

striated muscle *n*. Another name for a *striped muscle.
[From Latin *striatus* streaked, from *stria* a furrow or a flute of a column]

striatum *n*. A large mass of striped white and grey matter of the *forebrain or prosencephalon in front of and around the thalamus in each cerebral hemisphere, the afferent part of the basal ganglia, mainly involved in movement planning and control and habit formation. It includes the *putamen (connected mainly to the primary *somatosensory cortex, the primary *motor cortex, and the supplementary motor area) and the *caudate nucleus (connected to widespread cortical *association areas). Often confused with the corpus striatum, of which it is a part, or the striate cortex, to which it is unrelated. Also called the *neostriatum*.
[From Latin *corpus* body + *striatus* streaked, from *stria* a furrow or a flute of a column]

strictly competitive game *n.* A two-person *zero-sum game.

string length *n.* A measure of the complexity of an *average evoked potential or an *event-related potential corresponding to the length of a piece of string laid over a trace of the waveform, a longer string being required for a trace with many high-amplitude deviations from the baseline than for one with few lower-amplitude deviations in the first 250 or 500 ms following onset of the signal. The concept was introduced in 1980 in an article in the journal *Personality and Individual Differences* by A. E. and D. E. Hendrickson, who found a correlation of 0.72 between string length and Wechsler *IQ in a sample of school children, but hopes that this might provide a truly *culture-free measure of *intelligence were dashed by subsequent research, which failed to replicate this result. *Compare* N140, P200.

string variable *n.* In statistics and measurement theory, any *variable whose values contain letters or other characters instead of or in addition to numbers. Also called an *alphanumeric variable. Compare* numeric variable.

striped muscle *n.* Any voluntary muscle, capable of fast contraction, composed of long *myofibrils that have many nuclei and are transversely striped by alternating bands of *myosin and *actin, including all *skeletal muscles. Also *cardiac muscle, which is striped but is exceptional in being involuntary. Also called *striated muscle* or *voluntary muscle* (excluding cardiac muscle). *Compare* smooth muscle.

stroboscope *n.* A device that produces a bright, flashing light, the frequency of which can be synchronized with the frequency, or a multiple of the frequency, of rotation, vibration, or other movement of an object such as a piece of machinery, making it appear stationary and allowing it to be inspected in operation. It is also used as a form of illumination in nightclubs and discotheques. Also called a *strobe* or a *strobe light. See also* aliasing, wagon wheel illusion. **stroboscopic** *adj.*
[From Greek *strobos* a whirling + *skopeein* to view]

stroboscopic movement *n.* Another name for *beta movement.

stroke *n.* A blockage or (in about 20 per cent of cases) a haemorrhage of blood vessels in the brain, leading to a decreased supply of oxygenated blood to brain tissues normally perfused with blood by those vessels, lasting for more than 24 hours if the patient survives. The consequences depend on the site and extent of the stroke but often include *paralysis (especially *hemiplegia on the side of the body opposite the stroke), *homonymous hemianopia, *amnesia, *aphasia, *agraphia, *convulsions, or *coma. Also called *cerebrovascular accident* or *CVA. See also* aneurysm, internal capsule. *Compare* transient ischaemic attack (TIA).

strong AI *n.* An interpretation of *artificial intelligence according to which all thinking is computation, from which it follows that conscious thought can be explained in terms of computational principles, and that feelings of conscious awareness are evoked merely by certain computations carried out by the brain or (in principle at least) by a computer. A debatable implication of this view is that a computer that can pass the *Turing test must be acknowledged to be conscious. Also called *hard AI. See also* Chinese room, Gödel's theorem. *Compare* weak AI.

Strong–Campbell Interest Inventory *See* Strong Interest Inventory. **SCII** *abbrev.*

Strong Interest Inventory *n.* The revised version of the *Strong Vocational Interest Blank, an *occupational interest inventory, unified for men and women, comprising 317 items, each with the *response categories *Like/Indifferent/Dislike* or *Yes/?/No.* Since its 1974 revision it has been called the *Strong–Campbell Interest Inventory (SCII).* **SII** *abbrev.*
[Named after the US psychologist Edward K. Strong Jr (1884–1963)]

Strong Vocational Interest Blank *n.* One of the first widely used *occupational interest inventories, constructed by the US psychologist Edward K. Strong Jr (1884–1963) and published commercially in a version for men in 1927 and a version for women in 1938. The revised version was called the *Strong Interest Inventory. **SVIB** *abbrev.*

Stroop effect *n.* Delay and disruption in naming the colours of words printed in non-matching coloured ink, as when the word *red* is printed in blue ink, the word *blue* in green ink, and so on. To perform the task it is necessary to ignore the meanings of the printed words and to respond only to the colours in which they are printed, but with experienced adult readers *automatic processing tends to occur, causing interference in the processing of information and a significant (approximately 75 per cent) increase in the time required to name the colours, compared with the time taken to name the colours of meaningless strings of letters, and the effect cannot be suppressed voluntarily. The delay and disruption occur when naming the colours, but not when reading the words. This phenomenon provides a remarkable example of knowledge acting as a handicap: a person who could not read the words, through illiteracy or lack of knowledge of the language, for example, would not be slowed down. A commercial test of neuropsychological functioning based on this phenomenon is called the *Stroop Neuropsychological Screening Test (SNST)*. A simple demonstration of it can be constructed with a colour printer, or even with coloured pens. Prepare a page of colour names, such as *red*, *green*, *blue*, and *black*, in random order, each name printed in one of those colours at random, and then prepare another sheet, identical apart from the fact that the colour names are changed to nonsense words by moving each letter forward one place in the alphabet, so that *red* becomes *sfe*, and so on; then ask people to name all the colours in which the words are printed as quickly as possible, and compare the average times for the two sheets. [Named after the US psychologist J(ohn) Ridley Stroop (1897–1973) who first reported the effect in the *Journal of Experimental Psychology* in 1935]

structural equation *n.* An equation representing the strengths of hypothesized relations among a set of *variables in a formal *model.

structural equation modelling *n.* The construction of statistical models out of *structural equations. US *structural equation modeling*. *See also* analysis of covariance structures, path diagram. **SEM** *abbrev.*

structural gene *n.* A *gene specifying an *amino acid sequence of a *protein that is used for building body cells. *Compare* regulator gene.

structuralism *n.* **1.** An approach to linguistics, textual analysis, social anthropology, and psychology, inspired by the Swiss linguist Ferdinand de Saussure's (1857–1913) *Course in General Linguistics* (1916) and associated especially with the writings of the French anthropologist Claude Lévi-Strauss (born 1908) and the Swiss psychologist Jean Piaget (1896–1980), in which systems are analysed according to relations (such as equivalence and contrast) between their elements in order to determine the underlying structures below the surface manifestations of phenomena, and elements cannot be understood apart from their interrelations, because it is the network of interrelations that constitutes the meaningful structure of a system. *See also* deconstruction. **2.** A school of psychology, founded originally on the German psychologist Wilhelm (Max) Wundt's (1832–1920) book *Outlines of Psychology* (1896) and Edward Bradford Titchener's (1867–1927) book *An Outline of Psychology* (1896), devoted to studying mental experience by analysing its elements, notably sensations, but also ideas (images of memory and imagination), and feelings, their properties, and the way they combine with one another, using controlled methods of *introspection. Structuralism (in this sense) went into decline in Germany with the advent of Nazism in the 1930s and disappeared from US psychology shortly after Titchener's death in 1927. *See also* act psychology, content psychology, introspectionism, Würzburg school.

structuralist *adj. n.* A member or follower of the school of *structuralism (2), or one who advocates or practises *structuralism (1, 2); of or relating to structuralism.

structure from motion *n.* The process whereby the three-dimensional shape of an object is perceived by viewing it from different angles as it moves or the vantage point changes. Also called *depth from motion*. *See also* kinetic depth effect. **SFM** *abbrev.*

structure-of-intellect model *n.* Another name for *Guilford's cube. **SOI** *abbrev.*

strychnine *n.* A highly poisonous *alkaloid drug derived from the seeds of the *Strychnos nux-vomica* plant, in small doses functioning as a central nervous system *stimulant, exciting especially spinal reflexes, and sometimes being added to street drugs. It acts by binding to the neuroreceptor sites on *alpha motor

neurons to which *glycine molecules normally bind, causing *convulsions. It has been used, probably inappropriately, as an antidote for the respiratory and cardiovascular depression that occurs with barbiturate or anaesthetic poisoning. *Compare* curare, picrotoxin, tetanus toxin.
[From Greek *Strychnos* nightshade]

Student–Newman–Keuls procedure *n.* Another name for the *Newman–Keuls test.
[Named after Student, the pen name of the English statistician William Sealy Gosset (1876–1937) who published a statistic that is used in the test in 1908, the English statistician D. Newman, and the Dutch horticulturalist M. Keuls who published the test itself in 1952]

Student's *t* test *n.* The full name for the *t test. Although it was developed by Student (*see under* Student–Newman–Keuls procedure), it was later developed and modified by the English statistician Karl Pearson (1857–1936).

Study of Values *See* Allport–Vernon–Lindzey Study of Values.

stupor *n.* A state of lethargy and unresponsiveness with immobility and *mutism.
[From Latin *stupor* numbness, torpor, or senselessness]

stuttering *n.* A *communication disorder characterized by disturbed fluency and rhythm of speech, involving repetitions of sounds or syllables, prolongations, interjections, broken words, filled or unfilled pauses, word substitutions to avoid problem words, and excessive physical tension in pronouncing words, the speech disturbance interfering with scholastic, academic, or occupational achievement or social interaction and not being due solely to speech-motor or sensory deficit. Also called *stammering*. **stutter** *vb.*

stylometrics *n.* Another name for *stylostatistics.

stylostatistics *n.* The objective analysis of the relative frequencies of stylistic forms and patterns in the use of language, especially written texts. In practice, stylostatistical studies have focused on the frequency and distribution of a small number of stylistic features, such as parts of speech, the *type-token ratio,

the size and diversity of the author's *lexicon (2), the lengths of words and sentences, the author's preference between alternatives such as *on* versus *upon* and *while* versus *whilst*, rare and idiosyncratic constructions and usages. Stylostatistics has been used to settle issues of disputed authorship, and it has important applications in *forensic linguistics. Also called *stylometrics*. *See also* approximation to language.

stylostixis *n.* Another name for *acupuncture.
[From Greek *stylos* a pointed instrument + *stixis* a mark or spot]

subarachnoid *adj.* Below the *arachnoid membrane, in the space between it and the *pia mater. *See also* subarachnoid haemorrhage.
[From Latin *sub* under + *arachne* a spider, alluding to the membrane's delicate weblike structure]

subarachnoid haemorrhage *n.* Bleeding into the space between the *arachnoid membrane and the *pia mater and sometimes into the brain itself. The first symptom is a blinding headache that is initially highly localized and then spreads, followed rapidly by dizziness, rigidity of the neck, unequal pupil dilation, nausea, drowsiness, sweating, coma, and in the absence of urgent treatment death within hours or days. US *subarachnoid hemorrhage*. **SaH** *abbrev.*

subception *n.* Another name for *subliminal perception.
[A blend of *sub(liminal)* + *(per)ception*]

subcoerulear nucleus *n.* A cluster of neurons adjacent to the *locus coeruleus on either side of the *pons, involved in *REM atonia. Also spelt *subcerulear nucleus*. *See also* magnocellular nucleus.

subconscious *adj.* **1.** Operating or existing outside of *consciousness. *n.* **2.** In *psychoanalysis, a term used by Sigmund Freud (1856–1939) in a few very early publications to denote the *unconscious (2) but quickly abandoned because of its ambiguity. When it is used as a noun, it is usually another name for the *preconscious, but this is avoided in careful usage.

subcortical *adj*. Located beneath or below the *cerebral cortex, of or relating to structures or processes in the nervous system below the level of the cerebral cortex.
[From Latin *sub* under + *cortex* bark or outer layer + *-icalis* of, relating to, or resembling]

subdural *adj*. Below the *dura mater, between it and the *arachnoid membrane.
[From Latin *sub* under + *dura mater* hard mother, a literal translation of the Arabic name of the brain's outer membrane]

subdural haematoma *n*. *Subdural bleeding, creating a blood-filled space between the normally contiguous *dura mater and *arachnoid membrane, usually caused by a blow to the head or, especially in old people, by *cerebral arteriosclerosis, leading to various signs and symptoms including headaches, personality changes, convulsions, coma, and sometimes death. US *subdural hematoma*.
[From Greek *haima*, *haimatos* blood + *-oma* indicating an abnormality]

subfornical organ *n*. A small structure below the *fornix containing neurons that respond to the presence of *angiotensin II in the blood by exciting neural circuits that tend to initiate drinking. It is one of the *circumventricular organs. **SFO** *abbrev*.

subiculum *n*. A part of the hippocampal formation (*see* hippocampus) that is situated immediately below Ammon's horn (the hippocampus proper) between the detate gyrus and the entorhinal cortex and that projects to the entorhinal cortex and the fornix.
[From Latin *subicio* to lie under]

subitize *vb*. To perceive the number of items in a group without counting them. The maximum number of items that can be subitized under normal circumstances is about six, but *chunking can sometimes increase the number substantially. *See also* iconic store, magical number seven, span of apprehension. **subitization** *n*.
[From Latin *subitus* sudden, from *sub* below + *ire* to go + *-izare* to cause to become]

subjective colour *n*. A colour that is perceived in an *achromatic (1) stimulus. US *subjective color*. *See* Benham's top, pattern-induced flicker colour.

subjective contour *n*. Another name for an *illusory contour.

subjective equality *See* point of subjective equality.

subjective expected utility *n*. The *expected utility of an event or outcome calculated from subjective probabilities rather than from objective probabilities based on relative frequencies of observable events. **SEU** *abbrev*.

subjective expected utility theory *n*. A theory of decision making according to which a decision maker chooses an alternative or *strategy (2) that maximizes *subjective expected utility. It was introduced by the US decision theorist Leonard J(immie) Savage (1917–71) in his book *The Foundations of Statistics* (1954), and in the same year it was named and first studied empirically by the US psychologist Ward (Denis) Edwards (born 1927). *See also* Allais paradox, behavioural decision theory, common ratio effect, Ellsberg paradox, modified Ellsberg paradox, St Petersburg paradox. *Compare* expected utility theory, prospect theory, utility theory.

subjective probability *n*. Probability defined in terms of degree of belief rather than relative frequency of events (as in the classical interpretation of probability), widely used in *Bayesian inference, in which *prior probabilities (2) and *posterior probabilities are often interpreted as degrees of belief, and in *subjective expected utility theory. *See also* prospect theory, subjective expected utility, taxicab problem, Wells effect.

subjective utility *n*. The *utility (1) of an outcome or an event expressed in terms of an individual's personal judgement or degree of satisfaction rather than by *revealed preference. *See also* subjective expected utility, subjective expected utility theory.

subject (research or experimental) *n*. A person or other organism whose behaviour or mental experience is investigated in a research study. Also called a research or experimental *participant* or *volunteer*.
[From Latin *subiectus* thrown under, from *sub* under + *iacere* to throw]

subjunctive conditional *n*. A conditional statement or proposition (of the form *If p, then* *q*) in which both *p* and *q* are hypothetical. *See* conditional reasoning.

sublimation *n.* In *psychoanalysis, a *defence mechanism whereby a repressed or unconscious drive that is denied gratification is diverted into a more acceptable channel or form of expression, as when aggression is diverted into playing or watching violent sports or when *libido is diverted into artistic or creative activity. Sigmund Freud (1856–1939), in his book *Civilization and its Discontents* (1930, *Standard Edition*, XXI, pp. 64–145), attributed the highest expressions of civilization to the sublimation of the sexual instinct.
[From Latin *sublimare* to elevate, from *sublimis* lofty]

subliminal *adj.* Occurring without conscious awareness or below the *absolute threshold.
[From Latin *sub* below + Latin *limen* a threshold]

subliminal perception *n.* *Preconscious processing of stimuli below the intensity or duration of the *absolute threshold and therefore not eliciting conscious perception. It has been shown to occur for all sense modalities, and has been established experimentally by presenting stimuli of sufficiently low intensity or short duration as to be sub-threshold, and by *masking. Alarm was raised about subliminal advertising by the best-selling book *The Hidden Persuaders* (1957) by the US journalist Vance (Oakley) Packard (1914–96) and the essay *Brave New World Revisited* (1959) by the English novelist and essayist Aldous (Leonard) Huxley (1894–1963). Packard referred to a newspaper report in *The Times*: 'It cited the case of a cinema in New Jersey that it said was flashing ice-cream ads onto the screen during regular showings of film. These flashes of message were split-second, too short for people in the audience to recognize them consciously but still long enough to be absorbed unconsciously. A result, it reported, was a clear and otherwise unaccountable boost in ice-cream sales' (pp. 42–3). In 1957 the *New Yorker* magazine (21 September, p. 21) and the *Nation* magazine (5 October, p. 206) reported that the *motivational research practitioner James Vicary had carried out an experiment in a New Jersey cinema in which the messages *Drink Coca-Cola* and *Eat popcorn* (not ice-cream) had been flashed subliminally on alternate evenings and the sales of these products

during the intervals had reportedly risen by 18 per cent and 58 per cent respectively. However, Vicary admitted later that he had never actually carried out these experiments (*Advertising Age*, October 15, 1984, p. 46); in any event, the reported exposure time of 1/3,000 second was far too short to produce subliminal perception, and attempts to replicate the effect have uniformly failed. Research has shown that subliminal messages have only limited power to influence behaviour, and 'subliminal auditory tapes' that are marketed as a means of boosting IQ or helping people to lose weight, give up smoking, or achieve other self-help goals have proved ineffective when studied objectively. Also called *subception*. *See also* Poetzl phenomenon.

sublingual gland *See under* salivary gland.

submaxillary gland *See under* salivary gland.

submissive behaviour *n.* A form of *display (1) in which an animal that loses a fight, whether an *escalated fight or a *conventional fight, adopts a submissive posture to acknowledge defeat and to deter further attack. Human equivalents include *gestures (1) of *non-verbal communication such as holding up one's empty palms to communicate 'I give up'. US *submissive behavior*. *See also* emblem.

subspecies *n.* In biology, a *taxonomic group into which a *species is divided, containing organisms that are genetically differentiable from other members of the same species by the relative frequencies of their *polymorphic genes. Also called a *microspecies, race,* or *variety*.

substance abuse *n.* A maladaptive use of a *drug, resulting in impairment of functioning or distress, as manifested by: a failure to perform adequately at home, school, or work; repeated drug use in dangerous circumstances, such as when driving or operating machinery; repeated police arrests; or serious marital or interpersonal problems caused or exacerbated by the drug use. Preferred usage *substance misuse*. *See also* addiction, dependence (2), psychopharmacology, substance dependence, substance-induced disorders, substance-related disorders, substance use disorders.

substance dependence n. One of the major *substance use disorders, characterized by a maladaptive pattern of substance use leading to clinically significant impairment or distress, manifested by signs and symptoms such as *tolerance (3), *withdrawal, frequently taking larger amounts of the substance over a longer period than intended, persistent desire or effort to cut down on the substance use, excessive time spent on activities related to the substance use and its effects, often leading to the abandonment of social, occupational, or recreational activities, and continued substance use despite knowledge of problems likely to have been caused or exacerbated by it. See also dependence (2), substance-related disorders.

substance-induced disorders n. A class of *substance-related disorders including *substance intoxication, *substance withdrawal, and substance-induced forms of *delirium, persisting *dementia, persisting *amnestic disorder, *psychotic (1) disorders, *mood disorders, *anxiety disorders, *sexual dysfunctions, and *sleep disorders. Compare substance use disorders.

substance-induced persisting amnestic disorder See amnestic disorder.

substance intoxication n. A condition following administration of a *psychoactive substance or *drug resulting in disturbances of *consciousness, *cognition, *perception, *affect, or *behaviour.
[From Latin intoxicare to poison, from in in + toxicum poison + -ation indicating a process or condition]

substance intoxication delirium n. A form of *delirium associated with evidence from the case history, physical examination, or laboratory findings that the disturbance of *consciousness and change in *cognition developed during *substance intoxication or as a consequence of medication.

substance P n. An 11-member *peptide that is present in the brain, spinal cord, and peripheral nervous system and that functions as a *neurotransmitter, carrying afferent *pain signals, responding to painful stimuli by causing smooth muscles to contract, blood vessels to dilate, and mast cells to release *histamine. It is released by *free nerve endings after painful stimulation results in transmission of impulses not only in the normal *orthodromic direction to the central nervous system but also from points of bifurcation of their axons in the *antidromic direction into the neighbouring skin, where the nerve endings respond by releasing substance P. See also axon reflex, capsaicin.
[From substance + German P(ulver) powder, from Latin pulvis dust, sand, or ashes, because it was first extracted in 1931 as a powder]

substance-related disorders n. A class of *mental disorders resulting from *drug use (including alcohol), *side-effects of medication, or exposure to toxins. There are 11 groups of substances specifically discussed in *DSM-IV: *alcohol; *amphetamines and related *sympathomimetics; *caffeine; *cannabis; *cocaine; *hallucinogens; *inhalants; *nicotine; *opiates; *phencyclidine and related drugs; and *sedatives (2), *hypnotics, or *anxiolytics. However, many other substances, including heavy metals, rat poisons containing strychnine, carbon monoxide, and carbon dioxide can also lead to substance-related disorders. See alcohol-related disorders, amphetamine-related disorders, caffeine-related disorders, cannabis-related disorders, cocaine-related disorders, hallucinogen-related disorders, inhalant-related disorders, nicotine-related disorders, opioid-related disorders, phencyclidine-related disorders, sedative-, hypnotic-, or anxiolytic-related disorders. See also substance-induced disorders, substance use disorders.

substance use disorders n. A class of *substance-related disorders. See substance dependence, substance abuse. Compare substance-induced disorders.

substance withdrawal See withdrawal.

substance withdrawal delirium n. A form of *delirium associated with evidence from the case history, physical examination, or laboratory findings that the disturbance of consciousness and change in cognition developed during, or shortly after, an episode of *withdrawal.

substantia alba n. The technical name for the *white matter of the brain and spinal cord.
[From Latin substantia matter + alba white]

substantia gelatinosa *n.* Areas of *grey matter in the *posterior horns of the spinal cord, playing a part in *pain and temperature perception. They are packed with excitatory *interneurons, the *neurotransmitter of which is *glutamate, and inhibitory interneurons, the neurotransmitter of which is either *GABA for some interneurons or the endogenous opioid *enkephalin for others.
[From Latin *substantia* matter + *gelatina* gelatine, from *gelare* to freeze, alluding to its consistency]

substantia grisea *n.* The technical name for the *grey matter of the brain and spinal cord.
[From Latin *substantia* matter + *grisea* grey]

substantia nigra *n.* One of the *basal ganglia, implicated in motor control. It is a dark, pigmented area in the midbrain, just below the thalamus, containing neurons that synthesize and release *dopamine and project primarily to the striatum. Lesions in this area are associated with *Parkinson's disease. *See also* MPP$^+$.
[From Latin *substantia* matter + *nigra* black]

substantive *n.* **1.** Either a noun or some other word (often a pronoun) standing in place of a noun. *adj.* **2.** Of or relating to a word that is a *substantive (1). **3.** Of or relating to one of the classes of linguistic universals. *See* substantive universals.
[From Latin *substantia* substance, from *sub* under + *stare* to stand + *-ivus* indicating a tendency, inclination, or quality]

substantive universals *n.* One of the classes of *linguistic universals, consisting of the fundamental building blocks of languages, examples being the apparent existence in all languages of nouns and of vowels.

substitute formation *n.* In *psychoanalysis, the appearance of a *symptom, *parapraxis, or other psychological phenomenon that functions as a proxy or surrogate for an unconscious wish or idea following a process of *substitution. *See also* choice of neurosis, compromise formation, return of the repressed, symptom formation.

substitution *n.* The act or process of putting one thing in place of another. In *psychoanalysis, a *defence mechanism whereby an unattainable or unacceptable *instinctual object or *emotion is replaced by one that is more accessible or tolerable, resulting in *substitute formation.

substitution test *n.* Another name for a *coding test.

subthalamic fasciculus *n.* The small bundle of nerve fibres between the *subthalamic nucleus and the *globus pallidus.

subthalamic nucleus *n.* A structure belonging to the *basal ganglia, situated between each of the cerebral peduncles and one of the mammillary bodies, interconnected primarily with the *globus pallidus, functioning as a correlation centre for optical and vestibular impulses. *See also* ballism, hemiballism, jactation.

subthreshold *adj.* **1.** Insufficient to evoke a *response. **2.** Another word for *subliminal.

subtraction method *n.* A technique for estimating the duration of a psychological process by measuring the *reaction time for a task that incorporates the psychological process in question, and the reaction time for a task that does not incorporate it, and then subtracting the second from the first. It was introduced by the Dutch ophthalmologist Franciscus Cornelius Donders (1818–89) in his work on simple reaction time and choice reaction time, published in the *Archives of Anatomy and Physiology* in 1868. Also called the *subtractive method* or *Donders' method*.

subtractive colour mixture *n.* A colour formed from the absorption of light by *subtractive primary colorants, or the process of forming such a colour. US *subtractive color mixture*. *See also* colour mixing. *Compare* additive colour mixture.

subtractive primary *n.* Any of the colorants blue–green (cyan), deep purplish red (magenta), or yellow that can be subtracted from white light (usually by mixing pigments) to match any other spectral colour. They are the *complementary colours of red, green, and blue respectively. Also called a *primary colour*, though that term is ambiguous. *See also* primary colour (2). *Compare* additive primary, psychological primary.

subvocal rehearsal loop n. One of the two components of the *phonological loop of *working memory, functioning to keep information from decaying by mental repetition, and also translating visual information into phonological code where necessary for *short-term memory. Also called an *articulatory loop*, an *articulatory rehearsal loop*, or an *articulatory store*.

successive contrast n. The phenomenon whereby a sensation such as lightness, colour, or warmth tends to induce the opposite sensation in a stimulus that follows it. Successive warmth contrast can be demonstrated vividly by holding one's left hand in a bowl of cold water and one's right hand in a bowl of hot water for a minute and then transferring both hands to a bowl of lukewarm water, close to *physiological zero; the lukewarm water feels hot to the left hand and cold to the right hand. This experiment was first alluded to somewhat obscurely in 1690 by the English philosopher John Locke (1632–1704) in his *Essay Concerning Human Understanding* (Book 2, Chapter 8, section 21), as an argument that some physical properties that can be sensed must be secondary rather than *primary qualities, and in 1846 the experiment was described clearly and studied quantitatively by the German psychophysiologist Ernst Heinrich Weber (1795–1878). *See* colour contrast, contrast (2), lightness contrast, thermal adaptation, warmth contrast. *Compare* simultaneous contrast.

successive reproduction n. A technique for studying memory, popularized by the English psychologist Sir Frederic Charles Bartlett (1886–1969) in his book *Remembering: A Study in Experimental and Social Psychology* (1932, Chapter 5) in which a person reproduces learned material on a sequence of occasions over a period of time. Bartlett called it the *method of repeated reproduction*, and he used the technique to study *reconstructive memory. The technique had been introduced by the Welsh schoolteacher Philip Boswood Ballard (1865–1950) in the *British Journal of Psychology Monograph Supplements* in 1913, although Bartlett did not cite this earlier work. *See also* hypermnesia, reminiscence (2), War of the Ghosts. *Compare* serial reproduction.

success neurosis n. In *psychoanalysis, a term introduced in 1950 by the Hungarian psychoanalyst Sándor Lorand (1892–1987) to denote the phenomenon whereby a person responds to success with guilt and self-reproach. The condition was first identified by Sigmund Freud (1856–1939) in an article in 1916 on 'Some Character Types Met With in Psycho-Analytic Work', where he described people who were 'wrecked by success' (*Standard Edition*, XIV, pp. 311–33, at p. 316). *Compare* fate neurosis, fear of success.

sudorific adj. Sweat-producing. [From Latin *sudor* sweat]

suffix effect *See* auditory suffix effect.

suggestibility n. A propensity to be abnormally compliant with suggestions, commands, directions, instructions, or orders from another person, as in *hypnosis. **suggestible** adj. [From Latin *suggerere* to suggest, from *sub* under + *gerere* to bring + *-ibilitas* capacity, from *habilis* able]

suicide n. The act of killing oneself deliberately. Approximately fifteen per cent of people with *major depressive disorder or *bipolar disorder kill themselves each year, suicide being the ninth leading cause of death in the US according to official figures, which are widely believed to underestimate its incidence. The French sociologist Émile Durkheim (1858–1917), in his book *Suicide* (1897), used survey data purporting to show that egoistic suicide, resulting from feelings of self-reproach and sense of failure and more common among single than married people, arises from a lack of social cohesion; that altruistic suicide, carried out for the benefit of others and relatively common in Japan, arises from a sense of failure to society; and that anomic suicide, arising from a sense that life is pointless and rare among Catholics, arises from an absence of social norms that he called *anomie. *See also* depression. *Compare* parasuicide. **suicidology** n. The study of *suicide. [From Latin *sui* of oneself + *caedere* to kill]

sukra prameha *See* dhat.

suk yeong *See* koro.

sulcus n. Any of the grooves or furrows between the *gyri or convolutions of the brain, such as the *calcarine sulcus, *central sulcus,

*lateral sulcus, *longitudinal fissure, *parieto-occipital sulcus, or *superior temporal sulcus. Also called a *fissure*, especially when referring to one of the longer and deeper grooves. **sulci** *pl.*
[From Latin *sulcus* a furrow]

sulcus principalis *n.* Another name for the *longitudinal fissure.

sum *n.* In mathematics and statistics, a total arrived at by adding a set of numbers or scores together.
[From Latin *summa* the top or total, from *summus* highest]

summated ratings *n.* The method used to construct a *Likert scale.

summation tone *n.* A *combination tone whose frequency is equal to the sum of the frequencies of the two tones generating it. *Compare* difference tone.

sum of squares *n.* In statistics, a shortened expression for the sum of the squared deviations of a set of scores from their *arithmetic mean, to be distinguished from the sum of the squared scores, the meaning usually being clear from the context. The mean of the sum of the squared deviations, called the *mean square*, is used as an estimate of *variance.

sunk cost fallacy *n.* Another name for the *Concorde fallacy, especially among decision theorists.

superaesthesia *n.* Another name for *hyperaesthesia. US *superesthesia*.

superdominance *n.* Another name for *overdominance.

superego *n.* In *psychoanalysis, one of the three components of the human mental apparatus according to Sigmund Freud (1856–1939), after he replaced the *topography of the unconscious–preconscious–conscious by the structural model of id–ego–superego after 1920. The superego, which originates from a conflict between the *id and the *ego in the course of development, monitors and controls the ego like a judge or a censor. Freud introduced the concept in print for the first time in 1923 in his book *The Ego and the Id* (*Standard Edition*, XIX, pp. 12–66). In his

later book *New Introductory Lectures on Psycho-Analysis* (1932/3), he described its three functions as being 'of self-observation, of conscience and of the ideal' (1933, *Standard Edition*, XXII, pp. 5–182, at p. 66), and in the following key passage he referred to its long-term effects: 'Thus a child's super-ego is in fact constructed on the model not of its parents but of its parents' super-ego; the contents which fill it are the same and it becomes the vehicle of tradition and of all the time-resisting judgements of value which have propagated themselves in this manner from generation to generation' (p. 67). In the same work Freud explained its formation in both boys and girls as a consequence of the process of overcoming the *Oedipus complex (p. 129), and the superego is often described as the heir of the Oedipus complex. Some later theorists have claimed that its development occurs much earlier: the Hungarian psychoanalyst Sandor Ferenczi (1873–1933) argued in 1925 that prohibitions are internalized from the beginning of toilet training; the British-based Austrian psychoanalyst Melanie Klein (1882–1960) first claimed in 1933 that the superego develops during the *oral stage; and the Austrian psychoanalyst René A. Spitz (1887–1974) argued in 1958 that it develops gradually during infancy and childhood through *identification with the aggressor. Also spelt *super-ego. See also* ego ideal, superego lacuna.
[From German *Über-Ich*, over-I, from *über* over or above + *ich* I, following the precedent of *ego*]

superego lacuna *n.* In *psychoanalysis, a class of obviously immoral actions that are not forbidden by the *superego of a particular person, especially a person with *psychopathy or *antisocial personality disorder.
[From Latin *lacuna* a hollow or a cavity, from *lacus* a lake]

supergene *n.* A string of *genes along a *chromosome whose functions are generally unrelated but that tend to be inherited together because of their close proximity.

superior *adj.* Higher in any respect; towards the top of a body, organ, or part, or situated above another homologous structure. *Compare* inferior.
[From Latin *superior* higher, from *super* above]

superior colliculus *n.* Either of two small hillock-shaped bumps on the *tectum (the

roof of the midbrain), above and in front of the inferior colliculi, receiving some optic tract nerve fibres that bypass the lateral geniculate nucleus, involved in processing spatial aspects of visual information and eye movements in the direction of visual attention. The four colliculi are collectively called the corpora quadrigemina. **superior colliculi** *pl.*
[From Latin *superior* higher, from *super* above + *colliculus* a small hill from *collis* a hill]

superiority complex *n.* A non-technical name for *grandiose ideas or actions or a *grandiose delusion; more generally, an inflated estimate of one's own merit or importance.

superior longitudinal fasciculus *n.* A bundle of nerve fibres in each cerebral hemisphere linking the *frontal lobe to the *occipital lobe. *Compare* inferior longitudinal fasciculus. [From Latin *superior* higher + *longitudo* length, from *longus* long + *fasciculus* a little bundle, diminutive of *fasculus* a bundle]

superior oblique muscle *n.* The upper of the two *oblique muscles attached externally to the eyeball.

superior olivary nucleus *n.* Either of two collections of neuron cell bodies that are situated just above the inferior olivary nuclei in the pons and that receive signals from the *trapezoid bodies and project to the *inferior colliculi. They contain binaural neurons responding to inputs from both ears, the inputs reaching the superior olivary nuclei after the trapezoid bodies have amplified the left–right differences, and they are implicated in *sound localization based on binaural differences in both timing and sound intensity. Also called the *superior olivary complex* or the *superior olive*. *Compare* inferior olivary nucleus. **SON** *abbrev.*
[So called because it is olive-shaped and above the inferior olivary nuclei]

superior rectus *n.* The upper of the four *rectus muscles attached externally to the eyeball.

superior temporal gyrus *n.* The top *gyrus running horizontally on the lateral surface of the *temporal lobe, a small part of which (*Heschl's gyrus) is occupied by the primary auditory cortex. Also called the *temporal operculum*.

superior temporal sulcus *n.* The horizontal *sulcus near the top of each *temporal lobe, immediately below the superior temporal gyrus, believed to contain neurons that respond to visual images of faces. **STS** *abbrev.*

supernormal stimulus *n.* In ethology, an exaggerated *sign stimulus that evokes a stronger *fixed-action pattern than the normal sign stimulus. Thus, a yellow pencil with two red spots near its tip evokes even more pecking from a herring gull chick than its parent's bill, which is broader and has only one red spot.

supervised analysis *n.* Another name for a *control analysis.

supination *n.* Lying in a supine position (flat on one's back) or, if standing with one's hands at one's sides, turning the palms forwards. *Compare* pronation.
[From Latin *supinus* lying on the back + *-ation* indicating a process or condition]

supplementary motor area *See under* motor cortex. **SMA** *abbrev.*

supplementary sensory area *n.* Another name for the somatosensory association area. *See under* somatosensory cortex.

suppression *n.* Deliberate banishing from consciousness of selected thoughts, feelings, wishes, or memories, as in *thought stopping. In *psychoanalysis, it is a *defence mechanism in which emotional conflicts or *psychosocial stressors are dealt with by deliberately eliminating them from *consciousness. Unlike *repression, it is a conscious process, and the eliminated material ends up in the *preconscious rather than the *unconscious (2). Sigmund Freud (1856–1939) discussed it in his book *The Interpretation of Dreams* (1900, *Standard Edition*, IV–V, at pp. 235–7, 606n).

suppression amblyopia *n.* Another name for *amblyopia ex anopsia.

suprachiasmatic nucleus *n.* A collection of nerve cell bodies in each side of the *hypothalamus, above the optic chiasm and immediately adjacent to the supraoptic nucleus, receiving visual information via an accessory optic tract and projecting to the *pineal gland, involved in the regulation of *biological clocks and the control of *biological rhythms. **SCN** *abbrev*.

[From Latin *supra* above + Greek *chiasma* a cross, named after the shape of the upper-case letter chi (X), so called because of its location above the optic chiasm]

supranuclear palsy *See* progressive supranuclear palsy.

supraoptic nucleus *n*. A *nucleus (2) in each side of the *hypothalamus, above the optic chiasm and immediately adjacent to the suprachiasmatic nucleus, with nerve fibres projecting to the *posterior pituitary. Its stimulation causes *vasopressin to be released by the posterior pituitary.

[From Latin *supra* above + Greek *optikos* optic, from *optos* seen, alluding to the optic chiasm]

sure-thing principle *n*. A precept, first enunciated and named by the US decision theorist Leonard J(immie) Savage (1917–71) in his book *The Foundations of Statistics* (1954), according to which, if an alternative *A* is judged to be as good as another *B* in all possible states of the world and better than *B* in at least one, then a *rational decision maker will prefer *A* to *B*. Savage's illustration refers to a person deciding whether or not to buy a certain property shortly before a presidential election, the outcome of which could radically affect the property market. 'Seeing that he would buy in either event, he decides that he should buy, even though he does not know which event will obtain' (p. 21). This principle is accepted by virtually all decision theorists, although it appears counter-intuitive to some people in puzzles such as *Newcomb's problem, the *Prisoner's Dilemma game, and the *N-person Prisoner's Dilemma. A sure-thing alternative in a decision or a game of strategy is a *dominant alternative/strategy.

surface colour *n*. The appearance of colour when it is perceived as belonging to the surface of an object at a particular distance, with lines and/or edges present in the visual field. US *surface color*. *Compare* film colour.

surface dyslexia *n*. A form of *dyslexia characterized by an over-reliance on spelling-to-sound correspondences, making words whose spelling is irregular (such as *debt*, *busy*, and *yacht*) difficult or impossible to read. Also

called *phonological reading, reading by sound*. *See also* cognitive neuropsychology. *Compare* deep dyslexia.

surface structure *n*. A representation of a sentence together with labels and brackets to indicate the sentence's syntactic structure. In a famous example given by the US linguist and philosopher (Avram) Noam Chomsky (born 1928), the sentences *John is eager to please* and *John is easy to please* have similar surface structures but completely different *deep structures, because the first involves John pleasing someone and the second John being pleased by someone. *See also* transformational grammar.

surgency *n*. Another name for *extraversion.

surprise examination paradox *n*. Another name for the *unexpected hanging paradox.

survey research *n*. Research methods for investigating the distribution of attitudes, opinions, mental disorders, and other characteristics of individuals in specific sections of a population, or in a whole population, often broken down into demographic groups defined by geographical location, ethnic identity, age, sex, social class, marital status, education, and similar criteria. Surveys designed to compare different cultures or subcultures are called *cross-cultural surveys.

[From Latin *super* over + *videre* to see]

survival of the fittest *n*. An informal description of *natural selection, referring to the fact that the fittest organisms in the struggle for existence live longest and therefore transmit more of their genetic characteristics to future generations.

[The phrase was coined not by Charles (Robert) Darwin (1809–82) but by the English philosopher Herbert Spencer (1820–1903) in his *Principles of Biology* (1864, part III, Chapter 12)]

survivor guilt *n*. A feeling of guilt for surviving a tragedy in which others died, often associated with a sense of having been partly responsible for what happened. *See also* post-traumatic stress disorder, survivor syndrome.

survivor syndrome *n*. A term introduced by the US psychiatrist Robert Jay Lifton (born 1926) for a pattern of responses often seen in survivors of terrible ordeals, the most important symptoms being *anhedonia, chronic *anxiety, *depression, *dyssomnias, *nightmares (1), and in many cases *survivor guilt.

sustained responder n. Any of the *photoreceptors in the retina that respond to continuous stimulation by light rather than to changes in light stimulation. See also slowly adapting. Compare transient responder.

susto n. A *culture-bound syndrome found in Peru and other parts of Latin America and among Spanish-speaking communities in the United States and elsewhere, in which, following a frightening experience (sometimes weeks, months, or even years later), the soul is believed to have departed the body, resulting in symptoms such as *psychomotor agitation, *anorexia, *insomnia or *hypersomnia, *nightmares (1), and *depressed mood, together with somatic complaints such as muscle and joint pain, headaches, and diarrhoea. It is also called espanto (fright, terror), tripa ida (departing gut), perdida del alma (departure of the soul), or fallen fontanel syndrome.
[Spanish susto fright or scare]

sweat gland n. An *exocrine gland consisting typically of a coiled epithelial tube that secretes perspiration through a pore on to the surface of the *skin, present in humans in nearly all parts of the body.

sweet n. One of the primary tastes in *Henning's tetrahedron, the characteristic taste of sugar or *aspartame.

Sydenham's chorea n. A form of *chorea resulting from rheumatic fever, usually in children. Also called chorea minor, rheumatic chorea, Saint Vitus' dance.
[Named after the English physician Thomas Sydenham (1624–89) who first identified it]

syllogism n. A structured logical argument consisting of two assumed or given *propositions (1), functioning as *premises, and a third proposition, functioning as a conclusion, deduced from the premises. The premises each share a term in common with the conclusion and also a middle term with each other but not with the conclusion. There are 256 structurally distinct syllogisms, of which only 24 are valid. This syllogism is valid: All men are mortal; No gods are mortal; Therefore no men are gods. The following syllogism is invalid: Some

men are bald; some men like football; therefore some bald men like football. Since the Greek philosopher Aristotle (384–322 BC) popularized this form of reasoning in his Prior Analytics and Posterior Analytics, virtually all syllogisms that have been discussed are *categorical syllogisms, but see modal logic. See also atmosphere hypothesis, conversion hypothesis, deductive reasoning, logic, mood (3), sorites, Venn diagram. **syllogistic** adj.
[From Greek syllogismos a syllogism, from syllogizesthai to reckon together, from syn together + logizesthai to reckon or calculate, from logos word, discourse, or reason]

Sylvian aqueduct n. Another name for the *cerebral aqueduct.
[Named after the French anatomist Sylvius (1478–1555), also called Jacques Dubois, who discovered it]

Sylvian fissure n. Another name for the *lateral sulcus.
[Named after the Prussian physician Franciscus Sylvius (1614–72), also called Franz de le Boë, who apparently discovered it]

symbiosis n. A mutually beneficial relationship between two different species, especially between species living in close proximity to each other. **symbiotic** adj.
[From Greek syn together + bios life + -osis indicating a process or state]

symbol–digit test n. Another name for a *digit–symbol test.

symbolic interactionism n. A theoretical approach in social psychology and sociology, stemming largely from the writings of the US social psychologist George Herbert Mead (1863–1931), in which people are assumed to respond to elements of their environments according to the meanings they attach to those elements, such meanings being created and modified through social interaction involving symbolic communication with other people.

symbolic representation n. A form of *knowledge representation in which arbitrary symbols or structures are used to stand for the things that are represented, and the representations therefore do not resemble the things that they represent. Natural language (apart from onomatopoeic expressions)

is the most familiar example of symbolic representation. Also called *propositional representation*. Compare analogue (2).
[From Greek *symbolon* a token + *-ikos* of, relating to, or resembling]

symbolization *n*. In *psychoanalysis, a *defence mechanism whereby an unconscious idea is expressed in the form of a different idea, object, image, or concept, sometimes resulting in *symptom formation.

symbol-substitution test *n*. Another name for a *coding test.

Symmetrel *n*. A proprietary name for the dopamine agonist drug *amantadine.
[Trademark]

symmetry law *n*. A principle of *Gestalt psychology according to which perceptions tend to assume forms that are as symmetrical as the sensory input allows. *See also* Prägnanz.

sympathetic apraxia *n*. Another name for *unilateral limb apraxia. *See also* apraxia.

sympathetic ganglionic chain *n*. A string of *ganglia running down each side of the spinal cord throughout most of its length, containing cell bodies of neurons that belong to the *sympathetic nervous system and that project axons to muscles and glands, controlling the smooth muscles of the blood vessels, eyelids, hair follicles, sweat, tear, and salivary glands, respiratory organs, irises, and also the heart and other organs. Also called the *chain ganglia* or *sympathetic trunk*.
[From Greek *syn* with + *pathos* suffering + *ganglion* a cystic tumour]

sympathetic nervous system *n*. One of the two major subdivisions of the *autonomic nervous system, consisting of nerves originating from the cervical, thoracic, and lumbar regions of the spinal cord, supplying muscles and glands, concerned with general activation and mobilizing the body's fight or flight reaction to stress or perceived danger. It acts in opposition to and more diffusely than the *parasympathetic nervous system, accelerating pulse rate, dilating the pupils of the eyes and preparing them for *far vision, causing the sweat glands to secrete and urine to be retained, inhibiting the *smooth muscles of the *alimentary canal, diverting blood from the skin and intestines to the voluntary *striped muscles, and activating the *adrenal gland to secrete *adrenalin (epinephrine) and *noradrenalin (norepinephrine). *See also* sympathetic ganglionic chain. **SNS** *abbrev*.
[From Greek *syn* with + *pathos* suffering]

sympathetic trunk *n*. Another name for a *sympathetic ganglionic chain.

sympatholytic *adj. n*. (Of, relating to, or having an effect similar to) a drug or other agent that acts against or inhibits the activity of the *sympathetic nervous system. Compare parasympatholytic, sympathomimetic.
[From *sympathetic* + Greek *lysis* loosening + *-ikos* of, relating to, or resembling]

sympathomimetic *adj. n*. (Of, relating to, or having an effect similar to) any drug such as *amphetamine, *cocaine, *ephedrine, *phenmetrazine, *tyramine, or *yohimbine that mimics or increases the activity of *adrenalin (epinephrine), *noradrenalin (norepinephrine), and *dopamine, the major neurotransmitters of the *sympathetic nervous system, thereby acting as a central nervous system *stimulant, moderate dosages producing increased heart rate and general arousal, decreased fatigue and boredom, enhanced psychomotor performance, loss of appetite, and elevations in mood that are frequently described as euphoric, and higher dosages being associated with a variety of motor symptoms (twitching, restlessness, stereotyped movements), perceptual symptoms (distortion of time, tactile hallucinations or *formication), mood distortions (fear, paranoia, psychotic symptoms), and occasionally convulsions and death. Compare parasympathomimetic, sympatholytic.
[From Greek *syn* with + *pathos* suffering + *mimesis* imitation, from *mimeisthai* to imitate + *-ikos* of, relating to, or resembling]

symptom *n*. A subjective indication of a disorder reported by an afflicted person rather than being observed by an examiner. *See also* Present State Examination (PSE), SCAN, symptom formation, syndrome. Compare sign (1).
[From Greek *symptoma*, from *syn-* together + *piptein* to fall]

symptom formation *n*. In *psychoanalysis, the appearance of a *neurotic (1) or other *symptom, as a symbolic expression or manifestation of a mental conflict through the *return of the repressed. *See also* choice of neurosis, compromise formation, return of the repressed, substitute formation, symbolization.

synaesthesia *n.* **1.** A sensory experience elicited by a stimulus in a different sensory modality, as when particular sounds evoke sensations of colour. *See also* chromaesthesia, photism (1). **2.** The experience of a sensation in a different part of the body from the area of stimulation. *See also* referred pain. Also called *synaesthesis.* US *synesthesia, synesthesis.*
[From Greek *syn* together + *aisthesis* feeling + *-ia* indicating a condition or quality]

synapse *n.* **1.** The junction between two *neurons or between a neuron and a muscle or gland, where nerve impulses are relayed, usually by a *neurotransmitter, from the axon of a *presynaptic neuron to the axon, dendrite, or cell body of a *postsynaptic neuron, or sometimes from the dendrite of one to the dendrite of another, a typical synapse consisting of a *synaptic cleft approximately 20 nanometres (millionths of a millimetre) wide into which the neurotransmitter is released from *synaptic vesicles in the presynaptic neuron, triggering an *action potential in the postsynaptic neuron if the sum of all the signals reaching the postsynaptic neuron reaches a critical threshold (see illustration). Somatodendritic (cell body to dendrite) and

somatosomatic (cell body to cell body) synapses have also been identified but are very rare. The effect of the presynaptic neuron on the postsynaptic neuron, muscle, or gland may be either excitatory or inhibitory. *See* axoaxonic, axodendritic, axosomatic, dendro-dendritic. *See also* gap junction, synaptic receptor. *vb.* **2.** To form or play a part in a *synapse (1) as in *Motor neurons synapse directly on to muscles.* **synaptic** *adj.* Of, relating to, or consisting of a *synapse (1).
[From Greek *synapsis* contact or junction, from *syn* together + *haptein* to fasten]

synaptic bouton *n.* Another name for a *bouton. Also called an *end foot, end bulb,* or *synaptic terminal.*

synaptic cleft *n.* The narrow gap, typically 0.02 micrometres wide, between a *presynaptic neuron and a *postsynaptic neuron, muscle, or gland at a *synapse (1).

synaptic potential *n.* A change in the voltage difference across the membrane of a *postsynaptic cell, produced by the transmission of a nerve impulse across a *synapse (1). *See also* excitatory postsynaptic potential, inhibitory postsynaptic potential.

synaptic receptor *n.* A *neuroreceptor in a *postsynaptic neuron specialized to respond to a *neurotransmitter released from a *presynaptic neuron.

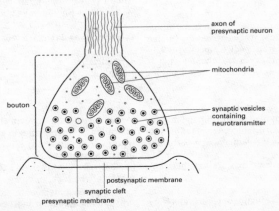

Synapse. Basic structure.

synaptic terminal *n*. Another name for a *bouton.

synaptic transmission *n*. The chemical process whereby a *presynaptic neuron passes a nerve impulse across a *synapse (1) to a *postsynaptic neuron, muscle, or gland.

synaptic vesicle *n*. A tiny sac in a synaptic *bouton containing a *neurotransmitter substance. When a nerve impulse arrives, it releases a small amount of the neurotransmitter across the *synapse (1).

synchronicity *n*. A term coined by Carl Gustav Jung (1875–1961) to denote a seemingly significant coincidence in time of two or more events that are related but not causally connected, as when a dream turns out to correspond to an external event or when close relatives or friends have similar thoughts, dreams, or experiences at the same time. *See also* analytical psychology.
[From Greek *synchronos* simultaneous, from *syn* together + *chronos* time + Latin -*itas* indicating a state or condition]

synchronized sleep *n*. Another name for *NREM sleep. **S sleep** *abbrev.*

synchronizer *n*. Another name for a *Zeitgeber.

syncope *n*. **1.** A brief loss of consciousness resulting from a fall in blood pressure or an interruption in the supply of oxygen to the brain, usually preceded by a sensation of lightheadedness and often preventable by lying down or placing one's head between one's knees. It may be caused by emotional stress, stimulation of the *vagus nerve, or a sudden change in posture or body temperature. **2.** In linguistics, another word for *haplology.
[From Greek *synkoptein* to cut short, from *syn* together + *koptein* to cut off]

syndrome *n*. A pattern of *signs (1) and *symptoms that tend to co-occur and may indicate a common origin, course, familial pattern, or indicated treatment of a particular disorder.
[From Greek *syndrome* from *syn*- together + *dromos* course]

synecdoche *n*. A *figure of speech involving the substitution of a word denoting a part of the thing referred to for the whole, or the whole for a part, as in the phrase *all hands on deck*, in which *hands* means sailors. *Compare* metonymy.
[From Greek *syn* together + *ekdoche* interpretation]

synergist *n*. A muscle that acts with another, or a substance that increases the effects of another. *See* agonist (2, 3).
[From Greek *synergia* cooperation, from *syn*- together + *ergon* work]

synonym *n*. A word that has approximately the same meaning as another word, such as *leap*, which is a synonym of *jump*. In *semantics, words are considered to be synonyms if they are close enough in meaning to be interchangeable in some contexts, although they may not be interchangeable in others: for example, in the sentence *This store offers a wide range of goods*, the word *choice* could be substituted for *range* without altering the meaning, and hence these two words are synonyms in that context; but in the sentence *This student displays a wide range of knowledge*, the word *choice* cannot be substituted and is not a synonym of *range*. *Compare* antonym. **synonymous** *adj*. **synonymy** *n*. The relationship between words that are *synonyms.
[From Greek *syn* together + *onoma* a name]

synonym test *n*. A type of *intelligence test item in which the respondent is presented with a word and is asked to supply a word with the same meaning to it, often by choosing from a set of response alternatives. *See also* synonym. *Compare* antonym test.

syntactic aphasia *See under* aphasia.

syntactics *n*. A term sometimes used, though not in linguistics, as a synonym for *syntax.

syntax *n*. The branch of *linguistics devoted to the study of the grammatical arrangement of words and *morphemes in sentences, and with the rules governing sentence structure in general. **syntactic** *adj*.
[From Greek *syn* together + *tassein* to arrange in order]

synthetic language *n*. Another name for an *inflecting language.

synthetic statement n. In *logic, a declarative statement in which the predicate asserts something that is not contained either explicitly or implicitly in the subject. Such a statement can be tested by observation or experience, and its negation is not self-contradictory. An example is the statement *All bachelors live alone*. The truth or falsity of a synthetic statement or proposition is *a posteriori. Also called a *synthetic proposition*. Compare analytic statement.
[From Greek *synthetikos* expert in putting together, from *syntithenai* to put together, from *syn-* together + *tithenai* to place]

SYSTAT abbrev. System for Statistics, a suite of statistical computer programs often used by psychologists, distributed by SYSTAT Inc. of Evanston, Illinois, USA. *Compare* BMDP, SAS, SPSS.

systematic desensitization n. A technique of *behaviour therapy, developed in the 1950s by the South African-born US psychiatrist Joseph Wolpe (1915–97) for treating *phobias in particular, in which each member of a hierarchy of increasingly anxiety-provoking imaginary situations involving the *phobic stimulus is repeatedly paired with a response that is physiologically incompatible with fear and anxiety, such as deep muscular relaxation, starting with the least frightening item and working up the hierarchy by degrees. An adaptation of the technique involving exposure to the actual phobic stimulus or situation is called *in vivo desensitization*. *See also* progressive relaxation, reciprocal inhibition.

systematized delusion n. An organized cluster of *delusions arising as ramifications of a single basic delusion in order to preserve a coherent or logical belief system.

System for Statistics *See* SYSTAT.

systems analysis n. The process of breaking down a complex task into its constituent parts and translating them into a form that enables a computer to carry out the task. **systems analyst** n. One who practises *systems analysis.

systems theory n. An approach to industrial relations, applied also to *family therapy and *group therapy, in which organizations, families, and other groups resemble organisms composed of interdependent parts, each with its own function and pattern of interrelationships with the others.

syzygy n. Conjunction or juxtaposition of opposites, as when the Earth and the moon lie in a straight line on opposite sides of the sun. In *analytical psychology, a pair of opposites, especially *anima and *animus (3). Carl Gustav Jung (1875–1961) was struck by the ubiquity of cultural symbols of syzygy, such as the Chinese *yin and yang. **syzygies** pl. **syzygial** adj.
[From Greek *syzygia* union or coupling, from *syn-* with or together + *zygon* a yoke]

Szondi test n. A *projective test consisting of 48 photographs of mental patients arranged in six groups, each group containing photographs of eight people representing eight basic psychological needs: a homosexual, a sadist, an epileptic, a hysteric, a catatonic schizophrenic, a paranoid schizophrenic, a depressive, and a manic patient. The respondent is asked to select the two most attractive and the two most repellent photographs from each group. The assumption underlying the test, based on the doctrine of *genotropism, is that the respondent will tend to be attracted to photographs of people with similar genetic predispositions and repelled by those with incompatible genes. The test provides measures (following the order of the photographs listed above) of need for tender, feminine love; need for aggression and masculinity; mode of dealing with aggression; need to exhibit emotions; narcissistic ego-needs; expansive tendencies of the ego; need to acquire and master objects; and need to cling to objects for enjoyment.
[Named after the Hungarian geneticist and psychoanalyst Lipot (Leopold) Szondi (1893–1986), who expounded the ideas behind his test in 1944 in a book entitled *Schicksalsanalyse* (Analysis of Destiny) and published the test itself shortly thereafter]

tabes dorsalis *n*. Another name for **locomotor ataxia.
[From Latin *tabes* wasting + *dorsalis* of the back, from *dorsum* the back]

tabula rasa *n*. A blank slate, a term introduced by the English philosopher John Locke (1632–1704) as a metaphor for the human mind at birth, the belief of Locke and the other British empiricists being that nothing is innate in the mind and that all knowledge comes through the senses. *See also* empiricism.
[From Latin *tabula* a tablet + *rasa* smoothed]

tachistoscope *n*. A device for exposing visual stimuli for very brief and carefully measured intervals, used in the study of visual perception, attention, and memory. **tachistoscopic** *adj*. Of or relating to a **tachistoscope.
[From Greek *tachistos* swiftest, from *tachys* swift + *skopeein* to view]

tachycardia *n*. Abnormally rapid pulse in the normal resting state, often taken to mean over 100 beats per minute. *Compare* bradycardia.
[From Greek *tachys* swift + *kardia* the heart]

tachygraphy *n*. Shorthand writing, especially of the type used in ancient Greece and Rome. *Compare* brachygraphy, stenography.
[From Greek *tachys* quick + *graphein* to write]

tachylalia *n*. Excessively rapid speech.
[From Greek *tachys* swift + *lalia* speech]

tachyphasia *n*. Another word for **tachylalia. Also called *tachyphresia*.
[From Greek *tachys* swift + *phasis* speech, from *phanai* to speak + *-ia* indicating a condition or quality]

tachyphrenia *n*. Racing thoughts or mental processes. It can be induced by extreme emotional states or **stimulant drugs.

[From Greek *tachys* swift + *phren* mind, originally midriff, the supposed seat of the soul + *-ia* indicating a condition or quality]

tachyphylaxis *n*. A form of drug **tolerance (3) that develops very rapidly, exemplified by the typical reaction to repeated dosages of **ephedrine, functioning by rapid emptying of **catecholamine neurotransmitter substances from **synaptic vesicles. **tachyphylactic** *adj*.
[From Greek *tachys* swift + *phylax* a guard, following the model of *prophylaxis*]

tact *n*. **1.** Consideration or politeness in dealing with others; diplomacy or skill in handling delicate negotiations. **2.** In the writings of the US psychologist B(urrhus) F(rederic) Skinner (1904–90), a verbal utterance that is elicited by an object or event in the external world. It differs from a **mand by being under the control of its antecedents rather than its consequences, but some non-Skinnerians have had difficulty understanding the concept. A typical example is the utterance: *Hello Hymie!* **3.** An almost obsolete term for the sense of touch.
[From Latin *tactus* a touching, from *tangere* to touch]

tactile *adj*. **1.** Of, relating to, or involving touch. *n*. **2.** A person whose characteristic style of mental imagery is tactile rather than visual, auditory, or motor. Also (rarely in psychology) called *tactual*. *Compare* audile (2), motile (2), visualizer.
[From Latin *tactilis* tactile, from *tactus* touched, from *tangere* to touch + *-il(is)* indicating capability or relationship]

tactile acuity *n*. The keenness or sharpness of the sense of touch, usually measured by the **two-point threshold. Also called *touch acuity*. *See also* acuity.

tactile agnosia n. Impaired ability to recognize or identify objects by touch alone. Also called *haptic agnosia*, *tactoagnosia*. *Compare* ahylognosia, amorphognosia.
[From Latin *tactilis* of or relating to touch, from *tangere* to touch + Greek *a-* without + *gnosis* knowledge + *-ia* indicating a condition or quality]

tactile aphasia n. A modality-specific naming impairment in which objects cannot be correctly named on the basis of touch alone so that a pair of scissors may be misnamed as a clock, or a ring as a balloon. This form of aphasia usually results from neurological damage resulting in disconnection between the tactile and language centres of the brain. *See also* aphasia, disconnection syndrome. *Compare* amorphognosia.

tactile corpuscle n. Another name for a *Meissner's corpuscle.

tactile disc n. Another name for a *Merkel cell. US *tactile disk*.

tactile egocentre n. Any of various points in the body where tactile sensations are perceived or felt to converge. US *tactile egocenter*. *See also* egocentre.

tactile hallucination n. A *hallucination of being touched or of something touching the skin, or quite commonly a feeling of electric shock or *formication.

tactile illusion n. Any *illusion of touch. *See* Aristotle's illusion, sensory saltation, size–weight illusion. *Compare* auditory illusion, visual illusion.

tactile receptor n. A generic name for *Meissner's corpuscle or a *Merkel cell. *See also* touch receptor.

tactoagnosia n. Another name for *tactile agnosia. *See under* agnosia.

tactor n. Another name for a *touch receptor.
[From Latin *tactus* a touching, from *tangere* to touch]

tactual adj. Another word for *tactile (1).

Tadoma method n. A technique devised in Norway in the 1890s to enable a person who is both blind and deaf to receive and interpret speech by placing a thumb lightly in contact with the speaker's lips and the fingers of the same hand on the speaker's jaw and neck, thereby detecting by touch the pattern of airflow from the speaker's mouth and nose, the articulatory movements, and the vibrations from the vocal tract, permitting a well-practised user of the system to achieve a modest comprehension of slow speech.
[Named after two deaf–blind children, Tad Chapman and Oma Simpson, who in the early 1960s were the first to use the system in the United States]

taijin kyofusho n. A *culture-bound syndrome found in Japan and included in the official Japanese classification of mental disorders, characterized by an intense and debilitating anxiety that one's body or its parts or functions are embarrassing, displeasing, repugnant, or offensive to others. Also called *shinkei-shitsu*. It is sometimes interpreted in Western cultures as a *body dysmorphic disorder.
[Japanese *taijin* confrontation + *kyofu-sho* phobia, from *kyofu* fear + *sho* nature or kind]

take-some game n. An experimental game used to represent a *resource dilemma.

Talbot–Plateau law n. Another name for *Talbot's law.

Talbot–Plateau spiral n. Another name for the *Plateau spiral. Also called the *Talbot–Plateau disc*.
[Named after the English photographer, physicist, and psychologist (William Henry) Fox Talbot (1800–77) who studied it and the Belgian physicist Joseph Antoine Ferdinand Plateau (1801–83) who published a major article on it in 1850]

Talbot's law n. The proposition that when two or more colours differing in *hue or *lightness are alternated, as on a rotating *Maxwell disc divided into contrasting sectors, there is a frequency beyond which perceived flicker ceases and an impression of uniform colour is created, and when a colour is mixed with black in this way, its lightness is proportional to the area of the disc that it fills. Also called the *Talbot–Plateau law*.
[Named after the English photographer, physicist, and psychologist (William Henry) Fox Talbot (1800–77) who published it in

1834, although the Belgian physicist Joseph Antoine Ferdinand Plateau (1801–83) had already formulated the underlying principle and published it in an obscure article in 1829]

Talwin n. A proprietary name for the narcotic analgesic *pentazocine.
[Trademark]

tandem reinforcement schedule n. A *compound reinforcement schedule in which *reinforcement (1) is delivered after an organism has completed two or more *simple reinforcement schedules in succession, no signal being given to indicate to the organism which schedule is operating at any particular time. Also called a *tandem schedule. See also* reinforcement schedule. *Compare* chained reinforcement schedule.
[From Latin *tandem* at length]

tangentiality n. Responding to questions obliquely rather than directly, without giving direct answers. Also called *tangential speech. Compare* circumstantiality, Ganser syndrome.
[So called because responses go off at a tangent to the questions]

tantrum n. A sudden outburst or fit of childish rage or temper. Also called a *temper tantrum.*

tanyphonia n. Thin, weak, metallic vocal quality resulting from tension in the muscles of the *vocal tract.
[From Greek *tanyzo* to stretch + *phone* a sound + -*ia* indicating a condition or quality]

tapetum n. **1.** The highly reflective layer that lies behind the retina of cats and other nocturnal animals and that provides the *photoreceptors with a second opportunity to respond to rays of light as they return through the retina after being reflected, thereby maximizing the eye's ability to respond to sparse light. It is the tapetum that causes cats' eyes to glow when caught in the beams of a car's headlamps. *Compare* pigment epithelium. **2.** The sheet of nerve fibres of the *corpus callosum above the lateral ventricles of the brain.
[From Latin *tapete* a carpet, from Greek *tapes* a carpet]

tarantism n. A nervous disorder characterized by *ataxia and frenzied *choreiform *hyperkinesis that began in southern Italy in the 15th century and spread northwards throughout Europe during the succeeding two centuries before dying out, initially believed to have been caused by a tarantula bite, and remedied by means of lively Neapolitan dances called *tarantellas*. Also called *dancing mania, tarantulism. See also* Saint Vitus' dance.
[From Latin *tarantula*, the large hairy venomous wolf spider, from *Taranto* the name of a port in southern Italy]

tardive dyskinesia n. Involuntary *choreiform, *athetoid, or rhythmic, stereotyped or writhing movements of the tongue, jaw, fingers, or hands, resulting as a *side-effect of *neuroleptic (1) medication and damage to the *basal ganglia. **TD** *abbrev.*
[From Latin *tardus* late + Greek *dys-* bad or abnormal + *kinesis* movement + -*ia* indicating a condition or quality]

target item n. A stimulus that a research participant or subject is searching for or trying to concentrate on, and that in research is often accompanied by *distractors.

taste n. One of the five classical *senses (1), stimulated by sapid (tastable) substances that are dissolved in water or capable of being dissolved in saliva and that stimulate approximately 9,000 *taste buds located principally in the *tongue but also in the soft palate, throat, pharynx, and inside of the cheeks, giving rise to sensations based on the primary tastes, usually assumed according to *Henning's tetrahedron to be sweet, sour, salty, and bitter (but *see also* umami). Also called *geusis* or *gustation. See also* aftertaste, ageusia, cacogeusia, chemoreceptor, flavour, hypergeusia, hypogeusia, miraculin, monosodium glutamate, redintegration, taste blindness.

taste aversion learning/conditioning See food aversion learning.

taste blindness n. An impaired ability to taste certain *sapid substances such as *PTC or *propylthiouracil (PROP), or less commonly a complete absence of taste (ageusia). *Compare* cacogeusia, dysgeusia, hypergeusia, hypogeusia, parageusia.

taste bud n. Any of approximately 9,000 *sensory receptors for taste that are abundantly present at the bases of *papillae in fissures or grooves of the *tongue and also in the soft palate, throat, pharynx, and insides of the cheeks. Sapid (tastable) substances dissolved either in water or saliva enter laterally through pores in the tongue's epithelial cells and make contact within each taste bud with receptor surfaces on the 50–150 *taste cells that are specialized to bind to molecules with particular structural features, the chemical property of the stimulus being converted into nerve impulses that are transmitted to the central nervous system and are experienced as the distinctive tastes sweet, sour, salty, or bitter. *See also* Henning's tetrahedron, PTC, taste, tongue.

taste cell *n.* A *neuron that is located in a *taste bud and is the actual *sensory receptor for taste. *See* gustatory receptor. Also called a *gustatory cell* or a *taste receptor*.

taste receptor *n.* Another name for a *taste cell, or sometimes for a *taste bud.

taster (PCT) *n.* A person with a hereditary capacity to taste *PTC.

taster (PROP) *n.* A person with a hereditary capacity to taste *propylthiouracil (PROP).

taste tetrahedron *n.* Another name for *Henning's tetrahedron.

TAT *abbrev.* Thematic Apperception Test, one of the best known *projective tests, consisting of 31 pictures (originally 20) of emotionally charged social events and situations printed on cards, from which the test administrator selects 20 depending on the age and sex of the respondent, plus a blank card that is presented last. For each picture, the respondent is asked to make up a story that the picture could illustrate, describing the relationship between the people, what has happened to them, what their present thoughts and feelings are, and what the outcome will be. The assumption underlying the test is that respondents tend to project their own circumstances, experiences, and preoccupations into their stories. The test was first introduced by the US artist/psychologist Christiana D(rummond) Morgan (1897–1967) and the US psychologist Henry Alexander Murray (1893–1988) in an article in the journal *Archives of Neurology and Psychiatry* in 1935, where they argued that 'when someone at-

tempts to interpret a complex social situation he is apt to tell as much about himself as he is about the phenomena on which attention is focused' (p. 289). An earlier version of the article by Morgan and Murray had been submitted to the *International Journal of Psycho-Analysis* but was rejected in 1934 by the editor, the Welsh psychoanalyst Ernest Jones (1879–1958). A new edition of the test, together with the first manual, were published in 1943 by Harvard University Press, the test being attributed to 'Henry A. Murray, M. D., and the Staff of the Harvard Psychological Clinic', although before Chris Morgan was airbrushed out of history the test had been generally known as the *Morgan–Murray Thematic Apperception Test*. The word *thematic* in its name derives from Murray's concept of a *thema*, an abstract representation of a situation combining a *press and a *need (3). *See also* apperception, Blacky pictures, Children's Apperception Test, Make-a-Picture-Story Test, personology.

TATA box *n.* In genetics, the sequence TATAAA of the bases thymine and adenine, approximately 25 base pairs upstream of a *start codon, involved in binding *RNA polymerase prior to transcription.

tau effect *n.* A relation between perceived space and time, demonstrated most simply by flashing three equidistant lights A, B, and C successively in the dark, with a shorter time interval between A and B than between B and C, creating the *space–time illusion that A and B are closer together in space than B and C. *Compare* kappa effect.

tau (Kendall's) *See* Kendall's tau.

taxicab problem *n.* The following problem of probability judgement, introduced in a book chapter in 1977 by the Israeli psychologists Amos Tversky (1937–96) and Daniel Kahneman (born 1934) to demonstrate the *base-rate fallacy. A taxicab was involved in a hit-and-run accident at night. Only the Green and Blue cab companies operate in the city, where 85 per cent of the cabs are Green and 15 per cent are Blue. A witness identified the cab as Blue, and when tested under similar conditions was able to identify 80 per cent of both Blue and Green cabs correctly. What is the probability that the cab involved in the accident was Blue? The modal and median judgement was 80 per cent, which coincides with the reliability of the witness but ignores the relative frequency of Blue and Green cabs (the base rate). The correct answer, worked out from *Bayes' theorem, is 0.41 or 41 per cent, which is much closer to the base rate.

taxon *n*. Any of the classes or categories belonging to a *taxonomy. Sometimes contrasted with a dimension or *continuum, as when a question is posed as to whether or not antisocial personality disorder is a taxon. *See also* type fallacy.
[Back formation from *taxonomy*]

taxonomy *n*. The branch of biology concerned with the classification of organisms; more loosely, any systematic classification. The conventional biological taxonomy includes the following, starting from the highest level: *kingdom (2), *phylum, *class (2), *order (3), *family (2), *genus, *species, *microspecies. A microspecies may be a *subspecies, a *race (2), or a *variety. *See also* taxon. **taxonomic** *adj*.
[From Greek *taxis* order + -*nomos* arranging]

Taylor Manifest Anxiety Scale *n*. Another name for the *Manifest Anxiety Scale.

Taylor–Woodhouse illusion *n*. Another name for the *hollow squares illusion.
[Named after the English optometrists Stephen P(hilip) Taylor (born 1951) and J(oy) Margaret Woodhouse (born 1948) who first published it in 1980]

Tay–Sachs disease *n*. A hereditary disorder transmitted through a *recessive gene, relatively common among Ashkenazi Jews, characterized by progressive accumulation of lipids in the brain, leading to blindness, convulsions, mental retardation, and death, usually before 5 years of age. Also called *amaurotic familial idiocy*. **TSD** *abbrev*.
[Named after the English ophthalmologist Warren Tay (1843–1927) who first identified it in 1881 and the US neurologist Bernard Sachs (1858–1944) who described it further in 1887]

T cell *n*. Another name for a *T lymphocyte.

teacher unit *n*. In *connectionism (1) and *parallel distributed processing, a unit with a predetermined level of activation that determines the levels of activation of other units in

order to achieve a target level according to the *delta rule. *See* back-propagation algorithm. *See also* neural network.

teacup illusion *n*. A visual illusion closely related to the *horizonal–vertical illusion that occurs when a person is invited to guess the depth of a teacup, relative to a teaspoon lying horizontally on the table, by grasping the teaspoon's handle at the point that would be opposite the top of the cup if the teaspoon were standing vertically in the cup (see illustration). Most people grossly overestimate the depth of the cup relative to the teaspoon.

Teacup illusion. If the teaspoon were standing upright in the teacup, which of the marks on the spoon would be exactly opposite the top of the cup? The answer is 1.

tear gas *n*. Any gas or vapour such as *CN gas, *CS gas, or *Mace that causes the eyes to smart and water, inducing temporary blindness, and is used for personal protection or as an *incapacitant in warfare or crowd control. Also called a *lacrimator*. *Compare* BZ gas, pepper spray.

technique, active *See* active technique.

technique, defensive *See* defensive technique.

tectal pathway *n*. The nerve fibres from the retinas of the eye that project via the *optic tract to the *superior colliculi. *Compare* pretectal pathway.
[So called because the superior colliculi are situated in the *tectum]

tectorial membrane *n*. The membrane in the *inner ear covering the *organ of Corti. Also called *Corti's membrane*.
[From Latin *tectorium* a covering, from *tectum* a roof or canopy]

tectum n. The structure at the base of the pons that forms the roof of the midbrain, on which are situated four hillock-shaped bumps, the two *inferior colliculi involved in hearing and the two *superior colliculi (the optic tectum) involved in vision, the four being known collectively as the corpora quadrigemina. In fishes, birds, amphibians, and reptiles it contains the main visual area. *See also* posterior cerebral commissure. **tectal** *adj.*
[From Latin *tectum* a roof or canopy]

tegmentum n. The tegmentum mesencephali, the intermediate region of the brainstem below the tectum, containing the motor pathways descending to the spinal cord, the sensory pathways ascending to the thalamus, part of the reticular formation, groups of nerve cell bodies such as the *substantia nigra, *red nucleus, and *locus coeruleus, and in its front part close to the substantia nigra, the *ventral tegmental area containing clusters of neurons that secrete dopamine.
[From Latin *tegmentum* a covering, from *tegere* to cover or conceal]

Tegretol n. A proprietary name for the antimanic drug *carbamazepine.
[Trademark]

telaesthesia n. Perception of objects or events that are beyond the range of the *sense organs, a conjectural *paranormal phenomenon. US *telesthesia*. *Compare* clairaudience, clairvoyance, precognition, telegnosis, telepathy. **telaesthetic** or **telesthetic** *adj.*
[From Greek *tele* far, from *telos* an end + *aisthesis* feeling + -*ia* indicating a condition or quality]

telalgia n. Another name for *referred pain.
[From Greek *tele* far, from *telos* an end + *algos* pain + -*ia* indicating a condition or quality]

teledildonics n. Computer-mediated sexual interaction between entities in *virtual reality. *See also* MUD.
[From Greek *tele* far + English *dildo* an artificial penis + Greek -*ikos* of, relating to, or resembling]

telegnosis n. Knowledge of distant objects or events obtained without use of the sense organs, a conjectural *paranormal phenomenon. *Compare* clairaudience, clairvoyance, precognition, telaesthesia, telepathy. **telegnostic** *adj.*
[From Greek *tele* far, from *telos* an end + *gnosis* knowledge]

telegraphic speech n. The typical speech of children from about 2 to 3 years of age, in which most utterances are about three or four words in length and *function words are usually omitted. Questions and commands as well as declarative sentences emerge, and typical utterances during this period are: *Daddy kick ball*, *Where Teddy going?*, and *Put car here*. *Compare* holophrase, pivot grammar.

telekinesis n. Movement of a body without the application of physical force, a conjectural *paranormal phenomenon. *See also* psychokinesis. **telekinetic** *adj.*
[From Greek *tele* far, from *telos* an end + *kinesis* movement]

telencephalon n. The top part of the forebrain or prosencephalon, comprising the *cerebral hemispheres together with the *olfactory lobes and *olfactory bulbs. *Compare* diencephalon.
[From Greek *tele* far, from *telos* end + *enkephalos* the brain, from *en* in + *kephale* the head]

teleonomy n. The science of *adaptation (1).
[From Greek *telos* the end + -*nomos* arranging]

teleopsia n. A visual abnormality in which objects appear further away than they are, sometimes arising from the ingestion of a drug such as *cannabis or *LSD.
[From Greek *tele* far, from *telos* an end + *ops* an eye + -*ia* indicating a condition or quality]

telepathy n. *Extra-sensory perception of another person's mental processes, a conjectural *paranormal phenomenon. *See also* psi, psi-missing. *Compare* clairvoyance, precognition. **telepathic** *adj.*
[From Greek *tele* far, from *telos* an end + *pathos* feeling]

telephone scatalogia n. A *paraphilia characterized by recurrent sexually arousing fantasies, sexual urges, or behaviour involving making obscene telephone calls to nonconsenting recipients.
[From Greek *skor, skatos* excrement + *logos* a word or discourse + -*ia* indicating a condition or quality]

telephone theory *n*. Another name for the *frequency theory of hearing.

telereceptor *n*. A *sensory receptor such as a *visual receptor or an *auditory receptor that can be stimulated by distant stimuli and that mediates a *far sense. Also called a *teleceptor*, a *teleoreceptor*, or a *teleoceptor*. Compare proximoreceptor.
[From Greek *tele* far, from *telos* an end + English *receptor*, from Latin *recipere, receptum* to receive, from *re-* back + *capere, ceptum* to take]

telesthesia *See* telaesthesia.

teletactor *n*. A device for deaf people that converts sound waves into vibrations that can be felt on the skin. The equivalent device for blind people is an *optacon or an *optohapt.
[From Greek *tele* far, from *telos* an end + Latin *tactus* a touching, from *tangere* to touch]

telomerase *n*. A short name for telomere terminal transferase, an *enzyme that helps to rebuild *telomeres in *germ line cells but is normally absent from *somatic cells, although it is present in most cancer cells and is largely responsible for their ability to proliferate indefinitely without manifesting cellular or replicative senescence.

telomere *n*. A segment of *DNA at the tip of every *chromosome that is thought to perform a protective function like the plastic or metal aglet at the end of a shoelace, preventing the chromosome from losing genetic information during replication. It is made up of thousands of repeating or stuttering units consisting of the bases thymine, adenine, and guanine in the sequence TTAGGG, a *consensus sequence found in widely divergent species of fish, amphibians, reptiles, birds, and mammals. Every time a cell divides, the telomeres get progressively shorter by about 70 base pairs, until the length eventually falls below a critical level and the cell enters a phase of replicative senescence during which cell division no longer occurs. Telomere shortening thus functions as a mitotic clock that regulates the number of divisions a cell can undergo, and it may be chiefly or at least partly responsible for the ageing process. *See also* telomerase. *Compare* centromere.
[From Greek *telos* end + *meros* part]

telophase *n*. The fourth and final phase of *mitosis, when the cell pinches in the middle and a nuclear membrane forms around the chromosomes at each end.
[From Greek *telos* end + *phasis* an aspect, from *phainein* to show]

temazepam *n*. A *sedative-hypnotic drug belonging to the class of *benzodiazepines, used in the treatment of insomnia. Also called *Restoril* (trademark).

temperament *n*. Character or *personality; the characteristic mode of behaviour or reaction of a person or an animal; originally character or personality determined by the particular mixture of the four *humours (3) in an individual's body. *See also* complexion (2). **temperamental** *adj*. Excitable, emotionally volatile, or easily upset.
[From Latin *temperamentum* a mixing in proportion, from *temperare* to temper or mingle]

temperament theory *n*. A popular typology of *personality, based on the *Myers–Briggs Type Indicator, focusing on four basic temperaments rather than the standard 16, namely SJ (sensing judges or *guardians*), SP (sensing perceivers or *performers*), NT (intuitive thinkers or *rationals*), and NF (intuitive feelers or *idealists*).

temperature receptor *n*. A type of *sensory receptor consisting of *free nerve endings that respond to stimulation by cold objects or substances in a *cold spot or to warm or hot objects or substances in a *warm spot. Also called a *thermoreceptor*.

temperature sense *n*. The mainly *cutaneous sense that responds to warm and cold stimuli. Also called *thermaesthesia* or the *thermal sense* or *thermic sense*. *See also* cold spot, warm spot.

temperature spot *n*. A generic name for a *cold spot or a *warm spot.

temper tantrum *See* tantrum.

template matching *n*. A hypothetical mechanism of visual recognition according to which forms or patterns are identified by matching them to stored forms or patterns (templates). This principle underlies *optical character recognition and most systems of *computer vision, but it is not the normal way in which recognition works in the visual system, and it fails to account for *shape constancy. Also called *prototype matching. See also* shape–slant invariance.

tempo *n.* The speed at which a piece or passage of music is played or an utterance or fragment of speech is delivered.
[From Italian *tempo* speed, from Latin *tempus* time]

temporal bone *n.* Either of the bones at the sides and base of the skull containing the *auditory canals.
[From Latin *temporalis* of the temple, from *tempus, temporis* a temple (on the side of the head)]

temporal lobe *n.* The bottom *lobe on the side of each cerebral hemisphere, separated on its lateral or outer surface from the frontal lobe and the parietal lobe by the *lateral sulcus and an imaginary line extending the sulcus horizontally towards the occipital lobe, and from the occipital lobe by an imaginary line from the top of the *parieto-occipital sulcus to the *pre-occipital notch. It is concerned with hearing, speech perception (especially in the left hemisphere), sexual behaviour, visual perception, musical interpretation (especially in the right hemisphere), memory, and social behaviour. Major lesions in the medial underlying part of this area can result in memory deficits and *temporal lobe epilepsy. *See also* global amnesia, Klüver–Bucy syndrome, limbic system, lobe, operculum, simultanagnosia, topographagnosia.

temporal lobe epilepsy *n.* A form of *epilepsy associated with abnormal electrical discharges radiating from the *temporal lobe, characterized by temporary impairment or loss of consciousness, sometimes accompanied by automatism, and abnormal or even antisocial or violent behaviour, without any apparent convulsions. Such an episode is often preceded by premonitory *auras (2), *derealization, *déjà vu, *jamais vu, or *cacosmia. Also called *psychomotor epilepsy* or *temporal lobe syndrome. See also* interictal syndrome. **TLE** *abbrev.*

temporal lobe seizure *n.* A *seizure of the type found in *temporal lobe epilepsy, without any evidence of a *convulsion. Also called a *psychomotor seizure.*

temporal operculum *See under* operculum.

temporal plane *n.* Another name for the *planum temporale.

temporal retina *n.* The half of the *retina that is nearest to the temple and from which nerve fibres are projected to the ipsilateral (same-side) cerebral hemisphere after passing through the *optic chiasm. *Compare* nasal retina.

temporal summation *n.* The successive impulses of afferent neurons combining additively in a *postsynaptic neuron to produce a *graded potential that may cause the neuron to transmit a nerve impulse or *action potential that could not be produced by a single afferent impulse. *See also* graded potential. *Compare* spatial summation.
[From Latin *temporalis* of or relating to time, from *tempus* time + -*alis* of or relating to]

temporary threshold shift *n.* A temporary change (usually an increase) in a sensory *threshold, the most familiar forms being the increase in auditory threshold resulting from the *acoustic reflex in response to loud noise and the increase in visual threshold resulting from the *pupillary light reflex in response to bright light. **TTS** *abbrev.*

tendon organ *n.* A shortened name for a *Golgi tendon organ.

tendon reflex *n.* Another name for a *deep tendon reflex.

tendon sense *n.* A form of *proprioception and *kinaesthesis mediated by receptors in or adjacent to the tendons. *See also* Golgi tendon organ.

tension headache *n.* A pain in the head associated with tension in the muscles of the neck, face, and shoulder, resulting from stress or overwork.

tensor tympani *n.* A muscle in the middle ear that reduces the movement of the *ossicles when it contracts and that acts in conjunction with the *stapedius in the *acoustic reflex to protect the ear from damage when exposed to loud sounds.
[From Latin *tensor* a stretcher from *tensus* tight, from *tendere* to stretch + *tympanum* a drum]

teonanactyl *n*. Any mushroom of the Agaricaceae family that contains the *hallucinogenic ingredient *psilocybin. Also called a *magic mushroom*.

[From Nahuatl *teotl* a god + *nanacatl* a mushroom]

teratogen *n*. Any substance, organism, or process that causes or increases the probability of a congenital disorder or birth defect in a baby, including a drug such as alcohol (*see* foetal alcohol syndrome), an infection such as German measles, or processes such as exposure to X-rays or other forms of ionizing radiation (*see* mutagen). **teratogenic** *adj*. **teratogenesis** *n*. The production of a congenital defect by a *teratogen.

[From Greek *teras*, *teratos* a monster + *genes* born]

terminal bouton *n*. Another name for a *bouton. Also spelt *terminal button*.

terminal insomnia *See under* insomnia.

terminal threshold *n*. The point along a *continuum of stimulus intensity beyond which further increases produce no further increases in sensation, although for some types of stimuli pain or damage to the *sensory receptors may be caused, or an analogous upper point along another stimulus dimension such as sound-wave frequency, the terminal threshold in that case being approximately 20,000 hertz for a person with normal hearing. Also called an *upper threshold*, though this usage causes confusion.

termination codon *n*. Another name for a *stop codon. Also called a *terminator codon*.

Ternus phenomenon *n*. A form of *apparent movement that is usually demonstrated with a row of four evenly spaced elements (dots or other identical shapes) labelled *A*, *B*, *C*, and *D* from left to right and presented in a sequence of brief flashes as follows: first *A*, *B*, and *C* all together, then *B*, *C*, and *D*, then *A*, *B*, and *C* again, and so on. If the *interstimulus interval is long, then no apparent movement is seen; with an intermediate interstimulus interval of about 200 milliseconds (under what Ternus called optimal conditions) *group movement* occurs as a single triplet of elements appears to move forwards and backwards in step without any appearance of two of the elements re-

maining fixed; and as the interstimulus interval is shortened further *element movement* occurs as *A* appears to hop forwards and backwards over *B* and *C*, which appear to remain stationary. Also called a *Ternus display*. *See also* apparent movement, phantom grating, random-dot kinematogram.

[Named after the German Gestalt psychologist Josef Ternus (1892–1959) who first described it in 1926]

territoriality *n*. The behaviour of certain animals and birds in marking out or defending their own territory against other members of the same species.

tertiary prevention *n*. Measures taken to alleviate the effects of a disorder, often through *rehabilitation. *Compare* primary prevention, secondary prevention.

tertiary projection area *n*. An area of the cerebral cortex that receives projections from a *secondary projection area. Also called an *association area*. *Compare* primary projection area.

test age *n*. In psychometrics, a *derived score, expressed in years, representing the average age at which children in the standardization sample achieved the raw score that the respondent achieved.

test anxiety *n*. A form of *state anxiety aroused by the event or prospect of taking a test or examination. Also called *examination anxiety*. **test-anxious** *adj*.

test battery *n*. In psychometrics, a set of tests standardized on the same population, enabling meaningful comparison or combination of scores on several tests.

test bias *n*. In psychometrics, the property of a psychological test, when administered to a particular group, such as an ethnic minority or one of the sexes, of yielding an average score that is either lower (in the case of negative bias) or higher (positive bias) than the average score for the total population, the disparity being due to a factor or factors other than a true difference in the attribute being measured. The last stipulation is often difficult to prove in practice, but without it an allegation of test bias is vacuous. Without it, one could argue that scales for weighing newborn babies are biased against black babies, because they yield lower average birth weights for black than white babies. *See also* item bias.

testee *n.* In psychometrics, a person being tested or responding to a test.

testing effect *n.* Any effect of taking tests on the respondents, a typical example being *test sophistication.

testis *n.* The technical word for a testicle, the male sex gland or *gonad, which produces *spermatozoa and secretes *androgens such as *androsterone and *testosterone into the bloodstream. *See also* Müllerian inhibiting substances, Wolffian duct. *Compare* ovary. **testes** *pl.*
[From Latin *testis* a witness, alluding to the fact that testes bear witness to a person's masculinity]

test item *n.* In psychometrics, an individual question or other element of a psychological test.

Test-Operate-Test-Exit *See* TOTE.

testosterone *n.* A potent male *steroid *sex hormone secreted mainly by the testes but also by the female ovaries (where it is required for the production of oestrogen) and adrenal glands, responsible for the development of the male sex organs and tending to stimulate competitiveness and aggression. *See also* DHEA, performance enhancer, sex hormone, Wolffian duct. *Compare* oestrogen.
[From *test(is)* + *ster(oid)* + *-one* indicating a ketone, from Greek *-one* a feminine name suffix]

test–retest reliability *n.* A measure of a test's *reliability, or more specifically its *stability, based on the correlation between scores of a group of respondents on two separate occasions.

test sophistication *n.* Knowledge of how to respond advantageously to psychological tests, acquired as a *testing effect by a person through extensive experience of taking similar tests. Also called *test wiseness*.

test wiseness *n.* A colloquial name for *test sophistication. **test-wise** *adj.*

tetanus toxin *n.* A substance that blocks the action of *glycine on *alpha motor neurons, causing convulsions. *Compare* picrotoxin, strychnine.

tetrachromatic theory *n.* Another name for the *opponent-process theory.
[From Greek *tetra-* four + *chroma, chromatos* a colour + *-ikos* of, relating to, or resembling]

tetracyclic antidepressant *n.* A class of *antidepressant drugs, the best known being *mianserin, that are used to treat depression, their mechanism of action being poorly understood. *Compare* monoamine oxidase inhibitor (MAOI), selective serotonin reuptake inhibitor (SSRI), St John's wort, tricyclic antidepressant.
[So called because they have four fused rings in their molecular structures]

tetrahydrocannabinol *n.* An abbreviated name for *delta-9-tetrahydrocannabinol (THC).

tetraplegia *n.* Another name for *quadriplegia. **tetraplegic** *adj.*
[From Greek *tetra-* four + *plege* a blow + *-ia* indicating a condition or quality]

tetrodotoxin *n.* A powerful *neurotoxin that is present in a species of puffer fish and that functions by blocking sodium channels in the neuronal membrane, thereby inactivating the *sodium pump. Tingling in the lips and tongue usually develop within 10–45 minutes of eating puffer fish, then the sensations spread rapidly to other parts of the body, and this is followed by excessive salivation, weakness, nausea, vomiting, diarrhoea, abdominal pain, paralysis, difficulty swallowing, convulsions, and sometimes death by respiratory paralysis. *See also* neurotoxin, zombie (2). **TTX** *abbrev.*
[From Greek *tetra-* four + *odous, odontos* a tooth + *toxikon* arrow-poison, from *toxon* a bow]

texture gradient *n.* A change in the appearance of the grain or microstructure of a surface, an abrupt or sudden change providing a cue for the perception of a *contour, and a gradual change (as when the blades of grass in a meadow appear widely spaced in the foreground and increasingly close together towards the background) being a form of *perspective that is related to *aerial

Texture gradient

perspective and *linear perspective and is one of the monocular cues of visual *depth perception (see illustration). *See also* visual cliff.

T-group *n.* A group of people who meet regularly and investigate patterns of authority and communication among themselves, as a technique of *group therapy and training developed in the 1940s by the Polish/German-born US psychologist Kurt Lewin (1890–1947). Also called a *human relations group* or a *sensitivity training group*. *Compare* encounter group.
[An abbreviation of (sensitivity) t(raining) group]

thalamencephalon *n.* The part of the *diencephalon that includes the *thalamus and *pineal gland.
[From *thalam(us)* + *(di)encephalon*]

thalamic syndrome *n.* A raised threshold (diminished sensitivity) for tactile sensations, which are felt as unpleasant if they are felt at all, resulting from a lesion in the *thalamus.

thalamus *n.* Either of a pair of large, golfball-sized capsules near the base of the brain in the diencephalon, forming a lateral wall of the third *ventricle, containing all the nerve fibres that ascend and descend between the cortex and the spinal cord, part of the *ascending reticular activating system, and relay stations such as the *lateral geniculate nuclei and *medial geniculate nuclei, and receiving all sensory inputs, except from the olfactory receptors, before they are relayed to areas in the cerebral cortex. Its *ventral anterior nuclei and *ventral lateral nuclei receive inputs from the globus pallidus and cerebellum and project to the prefrontal cortex and motor cortex, its *ventral posterior nuclei contain inverted *topographic maps of the body and project to the somatosensory cortex, and the *pulvinar at its back is implicated in atten-

tion. *See also* epithalamus, intralaminar nucleus, massa intermedia, neothalamus, thalamic syndrome. **thalami** *pl.* **thalamic** *adj.*
[From Greek *thalamos* an inner room or chamber, from *thalos* a vault]

thanatomania *n.* Another name for *voodoo death.
[From Greek *thanatos* death + *mania* madness]

thanatophobia *n.* A *specific phobia focused on fear of death or dying.
[From Greek *thanatos* death + *phobos* fear + -*ia* indicating a condition or quality]

Thanatos *n.* In *psychoanalysis, the unconscious drive towards dissolution and death, initially turned inwards on oneself and tending to self-destruction; later turned outwards in the form of aggression. Sigmund Freud (1856–1939), influenced by witnessing the ravages of the First World War, introduced the concept hesitantly and tentatively in 1920, in Chapter 6 of his book *Beyond the Pleasure Principle* (*Standard Edition*, XVIII, pp. 7–64), and he admitted in a later book *Civilization and its Discontents* (1930) that its existence was open to debate: 'Since the assumption of the existence of the instinct is mainly based on theoretical grounds, we must also admit that it is not entirely proof against theoretical objections' (*Standard Edition*, XXI, pp. 64–145, at pp. 121–2). The concept defies conventional biological assumptions, *natural selection favouring characteristics promoting survival and reproduction, and many psychoanalysts did indeed dissent, though others, notably the British-based Austrian psychoanalyst Melanie Klein (1882–1960) and her followers, assigned a major role to it, even in early childhood. Also called the *death instinct*. *See also* destructive instinct, destrudo, mortido, nirvana principle, object instinct, pain principle. *Compare* Eros.

[Named after Thanatos in Greek mythology, the personification of death and brother of Hypnos (the personification of sleep), from Greek *thanatos* death]

Thatcher illusion *n.* Another name for the *Margaret Thatcher illusion.

Thematic Apperception Test *See* TAT.

theobromine *n.* A white, crystalline, *alkaloid, *xanthine derivative, an isomer of theophylline (having the same chemical formula but a different arrangement of atoms within the molecule), that is found in tea, cocoa, and chocolate and that acts as a central nervous system *stimulant, being used in the treatment of headaches, as a diuretic, and as a myocardial stimulant in coronary heart disease. Formula: $C_7H_8N_4O_2$. *Compare* caffeine, theophylline.
[From Latin *Theobroma* the genus of tropical American cacao trees, literally food of the gods, from *theos* a god + *broma* food + -*ine* indicating an organic compound]

theophylline *n.* A white, crystalline, *alkaloid, *xanthine derivative and central nervous system *stimulant, an isomer of theobromine (having the same chemical formula but a different arrangement of atoms within the molecule), that is found in tea leaves and is used as a bronchodilator in the treatment of asthma and as a muscle relaxant, with pharmacological properties and medicinal uses similar to those of theobromine. Formula: $C_7H_8N_4O_2$. *Compare* caffeine, theobromine.
[From *theo(bromine)* or Latin *thea* tea + Greek *phyll(on)* a leaf + -*ine* indicating an organic compound]

theoretical research *n.* Another name for *basic research.

theory *n.* **1.** In logic and mathematics, a coherent system of primitive concepts, axioms, and rules of inference from which theorems may be derived. **2.** A *proposition (1) or set of propositions offered as a conjectured explanation for an observed phenomenon, state of affairs, or event. *Compare* hypothesis, model. **3.** Non-technically, any speculative or conjectural notion or opinion.
[From Greek *theoria* view or theory, from *theorein* to view or observe]

theory of games *See* game theory.

theory of mind *n.* People's intuitive understanding of their own and other people's minds or mental states, including beliefs and thoughts. It develops by degrees from a very early age in humans: by the age of 3 years children normally have a well-developed theory of mind but cannot yet understand, for example, that people's beliefs can be false: 3-year-olds who open a candy or chocolate box and are surprised to find pencils inside it consistently say that, before the box was opened, other people would have believed that there were pencils inside it and that they believed this also. Research has suggested that a theory of mind is fully developed only in human beings, but that people with *autistic disorder are severely impaired in their ability to understand mental states and to appreciate how mental states govern behaviour. Without a theory of mind, social behaviour is disrupted and the *cooperative principle breaks down. The specific inability to appreciate other people's mental states is called *mind-blindness*. **ToM** *abbrev.*

theory of planned behaviour *n.* An extended version of the *theory of reasoned action, incorporating a construct of perceived behavioural control and thus enabling predictions to be made of actions that are under incomplete volitional control. In the theory, perceived behavioural control is a function of one's beliefs about how likely it is that one has the resources and opportunities required to perform the behaviour. The theory was formulated by the Polish-born US psychologist Icek Ajzen (born 1942) and expounded in his book *Attitudes, Personality, and Behavior* (1988) and in an article in the journal *Organizational Behavior and Human Decision Processes* (1991). US *theory of planned behavior*.

theory of reasoned action *n.* A general theory of the relationship between attitudes and behaviour, according to which behaviour is determined by behavioural intentions, and behavioural intentions in turn are determined by *attitudes (1) to behaviour and subjective *norms (1). An attitude to behaviour is one's evaluation of the goodness or badness of performing the action in question, and a subjective norm is the perceived social pressure arising from one's perception of the extent to which significant others would like one to perform the action. Algebraically, $B(f)BI = w_1A_B + w_2SN$, where B denotes behaviour, f indicates a function, BI behavioural intention, A_B attitude towards the behaviour, and SN subjective norm; w_1 and w_2 are empirically determined weights representing the relative importance of the attitudinal and normative components. Attitude towards the behaviour (A_B) is determined by one's beliefs about the consequences of the behaviour multiplied by the evaluation of each consequence and then summed (see expectancy–value theory). Social norm (SN) is a function of one's perception of the preferences of significant others as to whether one should engage in the behaviour. The weights w_1 and w_2 reflect the relative influence on behavioural intention of attitude towards the behaviour and subjective norm. The theory was formulated by the US psychologist Martin Fishbein (born 1936) and the Polish-born US psychologist Icek Ajzen (born 1942) and published in their books *Belief, Attitude, Intention and Behavior: An Introduction to Theory and Research* (1975) and *Understanding Attitudes and Predicting Social Behavior* (1980). The theory is well supported by research findings, but a limitation of it is that it applies only to behaviour that is predominantly volitional or voluntary, and this limitation was addressed in the later *theory of planned behaviour.

therapeutic *adj.* Of or relating to the treatment of disorders. See also psychotherapy. **therapeutics** *n.* The aspect of medicine concerned with the treatment and cure of disorders. **therapeutist** *n.* An old-fashioned name for a therapist.
[From Greek *therapeuein* to heal or take care of, from *theraps* an attendant + *-itikos* resembling or marked by]

therapeutic alliance *n.* In *psychoanalysis, the implicit cooperative compact between an analyst and a patient whereby the analyst undertakes to offer *interpretations (2) and the patient undertakes to obey the *fundamental rule of psychoanalysis and to try to understand the analyst's interpretations.

therapeutic community *n.* A treatment facility in which the total environment, including the physical milieu, the other clients or patients, and the staff, is part of the treatment. See also milieu therapy. **TC** *abbrev.*

therapeutic index *n.* Any of several indices relating the clinical effectiveness of a drug to its safety factor, the most common being the *therapeutic ratio of the *median lethal dosage to the *median effective dosage (LD-50/ED-50). Other therapeutic indices include the ratio of the *minimum toxic dosage to the *minimum effective dosage, and the difference between the minimum effective dosage and the minimum toxic dosage.

therapeutic ratio *n.* An index relating the clinical effectiveness of a drug to its safety factor, introduced by the German bacteriologist and immunologist Paul Ehrlich (1854–1915), given by dividing the *median lethal dosage (LD-50) by its *median effective dosage (ED-50), whence therapeutic ratio = LD-50/ED-50, a drug often being considered safe only if its therapeutic ratio is at least 10. See also therapeutic index.

therapist *n.* A person who practises a *therapy.

therapy *n.* Any form of treatment for a disorder by a method other than surgery; such treatments in general. See also gene therapy, psychotherapy.
[From Greek *therapeuein* to heal or take care of, from *theraps* an attendant]

thermaesthesia *n.* Another name for the *temperature sense. US *thermesthesia*.
[From Greek *therme* heat + *aisthesis* feeling + *-ia* indicating a condition or quality]

thermal adaptation *n.* A form of *adaptation (2) whereby prolonged exposure to a stimulus that is warmer than *physiological zero tends to cause it to feel less warm, and prolonged exposure to a stimulus that is colder than physiological zero tends to cause it to feel less cold. It can be demonstrated by an experiment described under *successive contrast.

thermalgesia *n.* A condition in which *warm spots are hypersensitive and warm stimuli elicit pain responses. Also written *thermoalgesia*. Compare thermoanalgesia.
[From Greek *therme* heat + *algesis* sense of pain, from *algos* pain + *-ia* indicating a condition or quality]

thermalgia *n.* Another name for *causalgia.

thermal sense *n*. Another name for the *temperature sense. Also called the *thermic sense*.

thermoanaesthesia *n*. Insensitivity to warmth and coldness owing to a failure of the *temperature sense. US *thermoanesthesia*. Also called *thermanaesthesia* or *thermanesthesia*.
[From Greek *therme* heat + *an*- without + *aisthesis* feeling + *-ia* indicating a condition or quality]

thermoanalgesia *n*. A condition in which hot stimuli fail to elicit pain responses. Also called *thermanalgesia*. *Compare* thermalgesia.
[From Greek *therme* heat + *an*- without + *algesis* sense of pain, from *algos* pain + *-ia* indicating a condition or quality]

thermodynamics *n*. The study of the laws governing the interrelationships between heat, mechanical work, and other forms of energy and their effects on the behaviour of systems. The *first law of thermodynamics* (the law of the conservation of energy), states that when a system changes from one state to another, energy is converted to a different form but the total amount of energy remains unchanged or is conserved, making a perpetual-motion machine impossible; the *second law of thermodynamics* states that in any closed system (one that exchanges energy but not matter with the exterior) *entropy can only increase or in an idealized case remain unchanged; the *third law of thermodynamics* (the Nernst heat theorem) states that as a homogeneous system approaches a temperature of absolute zero its entropy tends to zero; and the *zeroth law of thermodynamics* states that if two bodies are each in thermal equilibrium with a third body, then they are in thermal equilibrium with each other.
[From Greek *therme* heat + *dynamikos* powerful, from *dynamis* strength + *-ikos* of, relating to, or resembling]

thermoform *n*. A raised or embossed representation of a map, diagram, or picture for tactile inspection by blind people.
[So called because it is made by shaping heated vinyl sheets]

thermoreceptor *n*. Another name for a *temperature receptor.

thermoregulation *n*. A form of *homeostasis whereby *homoiothermic animals such as humans maintain a constant internal body temperature.
[From Greek *therme* heat + Latin *regulare* to control + *-ation* indicating a process or condition]

theta wave *n*. A low-frequency (5–8 hertz) *EEG wave in the *hippocampus associated with relaxed wakefulness and REM sleep. Also called a *theta rhythm*.
[From *theta* (θ) the eighth letter of the Greek alphabet]

thiamine *See* vitamin B$_1$.

thing-presentation *n*. In *psychoanalysis, the type of non-linguistic and largely visual representation of memories that is characteristic of the *unconscious (2), whereas in the *preconscious and in *consciousness thing-presentations do not occur alone but are accompanied by or associated with *word-presentations. In a typical passage in an article on 'The Unconscious' (1915), Sigmund Freud (1856–1939) referred to this phenomenon: 'The conscious presentation comprises the presentation of the thing plus the presentation of the word belonging to it, while the unconscious presentation is the presentation of the thing alone' (*Standard Edition*, XIV, pp. 166–215, at p. 201).

thinking *n*. The act or process of having ideas or thoughts, including *reasoning, *problem solving, *decision making, the formation of *mental models, and the contemplation of *knowledge, *beliefs, and *opinions. *See also* absolute thinking, centipede effect, cognitive derailment, convergence–divergence, delusion, dereism, directed thinking, fantasy thinking, Humphrey's law, hyper-reflection, imageless thought, lateral thinking, logic, magical thinking, noesis, obsession, predicate thinking, problem solving, rational, thought disorder, thought stopping.

thinking type *n*. One of the subsidiary personality types in *analytical psychology. *See* function type.

thiopental *n*. Thiopental sodium, an ultra-short-acting *barbiturate drug used as an intravenous general anaesthetic and sometimes as a *truth drug. Also called *Pentothal* (trademark), *Sodium Pentothal*, or *thiopentone*.

thiopentone *See* thiopental.

thioridazine *n*. Thioridazine hydrochloride, a *neuroleptic (1) drug belonging to the class of *phenothiazines, prescribed in the treatment of *schizophrenia and other *psychotic (1) disorders, dysthymic disorder, childhood behavioural disorders, geriatric mental disorders, depressive disorders, and alcohol withdrawal. Also called *Mellaril* (trademark).

thiothixene *n*. A *neuroleptic (1) drug belonging to the group of *thioxanthenes, used (sometimes in its hydrochloride form) in the treatment of *schizophrenia and other *psychotic (1) disorders. Also called *Navane* (trademark).

thioxanthene *n*. Any of a group of *neuroleptic (1) drugs such as *thiothixene that have similar pharmacological effects to the *phenothiazines.
[From *thio-* indicating a chemical compound containing sulphur, from Greek *theion* sulphur + English *xanthene* a yellow crystalline compound used as a fungicide and as a dye, from Greek *xanthos* yellow + *-ene* indicating an unsaturated compound containing double bonds, from *-ene* a feminine name suffix]

third ear *n*. In *psychoanalysis, a term sometimes used to denote the analyst's faculty of *interpretation (2), which is supposed to enable the analyst to hear things in the patient's words that would not be apparent to an untrained listener with an ordinary pair of ears. The term was introduced by the Czechoslovakian-born psychoanalyst Theodore Reik (1888–1969) in the title of his book *Listening with the Third Ear* (1949).

third eyelid *n*. A non-technical name for a *nictitating membrane.

third ventricle *See under* ventricle.

thirst *n*. The physiological and psychological state or condition caused by dehydration or lack of drink, characterized by an urge to drink and a feeling of dryness in the mouth and throat. *See also* angiotensin II, baroreceptor, hypovolaemic thirst, intracellular thirst, subfornical organ.

Thorazine *n*. A proprietary name for the neuroleptic drug *chlorpromazine.
[Trademark]

thought broadcasting delusion *n*. A *delusion that one's thoughts are being disseminated in a way that enables others to know them.

thought disorder *n*. Any pathological disturbance of thought processes, including *delusions, *flight of ideas, *loosening of associations, or *perseveration (2), characteristic of certain mental disorders, notably *schizophrenia, and considered by some authorities, including the Swiss psychiatrist Eugen Bleuler (1857–1939), who coined the term *schizophrenia*, to be the defining feature of that disorder. Because of the difficulty of defining it objectively, *DSM-IV limits the term to disorganization of speech. *See also* overinclusiveness, proverbs test.

thought experiment *n*. Another name for a *Gedankenexperiment*.

thought insertion delusion *n*. A *delusion that certain of one's thoughts that are not one's own have been inserted into one's mind by an external agent.

thought stopping *n*. A technique of *cognitive behaviour modification in which patients or clients are trained to stop thinking about something as soon as it comes to mind, sometimes by self-administering a painful reminder, such as by snapping a rubber band worn round the wrist. It has been used to treat *obsessions, *phobias, *paraphilias, and *hallucinations. *See also* suppression.

Thouless ratio *n*. A modified version of the *Brunswik ratio of *perceptual constancy, influenced by Fechner's law, given by $(\log R - \log S)/(\log A - \log S)$, where R is the physical magnitude or intensity of the stimulus chosen as a match, S is the physical magnitude or intensity for a stimulus match with zero constancy, and A is the physical magnitude or intensity that would be chosen under 100 per cent constancy. The ratio is equal to zero when there is no perceptual constancy and 1 when there is perfect constancy.
[Named after the English psychologist Robert Henry Thouless (1894–1984) who proposed it in 1931]

three-colour theory *n*. Another name for the *trichromatic theory.

3-D model description n. In the *computational theory of vision pioneered in the late 1970s by the English psychologist David Courtenay Marr (1945–80), the third and final *representation (2), consisting of an abstract, object-centred three-dimensional representation enabling object recognition to occur, in contrast to the primitive *primal sketch and the viewer-centred *2$\frac{1}{2}$-D sketch.

3-hydroxytyramine See dopamine.

three Ps n. Pedantry, parsimony, and petulance. See anal character.

three–seven effect n. A phenomenon, based on *population stereotypes, that is often used by stage conjurors pretending to project their thoughts telepathically to their audiences. The performer says: 'I'm going to think of a two-digit number between one and fifty. I'll make both digits odd but not the same, so fifteen would be OK, but eleven wouldn't because the two odd digits are the same ... [pause]. Now how many of you got thirty-seven?' It usually turns out that more than one-third of the audience have thought of the number 37, partly because 3 and 7 are population stereotypes and partly because, surprisingly, the performer's instructions leave only seven possible two-digit numbers, apart from 15, which is effectively eliminated by being used as an example. It is often used in phoney demonstrations of telepathy.

threshold n. The lowest intensity at which a *stimulus (1) evokes a *response or at which two stimuli can be discriminated from each other. Intensity is interpreted broadly to include variable stimulus *attributes such as the length of a line or the pitch of a tone. Also called a limen. See absolute threshold, difference threshold. See also signal detection theory, subliminal perception, terminal threshold.

Thurstone scale n. A type of *attitude scale constructed by the *method of equal-appearing intervals, in which a large pool of candidate statements about an attitude object, ranging from strongly negative (Abortion is never justified) through neutral (There are arguments both for and against abortion) to strongly positive (Abortion is every woman's right), are sorted by a group of judges into eleven categories, assumed to appear equally spaced on the attitude *continuum, according to how favourable the statements are towards the attitude object, and items that yield the highest level of agreement among the judges as to their scale position, and that collectively represent an adequate range of contents and scale positions, are then selected for the final scale. Respondents to the scale endorse just those items with which they agree, and an individual respondent's score is calculated as the mean (or occasionally median) of the items endorsed, such scores being assumed to lie on an *interval scale of measurement. Also called an equal-appearing interval scale. Compare Guttman scale, Likert scale, semantic differential, unfolding technique, unobtrusive measure.
[Named after the US psychologist Louis Leon Thurstone (1887–1955) who introduced it in an article in the journal Psychological Bulletin in 1929]

thwasa n. The Xhosa name for *spell.
[From Xhosa ukuthwasa to appear or become visible]

thymine n. One of the constituent *bases (1) of *DNA, having an affinity for *adenine. **T** abbrev.
[From Greek thymos the thymus gland + -ine indicating an organic compound]

thymoleptic adj. n. (Of or relating to) an *antidepressant drug.
[From Greek thymos temper or emotion + lepsis a taking hold or seizure + -ikos of, relating to, or resembling]

thymus n. A double-lobed *endocrine gland situated just below the *thyroid gland at the base of the neck, formerly believed to be vestigial in adults but now known to have a crucial role in the lymphatic system and to be the source of *T lymphocytes.
[From Greek thymos the sweetbread or thymus gland]

thyroid gland n. An *endocrine gland, consisting in humans of two lobes near the base of the neck, that secretes the hormone *thyroxine, accelerating growth and metabolism and controlling body temperature. A deficiency of thyroxine leads to *hypothyroidism and can result in mental retardation, whereas an excess produces *hyperthyroidism and can lead to swelling of the eyeballs and exophthalmic goitre. The thyroid gland also secretes *calcitonin, which regulates calcium levels (*compare* parathyroid gland). *See also* thyroid-stimulating hormone, thyrotrophin-releasing hormone.

[From Greek *thyreoeides* a door-shaped shield, from *thyra* a door + *eidos* form, alluding to its appearance]

thyroid-stimulating hormone *n.* A hormone secreted by the anterior pituitary in response to *thyrotrophin-releasing hormone secreted by the hypothalamus. It stimulates the *thyroid gland to secrete *thyroxine. Also called *thyrotrophic hormone* or *thyrotropic hormone (TH)*. **TSH** *abbrev.*

thyrotrophin-releasing hormone *n.* A *releasing hormone synthesized and secreted by the hypothalamus, causing the secretion of *thyroid-stimulating hormone by the anterior pituitary. Also spelt *thyrotropin-releasing hormone*. **TRH** *abbrev.*

thyroxine *n.* A hormone secreted by the *thyroid gland, derived from the non-essential amino acid tyrosine, accelerating metabolism and growth and controlling body temperature. Its chemical name is tetraiodothyronine. Also spelt *thyroxin*.

tic *n.* A spasmodic, recurrent, non-rhythmic, stereotyped movement or vocalization, experienced as irresistible but capable of being temporarily suppressed, often made worse by stress and improved by distraction. Simple motor tics include eye blinking, neck twisting, shoulder shrugging, and facial grimacing, and simple vocal tics include throat clearing, grunting, snorting, and barking. Complex tics include facial and bodily gestures, repeating words or phrases, *coprolalia, *echolalia, and *palilalia. *See also* tic disorders, tic douloureux.

[French: origin obscure]

tic disorders *n.* A group of *mental disorders characterized by *tics. *See* chronic motor or vocal tic disorder, Tourette's disorder, transient tic disorder.

tic douloureux *n.* A disorder of the *trigeminal nerve, usually in a person over 60 years old, causing spasmodic stabbing pain in the forehead, nose, and scalp, the region between the nose, mouth and temple, or the lower face, depending on which of the three branches of the nerve is affected.

[From French *tic* a tic + *douloureux* painful, from *douleur* pain or suffering]

tickle *vb.* **1.** To touch, stroke, or poke a part of another person's body lightly, especially in certain sensitive areas such as the chest, stomach, genital area, or under the arms, in a manner that tends to produce *goose pimples, involuntary muscle spasms, and sensations that are partly pleasurable and partly aversive; hence, figuratively, to excite pleasurably (*She was tickled pink when she heard she was pregnant*). Self-tickling is difficult or impossible to achieve. *n.* **2.** The sensation produced by tickling.

tilt aftereffect *n.* A perceived inclination or slant in the parallel bars of a *grating as a result of gazing for half a minute or more at a different grating in which the parallel bars are slightly slanted in the opposite direction (see illustration). *See also* contingent aftereffect, figural aftereffect.

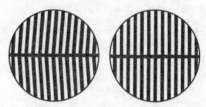

Tilt aftereffect. Run your eyes back and forth in the central channel of the left-hand figure for half a minute, then transfer your gaze to the central channel of the right-hand figure; the bars will appear to slope in the opposite direction to those on the left.

tilting-room test *n.* A test devised in the late 1940s by the US psychologist Herman A. Witkin (1916–79) to separate the gravitational cues from the *vestibular system from the visual cues that are used to judge one's orientation relative to the upright and to measure the cognitive style that came to be called *field dependence–independence. It consists of a small room that an experimenter can tilt to the left or right, containing a chair that the respondent can tilt to the left or right, the respondent's objective being to try to maintain an upright orientation. Field-independent people are able to bring the chair close to the vertical irrespective of how much the room is tilted, whereas field-dependent people tend to align themselves with the room, even when the room is tilted by as much as 35 degrees. Also called the *body adjustment test (BAT)*. *Compare* rod-and-frame test.

timbre *n*. The tone-colour or quality of a musical sound, the property that distinguishes the sound of a continuous tone played on two different musical instruments or sung by two different voices at the same pitch and intensity. In German it is called *Klangfarbe*, literally sound colour. In phonetics, it is the characteristic tonal quality distinguishing one *vowel from another.
[From French *timbre* the sound of a bell, from Latin *tympanum* a drum]

time series *n*. In statistics, any series of values of a variable taken at successive times or in a fixed order. For example, a person's pulse rate, measured every five minutes over a period of 24 hours, could be regarded as a time series. *See also* interrupted time-series design, noise (2), signal, signal-to-noise ratio, time-series analysis, white noise.

time-series analysis *n*. A set of statistical procedures for analysing *time series. *See* ARIMA, autocorrelation, autoregression, correlogram, Fourier analysis, moving average. *See also* aliasing, interrupted time-series design, white noise.

tinnitus *n*. Ringing, hissing, or rumbling noises in one or both ears, either of psychogenic origin or resulting from such physical causes as middle ear infection, the side-effects of certain drugs, including aspirin, or exposure to very loud noise.
[From Latin *tinnire* to ring]

tip-of-the-tongue phenomenon *n*. The recall of certain *attributes of an item of information being sought in memory without being able to recall the information itself. For example, a person trying to recall the capital of Nicaragua may recall that it begins with the letter M, and may know that it has three syllables, but may nevertheless not be able to recall its full name: *Managua*. If asked to guess, such a person might suggest names such as *Minorca*, *Montana*, or *Monica*. Apart from the initial letter or sound and number of syllables, which according to research are most often recalled when the phenomenon

occurs, the principal stressed syllable and the final letter or sound are also sometimes recalled—*see* serial position effect. The phenomenon was first investigated and named by the US psychologists Roger (William) Brown (1925–97) and David McNeill (born 1933) in an article in the *Journal of Verbal Learning and Verbal Behavior* in 1966. *See also* ugly sister effect. **TOT** *abbrev*.

Titchener circles *n*. Another name for the *Ebbinghaus illusion. Also called the *Titchener illusion*.
[Named after the English psychologist Edward Bradford Titchener (1867–1927) who published it in 1898]

tit for tat strategy *n*. A *programmed strategy for playing repeated *Prisoner's Dilemma games, also occasionally applied to other games, in which the program cooperates on the first trial and then, on each subsequent trial, chooses the strategy chosen by the co-player on the previous trial. It is often interpreted as a method of implementing *reciprocal altruism. **TFT** *abbrev*.

T lymphocyte *n*. A type of *lymphocyte synthesized in the *thymus gland that plays a crucial role in the *immune system. Two major subtypes are killer T cells that destroy cells infected by viruses and helper T cells that induce other cells, namely *B lymphocytes, to produce *antibodies. Also called a *T cell*. *See also* stem cell.
[From *t(hymus) lymphocyte*]

T-maze *n*. A simple *maze incorporating only one choice point with only two alternatives. It is shaped like the letter *T*, an animal entering the maze at the bottom and being rewarded for reaching the goal box at one end of the crossbar.

tocopherol *See* vitamin E.

Tofranil *n*. A proprietary name for the tricyclic antidepressant drug *amitriptyline.
[Trademark]

token *n*. **1.** An indication, sign, or symbol representing something else. **2.** A voucher or object that can be used as payment for goods or services. **3.** In linguistics, an instance or occurrence of a word or other linguistic unit in speech or writing, in contradistinction to the word or symbol (called a *type*) of which it is an instance. *See also* distractor, type-token ratio.

token distractor *See* distractor.

token economy *n.* A technique of *behaviour therapy sometimes used in hospitals and other institutions, in which inmates are given tokens (for example, poker chips) as *reinforcement (1) for the performance of certain target behaviour patterns (such as dressing or speaking normally or interacting with other patients on the ward), the tokens later being convertible into privileges such as special foods, cigarettes, or access to television.

tolerance *n.* **1.** The quality of being able or willing to accept the behaviour of others. **2.** The capacity to withstand extreme conditions or circumstances. **3.** In relation to drugs such as *narcotic analgesics, *dopamine antagonists, and *barbiturates, a tendency to require ever-increasing dosages of the drug to achieve a desired effect, or a markedly diminished effectiveness with continuation of the same dosages, caused by various mechanisms that reduce the number of drug molecules reaching neuroreceptor sites on target cells or that involve compensatory responses to the drug effects such as *enzyme induction or *neuromodulation. *See also* habituation (3), substance dependence, tachyphylaxis. *Compare* sensitization (reverse tolerance).
[From Latin *tolerare* to sustain or lift up]

tolerance of ambiguity *See* intolerance of ambiguity.

toluene *n.* A volatile flammable liquid derived from petroleum and coal tar, used as a *solvent in many household chemicals and often inhaled in *solvent abuse.
[From *tolu* an aromatic balsam, after *Santiago de Tolu*, from which it was exported + *-ene* indicating an unsaturated compound with double bonds, from Greek *-ene* a feminine name suffix]

tonal density *n.* A quality of sound associated with the perceived tightness or compactness of a tone, greater density usually occurring with higher frequency tones.

tone *n.* **1.** Any sound wave that is capable of being perceived as having a definite *pitch. *See also* complex tone, pure tone. *Compare* noise (1). **2.** A musical interval or difference in pitch equivalent to two *semitones or one-sixth of an *octave. Also called a *whole tone*.
[From Greek *tonos* a tone]

tone deafness *n.* A non-technical name for *asonia.

tongue *n.* The movable muscular structure situated on the floor of the mouth that functions as the principal organ of *taste and that plays an important part in the articulation of speech sounds, its epithelial covering being richly covered with *papillae, at the bases of which *taste buds are situated, maximal sensitivity for sweet tastes being located at the front, for sour tastes at the rear sides, for salty tastes at the front and front sides, and for bitter tastes at the front and especially in the soft palate above the back of the tongue. *See also* circumvallate papilla, filiform papilla, foliate papilla, fungiform papilla.
[From Old English *tunge*, cognate with Old High German *zunga*, Latin *lingua*]

tonic–clonic *adj.* Of or pertaining to a convulsion or spasm characteristic of *major epilepsy, beginning with a *tonic convulsion lasting up to a minute, then a *clonic convulsion for approximately a minute, often with clenched teeth, chewing movements, and loss of bladder or bowel control, then usually a period of relaxed unconsciousness followed by amnesia for the episode. Also called *grand mal*, *tonoclonic*. *Compare* absence.

tonic convulsion *n.* A prolonged and generalized contraction of the skeletal muscles. Also called *tonic immobility* or *tonic spasm*. *Compare* clonic convulsion, tonic–clonic.
[From Greek *tonos* tension, from *teinein* to stretch]

tonoclonic *adj.* A synonym for *tonic–clonic.

tonotopic map *n.* A *topographic map of the *basilar membrane in the *auditory cortex on *Heschl's gyrus. Also called a *cochleotopic map*.
[From Greek *tonos* a tone + *topos* a place + *-ikos* of, relating to, or resembling]

tonus *n.* The normal tension or elasticity of a resting muscle. Also called *muscle tone*. *See also* catalepsy, cataplexy (1), catatonia, decerebrate rigidity, dystonia, hypertonia, hypotonia, REM atonia. *Compare* atonia.
[From Greek *tonos* tension or tone]

topagnosia *n.* A form of agnosia involving an impaired ability to identify which part of one's body has been touched. Also called *topagnosis*. *See* agnosia. *See also* autotopagnosia.

[From Greek *topos* a place + *gnosis* knowing + *-ia* indicating a condition or quality]

top-down processing *n.* *Information processing that proceeds from information already stored in memory, especially general assumptions or presuppositions about the material being processed, as when a person forms a hypothesis on the basis of existing *schemata and prior experience about what an object might be and then uses sensory evidence to corroborate or disconfirm the hypothesis. In reading indistinct handwriting, for example, if the words *whisky and* . . . occur and the last word is illegible, a reader may use top-down processing and guess the last word to be *water*, checking the script for evidence to confirm or refute this guess, and if it is refuted, to guess that the word is *soda* and performing another check, and so on. A standard illustration of top-down processing is the phenomenon of reversal in an *ambiguous figure, which irresistibly oscillates between different interpretations. *Top-down theories* of perception are theories according to which perceptions are formed in this way. The term was introduced by the US psychologists Donald A. Norman (born 1935) and David E(verett) Rumelhart (born 1942) in their book *Exploration in Cognition* (1975). *See also* analysis by synthesis, constructive memory, constructivism, reconstructive memory. *Compare* bottom-up processing, feature detection theory.

top hat illusion *n.* A visual illusion, closely related to the *horizontal–vertical illusion, in which a drawing of a top hat, the height of which is equal to the width of its brim, appears much taller than it appears wide.

topographagnosia *n.* A form of agnosia involving an inability to find one's way around, read maps, draw plans, and perform similar functions, often associated with damage to the right hemisphere *parietal lobe. *See also* agnosia. *Compare* visuospatial agnosia (*see under* agnosia).

topographic map *n.* Any of the point-to-point representations of sensory fields, including especially the visual, auditory, and tactile

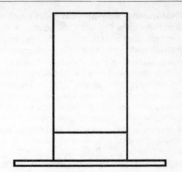

Top hat illusion. Its height is equal to the width of its brim.

fields, within particular areas of the brain, preserving the topological relationship between neighbouring points but often distorting relative distances. Also called a *topographical map* or a *topographic(al) (spatial) representation*. *See* auditory cortex, cerebellum, lateral geniculate nucleus, primary visual cortex, retinotopic map, somatosensory cortex, thalamus, tonotopic map, ventral posterior nucleus. *See also* somatosensory homunculus.

[From Greek *topos* a place + *graphein* to write + *-ikos* of, relating to, or resembling]

topography *n.* A detailed description of the major features of a region. In *psychoanalysis, a description of the layout of the mental apparatus, especially the first topography of Sigmund Freud (1856–1939) in terms of the *unconscious (2), *preconscious, and *consciousness, or his second structural model (from 1920 onwards) in terms of the *id, *ego, and *superego. *See also* metapsychology. **topographic** or **topographical** *adj.*

[From Greek *topos* a place + *graphein* to write]

topological psychology *n.* A largely discredited psychological geometry introduced in 1936 by the Polish/German-born US psychologist Kurt Lewin (1890–1947) to represent his *field theory, in particular the *life space, conceived as a *hodological space, and a person's locomotion within it.

[So called in reference to *topology, the branch of geometry concerned with the properties of a figure that remain unchanged when the figure is stretched, compressed, or bent]

torticollis *n.* A shortened name for *spasmodic torticollis.

total quality management *n.* An approach to management based on the principle that every member of staff should be involved in decision making and committed to achieving and maintaining high standards in all areas of the organization's activities. Additional assumptions are that success depends on giving the customers what they want at a price that they can afford, and that when one part of an organization supplies services to another it should treat the recipient as a customer. **TQM** *abbrev.*

TOTE *abbrev.* Test–Operate–Test–Exit, a *feedback loop proposed as the basic unit of behaviour by the US psychologist George A(rmitage) Miller (born 1920) and co-authors in their book *Plans for the Structure of Behavior* (1960). This hypothetical mechanism responds to a *stimulus (1) by testing it for incongruity, operates to remove the incongruity if any is found, tests again, and so on indefinitely until the incongruity is eliminated, then exits. The authors explained in a key passage that the TOTE is intended as a conceptual alternative to the *reflex arc: 'Obviously, the reflex arc is not the unit we should use as the element of behavior: the unit should be the feedback loop itself. If we think of the Test–Operate–Test–Exit unit—for convenience, we shall call it a TOTE unit—as we do of the reflex arc, in purely anatomical terms, it may describe reflexes, but little else. That is to say, the reflex should be recognized as only one of many possible actualizations of the TOTE pattern' (p. 27). It is not only energy that flows through the feedback loop, but also information and control, and it can be actualized at the cognitive level, as in the following example, especially apt for illustrating feedback: a person who is cooking tests a sauce for taste, notes an incongruity between the sensory input and the desired or expected taste, operates by adding various ingredients, tests again and repeats the cycle until no incongruity is found, then finally exits from the feedback loop.

totem *n.* A physical object having ritual significance, or a symbolic representation of such an object, especially a type of animal, plant, or natural structure representing a clan in certain cultures such as those of North American Indians. In *psychoanalysis, Sigmund Freud (1856–1939), in his book *Totem and Taboo* (1912–13, *Standard Edition*, XIII, pp. 1–162) interpreted it as a representation of the *primal father. *See also participation mystique*.

totem pole *n.* A pole on which *totems are hung.
[From Ojibwa *nintotem* mark of my family]

touch *n.* Originally one of the five classical *senses (1), now a generic term for several senses that respond to stimuli directly in contact with the *skin. *Dynamic touch is the ability to sense certain physical properties of an object by moving it around; *haptic touch is active exploration of objects or surfaces using the sense of touch, usually using the hands; and the *cutaneous senses are those responsible for the four sensations that may be felt when an object or surface touches the skin and that the Austrian physiologist Max von Frey (1852–1932) identified in 1904 as warmth, cold, pain, and pressure, although pressure is now known to include sensations of texture and vibration (*pallaesthesia*). *See also* aesthesiometer, cold spot, haphalgesia, paraesthesia, pressure-sensitive spot, sensory saltation, tactile acuity, touch receptor, two-point threshold, warm spot.

touch acuity *n.* Another name for *tactile acuity.

touch receptor *n.* A type of *sensory receptor, located in the *epidermis or the *dermis of the *skin, specialized for sensations of *touch. *See* free nerve ending, Golgi tendon organ, mechanoreceptor, Meissner's corpuscle, Merkel cell, Pacinian corpuscle, pain receptor, Ruffini corpuscle, temperature receptor. Also called a *tactor*.

tough-mindedness *n.* Practicality, lack of sentimentality, and determination, or obduracy and intractability. In the later writings (from 1975 onwards) of the German-born British psychologist Hans J(ürgen) Eysenck (1916–97) it is another name for *psychoticism.

Tourette's disorder *n.* A *tic disorder of genetic origin (located on chromosome 18) characterized by recurrent multiple motor tics and at least one vocal tic, causing significant distress or impairment in social or occupational functioning, the onset being before age 18 years, and the tics not being attributable to a stimulant drug or other substance or a *general medical condition. Contrary to common

misconception, *coprolalia or *copropraxia are present in only a minority of people with the disorder. Also called *Gilles de la Tourette's syndrome* (*GTS*) or *Tourette's syndrome* (*TS*).
[Named after the French physician Georges Gilles de la Tourette (1857–1904), who published case studies of eight patients with the disorder in 1885]

Tower of Hanoi *n*. A logical puzzle, frequently studied in cognitive psychology and used as a test of *problem-solving ability, consisting of three pegs, on one of which are placed a number of discs of varying diameter, the largest at the bottom and the smallest at the top (see illustration). The problem is to move the tower of disks over to one of the other pegs in the smallest number of moves, moving one disc at a time and using the third peg as a temporary way station as required, and never placing a larger disc on top of a smaller one. The puzzle is of ancient (possibly Indian) origin but was rediscovered by the French mathematician Edouard Lucas (1842–91) and marketed as a toy in 1883. Lucas proved that, for any number *n* of discs, the minimum number of moves is given by the formula $2^n - 1$. Hence 3 discs can be transferred in 7 moves, 4 discs in 15 moves, 5 discs in 31 moves, and so on. *See also* General Problem Solver.
[So called because of its supposed resemblance to a certain type of Vietnamese building, Lucas's toy having been described as a simplified version of the Tower of Brahma, which was said to contain 64 gold discs, and which would therefore require a minimum of $2^{64} - 1$ (more than 18 billion billion) moves to solve]

Tower of Hanoi

toxic *adj*. Of, relating to, or caused by a *toxin. *See also* toxic dosage. **toxicity** *n*. The state or quality of being *toxic; or the potency of a *toxin.
[From Greek *toxikon pharmakon* arrow-poison, from *toxon* a bow]

toxic dosage *n*. The minimum dosage of a drug required to produce signs or symptoms

of toxicity in an organism. **TD** *abbrev*. **toxic dosage 50** *n*. Another name for the *median toxic dosage. *See also* therapeutic index, therapeutic ratio. *Compare* effective dosage, lethal dosage. **TD-50** or **TD$_{50}$** *abbrev*.

toxicosis *n*. **1.** Any disorder or condition brought about by poisoning. **2.** Another name for *food aversion learning.
[From Greek *toxikon pharmakon* arrow-poison, from *toxon* a bow + *-osis* indicating a process or state]

toxin *n*. Any organic poison that stimulates an *immune response or the production of neutralizing *antibodies. More generally, any poison, but this meaning is avoided in careful usage.
[From Greek *toxikon pharmakon* arrow-poison, from *toxon* a bow]

trace conditioning *n*. A form of *conditioning (1) involving the repeated brief presentation of a *conditioned stimulus, followed by a period of time during which no stimulus is presented, and then the presentation of an *unconditioned stimulus, leading eventually to the development of a *conditioned response based on the memory of a previous stimulus. *Compare* delay conditioning.
[So called because it depends on a memory trace of the conditioned stimulus]

trace, memory *See* memory trace.

trachea *n*. The membranous tube, reinforced with cartilaginous rings, between the lungs and the *larynx, referred to non-technically as the *windpipe.
[From Greek *tracheia arteria* rough artery]

tragedy of the commons *See* commons dilemma.

trainable mentally retarded *adj*. An educational category equivalent to *moderate mental retardation. **TMR** *abbrev*.

training analysis *n*. A course of *psychoanalysis undergone by a student wishing to become an analyst. It was made obligatory at the Congress of the International Psycho-Analytical Association in 1922, although Sigmund Freud (1856–1939), the founder of psychoanalysis, believed that, for practical reasons, it could only be short and incomplete, and that its main objective should be to ensure that the student is suitable for further training ('Analysis Terminable and Interminable', 1937, *Standard Edition*, XXIII, pp. 216–53). *Compare* control analysis.

trait *n*. A characteristic or quality distinguishing a person or (less commonly) a thing, especially a more or less consistent pattern of behaviour that a person possessing the characteristic would be likely to display in relevant circumstances, typical examples being *shyness*, *honesty*, *tidiness*, and *stupidity*. The US psychologists Gordon W(illard) Allport (1897–1967) and Henry S(ebastian) Odbert (1909–95) carried out an exhaustive dictionary search (published in the journal *Psychological Monographs* in 1936) in which they found 17,953 trait names, and after eliminating synonyms that denoted essentially the same traits they were left with 4,505 distinct English trait names denoting psychological differences between people. *See also* 16PF, Big Five, Language Personality Sphere, trait centrality.
[From Old French *trait* a drawing or a stroke of the pen in a picture, from Latin *trahere*, *tractum* to draw]

trait anxiety *n*. A person's general or characteristic level of *anxiety. *See also* State-Trait Anxiety Inventory. *Compare* state anxiety.

trait centrality *n*. A tendency of certain personality *traits to have an overwhelming effect in *impression formation, even influencing the interpretation of other traits associated with the person being judged (an *atmosphere effect). The phenomenon was discovered in 1946 by the Polish-born US psychologist Solomon E(lliott) Asch (1907–96), who presented one group of judges with a description of a target person who was described as *intelligent*, *skilful*, *industrious*, *warm*, *determined*, *practical*, and *cautious* and another group of judges with a description that was identical apart from the replacement of *warm* with *cold*. The *warm/cold* trait turned out to be central in the sense of profoundly affecting the overall impression of the target person. When the list of traits contained *warm*, 91 per cent of judges guessed that the target person was also *generous*, compared with only 8 per cent when the list contained *cold*. When the stimulus list included *warm*, the target person tended to be perceived as also being *happy*,

humorous, *sociable*, and *popular*, but when the stimulus list included *cold*, most judges thought the stimulus person would not have those traits but would be *persistent*, *serious*, and *restrained*. Other traits, such as *reliable*, were not significantly affected by the *warm/cold* trait. Other trait pairs, such as *polite/blunt*, do not produce the same centrality effect. Central traits are believed to have the property of centrality by virtue of being highly correlated with other traits in the judges' *implicit personality theories. The phenomenon illustrates the property of a *Gestalt in which the whole is more than the mere sum of its parts. *See also* halo effect.

trait negativity bias *n*. A tendency for unfavourable information about a person to have more impact on impressions of that person than favourable information, so that, for example, even a single unfavourable comment in an otherwise supportive reference or testimonial may create a generally bad impression and undermine the candidate's chances. The effect presumably arises from the fact that information about people tends to be mostly positive or neutral, as a result of which negative information tends to have more *salience (1) and to contain more *information (2) in the sense of *information theory. *See also* Pollyanna effect.

trait validity *n*. In psychometrics, a form of *validity determined by the extent to which a test correlates more highly with different methods of measuring the same *construct than it does with similar methods of measuring different constructs. The concept was proposed by the US psychologist Donald T(homas) Campbell (1916–96) in an article in the journal *American Psychologist* in 1960, where it was distinguished from validity established through a *nomological network. *See also* multitrait–multimethod matrix.

trance *n*. An altered state of *consciousness, shown by a narrowing of awareness of events in the immediate surroundings, a suspension of the sense of personal identity, and diminution in the range of motor activity and speech. It is characteristic of certain forms of intoxication, some mental disorders, and (controversially) *hypnosis. *See also* dissociative trance disorder, possession trance.
[French *transe*, from Latin *transire* to go across or to die]

trance disorder, dissociative See dissociative trance disorder.

tranq n. A common street name for the depressant drug *phencyclidine.
[From tranquillizer]

tranquillizer n. Any drug that has a calming effect without causing any significant dulling of consciousness, usually because its sites of action are in subcortical structures, in contrast to a sedative or hypnotic drug that also has a calming effect but tends to produce significant hypnotic (sleep-inducing) or narcotic effects as well. The term was first introduced in 1953 to describe the psychotropic effects of reserpine but later came to refer to *anxiolytic and *sedative drugs. The major tranquillizers are the *neuroleptic (1) drugs, and the minor tranquillizers are the *anxiolytic drugs. US tranquilizer.
[From Latin tranquillus quiet, calm, or still]

trans See under cis–trans complementation test.

transactional analysis n. A theory of *personality and a form of *psychotherapy, originated by the Canadian-born psychoanalyst Eric Berne (1910–70), aimed primarily at improving interpersonal relations by adjusting the balance between the child, adult, and parent ego states that are assumed to coexist within the same personality. **TA** abbrev.

transactionalism n. An empiricist approach to perception adopted in the 1940s and 1950s by the US painter and psychologist Adelbert Ames, Jr (1880–1955) and his followers, according to which all stimuli are ambiguous, and perceptions are constructed largely from past experiences (transactions) with relevant stimuli, such phenomena as the *Ames room and the *trapezoidal window being cited as evidence for this interpretation, which can be traced to the Essay Towards a New Theory of Vision (1709) by the Irish philosopher Bishop George Berkeley (1685–1753).

transcendental meditation n. A spiritual exercise and form of *psychotherapy based on Hindu traditions, involving daily periods of relaxation and quiet meditation on a special word, called a mantra, given by an instructor or therapist. **TM** abbrev.

transcortical aphasia n. A generic term for transcortical motor aphasia, transcortical sensory aphasia, and mixed transcortical aphasia, all of which arise from lesions interfering with the transmission of nerve impulses across the cerebral cortex between the language and motor centres, leading to impairment of spontaneous speech with intact ability to repeat spoken language. See aphasia. Also called ideomotor aphasia.

transcriptase n. Another name for *RNA polymerase.

transcription n. **1.** The act or process of copying or rewriting a text. **2.** In genetics, the process whereby a molecule of *RNA is synthesized from a *DNA template. **transcribe** vb.
[From Latin trans across + scribere, scriptum to write + -ion indicating an action, process, or state]

transducer n. A device or instrument that converts one form of energy into another. All *sensory receptors are transducers inasmuch as they transform kinetic energy, light, sound, heat, and energy from chemical reactions into nerve impulses or *action potentials.
[From Latin transducere to lead across, from trans across + ducere to lead]

transducin n. An enzyme that is activated by molecules of visual pigment in the retina when they are stimulated by light and that in turn stops the action of *cyclic GMP in keeping open *sodium channels into the rods and cones.
[Alluding to the role of the visual receptors as *transducers of light into nerve impulses]

transduction n. **1.** The conversion of energy from one form into another by a *transducer. See also sensory transduction. **2.** In genetics, the transfer of *DNA from one bacterial cell to another by a bacteriophage (a virus that infects a bacterium).

transductive reasoning n. The term used by the Swiss psychologist Jean Piaget (1896-1980) to denote the type of thinking characteristic of children during the *pre-operational stage of development. It is so called because it focuses on concrete instances and does not follow the principles of either *induction (1) or *deductive reasoning. Also called *transductive logic*, but this is avoided in careful usage, because it is clearly not a form of *logic.

transfer-appropriate processing *n*. Another name for *encoding specificity.

transference *n*. In *psychoanalysis, a form of *displacement involving the redirection of emotions and attitudes from their original *instinctual object on to a substitute, especially as occurs in the dependent, child-like, and often both sexually and aggressively charged relationship that a person undergoing therapy usually forms with the analyst, generally having features carried over (transferred) from earlier relationships, especially with parents. The *interpretation (2) or *working through of the transference is an important aspect of psychoanalytic therapy in which aspects of past relationships are explored. Sigmund Freud (1856–1939) introduced and discussed this idea in 1914 in an article on 'Remembering, Repeating and Working-Through' (*Standard Edition*, XII, pp. 147–56). *See also* acting out (1), counter-transference, negative transference, positive transference, rapport, repetition compulsion, transference neurosis (1, 2).

transference neurosis *n*. **1.** In *psychoanalysis, a category of *psychoneuroses comprising *anxiety hysteria, *conversion hysteria, and *obsessional neurosis. It is distinguished from *narcissistic neurosis because *libido is not withdrawn into the *ego but is displaced or transferred on to external *instinctual objects. Sigmund Freud (1856–1939) expounded his taxonomy of neuroses to include transference neurosis in 1916–17 in his book *Introductory Lectures on Psycho-Analysis* (*Standard Edition*, XV–XVI, at pp. 387–91). **2.** More specifically, the artificial psychoneurosis that develops during psychoanalytic therapy, the *interpretation (2) of which is one of the techniques of psychoanalysis. In his article on 'Remembering, Repeating and Working-Through' (1914) Freud claimed that 'we regularly succeed in giving all the symptoms of the illness a new transference meaning and in replacing his [the patient's] ordinary neurosis by a "transference-neurosis" of which he can be cured by the therapeutic work' (*Standard Edition*, XII, pp. 147–56, at p. 154). *See also* transference.

transfer of training *n*. The facilitation or impairment of performance of a task resulting from prior training on a different but related task. Transfer tends to be positive when the two tasks involve different stimuli and similar responses, and it tends to be negative when the two tasks involve similar stimuli and different responses. When the two tasks involve different stimuli and different responses, there tends to be little or no transfer. *See* bilateral transfer, negative transfer, positive transfer.

transfer RNA *n*. A soluble form of *RNA that transports a specific *amino acid to a *ribosome during protein synthesis. Also called *soluble RNA*. *See also* frameshift suppression. *Compare* messenger RNA. **tRNA** *abbrev*.

transformation *n*. Any alteration in form, character, or substance. In statistics and measurement theory, a change of all the *raw scores in a data set by means of a mathematical function. Raw scores may be transformed to simplify computation, as when a constant is added to eliminate negative scores, to express the scores in dimensionless units of standard deviations, as when scores are transformed to *standard scores, to change the shape of the distribution of scores to meet the assumptions of a statistical test, as when *product–moment correlation coefficients are transformed to z scores by means of the *Fisher's r to z transformation, or for a variety of other reasons. Some transformations, such as the transformation of raw scores measured on an *interval scale to *ranks, are irreversible and involve loss of information, whereas others are reversible and involve no loss of information.

transformational grammar *n*. A representation of a language in terms of the rules through which structures or elements can be derived from others, and in particular the *deep structures of sentences can be converted into their *surface structures. *See also* binding problem, Chomskyan, competence (2), formal universals, government and binding, performance (2). *Compare* generative grammar.

transgenic *adj*. Of or relating to an *organism containing a *gene or genes transferred artificially from another organism.
[From Latin *trans* across + English *gene* + Latin *-icus* of, relating to, or resembling]

transient disparity n. Any instantaneous difference between the arrival times of a sound wave at the two ears, including interaural differences in the onset time of the sound, the termination time, and the time of any sudden change in pitch or intensity, but excluding ongoing or continuous *phase delay. It is used in conjunction with phase delay as a *cue (2) for localizing sounds below about 1,000 hertz (about two octaves above Middle C) having wavelengths greater than the diameter of the head, so that the sound waves bend round the head rather than being reflected from or absorbed by it, thus preventing a *sonic shadow from forming on the side furthest from the sound source. Sound waves reach the nearer ear fractionally before the further one, and in an open area with no reflecting surfaces, or a simulation of these conditions using earphones, low-pitched sounds can be localized easily within 10 degrees in the horizontal plane (using other cues in addition, the *minimum audible angle is nearer 2 degrees). Because sound travels through air at about 343 metres per second (1,240 kilometres per hour or 770 miles per hour), a simple calculation shows that people can detect time differences between the movements of their two eardrums of less than one ten-thousandth of a second. It is one of the *binaural time differences* or *interaural time differences* used in sound localization. *See also* binaural shift, biosonar, cone of confusion, sound localization. [From Latin *transiens* going over, from *transire* to go over, from *trans* across + *ire* to go]

transient global amnesia n. A sudden loss of memory, including both *anterograde amnesia and *retrograde amnesia, with full recovery within 24 hours, often resulting from *ischaemia in the *hippocampus or *fornix. *Compare* global amnesia. **TGA** *abbrev.*

transient ischaemic attack n. An episode similar to a *stroke but with full recovery within 24 hours, caused by a partial blockage of blood vessels in the brain leading to a decreased supply of oxygenated blood to brain tissues normally perfused with blood by those vessels, the symptoms typically including disturbance of vision in one eye, dizziness, weakness, numbness, *dysphasia, or unconsciousness. It is a warning sign of a stroke, which is 13 times more likely within a year of such an episode. US *transient ischemic attack*. **TIA** *abbrev.*

transient polymorphism n. A form of *genetic polymorphism occurring in the process of *natural selection, when an *allele has a selective advantage over another and is proceeding towards fixation at a relative frequency of $p = 1$ but has not yet reached that point. For the time being both alleles are present in the *gene pool, and some individuals *heterozygous for the *trait are present in the population. *See also* Hardy–Weinberg law. *Compare* balanced polymorphism. [From Latin *transiens* going over, from *trans* across + *ire* to go + Greek *polys* many + *morphe* a form or shape]

transient responder n. Any of a large number of *photoreceptors in the retina that show little or no response to a static stimulus but respond strongly to a change in the stimulus, such as a movement. *See also* rapidly adapting. *Compare* sustained responder.

transient tic disorder n. A *tic disorder characterized by one or more motor or vocal tics occurring many times a day for at least a month but no longer than a year and, apart from that, sharing the features of *Tourette's disorder.

transient tritanopia n. A temporary increase in the threshold for blue stimuli after a yellow adapting field is removed, relative to the threshold in the presence of the yellow adapting field. *See also* adaptation (2), chromatic adaptation (1), tritanopia.

transitional object n. In *psychoanalysis, a term introduced in 1953 by the English psychoanalyst Donald Woods Winnicott (1896–1971) to denote a familiar object, such as the hem of a blanket, from which an infant between 4 and 12 months old derives comfort, especially while falling asleep, its significance sometimes re-emerging in later life, especially in a period of depression. Winnicott considered it to lie 'between the thumb and the teddy bear' inasmuch as it is almost inseparable from the infant, like a thumb, yet in reality is an external object, like a teddy bear. Subsequent writers have generally interpreted the term to refer to an object that a child treats as something halfway between itself and another person, thus including a teddy bear as a typical example.

transitive preferences n. Preferences having the property that if one alternative is

preferred to a second, and the second is preferred to a third, then the first is preferred to
the third. It is often assumed to be an axiom of
*rational judgement. In a transitive prefer-
ence order, if x is preferred to y, and y is preferred to z, then x is preferred to z. Preferences
that are not transitive are said to be *intransitive*. *See also* Arrow's impossibility theorem,
Condorcet's paradox, lexicographic semiorder, money pump. *Compare* cyclic preferences, intransitive preferences.
[From Latin *transitivus* going over, from *transiens* going over, *transire* to pass over, from *trans*
across + *ire* to go + *-ivus* indicating a tendency,
inclination, or quality]

transmission deafness *n*. Another name for
*conductive deafness.

transmittance *See under* reflectance.

transmitter *n*. Anything that sends or conveys objects, substances, genes, information,
and so on; more specifically, a commonly used
abbreviation of *neurotransmitter.
[From Latin *trans* across + *mittere* to send]

transplantation of brain tissue *See* foetal
brain transplantation.

transposon *n*. In genetics, a fragment of
*DNA that is capable of migrating from one
*gene locus to another on the same or a dif-
ferent chromosome, causing a change in the
genetic constitution of the organism. *See also*
jumping gene.
[From Latin *transponere* to remove, from *trans*
across or beyond + *ponere* to place, on the
model of *codon*]

transsexual *n*. **1.** A person with a powerful
desire to adopt the physical attributes and to
play the role of a member of the opposite sex.
See also transsexualism. **2.** A person who has
undergone medical and surgical treatment to
alter the body's external sexual characteristics to those of the opposite sex.

transsexualism *n*. Severe *gender dysphoria,
accompanied by a persistent desire to live and
be accepted as a member of the opposite sex.
See also Diana complex. *Compare* fetishistic
transvestism, transvestism.

transverse plane *n*. A plane at right angles to
the long axis of any organ or organism, in the

human body often the same as the *horizontal plane. *Compare* coronal plane, sagittal
plane.
[From Latin *transversus* across]

transverse section *n*. A cutting through the
*transverse plane, in the human body gener-
ally equivalent to a *horizontal section.
Compare coronal section, sagittal section.

transvestic fetishism *See* fetishistic transvestism.

transvestism *n*. Dressing in the clothes
of a member of the opposite sex. Also
called *cross-dressing, eonism. See also* eonism,
fetishistic transvestism, gender identity disorder. **transvest** *vb*. **transvestite** *n*. A person
who is given to *transvestism.
[From Latin *trans* across + *vestire* to dress]

tranylcypromine *n*. The most stimulating,
dopaminergic, and relatively fast-acting of
the *monoamine oxidase inhibitor (MAOI)
drugs, chemically related to *amphetamine
and used in its sulphate form to treat severe
depression and panic disorder. Formula
$C_9H_{11}N$.
[From its chemical name *tran(s)* + *(phen)yl* +
cy(clo) + *pro(pyla)mine*]

trapezoidal window *n*. A visual illusion invented by the US painter and psychologist
Adelbert Ames, Jr (1880–1955) that consists of
a distorted window in the shape of a trapezium (US trapezoid) and that, when viewed
frontally from a distance, looks like a rectangular window turned at an angle, and when
rotated slowly about its vertical axis and
viewed monocularly from about 3 metres (10
feet) or binocularly from more than 6 metres
(20 feet) is perceived as a rectangular window
oscillating back and forth in a peculiar and
unnatural way. Also called the *Ames window*.
See also kinephantom, transactionalism.
Compare Ames room.
[From *trapezoid*, in US a quadrilateral having
two parallel sides of unequal length, from
Greek *trapezoeides* trapezium-shaped, from
trapeza a table + *-oeides* denoting resemblance
of form, from *eidos* shape or form]

trapezoid body *n*. Either of the two diamond-
shaped nuclei near the bottom of the *pons
that receive nerve impulses from the auditory
receptors and project to the *superior olivary

nucleus. Each trapezoidal body contains *interneurons that inhibit impulses from the ear on the same side and excite those from the opposite side, amplifying the left–right differences in the signals transmitted to the binaural neurons of the superior olivary nucleus and thereby facilitating *sound localization.
[From Greek *trapezion* a small table, diminutive of *trapeza* a table, from *tetra-* four + *peza* a foot]

trauma *n*. A physical injury or wound, or a powerful psychological shock that has damaging effects. **traumatic** *adj*. **traumata** or **traumas** *pl*. **traumatize** *vb*.
[From Greek *trauma* a wound]

trauma, birth *See* birth trauma.

traumatic neurosis *n*. Any *neurosis precipitated by a *trauma. The term was introduced in 1889 by the German neurologist Hermann Oppenheim (1858–1919). *See* post-traumatic stress disorder.

traumatic psychosis *n*. A *psychosis (1) resulting from a head injury causing brain damage.

traumatic shock *n*. The partial or total collapse of voluntary and involuntary bodily functions resulting from circulatory failure or a sudden drop in blood pressure brought about by physical *trauma, especially blood loss or injury to the spinal cord, *anaphylaxis, or intense psychological trauma or stress. *Compare* shock (1).

travel agent *n*. An intermediary who arranges trips for travellers; hence, figuratively, an informal name for a street drug dealer. *See also* trip.

travelling salesman problem *n*. The problem of finding the shortest path that passes through a given set of points once and only once, as when a travelling salesman needs to visit a number of specified cities exactly once, using the shortest possible route. The problem is notoriously difficult to solve, because the number of possible tours rises rapidly with the number of cities. For 10 cities, there are 3,628,800 different tours from which to choose, because there are ten cities available for the first visit, and for each of these there

are nine possibilities left for the second, hence there are $10 \times 9 = 90$ different ways in which the tour can begin with the first two cities, and for each of these there are eight possibilities left for the third visit, and so on, the total number of tours through the ten cities therefore being $10 \times 9 \times 8 \times 7 \times 6 \times 5 \times 4 \times 3 \times 2 \times 1 = 3,628,800$ tours. For 20 cities, the number of possible tours is 2,432,902,008,176,640,000, and for 30 cities it exceeds 265 thousand billion billion billion. Even the world's fastest supercomputer would take many billions of years to solve the travelling salesman problem for a tour of the 52 county towns of England and Wales or the 50 state capitals of the United States, but no efficient method of solving the problem has been found, and mathematicians have come very close to proving that it is impossible in principle to find an efficient solution to a problem of this type. US *traveling salesman problem*. *See also* bounded rationality, brute force algorithm. **TSP** *abbrev*.

travelling wave *n*. Any wave in which energy is transferred progressively in the direction of the wave propagation (in contrast to a standing wave); in particular a wave that is propagated from the *oval window along the *basilar membrane when the eardrum vibrates in response to a sound stimulus, the amplitudes of high-frequency components of the wave being greatest near the oval window and of low-frequency components furthest from the oval window. *See also* place theory.

treatment condition *n*. In experimental design, a level of an *independent variable or combination of levels of two or more independent variables. For example, in an experiment examining the effects of four different drugs on dreaming, research participants or subjects would receive a different drug in each treatment condition. Often shortened to *condition*.

tremor *n*. Any rhythmic vibration or shaking of the body or any of its parts. Two major classes are distinguished: *resting tremor, also called passive tremor, manifested when the affected body part is at rest, as in *parkinsonism, and *intention tremor, also called movement tremor, manifested only when the body part is moved deliberately, as in tremor arising from *alcohol dependence,

*cerebellar syndrome, or *senile dementia. *Postural tremor does not fall neatly into either category. *See also* cerebellar syndrome, delirium tremens, extrapyramidal syndrome, HIV dementia, kuru, multiple sclerosis, nervios, ocular tremor, punch-drunk, yips.
[From Latin *tremere* to tremble]

triad, anal *See* anal triad, three Ps.

triangular theory *See under* love.

triarchic theory of intelligence *n.* A theory of *intelligence, put forward in 1985 by the US psychologist Robert J(effrey) Sternberg (born 1949), according to which its three fundamental aspects are analytic, creative, and practical intelligence, only the first of which is measured adequately by conventional IQ tests. Analytic problems require the problem solver to analyse, evaluate, compare, contrast, judge, and so on; creative problems to create, invent, discover, imagine, and so on; and practical problems to apply, put into practice, use, implement, and so on. Unlike analytic problems, creative and practical problems tend to depend on problem recognition and formulation by the problem solver, to be poorly defined, to require information seeking, to have more than one acceptable solution, and to require everyday experience, motivation, and personal involvement.
[From Greek *triarchia* a triple rule, from *treis* three + *archein* to rule + *-ikos* of, relating to, or resembling]

triazolam *n.* A *benzodiazepine drug used mainly as a *hypnotic (2) in the short-term treatment of insomnia and as an *anxiolytic and *sedative. Also called *Halcion* (trademark).

tribar *n.* Another name for the *Penrose triangle.

tricarboxylic acid cycle *n.* Another name for the *Krebs cycle.
[Named after tricarboxylic acid, an acid having three carboxyl groups in each molecule, that plays a crucial role in the Krebs cycle]

triceps reflex *n.* A *deep tendon reflex occurring in response to a tap on the back of the elbow.
[Named after the triceps brachii muscle that controls it, from Latin *triceps* three-headed + *brachium* an arm]

trichotillomania *n.* An *impulse-control disorder characterized by repeated pulling out of one's hair (most often from the scalp, eyebrows, or eyelashes), resulting in visible hair loss, with an increasing sense of tension before pulling the hair, followed by pleasure, gratification, or relief after completing the act.
[From Greek *trichos* of hair, from *thrix* hair + *tillein* to pull + *mania* madness]

trichromacy *n.* The phenomenon discovered in 1704 by the English physicist and mathematician Sir Isaac Newton (1642–1727) whereby any spectral colour can be formed by the combination of red, green, and blue light, or in fact by any three wavelengths provided that they are well separated on the visible spectrum. *See also* primary colour (1), trichromatic theory, tristimulus values.
[From Greek *treis* three + *chroma* colour]

trichromatic theory *n.* A theory of colour vision specifically intended to take account of *trichromacy, according to which at each point on the retina of the eye there are three light-sensitive structures responsive to red, green, and blue light. The theory was formulated in 1802 by the English physician, physicist, and Egyptologist Thomas Young (1773–1829) and championed in 1852 by the influential German physiologist, physicist, and mathematician Hermann Ludwig Ferdinand von Helmholtz (1821–94), and in 1959 physiological research confirmed that the retina contains three types of *cones, each maximally responsive to a different wavelength, though with overlapping response curves. Also called the *three-colour theory* or the *Young–Helmholtz theory*. *Compare* opponent-process theory.

tricyclic antidepressant *n.* Any member of a class of *antidepressant drugs that block the reuptake mechanism of *noradrenalin (norepinephrine) and in some cases also of *serotonin, allowing these neurotransmitter substances to accumulate at *synapses (1) in the central nervous system. *See* amitriptyline, clomipramine, imipramine. *Compare* monoamine oxidase inhibitor (MAOI), selective serotonin reuptake inhibitor (SSRI), St John's wort, tetracyclic antidepressant. **TCA** *abbrev.*
[So called because they have three rings in their molecular structures]

trifluoperazine n. Trifluoperazine hydrochloride, a *neuroleptic (1) drug belonging to the group of *phenothiazines, used in the treatment of *schizophrenia and other *psychotic (1) disorders and anxiety disorders, also used as an anti-emetic. Also called *Stelazine* (trademark).

trigeminal chemoreception n. Another name for the *common chemical sense.

trigeminal lemniscus n. Either of the two bundles of nerve fibres within the *lemniscus running parallel to the *medial lemniscus and conveying information from one of the *trigeminal nerves to the *thalamus. *Compare* lateral lemniscus, medial lemniscus.

trigeminal nerve n. Either of the fifth pair of *cranial nerves whose three sensory branches supply (a) the skin of the forehead, nose, and scalp, (b) the region between the nose, mouth and temple, including the *mucous membranes of the mouth and nose, and (c) the lower face and teeth. It also has a motor root supplying the muscles involved in chewing. *See also* common chemical sense, corneal reflex, magnetic sense, tic douloureux.
[From Latin *trigeminus* a triplet, from *tres* three + *geminus* a twin]

trigeminal neuralgia n. Another name for *tic douloureux.

trigram n. A string of three letters, which may be a word (*cat*) or a *nonsense syllable (*kep*). *See also* CVC.
[From Greek *treis* + *gramma* a letter or character]

trigraph n. A three-letter combination representing a single speech sound, such as *sch* in the German word *Schule*. *Compare* trigram, triphthong.

trihexyphenidyl n. Trihexyphenidyl hydrochloride, an *anticholinergic drug that is used in the treatment of Parkinson's disease. *See also* antiparkinsonian.

Trilafon n. A proprietary name for the neuroleptic drug *perphenazine.
[Trademark]

trimmed mean n. In statistics, the *arithmetic mean calculated after eliminating a specified proportion or percentage of the largest and smallest scores, a common type being the *5 per cent trim. It is used occasionally when the set of scores contains values that are much smaller or much larger than the rest, because in such cases it yields a more useful indication of *central tendency than the untrimmed mean.

trip n. An excursion involving an outward and return journey; hence, figuratively, an experience induced by a *hallucinogenic drug. *See also* travel agent.

tripa ida n. Another name for *susto.
[From Spanish *tripa* intestine (believed in the past to be the seat of the soul) + *ida* departure]

triphthong n. A complex *vowel sound comprising a *glide from one vowel sound to a second and then a third within a single syllable, with movement of the tongue between the three sounds. In *Received Pronunciation there are five triphthongs, all of which consist of a *diphthong followed by a *schwa; they are the vowels in the words *layer, buyer, soya, flour*, and *mower*. *Compare* monophthong, diphthong, trigraph.
[From Greek *treis* three + *phthongos* sound]

triplegia n. Paralysis of three of the four limbs of the body, usually as a result of multiple lesions in the *motor cortex or *peripheral nervous system. *Compare* diplegia, hemiplegia, monoplegia, ophthalmoplegia, paraplegia, quadriplegia. **triplegic** adj.
[From Greek *treis* three + *plege* a blow + -*ia* indicating a condition or quality]

triplet code n. A sequence of three *bases (1) in a *DNA or an *RNA molecule, interpreted either as a single *amino acid during *protein synthesis or, if it is a *stop codon, as a signal to terminate translation. *See also* codon, codon family, genetic code.

Triptafen n. A proprietary name for the tricyclic antidepressant drug *amitriptyline. Often confused with *tryptophan.
[Trademark]

trisomy n. The condition of a human or other *diploid organism of having three rather than two *chromosomes of a particular type. *Autosomal trisomies are often associated

with *mental retardation, whereas trisomies of the sex chromosomes have variable psychological effects. *See* Klinefelter's syndrome, XXX syndrome, XYY syndrome. **trisomy 21** *n.* Trisomy of *chromosome 21, which underlies *Down's syndrome. **trisomic** *adj.*
[From Greek *treis* three + *soma* a body]

tristimulus values *n.* Three numbers, usually symbolized by x, y, and z, that together define a colour in terms of the proportions of three *additive primaries that match the given colour when mixed. *See also* CIE colour system, chromaticity, colour equation, Grassmann's laws (perception), primary colour (1), trichromacy.

tritanomaly *n.* A form of partial *colour-blindness caused by a deficiency in the *visual pigment that absorbs short-wave light, characterized by a decreased sensitivity to blue light and matches that deviate from the normal *Rayleigh equation. *Compare* deuteranomaly, protanomaly, tritanopia.
[From Greek *tritos* third, alluding to the third of the three *primary colours (1) red, green, and blue + *anomalos* uneven or inconsistent, from *an-* without + *homalos* even, from *homos* the same]

tritanopia *n.* A rare form of *anomalous dichromacy in which the *visual pigment associated with short-wave (blue) light is non-functional, causing a decreased sensitivity to blue light and a tendency to confuse blue with green. *See also* transient tritanopia. *Compare* deuteranopia, protanopia, tritanomaly.
[From Greek *tritos* third, alluding to the third of the three *primary colours (1) red, green, and blue + *anopia* blindness, from *an-* without + *ops* an eye + *-ia* indicating a condition or quality]

tritone *n.* A musical interval or difference in pitch of three whole tones (an augmented fourth), as between C and F# or between D and G#, the two sounds thus being separated in pitch by exactly half an *octave.

tritone paradox *n.* A phenomenon in the perception of musical tones that are clearly defined in terms of pitch class (the twelve notes of the octave that are normally labelled C, C#, D, . . . , B) but are ambiguous as regards the octaves to which they belong, each tone being composed of equal *sinusoidal waves

from octaves spanning the auditory range. If one such ambiguous tone is followed by a second, separated from the first by a tritone, then the sequence is clearly perceived as either rising or falling by half an octave, although the stimulus tones lack the cues required to determine pitch. It is a surprising phenomenon rather than a true *paradox. *See also* auditory illusion, auditory staircase illusion. *Compare* melodic paradox, semitone paradox.

trochlear nerve *n.* Either of the fourth pair of *cranial nerves supplying the superior *oblique muscles of the eyes. Paralysis of this nerve causes *diplopia when looking down, as when descending stairs.
[From Greek *trochalia* a pulley, referring to the fact that the superior oblique muscle passes through an eyelet and works like a pulley]

troilism *n.* Sexual activity involving three people.
[A blend of French *trois* three + English *dualism*]

Troland *n.* A unit of the intensity of light falling on the retina, calculated as the product of *luminance and pupil area. It is defined as the retinal illuminance produced by viewing a surface illuminated by 1 lumen per square metre through an artificial pupil with an area of 1 square millimetre centred on the natural pupil.
[Named after the US psychologist Leonard Thompson Troland (1889–1932) who introduced it before it was adopted by the Optical Society of America in 1944]

trompe l'oeil *n.* A visual illusion in a painting or other work of art creating an impression of reality, such as a painting that appears to be an open window or a T-shirt that gives the impression of a naked torso.
[French: a deception of the eye]

trophic hormone *n.* Any of a number of *hormones, such as *adrenocorticotrophic hormone, that is secreted by the *anterior pituitary and that controls the secretion of hormones by other *endocrine glands.
[From Greek *tropos* a turn, from *trepein* to turn]

Troxler effect *n.* The fading of an image in peripheral vision when a central stimulus is fixated with a steady gaze while attention is

shifted to the peripheral stimulus. Movement of the peripheral stimulus normally prevents it from fading. Also called *Troxler fading*.
[Named after the Swiss–German philosopher and physician Ignaz Paul Vitalis Troxler (1780–1866) who first reported it in 1804]

true self *n*. In the *neo-Freudian theory of the German-born US psychoanalyst Karen Horney (1885–1952), an underlying personality of unrealized potentials that is fundamentally good.

trust versus mistrust *See* basic trust versus basic mistrust.

truth drug *n*. Any sedative or analgesic drug such as *scopolamine or one of the short-acting *barbiturates, especially *thiopental (thiopentone or Sodium Pentothal), that is administered to a person who is to be interrogated in the belief that it might encourage free and truthful answers to questions. Also called a *truth serum*. *See also* hypermnesia.

truth functor *n*. A *sentence functor with a *truth table.
[From Latin *functio* a function, from *fungi* to perform]

truth table *n*. In *logic, an arrangement of rows and columns indicating the truth or falsity of a *proposition (1) for every combination of truth values (true or false) of its component propositions. It is a device for performing *logical analysis. *See also* sentence functor, truth functor.

tryptamine *n*. A crystalline *amine formed by decomposition of *tryptophan, functioning as a *biogenic amine belonging to the group of *indoleamines. *See also* DMT, melatonin, serotonin.
[From *trypt(ophan)* + *amine*]

tryptophan *n*. An essential *amino acid obtained from dietary milk, cheese, poultry, pineapple, and banana. It is metabolized into *5-hydroxytryptophan, which is able to cross the *blood–brain barrier, and then by brain neurons into *serotonin. Sometimes confused with *Triptafen. **Trp** *abbrev*.
[From Greek *trypsis* a rubbing + *phainein* to appear, alluding to trypsin, an enzyme first produced by rubbing the pancreas with glycerine]

tryptophan hydroxylase *n*. An enzyme involved in the synthesis of *serotonin, having a parallel action to tyrosine hydroxylase in the synthesis of catecholamines. **TPH** *abbrev*.

T score *n*. In psychometrics, a test score converted to an equivalent *standard score in a *normal distribution with a *mean of 50 and a *standard deviation of 10. *See also* derived score. *Compare* IQ, stanine score, sten score, *z* score.
[Probably an abbreviation of *true score*]

***t* test** *n*. In inferential statistics, a test most often used to establish the significance of the difference between the means of two samples of scores. It is calculated by dividing the difference between the means by the *standard error of this difference. Its full name is *Student's *t* test, because 'Student' was the pen name of the English statistician William Sealy Gosset (1876–1937) who developed the theory behind it in 1908 while working for the Guinness brewery in Dublin. The test itself was developed later by the English statistician Karl Pearson (1857–1936). Often written *t-test*, but the hyphen may be considered otiose, because analogous tests such as the χ^2 test and the *U* test are usually written without hyphens. *See also* independent samples *t* test, one-sample *t* test, related scores *t* test.
[Probably an abbreviation of *true test*]

tufted cell *n*. A type of vertically oriented neuron in the *olfactory bulb that receives inputs from olfactory neurons.

Tukey-HSD test *n*. In statistics, a method of *multiple comparisons in which a set of group means are ranked from smallest to largest, and then a statistic that is used to test for a significant difference between a pair of means is computed on the basis of the number of steps between the two means in the rank order. Its full name is the *Tukey honestly significant difference (HSD) test*. *Compare* Bonferroni correction, Duncan's multiple range test, least-significant difference test, Newman–Keuls test, Scheffé test.
[Named after the US statistician John Wilder Tukey (1915–2000) who developed versions of it in 1951 and 1952]

tumescence *n*. The process of becoming swollen or enlarged, especially with reference to the *penis during the excitement phase of the *sexual response cycle. *Compare* detumescence.

[From Latin *tumescere* to begin to swell, from *tumere* to swell]

tuning curve *n.* The response threshold of a single fibre of an auditory nerve, plotted as a function of the frequencies of the sounds to which it responds, the point at which the threshold is lowest, and therefore the responsiveness greatest, being the *characteristic frequency of the fibre. Also called the *frequency tuning curve* or *frequency threshold curve* *(FTC).*

tunnel vision *n.* A form of visual impairment in which the *visual field is decreased, creating the effect of looking down a narrow tube or tunnel, often resulting from advanced chronic *glaucoma. The American Foundation for the Blind defines a visual field subtending a *visual angle of 20 degrees or less as a criterion of *blindness.

Turing machine *n.* A hypothetical computing machine consisting of a movable head that reads, writes, or erases discrete symbols drawn from a finite set (often just 1 and 0), dealing with the symbols one at a time in separate frames marked on a tape of limitless length, and that always assumes one of a finite number of states, the activity of the machine being determined jointly by its current state and the symbol being read in the current frame, these two input variables in turn determining what symbol the machine writes in the current frame, what state it assumes next, and whether it moves one frame to the left, one frame to the right, or halts. A Turing machine usually consists of a table of instructions specifying what the machine does in every possible contingency, the input data being abbreviated by a pair of symbols such as $(S_1, 0)$ or represented by appropriately labelled rows and columns of a matrix, and an instruction being represented by a triplet of symbols such as $(1, S_3, R)$, this particular input pair and instruction triplet indicating that if the machine is in state S_1 and the symbol in the current frame is 0, then the machine writes the symbol 1 in the current frame (overwriting the 0), assumes state S_3, and moves one frame to the right. A *universal Turing machine* incorporates a coded description of a Turing machine in the form of a table of instructions and also a sequence of symbols that it encounters on the tape when it operates. For any possible computation, a Turing machine can, in principle, be constructed, and a universal Turing machine can compute anything computable, given sufficient time. *See also* algorithm, artificial intelligence, cellular automaton.

[Named after the English mathematician Alan Mathison Turing (1912–54) who first described it in an influential article in the *Proceedings of the London Mathematical Society* in 1936–7]

Turing test *n.* A hypothetical test or *Gedankenexperiment* to clarify the question as to whether computers can think. A person *A* and an interrogator in a different room engage in a dialogue by typing messages over an electronic link. At some point *A* is replaced by intelligent software that simulates human responses. Turing argued that if the remaining human being is free to ask probing questions (such as *Please write me a sonnet on the subject of the Forth Bridge*) but is unable to determine reliably whether the replies are generated by a human being or a computer, then the computer has passed the test. Turing considered the question *Can machines think?* to be 'too meaningless to deserve discussion' and argued that his test, which replaces it, poses a more meaningful problem; but passing the Turing test came to be interpreted by many of his followers as amounting to being able to think. The most sustained attacks on this approach have focused on the *Chinese room and *Gödel's theorem. *See also* artificial intelligence, strong AI.

[Named after the English mathematician Alan Mathison Turing (1912–54) who introduced it in an article in the journal *Mind* in 1950, where he called it the *imitation game*]

Turkish saddle *n.* Another name for the *sella turcica.

Turner's syndrome *n.* A congenital chromosomal aberration in a female who has only one X chromosome, leading to short stature, absence of functioning ovaries, underdeveloped breasts, uterus, and vagina, often moderate mental retardation, and various other signs and symptoms. Zygotes with just one Y chromosome are non-viable. Also called *monosomy X. Compare* trisomy.

[Named after the US physician Henry Hubert Turner (1892–1970) who first described it in 1938]

twilight vision *n.* A non-technical name for *scotopia.

twin study *n.* In behaviour genetics, an examination of the correlation between *monozygotic twins, and sometimes a comparison with the correlation between *dizygotic twins, on a measurable *trait in order to estimate the *heritability of that trait, the assumption being that the higher the heritability of the trait the greater will be the correlation between monozygotic twins and the more it will differ from the correlation between dizygotic twins, because monozygotic twins share identical genes and should therefore be more alike on a heritable trait than dizygotic twins who share only about half their genes in common. It can be shown mathematically that a rough estimate of heritability is provided by twice the difference between the monozygotic-twin and dizygotic-twin correlations. *See also* DF extremes analysis. *Compare* adoption study, kinship study.

twisted-cord illusion *n.* Any of several visual illusions that are created if a cord made by twisting dark and light strands together, or graphical representations of thin strips of diagonal stripes resembling such a twisted cord, are displayed against a chequered background, the alignment of the cords or strips appearing distorted and disordered (see illustration). The illusion is caused by the responses of *orientation-specific neurons in the visual cortex. The Scottish physician and psychologist James Fraser (1863–1936) discovered it in 1908, allegedly after observing wool made from strands of different colours lying on tartan fabric, and called it the 'twisted cord on chequer-work background illusion'. Also called a *Fraser illusion*. *See also* Fraser spiral.

Twisted-cord illusion. The lines outlining the letters are perfectly vertical or horizontal.

two-alternative forced-choice task *n.* In *signal detection theory, an experimental procedure designed to eliminate bias resulting from the observer's criterion level of sensory activation by presenting the observer with pairs of observation time intervals, only one interval in each pair containing the signal, the task being to choose the interval with the signal on each trial. The theory assumes that a particular level of sensory activation occurs in each observation interval and that the observer simply chooses the larger, and it has been shown that 76 per cent correct responses in this task equates to a *d prime of 1. **2AFC** *abbrev.*

2½-D sketch *n.* In the *computational theory of vision pioneered in the late 1970s by the English psychologist David Courtenay Marr (1945–80), the second stage in the perceptual process after the *primal sketch, incorporating orientation and depth cues relative to the viewpoint of the observer, but providing a *representation (2) that is insufficiently abstract for object recognition, because it is viewer-centred rather than being invariant with respect to the observer's viewpoint. *Compare* 3-D model description, primal sketch. [So called because although it is a three-dimensional representation, it provides insufficient information for visual recognition of three-dimensional objects]

2-4-6 problem *n.* A problem of concept formation in which people are given the ordered triple of numbers (2, 4, 6) and are invited to try to generate further examples of triples conforming to an unspecified rule that the example obeys, trying to home in on the correct rule on the basis of simple right/wrong feedback after every guess. The actual rule is *any ascending sequence*, but the example invites people to form more specific hypotheses, such as *ascending even numbers* or *numbers ascending by equal intervals*. It was introduced in 1960 by the English psychologist Peter C(athcart) Wason (born 1924), who found that people tend to try examples consistent with such more specific hypotheses, such as (10, 20, 30) and seldom try examples that would refute them such as (10, 11, 30), thus manifesting *confirmation bias and failing to find the right answer but often becoming increasingly convinced of the rightness of their incorrect hypotheses. Also called *Wason's 2-4-6 problem*. *See also* problem solving.

2-deoxyglucose *n*. A substance that stimulates hunger by blocking glucose metabolism in cells. **2-DG** *abbrev*.
[From Latin *de-* indicating a deprivation + English *oxygen* + Greek *glykys* sweet]

two-point threshold *n*. A measure of *tactile acuity defined as the smallest separation at which two points applied simultaneously to the *skin can be clearly distinguished from a single point. It varies from 1 or 2 millimetres in the finger pads and tongue to more than 60 millimetres on the upper arm, upper thigh, and back. *See also* aesthesiometer.

two-sample *t* test *n*. Another name for the *independent samples *t* test.

two-step flow *n*. A phenomenon of mass communication, first discovered in a *panel study of the 1944 US Presidential election and reported in *The People's Choice* (1944) by the Austrian-born US sociologist Paul Felix Lazarsfeld (1901–76) and several colleagues, according to which most rank-and-file members of a population are not directly influenced by messages conveyed through the mass media but are influenced by face-to-face contact with a relatively small number of recipients who do respond to mass media messages and are called *opinion leaders*. This explains why mass media messages often cause significant shifts in public opinion in spite of the fact that most individuals who are investigated show little or no direct response to them. The same phenomenon has been shown to occur in the diffusion of fashions and innovations, including the adoption of new drugs by general practitioners.

2-tailed probability *n*. In *inferential statistics, the probability of obtaining a result as extreme as the one observed, in either direction from the expected value, if the *null hypothesis is true. If the probability is small (by convention, often less than $p < 0.05$), then the null hypothesis may be rejected. *Compare* 1-tailed probability.
[The name refers to both tails of the relevant *probability distribution]

2-tailed test *See under* 1-tailed test.

two-way avoidance conditioning *n*. A form of *avoidance conditioning in which, typically, a *conditioned stimulus such as a light is presented in one end of an alley and is followed by the delivery of foot shock that the animal can avoid or escape by shuttling to the other end of the alley; but after a period of time, the conditioned stimulus is presented at the other end of the alley, so that the animal must return to the original location in order to avoid or escape the shock. The conflict in this situation interferes with learning to such an extent that a rat typically requires dozens or hundreds of responses to learn the task, and many do not learn it at all. Also called *two-way avoidance learning*.

Tycho's illusion *n*. A *cognitive illusion that caused the cosmology of the Danish astronomer Tycho Brahe (1546–1601) to appear physically impossible to his contemporary, the German astronomer Johannes Kepler (1571–1630), and to astronomers and cosmologists for the next four centuries, until its illusory quality was pointed out in 1998 in a letter to the journal *Nature* by the US political scientist Howard Margolis (born 1932). In Tycho's cosmology, which partially preserved Copernican heliocentrism but avoided the heresy of displacing the Earth from the centre of the universe, the planets revolve round the sun, but the sun together with its orbiting planets revolves round the Earth. When this is depicted diagrammatically, the orbits of Mars and the sun intersect, creating the impression that these bodies would collide with each other in the Tychonic system, whereas Margolis showed, by constructing a cardboard model, that the system implies no such collision.

tympanic membrane *n*. A membrane with a diameter of about 10 millimetres that separates the *middle ear from the *outer ear and that transmits sound vibrations to the *inner ear via the auditory *ossicles. Also called the *eardrum*, *membrana tympani*, or *tympanum*.

tympanic reflex *n*. Another name for the *acoustic reflex.

type distractor *See under* distractor.

type fallacy *n*. The widespread tendency to classify people or things into categories, even when the ways in which they differ are matters of degree rather than of kind. For example, people tend to think of one another as either being extraverts of introverts, whereas it is well established that *extraversion is a *continuum rather than a *taxon, with most people falling between the extremes. *See also* categorical perception.

Type I error *n*. In statistics, the error of rejecting the *null hypothesis when it is true. The significance level determined from a *statistical test is the probability of a Type I error. *Compare* Type II error, Type III error.

Type II error *n*. In statistics, the error of failing to reject the *null hypothesis when it is false. The probability of avoiding a Type II error is the *statistical power of the test, and it depends on the *alternative hypothesis. *Compare* Type I error, Type III error.

Type III error *n*. A term occasionally used to refer to an error arising from a misinterpretation of the nature of the scores being compared in a *significance test, as when a significant difference in an *interrupted time-series design is misinterpreted as relating to a comparison between the mean of the baseline scores and the mean of the post-intervention scores, whereas the true comparison is between *weighted* means of the raw scores, the weights depending on the components of the statistical model (such as autoregressions and/or moving averages; *see* ARIMA). *Compare* Type I error, Type II error.
[Named by the US psychologist Bradley E. Huitema (born 1938) by analogy with Type I and Type II errors]

type–token ratio *n*. In the study of texts, the ratio of the number of different words, called *types*, to the total number of words, called *tokens*. For example, in a particular text, the number of different words may be 1,000 and the total number of words 5,000, because common words such as *the* may occur several times, and in this case the type–token ratio would be 1/5 or 0.2. *See* token (3). *See also* stylostatistics. **TTR** *abbrev*.

tyramine *n*. An *amine with a *sympathomimetic action, synthesized in the body from *tyrosine and replacing *neurotransmitter substances at *adrenergic *neuroreceptors. It is found in ripe cheese, pickled herring, yeast extract, and certain red wines, all of which are forbidden to anyone taking a *monoamine oxidase inhibitor (MAOI) to avoid acute *hypertension. *See also* cheese effect.
[From *tyr(osine)* + *amine*]

tyrosine *n*. A non-essential *amino acid that is synthesized in the body from *phenylalanine and that acts as a precursor of adrenalin (epinephrine), noradrenalin (norepinephrine), dopamine, thyroxine, L-dopa, and melanin. **Tyr** *abbrev*.
[From Greek *tyros* cheese, from which it was first obtained + -*ine* indicating an organic compound]

tyrosine hydroxylase *n*. An enzyme involved in the synthesis of *catecholamines, having a parallel action to tryptophan hydroxylase in the synthesis of serotonin. *See also* alpha-methylparatyrosine. *Compare* tryptophan hydroxylase. **TH** *abbrev*.

ufufunyane *n*. A *culture-bound syndrome found mainly among young women in Zulu-speaking and Xhosa-speaking communities of southern Africa, and in Kenya where it is called *saka*, attributed locally to spirit possession, witchcraft, or magical potions administered by rejected lovers or enemies, characterized by shouting, sobbing, *pseudolalia, *paralysis, *convulsions, *nightmares (1) with sexual themes, and *trance or loss of *consciousness. It is feared and despised among local communities and is sharply distinguished from *thwasa* (*see* spell). Among Xhosa-speaking people the plural form *amafufunyane* is used to denote the syndrome.

[From Zulu *ufufunyane* a character or voice that has entered and taken control of a person, from *ukufuya* to possess (such things as herds of cattle) or to treat a person as a possession]

ugly sister effect *n*. A common feature of the *tip-of-the-tongue phenomenon, when a different but related *blocking memory pops into consciousness, impeding access to the required memory, and generally being difficult or impossible to dislodge.

[The name alludes to the ancient fairly tale in which Prince Charming tries to gain access to the beautiful Cinderella but is blocked by her ugly sisters, who pop up in her place]

Ultimatum game *n*. A two-person *game (1) in which a monetary prize is divided by one player making a one-off proposal for a division of the prize and the other player either accepting or rejecting it, neither player receiving anything if the proposal is rejected. Suppose the prize is $10 or £10. Player I first proposes a division (such as 60 per cent to Player I and 40 per cent to Player II); then Player II either accepts the proposal, in which case the prize is accordingly divided, or rejects it, in which case neither player receives anything. From a game-theoretic point of view, Player I should offer Player II one penny, and Player II should accept this offer because one penny is better than nothing. Numerous experiments by the US economist Richard H. Thaler (born 1945) and others have shown that human players appear to deviate sharply from *expected utility theory: Player I usually offers much more than one penny and often offers 50 per cent of the prize, and Player II usually rejects Player I's offer if it is less than about one-quarter of the prize, in which case it is perceived as too unfair or insulting to accept.

ultradian rhythm *n*. Any *biological rhythm such as a *circannual rhythm or a *menstrual cycle with a period longer than a day. *See also* biological clock, chronobiology. *Compare* circadian rhythm, infradian rhythm.

[From Latin *ultra* beyond + *dies* a day]

ultrasound *n*. A pressure wave of the same physical character as sound but with a frequency above the *audibility range, or above about 20,000 hertz, used in scanning devices for *ultrasound imaging* of internal body structures and unborn foetuses, which reflect some of the waves, and also for cleaning jewellery. Some frequencies of ultrasound can be perceived by animals such as bats, which use them for *biosonar, and dogs. *See also* audiogenic seizure, Galton whistle. *Compare* infrasound. **ultrasonic** *adj*.

[From Latin *ultra* beyond, from *ulter* distant + English *sound*]

ultraviolet *adj. n*. (Of or relating to) electromagnetic radiation with wavelengths shorter than the shortest radiation in the *visible spectrum but not as short as X-rays, hence within the range 5 to 390 nanometres, absorbed by glass but transmitted by quartz crystals (from which ultraviolet *lenses and

*prisms are therefore made), capable of causing genetic *mutations. *Compare* infra-red. **UV** *abbrev.*
[From Latin *ultra* beyond, from *ulter* distant + English *violet*]

Ulysses contract *n.* A form of *informed consent given in the form of an advance directive by people who have had *psychotic (1) episodes in the past and wish to precommit themselves to undergo appropriate treatment should they have similar crises in the future. Also called *voluntary involuntary treatment*.
[Named after an episode in Homer's *Odyssey* in which Ulysses binds himself to the masthead of a ship to avoid being drawn by the Sirens who bewitch men with their songs]

umami *n.* A fundamental taste in Japanese psychophysics, characteristic of the flavour enhancer *monosodium glutamate (MSG), supposedly not reducible to any combination of the traditional four primary tastes of *Henning's tetrahedron, namely sweet, sour, salty, and bitter.
[From Japanese *umami* delicious taste]

umlaut *n.* **1.** The diacritic mark in the form of a double dot or diaeresis placed over a letter representing a *vowel in German and some other languages to indicate a change in the quality of the vowel. **2.** In Germanic languages including English, the change in the sound quality of a vowel caused by the influence of a vowel in the following syllable, as when *gooses* changed to *geese*. *Compare* ablaut.
[From German *um* (changed) around + *Laut* sound]

Umweg problem *n.* Another name for a *detour problem.
[From German *Umweg* a detour, from *um* around + *Weg* a path or road]

Umwelt *n.* An umbrella term for all the environmental influences shaping an individual's behaviour, or the environment as it is experienced by the individual. The word was introduced in 1909 by the Estonian biologist Jacob Johann von Uexküll (1864–1944) in his book *Umwelt und Innenwelt der Tiere* (Environment and Inner World of Animals). In *phenomenology and *existentialism it is the environment as it is experienced. *See also* existential

analysis, existential therapy. *Compare* Eigenwelt, Mitwelt.
[From German *Umwelt* environment, from *um* around + *Welt* world]

unbalanced bilingual *n.* A person who can speak two languages but not with equal facility. Most bilinguals fall into this category, although rare cases of *balanced bilinguals have been confirmed by researchers.

uncertainty *n.* **1.** The state or condition of not being able to know or predict something accurately. **2.** The situation that exists when the outcome that will result from an action is not known with certainty, and even the probabilities associated with the possible outcomes are unknown or cannot be meaningfully estimated. A typical example would arise if a medical researcher were to test a new drug for the first time: various possible outcomes may be known, but there may be no meaningful way of assigning probabilities to them. *Risk (2) and uncertainty were first distinguished by the US economist Frank H. Knight (1885–1972) in his book *Risk, Uncertainty, and Profit* (1921), and the distinction is maintained in careful usage, although the terms are often used interchangeably. *See also* Ellsberg paradox, insufficient reason, modified Ellsberg paradox, uncertainty principle. **uncertain** *adj.*
[From Old English *un-* not + Latin *certus* sure or fixed, from *cernere* to discern or decide]

uncertainty principle *n.* The physical law, first propounded in 1927 by the German physicist Werner (Karl) Heisenberg (1901–76), that the position and momentum of a particle cannot both be determined with certainty, because neither can be measured without affecting the other. If the uncertainty of position is Δp, and the uncertainty of momentum is Δq, then $\Delta p \times \Delta q = h/4\pi$, where h is Planck's constant (6.6×10^{-34} Joule seconds). Because h is so small, the uncertainty is apparent only at the subatomic scale, but it has been argued by several brain scientists, and by the mathematical physicist Roger Penrose (born 1931) in *The Emperor's New Mind* (1989) and *Shadows of the Mind* (1994), that such subatomic events may occur in the *cytoskeletons of *neurons and may have important implications for psychological processes at the macroscopic level. Also called the *Heisenberg uncertainty principle* or *indeterminacy principle*.

uncinate fasciculus *n.* Either of two small bundles of nerve fibres in the cerebral cortex linking the *frontal lobe to the anterior *temporal lobe.
[From Latin *uncinatus* hooked, from *uncinus* a hooked structure, from *uncus* a hook + *fasciculus* a little bundle, diminutive of *fasculus* a bundle]

unconditional response *n.* An uncommon but more accurate name for an *unconditioned response.

unconditional stimulus *n.* An uncommon but more accurate name for an *unconditioned stimulus.

unconditioned reflex *n.* Another name for an *unconditioned response, presupposing that it consists of a *reflex arc. Also called an *unconditional reflex*.

unconditioned response *n.* In *classical conditioning, a *response such as salivation that follows an *unconditioned stimulus such as food naturally without any prior process of *conditioning (1). *Unconditioned* is a slight mistranslation of *unconditional*, the term originally used by the Russian physiologist Ivan Petrovich Pavlov (1849–1936), referring to a response that occurs unconditionally, that is, without conditioning. Also called an *unconditioned reflex* or an *unconditional reflex*, presupposing that it consists of a *reflex arc. *Compare* conditioned response. **UR** *abbrev.*

unconditioned stimulus *n.* In *classical conditioning, a *stimulus (1) such as food that naturally elicits an *unconditioned response such as salivation, without any prior process of *conditioning (1). It is a slight mistranslation of *unconditional stimulus*, the term originally used by the Russian physiologist Ivan Petrovich Pavlov (1849–1936) to denote a stimulus that elicits a particular response unconditionally, that is, without conditioning. *Compare* conditioned response. **US** *abbrev.*

unconscious *adj.* **1.** Lacking *consciousness or awareness of mental experiences such as perceptions, thoughts, or emotions; lacking deliberate intention (*an unconscious slip*). *Compare* conscious (1, 2). **ucs** *abbrev. n.* **2.** In *psychoanalysis, a part of the mind containing repressed instincts and their representative wishes, ideas, and images that are not

accessible to direct examination, its functions being governed by the mechanisms of the *primary process, especially *condensation and *displacement. The operation of *repression prevents the contents of the unconscious from entering either *consciousness or the *preconscious, and a barrier of *censorship exists between the unconscious and the preconscious–conscious system. Sigmund Freud (1856–1939) explicated his theory in 1912 in 'A Note on the Unconscious in Psycho-Analysis' (*Standard Edition*, XII, pp. 260–6) and in 1915 in an article on 'The Unconscious' (*Standard Edition*, XIV, pp. 166–215), but after 1920 he abandoned this *topography of the mind in favour of a structural model based on the concepts of the *id, *ego, and *superego. *See also* collective unconscious, id, personal unconscious, thing-presentation. **Ucs** *abbrev.*

uncus *n.* The anterior curved end of the hippocampal formation.
[From Latin *uncus* a hook, alluding to its hooklike appearance]

undecidable figure *n.* Another name for an *impossible figure.

underextension *n.* The interpretation of a word, usually by a child during the course of language development in the second or third year, to mean only part of what it normally means, for example, when a child understands the word *cup* to denote only a particular cup, as if the word were a proper noun. *See also* concept formation. *Compare* overextension, overgeneralization, mismatch.

undifferentiated schizophrenia *n.* One of the major types of *schizophrenia, defined negatively by the absence of signs and symptoms characteristic of *catatonic schizophrenia, *disorganized schizophrenia, or *paranoid schizophrenia.

undifferentiated somatoform disorder *n.* A *somatoform disorder characterized by one or more *somatic symptoms (most commonly chronic tiredness, loss of appetite, gastrointestinal or urinary complaints), lasting at least six months, causing significant distress or impairment in social, occupational, or other important areas of functioning, but below the threshold for a diagnosis of *somatization disorder.
[From Greek *soma* body + Latin *forma* form]

undinism *n.* Another name for *urophilia. [From *undine* a water spirit, from Latin *unda* a wave]

undoing *n.* In *psychoanalysis, a *defence mechanism whereby an emotional conflict associated with an action is dealt with by negating the action or attempting 'magically' to cause it not to have occurred by substituting an approximately opposite action. It differs from an ordinary act of making amends for an action that one regrets, inasmuch as the original action itself, and not merely its consequences, are negated. Sigmund Freud (1856–1939) introduced the concept briefly in his famous case study of the 'Rat Man' entitled 'Notes upon a Case of Obsessional Neurosis' (1909), where he describes *compulsive actions 'in two successive stages, of which the second neutralises the first' (*Standard Edition*, X, pp. 155–320, at p. 192). The Rat Man knocked his foot against a stone lying in the road and felt obliged to remove it in case a carriage containing his loved one struck it and caused her to come to grief; but a few minutes later he realized the absurdity of what he had done and felt obliged to put the stone back in its original position in the middle of the road. Freud discussed undoing at greater length in his book *Inhibitions, Symptoms and Anxiety* (1926), where he gave the clearest definition of it: 'An action which carries out a certain injunction is immediately succeeded by another action which stops or undoes the first one even if it does not go quite so far as to carry out its opposite' (*Standard Edition*, XX, pp. 77–175, at p. 113). Freud's daughter Anna Freud (1895–1982) discussed the phenomenon on page 36 of her book *The Ego and the Mechanisms of Defence* (1937).

unexpected hanging paradox *n.* A *paradox of prediction. Sentencing a man on Friday, a judge says: 'You will be hanged at noon on a day next week, but you will not know which day it is until the morning of the fateful day.' The prisoner reasons that he cannot be hanged next Saturday, because by Friday afternoon he would know that he was to be hanged the next day, and that he cannot be hanged on Friday because, with Saturday ruled out, by Thursday afternoon he would know that he was to be hanged on Friday, and that all the other days of the week can be excluded by the same argument, so he concludes with relief that he cannot be hanged

on any day next week and that therefore the judge's sentence cannot be correctly carried out. However, if he is hanged on Wednesday, the judge's sentence is correctly carried out, because the hanging would indeed be a surprise, given the prisoner's reasoning, because he appears to have ruled out every day including Wednesday. The paradox was discovered by the Swedish mathematician Lennart Ekbom (born 1919) and discussed with students in 1943 or 1944 after the Swedish broadcasting system announced that a civil defence drill would be held the following week but that no one would know in advance on which day it would take place. It was first discussed in print in 1948 by the British philosopher D(aniel) John O'Connor (born 1914) in an article in the journal *Mind*, where it was commented on by several eminent philosophers in subsequent issues, and it has generated by far the greatest attention of all epistemic paradoxes without producing anything resembling a consensus as to the right solution. At first the judge's sentence was interpreted as a classic *self-defeating prophecy (and O'Connor described the problem as 'rather frivolous'), but later commentators pointed out that if the hanging took place on Wednesday, then it would indeed be unexpected, which implies that the sentence is not self-defeating. Also called the *surprise examination paradox* or the *prediction paradox*. *See also* Oedipus effect.

unfaithful wives problem *See* muddy children problem.

unfinished business *n.* In *Gestalt therapy, an incomplete Gestalt arising from an experience with which a person has not come to terms; more generally an unresolved problem or issue in an interpersonal relationship.

unfolding technique *n.* A method of *scaling a set of stimuli without relying on any presupposed scale of measurement. Imagine a set of stimuli that are statements about capital punishment (*Capital punishment is never justified*, *People who commit murder should pay with their own lives*, and so on) arranged along a hypothetical scale, with anti-capital-punishment statements near the left and pro-capital-punishment statements near the right. Suppose an individual has judged the stimuli by the *method of paired comparisons and produced the rank-ordering of them, from anti-capital-punishment to pro-capital-punishment, and suppose that the judge's ideal point—in this example, the point corresponding to the judge's own attitude towards capital punishment—is marked on the scale with an X, yielding a *joint continuum* or *J* scale. An example of a hypothetical *J* scale with the positions of five stimuli (statements about capital punishment) *A*, *B*, *C*, *D*, and *E*, and the individual's ideal point *X*, might be as follows:

---A-----X---C----------B--------------D--------E---

From such a *J* scale, the individual's *I* scale could be obtained by imagining the *J* scale folded about the point *X*, so that the part of the scale to the left of the *X* is made to overlap the part to the right, yielding the following *I* scale:

X---C--A--------B--------------D--------E---

Reading from the *X* at the left, it is now clear that the individual's preference ordering of the five stimuli (attitude statements) is *CABDE*. If *X* had been closer to *A* than to *C* on the *J* scale, then the individual's preference order would have been *ACBDE*, and if *X* were to the right of the midpoint between *C* and *B*, then the order would have been *BCADE*. Any *I* scale may thus be viewed as a folded *J* scale, and from empirical data consisting in effect of observed *I* scales, *J* scales may therefore be recovered by unfolding the observed *I* scales. By unfolding the *I* scales of a number of judges who have ranked the five stimuli (statements), each with a different ideal position *X* on the hypothetical *J* scale, it is possible to infer not only the order of stimuli on the *J* scale, but also information about relative distances between them, and hence *interval scale information can be inferred from purely *ordinal scale input data, provided the judges behave consistently. For example, because the *J* scale depicted above induces the *I* scale *CABDE* and not *CBADE*, we can infer that the distance between *A* and *C* is less than the distance between *C* and *B*, although the data are purely ordinal. The technique was formulated by the US psychologist Clyde Hamilton Coombs (1912–88) and published in the journal *Psychological Review* in 1950, and is also called the *Coombs unfolding technique*. *See also* attitude scale, conjoint measurement theory, portfolio theory.

unidimensionality *n.* The property of having only one dimension. In psychometrics, the property of a test of measuring only one underlying *attribute or *construct. *See also* Guttman scale, reproducibility.

unilateral limb apraxia *n.* Another name for *left-sided apraxia. *See also* apraxia.

unilateral neglect *See* spatial neglect. Also called *unilateral spatial neglect*.

uniocular *n.* Another word for *monocular.

unipedophilia *n.* Another name for *acrotomorphilia.
[From Latin *unus* one + *pes, pedis* a foot + Greek *mania* madness]

unipolar depression *n.* A form of *depression that occurs within a *mood disorder with symptoms of depression only, without *manic episodes.
[From Latin *unus* one + *polaris* of or relating to a pole, from *polus* a pole]

unipolar neuron *n.* A *neuron that has a single *neurite, sometimes considered to be an axon and sometimes part axon and part dendrite. It has a *dendrite at one end and an *end organ at the other, attached to the cell body by a short process. Also called a *unipolar cell*, *monopolar neuron*, or *monopolar cell*. *Compare* bipolar cell, multipolar neuron.

unique colour *n.* Another name for a *psychological primary. US *unique color*. Also called a *unique hue*.

univariate statistics *n.* The branch of statistics devoted to analysing the effects of one or more *independent variables on a single *dependent variable. The *uni-* in the name refers to the dependent variable. *Compare* bivariate statistics, multivariate statistics.

universal grammar *n.* The set of formal grammatical features that all *natural languages, both actual and possible, must possess in order to have the properties of human languages, as proposed by the US linguist and philosopher (Avram) Noam Chomsky (born 1928) and his followers. *See also* formal universals, linguistic universals. **UG** *abbrev.*

universal quantifier *See* quantifier.

universals, linguistic *See* linguistic universals.

universal Turing machine *See under* Turing machine.

unobtrusive measure *n.* Any means of obtaining psychological or social science research data other than by interviews, questionnaires, or other direct approaches, that is, without the conscious cooperation of the research participants or subjects. It is considered useful where responses might be influenced by the respondents' awareness that their behaviour is being observed, the *validity of measurements in such circumstances demanding *non-reactive measures. The most common unobtrusive measures are *observational studies; studies of the physical traces of behaviour, such as the wear of floor tiles in front of museum exhibits as measures of the exhibits' popularity; and investigations based on archival records, including legal records, mass media, sales records, diaries, and other personal data. The term was popularized by the US psychologist Eugene J(ohn) Webb (1933–95) and several co-authors in their book *Unobtrusive Measures: Nonreactive Research in the Social Sciences* (1966), in which the idea itself is traced to the 1870s and attributed to the English explorer and scientist Sir Francis Galton (1822–1911). *See also* bogus pipeline, lost-letter technique.

unrealistic optimism *n.* A judgemental bias that tends to affect people's subjective estimates of the likelihood of future events in their lives, causing them to overestimate the likelihood of positive or desirable events and to underestimate the likelihood of negative or undesirable events. It was first reported in 1925 by the US psychologist F(rederick) H(ansen) Lund (1894–1965) and in 1938 by the US psychologist (Albert) Hadley Cantril (1906–69), and it came to prominence in 1980 when it was studied rigorously and named by the US psychologist Neil D(avid) Weinstein (born 1945) in an article in the *Journal of Personality and Social Psychology*. Weinstein asked students to estimate the relative likelihoods of various events happening to them, compared to the likelihoods of the same events happening to their peers, and his results showed that they rated their chances of experiencing positive events, such as *owning your own home, receiving a good job offer before graduation*, and *living past 80*, to be significantly above the average for students of the same sex at the same university, and their chances of experiencing negative events, such as *having a heart attack before age 40, being sued by someone*, and *being the victim of a mugging*, to be significantly below average. *See also* depressive realism, hypomanic episode. *Compare* overconfidence effect.

unweighted pair-group method using arithmetic averages *n.* Another name for the *average linkage between groups method of cluster analysis. **UPGMA** *abbrev.*

up-and-down method *n.* Another name for the *staircase method.

uppers *n.* A common street name for central nervous system *stimulant drugs in general. *Compare* downers.

upper threshold *n.* **1.** The higher of the two thresholds determined by the *method of limits. **2.** Another name for a *terminal threshold, though this usage can cause confusion.

uqamairineq *n.* A *culture-bound syndrome restricted mainly to Eskimo communities of North America and Greenland, characterized by a sensation of a peculiar sound or smell, followed by sudden *paralysis accompanied by *anxiety, *psychomotor agitation, or *hallucinations, usually lasting only minutes and attributed to soul loss or spirit possession. It is sometimes interpreted as a type of dissociative disorder.
[Inuit]

uracil *n.* One of the constituent *bases (1) of *RNA, having an affinity for *adenine. **U** *abbrev.*
[From *ur(ea)* + *ac(etic)* + Latin *-il(is)* indicating capability or relationship]

Urbach–Wiethe disorder *n.* A skin disorder, probably of genetic origin, believed to cause crystallization of the amygdala and consequent cognitive deficits in some cases.
[Named after the US dermatologist Erich Urbach (1893–1946) and the Austrian otologist Camillo Wiethe (1888–1949) who studied its features]

urban legend *n.* An apocryphal story, usually with either a nasty or a humorous twist in its tail, circulated by people who believe it actually to have happened to a 'friend of a friend'.

A typical example is the following, named the *Blind Man* urban legend by folklorists. A woman is taking a shower when she hears the doorbell ring. She calls out 'Who is it?' and a voice replies 'Blind man'. The woman is generous, and keen on helping people with disabilities, so she grabs some loose change and, without bothering to cover herself in front of a blind man, opens the door. The man looks at her with astonishment and says, 'Good day, madam. Now where do you want me to hang your blinds?' It is occasionally possible to establish beyond doubt that such a story is apocryphal, but more commonly internal evidence casts sufficient doubt on its veracity for it to be classified as a probable urban legend. The *Blind Man* is typical inasmuch as it appears plausible at first but does not bear closer scrutiny: a bathroom is unlikely to be situated close enough to a front door to enable a woman taking a shower to converse with a man outside; a man who installs blinds does not normally call himself a 'blind man'; everyone knows that a person describing himself as blind is not necessarily totally blind; a woman would normally cover herself to open the front door even to a caller she thought was totally blind, because other people may be passing in the street; and so on. Also called an *urban myth. See also* rumour.

urethral character *n.* In *psychoanalysis, a personality pattern determined by *fixation (2) of *urethral erotism, characterized by ambition and competitiveness, both being interpreted as reactions against shame. Also called the *urethral personality*.

urethral erotism *n.* In *psychoanalysis, a mode of *libidinal satisfaction through urinating, and focusing of *libido in that region during the *phallic stage. Sigmund Freud (1856–1939) linked it to *masturbation in his case study of 'Dora' entitled 'Fragment of an Analysis of a Case of Hysteria' (1901/5, *Standard Edition*, VII, pp. 7–122, at p. 74), and (symbolically) with fire-setting or *pyromania in an article on 'The Acquisition and Control of Fire' (1932, *Standard Edition*, 22, p. 185). The British-based Austrian psychoanalyst Melanie Klein (1882–1960), on page 186 of her book *The Psycho-Analysis of Children* (1932), stressed the aggressive, corrosive, and essentially sadistic fantasies associated with urination in both children and adults. Also called *urethral eroticism* or *urinary erotism* or *eroticism. See also*

urethral character. *Compare* urophilia. **urethral-erotic** *adj.*
[From Greek *ourethra* the urinary canal, from *ourein* to urinate]

urinary erotism *n.* Another name for *urethral erotism. Also called *urinary eroticism*.

uroboros *n.* An ancient circular symbol depicting a snake, or sometimes a dragon, swallowing its own tail, representing unity and/or infinity. Carl Gustav Jung (1875–1961) and his followers interpreted it as a metaphor for early development, when *Eros and *Thanatos are not differentiated and the infant cannot distinguish love from aggression or the feeder from the fed. **uroboric** *adj.*
[From Greek *drakon ouroboros* snake devouring its own tail]

urolagnia *n.* Another name for *urophilia.
[From Greek *ouron* urine + *lagneia* lust]

urophilia *n.* A *paraphilia characterized by recurrent sexually arousing fantasies, sexual urges, or behaviour involving urinating or being urinated on. Also called *undinism*, *urolagnia. Compare* urethral erotism.
[From Greek *ouron* urine + *philos* loving, from *philein* to love + *-ia* indicating a condition or quality]

utility *n.* **1.** A measure of the subjective desirability of an outcome or event, corresponding to the individual's preference for it. The concept was introduced in 1738 by the Swiss mathematician and physicist Daniel Bernoulli (1700–82), who explained the *St Petersburg paradox by pointing out that the values of things to a person are not simply equivalent to their monetary values, but the term *utility*, which Bernoulli called *moral worth*, became widespread only after the emergence of *expected utility theory in 1947. It is often used to represent the total gain or loss resulting from a particular course of action or the outcome of a strategic *game (1). *See also* expected utility, payoff, prospect theory, risk aversion, risk seeking, subjective expected utility, subjective utility, utility function, utility theory. **2.** The fact, character, or quality of being useful or serviceable. **3.** The capacity of any commodity to satisfy a human want. **4.** A public service, such as a bus system or an electricity, water, or gas supply.
[From Latin *utilitas* usefulness, from *utilis* useful, from *uti* to use]

utility function *n*. A rule specifying the relation between quantities of money or of any commodity and an individual's *utility (1). *See also* prospect theory.

utility theory *n*. A theory of decision making according to which a decision maker chooses an alternative or *strategy (2) that maximizes the *utility (1) of the outcome. The modern form of the theory was introduced in 1947 by the Hungarian-born US mathematician John von Neumann (1903–57) and the German-born US economist Oskar Morgenstern (1902–77). *See also* Allais paradox, common ratio effect, Ellsberg paradox, expected utility theory, modified Ellsberg paradox, prospect theory, revealed preference, St Petersburg paradox, subjective expected utility theory.

utricle *n*. The larger of the two sections of the *membranous labyrinth of the inner ear, functioning as an *otolith receptor in the *vestibular system. Also called a *utriculus*. *Compare* saccule. **utricular** *adj*.
[From Latin *utriculus* a little bag, diminutive of *uter* a bag]

uvula *n*. The small finger of fleshy tissue that hangs from the soft palate at the back of the throat.
[From Latin *uvula* little grape, diminutive of *uva* a grape]

uvular *adj*. In phonetics, of or relating to speech sounds whose *place of articulation is in the region of the *uvula, as in the pronunciation of the letter *r* in Parisian French.

vacuum activity *n*. Performance of a *fixed-action pattern in the absence of its normal *sign stimulus or *releaser, believed to result from a build-up of motivational energy breaking through the inhibitory function of the *innate releasing mechanism. A familiar example to cat owners is the slow rhythmic trampling by a cat with its front paws in its owner's lap, always accompanied by purring and often by dribbling, such behaviour being interpretable as a milk-treading fixed-action pattern normally triggered in a kitten by its mother lying down and exposing her nipples. Also called a *vacuum response* or an *overflow response*.

vagina *n*. The genital canal in females, extending from the vulva to the cervix of the uterus. *See also* Müllerian duct, Müllerian inhibiting substance. **vaginal** *adj*.
[From Latin *vagina* a sheath]

vagina dentata *n*. A fantasy of a toothed vagina, a legendary hazard associated with sexual intercourse. The Austrian psychoanalyst Otto Rank (1884–1939) first identified it, in his book *The Trauma of Birth* (1924), as a widespread cause of anxiety among neurotic men, and it was explored further by the Hungarian psychoanalyst Sandor Ferenczi (1873–1933). The counterpart fantasy among women, called *penis dentata* (toothed penis), is less commonly observed.
[From Latin *vagina* a sheath + *dentata* toothed, from *dens, dentis* a tooth]

vaginismus *n*. A *sexual dysfunction of women characterized by recurrent or persistent involuntary spasm of the perineal muscles surrounding the vagina when penetration is attempted with a penis, finger, tampon, or other object, interfering with sexual intercourse, causing significant distress or problems of interpersonal interaction. It is not diagnosed if it is attributable to a *general medical condition. *Compare* dyspareunia.
[From Latin *vagina* a sheath + *-ismus* indicating a state or condition]

vagus nerve *n*. Either of the tenth pair of *cranial nerves, the longest cranial nerve and the most important nerve of the *parasympathetic nervous system, a sensory part receiving sensations from the *mucous membranes of the digestive system and a motor part supplying the heart, lungs, and alimentary canal, controlling swallowing. One of the most striking effects of its stimulation is slowing of the heart. *See also Vagusstoff*.
[From Latin *vagus* wandering, alluding to its roundabout course]

Vagusstoff *n*. The name coined in 1921 by the German pharmacologist Otto Loewi (1873–1961) for what is now called *acetylcholine, following his pioneering experimental demonstration of the chemical nature of nervous transmission. Electrical stimulation of the *vagus nerve of a frog's heart, held in a beaker of saline solution and still beating, stimulated the release of a substance that, when pumped into a separate beaker containing a second frog's heart with its vagus nerve removed, caused the beating of the second heart to slow as if its vagus nerve had been stimulated.
[From German *Vagus* vagus + *Stoff* material or substance]

validation *n*. The act or process of making something valid, ratifying it, or checking that it satisfies certain standards or conditions. In psychometrics, the process of establishing the *validity of a test.
[From Latin *validus* valid, from *valere* to be strong + *-ation* indicating a process or condition]

validity n. The soundness or adequacy of something or the extent to which it satisfies certain standards or conditions. A research procedure or an interpretation of results obtained from a research study are considered valid if they can be justified on reasoned grounds. In psychometrics, it is the extent to which a test measures what it purports to measure, or the extent to which specified inferences from the test's scores are justified or meaningful. *Internal validity, *external validity, and *ecological validity (1) form a hierarchy in that order: an empirical investigation may produce results that have high internal validity and low external validity and ecological validity, or high internal validity and external validity and low ecological validity, but a higher form of validity is not possible without the lower forms. *See* concurrent validity, congruent validity, consensual validity, construct validity, content validity, convergent validity, criterion validity, cross-validation (1), discriminant validity, face validity (a priori validity), incremental validity, intrinsic validity, predictive validity, trait validity. *See also* nomological network, replication (2), validity coefficient, validity generalization. *Compare* reliability. **valid** *adj.*

validity coefficient n. A *correlation coefficient between scores on a test and a criterion of *validity, or a similar value taken as evidence of the test's validity. *Compare* reliability coefficient.

validity generalization n. Applying evidence of *validity obtained in a restricted range of circumstances to situations falling outside that range. This procedure is generally justified on the basis of *Bayesian inference, *meta-analysis, or other reasoned grounds. *See also* external validity, ecological validity (1).

Valium n. A proprietary name for the benzodiazepine drug *diazepam.
[Trademark]

value (of a variable) n. In mathematics and statistics, a specific number, amount, or magnitude attained by a *variable, or occasionally a state attained by a non-numerical variable such as sex, the possible values of which are male and female.
[From Latin *valere* to be worth]

vanishing point n. A point, usually located on the *horizon, towards which receding lines such as railway tracks appear to converge when depicted or viewed in *linear perspective.

vapours n. An almost obsolete word for the psychological condition later called *hysteria, formerly thought to arise from gases in the abdomen.

variability n. In statistics, the degree to which a set of scores is dispersed or scattered. Two sets of scores with identical *means (averages) may have widely different variabilities. The usual measures of variability are the *variance and the *standard deviation. *See also* interquartile range, probable error, range, semi-interquartile range.

variable n. Anything that is subject to variation; in psychological research, any *stimulus (1), *response, or extraneous factor that is changeable and that may influence the results of the research. *See also* dependent variable, extraneous variable, independent variable, intervening variable, mediating variable, value (of a variable), variate.

variable error n. In *psychophysics, any error of judgement or perception that is attributable to chance fluctuation and does not include any systematic bias. *Compare* constant error.

variable-interval schedule n. In *operant conditioning, a simple *reinforcement schedule in which reward follows the first response that the organism makes after a random time interval, and then the first response that it makes after another random time interval, and so on, the average length of the interval being specified in seconds as an affix to the abbreviation, hence *VI20* indicates a variable-interval schedule with an average interval of 20 seconds. Also called a *variable-interval reinforcement schedule. See also* simple reinforcement schedule. *Compare* fixed-interval schedule, fixed-ratio schedule, variable-ratio schedule. **VI** *abbrev.*

variable-ratio schedule n. In *operant conditioning, a simple *reinforcement schedule in which reward is delivered after the organism has made a random number of responses, and is then rewarded after a further random number of responses, and so on, the average number of responses before reinforcement being specified as an affix to the abbreviation, hence *VR50* indicates a variable-ratio schedule with an average of 50 responses between reinforcements. Also called a *variable-ratio reinforcement schedule*. *See also* simple reinforcement schedule. *Compare* fixed-interval schedule, fixed-ratio schedule, variable-interval schedule. **VR** *abbrev.*

variable stimulus *n.* In *psychophysics, a *stimulus (1) that is varied by the experimenter and is usually compared in magnitude to a *standard stimulus. Also called a *comparison stimulus*. **s** or **V** *abbrev.*

variable-sum game *n.* Another name for a *mixed-motive game.
[So called because the sum of the payoffs to the players varies from one outcome to another]

variance *n.* In descriptive statistics, a measure of the degree of dispersion, variability, or scatter of a set of scores. It is given by the mean (average) of the squared deviations of the scores from their mean. Also called a *mean square*. *See also* interquartile range, probable error, range, semi-interquartile range, standard deviation.
[From Latin *variare* to diversify]

variate *n.* In statistics, any *variable whose values can be predicted only probabilistically, such as a *dependent variable in a research design. The term is often used loosely to refer to any *variable. *See also* bivariate statistics, multivariate statistics, univariate statistics.

variety *n.* The quality or condition of being diversified, or a collection of unlike things. In biology, a *taxonomic group into which a *species is divided, containing organisms that are genetically differentiable from other members of the same species by the relative frequencies of their *polymorphic genes. Also called a *microspecies*, *race*, or *subspecies*.
[From Latin *varietas* variety, from *varius* various]

vascular dementia *n.* A form of *dementia associated with neurological signs and symptoms (such as exaggerated deep tendon reflexes) or laboratory findings indicating cerebrovascular disease (such as multiple cor-

tical *infarcts) that are judged to be responsible for the disorder. Also called *arteriosclerotic dementia*, *multi-infarct dementia* (*MID*).
[From Latin *vasculum* a little vessel, diminutive of *vas* a vessel]

vascular tunic *n.* The middle layer of the eyeball, including the *ciliary body.

vasoconstrictor *n.* Any drug, hormone, or nerve that causes blood vessels to narrow or contract. **vasoconstriction** *n.* Narrowing of blood vessels. *See also* ergot, vasopressin. *Compare* vasodilator.
[From Latin *vas* a vessel + *constringere*, *constrictum* to bind together or compress]

vasodilator *n.* Any drug, hormone, or nerve that causes blood vessels to expand. **vasodilation** *n.* Expansion or widening of blood vessels. *Compare* vasoconstriction.
[From Latin *vas* a vessel + *dilatare* to spread out, from *dis-* apart + *latus* wide]

vasomotor *adj.* Of or relating to a drug, hormone, or nerve that can cause blood vessels to constrict or dilate. *See* vasoconstrictor, vasodilator.
[From Latin *vas* a vessel + *motor* a mover, from *movere* to move]

vasopressin *n.* A hormone produced by the *hypothalamus and stored in the *posterior pituitary, also synthesized artificially. It is released from the posterior pituitary in response to a decrease in blood volume detected by *baroreceptors or *blood-flow receptors, or in response to an increase of sodium or of certain other substances in the blood detected by *osmoreceptors (2), or as a reaction to pain, stress, or the action of certain drugs such as nicotine, whereupon it stimulates smooth muscle contraction and causes constriction of small blood vessels and release of *renin by the kidneys, thereby raising blood pressure and inducing water retention in the kidney tubules. It also functions as a *neurotransmitter in the brain, where it is thought to have a role in memory, and it is sometimes inhaled via a nasal spray as a *smart drug, supposedly improving attention, concentration, and memory. Also called *antidiuretic hormone* or *ADH*.
[From *Vasopressin* a trademark, from Latin *vas* a vessel + *pressare* to keep pressing, from *premere*, *pressum* to press]

Vater–Pacini corpuscle n. Another name for a *Pacinian corpuscle.

[Named after the German anatomist Abraham Vater (1684–1751) who discovered it some time prior to 1741 and the Italian anatomist Filippo Pacini (1812–83) who rediscovered it in 1835 and gave a full description of it in 1840]

vault n. Another name for the *fornix, so called because of its arched appearance; or more generally an arched roof or ceiling, or a room, chamber, or cellar with such a structure.

[From Old French voute a vault, from Latin volvere, volutum to roll]

vection n. An illusion of *passive movement arising from the perception of motion in the surrounding environment, as when a person sitting in a stationary train sees another train on an adjacent track begin to move and experiences an illusory sensation of being moved in the opposite direction. The phenomenon was first identified and studied quantitatively in 1929 by the German psychologist Karl Duncker (1903–40). Also called induced motion. See also audiogyral illusion. Compare apparent movement.

[From Latin vector a bearer or carrier, from vehere, vectum to convey + -ion indicating an action, process, or state]

vegetative state See persistent vegetative state.

velar adj. Of or relating to speech sounds articulated with the back of the tongue against the soft palate, as in the final *phonemes in the words wick, wig, and wing. See also place of articulation.

[From velum the soft palate, from Latin velum a veil]

velocity constancy n. A form of *perceptual constancy according to which if an object is moving with constant velocity its perceived velocity also remains constant despite changes in the velocity of its images on the viewer's retinas, as when a viewer standing by the side of a road watches a car approaching at constant speed, the retinal image moves slowly when the car is far away and much more rapidly as it passes the viewer, and movements of the viewer's eyes add erratic movements to the retinal images, but the viewer nevertheless perceives the car moving at a constant speed.

Venn diagram n. A pictorial representation of logical *propositions (1) or *sets (1) by overlapping circles depicting all possible combinations of set membership within different areas of the diagram. It is useful for clarifying and checking logical arguments. Any area that contains no members is shaded, an x is placed within any area containing at least one member, and an x is placed on the border between any two areas at least one of which contains members. For example, the proposition All A are B is depicted by two overlapping circles representing A and B, with the area of A that does not overlap B being shaded to show that it is empty; the proposition Some A are C is depicted by two overlapping circles representing A and C, with an x in the area where A and C overlap; and so on. Compare Euler diagram.

[Named after the English logician John Venn (1834–1923) who introduced it in 1880]

ventral adj. Of, relating to, or situated towards the same side of the body as the belly, except in the brain, where ventral is synonymous with inferior or bottom, as if humans walked on all fours and the cerebrum were not bent forwards 80° relative to the brainstem to keep it horizontally oriented when standing upright. Compare dorsal.

[From Latin venter, ventris the belly]

ventral anterior nucleus n. A cluster of nerve cell bodies near the front of the lower part of each *thalamus, receiving inputs from the globus pallidus and projecting to the prefrontal cortex. Compare ventral lateral nucleus, ventral posterior nucleus.

ventral lateral nucleus n. A cluster of nerve cell bodies at the side of the lower part of each *thalamus, receiving inputs from the globus pallidus and the cerebellum and projecting to the motor cortex and the supplementary motor area. Compare ventral anterior nucleus, ventral posterior nucleus.

ventral posterior nucleus n. A cluster of nerve cell bodies behind the ventral lateral nucleus of each *thalamus, containing an inverted *topographic map of the body with a disproportionate amount of space devoted to the face and especially the tongue, receiving inputs from the medial lemniscus and the trigeminal lemniscus and projecting to the somatosensory cortex. *Compare* ventral anterior nucleus, ventral lateral nucleus.

ventral root *n*. The short pathways into which a *spinal nerve divides near its point of attachment to the front of the *spinal cord, containing efferent or motor fibres emerging from the front of the spinal cord. *See also* Bell–Magendie law. *Compare* dorsal root.

ventral tegmental area *n*. The lower part of the *tegmentum alongside the substantia nigra, containing nerve cell bodies that release *dopamine, projecting to various parts of the *limbic system and the *prefrontal cortex, implicated in emotional responsiveness and possibly, when overactive, linked to schizophrenia. *See also* mesocortical system. **VTA** *abbrev*.

ventricle *n*. Any of a number of small cavities in the body, especially the two lower contractile chambers of the heart, which are filled with blood, and the four major cavities in the brain, which are filled with *cerebrospinal fluid. The two lateral ventricles in the forebrain, the main parts of which lie in the temporal lobes immediately below the corpus callosum and above the thalamus, are separated by the *septum pellucidum and are connected by the *foramen of Monro to the third ventricle in the midline of the brainstem, and the third ventricle is connected in turn by the *cerebral aqueduct to the fourth at the level of the pons and cerebellum. Also called a *lumen*. *See also* area postrema, encephalogram, ependyma, ependymal cell, hydrocephalus, lumen (2), Magendie's foramen, organum vasculosum lamina terminalis, pneumoencephalogram. **ventricular** *adj*.
[From Latin *ventriculus* a little belly, diminutive of *venter, ventris* a belly]

ventriloquism effect *n*. An *auditory illusion in which sound is misperceived as emanating from a source that can be seen to be moving appropriately when it actually emanates from a different invisible source. The effect is most powerful for speech sounds, and it arises from *visual dominance over auditory information. It is exploited by stage ventriloquists who practise the art of speaking without moving their lips while manipulating the movements of a puppet or dummy.
[From Latin *venter* the belly + *loqui* to speak]

ventromedial hypothalamic syndrome *n*. A constellation of signs and symptoms associated with a lesion in both sides of the *ventromedial hypothalamus, especially *hyperphagia, *bulimia (1), and *aggression or rage. Also called *hypothalamic hyperphagia*. *Compare* lateral hypothalamic syndrome.

ventromedial hypothalamus *n*. The lower middle part of each side of the *hypothalamus, responsible for the feeling of satiation after eating, stimulation of which inhibits eating and destruction increases eating, also implicated in the control of anger and aggression. Also called the *satiety centre*. *See also* appestat. *Compare* lateral hypothalamic feeding centre. **VMH** *abbrev*.
[From Latin *ventris* a belly + *medialis* situated in the middle, from *medius* the middle]

ventromedial tract *n*. Part of the *corticospinal tract controlling trunk movements that does not decussate but stays on the same side of the body midline.

verbal ability *n*. Another name for *verbal intelligence.

verbal intelligence *n*. One of the fundamental *factors (2) of human intelligence, derived from *factor analysis, corresponding roughly to *crystallized intelligence. Also called *verbal ability*. *See also* British Ability Scales, Mill Hill Vocabulary scale, Wechsler scales.

verbal rating scale *n*. Any *rating scale in which the *response categories are labelled with words, such as *Strongly Disagree, Disagree, Neutral, Agree, Strongly Agree*. *Compare* graphic rating scale, numerical rating scale.

verbal transformation effect *n*. An *auditory illusion involving radical changes in what is heard in a clear recording of a word or phrase repeated many times on a loop of audiotape. If a single word is repeated 360 times in three minutes, the average young adult listener experiences substantial distortions and hears about 30 changes involving about six different word forms. In a classic experiment in which the word *tress* was used, listeners heard such words as *dress, stress, Joyce, florist, purse*, and even phonetically unrelated words such as *lunchtime*. Children under six years experience few if any transformations, and susceptibility to the effect declines slowly in middle age. The phenomenon was discovered by the US psychologist Richard M. Warren (born 1925) and the English psychologist Richard L(angton) Gregory (born 1923) and published in the *American Journal of Psychology* in 1958, a more detailed account being provided by Warren in the journal *Psychological Bulletin* in 1968. *Compare* semantic satiation.

vergence *n.* Inward or outward turning of the eyes; a generic term for both *ocular convergence and *ocular divergence.
[From Latin *vergere* to incline]

vermis *n.* The wormlike central strip connecting the two halves of the *cerebellum along its midline, involved in the coordination of trunk and eye movements and probably in the regulation of motivation. *See also* attention-deficit/hyperactivity disorder.
[From Latin *vermis* a worm]

vernacular *n.* The indigenous language or *dialect commonly spoken by members of a community. *See also* Black English Vernacular.
[From Latin *vernaculus* belonging to a household slave, from *verna* a household slave]

vernier acuity *n.* *Visual acuity expressed in terms of the minimum *visual angle of displacement that can be detected between two bars or lines that are almost, but not quite, aligned.
[From *vernier scale* an auxiliary device for making fine adjustments to a measuring instrument, named after the French mathematician Paul Vernier (1580–1637) who invented it]

Verstehen *n.* A method of interpreting or understanding other people through an intuitive understanding of symbolic relationships derived from adopting the point of view of the people being studied. It was originally put forward by the German philosopher Wilhelm Dilthey (1833–1911) who argued that the ultimate goal of the human or mental sciences (*Geisteswissenschaften*) is understanding, whereas that of the natural sciences (*Naturwissenschaften*) is explanation (*Erklärung*). *See also* hermeneutics (1).
[From German *verstehen* to understand]

vertebrate *n.* **1.** An animal with a spinal column or backbone, belonging to the subphylum Vertebrata, characterized by a relatively well-developed brain, including fish, amphibians, reptiles, birds, and mammals in the phylum Chordata. *Compare* invertebrate (1). *adj.* **2.** Of or relating to a *vertebrate (1). *Compare* invertebrate (2).
[From Latin *vertebra* a spinal joint, from *vertere* to turn]

vertical décalage *See under* décalage.

vertical icicle plot *n.* In statistics, a graphical representation of the formation of clusters during successive steps of a *cluster analysis. The steps of the analysis are represented in the display by the rows, and the individuals or cases by the columns, with individuals or cases in the same cluster being joined by a horizontal line. *Compare* horizontal icicle plot.
[Named after its resemblance to a row of icicles hanging from a windowsill]

vertical thinking *See under* lateral thinking.

vertigo *n.* A sensation of dizziness or of the external world or one's body whirling around, usually caused by damage to the *vestibular system. Sometimes used to denote a pathological fear of heights, more correctly called *acrophobia.
[From Latin *vertigo* a whirling around, from *vertere* to turn]

vesicle *n.* Any small sac or cavity, including any of the *ventricles of the brain, or the *prosencephalon, *mesencephalon, or *rhombencephalon of the developing foetus. *See also* synaptic vesicle.
[From Latin *vesicula* a little bladder or blister, diminutive of *vesica* a bladder or blister]

vestibular nerve *n.* One of the two major branches of the *vestibulocochlear nerve, transmitting information related to balance from the *vestibular system.
[From Latin *vestibulum* a forecourt]

vestibular nystagmus *n.* Any form of *nystagmus controlled by the *vestibular system and activated by head movements. *See also* post-rotational nystagmus, vestibulo-ocular reflex.

vestibular sense *n.* The sense of balance and orientation, governed by the *vestibular system. *See also* Aubert effect, vestibulocochlear nerve.

vestibular system n. An organ in the *membranous labyrinth of the *inner ear mediating sensations of balance, orientation, and movement, containing the *otolith (or statolith) organs that are responsive to linear acceleration (including gravity) and the *semicircular canals that are responsive to angular acceleration. When the head is accelerated rapidly in a straight line, a gelatinous membrane covered with heavy *otoconia crystals of calcium carbonate tends to remain stationary through inertia, bending or displacing *hair cells that project into the fluid at different angles from the *maculae of the *utricle and *saccule, causing the hair cells to trigger nerve impulses that are sent to the brainstem and cerebellum, leading to reflex movements of muscles of the eyes, neck, limbs, and trunk, and exciting neurons in the central nervous system that mediate the perception of motion and orientation in space. The otolith organs also respond to gravity, which according to the general theory of relativity is equivalent to accelerating an object upwards at 9.8 metres per second squared. The three semicircular canals detect angular acceleration by means of hair cells that project into the gelatinous membrane of the *cupula where a fluid (endolymph) acts as an inertial mass resisting angular acceleration, displacing the hair cells in the direction opposite to the direction of movement and causing adjoining neurons to send nerve impulses to the brainstem and cerebellum. Also called the *vestibular apparatus. See also Aubert effect, kinaesthesis, mechanoreceptor, proprioception, vestibular nerve, vestibular nystagmus, vestibular sense, vestibulo-ocular reflex.
[From Latin *vestibulum* a forecourt or entrance]

vestibule n. An entrance hall, or a cavity positioned at the entrance to another, especially the *vestibular system of the inner ear. **vestibular** adj.

vestibulitis n. Inflammation of the *labyrinth and *cochlea of the inner ear, causing ataxia, deafness, and vertigo.

vestibulocerebellum n. The functional area of the *cerebellum, comprising the *vermis, *flocculonodular lobe, and associated nuclei, having two-way connections with *Deiters' nucleus in the *medulla oblongata. Lesions in this area lead to *nystagmus and *ataxia,

especially involving trunk movements. See also cerebellar syndrome. Compare neocerebellum, spinocerebellum.
[So called because it is a part of the cerebellum connected to Deiters' nucleus, which receives inputs mainly from the vestibular system]

vestibulocochlear nerve n. Either of the eighth pair of *cranial nerves, supplying the organs of hearing and balance in the *inner ear. It has two principal branches: the vestibular nerve, which transmits information related to balance from the *vestibular system, and the cochlear nerve, which transmits auditory information from the *organ of Corti in the cochlea of the inner ear to the *inferior colliculus and thence to the *auditory cortex. Also called the *auditory nerve* or the *acoustic nerve*.

vestibulo-ocular reflex n. A reflex rotation of the eyes activated by the *vestibular system in response to a movement of the head, keeping the retinal image stable, also activated by stimulation of the external auditory canal with warm fluid, eliciting rotatory nystagmus towards the stimulated side, or cold fluid eliciting rotation away from the stimulated side. See also Bárány test, caloric nystagmus. **VOR** abbrev.

Viagra n. The proprietary name of the drug sildenafil citrate, introduced in 1998 for the treatment of *impotence (2) or *male erectile disorder. It acts by selectively inhibiting the enzyme phosphodiesterase type 5 (PDE5) that metabolizes *cyclic GMP in the *corpora cavernosa of the penis, increasing the bioavailability of cyclic GMP and thereby increasing the inflow and decreasing the outflow of blood in these erectile tissues, the effects becoming apparent within half an hour or an hour of oral administration.
[Trademark, a blend of *vi(gour)* + *(Ni)ag(a)ra*, suggesting a combination of power or stamina and unstoppable flow, coined by the drug company Pfizer in spite of the fact that the name *Niagara* has connotations of falls rather than rises]

vibration receptor n. A *sensory receptor that responds to rapid oscillatory movements and that mediates the *vibratory sense. See Meissner's corpuscle, Pacinian corpuscle. See also mechanoreceptor.

vibratory sense *n*. The faculty for sensing vibration, mediated by *vibration receptors, also involved in the *tactile sensation of texture when the fingers are moved across a surface. Also called *vibrotactile perception*. *See also* pallaesthesia, touch.

Vierordt's law *n*. The proposition that short time intervals tend to be overestimated and long ones underestimated, the *indifference interval* being the intermediate length that is neither overestimated nor underestimated, usually found by experiment to be in the region of 0.7 second.
[Named after the German physiologist Karl von Vierordt (1818–84) who formulated it in 1868]

vigilance *n*. The state or condition of being alert and attentive. It is studied in psychology by measuring the speed and accuracy with which a person can respond to stimuli, the stimuli usually being infrequent and difficult to detect against a background of *noise (2). *See also* signal detection theory.
[From Latin *vigilans* keeping awake, from *vigilare* to be watchful, from *vigil* awake]

vignette *n*. A word-picture, a brief verbal outline of a scenario, or a short story about hypothetical characters in a particular situation, to which research participants or interviewees are asked to respond. Vignettes are used in various areas of psychological research including studies related to *attribution theory, and they are also used to elicit opinions, attitudes, beliefs, or judgements.
[From French *vignette* a small vine, from *vigne* a vine, from Latin *vinea* a vine, alluding to the original meaning, a design of vine-leaves and tendrils used on the title-page of a book or manuscript]

Vigotsky blocks *See* Vygotsky blocks.

Vineland Social Maturity Scale *n*. A scale designed to measure social competence, defined as a functional composite of human traits that subserve social usefulness and are reflected in self-sufficiency and in service to others, from birth to 30 years of age. It measures eight categories of behaviour: self-help general, self-help eating, self-help dressing, locomotion, occupation, communication, self-direction, and socialization. An interview is conducted with a parent, sibling, or other third party who is familiar with the person being assessed, and scores are assigned according to the behaviours that are reported to be customarily exhibited, the assessment being expressed in terms of *social age or *social quotient. It was developed by the US psychologist Edgar (Arnold) Doll (1889–1968), originally published in 1936, and discussed in Doll's booklet *Your Child Grows Up* in 1950.

virtual reality *n*. A computer-generated perceptual simulation of a three-dimensional image or environment with which the viewer can interact, often requiring a headset or goggles providing visual stimuli and gloves or other bodily attachments fitted with sensors. In a typical virtual reality display, turning the head produces an appropriate change in what is seen, and moving a hand activates a corresponding movement of an image of a hand in the display. The term, which became popular in the 1980s, is based on the concept of a *virtual image* in optics, which is an image of the kind seen in a mirror and formed from light rays apparently diverging from an object or surface, in contradistinction to an actual image formed from light rays actually diverging from an object or surface. *See also* MUD, teledildonics. **VR** *abbrev*.

virtual self *n*. In *self-psychology, an image of the neonate's self in the mind of a parent.

virus *n*. A submicroscopic particle of *RNA or *DNA, coated with *protein and capable of self-replication within the cells of an organism, where its effects are often *pathogenic.
[From Latin *virus* venom]

viscera *n. pl*. A generic term for the large internal organs of the abdominal cavity. **viscus** *sing*. **visceral** *adj*.
[From Latin *viscera* entrails, plural of *viscus* an internal organ]

visceral afferent fibres *n*. Nerve fibres that arise from neuron cell bodies in *dorsal root ganglia and that transmit impulses from the internal organs of the body to the spinal cord. *Compare* visceral efferent fibres.
[From Latin *viscera* entrails, plural of *viscus* an internal organ + *aferre* to carry to, from *ad* to + *ferre* to carry]

visceral efferent fibres *n*. Nerve fibres that belong to the sympathetic and parasympathetic divisions of the *autonomic nervous system and that transmit impulses from the spinal cord to smooth muscles and glands.

[From Latin *viscera* entrails, plural of *viscus* an internal organ + *eferre* to carry off, from *e* from + *ferre* to carry]

visceroreceptor *n*. A *sensory receptor located in the *viscera. Also called a *visceroceptor*. *See also* interoceptor.

visible spectrum *n*. The part of the *spectrum of light that stimulates *photoreceptors in the eye and produces visual sensations, with wavelengths ranging from about 390 to 740 nanometres corresponding to the *bandwidth of the visual system.

vision *n*. **1.** One of the five classical *senses (1), stimulated by light and mediated by *photoreceptors in the retinas of the eyes. It consists of three largely independent systems that analyse information about shape, colour, and movement, respectively, and that feed sensory signals from photoreceptors along three separate visual pathways to different processing systems in the *visual cortex, rather than a single hierarchical system that processes them all together. *See also* magnocellular system, parvocellular system. **2.** An unusually vivid mental *image (3). **3.** A mystical or religious experience or divine revelation involving supernatural or paranormal perception (*the vision of St John of the Cross*). **4.** The experience of perceiving an apparition or ghost (*I had a vision of my late father*). **5.** The faculty of wise judgement or foresight (*We need a leader with vision*). **visual** *adj*. Of or relating to *vision (1) or the eyes.

[From Latin *visio* sight, from *videre* to see + *-ion* indicating an action, process, or state]

visual accommodation *n*. Another name for *accommodation (1).

visual acuity *n*. The keenness or sharpness of *vision (1), measured by various devices such as an *acuity grating, *Landolt circles, *König bars, or a *Snellen fraction. *See also* acuity, dynamic visual acuity, minimum separable, minimum visible, stereoscopic acuity, vernier acuity.

visual adaptation *n*. A generic term for *chromatic adaptation (1), *dark adaptation, *light adaptation, *prism adaptation, *transient tritanopia, or any other form of *adapta-

tion (2) affecting *vision (1). *See also* field adaptation, visual aftereffect.

visual aftereffect *n*. Any visual experience that follows and is caused by an earlier visual stimulus, including *afterimages and an important class of *visual illusions. *See* Aubert effect, contingent aftereffect, figural aftereffect, McCollough effect, motion aftereffect, spiral aftereffect, successive contrast, tilt aftereffect, waterfall illusion.

visual angle *n*. The angle subtended at the nodal point of the eye's crystalline lens by a visual stimulus, determined jointly by the size of the stimulus and its distance from the observer. The visual angle subtended by the moon in the night sky is almost exactly one-half of a degree or 30 minutes of arc, this being the *angular size* of the stimulus. Labelling the visual angle θ (degrees), if the linear size (height, width, or diameter) of the stimulus is h and its distance from the observer is d, where h and d are measured in any units provided they are the same, then according to simple trigonometry $\tan(\theta/2) = (h/2)/d$. Hence for the image of a person 6 feet tall at a distance of 100 feet, $h = 6$, $d = 100$, and $\tan(\theta/2) = 3/100 = 0.03$. Using an inverse tangent button ($\tan^{-1}$) on a pocket calculator or a table of tangents, we can determine that $\theta/2 = 1.72$, therefore the visual angle θ subtended by the object is 3.44 degrees or 3 degrees and 26 minutes of arc. For small visual angles, the approximation $\tan\theta \approx h/d$ may be used, yielding in this example $\tan\theta = 0.06$ and $\theta = 3.43$ degrees, which also rounds to 3 degrees and 26 minutes of arc. The moon's diameter is 2,160 miles and its average distance is 238,900 miles, therefore $\tan\theta \approx 2,160/238,900$, yielding an angular size of $\theta \approx 0.52$. The sun's diameter is approximately 400 times that of the moon and it is 400 times further away, so by a remarkable coincidence, it subtends almost exactly the same angle at the eye. *See also* Aubert–Förster phenomenon, Emmert's law, König bars, minimum separable, minimum visible, size constancy.

visual aphasia *n*. Another name for *alexia. *See also* aphasia.

visual area *See* visual cortex.

visual association cortex *See under* visual cortex.

visual cliff *n*. An experimental apparatus for studying depth perception in infants, introduced by the US psychologists Eleanor J(ack) Gibson (1910–2002) and Richard D(avid) Walk (1920–1999) and published in the journals *Science* in 1957 and *Scientific American* in 1960, consisting of a narrow wooden board laid across the middle of a sheet of heavy glass, with a chequered material immediately beneath the glass on one side of the board and several feet below it on the other side. Although the glass surface is palpably flat and solid on both sides, the chequered pattern provides a *texture gradient indicating a deep cliff on one side of the central board, and an infant as young as 6 months who is placed on the board will happily crawl across the glass to its mother on the shallow side but will almost invariably refuse to cross the deep side in spite of strong coaxing and tactile evidence that the glass provides a solid surface. The effect has also been found in several other species, such as kittens that have just learned to walk at about 4 weeks of age and that never cross the visual cliff, and chicks less than a day old that also never cross the cliff, suggesting that depth perception is innate rather than learned by experience.

visual cortex *n*. The areas of the *cerebral cortex devoted to processing visual information from the eyes, including the *primary visual cortex and the visual association cortex. The primary visual cortex, occupying the gyri on both sides of the deep *calcarine sulcus in the *occipital cortex, is known technically as Area V1 (for Visual Area 1), and it is sometimes called the striate cortex, because it contains white bands of myelin within the cortical layers of grey matter that give it a striped appearance. Neurons in Area V1 have the smallest *receptive fields in the visual cortex. The visual association cortex, now generally called the prestriate cortex, occupies areas successively further outward from the primary visual cortex. Area V2, immediately adjacent to V1, is characterized by thin stripes responsive to colour information and thick stripes responsive to directional motion and form, separated by paler interstripes responsive only to form, and it receives inputs concerning form from layers 2 and 3 of Area V1 and relays them to Area V3; it also receives inputs concerning colour from *blobs in Area V1 and relays them to Area V4; and it receives inputs concerning movement and stereopsis

from layer 4B of Area V1 and relays them to Area V5 (also called *MT* because it is situated towards the back of the *middle temporal gyrus). Area V3, which surrounds V1 and V2, is specialized for monochromatic pattern perception, and Area V3A, which surrounds V3, is specialized for dynamic or moving form; Area V4, which occupies the *fusiform gyrus, is specialized for colour vision and form perception; and Area V5 (or MT) is specialized for the perception of visual motion and stereopsis. There are further projections from Areas V3, V4, and V5 to specialized visual areas, such as the *inferior temporal gyrus specialized for recognizing certain types of patterns, perhaps including hands, a part of the *superior temporal sulcus containing neurons that respond selectively to faces, and the *pulvinar at the back of the thalamus concerned with attention. Area V7, adjacent to V3A, has an unknown function, Area V8, adjacent to V4 at the back of the inferior temporal gyrus, processes colour vision, and an area labelled V6 has been identified only in monkeys.

visual disparity *n*. Another name for *binocular disparity.

visual dominance *n*. The tendency for visual information to determine what is perceived when there is a conflict between the visual information and information from another sensory modality, as in the *ventriloquism effect.

visual egocentre *n*. The point either midway between the eyes or at the centre of the skull where visual sensations are perceived or felt to converge. US *visual egocenter*. *See also* egocentre.

visual evoked potential *n*. An *evoked potential elicited by a visual stimulus. *See also* nerve conduction velocity. **VEP** *abbrev*.

visual field *n*. The entire area of space supplying stimuli to the visual receptors at a given time. In humans, the visual field of each eye subtends a *visual angle of about 170 degrees in the horizontal plane and there is almost complete overlap between the visual fields of the two eyes. The part of the visual field to the left of the point on which gaze is fixated is called the *left visual field (lvf)* and the area to the right the *right visual field (rvf)*, each of these areas being a *hemifield*. Also called *field of vision* or a *visual perceptual field*. *See also* appurtenance, divided visual field, Ganzfeld, homonymous hemianopia, perimetry, tunnel vision. *Compare* receptive field.

visual fixation *n*. The act or process of *fixating (1) or training one's eyes on an object or point in the visual field so that its image falls on the *foveas of the eyes.

visual hallucination *n*. A *hallucination of vision, either of fully formed images of people or objects, or of unformed visual sensations such as flashes of colour or movement.

visual illusion *n*. Any of a diverse and heterogeneous group of *illusions in the visual domain, also called *optical illusions*, the most significant of which fall into the following inexact and overlapping categories: *ambiguous figures*, which are not strictly illusory but are generally included in discussions of visual illusions, *see* Mach illusion, Necker cube, reversible goblet, Schröder staircase, Scripture's blocks, young girl/old woman figure; *associative illusions*, *see* Baldwin illusion, Craik–O'Brien effect, curvature illusion, Delboeuf illusion, Ebbinghaus illusion, Ehrenstein's brightness illusion, Ehrenstein's square illusion, filled-space illusion, filling-in illusion, Fraser spiral, Helmholtz illusion, Hering illusion, Hermann grid, hollow squares illusion, horizontal–vertical illusion, irradiation illusion, Jastrow illusion, Land effect, Margaret Thatcher illusion, Morinaga misalignment illusion, Müller-Lyer illusion, Münsterberg illusion, Orbison illusion, Ouchi illusion, pattern-induced flicker colour, Poggendorff illusion, Ponzo illusion, Sander parallelogram, star illusion, teacup illusion, top hat illusion, twisted-cord illusion, Wundt illusion, Zanforlin illusion, Zöllner illusion; *illusory contours*, *see* Ehrenstein's brightness illusion, Kanizsa triangle, random-dot stereogram; *impossible figures*, *see* Freemish crate, impossible trident, Penrose triangle, staircase illusion; *movement illusions*, *see* apparent movement (alpha movement, beta movement, gamma movement, delta movement), autokinetic effect, Cheshire cat effect, kinetic depth effect, Lissajous figure, motion capture, oculogyral illusion, optimal movement, Ouchi illusion, partial movement, phantom grating, phi movement, random-dot kinematogram, rotating head illusion, spiral aftereffect, Ternus phenomenon, vection, wagon wheel illusion, waterfall illusion, windmill illusion; *perspective illusions*, *see* Ames room, corridor illusion, horizontal–vertical illusion, moon illusion, Ponzo illusion, teacup illusion, trapezoidal window; *space-time illusions*, *see* kappa effect, tau effect; *stereoscopic illusions*, *see* anaglyph, Cheshire cat effect, floating-finger illusion, hole-in-the-hand illusion, Lissajous figure, Pulfrich effect, random-dot kinematogram, random-dot stereogram; *visual aftereffects*, *see* Aubert effect, contingent aftereffect, figural aftereffect, McCollough effect, motion aftereffect, spiral aftereffect, successive contrast, tilt aftereffect, waterfall illusion. *See also* carpentered world, Honi phenomenon, naive realism, Pepper's ghost, *trompe l'oeil*, Vierordt's law. *Compare* auditory illusion, postural aftereffect, tactile illusion.

visual image *See* image (1, 2, 3).

visual impairment *n*. Any defect of vision, especially one falling short of total blindness. *See* blindness.

visual induction *n*. A form of *induction (3) in the visual modality in which stimulus elements associated with one part of the visual field or of an object or image affect what is perceived in another. *See* associative illusion, colour contrast, lightness contrast.

visualizer *n*. A person whose characteristic style of mental imagery is visual rather than auditory, tactile, or motor. *Compare* audile (2), motile (2), tactile (2).

visual masking *n*. A reduction or elimination of the detectability of a brief (shorter than 100 milliseconds) visual stimulus called the *test stimulus* by the presentation of a second stimulus called the *masking stimulus* either before the test stimulus (*forward masking), at the same time as the test stimulus (*simultaneous masking), or after the test stimulus (*backward masking). When the test stimulus and masking stimulus do not overlap spatially, forward masking is called *paracontrast and backward masking is called *metacontrast. The term was introduced in 1925 by the French experimental psychologist Henri Piéron (1881–1964). *See also* brightness masking, central masking, dichoptic masking, inspection time, masking, Perky phenomenon.

Visual–Motor Gestalt Test *See* Bender Gestalt Test. **VMGT** *abbrev*.

visual pigment *n*. Any of four different *pigments that are contained in *rods and *cones in the retinas of the eyes and that absorb light over a broad range of the *visible spectrum but are maximally sensitive to either short wavelengths (blue light), medium wavelengths (green light), or long wavelengths (red, orange, and yellow light), the rod pigment *rhodopsin having peak sensitivity to light of approximately 510 nanometres in the green part of the spectrum and the *cone pigments having peak sensitivity at approximately 430 nm, 530 nm, and 560 nm, usually called blue, green, and red pigments respectively, although light of these wavelengths actually looks violet, blue–green, and yellowish-green. *See also* Bunsen–Roscoe law, chromophore.

visual purple *n*. Another name for *rhodopsin.

visual receptor *n*. Any of the *rods or *cones in the *retina of the eyes that function as *sensory receptors by converting light stimuli into nerve impulses. Also called a *photoreceptor*.

visual search *n*. An experimental task, the objective of which is to find a particular element in a visual display, as when all occurrences of the letter *e* have to be located and crossed out as quickly as possible in a page of text. *See also* multiframe task, single-frame task.

visual suppression *n*. Momentary suspension of visual perception during a *saccade, triggered by *feedforward of the efferent output of the extra-ocular muscles, eliminating the impression of movement that would otherwise be created by the motion of the eyes, which cause movements of the images across the retinas. If a visual display linked to an automatic eye-movement tracker is altered only during saccades, the viewer does not perceive the changes occurring but may eventually become conscious of the fact that the image is no longer the same as it was. Also called *saccadic suppression*.

visual system *n*. A generic name for the totality of structures of the nervous system involved in vision.

visual violet *n*. Another name for *iodopsin.

visual word-form dyslexia *n*. A generic name for *attentional dyslexia, *neglect dyslexia, and *spelling dyslexia. Also called *peripheral dyslexia*.

visuospatial sketchpad *n*. A subsystem of *working memory that functions as a *buffer store for visually coded information.

vitamin *n*. Any of a number of organic substances (thus excluding trace minerals) that are present in foods in small quantities (thus excluding fats, carbohydrates, and proteins) and are necessary for normal *metabolism. **vitamin A** *n*. *Retinol, a fat-soluble *vitamin necessary for *scotopic vision, formed by *hydrolysis of beta-carotene (*see under* carotene), which is found in carrots and other yellow and green vegetables, butter, eggs, fish oil. **vitamin B complex** *n*. A group of water-soluble *vitamins found especially in yeast and liver, necessary for the normal function of the cardiovascular and nervous systems, including thiamine (vitamin B_1), riboflavin (vitamin B_2 or, especially in the US, vitamin G), pyridoxine (vitamin B_6), and cyanocabalamin (vitamin B_{12}). **vitamin C** *n*. Ascorbic acid, a white, crystalline, water-soluble *vitamin found in citrus fruits, tomatoes, green vegetables, and potatoes, necessary for repair of fibrous tissue, as an antioxidant scavenging *free radicals that can damage cells, and as a cofactor in the synthesis of *adrenalin (epinephrine) and *noradrenalin (norepinephrine); the human body cannot store it and a deficiency causes scurvy. **vitamin D** *n*. A group of fat-soluble *vitamins found in cod-liver oil and other fish oils, milk, butter, and eggs, also synthesized from cholesterol in the skin when exposed to sunlight, a deficiency causing rickets and osteoporosis. **vitamin E** *n*. Tocopherol, a group of fat-soluble *vitamins found in wheatgerm, lettuce, nuts, soybean, and eggs, necessary for normal reproduction and for maintaining *pituitary gland, *adrenal gland, and *sex hormones. **vitamin G** *n*. Another name for vitamin B_2. **vitamin H** *n*. Another name (especially in US) for biotin, one of the B complex vitamins. **vitamin K** *n*. A group of fat-soluble *vitamins found in green vegetables, eggs, fish-liver oils, necessary for blood clotting, also called *quinones*. **vitamin P** *n*. A group of water-soluble *vitamins found in citrus fruits, blackcurrants, and rosehips, necessary for maintaining the permeability of the blood capillaries, also called *bioflavinoids*.

[From Latin *vita* life + English *amine*, from *am(monium)* + Greek *-ine* indicating an amine, first identified and named in 1912 by the Polish-born US biochemist Casimir Funk (1884–1967) in the mistaken belief that they are amines]

vitamin therapy *See* orthomolecular therapy.

vitreous humour *n*. The transparent gelatinous substance that fills the eyeball between the crystalline lens and the retina. US *vitreous humor*.
[From Latin *vitreus* made of glass, from *vitrum* glass, probably related to *videre* to see]

VNTR *abbrev*. Variable number of tandem repeats. VNTR genetic loci are those containing *repetitive DNA.

vocal cords *n*. Two pairs of membranes in the *larynx. The upper pair are called false vocal cords and are not involved in speech production; the lower pair (true vocal cords) are the *vocal folds.

vocal folds *n*. A pair of membranes, resembling lips, stretched across the *larynx from front to back and capable of closing and opening to form a space called the *glottis. During speech production, the airstream from the lungs causes them to vibrate, and this vibration, amplified by resonators of the chest, throat, mouth-cavity, nose-cavity, and sinuses, results in the production of vocal sounds. Also called *(true) vocal cords*.

vocal tic disorder *n*. Any *tic disorder in which the predominant symptom is a vocal tic. *See also* tic.

vocal tract *n*. The part of the air passage from the lungs that lies above the *larynx. The part of the air passage below the larynx is the *trachea.

vocational aptitude test *n*. In psychometrics, any *aptitude test designed to predict how successful the respondent is likely to be in a particular occupation.

voice box *n*. A non-technical name for the *larynx.

voiceprint *n*. A *sound spectrograph of a person's voice. It was claimed in the 1960s that voiceprints are as distinctive as fingerprints, and people were convicted in courts of law on the evidence of voiceprint identification. Experiments subsequently established that the technique is less reliable than had originally been thought, and much less reliable than fingerprints or genetic fingerprints, but more advanced and reliable techniques of voice recognition have replaced it. *See also* sound spectrogram.

void mode *n*. A manner of viewing a coloured surface through a small aperture so that only a small and isolated area of the surface is visible at one time. Under these conditions the *Land effect disappears, and some *non-spectral colours such as brown cannot be perceived at all, the appearance of brown arising only when a yellow surface is darker than its surround. *See also* retinex theory. *Compare* anorthoscopic, reduction screen.

volaemic thirst *n*. Another name for *hypovolaemic thirst. US *volemic thirst*.

volley theory *n*. A refinement of the *frequency theory of pitch perception, first proposed in 1939 by the US psychologist Ernest Glen Wever (1902–91), according to which the ear converts acoustic vibrations into nerve impulses for frequencies between about 500 hertz (the maximum firing rate of individual auditory neurons) and 5,000 hertz (above which the *place theory provides an adequate explanation) by causing groups of neurons to fire repeatedly and slightly out of phase with one another, producing a stream of nerve impulses more rapid than the firing rate of any individual neuron, analogously to volleys of arrows from a group of asynchronous archers arriving at their target more frequently than the maximum firing rate of any individual archer. Also called the *platoon-volley theory*. *Compare* frequency theory, place theory.

voltage-gated ion channel *n*. An *ion channel, the permeability of which is regulated by changes in the cell's *membrane potential. *Compare* chemically gated ion channel.

volume *n*. **1.** The magnitude of the three-dimensional space occupied by a solid or a quantity of fluid (*brain volume, blood volume*); hence, figuratively, a quantity or amount of anything (*volume of trade*). **2.** The perceived magnitude of space filled by a sound, loud and

low-pitched sounds generally appearing to fill more space than soft and high-pitched sounds. **3.** Another name for *loudness, but this sense is avoided in careful usage. **4.** A bound book, especially one belonging to a series.
[From Latin *volumen* a roll or book, from *volvere* to turn or roll up]

volume colour *n.* Another name for *film colour. US *volume color.*
[So called in contrast to surface colour]

volumetric thirst *n.* Another name for *hypovolaemic thirst.
[From Greek *volumen* a roll + *metron* a measure + *haima* blood]

voluntary involuntary treatment *n.* Another name for a *Ulysses contract.

voluntary muscle *n.* Any muscle controlling voluntary functions and consisting of *striped muscle tissue, including any *skeletal muscle. The *cardiac muscle, though striped, is an exception in not being a voluntary muscle. *See also* muscle. *Compare* involuntary muscle.

volunteer (research or experimental) *n.* Another name for a *subject (research or experimental) or *participant (research or experimental).

vomeronasal organ *n.* A slender horizontal groove ending in a blind pouch in the nasal *mucous membrane on each side of the septum separating the nostrils in most mammals. In non-human mammals and reptiles it is highly developed and functions as a sensitive olfactory organ that responds to *pheromones, but in human adults it is rudimentary and possibly vestigial, though there is some evidence that it functions as a receptor for *steroid molecules and mediates the *Whitten effect, even in humans. Also called *Jacobson's organ*. **VNO** *abbrev.*
[From *vomer* the bone separating the nasal passages in mammals, from Latin *vomer* a ploughshare + *nasalis* of or relating to the nose, from *nasus* the nose]

von Osten's horse *See* Clever Hans.

von Restorff effect *n.* A tendency, when attempting to recall a list of words or other items that have been learned, to show superior recall for any item that has a high degree of *salience (1), a typical example being a word printed in differently coloured ink. Also called the *Restorff effect* or the *isolation effect*. *See also* next-in-line effect.
[Named after the German psychologist Hedwig von Restorff (1906–62) who first reported it in 1933]

voodoo death *n.* Death or apparent death resulting from the effects of voodoo, a set of religious beliefs and practices of West African origin, surviving in Haiti and other parts of the Caribbean and in scattered communities in the southern United States. Voodoo formerly involved human sacrifice and cannibalism; it now involves sorcery and curses so frightening that they are believed to be capable of causing the death of their victims, though some of the deaths may be apparent rather than real and may result from poisoning by sorcerers attempting zombification—*see* zombie (2). In Haitian voodoo (or vodun), the physical parts of a human being are the *corps cadavre* (mortal flesh), which decays after death, and the *n'âme* (spirit of the flesh), which passes into the soil. The spiritual parts are the *z'étoile* (star of destiny) and the two components of the soul, namely the *gros-bon-ange* (great good angel) and the *ti-bon-ange* (little good angel), both of which survive death and are susceptible to sorcery. Also called *thanatomania*. *See also* zombie (2).
[From Louisiana French *voudou*, from West African Ewe *vodu* a guardian spirit]

voting paradox *n.* Another name for *Condorcet's paradox.

vowel *n.* A speech sound, almost invariably forming the main part of a syllable, that involves no significant obstruction of the airstream through the *vocal tract. Various features distinguish the sound of one vowel from another, notably whether the front, central part, or back of the tongue is raised, leading to *front vowels, *central vowels, and *back vowels respectively, and how high the tongue is raised towards the roof of the mouth, leading to *close vowels, *mid vowels, and *open vowels. These features are often portrayed on a *vowel quadrilateral* representing the mouth schematically (see illustration overleaf). *Compare* consonant, semivowel.
[French *voyelle*, from Latin *vox* a voice]

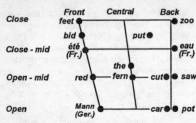

Vowel quadrilateral

voyeurism *n.* A *paraphilia characterized by recurrent, intense sexual fantasies, urges, or behaviour involving the surreptitious observation of people who are naked, undressing, or engaging in sexual activity. *See also* scopophilia. **voyeur** *n.* A person given to *voyeurism, often referred to non-technically as a *peeping Tom. *Compare* écouteur.
[From French *voyeur* one who observes or sees]

vulva *n.* The orifice of the *vagina, constituting the external genitalia of a human female, including the labia majora, labia minora, and clitoris.
[From Latin *vulva* a covering or womb]

VX *abbrev.* The chemical name of methylphosphonothioic acid, a colourless and odourless liquid that was developed in the UK in 1949, that turns into a potent *nerve gas when exposed to air, and that is stockpiled by the United States and other countries as a potential chemical weapon. It blocks the transmission of nerve impulses in the central nervous system, causing convulsions and respiratory failure, its effect being immediate. Just 10 milligrams on the skin is enough to kill an average adult male. Formula: $C_{11}H_{26}NO_2PS$.

Vygotsky blocks *n.* A test of *concept formation in which the respondent is presented with 32 blocks differing in shape, colour, width, and height and is asked to sort them into categories according to codes written on their undersides. The respondent is not told the meaning of the codes, but blocks with the same code belong to the same category, one code being used for all tall and wide blocks, a second code for short and wide blocks, a third code for tall and thin blocks, and a fourth code for short and thin blocks, colour and shape being irrelevant. Also spelt *Vigotsky blocks*, and sometimes referred to as the *Vygotsky test* or *Vigotsky test*.
[Named after the Russian psychologist Lev Semyonovich Vygotsky (1896–1934) who used them extensively in his research, though he credited their development to his colleague L. S. Sakharov]

Wada test *n*. A procedure for determining which cerebral hemisphere is dominant for speech production by injecting an anaesthetic (sodium amytal) into one of the carotid arteries that supply blood to the brain and noting whether speech is immediately disrupted, indicating that the anaesthetized hemisphere is dominant for speech.
[Named after the Japanese-born Canadian physician Juhn Atsushi Wada (born 1924) who introduced it in 1949]

waggle dance *n*. One of two patterns of movement, described by the Austrian zoologist Karl von Frisch (1886–1982) in a series of publications from 1924 onwards, through which a female honey-bee communicates to other members of her hive the direction and distance of a source of nectar or a new nesting site more than a certain distance away—more than about 5–80 metres away, depending on the bee species or subspecies. The bee describes a repeated figure of eight on the (usually) vertical surface of a honeycomb, moving in a straight line while waggling her abdomen swiftly (3–15 hertz) from side to side, looping back to perform another straight waggling run from the same point, then looping back for a further straight waggling run, and so on, alternating the return loops between left (anticlockwise) and right (clockwise) (see illustration). The direction of the waggling run relative to the perpendicular indicates the direction of the target relative to the position of the sun, the liveliness and length of the dance, how rich the food source is; and the tempo of the dance, the distance of the food source—for example, in the giant honey-bee *Apis dorsata*, 40 complete figures of eight per minute indicates 15 metres, 27 per minute indicates 30 metres, and 19 per minute indicates 610 metres. This comes closer to being a *language (1) than any other non-human communication system. *Compare* round dance.

[Translated from von Frisch's German *Schwänzeltanz* literally tail-wagging dance, from *schwänzeln* to wag one's tail, from *Schwanz* a tail + *Tanz* a dance]

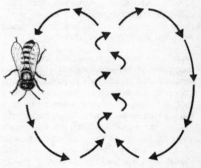

Waggle dance

Wagner–Meissner corpuscle *n*. Another name for *Meissner's corpuscle.
[Named after the German anatomists Rudolf Wagner (1805–64) and Georg Meissner (1829–1905) who both studied it]

wagon wheel illusion *n*. A visual illusion caused by *aliasing in which a rotating wheel or other object, when viewed in a cinema or television picture or under *stroboscopic illumination, appears to turn slowly one way, then slowly the other way as its rotation gathers speed. If the picture or stroboscopic frequency is exactly synchronized to a multiple of the rotation frequency, then the rotating object appears stationary. *Compare* windmill illusion.

Wald–Wolfowitz runs test *n*. In statistics, a *non-parametric and *distribution-free test of the randomness of an ordered sequence of binary or dichotomous observations, in which the number of *runs expected on the basis of chance is calculated and compared with the observed number of runs. Also called the *runs test*.

[Named after the Romanian-born US statistician Abraham Wald (1902–50) and the Polish-born US statistician Jacob Wolfowitz (1910–81) who developed it in 1940]

Wallerian degeneration *n*. Disintegration of a nerve fibre following injury or disease distal to the nerve cell body, progressing from the site of the lesion along the axon away from the nerve cell body, leaving the segment between the nerve cell body and the site of the injury intact. It is sometimes induced experimentally to trace projections from particular areas to unknown destination sites. Also called *anterograde degeneration*.

[Named after the English physiologist Augustus V(olney) Waller (1816–70)]

Ward's method *n*. In statistics, a widely used technique of *cluster analysis that begins with isolated individuals or cases and progressively combines them into clusters, and then combines clusters, until every individual is in the same cluster. At each stage in the analysis individuals or clusters that merge are those that result in the smallest increase in the sum of the squared distances of each individual from the mean of its cluster. Ward's method is a form of *agglomerative hierarchical clustering.

[Named after the US educational psychologist Joe Henry Ward, Jr (born 1926), who developed the technique in 1963]

warm/cold effect *See* trait centrality.

warm spot *n*. A small area of the *skin supplied by *free nerve endings that transmit sensations of warmth when touched by warm stimuli. *See also* paradoxical warmth, paradoxical heat. *Compare* cold spot.

warmth contrast *n*. The apparent increase in the warmth of a stimulus when it is juxtaposed with or follows shortly after a cooler stimulus, or its apparent decrease in warmth if it is juxtaposed with or follows a warmer stimulus. *See also* contrast (2), simultaneous contrast, successive contrast, thermal adaptation.

War of the Ghosts *n*. A haunting native American folk tale that has been widely used

to study memory since the English psychologist Sir Frederic Charles Bartlett (1886–1969) introduced it into psychology for his experiments on *serial reproduction and *successive reproduction and recorded it in his book *Remembering: A Study in Experimental and Social Psychology* (1932). He chose it because of its capacity to arouse vivid imagery and because it was taken from a radically different culture and 'seemed likely to afford good material for persistent transformation' (p. 64). This is the story exactly as Bartlett presented it, apart from new paragraphs, which have been suppressed for reasons of space: 'One night two young men from Egulac went down to the river to hunt seals, and while they were there it became foggy and calm. Then they heard war-cries, and they thought: "Maybe this is a war party". They escaped to the shore, and hid behind a log. Now canoes came up, and they heard the noise of paddles, and saw one canoe coming up to them. There were five men in the canoe, and they said: "What do you think? We wish to take you along. We are going up the river to make war on the people". One of the young men said: "I have no arrows". "Arrows are in the canoe", they said. "I will not go along. I might be killed. My relatives do not know where I have gone. But you", he said, turning to the other, "may go with them." So one of the young men went, but the other returned home. And the warriors went on up the river to a town on the other side of Kalama. The people came down to the water, and they began to fight, and many were killed. But presently the young man heard one of the warriors say: "Quick, let us go home: that Indian has been hit". Now he thought: "Oh, they are ghosts". He did not feel sick, but they said he had been shot. So the canoes went back to Egulac, and the young man went ashore to his house, and made a fire. And he told everybody and said: "Behold I accompanied the ghosts, and we went to fight. Many of our fellows were killed, and many of those who attacked us were killed. They said I was hit, and I did not feel sick". He told it all, and then he became quiet. When the sun rose he fell down. Something black came out of his mouth. His face became contorted. The people jumped up and cried. He was dead.' (p. 65)

Wason selection task *n*. A simple but tricky logical puzzle introduced in 1966 by the English psychologist Peter C(athcart) Wason (born 1924) and widely used to study *problem solving. Four cards are laid on a table with their uppermost faces showing the following letters and numbers: E, K, 4, 7. The respondent is told that each card has a number on one side and a letter on the other. The following rule may or may not be true: *If a card has a vowel on one side, then it has an even number on the other side*. Which cards would have to be turned over to determine whether or not the rule is true? The vast majority of respondents choose only the card showing E, or the card showing E and the card showing 4. The correct answer is E and 7. If the card showing E turned out to have an odd number on the other side, or if the card showing 7 turned out to have a vowel on the other side, that would disprove the rule. But the card showing 4 is irrelevant, because the rule does not state that a card with an even number on one side must have a vowel on the other, and therefore turning over this card could neither prove nor disprove the rule. The failure of most respondents to select the card showing 7, which could disprove the rule, and their tendency to select the irrelevant card showing 4, were interpreted by Wason as evidence of a *confirmation bias. According to some researchers, errors in this task may also be due partly to a *matching bias—a tendency to focus attention on evidence that contains the letters and numbers mentioned explicitly in the rule that is being tested. The problem can be framed in realistic rather than abstract terms. In one influential Italian experiment, participants were shown a sealed and an unsealed envelope face down, and an envelope with a 50-lire stamp and an envelope with a 40-lire stamp face up, and were asked which envelopes would be turned over to prove or disprove the rule: *If a letter is sealed, then it has a 50-lire stamp on it*. This is the identical problem; but when it is presented in this way, most people solve it easily—a classical *framing effect. Also called *Wason's four-card selection task* or simply the *four-card problem*.

Wason's 2-4-6 problem *See* 2-4-6 problem.

waterfall illusion *n.* A visual illusion of *apparent movement created by gazing for a period of time at a fixed point in a waterfall and then looking at a stationary object, which appears to move upwards. It is usually produced in the laboratory by means of an endless belt of horizontal stripes or dots at which a viewer is instructed to stare fixedly. If the belt is stopped

after about 30 seconds, the vivid illusion is created that it is drifting backwards, but in a strange manner, appearing to move without changing position. The illusion was first discussed in print by the Greek philosopher Aristotle (384–322 BC) in the *Parva Naturalia* in the essay *On Dreams*, although Aristotle did not mention waterfalls: 'When people turn away from looking at objects in motion, for example rivers, and especially those that flow very rapidly, things really at rest are then seen as moving' (Chapter 2, Bekker edition, p. 459b). Also called the *waterfall effect. See also* motion after-effect. *Compare* Plateau spiral.

water intoxication *n.* A condition of irritability, lethargy, and confusion, sometimes followed by convulsions and coma, caused by drinking an excessive quantity of water, leading to an abnormally low concentration of *sodium in the blood.

water-jar problem *n.* Any logical problem involving the measurement of a specified volume of liquid using jars of different capacity, first introduced into cognitive psychology in 1942 by the US psychologist Abraham S(amuel) Luchins (born 1914) to study *Einstellung effects in *problem solving. A typical complex water-jar problem requiring an indirect solution is as follows. Given empty jars holding 21 quarts, 127 quarts, and 3 quarts, obtain 100 quarts of water; this is solved by filling the 127-quart jar and then from it filling the 21-quart jar once and the 3-quart jar twice, leaving 100 quarts as required in the 127-quart jar. A simple water-jar problem such as the following can be solved directly. Given empty jars holding 15 quarts, 39 quarts, and 3 quarts, obtain 18 quarts of water; this can be solved directly by filling the 15-quart and 3-quart jars and then emptying their contents into the 39-quart jar. In an experiment with college students, Luchins found that after solving several complex problems, 81 per cent of the students used the same indirect procedure with simple problems that could be solved directly, and only 17 per cent used the direct approach, whereas 100 per cent of students who had not been exposed to the complex problems solved the simple problems directly. Previous success with the indirect technique apparently created an *Einstellung* or *set (2) that blinded students to the direct approach. *See also* Aufgabe, General Problem Solver, set (2).

water on the brain *n.* A non-technical name for *hydrocephalus.

wavelength *n.* The distance between successive peaks of a wave, measured in the direction of propagation. Wavelength (λ) is equivalent to the velocity of propagation (v) divided by wave frequency (f): $\lambda = v/f$. The *visible spectrum of light extends from a wavelength of about 390 nanometres at the violet end to about 740 nm at the red end, and the *audibility range of sound waves from about 21.44 metres at the low end to 1.72 centimetres at the high end.

W cell *n.* A type of ganglion cell with a slow-conducting axon found in the retina and the lateral geniculate nuclei, not clearly classifiable as an X cell or a Y cell, projecting to cells lying in the *parvocellular system of the *lateral geniculate nucleus concerned with colour vision and from there to *blobs in the upper layers of the *primary visual cortex.

weak AI *n.* An interpretation of *artificial intelligence according to which conscious awareness is a property of certain brain processes, and whereas any physical behaviour can, in principle at least, be simulated by a computer using purely computational procedures, computational simulation cannot in itself evoke conscious awareness. *See also* Chinese room, Gödel's theorem. *Compare* strong AI.

weal response *See under* axon reflex.

weapon focus *n.* A tendency for eyewitnesses to a crime involving a firearm to concentrate their attention on the weapon and as a consequence to show relatively poor subsequent recall of other aspects of the incident, in particular poor ability to identify the offender. The underlying psychological mechanism responsible for this phenomenon is *sharpening.

Weber–Fechner law *n.* Another name for *Fechner's law, Fechner himself having called it Weber's law, acknowledging the contribution to its development of the German psychophysiologist Ernst Heinrich Weber (1795–1878).

Weber fraction *n.* In *psychophysics, a ratio, differing from one type of sensory experience to another, representing the smallest increment in the magnitude of a stimulus that can be detected under ideal testing conditions, and that is a constant for each type of sensation according to *Weber's law. Its value has been determined experimentally as $k = 1/62$ for visual brightness discrimination, $k = 1/333$ for auditory pitch discrimination, $k = 1/11$ for auditory loudness discrimination, $k = 1/53$ for weight discrimination, and so on. *See also* Weber's law.
[Named after the German psychophysiologist Ernst Heinrich Weber (1795–1878) who discovered it and published it in Latin in 1834 and in German in 1846]

Weber's law *n.* In *psychophysics, the proposition that the smallest detectable difference in the magnitude of a stimulus (the *Weber fraction) is proportional to the magnitude of the lesser stimulus. Thus, for example, the smallest difference in weight that can be detected is proportional to the original weight, so that most people can just barely feel the difference in weight between an object of 530 grams and one of 540 grams, or between 1,060 grams and 1,080 grams, the *Weber fraction being 1/53 for weight discrimination according to experimental tests. The law is usually expressed by the equation $(\Delta I)/I = k$, where ΔI is the *difference threshold in physical magnitude, I is the magnitude of the lesser stimulus, and k is the Weber fraction, which is a constant for any type of sensation but that varies from one type of sensation to another. The law is accurate over most of the usable ranges for most sensory modalities (across 99.9 per cent of the range of visual brightness intensities that can be tested without damaging people's eyes, across 999,999-millionths of the usable range of auditory loudness intensities, and so on) but it breaks down at the extremes, and for auditory pitch perception the Weber fraction remains constant above 500 hertz but is slightly larger for lower pitches. *Compare* Fullerton–Cattell law.
[Named after the German psychophysiologist Ernst Heinrich Weber (1795–1878) who formulated it in 1834]

Wechsler Adult Intelligence Scale *See under* Wechsler scales.

Wechsler Intelligence Scale for Children *See under* Wechsler scales.

Wechsler Preschool and Primary Scale of Intelligence *See under* Wechsler scales.

Wechsler scales *n.* A suite of *intelligence tests based on a test originally developed in 1939 as the Wechsler–Bellevue (WB) scale by the Romanian-born US psychologist David Wechsler (1896–1981). The *Wechsler Adult Intelligence Scale* (third revision) or WAIS-III and the *Wechsler Intelligence Scale for Children* or WISC-III are among the most highly regarded intelligence tests, and the *Wechsler Preschool and Primary Scale of Intelligence* or WPPSI and the *Wechsler Abbreviated Scale of Intelligence* or WASI are also well known. Each of these scales has to be administered individually by a trained tester, and each yields three separate scores: verbal IQ, performance IQ, and full scale IQ. The verbal subtests of the WAIS-III and WISC-III include information (general knowledge), digit span (repeating back a string of numbers that are read out), vocabulary (explaining the meanings of words), arithmetic (solving arithmetic problems), comprehension (explaining the reasons for everyday things), and similarities (explaining what things have in common). The performance subtests include picture completion (pointing out missing elements in several line drawings, such as the numeral 8 missing from a clock face or a leg missing from a crab), picture arrangement (arranging a number of pictures into a sequence that tells a meaningful story), block design (arranging painted wooden blocks to copy designs formed by the examiner), object assembly (fitting a number of shapes together like large jigsaw pieces to make recognizable objects), and digit symbol (learning a code in which each digit is represented by a symbol, and then substituting the correct symbols for a series of digits as quickly and accurately as possible). The *correlations between scores on the subtests are all moderate or high.

weed *n.* Any useless or unwanted plant. Also, a common street name for *cannabis, especially in the form of *marijuana.

Weigl–Goldstein–Scheerer tests *See* Goldstein–Scheerer tests.

Weismannism *n.* The doctrine of the continuity of the *germ plasm and its rigid segregation from the mortal bodies in which it resides, including the notion that the *germ line can influence the body but not vice versa. *See also* central dogma.
[Named after the German biologist August Friedrich Leopold Weismann (1834–1914) who expounded it in a series of articles in 1889–92]

well-defined problem *n.* In the study of *problem solving, any problem in which the initial state or starting position, the allowable operations, and the goal state are clearly specified, and a unique solution can be shown to exist. Typical examples are the *Tower of Hanoi, *Wason selection task, and *water-jar problems. A problem that lacks one or more of these specified properties is an *ill-defined problem, and most problems that are encountered in everyday life fall into this category. Also called a *well-structured problem. See also* problem-solving stages.

Wells effect *n.* A reluctance to make judgements of legal liability on the basis of naked statistical evidence alone. In the original experiments, evidence from tyre tracks providing an 80 per cent probability that a particular bus company was responsible for running over a dog persuaded fewer than 20 per cent of experienced judges and people without legal training to rule against the bus company, although they were instructed to decide on the balance of probabilities. In contrast, evidence that the particular bus company was responsible for running over the dog, based on an analysis of tyre tracks that was said to be 80 per cent reliable, persuaded almost 70 per cent to rule against the company. Thus, evidence that is 80 per cent reliable is sufficient to persuade most people, but naked statistical evidence of an 80 per cent probability is not, although the mathematical probability is the same in both cases. *See also* base-rate fallacy, subjective probability, taxicab problem.
[Named after the US psychologist Gary L(eroy) Wells (born 1950) who first drew attention to the phenomenon in 1992]

well-structured problem *n.* Another name for a *well-defined problem.

Weltanschauung *n.* A world view, philosophy, or distinctive outlook of a particular individual or group.
[From German *Welt* world + *Anschauung* view or opinion]

wendigo *n.* A variant spelling of *windigo.

Wernicke–Korsakoff syndrome *n.* A generic name for disorders of the *central nervous system resulting from a deficiency of thiamine (vitamin B_1), usually caused by chronic *alcohol dependence, with the signs and symptoms of *Wernicke's encephalopathy and/or *Korsakoff's psychosis.

Wernicke's aphasia *See under* aphasia.

Wernicke's area *n.* A region of the *cerebral cortex towards the back of the *superior temporal gyrus (temporal operculum), between Heschl's gyrus and the angular gyrus, usually in the left *cerebral hemisphere, involved in the comprehension of both spoken and written language. Lesions in this area are associated either with Wernicke's aphasia, also called *auditory aphasia*, *receptive aphasia*, or *sensory aphasia* (*see under* aphasia), or with logagnosia (*see under* agnosia). *See also* planum temporale. *Compare* Broca's area.
[Named after the German neuropsychiatrist Karl Wernicke (1848–1905) who discovered it in 1874]

Wernicke's encephalopathy *n.* A degenerative brain disorder resulting from a deficiency of thiamine (vitamin B_1), usually caused by chronic *alcohol dependence, characterized by lesions in the hypothalamus and elsewhere, causing *diplopia, *nystagmus, *dyskinesia, and intellectual impairment.
[Named after the German neurologist Karl Wernicke (1848–1905) who first described it in 1881]

Wertherism *n.* Morbid sentimentality. *See also* Werther syndrome. **Wertherian** *adj.*
[Named after the hero of Goethe's novel *The Sorrows of Young Werther* (1774), the publication of which led to a spate of suicides among young men]

Werther syndrome *n.* A pattern of imitative *cluster suicides following the well-publicized suicide of a famous person.

Wheatstone–Panum limiting case *n.* Another name for *Panum's limiting case.
[Named after the English physicist and inventor Sir Charles Wheatstone (1802–75) who discovered and reported it in 1838 and the Danish physician and physiologist Peter Ludvig Panum (1820–85) who rediscovered it in 1858]

whistled speech *n.* A form of human communication by whistling used by certain communities in Central and South America, the Canary Islands, and Turkey. When used for this purpose, whistling follows closely the rhythms and intonation contours of speech, allowing the listener to translate the whistled tones into ordinary language.

white blood cell *n.* Another name for a *leucocyte. Also called a *white blood corpuscle*.

white matter *n.* The whitish tissue of the brain and spinal cord, composed chiefly of myelinated neurons, the whiteness being due to the *myelin and not the nerve tissue, which is grey. Also called (technically) the *substantia alba*. *Compare* grey matter.

whiteness constancy *n.* Another name for *lightness constancy.

white noise *n.* A sound wave or any other *time series that is essentially random, all frequencies within a specified range being represented with equal intensity or energy. The sound of a radio or television receiver tuned between stations is white noise. The Russian statistician Evgeny Evgenievich Slutsky (1880–1948) proved in 1927 that a time series with a periodic structure can be transformed into white noise by passing it through a linear filter such as a *moving average, and white noise can be transformed back into the periodic time series by passing it through the reverse linear filter, and this theorem is the basic principle of time-series modelling. *See also* noise (2). *Compare* coloured noise, frozen noise, pink noise.
[So called by analogy with white light, which contains all spectral frequencies in equal proportion]

whitigo *n.* Another name for *windigo.

Whitten effect *n.* The synchronization of the *oestrous cycles of a group of females living together, occurring only when a male or his *pheromone is present. It has been observed in rats, hamsters, voles, goats, cows, sheep, and humans, and is believed to operate via the *vomeronasal organ. Also called the *male mouse effect*. *Compare* Lee–Boot effect.

[Named after the Australian reproductive biologist Wes (Wesley Kingston) Whitten (born 1918) who first reported it in 1959]

whole object n. In *Kleinian analysis, any person or other entity that serves as an *instinctual object satisfying another person's sexual *instinct (3), the first instance in human development usually being the mother. It is distinguished from a *part object that is a portion of a whole object serving the same function, such as the mother's breast. See also depressive position, good object, instinctual object, object relations, splitting of the object.

whole tone n. Another name for a *tone (2).

whole-word method n. A method of teaching reading by encouraging children to recognize the shapes of entire words rather than individual letters and their associated sounds. Also called look-and-say method. Compare phonics (2).

Whorfian hypothesis n. Another name for the *Sapir–Whorf hypothesis.

Widrow–Hoff rule n. Another name for the *delta rule.

wife/mother-in-law figure n. Another name for the *young girl/old woman figure. Also called the wife-mistress figure.

Wilcoxon matched-pairs test n. In statistics, a popular *significance test that is used with two related samples to test the *null hypothesis that the distributions of two variables are identical. It makes no assumptions about the shapes of the distribution of the two variables and it is therefore a *distribution-free test. It involves calculating the absolute values of the differences between the two variables for each individual or case and then converting these differences to *ranks, and the test statistic is computed from the sums of ranks for negative and positive differences. The distribution-dependent alternative is the *related scores t test.
[Named after the Irish statistician Frank Wilcoxon (1892–1965) who developed the test in 1945]

Wilcoxon rank-sum test n. An alternative name for the *Mann–Whitney U test, not to be

confused with the *Wilcoxon matched-pairs test.

Wild Boy of Aveyron n. A boy, about 10 years old, discovered in 1798 by a group of hunters near Aveyron in France, after living in the forest, roaming about almost naked, apparently without human contact. He was studied in detail by the French physician Jean Marie Gaspard Itard (1774–1838) and is considered a classic example of a *feral child.

wild psychoanalysis n. A term introduced in 1910 by Sigmund Freud (1856–1939), in an article entitled ' "Wild" Psycho-Analysis' (Standard Edition, XI, pp. 221–7), to denote amateur attempts at *psychoanalysis based on ignorance or misunderstandings of its fundamental ideas, such endeavours being characterized by attempts to rush the process of analysis through premature *interpretations (2) conveyed to the patient without proper *working through and without regard for *resistance and *transference. Appropriately, Freud's article was published in the same year that the International Psycho-Analytic Association was founded.

Williams syndrome n. A rare condition (estimated to occur in 1 out of 20,000 births) characterized by delayed physical and mental development, leading to *mild mental retardation, coupled with strengths in such areas of functioning as language usage, face recognition, social skills, and musical performance. It was discovered in 1993 that the syndrome is caused by the deletion of the gene that directs the manufacture of elastin, a protein providing strength and elasticity to blood vessels, from one of the two copies of chromosome 7 present in every body cell. People with this syndrome, who are often called Williams people or Williams children, have facial features reminiscent of elves or pixies, hoarse voices, *hyperacusis or extreme sensitivity to noise, cardiovascular problems, and elevated levels of calcium in the blood. Compare Down's syndrome.
[Named after the New Zealand cardiologist John Cyprian Phipps Williams (born 1922) who first described it in 1961]

will therapy n. A type of *psychotherapy, introduced by the Austrian *psychoanalyst Otto Rank (1884–1939) in his book Will Therapy and Truth and Reality (1945), in which the patient is encouraged to exert will power in order to develop autonomy and independence.

will to power *n.* In *individual psychology, a term introduced by the Austrian psychiatrist Alfred Adler (1870–1937) to denote the need, especially in men, to outdo and to dominate others.

windigo *n.* A rare *culture-bound syndrome found among North American Indian tribes in the subarctic cultural area, characterized by symptoms such as depression, homicidal or suicidal thoughts, and a compulsive desire to eat human flesh, often prompting warnings to family and friends to get as far away as possible, followed by the afflicted person turning into a cannibal, regarded locally as a monster and generally ostracized or put to death. The reality of this syndrome, as opposed to its status as a localized folk myth, is controversial. Also spelt *wendigo, whitigo*.
[From Ojibwa *wintiko* a flesh-eating monster]

windmill illusion *n.* A visual illusion first described by the English mathematician Robert Smith (1689–1768) in his book *A Compleat System of Opticks* (1738), in which the blades of a windmill, seen from a distance silhouetted against the sky, appear to reverse their direction of rotation. The direction of rotation sometimes becomes indeterminate, and Smith pointed out that the illusion can also be observed in weather-cocks and flags. It should not be confused with the *wagon wheel illusion but is closely related to the *kinetic depth effect.

windpipe *n.* A non-technical name for the *trachea.

winner's curse *n.* A tendency for the highest bid at an auction to exceed the true market value of the lot or prize. It arises from the fact that the bidders' estimates of the value of the prize are unreliable; some bidders are likely to underestimate the value and others to overestimate it, and it is the bidder who overestimates it the most who is likely to make the highest bid and to win the prize, in which case the winner is, in this sense, a loser. The effect has been confirmed by both experimental and field studies. It can be explored with the following demonstration, based on a classic experiment published in the *Journal of Conflict Resolution* in 1983. Fill a jar with coins

and auction it off to the highest bidder among a group of friends. The average bid will probably be less than the value of the coins, because of *risk aversion among bidders, but the winning bid will probably exceed the value of the coins, dramatically illustrating the winner's curse and providing a small profit for the auctioneer. The phenomenon was first discussed in an article on the purchase of oil-drilling rights in the *Journal of Petroleum Technology* in 1971 and was subsequently analysed in depth by the US economist Richard H. Thaler (born 1945).

Winnicottian *adj.* Of or relating to the theories and practices of the English psychoanalyst Donald Woods Winnicott (1896–1971). *See* good-enough mother, object-relations theory, squiggle game, transitional object. *See also* basic trust versus basic mistrust.

win-stay, lose-change strategy *n.* A simple strategy, applicable to any sequential decision task or *game (1), according to which the first decision or move is chosen arbitrarily, and thereafter, whenever a choice leads to reward or a satisfactory outcome the player repeats it on the following occasion, and whenever it leads to punishment or an unsatisfactory outcome the player switches to a different option on the following occasion. If applied to the *minimal social situation, it leads to mutually rewarding choices after only three rounds. It amounts to an implementation of the *law of effect. It was first suggested in 1962 by the US psychologist Harold H. Kelley (born 1921) and several colleagues in the journal *Psychological Monographs*. It has also been called PAVLOV because of its simple reflex properties.

Wisconsin Card Sorting test *n.* A widely used test of abstract thinking, planning, and ability to alter mental *set (2) as circumstances require. The test consists of 128 cards differing in colour, form, and number of design markings, and the respondent tries to match them to four target cards, the test administrator telling the respondent merely whether each sort is right or wrong but not what the rule is, and in the latter stages of the test the sorting rule is changed without warning, requiring the respondent to show flexibility. The test was developed at the University of Wisconsin by the US psychologist David A(lexander) Grant (born 1916) and Esta A. Berg and first published in the *Journal of General Psychology* in 1948. It is regarded as a good indicator of *frontal lobe damage, and is especially useful for identifying *perseveration (1, 2). **WCST** *abbrev.*

Wisconsin General Test Apparatus *n.* A device incorporating a presentation tray and a moveable screen for studying learning and perception in rhesus monkeys. Several objects are placed on the tray, just outside the cage, and the monkey selects one of them, then the screen is lowered, the placement of the objects is altered, and then the screen is lifted and the monkey chooses again, and so on. **WGTA** *abbrev.*
[So called because it was developed at the University of Wisconsin]

wish fulfilment *n.* Satisfaction of a desire, especially, in *psychoanalysis, the satisfaction of an *unconscious (1) desire in a disguised way such as a *fantasy (2), *dream (1), *symptom, or *parapraxis. *See also* dream analysis.

withdrawal *n.* A constellation of *signs (1) and *symptoms manifested by a person with drug *dependence (2) or *addiction after ceasing to take the drug or reducing the dosage, varying from one drug to another but often including agitation, anxiety, delirium, insomnia, dysphoria, running nose, muscle pains, sweating, fever, tremor, formication, and nausea. Also called *abstinence syndrome*. *See also* nalorphine, substance dependence, substance withdrawal delirium.

withdrawal of cathexis *n.* Another name for *decathexis.

within-subjects design *n.* Any research design in which the same research participants or subjects are tested under different *treatment conditions. *See also* Latin square, related scores *t* test, repeated-measures analysis of variance. *Compare* between-subjects design.

Witzelsucht *n.* A pattern of verbal punning and inappropriate jocularity often observed in people with *frontal lobe lesions.
[From German *witzeln* joking + *Sucht* sickness or mania]

Wolffian duct *n.* Either of the pair of ducts that are present in a human *embryo, along-side the pair of *Müllerian ducts, and that develop into the male internal reproductive tract if embryonic *testes are present and secrete *testosterone and *Müllerian inhibiting substance. In a female embryo the default development occurs: the Wolffian ducts atrophy and disappear because of the absence of testosterone, while in the absence of Müllerian inhibiting substance the Müllerian ducts develop into Fallopian tubes, uterus, and the upper part of the vagina.
[Named after the German anatomist Kaspar Friedrich Wolff (1733–94)]

Wolf Man *n.* The nickname given in the literature of *psychoanalysis to a 23-year-old Russian patient analysed in 1910–14 by Sigmund Freud (1856–1939) and discussed in 1918 in a case study entitled 'From the History of an Infantile Neurosis' (*Standard Edition*, XVII, pp. 7–122). The nickname refers to a terrifying dream about wolves that the patient had experienced at the age of $3\frac{1}{2}$, which Freud interpreted as a symbolic representation of the *primal scene of parental intercourse that he had witnessed two years earlier. The case generated a great deal of material that appeared to confirm Freud's theories and refute those of the Austrian psychiatrist Alfred Adler (1870–1937) and the Swiss psychologist Carl Gustav Jung (1875–1961), who had defected from the psychoanalytic movement in 1911 and 1913 respectively.

woman, phallic *See* phallic woman.

woolsorter's disease *n.* An obsolescent name for *anthrax.
[So called because woolsorters used to be at risk of contracting it from sheep]

word-association test *n.* A research technique pioneered by the English explorer, amateur scientist, and psychologist Sir Francis Galton (1822–1911) and published in 1879/80 in the journal *Brain*, then reinvented in 1904 as a diagnostic aid or *projective test by the Swiss psychologist Carl Gustav Jung (1875–1961). In the technique popularized by Jung, a list of (usually 100) stimulus words is read out, the patient or subject responding to each stimulus word as quickly as possible with the first response word that comes to mind, and then the exercise is repeated a second time with the same list of words. The stimulus words are selected to cover a wide range of topics and generally include a number of *critical words* that are likely to have particular psychological significance (Jung's original list included such critical words as *beat*, *dead*, *fear*, *kiss*, *pure*, *ridicule*, and *sick*), and the person's responses, occurring before *defence mechanisms have time to intervene, are assumed to reveal aspects of unconscious mental processes and especially *complexes (2), enabling the analyst to focus in on the key areas of unconscious conflict. According to Jung, the major *complex indicators* are unusual reactions such as laughing or blushing, abnormally long reaction times, repetition of the stimulus word, absurd or far-fetched associations, and failure to respond to a stimulus word. Jung published an account of the technique as a *lie detector test in an article entitled 'The Association Method' in the *American Journal of Psychology* in 1910 and expounded it in detail in his book *Studies in Word-Association* (1919), after he had founded his school of *analytical psychology. *See also* experimentally induced false memory, Kent–Rosanoff Free Association Test, Marbe's law. **WAT** *abbrev.*

word blindness *n.* A non-technical name for *alexia or *dyslexia. It was the original term used by the German physician Adolf Kussmaul (1822–1902), who first described dyslexia in 1877.

word-building test *n.* A cognitive task in which a respondent is given a set of letters from which to construct as many words as possible.

word completion task *n.* Another name for a *word-stem completion task.

word constancy *n.* A form of *perceptual constancy according to which a spoken word tends to sound recognizably the same despite wide variations both between and within speakers in *paralanguage, including *accent (1), *loudness, *pitch, *prosody, *rhythm, *tempo, and *timbre.

word deafness *n.* An impaired ability to understand spoken language; another name for Wernicke's aphasia. Also called *word meaning deafness*. *See under* aphasia.

word-form dyslexia *See* visual word-form dyslexia.

word-length mnemonic *n.* A memory aid based on the numbers of letters in a sequence of words. *See under* mnemonic.

word-presentation *n.* In *psychoanalysis, the linguistic and largely auditory representation of memories accompanying non-linguistic *thing-presentations in the *preconscious and *consciousness, in contrast to the purely thing-presentations in the *unconscious (2). Sigmund Freud (1856–1939) argued that in *schizophrenia, word-representations are sometimes treated like thing-representations, and in an article entitled 'A Metapsychological Supplement to the Theory of Dreams' (1915/17) he described a similar phenomenon occurring in dreams: 'Where the word-presentations occurring in the day's residues are recent and current residues of *perceptions*, and not the expressions of thoughts, they are themselves treated like thing-presentations' (*Standard Edition*, XIV, pp. 217–36, at p. 228).

word salad *n.* A non-technical name for *incoherence.

word-stem completion task *n.* A cognitive task in which the respondent is given the first few letters of a word (such as *VIK . . .*) and tries to complete the word as quickly as possible. Also called a *word completion task* or a *stem completion task*.

word superiority effect *n.* A *configural superiority effect, making a letter more easily recognizable when it is seen in the context of a word than on its own. Thus, if several observers are shown brief *tachistoscopic exposures and are asked to press one button if the word *fact* appears and another button if the word *fast* appears, they will tend to respond quicker and more accurately than if the stimuli are the letter *c* and the letter *s* presented in isolation. This type of *context effect presents a serious challenge to researchers who believe that letters must be recognized in order to identify words. **WSE** *abbrev.*

working memory *n.* According to a theory put forward by the English psychologists Alan (David) Baddeley (born 1934) and Graham J(ames) Hitch (born 1946) in a book chapter in 1974, a temporary store for recently activated items of information that are currently occupying consciousness and that can be manipulated and moved in and out of *short-term memory. It consists of a *central executive and two *buffer stores, called the *phonological loop and the *visuospatial sketchpad, its functions are carried out largely in the *prefrontal cortex of the brain, and it is tested in a variety of organisms by means of *delayed-response tasks and tests of *object permanence. *See also* ACT*.

working through *n.* In *psychoanalysis, the process by which an *interpretation (2) is conveyed to a patient, overcoming the *resistance that it has previously generated and enabling the patient to accept repressed ideas or wishes underlying *symptoms. Sigmund Freud (1856–1939) described this process most fully in his article on 'Remembering, Repeating and Working-Through' (1914, *Standard Edition*, XII, pp. 147–56).

work psychology *n.* An umbrella term for all aspects of *occupational psychology and *industrial/organizational psychology.

W process *n.* In *psychoanalysis, a term used by Sigmund Freud (1856–1939) to denote any function of the *perception–consciousness system. Also called a *ω process* or a *Pcpt-Cs process*.

writing disorder *See* written expression, disorder of.

written expression, disorder of *n.* A *learning disability characterized by substantially below-average writing skills for the given age, intelligence, and education, interfering substantially with scholastic or academic achievement or everyday life and not being due merely to a sensory deficit.

wryneck *n.* A non-technical name for *spasmodic torticollis.

Wundt illusion *n.* A visual illusion in which a pair of straight lines appear to be bowed inwards when superimposed on a pattern of lines converging to points on either side of them. It is closely related to the *Hering illusion.
[Named after the German psychologist Wilhelm (Max) Wundt (1832–1920) who first published it in 1896]

Würzburg school *n.* A school of psychological thought that flourished under the leadership of the Latvian-born German psychologist Oswald Külpe (1862–1915) from 1894 until his death in 1915. Külpe worked in Leipzig for eight years with the founder of the structuralist school Wilhelm (Max) Wundt (1832–1920) before moving to Würzburg in 1894, where he founded the school that became an important rival to the *structuralism (2) of Leipzig. Whereas Wundt discouraged experimental research into higher mental processes such as thinking, Külpe and his followers concentrated their research largely on thinking, attention, and aesthetic responses. The Würzburg school is remembered chiefly for claiming to have discovered *imageless thought.

Xanax *n.* A proprietary name for the benzodiazepine drug *alprazolam.
[Trademark]

xanthine *n.* The white, crystalline compound methylxanthine or any substituted derivative of it, especially the three methylated derivatives *caffeine, *theobromine, and *theophylline that are pharmacologically active as central nervous system *stimulants, acting through increasing the permeability of neuron cell membranes to calcium, the major psychological effects at low doses being a decrease in fatigue and drowsiness, an increase in speed and efficiency, and a decrease in the number of errors (especially in an overlearned task such as typing). Formula: $C_5H_4N_4O_2$.
[From Greek *xanthos* yellow, alluding to the lemon-yellow residue that it leaves when evaporated with nitric acid]

xanthopsia *n.* A visual defect in which everything in the visual field appears to have a yellow hue. It can be induced temporarily by prolonged exposure to blue light, and it is sometimes associated with jaundice or poisoning with *digitalis or foxglove. *See also* chromatic adaptation (1).
[From Greek *xanthos* yellow + *ops* an eye + *-ia* indicating a condition or quality]

X cell *n.* A type of ganglion cell belonging to the *parvocellular system, present in the retina and the lateral geniculate nuclei. Also called a *P cell*.

X chromosome *n.* A type of *sex chromosome present in pairs in all of the diploid cells of females, and present singly, paired with a *Y chromosome, in all diploid cells of males.
[So called because of its resemblance to the letter X]

xenoglossia *n.* A facility claimed by some spirit mediums, clairvoyants, and other psychics to speak in languages that they have never learnt. Xenoglossia should be distinguished carefully from *glossolalia.
[From Greek *xenos* foreign + *glossa* a tongue + *-ia* indicating a condition or quality]

X-linked *adj.* Of or relating to a gene situated on the *X chromosome or a *character (2) or *trait determined by such a gene. Most X-linked disorders and conditions, including *Duchenne muscular dystrophy, haemophilia, and various forms of *colour-blindness, are determined by *recessive genes carried by females on an X chromosome but expressed predominantly in males who have only one X chromosome, preventing *complementation from occurring. A female can inherit such a gene, but its effects are normally masked by a normal *dominant *allele, unless the female inherits the abnormal allele from both parents. *See also* daltonism, hologynic, Horner's law, sex-linked. *Compare* Y-linked. **X-linkage** *n.*

XTC *n.* A street name for *ecstasy (2).
[From the similarity in sound; not an abbreviation]

XXX syndrome *n.* A chromosomal abnormality in which a woman has three *X chromosomes instead of the usual two, leading to deficits in auditory and language comprehension, and usually sterility. *Compare* Klinefelter's syndrome, XYY syndrome.

XXY syndrome *n.* Another name for *Klinefelter's syndrome.

XYY syndrome *n.* A chromosomal abnormality in which a man has an extra *Y chromosome, often leading to antisocial behaviour and violence. *Compare* antisocial personality disorder, Klinefelter's syndrome, Turner's syndrome, XXX syndrome.

yang See under yin and yang.

Yates' correction for continuity n. In statistics, a correction sometimes applied before performing the *chi-square test on data in a 2 × 2 contingency table to improve the approximation to the theoretical distribution, which is a continuous distribution in contrast to the discrete scores being analysed. Corrected chi-square values are always smaller than uncorrected values.
[Named after the English statistician Frank Yates (1902–94) who published the correction in 1934]

YAVIS abbrev. Young, attractive, verbal, intelligent, successful, the syndrome of personal qualities that counsellors, therapists, and people in general supposedly find most appealing in their clients or associates. This idea first appeared in 1964 in the book Psychotherapy: The Purchase of Friendship by the US psychologist William Schofield (born 1921). Compare HOUND.

Y cell n. A type of ganglion cell belonging to the *magnocellular system, present in the retina and the lateral geniculate nuclei. Also called an M cell.

Y chromosome n. A *sex chromosome occurring in all of the diploid cells of males, paired with an *X chromosome.
[So called because of its resemblance to the upper-case letter Y]

yellow bile See under humour (3).

yellow bullets n. A street name for the barbiturate drug *pentobarbital (pentobarbitone).

yellow-sighted adj. Experiencing *xanthopsia.

yellow spot n. Another name for the *macula lutea.

Yerkes–Dodson law n. The proposition that optimal task performance occurs at an intermediate level of *arousal, with relatively poorer performance at both lower and higher arousal levels, leading to an inverted U relation between arousal and performance. It is often accompanied by the proposition that the peak occurs at a lower level of arousal for easy than for difficult tasks. **YDL** abbrev.
[Named after the US psychologists Robert Mearns Yerkes (1876–1956) and John Dillingham Dodson (1879–1955) who published an article in the Journal of Comparative Neurology and Psychology in 1908 on the 'Relation of Strength of Stimulus to Rapidity of Habit-formation', though they did not enunciate the law explicitly or attempt to test it directly]

Yerkish n. An artificial language, using a computer console with keys bearing geometrical symbols for words, developed by the US primatologists Duane Rumbaugh (born 1929) and Sue Savage-Rumbaugh (born 1946) for communicating with chimpanzees.
[Named after the Yerkes Regional Research Center in Georgia, US, where the language was developed, which in turn is named after the US psychologist Robert Mearns Yerkes (1876–1956), who founded the parent laboratory in Florida in 1919]

yin and yang n. In traditional Chinese philosophy, two complementary principles of the universe, yin being a passive female principle that is cold, wet, dark, and earthly, and yang being an active male principle that is hot, dry, light, and heavenly. Their balance is believed to maintain the harmony of the universe and of everything in it, including human bodies and minds. See also syzygy.
[From Chinese yin dark + yang bright]

yips *n.* A type of focal *dystonia associated with psychological tension or anxiety, common among golfers but, for reasons unknown, seldom afflicting snooker, pool, or billiards players, usually experienced as a *tremor, *spasm, or weakness in the fingers or hands before making a shot (especially a golfing putt) and described as *having the yips.* [Origin unknown]

Y-linked *adj.* Of or relating to a gene situated on the *Y chromosome or a characteristic or *trait determined by such a gene, such as hirsutism of the ears and certain other characteristically masculine traits. No significant Y-linked disorders are known. *See also* holandric, sex-linked. *Compare* X-linked. **Y-linkage** *n.*

yohimbine *n.* A crystalline alkaloid, found in the bark of the tropical African yohimbe tree *Corynanthe yohimbe,* that acts as a noradrenalin (norepinephrine) *agonist (3) and is taken as a *sympathomimetic central nervous system *stimulant drug and, in its hydrochloride form, as an *aphrodisiac. Formula $C_{21}H_{26}N_2O_3$. [From Bantu *yohimbé* the yohimbe tree + *-ine* indicating an organic compound]

yoked control *n.* In experimental designs in which members of an *experimental group and a *control group are paired, the control group members receiving the same stimuli, reinforcements, or punishments as the experimental group members but without the possibility of influencing these effects through their own behaviour, the effects being controlled by the experimental group members alone.

young girl/old woman figure *n.* A popular *ambiguous figure that does not depend on

Young girl/old woman figure

figure-ground reversal and that appears as a portrait of a young girl or an old woman (see illustration). It was copied from an anonymous German postcard issued in 1888 and published as a cartoon by the US artist William Ely Hill (1887–1962) in *Puck* magazine in 1915 under the title *My Wife and My Mother-in-law. They are Both in this Picture—Find Them,* then it was adapted and republished in 1930 by the US psychologist Edwin Garrigues Boring (1886–1968), to whom it is often wrongly attributed. In 1961 the US psychologist Jack Botwinik (born 1923) published a version equally as unflattering to old men entitled *Husband and Father-in-law.* Also called the *old woman/young girl figure,* the *wife/mistress* figure, or (misleadingly) the *Boring figure.*

Young–Helmholtz theory *n.* Another name for the *trichromatic theory of colour vision. [Named after the English physician, physicist, and Egyptologist Thomas Young (1773–1829) who proposed it in 1802 and the German physiologist, physicist, and mathematician Hermann Ludwig Ferdinand von Helmholtz (1821–94) who subsequently championed it]

Zanforlin illusion *n.* A visual illusion in which a straight line extending between the most distant points on the circumferences of two circles appears shorter than a line of the same length extending between the nearest points on the circumferences of two similar circles (see illustration). It is closely related to the *Baldwin illusion and possibly also the *Müller-Lyer illusion.
[Named after the Italian psychologist Mario Zanforlin who first described it in 1967]

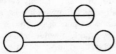

Zanforlin illusion. The horizontal straight lines are equal in length.

zar *n.* A *culture-bound syndrome found in Ethiopia and other areas of North Africa, and among Arab communities in various parts of the Middle East, characterized by episodes of *dissociation that are locally attributed to spirit possession and are associated with signs and symptoms such as shouting, laughing, self-injury or self-mutilation, singing and weeping, often followed by apathy and withdrawal. The condition is traditionally dealt with through elaborate ceremonies of exorcism involving singing, dancing, and drinking the blood of a sacrificed ram. Also called *sar* in Somalia and elsewhere.
[Amharic *zar* an evil spirit]

Z-disc *n.* A dark line separating two *sarcomeres of muscle tissue, being the membranes to which the *actin filaments of the sarcomere are attached. US *Z-disk.* Also called a *Z-line.*

Zeigarnik effect *n.* The tendency for interrupted tasks to be recalled better than com-

pleted tasks. The effect is temporary and does not occur with all types of tasks.
[Named after the Russian psychologist Bluma Zeigarnik (1900–88), who first reported it in the journal *Psychologische Forschung* in 1927]

Zeitgeber *n.* An environmental cue as to the passage of time, such as the *diurnal cycle of light and dark, that tends to calibrate and synchronize a *biological clock to the external passage of time. Also called a *synchronizer*. *See also* entrainment.
[From German *Zeitgeber* a timer, from *Zeit* time + *geben* to give]

Zener cards *n.* A deck of 25 cards used in research into *extra-sensory perception. On the face of each card is printed one of five symbols (circle, cross, square, star, or wavy lines); therefore, the chance probability of a hit is 1/5 for an individual card, and the number of hits expected on the basis of chance alone for the complete pack is five. Also called *ESP cards.*
[Named after the US psychologist Karl E. Zener (1903–64) who devised them at Duke University in 1930 and objected in vain to their being named after him]

zenith distance *n.* The direction of an object or image in a vertical plane relative to a point directly overhead. *Compare* azimuth.
[From Old Spanish *zenit* zenith, from Arabic *samt*, short for *samt-al-ras* overhead, from *samt* direction + *al* the + *ras* head]

zero-crossing *n.* In *computational theories of vision, a location where the *luminance in a smoothed or blurred visual image changes abruptly. Zero-crossing segments that align with one another for different levels of smoothing form the basis of *contours in the *primal sketch.
[So called because in mathematical terms it is a region where the second derivative of the

luminance function changes from positive through zero to negative or from negative through zero to positive]

zero-order approximation to language *See* approximation to language.

zero-sum game *n.* In *game theory, a game in which the sum of the players' payoffs is equal to zero in every outcome of the game. Two-person zero-sum games are *strictly competitive games*, in which the players' interests are directly opposed, one player's gain invariably being equal to the other's loss. *See also* minimax theorem. *Compare* mixed-motive game.

Zipf's laws *n.* **1.** A law of linguistics stating that the rank (r) of a word on a frequency list multiplied by the frequency (f) with which the word is used is a constant (C), hence $rf = C$. For example, in the London–Lund corpus of spoken English, the words *see*, *which*, and *get* are the 45th, 55th, and 65th most frequently used words, and their frequencies are 674, 563, and 469 respectively; thus $45 \times 674 = 30,330$, $55 \times 563 = 30,965$, and $65 \times 469 = 30,485$; in each case $rf = 30,500$ approximately. This relationship has been confirmed in many languages, but it is now known that it tends to break down for words at both extremes of the frequency range. **2.** A law of linguistics stating the existence of an inverse relation between the lengths of words and their frequency, resulting presumably from the fact that frequently used words tend to be shortened, so that *pianoforte* becomes *piano*, *omnibus* becomes *bus*, *television* becomes *telly*, *zoological garden* becomes *zoo*, and so on.
[Named after the US philologist George Kingsley Zipf (1902–50) who formulated both laws]

Zöllner illusion *n.* A visual illusion in which parallel straight lines appear to converge and diverge alternately when intersected by a herring-bone pattern of oblique stripes (see illustration).
[Named after the German astronomer Johann Karl Friedrich Zöllner (1834–82) who first reported it in 1860 after observing it in the pattern of a piece of dressmaking fabric]

Zoloft *n.* A proprietary name for the antidepressant drug *sertraline.
[Trademark]

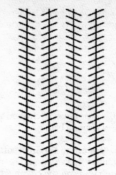

Zöllner illusion. The long lines are straight and parallel.

zombie *n.* **1.** In informal usage, a person who appears to be lifeless, apathetic, and unresponsive to the external environment, or one who behaves like an *automaton. **2.** A being believed to belong to the living dead, a corpse resurrected by witchcraft, especially in the voodoo cult of Haiti and in certain West African religions from which it is derived. In Haitian voodoo, a person who has been given a *coup poudre* (magic powder) by a voodoo sorcerer, called a *bokor*, appears to die, is buried, and is exhumed a few days later as an apparently soulless zombie to work as the *bokor*'s slave. In 1982 the Irish–Canadian ethnobiologist (Edmund) Wade Davis (born 1953) discovered that *coup poudre* is made from puffer fish and other ingredients containing the powerful neurotoxin *tetrodotoxin (TTX), and in his book *The Serpent and the Rainbow* (1985) he put forward a theory of zombiism according to which ingestion of a barely sub-lethal dosage of the poison results in a deep coma resembling death, and both the poison and the live burial cause extensive neurological damage, so that the victim who is later exhumed and revived has few intact memories or mental capacities and no power of speech and usually adopts the shuffling gait and blank facial expression characteristic of a zombie. Although this theory has been widely accepted, there is evidence that some zombies, at least, are simply people with severe or profound *mental retardation. Also spelt *zombi*. *See also* voodoo death. **zombify** *vb.* To turn someone into a *zombie (1, 2), or deprive a person of vitality or spirit.
[From Kikongo *zumbi* a fetish, from *nzambi* a spirit of a dead person]

zona fasciculata *n*. The middle portion of the *adrenal cortex, where *glucocorticoids and other hormones are produced.
[From Latin *zona* a girdle or belt + *fasciculus* a small bundle, diminutive of *fascis* a bundle]

zona glomerulosa *n*. The outer, knotty portion of the *adrenal cortex, where *mineralocorticoids are produced.
[From Latin *glomerulus* a cluster or knot, diminutive of *glomus* a ball]

zona granulosa *n*. The granular portion of a *Graafian follicle, where the *ovum is embedded.
[From Latin *granulum* a little grain, diminutive of *granum* a grain]

zona incerta *n*. A small ribbon of nerve cell bodies on each side of the *hypothalamus that control drinking. Stimulation in this area instigates *polydipsia or excessive drinking, and a lesion can result in *adipsia or cessation of drinking.
[From Latin *zona* a girdle or belt + *incertus* uncertain or obscure, so called because its function was unknown for a long time after its discovery]

zona reticularis *n*. The innermost netlike portion of the *adrenal cortex, acting together with the *zona fasciculata to produce *glucocorticoids and other hormones.
[From Latin *zona* a girdle or belt + *reticulum* a little net, diminutive of *rete* a net]

zone of proximal development *n*. A term introduced in 1931 by the Russian psychologist Lev Semyonovich Vygotsky (1896–1934) to denote the distance between a child's 'actual developmental level as determined by independent problem solving [and the higher level of] potential development as determined through problem solving under adult guidance or in collaboration with more capable peers'. Vygotsky believed that it is most likely to emerge during play. *See* dynamic testing. Also called the *zone of potential development*. **ZPD** *abbrev.*

zonule of Zinn *n*. The ligament from which the *crystalline lens of the eye is suspended. Also called the *ciliary zonule* or the *zonula ciliaris*.
[Named after the German anatomist Johann Gottfried Zinn (1727–59) who discovered it]

zooerasty *n*. Another name for *bestiality (1).
[From Greek *zoion* and animal + *erastes* a lover]

zoophilia *n*. A *paraphilia characterized by recurrent sexually arousing fantasies, sexual urges, or behaviour involving erotic attraction of a person to an animal; more specifically, another name for *bestiality (1).
[From Greek *zoion* an animal + *philos* loving, from *phileein* to love + *-ia* indicating a condition or quality]

zoösemiotics *n*. The study of animal communication systems.
[From Greek *zoion* an animal + *semiotics*]

z score *n*. In statistics, any score expressed in units of *standard deviations of the distribution of scores in the population, with the mean set at zero and standard deviation equal to 1. Also called a *standard score* or *sigma score* or sometimes a *deviation score*. *See* standard score. *See also* derived score. *Compare* IQ, stanine score, sten score, T score.

Zwaardemaker olfactometer *n*. A device for measuring olfaction, consisting of a glass tube through which an odorant is drawn into the nostril, the amount of odour being determined by the length of the tube.
[Named after the Dutch physiologist Hendrik Zwaardemaker (1857–1930) who devised it in 1888]

Zwaardemaker smell system *n*. A scheme for classifying smells based on nine fundamental or primary odours: ethereal (like ether or beeswax), aromatic (like spice or camphor), fragrant (like lavender or rose petals), ambrosiac (like amber or musk), alliaceous (like garlic or onion), empyreumatic (like roasted coffee or tobacco smoke), hircine (like strong cheese or rancid food), foul (like bedbugs or coriander flower), and nauseous (like faeces or rotten eggs). *Compare* Crocker–Henderson system, Henning's prism.
[Named after the Dutch physiologist Hendrik Zwaardemaker (1857–1930) who published it in 1895]

zygote *n*. A fertilized *ovum or egg. *See also* blastocyst, embryo, foetus, morula.
[From Greek *zygotos* yoked, from *zygon* a yoke]

Zyprexa *n*. A proprietary name for the atypical antipsychotic drug *olanzapine.
[Trademark]

Appendixes

Appendix I: Phobias and phobic stimuli

A phobia is a persistent, irrational fear of an object, event, activity, or situation, called the *phobic stimulus*, resulting in a compelling desire to avoid it—a more detailed definition is given under the headword **phobia** in the main body of the dictionary, and the correct term for irrational fears that do not qualify as true phobias is defined under the headword **paraphobia**. This is probably a more comprehensive inventory of phobias and their etymologies than any previously published, but it has no pretensions to completeness. Virtually anything is capable of becoming a phobic stimulus, and names of phobias are often coined as nonce words, hence the number of potential phobias is unlimited, and any attempt to list them exhaustively would be futile. The entries in this appendix are restricted to phobias that have been discussed in serious publications or catalogued in general or specialist reference works. In addition to etymologies, the table includes cross-references and occasional comments on usage. Phobias with separate entries in the main body of the dictionary are flagged.

The names of most phobias are formed by combining a Greek prefix denoting the phobic stimulus with the suffix *-phobia* (from Greek *phobos* fear + *-ia* indicating a condition or quality). But many names of phobias are neoclassical hybrids, combining a Latin prefix with the Greek suffix, a typical example—one is tempted to say a classic example—being *claustrophobia*. Although frowned on by linguistic purists, this type of word-formation is well established in contemporary English: compare *sociology*, *television*, *monolingual*. There are also a few phobias that are named by combining an English (or other modern language) prefix with the Greek suffix, for example *computerphobia*.

What follows is a double-entry list. Each phobia can be looked up either under its technical name, where the phobic stimulus is specified and a brief etymology is given, or (excepting *panphobia*) under its distinguishing phobic stimulus or stimuli—spiders, confined spaces, heights, and so on—where the name of the corresponding phobia will be found. After looking up the name of a phobia, the entry under the corresponding phobic stimulus may then be consulted for alternative names, if any, of the same phobia; or after looking up a phobic stimulus, the entry under the corresponding phobia may be consulted for further information, including its etymology and occasional cross-references.

ablutophobia Bathing.
[From Latin *ablutio* the act of washing, from *abluere* to wash away]

acarophobia Bugs, mites, and other small creatures. *Compare* microphobia, parasitiophobia.
[From Greek *akaris* a mite]

accidents Dystychiphobia.

acerbophobia Sour tastes. Also spelt *acerophobia*.
[From Latin *acerbus* sour, from *acer* sharp]

achluophobia Darkness.
[From Greek *achlys* mist]

acousticophobia Noise.
[From Greek *akoustikos* relating to sound, from *akouein* to hear + *-itikos* resembling or marked by]

acrophobia Heights. *Compare* bathophobia.
[From Greek *akros* highest]

action Ergasiophobia.

aelurophobia *See* ailurophobia.

aeronausiphobia Flying in an aircraft. *Compare* aviophobia.
[From Greek *aer* air + *naus* a ship]

aerophobia Draughts or (loosely) flying.
[From Greek *aer* air]

ageing Gerascophobia.

agoraphobia Public places, crowds, travelling alone, or being away from home (for more detail, see the entry in the main body of the dictionary).
[From Greek *agora* a market-place]

aichmophobia Sharp or pointed objects or knives.
[From Greek *aichme* the point of a spear]

ailurophobia Cats. Also spelt *aelurophobia*. Also called *gatophobia* or (not quite accurately) *galeophobia*.
[From Greek *ailouros* a cat]

aircraft (flying in) Aeronausiphobia or (loosely) aerophobia.

alcoholic drinks Potophobia or dipsophobia.

alektorophobia Chickens.
[From Greek *alektor* a rooster]

algophobia Pain.
[From Greek *algos* pain]

alliumphobia Garlic.
[From Latin *allium* garlic]

alone (being) Autophobia, eremophobia, or monophobia.

amathophobia Dust.
[From Greek *amathos* sand]

amaxophobia Vehicles or travelling in a vehicle. *Compare* hodophobia.
[From Greek *amaxa* a wagon]

amnesia Amnesiophobia.

amnesiophobia Amnesia or forgetting.
[From Greek *amnesia* oblivion]

amychophobia Being scratched.
[From Greek *mychia* a scratch]

androphobia Men.
[From Greek *andros* of a man]

anemophobia Wind, draughts, or cyclones.
[From Greek *anemos* wind]

anginophobia Choking or suffocation.
[From Latin *angina* of the chest]

Anglophobia England or English people or culture.
[From Latin *Anglus* English]

animals Zoophobia.

anthophophobia Flowers.
[From Greek *anthos* a flower]

anthrophobia An aberrant form of *anthropophobia*.

anthropophobia Humanity or human beings. Also written *phobanthropy*.
[From Greek *anthropos* human]

antlophobia Floods.
[From Greek *antlia* a pump]

ants Myrmecophobia.

anus Proctophobia.

apeirophobia Infinity or endlessness.
[From Greek *apeiros* endless or infinite, from *a-* without + *peiron* an end]

aphephobia An alternative spelling of *haphephobia*.

apiphobia Bees.
[From Latin *apis* a bee]

aquaphobia Water.
[From Latin *aqua* water]

arachibutyrophobia Peanut butter, especially fear of peanut butter sticking to the roof of the mouth.
[From Latin *arachis* a leguminous plant, from Greek *arachos*, *arakis* leguminous plants + *boutyron* butter, from *bous* ox + *tyros* cheese]

arachnophobia Spiders. Also spelt *arachnephobia* or *arachniphobia*.
[From Greek *arachne* a spider]

arithmophobia Numbers.
[From Greek *arithmos* a number]

asthenophobia Weakness.
[From Greek *a-* without + *sthenos* strength]

astraphobia Thunder and lightning.
[From Greek *astrape* lightning]

astrophobia The influence of the stars. Also spelt *astrapophobia*.
[From Greek *astron* a star]

atax(i)ophobia Disorder.
[From Greek *ataxia* disorder, from *a-* without + *taxis* order]

atelophobia Incompleteness or imperfection.
[From Greek *ateles* incomplete]

attention (being the focus of) Social phobia.

atychiphobia Failure.
[From Greek *atyches* unfortunate]

aulophobia Flutes and similar wind instruments.
[From Greek *aulos* an ancient Greek wind instrument]

aurophobia Gold or money.
[From Greek *aurum* gold]

automobiles Amaxophobia.

automysophobia Being dirty.
[From Greek *autos* self + *mysos* defilement]

autophobia Oneself or being alone. *Compare* eremophobia.
[From Greek *autos* self]

aviophobia Flying. *Compare* aeronausiphobia.
[From Latin *avis* a bird]

away from home (being) Agoraphobia.

bacilli Bacillophobia or bacteriophobia.

bacillophobia Bacteria or bacilli.
[From Latin *bacillus* a little rod]

bacteria Bacillophobia or bacteriophobia.

bacteriophobia Bacteria or bacilli.
[From Greek *bakterion* a little stick]

bad luck Dystychiphobia.

bad people Scelerophobia.

baldness Phalacrophobia.

ballistophobia Projectiles, missiles, or thrown objects.
[From Greek *ballein* to throw]

basiphobia Walking.
[From Greek *basis* a step from *bainein* to step or go]

bathing Ablutophobia.

bathmophobia Stairs or escalators.
[From Greek *bathmos* a step]

bathophobia Depth or looking down from high places.
[From Greek *bathos* depth]

bathysiderodromophobia Subways or underground trains.
[From Greek *bathys* deep, from *bathos* depth + *sideros* iron + *dromos* running]

batrachophobia Frogs, toads, and newts.
[From Greek *batrachos* a frog]

beards or bearded men Pogonophobia.

bed (going to) Clinophobia.

bees Apiphobia or melissophobia.

behaviour Ergasiophobia.

belonephobia Sharp, pointed objects.
[From Greek *belone* a needle]

bibliophobia Books.
[From Greek *biblion* a book]

bicycling Cyclophobia.

birds Ornithophobia.

black people Colorphobia (US), Negrophobia.

blennophobia Slime or mucus. *Compare* myxophobia.
[From Greek *blennos* mucus]

blind spots Scotomaphobia.

blood Haematophobia or haemophobia.

blushing Erythrophobia.

body odour Bromidrosiphobia.

bogeyphobia Bogies.
[From the Scots *bogle* a spectre or goblin]

bogeys Bogeyphobia or bogyphobia.

bogyphobia An alternative spelling of *bogeyphobia*.

books Bibliophobia.

boys Paedophobia.

breasts Kolpophobia.

bridges Gephyrophobia.

bromidrosiphobia Body odour. *Compare* osmophobia.
[From Greek *bromos* a stink + *drosos* moisture]

brontophobia Thunder or thunderstorms.
[From Greek *bronte* thunder]

bugs Acarophobia.

bulls Taurophobia.

burglary Kleptophobia.

burial alive Taphophobia.

caenophobia Novelty or new things or ideas. Also spelt *cainophobia*, *caenotophobia*, *cainotophobia*, *cenophobia*, *cenotophobia*, *kainophobia*, *kainotophobia*. *Compare* neophobia.
[From Greek *kainos* new]

caino(to)phobia *See* caenophobia.

cancer Cancer(o)phobia, carcinomatophobia, or carcinophobia.

cancerphobia Cancer. Also spelt *cancerophobia*.
[From English *cancer*, from Latin *cancer* a crab, alluding to the manner in which it creeps]

canophobia Dogs.
[From Latin *canis* a dog]

carcinophobia Cancer. Also spelt *carcinomatophobia*.
[From Greek *karkinos* a crab]

cardiophobia Heart disease or heart attacks.
[From Greek *kardia* heart]

carnophobia Meat.
[From Latin *caro, carnis* meat]

cars Amaxophobia.

catagelophobia Ridicule or humiliation.
[From Greek *kata* down + *gelaein* to laugh]

catapedaphobia Jumping.
[From Greek *kata* down + Latin *pes, pedis* a foot]

cathisophobia Sitting down. Also spelt *kathisophobia*.
[From Greek *kata* down + *hizein* to seat]

catoptrophobia Reflections or mirrors. Also called *spectrophobia*.
[From Greek *katoptron* a mirror, from *kata* back and *optos* seen]

cats Ailurophobia or gatophobia.

Celtophobia Celts.
[From English *Celt*, from Latin *Celtae* the Celts]

Celts Celtophobia.

cemeteries Coimetrophobia.

cenotophobia *See* caenophobia.

chaerophobia *See* cherophobia.

chairophobia *See* cherophobia.

change Tropophobia.

cheimaphobia Cold weather. Also spelt *cheimatophobia*.
[From Greek *cheimon* winter]

cherophobia Gaiety or fun. Also spelt *chaerophobia*, *chairophobia*.
[From Greek *chero* to be pleased]

chickens Alektorophobia.

childbirth or labour Maieusiophobia, parturiphobia, or tocophobia.

children Paedophobia.

China or Chinese people or culture Sinophobia.

chins Geniophobia.

chionophobia Snow.
[From Greek *chion* snow]

choking Anginophobia, pnigophobia, or pnigerophobia.

cholera Cholerophobia.

cholerophobia Cholera.
[From Greek *cholera* jaundice, from *chole* bile]

chorophobia Dancing.
[From Greek *choros* a dance]

chrematophobia Wealth or money.
[From Greek *chrema, chrematos* money]

chrom(at)ophobia A particular colour or colours.
[From Greek *chroma, chromatos* colour]

chronophobia Time.
[From Greek *chronos* time]

church Ecclesiophobia.

cibophobia Food.
[From Latin *cibus* food]

claustrophobia Confined spaces.
[From Latin *claustrum* an enclosed space]

cleisiophobia Closed spaces.
[From Greek *kleistos* closed]

climacophobia Stairs.
[From Greek *klimax* a ladder]

clinophobia Going to bed.
[From Greek *kline* a bed]

closed spaces Claustrophobia or cleisiophobia.

clouds Nephophobia.

cnidophobia Nettle stings or stings in general.
[From Greek *knide* a nettle or sea-anemone]

coimetrophobia Cemeteries.
[From Greek *koimeterion* a room for sleeping, from *koiman* to put to sleep]

coitophobia Sexual intercourse. *Compare* cypridophobia.
[From Latin *coitio* coitus, from *co-* together + *ire, itum* to go]

cold Cheimaphobia, cheimatophobia, frigophobia, or psychrophobia.

colorphobia Coloured people or black people (US).
[From English *color*, US spelling of *colour*, from Latin *color* colour or complexion]

colour (particular) Chrom(at)ophobia.

coloured people Colorphobia (US), Negrophobia.

cometophobia Comets.
[From English *comet*, from Greek *kometes* longhaired, from *kome* hair]

comets Cometophobia.

computerphobia Computers.
[From English *computer*, from Latin *computare* to calculate, from *com-* together + *putare* to reckon]

computers Computerphobia or cyberphobia.

confined spaces Claustrophobia or cleisiophobia.

constipation Coprostasophobia.

contamination Mysophobia, rhypophobia, or scatophobia.

coprophobia Faeces (feces) or dung.
[From Greek *kopros* dung]

coprostasophobia Constipation.
[From Greek *kopros* dung + *stasis* a standstill]

corpses Necrophobia.

cremnophobia Precipices or steep places.
[From Greek *kremannynai* to hang]

criticism Enissophobia.

criticophobia Critics.
[From English *critic*, from Greek *kritikos* of or relating to judgement, from *krinein* to judge]

critics Criticophobia.

crossing streets Dromphobia.

crowds Agoraphobia, demophobia, ochlophobia.

crucifixes Staurophobia.

cryophobia Frost or ice.
[From Greek *kryos* frost]

cyberphobia Another name for *computerphobia*.
[From Greek *kybernetes* a steersman]

cycling or cyclists Cyclophobia.

cyclones Anemophobia.

cyclophobia Cycling or cyclists.
[From English *cycle*, from Greek *kyklos* a wheel]

cynophobia Another name for *canophobia*.
[From Greek *kynos* a dog]

cyprianophobia Prostitutes.
[From Greek *Kypris* Venus, the goddess of love]

cypridophobia Venereal disease and sexual activity. *Compare* coitophobia, genophobia.
[From Greek *Kypris* Venus, the goddess of love]

daemonophobia *See* demonophobia.

dampness Hygrophobia.

dancing Chorophobia.

darkness Achluophobia, nyctophobia, scotophobia.

dawn Eosophobia.

daylight Phengophobia.

death and dying Thanatophobia, necrophobia.

decidophobia Decisions or decision making.
[From English *decide*, from Latin *decidere* to decide, from *de* away + *caedere* to cut]

decisions Decidophobia.

defecation Rhypophobia.

deformity Dysmorphophobia.

deipnophobia Dinner-parties or dining.
[From Greek *deipnon* dinner]

demonophobia Demons. Also spelt *daemonophobia*.
[From Greek *daimon* a spirit or deity]

demons Demonophobia.

demophobia Crowds.
[From Greek *demos* the people]

dendrophobia Trees.
[From Greek *dendron* a tree]

depth Bathophobia.

dermatopathophobia Skin disease.
[From Greek *derma, dermatos* skin + *pathos* suffering]

dermatophobia Skin. *Compare* doraphobia.
[From Greek *derma, dermatos* skin]

deserted places Eremophobia.

design (doctrine of) Teleophobia.

destitution Peniaphobia.

devil Satanophobia.

diabetes Diabetophobia.

diabetophobia Diabetes.
[From English *diabetes*, from Greek *diabetes* a siphon, from *dia* through + *banein* to go]

dinner parties or dining Deipnophobia.

dipsophobia Drinks or drinking.
[From Greek *dipsa* thirst]

dirt Coprophobia, mysophobia, rhypophobia, scatophobia.

dirty (being) Automysophobia.

disease Pathophobia.

disease (contracting a specific) Nosophobia or monopathophobia.

disorder Ataxiophobia or ataxophobia.

doctors Iatrophobia.

dogs Canophobia or cynophobia.

domatophobia Being confined at home. *Compare* oikophobia.
[From Greek *domation* diminutive of *doma* a house]

doraphobia Fur. *Compare* dermatophobia.
[From Greek *dora* skinning]

drafts Aerophobia or anemophobia.

draughts Aerophobia or anemophobia.

drinking Dipsophobia, phobodipsia, potophobia.

dromophobia Crossing streets.
[From Greek *dromos* a public way]

drugs (medicinal) Pharmacophobia.

dung Coprophobia, rhypophobia, or scatophobia.

dust Amathophobia.

duty (neglecting) Paraleipophobia.

dysmorphophobia Any personal physical deformity (for more detail, see the entry in the main body of the dictionary).
[From Greek *dys* bad or abnormal + *morphe* form]

dystychiphobia Accidents or bad luck.
[From Greek *dys* bad or abnormal + *tyche* luck]

eating Cibophobia, phagophobia.

ecclesiophobia The Church and its traditions.
[From Greek *ekklesia* the church]

economic globalization Globaphobia.

ecophobia *See* oikophobia.

emetophobia Vomiting.
[From Greek *emetikos* causing vomiting, from *emeein* to vomit + *-itikos* resembling or marked by]

empty spaces Kenophobia.

endlessness Apeirophobia.

England or English people or culture Anglophobia.

enissophobia Criticism.
[From Greek *enisso* attack or reproach]

entomophobia Insects.
[From Greek *entomon* an insect]

eosophobia Dawn or sunrise.
[From Greek *eos* dawn]

epistemophobia Knowledge.
[From Greek *episteme* knowledge]

equinophobia Another name for hippophobia.
[From Latin *equinus* of or pertaining to horses, from *equus* a horse]

erection (loss of during intercourse) Mesomalacophobia.

eremophobia Solitude, loneliness, or deserted places.
[From Greek *eremos* a desert]

ergasiophobia Behaviour or action. *Compare* ergophobia, ponophobia.
[From Greek *ergasia* work or business]

ergophobia Work. *Compare* ergasiophobia, ponophobia.
[From Greek *ergon* work]

erotica Cypridophobia, erotophobia, or pornophobia.

erotophobia Sex. *Compare* genophobia.
[From Greek *Eros* the god of love]

erythrophobia Blushing or the colour red.
[From Greek *erythros* red]

escalators Bathmophobia.

Europe or the European Union (EU) Europhobia.

Europhobia Europe or (more commonly) the European Union (EU).
[From English *Europe*, from *Europa* a princess of Tyre in Greek mythology]

everything Pantophobia.

evil eye Ommatophobia.

evil people Scelerophobia.

exhaustion Kopophobia.

eyes Ommatophobia.

faeces Coprophobia, rhypophobia, or scatophobia.

failure Atychiphobia or kakorraphiophobia.

Fathers (of the early Church) Paterophobia.

fatigue Kopophobia.

fear Phobophobia.

feathers Pteronophobia.

febriphobia Fever. Also applied to a generalized fear resulting from a rise in body temperature.
[From Latin *febris* fever]

feces Coprophobia, rhypophobia, or scatophobia.

feminophobia Women.
[From Latin *femina* a woman]

fever Febriphobia or pyrexiophobia.

filth Coprophobia, mysophobia, rhypophobia, scatophobia.

final causes (doctrine of) Teleophobia.

fire Pyrophobia.

fish Ichthyophobia.

flashing lights Selaphobia.

flogging Mastigophobia.

floods Antlophobia.

flowers Anthophophobia.

flutes Aulophobia.

flying Aeronausiphobia, aerophobia, or aviophobia.

fog Homichlophobia, nebulophobia.

food Cibophobia, sitophobia, or sitiophobia.

foreigners Xenophobia.

foreign languages Xenoglossophobia.

forests Hylephobia or xylophobia.

forgetting Amnesiophobia.

France or French people or culture Francophobia or Gallophobia.

Francophobia France or French people or culture.
[From Latin *Francus* a Frank]

Friday the 13th Parascevedekatriaphobia.

fright Hormephobia.

frigophobia Cold (for a specific Chinese form, see *pa-leng* in the main body of the dictionary).
[From Latin *frigus* cold]

frogs Batrachophobia.

frost Cryophobia.

fun Cherophobia or hedonophobia.

fur Doraphobia.

gaiety Cherophobia.

galeophobia Weasels, martens, or (loosely) cats.
[From Greek *galee* a weasel or marten]

Gallophobia France or French people or culture.
[From Latin *Gallus* a Gaul]

gamophobia Marriage.
[From Greek *gamos* marriage]

garlic Alliumphobia.

gatophobia Cats.
[From Spanish *gato* a cat]

gelophobia Laughter.
[From Greek *gelaein* to laugh]

geniophobia Chins.
[From Greek *genus* a jaw]

genophobia Sex or sexual intercourse.
[From Greek *genos* begetting or producing]

gephyrophobia Bridges or crossing bridges.
[From Greek *gephyra* a bridge]

gerascophobia Ageing or old age.
[From Greek *geras* old age]

Germanophobia Germany or German people or culture.
[From English *German*, from Latin *Germanus* German]

Germany or German people or culture Germanophobia, Teutonophobia, Teutophobia.

germs Bacillophobia or bacteriophobia.

gerontophobia Old people or old age.
[From Greek *geron, gerontos* an old man]

geumaphobia Tastes.
[From Greek *geume* taste]

ghosts Phasmaphobia.

girls Parthenophobia.

glass Hyalophobia.

globalization Globaphobia.

globaphobia Globalization.
[From Latin *globus* a globe or sphere]

glossophobia Speaking.
[From Greek *glossa* a tongue]

God Theophobia.

gold Aurophobia.

graphophobia Writing.
[From Greek *graphein* to write]

Greek language, people, or culture Hellenophobia.

Greek terminology Hellenologophobia.

gymnophobia Nudity.
[From Greek *gymnos* naked]

gynephobia Women. Also spelt *gynophobia*.
[From Greek *gyne* a woman]

hadephobia Hell.
[From Greek *Hades* the underworld abode of the dead]

haematophobia Blood or the sight of blood. Also spelt *haemophobia, hematophobia, hemophobia*.
[From Greek *haima* blood]

haemophobia Blood or the sight of blood. Also spelt *haematophobia, hematophobia, hemophobia*.
[From Greek *haima* blood]

hair (excessive or unwanted) Hypertrichophobia, trichopathophobia or trichophobia.

hamartophobia Sin. *Compare* peccatophobia.
[From Greek *hamartia* sin or error of judgement]

haphephobia Being touched by another person. Also spelt *aphephobia*.
[From Greek *haphe* touch]

haptephobia Being touched by another person.
[From Greek *haptein* to touch]

heart disease or heart attacks Cardiophobia.

heat Thermophobia.

heaven Uranophobia.

hedonophobia Pleasure.
[From Greek *hedone* pleasure]

heights Acrophobia, hypsosophobia.

heliophobia The sun or sunlight. *Compare* phengophobia, photophobia.
[From Greek *helios* the sun]

hell Stygiophobia, hadephobia.

hellenologophobia Greek terminology or scientific jargon.
[From Greek *Hellen* a Greek + *logos* word, discourse, or reason]

Hellenophobia Greek people or culture.
[From Greek *Hellen* a Greek]

helminthophobia Worms.
[From Greek *helmins, helminthos* a worm]

hematophobia US spelling of *haematophobia*.

hemophobia US spelling of *haemophobia*.

hereditary disorders Patriophobia.

heresy Heresyphobia.

heresyphobia Heresy.
[From Greek *hairesis* school of thought, from *haireein* to take]

herpetophobia Reptiles.
[From Greek *herpeton* a reptile, from *herpein* to creep]

hierophobia Religion or the objects and rituals associated with religion.
[From Greek *hieros* sacred]

hippophobia Horses.
[From Greek *hippos* a horse]

hodophobia Travelling. *Compare* agoraphobia, amaxophobia.
[From Greek *hodos* a way]

home Domatophobia, oikophobia.

home (being away from) Agoraphobia.

homichlophobia Fog or mist.
[From Greek *omichle* fog or mist]

homilophobia Sermons or sermonizing.
[From Greek *homilia* a sermon, from *homos* the same + *ile* a company]

homophobia Homosexuals or homosexuality.
[From English *homo(sexual)*, from Greek *homos* the same + Latin *sexus* sex]

homosexuals or homosexuality Homophobia.

hormephobia Shock or fright.
[From Greek *hormaein* to stir up]

horses Equinophobia or hippophobia.

hospitals Nosocomephobia.

house (one's) Oikophobia. *Compare* domatophobia, ecophobia.

human beings or humanity Anthropophobia.

humiliation Catagelophobia.

hurricanes Lilapsophobia.

hyalophobia Glass.
[From Greek *hyalos* glass]

hydrophobia Water. As a symptom of rabies, hydrophobia is an inability to swallow water as a result of a contraction of the throat. *Compare* hydrophobiaphobia.
[From Greek *hydor* water]

hydrophobiaphobia Rabies. *Compare* hydrophobia.
[From English *hydrophobia*]

hygrophobia Dampness or moisture.
[From Greek *hygros* wet]

hylephobia Forests or wood. Also spelt *hylophobia*.
[From Greek *hyle* wood]

hypaegiaphobia Responsibility.
[From Greek *hypo* under + *aigis* the shield of Zeus]

hypengyophobia Responsibility.
[From Greek *hypo* under + *engys* close]

hypertrichophobia Excessive personal bodily hair. *Compare* trichopathophobia, trichophobia.
[From Greek *hyper* over + *trichos* of hair]

hypnophobia Falling asleep.
[From Greek *hypnos* sleep]

hypsosophobia Heights.
[From Greek *hypsos* height]

iatrophobia Doctors or visiting a doctor.
[From Greek *iatros* a physician]

ice Cryophobia.

ichthyophobia Fish.
[From Greek *ichthys* a fish]

iconophobia Images.
[From Greek *eikon* an image, from *eikenai* to be like]

illness Pathophobia.

illness (contracting a specific) Nosophobia.

images Iconophobia.

imperfection Atelophobia.

impotence during intercourse Mesomalacophobia.

incompleteness Atelophobia.

infinity Apeirophobia.

injury Traumatophobia.

inoculation (performing) Vaccinophobia.

insanity Lyssophobia or phrenophobia.

insects Entomophobia.

intercourse (sexual) Genophobia.

iophobia 1. Being poisoned. **2.** Rusty objects.
[From Greek *ios* poison or rust]

iron Siderophobia.

Italophobia Italy or Italian people or culture.
[From Greek *Italia* Italy]

Italy or Italian people or culture Italophobia.

jealousy Zelophobia.

Judaeophobia Judaism.
[From Latin *iudaicus* pertaining to Judaism, from *Iuda* Judah, a son of Israel]

Judaism Judaeophobia.

jumping Catapedaphobia.

kaino(to)phobia *See* caenophobia.

kakorr(h)aphiophobia Failure.
[From Greek *kakos* bad + *raphi* a shelf]

katagelophobia Ridicule or being laughed at.
[From Greek *kata* down + *gelaein* to laugh]

kathisophobia Sitting down. Also spelt *cathisophobia*.
[From Greek *kata* down + *hizein* to seat]

kenophobia Empty spaces.
[From Greek *kenos* empty]

keraunophobia Thunder.
[From Greek *keraunos* a thunderbolt]

kinesophobia Motion or movement. Also spelt *kinetophobia*.
[From Greek *kinesis* movement, from *kineein* to move]

kissing Philemaphobia.

kleptomaniac (becoming) Kleptophobia.

kleptophobia Thieves, thieving, burglary, or becoming a kleptomaniac.
[From Greek *kleptein* to steal]

knives Aichmophobia.

knowledge Epistemophobia.

kolpophobia Breasts.
[From Greek *kolpos* a breast]

kopophobia Becoming tired or exhausted.
[From Greek *kopos* fatigue]

kymophobia Waves.
[From Greek *kyma* a wave]

laevophobia The left-hand side of one's body or other objects. Also spelt *levophobia*.
[From Latin *laevus* left]

lakes Limnophobia.

laliophobia Speaking or making errors while speaking. Also spelt *lalophobia*.
[From Greek *lalia* chatter, from *lalein* to babble]

large objects Macrophobia or megalophobia.

laughed at (being) Katagelophobia.

laughter Gelophobia.

learning Sophophobia.

left-hand side Laevophobia or levophobia.

lepraphobia Another name for *leprophobia*.

leprophobia Leprosy.
[From English *leprosy*, from Greek *lepros* scaly, from *lepis* a scale, from *lepein* to peel]

leprosy Lepraphobia or leprophobia.

levophobia US spelling of *laevophobia*.

lice Pediculophobia.

lies Mythophobia.

light Photophobia. *Compare* heliophobia, phengophobia, selaphobia.

lightning Astraphobia, selaphobia.

lilapsophobia Hurricanes or tornadoes.
[From Greek *lailapas* a hurricane]

limnophobia Lakes, ponds, or pools.
[From Greek *limne* a body of water enclosed by land]

logophobia Words.
[From Greek *logos* word]

loneliness Autophobia, eremophobia, monophobia.

long words Hellenologophobia or sesquipedalophobia.

looked at (being) Scopophobia.

looking down from a high place Bathophobia.

lousiness Pediculophobia.

love Philophobia.

luck (bad) Dystychiphobia.

lyssophobia Madness, hydrophobia, or rabies.
[From Greek *lyssa* madness or rabies]

machines Mechanophobia.

macrophobia Large objects.
[From Greek *makros* large]

madness Lyssophobia or phrenophobia.

maieusiophobia Childbirth or labour.
[From Greek *maieutikos* relating to midwifery, from *maia* a midwife]

male sex Androphobia.

many things Polyphobia.

marriage Gamophobia.

martens Galeophobia.

mastigophobia Being flogged or whipped.
[From Greek *mastix* a whip]

meat Carnophobia.

mechanophobia Machines or machinery.
[From Greek *mechane* a contrivance]

medicines Pharmacophobia.

megalophobia Large objects.
[From Greek *megale* large]

melissophobia Bees.
[From Greek *melissa* a bee]

melophobia Music.
[From Greek *melos* a song]

men Androphobia.

menophobia Menstruation.
[From Greek *men* a month]

menstruation Menophobia.

mesomalacophobia Loss of erection or impotence during intercourse.
[From Greek *mesos* middle + *malakos* soft]

metal Metallophobia.

metallophobia Metal. *Compare* siderophobia.
[From Greek *metallon* a mine]

meteorophobia Meteors or one's success being short-lived (overnight success).
[From English *meteor*]

meteors Meteorophobia.

metrophobia Poetry.
[From Greek *metron* a measure]

mice Muriphobia or musophobia.

microphobia Small objects or creatures. *Compare* acarophobia, parasitiophobia.
[From Greek *mikros* small]

mirrors Catoptrophobia, spectrophobia.

missiles Ballistophobia.

mist Homichlophobia, nebulophobia.

mites Acarophobia.

mobs Demophobia or ochlophobia.

moisture Hygrophobia.

money Aurophobia or chrematophobia.

monopathophobia Contracting a specific disease.
[From Greek *monos* single + *pathos* suffering]

monophobia Being alone.
[From Greek *monos* single or alone]

monsters Teratophobia.

moon Selenophobia.

motion or movement Kinesophobia or kinetophobia.

mucus Blennophobia or myxophobia.

muriphobia Mice.
[From Latin *mus, muris* a mouse]

mushrooms Mycophobia.

music Melophobia or musicophobia.

musicophobia Music.
[From English *music*]

musophobia Mice.
[From Latin *mus, muris* a mouse]

mycophobia Mushrooms.
[From Greek *mykes* a mushroom]

myrmecophobia Ants.
[From Greek *myrmex* an ant]

mysophobia Contamination or dirt.
[From Greek *mysos* defilement]

mythophobia Lies.
[From Greek *mythos* a myth]

myxophobia Mucus. *Compare* blennophobia.
[From Greek *myxa* mucus]

name (a particular) Onomatophobia.

nautophobia The sea.
[From Greek *nautes* a sailor, from *naus* a ship]

nebulophobia Fog or mist.
[From Greek *nephele* cloud or mist]

necrophobia Death or corpses.
[From Greek *nekros* dead or dead body]

needles Belonephobia.

neglecting work or duty Paraleipophobia. Also spelt *paralipophobia*.

Negroes Colorphobia (US), Negrophobia.

Negrophobia Black people or Negroes.
[From English *Negro*, from Latin *nigrum* black]

neophobia New or novel foods (**dietary neophobia**) or other things. *Compare* caenophobia.
[From Greek *neos* new]

nephophobia Clouds.
[From Greek *nephos* a cloud]

nettle stings Cnidophobia.

new things or ideas Caenophobia or neophobia.

newts Batrachophobia.

night Nyctophobia.

noise Acousticophobia.

nosocomephobia Hospitals.
[From Greek *nosokemeion* a hospital, from *nosos* a disease + *komein* to tend]

nosophobia Disease or contracting a disease. [From Greek *nosos* a disease]

novelty Caenophobia, neophobia.

nudity Gymnophobia.

numbers Arithmophobia.

nyctophobia The night or darkness. [From Greek *nyx*, *nyktos* the night]

obscenity Pornophobia.

ochlophobia Crowds or mobs. [From Greek *ochlos* a crowd]

odontophobia Teeth or having one's teeth worked on by a dentist. [From Greek *odon* a tooth]

odour (body) Bromidrosiphobia.

odours Osmophobia.

odynophobia Pain. [From Greek *odyne* pain]

oecophobia *See* oikophobia.

oikophobia One's house or home. *Compare* domatophobia. [From Greek *oikos* a house]

old age Gerontophobia or gerascophobia.

old people Gerontophobia.

ombrophobia Rain or rainstorms. Applied more often to plants than to human beings. [From Greek *ombros* a rainstorm]

ommatophobia Eyes or the evil eye. [From Greek *omma* an eye]

oneself Autophobia.

onomatophobia A particular name or word. [From Greek *onoma* a name]

ophidiophobia Snakes. [From Greek *ophis* a snake]

ornithophobia Birds. [From Greek *ornis* a bird]

osmophobia Odours or smells. *Compare* bromidrosiphobia. [From Greek *osme* a smell]

osphresiophobia Odours or smells. *Compare* bromidrosiphobia. [From Greek *osphresis* smell]

ostraconophobia Shellfish. [From Greek *ostrakon* a shell]

overnight success Meteorophobia.

overwork Ergophobia or ponophobia.

paedophobia Children or boys. Also spelt *pedophobia* or *pediophobia*. *Compare* parthenophobia. [From Greek *pais*, *paidos* a child or a boy]

pain Algophobia or odynophobia.

pamphobia A variant spelling of *panphobia*.

panophobia A variant spelling of *panphobia*.

panphobia Sudden causeless fear or panic, hence a phobia without a phobic stimulus. Often misdefined and misinterpreted as fear of everything, on a mistaken assumption (a folk etymology) that it derives from the Greek *pan* all. *Compare* pantophobia, polyphobia. [From Greek *Pan* the god of pastures, flocks, and woods, who supposedly inspired fears]

pantophobia Everything. Often confused with *panphobia*, which has a different meaning and etymology. *Compare* polyphobia. [From Greek *pantos* all]

papaphobia The pope or popery. [From Latin *papa* a pope]

paper Papyrophobia.

papyrophobia Paper. [From Greek *papyros* the paper-reed]

paraleipophobia Neglecting work or duty. Also spelt *paralipophobia*. [From Greek *paraleipein* to leave aside, from *para* beside + *leipein* to omit]

parascevedekatriaphobia Friday the 13th. Also spelt *paraskevedekatriaphobia* or *paraskevi-dekatriaphobia*. *Compare* triskaidekaphobia.

[From Latin *parasceve* and Greek *paraskeye* Friday or the day of preparation (for the Jewish sabbath), from Greek *para* beside or beyond + *skeyos* a utensil + *dekatreis, dekatria* thirteen, from *deka* ten + *treis, tria* three]

parasites Parasitiophobia.

parasitiophobia Parasites. *Compare* acarophobia, microphobia.
[From Greek *parasitos* a parasite, from *para* beside + *sitos* corn]

parthenophobia Virgins or young girls. *Compare* pedophobia or pediophobia.
[From Greek *parthenos* a virgin]

parturiphobia Childbirth or labour.
[From Latin *parturire* to be in labour]

paterophobia Fathers (of the early Church).
[From Greek *pater* a father]

pathophobia Disease.
[From Greek *pathos* suffering]

patriophobia Hereditary disorders.
[From Greek *patrios* ancestral or native]

peanut butter Arachibutyrophobia.

peccatophobia Sinning. Also spelt *peccatiphobia*. *Compare* hamartophobia.
[From Latin *peccare* to sin]

pediculophobia Lousiness or infestation of lice.
[From Latin *pediculus* a little louse]

pedophobia Children or boys. Also spelt *pediophobia* or *paedophobia*. *Compare* parthenophobia.
[From Greek *pais, paidos* a child or a boy]

peniaphobia Poverty or destitution.
[From Greek *penes* a destitute or needy person]

penises Phallophobia.

phagophobia Eating.
[From Greek *phagein* to eat]

phalacrophobia Baldness.
[From Greek *phalakros* bald-headed]

phallophobia Penises.
[From Greek *phallos* a penis]

phantoms Phasmaphobia.

pharmacophobia Medicines or medicinal drugs.
[From Greek *pharmakon* a drug]

phasmaphobia Ghosts or phantoms. Also spelt *phasmophobia*.
[From Greek *phasma* a spectre]

phengophobia Daylight. *Compare* heliophobia, photophobia, selaphobia.
[From Greek *phengos* daylight]

philemaphobia Kissing.
[From Greek *phili, philema* a kiss]

philophobia Love.
[From Greek *phileein* to love]

philosophobia Philosophy or philosophers.
[From English *philosophy*, from Greek *philos* friend, from *phileein* to love + *sophia* wisdom]

philosophy or philosophers Philosophobia.

phobanthropy *See* anthropophobia.

phobias Phobophobia.

phobodipsia Drinking.

phobophobia Fear or phobias.
[From Greek *phobos* fear]

phonophobia Sounds or speaking aloud.
[From Greek *phone* a sound or voice]

photophobia Light. This word more usually denotes a physiological hypersensitivity to light caused by conjunctivitis, etc. *Compare* heliophobia, phengophobia, selaphobia.
[From Greek *phos, photos* light]

phrenophobia Thinking or madness.
[From Greek *phren* mind, originally midriff, the supposed seat of the mind]

phronemophobia Thinking.
[From Greek *phroneein* to think]

phthisiophobia Tuberculosis.
[From English *phthisis* tuberculosis]

places (certain) Topophobia.

pneumatophobia Spiritual things.
[From Greek *pneuma* spirit]

pnigophobia Choking or suffocating. Also spelt *pnigerophobia*.
[From Greek *pnygyros* choking]

poetry Metrophobia.

pogonophobia Beards or bearded men.
[From Greek *pogon* a beard]

poinephobia Punishment. *Compare* rhabdophobia.
[From Greek *poinikos* punitive]

pointed objects Aichmophobia or belonephobia.

poison or poisoning Iophobia or toxiphobia.

politicophobia Politics or politicians.
[From English *politics*, from Greek *politikos* of the people, from *polites* a citizen]

politics or politicians Politicophobia.

polyphobia Many things. *Compare* pantophobia.
[From Greek *polys* many]

ponds Limnophobia.

ponophobia Overwork. *Compare* ergasiophobia, ergophobia.
[From Greek *ponos* toil]

pools Limnophobia.

pope or popery Papaphobia.

pornophobia Prostitutes or obscenity.
[From Greek *porne* a prostitute]

porphyrophobia Purple.
[From Greek *porphyra* purple dye]

potamophobia Rivers.
[From Greek *potamos* a river]

potophobia Drinks or drinking.
[From Latin *potare* to drink]

poverty Peniaphobia.

precipices Cremnophobia.

proctophobia The anus or rectum.
[From Greek *proktos* the anus]

projectiles Ballistophobia.

prostitutes Cyprianophobia or pornophobia.

psellismophobia Stuttering or stammering.
[From Greek *psellos* stammering]

psychrophobia Cold.
[From Greek *psychros* cold]

pteronophobia Feathers.
[From Greek *pteron* a wing]

public places Agoraphobia.

punishment Poinephobia.

purple Porphyrophobia.

pyrexiophobia Fever.
[From Greek *pyrexis* fever, from *pyr* fire]

pyrophobia Fire.
[From Greek *pyr* fire]

rabies Hydrophobiaphobia, lyssophobia.

railways Siderodromophobia or sideromophobia.

rain or rainstorms Ombrophobia.

rectum Proctophobia.

red (colour) Erythrophobia.

reflections Catoptrophobia, spectrophobia.

relatives Syngenesophobia.

religion Hierophobia.

reptiles Herpetophobia.

responsibility Hypaegiaphobia or hypengyophobia.

rhabdophobia Being beaten with a rod. *Compare* poinephobia.
[From Greek *rhabdos* a rod]

rhypophobia Dirt, defecation, or faeces. Also spelt *rupophobia*.
[From Greek *rhyparos* dirty]

rhytiphobia Wrinkles.
[From Greek *rhytis* a wrinkle]

ridicule Catagelophobia or katagelophobia.

rivers Potamophobia.

rods (being beaten with) Rhabdophobia.

Russia or Russian people or culture Russophobia.

Russophobia Russia or Russian people or culture.
[From English *Russia*]

rusty objects Iophobia.

Satan Satanophobia.

Satanophobia Satan or the devil.
[From Greek *Satan* the Devil, from Hebrew *satan* an enemy]

scabies Scabiophobia.

scabiophobia Scabies.
[From English *scabies*, from Latin *scabere* to scratch]

scatophobia Contamination by faeces.
[From Greek *skatos* dung]

scelerophobia Bad or evil people.
[From Latin *scelus, sceleris* a crime]

school School phobia.

school phobia School or attending school.
[From English *school*, from Greek *schole* a lecture or a school]

scientific terminology Hellenologophobia.

sciophobia Shadows.
[From Greek *skia* a shadow]

scopophobia Being looked at.
[From Greek *skopeein* to look at]

Scotland or Scots people or culture Scotophobia.

scotomaphobia Blind spots in the visual field.
[From Greek *skotos* darkness]

scotophobia Darkness. Not to be confused with *Scotophobia*.
[From Greek *skotos* darkness]

Scotophobia Scotland or Scots people or culture. Not to be confused with *scotophobia*.
[From English *Scot*, from Latin *Scotus* a Scot]

scratched (being) Amychophobia.

scrutiny by other people Social phobia.

sea Thalassophobia.

selaphobia Flashing lights or lightning.
[From Greek *selas* brightness]

selenophobia The moon.
[From Greek *selene* the moon]

semen Spermatophobia.

sermonizing Homilophobia.

sesquipedalophobia Long words.
[From Latin *sesqui-* one and a half + *pedalis* of the foot]

sexual activity Cypridophobia, erotophobia, or genophobia.

sexual intercourse Coitophobia, cypridophobia, erotophobia, or genophobia.

shadows Sciophobia.

sharp objects Aichmophobia or belonephobia.

shellfish Ostraconophobia.

shock Hormephobia.

short-lived success Meteorophobia.

siderodromophobia Railways or trains. Also called *sideromophobia*.
[From Greek *sideros* iron + *dromos* running]

sideromophobia Railways or trains. Also called *siderodromophobia*.
[From Greek *sideros* iron]

siderophobia Iron. More often in reference to a property of chemicals than people. *Compare* metallophobia.
[From Greek *sideros* iron]

sinning Hamartophobia, peccatophobia.

Sinophobia China or Chinese people or culture.
[From Greek *Sinai* Chinese (*pl.*)]

sitiophobia Another name for *sitophobia*.

sitophobia Food.
[From Greek *sitos* grain or food]

sitting down Cathisophobia, kathisophobia.

skin Dermatophobia.

skin disease Dermatopathophobia.

sleep Hypnophobia.

slime Blennophobia or myxophobia.

small creatures Acarophobia.

small objects Microphobia.

smell (body) Bromidrosiphobia.

smells Osmophobia or osphresiophobia.

snakes Ophidiophobia.

snow Chionophobia.

social embarrassment Social phobia.

social phobia Scrutiny by other people, being the focus of attention, or social embarrassment (for more detail, see the entry in the main body of the dictionary).
[From English *social*, from Latin *socius* a companion]

solitude Eremophobia.

sophophobia Learning or wisdom.
[From Greek *sophia* wisdom]

sounds Phonophobia.

sour tastes Acerbophobia or acerophobia.

speaking Glossophobia, phonophobia, or laliophobia.

spectrophobia Mirrors or one's own reflection. Also called *catoptrophobia*.
[From Latin *spectrum* an appearance, from *specere* to look at]

speech errors Laliophobia.

speed Tachophobia.

sperm Spermatophobia.

spermatophobia Sperm or semen.
[From Greek *sperma, spermatos* seed or semen, from *speirein* to sow]

spheksophobia Wasps.
[From Greek *spheka* a wasp]

spiders Arachnophobia.

spiritual things Pneumatophobia.

stairs Bathmophobia, climacophobia.

stammering Psellismophobia.

standing upright Stasiphobia or stasibasiphobia.

stars (the influence of) Astrophobia.

stasibasiphobia Standing and walking upright. Also spelt *stasobasophobia*.
[From Greek *stasis* a standing + *basis* a step, from *bainein* to step or go]

stasiphobia Standing. Also spelt *stasophobia*.
[From Greek *stasis* a standing]

staurophobia Crucifixes.
[From Greek *stauros* a cross]

stealing Kleptophobia.

steep places Cremnophobia.

stings Cnidophobia.

strangers Xenophobia.

streets (crossing) Dromophobia.

stuttering Psellismophobia.

stygiophobia Hell.
[From Greek *Styx* one of the rivers of Hades, from *stygein* to hate]

subways Bathysiderodromophobia.

suffocation Anginophobia, pnigophobia, or pnigerophobia.

sun or sunlight Heliophobia, phengophobia, photophobia.

surgery Tomophobia.

symbolophobia Symbols or symbolic representations.
[From English *symbol*, from Greek *symbolon* a token, from *syn* together + *ballein* to throw]

symbols Symbolophobia.

symmetrophobia Symmetry.
[From Greek *symmetria* symmetry, from *syn* together + *metron* a measure]

symmetry Symmetrophobia.

syngenesophobia Relatives.
[From Greek *syn* together + *genesis* generation]

syphilis Syphilophobia.

syphilophobia Syphilis.
[From the title of Fracastoro's Latin poem of 1530, whose hero *Syphilus* is infected]

tachophobia Speed.
[From Greek *tachos* speed]

taeniophobia Tapeworms. Also spelt *taeniphobia*. *Compare* trichinophobia.
[From Greek *tainia* a band]

talking Glossophobia, laliophobia, or phonophobia.

tapeworms Taeniophobia.

taphophobia Being buried alive. Also spelt *taphephobia*.
[From Greek *taphos* a grave]

tastes Geumaphobia.

taurophobia Bulls.
[From Greek *tauros* a bull]

technology Technophobia.

technophobia Technology.
[From English *techno(logy)*, from Greek *techne* art or skill]

teeth Odontophobia.

teleophobia The doctrine of design or final causes in nature.
[From Greek *telos* end]

teniophobia An alternative spelling of *taeniophobia*.

teratophobia Monsters or giving birth to a monster.
[From Greek *teras*, *teratos* a monster]

Teutonophobia Germany or German people or culture.
[From Latin *Teutoni* the Teutons]

Teutophobia Another name for *Teutonophobia*.

thalassophobia The sea. Also spelt *thalassiophobia*.
[From Greek *thalassa* the sea]

thanatophobia Death and dying (for more detail, see the entry in the main body of the dictionary).
[From Greek *thanatos* death]

theatres and theatre-going Theatrophobia.

theatrophobia Theatres and theatre-going.
[From English *theatre*, from Greek *theatron* a theatre, from *theaesthai* to see]

theophobia God.
[From Greek *theos* a god]

thermophobia Heat.
[From Greek *therme* heat]

thieves or thieving Kleptophobia.

thinking Phronemophobia or phrenophobia.

thirteen (the number) Triskaidekaphobia.

thrown objects Ballistophobia.

thunder or thunderstorms Astraphobia, brontophobia, keraunophobia.

time Chronophobia.

toads Batrachophobia.

tocophobia Childbirth or labour. Also spelt *tokophobia*.
[From Greek *tokos* childbirth, from *tiktein* to bear]

tomophobia Surgery.
[From Greek *tomos* a slice]

topophobia Certain places.
[From Greek *topos* a place]

tornadoes Lilapsophobia.

touching by another person Haptephobia or (h)aphephobia.

toxiphobia Poison or being poisoned. Also spelt *toxicophobia* or *toxophobia*.
[From Greek *toxikon* arrow-poison, from *toxon* a bow]

trains Siderodromophobia or sideromophobia.

traumatophobia Injury or wounds.
[From Greek *trauma* a wound]

travelling Hodophobia.

travelling alone Agoraphobia.

travelling in a vehicle Amaxophobia.

trees Dendrophobia.

trembling Tremophobia.

tremophobia Trembling. Also spelt *tremaphobia*.
[From English *trem(ble)*, from Latin *tremere* to shake]

trichinophobia Trichinosis or infestation by trichinae worms. *Compare* taeniophobia.
[From Greek *trichinos* of hair, from *thrix, trichos* hair]

trichinosis Trichinophobia.

trichopathophobia Hair growing where it is unwanted. *Compare* hypertrichophobia, trichophobia.
[From Greek *trichos* of hair + *pathos* suffering]

trichophobia Hair. *Compare* hypertrichophobia, trichopathophobia.
[From Greek *trichos* of hair]

triskaidekaphobia The number thirteen. *Compare* parascevedekatriaphobia.
[From Greek *tr(e)iskaideka* thirteen]

tropophobia Change.
[From Greek *tropos* a turn]

tuberculophobia Tuberculosis.
[From English *tuberculo(sis)*, from Latin *tuberculum* a little tube, from *tuber* a tube]

tuberculosis Phthisiophobia or tuberculophobia.

tyrannophobia Tyrants.
[From English *tyran(t)*, from Latin *tyrannus* and Greek *tyrannus* a tyrant]

tyrants Tyrannophobia.

underground trains Bathysiderodromophobia.

uranophobia Heaven.
[From Greek *ouranos* heaven]

vaccination Vaccinophobia.

vaccinophobia Performing a vaccination or being vaccinated.
[From English *vaccin(ation)*, from Latin *vaccinus* a vaccine, from *vacca* a cow]

vehicles Amaxophobia.

venereal disease Cypridophobia.

vermin Vermiphobia.

vermiphobia Vermin or worms.
[From Latin *vermis* a worm]

virgins Parthenophobia.

vomiting Emetophobia.

walking or walking upright Basiphobia or stasibasiphobia.

wasps Spheksophobia.

water Aquaphobia or hydrophobia.

waves Kymophobia.

weakness Asthenophobia.

wealth Chrematophobia.

weasels Galeophobia.

whipping Mastigophobia.

wind Anemophobia.

wind instruments Aulophobia.

wisdom Sophophobia.

women Feminophobia or gynephobia.

wood Hylephobia or xylophobia.

word (particular) Onomatophobia.

words Logophobia.

work Ergophobia, ergasiophobia, or pono-phobia.

work (neglecting) Paraleipophobia.

worms Helminthophobia, taeniophobia, trichinophobia, or vermiphobia.

wounds Traumatophobia.

wrinkles Rhytiphobia.

writing Graphophobia.

xenoglossophobia Foreign languages.
[From Greek *xenos* foreign + *glossa* a tongue or language]

xenophobia Foreigners or strangers or their cultures.
[From Greek *xenos* foreign]

xylophobia Forests or wood.
[From Greek *xylon* wood]

young girls Parthenophobia.

zelophobia Jealousy.
[From Greek *zelotypia* jealousy, from *zelos* zeal + *typtein* to strike]

zenophobia A rare spelling of *xenophobia*.

zoophobia Animals.
[From Greek *zoion* an animal]

Appendix II: Abbreviations and symbols

Terms that are more commonly used in their abbreviated forms, such as IQ, RNA, and PET scan, are cross-referenced to the main body of the dictionary where full entries are to be found.

α *See* adrenergic receptor, alpha fibre/motor neuron, alpha male, alpha movement, Cronbach's alpha.

β *See* adrenergic receptor, beta coefficient, beta-endorphin, beta-lipotropin, beta movement, likelihood ratio (2).

γ *See* gamma fibre/motor neuron, gamma movement, Goodman–Kruskal gamma.

δ *See* delta fibre, delta movement.

η *See* correlation ratio.

κ **effect** *See* kappa effect.

K *see* Kappa statistic.

λ *See* Goodman–Kruskal lambda.

ρ *See* Spearman rank correlation coefficient, Spearman's rho.

σ *See* sigma score, standard deviation.

τ **effect** *See* Kendall's tau, tau effect.

ϕ *See* phi coefficient.

Φ *See* luminous flux.

χ^2 *See* chi-square distribution, chi-square test.

ω *See* omega process, perception–consciousness system.

2AFC *See* two-alternative forced-choice task.

2-DG *See* 2-deoxyglucose.

5-HIAA *See* 5-hydroxyindoleacetic acid.

5-HT 5-hydroxytryptamine. *See* serotonin.

5-HTP *See* 5-hydroxytryptophan.

6-OHDA *See* 6-hydroxydopamine.

16PF Sixteen Personality Factor Questionnaire. *See* 16PF in the main body of the dictionary.

A *See* adenine, response amplitude.

A-A *See* axoaxonic.

ABC Activating event, beliefs, consequences; or antecedent, behaviour, consequence. *See* ABC in main body of the dictionary.

ABH Actual bodily harm. *See under* GBH (1).

Ac Achievement via conformance. *See under* California Psychological Inventory.

ACh *See* acetylcholine.

AChE *See* acetylcholinesterase.

ACL *See* Adjective Check List.

ACT* *See* ACT* in main body of dictionary.

ACTH *See* adrenocorticotrophic hormone.

ACTP *See* American College Testing Program.

AD *See* Alzheimer's disease.

A-D *See* axodendritic.

ADC AIDS dementia complex. *See* HIV dementia.

ADD Attention-deficit disorder. *See* attention-deficit/hyperactivity disorder.

ADH Antidiuretic hormone. *See* vasopressin.

ADHD *See* attention-deficit/hyperactivity disorder.

ADP Adenosine diphosphate. *See* ADP in main body of the dictionary.

AEP *See* average evoked potential.

AER Average evoked response. *See* average evoked potential.

AF *See* audibility function.

AFF *See* auditory flutter fusion.

afp *See* alpha-foetoprotein.

AGCT *See* Army General Classification Test.

AI *See* artificial intelligence.

Ai Achievement via independence. *See under* California Psychological Inventory.

AIDS Acquired immune (or immuno-) deficiency syndrome. *See* AIDS in main body of the dictionary.

AKI Autokinetic illusion. *See* autokinetic effect.

AL *See* adaptation level.

ALS *See* amyotrophic lateral sclerosis.

AMH *See* anti-Müllerian hormone.

AMP Adenosine monophosphate. *See* AMP in main body of the dictionary.

AMPT *See* alpha-methylparatyrosine.

ANCOVA *See* analysis of covariance.

ANN Artificial neural network. *See* neural network.

ANOVA *See* analysis of variance.

ANS *See* autonomic nervous system.

AOC *See* attention operating characteristic.

APA American Psychiatric Association, American Psychological Association.

APD *See* antisocial personality disorder.

ARAS *See* ascending reticular activating system.

ARC *See* AIDS-related complex.

ARIMA Autoregressive integrated moving average. *See* ARIMA in the main body of the dictionary.

ARP *See* Argyll Robertson pupil.

A-S Anti-Semitism, ascendance–submissiveness, axosomatic. *See* A–S scale, A–S Reaction Study, axosomatic.

A/S Association/sensation. *See* A/S ratio in the main body of the dictionary.

ASC *See* altered state of consciousness.

ASL *See* American Sign Language.

Asp *See* aspartic acid.

AT *See* attribution theory.

ATP Adenosine triphosphate. *See* ATP in main body of the dictionary.

ATPase Adenosine triphosphatase, *See* ATPase in main body of the dictionary.

BAP Beta-amyloid protein. *See* amyloid plaque.

BAC *See* blood alcohol concentration.

BAL Blood alcohol level. *See* blood alcohol concentration.

BAS *See* British Ability Scales.

BASIC-ID Behaviours, affective processes, sensations, images, cognitions, and interpersonal relationships springing from drugs. or biological factors. *See* BASIC-ID in main body of the dictionary.

BAT *See* body adjustment test.

BBB *See* blood–brain barrier.

BCS *See* battered child syndrome.

BDD *See* body dysmorphic disorder.

BDI *See* Beck Depression Inventory.

BDT *See* behavioural decision theory.

BEV *See* Black English Vernacular.

BGT *See* Bender Gestalt Test.

BMDP Bio-Medical Data Package. *See* BMDP in the main body of the dictionary.

BMR *See* basal metabolic rate.

BOSS Basic Orthographic Syllabic Structure. *See* BOSS in main body of the dictionary.

BPD *See* borderline personality disorder.

BPS British Psychological Society.

BRAC *See* basic rest–activity cycle.

BSE Bovine spongiform encephalopathy. *See* BSE in main body of the dictionary.

BSL *See* British Sign Language.

BSRF Brainstem reticular formation. *See* reticular formation.

BWS *See* battered wife syndrome.

BZ Benzilic acid. *See* BZ gas in the main body of the dictionary.

C *See* C fibre, Cochran's *C*, Cramér's *C*, cytosine.

Ca *See* calcium.

CA *See* catecholamine, chronological age, conversation analysis.

CAGE Cut, annoyed, guilty, eye-opener. *See* CAGE in main body of the dictionary.

Cal. *See* Calorie.

cal. *See* calorie.

cAMP *See* cyclic AMP.

CAPD *See* central auditory processing disorder.

CAT *See* Children's Apperception Test. Also computed (or computerized, or computer-aided, or computer-assisted) axial tomography: *see under* CT scan.

C–B Cost–benefit. *See* cost–benefit analysis.

CBA *See* cost–benefit analysis.

CBF *See* cerebral blood flow.

CBM *See* cognitive behaviour modification.

CBT Cognitive behaviour therapy. *See* cognitive behaviour modification.

CCC Consonant–consonant–consonant. *See* CCC trigram.

CCFT *See* Cattell Culture-Fair Test.

CCK *See* cholecystokinin.

cd *See* candela.

cDNA *See* complementary DNA.

CDP *See* chlordiazepoxide.

CE *See* constant error.

CER *See* conditioned emotional response.

CF *See* characteristic frequency.

cff *See* critical flicker frequency.

CFQ *See* Cognitive Failures Questionnaire.

CFS *See* chronic fatigue syndrome.

cGMP Cyclic guanosine monophosphate. *See* cyclic GMP.

CHS *See* Clinical History Schedule.

CIE Commission Internationale de l'Éclairage. *See* CIE colour system.

CJD *See* Creutzfeldt–Jakob disease.

CM *See* cochlear microphonic.

Cm Community. *See under* California Psychological Inventory.

CN Chloroacetophenone. *See* CN gas in the main body of the dictionary.

CNS *See* central nervous system.

CNV *See* contingent negative variation.

Co Comparison stimulus. *See* variable stimulus.

COMT *See* catechol-*o*-methyl-transferase.

CPI *See* California Psychological Inventory.

CPU *See* central processing unit.

CR *See* conditioned response.

CRE *See* common ratio effect.

CRF Corticotrophin-releasing factor. *See* corticotrophin-releasing hormone.

CRH *See* corticotrophin-releasing hormone.

CRT *See* choice reaction time.

CS *See* conditioned stimulus, CS gas.

Cs *See* consciousness. Also capacity for status: *see under* California Psychological Inventory.

CSEI *See* Coopersmith Self-Esteem Inventories.

CSF *See* cerebrospinal fluid, contrast sensitivity function.

CST *See* corticospinal tract.

CT Computed (or computerized) tomography. *See* CT scan in main body of the dictionary.

CV Consonant-vowel. *See* CV digram.

CVA Cerebrovascular accident. *See* stroke.

CVC Consonant–vowel–consonant. *See* CVC in main body of the dictionary, and CVC trigram.

D *See* Cook's *D*, drive strength, Somers' *D*. Also depression: *see under* MMPI; desynchronized: *see* REM sleep.

d′ Detectability or discriminability. *See* d prime.

DA *See* discourse analysis, dopamine.

DAF *See* delayed auditory feedback.

DAM *See* Draw-a-Man test.

DAP *See* Draw-a-Person test.

DAT *See* Differential Aptitude Tests. Also dementia of the Alzheimer type: *see* Alzheimer's disease.

dB *See* decibel.

dB SPL Decibel sound pressure level. *See under* decibel.

DCT *See* dual-code theory.

DD *See* dissociative disorders.

D-D *See* dendrodendritic.

df *See* degrees of freedom.

DF DeFries and Fulker. *See* DF extremes analysis in main body of the dictionary.

DFA *See* discriminant function analysis.

DHEA Dehydroepiandrosterone. *See* DHEA in main body of the dictionary.

DID *See* dissociative identity disorder.

DIMS Disorders of initiating and maintaining sleep. *See* dyssomnias.

DL Difference limen. *See* difference threshold.

DMD *See* Duchenne muscular dystrophy.

DMT Dimethyltryptamine. *See* DMT in the main body of the dictionary.

DNA Deoxyribonucleic acid. *See* DNA in main body of the dictionary.

Do Dominance. *See under* California Psychological Inventory.

DOES Disorder of excessive somnolence. *See* primary hypersomnia.

DOM Dimethoxy-methylamphetamine. *See* STP.

DQ *See* developmental quotient.

DRH *See* differential reinforcement of high response rates.

DRL *See* differential reinforcement of low response rates.

DRO *See* differential reinforcement of other responses.

DRP *See* differential reinforcement of paced responses.

DRT *See* discrimination reaction time.

DS *See* Down's syndrome.

DSM Diagnostic and Statistical Manual of Mental Disorders. *See* DSM-IV in main body of the dictionary.

DSPS *See* delayed sleep-phase syndrome.

DST *See* dexamethasone suppression test.

DT *See* decision theory.

DTR *See* deep tendon reflex.

DTs *See* delirium tremens.

DV *See* dependent variable.

DZ *See* dizygotic, dizygotic twins.

DZP *See* diazepam.

E *See* epinephrine, ecstasy (2), E scale (ethnocentrism).

e² *See* environmentability.

EBA *See* elimination by aspects.

EBS *See* electrical brain stimulation.

ECF *See* extracellular fluid.

ECS electroconvulsive shock. *See* electroconvulsive therapy.

ECT *See* electroconvulsive therapy.

ED *See* effective dosage: ED-1 is the dosage that produces a specified effect in one per cent of the population, ED-2 is the dosage that produces a specified effect in two per cent of the population, and so on. Also erectile dysfunction or erectile disorder: *see* male erectile disorder, impotence (2).

ED-50 Effective dosage 50. Also written ED_{50}. *See* median effective dosage.

EDA *See* exploratory data analysis.

EDR Electrodermal response. *See* galvanic skin response.

EEG Electroencephalogram. *See* EEG in main body of the dictionary.

EFT *See* embedded-figures test.

ELM *See* elaboration likelihood model.

EMDR *See* eye-movement desensitization and reprocessing.

EMG *See* electromyogram.

EMR *See* educable mentally retarded.

EOG *See* electro-oculogram.

EP *See* evoked potential.

EPI *See* Eysenck Personality Inventory.

EPO *See* erythropoietin.

EPP *See* end-plate potential.

EPPS *See* Edwards Personal Preference Schedule.

EPQ *See* Eysenck Personality Questionnaire.

EPSP *See* excitatory postsynaptic potential.

EQ *See* emotional quotient, encephalization quotient.

ER *See* endoplasmic reticulum.

ERG *See* electroretinogram.

ERP *See* event-related potential.

ESN *See* educationally subnormal.

ESP *See* extra-sensory perception.

ESS *See* evolutionarily stable strategy.

ESSB *See* electrical self-stimulation of the brain.

EST Electric shock therapy. *See* electroconvulsive therapy.

est Erhard Seminars Training. *See* est in main body of dictionary.

EU *See* expected utility.

EV *See* expected value.

F Potentiality for fascism. *See* F scale in main body of the dictionary.

F *See* Bartlett–Box *F* test, *F* statistic in main body of dictionary. Also validity: *see under* MMPI.

F₁ First filial generation. *See* filial generation.

FAE *See* figural aftereffect.

fan Facts associated with node. *See* fan effect.

FAP *See* fixed-action pattern.

FAS *See* foetal alcohol syndrome.

FC *See* facilitated communication.

fc *See* foot-candle.

FCM *See* feature comparison model.

FCT Facilitated communication training. *See* facilitated communication.

FD-I *See* field dependence-independence.

Fe Femininity. *See under* California Psychological Inventory.

FEF Frontal eye field. *See under* motor cortex.

fff Flicker fusion frequency. *See* critical flicker frequency.

FFI *See* fatal familial insomnia.

FG Fast glycolytic. *See* fast glycolytic fibre.

FI Fixed-interval. *See* fixed-interval schedule.

F_{ij} *See* coefficient of consanguinity.

F max *See* Hartley's *F* max.

fMRI Functional magnetic resonance imaging. *See under* MRI.

FMS *See* false memory syndrome.

FOG Fast oxidative glycolytic. *See* fast oxidative glycolytic fibre.

FR Fixed-ratio. *See* fixed-ratio schedule.

FRT *See* fixed-role therapy.

FSH *See* follicle-stimulating hormone.

FTC Frequency threshold curve or frequency tuning curve. *See* tuning curve.

ft-L *See* foot-lambert.

Fx Flexibility. *See under* California Psychological Inventory.

FXT *See* fluoxetine.

G *See* guanine. Also Gräfenberg: *see* G spot in main body of the dictionary.

g General ability or intelligence. *See* g in main body of the dictionary.

GA *See* Golgi apparatus.

GABA Gamma-aminobutyric acid. *See* GABA in main body of the dictionary.

GAD *See* glutamic acid decarboxylase, generalized anxiety disorder.

GAS *See* general adaptation syndrome.

GB *See* government and binding.

GBH Grievous bodily harm. *See* GBH in the main body of the dictionary.

Gc *See* crystallized intelligence.

Gf *See* fluid intelligence.

GH *See* growth hormone.

GHB Gamma-hydroxybutyrate. *See* GHB in the main body of the dictionary.

GHQ *See* General Health Questionnaire.

GHRH *See* growth hormone releasing hormone.

GI *See* gastrointestinal.

Gi Good impression. *See under* California Psychological Inventory.

GIGO Garbage in, garbage out (computer slang).

Glu *See* glutamic acid.

Gly *See* glycine.

GM *See* genetically modified.

GMP Guanosine monophosphate. *See* cyclic GMP.

GnRH *See* gonadotrophin-releasing hormone.

GPI *See* general paralysis (paresis) of the insane.

GPS *See* General Problem Solver.

GSR *See* galvanic skin response.

GSS *See* Gerstmann–Sträussler–Scheinker syndrome.

GST *See* general systems theory.

GTS Gilles de la Tourette's syndrome. *See* Tourette's disorder.

GWS *See* Gulf War Syndrome.

H *See* heroin.

h^2 *See* heritability.

Hb *See* haemoglobin.

HD *See* Huntington's disease.

HIT *See* Holtzman Inkblot Technique.

HIV Human immunodeficiency virus. *See* HIV in main body of the dictionary.

HOUND Humble, old, unattractive, non-verbal, dumb. *See* HOUND in main body of the dictionary.

HPA axis Hypothalamic–pituitary–adrenal axis. *See* HPA axis in main body of the dictionary.

HPD *See* histrionic personality disorder.

Hs Hypochondriasis. *See under* MMPI.

HSD Honestly significant difference. *See* Tukey-HSD test.

HSE *See* herpes simplex encephalitis.

H–T–P *See* House–Tree–Person technique.

Hy Hysteria. *See under* MMPI.

Hz *See* hertz.

I *See* luminous intensity. Also Induction (intelligence factor): *See under* primary mental abilities.

Ia *See* Ia fibre.

IAS *See* Internet addiction syndrome.

Ib *See* Ib fibre.

ICD International Classification of Diseases and Related Health Problems. *See* ICD-10 in main body of the dictionary.

ICF *See* intracellular fluid.

ICSH Interstitial-cell-stimulating hormone. *See* luteinizing hormone.

Ie Intellectual efficiency. *See under* California Psychological Inventory.

I–E *See* internal–external scale.

Ig *See* immunoglobulin.

IgA, IgG, IgM *See under* immunoglobulin.

IGC *See* Item Group Checklist.

IHC *See* inner hair cell.

II *See* II fibre.

IID *See* interaural intensity difference.

INDSCAL Individual differences scaling. *See* INDSCAL in the main body of the dictionary.

I/O *See* industrial/organizational psychology.

ION *See* inferior olivary nucleus.

IPA *See* interaction process analysis, International Phonetic Alphabet.

IPSP *See* inhibitory postsynaptic potential.

IQ Intelligence quotient. *See* IQ in main body of the dictionary.

IQR *See* interquartile range.

IR *See* infra-red.

IRM *See* innate releasing mechanism.

IRT *See* item response theory.

ISI *See* interstimulus interval.

IT *See* Information technology, inspection time.

ITA *See* Initial Teaching Alphabet.

ITC Inferior temporal cortex. *See* inferior temporal gyrus.

ITD *See* interaural time difference.

ITG *See* inferior temporal gyrus.

ITPA *See* Illinois Test of Psycholinguistic Abilities.

IU *See* interval of uncertainty.

IV *See* independent variable.

IVF *See* in vitro fertilization.

JDI *See* Job Descriptive Index.

jnd Just noticeable difference. *See* difference threshold.

K *See* incentive motivation.

K *See* kappa statistic, potassium. Also correction factor: *see under* MMPI.

kcal Kilocalorie. *See under* Calorie.

KDE *See* kinetic depth effect.

KPR *See* Kuder Preference Record.

KPR–V Kuder Preference Record–Vocational. *See* Kuder Preference Record.

KR *See* knowledge representation.

K-R 20 Kuder–Richardson 20 formula. *See* Kuder–Richardson coefficient.

K-R 21 Kuder–Richardson 21 formula. *See* Kuder–Richardson coefficient.

L *See* luminance. Also Lie scale: *see under* MMPI.

LAD *See* language acquisition device.

LAS Language acquisition system. *See* language acquisition device.

L_B *See* Goodman–Kruskal lambda.

LD *See* learning disability, lethal dosage.

LD-50 Lethal dosage 50. Also written LD_{50}. *See* median lethal dosage.

L-dopa Laevo-dihydroxyphenylalanine. *See* L-dopa in main body of the dictionary.

LDT *See* lexical decision task.

LEM *See* lateral eye movement.

LGN *See* lateral geniculate nucleus.

LH *See* luteinizing hormone.

LH-RH *See* luteinizing-hormone releasing hormone.

LI *See* latent inhibition.

LLPDD *See* late luteal phase dysphoric disorder.

lm *See* lumen.

LOP *See* levels of processing.

LPAD *See* Learning Potential Assessment Device.

LSD Lysergic acid diethylamide. *See* LSD in the main body of the dictionary.

LTH Luteotrop(h)ic hormone. *See* prolactin.

LTM *See* long-term memory.

LTP *See* long-term potentiation.

LTS *See* long-term store.

lvf Left visual field. *See under* visual field.

M Magnocellular, mean, memory (intelligence factor). *See under* magnocellular system, M cell, mean, primary mental abilities.

MA *See* mental age.

Ma Hypomania. *See* MMPI.

MAA *See* minimum audible angle.

MADM *See* multi-attribute decision making.

MAE *See* motion aftereffect.

MAF *See* minimum audible field.

MANOVA *See* multivariate analysis of variance.

MAO *See* monoamine oxidase.

MAOI *See* monoamine oxidase inhibitor.

MAP *See* minimum audible pressure.

MAPS *See* Make-a-Picture-Story Test.

MAS *See* Manifest Anxiety Scale.

MBD Minimal brain dysfunction. *See* attention-deficit/hyperactivity disorder.

MBPS Munchausen by proxy syndrome. *See* factitious disorder by proxy.

MBTI *See* Myers–Briggs Type Indicator.

MDA Methyl-dioxy amphetamine. *See* MDA in the main body of the dictionary.

MDD *See* major depressive disorder.

MDMA 3,4-methylene-dioxy-methamphetamine. *See* MDMA in the main body of the dictionary.

MDP *See* manic–depressive psychosis.

MDS *See* multidimensional scaling.

ME Myalgic encephalomyelitis. *See* chronic fatigue syndrome.

MED *See* minimum effective dosage.

MED-50 Median effective dosage, 50 per cent. *See* MED-50 in the main body of the dictionary.

MEG *See* magnetoencephalography.

MEPP *See* miniature end-plate potential.

Mf Masculinity-femininity. *See under* MMPI.

MFB *See* medial forebrain bundle.

MFFT *See* Matching Familiar Figures Test.

MGN *See* medial geniculate nucleus.

MHPG 3-methoxy-4-hydroxyphenylethylene glycol. *See* MHPG in the main body of the dictionary.

MHV *See* Mill Hill Vocabulary scale.

MID Multi-infarct dementia. *See* vascular dementia.

MIS *See* Müllerian inhibiting substance.

MLD *See* minimum lethal dosage.

MLU *See* mean length of utterance.

MMPI *See* MMPI in the main body of the dictionary.

MMT *See* multimodal therapy.

MND *See* motor neuron disease.

MOC *See* memory operating characteristic.

MOP *See* memory organization packet.

MPB *See* meprobamate.

MPD Multiple personality disorder. *See* dissociative identity disorder.

MPI *See* Maudsley Personality Inventory.

MPP⁺ Methylphenylpyridine. *See* MPP⁺ in the main body of the dictionary.

MPPP 1-Methyl-4-phenyl-4-propionoxy-piperidine. *See* MPPP in the main body of the dictionary.

MPTP 1-Methyl-4-phenyl-1,2,3,6-tetrahydropyridine. *See* MPTP in the main body of the dictionary.

MR *See* motivational research.

MRH Müllerian regression hormone. *See* Müllierian inhibiting substance.

MRI Magnetic resonance imaging. *See* MRI in main body of the dictionary.

mRNA *See* messenger RNA.

MS *See* multiple sclerosis.

MSG *See* monosodium glutamate.

MSH *See* melanocyte-stimulating hormone.

MT Median or middle temporal. *See* MT in main body of the dictionary.

MTD *See* minimum toxic dosage.

mtDNA *See* mitochondrial DNA.

MTF Modulation transfer function. *See* contrast sensitivity function.

MTMM *See* multitrait–multimethod matrix.

MUD Multi-user dungeon, or multi-user dimension. *See* MUD in main body of the dictionary.

MZ *See* monozygotic.

n Often used for the number in a subsample. *Compare N.*

N Often used to represent the total number of scores in a data set or total number of research participants or subjects in an experiment or investigation. *Compare n.* Also Number (intelligence factor): *see under* primary mental abilities.

N140 Negative deflection, 140 milliseconds. *See* N140 in main body of the dictionary.

N₂O *See* nitrous oxide.

NA *See* noradrenalin.

Na *See* sodium.

N Ach *See* need for achievement. Also written *nAch.*

N Aff *See* need for affiliation. Also written *nAff.*

Na⁺–K⁺ Sodium–potassium. *See* sodium pump.

NANC Non-adrenergic, non-cholinergic. *See* NANC in main body of the dictionary.

nbM *See* nucleus basalis of Meynert.

NCV *See* nerve conduction velocity.

NE Norepinephrine. *See* noradrenalin.

NEO Neuroticism, Extraversion, Openness to experience. *See* NEO in the main body of the dictionary.

NEO-FFI Neuroticism, Extraversion, Openness to experience Five-Factor Inventory. *See under* NEO in the main body of the dictionary.

NEO-PI-R Neuroticism, Extraversion, Openness to experience Personality Inventory-Revised. *See under* NEO in the main body of the dictionary.

NFT *See* neurofibrillary tangle.

NGF *See* nerve growth factor.

NHST Null hypothesis significance testing. *See* null hypothesis, significance, significance test.

NLP *See* neurolinguistic programming.

nm *See* nanometre.

NMR *See* nuclear magnetic resonance.

NO *See* nitric oxide.

NPD *See* narcissistic personality disorder, *N*-person Prisoner's Dilemma.

NREM Non-rapid-eye-movement. *See* NREM sleep in main body of the dictionary.

NSB *See* nigrostriatal bundle.

NUD*IST Non-numerical unstructured data indexing. *See* NUD*IST in the main body of the dictionary.

NVC *See* non-verbal communication.

nvCJD New-variant CJD. *See under* Creutzfeldt–Jakob disease.

OBE *See* out-of-body experience.

OBS Organic brain syndrome. *See* organic disorders.

OC Oleoresin capsicum. *See* pepper spray.

OCD *See* obsessive–compulsive disorder.

OCR *See* optical character recognition.

OEE *See* overtraining extinction effect.

OHC *See* outer hair cell.

OKN *See* optokinetic nystagmus.

OOBE *See* out-of-body experience.

OP *See* organophosphate.

OR *See* operational research.

ORE *See* overtraining reversal effect.

OT *See* occupational therapy.

OTC Over-the-counter, in contradistinction to prescription drugs.

OVLT *See* organum vasculosum lamina terminalis.

P Parvocellular, perceptual speed (intelligence factor). *See under* P cell in main body of the dictionary, and primary mental abilities.

p Probability. *See p* value in the main body of the dictionary.

P200 Positive deflection, 200 milliseconds. *See* P200 in main body of the dictionary.

P300 Positive deflection, 300 milliseconds. *See* P300 in main body of the dictionary.

PA *See* paired-associate learning.

Pa Paranoia. *See under* MMPI.

PAG *See* periaqueductal grey matter.

PAL *See* paired-associate learning.

PAM Precategorical acoustic memory. *See* precategorical acoustic store.

PAR *See* participatory action research.

PAS *See* precategorical acoustic store.

PC *See* politically correct. Also an abbreviation of *personal computer*.

PCA *See* principal-components analysis.

PCP *See* phencyclidine.

p-CPA *See* parachlorophenylalanine. Also written **PCPA**.

Pcpt-Cs *See* perception-consciousness system.

PCR *See* polymerase chain reaction.

Pcs *See* preconscious.

pcs *See* preconscious.

PCT *See* personal construct theory.

PD *See* panic disorder, Parkinson's disease, Prisoner's Dilemma game.

Pd Psychopathic deviate. *See under* MMPI.

PDE5 *See* phosphodiesterase type 5.

PDG *See* Prisoner's Dilemma game.

PDP *See* parallel distributed processing.

PE *See* probable error.

PEA *See* phenylethylamine.

PEC Political and economic conservatism. *See* PEC scale.

PET scan Positron emission tomography scan. *See* PET scan in main body of the dictionary.

PFA *See* Panum's fusion area.

PG *See* Prostaglandin. Different prostaglandins are given names such as PGA, PGB, PGF_α, and so on.

PGHS Prostaglandin H_2 synthase. *See* prostaglandin.

PGO Pontogeniculo-occipital. *See* PGO spike in main body of the dictionary.

PGR Psychogalvanic response. *See* galvanic skin response.

pH Potential of hydrogen. *See* pH in main body of the dictionary.

Phe *See* phenylalanine.

PI *See* parental investment, proactive interference.

PIFC *See* pattern-induced flicker colour.

PK *See* psychokinesis.

PKC *See* protein kinase C.

PKU *See* phenylketonuria.

PMA *See* primary mental abilities.

PMC Premotor cortex. *See under* motor cortex.

PMDD Premenstrual dysphoric disorder. *See* premenstrual syndrome.

PMS *See* premenstrual syndrome.

PMT *See* Porteus Maze Test. Also premenstrual tension: *see* premenstrual syndrome.

PNI *See* psychoneuroimmunology.

PNMT Phenylethanolamine-*N*-methyltransferase. *See* PNMT in main body of the dictionary.

PNS *See* parasympathetic nervous system, peripheral nervous system.

POC *See* performance operating characteristic.

POMC Pro-opiomelanocortin. *See* POMC in main body of the dictionary.

PONS Profile of non-verbal sensitivity. *See* PONS in the main body of the dictionary.

PPVT *See* Peabody Picture Vocabulary Test.

PPVT-R Peabody Picture Vocabulary Test-Revised. *See* Peabody Picture Vocabulary Test.

PR *See* partial reinforcement.

PRE *See* partial reinforcement effect.

PrL *See* prolactin.

PROP *See* propylthiouracil.

PRP Psychological refractory period. *See* refractory period (3).

PrP Prion protein. *See* PrP in main body of the dictionary.

PSE *See* point of subjective equality, Present State Examination.

PSP *See* progressive supranuclear palsy.

P system *See* parvocellular system.

Pt Psychasthenia. *See under* MMPI.

PTC Phenylthiocarbamide. *See* PTC in the main body of the dictionary.

PTH *See* parathyroid hormone.

PTSD *See* post-traumatic stress disorder.

PVS *See* persistent vegetative state.

Py Psychological-mindedness. *See under* California Psychological Inventory.

Q *See* Cochran's Q, Q-methodology, Q-sort.

R *See* Reiz, response, R-methodology. Also reasoning (intelligence factor): *See under* primary mental abilities.

R *See* multiple correlation coefficient.

r *See* coefficient of relationship, product–moment correlation coefficient.

R^2 *See* coefficient of determination.

RA *See* rapidly adapting.

RAS Reticular activating system. *See* ascending reticular activating system.

RBD *See* REM behaviour disorder.

rCBF *See* regional cerebral blood flow.

RCT *See* randomized controlled trial.

RDD *See* random digit dialling.

Re Responsibility. *See under* California Psychological Inventory.

REBT *See* rational emotive behaviour therapy.

REM *See* rapid eye movement. *See also* REM atonia, REM behaviour disorder, REM rebound, and REM sleep in main body of the dictionary.

Rep *See* reproducibility. Also Repertory: *See* Repertory Grid Test.

RER Rough endoplasmic reticulum. *See under* endoplasmic reticulum.

RET *See* rational emotive therapy.

RF *See* reticular formation.

RFT *See* rod-and-frame test.

RHP *See* resource-holding potential.

RI *See* retroactive interference.

RISB *See* Rotter Incomplete Sentences Blank.

RL *Reiz* limen. *See* absolute threshold.

RNA Ribonucleic acid. *See* RNA in main body of dictionary.

ROC *See* receiver operating characteristic.

RP *See* Received Pronunciation.

RPFS *See* Rosenzweig Picture-Frustration Study.

RPM *See* Raven's Progressive Matrices.

R–S *See* repression–sensitization scale.

RT *See* reaction time.

rvf Right visual field. *See under* visual field.

S *See* stimulus, standard stimulus. Also Spatial ability (intelligence factor): *see under* primary mental abilities; synchronized: *see* NREM sleep.

s *See* variable stimulus.

SA *See* slowly adapting, social age.

Sa Self-acceptance. *See under* California Psychological Inventory.

SAD *See* seasonal affective disorder.

SaH *See* subarachnoid haemorrhage. Also written **SAH**.

SAS Statistical Analysis System. *See* SAS in the main body of the dictionary.

SAT *See* Scholastic Aptitude Test.

S–B *See* Stanford–Binet intelligence scale.

Sc Schizophrenia. *See under* MMPI. Also self-control: *see under* California Psychological Inventory.

SCAN Schedules for Clinical Assessment in Neuropsychiatry. *See* SCAN in the main body of the dictionary.

SCII Strong–Campbell Interest Inventory. *See* Strong Interest Inventory.

SCN *See* suprachiasmatic nucleus.

SCR *See* skin conductance response.

SCT *See* social cognitive theory.

SD *See* semantic differential, standard deviation.

SDAT Senile dementia of the Alzheimer type. *See* senile dementia and SDAT in main body of the dictionary.

SDT *See* sensory decision theory, signal detection theory.

SE *See* standard error.

SEM *See* structural equation modelling.

SER Smooth endoplasmic reticulum. *See under* endoplasmic reticulum.

$_s\bar{E}_R$ *See* net reaction potential.

$_sE_R$ *See* generalized reaction potential.

SEU *See* subjective expected utility.

SFH *See* sematic-feature hypothesis.

SFM *See* structure from motion.

SFO *See* subfornical organ.

$_sH_R$ *See* habit strength.

$_s\bar{H}_R$ *See* generalized habit strength.

Si Social introversion. *See under* MMPI.

SII *See* Strong Interest Inventory.

SIS Sensory information store. *See* sensory register.

SIT *See* social identity theory.

SL *See* sensation level.

SLD *See* specific learning disability.

$_sL_R$ *See* reaction threshold.

SLT *See* social learning theory.

SM *See* sadomasochism.

SMA Supplementary motor area. *See under* motor cortex.

snRNP Small nuclear ribonucleoprotein. *See* snurp.

SNS *See* somatic nervous system, sympathetic nervous system.

SNST Stroop Neuropsychological Screening Test. *See* Stroop effect.

SO Slow oxidative. *See* slow-twitch fibre.

So Socialization. *See under* California Psychological Inventory.

SOA *See* span of apprehension, stimulus onset asynchrony.

SOD Sexual orientation disturbance. *See* ego-dystonic sexual orientation.

SOI Structure of intellect. *See* Guilford's cube.

SON *See* superior olivary nucleus.

$_sO_R$ *See* behavioural oscillation.

Sp Social presence. *See under* California Psychological Inventory.

SPECT Single photon emission computed tomography. *See* SPECT scan in main body of the dictionary.

SPET Single photon emission tomography. *See* SPECT scan in the main body of the dictionary.

SPL *See* sound pressure level.

SPSS Statistical Product and Service Solutions, or (formerly) Statistical Package for the Social Sciences. *See* SPSS in the main body of the dictionary.

SQ *See* social quotient.

SQUID Superconducting quantum interference device. *See* SQUID in main body of the dictionary.

SRIF *See* somatotrophin release inhibiting factor.

SRO Steele-Richardson-Olszewski syndrome. *See* progressive supranuclear palsy.

SRS *See* simple random sample.

SSRI *See* selective serotonin reuptake inhibitor.

SST *See* social skills training.

St *See* standard stimulus.

STAI *See* State-Trait Anxiety Inventory.

STM *See* short-term memory.

$_st_R$ *See* reaction latency.

STRH *See* somatotrophin releasing hormone.

STS *See* short-term store, superior temporal sulcus.

STX *See* saxitoxin.

SUD Subjective Units of Distress. *See under* eye-movement desensitization and reprocessing.

SVIB *See* Strong Vocational Interest Blank.

SWS *See* slow-wave sleep.

Sy Sociability. *See under* California Psychological Inventory.

SYSTAT System for Statistics. *See* SYSTAT in the main body of the dictionary.

T *See* thymine, T-maze. Also true: *see* T score; thymus: *see* T lymphocyte; training: *see* T-group.

t True. *See* one-sample *t* test, paired samples *t* test, related scores *t* test, *t* test.

TA *See* transactional analysis.

TAT Thematic Apperception Test. *See* TAT in the main body of the dictionary.

TATA Thymine adenine thymine adenine. *See* TATA box in main body of the dictionary.

TC *See* therapeutic community.

TCA *See* tricyclic antidepressant.

TD *See* tardive dyskinesia, toxic dosage.

TD-50 Toxic dosage 50. Also written TD_{50}. *See* median toxic dosage.

TFT *See* tit for tat strategy.

TGA *See* transient global amnesia.

TH *See* tyrosine hydroxylase. Also thyrotrophic hormone: *see* thyroid-stimulating hormone.

THC *See* delta-9-tetrahydrocannabinol.

TIA *See* transient ischaemic attack.

TLE *See* temporal lobe epilepsy.

TM *See* transcendental meditation.

TMR *See* trainable mentally retarded.

To Tolerance. *See under* California Psychological Inventory.

ToM *See* theory of mind.

TOT Tip of the tongue. *See* tip-of-the-tongue phenomenon.

TOTE Test–Operate–Test–Exit. *See* TOTE in the main body of the dictionary.

TPH *See* tryptophan hydroxylase.

TQM *See* total quality management.

TRH *See* thyrotrophin-releasing hormone.

tRNA *See* transfer RNA.

Trp *See* tryptophan.

TS Tourette's syndrome. *See* Tourette's disorder.

TSD *See* Tay–Sachs disease.

TSH *See* thyroid-stimulating hormone.

TSP *See* travelling salesman problem.

TTR *See* type-token ratio.

TTS *See* temporary threshold shift.

TTX *See* tetrodotoxin.

Tyr *See* tyrosine.

U *See* Mann-Whitney *U* test, uracil.

Ucs *See* unconscious (2).

ucs *See* unconscious (1).

UG *See* universal grammar.

UPGMA Unweighted pair-group method of analysis. *See* UPGMA in the main body of the dictionary.

UR *See* unconditioned response.

US *See* unconditioned stimulus.

UV *See* ultraviolet.

V *See* Cramér's *V*, stimulus intensity dynamism, variable stimulus. Also Verbal comprehension (intelligence factor): *see under* primary mental abilities.

V1 Visual area 1, the primary visual cortex. Also **V2**, **V3**, **V3A**, **V4**, **V5**, **V6**, **V7**, **V8**. *See under* visual cortex.

VEP *See* visual evoked potential.

VI Variable interval. *See* variable-interval schedule.

VMGT *See* Visual-Motor Gestalt Test.

VMH *See* ventromedial hypothalamus.

VNO *See* vomeronasal organ.

VNTR Variable number of tandem repeats. *See* repetitive DNA and VNTR in main body of the dictionary.

VOR *See* vestibulo-ocular reflex.

VR *See* variable ratio schedule, virtual reality.

VTA *See* ventral tegmental area.

VX Methylphosphonothioic acid. *See* VX in main body of the dictionary.

W *See* perception-consciousness system, Kendall coefficient of concordance. Also

Word fluency (intelligence factor): *see under* primary mental abilities.

WAIS Wechsler Adult Intelligence Scale. *See* Wechsler scales.

WASI Wechsler Abbreviated Scale of Intelligence. *See* Wechsler scales.

WAT *See* word-association test.

WB Wechsler–Bellevue. *See under* Wechsler scales.

Wb Sense of well-being. *See under* California Psychological Inventory.

WCST *See* Wisconsin Card Sorting test.

WGTA *See* Wisconsin General Test Apparatus.

WISC Wechsler Intelligence Scale for Children. *See* Wechsler scales.

WPPSI Wechsler Preschool and Primary Scale of Intelligence. *See* Wechsler scales.

WSE *See* word superiority effect.

X *See* X chromosome in the main body of the dictionary. Also parvocellular system cell: *see* parvocellular system.

XTC *See* ecstasy (2).

XYZ Euclidian coordinates. *See* CIE colour system.

Y *See* Y chromosome in the main body of the dictionary.

YAVIS Young, attractive, verbal, intelligent, successful. *See* YAVIS in main body of the dictionary.

YDL *See* Yerkes–Dodson law.

z *See* standard score.

ZPD *See* zone of proximal development.

Principal sources

Abercombie, M., Hickman, C. J., & Johnson, M. L. (1973). *A dictionary of biology* (6th ed.). Harmondsworth: Penguin.

Aiken, L. R. (1999). *Personality assessment methods and practices* (3rd ed.). Kirkland, WA: Hogrefe & Huber.

American Psychiatric Association. (1987). *Diagnostic and statistical manual of mental disorders* (3rd ed., revised). Washington, DC: Author.

American Psychiatric Association. (1994). *Diagnostic and statistical manual of mental disorders* (4th ed.). Washington, DC: Author.

American Psychological Association. (1985). *Standards for educational and psychological testing.* Washington, DC: Author.

American Psychological Association. (1994). *Publication manual of the American Psychological Association* (4th ed.). Washington, DC: Author.

Anderson, B. F., Deane, D. H., Hammond, K. R., & McClelland, G. H. (1981). *Concepts in judgement and decision research: Definitions, sources, interrelations, comments.* New York: Praeger.

Anderson, K. N., Anderson, L. E., & Glanze, W. D. (Eds.). (1994). *Mosby's medical, nursing, and allied health dictionary* (4th ed.). St Louis, MO: Mosby.

Argyle, M., & Colman, A. M. (Eds.). (1995). *Social psychology.* London and New York: Longman.

Atkinson, R. C., Herrnstein, R. J., Lindzey, G., & Luce, R. D. (Eds.). (1988). *Stevens' handbook of experimental psychology* (2nd ed.). New York: Wiley.

Beaumont, J. G., Kenealy, P. M., & Rogers, M. J. C. (Eds.). (1996). *The Blackwell dictionary of neuropsychology.* Oxford: Blackwell.

Best, J. B. (1995). *Cognitive psychology* (4th ed.). St Paul. MN: West.

Biographical Dictionary of Parapsychology. (1996). New York: Garrett.

Boneau, C. A. (1990). Psychological literacy: A first approximation. *American Psychologist, 45*, 891–900.

Boring, E. G. (1942). *Sensation and perception in the history of experimental psychology.* New York: Appleton-Century-Crofts.

Boring, E. G. (1957). *A history of experimental psychology* (2nd ed.). New York: Appleton-Century-Crofts.

Bowman, W. C., Bowman, A., & Bowman, A. (1986). *Dictionary of pharmacology.* Oxford: Blackwell.

Bryant, P. E., & Colman, A. M. (Eds.). (1995). *Developmental psychology.* London and New York: Longman.

Campbell, R. J. (1996). *Psychiatric dictionary* (7th ed.). New York: Oxford University Press.

Carlson, N. R. (1994). *Physiology of behavior* (5th ed.). Boston: Allyn & Bacon.

Colman, A. M. (1988). *What is psychology? The inside story* (2nd ed.). London: Unwin Hyman.

Colman, A. M. (Ed.). (1994). *Companion encyclopedia of psychology* (2 vols). London: Routledge.

Colman, A. M. (Ed.). (1995). *Applications of psychology.* London and New York: Longman.

Colman, A. M. (Ed.). (1995). *Controversies in psychology.* London and New York: Longman.

Colman, A. M. (Ed.). (1995). *Psychological research methods and statistics.* London and New York: Longman.

Cooper, J. E. (Ed.). (1994). *Pocket guide to the ICD-10 classification of mental and behavioural disorders: With glossary and diagnostic criteria for research.* Edinburgh: Churchill Livingstone.

Corsini, R. J., & Auerbach, A. J. (Eds.). (1996). *Concise encyclopedia of psychology* (2nd ed.). New York: Wiley.

Crystal, D. (1987). *The Cambridge encyclopedia of language.* Cambridge: Cambridge University Press.

Crystal, D. (1997). *A dictionary of linguistics and phonetics* (4th ed.). Oxford: Blackwell.

Daintith, J., & Nelson, R. D. (1989). *The Penguin dictionary of mathematics.* London: Penguin.

Deutsche bibliographische Enzyklopädie: DBE. (1998). München: Saur.

Domjan, M., & Burkhard, B. (1986). *The principles of learning & behavior* (2nd ed.). Monterey, CA: Brooks/Cole.

Edgerton, J. E., & Campbell, R. J., III. (Eds.). (1994). *American psychiatric glossary* (7th ed.). Washington, DC: American Psychiatric Press.

Ellenberger, H. F. (1970). *The discovery of the unconscious: The history and evolution of dynamic psychology.* New York: Basic Books.

Ellis, W. D. (Ed.). (1938). *A source book of Gestalt psychology.* London: Routledge & Kegan Paul.

English, H. B., & English, A. C. (1958). *A comprehensive dictionary of psychological and psychoanalytical terms: A guide to usage.* New York: David McKay.

Eysenck, M. W. (Ed.). (1990). *The Blackwell dictionary of cognitive psychology.* Oxford: Blackwell.

Feldman, R. S., & Quenzer, L. F. (1984). *Fundamentals of neuropsychopharmacology.* Sunderland, MA: Sinauer.

Feltham, C., & Dryden, W. (1993). *Dictionary of counselling.* London: Whurr.

Fisher, R. B., & Christie, G. A. (1982). *A dictionary of drugs*. London: Paladin.

FitzGerald, M. J. T. (1996). *Neuroanatomy: Basic and clinical* (3rd ed.). London: W. B. Saunders.

Flew, A. (Ed.). (1979). *A dictionary of philosophy* (3rd ed.). London: Pan.

French, C. C., & Colman, A. M. (Eds.). (1995). *Cognitive psychology*. London and New York: Longman.

Freud, S. (1953–74). *The standard edition of the complete psychological works of Sigmund Freud* (Vols 1–24, J. Strachey, Ed. and Trans.). London: Hogarth Press. (Original works published 1886–1938)

Freund, J. E., & Williams, F. J. (1966). *Dictionary/outline of basic statistics*. New York: McGraw-Hill.

Gove, P. B. (Ed.). (1993). *Webster's third new international dictionary of the English language unabridged*. Springfield, MA: Merriam-Webster.

Gregory, R. L. (1981). *Mind in science: A history of explanations in psychology and physics*. Harmondsworth: Penguin.

Gregory, R. L. (Ed.). (1987). *The Oxford companion to the mind*. Oxford: Oxford University Press.

Gregory, R. L., & Colman, A. M. (Eds.). (1995). *Sensation and perception*. London and New York: Longman.

Grosser, G. S., & Spafford, C. S. (1995). *Physiological psychology dictionary: A reference guide for students and professionals*. New York: McGraw-Hill.

Groves, P. M., & Rebec, G. V. (1992). *Introduction to biological psychology* (4th ed.). Dubuque, IA: Wm. C. Brown.

Hamilton, L. W., & Timmons, C. R. (1990). *Principles of behavioral pharmacology: A biopsychological perspective*. Englewood Cliffs, NJ: Prentice-Hall.

Hampson, S. E., & Colman, A. M. (Eds.). (1995). *Individual differences and personality*. London and New York: Longman.

Harré, R., & Lamb, R. (Eds.). (1986). *Dictionary of ethology and animal learning*. Oxford: Blackwell.

Hearnshaw, L. S. (1987). *The shaping of modern psychology*. London: Routledge & Kegan Paul.

Herrnstein, R. J., & Boring, E. G. (Eds.). (1965). *A source book in the history of psychology*. Cambridge, MA: Harvard University Press.

Heymer, A. (1977). *Ethological dictionary*. New York: Garland.

Hinshelwood, R. D. (1991). *A dictionary of Kleinian thought* (2nd ed.). Northvale, NJ: Jason Aronson.

Howells, J. G., & Osborn, M. L. (1984). *A reference companion to the history of abnormal psychology*. Westport, CT: Greenwood Press.

Hubel, D. H. (1988). *Eye, brain, and vision*. New York: W. H. Freeman.

Impara, J. C., Plake, B. S., & Murphy, L. L. (Eds.).

(1998). *The thirteenth mental measurements yearbook*. Lincoln, NB: University of Nebraska Press.

Isaacs, A., Daintith, J., & Martin, E. (Eds.). (1991). *Concise science dictionary* (2nd ed.). Oxford: Oxford University Press.

Julien, R. M. (1992). *A primer of drug action: A concise, nontechnical guide to the actions, uses, and side effects of psychoactive drugs* (6th ed.). New York: W. H. Freeman.

Jung, C. G. (1953–71). *The collected works of C. G. Jung* (H. Read, M. Fordham, & G. Adler Eds.). London: Routledge, & Princeton, NJ: Princeton University Press.

Kalat, J. W. (1995). *Dictionary of biological psychology* (5th ed.). Pacific Grove, CA: Brooks/Cole.

Kendall, M. G., & Buckland, W. R. (1982). *A dictionary of statistical terms* (4th ed.). London: Longman.

Kendall, M. G., & Doig, A. G. (1962). *Bibliography of statistical literature 1950–1958*. Edinburgh: Oliver & Boyd.

Kendall, M. G., & Doig, A. G. (1965). *Bibliography of statistical literature 1940–1949*. Edinburgh: Oliver & Boyd.

Kendall, M. G., & Doig, A. G. (1965). *Bibliography of statistical literature pre-1949 with supplements to the volumes for 1940–49 and 1950–58*. Edinburgh: Oliver & Boyd.

Kendell, R. E., & Zealley, A. K. (Eds.). *Companion to psychiatric studies* (5th ed.). Edinburgh: Churchill Livingstone.

Kimble, D. P. (1988). *Biological psychology*. New York: Holt, Rinehart and Winston.

Kimble, D., & Colman, A. M. (Eds.). (1995). *Biological aspects of behaviour*. London and New York: Longman.

Kolb, B., & Whishaw, I. Q. (1980). *Fundamentals of human neuropsychology*. San Francisco: W. H. Freeman.

Kuper, A., & Kuper, J. (Eds.). (1996). *The social science encyclopedia* (2nd ed.). London: Routledge.

Laplanche, J., & Pontalis, J.-B. (1988). *The language of psycho-analysis* (Trs. D. Nicholson-Smith). London: Karnac Books and the Institute of Psycho-Analysis. [Original work in French published 1973]

Lawrence, E. (1989). *Henderson's dictionary of biological terms*. London: Longman.

Lazarus, A. A., & Colman, A. M. (Eds.). (1995). *Abnormal psychology*. London and New York: Longman.

Levine, M. W., & Shefner, J. M. (1981). *Fundamentals of sensation and perception*. Reading, MA: Addison-Wesley.

Mackintosh, N. J., & Colman, A. M. (Eds.). (1995). *Learning and skills*. London and New York: Longman.

MacRae, S. (1994). *Describing and interpreting data*. Leicester: The British Psychological Society.

MacRae, S. (1994). *Drawing inferences from statistical data*. Leicester: The British Psychological Society.

MacRae, S. (1994). *Models and methods for the behavioural sciences*. Leicester: The British Psychological Society.

Manstead, A. S. R., & Hewstone, M. (Eds.). (1995). *The Blackwell encyclopedia of social psychology*. Oxford: Blackwell.

Martin, E. A., Ruse, M., & Holmes, E. (1996). *A dictionary of biology* (3rd ed.). Oxford: Oxford University Press.

McCarthy, R. A., & Warrington, E. K. (1990). *Cognitive neuropsychology: A clinical introduction*. San Diego, CA: Academic Press.

Miller, P. M., & Wilson, M. J. (1983). *A dictionary of social science methods*. New York: Wiley.

Moore, B. E., & Fine, B. D. (Eds.). (1990). *Psychoanalytic terms and concepts*. New Haven, CT: The American Psychoanalytic Association and Yale University Press.

Palfai, T., & Kankiewicz, H. (1991). *Drugs and human behavior*. Dubuque, IA: Wm. C. Brown.

Parchi, P., & Gambetti, P. (1995). Human prion diseases. *Current opinion in neurology, 8*, 286–293.

Parkinson, B., & Colman, A. M. (Eds.). (1995). *Emotion and motivation*. London and New York: Longman.

Pearsall, J. (Ed.). (1998). *The new Oxford dictionary of English*. Oxford: Clarendon Press.

Reber, A. S. (1995). *The Penguin dictionary of psychology* (2nd ed.). Harmondsworth: Penguin.

Roach, P. (1992). *Introducing phonetics*. Harmondsworth: Penguin.

Rosenzweig, M. R., & Leiman, A. L. (1989). *Physiological psychology* (2nd ed.). New York: Random House.

Rycroft, C. (1968). *A critical dictionary of psychoanalysis*. London: Nelson. [With amendments for 1994 revision]

Samuels, A., Shorter, B., & Plant, F. (1986). *A critical dictionary of Jungian analysis*. London: Routledge & Kegan Paul.

Sarle, W. (1995). What is measurement theory? In *Disseminations of the International Statistical Institute* (4th ed., pp. 61–66). Wichita, TX: ACG Press.

Schiff, W. (1980). *Perception: An applied approach*. Boston, MA: Houghton Mifflin.

Schiffman, H. R. (1996). *Sensation and perception: An integrated approach* (4th ed.). New York: Wiley.

Schwandt, T. A. (1997). *Qualitative inquiry: A dictionary of terms*. Thousand Oaks, CA: Sage.

Schwarz, C. (Managing Ed.). (1994). *The Chambers dictionary*. Edinburgh: Chambers Harrap.

Scriven, M. (1991). *Evaluation thesaurus* (4th ed.). Newbury Park, CA: Sage.

Sekuler, R., & Blake, R. (1994). *Perception* (3rd ed.). New York: McGraw-Hill.

Sheehy, N., Chapman, A. J., & Conroy, W. A. (Eds.). (1997). *Biographical dictionary of psychology*. London: Routledge.

Siegel, S., & Castellan, N. J., Jr. (1988). *Nonparametric statistics for the behavioral sciences* (2nd ed.). New York: McGraw-Hill.

Simpson, J. A., & Weiner, E. S. C. (Eds.). (1989). *The Oxford English dictionary* (2nd ed.). Oxford: Oxford University Press.

SPSS for Windows: Release 8.0 [Computer software]. (1999). Chicago, IL: SPSS Inc.

Sternberg, R. J. (1996). *Cognition*. New York: Harcourt Brace.

Stevens, S. S. (Ed.). (1951). *Handbook of experimental psychology*. New York: Wiley.

Stuart-Hamilton, I. (1995). *Dictionary of cognitive psychology*. London: Jessica Kingsley.

Stuart-Hamilton, I. (1995). *Dictionary of developmental psychology*. London: Jessica Kingsley.

Sutherland, S. (1995). *The Macmillan dictionary of psychology* (2nd ed.). London: Macmillan.

Tabachnick, B. G., & Fidell, L. S. (1989). *Using multivariate statistics* (2nd ed.). New York: HarperCollins.

Tootill, E. (Ed.). (1990). *The Pan dictionary of biology*. London: Pan Books.

Trask, R. L. (1996). *A dictionary of phonetics and phonology*. London: Routledge.

Treffry, D. (Editorial Director). (1998). *Collins English dictionary* (4th ed.). Glasgow: HarperCollins.

Tulloch, S. (1992). *The Oxford dictionary of new words: A popular guide to words in the news*. Oxford: Oxford University Press.

Vogt, W. P. (1993). *Dictionary of statistics and methodology: A nontechnical guide for the social sciences*. Newbury Park, CA: Sage.

Walker, A. Jr. (Ed.). (1994). *Thesaurus of psychological index terms* (7th ed.). Washington, DC: American Psychological Association.

Walsh, K. (1987). *Neuropsychology: A clinical approach*. Edinburgh: Churchill Livingstone.

Wardhaugh, R. (1995). *Understanding English grammar: A linguistic approach*. Oxford: Blackwell.

Watson, R. I. (Ed.). (1979). *Basic writings in the history of psychology*. New York: Oxford University Press.

Wilson, R. A., & Keil, F. C. (Eds.). (1999). *The MIT encyclopedia of cognitive sciences*. Cambridge, MA: MIT Press.

Wing, J. K., Cooper, J. E., & Sartorius, N. (1974). *Measurement and classification of psychiatric symptoms: An instruction manual for the PSE and Catego program*. Cambridge: Cambridge University Press.

Woodworth, R. S., & Schlosberg, H. (1955).

Experimental psychology (3rd ed.). London: Methuen.

World Health Organization. (1993). *The ICD-10 classification of mental and behavioural disorders: Diagnostic criteria for research*. Geneva: Author.

World Health Organization Division of Mental Health. (1994). *SCAN schedules for clinical assessment in neuropsychiatry: Glossary: Differential definitions of SCAN items and commentary on the SCAN text*. Geneva: Author.

Yaremko, R. M., Harai, H., Harrison, R. C., & Lynn, E. (1982). *Reference handbook of research and statistical methods in psychology: For students and professionals*. New York: Harper & Row.

Youngman, M. B. (1979). *Analysing social and educational research data*. Maidenhead: McGraw-Hill.

Great value ebooks from Oxford!

An ever-increasing number of Oxford subject reference dictionaries, English and bilingual dictionaries, and English language reference titles are available as ebooks.

All Oxford ebooks are available in the award-winning Mobipocket Reader format, compatible with most current handheld systems, including Palm, Pocket PC/Windows CE, Psion, Nokia, SymbianOS, Franklin eBookMan, and Windows. Some are also available in MS Reader and Palm Reader formats.

Priced on a par with the print editions, Oxford ebooks offer dictionary-specific search options making information retrieval quick and easy.

For further information and a full list of Oxford ebooks please visit: www.askoxford.com/shoponline/ebooks/

Oxford Paperback Reference

A Dictionary of Psychology
Andrew M. Colman

Over 10,500 authoritative entries make up the most wide-ranging dictionary of psychology available.

'impressive ... certainly to be recommended'
Times Higher Educational Supplement

'Comprehensive, sound, readable, and up-to-date, this is probably the best single-volume dictionary of its kind.'
Library Journal

A Dictionary of Economics
John Black

Fully up-to-date and jargon-free coverage of economics. Over 2,500 terms on all aspects of economic theory and practice.

A Dictionary of Law

An ideal source of legal terminology for systems based on English law. Over 4,000 clear and concise entries.

'The entries are clearly drafted and succinctly written ... Precision for the professional is combined with a layman's enlightenment.'
Times Literary Supplement

Oxford Paperback Reference

A Dictionary of Chemistry

Over 4,200 entries covering all aspects of chemistry, including physical chemistry and biochemistry.

'It should be in every classroom and library ... the reader is drawn inevitably from one entry to the next merely to satisfy curiosity.'

School Science Review

A Dictionary of Physics

Ranging from crystal defects to the solar system, 3,500 clear and concise entries cover all commonly encountered terms and concepts of physics.

A Dictionary of Biology

The perfect guide for those studying biology – with over 4,700 entries on key terms from biology, biochemistry, medicine, and palaeontology.

'lives up to its expectations; the entries are concise, but explanatory'

Biologist

'ideally suited to students of biology, at either secondary or university level, or as a general reference source for anyone with an interest in the life sciences'

Journal of Anatomy

Oxford Paperback Reference

Concise Medical Dictionary

Over 10,000 clear entries covering all the major medical and surgical specialities make this one of our best-selling dictionaries.

'"No home should be without one" certainly applies to this splendid medical dictionary'

Journal of the Institute of Health Education

'An extraordinary bargain'

New Scientist

'Excellent layout and jargon-free style'

Nursing Times

A Dictionary of Nursing

Comprehensive coverage of the ever-expanding vocabulary of the nursing professions. Features over 10,000 entries written by medical and nursing specialists.

An A-Z of Medicinal Drugs

Over 4,000 entries cover the full range of over-the-counter and prescription medicines available today. An ideal reference source for both the patient and the medical professional.